EARLIER PUBLICATIONS IN THIS SERIES

Edited by Oscar Krisen Buros

Educational, Psychological, and Personality Tests of 1933 and 1934

Educational, Psychological, and Personality Tests of 1933, 1934 and 1935

Educational, Psychological, and Personality Tests of 1936

The Nineteen Thirty-Eight Mental Measurements Yearbook

The Nineteen Forty Mental Measurements Yearbook

The Third Mental Measurements Yearbook

The Fourth Mental Measurements Yearbook

The Fifth Mental Measurements Yearbook

Tests in Print

The Sixth Mental Measurements Yearbook

READING
TESTS AND REVIEWS

READING

TESTS AND REVIEWS

Including a Classified Index to
The Mental Measurements Yearbooks

Edited by
OSCAR KRISEN BUROS

THE GRYPHON PRESS
HIGHLAND PARK · NEW JERSEY

Table of Contents

Contributing Test Reviewers

Ira E. Aaron   6:830, 6:831, 6:834
Janet G. Afflerbach   5:693
Lois Grimes Afflerbach   5:693
Irving H. Anderson   1:1095, 1:1097,
    1:1104, 3:514, 3:518, 3:519, 3:521
Mary C. Austin   6:848
Warren R. Baller   4:583
Thomas C. Barrett   6:795, 6:814
Robert M. Bear   3:497,
    3:509, 4:575, 4:586
Emmett Albert Betts   6:810, 6:831
L. B. Birch   6:833
Emery P. Bliesmer   6:826, 6:832, 6:842
Paul Blommers   3:530
Joan Bollenbacher   5:675, 5:679
Guy L. Bond   2:1533, 2:1548
Ivan A. Booker   1:1105, 1:1110, 2:1547,
    2:1581, 3:505, 3:532, 3:534, 4:544, 4:558
M. Alan Brimer   6:843
M. E. Broom   2:1534
Charles M. Brown   6:829, 6:834
N. Dale Bryant   5:649,
    5:676, 6:821, 6:824
Guy T. Buswell   2:1559
Harold D. Carter   4:559
Stella S. Center   1:1108
W. V. Clemans   6:806
William E. Coffman   6:786
Thomas E. Culliton, Jr.   6:820, 6:836
Reginald R. Dale   5:652
Frederick B. Davis   1:1107, 1:1114, 2:1529,
    2:1563, 3:480, 3:489, 3:507, 4:531
Robert A. Davis   3:536
Stanley E. Davis   6:865
James Deese   5:688, 5:697
Gabriel M. Della-Piana   6:824
Clarence Derrick   5:649, 6:815

Joseph C. Dewey   1:1105,
    1:1110, 1:1115, 2:1539
Jerome E. Doppelt   5:644
Lydia A. Duggins   5:671, 5:672
S. S. Dunn   5:631, 5:677, 5:679
Henry S. Dyer   5:621
Robert L. Ebel   4:582, 5:696, 5:698
William Eller   6:792, 6:836
Alvin C. Eurich   2:1578
Ethel M. Feagley   3:536, 3:543
Leonard S. Feldt   5:687
John C. Flanagan   4:530
C. M. Fleming   4:537
W. G. Fleming   6:806, 6:865
Gustav J. Froehlich   4:577
Edward B. Fry   6:787, 6:808
Eric F. Gardner   4:570, 5:653
J. Raymond Gerberich   2:1555,
    4:581, 6:815
    5:666, 5:699
Marvin D. Glock   2:1557
Hans C. Gordon   5:637
Neil Gourlay
William S. Gray   1:1099,
    3:486, 3:493, 4:535, 4:568
W. E. Hall   3:480, 3:528
Albert J. Harris   3:496,
    3:511, 3:530, 6:826, 6:842
J. Thomas Hastings   4:560, 5:691
A. N. Hieronymus   5:690, 6:791
Walker H. Hill   5:691, 5:700
James R. Hobson   2:1539, 2:1567,
    3:498, 3:501, 4:530,
    4:543, 4:555, 5:653, 5:665, 5:678
Dorothy E. Holberg   3:487
Kenneth D. Hopkins   6:790
Carl I. Hovland   5:700
Duncan Howie   5:694

ix

READING
TESTS AND REVIEWS

Preface

P LANS for the publication of this monograph were first announced twenty-seven years ago in the Preface of *The 1940 Mental Measurements Yearbook*. In November 1940, I wrote:

In order to make the material in the yearbooks more easily accessible to individuals who are interested in only a small part of each volume, a new series of monographs is being planned. If the first two or three monographs prove successful, others will eventually be prepared to cover tests in each of the following fields: business education, character and personality, elementary education, English and reading, fine arts, foreign languages, health and physical education, home economics, industrial arts, intelligence, mathematics, sciences, social studies, and vocational aptitudes. The first publication in each field will include: a comprehensive bibliography of all standard tests in print in that area; a reprinting, in part or in full, of all reviews of these tests which have appeared in previous yearbooks or in the journal literature; new reviews written especially for the monograph (to be, in turn, reprinted, in part or in full, in the following yearbook); and an extensive list of references on the construction, validation, use, and limitations of the tests. Separates in each field will be issued every four, six, or eight years depending upon the frequency of test publication. These monographs will range in size from fifty to two hundred pages. This new series will make it possible for an individual to purchase at a nominal cost every four, six, or eight years a monograph devoted solely to the tests and reviews of most interest to him. These separates will greatly extend the range of service of the yearbooks. The first monograph will be devoted to tests in English and reading and will be published in late 1941 or early 1942. Other titles will be planned for publication at the rate of two monographs each year.

Considerable work was actually done in 1940 and 1941 on the preparation of the first monograph to cover English and reading. Unfortunately, we just didn't have the financial resources to complete the preparation and publication of a single one of the planned monographs. It was constantly touch and go even to get out another MMY, let alone the supplementary monographs. At no time, however, did we give up our dreams of launching the monograph series. Even though it has taken us over a quarter of a century to prepare and finance this volume, we are both pleased and surprised that we have finally succeeded.

The major objective of this monograph is to make readily available to reading teachers and specialists the wealth of material to be found in the reading sections of the first six *Mental Measurements Yearbooks*. The monograph also presents a comprehensive bibliography of all reading tests known to be in print as of May 1, 1968.

In addition to the material on reading tests and reviews, this monograph includes—as will other monographs in the series—a classified index to all tests and reviews in the six MMY's. This classified index, called the MMY Test Index, is a master index or key to all tests, reviews, excerpts, and references to be found in *The Mental Measurements Yearbooks*. The MMY Test Index should prove extremely useful in locating critical information about tests in areas other than reading.

The next monograph in this series will be *Personality Tests and Reviews* to be published early in 1969. Because of the tremendous output of personality tests and publications on personality tests, the next monograph will be a volume very nearly the size of *The Sixth Mental Measurements Yearbook*. Later in 1969, we hope to publish similar monographs in the areas of intelligence and vocations. The 7th MMY is scheduled for publication in 1971 followed by a new edition of *Tests in Print*. If the monographs prove as useful as we anticipate, monographs in other areas such as English, foreign languages, mathematics, sciences, and social studies will be published shortly after the appearance of the 7th MMY.

I wish to acknowledge the assistance which I have received from members of my editorial and secretarial staff in preparing the manuscript for this monograph and in seeing the volume through the press. Mr. Clement Haimowitz served as a part-time editorial assistant during the academic year 1966–67. Miss Ethel Kersting, the only full-time member on my staff, has been especially helpful as an editorial assistant. Mrs. Augusta D. Fleagle, Mrs. Doris G. McCan, and Mrs. Ann Mary Volpe have competently carried out a variety of activities—typing, copyreading, indexing, and proofreading. I am grateful for the painstaking care which both the editorial and secretarial staff members have taken to make this monograph

as accurate as possible. My greatest debt is to my wife, Luella, who has worked in various capacities on all the MMY's and related publications over the past thirty-five years.

I wish to thank those publishers who have provided us with information and specimen sets of their tests for editorial processing and review. Our work would be greatly facilitated if all publishers would do likewise. We still have considerable difficulty in getting information from some test publishers—three small publishers even refuse to give or sell tests to us and ignore all requests for information. Other publishers probably mean well but do not reply to our requests for information and specimen sets of tests or do so only after repeated inquiries.

I hope that readers will inform me of errors and omissions found in this monograph.

OSCAR KRISEN BUROS

Highland Park, N.J.
July 17, 1968

Introduction

PRIOR to 1938 there was no source to which test users could go to obtain information about the merits and limitations of the hundreds of standardized tests published for use by teachers, psychologists, and personnel workers in industry. Rarely were tests reviewed in the professional journals. Textbooks did little more than describe in an uncritical manner the most commonly used tests. Test manuals were generally much less informative than they are today. Poorly constructed tests having little or no validity could be marketed without fear of published criticism. There was a crying need for some sort of a bureau of standards to point out the weaknesses and strengths of competing tests.

SERVICE FOR TEST USERS

For a time, I hoped that I might be instrumental in the establishment of such a test-the-tests research organization back in the thirties. It was only after I failed in repeated attempts to get the financial support needed to launch a test consumers research organization that I conceived the idea of setting up a test reviewing service with the cooperation of hundreds of specialists in education, industry, and psychology who would contribute frankly critical reviews of tests for publication in a series to be called *The Mental Measurements Yearbooks.*

For the past thirty years *The Mental Measurements Yearbooks* have provided test users with critical information about the merits and limitations of tests of every description—achievement, aptitude, intelligence, personality, and vocational. Since each succeeding volume supplements rather than supplants earlier volumes, the six MMY's published to date present a tremendous amount of useful information for all who make, sell, buy, or use tests. Each of the "yearbooks"—published at intervals of three to six years—consists of two major sections: "Tests and Reviews" and "Books and Reviews."

MMY OBJECTIVES

The objectives of the section Tests and Reviews—the heart of the MMY's—have remained essentially unchanged since this cooperative test reviewing service was first initiated thirty years ago. The major objectives of the test section are:

a) To provide comprehensive bibliographies of all standardized tests published in English-speaking countries.

b) To provide frankly critical evaluations of tests, written by competent specialists representing a variety of viewpoints, to assist test users to choose the tests which will best meet their needs.

c) To provide comprehensive bibliographies of articles, books, and theses dealing with the construction, validity, use, and limitations of specific tests.

d) To impel test authors and publishers to place fewer but better tests on the market and to provide test users with detailed information on the validity and limitations of their tests at the time the tests are first published.

e) To suggest to test users better methods of arriving at their own appraisals of both standardized and nonstandardized tests in light of their own particular values and needs.

f) To stimulate contributing reviewers to reconsider and think through more carefully their own beliefs and values relevant to testing.

g) To inculcate upon test users a keener awareness of both the values and dangers involved in the use and non-use of standardized tests.

h) To impress test users with the desirability of suspecting all standardized tests—even though prepared by well-known authorities—unaccompanied by detailed data on their construction, validity, uses, and limitations.

The two major objectives of the book section are:

a) To present bibliographies of recent books on measurements and closely associated fields published in all English-speaking countries.

b) To make readily available evaluative excerpts from hundreds of book reviews appearing in a great variety of journals in this country and abroad to assist test users in making more discriminating selections of books for study and purchase.

THE SIX MMY'S AND TIP

One hundred and thirty-three specialists contributed 331 original test reviews to *The 1938 Mental Measurements Yearbook*,[1] the first publication to provide test users with critical information regarding standardized tests of every description. This 430-page volume was widely hailed as a landmark in the history of testing. Its publication marked the end of the days when tests having either no validity or unknown validity could be published without fear of criticism. *The 1938 Yearbook*—hereafter referred to as *The First Mental Measurements Yearbook*—presents information on 314 tests, most of which were published within the period of 1933–37. *The First Yearbook* also includes excerpts from 776 reviews of 241 books on testing and closely related subjects.

Two hundred and fifty cooperating reviewers contributed 503 original reviews to *The 1940 Mental Measurements Yearbook*,[2] a 699-page volume published in 1941. *The 1940 Yearbook* —hereafter referred to as *The Second Mental Measurements Yearbook*—lists 524 tests, most of which were published in 1938–40. *The Second Yearbook* also includes excerpts from 13 test reviews first published in journals and excerpts from 735 reviews of 368 books on testing.

Comprehensive bibliographies—including a total of 1511 references on the construction, validity, and use of specific tests—were introduced for the first time in *The Second Yearbook*. Except for unpublished theses, all references in the specific test bibliographies in this and later MMY's were examined at first hand to make sure that they were relevant and that the listings were accurate. The introduction of these comprehensive and carefully screened bibliographies added greatly to the usefulness of the series.

The Third Mental Measurements Yearbook,[3] a 1062-page volume published in 1949, presents buying information on 663 tests, most of which were published during the period 1941–47. Three hundred and twenty cooperating reviewers contributed 713 original reviews. *The Third Yearbook* also includes excerpts from 79 test reviews first published in journals, excerpts from 785 reviews of 549 books on testing, and 3368 references on the construction, validity, and use of specific tests.

The Fourth Mental Measurements Yearbook,[4] a 1188-page volume published in 1953, lists 793 tests, most of which were published during the years 1948–51. Three hundred and eight specialists cooperated in the preparation of this volume by contributing 596 original test reviews. *The Fourth Yearbook* also presents excerpts from 53 test reviews, excerpts from 758 reviews of 429 books on testing, and 4417 references in its bibliographies on specific tests.

The first three MMY's presented information on tests commercially available as separates in English-speaking countries. The scope of the fourth and later yearbooks was expanded to include tests available only as a part of highly restricted programs such as the tests of the College Entrance Examination Board.

The Fifth Mental Measurements Yearbook,[5] a 1321-page volume published in 1959, presents information on 957 tests, most of which were published in the years 1952–58. Three hundred and fifty reviewers contributed 698 original test reviews. *The Fifth Yearbook* also presents excerpts from 48 test reviews, excerpts from 535 reviews of 485 books on testing, and 6468 references in the test bibliographies.

1 BUROS, OSCAR KRISEN, EDITOR. *The Nineteen Thirty-Eight Mental Measurements Yearbook*, New Brunswick, N.J.: Rutgers University Press, 1938. Pp. xv, 415. Out of print. A reprint is scheduled for publication by Johnson Reprint Corporation, 111 Fifth Ave., New York, N.Y. 10003. Xerographic prints are available from University Microfilms, Inc., 313 North First St., Ann Arbor, Mich. 48103.
2 BUROS, OSCAR KRISEN, EDITOR. *The Nineteen Forty Mental Measurements Yearbook*. Highland Park. N.J.: Gryphon Press, 1941. Pp. xxv, 674. Out of print. A reprint is scheduled for publication by Johnson Reprint Corporation, 111 Fifth Ave., New York, N.Y. 10003. Xerographic prints are available from University Microfilms, Inc., 313 North First St., Ann Arbor, Mich. 48103.

3 BUROS, OSCAR KRISEN, EDITOR. *The Third Mental Measurements Yearbook*. Highland Park, N.J.: Gryphon Press, 1949. Pp. xv, 1047.
4 BUROS, OSCAR KRISEN, EDITOR. *The Fourth Mental Measurements Yearbook*. Highland Park, N.J.: Gryphon Press, 1953. Pp. xxv, 1163.
5 BUROS, OSCAR KRISEN, EDITOR. *The Fifth Mental Measurements Yearbook*. Highland Park, N.J.: Gryphon Press, 1959. Pp. xxix, 1292.

Since each yearbook supplements rather than supplants earlier volumes in the series, the publication of successive volumes made it necessary for the reader to search through several volumes to locate the information wanted. Despite the numerous cross references to reviews, excerpts, and bibliographic references in earlier volumes, it was becoming increasingly difficult to locate quickly the relevant material with the publication of each new volume. Furthermore, there was no way of knowing whether a test listed in an earlier volume but not in the latest MMY was still in print. Then again publishers and their addresses were constantly changing. Clearly, something needed to be done to facilitate the use of the five MMY's published through 1959.

Tests in Print,[6] a master index to the contents of the first five yearbooks and a comprehensive bibliography of standard tests, was published in 1961. This volume lists 2967 tests, 2126 of which were in print early in 1961. When information is wanted from the first five MMY's, the reader is well advised to consult *Tests in Print* first. TIP indicates which of the first five MMY's presents the most recent listing of a test along with information regarding its in print status, the number of reviews it received, the names of the reviewers, the number of references on its construction, validity, and use, and the number of excerpts reprinted from test reviews in journals. The dual function served by TIP—a comprehensive bibliography of tests in print and a master index to the wealth of material in the first five MMY's—makes it an indispensable tool for all who wish to derive the maximum benefit from the MMY's in the shortest possible time.

The Sixth Mental Measurements Yearbook,[7] a 1751-page volume published in late 1965, presents purchasing information on 1219 tests, most of which were published in the years 1959–64. Three hundred and ninety-six specialists prepared 795 original reviews for this volume. *The Sixth Yearbook* also includes excerpts from 377 book reviews, excerpts from 97 test reviews, and 8001 references on the construction, validity and use of specific tests. In addition to the 1219 tests for which ex-

tensive information, references, and reviews were presented, the 6th MMY lists by title all other tests known to be in print as of mid-1964. Each of these tests listed by title only appears in both the Classified Index of Tests and in the Title Index with a cross reference to its listing in *Tests in Print*. Thus, used together, the 6th MMY and TIP provide a comprehensive bibliography of all tests known to be in print as of mid-1964.

READING TESTS AND REVIEWS

Many test users are primarily interested in obtaining critical information about tests in only one or two of the following areas: English, foreign languages, intelligence, mathematics, personality, reading, sciences, social studies, or vocational aptitudes. In order to make the MMY reviews more easily accessible to specialized groups interested in only one or two sections of the yearbooks, we are initiating a series of monographs, of which this volume, *Reading Tests and Reviews*, is the first in the series. The second volume will be *Personality Tests and Reviews* followed by *Intelligence Tests and Reviews* and then *Vocational Aptitude Tests and Reviews*.

Each volume will present for the field covered: (*a*) a comprehensive bibliography of tests in print; (*b*) a reprinting of the corresponding test review sections in the MMY's; (*c*) a classified index to the tests and reviews in all MMY's published to date; (*d*) a directory of publishers; and (*e*) title and name indexes. The monographs will make it possible for a test user to have in a single volume all the MMY material of most interest to him as well as to have classified, name, and title indexes to all other tests and reviews in the *Mental Measurements Yearbooks* published to date. Later monographs in the series will be very similar to *Reading Tests and Reviews* but with several improvements growing out of our experience in preparing this volume.

READING TEST INDEX

This chapter presents: (*a*) a comprehensive bibliography of reading tests known to be in print in English-speaking countries as of May 1, 1968; (*b*) a bibliography of reading tests

6 Buros, Oscar Krisen, Editor. *Tests in Print: A Comprehensive Bibliography of Tests for Use in Education, Psychology, and Industry.* Highland Park, N.J.: Gryphon Press, 1961. Pp. xxix, 479.
7 Buros, Oscar Krisen, Editor. *The Sixth Mental Measurements Yearbook.* Highland Park, N.J.: Gryphon Press, 1965. Pp. xxxvii, 1714.

now out of print but once listed and possibly reviewed in one or more MMY's; and (c) an index to the contents (reviews, references, and long test entries) of the next chapter, Reading Test Reviews, which consists of a reprinting of the reading sections of the first six *Mental Measurements Yearbooks*.

The Reading Test Index lists a total of 292 tests, 209 in print tests and 83 out of print tests. A statistical breakdown by kinds of reading tests—in print, out of print, and total—is presented in Table 1. The percentages of all read-

TABLE 1

CLASSIFICATION OF TESTS IN THE READING TEST INDEX

Classification	In Print	Out of Print	Total Number	Total Percentage
General	89	27	116	39.7
Diagnostic	27	5	32	11.0
Miscellaneous	13	4	17	5.8
Oral Reading	11	5	16	5.5
Readiness	29	5	34	11.6
Special Fields	18	5	23	7.9
Speed	2	4	6	2.1
Study Skills	20	28	48	16.4
Total	209	83	292	100.0

ing tests in the various categories may be arrayed as follows: general, 39.7; study skills, 16.4; readiness, 11.6; diagnostic, 11.0; special fields, 7.9; miscellaneous, 5.8; oral reading, 5.5; and speed, 2.1.

For each test, the following information is presented: title, population for which the test is suitable, range of publication dates, number and description of scores, authors, publisher, cross references to the reviews which the test received in the six MMY's, names of persons who have written original reading test reviews for the *Mental Measurements Yearbooks,* number of references presented in each yearbook on the construction, validity, and use of the test, and the number of excerpts reprinted from journal reviews of the test. A star (★) preceding a test title denotes a new test not previously listed in a *Mental Measurements Yearbook.* As shown in Table 2, one out of four of the 209 in print tests are new tests. An asterisk (*) preceding a test title indicates that the test has either been revised or supplemented in some way (e.g., a new form or a revised manual) since the test was last included in an MMY. Approximately one out of six of the 209 in print tests has been revised or supplemented. Although the interval between the closing dates of *The Sixth Mental Measurements Yearbook*

TABLE 2

NEW AND REVISED (OR SUPPLEMENTED) TESTS AMONG THE READING TESTS IN PRINT

Classification	In Print Tests	Percentage New	Percentage Revised	Percentage Total
General	89	23.6	27.1	41.6
Diagnostic	27	25.9	22.2	48.1
Miscellaneous	13	30.8	30.8	61.5
Oral Reading	11	0	0	0
Readiness	29	48.3	20.7	69.0
Special Fields	18	27.8	16.7	44.4
Speed	2	0	0	0
Study Skills	20	5.0	5.0	10.0
Total	209	24.9	17.2	42.1

and *Reading Tests and Reviews* is slightly less than four years, 42 per cent of the 209 tests currently in print are classified as new, revised, or supplemented since the 6th MMY.

Within each of the eight categories in which the reading tests have been classified, the in print tests are listed first in alphabetical order followed by the out of print tests. Cross references to reviews, references, and excerpts in the six MMY's are also references to material in the next chapter, Reading Test Reviews. A cross reference such as 1:1100 refers to test 1100 reprinted from the 1st MMY; 3:476 refers to test 476 reprinted from the 3rd MMY; and 6:783 refers to test 783 reprinted from the 6th MMY. To facilitate the location of the tests and reviews in the next chapter, these numbers are printed as catchwords in the running heads next to the outside margins.

In summary, the Reading Test Index answers such questions as: What reading tests are currently available in English-speaking countries? Which of the reading tests listed in an MMY are now out of print? Which of the yearbooks contain reviews of a given reading test? Which of the MMY's present references on the construction, validity, and use of a given reading test? Who are the reading and testing specialists who have reviewed a particular test? In addition, the Index presents the following information for each test: title, age or grade range for which suitable, range of copyright or publication dates, scores obtainable from the test, authors, and publisher.

READING TEST REVIEWS

This chapter presents 349 critical reviews of 158 tests by 154 specialists in reading and testing, 38 excerpts from reading test reviews originally published in professional journals, and 608 references on the construction, validity, and use of specific reading tests. All the material in this chapter originally appeared in the first (26 reviews, 1 excerpt), second (42 reviews, 13 excerpts), third (86 reviews, 13 excerpts), fourth (47 reviews, 6 excerpts), fifth (76 reviews), and sixth (72 reviews, 5 excerpts) *Mental Measurements Yearbooks*. Although the reviews reprinted from the last four MMY's are of the greatest value, some of the reviews reprinted from the first two MMY's still have value apart from their historical interest—see, e.g., the reviews of 1:1099, 1:1105, and 1:1108.

The reading sections of the six yearbooks are presented in the order of their publication. The reading section from the 1st MMY appears first, the reading section of the 2nd MMY appears next, then the reading sections of the 3rd, 4th, 5th, and 6th MMY's. Because of the smaller page size, copy for the 1st MMY had to be reset; the remaining reading sections have been reproduced by offset with only the running heads changed. Page numbers are given next to the inside margins; the entry numbers of tests are presented as catchwords next to the outside margins with a yearbook designation added. Thus, 1:1166 refers to test 1166 in the 1st MMY; 3:543 refers to test 543 in the 3rd MMY; and 6:865 refers to test 865 in the 6th MMY. To locate the reviews which a test has received, first consult the preceding chapter, Reading Test Index. The Index is not only a comprehensive bibliography of all reading tests in print as of May 1, 1968, it is also a convenient index to the reviews, excerpts, and references which are presented in this chapter.

TEST ENTRIES

The descriptive information given for each test preceding the reviews has been increased slightly in each succeeding yearbook. For a full understanding of these test entries, it is important that the user of this monograph understand the basis and nature of the information provided. Since the 6th MMY presents the fullest entries, a description of the information provided for each test will suffice for all the MMY's. This information follows:

a) TITLE. Test titles are printed in boldface type. Secondary or series titles are set off from main titles by a colon. Titles are always presented exactly as reported in the test materials. When the titles on the test booklet and manual differ, the better known title is given in boldface; the second title is generally given in italic type within the entry. Entry titles which differ from those reported in the test materials (generally because no definitive title is used) are enclosed in brackets. Stars (★) precede titles of tests which have never before been listed in an MMY; asterisks (*) precede titles of tests which have been revised or supplemented since their last MMY listing.

b) DESCRIPTION OF THE GROUPS FOR WHICH THE TEST IS INTENDED. The grade, chronological age, or semester range, or the employment category is usually given. "Grades 1.5–2.5, 2–3, 4–12, 13–17" means that there are four test booklets: a booklet for the middle of the first grade through the middle of the second grade, a booklet for the beginning of the second grade through the end of the third grade, a booklet for grades 4 through 12 inclusive, and a booklet for undergraduate and graduate students in colleges and universities. "First, second semester" means that there are two test booklets: one covering the work of the first semester, the other covering the work of the second semester. "1, 2 semesters" indicates that the second booklet covers the work of the two semesters. Hyphens separate years and months. For example, "ages 10-2 to 11-11" means ages 10 years 2 months to 11 years 11 months; "grades 4-6 to 5-9" means the sixth month in the fourth grade through the ninth month in the fifth grade. Commas are used to separate levels. "High school and college" denotes a single test booklet for both levels; "High school, college" denotes two test booklets, one for high school and one for college.

c) DATE OF COPYRIGHT OR PUBLICATION. The inclusive range of copyright dates (or publication dates if not copyrighted) for the various forms, accessories, and editions of a test is reported. When the publication date differs from the copyright date, both dates are given; e.g., "1948, c1946–48" means that the test was copyrighted both in 1946 and in 1948 but was not published until 1948. When publication or copyright dates do not appear on the materials and the date has been secured through correspondence with the publisher, it is enclosed in brackets.

d) PART SCORES. The number of part scores is presented along with their titles or descriptions of what they presumably represent.

e) INDIVIDUAL OR GROUP TEST. All tests are group tests unless otherwise indicated.

f) MACHINE SCORABLE TESTS. Tests which may be scored by scoring machines which may be purchased or for which machine scoring services are available independently of the test publisher are marked in one of the following ways: "IBM" means either that the test may be scored by *IBM Test Scoring Machine* or that it may be scored by *IBM Optical Mark Scoring Reader;* "Digitek" means that the test may be scored by *Digitek Optical Test Scoring and Document Scanning System;* "Grade-O-Mat" means that the test may be scored by *Grade-O-Mat;* "Hankes" means that *Hankes Answer Sheets* and scoring services are available; "MRC" means that Measurement Research Center answer sheets and scoring services are available; and "NCS" means that National Computer Systems answer sheets and scoring services are available. "IBM" may refer to either IBM 805 or IBM 1230 answer sheets; no attempt has been made to specify which type answer sheet is available. Some publishers have developed special types of answer sheets and scoring services which are available only for their own tests; such machine scorable features are not mentioned at this point in the entry but are noted in the price information given for answer sheets. As entries for *The Sixth Yearbook* were being prepared, many publishers—most of the larger ones—were in the process of revising and expanding upon the machine scoring accessories available for their tests. For up-to-date information on machine scoring features, the latest catalogs of test publishers should be consulted.

g) FORMS, PARTS, AND LEVELS. All available forms, parts, and levels are listed with the most recent date of publication.

h) PAGES. The number of pages on which print occurs is reported for test booklets, manuals, technical reports, profiles, and other nonapparatus accessories. Blank pages and pages containing only material not related to the test (e.g., advertising pages and pages containing only printer's marks) have not been counted. Self-covers have been counted only when the cover is not duplicated by a title page inside.

i) RELIABILITY AND VALIDITY. The complete absence of data in a test manual is indicated. It was originally intended to include in the entries the statement "reliability data for raw scores only" wherever appropriate. However, since it soon became apparent that almost all tests still report only raw score reliability data rather than data on reliability of normed scores, the idea of including such a statement was abandoned.

j) COST. Both test package and specimen set prices are given. A statement such as "$3 per 35 tests" means that all accessories are included unless otherwise indicated by the reporting of separate prices for accessories. Such a statement also means 35 tests of one level, one edition, or one part unless we say otherwise. Discounts that may be available for purchasing in large quantities and special discounts that may be available to professional groups are not reported. Specimen set prices mean specimen sets of all levels, all editions, all parts—but not all forms—unless otherwise indicated. Price information is believed to be correct as of mid-1964. Although every precaution has been taken to ensure accuracy, some prices may be in error and other prices may have changed. For full and up-to-date information on test prices, the latest catalogs of test publishers should be consulted.

k) TIME. The number of minutes of actual working time allowed examinees and the approximate length of time needed for administering a test are reported whenever obtainable. The latter figure is always enclosed in parentheses. Thus, "50(60) minutes" indicates that the examinees are allowed fifty minutes of working time and that a total of sixty minutes is needed to administer the test. When the time necessary to administer a test is not reported or suggested in the test materials but has been obtained through correspondence with the test publisher or author, the time is enclosed in brackets.

l) AUTHOR. For most tests, all authors are reported. In the case of tests which appear in a new form each year, only authors of the most recent forms are listed. Names are reported exactly as printed on test booklets. Names of editors are generally not reported.

m) PUBLISHER. The name of the publisher or distributor is reported for each test. Publishers' names which do not appear on the test materials are enclosed in brackets. For addresses of publishers and distributors, see the Publishers Directory and Index.

n) SUBENTRIES. Levels, editions, subtests, or parts of a test which are available in separate booklets are presented as subentries with titles set in small capitals. Sub-subentries are indented with titles set in italic type.

TEST BIBLIOGRAPHIES

Immediately following each test entry, all known references—published articles and books and unpublished theses—on the construction, validity, use, and limitations of the test are reported. These references are arranged in chronological order by year of publication and alphabetically by authors within years. The test bibliographies are believed to be fairly complete through 1963. In order to assist students who wish to do selected reading on a particular test, references are given to abstracts in *Dissertation Abstracts* and in *Psychological Abstracts*. For example, "(*DA* 33:6843)" refers to a thesis abstract beginning on page 6843 in volume 33 of *Dissertation Abstracts;* and "(*PA* 37:416)" refers to abstract number 416 in volume 37 of *Psychological Abstracts*. References are numbered consecutively through all MMY volumes. References which appeared in earlier volumes are referred to but are not repeated. For example, "1–5. See 5:622" means that the first five references for the test will be found under entry 622 in this monograph in the section reprinted from *The Fifth Mental Measurements Yearbook*. The total number of references reported for specific reading tests in the first six MMY's is 608, 2.57 per cent of all references listed in the MMY's to date.

SUGGESTIONS TO REVIEWERS

A sheet entitled "Suggestions to Reviewers" was enclosed with each letter inviting a person to review for an MMY. The suggestions have been essentially the same for all six MMY's. To properly understand the viewpoint from which the test reviews were written, readers are urged to study the following suggestions which were sent to persons who reviewed for the 6th MMY.

1) Reviews should be written with the following major objectives in mind:

a) To provide test users with carefully prepared appraisals of tests for their guidance in selecting and using tests.

b) To stimulate progress toward higher professional standards in the construction of tests by commending good work, by censuring poor work, and by suggesting improvements.

c) To impel test authors and publishers to present more detailed information on the construction, validity, reliability, uses, and possible misuses of their tests.

2) Reviews should be concise, the average review running from 500 to 1000 words in length. The average length of the reviews written by one person should not exceed 800 words. Except for reviews of achievement batteries, multi-factor batteries, and tests for which a literature review is to be made, longer reviews should be prepared only with the approval of the editor.

3) Reviews should be frankly critical, with both strengths and weaknesses pointed out in a judicious manner. Descriptive comments should be kept to the minimum necessary to support the critical portions of the review. Criticism should be as specific as possible; implied criticisms meaningful only to testing specialists should be avoided. Reviews should be written primarily for the rank and file of test users. An indication of the relative importance and value of a test with respect to competing tests should be presented whenever possible. If a reviewer considers a competing test better than the one being reviewed, the competing test should be specifically named.

4) If a test manual gives insufficient, contradictory, or ambiguous information regarding the construction, validity, and use of a test, reviewers are urged to write directly to authors and publishers for further information. Test authors and publishers should, however, be held responsible for presenting adequate data in test manuals—failure to do so should be pointed out. For comments made by reviewers based upon unpublished information received personally from test authors or publishers, the source of the information should be clearly indicated.

5) Reviewers will be furnished with the test entries which will precede their reviews. Information presented in the entry should not be repeated in reviews unless it is done for evaluative purposes.

6) The use of sideheads is optional with reviewers.

7) Each review should conclude with a paragraph presenting a concise summary of the reviewer's overall evaluation of the test. The summary should be as explicit as possible. Is the test the best of its kind? Is it recommended for use? If other tests are better, which of the competing tests is best?

8) A separate review should be prepared for each test. Each review should begin on a new sheet. The test and forms reviewed should be clearly indicated. Your name, title, position, and address should precede each review, e.g.: John Doe, Professor of Education and Psychology, University of Maryland, College Park, Maryland. The review should begin a new paragraph immediately after the address.

9) All reviews should be typed *double spaced* and *in triplicate. Two copies* of each review should be submitted to THE MENTAL MEASUREMENTS YEARBOOK; *one copy* should be retained by the reviewer.

10) If for any reason a reviewer thinks he is not in a position to write a frankly critical review in a scholarly and unbiased manner, he should request the editor to substitute other tests for review.

11) Reviewers may not invite others to collaborate with them in writing a review unless permission is secured from the editor.

12) Most tests will be reviewed by two or more persons in order to secure better representation of various viewpoints. Noncritical content which excessively overlaps similar material presented by another reviewer may be deleted. Reviews will be carefully edited, but no important changes will be made without the consent of the reviewer. Galley proofs (unaccompanied by copy) will be submitted to reviewers for checking.

13) The editor reserves the rights to reject any review which does not meet the minimum standards of the yearbook series.

14) Each reviewer will receive a complimentary copy of THE SIXTH MENTAL MEASUREMENTS YEARBOOK.

MMY TEST INDEX

Many readers of this monograph will be interested in consulting *The Mental Measurements Yearbooks* for information about tests in areas other than reading such as achievement, aptitudes, intelligence, interests, personality, and sensory-motor. This chapter provides a master guide and classified index to the contents of the test sections in the first six MMY's. The MMY Test Index makes it possible for the reader to turn quickly to the appropriate MMY to learn where further information may be obtained about the tremendous wealth of information to be found in the test sections of the first six *Mental Measurements Yearbooks.*

Table 3 presents a summary of what is presented in the test sections of the first six MMY's: 2,802 tests, 3,573 original test reviews, 358 excerpted test reviews, and 23,744 references on the construction, validity, and use of specific tests. The reading sections of the first six MMY's make up less than ten per cent of the total test sections: 8.0 per cent of the

TABLE 3

Tests, Reviews, Excerpts, and References in the First Six MMY's by Major Classifications

Classification	Tests	Reviews	Excerpts	References
Achievement Batteries	54	174	5	462
Business Education	69	59	5	41
English	255	259	13	520
Fine Arts	43	72	2	288
Foreign Languages	164	156	5	191
Intelligence	290	483	64	5,494
Mathematics	247	312	6	181
Miscellaneous	297	177	25	713
Multi-Aptitude	25	77	10	680
Personality	386	649	135	11,195
Reading	224	351	31	601
Science	163	186	12	186
Sensory-Motor	60	29	11	467
Social Studies	160	154	4	75
Vocations	365	435	30	2,650
Total	2,802	3,573	358	23,744

tests, 9.8 per cent of the original test reviews, 8.7 per cent of the excerpted reviews, and 2.6 per cent of the test references.

The title last used in an MMY is presented for each test along with a listing of the names of persons who have reviewed the test in an MMY, the number of references on the construction, validity, and use of the test, and the number of reviews excerpted from journals. *The MMY Test Index does not indicate whether a test is currently in print; nor does it list tests published since the 6th MMY;* it is a master index to the tests, reviews, references, and excerpts to be found in the first six *Mental Measurements Yearbooks.* Within each classification, tests are listed in alphabetical order. If information is wanted about tests in a particular area, consult the key to the classification presented at the beginning of the MMY Test Index; if information is wanted about a particular test, consult the title index (superseded titles are also listed in the title index); if information is wanted about the tests reviewed by a particular person, consult the name index.

PUBLISHERS DIRECTORY AND INDEX

The Publishers Directory and Index lists all publishers of reading tests listed in the Reading Test Index. Out of print tests are so designated. Addresses are presented only for those publishers known to have one or more reading tests in print as of May 1, 1968. Publishers issuing catalogs devoted entirely or in large part to tests are marked by a star.

The number of publishers of reading tests is surprisingly large. Considering only publishers of reading tests in print, there are 86 publishers: 69 in the United States, 10 in Great Britain, 2 in Australia, 2 in Canada, 1 in New Zealand, 1 in South Africa, and 1 in Sweden. In addition, there are 20 publishers with only out of print reading tests.

Fifty of the 86 publishers publish only 1 reading test, 15 publish 2 tests, 4 publish 3 tests, 6 publish 4 tests, 2 publish 5 tests, 1 publishes 6 tests, 2 publish 7 tests, and 6 publish 8 or more tests. The 6 publishers with 8 or more tests are: Bobbs-Merrill Co., Inc., 14 tests; Harcourt, Brace & World, Inc., 14 tests; Houghton Mifflin Co., 10 tests; Science Research Associates, Inc., 10 tests; California Test Bureau, 8 tests; and Psychometric Affiliates, 8 tests.

INDEX OF TITLES

The Index of Titles is the most comprehensive listing of test titles available to test users. In addition to listing all reading tests known to be in print as of May 1, 1968, the index includes all tests which have been in one or more of the first six *Mental Measurements Yearbooks* or in *Tests in Print.* References are to entry numbers, not to page numbers. Numbers not preceded by a letter refer to test entries in the Reading Test Index; numbers preceded by a letter refer to test entries in the MMY Test Index; and numbers preceded by the acronym TIP refer to test entries in *Tests in Print.* Superseded titles are followed by the word "see" before the entry number reported for the test title last used in an MMY. In summary, the index of well over three thousand titles lists all reading tests known to be in print and all tests—reading and otherwise—which have been listed in either an MMY or TIP.

INDEX OF NAMES

The Index of Names lists: (*a*) authors of reading tests currently in print and all reading tests now out of print but once listed in an MMY or in TIP; (*b*) authors of reading test reviews written for an MMY; (*c*) authors of excerpted reading test reviews; (*d*) authors of references reported for specific reading tests in the first six MMY's; (*e*) persons mentioned in footnotes in the reading sections of the MMY's; and (*f*) authors of other test reviews written for an MMY. Each of the entry numbers is clearly marked to indicate whether the reference is to an author of a test, review, excerpt, or reference, or whether the reference is to the listing of a name in a footnote.

Reading Test Index

THIS chapter presents a classified listing of all reading tests known to be in print in English-speaking countries as of May 1, 1968. In addition, the Reading Test Index lists all out of print tests which were once listed in one or more of the six *Mental Measurements Yearbooks*. Consequently, the Index serves not only as a ready reference guide to the available reading tests but also as a guide to the reading sections reprinted in the next chapter, Reading Test Reviews, from the first six MMY's. For each test the following information is presented: title, population for which suitable, range of publication dates, number and description of scores, authors, publisher, names of persons who have written original test reviews for a *Mental Measurements Yearbook,* the number of references presented on the test's construction, validation, and use, and the number of reviews excerpted in the MMY from other publications. A star preceding a test title denotes a new test not previously listed in an MMY; an asterisk indicates a test revised since it was last listed in an MMY. The asterisk following the entry indicates that the test entry was prepared from an actual examination of the test. Within each classification, in print tests are listed first in alphabetical sequence by title followed by out of print tests. Since the next chapter is a reprinting of the reading sections of the first six MMY's, all cross references such as 2:1530, 4:531, and 5:665 refer to material presented in the next chapter. This chapter lists 292 reading tests. Of the 209 reading tests currently in print, 52 tests (24.9 per cent) are new tests not previously listed in an MMY and 36 tests (17.2 per cent) have been revised or supplemented since last listed in an MMY.

CLASSIFICATION

[1]

★**A.C.E.R. Lower Grades Reading Test: Level 1, Second Edition.** Grade 1; 1962–64; for schools in New South Wales; M. L. Clark, N. E. Morison, and J. L. A. Russell; Australian Council for Educational Research. *

[2]

A.C.E.R. Silent Reading Tests, Forms A and B. Ages 9–11; 1933–57; Australian Council for Educational Research. *
a) PART 1, WORD KNOWLEDGE.
b) PART 2, SPEED OF READING.
c) PART 3, READING FOR GENERAL SIGNIFICANCE.
d) PART 4, READING TO NOTE DETAILS.
e) PART 5, READING FOR INFERENCE.
For additional information and a review by Fred J. Schonell, see 5:616.

[3]

A.C.E.R. Silent Reading Tests, Forms C and D. Ages 10–13; 1946–63; Australian Council for Educational Research. *
a) PART 1, WORD KNOWLEDGE.
b) PART 2, SPEED OF READING.
c) PART 3, READING FOR MEANING.
For additional information, see 6:782 (1 reference); for reviews by Fred J. Schonell and D. K. Wheeler, see 5:617.

[4]

A.C.E.R. Silent Reading Tests: Standardized for Use in New Zealand. Ages 9–12; 1955; tests for a and c identical with corresponding parts of *A.C.E.R.*

Silent Reading Test, Form C; test for *b* identical with corresponding part of *A.C.E.R. Silent Reading Tests,* Form B; A. E. Fieldhouse (manual); New Zealand Council for Educational Research. *
a) PART 1, WORD KNOWLEDGE.
b) PART 2, SPEED OF READING.
c) PART 3, READING FOR MEANING.
For additional information, see 5:618.

[5]
Achievement Test in Silent Reading: Dominion Tests. Grades 1, 2, 2–3, 3–4, 4–6, 5–6; 1941–57; Department of Educational Research, Ontario College of Education, University of Toronto; distributed by Guidance Centre. *
a) TYPE 1, WORD RECOGNITION. Grade 1; 1941–57.
b) TYPE 2, PHRASE AND SENTENCE READING. Grade 1; 1941–53.
c) TYPE 3, PARAGRAPH READING. Grade 1; 1943–53.
d) TYPE 4, DIAGNOSTIC TEST IN WORD RECOGNITION. Grade 1; 1943–53.
e) TYPE 1, VOCABULARY. Grades 2–3, 4–6; 1943–56. *Out of print.*
f) TYPE 2, DIAGNOSTIC TEST IN PARAGRAPH READING. Grades 2, 3–4, 5–6; 1943–56.
For additional information and reviews by Harry L. Stein and Magdalen D. Vernon, see 5:619; for a review by Henry P. Smith, see 4:529; for a review by Margaret G. McKim, see 3:476.

[6]
American School Achievement Tests: Part 1, Reading. Grades 2–3, 4–6, 7–9; 1941–63; subtest of the *American School Achievement Tests;* 3 scores: sentence and word meaning, paragraph meaning, total; Willis E. Pratt, Robert V. Young, and Clara E. Cockerille; Bobbs-Merrill Co., Inc. *
For additional information, see 6:783; for reviews by Russell G. Stauffer and Agatha Townsend, see 5:620. For reviews of the complete battery, consult the 6th, 5th, 4th, and 3rd MMY's.

[7]
American School Reading Tests. Grades 10–13; 1955; 3 scores: vocabulary, reading rate, comprehension; Willis E. Pratt and Stanley W. Lore; Bobbs-Merrill Co., Inc. *
For additional information and reviews by Henry S. Dyer and Donald E. P. Smith, see 5:621.

[8]
*Buffalo Reading Test for Speed and Comprehension. Grades 9–16; 1933–65; 3 scores: speed, comprehension, total; Mazie Earle Wagner and Daniel S. P. Schubert (manual); Mazie Earle Wagner. *
For additional information and reviews by Holland Roberts and William W. Turnbull, see 3:477.

[8.1]
★Burnett Reading Series: Survey Test. Grades 1.5–2.4, 2.5–3.9, 4.0–6.9, 7.0–9.9, 10.0–12.9; 1966–68; Richard W. Burnett; Scholastic Testing Service, Inc. *
a) PRIMARY 1. Grades 1.5–2.4; 1966–67; 4 scores: word identification, word meaning, comprehension, total.
b) PRIMARY 2. Grades 2.5–3.9; 1966; scores as for Primary 1.
c) INTERMEDIATE. Grades 4.0–6.9; 1966–67; scores as for Primary 1.
d) ADVANCED. Grades 7.0–9.9; 1967; 4 scores: vocabulary, comprehension, total, rate and accuracy.
e) SENIOR. Grades 10.0–12.9; 1968; scores as in Advanced.

[9]
[Burt's Reading Tests.] Ages 6–14, 7–14; 1921; reprinted from the author's *Mental and Scholastic Tests;* Cyril Burt; Staples Press Ltd. *
a) TEST 3, READING SPEED AND ACCURACY: DISCONTINUOUS UNGRADED TEST: TWO- AND THREE-LETTER MONOSYLLABLES. Ages 6–14 with reading handicaps.
b) TEST 5, READING COMPREHENSION. Ages 7–14; 3 scores: speed, accuracy, comprehension.

[10]
California Reading Test, 1957 Edition With 1963 Norms. Grades 1–2, 2.5–4.5, 4–6, 7–9, 9–14; 1933–63; subtest of *California Achievement Tests;* formerly called *Progressive Achievement Tests;* 3 scores: vocabulary, comprehension, total; Ernest W. Tiegs and Willis W. Clark; California Test Bureau. *
For additional information, see 6:784 (13 references); see also 5:622 (5 references); for reviews by John C. Flanagan and James R. Hobson of an earlier edition, see 4:530 (1 excerpt); for a review by Frederick B. Davis, see 2:1563; for reviews by Ivan A. Booker and Joseph C. Dewey, see 1:1110. For reviews of the complete battery, consult the 6th, 5th, 4th, 3rd, 2nd, and 1st MMY's.

[11]
*Canadian English Achievement Test (CEAT): Part 1, Reading Comprehension. Grades 8–9; 1959–64; Department of Educational Research, Ontario College of Education, University of Toronto; distributed by Guidance Centre. *
For additional information and reviews of the complete battery, consult the 6th MMY.

[12]
Commerce Reading Comprehension Test. Grades 12–16 and adults; 1956–58; Irma T. Halfter and Raymond J. McCall; Department of Psychological Testing, DePaul University. *
For additional information, see 5:624.

[13]
Comprehension Test for Training College Students. Training college students and applicants for admission; 1962; E. L. Black; distributed by National Foundation for Educational Research in England and Wales. *
For additional information, see 6:785.

[14]
★Comprehensive Primary Reading Scales. Grade 1; 1956–60; M. J. Van Wagenen, Mary A. Van Wagenen (Part 1), and Maximilian L. G. Klaeger (Part 2); Van Wagenen Psycho-Educational Research Laboratories. *
a) PART 1, READING COMPREHENSION SCALE.
b) PART 2, PICTURE READING VOCABULARY SCALE.
c) PART 3, MEANING READING VOCABULARY SCALE.
d) PART 4, WORD RECOGNITION VOCABULARY SCALE.

[15]
★Comprehensive Reading Scales. Grades 4, 5, 6, 7, 8, 9–10, 11–12; 1948–53; M. J. Van Wagenen; Van Wagenen Psycho-Educational Research Laboratories. *

[16]
*Cooperative Reading Comprehension Test, Form Y. Secondary forms 5–6; 1958, c1940–64; Australian adaptation (spelling only) of Form Y of *Reading Comprehension: Cooperative English Test, Higher Level C2;* 4 scores: vocabulary, speed of comprehension, level of comprehension, total; Frederick B. Da-

vis, Clarence Derrick, Jeanne M. Bradford, and Geraldine Spaulding; Australian Council for Educational Research. *

[17]

*Cooperative Reading Comprehension Test, Forms L and M. Secondary forms 2–4; 1960–67; Australian adaptations of Forms 2A, 2B, and 2C of *Reading Comprehension: Cooperative English Test, 1960 Revision;* 3 scores: vocabulary, level of comprehension, speed of comprehension; Clarence Derrick, David P. Harris, and Biron Walker; Australian Council for Educational Research. *

[18]

Davis Reading Test. Grades 8–11, 11–13; 1956–62; 2 scores: level of comprehension, speed of comprehension; Frederick B. Davis and Charlotte Croon Davis; Psychological Corporation. *
For additional information and reviews by William E. Coffman and Alton L. Raygor, see 6:786 (2 references); for a review by Benjamin Rosner of the lower level, see 5:625.

[19]

★Delaware County Silent Reading Test, Second Edition. Grade 1², 2¹, 2², 3¹, 3², 4, 5, 6, 7, 8; 1965; 5 scores: interpretation, organization, vocabulary, structural analysis, total; Judson E. Newburg and Nicholas A. Spennato; Delaware County Reading Consultants Association. *

[20]

Detroit Word Recognition Test. Grades 1–3; 1925–29; Eliza F. Oglesby; Harcourt, Brace & World, Inc. *

[21]

*Developmental Reading Tests. Grades 1–2.5, 2.5–3, 4–6; 1955–65; test booklet title for grades 1–3 is *New Developmental Reading Tests;* Guy L. Bond, Bruce Balow (a and b), Theodore Clymer (c), and Cyril J. Hoyt; Lyons & Carnahan. *
a) LOWER PRIMARY READING. Grades 1–2.5; 1955–65; 4 scores: vocabulary, general comprehension, specific comprehension, total.
b) UPPER PRIMARY READING. Grades 2.5–3; 1955–65; same scores as for a.
c) [INTERMEDIATE READING.] Grades 4–6; 1959; 6 scores: basic vocabulary, reading to retain information, reading to organize, reading to evaluate-interpret, reading to appreciate, average comprehension.
For additional information and reviews by Edward B. Fry and Agatha Townsend, see 6:787.

[22]

Diagnostic Examination of Silent Reading Abilities. Grades 4–6, 7–9, 10–13; 1939–54; 3 parts, parts 2 and 3 are in 1 booklet; August Dvorak (Parts 2 and 3) and M. J. Van Wagenen; Van Wagenen Psycho-Educational Laboratories. *
a) PART 1, VAN WAGENEN RATE OF COMPREHENSION SCALE. 1939–53.
b) PART 2. 1939–52; 4 scores: perception of relations, vocabulary (context, isolation), information.
c) PART 3. 1939–54; also published separately under the title *Van Wagenen Analytical Reading Scales;* 6 scores: central thought, single details, related ideas, inferences, interpretation, total.
d) PART 4, READING FOR IDEAS. 1952–53; rate of reading.
For additional information and reviews by Frederick B. Davis, W. E. Hall, and J. B. Stroud, see 3:480 (2 references); see also 2:1532 (1 excerpt).

[23]

*Elementary Reading: Every Pupil Achievement Test. Grades 4–6, 7–8; 1928–68; series formerly called *Every Pupil Scholarship Test;* new form usually issued each January and April; Gene E. Plank (1964–67 tests); Bureau of Educational Measurements. *
For additional information, see 6:788.

[24]

*Emporia Elementary Reading Test. 1, 2 semesters in grades 2–3; 1964, c1962–64; first published in the Every Pupil Scholarship series; Marjorie Barnett and M. W. Sanders; Bureau of Educational Measurements. *

[25]

★Emporia Intermediate Reading Test. 1, 2 semesters in grades 4–6; 1964, c1962–64; first published in the Every Pupil Scholarship series; Donald E. Carline, Angie Seybold, Ed. L. Eaton, and M. W. Sanders; Bureau of Educational Measurements. *

[26]

★Emporia Junior High School Reading Test. 1, 2 semesters in grades 7–8; 1964, c1962–64; first published in the Every Pupil Scholarship series; Donald E. Carline, Stafford S. Studer, Ed. L. Eaton, and M. W. Sanders; Bureau of Educational Measurements. *

[27]

★Emporia Primary Reading Test. 1, 2 semesters grade 1; 1964, c1962–64; first published in the Every Pupil Scholarship series; Marjorie Barnett and M. W. Sanders; Bureau of Educational Measurements. *

[28]

Emporia Silent Reading Test. Grades 3–8; 1933–35; H. E. Schrammel and W. H. Gray; Bureau of Educational Measurements. *
For additional information and reviews by M. E. Broom and Harriet Barthelmess Morrison, see 2:1534.

[29]

★GAP Reading Comprehension Test. Grades 2–7; 1965–67; cloze technique with approximately every tenth word omitted; J. McLeod; Heinemann Educational Books Ltd. *

[30]

*Gates-MacGinitie Reading Tests. Grades 1, 2, 3, 2–3, 4–6, 7–9; 1926–65; Primary A is a revision of the *Gates Primary Reading Tests,* Primary B is a revision of the *Gates Advanced Primary Reading Tests,* the other tests in this series are revisions of the *Gates Reading Survey;* Arthur I. Gates and Walter H. MacGinitie; Teachers College Press. *
a) PRIMARY A. Grade 1; 1926–65; 2 scores: vocabulary, comprehension.
b) PRIMARY B. Grade 2; 1926–65; 2 scores: vocabulary, comprehension.
c) PRIMARY C. Grade 3; 1939–65; 2 scores: vocabulary, comprehension.
d) PRIMARY CS. Grades 2–3; 1926–65; speed and accuracy.
e) SURVEY D. Grades 4–6; 1939–65; 3 scores: speed and accuracy, vocabulary, comprehension.
f) SURVEY E. Grades 7–9; 1964–65; 3 scores: speed and accuracy, vocabulary, comprehension.
For additional information and reviews by William Eller and Coleman Morrison of *Gates Primary Reading Tests,* see 6:792 (1 reference); see also 5:632 (2 references); for reviews by William S. Gray and George Spache of an earlier edition, see 3:486 (7 ref-

erences). For additional information and a review by Kenneth D. Hopkins of *Gates Advanced Primary Reading Tests,* see 6:790 (1 reference) ; see also 5:630 (3 references) ; for reviews by Virginia Seavey and George Spache of an earlier edition, see 3:484. For additional information and reviews by George Spache and Morey J. Wantman of *Gates Reading Survey,* see 6:793 (7 references) ; for reviews by Dorothy E. Holberg and Herbert F. Spitzer of an earlier edition, see 3:487.

[31]

Group Achievement Tests: Dominion Tests: Niagara Edition: Test 2, Diagnostic Paragraph Comprehension. Grade 8; 1950; 4 scores: general significance, detail, inference, total; F. W. Minkler, C. Howitt, C. R. MacLeod, W. A. Marshall, M. F. Pummell, N. Wightman, and the Department of Educational Research, Ontario College of Education, University of Toronto; distributed by Guidance Centre. *

For additional information, consult the 5th MMY.

[32]

★**Group Reading Assessment.** End of first year junior school; 1964; c1962–64; Frank A. Spooncer; University of London Press Ltd. *

[33]

High School Reading Test: National Achievement Tests. Grades 7–12; 1939–52; 6 scores: vocabulary, word discrimination, sentence meaning, noting details, interpreting paragraphs, total; Robert K. Speer and Samuel Smith; Psychometric Affiliates. *

For additional information and a review by Victor H. Noll, see 5:634; for a review by Holland Roberts, see 4:536; for a review by Robert L. McCaul, see 3:488.

[34]

Iowa Silent Reading Tests. Grades 4–8, 9–14; 1927–56; H. A. Greene, A. N. Jorgensen, and V. H. Kelley; Harcourt, Brace & World, Inc. *

a) ELEMENTARY TEST. Grades 4–8; 1933–56; 9 scores: rate, comprehension, directed reading, word meaning, paragraph comprehension, sentence meaning, alphabetizing, use of index, total.

b) ADVANCED TEST. Grades 9–14; 1927–43; 10 scores: rate, comprehension, directed reading, poetry comprehension, word meaning, sentence meaning, paragraph comprehension, use of index, selection of key words, total.

For additional information and a review by Worth R. Jones, see 6:794 (40 references) ; for reviews by Frederick B. Davis and William W. Turnbull, see 3:489 (21 references, 2 excerpts) ; for reviews by Ivan A. Booker and Holland D. Roberts of an earlier edition, see 2:1547 (6 references).

[35]

Kelley-Greene Reading Comprehension Test. Grades 9–13; 1953–55, c1952–55; 5 scores: paragraph comprehension, directed reading, retention of details, reading rate, total; Victor H. Kelley and Harry A. Greene; Harcourt, Brace & World, Inc. *

For additional information and reviews by Russell P. Kropp and Magdalen D. Vernon, see 5:636 (1 reference).

[36]

Kelvin Measurement of Reading Ability. Ages 8–12; 1933; C. M. Fleming; Robert Gibson & Sons (Glasgow), Ltd. *

For additional information, see 1:1103.

[37]

The Kingston Test of Silent Reading. Ages 7–11; 1953–54; M. E. Hebron (formerly M. E. Highfield) ; George G. Harrap & Co. Ltd. *

For additional information and reviews by Neil Gourlay and Magdalen D. Vernon, see 5:637.

[38]

Lee-Clark Reading Test. Grades 1, 1–2; 1931–58; J. Murray Lee and Willis W. Clark; California Test Bureau. *

a) PRIMER. Grade 1; 4 scores: auditory stimuli, visual stimuli, following directions, total.

b) FIRST READER. Grades 1–2; 6 scores: same as for primer level plus completion, inference.

For additional information and reviews by Thomas C. Barrett and Coleman Morrison, see 6:795; for a review by Ruth Lowes of the 1943 edition of the primer level, see 3:490.

[39]

Los Angeles Elementary Reading Test. Grades 3–8; 1926–31; Jessie E. Ingraham; California Test Bureau. *

For additional information and a review by Henry P. Smith, see 4:541.

[39.1]

★**McGrath Test of Reading Skills, Second Edition.** Grades 1–13; 1965–67; 4 scores: word recognition, oral reading, vocabulary, oral reading rate; Joseph E. McGrath; McGrath Reading Clinic. *

[40]

★**McMenemy Measure of Reading Ability.** Grades 3, 5–6, 7–8; 1964–68; Richard A. McMenemy; the Author. *

a) PRIMARY. Grade 3; 1964–68.

b) INTERMEDIATE. Grades 5–6; 1966–68.

c) ADVANCED. Grades 7–8; 1965–68.

[41]

★**Maintaining Reading Efficiency Tests.** Grades 9–12 and college; 1966; reprinted from the 1966 edition of *Maintaining Reading Efficiency* by Lyle L. Miller; 3 scores: rate, comprehension accuracy, reading efficiency; 2 forms labeled Tests 1 (*History of Brazil*), 2 (*History of Japan*) ; Wiley E. Peeples (Test 1) and Jeanne K. Taylor (Test 2); Developmental Reading Distributors. *

[42]

Manchester Reading Comprehension Test (Sen.) 1. Ages 13.5–15; 1959; Stephen Wiseman and Jack Wrigley; University of London Press Ltd. *

For additional information, see 6:796 (1 reference).

[43]

Metropolitan Achievement Tests: Reading. Grades 2, 3–4, 5–6, 7–9; 1932–62; subtest of *Metropolitan Achievement Tests;* catalog uses the title *Metropolitan Reading Tests;* 2–3 scores: word knowledge, word discrimination (grade 2 only), reading; Walter N. Durost, Harold H. Bixler, Gertrude H. Hildreth, Kenneth W. Lund, and J. Wayne Wrightstone; Harcourt, Brace & World, Inc. *

For additional information and a review by H. Alan Robinson, see 6:797 (4 references) ; for reviews by James R. Hobson and Margaret G. McKim of the 1947 edition, see 4:543; for a review by D. A. Worcester of an earlier edition, see 2:1551; for reviews by Ivan A. Booker and Joseph C. Dewey, see 1:1105. For reviews of the complete battery, consult the 6th, 4th, 2nd, and 1st MMY's.

[44]

Minnesota Reading Examination for College Students. Grades 9–16; 1930–35; 2 scores: vocabulary, paragraph reading; Melvin E. Haggerty and Alvin C. Eurich; University of Minnesota Press. *

For additional information and a review by James M. McCallister, see 3:491 (3 references); for a review by W. C. McCall, see 2:1554 (3 references); for a review by Ruth Strang, see 1:1106.

[45]

Monroe's Standardized Silent Reading Test. Grades 3–5, 6–8, 9–12; 1919–59; 2 scores: rate, comprehension; Walter S. Monroe; Bobbs-Merrill Co., Inc. *

For additional information and reviews by Charles R. Langmuir and Agatha Townsend, see 6:798 (5 references).

[46]

N.B. Silent Reading Tests (Beginners): Reading Comprehension Test. Standard 1 (grades 1–2); 1961; National Bureau of Educational and Social Research. *

For additional information, see 6:799.

[47]

The Nelson-Denny Reading Test: Vocabulary and Paragraph. Grades 9–16; 1929–38; 3 scores: vocabulary, paragraph comprehension, total; M. J. Nelson and E. C. Denny; Houghton Mifflin Co. * *Out of print.* For the revised edition, see 48.

For additional information and a review by Ivan A. Booker, see 4:544 (17 references); for a review by Hans C. Gordon, see 2:1557 (6 references); for references to reviews of a later edition, see 48.

[48]

The Nelson-Denny Reading Test: Vocabulary-Comprehension-Rate. Grades 9–16 and adults; 1929–60; 4 scores: vocabulary, comprehension, total, rate; original edition by M. J. Nelson and E. C. Denny; revision by James I. Brown; Houghton Mifflin Co. *

For additional information and reviews by David B. Orr and Agatha Townsend, see 6:800 (13 references, 1 excerpt); for references to reviews of an earlier edition, see 47.

[49]

The Nelson Reading Test, Revised Edition. Grades 3–9; 1931–62; revision of *The Nelson Silent Reading Test: Vocabulary and Paragraph;* previous edition (see 50) still available; 3 scores: vocabulary, paragraph comprehension, total; M. J. Nelson; Houghton Mifflin Co. *

For additional information and a review by H. Alan Robinson, see 6:802; for references to reviews of earlier editions, see 50.

[50]

The Nelson Silent Reading Test: Vocabulary and Paragraph: The Clapp-Young Self-Marking Tests. Grades 3–9; 1931–39; for revised edition, see *Nelson Reading Test;* 5 scores: vocabulary, general paragraph comprehension, ability to note details, ability to predict probable outcome, total; M. J. Nelson; Houghton Mifflin Co. *

For additional information and a review by William D. Sheldon of an earlier edition, see 4:545 (1 reference); for a review by Constance M. McCullough, see 3:492; see also 2:1558 (1 excerpt); for reference to a review of a later edition, see 49.

[51]

Pressey Diagnostic Reading Tests. Grades 3–9; 1929; 4 scores: speed, vocabulary, paragraph meaning, total; S. L. Pressey and L. C. Pressey; Bobbs-Merrill Co., Inc. *

[52]

*Primary Reading: Every Pupil Achievement Test.** Grades 1, 2–3; 1935–67; series formerly called *Every Pupil Scholarship Test;* new form usually issued each January and April; Marjorie Barnett (1961–67 tests); Bureau of Educational Measurements. *

For additional information, see 6:803.

[53]

Primary Reading Test: Acorn Achievement Tests. Grades 2–3; 1943–57; 5 scores: word recognition, words-similar meaning, word meaning-opposites, story-paragraph-sentence meaning, total; Winifred E. Stayton, Frances C. Ranson, and Roland L. Beck; Psychometric Affiliates. *

For additional information, see 5:642; for a review by Alice N. Jameson, see 3:495.

[54]

★**Primary Reading Test 2.** 2–4 years primary school; 1967–68; published for the National Foundation for Educational Research in England and Wales; Newnes Educational Publishing Co. Ltd. *

[55]

The Purdue Reading Test. Grades 7–16; 1928–53; H. H. Remmers, John M. Stalnaker, and P. C. Baker; State High School Testing Service for Indiana. *

For additional information, see 5:643; for a review by Albert J. Harris, see 3:496.

[56]

Reading Comprehension: Cooperative English Tests. Grades 9–12, 13–14; 1940–60; separate booklet edition of reading subtest of *Cooperative English Tests;* 4 scores: vocabulary, level of comprehension, speed of comprehension, total; revision by Clarence Derrick, David P. Harris, and Biron Walker; Cooperative Test Division. *

For additional information and reviews by W. V. Clemans and W. G. Fleming, see 6:806 (12 references); see also 5:645 (21 references) and 4:547 (20 references); for reviews by Robert Murray Bear and J. B. Stroud of an earlier edition, see 3:497 (15 references); see also 2:1564 (2 references). For reviews of the complete battery, consult the 6th and 3rd MMY's.

[57]

★**Reading Comprehension Test.** College entrants; 1963–68; William A. McCartney; the Author. *

[58]

Reading Comprehension Test: National Achievement Tests [Crow, Kuhlmann, and Crow]. Grades 4–6, 4–9; 1953–57; Lester D. Crow, Martha J. Kuhlmann, and Alice Crow; Psychometric Affiliates. *

For additional information, see 5:647.

[59]

Reading Comprehension Test: National Achievement Tests [Speer and Smith]. Grades 3–8; 1938–57; 4 scores: following directions, sentence meaning, paragraph meaning, total; Robert K. Speer and Samuel Smith; Psychometric Affiliates. *

For additional information, see 5:646; for a review by James R. Hobson, see 3:498.

[60]
★**Reading Comprehension Test 1.** Fourth year junior and first year secondary; 1963–67; E. L. Barnard; published for the National Foundation for Educational Research in England and Wales; Newnes Educational Publishing Co. Ltd. *

[61]
★**Reading for Understanding Placement Test.** Grades 3–16, 8–12; 1959–65; designed for use with the self-teaching reading exercises prepared by the same author; Thelma Gwinn Thurstone; Science Research Associates, Inc. *
a) [JUNIOR AND GENERAL EDITION.] Grades 3–16; 1959–63.
b) SENIOR EDITION. Grades 8–12; 1963–65.

[62]
Reading: Public School Achievement Tests. Grades 3–8; 1928–59; subtest of *Public School Achievement Tests;* Jacob S. Orleans; Bobbs-Merrill Co., Inc. *
For additional information, see 6:807. For reviews of the complete battery, consult the 2nd MMY.

[63]
Reading: Seven Plus Assessment: Northumberland Series. Ages 7–8; 1951; C. M. Lambert; University of London Press Ltd. *
For additional information, see 4:548. For a review of the complete battery, consult the 4th MMY.

[64]
Reading Test (Comprehension and Speed): Municipal Tests: National Achievement Tests. Grades 3–6, 6–8; 1938–57; subtest of *Municipal Battery;* 5 scores: following directions, sentence meaning, paragraph meaning, reading speed, total; Robert K. Speer and Samuel Smith; Psychometric Affiliates. *
For additional information, see 5:648. For reviews of the complete battery, consult the 5th, 4th, and 2nd MMY's.

[65]
*****SRA Achievement Series: Reading.** Grades 1–2, 2–4, 3–4, 4–9; 1954–67; subtest of *SRA Achievement Series* (6:21); 4 levels; 2 editions; Louis P. Thorpe, D. Welty Lefever, and Robert A. Naslund; Science Research Associates, Inc. *
a) [ORIGINAL EDITION.] Grades 1–2, 2–4, 4–9; 1954–64; 3 levels.
  1) *Grades 1–2.* 1954–63; 5 scores: verbal-pictorial association, language perception, comprehension, vocabulary, total.
  2) *Grades 2–4.* 1954–64; 3 scores: comprehension, vocabulary, total.
  3) *Grades 4–9 (Multilevel Edition).* 1963–64; 3 scores: comprehension, vocabulary, total.
b) MACHINE-SCORABLE EDITION. Grades 1–2, 3–4; 1954–67; 2 levels.
  1) *Grades 1–2.* 1954–67; 5 scores as in original edition; uses same content as original edition but with some differences in timing, sequence of items, and combinations of stems, responses, and items.
  2) *Grades 3–4.* 1954–66; 3 scores as in original edition; based upon material from the original editions.
For additional information and a review by Edward B. Fry, see 6:808; for reviews by N. Dale Bryant and Clarence Derrick, see 5:649. For reviews of the complete battery, consult the 6th and 5th MMY's.

[66]
SRA Reading Record. Grades 6–12; 1947–59; 5 scores: reading rate, comprehension, everyday reading skills, vocabulary, total; Guy T. Buswell; Science Research Associates, Inc. *
For additional information and a review by William W. Turnbull, see 4:550 (2 references); for a review by Frances Oralind Triggs, see 3:502 (1 excerpt).

[67]
Schrammel-Gray High School and College Reading Test. Grades 7–16; 1940–42; 3 scores: gross-comprehension, comprehension-efficiency, rate; H. E. Schrammel and W. H. Gray; Bobbs-Merrill Co., Inc. *
For additional information and reviews by James M. McCallister and Robert L. McCaul, see 3:500 (1 excerpt).

[68]
★**Secondary Reading Tests 1–3.** First four years of secondary schooling; 1961–66; S. M. Bate; published for the National Foundation for Educational Research in England and Wales; Newnes Educational Publishing Co. Ltd. *
a) TEST 1, VOCABULARY. 1961.
b) TEST 2, COMPREHENSION. 1961.
c) TEST 3, CONTINUOUS PROSE. 1965.

[69]
Sentence Reading Test 1. Ages 7-6 to 11-1; 1956–60; A. F. Watts; published for the National Foundation for Educational Research in England and Wales; Newnes Educational Publishing Co. Ltd. *
For additional information, see 6:809; for reviews by Reginald R. Dale and Stephen Wiseman, see 5:652.

[70]
Sequential Tests of Educational Progress: Reading. Grades 4–6, 7–9, 10–12, 13–14; 1956–63; Cooperative Test Division. *
For additional information and reviews by Emmett Albert Betts and Paul R. Lohnes, see 6:810 (6 references); for reviews by Eric F. Gardner, James R. Hobson, and Stephen Wiseman, see 5:653. For reviews of the complete battery, consult the 6th and 5th MMY's.

[71]
Silent Reading Comprehension: Iowa Every-Pupil Tests of Basic Skills, Test A. Grades 3–5, 5–9; 1940–47; 3 scores: reading comprehension, vocabulary, total; H. F. Spitzer, Ernest Horn, Maude McBroom, H. A. Greene, and E. F. Lindquist; Houghton Mifflin Co. *
For additional information, see 4:554; for reviews by James R. Hobson and Constance M. McCullough, see 3:501. For reviews of the complete battery, consult the 4th, 3rd, and 1st MMY's.

[72]
Silent Reading Tests. Standards 1–3 (ages 7–10), 3–8 (ages 10–15), 6–10 (ages 13–17); 1947–63; National Bureau of Educational and Social Research. *
a) SILENT READING TEST (ELEMENTARY). Standards 1–3; 1947–63; 4 tests.
  1) *Paragraphs.*
  2) *Sentences.*
  3) *Vocabulary.*
  4) *Speed.*
b) SILENT READING TESTS (REVISED EDITION). Standards 3–8, 6–10; 1947–63; 3–4 scores: vocabulary, paragraphs, sentences (junior level only), language usage.
For additional information, see 6:811.

[73]

Southgate Group Reading Tests. Ages 6-0 to 7-6, 7-0 to 8-11; 1960–62, c1959–62; Vera Southgate; University of London Press Ltd. *
a) TEST 1—WORD SELECTION. Ages 6-0 to 7-6; 1960–61, c1959.
b) TEST 2—SENTENCE COMPLETION TEST. Ages 7-0 to 8-11; 1962.
For additional information and reviews by M. L. Kellmer Pringle and Magdalen D. Vernon, see 6:812 (1 excerpt).

[74]

★**Stanford Achievement Test: High School Reading Test.** Grades 9–12; 1965–66; a subtest of the *Stanford Achievement Test: High School Battery;* catalog uses the title *Stanford High School Reading Test;* Eric F. Gardner, Jack C. Merwin, Robert Callis, and Richard Madden; Harcourt, Brace & World, Inc. *

[75]

★**Stanford Achievement Test: Reading Tests.** Grades 1.5–2.5, 2.5–4.0, 4–5.5, 5.5–6.9, 7–9; 1922–66; catalog uses the title *Stanford Reading Tests;* Truman L. Kelley, Richard Madden, Eric F. Gardner, and Herbert C. Rudman; Harcourt, Brace & World, Inc. *
a) PRIMARY I READING TESTS. Grades 1.5–2.5; 4 scores: word reading, paragraph meaning, vocabulary, word study skills.
b) PRIMARY 2 READING TESTS. Grades 2.5–4.0; 3 scores: word meaning, paragraph meaning, word study skills.
c) INTERMEDIATE I READING TESTS. Grades 4–5.5; 2 scores: word meaning, paragraph meaning.
d) INTERMEDIATE 2 READING TESTS. Grades 5.5–6.9; 2 scores: word meaning, paragraph meaning.
e) ADVANCED PARAGRAPH MEANING TEST. Grades 7–9.
For additional information, see 6:813 (1 reference); for reviews by Helen M. Robinson and Agatha Townsend of an earlier edition, see 5:656; for a review by James R. Hobson, see 4:555 (4 references); for a review by Margaret G. McKim, see 3:503. For reviews of the complete battery, consult the 6th, 5th, 4th, and 3rd MMY's.

[76]

★**Survey of Primary Reading Development.** Grades 1–2, 2–4; 1957–64; Richard Harsh and Dorothy Soeberg; Educational Testing Service (Western Office). *
a) FORMS A AND B. Grades 1–2; 1957.
b) FORMS C AND D. Grades 2–4; 1964.
For additional information and reviews by Thomas C. Barrett and Russell G. Stauffer, see 6:814.

[77]

Survey of Reading Achievement: California Survey Series. Grades 7–9, 9–12; 1959; all items from *California Reading Test, 1957 Edition;* Ernest W. Tiegs and Willis W. Clark; California Test Bureau. *
For additional information and reviews by Clarence Derrick and J. Raymond Gerberich, see 6:815.

[78]

Survey Tests of Reading. Grades 3–6, 7–13; 1931–32; L. J. O'Rourke; Psychological Institute. *
a) CENTRAL THOUGHT TEST. Grades 3–6, 7–13; 1931–32.
b) POWER TEST. Grades 3–13; 1931.

[79]

★**Tests of Academic Progress: Reading.** Grades 9, 10, 11, 12; 1964–65; a subtest of *Tests of Academic Progress;* 4 levels in a single booklet; Henry P. Smith under the direction of Dale P. Scannell; Houghton Mifflin Co. *

[80]

★**Tests of Reading: Cooperative Inter-American Tests.** Grades 1–3, 4–7, 8–13; 1950–67; a series of parallel tests and manuals in English and Spanish; for revised edition, see *Tests of Reading: Inter-American Series;* 3 scores: vocabulary, comprehension, total; Herschel T. Manuel; Guidance Testing Associates. *
a) PRIMARY LEVEL. Grades 1–3; 1950.
b) INTERMEDIATE LEVEL. Grades 4–7; 1950.
c) ADVANCED LEVEL. Grades 8–13; 1950.
For additional information, see 6:818 (4 references); for reviews by Jacob S. Orleans and Frederick L. Westover, see 4:557 (4 references).

[81]

★**Tests of Reading: Inter-American Series.** Grades 1–2, 2–3, 4–6, 7–9, 10–13; 1950–67; revision of *Tests of Reading; Cooperative Inter-American Tests;* earlier edition (see 80) still available; a series of parallel tests and manuals in English and Spanish; Herschel T. Manuel; Guidance Testing Associates. *
a) LEVEL 1, PRIMARY. Grades 1–2; 1966; 3 scores: vocabulary, comprehension, total.
b) LEVEL 2, PRIMARY. Grades 2–3; 1962; 5 scores: vocabulary, comprehension (level, speed, total), total.
c) LEVEL 3, ELEMENTARY. Grades 4–6; 1962; 5 scores as in *b.*
d) LEVEL 4, INTERMEDIATE. Grades 7–9; 1962; 5 scores as in *b.*
e) LEVEL 5, ADVANCED. Grades 10–13; 1962; 5 scores as in *b.*
For additional information concerning an earlier edition, see 6:818 (4 references).

[82]

★**Traxler High School Reading Test, Revised.** Grades 10–12; 1938–67; the revised test booklets copyrighted in 1966 are identical to the original 1938 and 1939 booklets except for minor changes in 3 items; 5 scores: rate, story comprehension, main ideas, total comprehension, total; Arthur E. Traxler; Bobbs-Merrill Co., Inc. *
For additional information and a review by Harold D. Carter, see 4:559 (4 references); for reviews by Alvin C. Eurich, Constance M. McCullough, and C. Gilbert Wrenn, see 2:1578 (2 excerpts).

[83]

Traxler Silent Reading Test. Grades 7–10; 1934–42; 6 scores: reading rate, story comprehension, word meaning, paragraph meaning, total comprehension, total; Arthur E. Traxler; Bobbs-Merrill Co., Inc. *
For additional information and a review by J. Thomas Hastings, see 4:560 (2 references); for reviews by Robert L. McCaul and Miles A. Tinker, see 2:1579 (3 references, 1 excerpt); for reviews by Frederick B. Davis and Spencer Shank, see 1:1114.

[84]

★**Van Wagenen Analytical Reading Scales.** Grades 4–6, 7–9, 10–13 for Form M; grades 5–7, 7–9, 9–11 for Form N; 1953–54; 6 or 7 scores: central thought, simple details, complex ideas, inferences, interpretation, total, word meaning (Form M only); M. J. Van Wagenen; Van Wagenen Psycho-Educational Laboratories. *
a) INTERMEDIATE DIVISION. Grades 4–6, 5–7; 1953.
b) JUNIOR DIVISION. Grades 7–9; 1953.
c) SENIOR DIVISION. Grades 10–13, 9–11; 1953–54.

[85]

★**W.A.L. English Comprehension Test.** High school; 1962–65; 4 scores: recognition vocabulary,

recall vocabulary, reading comprehension, total; Australian Council for Educational Research. *
For additional information, see 6:819.

[86]

Williams Primary Reading Test. Grades 1, 2–3; 1926–55; Allan J. Williams; Bobbs-Merrill Co., Inc. *
For additional information, see 5:658; for a review by Alice N. Jameson, see 3:508.

[87]

Williams Reading Test for Grades 4–9. Grades 4–9; 1929; Allan J. Williams; Bobbs-Merrill Co., Inc. *

OUT OF PRINT

[88]

[Ballard's Reading Tests.] Ages 6–10, 9–14; 1920–23; P. B. Ballard; University of London Press Ltd. *
Out of print.
a) ONE-MINUTE READING SCALE. Ages 6–10; 1920–23; reprinted from the author's *The New Examiner.*
b) SILENT READING TEST A. Ages 9–14; 1920; reprinted from the author's *Mental Tests.*
c) SILENT READING TEST B. Ages 9–14; 1923; reprinted from the author's *The New Examiner.*

[89]

Basic Reading Tests. Grades 1, 1–2, 2–3; 1935–36; 2 scores: word recognition, word attack; E. W. Dolch and W. S. Gray; Scott, Foresman & Co. * *Out of print.*
For additional information, see 1:1096.

[90]

The "Brighton" Reading Tests. Ages 8–14, 9–14; 1931; Educational Research Sub-Committee of the Brighton and Hove Teacher's Association; University of London Press Ltd. * *Out of print.*
For additional information and a review by Frederick B. Davis, see 2:1529.

[91]

Chapman Reading Comprehension Test. Grades 5–12; 1924–53; formerly called *Chapman Unspeeded Reading Comprehension Test;* J. C. Chapman; Educational Test Bureau. * *Out of print.*
For additional information and a review by Russell P. Kropp, see 5:623.

[92]

Chicago Reading Tests. Grades 1–2, 2–4, 4–6, 6–8; 1939–40; Max D. Engelhart and Thelma Gwinn Thurstone; E. M. Hale & Co. * *Out of print.*
a) TEST A. Grades 1–2; 6 scores: words, phrases, sentences, directions, paragraphs, total.
b) TEST B. Grades 2–4; 5 scores: words, sentences, story-directions-paragraphs, total, rate.
c) TEST C. Grades 4–6; 5 scores: words, sentences, story-maps-paragraphs, total, rate.
d) TEST D. Grades 6–8; 5 scores: words, sentences, story-maps-graphs-paragraphs, total, rate.
For additional information, see 3:478 (1 reference, 1 excerpt); for reviews by Robert Lawrence McCaul and W. J. Osburn, see 2:1531.

[93]

DeVault Primary Reading Test. Grades 1–2; 1931; Nellie N. DeVault; California Test Bureau. * *Out of print.*
For additional information and a review by Alice N. Jameson, see 3:479.

[94]

Elementary Reading: Every Pupil Test. Grades 4–6; 1936–65; Ohio Scholarship Tests. * *Out of print.*
a) GENERAL ABILITY.
b) SPEED AND COMPREHENSION. 2 scores: speed, comprehension.
For additional information, see 6:789.

[95]

English No. 1, Reading Comprehension: Midland Attainment Tests. Ages 6–14; [1938]; Raymond B. Cattell; University of London Press Ltd. * *Out of print.*
For additional information, see 1:1101.

[96]

Garrison First Year Reading Test. Grades 1B, 1A; 1938; title on test is *First Year Reading Test;* 5 scores: visual discrimination, auditory-visual discrimination, phrases and sentences, comprehension, total; Marie Garrison; C. A. Gregory Co. * *Out of print.*
For additional information and a review by Ruth Lowes, see 3:483 (2 references).

[97]

Garvey Primary Reading Test. Grades 1–3; 1931–36; Helen Sue Read and May V. Seagoe; California Test Bureau. * *Out of print.*
For additional information, see 4:533.

[98]

Gates Basic Reading Tests. Grades 3.5–8; 1926–58; revision of *Gates Silent Reading Tests;* Arthur I. Gates; Teachers College Press. * *Out of print.*
a) TYPE GS, READING TO APPRECIATE GENERAL SIGNIFICANCE.
b) TYPE UD, READING TO UNDERSTAND PRECISE DIRECTIONS.
c) TYPE ND, READING TO NOTE DETAILS.
d) TYPE RV, READING VOCABULARY.
e) TYPE LC, LEVEL OF COMPREHENSION.
For additional information and reviews by Albert N. Hieronymus and Arthur E. Traxler, see 6:791 (1 reference); for a review by S. S. Dunn, see 5:631 (1 reference); for reviews by George Spache, Herbert F. Spitzer, and T. L. Torgerson, see 3:485 (2 references); for reviews by Joseph C. Dewey and James R. Hobson, see 2:1539 (5 references, 1 excerpt).

[99]

General Reading Test: Ohio Senior Survey Tests. Grade 12; 1934–53; 4 scores: paragraph meaning, general vocabulary, outlining, total; S. L. Pressey and Maurice E. Troyer; Ohio Scholarship Tests. * *Out of print.*
For additional information, see 4:534.

[100]

Haggerty Reading Examination. Grades 1–3, 6–12; 1920–29; M. E. Haggerty, Margaret E. Noonan, and Laura C. Haggerty; Harcourt, Brace & World, Inc. * *Out of print.*
For additional information and a review by William S. Gray, see 4:535 (5 references).

[101]

Ingraham-Clark Diagnostic Reading Tests. Grades 1–3, 4–8; 1929; Jessie E. Ingraham and Willis W. Clark; California Test Bureau. * *Out of print.*
For additional information and a review by Katherine G. Keneally, see 4:538.

[102]

Kansas Primary Reading Test. Grades 1–3; 1935; 4 scores: sentence reading, word knowledge, paragraph comprehension, total; Alma Hoag, Emma Humble, Bertha Robinson, Adeline Wipf, and H. E. Schrammel; Bureau of Educational Measurements. * *Out of print.*

For additional information and a review by Nila Banton Smith, see 4:539; for a review by Alice K. Liveright, see 2:1549.

[103]

Los Angeles Primary Reading Test. Grades 1–3; 1925; Jessie E. Ingraham; California Test Bureau. * *Out of print.*

For additional information and a review by Nila Banton Smith, see 4:542 (1 reference).

[104]

Nelson-Lohmann Reading Test. Grades 4, 5, 6, 7, 8; 1946–54; identical with reading sections of *Coordinated Scales of Attainment;* Ethel V. Nelson and Victor L. Lohmann; Educational Test Bureau. * *Out of print.*

For additional information and a review by Jason Millman, see 6:801.

[105]

Primary Reading: Every Pupil Test. Grades 2–3; 1936–65; Ohio Scholarship Tests. * *Out of print.*

For additional information, see 6:804; for reviews by William S. Gray and Virginia Seavey of the 1946 forms, see 3:493.

[106]

Primary Reading Test. Grade 1; 1939–40; 5 scores: word recognition, word meaning, sentence meaning, paragraph meaning, total; Albert G. Reilley; Houghton Mifflin Co. * *Out of print.*

For additional information and a review by Ruth Lowes, see 3:494 (1 reference).

[107]

Sangren-Woody Reading Test. Grades 4–8; 1927–28; 8 scores: word meaning, rate, fact material, total meaning, central thought, following directions, organization, total; Paul V. Sangren and Clifford Woody; Harcourt, Brace & World, Inc. * *Out of print.*

For additional information and a review by David H. Russell, see 4:551; for a review by Alice K. Liveright, see 2:1565 (7 references).

[108]

Shank Tests of Reading Comprehension. Grades 3–6, 7–9, 10–12; 1929; Spencer Shank; C. A. Gregory Co. * *Out of print.*

For additional information and a review by William D. Sheldon, see 4:553; for a review by James R. Hobson, see 2:1567 (3 references).

[109]

Stone-Webster Test in Beginning Reading. Grade 1; 1936–37; 3 scores: word recognition, sentence comprehension, total; Clarence R. Stone; Webster Publishing Co. * *Out of print.*

For additional information and a review by Ruth Lowes, see 3:504 (1 reference).

[110]

Techniques in Reading Comprehension: Every Pupil Test. Grades 7–9, 10–12; 1937–65; test booklet titles vary; Ohio Scholarship Tests. * *Out of print.*

For additional information, see 6:816; for reviews by Ivan A. Booker and James M. McCallister, see 3:505.

[111]

Thorndike-Lorge Reading Test. Grades 7–9; 1941–47; E. L. Thorndike and Irving Lorge; Teachers College Press. * *Out of print.*

For additional information and a review by Ivan A. Booker, see 4:558 (1 reference); for a review by Robert L. McCaul, see 3:506 (1 excerpt).

[112]

Unit Scales of Attainment in Reading. Grades 1B, 1A, 2B, 2A, 3, 3–4, 5–6, 7–8, 9–12; 1932–43; subtest of *Unit Scales of Attainment;* 1 or 2 scores: vocabulary (grades 1–3), comprehension; M. J. Van Wagenen; Educational Test Bureau. * *Out of print.*

For additional information and reviews by Ivan A. Booker and J. Wayne Wrightstone, see 2:1581; for a review by Joseph C. Dewey, see 1:1115.

[113]

Whipple's High-School and College Reading Test. Grades 9–16; 1925; Guy M. Whipple; Public School Publishing Co. * *Out of print.*

For additional information and a review by Frederick B. Davis, see 3:507 (3 references).

[114]

Ypsilanti Reading Test. Grades 6–8; 1940; 4 scores: rate, comprehension, vocabulary, total; B. H. Vanden Belt and Thelma McAndless; Hillsdale School Supply Co. * *Out of print.*

For additional information, see 2:1583.1.

DIAGNOSTIC

[115]

California Phonics Survey. Grades 7–12 and college; 1956–63; shortened version of *Stanford Diagnostic Phonics Survey, Research Edition* (see 5:670); 9 error analysis scores for Form 1 (Form 2 yields total score only): long-short vowel confusion, other vowel confusion, consonants-confusion with blends and digraphs, consonant-vowel reversals, configuration, endings, negatives-opposites-sight words, rigidity, total; Grace M. Brown and Alice B. Cottrell; California Test Bureau. *

For additional information and a review by Thomas E. Culliton, Jr., see 6:820 (1 reference).

[116]

★**Classroom Reading Inventory.** Grades 2–8; 1965; 6 scores: word recognition, independent reading level, instructional reading level, frustration level, hearing capacity level, spelling; Nicholas J. Silvaroli; Wm. C. Brown Book Co. *

[117]

★**The Denver Public Schools Reading Inventory.** Grades 1–8; 1965; 2 scores (instructional level, independent level) and ratings of areas of both strength and weakness; reading selections taken from the *Sheldon Basic Reading Series;* Department of General Curriculum Services, Denver Public Schools. *

[118]

Diagnostic Reading Examination for Diagnosis of Special Difficulty in Reading. Grades 1–4; [1928–29]; a combination of assessment procedures consisting of the *Revised Stanford-Binet Scale,* Gray's *Standardized Oral Reading Paragraphs, Monroe's Standardized Silent Reading Tests,* an adaptation of *Ayres Spelling Scale,* the arithmetic computation subtest of *Stanford Achievement Test: Arithmetic,* and 9 additional tests: alphabet repeating and reading, *Iota Word Test,* letter naming, recognition of orientation, mirror reading, mirror writing, number reversals, word discrimination, sounding; Marion Monroe [Cox]; C. H. Stoelting Co. *

[119]

Diagnostic Reading Scales. Grades 1–8 and retarded readers in grades 9–12; 1963; 10 or 11 scores: word recognition, instructional level (oral reading), independent level (silent reading), rate of silent reading (optional), potential level (auditory comprehension), and 6 phonics scores (consonant sounds, vowel sounds, consonant blends, common syllables, blending, letter sounds); George D. Spache; California Test Bureau. *

For additional information and a review by N. Dale Bryant, see 6:821.

[120]

Diagnostic Reading Test: Pupil Progress Series. Grades 1.9–2.1, 2.2–3, 4–6, 7–8; 1956–65; various titles used by publisher; catalog uses the title *PPS Diagnostic Reading Tests;* some subtests also appear in *Scholastic Diagnostic Reading Test* for Catholic schools; Oliver F. Anderhalter, R. Stephen Gawkoski, and Ruth Colestock; Scholastic Testing Service, Inc. *
a) PRIMARY TEST 1. Grades 1.9–2.1; 9 scores: vocabulary (word recognition, word to content relation, words in use, total), rate of reading for meaning, comprehension (recalling information, locating information, reading for descriptions, total).
b) PRIMARY TEST 2. Grades 2.2–3; 10 scores: vocabulary (words in use, word meaning, total), rate of reading for meaning, comprehension (same as for *a* plus following directions, reading for meaning).
c) ELEMENTARY TEST. Grades 4–6; 13 scores: knowledge and use of sources (functions, best sources, use of index, use of table of contents, total), rate of reading for meaning, comprehension (same as for *a* plus word meaning, reading for meaning, reading for directions or procedures).
d) ADVANCED TEST. Grades 7–8; 13 scores: same as for *c*.

For additional information and a review by Agatha Townsend, see 6:822.

[121]

Diagnostic Reading Tests. Various grades kgn–13; 1947–66; Committee on Diagnostic Reading Tests, Inc. *
a) DIAGNOSTIC READING TESTS: KINDERGARTEN THROUGH FOURTH GRADES. Various grades kgn–4 (except for section 4, part 1); 1957–63.
　1) *Survey Section.* Grades kgn–1, 1, 2, 3–4; 1957–63.
　　(*a*) Reading Readiness Booklet. Grades kgn–1; 5 scores: relationships, eye-hand coordination, visual discrimination, auditory discrimination, vocabulary.
　　(*b*) Booklet 1. Grade 1; 12 scores: visual discrimination, auditory discrimination (3 subscores plus total), vocabulary (3 subscores plus total), story reading (2 subscores plus total).
　　(*c*) Booklet 2. Grade 2; 3 scores: word recognition, comprehension, total.
　　(*d*) Booklet 3. Grades 3–4; scores same as for (*c*) above.
　2) *Section 4: Word Attack, Part 1: Oral.* Grades 1–8; 1958.
b) DIAGNOSTIC READING TESTS: LOWER LEVEL. Grades 4–8; 1947–63.
　1) *Survey Section.* Grades 4–8; 1952–63. Also distributed by Science Research Associates, Inc.
　　(*a*) Booklet 1: Part 1, Word Recognition and Comprehension. 2 scores: word recognition, comprehension.
　　(*b*) Booklet 2: Parts 2 and 3, Vocabulary-Story Reading. 3 scores: vocabulary, rate of reading, story comprehension.
　2) *Section 4: Word Attack.* Various grades 1–13; 1947–63.
　　(*a*) Part 1, Oral. Grades 1–8; see *a*2 above.
　　(*b*) Part 2, Silent. Grades 4–13; 3 scores: identification of sounds, syllabication, total.
c) DIAGNOSTIC READING TESTS: [UPPER LEVEL]. Grades 7–13; 1947–66.
　1) *Survey Section.* 1947–66; the 1966 revisions of Forms A and B are identical to the original 1947 tests except for the substitution of a new reading selection in Part 3; 5 scores: rate of reading, comprehension check, vocabulary, total comprehension, total. Also distributed by Science Research Associates, Inc.
　2) *Section 1: Vocabulary (Revised).* 1947–63; 5 scores: English, mathematics, science, social studies, total.
　3) *Section 2: Comprehension: Silent and Auditory.* 1947–63; may be administered as a listening comprehension test.
　4) *Section 3: Rates of Reading: Part 1, General.* 1947–63; 4 scores: normal rate of reading, comprehension at normal rate, maximum rate of reading, comprehension at maximum rate.
　5) *Section 4: Word Attack.* 1947–63.
　　(*a*) Part 1, Oral. 1948–58.
　　(*b*) Part 2, Silent. Grades 4–13; see *b*2(*b*) above.
For additional information and reviews by Albert J. Kingston and B. H. Van Roekel, see 6:823 (21 references); for reviews by Frederick B. Davis, William W. Turnbull, and Henry Weitz, see 4:531 (19 references).

[122]

Doren Diagnostic Reading Test of Word Recognition Skills. Grades 1–9; 1956–64; 12 scores: letter recognition, beginning sounds, whole word recognition, words within words, speech consonants, ending sounds, blending, rhyming, vowels, sight words, discriminate guessing, total; Margaret Doren; American Guidance Service, Inc. *

For additional information and reviews by B. H. Van Roekel and Verna L. Vickery, see 5:659.

[123]

Durrell Analysis of Reading Difficulty, New Edition. Grades 1–6; 1937–55, c1933–55; Donald D. Durrell; Harcourt, Brace & World, Inc. *

For additional information and reviews by James Maxwell and George D. Spache, see 5:660; for a review by Helen M. Robinson, see 4:561 (2 references); for reviews by Guy L. Bond and Miles A. Tinker, see 2:1533; for a review by Marion Monroe [Cox], see 1:1098.

[124]

Gates-McKillop Reading Diagnostic Tests. Grades 2–0 to 6–0; 1926–62; revision of *Gates Reading Diagnostic Tests;* 28 scores: omissions, additions, repetitions, 8 mispronunciation scores (reversals, partial reversals, total reversals, wrong beginnings, wrong middle, wrong ending, wrong in several parts, total mispronunciations), oral reading total, words—flash presentation, words—untimed presentation, phrases—flash presentation, recognizing and blending common word parts, giving letter sounds, naming capital letters naming lower-case letters, 4 scores for recognizing the visual form of sounds (nonsense words, initial letters final letters, vowels), auditory blending, spelling, oral vocabulary, syllabication, auditory discrimination; Arthur I. Gates and Anne S. McKillop; Teachers College Press. *

For additional information and reviews by N. Dale Bryant and Gabriel M. Della-Piana, see 6:824 (2 references); for a review by George D. Spache, see 5:662; for a review by Worth J. Osburn, see 4:563 (2 references); for related reviews, see 4:564 (2 excerpts); for a review by T. L. Torgerson, see 3:510 (3 references).

[125]

Group Diagnostic Reading Aptitude and Achievement Tests. Grades 3–9; 1939; 15 scores: reading (paragraph understanding, speed), word discrimination (vowels, consonants, reversals, additions and omissions), arithmetic, spelling, visual ability (letter memory, form memory), auditory ability (letter memory, discrimination and orientation), motor ability (copying text, crossing out letters), vocabulary; Marion Monroe [Cox] and Eva Edith Sherman; C. H. Nevins Printing Co. *

For additional information, see 6:825.

[126]

Individual Reading Test. Ages 5.6–9.6; 1935–36; 3 scores: oral word reading, comprehension, speed; L. W. Allen; Australian Council for Educational Research. *

For additional information and a review by R. W. McCulloch, see 5:663.

[127]

*McCullough Word-Analysis Tests. Grades 4–6; 1962–63, c1960–63; 10 scores: initial blends and digraphs, phonetic discrimination, matching letters to vowel sounds, sounding whole words, interpreting phonetic symbols, phonetic analysis total, dividing words into syllables, root words in affixed forms, structural-analysis total, total; Constance M. McCullough; Personnel Press, Inc. *

For additional information and reviews by Emery P. Bliesmer and Albert J. Harris, see 6:826.

[128]

*OC Diagnostic Syllabizing Test. Grades 4–6; 1960–62; formerly called OC Diagnostic Syllable Test; Katherine O'Connor; O'Connor Reading Clinic Publishing Co. *

For additional information, see 6:827.

[129]

*Ohio Diagnostic Reading Test. Grades 2.5–4.5, 4.5–8.5; 1966; although not so identified, this test is made up of 3 subtests taken from Form W and 4 or 5 subtests taken from Form X of the Stanford Diagnostic Reading Test; Bjorn Karlsen, Richard Madden, and Eric F. Gardner; Ohio Testing Services. *

a) LEVEL 1. Grades 2.5–4.5; 7 scores: comprehension, vocabulary, auditory discrimination, syllabication, beginning and ending sounds, blending, sound discrimination; 3 subtests from the Stanford Form W and 4 from Form X.

b) LEVEL 2. Grades 4.5–8.5; 8 scores: comprehension (literal, inferential, total), vocabulary, syllabication, sound discrimination, blending, rate; 3 subtests from the Stanford Form W and 5 from Form X.

[130]

Phonics Knowledge Survey. Grades 1–6; 1964; Dolores Durkin and Leonard Meshover; Teachers College Press. *

For additional information, see 6:828.

[131]

Phonovisual Diagnostic Test. Grades 3–12; 1949–58; formerly called Phonovisual Diagnostic Spelling Test; phonetic weaknesses; Lucille D. Schoolfield and Josephine B. Timberlake; Phonovisual Products, Inc. *

For additional information and reviews by Charles M. Brown and George D. Spache, see 6:829.

[132]

*Primary Reading Profiles. Grades 1, 2; 1953–68, c1953–57; 6 scores: reading aptitude, auditory association, word recognition, word attack, reading comprehension, total; the 1967 machine scored (MRC) edition is identical in content with the 1957 hand scored edition; James B. Stroud, Albert N. Hieronymus, and Paul McKee; Houghton Mifflin Co. *

For additional information and reviews by James R. Hobson and Verna L. Vickery, see 5:665.

[133]

★Reading Skills Diagnostic Test. Grades 2–8; 1967; 9 scores: letter identification, letter-sound identification, phonetic sounds, phonetic words, inconsistent words, consistent phrases, inconsistent phrases, letters in context, words in context; Richard H. Bloomer; Brador Publications, Inc. *

[134]

Roswell-Chall Auditory Blending Test. Grades 1–4; 1963; Florence G. Roswell and Jeanne S. Chall; Essay Press, Inc. *

For additional information and reviews by Ira E. Aaron and B. H. Van Roekel, see 6:830 (2 references).

[135]

Roswell-Chall Diagnostic Reading Test of Word Analysis Skills. Grades 2–6; 1956–59; Florence G. Roswell and Jeanne S. Chall; Essay Press, Inc. *

For additional information and reviews by Ira E. Aaron and Emmett Albert Betts, see 6:831 (1 reference); for a review by Byron H. Van Roekel, see 5:667.

[136]

The Schonell Reading Tests. Ages 5–15, 6–9, 7–11, 9–13; 1942–55; Fred J. Schonell; Oliver & Boyd Ltd. *

a) TEST R1, GRADED WORD READING TEST. Ages 5–15; 1942; also called Graded Reading Vocabulary Test.
b) TEST R2, SIMPLE PROSE READING TEST. Ages 6–9; 1942; also called My Dog Test.
c) TEST R3, SILENT READING TEST A. Ages 7–11; 1942.
d) TEST R4, SILENT READING TEST B. Ages 9–13; 1942.
e) TEST R5, TEST OF ANALYSIS AND SYNTHESIS OF WORDS CONTAINING COMMON PHONIC UNITS.
f) TEST R6, TEST OF DIRECTIONAL ATTACK ON WORDS.
g) TEST R7, VISUAL WORD DISCRIMINATION TEST.

For additional information and a review by R. W. McCulloch, see 5:651 (4 references); for a review by M. L. Kellmer Pringle, see 4:552 (3 references); for a review by Edith I. M. Thomson, see 3:499.

[137]

Silent Reading Diagnostic Tests: The Developmental Reading Tests. Grades 3–8; 1955; 20 scores: recognition pattern (6 scores), error analysis (4 scores), recognition techniques (9 scores), word synthesis; Guy L. Bond, Theodore Clymer, and Cyril J. Hoyt; Lyons & Carnahan. *

For additional information and reviews by Emery P. Bliesmer and Albert J. Kingston, see 6:832 (1 reference).

[138]
★**Standard Reading Inventory.** Grades 1–7; 1966, c1963–66; 4 scores (independent reading level, minimum instructional level, maximum instructional level, frustration level), 6 to 9 subtest scores (vocabulary in isolation, vocabulary in context, oral word recognition errors, total oral errors, recall after oral reading, recall after silent reading, total comprehension, oral speed, silent speed) at each of 11 reading levels, and various ratings and checklistings; Robert A. McCracken; Pioneer Printing Co. *

[139]
The Standard Reading Tests. Reading ages up to 9-0; 1958; J. C. Daniels and Hunter Diack; Chatto & Windus Ltd. *
a) TEST 1, THE STANDARD TEST OF READING SKILL.
b) TEST 2, COPYING ABSTRACT FIGURES.
c) TEST 3, COPYING A SENTENCE.
d) TEST 4, VISUAL DISCRIMINATION AND ORIENTATION TEST.
e) TEST 5, LETTER-RECOGNITION TEST.
f) TEST 6, AURAL DISCRIMINATION TEST.
g) TEST 7, DIAGNOSTIC WORD-RECOGNITION TESTS.
h) TEST 8, ORAL WORD-RECOGNITION TEST.
i) TEST 9, PICTURE WORD-RECOGNITION TEST.
j) TEST 10, SILENT PROSE-READING AND COMPREHENSION TEST.
k) TEST 11, GRADED SPELLING TEST.
l) TEST 12, GRADED TEST OF READING EXPERIENCE.
For additional information and a review by L. B. Birch, see 6:833 (1 reference).

[140]
★**Stanford Diagnostic Reading Test.** Grades 2.5–4.5, 4.5–8.5; 1966; Bjorn Karlsen, Richard Madden, and Eric F. Gardner; Harcourt, Brace & World, Inc. *
a) LEVEL 1. Grades 2.5–4.5; 7 scores: comprehension, vocabulary, auditory discrimination, syllabication, beginning and ending sounds, blending, sound discrimination.
b) LEVEL 2. Grades 4.5–8.5; 8 scores: comprehension (literal, inferential, total), vocabulary, syllabication, sound discrimination, blending, rate.

[141]
★**Test of Individual Needs in Reading, Sixth Edition.** Grades 1–6; 1961–66; test booklet title is *John Bidwell and the Trail to California;* 20 scores: oral reading, comprehension, rate, word analysis (use of context, words beginning alike, beginning consonants, ending consonants, consonant substitutions, speech consonants, consonant blends, reversals, long and short vowels, vowel blends, blending letter sounds, prefixes, suffixes, compound words, recognizing syllables, syllabication, total); Hap Gilliland; Montana Reading Clinic Publications. *

OUT OF PRINT

[142]
Hildreth Diagnostic Reading Record. Grades 1–16; 1939; a blank to help summarize data of reading disability cases; Gertrude Hildreth; Psychological Corporation. * *Out of print.*
For additional information, see 2:1541.

[143]
McGuffey Diagnostic Reading Test. Grades 4–6; 1955; 5 scores: syllables, sound value recognition, vocabulary, appreciation, understanding; Ullin W. Leavell; American Guidance Service, Inc. * *Out of print.*
For additional information, see 5:664.

[144]
Reading Diagnostic Record for High School and College Students. High school and college; 1938–52; formerly called *Examiner's Reading Diagnostic Record for High School and College Students;* Ruth Strang with the assistance of Margaret M. Conant, Margaret G. McKim, and Mary Alice Mitchell; Teachers College Press. * *Out of print.*
For additional information and reviews by Marvin D. Glock and Donald E. P. Smith, see 5:666; for reviews by Robert Murray Bear and Carolyn M. Welch, see 3:509; for a review by Henry D. Rinsland, see 2:1535 (3 excerpts).

[145]
Record for Reading Diagnosis. Grades 1–8; 1936; C. R. Stone; Webster Publishing Co. * *Out of print.*
For additional information and a review by Carolyn M. Welch, see 3:512.

[146]
Scholastic Diagnostic Reading Test. Grades 1–3, 4–6, 7–9; 1953–55; for Catholic schools; some subtests also appear in *Diagnostic Reading Test: Pupil Progress Series* for non-Catholic schools; Oliver F. Anderhalter, Ruth Colestock, and R. Stephen Gawkowski; Scholastic Testing Service, Inc. * *Out of print.*
a) PRIMARY TEST. Grades 1–3; 11 scores: vocabulary (word recognition, word meaning, word use, total), rate, comprehension (reading for recall, reading for location of information, reading for meaning, reading for directions or procedures, reading for descriptions, total).
b) ELEMENTARY TEST. Grades 4–6; 13 scores: knowledge and use of sources (functions, best sources, use of index, use of table of contents, total), rate of reading for meaning, comprehension (same as for *a* plus word meaning).
c) ADVANCED TEST. Grades 7–9; 13 scores: same as for *b.*
For additional information and reviews by Russell G. Stauffer and Arthur E. Traxler, see 5:650.

MISCELLANEOUS

[147]
Basic Sight Word Test. Grades 1–2; 1942; Edward W. Dolch; Garrard Publishing Co. *

[148]
*★Botel Reading Inventory.** Grades 1–12; 1961–66; reading instructional level and placement of reading materials; 3 tests; *b* and *c* yield 4 ratings: free reading level, highest instructional level, highest potential level, frustration level; Morton Botel; Follett Publishing Co. *
a) PHONICS MASTERY TEST. 4 areas: consonants, vowels, syllabication, nonsense words.
b) WORD RECOGNITION TEST.
c) WORD OPPOSITES TEST. May be administered as a reading or listening test.
For additional information and reviews by Ira E. Aaron and Charles M. Brown, see 6:834.

[149]
Cumulative Reading Record, 1956 Revision. Grades 9–12; 1933–56; revision of a record by Margaret M. Skinner; National Council of Teachers of English. *

[150]

Durrell-Sullivan Reading Capacity and Achievement Tests. Grades 2.5–4.5, 3–6; 1937–45; 3–5 scores: word meaning, paragraph meaning, total, spelling (optional), written recall (optional); Donald D. Durrell and Helen Blair Sullivan; Harcourt, Brace & World, Inc. *
a) READING CAPACITY TEST.
b) READING ACHIEVEMENT TEST.
For additional information and a review by James Maxwell, see 5:661 (5 references); for a review by Helen M. Robinson, see 4:562 (4 references); for reviews by William S. Gray and Marion Monroe [Cox], see 1:1099 (1 excerpt).

[151]

Functional Readiness Questionnaire for School and College Students. Grades 1–16; 1957; reports by pupil and teacher on physical and emotional problems related to reading difficulties and school problems; Earl A. Taylor and Harold A. Solan; Taylor Center for Controlled Reading and Research. *
For additional information, see 6:835.

[152]

★**Gilliland Learning Potential Examination.** Ages 6 and over; 1966; an intelligence test "for use with remedial readers and the culturally disadvantaged"; 4 scores: nonreading and noncultural, predicted comprehension, total, visual memory; Hap Gilliland; Montana Reading Clinic Publications. *

[153]

*****Learning Methods Test.** Grades kgn, 1, 2, 3; 1954–54; comparative effectiveness of four methods of teaching new words: visual, phonic, kinesthetic, combination; Robert E. Mills; Mills Center, Inc. *
For additional information and reviews by Thomas E. Culliton, Jr. and William Eller, see 6:836 (1 reference).

[154]

*****The Reader Rater With Self-Scoring Profile.** Ages 15 and over; 1959–65; self-administered survey of reading skills; 12 scores: speed, comprehension, reading habits, reading for details, reading for inferences, reading for main ideas and adjusting speed, summarizing, skimming, recall of information read, unspeeded vocabulary, speeded vocabulary, total; designed for use either with the Rapid Reading Kit or separately; Better Reading Program, Inc. *
For additional information, see 6:837.

[155]

★**The Reader's Inventory.** Entrants to a reading improvement course for secondary and college students and adults; 1963; information concerning a student's reading interests, attitudes, habits, visual conditions, educational and vocational background, and what he expects to gain from a reading course; George D. Spache and Stanford E. Taylor; Educational Developmental Laboratories, Inc. *

[156]

The Reading Eye. Grades 1, 2, 3, 4, 5, 6, 7–8, 9–16 and adults; 1959–60; an eye-movement camera with test materials; 5 reading component scores (fixations, regressions, average span of recognition, average duration of fixation, rate with comprehension), 3 ratings (grade level of fundamental reading skill, relative efficiency, directional attack), and 2 diagnostic categories (visual adjustment, general adjustment to reading); Stanford E. Taylor and [Helen Frackenpohl]; Educational Developmental Laboratories, Inc. *

For additional information and reviews by Arthur S. McDonald and George D. Spache, see 6:838 (3 references).

[157]

*****Reading Versatility Test.** Grades 5–8, 6–10, 8–12, 12–16; 1961–68; reading flexibility; Arthur S. McDonald, Mary Alodia (*a, b*), Stanford E. Taylor (*a*2), Harold M. Nason (*b*), George Zimny (*c*), and James Byrne (*c*); Educational Developmental Laboratories, Inc. *
a) BASIC.
  1) [*Paper and Pencil Edition.*] Grades 5–8; 1961–67; 8 scores: rate of reading (2 scores), comprehension (2 scores), skimming (rate, comprehension), scanning (rate, comprehension).
  2) [*Reading Eye Edition.*] Grades 6–10; 1961–62; administered using the publisher's eye-movement camera; 29 scores: 5 scores (comprehension, rate, fixations per 100 words, duration of fixation, apparent number of lines) for each of 5 exercises, and 2 scores (regressions per 100 words, span of recognition) for each of 2 exercises.
b) INTERMEDIATE. Grades 8–12; 1962–68; 8 scores: same as for *a*1.
c) ADVANCED. Grades 12–16; 1962–68; 8 scores: same as for *a*1.
For additional information, see 6:839 (1 reference).

[158]

★**SRA Reading Checklist.** Grades 1–8; 1966; 38 ratings by teachers in 3 categories: preparation for reading, values in reading, mechanics of reading; Science Research Associates, Inc. *

[159]

★**Screening Tests for Identifying Children With Specific Language Disability.** "Average to high IQ" children in grades 1–2.5, 2–3.5, 3.5–4; 1964–67; c1962–67; 8 tests (visual copying—far point, visual copying—near point, visual perception memory for words, visual discrimination, visual perception memory in association with kinesthetic memory, auditory recall, auditory perception of beginning and ending sounds, auditory associations) with 7 scores for each (right, wrong, total, recall confusion—self-correction, reversals, letter form errors, omission errors), plus echolalia test (individual and optional); Beth H. Slingerland; Educators Publishing Service, Inc. *

OUT OF PRINT

[160]

Instructional Reading Tests for the Intermediate Grades. Grades 4, 5, 6; 1938–39; 4 scores: general significance, details, logical outcomes, vocabulary; M. J. Nelson; Houghton Mifflin Co. * *Out of print.*
For additional information, see 2:1543.

[161]

Inventory of Reading Experiences. Grades 9–16; 1940, c1938–40; 2 scores: quality, quantity; Frederick L. Pond; Stanford University Press. * *Out of print.*
For additional information and a review by Albert J. Harris, see 3:511 (2 references).

[162]

The Master Ophthalmograph. Grades 1–16 and adults; 1936–47; a camera, using 35 mm. standard motion picture film, for photographing eye movements while the examinee reads; developed by the Bureau of Visual Science of the American Optical Company and the Research Division of the Eastman Kodak Company; American Optical Co. * *Out of print.*

For additional information and a review by Miles A. Tinker, see 4:660 (8 references); see also 3:470 (15 references); for a review by G. T. Buswell of an earlier model, see 2:1559 (2 references, 2 excerpts); for reviews by Stella S. Center, David Kopel, Marion Monroe [Cox], Joseph Tiffin, and Miles A. Tinker, see 1:1108 (1 excerpt).

[163]

SRA Achievement Series: Language Perception. Grades 2–4; 1954–57; title on test is *Are These the Same?*; 3 scores: auditory discrimination, visual discrimination, sight vocabulary; Louis P. Thorpe, D. Welty Lefever, and Robert A. Naslund; Science Research Associates, Inc. * *Out of print.*
For additional information, see 5:668.

ORAL

[164]

Flash-X Sight Vocabulary Test. Grades 1–2; 1961; 2 scores: sight vocabulary, experience vocabulary; George D. Spache and Stanford E. Taylor; Educational Developmental Laboratories, Inc. *
For additional information, see 6:841.

[165]

Gilmore Oral Reading Test. Grades 1–8; 1951–52; 3 scores: accuracy, comprehension, rate; John V. Gilmore; Harcourt, Brace & World, Inc. *
For additional information and reviews by Lydia A. Duggins and Maynard C. Reynolds, see 5:671 (1 reference).

[166]

Graded Vocabulary Tests. Ages 5–21; 1921–38; pronunciation; University of London Press Ltd. *
a) THE BURT (REARRANGED) WORD READING TEST. Ages 5–14; 1921–38; rearrangement for Scottish schools by Philip E. Vernon; original test by Cyril Burt.
b) GRADED WORD READING TEST. Ages 5–21; 1938; for use in Scottish schools.

[167]

Gray Oral Reading Test. Grades 1–16 and adults; 1963–67; the 1967 revised manual is identical to the original manual except for new norms for grade 1 and a table of norms for boys and girls combined; edited by Helen M. Robinson; William S. Gray; Bobbs-Merrill Co., Inc. *
For additional information and reviews by Emery P. Bliesmer, Albert J. Harris, and Paul R. Lohnes, see 6:842.

[168]

Holborn Reading Scale. Ages 5.5–11.0; 1948; 2 scores: word recognition, comprehension; A. F. Watts; George G. Harrap & Co. Ltd. *
For additional information and a review by Stanley Nisbet, see 5:635 (1 reference); for a review by C. M. Fleming, see 4:537.

[169]

Neale Analysis of Reading Ability. Ages 6–12; 1957–58; 3 scores (accuracy, comprehension, rate of reading) plus 3 optional supplementary tests (names and sounds of letters, auditory discrimination through simple spelling, blending and recognition of syllables); Marie D. Neale; Macmillan & Co. Ltd. * (United States publisher: St Martin's Press, Inc.)

For additional information and reviews by M. Alan Brimer and Magdalen D. Vernon, see 6:843 (1 excerpt).

[170]

Oral Diagnostic Test of Word-Analysis Skills, Primary: Dominion Tests. Grades 1–2; 1947; Department of Educational Research, Ontario College of Education, University of Toronto; distributed by Guidance Centre. *
For additional information and a review by S. A. Rayner, see 5:673; for a review by Nila Banton Smith, see 4:565.

[171]

Oral Word Reading Test. Ages 7–11; 1952; A. E. Fieldhouse; New Zealand Council for Educational Research. *
For additional information and reviews by S. A. Rayner and D. K. Wheeler, see 5:674.

[172]

Slosson Oral Reading Test (SORT). Grades 1–8 and high school; 1963; Richard L. Slosson; Slosson Educational Publications. *
For additional information, see 6:844.

[173]

Standardized Oral Reading Check Tests. Grades 1–2, 2–4, 4–6, 6–8; 1923–55; 2 scores: rate, accuracy; William S. Gray; Bobbs-Merrill Co., Inc. *
For additional information and reviews by David H. Russell and Clarence R. Stone, see 2:1570 (1 reference).

[174]

Standardized Oral Reading Paragraphs. Grades 1–8; 1915; William S. Gray; Bobbs-Merrill Co., Inc. *
For additional information and reviews by David Kopel and Clarence R. Stone, see 2:1571 (7 references).

OUT OF PRINT

[175]

Articulation Test With Reading Disability Feature. Grades 3–12; no date; I. Sherman; the Author. * *Out of print.*
For additional information and a review by Irving H. Anderson, see 1:1095.

[176]

Graded Word Reading Test, Test 1. Ages 4–14; 1921; pronunciation; reprinted from the author's *Mental and Scholastic Tests;* Cyril Burt; Staples Press Ltd. * *Out of print.*

[177]

Jenkins Oral Reading Test: Individualized Oral Diagnostic Test for Children With Serious Reading Difficulties. Children whose reading ability falls within the range of normal children in grades 1–3; 1939; Frances Jenkins; C. A. Gregory Co. * *Out of print.*
For additional information and reviews by Guy L. Bond, David Kopel, and Clarence R. Stone, see 2:1548.

[178]

Kindergarten-Primary Articulation Test. 1935–37; I. Sherman and B. Kenevan; the Authors. * *Out of print.*
For additional information and a review by Irving H. Anderson, see 1:1104.

[179]

Leavell Analytical Oral Reading Test. Grades 1–10; 1952–53; [Ullin W. Leavell]; American Guidance Service, Inc. * *Out of print.*

For additional information and reviews by Lydia A. Duggins and Maynard C. Reynolds, see 5:672.

READINESS

[179.1]

★**The ABC Inventory to Determine Kindergarten and School Readiness.** Entrants to kgn and grade 1; 1965; Normand Adair and George Blesch; Research Concepts. *

[180]

*****American School Reading Readiness Test, Revised.** First grade entrants; 1941–64; 1964 revision (Form X) is identical with Forms A ('41) and Forms D ('55) except for changes in the titles and sequence of subtests and slight changes in format and drawings; Willis E. Pratt, George W. Stouffer (Form X), Robert V. Young (Forms A and D), and Carroll A. Whitmer (Forms A and D); Bobbs-Merrill Co., Inc. *

For additional information and reviews by Joan Bollenbacher and Helen M. Robinson, see 5:675 (3 references); for reviews by David H. Russell and Paul A. Witty, see 3:513.

[181]

The Anton Brenner Developmental Gestalt Test of School Readiness. Ages 5–6; 1964; Anton Brenner; Western Psychological Services. *

For additional information, see 6:844a (8 references).

[182]

Binion-Beck Reading Readiness Test for Kindergarten and First Grade. Grades kgn–1; 1945; Harriet Seay Binion and Roland L. Beck; Psychometric Affiliates. *

For additional information and reviews by Irving H. Anderson and Paul A. Witty, see 3:514 (1 reference).

[182.1]

★**Clymer-Barrett Prereading Battery.** First grade entrants; 1966–67; 4 scores: visual discrimination, auditory discrimination, visual-motor, total; short screening form consisting of 2 of the 6 subtests yields a single score; Theodore Clymer and Thomas C. Barrett; Personnel Press, Inc. *

[183]

★**Early Detection Inventory.** Preschool children; 1967; school readiness; 4 scores: school readiness tasks, social-emotional behavior responses, motor performance, total; medical history and family background supplied by parent; F. E. McGahan and Carolyn McGahan; Follett Publishing Co. *

[184]

*****Gates-MacGinitie Reading Tests: Readiness Skills.** Grades kgn–1; 1939–68; revision of *Gates Reading Readiness Test* (see 6:845); 9 scores: listening comprehension, auditory discrimination, visual discrimination, following directions, letter recognition, visual-motor coordination, auditory blending, word recognition, total; Arthur I. Gates and Walter H. MacGinitie; Teachers College Press. *

For a review by F. J. Schonell of the original edition, see 4:566; for reviews by Marion Monroe Cox and Paul A. Witty, see 3:516 (3 references); see also 2:1537 (5 references, 2 excerpts).

[185]

Group Test of Reading Readiness: The Dominion Tests. Grades kgn, kgn–1; 1949–59; Department of Educational Research, Ontario College of Education, University of Toronto; distributed by Guidance Centre. *

a) [LONG FORM.] Grades kgn–1; 1949–59; 6 scores: discrimination of objects-symbols-words, listening-remembering-observing, familiarity with word forms, memory for word forms, motor coordination, total.

b) [SHORT FORM.] Grade kgn; 1954–55; 2 editions: Subtest Type and Omnibus Type. *Out of print.*

For additional information and a review by N. Dale Bryant, see 5:676.

[186]

The Harrison-Stroud Reading Readiness Profiles. Grades kgn–1; 1949–56; 7 scores: using symbols, making visual discriminations (2 scores), using the context, making auditory discriminations, using context and auditory clues, giving the names of letters; M. Lucile Harrison and James B. Stroud; Houghton Mifflin Co. *

For additional information and a review by S. S. Dunn, see 5:677 (2 references); for a review by William S. Gray, see 4:568.

[186.1]

★**Keystone Ready to Read Tests.** School entrants; 1954; visual readiness "to read books at the usual distance"; 3 test cards (1, 2, and 4 pass-fail scores, respectively) using Keystone Telebinocular No. 46: near-point fusion, lateral and vertical posture, usable vision; no data on reliability or validity; Keystone View Co. *

[187]

Lee-Clark Reading Readiness Test, 1962 Revision. Grades kgn–1; 1931–63; 4 scores: letter symbols, concepts, word symbols, total; J. Murray Lee and Willis W. Clark; California Test Bureau. *

For additional information, see 6:846 (9 references); for a review by James R. Hobson of an earlier edition, see 5:678; for reviews by Marion Monroe Cox and David H. Russell, see 3:517.

[187.1]

★**Lippincott Reading Readiness Test (Including Readiness Check List).** Grades kgn–1; 1965; Pierce H. McLeod; J. B. Lippincott Co. *

[188]

★**McHugh-McParland Reading Readiness Test.** Grades kgn–1; 1966–68; 5 scores: rhyming words, beginning sounds, visual discrimination, identifying letters, total; Walter J. McHugh and Myrtle McParland; Cal-State Bookstore. *

[189]

Maturity Level for School Entrance and Reading Readiness. Grades kgn–1; 1950–59; revision of *School Readiness Inventory;* behavior checklist completed by teachers; 2 scores: maturity level, reading readiness; Katharine M. Banham; American Guidance Service, Inc. *

For additional information, see 6:847; for a review by David H. Russell, see 4:572.

[190]

*Metropolitan Readiness Tests. First grade entrants; 1933–66; 7 or 8 scores: word meaning, listening, matching, alphabet, numbers, copying, total, drawing a man (optional); Gertrude H. Hildreth, Nellie L. Griffiths, and Mary E. McGauvran; Harcourt, Brace & World, Inc. *

For additional information and a review by Eric F. Gardner of an earlier edition, see 4:570 (3 references, 1 excerpt); for a review by Irving H. Anderson, see 3:518 (5 references); for a review by W. J. Osburn, see 2:1552 (10 references).

[191]

*Murphy-Durrell Reading Readiness Analysis. First grade entrants; 1949–65, c1947–65; revision of Murphy-Durrell Diagnostic Reading Readiness Test; 6 scores: sound recognition, letter naming (capitals, lower case, total), learning words, total; Helen A. Murphy and Donald D. Durrell; Harcourt, Brace & World, Inc. *

For additional information and reviews by Joan Bollenbacher and S. S. Dunn, see 5:679 (2 references); see also 4:571 (2 references).

[192]

*Perceptual Forms Test. Ages 6–8.5; 1955–67; revision of Children's Perceptual Achievement Forms; visual development; Publication Committee, Winter Haven Lions Club; Winter Haven Lions Research Foundation, Inc. *

For additional information and a review by Mary C. Austin, see 6:848 (6 references).

[192.1]

★Primary Academic Sentiment Scale. Ages 4-4 to 7-3; 1968; motivation for learning and level of maturity and parental independence; 2 scores: sentiment, dependency; Glen Robbins Thompson; Priority Innovations, Inc. *

[193]

Reading Aptitude Tests. Grades kgn–1; 1935; also called Monroe Reading Aptitude Tests; 5 scores: visual, auditory, motor, articulation, language; Marion Monroe [Cox]; Houghton Mifflin Co. *

For additional information and a review by Irving H. Anderson, see 3:519 (5 references).

[194]

Reversal Test. Age 6.5; 1954; Åke W. Edfeldt; Skandinaviska Testförlaget AB. *

[195]

★School Readiness: Behavior Tests Used at the Gesell Institute. Ages 5–10; 1964–65; readiness to start school; Francis L. Ilg and Louise Bates Ames; Programs for Education. *

[195.1]

★The School Readiness Checklist, Research Edition. Ages 4–6; 1963; booklet title is Ready or Not; checklist to be used by parents; John J. Austin and J. Clayton Lafferty; Research Concepts. *

[196]

★School Readiness Survey. Ages 4–6; 1967; to be administered and scored by parents with school supervision; F. L. Jordan and James Massey; Consulting Psychologists Press, Inc. *

[196.1]

★Screening Test for the Assignment of Remedial Treatments. Ages 4-6 to 6-5; 1968; 5 scores: visual memory, auditory memory, visual copying, visual discrimination, total; A. Edward Ahr; Priority Innovations, Inc. *

[197]

★Screening Test of Academic Readiness. Ages 4–6.5; 1966; 9 scores: picture vocabulary, letters, picture completion, copying, picture description, human figure drawings, relationships, numbers, total (IQ); A. Edward Ahr; Priority Innovations, Inc. *

[198]

★The Steinbach Test of Reading Readiness. First grade entrants; 1965–66; 5 scores: letter identification, word memory, auditory discrimination, language comprehension, total; M. Nila Steinbach; Scholastic Testing Service, Inc. *

[199]

★Valett Developmental Survey of Basic Learning Abilities. Ages 2–7; 1966; largely a selection and adaptation of items from many scales, particularly the Gesell Developmental Schedules; 7 age scores: motor integration and physical development, tactile discrimination, auditory discrimination, visual-motor coordination, visual discrimination, language development and verbal fluency, conceptual development; Robert E. Valett; Consulting Psychologists Press. *

[200]

*Van Wagenen Reading Readiness Scales. First grade entrants; 1933–58; Van Wagenen Psycho-Educational Research Laboratories. *

a) PART 1, LISTENING VOCABULARY. 1954–58; Maximilian L. G. Klaeger and M. J. Van Wagenen.

b) PART 2. 1933–58; test items same as in earlier edition published in 1938 under the title Reading Readiness Test (see 3:520); 7 scores: range of information, perception of information, opposites, memory span for ideas, word discrimination, word learning, verbal IQ; M. J. Van Wagenen.

For additional information and a review by David H. Russell of an earlier edition of Part 2, see 3:520 (4 references).

[201]

Watson Reading-Readiness Test. Grades kgn–1; 1960; 3 scores: subjective test (teacher's ratings of physical, social, emotional, and psychological readiness), objective test, total; G. Milton Watson; Book Society of Canada Ltd. *

For additional information, see 6:851.

OUT OF PRINT

[202]

Classification Test for Beginners in Reading. First grade entrants; 1933; Clarence R. Stone and Clifford C. Grover; Webster Publishing Co. * Out of print.

For additional information and reviews by Marion Monroe Cox and David H. Russell, see 3:515 (2 references).

[203]

Reading Readiness Test. Grades kgn–1; 1957; David F. Votaw, Sr. and Peggy Lou Moses; Steck-Vaughn Co. * Out of print.

For additional information and a review by David A. Payne, see 6:849 (1 reference).

[204]

Scholastic Reading Readiness Test. First grade entrants; 1953–60; various titles, including STS Read-

ing Readiness Test, used by the publisher; Oliver F. Anderhalter and Ruth Colestock; Scholastic Testing Service, Inc. * *Out of print.*

For additional information and a review by David A. Payne, see 6:850.

[205]

Stevens Reading Readiness Test. First grade entrants; 1938–44; Avis Coultas Stevens; Harcourt, Brace & World, Inc. * *Out of print.*

For additional information and reviews by Irving H. Anderson and Marion Monroe Cox, see 3:521.

[206]

Webster Reading-Readiness Test. Grades kgn–1.5; 1950; 5 scores: verbal discrimination, memory of word forms, auditory discrimination, vocabulary and comprehension, total; Clarence R. Stone and Mary Nila; Webster Publishing Co. * *Out of print.*

For additional information, see 5:682.

SPECIAL FIELDS

[207]

Ability to Interpret Reading Materials in the Natural Sciences: The Iowa Tests of Educational Development, Test 6. Grades 9–12; 1942–61; prepared under the direction of E. F. Lindquist; Science Research Associates, Inc. *

For additional information, see 6:853. For reviews of the complete battery, consult the 6th, 5th, 4th, and 3rd MMY's.

[208]

Ability to Interpret Reading Materials in the Social Studies: The Iowa Tests of Educational Development, Test 5. Grades 9–12; 1942–61; prepared under the direction of E. F. Lindquist; Science Research Associates, Inc. *

For additional information, see 6:852. For reviews of the complete battery, consult the 6th, 5th, 4th, and 3rd MMY's.

[209]

★**The Adult Basic Reading Inventory.** Functionally illiterate adolescents and adults; 1966; test booklets with the title *Basic Reading Inventory* are available for school use; scores in 5 areas: sight words, sound and letter discrimination, word meaning (reading), word meaning (listening), context reading; Richard W. Burnett; Scholastic Testing Service, Inc. *

[210]

*Interpretation of Reading Materials in the Natural Sciences: Tests of General Educational Development, Test 3.** High school, college; 1944–68; college level out of print; tests administered only at Official GED Centers; General Educational Development Testing Service of the American Council on Education.

For additional information, see 5:683. For reviews of earlier editions of the complete battery, consult the 5th, 4th, and 3rd MMY's.

[211]

*Interpretation of Reading Materials in the Social Studies: Tests of General Educational Development, Test 2.** High school, college; 1944–68; college level out of print; tests administered only at Official GED Centers; General Educational Development Testing Service of the American Council on Education.

For additional information, see 5:684; for reviews by W. E. Hall and C. Robert Pace of the college level, see 3:528 (1 reference). For reviews of earlier editions of the complete battery, consult the 5th, 4th, and 3rd MMY's.

[212]

Lorimer Braille Recognition Test: A Test of Ability in Reading Braille Contractions. Students (ages 7–13) in grade 2 Braille; 1962; John Lorimer; College of Teachers of the Blind. *

For additional information, see 6:854 (1 reference).

[213]

Purdue Reading Test for Industrial Supervisors. Supervisors; 1955; Joseph Tiffin and Roy Dunlap; University Book Store, West Lafayette, Ind. *

For additional information and reviews by Jerome E. Doppelt and Louis C. Nanassy, see 5:644 (1 reference).

[214]

RBH Reading Comprehension Test. Business and industry; 1951–63; Richardson, Bellows, Henry & Co., Inc. *

For additional information, see 6:817.

[215]

★**RBH Scientific Reading Test.** Engineers and executives in technical companies; 1950–62; Richardson, Bellows, Henry & Co., Inc. *

[216]

*Reading Adequacy "READ" Test: Individual Placement Series.** Adults in industry; 1961–66; 3 scores: reading rate, per cent of comprehension, corrected reading rate; J. H. Norman; Personnel Research Associates, Inc. *

For additional information, see 6:805.

[217]

★[**Reading: Adult Basic Education Student Survey, Parts 1 and 2.**] Poorly educated adults; 1966–67; 2 scores: comprehension, vocabulary; Elvin Rasof and Monroe C. Neff; Follett Publishing Co. *

[218]

★**Reading Comprehension Test for Personnel Selection.** Applicants for technical training programs with high verbal content; 1965–66; L. R. C. Haward; University of London Press Ltd. *

[219]

[**Robinson-Hall Reading Tests.**] College; 1940–49; Francis P. Robinson and Prudence Hall; University Publications Sales, Ohio State University. *
a) A TEST OF READING ABILITY FOR ART.
b) A TEST OF READING ABILITY FOR GEOLOGY.
c) A TEST OF READING ABILITY FOR HISTORY.
d) A TEST OF READING ABILITY FOR FICTION.

For additional information and a review by Robert Murray Bear, see 4:575 (2 references); see also 3:533 (3 references).

[220]

★**SRA Reading Progress Test.** Employees; 1962–63; test booklet title is *Reading Progress Test;* 4 scores: vocabulary, logical thinking, reading for information, rate; Science Research Associates, Inc. *

[221]

Tests of Natural Sciences: Vocabulary and Interpretation of Reading Materials: Cooperative Inter-American Tests. Grades 8–13; 1950; English and Spanish editions; 3 scores: vocabulary, interpretation of reading materials, total; Committee on Modern Languages of the American Council on Education; Guidance Testing Associates. *

For additional information and a review by Clarence H. Nelson, see 4:576 (4 references).

[222]

Tests of Social Studies: Vocabulary and Interpretation of Reading Materials: Cooperative Inter-American Tests. Grades 8–13; 1950; English and Spanish editions; 3 scores: vocabulary, interpretation of reading materials, total; Committee on Modern Languages of the American Council on Education; Guidance Testing Associates. *

For additional information and reviews by Gustav J. Froehlich and Martha E. Layman, see 4:577 (4 references).

[223]

Tooze Braille Speed Test: A Test of Basic Ability in Reading Braille. Students (ages 7–13) in grades 1 or 2 Braille; 1962; F. H. G. Tooze; College of Teachers of the Blind. *

For additional information, see 6:855.

[224]

Understanding Communication (Verbal Comprehension). Industrial employees at the skilled level or below; 1959, c1956–59; Thelma G. Thurstone and Measurement Research Division, Industrial Relations Center, University of Chicago; Education-Industry Service. *

For additional information and reviews by C. E. Jurgensen and Donald E. P. Smith, see 6:840.

OUT OF PRINT

[225]

Mathematics, Biology, Physical Science. Grades 10–16; 1938; 5 reading comprehension scores: mathematics, biology, physics and astronomy, chemistry and geology, total science; English Commission of the Association of Georgia Colleges; the Association. * *Out of print.*

For additional information, see 2:1550.

[226]

Reading Scales in History. Grades 7–12; 1938–39; M. J. Van Wagenen; Educational Test Bureau. * *Out of print.*

For additional information and reviews by Paul Blommers and Albert J. Harris, see 3:530.

[227]

Reading Scales in Literature. Grades 7–12; 1939; M. J. Van Wagenen; Educational Test Bureau. * *Out of print.*

For additional information, see 3:531.

[228]

Reading Scales in Science. Grades 7–12; 1938; M. J. Van Wagenen; Educational Test Bureau. * *Out of print.*

For additional information and a review by Ivan A. Booker, see 3:532.

[229]

Southeastern Problems and Prospects: Social Studies and English. Grades 10–16; 1938; 2 reading comprehension scores: English, social studies; English Commission of the Association of Georgia Colleges; the Association. * *Out of print.*

For additional information, see 2:1569.

SPEED

[230]

Minnesota Speed of Reading Test for College Students. Grades 12–16; 1936; Alvin C. Eurich; University of Minnesota Press. *

For additional information and a review by J. R. Gerberich, see 2:1555 (2 references); for reviews by Frederick B. Davis and Ruth Strang, see 1:1107.

[231]

Tinker Speed of Reading Test. Grades 7–16 and adults; 1955, c1947–55; Miles A. Tinker; University of Minnesota Press. *

For additional information and a review by Leonard S. Feldt, see 5:687.

OUT OF PRINT

[232]

Chapman-Cook Speed of Reading Test. Grades 4–8; 1923–24; J. C. Chapman and Sidney Cook; Educational Test Bureau. * *Out of print.*

For additional information and a review by Eason Monroe, see 3:522 (1 reference).

[233]

Michigan Speed of Reading Test. Grades 6–16; 1932–37; Edward B. Greene; Psychological Corporation. * *Out of print.*

For additional information and a review by Eason Monroe, see 3:523 (1 reference); see also 2:1553 (2 references); for reviews by Richard Ledgerwood and M. R. Trabue, see 1:1171.

[234]

Reading Speed and Comprehension: Ohio Senior Survey Tests. Grade 12; 1935–53; 2 scores: speed, comprehension; S. L. Pressey and J. W. Sherburne; Ohio Scholarship Tests. * *Out of print.*

For additional information and reviews by J. B. Stroud and Miles A. Tinker, see 3:524.

[235]

Reading Speed Test: National Achievement Test. Grades 3–8; 1938–39; Robert K. Speer and Samuel Smith; Acorn Publishing Co. * *Out of print.*

For additional information and a review by Eason Monroe, see 3:525.

STUDY SKILLS

[236]

California Study Methods Survey. Grades 7–13; 1958; 5 scores: attitudes toward school, mechanics of study, planning and system, total, verification; Harold D. Carter; California Test Bureau. *

For additional information and reviews by John D. Krumboltz and Donald E. P. Smith, see 6:857 (2 references, 2 excerpts); see also 5:689 (7 references).

[237]

Evaluation Aptitude Test. Candidates for college and graduate school entrance; 1951–52; 5 scores: neutral syllogisms, emotionally toned syllogisms, total, emotional bias, indecision; DeWitt E. Sell; Psychometric Affiliates. *

For additional information and reviews by J. Thomas Hastings and Walker H. Hill, see 5:691.

[238]

Logical Reasoning. Grades 9–16 and adults; 1955; Alfred F. Hertzka and J. P. Guilford; Sheridan Psychological Services, Inc. *
For additional information and reviews by Duncan Howie and Charles R. Langmuir, see 5:694 (1 reference).

[239]

Nationwide Library Skills Examination. Grades 4–12; 1962–63; [Donald R. Honz]; Educational Stimuli. *
For additional information, see 6:860.

[240]

OC Diagnostic Dictionary Test. Grades 5–8; 1960; Katherine O'Connor; O'Connor Reading Clinic Publishing Co. *
For additional information, see 6:861.

[241]

Peabody Library Information Test. Grades 4–8, 9–12, 13–16; 1938–40; Louis Shores and Joseph E. Moore; American Guidance Service, Inc. *
a) ELEMENTARY LEVEL. Grades 4–8; 1940.
b) HIGH SCHOOL LEVEL. Grades 9–12; 1940.
c) COLLEGE LEVEL, REVISED EDITION. Grades 13–16; 1938–40; 9 scores: the book, arrangement of books, catalog, dictionary, encyclopedia, periodicals and indexes, special reference books, bibliography, total.
For additional information and a review by Douglas E. Scates, see 3:538 (2 references, 2 excerpts).

[242]

Pictographic Self Rating Scale. High school and college; 1955–57; attitude toward classroom and study activities; Einar R. Ryden; Psychometric Affiliates. *
For additional information, see 5:695 (2 references).

[243]

SRA Achievement Series: Work-Study Skills. Grades 4–6, 6–9; 1954–64; subtest of *SRA Achievement Series;* 2–3 scores: references, charts, total (Forms C and D only); Louis P. Thorpe, D. Welty Lefever, and Robert A. Naslund; Science Research Associates, Inc. *
For additional information, see 6:862; for reviews by Robert L. Ebel and Ruth M. Strang, see 5:696. For reviews of the complete battery, consult the 6th and 5th MMY's.

[244]

Spitzer Study Skills Test: Evaluation and Adjustment Series. Grades 9–13; 1954–55; 6 scores: dictionary, index, graphs-tables-maps, sources of information, total, note taking; Herbert F. Spitzer; Harcourt, Brace & World, Inc. *
For additional information and a review by Alton L. Raygor, see 6:864 (1 reference); for a review by James Deese, see 5:697.

[244.1]

★**Study Habits Checklist.** Grades 9–16; 1957–67; Ralph C. Preston and Morton Botel; Science Research Associates, Inc. *

[245]

Study Habits Inventory, Revised Edition. Grades 12–16; 1934–41; C. Gilbert Wrenn; Consulting Psychologists Press, Inc. *
For additional information and a review by Douglas E. Scates, see 3:540 (8 references); for reviews by Edward S. Jones and William A. McCall, see 2:1574.

[246]

Study Performance Test. High school and college; 1934–43; Herbert A. Toops, Grace Shover, and others; Wilbur L. Layton. *

[247]

The Study Skills Counseling Evaluation. High school and college; 1962; George Demos; Western Psychological Services. *
For additional information and reviews by Stanley E. Davis and W. G. Fleming, see 6:865.

[248]

★**Survey of Study Habits and Attitudes.** Grades 7–12, 12–14; 1953–67; 7 scores: study habits (efficiency, promptness, total), study attitudes (toward teachers, educational objectives, total), total; William F. Brown and Wayne H. Holtzman; Psychological Corporation. *
a) FORM H. Grades 7–12; 1967.
b) FORM C. Grades 12–14; 1965.
For additional information, see 6:856 (12 references); for reviews by James Deese and C. Gilbert Wrenn (with Roy D. Lewis) of the original edition, see 5:688 (14 references).

[249]

Survey of Study Habits, Experimental Edition. Grades 8–14; 1944; Arthur E. Traxler; Educational Records Bureau. *
For additional information and a review by Warren R. Baller, see 4:583 (1 reference).

[250]

A Test on Use of the Dictionary. High school and college; 1955–63; 6 scores: pronunciation, meaning, spelling, derivation, usage, total; George D. Spache; Reading Laboratory and Clinic. *
For additional information, see 6:866.

[251]

Tyler-Kimber Study Skills Test. Grades 9–16; 1937; 9 scores: finding what you want in a book, using an index, using general reference books, recognizing common abbreviations, using the library card catalog, interpreting maps, current periodical literature, interpreting graphs, total; Henry T. Tyler and George C. Kimber; Consulting Psychologists Press, Inc. *
For additional information and reviews by William A. McCall and Rachel Salisbury, see 2:1580 (1 reference); for reviews by Edward S. Jones and C. Gilbert Wrenn, see 1:1166.

[252]

Use of Sources of Information: The Iowa Tests of Educational Development, Test 9. Grades 9–12; 1942–61; prepared under the direction of E. F. Lindquist; Science Research Associates, Inc. *
For additional information, see 6:858. For reviews of the complete battery, consult the 6th, 5th, 4th, and 3rd MMY's.

[253]

Watson-Glaser Critical Thinking Appraisal. Grades 9–16 and adults; 1942–64; formerly called *Watson-Glaser Tests of Critical Thinking;* 6 scores: inference, recognition of assumptions, deduction, interpretation, evaluation of arguments, total; Goodwin Watson and Edward M. Glaser; Harcourt, Brace & World, Inc. *
For additional information, see 6:867 (24 references); for reviews by Walker H. Hill and Carl I.

Hovland, see 5:700, (8 references); for a review by Robert H. Thouless, see 3:544 (3 references, 1 excerpt).

[254]

Work-Study Skills: Iowa Every-Pupil Tests of Basic Skills, Test B. Grades 3–5, 5–9; 1940–47; 6 scores: map reading, use of references, use of index, use of dictionary, alphabetizing (grades 3–5) or graphing (grades 5–9), total; H. F. Spitzer, Ernest Horn, Maude McBroom, H. A. Greene, and E. F. Lindquist; Houghton Mifflin Co. *
For additional information, see 4:588; for a review by J. Wayne Wrightstone, see 3:545. For reviews of the complete battery, consult the 4th, 3rd, and 1st MMY's.

OUT OF PRINT

[255]

Analysis of Controversial Writing: Test 5.31. Grades 10–12; 1939; 10 scores: general objectivity, nonrecognition of conflicting points of view, misconception of author's purposes, defense of author, suggestibility, identifying propaganda devices, confusion of propaganda devices, uncritical toward the use of propaganda devices, recognition of desirable forms of argument, gullibility; Evaluation in the Eight Year Study, Progressive Education Association. * *Out of print.*
For additional information, see 2:1527.

[256]

Application of Certain Principles of Logical Reasoning: Test 5.12. Grades 10–12; 1939–40; Evaluation in the Eight Year Study, Progressive Education Association. * *Out of print.*
For additional information, see 2:1528.

[257]

Applied Reading for Junior-Senior High School: Every Pupil Test. Grades 7–12; 1943–51; 4 scores: use of an index, use of running heads in a dictionary, vocabulary, total; Marion Steele and Margaret Egeland; 1948–51 forms: Clara B. Martin, Mabel Murray, C. A. Woods, S. H. Dillon; Ohio Scholarship Tests. * *Out of print.*
For additional information and a review by Ivan A. Booker, see 3:534.

[258]

Bennett Use of Library Test. High school and college; 1947; Alma Bennett and H. E. Schrammel; Bureau of Educational Measurements. * *Out of print.*
For additional information and a review by Louis Shores, see 4:578.

[259]

Cooperative Dictionary Test. Grades 7–12; 1951–52; 5 scores: alphabetizing, spelling, pronunciation, meaning, total; S. D. Melville, Clarence Derrick (manual), and Frances Swineford (manual); Cooperative Test Division. * *Out of print.*
For additional information and a review by A. N. Hieronymus, see 5:690.

[260]

Critical Classification of Magazines and Newspapers. Grades 10–18; 1937; 4 scores: types of newspapers and magazines, newspaper policies, magazine policies, total; Karl C. Pratt; Cooperative Bureau of Educational Research. * *Out of print.*
For additional information, see 1:1163.

[261]

Critical-Mindedness in the Reading of Fiction: Test 3.7. Grades 9–12; 1938; 4 scores: judicious, hypercritical, uncritical, uncertain; Evaluation in the Eight Year Study, Progressive Education Association. * *Out of print.*
For additional information, see 2:1530 (1 reference).

[262]

Edmiston How to Study Test. Grades 7–13; 1947–49; R. W. Edmiston; the Author. * *Out of print.*
For additional information, see 4:580.

[263]

Information Concerning Library Processes. Grades 10–18; 1937; Charles V. Park; Cooperative Bureau of Educational Research. * *Out of print.*
For additional information, see 1:1164.

[264]

Interpretation of Data Test: General Education Series. Grades 7–12, 12–14; 1939–50; Evaluation in the Eight Year Study, Progressive Education Association; Cooperative Test Division. * *Out of print.*
For additional information and reviews by J. Raymond Gerberich and Victor H. Noll, see 4:581 (5 references); for a review by J. Wayne Wrightstone, see 3:535 (4 references); see also 2:1544 (9 references).

[265]

Interpretation of Data: Test 2.71. Grades 7–9; 1940; Evaluation in the Eight Year Study, Progressive Education Association. * *Out of print.*
For additional information, see 2:1545 (4 references).

[266]

A Library Orientation Test for College Freshmen. Grade 13; 1950–61; Ethel M. Feagley, Dorothy W. Curtiss, Mary V. Gaver, and Esther Greene; Teachers College Press. * *Out of print.*
For additional information and a review by Morey J. Wantman, see 6:859 (1 reference); for reviews by Janet G. Afflerbach (with Lois Grimes Afflerbach) and J. Wayne Wrightstone, see 5:693.

[267]

Library Test for Junior High Schools. Grades 7–9; 1942; 6 scores: the book, arrangement of books, card catalog, dictionary and encyclopedia, miscellaneous books, total; Committee on Tests of the School Library Association of California; California Test Bureau. * *Out of print.*
For additional information and reviews by Robert A. Davis and Ethel M. Feagley, see 3:536.

[268]

Library Usage Test. Grades 11–13; 1940; Elmer R. Smith; Turner E. Smith & Co. * *Out of print.*
For additional information and a review by J. Wayne Wrightstone, see 3:537.

[269]

Logical Reasoning Test: General Education Series. Grades 10–12; 1939–50; Evaluation in the Eight Year Study, Progressive Education Association; Cooperative Test Division. * *Out of print.*
For additional information and a review by Robert L. Ebel, see 4:582 (1 reference); see also 2:1528 (4 references).

[270]

Nature of Proof: Test 5.22. Grades 10–12; 1939–40; 6 scores: recognizing relevancy, recognizing statements which support conclusion, recognition of weak points, standard of proof, qualifying judgments, general accuracy; Evaluation in the Eight Year Study, Progressive Education Association. * *Out of print.*

For additional information, see 2:1556 (3 references).

[271]

Parr Skill-Ability Tests. Grades 9–16; 1938–41; Frank W. Parr; Cooperative Book Store. * *Out of print.*
a) CONCENTRATION. 1940; 3 scores: accuracy, speed, efficiency.
b) OUTLINING. 1938; 3 scores: accuracy, speed, efficiency.
c) READING. 1940; 2 scores: comprehension, rate.
d) VOCABULARY. 1941; 9 scores: roots, prefixes, suffixes, synonyms, antonyms, analogies, word construction, word usage, total.

For additional information, see 2:1559.1.

[272]

Poley Precis Test: A Test by Paragraph Summaries of Reading Comprehension. Grades 9–12; 1927; Irvin C. Poley; Public School Publishing Co. * *Out of print.*

For additional information and a review by Edward A. Tenney, see 2:1561.

[273]

Reading and Construction of Tables and Graphs. Grades 10–18; 1936; 5 scores: reading graphs, making graphs, reading tables, making tables, total; Clifford Woody and Almon Vedder; Cooperative Bureau of Educational Research. * *Out of print.*

For additional information, see 1:1165.

[274]

Senior High School Library and Reference Skills Test. Grades 9–12; 1960; 8 scores: alphabetization, uses of the dictionary, the card catalogue, research vocabulary, reference books, Dewey Decimal System, periodicals, total; Claude E. Stephenson; Perfection Form Co. * *Out of print.*

For additional information, see 6:863.

[275]

Special Reading Test: Ohio Senior Survey Tests. Grade 12; 1935–41; 5 scores: English vocabulary, foreign words, dictionary, graphs and maps, total; S. L. Pressey and J. W. Sherburne; Ohio Scholarship Tests. * *Out of print.*

For additional information and a review by Miles A. Tinker, see 3:539.

[276]

Stanford Achievement Test: Study Skills. Grades 5–6, 7–9; 1953–54, c1952–54; Truman L. Kelley, Richard Madden, Eric F. Gardner, Lewis M. Terman, and Giles M. Ruch; Harcourt, Brace & World, Inc. * *Out of print.*

For additional information and reviews by Robert L. Ebel and Ruth M. Strang, see 5:698.

[277]

Student Skills Inventory, Experimental Edition. College; 1939; Norman M. Locke; Psychological Corporation. * *Out of print.*

For additional information, see 2:1573 (1 reference).

[278]

Study Outline Test. Grades 9–16; 1926; 4 scores: coordination, subordination, elaboration, total; F. Dean McClusky and Edward William Dolch; Public School Publishing Co. * *Out of print.*

For additional information and a review by Harriet Barthelmess Morrison, see 2:1575 (1 reference).

[279]

Test of Critical Thinking. Grades 7–9; 1951; 7 scores: inquiry, interest, relationships, openmindedness, generalizations, accuracy, total; M. T. Macy and Hugh B. Wood; [Curriculum Bulletin]. * *Out of print.*

For additional information, see 4:584.

[280]

A Test of Study Skills. Grades 4–9; 1940–41; J. W. Edgar and H. T. Manuel; Steck-Vaughn Co. * *Out of print.*

For additional information and a review by Marvin D. Glock, see 5:699; for a review by Douglas E. Scates, see 3:542.

[281]

Test on the Use of Books and Libraries: General Education Series. Grades 7–12; 1939–50; Evaluation in the Eight Year Study, Progressive Education Association; Cooperative Test Division. * *Out of print.*

For additional information and reviews by Henry D. Rinsland and Louis Shores, see 4:585 (1 reference).

[282]

The Use of Library and Study Materials. Grades 9–16; 1939–41; Mary S. Kirkpatrick, Lola Rivers Thompson, and Helen Tomlinson; Steck-Vaughn Co. * *Out of print.*

For additional information and a review by Robert Murray Bear, see 4:586 (1 reference); for a review by Ethel M. Feagley, see 3:543.

Reading Test Reviews

THE reading sections of the first six *Mental Measurements Yearbooks* are presented in this chapter in order of publication. The reading section of *The 1938 Mental Measurements Yearbook*—hereafter, referred to as *The First Mental Measurements Yearbook*—appears first; the reading section of *The 1940 Mental Measurements Yearbook* —hereafter, referred to as *The Second Mental Measurements Yearbook*—appears next; then the reading sections of the third, fourth, fifth, and sixth MMY's. Because of differing page sizes, copy from the First MMY had to be reset; the remaining reading sections have been reproduced by offset with only the running heads changed. Page numbers are given next to the inside margins; the entry numbers of tests are given next to the outside margins.

Read 2:1530 as test number 1530 in *The Second Mental Measurements Yearbook;* 6:812 as test number 812 in *The Sixth Mental Measurements Yearbook*. Reference to the tests and reviews in this chapter will be facilitated by first referring to the previous chapter, Reading Test Index. The Index lists all reading tests listed in the first six *Mental Measurements Yearbooks* and all other reading tests in print as of May 1, 1968. For each test, the Index refers to the last listing in an MMY and to all reviews received by the test in the first six MMY's. The Reading Test Index answers such questions as: What reading tests are currently available? Which of the reading tests listed in an MMY are out of print? What is the latest listing of a test in an MMY? By whom has a test been reviewed?

CHAPTER CONTENTS

READING—FIRST MMY

REVIEWS BY *Irving H. Anderson, Ivan A. Booker, Stella S. Center, Frederick B. Davis, Joseph C. Dewey, William S. Gray, Edward S. Jones, David Kopel, Marion Monroe Cox, Spencer Shank, Ruth Strang, Joseph Tiffin, Miles A. Tinker, Guy Wagner, and C. Gilbert Wrenn.*

[1095]

Articulation Test with Reading Disability Feature. Grades 3–12; a booklet containing sentences with initial, medial and final sounds to be tested for articulation and also key words for detecting various types of reading disabilities; $1.50 per examiner's booklet (nonconsumable) ; I. Sherman ; the Author, Winona Public Schools, Winona, Minn.

Irving H. Anderson, Harvard University. In this test the pupil is required to read sentences which contain the sounds for which his articulation is being tested. Each sound occurs in the initial, medial, and final positions. The sounds are arranged in the order of the frequency with which they are mispronounced. In addition to recording errors of articulation, the teacher records various other errors of oral reading. The articulation test is somewhat limited by the fact that at each grade level only one sentence is used for each sound. The reading disability feature is but poorly standardized.

[1096]

Basic Reading Tests. Grades 1B, 1A–2B, 1A–2A, 2B–3B, 2A–3A ; c1935–36 ; 1 form ; by testing for different words, the same test sheet can be used as four equivalent test forms ; 5 levels ; although specifically planned for use with the Elson-Gray Basic Readers, the tests may be used with any reading series ; 60¢ per 25 tests ; 20¢ per manual ; sample copies free ; E. W. Dolch and W. S. Gray ; Scott, Foresman & Co.
a) WORD-RECOGNITION TESTS. Grades 1B, 1A–2B.
b) WORD-ATTACK TESTS. Grades 1A–2A, 2B–3B, 2A–3A.

[1097]

Betts Ready to Read Tests. Pre-school through college ; c1934–38 ; Case Study Forms, 1936 Edition : 5¢ per blank ; Key Record Form No. 1 for Secondary Schools : 35¢ per 50 blanks ; Survey Forms, 1938 Edition : 3¢ per blank ; Visual Survey Record Form, 1938 Edition : 35¢ per 50 blanks ; quantity discounts on record forms ; E. A. Betts ; Keystone View Co.
a) CLINIC UNIT. c1934–38 ; a battery of tests for determining psychological and physiological reading readiness and for analysis and remediation of reading difficulties ; individual ; $105 per case of accessories including the improved *Keystone Visual Safety Telebinocular.*
b) VISUAL SURVEY UNIT. c1937–38 ; a battery of tests for determining physiological reading readiness and an analysis of visual efficiency from the first grade through college ; individual ; $85 per case of accessories including the improved *Keystone Visual Safety Telebinocular;* quantity discounts on record forms.

I. H. Anderson, Harvard University. Readiness to read is measured by these tests in terms of the maturation of certain visual functions. The tests consist of a series of stereoscopic slides which are administered by means of an instrument known as the *Ophthalmic Telebinocular.*

David Kopel, Northwestern University. The *Betts Ready to Read Tests* comprise visual readiness tests, auditory tests, visual sensation and perception tests, and oculomotor and perception tests.

The visual readiness tests consist of a series of large cards used in gauging a child's ability to discriminate visually among readily reversed or confused letters, words, and phonetic elements. With the auditory series, it is possible to make appraisals of the child's span or memory (as sentences of varying length are presented), of fusion (of isolated sounds, to be combined into words), of perception (—repetition of sounds pronounced by the examiner), and of acuity (—repetition of digits expressed in a low voice by the examiner). Responses to these readiness tests may be compared with norms to determine children's probable success in reading situations.

The tests of visual sensation and perception are mounted on eleven stereoscopic slides which are viewed in the Keystone Ophthalmic Telebinocular. These tests provide measures of visual efficiency (acuity) of the right, left, and both eyes ; sharpness of image in each eye (astigmatism) ; level of eye co-ordination (degree of stereopsis or depth perception) ; imbalance of the vertical and lateral eye muscles ; and fusion of images at reading distance and at infinity.

In the usual school examination of vision only acuity is appraised, with the Snellen chart. Sometimes astigmatism also is tested. The various other ocular functions and their interrelationships, which are very important in determining visual efficiency and comfort, are unjustifiably ignored. The school needs a practical technique for identifying quickly and reliably the presence of refractive errors, or of functional disturbances in vision. (These cases must then be referred to eye specialists.) This need is probably fulfilled best at present by the Betts tests of visual sensation and perception.

"Oculomotor and perception habits" are studied also by means of a series of stereoscopic slides which contain many reversible, isolated words, letters, and numbers. Adequate responses are dependent upon good eye co-ordination, fusion, and depth perception. Norms are provided. The tests are useful in diagnosis of reading difficulty at the elementary school level.

Marion Monroe, Pittsburgh Public Schools. These tests are designed to measure certain visual and auditory abilities in beginning pupils for prognosis in reading. The tests consist of four parts : visual tests of ability to discriminate similarities and differences in letters and word forms ; auditory tests of memory-span and sound-blending ; tests of dominance in hand and eye preferences ; and tests of visual sensation as measured by the Betts *Ophthalmic Telebinocular.* The *Telebinocular* is an instrument resembling a stereoscope mounted on a stand. Stereoscopic slides are inserted in the instrument and indicate pupil's difficulties in binocular acuity, right and left eye acuity, far and near point fusion, stereopsis, vertical and lateral imbalance, and ametropia.

The tests are not designed to diagnose or define visual defects with sufficient exactness for prescription. They have value rather as an initial screen to select children who need to be referred for further examination of vision by an eye specialist. When used in this way, the *Telebinocular* enables teachers to discover eye-defects with greater accuracy than would be obtained by teacher-judgment or the usual visual charts. The *Telebinocular* does not detect all types of visual defects, however, and children having certain difficulties, such as unequal size of retinal images, anomalies of visual fields, etc., may escape detection. It would be helpful to examiners using the instrument had the author given reliability coefficients of the tests and discussed validity in terms of the amount of agreement found between the *Telebinocular* tests and later complete eye-examinations by eye-specialists.

As an instrument for discovering children needing eye-examinations, the *Telebinocular* has considerable value. As a measure of reading-readiness, however, the *Betts Ready to Read Tests* do not give as much statistical information as to their standardization and predictive value as would be desired by clinical examiners. They should prove helpful to teachers, however, in pointing out at least a large proportion of the children who are suffering from eye defects and who need to have such defects corrected in early school life.

Guy Wagner, State Normal School, Oswego, New York. Studies of the *Betts Ready to Read Tests* have dealt almost exclusively with only one of the four sets of tests which comprise the complete series. This set, the Visual Sensation and Perception Tests, measures certain anomalies of the eyes when both eyes are seeing. As a result, the appraisals made by different investigators have carried the impression that the Betts tests were concerned only with peripheral visual factors. Although these tests lay emphasis upon the value of effective and comfortable vision in the reading process, a study of the entire series reveals the tests as also measuring certain central factors and auditory factors which are deemed to be important in analysis of a subject's readiness for reading.

The first set of tests measures visual readiness by checking the ability of the subject to match letters, words, and phonetic elements and to recognize letters. The telebinocular is not used here and thus the measurement is not concerned with binocular vision. On the grounds that children who are unable to recognize similarities in letters and words are probably too immature to enter the work of beginning reading the inclusion of these tests in the series appears to be justified. Results of a study by Wilson and Burke[1] of the relationships between reading readiness test scores and measures of reading ability present evidence "that certain abilities with letter forms and sounds were strikingly related to the reading process, namely : naming letters, giving phonic combinations, giving letter sounds, and writing words."

The second set of tests measures auditory readiness and is concerned not only with auditory efficiency but measures such central factors

[1] Wilson, Frank T., and Burke, Agnes. "Reading Readiness in a Progressive School." *Teach Col Rec* 38:565–80 Ap '37.

as auditory memory span and auditory fusion. In addition, facility in the interpretation of language and background of experiences are apparently measured by this test. In a study of the relation of reading comprehension and retention to hearing comprehension and retention, Young [2] states that his findings "justify somewhat the implication that in any case of reading disability the first step should be to ascertain the language difficulties of the case."

The third set of tests is designed to detect visual refractive errors and certain anomalies of binocular co-ordination. An evaluation of these tests focuses attention on two problems: first, Are the eye defects and anomalies which are measured related to efficient, comfortable, and sustained reading?; second, Does the use of the *Ophthalmic Telebinocular* produce valid and reliable results?

In answer to the first question, studies by Betts,[3] Clark,[4] Eames,[5] Farris,[6] Fendrick,[7] Kanarik and Manwiller,[8] Selzer,[9] Taylor,[10] and Wagner [11] appear to justify the belief that inadequate vision is associated with inefficient reading although the differences in visual functioning between good and poor readers are small. There is a variation in findings as to the binocular anomalies that are most closely associated with reading deficiency but consistency in reports that refractive errors affect reading efficiency.

Swanson and Tiffin [12] and Witty and Kopel [13]

have reported results with this set of the Betts Tests which show that the poor readers are not characterized by a greater incidence of visual defects and anomalies than the good readers. However, these investigators stress in their conclusions the importance of good vision for optimum physical efficiency and achievement of both poor and good readers. Witty and Kopel conclude that "visual defects may, in individual cases, seriously impede the reading process or contribute to its disfunction." Swanson and Tiffin state that they "do not wish to discourage a broad program of eye examination in the elementary schools. Betts' test will undoubtedly shed light on occasional individual cases where a student is handicapped in reading by a visual defect."

The question as to the validity and reliability of this set of the Betts test awaits a final answer. Betts [14] states that "School people and doctors in the Cleveland area gave full cooperation in the validation of the *Betts Ready to Read Tests*." A study by Uhl [15] presents evidence that "many pupils have deficiencies that can be detected readily through the use of these tests." Gates and Bond [16] found significant variations in results when the tests were given at frequent intervals to twenty-six first grade children. These inconsistencies were attributed to lack of experience in test taking on the part of the children. The investigators indicated that the results would be more reliable with older children. The experience of the writer in working with students in giving these tests leads to the belief that the reliability of the tests is high when the tests are administered by an experienced and careful worker.

The fourth set of tests measure word recognition at various levels while the subject is experiencing two-eyed vision. Success in this test is dependent not only on efficient oculomotor control but upon ability to recognize words. Thus, while subjects with normal oculomotor control will pass the Visual Sensation and Perception Tests, lacks in word recognition skills will be detected by these tests of Oculomotor and Perception Habits. These tests show that

2 Young, William E. "The Relation of Reading Comprehension and Retention to Hearing Comprehension and Retention." *J Exp Ed* 5:30–9 S '36.
3 Betts, Emmett A. "Prevention and Correction of Reading Disabilities." *Elem Engl R* 12:25–32 F '35.
4 Clark, Brant. "Additional Data on Binocular Imbalance and Reading." *J Ed Psychol* 27:473–5 S '36.
5 Eames, T. H. "Improvements in Reading Following the Correction of Eye Defects of Non-readers." *Am J Ophthal* 17:324–5 Ap '34.
6 Farris, L. P. "Visual Defects as Factors Influencing Achievement in Reading." *Jr-Sr H S Clearing House* 9:226–8 D '34.
7 Fendrick, Paul. *Visual Characteristics of Poor Readers.* Columbia University, Teachers College, Contributions to Education, No. 656. New York: Bureau of Publications, the College, 1935. Pp. 54.
8 Kanarik, Rosella, and Manwiller, C. E. "How a High School Attacks Its Learning Difficulties in Reading and Arithmetic." *Pittsburgh Sch* 11:94–116 Ja-F '37.
9 Selzer, Charles A. *Lateral Dominance and Visual Fusion.* Harvard Monographs in Education, No. 12. Cambridge, Mass.: Harvard University Press, 1933. Pp. 119.
10 Taylor, Earl A. *Controlled Reading: A Correlation of Diagnostic, Teaching, and Corrective Techniques.* Chicago, Ill.: University of Chicago Press, 1937. Pp. xxviii, 368.
11 Wagner, Guy W. "The Maturation of Certain Visual Functions and the Relationship Between These Functions and Success in Reading and Arithmetic," pp. 108–46. In *Studies in Psychology of Reading, Volume 1.* University of Iowa Studies in Psychology, No. 21; Psychological Monographs, Vol. 48, No. 3, Whole No. 215. Princeton, N.J.: Psychological Review Co., 1937.
12 Swanson, Donald E., and Tiffin, Joseph. "Betts' Physiological Approach to the Analysis of Reading Disabilities as Applied to the College Level." *J Ed Res* 29:443–8 F '36.
13 Witty, Paul A., and Kopel, David. "Studies of Eye-Muscle Imbalance and Poor Fusion in Reading Disability: An Evaluation." *J Ed Psychol* 27:663–71 D '36.

14 Betts, Emmett A. *The Prevention and Correction of Reading Difficulties.* Evanston, Ill.: Row, Peterson & Co., 1936.
15 Uhl, Willis L. "Apparatus for Diagnosis of Reading Disabilities," pp. 183–6. In *The Role of Research in Educational Progress: Official Report of the Meetings Held at New Orleans, Louisiana, February 20–24, 1937.* National Education Association. American Educational Research Association. Washington, D.C.: the Association, May 1937. Pp. 225.
16 Gates, Arthur I., and Bond, Guy L. "Reliability of Telebinocular Tests of Beginning Pupils." *J Ed Psychol* 28:31–6 Ja '37.

a substantial number of intermediate grade children recognize only a few words at the primary levels corresponding to grades one, two, and three. In many cases reversal or confusion of letter and word forms are evidenced. Although no investigations of these tests are known to the writer, the value of information regarding the vocabulary level and specific word recognition difficulties of individual pupils seem important in a reading program which cares for the problems of the retarded reader. .

[1098]
Durrell Analysis of Reading Difficulty. Grades 1–6; p1937, c1933–37; a battery of individual tests; 1 form; (30) minutes; $1.50 per 25 individual record blanks; 50¢ per booklet of reading paragraphs; 50¢ per tachistoscope; 25¢ per manual of directions; $1.65 per examiner's kit (including 5 record blanks); D. D. Durrell; World Book Co.

Marion Monroe, Pittsburgh Public Schools. These tests consist of oral reading and recall, silent reading and recall, word analysis as measured by tachistoscopic exposures compared with long-time exposures, rate of reading, phonetic abilities, handwriting and spelling. A check list of difficulties is provided so that after each test has been administered, the examiner may record observations on errors and note various difficulties and mannerisms during reading. Norms are provided for each test in terms of three levels for each grade, low, medium, and high. A profile of abilities is given on the face sheet of the test. This battery of tests provides an especially helpful instrument for observation and recording of specific difficulties in reading and should prove of value to teachers and clinical psychologists.

[1099]
Durrell-Sullivan Reading Capacity and Reading Achievement Tests. Grades 3–6; c1937; 1 form; 45¢ per complete specimen set; 15¢ per manual; D. D. Durrell and H. B. Sullivan; World Book Co.
a) READING CAPACITY TEST: INTERMEDIATE TEST. $1.10 per 25 tests; 25¢ per specimen set.
b) READING ACHIEVEMENT TEST: INTERMEDIATE TEST. $1.25 per 25 tests; 30¢ per specimen set.

William S. Gray, University of Chicago. One of the basic steps involved in the diagnosis of most cases of reading disability is to determine whether the present reading achievement of a pupil is as great as might be expected in the light of his ability to learn. As an aid in this connection, either individual or group tests of mental ability have been used widely. Unfortunately each of these types of tests is open to serious limitations when used as part of a diagnostic battery. In the case of individual tests the time required to administer them makes their use prohibitive for most classroom teachers. In the case of group tests the interpretation of the scores is difficult because reading is usually involved to a greater or lesser extent in taking the test. The situation is further complicated by the fact that the content and language forms involved in any combination of reading and mental tests differ so widely, as a rule, that factors other than difficulties in reading influence variations from expectancy in the results. The need has been urgent, therefore, for a battery of tests which will enable teachers and clinicians to determine accurately the extent of the reading disability of poor readers, after general intelligence and language mastery have been accounted for.

In response to the foregoing need, a battery of reading capacity and reading achievement tests have been developed by Donald D. Durrell and Helen Blair Sullivan. The *Reading Capacity Test* is a group test "measuring the child's capacity to learn to read in terms of his ability to understand spoken language." The test material consists entirely of pictures and comprises two subtests: Test I, Word Meaning, which measures ability to understand spoken words; and Test II, Paragraph Meaning, which measures comprehension of spoken discourse. The *Reading Achievement Test* is a group test which has been organized to give an analytical measure of reading achievement. It parallels the *Reading Capacity Test* in organization and content and has been standardized on the same school population. Test I provides a measure of word meaning and Test II of paragraph meaning. Optional tests of spelling and written recall have also been provided.

When used together the *Durrell-Sullivan Reading Capacity and Achievement Tests* supply data of value in answering the following questions: (1) "Can the child understand the written word as well as he can understand spoken language?" Norms are available for each of the two tests used. In addition, tables are provided which show roughly "the significance of the difference between the score on the *Capacity Test* and the score on the *Achievement Test.* (2) "Is the child's difficulty in reading primarily one of vocabulary or does it involve longer units of speech?" (3) "In which of the following phases of silent reading does the child show special disability?" understanding sentences, understanding words in context, noting details, getting the central thought, locating specific information.

The optional tests in spelling and written recall show also whether the child has difficulty in spelling and whether he is able to make a satisfactory written summary of materials which he reads, without the benefit of repeated access to these materials.

The basic assumption underlying these tests is "that serious reading disabilities can be discovered by revealing discrepancies between the child's understanding of spoken language and his understanding of the printed word." It is obvious that if a child can understand spoken words or sentences and cannot grasp their meaning in written or printed form that some form of reading difficulty is involved. In order to insure that the discrepancy revealed is not due to differences in the inherent difficulty of the test materials, the authors developed experimentally lists of words and sentences which were comparable in difficulty when presented orally. These tests were then split into two series of approximately equal difficulty and used in the reading capacity and the reading achievement tests. The reliability coefficients which were secured indicated that the tests were highly satisfactory. It remains to determine how readily and efficiently the tests can be administered under practical classroom conditions.

A controversial issue relates to the validity of calling the first of the two instruments a reading capacity test. The authors doubtless assume that the mental processes involved in understanding spoken language comprise the essential factors involved in learning to read. No analysis of the two learning activities is presented in support of their assumption. It may be argued that essential factors which differentiate the two activities are adequate auditory acuity and memory on the one hand, and adequate visual acuity and memory on the other hand. Detailed analysis may reveal other distinguishing characteristics of considerable importance. Undoubtedly the difference in achievement on the two tests reveals a fact of large significance in diagnosing severe cases of reading disability.

A second question relates to the validity of using a different device for checking meaning in the two tests. In the case of both word meaning and paragraph meaning, pictures are used in the *Reading Capacity Test* and printed words or phrases in the *Reading Achievement Test*. The obvious assumption is that these methods are equivalent or at least make the same demand for interpretation upon the reader. No data was presented in support of this view. It is reasonable to assume that identifying the meaning of a spoken word with one of several pictures may be a radically different process from identifying the meaning of a printed word with one of several other printed words. In the latter case failure to respond accurately may be due to difficulty in recognizing the word or phrase which represents the meaning of the test word or passage. It appears, therefore, that the two tests might have been more comparable if pictures had been used in both tests rather than pictures in one and printed words in the other.

Marion Monroe, Pittsburgh Public Schools. This attractive and unique combination of tests will undoubtedly catch the interest of examiners in the field of reading disabilities. The tests consist of two batteries. The *Reading Capacity Test* is designed to measure a child's ability to respond to words and paragraphs presented orally, the pupil marking pictures which illustrate the text read aloud by the teacher. The *Reading Achievement Test* is a reading test for vocabulary and paragraph comprehension measured by the multiple-choice technique. Both tests are standardized on the same populations and are scored in comparable grade units. The tests are well set up, are statistically satisfactory, and the manual of directions is explicit and well written.

The assumption underlying the tests is that reading disabilities can be discovered by revealing a discrepancy between a child's ability to understand spoken language and his ability to understand printed language. This assumption will probably be challenged to some extent by investigators who regard some types of reading disabilities as a phase of a general linguistic handicap. Many poor readers do well on performance-type intelligence tests, but less well on verbal intelligence tests such as the Binet. They would probably be handicapped somewhat in demonstrating their capacity on a test which stresses the understanding of verbal concepts as a criterion of capacity. Such children might fail to do well on both the *Reading Capacity Test* and the *Reading Achievement Test* because of a disability in a verbal function common to both tests. The types of reading disabilities revealed by the tests would, therefore, be limited somewhat by this assumption underlying the tests. The *Reading Capacity Test* also utilizes very tiny pictures. Although the authors recognize that these pictures are tiny, they did not find that the size of the pictures was a handicap to an experimental group of normal children who tried out both large and small pictures. It would seem desirable, however, to determine also whether children who possess eye defects are in any way handicapped by the small size of the pictures. These two comments on the tests should not be taken in any way to minimize the real value of the tests. The tests are an original and helpful contribution to the problem of the selection of cases for remedial instruction in reading. They will undoubtedly receive wide use and will prove helpful in discovering many children in need of remedial work who might otherwise be overlooked.

[1100]

Elementary Reading: Every Pupil Test, December 1937 and April 1938. Grades 4–6; c1937–38; a new form is scheduled for publication each December and April; 2¢ per test; 1¢ per key; specimen set free; S. Shank; sketches by J. Hunter; Ohio Scholarship Tests.

[1101]

English No. 1, Reading Comprehension: Midland Attainment Tests. Ages 6–14; p1938; 1 form; 2d. per test; 1s. 6d. per 12 tests; 2s. 9d. per 25 tests; 8s. 6d. per 100 tests; 6d. per manual; 1s. 3d. per specimen set (including English tests Nos. 2, 4, and 5 in the same series); 10(15) minutes; R. B. Cattell; University of London Press, Ltd.

[1102]

Junior-Senior High School Reading: Every Pupil Test, December 1937 and April 1938. Grades 7–12; c1937–38; a new form is scheduled for publication each December and April; 2¢ per test; 1¢ per key; specimen set free; S. Shank; Ohio Scholarship Tests.

[1103]

Kelvin Measurement of Reading Ability. Ages 8–12; 1 form; 2s. 6d. per 20 tests; 3d. per specimen set; quantity discounts; 20(30) minutes; C. M. Fleming; Robert Gibson and Sons (Glasgow), Ltd.

[1104]

Kindergarten-Primary Articulation Test. c1935–37; a booklet of pictures to be identified orally by examinees; the sequence of pictures is based upon the frequency with which the sound represented is mispronounced; $1.50 per examiner's booklet (nonconsumable); I. Sherman and B. Kenevan; the Authors, Winona Public Schools, Winona, Minn.

Irving H. Anderson, Harvard University. In this test the ability to articulate sounds is tested by requiring the child to name familiar objects portrayed in drawings. The objects used in the drawings are so selected that the child is required to pronounce each sound in the initial, medial, and final positions. The sounds are arranged in the order of the frequency with which they are mispronounced. As the child names each object, the teacher records the errors made on a specially prepared record sheet. The objects as drawn seem to be sufficiently legible and familiar to control the child's responses as intended. Apparently, there are no norms available.

[1105]

Metropolitan Achievement Tests [Reading]. p1933–35, c1931–35; edited by J. S. Orleans; World Book Co.
a) PRIMARY READING TEST. Grades 1–3; p1933–34, c1931–33; 3 forms; $1.25 per 25; 15¢ per specimen set; 40(60) minutes; G. H. Hildreth. Same test as the combined reading tests in the Primary Batteries of the Metropolitan Achievement Tests.
b) INTERMEDIATE READING TEST. Grades 4–6; p1933–35, c1932–35; 3 forms; $1 per 25; 10¢ per specimen set; 37(45) minutes; R. D. Allen, H. H. Bixler, W. L. Connor, F. B. Graham and J. S. Orleans.
c) ADVANCED READING TEST. Grades 7–8; p1933–35, c1932–35; 3 forms; $1 per 25; 10¢ per specimen set; 37(45) minutes; R. D. Allen, H. H. Bixler, W. L. Connor, F. B. Graham and J. S. Orleans.

Ivan A. Booker, National Education Association. The Metropolitan reading tests, part of the comprehensive *Metropolitan Achievement Tests* for grade school children, are intended primarily as measures of general level of reading achievement. They measure separately the ability to read continuous material and the ability to recognize single words, but they do not purport to give an accurate and detailed diagnosis of specific reading disabilities. There is no measure either of rate of continuous reading or of *power* of comprehension. Each test has relatively few parts, with a substantial number of similar items in each. From the standpoint of reliability and equality of the various forms the Metropolitan reading tests are as satisfactory as most achievement tests. They are published not only as part of the comprehensive test battery but also in three separate booklets: (1) the primary reading test for grades 1, 2, and 3; (2) the intermediate test for grades 4, 5, and 6; and (3) the advanced test for grades 7 and 8.

To test ability to read continuous material the Metropolitan reading tests rely heavily on completion exercises. Both the intermediate and advanced tests use this technic to measure general reading achievement. Sometimes the student must insert an omitted word in the sentence or paragraph he is reading. In other exercises, he must read a paragraph and then answer questions by supplying words or short phrases in the blanks provided. This type of exercise is not entirely objective. For example, one exercise states, "Some trees that are still growing in the West had already reached a large size before Julius Caesar was _____." All right! What would you say? How many right answers can you name? The key gives three: "born," "alive," "living." But scorers are told to give credit for all answers that are unmistakably correct. Thus, scoring is somewhat subjective. Moreover, the process of scoring must be slower than with a test where each item has one and only one possible answer, for the student's response often must be compared with a list of right responses and then perhaps rated on its own merits without reference to the key. Furthermore, although the speed at which pupils can supply missing words in completion exercises probably is an important index of reading skill, such exercises are not representative of the reading situations that pupils regularly encounter.

The vocabulary parts of the Metropolitan reading tests make use of the multiple-choice technic and a majority of the items seem well constructed. However, the test words are not presented in context, as some believe they should be in any measure of the pupil's *reading vocabulary*. Moreover, throughout the vocabulary test there are occasional items which seem to require an unreasonable amount of discrimination in word meaning. A few samples will illustrate this point. In one exercise the choice is between *superior* and *overbearing* as synonyms for *imperious*. Webster's *New International Dictionary* gives the word *domineering* as a synonym for all three of these words. In another, *prudent* must be defined either as *sensible* or *careful*. Which would you say? Webster's dictionary defines prudent as *cautious, highly sensible,* etc., but in no place uses the word *careful*. According to the scoring key, however, *careful* is correct. Is it? The question is, Should any test item offer alternatives so closely identified in meaning that each of them and the test word are defined in standard dictionaries by the use of some common synonym? In the vocabulary section of the primary reading test, especially, some of the suggested synonyms seem rather poorly to define the test word. For example, is *good* an accurate synonym for *kind?* Or again, Does the classification

of a word explain its meaning better than an analogy? For example, Does *cook* or *fry* mean "most nearly the same as" *bake?*

The primary reading test booklet contains six tests. The first three are intended particularly for the first grade and the poorer readers in the next two grades; the last three, for superior readers in the first grade and ordinary pupils in the second and third grades. The manual emphasizes the fact that teachers may administer "any selection of the six tests in the booklet, or all of them," according to the abilities of the pupils. Age and grade norms are given for each of the six parts of the test. The composite score suggested is the average reading grade equivalent. This could be obtained, of course, whether all six tests had been administered or only two of them. In all comparisons of average ratings, therefore, it is quite essential to know whether the same number of tests, and, indeed, the same ones, have been administered to all pupils. Furthermore, unless one can appropriately use all six of the tests, it is somewhat wasteful to purchase a sixteen-page test booklet and use only part of it.

The third section of the primary test booklet requires the pupil to identify and mark either two or three words of similar class in each series of six. The words marked in one case are "everything that grows"; in another, "the things that fly"; etc. A mechanical weakness in connection with this exercise is the fact that items are numbered 1–3; 4–5; 6–8; etc. This shows how many words should be marked. In addition, the examiner cannot readily refer to the items by number. Pupils are expected to work on each test item simultaneously, being allowed just 20 seconds for each item. But the examiner cannot say, "Now look at row 4." He must keep them together by saying, "Look at the next row of words. Mark everything that grows," etc. The "next row" is quite indefinite for slow workers—consistently behind time—and for pupils who have gone back to some previous item that was left unfinished. If directions are followed as given in the manual, a number of pupils are likely to become hopelessly lost on this exercise.

For general survey purposes, the Metropolitan reading tests offer many advantages. As a result of wide use of the test, the age and grade norms are significant. Comparable forms make it possible to retest and determine what progress has been made during a semester or year. The tests are easy to administer and re-quire less than an hour of working time.

Joseph C. Dewey, Westminster College. Se-lected portions of the complete test battery were used in these separately published reading tests. It appears that the tests provide a rather in-adequate measurement of total reading ability because of the failure to test the various read-ing skills. The primary test seems superior to the others in this respect. A valuable feature of the tests on reading comprehension is the effort to measure the pupil's ability to make inferences from the material read. However, portions of the tests may measure intelligence rather than reading ability. No provision is made for diagnosis of reading difficulties nor the measurement of the rate of reading.

[1106]

Minnesota Reading Examination for College Students. c1930–35; 2 forms; only the examiner's manual revised in 1935; 46(55) minutes; $6 per 100 tests, including examiner's manual and scoring key; 35¢ per specimen set; M. E. Haggerty and A. C. Eurich; University of Minnesota Press.

Ruth Strang, Columbia University. DESCRIP-TION OF TEST. The first part tests vocabulary and is made up of one hundred words. The second part tests paragraph reading and con-tains ten paragraphs of increasing difficulty with a series of exercises based on each. This test is one of the most frequently reported tests in the literature on reading and also one of the most widely used reading tests in colleges as judged by a survey of reading in eighty-three colleges and universities.

RELIABILITY. The reliability coefficients of the two parts of the test vary. Coefficients ob-tained by the split-halves method and corrected by the Spearman-Brown formula have been reported as .93 and .95 for Part I, and .69 and .61 for Part II. Retest methods give coefficients of .91 for Part I and .78 for Part II and .87 for the total score. Correlations between the two parts cluster around .50.

CORRELATION WITH OTHER FACTORS. The ex-amination shows correlation with intelligence tests ranging from .55 to .75. Vocabulary shows a slightly higher correlation with intelligence tests than does paragraph meaning.

The correlations reported between scores on this reading test and college scholarship are approximately .50 or lower, the vocabulary scores correlating about the same as the para-graph reading scores in spite of their differ-ences in reliability.

The test appears to be a good measure of "general" reading ability as judged by correla-tions of .84 and .75, respectively, for the vo-cabulary and paragraph meaning parts of the test, with a composite standard score for four reading tests. With individual reading tests the correlations for the Minnesota paragraph read-ing test are, in general, less than .50. The vo-cabulary test, however, seems to correlate higher with both the total score on tests and scores on paragraph comprehension of other tests than does the paragraph meaning section of the Minnesota test.

REACTION OF THE STUDENT TO THE TEST. The reactions of students to this test are favorable. "This test seems to be a real challenge to college students. The words and paragraphs are inter-esting." The difficult paragraphs were con-sidered to be stimulating and the material really of the sort students are required to read in college.

DIAGNOSTIC VALUE. Considerable diagnostic value may be extracted for a student with the study of the specific errors which he made.

[1107]

Minnesota Speed of Reading Test for College Students. c1936; 2 forms; 6(15) minutes; $2.75 per 100 tests, including directions; 35¢ per specimen set; A. C. Eurich; University of Minnesota Press.

Frederick B. Davis, Avon Old Farms, Avon, Connecticut. This test appears to measure the same reading skills tested by the familiar *Chap-man-Cook Speed of Reading Tests.* The items cover a wider range of difficulty and the time limit is longer than that of the Chapman-Cook test. When more adequate norms are provided, extending over a wide range of grade levels, this test ought to prove very useful. At present, data regarding its reliability and its correlation with other reading tests are unfortunately not available.

Ruth Strang, Columbia University. DESCRIP-TION OF TEST: It consists of thirty-eight short paragraphs on different subjects, each contain-ing an absurdity to be crossed out. RELIABILITY: The correlations between Forms A and B for each grade and for all grades combined center around .85. CORRELATION WITH OTHER FACTORS: Correlations of the test with Army Alpha (Form A) and the Minnesota College Ability Examination were .45 and .58, respectively.

DIAGNOSTIC VALUE: The scores of speed tests are difficult to interpret because the speed varies with the material and with the attitude and purpose of the reader.

[1108]

Ophthalm-O-Graph. 1936; a portable camera, using 35 mm. standard motion picture film, which photographs eye movements while the examinee is engaged in the act of reading; for A.C. or D.C., $275; Form R records cards, 65¢ per 100; all prices are F.O.B. factory and are subject to a 1% cash discount for payment by the 10th of the month following delivery; American Optical Co.

Stella S. Center, New York University. The binocular reading graph, or eye-movement photograph secured in the act of reading, furnishes objective information concerning the way in which the pupil attacks the printed page. Its validity as a diagnostic and prognostic test is based upon the well established assumption that the form, characteristics, and maturity of the reading habit, together with the nature of the ocular co-ordinations involved, are reflected by the behavior of the eyes during an actual reading performance.

David Kopel, Northwestern University. The eye-movement records obtained from its use reveal patterns which reflect reading status; rarely do the photographs disclose causal factors not previously known or identified by more simple means. The *Ophthalm-O-Graph* should prove of value in eye-movement research; but it is not "the only device that furnishes [in the photographic record] objective information concerning the maturity of the reading habit, or the functional efficiency of the subject in the reading situation."

Marion Monroe, Pittsburgh Public Schools. The camera uses a film upon which a photographic record is made showing fixations per line, regressive movements, speed of reading and co-ordination of the two eyes during reading. The photograph supplements the usual eye-examination by showing the actual behavior of the eye while at work. The information obtained from such records may be used in the selection of appropriate remedial methods. Repeated photographs at intervals during remedial work serve as an objective record of progress in acquiring satisfactory eye-movements during reading. The *Ophthalm-O-Graph* is a useful contribution to the reading laboratory. Some training on the part of examiners is required

for satisfactory use and interpretation. The instrument has its greatest value when used in conjunction with eye-examinations by an eye-specialist and other diagnostic reading tests, since it measures only one aspect of reading.

Joseph Tiffin, Purdue University. The *Ophthalm-O-Graph* makes available to clinicians and research workers a simple and effective method of obtaining a photographic record of eye-movements in reading. Various eye-movement characteristics such as number of fixations per line, duration of fixations and number and extent of regressions may be readily determined from the records. The camera is rugged in construction and so simple in operation that anyone can use it effectively with twenty or thirty minutes' practice. It is the only commercial apparatus for recording eye-movements that can be readily operated by the average public school reading clinician.

The value of the camera in clinical work with retarded readers depends primarily upon the point of view of the clinician and the therapeutic methods which he favors. To those who feel that eye-movement characteristics are habits which determine the level of skill in reading, the camera is a real boon for it offers a simple clinical method of recording these movements. To those who feel, with this reviewer, that in the majority of cases eye-movement behavior reflects the central processes involved in reading, the uses of the camera are obviously more limited. It is hoped that the ease of eye-movement photography which this camera affords will not cause clinicians to ascribe a more important role to eye-movements as causative factors in poor reading than is justified by the evidence from impartial studies.

An application of the camera which should appeal to all reading clinicians as well as to research workers is in the recording and measurement of such factors as lateral inco-ordination, nonsimultaneous movement, speed of movement, and similar elements which might be thought of as limiting physiological characteristics and which, in certain cases, probably cause reading retardation.

Miles A. Tinker, University of Minnesota. Although research on eye-movements in reading began some time before the turn of the century, widespread use of research results in practical situations has been prevalent for only about 20 years. At present eye-movement records find application not only in treatises on reading but also in reading clinics and by school teachers and optometrists. It is becoming increasingly evident that many tend to interpret and to employ results from eye-movement records indiscriminately. It seems desirable that there be a clear understanding of the eye-movement apparatus and of the uses and limitations of photographic measures of reading, especially as applied to remedial reading in high schools and colleges.

The *Ophthalm-O-Graph* is an expertly devised eye-movement camera that has several advantages over the more elaborate equipment employed in most research laboratories. Its portable size makes its use in the school, the office, the clinic and in the laboratory practical. The operation of the machine is so simple that it may be used by the remedial teacher, the doctor or the researcher with a minimum amount of practice. It produces excellent records that are easily read for tabulation of results. The eye-movement measures obtained from the records are: (1) number of fixation pauses per line, per selection or per 100 words; (2) number of backward movements (regressions) per line, per selection or per 100 words; and (3) total reading time. All eye-movement measures are highly consistent (reliable) providing approximately 20 lines of print are read. Both reading time and fixation frequency have high validity, i.e., they are true measures of reading speed. Regression frequency has only fair validity.

There is ample evidence to show that eye-movement patterns (i.e., frequency, regularity and duration of the fixation pauses) are external manifestations of perception and assimilation during reading. Hence they reflect reading status rather than determine proficiency of reading. The term "rhythm reading" and the implication that rhythmic eye-movements produce efficient reading are unfortunate because they are misleading. There is no evidence that "pacing" eye-movements as such develops effective oculomotor habits which improve reading ability as is assumed in the concept of "rhythm reading." In diagnostic and remedial work the clinician should emphasize the central factors of perception and assimilation rather than behavior of the eyes.

In the school or college reading clinic there are two principal means of measuring reading

proficiency: (1) by standardized reading tests, and (2) by photographing eye-movements. Results from these two methods correlate highly (i.e., they are equivalent) and hence the more convenient technique may be employed. The standardized tests are less expensive and easier to use.

Research has shown that poor readers make an excessively large number of fixation pauses, many regressions and frequently do not move far enough to the left in the return sweep from the end of one line to the beginning of the next. Research also shows that when reading proficiency improves through instruction that does not include training of oculomotor habits, the eye-movements readily adjust themselves to the changed conditions of perception and assimilation. That is, there are fewer fixations and regressions.

Eye-movement records may be employed to supplement results from reading tests. They reveal to the poor reader in a convincing manner the irregular and frequent fixations which are symptoms of his laborious and ineffective reading. The oculomotor patterns furnish important clues to the location of special difficulty in comprehending difficult words, formulas and the like. They also show inaccuracies in the return sweep. Lack of binocular coordination of the eyes in reading due to muscular imbalance is easily discovered by photographing the eyes during reading. This fact, however, should have been discovered by an oculist.

The *Ophthalm-O-Graph* is well adapted for photographing eye-movements by the clinician in elementary schools, high schools, and colleges *as far as ease of operation and reading the records are concerned*. The main questions are (1) whether the user of the apparatus can evaluate the records properly and (2) whether the information gained from the records justify the use of this technique. Critical analysis of all evidence available indicates that photographing eye-movements in the reading clinic may be dispensed with without lessening the effectiveness of diagnosis and instruction. Adequate methods are available for satisfactory diagnosis and remedial treatment without employing either eye-movement records of "pacing" or eye-movements. In fact, a too heavy emphasis upon peripheral factors such as oculomotor habits and eye disabilities may divert proper attention from the highly important central factors of perception and assimilation. Nevertheless, the final decision on the use of eye-move-ment photography in the clinic is up to each clinician. If the supplementary information to be gained from eye-movement records is con-sidered important enough, use of the technique may be justified.

Imus, Henry A., Rothney, John W. M., Bear, Robert M. An Evaluation of Visual Factors in Reading. Hanover, New Hampshire: Dart-mouth College Publications. Pp. xiv, 144. [The eye-movement camera referred to in this study is the Ophthalm-O-Graph] * The study to be reported herewith was begun by the Clinical Division of the Dartmouth Eye Institute in September 1936. * A staff of eight members drawn from the Dartmouth Eye Institute and the Department of Psychology began the visual survey, of which this monograph is a prelimi-nary report, by obtaining the data upon 636 members of the Class of 1940 of Dartmouth College. * inferior and superior students make almost the same number of regressions, while the average students make fewer regressions than either group * It would appear then that an increased number of regressions (as meas-ured by the eye-movement camera) is not an academic handicap for students of high scholas-tic aptitude. If the number of regressions were measured reliably by the eye-movement cam-era, we might even argue that an increase in regressive movements is desirable, that the regressions are made for reasons other than those usually implied (faulty reading habits) and that they serve as desirable procedures for the superior students. Since, however, the re-testing coefficient of regressive performances on the eye-movement camera is only 0.60, we cannot emphasize this finding. * It is generally assumed that the photographic record of eye-movements produces a true picture, in an ob-jective manner, of the actual reading habits of the subject. It is claimed that the records pro-vide a means for diagnosing difficulty in read-ing and that groups may be selected for re-medial treatment on the basis of such records. * In order to determine the reliability of the eye-movement camera record we have computed the correlations between scores [regressions, fixations, and speed] obtained by a group of our subjects on first and second, first and third, and second and third repetitions of the reading. * The retesting coefficients vary from 0.592 to 0.720. These figures are *not* high enough for the purpose of individual diagnosis. * the

records, if they are to be of use in individual diagnosis, should be increased to a minimum of 250 words, and a record of 300 words would permit still greater accuracy. We have no hesi-tation in stating that before individual diagnosis of reading difficulty is made on the basis of eye-movement camera scores, the subject should be required to read 5 to 7 times as much ma-terial as he now reads. Comprehension of read-ing on the eye-movement camera is presumed to be measured by means of ten statements covering the material read to which the subject responds by circling a "yes" or "no" to indicate the truth or falsity of the statement. It is rather startling, at our present state of knowledge concerning the measurement of comprehension, to find "yes—no" questions used without cor-rection for guessing. In order to determine the value of such a technique, we required students to answer the questions *before* they had read the paragraphs and then took the scores of stu-dents *after* they had read them for comparison. * the comprehension score cannot be used as evidence that the subject understood what he had read, since he can do almost as well *before* as *after* he has read it * The reason....may be found in the failure to correct for guessing, in using material which is known rather generally by college students, by generally inadequate knowledge of how to examine for comprehen-sion, and in inadequate sampling, all of which has resulted in inexpert test construction. * we find that the speed of reading as measured by the eye-movement camera, the number of fixa-tions and the number of regressions are corre-lated with ability in reading as measured by the Iowa comprehension test to the extent indicated by coefficients of only 0.315, 0.379 and 0.247 respectively * any claim which is made con-cerning its [the camera's] diagnostic value must be followed by a statement that the diag-nosis is likely to be highly unreliable since the presence of difficulties in reading presumed to be measured by the eye-movement camera are not potent factors in determining the effective-ness of the process of reading as measured by the Iowa test * the three eye-movement camera records predict academic success to the extent of less than one per cent greater than could be done by throwing dice. It is important that the figures given above be kept in mind because the implication in so much of the eye-move-ment camera work is that there is a relationship between academic achievement and eye-movement camera score. * the correlation between speed as measured by the Iowa Test of Silent Reading is related to eye-movement camera speed only to the extent indicated by the correlation coefficient of 0.385 * one must question seriously the value of any reading program which is designed to increase speed of reading, as measured by the eye-movement camera or other tests of reading, *so that* it will improve achievement in college * students of high scholastic aptitude made more regressions, as measured by the eye-movement camera, as well as higher academic point scores. The interpretation that better students regress oftener so that they can read more carefully is, at least, worth consideration. These and other findings reported suggest that regressions *per se* are not undesirable. Consideration, however, of the size of the re-testing coefficients reported above will show how tenuous are all these arguments. * The relationship between the number of fixations per hundred words and comprehension scores on the Iowa Test, the scholastic aptitude test and academic points are 0.379, 0.266 and 0.197 respectively. These coefficients indicate that the number of fixations, as measured by the eye-movement camera, do not differentiate groups on these three tests. They certainly cannot be used as indicators of the type of achievement which these tests measure * We have presented some rather convincing evidence concerning the lack of reliability and validity of the eye-movement camera procedure. The following section includes a report of an attempt to use it as a diagnostic instrument in The Eye Clinic. The statements presented herewith were written by a clinician from the regular staff before the study of the reliability and validity reported above was made. It may, therefore, be considered as an independent and clinical, rather than statistical, appraisal of the instrument. * While this study is by no means exhaustive, it is fairly evident from these repeated pictures that an individual does vary in his eye-movement camera performance on successive tests. This is important in that, if a person varies from fifth grade level to college level merely by taking another picture, we must be skeptical when (after remedial reading training or lenses have been prescribed) the eye-movement camera record indicates that the patient's reading ability has been improved. * It is probable that the eye-movement camera may be a useful instrument, that it may be one

used successfully for other age and grade levels than those used in our study, that it can be improved and that it furnishes an objective record which may be of some use other than the prediction of reading performance. It must be stated with considerable emphasis, however, that for our group it is unreliable, that it is not a valid measure of ability in reading if we use tests of reading as criteria, that the scores obtained from it are not closely related to the academic achievement of our subjects, that it cannot be used for individual diagnosis and, therefore, it cannot be used for differentiation of groups for the purpose of administering instruction in remedial reading. We have made several constructive criticisms to conclude this very negative report. Among them are included, first, the increase of the length of the selection read from 5 to 7 times that of the present selection; the more adequate measurement of comprehension by better tests; the selection of material from other sources than the kind now used; some attempt to remove the artificiality of the situation for reading (or presentation of evidence that the situation in the eye-movement camera is closely related to that in the usual situation for reading) and adequate reporting of data from which normative material is prepared. *

[1109]

Primary Reading: Every Pupil Test, December 1937 and April 1938. Grades 2–3; c1937–38; a new form is scheduled for publication each December and April; 2¢ per test; 1¢ per key; specimen set free; S. Shank; sketches by J. Hunter; Ohio Scholarship Tests.

[1110]

Progressive Reading Tests. Grades 1–3, 3–6, 7–9, 9–13; c1934–37; 4 levels; 75¢ per 25 tests; 15¢ per specimen set of any one level; E. W. Tiegs and W. W. Clark; [California Test Bureau].
a) PRIMARY BATTERY. Grades 1–3; c1934–37; 3 forms; 35(40) minutes.
b) ELEMENTARY BATTERY. Grades 3–6; c1934–37; 3 forms; 35(40) minutes.
c) INTERMEDIATE BATTERY. Grades 7–9; c1934–37; 3 forms; 50(55) minutes.
d) ADVANCED BATTERY. Grades 9–13; c1934–36; 2 forms; 50(55) minutes.

Ivan A. Booker, National Education Association. These reading tests are designed to measure two general types of ability, namely, reading vocabulary and reading comprehension. The 1937 norms are "derived from tests given to over 100,000 pupils in schools throughout the United States." In view of the number of test forms and grade levels involved, however, each form has been standardized on fewer cases than many readers would infer from the foregoing statement. Norms for the advanced battery, for example, are based on test results from only "1500 pupils in Grades 9, 10, 11, 12, and 13 in seven schools." The tests have been validated by customary intercorrelation with other reading tests but more especially by selecting test situations which "represent the essential elements of the basic skills which are needed for success" in the work of the grades for which the battery is appropriate. Although the value of the latter method is apparent when it is skillfully employed, its subjectivity and obvious limitations should also be recognized. Reliability coefficients reported by the authors for each major division of the four test units in the series—i.e., the batteries for various grade levels—range from about .86 to .96, most of them falling above .90. When reliability is determined, not for the entire series of grades for which each test battery is designed but for pupils in a single grade, the coefficients usually are somewhat lower, ranging from .77 to about .96.

The vocabulary test for primary grades is subdivided into three parts and the corresponding test for later grades into four parts. Each comprehension test in the series likewise is made up of three distinct parts. The tests are organized in this way to provide a diagnosis of specific weaknesses. The interpretation of the test includes the development of individual profile charts for all the pupils tested. Although the organization of the test undoubtedly is helpful to teachers who are interested in the types of errors which their pupils make, the authors and publishers do not claim high reliability for each of the six, or seven, subdivisions of the various test batteries. A number of schools which regularly use the *Progressive Reading Tests* disregard all scores except for total-vocabulary, total-comprehension, and total-reading scores. This does not mean, however, that the teachers in these schools find no diagnostic help in the tests. It indicates only that the scores on the shorter subdivisions seem inadequate for purposes of permanent records and for statistical analyses.

A feature of the *Progressive Reading Tests,* thought to be a weakness by some who have made extensive use of them, is the indefinite time limit recommended. Examiners are directed to let pupils work on each part of the test until about 90 per cent of the pupils have finished. This is done because the test is designed to measure the *power* rather than *speed.* With some justification, however, it is claimed that inconsistencies on the part of examiners—some allowing more time than others—partially invalidate any comparison of the results obtained in different schools.

The vocabulary tests for primary and elementary grades require the pupils (1) to recognize when two similar words are the same, or mean the same; (2) to recognize the printed form of words pronounced by the examiner; and (3) to identify words having *same* or *opposite* meanings. The vocabulary tests in the intermediate and advanced batteries require the selection of synonyms, using a 4-item, multiple-choice technic. Twenty to twenty-five test words appear in each of the four parts and the parts are designated: (1) mathematics, (2) science, (3) social science, and (4) literature. This raises the issue as to whether familiarity with more or less technical words, or proficiency in the use of general nontechnical words, is the more significant indication of reading ability. If one is interested primarily in general vocabulary, the *Progressive Reading Tests* obviously would not be selected.

The comprehension tests require pupils (1) to follow directions, (2) to interpret meaning, and (3) to organize materials. In common with most comprehension tests, some of the items are open to criticism on the ground that they could be answered correctly by many pupils without having read the test paragraphs on which they depend. Some of the most interesting innovations occur in connection with items designed to test ability to organize materials.

The general format of the test makes for ease of scoring. Interpretation helps include (1) the individual profile charts already mentioned, based on the pupil's percentile rank for grade, (2) grade placement norms, and (3) age norms. Anyone interested primarily in a general survey of reading achievement plus some preliminary diagnosis of reading disabilities may well include the *Progressive Reading Tests* among those to be considered for possible use.

Joseph C. Dewey, Westminster College. A valuable feature of these tests is an analysis of learning difficulties and a diagnostic profile which are found on the front page of each test booklet, which enable the teacher to analyze pupil difficulties quickly in order that remedial work may be given, as well as to determine grade placement in' reading.

Another valuable feature of the vocabulary tests is the use of lower-case printed words, and words printed in script, capitals, and italics. This enables the teacher to measure the pupil's ability to recognize words in various forms.

The primary test consists of: (1) reading vocabulary (word forms, word recognition, and the meaning of opposites); and (2) reading comprehension (following directions, directly stated facts, and interpretations).

Although the authors state that they seek to measure the ability of pupils to interpret what is read and to make inferences, it appears that the questions used for this purpose require the reproduction of facts stated directly in the reading context rather than inferences made from these facts. The directions, "Draw a line under the right words below," in the multiple-choice items do not seem adequate for primary children.

The questions on the table of contents seem exceedingly difficult for primary children. For example, the children are asked what would be found on certain pages when this is not stated directly in the data given. If this exercise is suitable for primary children it is difficult to understand why the authors in the same exercise for the intermediate grades use two out of three questions the answers to which can be found stated directly in the table of contents given.

The elementary test consists of: (1) reading vocabulary (word form, word recognition, meaning of opposites, and meaning of similarities); and (2) reading comprehension (following directions, interpretations, and organization).

Again the authors provide very little in the way of testing ability to make inferences. A large majority of the test items deal with directly stated facts while others operate as vocabulary tests in that they require the pupils to know synonyms for various words given in the reading context. Question 8 in the section on interpretations does not seem clear either in Form A on Alaska or Form B on Canada.

The intermediate test consists of (1) reading vocabulary (mathematics, science, social science, and literature); and (2) reading comprehension (following directions, organization, and interpretation).

The vocabulary test seems valuable because it seeks to measure the pupil's knowledge of the vocabulary of the various subject matter fields. This should give some estimate of the pupil's ability to do the reading necessary in high school work.

The section on interpretations is subject to the same criticism as that given previously. This section may test interpretation, but it does not seem to test the pupil's ability to make inferences from the material read.

An excellent manual of directions is provided for each of the grade levels which provides directions for administering the tests as well as adequate norms for determining grade placement in reading. According to the manuals the reliabilities of the tests are high, ranging from .840 to .962.

On the whole these tests should provide a valuable instrument for teachers who wish a test which may be used for diagnostic as well as for survey purposes. The tests, however, make no provision for measuring the speed of reading.

[1111]

Reading Comprehension Test: National Achievement Tests. Grades 3–8; c1938; 1 form; $1.50 per 25 tests; 100 or more, 4½¢ per test; 5¢ per specimen set; nontimed (30) minutes; R. K. Speer and S. Smith; Acorn Publishing Co.

[1112]

Reading Speed Test: National Achievement Tests. Grades 3–8; c1938; 1 form; $1.25 per 25 tests; 100 or more, 4¢ per test; 5¢ per specimen set; R. K. Speer and S. Smith; Acorn Publishing Co.

[1113]

Record for Reading Diagnosis. Elementary grades; c1936; 1 to 99 copies, 2¢ per folder; 100 or more copies, 1½¢ per folder; C. R. Stone; Webster Publishing Co.

[1114]

Traxler Silent Reading Test. Grades 7–10; c1934; 2 forms; $1.50 per 25; 15¢ per Teacher's Handbook; 30¢ per specimen set; 46(50) minutes; A. E. Traxler; Public School Publishing Co.

Frederick B. Davis, Avon Old Farms, Avon, Connecticut. This test is so designed that, in addition to supplying a single measure of reading ability, "pupils who are in need of special remedial attention can be identified and the general nature of their needs can be stated." (*Teacher's Handbook,* p. 3.) For these purposes, norms are provided for scores on each of the four parts of the test as well as for two composite scores, one for the whole test and one for the three comprehension sections taken together.

Mr. Traxler discusses the validity of the part scores in the accompanying *Teacher's Handbook,* citing statistical data which are indicative of their validity. Subjective examination of the test blank leads one to the conclusion that the four subtests are about as valid as most reading tests are.

The validity of the total score is, however, open to question. Because of the nature of the rate score and its heavy weighting in the determination of the composite total score, the latter should, in my opinion, be used for individual measurement only with great care and then only when the part scores are taken into consideration. With the present scoring system it is possible for a rapid careless reader to race through the *rate* test with no real intention of understanding the material, to make a very low score on the *story comprehension* test, and to obtain a high *total score.*

To illustrate the weighting of the part scores in computing the *total score,* the average raw scores for grade seven, as given in the *Teacher's Handbook,* together with the percentage of the *total score* which each part constitutes, are presented here: Part I; *rate,* 35 points or 49%; Part I; *story comprehension,* 10 points or 14%; Part II; *word meaning,* 13 points or 18%; Part III; *power of comprehension,* 14 points or 19%; *Total Score,* 72 points or 100%.

Without considering the difficult problem of what percentage of a composite reading test score should be assigned to rate of reading, it seems reasonable to conclude that in this particular test the story *comprehension* section of Part I should be weighted more heavily so that rapid, careless, or superficial reading would be penalized equally in the scoring with laboriously careful slow reading.

Although the validities of the part scores seem reasonably well established, the standard errors of obtained scores on the several parts of the test are far larger than we should like to have them for use in individual diagnosis. On the *rate* test, for example, which has the highest reliability coefficient of any of the parts (.82 in grade nine), the standard error of an obtained raw score is 5 points among a group of 655 ninth grade pupils tested last fall in the Educational Records Bureau independent schools testing program. This standard error may be compared with the standard deviation

of the distribution of raw scores in the ninth grade which was 11.8.

If this test were to be used for individual diagnosis, the differences among the four part scores would have to be extraordinarily large before they could be taken as evidence of real differences in ability. This greatly limits the utility of the test in the diagnosis of individual reading difficulties and, unfortunately, the author has given no consideration to this fundamental limitation of the test in the *Teacher's Handbook.* It is only fair to state that other reading tests are similarly limited by the unreliability of their part scores.

Finally, the norms presented in the *Teacher's Handbook* do not cover a sufficiently wide range; it is, therefore, impossible to obtain grade scores for either good or poor readers at the junior high school level. However, the author implies that senior high school norms will be made available later. It will be of great value to find out to what extent the test will differentiate between tenth, eleventh, and twelfth grade readers.

It seems fair to conclude that this test is of very limited value in the diagnosis of individual reading difficulties when used alone. It appears likely that for a single measure of an individual's reading ability the total comprehension score, rather than the total score, should be employed. Its principal value probably lies in group measurement of the functions tested by its four component sections.

Spencer Shank, University of Cincinnati. A critical examination of the two available forms and the manual of the *Traxler Silent Reading Test* will readily show two things: (a) that the phases of reading employed in the procedures and content of the test are most desirable, (b) but that certain qualities (expected of a modern, standardized test) leave something to be desired, as they apply or function in the Traxler test.

By means of the test, answers are sought to four questions: (1) how fast can pupils read, (2) how good is their understanding of words, (3) how good is their comprehension of important points *from a single reading* of materials, and (4) how able are they to comprehend reading materials which steadily increase in difficulty, with repeated readings possible. These four phases of reading—speed, vocabulary and two types of comprehension—do not cover all that is inherent in silent reading, but they are essential and are of great importance. If all other factors were maintained at a desirable level, a test built upon these phases of reading should give a good measure of reading ability. However, such a test could be diagnostic only to a very limited degree, if diagnosis were to be used as a point of departure for remedial work with remediable cases.

Mention was made above of certain qualities of the Traxler test that left something to be desired. This opinion is based upon information from two sources—the *Teacher's Handbook* and a detailed analysis of the two available forms of the test. According to Traxler, statistical determination of validity was secured by correlating various phases of the test with selected criteria. Of these phases, the most important—comprehension—has the lowest correlation (.799) with its criterion, which was a combination of scores on the *Monroe Silent Reading Test,* the *Thorndike-McCall Reading Scale,* and the paragraph-meaning part of the *Stanford Achievement Test.* Either the criterion was poorly chosen or it must be said that the Traxler test *only approaches* doing as good a job of measuring as the three other reading tests combined. An application of the coefficient of alienation (k) to the data on validity will bring out the force of this statement.

In the matter of reliability (Forms 1 and 2), the coefficients are as follows: rate, .848; word meaning, .860; story comprehension, .612; power of comprehension, .728; total comprehension, .926; and total score, .908. The reliability coefficients on the two phases of comprehension are definitely low. None of these data are for more than one grade, either 8 or 9. What the data on all grades would be is left either to conjecture or one's own investigation.

Why the reliability coefficients on the two phases of comprehension are low, and why the "validity coefficient" between the same phases combined and the criterion with which they were correlated is only .799, Traxler does not suggest. However, if the Traxler tests on comprehension are broken down, it will be shown that comprehension of the paragraphs is measured by asking for: (a) details directly stated in the content, (b) details implied in the content (involving multiple-choice technique), (c) "yes" "no" answers, (d) total meanings, (e)

central thought, etc. These techniques have long been proven good, but their application to the paragraphs in either of the forms is not consistent. Some paragraphs are followed by only one type of question, others by two or three, seemingly without plan. In addition, if the two forms are compared, the inconsistency is increased more than ever. Another way of putting this point is to inquire, What is paragraph comprehension? Is it something that is to be measured only through details in one instance, and a combination of several different techniques in another? It is suggested that herein lie some of the explanations of the statistical data on validity and reliability of the Traxler test.

Finally, if testing is to be followed by remedial work, a thorough diagnosis is imperative. The Traxler test *does not provide* the machinery for such a diagnosis. Four scores are available: speed, vocabulary, story comprehension and paragraph comprehension. If a pupil's score is low in either of the last two, there is no way in determining why. Furthermore, there is no suggestion as to what would be needed to strengthen these phases. The Traxler test may give broad, general indications of a pupil's reading; it will not indicate in detail the expert services so essential in the improvement needed.

[1115]

Unit Scales of Attainment, Reading. Grades 1B, 1A, 2B, 2A, 3, 3–4, 4–6, 7–8, 9–12; c1932–34; 3 forms; 9 levels; same as reading comprehension tests in the Unit Scales of Attainment; 75¢ per 25 tests; 20¢ per specimen set; nontimed (40–45) minutes; M. J. Van Wagenen; Educational Test Bureau, Inc.

Joseph C. Dewey, Westminster College. This series is concerned largely with measuring pupils' ability to understand paragraphs read. Since the items have been scaled, the teacher can determine how difficult material each pupil can understand. An excellent feature is the attempt to measure pupils' ability to make inferences from material read which is an important phase of reading comprehension ability. However, the author seems to have neglected to measure several other skills commonly thought a part of total reading ability. Thus, this series seems an excellent survey instrument for paragraph comprehension but less valuable as a measure of total reading ability or as a diagnostic instrument.

STUDY SKILLS

[1163]

Critical Classification of Magazines and News-papers. Grades 10–18; p1937; 1 form; 90¢ per 25 tests; 6¢ per sample test; 30(35) minutes; mimeographed; K. C. Pratt; Cooperative Bureau of Educational Research.

[1164]

Information Concerning Library Processes. Grades 10–18; p1937; 1 form; 75¢ per 25 tests; 6¢ per sample test; (15–20) minutes; mimeographed; C. V. Park from a test developed by the Class Librarianship, University of California at Los Angeles, Summer Session, 1935; Cooperative Bureau of Educational Research.

[1165]

Reading and Construction of Tables and Graphs. Grades 10–18; p1936; 2 forms; $1.10 per 25 tests; 15¢ per sample test, both forms; 80(85) minutes; lithotyped; C. Woody and A. Vedder; Cooperative Bureau of Educational Research.

[1166]

Tyler-Kimber Study Skills Test. Grades 9–16; c1937; 1 form; nontimed (90) minutes; $2 per 25 tests; $3.50 per 50; $6 per 100; 500 or more copies, $5 per 100; 15¢ per specimen set; H. T. Tyler and G. C. Kimber; Stanford University Press.

Edward S. Jones, University of Buffalo. This test has been standardized and completely treated by the usual statistical devices. The reliability is high (.90), and the validity, as measured by grade-point ratio in college, is unusually high as such tests go (.51). It differentiates high from low scholarship students, but shows little difference between the junior college classes separated by semesters in college.

It is possible that the title of the test is misleading, since the majority of habits usually thought of as a part of studying are not measured,—e.g., quality and amount of note-taking, getting the meat out of difficult passages, etc. The authors are perhaps fortunate in choosing other kinds of abilities, mainly involving use of factual information about books. The various subtitles of the test include finding what you want in a book, using an index, using general reference books, recognizing common abbreviations, using library card catalogue, interpreting maps, knowing current periodical literature, interpreting graphs.

Apparently the test correlates significantly higher with the *A.C.E. Psychological Examination* (.65) than with grade-point ratio. It might be characterized as a reading-library-intelligence test, and would doubtless compare closely with the *Nelson-Denny Reading Test* or one of the Ohio State University intelligence tests. It should be useful in a how-to-study course.

C. Gilbert Wrenn, University of Minnesota. This test is designed to measure eight different study skills that presumably enter into scholastic work at the college level. These study skills are as follows: (1) finding what you want in a book; (2) using an index; (3) using general reference books; (4) recognizing common abbreviations; (5) using the library card catalogue; (6) interpreting maps; (7) knowing current periodical literature; and (8) interpreting graphs.

This is a power test, taking ordinarily between sixty and ninety minutes. The fact that it is a power test and that many students work over one class period makes it somewhat awkward in administration. The interpretation of the test is given in terms of percentile scores based on junior college students. The percentile scores for each semester of the junior college period are given. In addition, part scores on each of the eight parts are given in terms of quartiles presumably found on the entire college population.

Two assumptions that are made by this test raise questions. Although the test has been used only with junior college students in terms of both composition and standardization, the manual indicates that the test "is suitable for use with high school and college students, i.e., for grades 9–16, inclusive." This is very questionable, since much of the wording of the test and many of the illustrations used are entirely too mature for high school freshmen or sophomores. The wording is often too difficult for any but college students, and many of the references used as illustrations to determine study skills are beyond the scope of high school students. It is rather doubtful that one should expect high school freshmen to be acquainted with such periodicals as the following: *Readers' Guide to Periodical Literature,* the *Monthly Labor Review, Social Science Abstracts, Survey,* the *Congressional Record,* or *Forum.* Only the exceptional freshmen students at the high school level would know of these periodicals and would, therefore, be adequately tested on those portions of the test. Part VIII on interpreting graphs is obviously intended for college students and should prove a stiff measure of interpretational ability of even the best of college freshmen.

The test presumes to measure study skills, and yet the factor of intelligence is not held constant. The correlation coefficient between the *Study Skills Test* and the *American Council on Education Psychological Examination* is .65, higher than the correlation between the *Skills Test* and grade-point ratio, which is .51. The fact that intelligence is a large factor in scores on the *Study Skills Test* is indicated by a correlation of .26 between Study Skills score and grade-point ratio when the psychological examination score is held constant. It is true that both intelligence and work habits enter into scholarship. The extent to which this test measures work habits as such is indicated by the correlation coefficient of .26.

The criticism just given should not be held to invalidate the test. It should, however, indi-cate that the test measures both intelligence and work habits and is not a separate measure of work habits as such. The critical ratio between the mean *Study Skills* score of one hundred high scholarship students and the mean score of two hundred and twenty-five junior college probation students is 15.9, which is quite adequate to indicate that whatever the test measures is a significant factor in scholarship.

This is a valuable instrument, but it is not equally suitable for high school and junior college levels, nor does it measure study skills alone. The correlation coefficients indicate that intelligence is at least as large a factor in the score secured as is the presence or absence of certain work habits. All statistical computations were made upon Sacramento Junior College students.

READING—SECOND MMY

Reviews by Guy L. Bond, Ivan A. Booker, M. E. Broom, G. T. Buswell, Frederick B. Davis, Joseph C. Dewey, Alvin C. Eurich, J. R. Gerberich, Hans C. Gordon, James R. Hobson, Edward S. Jones, David Kopel, Alice K. Liveright, W. C. McCall, William A. McCall, Robert L. McCaul, Constance M. McCullough, Harriet Barthelmess Morrison, W. J. Osburn, Henry D. Rinsland, Holland D. Roberts, David H. Russell, Rachel Salisbury, Clarence R. Stone, Edward A. Tenney, Miles A. Tinker, D. A. Worcester, C. Gilbert Wrenn, and J. Wayne Wrightstone.

[1527]

Analysis of Controversial Writing: Test 5.31. Grades 10-12; 1939; 1 form; revision of Test 5.3; 15¢ per test; 1½¢ per machine-scorable answer sheet; 5¢ per explanation sheet and interpretation guide; $1.50 per set of stencils for machine scoring; Chicago, Ill.: Evaluation in the Eight Year Study, Progressive Education Association.

[1528]

Application of Certain Principles of Logical Reasoning: Test 5.12. Grades 10-12; 1939-40; 1 form; revision of Tests 5.1 and 5.11; 5¢ per test; 1¢ per machine-scorable answer sheet; 5¢ per explanation sheet and interpretation guide; $1 per set of stencils for machine scoring; Chicago, Ill.: Evaluation in the Eight Year Study, Progressive Education Association.

REFERENCES

1 RATHS, LOUIS E. "Evaluating Some Aspects of Proof." *Ed Res B* 17:108-14 Ap '38.
2 RATHS, LOUIS E. "Evaluating the Program of Lakeshore School." *Ed Res B* 17:57-84 Mr 16 '38.
3 RATHS, LOUIS E. "Measuring the Ability to Apply Scientific Principles." *Ed Res B* 17:86-98 Ap 13 '38.
4 *The Evaluation of Abilities Involved in Dealing with Quantitative Relationships.* Chicago, Ill.: Evaluation in the Eight Year Study, Progressive Education Association, March 1939. Pp. [24]. Paper, mimeographed. Out of print.

[1529]

"Brighton" Reading Tests. Ages 8-14 or 9-14; 1931; 6 forms; 1s. 9d. per 50 test papers (nonconsumable); 1s. 9d. per 50 question papers; 6d. per manual; 1s. 3d. per specimen set; Educational Research Sub-Committee of the Brighton and Hove Teacher's Association; London: University of London Press, Ltd.

a) MACAULAY TEST. Ages 8-14; 40(45) minutes.
b) BEE TEST. Ages 8-14; time limit not reported.
c) STEVENSON TEST. Ages 9-14; 34(40) minutes.
d) STURLUNGA TEST. Ages 9-14; 32½(40) minutes.
e) PEPYS TEST. Ages 9-14; 27½(35) minutes.
f) WALPOLE TEST. Ages 9-14; 30(35) minutes.

Frederick B. Davis, Reading and Professional Education Editor, Cooperative Test Service, New York, New York; and Educational Psychologist and Head of the Remedial Department, Avon Old Farms, Avon, Connecticut. The purposes of these tests, as stated in the accompanying manual of instructions, are as follows: "It is the double purpose of these tests to enable a teacher to compare a child's powers of understanding a passage which he has read silently, with the normal powers of children of his age, and later, after an interval, to ascertain whether the child's powers in that respect are improving or not."

The tests include six forms, for each of which separate question papers and norms are provided. When one of the forms is administered, the pupils are given ten minutes in which to read the passage, after which the papers are collected and the question sheets are distributed. At the expiration of a second time limit, which varies from 22½ to 30 minutes, the question sheets are collected. The directions provided in the manual are sufficiently clear, but the time limit for one of the question sheets has been omitted.

No information is given regarding the construction of the tests; there is no statement concerning the specific reading skills which they are intended to measure. As a matter of fact, it seems questionable to call them "reading" tests because the method of administration introduces a memory factor which must greatly influence the scores and affect their validity as measures of comprehension. A rough classification of the 100 items included in the six question papers reveals the following distribution of items:

Items testing factual content 41
Items requiring inference 41
Items testing vocabulary 12
Items testing background knowledge ... 5
Unanswerable item 1

The last item in the list occurs in the *Macaulay Test* and reads as follows: "What was the longest day's journey you could make from London in the coach which took the Great North Road? I do not mean the longest day's journey."

Unfortunately, the items in the various categories listed above are not evenly distributed among the six forms; that is, one form consists almost wholly of fact items, another form almost wholly of inference items. In view of the low correlations which have been found experimentally between scores on these two types of items, one must conclude that the several forms of the *"Brighton" Reading Tests* are not comparable since they do not measure the same functions. For this reason, successive testings with the various forms could not properly be used to accomplish the second purpose of the test as stated in the manual; namely, the measurement of growth to discover the effect of practice.

The manual contains no information about the reliability coefficients of the various forms. Age norms ranging from ages eight to fourteen for two tests and from nine to fourteen for four tests are provided, but the variability of the scores at each age level is not mentioned and the number of cases is not stated. The extent to which the test discriminates between the various age levels can, therefore, only be estimated by an inspection of the raw-score differences between the age norms. On the best-discriminating test the average raw-score difference between grades is 1.6 points but between ages thirteen and fourteen the raw-score difference is only .3 of a point. On the least-discriminating test there is an average raw-score difference of .6 of a point between grades. On the *Sturlunga Test,* which includes

fifteen questions, there is no raw-score difference between the norms for ages nine and ten, the total raw-score difference over the entire range of the test from ages nine to fourteen being only 3.3 points. From these data we can conclude with considerable assurance that most of the differences between the age norms are too small to be significant for individual measurement. It is probable that an individual's score could easily vary by pure chance over the entire range of norms provided. Hence, we must conclude that the tests cannot be used singly to accomplish the first purpose stated in the manual, that of comparing a child's power of understanding a passage with the normal powers of children of his age.

SUMMARY. These tests do not seem to be valid reading-comprehension tests. Furthermore, their apparent lack of discriminating power between the ages for which norms are provided and their probable lack of reliability and comparability combine to make them poor tests of the combination of memory ability and reading-comprehension skills which they appear to measure.

[1530]

Critical-Mindedness in the Reading of Fiction: Test 3.7. Grades 9-12; 1938; an experimental form; 5¢ per test; 1¢ per machine-scorable answer sheet; 2¢ per summary sheet; nontimed (40) minutes; Chicago, Ill.: Evaluation in the Eight Year Study, Progressive Education Association.

REFERENCES

A Descriptive Summary of Evaluation Instruments in the Field of English. Chicago, Ill.: Evaluation in the Eight Year Study, Progressive Education Association, March 1939. Pp. 10. Paper, mimeographed. Out of print.

[1531]

Chicago Reading Tests. Grades 2-4, 4-6, 6-8; 1939; 2 forms, 4 levels; $1.00 per 25; 60¢ per specimen set; Max D. Engelhart and Thelma Gwinn Thurstone; Milwaukee, Wis.: E. M. Hale and Co.

a) TEST A. Grades 1-2; 31(40) minutes.
b) TEST B. Grades 2-4; 42(60) minutes.
c) TEST C. Grades 4-6; 45(55) minutes.
d) TEST D. Grades 6-8; 45(55) minutes.

REFERENCES

1 ENGELHART, MAX D., AND THURSTONE, THELMA G. "Chicago Reading Tests." *Chicago Sch J* 20:74-81 N '38.

Robert Lawrence McCaul, Instructor of Remedial Reading in the Laboratory Schools and the College, The University of Chicago. [Review of Tests B, C, and D.] Underlying the construction of the *Chicago Reading Tests* is a philosophy consisting of two main principles: (a) reading ability is a composite of many abilities and skills, each of which must be measured by an adequate reading test; and (b) the materials of a reading test should correspond to the materials of those courses of the school curriculum which entail reading. As a theory of the nature of reading, the first principle may easily be carried to extremes. Its proponents often consider reading ability a loose conglomeration of independent abilities and skills and ignore the interdependence of these components and the fused unitary way in which they function in normal reading activity. Tests constructed upon this theory customarily afford measurements of a large number of what the authors subjectively judge to be important component reading abilities and skills, and these tests forthwith are labeled "diagnostic." However the reliability of their subtests is usually such that they cannot be safely employed for individual diagnosis. There also remains a question of whether a total measure secured from relatively unanalytical tests, like the *New Stanford Reading Test* or the *Nelson-Denny Reading Test,* is not more valid than a total measure secured from an analytical test where the measures of many subtests are lumped together. So much in general for the theory.

Their adherence to the first principle has caused the authors to make the Chicago tests very broad in sampling. Test C, for example, assesses vocabulary, sentence comprehension, speed, story comprehension, map reading, skimming, paragraph comprehension, drawing conclusions, discerning central ideas, knowledge of details, and interpretation. To facilitate diagnosis, at the end of each of the three tests is a profile chart for numerical and graphic records of the derived scores earned by the pupils from subtests and the whole test. Unfortunately for the diagnostician no reliabilities of the subtests are reported, nor are there probable or standard errors which would enable him to determine when variations in achievement upon the subtests are of real significance. Owing to their espousal of the second principle, the authors have incorporated within the tests literary, social studies, science, health, and other course materials. This is a distinct advantage, for the pupils' ability to read their curricula books is appraised by material analogous to that in their texts.

Preliminary work upon the tests, including the evaluation and final choice of items, appears to have been carefully done. Especially good are the picture items of Test B. They are not subject to the ambiguity which in the case of some tests, notably *Gates Primary Reading Test,* leads a child now and then to fail certain items because he misinterprets the pictures rather than because he misreads the words to be paired with the pictures. Frequently the word choices of vocabulary items in the Chicago tests may not demand precise discrimination. A bright child with a modicum of phonics might be able to answer the items correctly even though he could recognize in context none of the words.

The *Chicago Reading Tests* were tentatively standardized by administering them to approximately 25,000 pupils of grades two to eight in "a representative sample of thirty Chicago Elementary Schools." Before applying the norms to his own pupils, the non-Chicago schoolman should know more about this population and especially more about what is meant by "representative" than he is told by the authors. Grade norms for the subtests of Test B extend from 2.0 to 4.9, for the subtests of Test C they extend from grades 4.0 to 6.9, and for the subtests of Test D the norms extend from grades 6.0 to 8.9. Certain percentages of children will assuredly earn scores entitling them to reading grade placements below the lowest grade norm or above the highest grade norm of the particular subtest that they take. Consequently, no grade ratings of their reading abilities and skills can be obtained unless another reading test, at a lower or higher level, is administered. It would be both a convenience and an economy for the user of these tests were the norms of the subtests expanded by one or more grades above and below their present extremes. This likewise would serve to extricate the authors from the anomalous position in which they place themselves when they recommend that Test B (published as being for grades 2, 3, and 4) be given ordinarily only in grades 2 and 3 and Test C (published as being for grades 4, 5, and 6) be given ordinarily only in grades 4 and 5.

Two final comments about the tests are warranted. First, the skimming sections could be improved by placing the information asked of the pupil less consistently in the same location within the test paragraphs. Second, for the benefit of pupil and scorer the test items might be numbered.

W. J. Osburn, Professor of Education, The University of Washington. [Review of Tests B, C, and D.] Two sittings are recommended for each test. Each test covers comprehension of words, comprehension of sentences, comprehension of paragraphs, and rate. Story comprehension and following directions are found in Test B. Story comprehension and map comprehension in Test C. Story comprehension, map comprehension, and graph comprehension in Test D. The tests show that they have been constructed with a great amount of care. In general, they are well graded so far as vocabulary is concerned. Vocabulary is directly measured under word comprehension. The tests are unique in that they include the interpretation of maps, graphs, and statistical tables. Tests C and D contain a generous amount of material which involves skimming. The exercises in Test D in which a pupil is required to read a paragraph in order to find (*a*) a statement that is true, and (*b*) a statement that is false, are of particular interest.

The tests are of unusual importance because of their possibility as diagnostic instruments. By using them, it is possible to diagnose vocabulary, skimming, and the ability to locate details, antecedents, and central thoughts. In addition there is extensive material dealing with interpretation and inference. The reviewer knows of no other test which includes so many types of reading. Consequently, these tests are to be recommended as among the best of our diagnostic reading instruments.

Standard scores are supplied which are based upon the test papers of more than eight thousand Chicago school pupils. Answer sheets and class record sheets are furnished.

On the adverse side there are only a few things to say. It would be quite an advantage if the questions were numbered. A few of the test items are questionable. In Test B, page 10, the child is invited to respond that "one time a big dog chased Uncle Toby," but the paragraph hardly warrants this inference. On the same page there are two possible answers to page 4 of the same test, "red" and "color" are presented as synonyms. In Test C, page 4, the pupil is required to identify "doubt" and "question" as synonyms. In the same test, page 10, a neighbor is identified as "one who lives in the next village." Elements of this sort seem to contribute to fuzzy thinking. They could easily be eliminated.

There are some evidences that more attention should have been given to the matter of scaling in the separate tests. For example, in Test B which applies to grades 2-4, most of the words are on the first-grade level. A few more are on the second-grade level. The test closes with two words on the fifth-grade level, but no words at all are included for the third and fourth grades. Furthermore, the word "rapidly" is one upon which we do not have accurate information as to its grade level. Possibly it should have been omitted.

While the test contains an unusually wide sample of different types of reading, the frequencies are not so well balanced. In Test B there are only two questions each for "detail" and "central thought," while there are twenty which are concerned with interpretation. Special emphasis upon interpretation is found in all the tests, with consequent neglect of other types. Test D has no questions relating to antecedents and only one relating to central thought. The tests overlap with reference to grade levels, but there is no overlapping of content. This would not be a disadvantage, if the overlapping areas were carefully matched, but no evidence is given on that point. No discussion of validity is presented although an inspection of the tests assures one that that quality has not been overlooked. Grade standards are available, but the T-score technique is not used.

In spite of all this, the tests are well worth what they cost. Indeed, with respect to some features such as map interpretation, graph interpretation, and skimming, they stand almost alone in the field.

[1532]

Diagnostic Examination of Silent Reading Abilities. Grades 4-6, 7-9, 10-16; 1939; 1 form, 3 levels; 10¢ per test; 5¢ per machine-scorable answer sheet; 10¢ per manual; $1 per scoring key for any one level; 25¢ per specimen set; part timed, part nontimed (110-140) minutes; M. J. Van Wagenen and August Dvorak; Minneapolis, Minn.: Educational Test Bureau, Inc.

a) INTERMEDIATE DIVISION. Grades 4-6.
b) JUNIOR DIVISION. Grades 7-9.
c) SENIOR DIVISION. Grades 10-16.

Univ Wash Col Ed Rec 6:80 Mr '40. Worth J. Osburn. This is one of the few "diagnostic tests" which really diagnoses. It can be used also for general survey purposes. The diagnostic features apply to "ten silent reading abilities" which is a larger number than any other test presents. The tests for each division are presented in three parts: Part I tests Rate of Comprehension; Part II includes vocabulary of two types, word relations and general information; Part III furnishes a basis for the diagnosis of "ability to group the central thought of the paragraph, ability to note the clearly stated details, ability to interpret the content of the paragraph, ability to grasp an idea when spread through several sentences and the ability to draw inferences from the ideas of a paragraph." * In the opinion of the reviewer, the authors could have improved their excellent test further by informing the teacher what diagnostic value each question in Part III has. They could also have enhanced the attractiveness of their test by explaining and emphasizing the diagnostic value of those tests which relate to vocabulary, word relationships, and general information. Their presentation of these tests is overly modest. If the authors have been a bit reticent and modest, the fact remains that they have given us a test that has high validity as a diagnostic instrument. No one truly interested in the diagnosis of reading ability can afford to be without it.

[1533]

Durrell Analysis of Reading Difficulty. Grades 1-6; 1933-37; 1 form; individual; $1.50 per 25 individual record blanks; 50¢ per booklet of reading paragraphs; 50¢ per tachistoscope; 80¢ per 30 blank tachistoscope cards; 25¢ per manual; $1.65 per examiner's kit, including 5 record blanks; a minimum of (30) minutes; Donald D. Durrell; Yonkers, N. Y.: World Book Co.

Guy L. Bond, Associate Professor of Education, The University of Minnesota. In diagnosing a reading disability case, it is necessary to locate any discrepancy that exists between the various reading attainments as well as to locate the factors associated with the cause of the disability. These discrepancies indicate the nature of the remedial work while the causal factors indicate the adjustments of instruction needed. The worth of a diagnostic battery is determined, in no small degree, by the insight into the disability derived from a comparison of the relative proficiency in the attainments measured. The worth is also determined by the insight it gives as to the causal factors.

The *Durrell Analysis of Reading Difficulty* test makes possible some revealing comparisons between various reading attainments. The specific abilities measured are: oral reading and recall, silent reading and recall, flash recognition of words, word pronunciation, and difficulties in writing and spelling. Although each of the comparisons that can be made between the parts of this battery of tests give valuable results, the real contribution is in the use of a simple tachistoscopic technique for comparing flash recognition of words with word pronunciation under long time exposure conditions. This latter comparison gives, among other things, an indication of any tendency toward overanalysis.

The areas in which this instrument seems to be weakest are those of isolating differences in the various sensory capacities and of appraising certain personality characteristics and interests which would prove helpful in formulating remedial instruction. The remedial worker may find the results of the appraisals do not give data to indicate the adjustment of instruction that is needed for some of the more stubborn cases. For the vast majority of cases, however, the analysis will give sufficient information to prescribe the remedial instruction.

A comprehensive check list of difficulties has been included in the individual record blank. Observational methods and subjective judgment must be used in making most of the entries. Nevertheless, the list should aid the diagnostician in making a complete analysis of the difficulties.

Miles A. Tinker, Associate Professor of Psychology, The University of Minnesota. This test consists of materials designed to measure comprehension, recall, and speed for oral and silent reading as well as phonetic ability and word analysis. Difficulties in spelling are also checked. It is suggested that these results may well supplement those on reading capacity and achievement tests.

Important criteria for an adequate reading test might well include: (a) satisfactory standardization, (b) data on consistency of measurement, and (c) proven validity.

This test was standardized on approximately one thousand children. Use of the norms is not clear in some instances. For paragraphs designed to measure comprehension in oral reading, only rate of reading norms are presented although errors in reading and comprehension are tabulated. In the manual of instructions, it is stated that inability to answer, or wrong answers to two questions on a given paragraph indicates low comprehension. It is, of course, contrary to good practice to use rate of reading to determine reading grade when comprehension is being measured. Is grade location determined by noting the place of the rate score for the most difficult paragraph that is read with no more than two comprehension questions missed? Or is it based upon rate for paragraph established as the "upper level"? Similar difficulties are encountered in using norms for oral recall on oral reading. For written recall on silent reading the norms for oral recall are used although the author admits that they may not be equivalent. He suggests, however, that they are adequate for rough analysis. The norms for word recognition, pronunciation, spelling, and handwriting are readily interpreted. Use of the profile chart furnished in the record blank involves the difficulties inherent in interpretation of the norms.

No reliability coefficients are furnished with the test nor are any other indications of consistency of measurement given. Also little concerning validity is cited. It is stated that after standardization, 3,000 tests were given to children with reading difficulties and the norms were found to check satisfactorily against other tests of reading ability. No correlations or other figures are given.

Directions for procedure in giving the test are clearly stated. The author correctly emphasizes the usefulness of the test for standard observation of errors and faulty reading habits and that these are more important than the norms. The check list of difficulties is extensive and well selected with the exception of those items concerning eye movements which are of dubious value.

For a review by Marion Monroe, see 1098.

[1534]

Emporia Silent Reading Test. Grades 3-8; 1933-34; 4 forms; 50¢ per 25; 15¢ per specimen set; 15(20) minutes; H. E. Schrammel and W. H. Gray; Emporia, Kan.: Bureau of Educational Measurements, Kansas State Teachers College.

M. E. Broom, Assistant Superintendent of Schools, El Paso, Texas. Each of the four forms of this test includes fifteen paragraphs and a total of forty-one scorable answers, presented in multiple-response form. The test content is largely taken from literary and social science materials, with some content from sci-

ence. A good reading test should include variety in its content, in the types of reading skills measured, and in the form of the exercises used in measuring the varied reading skills. This test does not do these things sufficiently. Furthermore, no test with only forty-one scorable items can measure adequately over a six-grade range, yielding discriminative scores at all levels. The percentile norms bear this out, since on three of the four forms one per cent of third-grade pupils at midyear earn scores of zero, while one per cent of these pupils earn scores above 33. From one to three per cent of the pupils in grades seven and eight at midyear earn perfect scores.

The tables of percentile norms raise some question as to the equivalence of the forms. For example, tracing the percentile equivalents for scores of 10, 20, and 30 for both midyear and end-of-year testing for the four forms shows marked differences in the percentile equivalents for each of these three score values among the four forms.

Reliability coefficients were obtained in each of the six grades by the Spearman-Brown technique, based on odd versus even scores for Forms A and B separately. The average of the six coefficients for Form A was .88; for Form B, .86. The numbers of cases are not given in the manual. Sufficient evidence as to the reliability of this test is not given.

Validity was determined, using the *Burgess Silent Reading Scale,* the *Los Angeles Reading Test,* and the *Thorndike-McCall Reading Scale* as criteria. The average of the coefficients between the test and the criterion was .86. At least one of the criterion instruments, the *Los Angeles* test, has not been sufficiently identified; there are several Los Angeles reading tests. Furthermore, a better choice of criterion instruments might have been made, including such tests as the *Sangren-Woody Reading Test,* the *Gates Silent Reading Tests,* the *Ingraham-Clark Diagnostic Reading Tests,* etc.

Norms are based on 25,000 cases. Forms A and C were used for midyear testing, and the end-of-year norms were computed statistically from the midyear scores. Forms B and D were used for end-of-year testing, and the midyear norms were computed statistically from the end-of-year scores.

Distinctly better reading tests than the *Emporia Silent Reading Test* are available for use in grades three to eight.

Harriet Barthelmess Morrison, Research Assistant, Bureau of Reference, Research, and Statistics, Public Schools, New York, New York. Each form consists of fifteen paragraphs arranged according to difficulty and 41 questions based thereon, of the usual multiple-response type. The highly satisfactory two-column arrangement is used, the paragraph on the left, and the questions on the right.

The test is attractive in appearance, well edited, easy to administer, and simple to score, with the answer key arranged to fit the pupil's answers spacially.

The content is varied and interesting. The questions are well chosen, and the multiple answers have been carefully constructed so that usually the pupil cannot—except by chance—choose the correct answer without reading the paragraph. Form A, however, is less satisfactory in this respect than the other forms. The score yielded is an undifferentiated score of general comprehension, no provision being made for specific types of reading skills.

The validity of the test for measuring general reading comprehension appears, from inspection of the test, to be high. This judgment is confirmed by the statistical validity, which is shown by an average correlation of .72 per grade with the *Thorndike McCall Reading Scale*, the *Burgess Silent Reading Scale,* and the *Los Angeles Reading Test.* The number of cases involved in this validating is not stated in the manual nor are the separate correlations given.

The reliability is indicated by an (*a*) average correlation of .71 per grade (grades 4-6) between Form A and Form B, (*b*) reliability coefficients ranging between .82 and .93 and averaging at .88 per grade in grades 3 to 8 inclusive, secured by the odd-versus-even method on Form A, (*c*) results similar to the foregoing, based on Forms B, C, and D. The separate correlations are not stated in the manual. These reliabilities are not high enough to warrant using one form of the test alone for individual diagnosis, but they do not lessen the usefulness of one form as a survey instrument.

Percentile norms for each grade, midyear and end-of-term, are reported for grades 3 to 8 inclusive, for each of the four forms. These are based on "the scores made by 25,000 pupils." Analysis indicates that this means about 900 pupils per grade for each of Forms A, B, and C, and 1,600 for Form D. Comparison of pupil progress by the use of different forms in successive testings rests on the questionable assumption of the equality of the samplings used for the norms for the various forms and grades.

The test should not be used in grade 3 in a normal situation since approximately half the children at midyear can get a score of 10, which is within the area of chance.

The usefulness of the test is impaired by its inadequate standardization. When the four forms have been equated on identical groups, with the practice factor controlled, the test should provide one of the most useful general reading tests available.

[1535]

Examiner's Reading Diagnostic Record for High School and College Students. 1938-39; 20¢ per record blank, 10 or more; 25¢ per specimen set; Ruth Strang with the assistance of Margaret E. Martin, Margaret G. McKim, and Mary Alice Mitchell; New York: Bureau of Publications, Teachers College, Columbia University.

Henry D. Rinsland, Director of the Bureau of Educational Research, and Professor of School Measurements, The University of Oklahoma. The record is a 20-page booklet for recording the following: (*a*) identifying data with names of parents, language spoken at home, and so forth; (*b*) summary of results of standardized tests including intelligence, achievement and reading, with space for observations and analyses; (*c*) summary of scholastic achievement giving general trends, years covered in each subject, and attitude of student toward each subject; (*d*) medical examination and reports of physical conditions, which includes a report of oculist, results of Betts' tests, and photographic record of eye movements; (*e*) development and educational history, most of which concern reading and its influences on activities and interests; (*f*) present interests in reading, with lists of books recently read, and reading habits as they concern reading newspapers, magazines and books; (*g*) other interests and activities; (*h*) present reading status, which includes an analysis of reading ability through interview, oral reading of four paragraphs with analysis of reading errors, speed of reading, likes and dislikes of materials in the paragraphs, and a practical test of looking up words in the dictionary; (*i*) summary; (*j*) recommendations; and (*k*) follow-up.

It is obvious that the record is very thorough. The questions provided under many headings are just the type to bring into consideration factors which indicate reading habits and interests; as, "How does the student spend his week end?" and "What things and activities apparently give the student the keenest pleasure and satisfaction?" One regrets that the oral reading paragraphs are not standardized in a manner similar to the *Standardized Oral Reading Check Tests* by Gray for the elementary school, and that a diagnostic record of the kinds of errors is not provided. More anecdotal records of this nature, combining life history and results of tests and scales, are needed in other high school subjects, especially English.

Ed Res B 19:118 F 14 '40. * The unusual attribute of this diagnostic record is the part played by an oral-reading test. In the reviewer's opinion the quickest and surest way to detect a student's reading difficulties is for a discriminating listener to hear him read aloud.

Loyola Ed Digest 15:7-8 N '39. Austin G. Schmidt. Contains a number of tests, including passages for oral reading, designed to obtain a complete measure of a student's reading ability and interests. The record is diagnostic in the sense that it calls for data on significant factors, but neither the record itself nor the accompanying manual gives the examiner much assistance in interpreting the data obtained.

Q J Speech 25:685-6 D '39. Seth A. Fessenden. * The blank, when scored by one trained in clinical observation and interpreted by one trained in reading diagnosis, should be of very considerable value for diagnostic work. It would have little value, except to point out the complexity of reading diagnosis, in the hands of the untrained teacher or administrator. The form should be of primary value for individual analyses of cases of reading disability in which the cause is in question, and its use should do much to show that remedial reading work is clinical in nature rather than subject to group classification.

[1536]

First Year Reading Test. Grades 1B, 1A; 1938; 2 levels; 75¢ per 25; 10¢ per specimen set; part non-timed (30-35) minutes; Marie Garrison; Cincinnati, Ohio: C. A. Gregory Co.

a) TEST I, MID-YEAR.
b) TEST II, END OF YEAR.

REFERENCES

1 EVANS, MARIE GARRISON. *The Revision and Standardization of a First Grade Reading Test.* Unpublished master's thesis, University of Michigan, 1938.

[1537]

Gates Reading Readiness Tests. Grade 1; 1939; 1 form; $3.75 per 100; 25¢ per specimen set; (50) minutes; Arthur I. Gates; New York: Bureau of Publications, Teachers College, Columbia University.

REFERENCES

1 GATES, ARTHUR I., AND BOND, GUY L. "Reading Readiness: A Study of Factors Determining Success and Failure in Beginning Reading." *Teach Col Rec* 37:679-85 My '36.
2 WILSON, FRANK T.; FLEMMING, CECILE WHITE; BURKE, AGNES; AND GARRISON, CHARLOTTE G. "Reading Progress in Kindergarten and Primary Grades." *El Sch J* 38:442-9 F '38.
3 GATES, ARTHUR I. "Basal Principles in Reading Readiness Testing." *Teach Col Rec* 40:495-506 Mr '39.
4 GATES, ARTHUR I. "An Experimental Evaluation of Reading-Readiness Tests." *El Sch J* 39:497-508 Mr '39.
5 GATES, A. I.; BOND, G. L.; AND RUSSELL, D. H.; ASSISTED BY EVA BOND, ANDREW HALPIN, AND KATHRYN HORAN. *Methods of Determining Reading Readiness.* New York: Bureau of Publications, Teachers College, Columbia University, 1939. Pp. iv, 55. $0.60. Paper.
6 GATES, ARTHUR I. "A Further Evaluation of Reading-Readiness Tests." *El Sch J* 40:577-91 Ap '40.

Loyola Ed Digest 15:8 N '39. Austin G. Schmidt. It is interesting to note how frequently psychology, after losing itself in dark labyrinths, finally works out into clear open spaces. Convinced some years ago that the possession of a mental age of six and a half years was not a sufficient guarantee that a child would succeed in reading, research workers analyzed the physical, mental, emotional, and social factors involved in reading and developed such a multiplicity of tests that teachers were baffled in their search for a simple and scientifically reputable index of reading readiness. Dr. Gates with that simplicity which is one of the secrets of his success, concludes that the only safe index of ability to go forward in reading is previous success in those approaches toward reading to which the natural environment invites every child. His test consists of five parts. In the first part the child is shown pictures and required to make certain marks according to the directions given by the examiner. This requires ability to listen, to understand, and to remember. In the second test the child is required to find among four words two that are identical. In the third he is required to find among four printed words one that is identical with the one printed on a card shown by the examiner. In the fourth he is shown pictures in sets of four and required to find one the name for which sounds almost the same as the first. In the fifth he names as many as he can of the letters of the alphabet and the numbers. The author does not propose any score as an index of reading readiness. The percentile standing shows whether the testee can be expected to experience less or greater difficulty than the average child. The mental age merely accentuates for better or for worse whatever condition is found to exist.

Sight-Saving R 10:165-6 Je '40. * In the first test it is necessary to have many details in the pictures. These may at first prove somewhat confusing to the young child who is not used to close eye work. The examiner will do well to take this into consideration. The printing and the pictures of the other tests are in good size and the type is clear and well chosen. * should be of great value to those interested in beginning reading.

[1538]

Gates Reading Survey for Grades 3 to 10: Vocabulary, Level of Comprehension, Speed, and Accuracy. 1939; 2 forms; $5.25 per 100; 20¢ per specimen set; part timed and part nontimed (60-90) minutes; Arthur I. Gates; New York: Bureau of Publications, Teachers College, Columbia University.

[1539]

Gates Silent Reading Tests. Grades 3-8; 1926-35; 3 forms, 4 parts; $2.10 per 100; 25¢ per specimen set; Arthur I. Gates; New York: Bureau of Publications, Teachers College, Columbia University.
a) TYPE A, READING TO APPRECIATE GENERAL SIGNIFICANCE. 6(12) minutes.
b) TYPE B, READING TO PREDICT THE OUTCOME OF GIVEN EVENTS. 8(15) minutes.
c) TYPE C, READING TO UNDERSTAND PRECISE DIRECTIONS. 8(15) minutes.
d) TYPE D, READING TO NOTE DETAILS. 8(15) minutes.

REFERENCES

1 FORAN, T. G. *The Present Status of Silent Reading Tests:* Part II, The Measurement of Rate of Reading. Catholic University of America, Educational Research Bulletin, Vol. 2, No. 2. Washington, D. C.: Catholic Education Press, February 1927. Pp. 27. $0.50. Paper.
2 GATES, ARTHUR I. "Methods of Constructing and Validating the Gates Reading Tests." *Teach Col Rec* 29:148-59 N'27.
3 FORAN, T. G., AND ROCK, ROBERT T., JR. *The Reliability of Some Silent Reading Tests.* Catholic University of America, Educational Research Bulletin, Vol. 5, No. 6. Washington, D. C.: Catholic Education Press, June 1930. Pp. 23. $0.35. Paper.
4 GATES, ARTHUR I. *The Improvement of Reading,* Revised edition. New York: Macmillan Co., 1935. Pp. xvii, 668. $2.50. (London: Macmillan & Co., Ltd. 8s. 6d.)
5 LANDRY, HERBERT. "The Disparity of Test Norms," pp. 208-17. In Yearbook of the New York Society for the Experimental Study of Education, 1938. New York: the Society (c/o C. Frederick Pertach, Sec.-Treas., 500 Park Ave.). Pp. vii, 228. $1.00. Paper.

Joseph C. Dewey, Head of the Department of Education and Psychology, Westminster College. These tests consist of four different types each designed to measure one specific reading skill. Each type test contains three forms called equivalent by the author but no evidence is submitted to show that this is true. An excellent manual provides clear and careful directions for using the tests for individual and group diagnosis. Regular age and grade norms are provided as well as those for the lower and upper quartiles. The manual provides the answers to the various tests but no actual answer keys seem to be provided.

The manual states that each test measures a type of reading ability that is important. No evidence is submitted to support this contention. Evidently test makers do not agree on what are the important skills.

These tests provide such small bits of reading material in each case that test results may not give a true picture of what children can do reading longer selections.

Little or no provision is made for measuring speed of reading. It is possible to get some measure of speed of reading from the number of attempts made but no norms are provided to show how fast children should read this material.

No statements regarding validity or reliability coefficients are given in the manual although the author does state that the reliability of the tests depend upon how carefully they are given.

The reading material seems better adapted for third-grade pupils than for eighth graders and seems to possess little literary quality and might prove rather uninteresting to upper-grade pupils.

It is doubtful if these tests give an accurate picture of reading ability since they are almost entirely verbal in nature and there is evidence available that pencil-and-paper verbal tests give distorted pictures of children's reading ability when checked against picture and object tests and by individual interviews.

Certainly the ability to read to appreciate the general significance as found in the Type A test is a valuable reading skill. However, one wonders if each of the various paragraphs of reading material is equal in difficulty so as to give equal credit for each correct response. The reading material in this test apparently lacks variety as the pupil is always asked how some one feels about something. Is the general significance of a paragraph only how one feels about something?

The Type B test, Reading to Predict the Outcomes of Given Events, seems to be the only test in the series wherein the pupil is expected to make inferences concerning his reading. This is again a valuable skill in reading and as such this test is valuable. The alternate responses used are often rather obvious and the pupils are presented with an even chance of guessing correctly in some cases.

The Type C test, Reading to Understand Precise Directions, seems a great deal like the type of reading found in the Type D test, Reading to Note Details. Both tests seem to test ability to understand detail in the reading material. This test makes use of pictures many of which are rather poorly drawn or are printed from old plates. Some of the pictures might not convey to children intended meanings.

The Type D test is entitled Reading to Note Details. To be able to read carefully and accurately to get the details is no doubt an important skill in reading. However, in this test the test paragraphs are so short, especially for upper-grade pupils, that there are few details to note. Some of the material is so well known to the children that they might answer questions correctly even though they did not read the material carefully.

It appears that Gates has provided a rather valuable instrument for measuring the specific phases of reading that he thinks are important. However, one must not conclude that these tests will give an accurate and complete measure of reading ability as there is no provision for measuring how difficult reading the pupils can do nor how fast they can read. There is no assurance that if a pupil excels in these reading skills he will excel in general all-around reading ability. We must also recognize that these tests have the weakness inherent in all verbal tests that pupils may answer in words and not actually understand what the responses mean.

James R. Hobson, Director of Child Placement, Public Schools, Brookline, Massachusetts. This series of four separate tests is referred to by the author as a "team of tests" and is designed to serve two purposes—namely, to furnish a "general measure of silent reading ability" and to provide "an intelligible diagnosis of special needs for follow-up work." The four skills measured by this team of tests were selected from the list of silent reading skills generally recognized because, according to the author, each measures a particular kind of reading ability which is important and which can be acquired. Considerable emphasis is

placed upon the differences in difficulty for the average child of these four types of reading as well as the differences in probable and desirable rates of speed in reading for each of the four purposes indicated.

Unlike most tests of reading comprehension the paragraph units in this series apparently do not increase in difficulty from the beginning to the end of each test. Each pupil's proficiency in each of the four abilities tested is not measured in terms of the depth of his power of comprehension but rather on the basis of the number of test units attempted, the number correct, and the percentage of accuracy. Although this team of tests covers a range of six grades, each paragraph in them is within the ability range of the average third-grade pupil.

The manual which accompanies this test series goes into considerable detail in giving directions for the diagnosis of both individual and group difficulties in reading through the use of these tests in conjunction with other measures. Complete norms based upon more than 300,000 cases in all parts of the United States are given in terms of grade level, reading age, and percentiles.

Despite the wide use and evident popularity of this series of tests, there are many questions about their construction and use and several features of their physical make-up upon which more light needs to be thrown. To begin with, no reasons are given in the manual for the selection of the four types of reading skills measured by these tests. No experimental evidence is produced to show that these are the basic silent reading skills in grades 3-8. There seems to have been no attempt made to validate these tests and no reliability coefficients are reported in the manual. If data on these points are available they should be reported in the manual.

Each of the twenty-four questions in Reading to Appreciate General Significance asks the pupil to select one from among five words which best describes the feelings of some person or character mentioned in the paragraph. This appears to the reviewer to be a very narrow delimitation of "reading to appreciate general significance."

A valid criticism of any reading comprehension test, which requires specially written paragraphs or a special physical make-up in order to permit questions of a certain type to be asked about it, is that the kinds of comprehension which a pupil needs in order to gain meaning from textbook material or from general literature are not being measured. When a pupil reads a paragraph in normal reading he is not ordinarily reading it for one narrow specific purpose. Reading of this type is valuable as a practice exercise to develop a somewhat specific ability, but such an ability is genuine only if it can be demonstrated in a normal reading situation.

Finally, it seems to the writer that a series of tests covering a range of six grades in which each paragraph is entirely within the comprehension range of a pupil in the lowest grade cannot measure anything except the speed of comprehension and cannot be classed as "an accurate measure of reading ability in general." Important as speed of reading admittedly is, the increase in reading comprehension from grade to grade cannot be measured without measuring the increase in "depth of power of comprehension." In this series of tests there is nothing to prevent a rapid reader in grade four or five from attaining a higher score than a reader of average speed but great power in grade eight. Yet his true ability in reading comprehension of any one of the types measured would normally be much less.

The greatest usefulness of this group of tests appears to lie in their ability to detect lack of facility in four of the reading comprehension skills and to point the way to needed teaching of these skills, rather than as a measure of general reading ability.

Dolch, Edward William. A Manual for Remedial Reading, pp. 137-8. (Champaign, Ill.: Garrard Press, 1939. Pp. x, 166. $2.00.) * The reading matter in the Gates Silent Reading Tests, though intended for grades 3 to 8, is all at one level of difficulty, about grades 4 or 5. Therefore these tests are excellent for use with children whose actual reading ability ranges from fourth grade to sixth grade. Readers at lower reading levels find too many hard words and therefore do too much guessing. High school teachers who have readers as low as fourth to sixth grades can use these tests to advantage. For first testing of a large group only one type needs to be used as this makes the testing quite inexpensive. It is recommended that type D, "Reading for Details," be chosen because it is perhaps closest to the kind of thing these children are supposed to be doing with their high school textbooks. If, however, the teacher is concerned with the child's outside reading she would choose type A, "Reading to Predict Coming Events." For a remedial case, the "Reading to Follow Directions" is probably best because one can watch best the child's thought processes. Here is a clear case in which the teacher's purpose influences her choice of tests. For better understanding of the remedial cases, all four of the Gates Tests are helpful. *

[1540]

High School Reading Test: National Achievement Tests. Grades 7-12; 1939; 1 form; $2.50 per 25; 15¢ per specimen set; nontimed (40) minutes; Robert K. Speer and Samuel Smith; Rockville Centre, N. Y.: Acorn Publishing Co.

[1541]

Hildreth Diagnostic Reading Record. Grades 1-16; 1939; $1.25 per 25; 25¢ per specimen set; Gertrude Hildreth; New York: Psychological Corporation.

[1542]

Individual Reading Test. Grades 1-3; [1933?]; 1 form, 3 parts; individual; 2s. 6d. per set of cards for testing; 3d. per manual; L. W. Allen; Melbourne, Australia: Australian Council for Educational Research.
a) WORD READING TEST.
b) READING COMPREHENSION TEST.
c) SPEED OF READING.

[1543]

Instructional Reading Tests for the Intermediate Grades. Grades 4, 5, 6; 1938-39; 3 forms, 3 levels; 50¢ per 25; single specimen set free; 15(20) minutes; M. J. Nelson; Boston, Mass.: Houghton Mifflin Co.

[1544]

Interpretation of Data: Tests 2.51 and 2.52. Grades 9-12; 1939-40; 2 forms (Tests 2.51 and 2.52); revision of Test 2.5; 5¢ per test; 1¢ per machine-scorable answer sheet; 5¢ per explanation sheet and interpretation guide; $1.50 per set of stencils for machine scoring; nontimed (90) minutes; Chicago, Ill.: Evaluation in the Eight Year Study, Progressive Education Association.

REFERENCES

1 HARTUNG, M. L. *Interpretation of Data.* Progressive Education Association, Evaluation in the Eight Year Study, Bulletin No. 3. Chicago, Ill.: the Study, October 1935. Pp. 11. Paper, mimeographed. Out of print.
2 RATHS, LOUIS E. "Evaluating Some Aspects of Proof." Ed Res B 17:108-14 Ap 13 '38.
3 RATHS, LOUIS, "Evaluating the Program of Lakeshore School." Ed Res B 17:57-84 Mr 16 '38.
4 RATHS, LOUIS E. "Measuring the Interpretation of Data." Ed Res B 17:98-107 Ap 13 '38.
5 *Evaluation Materials Developed for Various Aspects of Thinking.* Chicago, Ill.: Evaluation in the Eight Year Study, Progressive Education Association, March 1939. Pp. [22]. Paper, mimeographed. Out of print.
6 *The Evaluation of Abilities Involved in Dealing with Quantitative Relationships.* Chicago, Ill.: Evaluation in the Eight Year Study, Progressive Education Association, March 1939. Pp. [24]. Paper, mimeographed. Out of print.
7 AMSTUTZ, WADE S. "A Study of Characteristics of Education Freshmen Who Entered Ohio State University in 1938." J Exp Ed 8:289-92 Mr '40.
8 AMSTUTZ, WADE S., AND KOENINGER, RUPERT C. "A Study of a Test for Measuring Skill in the Interpretation of Data." J Exp Ed 8:251-5 Mr '40.
9 CAHOW, ARTHUR C. "Relationships of Test Scores of Education College Freshmen to Grades in Selected Courses." J Exp Ed 8:284-9 Mr '40.

[1545]

Interpretation of Data: Test 2.71. Grades 7-9; 1940; 1 form; revision of Test 2.7; 5¢ per machine-scorable answer sheet; $1.50 per set of stencils for machine scoring; nontimed (60) minutes; Chicago, Ill.: Evaluation in the Eight Year Study, Progressive Education Association.

REFERENCES

1 HARTUNG, M. L. *Interpretation of Data.* Progressive Education Association, Evaluation in the Eight Year Study, Bulletin No. 3. Chicago, Ill.: the Study, October 1935. Pp. 11. Paper, mimeographed. Out of print.
2 *Evaluation Materials Developed for Various Aspects of Thinking.* Chicago, Ill.: Evaluation in the Eight Year Study, Progressive Education Association, March 1939. Pp. [22]. Paper, mimeographed. Out of print.
3 *The Evaluation of Abilities Involved in Dealing with Quantitative Relationships.* Chicago, Ill.: Evaluation in the Eight Year Study, Progressive Education Association, March 1939. Pp. [24]. Paper, mimeographed. Out of print.
4 *Social Sensitivity:* An Approach to Evaluation in Social Studies. Chicago, Ill.: Evaluation in the Eight Year Study, Progressive Education Association, March 1939. Pp. [34]. Paper, mimeographed. Out of print.

[1546]

Inventory of Reading Experiences. Grades 9-16; 1938-40; 1 form; $1.75 per 25; Frederick L. Pond; Stanford University, Calif.: Stanford University Press.

REFERENCES

1 POND, FREDERICK L. "A Qualitative and Quantitative Appraisal of Reading Experiences." *J Ed Res* 33:241-52 D '39.

[1547]

Iowa Silent Reading Tests, New Edition. Grades 4-9, 9-13; 1929-39; 2 forms, 2 levels; Yonkers, N. Y.: World Book Co.
a) ELEMENTARY TEST. Grades 4-9. $1.25 per 25; 25¢ per specimen set; 50(65) minutes. H. A. Greene and V. H. Kelley.
b) ADVANCED TEST. Grades 9-13. $1.60 per 25; 35¢ per specimen set; 5¢ per machine-scorable answer sheet; 47(60) minutes. H. A. Greene, A. N. Jorgensen, and V. H. Kelley.

REFERENCES

1 JORGENSEN, A. N. *Iowa Silent Reading Examinations.* University of Iowa. Studies, First Series No. 130; Studies in Education, Vol. 4, No. 3. Iowa City, Iowa: the University, May 1927. Pp. 76. $0.75. Paper.
2 STRANG, RUTH. "An Evaluation of Reading Tests for College Students (Abstract)," pp. 35-7. In *The Role of Research in Educational Progress:* Official Report, American Educational Research Association, A Department of the National Education Association, New Orleans, Louisiana, February 20-24, 1937. Washington, D. C.: the Association, May 1937. Pp. 255. $1.50. Paper.
3 DEARBORN, W. F., AND GORES, H. B. "Adult Reactions to a Silent Reading Test." *Harvard Ed R* 8:38-43 Ja '38.
4 LANDRY, HERBERT. "The Disparity of Test Norms," pp. 208-17. In *Yearbook of the New York Society for the Experimental Study of Education,* 1938. New York: the Society (c/o C. Frederick Pertach, Sec.-Treas., 500 Park Ave.). Pp. vii, 228. $1.00. Paper.
5 TRAXLER, ARTHUR E. "One Reading Test Serves the Purpose." *Clearing House* 14:419-21 Mr '40.
6 TRAXLER, ARTHUR E. "A Study of the New Edition of the Iowa Silent Reading Test for High Schools and Colleges," pp. 39-47. In *1939 Fall Testing Program in Independent Schools and Supplementary Studies.* Educational Records Bulletin, No. 29. New York: Educational Records Bureau, January 1940. Pp. x, 50. $1.00. Paper.

Ivan A. Booker, Assistant Director of the Research Division, National Education Association, Washington, D. C. An agreeable surprise but perhaps some measure of disappointment, too, is in store for test users who have long been familiar with the *Iowa Silent Reading Test* but have not yet made the acquaintance of the new, 1939 edition of it. Although in general scope and purpose the new edition

closely resembles the earlier test battery, it differs from it both in appearance and in the technics of measurement employed.

The new edition of the *Iowa Silent Reading Test,* in common with its predecessor, is made up of several subtests. The types of subtests, however, are by no means the same. The new Elementary Test consists of: (*a*) a combined measure of rate and comprehension, (*b*) a test of "directed reading," (*c*) a vocabulary test, (*d*) a measure of paragraph comprehension, (*e*) a test of "sentence meaning," and (*f*) an exercise involving the "location of information." The Advanced Test contains all the foregoing subtests and an additional one on "poetry comprehension."

The directions for administering and scoring the new Iowa test are clear and easy to follow. Pupils should find it easy, too, to follow directions in doing the exercises. All the tests in the series are quite objective. The scoring is less time consuming and laborious than for most test batteries of comparable length. The test manual says nothing about the possibility of scoring the tests on the electrical test-scoring machines now available, but apparently the tests have been set up with that possibility in mind.

Strict and relatively brief time limits are enforced in administering the Iowa tests. Consequently, rate of work affects not only the pupils' rate scores but, to some extent, their scores on all parts of the test. Slow workers do not have time to finish the exercises, whereas rapid workers not only finish but have time to discover and correct their errors.

Each subtest yields a point score which is converted, by reference to a table of values in the test manual, into a standard score. The pupil's *median standard score* on the six (or seven) subtests is then computed and used as *the measure* of his silent reading ability. Tabled values are given for converting these median standard scores into age and grade equivalents or percentile ranks. The test manual points out, however, that the norms given are not valid as a basis for converting any given subtest score into an age-grade or percentile equivalent. For this reason the *Iowa Silent Reading Test* is, at present, primarily a survey test, affording a measure of the general level of silent reading achievement. In the absence of norms for each subtest, its potential diagnostic value can be realized only by test users who are willing and able to establish their own standards of achievement for the various parts of the test battery.

The information given in the new manual of directions is disappointingly scant with reference to procedures followed in constructing and standardizing the test—perhaps due to the newness of the revision. The only available data on the reliability of the Elementary Test were obtained by applying the Spearman-Brown formula to the scores of 120 seventh-grade pupils on Form A of the test. Similarly, the reliability of the Advanced Test is given in terms of the chance-half correlation of the scores of only 160 tenth-grade pupils. No data are presented on the equality of Forms A and B. Validity is established only by comparing the titles of the subtests included with a single outline of silent reading skills which was developed some fifteen years ago. Statements with reference to the basis for the age, grade, and percentile norms are too indefinite, vague, or general to admit of critical evaluation.

The suggestions given on interpreting the scores of individuals and groups of pupils on the new Iowa test also suffer by comparison with the corresponding helps given with the earlier form of the test. Much is left to the skill and ingenuity of the test giver in finding out what the test results mean in terms of pupil adjustment and corrective teaching.

Some of the least useful tests in the earlier edition have been abandoned, among them the exercise on "paragraph organization." Different technics have been introduced into other parts of the test which should result in definite improvement, particularly the technic of measuring reading rate and that of testing paragraph comprehension.

The new rate-comprehension subtest makes use of a technic which resembles, but is not quite identical with, the technic used in the *Traxler Silent Reading Test,* designed for junior high-school pupils. The student is required to read each of two selections ranging in length, in the different forms and at different grade levels, from 374 to 635 words. At the end of one minute he marks the word being read and continues to read for two more minutes. Then a check on comprehension is made by having him respond to 10 to 20 multiple-choice questions based on the selection. His rate score is based on the *sum of the number of sentences read in one minute for the*

two selections; his comprehension score, on the total number of questions answered correctly. The scoring key makes it possible to obtain, also, a rate score in terms of number of words per minute. But the manual advises against this procedure, referring to it as an "unnecessary and probably an unjustified refinement." The type of comprehension measured by this particular exercise is perhaps best described as the *immediate recall of more or less significant details.*

The subtest, entitled "Directed Reading," makes use of the same identical selections used in the rate-comprehension part which precedes it. According to the manual, the purpose is "to measure the student's ability to comprehend general and specific situations expressed in the content without unduly stressing memory." Although no explanation is given as to why the same selections used in Subtest 1 are preferable to new material for use in Subtest 2, the purpose probably is to make it as easy as possible for students to *skim* the material, looking for the sentences pertinent to the questions asked. In this exercise the student is confronted with 20 questions to which he responds by giving the number of the sentence in the test selection in which the answer is found. In this exercise, the answer always is given in one of the five sentences occupying approximately the same horizontal plane as the question—a fact which automatically limits the students' search to those items. There is little difference in the type of question asked in Subtests 1 and 2. In Subtest 1, for example, the student may be asked to state from memory: "In what kind of climate does sugar cane grow best? 1 cool, 2 temperate, 3 very warm." Then in Subtest 2 he must find and give the number of the sentence which answers the question: "Does sugar cane grow better in a hot or a cold country?" The remainder of the subtests follow either the same technics employed in the original *Iowa Silent Reading Tests* or other technics commonly employed in reading scales. The subtest on "poetry comprehension" in the new Advanced Test represents an improvement over the earlier form but, in the judgment of this reviewer, is still one of the least valid and significant of the seven subtests.

The vocabulary section of the Advanced Test represents the "technical vocabulary" of four special fields: social science, science, mathematics, and English. Whether a test of technical vocabulary or one of general vocabulary is the more significant measure of reading achievement is a question on which authorities differ. It is pertinent here merely to point out that the Advanced Test includes only a test of technical vocabulary. In the Elementary Test, the first half is concerned with "general vocabulary"; the last, with "subject-matter vocabulary."

The tests of sentence meaning in both the elementary and advanced divisions measure reasoning power, and perhaps general information and intelligence, rather than ability to understand sentences of increasing complexity —as the title, "sentence meaning," might suggest. No sentence requires more than a single line of type. Each test exercise is a brief question, such as: "Should free people be expected to work for nothing?" This does not imply a criticism of the sentence meaning subtest, but is a fact which should be kept in mind in interpreting the test results.

In spite of certain obvious limitations, such as are more or less typical of new tests, the revised edition of the *Iowa Silent Reading Test* merits the attention and study of those who need both a comprehensive and diagnostic measure of silent reading achievement.

Holland D. Roberts, Associate Professor of Education, Stanford University. [Review of the Advanced Test.] This 1939 issue of a widely-used standard reading test for high schools and colleges follows the general form and approach of the earlier editions, using new material and improved methods. It is based essentially upon the traditional educational philosophy of the earlier test. The new work materially improves the effectiveness but does not substantially change its purposes or scope.

In constructing it the authors have made "an effort to go beyond the ordinary general survey of a single phase of silent reading ability." They state that it "measures three major aspects of silent reading ability; namely, (1) Rate of Reading at a Controlled Level of Comprehension, (2) Comprehension of Words, Poetry, Sentences, Paragraphs, and Longer Articles, and (3) Ability to Use Skills Required in Locating Information." To realize these purposes ten different types of tests are to be used in a 60- to 65-minute period.

This new Iowa test is one of the leading standardized instruments for diagnosis and evaluation of work type reading available at the time of publication. It is the work of thoroughly experienced test makers whose previous tests have given some years of satisfactory service. However, further study and insight would have resulted in significant improvements.

In this Iowa test, rate of reading and comprehension are checked for prose with short science and social studies selections. *Rate* consequently includes a measure of the total study-reading-response act and is not comparable to *rate* in words or lines per minute. The directions "Read this story about 'glass' very carefully so that you can answer questions about it" may produce word by word reading and increased regression.

Formal, religious verse of little significance to modern youth is used to test poetry comprehension. The archaic language of John Pryor's "knowledge" and the intensive analysis of the comprehension test are in disrepute among leading teachers of English as means of evaluating the "ability to read and interpret poetry." To realize that aim modern verse and an oral test are needed.

The vocabulary test is subject matter centered and designed to measure a pupil's understanding of significant words in social science, science, mathematics, and English. The large life areas of youth: sports, movies, radio, automobiles, aviation, adventure, friendship, and romance are not represented. The choice of material for the four subject-matter areas is traditional and does not recognize the important changes that have taken place within subject matter organization and viewpoint. Testing word meaning in the English section is chiefly through recognition of terms of formal grammar and literary form, such as "objective," "prologue," and "allegory." Clearly the authors have not realized their aim of cataloguing "the important concepts in that subject."

Tests of both word and sentence meaning are constructed of sentences presenting similar comprehension problems, and it seems probable that both measure the same interrelated abilities. Simple history, geography, and agriculture provide the content for testing paragraph comprehension. Item 3 perpetuates our current textbook mythology about the Eskimo exposed some years ago by Stefansson in *Adventures in Error*. Finding material in an index is used to test ability to locate information. It seems to be an excellent test of the mechanical skill of finding correct answers to questions in an index when neither the questions nor the answers are of interest or importance, and the student is motivated by the stop watch and the fear of a low score in the record. Such abilities as how to find the most interesting radio, theater, or movie programs, your friend's address or telephone number in a strange city, or how to find the best quality goods for the lowest price are not tested.

Scoring the test, except for rate, has been made simple and rapid by means of a perforated stencil scoring key. Percentile norms are based on some 10,000 cases and apply to the end of the school year. They are based upon "a random sampling of the entire school population of Iowa plus all the children in the requisite grades in two Eastern communities."

All standard reading tests now available have certain fundamental limitations which should be considered in evaluating this test.

1. The test experience is not one of the reading experiences which are frequently met in daily life situations. From the student viewpoint taking such a test does not meet his own needs and is nonfunctional. There is a serious question whether the reading power which we employ when we are striving to satisfy our own desires is operative when the motivation is external and compulsive as it necessarily is in standard tests. Standardized reading with teacher interruptions at the end of a minute, or a few minutes at most, obviously formalizes the reading process.

2. The content lacks significance in the life of the student. Neither the subject matter of the parts nor the form is unified, and there is a consequent handicap to those who have been prepared to look for related meanings in developmental reading and study.

3. The test makers do not guide the users to see the functional relationships of the test data in a complete diagnosis of the reading capacities of a student. Accordingly many teachers and schools base their entire reading programs on the necessarily incomplete data which the most satisfactory of tests give. For example, the test data provides no direct information on such crucial aspects of reading as attitudes and interests, habits, long-term concentration, and

scope and penetration in past reading experience.

4. The testing is upon specific forms of study reading, and excludes reading for enjoyment.

5. There is always the possibility that "test shock" may inhibit a student, and that the scores will not reflect actual power in daily life situations nor provide comparable measures.

It should be emphasized that these limitations do not invalidate a test when it is used for specific purposes as a part of a complete program of evaluation. They should qualify its use.

[1548]

Jenkins Oral Reading Test: Individualized Oral Diagnostic Test for Children with Serious Reading Difficulties. Children whose reading ability falls within the range of normal children in grades 1-3; 1939; 2 forms; 75¢ per 25; 10¢ per specimen set; Frances Jenkins and students; Cincinnati, Ohio: C. A. Gregory Co.

Guy L. Bond, Associate Professor of Education, The University of Minnesota. This test consists of eleven paragraphs of increasing difficulty. The pupil reads each paragraph orally until he reaches a paragraph where he has to be told ten words by the examiner. There are questions to measure comprehension. The test has some merit as an oral reading test but can hardly lay claim to giving a diagnosis of the difficulties. The examiner is supposed to estimate whether the reader is reading words or phrases. It is upon this estimate that the diagnosis rests. There is a rough scale given for locating the reader's approximate oral reading grade.

David Kopel, Department of Education, Chicago Teachers College. The Jenkins test is similar to and merits comparison with the better known *Standardized Oral Reading Paragraphs* by William S. Gray. Like the Gray, the Jenkins test consists of a series of increasingly difficult paragraphs, eleven in number. The material ranges in difficulty from primer to the fourth-grade level. The paragraphs are desirably longer and more episodic in character than those in the Gray test; they are followed by several "comprehension" questions which yield a percentage score. Unlike the Gray, this test is not timed. A record is kept, instead, of whether words are read singly or in groups. Number of errors is also recorded and the test continues until the child has to be told ten words in one paragraph. His test score is that of the selection preceding this.

This instrument possesses some of the obvious values and limitations mentioned in the writer's review of the Gray test. Thus it provides an opportunity for observing a child's reading and behavior in a "standardized" situation. The meaning of the test score must be validated in every instance, however, by observing the child's actual reading performance with several types of material.

The test suffers from a number of limitations. Not very serious is the poor typography: irregularities in inking, margination, and spacing between lines. More important is the omission of standardization data in the record sheet and manual which accompanies the test, although the chronological ages and grade scores on both the Jenkins and Gray tests are given for 36 pupils whose IQ's range from 51 to 99 (a non-representative group in terms of the intelligence distribution of poor readers generally). Comparative test scores are reported for several other retarded readers.

Perhaps the most serious criticism of the test is its oversimplification of the problem of diagnosis and remediation. The title page of the test bears several suggestions under the heading "Diagnosis and Remedial Measures." When one finds "sight words lacking"—presumably in the child's test performance—one should, it is to be inferred, provide "drill on small number of sight words from standard lists." As though children don't know "sight words" because they haven't had drills (usually countless drills) on words taken from "standard lists"! The approach in this test exemplifies that narrow point of view still held by some workers who (a) analyze reading problems into some of their superficial components (or symptoms) and (b) then proceed with "remedial" work by attempting to improve or strengthen these elementalistic skills through isolated and largely meaningless drill. Extensive studies and reviews of the literature by Jastak, Tinker, Gates, Gray, Bennett, Hildreth, Strang, Harrison, Witty and others have demonstrated the complexity of causation in reading disability—the lack of single "causes" —and the correlative need (a) in diagnosis, of a comprehensive study of the individual's development, and (b) in remedial work, for the use of techniques which are individually appro-

priate and which may contribute to the individual's progress in reading for meaning.

Clarence R. Stone, 2140 Los Angeles Avenue, Berkeley, California. This is a power test consisting of eleven short units ranging in difficulty from easy primer material to material on about college level. Consequently this test increases in difficulty more gradually than does Gray's test entitled *Standardized Oral Reading Paragraphs Test.* Apparently the material has been carefully selected and graded. The reader has no information as to the basis for gradation with respect to vocabulary or other factors. In this test no time record of the oral reading is taken as in the Gray test. Instead, the examiner indicates for each unit whether or not in his judgment the pupil reads word by word or in word groups. The examiner also records for each unit the number of words the examiner tells the child during the course of his oral reading of the unit. Immediately following the oral reading of the unit the child responds with pencil to one or more comprehension questions. The examiner records for each unit the percentage of correct answers. The child reads until he has to be told ten words in his oral reading of the unit. The score for the whole test is based on his record for the unit preceding this one.

While this test is somewhat easier to administer than the Gray test and is superior in construction in that it increases in difficulty more gradually and is apparently more carefully standardized as to the difficulty of the units, the reviewer's judgment is that this test will not yield sufficient information for an adequate diagnosis with respect to the oral reading of poor readers. A plan of recording on the test sheets different types of errors as is done in the Gray tests would greatly improve this test.

[1549]

Kansas Primary Reading Test. Grades 1-3; 1935; 2 forms; 40¢ per 25; 15¢ per specimen set; 12(20) minutes; Alma Hoag, Emma Humble, Bertha Robinson, Adeline Wipf, and H. E. Schrammel; Emporia, Kan.: Bureau of Educational Measurements, Kansas State Teachers College.

Alice K. Liveright, Principal of the Logan Demonstration School, Public Schools, Philadelphia, Pennsylvania. The *Kansas Primary Reading Test* is intended both as a survey and diagnostic measure of silent reading in grades 1-3. It comprises three distinct parts, so that ability in sentence reading, word knowledge, and paragraph reading may each be tested separately.

As a survey instrument the test appears to have many admirable features. It possesses adequate validity and a high degree of reliability. Norms available both for each part of the test and for the whole, as well as a table of percentile scores, assist the teacher in interpretation of results. Two forms render the repeated use of the test practicable. The brevity of the test, twelve minutes reading time, saves the time of the teacher and avoids fatigue of the young readers. As the method of registering response, underlining words, is simple and as the same response is used in all three parts, the reader's attention may be focused upon the reading problem solely and the scoring is simplified for the teacher. The test may be given to large numbers without great expenditure of money as it costs but $1.50 for one hundred copies.

The norms and the percentile scale records indicate that most first grade pupils receive quite low scores. This seems to indicate that the material is so difficult for pupils in the first grade as to prove very discouraging to them. As a survey measure, the test might well be delayed beyond the first year.

As an instrument for diagnosis it is probably as valuable as any short group test could be. In each part the material is well scaled from the simple to the more difficult so that the teacher can ascertain at a glance the level at which each pupil can attain success.

The multiple-choice method is used for indicating the response. The child must choose from among five words. This seems an unnecessarily long list. Many similar tests for older pupils use lists of four words only.

Part II is designed to test word knowledge. The words, however, are used in sentences. One who lacks ability to read the sentences, fails in this part of the test. There are ways of testing the word knowledge of young children without resorting to sentences. The ability required to succeed in Part II appears not to vary greatly from that required in Part I.

In Part III, two statements follow each paragraph. In each statement the child chooses the word from among three which makes the statement correct. The responses indicate both the understanding of the selection and grasp of details.

As a result of administering this test, the teacher knows the child's reading level. No causes of lack of ability are revealed. However, it should be said that it is difficult to find a short group test which diagnoses reading failures adequately.

In format the test is pleasing. It is likewise convenient to handle. The type is clear and bold. The spacing is good, with the exception of the first page of Part III, Form B. Here there is less space than in the similar portion of Form A, and the crowding might cause confusion to the reader. The format would be improved by the use of slightly thicker paper. The print from one side of a sheet shows somewhat on the other.

[1550]

Mathematics, Biology, Physical Science [Reading Test]: Booklet No. 2. Grades 10-16; 1938; 8¢ per test; 2¢ per machine-scorable answer sheet; 12¢ per sample test; 180(190) minutes; English Commission of the Association of Georgia Colleges; Athens, Ga.: the Association, c/o F. S. Beers, Memorial Hall.

[1551]

Metropolitan Achievement Tests in Reading. Grades 1, 2-3, 4-6, 7-8; 1931-35; 3 forms, 4 levels; edited by Jacob S. Orleans; Yonkers, N. Y.: World Book Co.
a) PRIMARY READING TEST. Grades 1-3; 1931-34; $1.25 per 25; 15¢ per specimen set; 40(60) minutes; Gertrude H. Hildreth.
b) INTERMEDIATE READING TEST. Grades 4-6; 1932-35; $1.00 per 25; 10¢ per specimen set; 37(45) minutes; Richard D. Allen, Harold H. Bixler, William L. Connor, and Frederick B. Graham.
c) ADVANCED READING TEST. Grades 7-8; 1932-35; $1.00 per 25; 10¢ per specimen set; 37(45) minutes; same authors as for *b*.

D. A. Worcester, Chairman of the Department of Educational Psychology and Measurements, The University of Nebraska. The primary test includes six subtests measuring respectively: word picture, word recognition, word meaning, reading completion, paragraph reading, and vocabulary. The intermediate and advanced tests measure reading and vocabulary, the reading subtest being divided into exercises requiring the supplying of missing words in paragraphs and the answering of questions on the content of paragraphs. No evidence of reliability or validity is presented in the directions for administering or other material contained in the specimen package.

Each of the subtests in the primary test is scored separately, and it is assumed that an accurate measure can be obtained from any one or any combination of the tests. The reader is told, moreover, that if a child's score exceeds a certain value, this test should not be used in obtaining his average reading grade equivalent. It is interesting to note that on this basis four of the six tests do not offer a sufficient range to measure the completion of the third grade, the highest grade equivalents which can be used for a general score being 3.1, 2.10, 3.7, 3.7, 4.7, and 5.4. If a child should make the highest score allowable on all six tests, his average reading equivalent would be 3.7, although on the two tests which allow a wider range, he would secure the equivalent of 4.7 and 5.4, respectively.

The instructions for the primary test present an interesting combination of the desire to appear very scientific and at the same time to be sensible. Paragraph five of the general directions, for example, says "Accurate administering requires implicit following of instructions. The precise wording of directions has been worked out with great care and any marked deviation may invalidate the results." Later in the same paragraph we read "Not all pupils respond in the same way to testing. Pupils totally unfamiliar with testing will need more preliminary help than others, and dull children may be expected to require more assistance. . . The examiner's own good sense must be relied upon to make necessary adaptions in the testing program"; then in paragraph six, "These tests are designed as measures of achievement of pupils—*not* tests of following directions. Consequently any method of making clear to the pupil what he is expected to do is allowable." Still later it is emphatically stated that the child may not ask questions during the examination, although it is pointed out that the examiner may walk about the room to see that the pupils are marking the answers instead of writing words, and so on. Why the child should not be allowed to ask if he is doing it rightly is, therefore, not made very clear.

The intermediate and advanced tests are not only very limited as to their diagnostic value, but are very similar in content. Twelve of the seventeen paragraphs in Part I of the reading test for grades 7-8, three of the four paragraphs in Part II, and forty of the sixty-five words in the vocabulary test are the same as those used in the test for grades 4-6. In addition to this similarity in test material, the table of grade equivalents for the intermediate test gives values from grade 4.0 to grade 9.0 (scores outside of these limits are extrapolated). There

scarcely seems to be, therefore, justification for the publication of the advanced form.

The scoring of the intermediate and advanced tests is quite largely subjective. The keys list several correct answers for some items but do not include all of the answers which may be correct, and do not suggest the possibility of several answers in some instances where the possibility exists. A single difference in the number of correct answers, however, may make as much as two months difference in a child's reading age equivalent.

The tests appear to this reviewer to be decidedly inferior to several other tests which are easily available; for example, the *Iowa Silent Reading Test* or the *Progressive Achievement Test in Reading*.

For reviews by Ivan A. Booker and Joseph C. Dewey, see 1105. For reviews by Jack W. Dunlap, Richard Ledgerwood, E. V. Pullias, and Hugh B. Wood of the total battery, see 874 and 1189.

[1552]

Metropolitan Readiness Tests. Kindergarteners and first-grade entrants; 1933-39; 1 form; $1.20 per 25; 15¢ per specimen set; (70) minutes; Gertrude H. Hildreth and Nellie L. Griffiths; Yonkers, N. Y.: World Book Co.

REFERENCES

1 HILDRETH, GERTRUDE. "Number Readiness and Progress in Arithmetic." *J Exp Ed* 4:1-6 S '35.
2 WRIGHT, WENDELL W. *Reading Readiness*: A Prognostic Study. Bulletin of the School of Education, Indiana University, Vol. 12, No. 3. Bloomington, Ind.: Indiana University Bookstore, June 1936. Pp. 46. $0.50. Paper.
3 CALVERT, EVERETT T. "Predicting Accomplishment in Beginning Reading." *Calif J El Ed* 6:34-44 Ag '37.
4 GRANT, ALBERT. "A Comparison of the Metropolitan Readiness Tests and the Pintner-Cunningham Primary Mental Test." *El Sch J* 38:118-26 O '37.
5 SENOUR, A. C. "A Comparison of Two Instruments for Measuring Reading Readiness," pp. 178-83. In *The Role of Research in Educational Progress*: Official Report, American Educational Research Association, A Department of the National Education Association, New Orleans, Louisiana, February 20-24, 1937. Washington, D. C.: the Association, May 1937. Pp. 255. $1.50. Paper.
6 FENDRICK, PAUL, AND MCGLADE, CHARLES A. "A Validation of Two Prognostic Tests of Reading Aptitude." *El Sch J* 39:187-94 N '38.
7 GRANT, ALBERT. "The Comparative Validity of the Metropolitan Readiness Tests and the Pintner-Cunningham Primary Mental Tests." *El Sch J* 38:599-605 Ap '38.
8 HUGGETT, A. J. "An Experiment in Reading Readiness." *J Ed Res* 32:263-70 D '38.
9 KAWIN, ETHEL. "Implications of Individual Differences at the First Grade Level." Discussion by S. J. Beck. *Am J Orthopsychiatry* 8:654-72 O '38.
10 RANSOM, KATHARINE A. "A Study of Reading Readiness." *Peabody J Ed* 16:276-84 Ja '39.

W. J. Osburn, Professor of Education, The University of Washington. It is futile as well as dangerous to try to teach children who are not ready to learn what is taught. It is stupid to subject little children to impossible tasks upon their first contact with the school. Yet we have been doing just those things year after year with 25 per cent of our first grade children. It does no good to ascribe the high mortality in the first grade to such vague concepts as "lack of cooperation," "lack of interest," "naughtiness," "lack of attention," and the like when the real cause of the trouble is immaturity.

For these reasons all tests which purport to measure readiness are of major interest and importance. The *Metropolitan Readiness Tests* have been widely and successfully used as an objective means of identifying the children who are not yet mature enough to profit by ordinary first grade instruction.

In these tests maturity is defined in terms of perception vocabulary, the understanding and correct reaction to oral directions, number knowledge, information, and ability in drawing. While the total time required is 70 minutes at least four "sittings" are recommended. In addition the examiner is warned to stop at the end of any test when there is evidence of undue fatigue. The tests are to be used either at the close of the kindergarten or at the beginning of the first grade. Children who fail to score 60 points on the entire test are considered unready for ordinary reading instructions. The norms are based upon more than 7,000 cases.

The tests are entirely free from reading content. Test 1 is concerned with similarities in pictures. Test 2 requires the copying of forms. Tests 3 and 4 test vocabulary and the understanding of sentences by the use of pictures. Test 5 contains forty items involving ability in "number vocabulary, counting, ordinal numbers, recognition of written numbers, writing numbers, interpreting number symbols, the meaning of number terms, the meaning of fractional parts, recognition of forms, telling time, and the use of numbers in simple problems," all of which are markedly absent from most of our primary number tests. Test 6 is informational and Test 7 is concerned with freehand drawing.

It is obvious that the authors of the test would readily admit that their technique for the testing of readiness is far from perfect. With only one form they are unable to furnish measures of improvement in readiness. The validity problem is not solved adequately as yet. The ever difficult problem of reliability when testing very young children in groups is still with us. The authors warn clearly that some children who fail to achieve a total score of 60 are nevertheless ready to read. On the other hand some who achieve more than 60 are still unready.

Imperfections such as these are to be expected in all pioneer testing. In spite of them, however, the *Metropolitan Readiness Tests* are emphatically worth while.

[1553]

Michigan Speed of Reading Test, 1937 Revision. Grades 3-16; 1932-37; 2 forms; $1 per 25; 10¢ per specimen set; 7(15) minutes; Edward B. Greene; New York: Psychological Corporation.

REFERENCES

1 GREENE, EDWARD B. "Michigan Speed of Reading Tests." *J Ed Res* 28:283-8 D '34.
2 STRANG, RUTH. "An Evaluation of Reading Tests for College Students (Abstract)," pp. 35-7. In *The Role of Research in Educational Progress*: Official Report, American Educational Research Association, A Department of the National Education Association, New Orleans, Louisiana, February 20-24, 1937. Washington, D. C.: the Association, May, 1937. Pp. 255. $1.50. Paper.

[1554]

Minnesota Reading Examinations for College Students. Grades 9-16; 1930-35; 2 forms; $6 per 100; 35¢ per specimen set; 46(55) minutes; Melvin E. Haggerty and Alvin C. Eurich; Minneapolis, Minn.: University of Minnesota Press.

REFERENCES

1 EURICH, ALVIN C. *The Reading Abilities of College Students*: An Experimental Study, pp. 17-40. Minneapolis, Minn.: University of Minnesota Press, 1931. Pp. xv, 208. $2.50.
2 STRANG, RUTH. "An Evaluation of Reading Tests for College Students (Abstract)," pp. 35-7. In *The Role of Research in Educational Progress*: Official Report, American Educational Research Association, A Department of the National Education Association, New Orleans, Louisiana, February 20-24, 1937. Washington, D. C.: the Association, May 1937. Pp. 255. $1.50. Paper.
3 PATERSON, DONALD G.; SCHNEIDLER, GWENDOLEN G.; AND WILLIAMSON, EDMUND G. *Student Guidance Techniques*, pp. 91-4. New York: McGraw-Hill Book Co., Inc., 1938. Pp. xviii, 316. $3.00. (London: McGraw-Hill Publishing Co., Ltd. 18s.)

W. C. McCall, Director of the Personnel Bureau and Associate Professor of Education, University of South Carolina. This test contains two parts, the first is devoted to vocabulary measurement and the second to measuring silent reading comprehension through the medium of paragraph reading. The vocabulary part consists of a 100-word multiple-choice test, derived mostly from the *Haggerty Reading Examination, Sigma 3*, with additional items and arrangement of items in terms of difficulty. The time allowance is six minutes. The paragraph reading part consists of ten independent passages typical of textbook content at the college level. Three or four questions are attached to each passage, a total of 35 questions in all, devoted to testing grasp of factual information, comprehension of organization, and understanding of thought content. The time allowance for the ten paragraphs and 35 questions is 40 minutes.

The manual warns that timing must be adhered to precisely since "few pupils" are able to finish the vocabulary part within 6 minutes. The manual states, however, in reference to the paragraphs that "practically every pupil should finish in the time allowed." Thus, the test yields two part scores, the first of which, due to the short time limit, must be interpreted as a combined measure of vocabulary, rate of work, and "intelligence," and the second as essentially a power measure of silent reading comprehension.

That the vocabulary part measures "intelligence" to some extent, as is done by typical group intelligence tests, would naturally be assumed on the basis of the common characteristics of language content and speed emphasis. This assumption is supported by correlations cited in the manual which indicate that the "vocabulary" scores on Form A correlate with group intelligence tests to the extent of approximately .73. (Direct average of three correlations reported in the manual.) The authors report a reliability of .93 for the vocabulary part of Form A, based upon high school seniors' scores.

For the paragraph-reading part of Form A, the authors report a reliability coefficient of .78, based upon college juniors and seniors. The reliability for high school seniors is reported as only .69, an indication that the paragraph reading material is better suited to the upper-college level. The intercorrelation of the vocabulary and paragraph-reading parts is given in the manual as .54, based upon testing of high school seniors. It seems reasonable, therefore, to conclude that the paragraph-reading measure afforded by the *Minnesota Reading Examination* is a useful but not highly reliable index of a college student's ability to grasp facts and thought content in work-study reading material. From the intercorrelations it is evident that the two parts of the test measure partially separate abilities and it is therefore suggested that Part I scores may be used as rough indicators of whether or not respective pupils are as proficient in reading paragraphs as their "vocabulary-speed" scores would seem to warrant.

The extent to which total scores on Form A predict college marks is indicated by two correlations reported in the manual. These correlations seem to justify an average correlation expectation of approximately .50 between total scores on the reading test and marks on college courses when marks are formulated independently by various instructors and reported in traditional five-letter symbolism. Thus, it is apparent that the test as a whole predicts college marks about as well as group intelligence tests usually predict.

All correlation studies reported in the manual are for Form A scores. Form B was constructed several years after Form A and both the item analysis and the standardization of Form B were based upon later generations of students. The manual contains tables of corresponding percentile ranks and standard scores for Forms A and B, based upon examining large numbers of separate generations of college sophomores, juniors, and seniors. Corresponding percentile ranks show only small differences in raw scores for the two forms and so the authors accordingly claim that "a high degree of comparability of total scores is apparent." The large numbers of cases on which the comparability tables are based obviously lend considerable support to their claim but the method of standardization was clearly faulty.

In several respects the format of the test and the scoring key suggest possibilities of improvement. The questions following the paragraphs are printed in type so small as to create eye strain for some students, especially if the lighting in the examination room is not entirely ideal. Also, the provisions for recording responses to the questions on paragraph reading invite scoring errors in that the alternatives are not numbered and the student is requested to check in some instances and to underscore in others. With answers thus falling in various positions on the paper, scoring is rendered laborious. The scoring key is of the old-fashioned strip-cut variety. A stencil-type key is needed to bring the answers conveniently adjacent to the recorded responses in the test booklet. Better still, the alternatives might be numbered and students directed to record their choices within parentheses in column, thereby making possible use of an easily manipulated fan-type key.

The examiner's manual is well written, conservative in claims for the test, instructive in discussion of reading and testing, and critical in analysis of what the Minnesota test accomplishes. The manual contains extensive norms data for Form A and reports a number of correlation studies, only a few of which have been referred to in this paper.

In conclusion, it may be said that the *Minne-*

sota Reading Examination for College Students is a useful instrument but that the test leaves much to be 'desired in that it is only roughly diagnostic to the extent of enabling description of a student's "reading" capability in terms of a "vocabulary" measure which is beclouded with emphasis upon speed and a measure of paragraph reading which is rather low in reliability and general in meaning. It is the writer's belief that much improvement could be made by increasing the time limit for Part I, increasing the content (and time allowance accordingly) of Part II, revising the format to facilitate scoring and reduce eye strain, and restandardizing Forms A and B as thus revised.

For a review by Ruth Strang, see 1106.

[1555]
Minnesota Speed of Reading Test for College Students. Grades 12-16; 1936; 2 forms; $2.75 per 100; 35¢ per specimen set; 6(15) minutes; Alvin C. Eurich; Minneapolis, Minn.: University of Minnesota Press.

REFERENCES
1 EURICH, ALVIN C. *The Reading Abilities of College Students*: An Experimental Study, pp. 54-61, Minneapolis, Minn.: University of Minnesota Press, 1931. Pp. xv, 208. $2.50.
2 PATERSON, DONALD G.; SCHNEIDLER, GWENDOLEN G.; AND WILLIAMSON, EDMUND G. *Student Guidance Techniques*, pp. 87-8. New York: McGraw-Hill Book Co., Inc., 1938. Pp. xviii, 316. $3.00. (London: McGraw-Hill Publishing Co., Ltd. 18s.)

J. R. Gerberich, Director of the Bureau of Educational Research and Statistical Service and Associate Professor of Education, University of Connecticut. Thirty-eight short paragraphs of material from such fields as history, geography, economics, government, psychology, education, and the sciences make up this test for measuring the reading speed of college students. The paragraphs, from 40 to 60 words in length, are sufficiently simple that the comprehension factor, which usually has variable and unpredictable influence on speed of reading test results, is largely controlled. Each paragraph contains an absurd phrase through which the student is to draw a line. The absurdities are on the whole rather cleverly worded and keyed to the context, so that a certain degree of comprehension is necessary on the part of the reader if the absurdity is to be detected. Students work as far through the thirty-eight paragraphs as they can during the six minutes for which the test is timed.

The manual for the test consists of eleven pages of mimeographed material in which are included directions for administration, directions for scoring, scoring keys for both Forms

A and B, and norms for both Forms A and B. No information of any kind is given concerning the validity or reliability of the instrument. Tables for converting raw scores to percentiles and to "scale values," which express deviations from the median in terms of the standard deviation, are based on college sophomores and juniors at the University of Minnesota, but the user of the test is left to conjecture concerning the number of such students upon which the norms are based. Obviously, the sampling is not likely to be highly representative of college students.

Although the manual makes no mention of any supplementary source of information, Eurich's, *The Reading Abilities of College Students*,[1] 1931 copyright, contains a chapter devoted to the development and standardization of the instrument. That the test is the same seems certain, despite the 1936 copyright of the test, because the manual contains tables of grade norms which are taken bodily from tables in the chapter of the book. The following data concerning reliability and validity are taken from the 1931 source. Reliability coefficients between the two forms of the test are reported as ranging from .81 for tenth grade pupils to .87 for graduate students in college. Correlation coefficients between scores on the two forms of the *Chapman-Cook Speed of Reading Test* and the two forms of the *Minnesota Speed of Reading Test for College Students* are reported as ranging from .63 to .76, while coefficients between scores on an informal reading exercise measuring words read per minute and on the two forms of the Minnesota test were .39 and .63. Eurich states that the validity coefficients listed above lead one "to the conclusion that the Minnesota Speed Test has marked validity as an instrument to measure the rate at which college students read."

Even though different speed of reading tests doubtless place varying emphases upon the speed and comprehension outcomes (by means of variations in difficulty of content, directions to the students, scoring methods, etc.), which justifies the acceptance of relatively low degrees of relationship between scores on such tests as evidence of satisfactory validity, it seems probable that a change in the placement of some of the absurdities in the paragraphs might well result in more valid scores. For example, in the 76 paragraphs from the combined

Forms A and B, 69 of the absurdities occur in whole or in part in the last two lines of the paragraphs. No paragraph has less than six lines, while the mode appears to be seven lines. It seems certain that at least occasional students would decide after brief experience with the test that reading the first parts of the selections is a waste of time, and would then go immediately to the last two or three lines of each paragraph through the remainder of the test. The comprehension level of the paragraphs is such that the absurdities can rather readily be detected without knowing the entirety of the context, so that such a technique might well effect a marked increase in rate scores for such students.

This test, despite the glaring inadequacy of the manual, the too-homogeneous sampling of college students used in establishing the norms, and validity which cannot be classed as high, appears to have considerable merit. The least improvement which would make the test acceptable as a scientific instrument would be the amplification of the manual to provide the information to which a test user is entitled or to indicate where such information is to be obtained.

For reviews by Frederick B. Davis and Ruth Strang, see 1107.

[1556]

Nature of Proof: Test 5.22. Grades 10-12; 1939-40; 1 form; revision of Tests 5.2a and 5.21; 5¢ per test; 1¢ per machine-scorable answer sheet; 5¢ per explanation sheet and interpretation guide; $1.50 per set of stencils for machine scoring; Chicago, Ill.: Evaluation in the Eight Year Study, Progressive Education Association.

REFERENCES

1 RATHS, LOUIS. "Evaluating the Program of Lakeshore School." *Ed Res B* 17:67-84 Mr 16 '38.
2 *Evaluation Materials Developed for Various Aspects of Thinking.* Chicago, Ill.: Evaluation in the Eight Year Study, Progressive Education Association, March 1939. Pp. [22]. Paper, mimeographed. Out of print.
3 *The Evaluation of Abilities Involved in Dealing with Quantitative Relationships.* Chicago, Ill.: Evaluation in the Eight Year Study, Progressive Education Association, March 1939. Pp. [24]. Paper, mimeographed. Out of print.

[1557]

Nelson-Denny Reading Test. Grades 9-16; 1929-30; 2 forms; $1.65 per 25 tests including 25 answer booklets; 75¢ per 25 answer booklets; single specimen set free; 30(35) minutes; M. J. Nelson and E. C. Denny; Boston, Mass.: Houghton Mifflin Co.

REFERENCES

1 THORNDIKE, E. L. *A Teacher's Word Book.* New York: Bureau of Publications, Teachers College, Columbia University, 1921. Pp. 134. $0.80.
2 HORN, ERNEST. *A Basic Writing Vocabulary: 10,000 Words Most Commonly Used in Writing.* State University of Iowa, Monographs in Education, Series 1, No. 4. Iowa City, Iowa: the University, 1926. Pp. 225. Cloth, $2.25; paper, $1.75.
3 STRANG, RUTH. "An Evaluation of Reading Tests for College Students (Abstract)," pp. 35-7. In *The Role of Research in Educational Progress:* Official Report, American Educational Research Association, A Department of the National Education Association, New Orleans, Louisiana, February 20-24, 1937. Washington, D. C.: the Association, May 1937. Pp. 255. $1.50. Paper.
4 HELD, OMAR C. "Nelson-Denny Reading Test as an English Placement Test." *Sch and Soc* 49:64 Ja 14 '39.
5 TRAXLER, ARTHUR E. "One Reading Test Serves the Purpose." *Clearing House* 14:419-21 Mr '40.
6 UPSHALL, C. C. "Reading Ability and Success in First Year College History." *Univ Wash Col Ed Rec* 6:33-6 Ja '40.

Hans C. Gordon, Division of Educational Research, Public Schools, Philadelphia, Pennsylvania. The vocabulary test contains 100 items which are short sentence completions with five answers from which to choose. The time for the vocabulary part is only ten minutes. Consequently, there is a large element of speed involved in answering 100 items. In addition, the student is obliged to find the proper place for the answer on a separate answer sheet. The fact that the time limits are quite short is evidenced in the norms reported. Thus, with 100 five-choice items an average score attained by marking answer spaces at random on the answer sheet would be 20 items right. There is no correction for wrong answers. The median for grade 9 is only 18 or two points less than a random or chance score. For grade 10 the vocabulary median is 21.

Most of the words in the vocabulary test were chosen from the Thorndike [1] and Horn [2] lists. The basis of choice is not described. The test follows good vocabulary test form in that the word given in the sentence occurs less frequently than the words given in the choices for the answers. It is evident, however, that in this vocabulary test other traits than breadth of vocabulary are measured, especially reading speed and clerical facility.

The paragraph test consists of nine selections of 200 words each followed by four multiple-choice questions (five choices). The time allowed for this section of the test is twenty minutes. Here again the comprehending reading rate is an important element in attaining high scores. In order to finish the test and to spend approximately half time on seeking and writing answers it is necessary for the student to read at the rate of 300 words a minute. Accordingly, high scores are attained by those who read rapidly and who after reading are able to answer relatively simple questions of fact. The paragraph selections are largely from college reading material. It is possible in some cases for a student with an adequate acquaintance with the general content of the selection to answer some questions without reading the selection carefully.

The first listed purpose of the test is "to predict probable success in college." Evidence of the value of the test for this purpose is cited in an *r* of .70 for the total scores correlated with an objective test in child psychology. In another reported study the test predicted "general scholastic success about as well or better than the better intelligence tests." Additional criteria for prediction of success in college are always welcome but, in view of the mass of evidence available in cumulative records and from scholastic aptitude tests, the addition of this test of reading is justified only when other evidence is quite meagre.

The second purpose of the test is listed: "to section incoming college or high-school classes." In view of the reported correlation between the test and at least one kind of college work, the value of this reading test for this purpose may be important. However, no suggestions are offered as to how the test may be used. The authors' satisfaction with the situation expressed in the high correlation coefficients might be interpreted to mean that the authors considered the test sufficiently accurate to be the sole criterion for sectioning. Where it is possible, it would seem to be a much more desirable procedure, however, to use a wider basis of fact in organizing classes in college or high-school subjects. Since these classes are usually organized separately in specific subjects, it is probably better to select those predictors which are of greatest value in the subject under consideration. It is hardly credible that any predictor will be equally valuable in all subjects.

The third purpose listed is diagnosis. The author makes no suggestion as to how the test might be used for this purpose. Since the vocabulary and reading tests involve a very considerable element of speed of reading which is not differentiated in score, it is obvious that the blend of reading ability indexed in the part score is not a satisfactory clue as to whether unusual pains should be taken to broaden the vocabulary or to deepen the power of paragraph comprehension. No reliability coefficients are reported for the part scores. The total test shows an *r* of .91 between Forms A and B for college freshmen. The *PE* of a score is about one-half year in grade norms.

Norms are reported for all grades from the third grade to the senior class in college. The value of some of these norms may be questioned in view of the fact that a random or chance score on the total test is 34 which is the same as the norm for the eighth grade.

[1558]

Nelson Silent Reading Test. Grades 3-9; 1931-39; 3 forms; $1.65 per 25 tests including answer booklets; 75¢ per 25 answer booklets; single specimen set free; 30(35) minutes; M. J. Nelson; Boston, Mass.: Houghton Mifflin Co.

REFERENCES

1 GRANT, ALBERT. "Results of Nelson Silent Reading Test in Grade IX." *Sch R* 48:34-9 Ja '40.

Sch R 48:34-9 Ja '40. Albert Grant. "Results of Nelson Silent Reading Test in Grade IX." This report analyzes the results of the Nelson Silent Reading Test for more than three thousand ninth-grade pupils in Cincinnati. The Nelson test was originally issued as suitable for Grades III-VIII, inclusive. Recently, however, it has been described by the publishers as also suitable for Grade IX. The *Teacher's Manual* gives norms for Grade IX but gives no information on the size and the nature of the ninth-grade population used in the derivation of the norms. The author of the test, in a letter to the writer, states that he had been unable to secure the results of the test for the ninth-grade population of any large city. This dearth of information on the results of the test at the ninth-grade level suggested to the writer that an analysis of the results for the entire ninth grade of a large city might prove helpful to future users of the test. The test was given on a city-wide basis in Grade IX in Cincinnati during January, 1939. * The Nelson test consists of two parts, a vocabulary test and a paragraph test. The latter contains twenty-five paragraphs, each followed by three questions. Each question is intended to measure a distinct aspect of reading ability. Thus "A" questions are intended to measure ability to understand the general significance of the paragraph; "B" questions deal with ability to note details; and "C" questions have to do with ability to predict the probable outcome. The test is scored separately for each type of question—a fact which greatly increases the total scoring time required. The separate scores are intended to make possible a diagnosis of the pupil's status with respect to the three types of reading ability mentioned. The *Teacher's Manual* suggests ways in which these separate scores may be used as a basis for planning remedial work. * the coefficients of correlation between scores on Subtests A, B, and C were determined for a sampling of three hundred cases. The correlation between subtests A and B was found to be .91 ± .007; between Subtests A and C, .91 ± .007; and between Subtests B and C, .92 ± .006. Since all coefficients are above .90, close relationship is indicated. In fact, it is doubtful whether the coefficients of reliability for these subtests are any higher. In other words, the subtests correlate as closely with one another as they correlate with themselves. These findings definitely suggest that the various parts of the paragraph test measure functions which are either practically identical or closely related. It follows that the extra scoring time required to secure a score on the individual subtests is essentially wasted, since these scores yield no information which cannot be secured directly from the pupil's total score on the paragraph test. * This report gives a statistical analysis of results of the Nelson Silent Reading Test for more than three thousand ninth-grade pupils in Cincinnati. The essential findings are as follows: (1) The test is sufficiently difficult so that few ninth-grade pupils get maximum or nearly maximum scores. (2) In Grade IX the test yields scores the variability of which is as great as the variability of scores made by pupils in grades below the ninth. (3) The ninth-grade norms given in the *Teacher's Manual* agree closely with the median scores of the ninth-grade population of a large city (Cincinnati). (4) The three subtests of the paragraph test, which are intended to measure distinct aspects of reading ability, really measure functions which are closely related. Individual scores on these subtests yield little diagnostic information which cannot be secured from the total paragraph score.

[1559]

Ophthalm-O-Graph. 1936; a portable camera, using 35 mm. standard motion picture film, which photographs eye movements while the examinee is engaged in the act of reading; for A.C. or D.C., $275; Form R record card, 65¢ per 100; Southbridge, Mass.: American Optical Company.

REFERENCES

1 IMUS, HENRY A.; ROTHNEY, JOHN W. M.; AND BEAR, ROBERT M. *An Evaluation of Visual Factors in Reading.* The Dartmouth Eye Institute of the Dartmouth Medical School, Hanover, N. H.: Dartmouth College Publications, 1938. Pp. xiv, 144. $1.50. Paper.
2 DOLCH, EDWARD WILLIAM. *A Manual for Remedial Reading,* pp. 159-62. Champaign, Ill.: Garrard Press, 1939. Pp. x, 166. $2.00.

G. T. Buswell, Professor of Educational Psychology, The University of Chicago. The *Ophthalm-O-Graph* is a portable eye-movement camera patented by the American Optical

Company. In common with most cameras built for this purpose, it has two lenses which may be used for photographing both eyes or one eye plus a head line. The instrument is suitable for ordinary clinical purposes but is not suitable for precise scientific work. The principal criticisms of the *Ophthalm-O-Graph* as a scientific instrument for the reading clinic are three in number.

First, the apparatus lacks a precise timing device, the only means of measuring the duration of a pause of the eye being to measure the length of the eye-line on the film and then translate this into units of time. Although a synchronous motor is used, the film runs slowly which allows a considerable margin of error in measuring brief pauses. Still more serious is the fact that precise measurement is impossible where there are vertical movements of the head, since these elongate or shorten the eye-line. The errors may compensate in computing averages, but the apparatus is not reliable for measuring duration of individual pauses.

A second criticism of the apparatus is that the material to be read is placed below the lenses in such a position that only a very short sample of reading material can be used. The reliability of such short records is open to serious question. There are various ways in which a camera might be constructed to obviate this difficulty. Longer samples of reading are necessary for either scientific study or accurate diagnosis.

A third criticism applies to the head rest device. In all of the models which the reviewer has seen, a chin rest has been used. This is the worst possible position to support the head, because any tendency to vocalize is immediately translated into vertical head movements which, in turn, cause errors in measuring the duration of fixations and in determining the exact position of a fixation.

Aside from the foregoing criticisms the apparatus is a convenient portable device for use in a reading clinic. It is compact, light in weight, and reasonably substantial in construction.

In order to use the *Ophthalm-O-Graph* for purposes of diagnosing reading ability, reliable standards are needed for studying growth from grade to grade. The writer has been unable to find the scientific data underlying the standards which appear in the advertising material distributed by the American Optical Company.

Furthermore, the reading materials on which the "norms" are based are not shown nor is there a description of precise conditions under which they were obtained. Without these qualifying facts the norms are scientifically useless. The nearest to a body of data of the type needed appeared in the Dartmouth College study.[1] However, the reliability of the samples in this study is open to serious criticism.

Since the research laboratory ordinarily develops and standardizes its own materials, the lack of adequate norms supplied by the distributor of the apparatus is not important. However, in view of the fact that by far the largest number of *Ophthalm-O-Graphs* used for educational purposes are found in schools where there are no adequately trained technicians, the absence of carefully standardized norms and reading materials is so serious that little educational value can result from the investment. An eye-movement camera is essentially a scientific rather than a clinical instrument.

The *Ophthalm-O-Graph* has certain values for the medical clinic quite apart from its value in the reading clinic. The criticisms expressed above apply to the employment of the *Ophthalm-O-Graph* as an instrument for use in the school.

Sch and Soc 52:205-8 S 14 '40. M. E. Broom. "The Reliability of the Reading Graph Yielded by the Ophthalmograph." * 1. The reliability coefficients of the tests of fixations, regressions and reading speed are too low in value to permit the use of these measures with individuals. 2. The reliability of the comprehension test is such that this test should never be used for the measurement of comprehension during silent reading. This is a minor defect, however, since this test functions primarily to motivate the subjects' actual reading performance. 3. The present information concerning the reliability of the tests is of doubtful value, and the truth as to the reliability of these measures probably will not be known until studies are made in which the same card is used for both the initial test and the re-test of the same individuals, and possibly not until adequately standardized duplicate and equivalent card materials are available for use with the ophthalmograph. While the present card test materials are not sufficiently reliable, they have served education through bringing before the public a better knowledge of the approximate recognition span that is found at various grade, and maturity, levels. The present card tests have rendered also a service in permitting the determination of gross progress made by groups of pupils. The writer still believes that the ophthalmograph has definite values as a prognostic and clinical instrument, but it is doubtful whether the full value of the instrument will be known until the card test materials have been scientifically standardized.

Dolch, Edward William. A Manual for Remedial Reading, pp. 159-62. (Champaign, Ill.: Garrard Press, 1939. Pp. x, 166. $2.00.) For many years, laboratories which studied reading problems have photographed eye movements. The machine used contained the usual 35-mm. motion-picture film which moved at a constant rate behind a pair of lenses. Each lens focused upon the film spots of light reflected from the reader's eyeballs and which were cast on the eye by a light shining through a small hole in a box which contained an electric bulb. Every movement of the pair of eyes was recorded upon the film by the movement of the spots of light reflected from the eyeballs. The standard procedure was to ask the subject to read five or six lines on a card placed at the proper reading distance and thus to secure on the film a record of the eye movements during this reading. The purpose of photographing the eye movements has been to study what were called "reading habits." It was assumed that the eyes of each individual moved in certain habitual ways during reading. If then a record of the eyes' habitual movements could be secured, it was assumed that remedial exercises could be given to change these habits. There has now been put on the market a very compact and effective machine for making eye movement photographs. Reading clinics everywhere have these machines and they are also found in the offices of school psychologists and others interested in the problems of poor readers. Many schools are wondering whether they should possess one of these machines or, if they have one, how they should use it. First of all, it must be said that no one should imagine, when he has secured an eye movement photograph for a child that he has fully adequate material for a diagnosis of that child's reading difficulties. The eye movement photograph tells what the child's eyes did in reading a certain short selection at a certain time. It does not tell what the child's eyes do in reading at all times. Two variables must be always kept in mind. (1) The child's reading changes as the material changes. The photograph shows the reading of a certain test card. Suppose an easier card had been used, or a harder one. It is easily shown in the photographing of the eye movement that we can change the record on the film in many ways by changing the material that the child is asked to read. This does not mean that the child does not have eye movement habits. Instead it shows either that he has various habits or that his habits change with changing conditions. (2) The other variable is the child's purpose, we find that we can change the record on the film by telling the child to read rapidly or to read very carefully or in some other special way. The standard directions for photographing eye movements are: You should read as rapidly as you can, remembering that you will answer a few questions about what you have read. It has been found that the direction "read rapidly" registers strongly with some children and causes them to hurry more than usual; while the warning about a "few questions" registers with others and causes them to slow down. These two limitations of the photograph secured by use of the machine are very important when we think of the kind of reading we are going to have the remedial case do. We are not going to have him read these standard cards with these standard directions. We are going to give him school books and other books of various degrees of difficulty and of interest for him. We are going to give him many purposes in reading and ask him all sorts of questions. Therefore, the eye movement photograph showing reading of a certain piece of text, following certain directions, is a *sample* of the child's eye movement. It is a *special* sample which must be taken as such. It is valuable if one remembers exactly the card the child was reading and the exact conditions which surrounded that reading. The photograph is valuable especially to a person who has personally taught many remedial cases how to read. Such a person understands how the child's mind works and what effects him and how. As a part of this total understanding of the remedial process, the sample given by the photograph is helpful. But a study of eye movement

photographs, apart from the child's total situation, is definitely misleading and may be clearly harmful. The concept that the child has a single reading habit, supposed to be very like a habit of handwriting, leads to mechanical exercises which may not at all fit the whole complicated situation. Such a partial and distorted view of the use of eye movement photographs is by all means to be avoided. Second, we wish to point out that eye movement photographs need to be interpreted in detail. Common practice is to count the forward movements, count the regressive movements, and give averages, including fixations per 100 words, regressions per 100 words, duration of fixations per 100 words, number of words per fixation, and number of words per minute. These averages may or may not be very significant depending upon how uniform the child's performance was during the reading of the lines. But in a reading case the chances are against uniform performance. One line may consist of familiar words and may be read with ease. Another line may contain an unknown word which causes great confusion, with many regressions, long fixations, or a mere wavering of the eyes back and forth. And still another line may contain an unfamiliar idea which causes a mental confusion which shows itself in hesitating and confused eye movements. Therefore, to interpret a strip of film showing the reading of a number of lines of print, one must lay down beside the film the card which was read and compare the two line by line to try to discover the causes for the many kinds of movement which the film shows. While doing this one must remember the question raised above, whether the particular card was probably easy for the child to read, hard for him to read, contained certain unknown words or the like. It is in this interpretation of eye movement records that there has been the greatest failure to make proper use of them. Third, we must call attention to the check on comprehension which accompanies the usual photographing of eye movements. The standard procedure gives ten statements on the back of each card which is read. Immediately after the photographing, these statements are read to the child, and he answers "yes" or "no" depending on whether the statements agree with the paragraph just read. Thus the check on comprehension is planned to be immediate memory as determined by true or false statements. The percentage of statements which the pupil gets right is called his comprehension score. Several comments need to be made concerning this comprehension score. First, it is obvious that mere chance would give on the average a comprehension score of 50 per cent. This fact is keenly appreciated by all workers in education who use true and false or yes-no tests. It must not be forgotten here. Second, we must point out that many of the questions can be answered from previous knowledge. This has been found to be an especial difficulty with some of the cards which deal with facts in history. It is to some extent a difficulty with all the cards because about half of the statements are always false, and common sense or general experience will often detect falsity even without the reading of the cards. Third, it is found that the child, when first photographed, generally paid so much attention to the unusual experience that he was not trying hard enough to remember details. But after having tried to answer ten questions on one card he will be more cautious next time in his reading and therefore be able to answer more questions. We should know, therefore, whether an eye movement photograph is the first one made or whether it had been preceded by others. Finally, we must raise the question whether the kind of reading in which a child tries to remember ten details from six lines of text is the kind we are trying to teach in remedial reading. This is really part of the question which we raised in the last section, whether the type of reading done with the eye photographing machine is typical of the type of reading we are planning on teaching.

For reviews by Stella S. Center, David Kopel, Marion Monroe, Joseph Tiffin, and Miles A. Tinker, see 1108.

[1559.1]
Parr Skill-Ability Tests. Grades 9-16; 1938-40; 4 parts; Frank W. Parr; Corvallis, Ore.: O. S. C. Cooperative Association.
a) CONCENTRATION. 1940; 1 form; 4¢ per test, 50 or more.
b) OUTLINING. 1938; 1 form; 8¢ per test, 50 or more.
c) READING. 1938; 2 forms; 6¢ per test, 50 or more.
d) VOCABULARY. 1938; 2 forms; 10¢ per test, 50 or more; 28(35) minutes.

[1560]
Peabody Library Information Test, Revised Edition. Grades 13-16; 1938; 1 form; $1.25 per 25; 20¢ per specimen set; 32(40) minutes; Louis Shores and Joseph E. Moore; Minneapolis, Minn.: Educational Test Bureau, Inc.

[1561]
Poley Précis Test: A Test by Paragraph Summaries of Reading Comprehension. Grades 9-12; 1927; 2 forms; 75¢ per 25; 15¢ per specimen set; 40(45) minutes; Irvin C. Poley; Bloomington, Ill.: Public School Publishing Co.

Edward A. Tenney, Associate Professor of English, Cornell University. The *Poley Précis Test* is a sound device for determining a student's ability to read intelligently. In it, a student must judge the accuracy of forty précis (five each for eight selections), and he must label each précis as "right," "inadequate," or "wrong." The usefulness of the test is not confined to those who have studied précis-writing; it can readily be used to test anyone's ability to understand what he reads. A further advantage is that ample time is allowed. In consequence the ability to read rather than speed of reading is tested.

The publishers assert that "the test is also useful in diagnosing individual reading difficulties. . . . The eight selections in the test exemplify widely different fields of interest." The truth of this assertion is questionable, for six of the selections are literary; two are scientific. One of these two (Selection VI) by reason of its elaborate concluding simile is as "literary" as it is "scientific." Before a trustworthy diagnosis can be made, a series of précis tests including the same number of selections from poetry, from prose fiction, from expository prose, from argumentative prose, and from philosophical and scientific prose must be given.

This reviewer thinks that the attempt to carry the diagnosis to so fine a point is both futile and unnecessary. The ability to understand any passage of general writing, poetry or prose, literary or scientific, is based upon the accuracy and extent of the reader's vocabulary, upon his knowledge of the structure of sentences and paragraphs, and upon his ability to follow a logical argument or to imagine characters and scenes. If this is true, a diagnostic reading test should try to discover whether some one of these powers is weaker than another; for when they are well developed in a reader, he can encompass the meaning of all kinds of general writing. The *Poley Précis Test* does test these powers and is therefore useful; but it is not, in my opinion, a very accurate diagnosis of a student's capacity to interpret different kinds of literature.

Those who are interested in testing not the speed at which a student reads nor his special powers but his general capacity to get the exact sense of what he reads will find these précis tests very useful.

[1562]

Primary Reading Test. Grade 1; 1939; 1 form; 85¢ per 25; single specimen set free; nontimed (40-55) minutes; Albert G. Reilley; Boston, Mass.: Houghton Mifflin Co.

[1563]

Progressive Reading Tests. Grades 1-3, 3-6, 7-9, 9-13; 1934-39; identical to the reading tests in the battery *Progressive Achievement Tests*; 4 levels; 75¢ per 25; 15¢ per specimen set of any one level; 2¢ per machine-scorable answer sheets; Ernest W. Tiegs and Willis W. Clark; Los Angeles, Calif.: California Test Bureau.
a) PRIMARY. Grades 1-3; 1934-37; 3 forms; 35(40) minutes.
b) ELEMENTARY. Grades 3-6; 1934-39; 3 forms; 35(40) minutes; *Machine Scoring Edition*: 2 forms; 5¢ per test.
c) INTERMEDIATE. Grades 7-9; 1934-39; 3 forms; 50(55) minutes; *Machine Scoring Edition*: 2 forms; 5¢ per test.
d) ADVANCED. Grades 9-13; 1934-39; 2 forms; 50(55) minutes; *Machine Scoring Edition*: 2 forms; 5¢ per test.

Frederick B. Davis, Reading and Professional Education Editor, Cooperative Test Service, New York, New York; and Educational Psychologist and Head of the Remedial Department, Avon Old Farms, Avon, Connecticut. The *Progressive Reading Tests* appear to be well-planned and carefully constructed measures of reading ability. In each manual particular emphasis is placed upon the fact that subtest scores, valuable for individual diagnosis, may be obtained in addition to the total score. On the cover of each test booklet is printed a diagnostic profile for graphic presentation of the subtest scores and a classification of the test items. These are unquestionably useful, but it is unfortunate that the manual contains no warning of the inevitable unreliability of subtest scores based on only a small number of items.

The writer consulted the manual for the Advanced Battery and, using data concerning the reliabilities of the tests and distributions of the scores at the eleventh grade level, estimated the standard errors of measurement for the vocabulary test and its four subtests and for the reading-comprehension test and its three subtests. The results of these calculations are somewhat discouraging because it appears that only the total reading score may be regarded as reasonably accurate in individual measurement. Subtest scores near the median may readily vary as much as thirty percentile-rank points on the diagnostic profile by pure chance.

It is clear that such great inaccuracy in the subtest scores means that the profile chart should be regarded as merely suggestive of possible variations in an individual pupil's reading skills. As such, it is of some value. Incidentally, the chart could be improved simply by relocating the percentile points in terms of the distances corresponding to standard deviation units.

The directions for all of the tests specify that pupils are to be stopped on each test when 90 per cent of the group has finished. Because the tests measure power rather than speed these directions are possible. However, the fact that the tests are often administered in schools where the practice of ability grouping is followed makes this kind of time limit undesirable. The better pupils in a low-ability group have an advantage over the poorer pupils in a high-ability group. For example, consider the case of two pupils of equal reading ability; one takes the test with a group of poor readers, the other takes the test with a group of good readers. The pupil in the group of poor readers is likely to obtain a higher score on the test simply because his companions take a longer time to finish.

Users of the Intermediate Battery should make sure that they have the proper norms. The most recent edition can be identified by the heading of the table on page 10, which should read: Norms (1937 Revision) : Including revised extension of norms above 9.5 in 1939. One of the earlier editions, printed on pink paper, contained two misprints on page 10. At grade level 11.0 in the reading vocabulary norms, 99 should be read for 79; at grade level 15.0 in the age norms, 241 should be read for 214.

SUMMARY. The total reading test score derived from each of the four *Progressive Reading Tests* appears to be a valid and reliable index of reading ability. The Diagnostic Profile, however, is useful in individual measurement only to provide possible clues for remedial work or as the basis for further diagnostic testing.

For reviews by Ivan A. Booker and Joseph C. Dewey, see 1110. For reviews by D. Welty

Lefever, C. W. Odell, and Hugh B. Wood of the complete battery, see 876 and 1193.

[1564]

Reading Comprehension: Cooperative English Test, Tests C1 and C2. Grades 7-12, 11-16; 1940; 2 levels; Form Q; 5¢ per test, 10 to 99 copies; 1½¢ per machine-scorable answer sheet; 25¢ per specimen set; 40(45) minutes; Frederick B. Davis, F. S. Beers, Warner F. Gookin, D. G. Paterson, and Mary Willis with the cooperation of Walter F. Dearborn, Donald D. Durrell, Daniel D. Feder, William S. Gray, Arthur E. Traxler, and Louis C. Zahner; New York: Cooperative Test Service.

a) TEST c1, LOWER LEVEL. Grades 7-12.
b) TEST c2, UPPER LEVEL. Grades 11-16.

REFERENCES

1 Cooperative Test Service. *The Cooperative Reading Comprehension Tests*: Information Concerning their Construction, Interpretation, and Use. New York: Cooperative Test Service, 1940. Pp. 4. Gratis. Paper.
2 TRAXLER, ARTHUR. "The Cooperative English Test, Form Q: Correlations with School Marks and Intercorrelations," pp. 42-50. In *1940 Achievement Testing Program in Independent Schools and Supplementary Studies*. Educational Records Bureau Staff. Educational Records Bulletin, No. 30. New York: the Bureau, June 1940. Pp. xii, 76. $1.50. Paper, lithotyped.

[1565]

Sangren-Woody Reading Test. Grades 4-8; 1927-28; 2 forms; $1.25 per 25; 15¢ per specimen set; 27(35-40) minutes; Paul V. Sangren and Clifford Woody; Yonkers, N. Y.: World Book Co.

REFERENCES

1 SANGREN, PAUL V. "The Need for More Adequate Measures of Achievement in Silent Reading." *J Ed Res* 17:365-71 My '28.
2 DOUGLAS, JOSEPHINE, AND LAWSON, J. W. "Measurement of Reading Skills in Ability Groups." *J Appl Psychol* 13:494-8 O '29.
3 SANGREN, PAUL V. "The Sangren-Woody Silent Reading Test." *J Ed Res* 19:233-4 Mr '29.
4 FORAN, T. G., AND ROCK, ROBERT T., JR. *The Reliability of Some Silent Reading Tests.* Catholic University of America, Educational Research Bulletin, Vol. 5, No. 6. Washington, D. C.: Catholic Education Press, June 1930. Pp. 23. $0.35. Paper.
5 BROOM, M. EUSTACE; DOUGLAS, JOSEPHINE; AND RUDD, MARION. "On the Validity of Silent Reading Tests." *J Appl Psychol* 15:35-8 F '31.
6 "Report on Sangren-Woody Reading Test." *Pittsburgh Sch* 6:3-67 S '31.
7 SANGREN, PAUL V. Chapter 9, "Critical Study of a Silent Reading Test," pp. 165-76. *Improvement of Reading Through the Use of Tests.* Kalamazoo, Mich.: Extension Department, Western State Teachers College, 1932. Pp. 207. Paper. Out of print.

Alice K. Liveright, Principal of the Logan Demonstration School, Public Schools, Philadelphia, Pennsylvania. The *Sangren-Woody Reading Test* is admirably suited both for diagnostic purposes and to provide a comprehensive survey of silent reading ability. It consists of seven tests each of which deals with a distinct phase of the reading process. Silent reading vocabulary is tested through Part I, Word Meaning. The child indicates his knowledge of the meaning of a word by choosing from among four words that which best shows the use of the original word in a sentence.

In Part II, Rate, the child is asked to read a selection of about four hundred words as rapidly as is consistent with understanding. Rate is indicated by the number of words read during the first minute.

In Part III, Fact Material, the selection is the same as that used in Part II. Each paragraph, however, is followed by one or more factual questions. The answer, one or a few words, is written in the space provided.

Part IV, Total Meaning, likewise consists of a series of short paragraphs. Each is followed by a question which asks about the total meaning. Each question in turn is followed by four words. The pupil is asked to underline the word which best answers the question.

Part V, Central Thought, consists of paragraphs each followed by four statements. The pupil is expected to check the statement which expresses the central or important thought of the paragraph.

Part VI, Following Directions, contains ten paragraphs, each of which comprises one or more simple directions. The child's responses indicate whether he has understood the directions.

Part VII, Organization, consists of a number of sets of paragraphs with each set followed by a series of four statements in disarranged order. The pupil numbers them to indicate their correct order.

The authors have exercised great care to insure validity and reliability. A table of grade equivalents derived from the results of a huge number of pupils contains not only median scores for grades, but also for each month of the grade. Alternate forms are available.

Considering the comprehensive scope of the test, it is both short and simple to administer. The total time required is less than forty minutes. If necessary, the test may be given in two sittings. The scoring key may be fitted to each part of the test and the scoring is thus simplified as much as possible. Part VII alone is a bit complicated in arrangement and cumbersome to score. It requires the pupil to turn the paper both upside down and back and forward. This does prove confusing to some pupils and renders the scoring tedious.

Each test booklet includes a profile chart. The scores for each part of the test when indicated as directed on this chart form an individual reading profile. The pupil, parent, and teacher can at a glance note from the profile in which abilities the pupil is weak and in which he is strong. Pupils take a keen interest in the chart. They understand their reading strengths and weaknesses.

As the scores correlate well with those of shorter survey tests, the Sangren-Woody may be used for survey purposes. Its unique feature is its excellent diagnostic value. The most important skills required in study reading are all included. The organization test, however, covers one factor in organization only. To organize requires abilities other than arranging statements in proper sequence. The test is on the whole, nevertheless, quite comprehensive.

Both pupils and teachers receive the test enthusiastically. The child learns both his reading strengths and weaknesses. As few normal pupils fail in all parts, discouragement is avoided. After the test has been administered, each child may receive the special type of remedial exercise he needs and each may read with the specific purpose of making good his particular type of deficiency. When the teacher has administered the test, she is no longer satisfied with merely assigning more miscellaneous so-called remedial exercises. She helps each child to find the specific type of remedial exercise he requires.

[1566]

Schrammel-Gray High School and College Reading Test. Grades 7-13; 1940; 1 form; $1.50 per 25; 30¢ per specimen set; 25(30) minutes; H. E. Schrammel and W. H. Gray; Bloomington, Ill.: Public School Publishing Co.

[1567]

Shank Tests of Reading Comprehension. Grades 3-6, 7-9, 10-12; 1929; 3 forms, 3 levels; $3.20 per 25; 30¢ per manual;[1] 30¢ per specimen set, not including manual; quantity discounts; Spencer Shank; Cincinnati, Ohio: C. A. Gregory Co.
a) TEST I. Grades 3-6. 18(28) minutes.
b) TEST II. Grades 7-9. 20(30) minutes.
c) TEST III. Grades 10-12. 20(30) minutes.

REFERENCES

1 SHANK, SPENCER. *Student Responses in the Measurement of Reading Comprehension:* A Manual of Directions for the Shank Reading Tests. Cincinnati, Ohio: C. A. Gregory Co., 1929. Pp. 69. $0.30. Paper.
2 SHANK, SPENCER. "Student Responses in the Measurement of Reading Comprehension." *J Ed Res* 22:119-29 S '30.
3 TRAXLER, ARTHUR E. "One Reading Test Serves the Purpose." *Clearing House* 14:419-21 Mr '40.

James R. Hobson, Director of Child Placement, Brookline Public Schools, Brookline, Massachusetts. The author of this series of tests started with the assumption that reading comprehension is a composite of many separate but perhaps related abilities which cannot be measured by any single type of test response.

A complete analysis of forty-five reading tests then available for use in grades three through twelve showed that attempts had been made to measure at least seven general kinds of reading comprehension skills as indicated by the types of student response called for in the various tests.

The question of deciding which types of student response should be called for in the series under construction was solved partly by the logical consideration of the practical problems involved and partly by the construction and administration of two experimental forms of the test. Types of response which bore no relation to the content of the paragraph were eliminated as were also types of response requiring a particular kind of content and types requiring a special physical setup of the test. The response types remaining which are applicable to the reading of paragraph units as found in general literature are listed by the author as follows: (*a*) responses based upon giving details stated directly in the reading content, (*b*) responses based upon giving details implied in the content, (*c*) responses based upon giving thought implied in the content as a whole, (*d*) responses based upon determining whether or not the content stated a certain given idea, (*e*) responses based upon giving objects or thoughts to which given words refer, (*f*) responses based upon determining whether given statements are true or false, and (*g*) responses based upon selecting words of synonymous or similar meanings.

The next step in the development of this series of tests was an attempt to measure the effectiveness with which each of the above types of response measures reading comprehension when applied to the same paragraph. This was done by correlating the scores obtained from each response type with (*a*) the scores obtained from a test made up of all types, (*b*) teachers' marks, and (*c*) intelligence quotients. The results of these comparisons obtained through the administration of two experimental forms of the test series showed definite trends in the correlation of each of the types of comprehension skills included in the test with each of the three criteria chosen as a check on the validity of the test. These comparisons also revealed certain tendencies concerning the varying effectiveness from grade to grade with which each of the types of response included in the test measured reading comprehension. For example, it is of interest to note that Type *f* correlated highest on the whole with all three of the criteria while the correlation of Type *g* with each of the criteria increased with the increase in grade level. Apparently these results were used to justify the inclusion of four questions of Type *f* on each test paragraph as compared with one question requiring each of the other types of response. The trend just mentioned in regard to Type *g* as well as the fact that it was the only type to correlate more highly with IQ than with teachers' marks in reading resulted in the exclusion of questions of this type from Test I for grades 3-6.

The validity of the completed form of the test is indicated by mean *r*'s of .69, .62, and .63 between total test scores and average academic marks for Tests I, II, and III respectively, and by mean *r*'s of .66, .69, and .66 between total test scores and average IQ for the same tests. Multiple *R*'s from total scores, academic achievement marks, and IQ's averaged above .75. The number of cases in each grade averaged about 65.

The coefficient of reliability for each test obtained by the intercorrelation of the three forms of each test on more than 100 cases at each grade level is .90. The equivalence of the three forms of each test is indicated by the average score obtained from the administration of these three forms to an unmentioned number of pupils over the whole grade range of each test. No data are given regarding their equivalence from grade to grade. Age and grade norms based upon the administration of the three tests to approximately 5,000 pupils in grades 3-12 are given. These pupils represent both urban and rural districts in three states. The grade norms given are for the end of the semester in each case. The number of pupils in each grade or at each age upon which the norms are based is not given.

Criticisms of such well-constructed and altogether usable instruments as these tests must necessarily be minor ones. It does not appear to this reviewer that the evidence presented warrants four true-false questions about each paragraph as contrasted with one question of each of the other types. Incidentally, this would serve to make the correlation between Type *f* and the whole test spuriously high. The method of scoring the responses to this type of question is not in line with current practice and does not appear to be defended satisfactorily. The use of negative statements when false statements are to be marked introduces the idea of the double negative which is unnecessarily confusing to children in the elementary grades. The reasons for the elimination of certain response types which are included in other instruments of recognized value in this field seem in some instances at least to be trival and inconclusive.

There is no question, however, but that this series of tests will rate highly as judged by any objective check list of desirable test qualities which may be applied to them. Their diagnostic features should appeal to classroom teachers while such features as careful selection and editing of content and gradation of vocabulary and concept level make them interesting to the pupils to whom they are administered. The thoroughness and scientific nature of the procedures followed in the development of this series of tests may well serve as an example to test authors. The steps taken in the conception, development, and standardization of these tests are explained in detail in the manual which accompanies them. The completeness and objective quality of this report should commend this series of tests to the test consumer who objects to buying on faith alone.

[1568]

Silent Reading Comprehension: Iowa Every-Pupil Tests of Basic Skills, Test A. Grades 3-5, 6-8; 1940; Form L, 2 levels; 30¢ per manual; 12¢ per booklet of norms; 40¢ per 25 record cards; single specimen set free; H. F. Spitzer in collaboration with Ernest Horn, Maude McBroom, H. A. Greene, and E. F. Lindquist with the assistance of the faculty of the University Experimental Schools, State University of Iowa; Boston, Mass.: Houghton Mifflin Co.
a) ELEMENTARY BATTERY. Grades 3-5; $1.15 per 25; 44(50) minutes.
b) ADVANCED BATTERY. Grades 6-8; $1.25 per 25; 67(85) minutes.

[1569]

Southeastern Problems and Prospects, Social Studies and English [Reading Test]: Booklet No. 1. Grades 10-16; 1938; 8¢ per test; 2¢ per machine-scorable answer sheet; 12¢ per sample test; 180(190) minutes; English Commission of the Association of Georgia Colleges; Athens, Ga.: the Association, c/o F. S. Beers, Memorial Hall.

[1570]

Standardized Oral Reading Check Tests. Grades 1-2, 2-4, 4-7, 6-8; 1923; 5 forms, 4 levels; $1.50 per 20 tests, including all 5 forms; 50¢ per specimen set; 15¢ per specimen set of any one set; nontimed (1-3) minutes; William S. Gray; Bloomington, Ill.: Public School Publishing Co.
a) SET I. Grades 1-2.
b) SET II. Grades 2-4.
c) SET III. Grades 4-7.
d) SET IV. Grades 6-8.

REFERENCES

1 CAMP, CORDELIA, AND ALLEN, C. H. "How Oral Reading Was Improved through the Use of Gray's Check Tests." *El Sch J* 30:132-5 O '29.

David H. Russell, Assistant Professor of Education, The University of Saskatchewan. These tests consist of four sets, each containing five tests of approximately equal difficulty. Each test consists of a paragraph or paragraphs to be read orally in the presence of an examiner who records errors and the time required. One commendable feature of the tests, then, is the fact that the four sets allow testing at a reading level closer to the child's actual reading ability than is usually obtained in a reading test which is part of an achievement battery. Another advantage of the test is the availability of five forms of approximately equal difficulty, thus allowing for frequent retesting. These values are somewhat impaired for the test reviewer (if not the test user) by the fact that little information is given on how the material for the tests was selected or how the tests in any one set were equated. In the ten-line description of the construction of the tests it is stated that the tests "have been revised three times after each test of a set was given to no less than 120 pupils each time." There is no further statement on the sheet of directions regarding efforts to determine the validity or reliability of these tests at the four levels. The description states rather conservatively, then, that "the standard scores for rate and accuracy which follow are more or less tentative."

The uses to which a reading test may be put are probably at least as important as its material or grading. The *Standardized Oral Reading Check Tests* aim, first, to be a measure of oral reading. They probably accomplish this as well as other available oral reading tests but, like other tests, they make no attempt to measure such factors as rhythm, phrasing, interpretation, bodily position, etc., which, after all, are significant to the effectiveness of oral reading in the audience situation. Another weakness of the test is that there is no check on the comprehension of what is read. The accuracy records might include more than the actual errors made.

The second use that is suggested for these tests is to determine the specific nature of a pupil's difficulties. The diagnostic value of these, and certain other oral reading tests, would seem to be much greater than that of most silent reading tests. The Individual Record Sheet that accompanies the tests gives rather complete instructions for recording mis-

pronunciations, omissions, substitutions, repetitions, and insertions of words or parts of words. Space is provided for tabulating these errors on this sheet. Such a procedure should be valuable to the diagnostician. This value could be greatly enhanced, however, by additional information as to the seriousness of the number of these errors in relation to the number of errors usually made by children at a particular reading level. For example, the poor reader may make many more omissions and mispronunciations than insertions or repetitions on these tests, but this may not be atypical at his level, and so no hints as to causes of retardation can be obtained. The *Gates Oral-Context Test VI, 2* in the *Gates Reading Diagnosis Tests,* for example, allows for such comparisons and also analyzes types of mispronunciation more fully. The practised diagnostician, however, should find the analysis of errors on the Individual Record Sheet of considerable value.

The prospective purchaser of these tests should not confuse them with Gray's *Standardized Oral Reading Paragraphs* published by the same company.

Clarence R. Stone, 2140 Los Angeles Avenue, Berkeley, California. There are four sets or levels of these tests ranging from first-grade to seventh- or eighth-grade material. Each set or level has five forms of the test constructed to be of equal difficulty, thereby making possible repeated tests at intervals to measure progress. A very satisfactory plan of recording the child's errors on a copy of the test is provided. The reviewer has found these tests very valuable for measuring progress and for stimulating interest on the part of the individual in improving his oral reading. The progress can be easily graphed in terms of decreasing errors.

These tests were constructed before we had any graded vocabulary lists. Consequently, the series could now be improved by the use of graded vocabulary lists available and by providing one set or level for each school grade.

[1571]

Standardized Oral Reading Paragraphs. Grades 1-8; 1915; individual; 1 form; $1.00 per 100; 6¢ per specimen set; nontimed (5-15) minutes; William S. Gray; Bloomington, Ill.: Public School Publishing Co.

REFERENCES

1 GRAY, WILLIAM S. *A Tentative Scale for the Measurement of Oral-Reading Achievement.* Unpublished master's thesis, Columbia University, 1914.

2 GRAY, WILLIAM SCOTT. *Studies of Elementary-School Reading through Standardized Tests.* University of Chicago, Supplementary Educational Monographs, Vol. 1, No. 1. Chicago, Ill.: University of Chicago Press, 1917. Pp. viii, 157. Paper. Out of print.

3 MONROE, WALTER S. "A Simplified Method of Determining a Pupil's Score on Gray's Oral Reading Test." *Sch and Soc* 15:538 40 My 12 '22.

4 PAYNE, C. S. *The Derivation of Tentative Norms for Short Exposures in Reading.* Harvard Monographs in Education, No. 10. Cambridge, Mass.: Harvard University Press, 1930. Pp. 84. $1.00. Paper. (London: Oxford University Press. 4s. 6d.)

5 GATES, ARTHUR I. *The Improvement of Reading*: Revised edition, p. 533. New York: Macmillan Co., 1935. Pp. xvii, 668. $2.50. (London: Macmillan & Co., Ltd. 8s. 6d.)

6 BUCKINGHAM, B. R., AND DOLCH, E. W. *A Combined Word List.* Boston, Mass.: Ginn and Co., 1936. Pp. iii, 185. $1.50.

7 STONE, CLARENCE R. *Graded Vocabulary for Primary Reading.* St. Louis, Mo.: Webster Publishing Co., 1936. Pp. 61. $0.50. Paper.

David Kopel, Department of Education, Chicago Teachers College. This widely used individual test consists of twelve brief paragraphs arranged in order of difficulty of content. The first paragraph is primer material; each succeeding paragraph appears to represent an increment in difficulty of approximately one grade. The scoring of each paragraph is based upon the speed of reading and number of errors. The composite score is interpreted by reference to a table of norms or standards which are available for grades 1-8.

Several desirable qualities are to be found in the test. Its administration requires but a few minutes; directions are rather simple and easily learned; scoring is fairly objective (examiners will differ occasionally as to what represents an "error" and as to the meaning of "several seconds"—the amount of time one should wait before helping the child with a word he cannot pronounce). Use of the instrument yields a grade score which crudely classifies a child as to grade level of reading ability. An important by-product is the opportunity to observe many characteristics of the child's reading: type and frequency of errors, fluency and meaningfulness of reading, use of punctuation devices, skill in recognizing and analyzing words in context, emotional reactions to oral reading of increasingly difficult materials and to possible frustrating experiences that may be involved. Observations made during the test may have considerable diagnostic value as well as definite implications for therapy.

The following limitations in the test should be noted. Comparable forms of the test are not available; hence one must estimate practice effect when it is used more than once. Standardization data are not given in the manual provided by the publisher. However, Gates[5] states that grade scores on the test are usually equivalent to mental grades and reading grades established on other tests. Comprehension of the material read must be checked informally. The validity of the test can and should be determined for the individual with whom it is being employed by having him read aloud *episodes* from various types of graded material chosen in accord with the test finding. An experienced teacher or clinician can readily and meaningfully determine in this manner the real status of the child's ability.

Clarence R. Stone, 2140 Los Angeles Avenue, Berkeley, California. This is a power test with one form consisting of twelve short units of reading matter increasing in difficulty from the primer level to the college level. The score on each unit depends upon the rate of reading and the number of errors made. An excellent plan of recording errors on a copy of the reading material is set forth in the directions. With this test it is possible to determine the level of material the child can read with reasonable accuracy and fluency. Since the test was constructed before we had available any standardized word lists, the material no doubt could be improved by a revision in which the vocabulary would be checked, level by level, against *Graded Vocabulary for Primary Reading*[7] and *A Combined Word List.*[6] The test would also be improved by a more gradual increase in the difficulty of the material.

[1572]

Stevens Reading Readiness Test. Grade 1; 1938; part individual; 1 form; $1 per 25; 10¢ per manual; 15¢ per specimen set; 10 daily sittings over a 2-week period; Avis Coultas Stevens; Columbus, Ohio: American Education Press, Inc.

[1573]

Student Skills Inventory. Experimental Edition. College; 1939; $1 per 25; 15¢ per specimen set; nontimed; Norman M. Locke; New York: Psychological Corporation.

REFERENCES

LOCKE, NORMAN M. "The Students Skills Inventory: A Study Habits Inventory." *J Appl Psychol* 24:493-504 Ag '40.

[1574]

Study-Habits Inventory. Grades 12-16; 1933-34; 1 form; $1.25 per 25; 25¢ per 25 sheets "What Your Score Means"; 10¢ per specimen set; nontimed (10-20) minutes; C. Gilbert Wrenn, assisted by R. B. McKeown; Stanford University, Calif.: Stanford University Press.

Edward S. Jones, Professor of Psychology and Director of Personnel Research, The University of Buffalo. This inventory is made up of a set of thirty items carefully selected from a much larger list of statements and attitudes previously submitted to 220 students at Stanford University. Half of them were in the upper 10 per cent of scholarship and the other half in the lower 20 per cent, the students being paired with each other on the basis of intelligence test scores, so that the difference would not be one of intelligence but a scholastic difference entirely. The 30 items are obviously related to attitudes or situations conducive to study. In fact, nearly half of them beg the question, such as: "I find myself too tired, sleepy, and listless to study efficiently," "I am conscious that I have been out of school too long, or took basic subjects too long ago," and "I read so slowly that I cannot get over all the assignments and outside readings." Naturally, some of the assignments have much greater weight than others. The item of greatest weight is, "My time is unwisely distributed; I spend too much time on some things and not enough on others." Obviously, the use of the adverb "too" presupposes that students knowing that they are good will be inclined to answer corresponding to their particular accomplishments. It is not amazing, therefore, that Wrenn comes out with scores in his tests such that the lowest quartile of the high-scholarship group is definitely above the highest quartile of the low-scholarship group.

It would seem to the reviewer much more satisfactory if a study-habits inventory could be worked up to include greater objectivity, one which could be applied to students before they know what kind of success they are going to achieve in college. Most of the attempts of this type, however, have not proved very diagnostic in differentiating between students because there are so many different standards of mental effort, and because intellectual background and motivation are more important than particular methods of work.

William A. McCall, Professor of Education, Columbia University. This inventory lists thirty habits of study, some good, some bad, and the student indicates whether each habit characterizes him rarely, sometimes, or often. Positive or negative scores of varying amounts are provided for each answer for each item.

The author evidently adopted the inventory instead of the test technique partly because some habits do not readily lend themselves to testing on paper. The inclusion of such habits is easily justified. Such, for example, is Item

27: "I study carefully the outlines in all courses where they are given."

Also the inventory method permits the author to cover much territory rapidly and inexpensively. Consider, for example, Item 5: "I read so slowly that I cannot get over all the assignments and outside readings." It would require much time to test this point, but there will be persons who believe that the more time-consuming procedure is preferable.

The entire inventory must depend upon the student for a truthful report, and, assuming his honesty, must further depend upon his being aware of what the truth is. In Item 8, the student is required to state whether his grades are lowered by faulty command of fundamental subjects. The student may not honestly know. The author commendably suggests uses for the inventory that encourage frank cooperation, thereby weakening somewhat the force of the former of these criticisms.

The items used are the thirty out of sixty-nine which discriminated best between high- and low-scholarship students whose intelligence test scores were approximately equal. Such correlation, even with intelligence partialed out, does not imply causation, yet the author makes several statements in his manual which fail to recognize this fact. If statements are properly guarded, the author is entitled to some leeway in this matter, pending an experimental proof of causal connection between these thirty habits and scholarship.

This reviewer is troubled about those discarded thirty-nine items. The technique of selection condemns these as being relatively unimportant. But are they? The possession of a brain may not distinguish a Nordic from a Mediterranean type but who would suggest therefore, that a brain is not important to a Nordic, and similarly for study-habit items. What better could the author have done? Without more reflection, and possibly with, the reviewer does not know.

Most serious of all, though we can scarcely blame the author for it, Item 23 and the atmosphere of many other items assume the indefensible *status quo* in college education. This is Item 23: "I study with others rather than by myself." When the long overdue revolution occurs in college education such an item, when answered with *often,* will not be heavily penalized. On the contrary, the student who answers *often* will be commended, and rewarded with a positive score, for in such education statistical considerations will be required to serve philosophical considerations.

[1575]

Study Outline Test. Grades 9-16; 1926; 1 form, 3 levels; 75¢ per package containing 25, 15, and 10 copies respectively of Tests I, II, and III; 10¢ per specimen set; nontimed; F. Dean McClusky and Edward William Dolch; Bloomington, Ill.: Public School Publishing Co.
a) TEST I.
b) TEST II. For examinees failing Test I.
c) TEST III. For examinees failing Test II.

REFERENCES

1 McCLUSKY, F. DEAN, AND DOLCH, EDWARD WILLIAM. "A Study Outline Test." *Sch R* 32:757-72 D '24.

Harriet Barthelmess Morrison, Research Assistant, Bureau of Reference, Research and Statistics, Public Schools, New York, New York. The test content consists of a three-paragraph selection. The testee is to designate for each sentence the appropriate number or letter to indicate its position in the outline presumably used by the author. A sample outline indicating the coordinate and subordinate letters and figures to be used is to be put on the blackboard.

The same content is used in all three tests, but with differing degrees of help on the part of the author in the way of "signs" of structure. Test I, the most difficult, is given first. Those pupils not getting a perfect score are given drill on outlining, and then are tested on Test II. Those unable to get a perfect score on this have more drill and then are given Test III, the easiest test. Diagnostic scores for coordination, subordination, and elaboration "give the clue as to the type of drill needed."

Neither the direction sheet nor the publisher's catalog gives any indication of validity or reliability. Nor do we know to what degree the results are conditioned by general reading ability.

The way in which the text is to be outlined is artificial and the pupil results may or may not be indicative of outlining ability in a more functional situation. Nor does the length of the test seem to offer high reliability. However, the development of the same content in three degrees of structural difficulty is ingenious and useful as a teaching aid.

Testing material in this field is limited and the type of test developed here deserves further experimentation.

[1576]

Test of Study Skills. Grades 4-9; 1940; 2 forms; $1.50 per 30, including 30 machine-scorable answer sheets; $1.50 per 100 machine-scorable answer sheets; 10¢ per specimen set; 60(70) minutes; J. W. Edgar and H. T. Manuel; Austin, Tex.: Steck Co.

[1577]

Test on the Use of Books and Libraries: Test 7.3. Grades 7-10; 1939; 2 forms; 10¢ per test; 1¢ per machine-scorable answer sheet; $1 per set of stencils for machine scoring; nontimed (60) minutes; Chicago, Ill.: Evaluation in the Eight Year Study, Progressive Education Association.

[1578]

Traxler High School Reading Test. Grades 10-12; 1938-39; 2 forms; $1.50 per 25; 10¢ per manual; 25¢ per specimen set; adapted to machine scoring; 50(55) minutes; Arthur E. Traxler; Bloomington, Ill.: Public School Publishing Co.

REFERENCES

1 TRAXLER, ARTHUR E. "Relationship between the Length and the Reliability of a Test of Rate of Reading." *J Ed Res* 32:1-2 S '38.

Alvin C. Eurich, Professor of Education, Stanford University. Like the authors of most of the available measures of reading ability, Traxler, in constructing this test, aimed to measure reading rate, understanding, and the ability to locate the central thought in reading a paragraph. The student is asked to read four and a half uninteresting looking pages of fairly easy social science material. The number of words read in five minutes translated into words read per ten seconds, gives the rate score. The understanding of the material read is tested by twenty items, each involving a choice of one of four possible answers. Part II, on finding the main ideas in paragraphs, consists of thirty short paragraphs, each followed by four statements, one of which the student designates as giving the central idea.

The validity of each comprehension question was determined by calculating the degree to which it distinguished the good readers or those in the top fourth of the distribution of total scores, from the poor readers, or those in the lowest fourth.

By discounting the coefficient of reliability derived through the use of the Spearman-Brown formula, the author estimates the reliability of the rate score to be .90. The reliability of the story comprehension score is only .72 for a group of tenth grade pupils. The author is to be commended for recognizing in the Manual that this part of the test is "reliable enough for group studies, but is of limited value for individual prediction." Few authors are so forthright in acknowledging the weaknesses of the instruments they produce. The reliability of Part II, on finding the main ideas in paragraphs is .80 for a group of twelfth grade students. Curiously, and with no explicit reason, the author combines the rate and comprehension scores into a total score for which he did not determine either the reliability or its meaning. The reviewer, therefore, is unable to interpret this total score. It appears much the same as adding up the distance run and the time taken to run it.

Norms for Part II were based on sixteen hundred high school pupils, and for Part I on twenty-one hundred. Percentiles for part scores are given for grades 10, 11, and 12. The directions for administering and scoring the test are clearly stated, and answer sheets are available for machine scoring.

Clearly the understanding and comprehension sections of this test are not as reliable as available reading tests for high school students, such as the *Iowa Silent Reading Test* and the *Nelson-Denny Reading Test*. The rate section, mainly because it is longer than other similar tests, is slightly more reliable. On the whole, the Traxler test does not provide a better instrument for measuring reading ability than those already available; in fact, it is not as good.

Constance M. McCullough, Assistant Professor of Education, Western Reserve University. This test is an upward extension of the *Traxler Silent Reading Test* for grades 7 through 10. Part I, Reading Rate and Story Comprehension, consists of rather easy story material of social studies content. The pupil is asked to read for understanding in order to answer questions at the end of his reading, and to mark his position when the examiner says, *mark* (after 150 and after 300 seconds). This part yields a score on the rate the pupil has chosen to read the passage with understanding. The twenty multiple-choice statements to which the pupil must respond without a second reading of the passage appear to refer to twelve of the twenty paragraphs and cover the "more important points" of the selection. A few concern main ideas; a few, simple inference; and the majority, important details. The score derived from these questions is labeled Story Comprehension. The time limit is generous and flexible so that all may finish responding to the statements.

Part II, Main Ideas in Paragraphs, comprises thirty paragraphs, each followed by four multiple-choice statements, one of which is to be selected as representative of the main idea. Groups of five paragraphs on history alternate with groups of five dealing with natural science. Various kinds of paragraph construction are represented, but none in which the main idea must be inferred. Of the multiple-choice statements, one is a main idea, three are details. The pupil is free to reread the paragraph if necessary. The time limit is generous.

The manual of directions is admirably frank, thorough, and practical. The validity of the test items was established on the performance of the 25 highest and 25 lowest scorers among 400 pupils in grades 10 and 11.

Tentative reliability indices based upon limited data are presented. From data secured by correlating the rates of reading during the first and second 2½-minutes of reading, the author estimates the reliability coefficient to be approximately .90 for pupils in grade 10. For the same group of pupils the reliability of the Story Comprehension score is .72. For the subtest, Main Ideas in Paragraphs, a reliability coefficient of .80 is reported for a group of twelfth grade pupils.

The tentative norms are based upon the scores of sixteen hundred public school pupils in the case of Part I and twenty-one hundred pupils in the case of Part II. Percentile norms for the subtest, Story Comprehension and Main Ideas, are given separately for each grade. The differences in rate among the three grades are so slight that percentile norms for Rate of Reading are given for the three grades combined.

The test may be scored by machine. However, a hand-scoring key is provided. The class record sheet is designed to show individual and class achievement on the parts of the test. Space is given in a column after the individual's name for recording the IQ. It would seem desirable in view of the part reading ability plays in tests of verbal intelligence to have two columns here, one for verbal intelligence scores and one for nonverbal.

Test users should hold certain facts in mind in considering this test. The rate score is more reliable than the rate scores of most speed of reading tests. The Story Comprehension section is practically the only standardized reading examination which tests pure rate of continuous reading for meaning. The reliabilities of the Story Comprehension and Main Ideas sections suggest that test users should not attempt interpretation of individual scores on these parts. However, if an individual conference can be held shortly after the administration of the examination, the pupil's reasons for various responses will give greater meaning to his score and fuller understanding of his particular difficulties.

Because the vocabulary of the test is not particularly difficult, the comprehension scores are chiefly measures of the pupil's ability to understand thought patterns in the social studies and natural science fields. Students of ancient history, however, may be familiar with the content of Part I and may profit by that familiarity in answering the comprehension items. The varied content of Part II would probably not give advantage to any particular pupil. As the entire test is concerned exclusively with materials in the social and natural science fields, it should be used to determine a student's reading abilities only in these types of subject matter.

Part I may be said to test a pupil's ability to identify from memory statements of the significant points of a story of social studies content, which he has just read at a rate freely chosen for the purpose of reading with understanding. Since no questions are given the pupil before the reading of the story, he must set his own standard of careful reading. Thus the score in Part I indicates his standard of careful reading modified by his ability to maintain it. It tests his reading judgment, which is of tremendous importance to efficient scholarship.

Part II is a test of the pupil's ability to recognize the main idea from among several details in a paragraph of social and natural science material. It could be wished that some multiple-choice statements in this section had included faulty statements of the main idea, such as overstatement, understatement, and the misinterpretation of the main idea, so that the test would involve more than the distinction between details and main ideas.

However, while Traxler has limited the scope of his test to a few rather specific reading abilities functioning in two special types of material, he has provided a diagnostic measure more thorough and explicit than most of the tests in this field can claim to be. His contribu-

tion is a reminder that reading abilities are many and varying, and that a 40-minute test which attempts to touch upon more than two or three abilities through a given type of material forfeits reliability in its parts and its utility in the schools. The test users need to recognize this fact and to select tests according to their appropriateness to specific situations. If they wish to survey a broad range of reading abilities with varied materials, they must be ready to devote more than an hour's time to testing.

C. Gilbert Wrenn, Professor of Educational Psychology, The University of Minnesota. The mechanical form of this test deserves first and favorable consideration. The inverted-page technique of questions on material read for rate is used but the reviewer found the familiar lack of relationship between comprehension and rate in computing rate of reading. Rate is determined *only* by the student's marking how far he has gone at the end of two and one-half and five minutes, but if he has skimmed or read absent-mindedly he still gets credit for what his eyes have covered mechanically since the questions on the material are figured in the "comprehension score" only. In other words, a "rate" score on a reading test would be much more significant if the comprehension has been perfect (in terms of the questions asked on the material) than if comprehension has been poor. Complete separation of "rate" and "comprehension" scores is artificial. The reviewer has had experience in trying to construct a test that would make a rate score more functionally meaningful in a test that was eventually built for use at Stanford University, and he knows full well the difficulty of the assignment. This is a task in test construction that still challenges and that the Traxler test has not solved. The rate section of this test is too short (62 lines) although the time limits are generous and the materials were taken from a selection that would not normally have been previously read by high school students. These are important factors.

Nine of the twenty questions on the rate section are so specific as to require the recall of one of a series of proper names, specific nouns, or figures. This is an unfortunately large proportion. The paragraph comprehension section follows the familiar form of multiple-choice questions on the main idea contained in short paragraphs. There are thirty of these paragraphs which is a much more satisfactory sample than the paragraph comprehension section of many other tests.

Simple reading rate, and comprehension of sixty-two lines of continuously read material and of thirty discrete paragraphs make up the test. We can be sure that these comprise the important elements of a reading test *only if* data are given as to the validity of the parts or totality of the test. This is lacking for the test under discussion. In fact validity data of any sort are lacking except for the selection of items in terms of internal consistency. Relationship of the test to intelligence test scores, scholarship groups or other external criteria leave one in doubt as to just what the test measures. Very tentative reliability coefficients are given but the number of cases involved is not stated. Reliability coefficients of .72 and .80 are quoted for the two comprehension sections. (The method of computing reliability is not given.) Percentile norms on sixteen hundred high school students are given but the number of cases for the norms of each of the three grades, 10, 11, and 12, is not stated. The medians and standard deviations for the three grades are provided and these show consistent rise in medians and fall in sigmas from grades 10 to 12, which may be considered an aspect of validity.

This test will be useful in senior high schools, particularly to those educators who have found the Traxler test for grades 7 to 10 helpful. Its value over other published tests will be more apparent when further standardization data are made available. It is a carefully made test of conventional form which adds but little to our knowledge of reading-test techniques.

Ed Res B 18:117-8 Ap '39. J. Wayne Wrightstone. * In measuring comprehension of the main ideas in paragraphs, the author has provided a sample of paragraphs based upon content found in typical social-science and natural-science textbooks. The method for presenting alternative responses is novel. * The author is to be commended because he has stated as precisely as he can the aspects of the reading process which various parts of his test measure. The test may be recommended for the measurement of the selected aspects of silent reading of high-school students that it purports to measure. It does not purport to measure

all phases of silent reading. The test is carefully constructed and easily administered, but the format of the story-comprehension part might be improved. *

Teach Col J 10:147 Jl '39. E. L. Abell. * The material and arrangement of this test seem to be very good, and the validity of each item in the comprehension test has been established by Ruch's commonly used method. Reliabilities of .92, .72, and .80 for the three tests would indicate, for this type of test very satisfactory consistency. * The test would seem to be a desirable addition to the list of high school reading tests.

[1579]

Traxler Silent Reading Test. Grades 7-10; 1934-39; 2 forms; $1.50 per 25; 15¢ per manual; 30¢ per specimen set; adapted to machine scoring; (50-55) minutes; Arthur E. Traxler; Bloomington, Ill.: Public School Publishing Company.

REFERENCES

1 RUCH, G. M., AND STODDARD, GEORGE D. *Tests and Measurements in High School Instruction,* p. 120. Yonkers, N. Y.: World Book Co., 1927. Pp. xxi, 381. $2.20.
2 TRAXLER, ARTHUR E. *The Measurement and Improvement of Silent Reading at the Junior High School Level.* Chicago, Ill.: University of Chicago Libraries, 1932. Pp. 218. Paper, lithotyped. Out of print.
3 TRAXLER, ARTHUR E. "One Reading Test Serves the Purpose." *Clearing House* 14:419-21 Mr '40.

Robert L. McCaul, Instructor of Remedial Reading in the Laboratory Schools and College of the University of Chicago. In *The 1938 Mental Measurements Yearbook* this test was thoroughly evaluated (*see* 1114). Last year's reviewers criticized: (*a*) The disproportionately heavy weighting of the rate score in determining total score; (*b*) The way in which the rate selection could be read superficially, no penalty being exacted; (*c*) The large standard errors of the part tests; (*d*) The coefficient of .80 obtained by correlating the comprehension parts of the test with their criterion of validity: a combination of scores from the *Monroe Standardized Silent Reading Test,* the *Thorndike-McCall Reading Scale,* and the paragraph-meaning part of the *New Stanford Achievement Test;* (*e*) The narrow range of the tentative norms contained in the teacher's handbook; (*f*) The limited value of the test for individual diagnosis, when used alone; and (*g*) The inconsistent sampling of the comprehension items.

His experience in administering and interpreting the Traxler test causes the present reviewer to agree with the criticism of the test's limitations for individual diagnosis and of the inadequacy of its norms. To these criticisms he would add that the vocabulary part test includes too large a percentage of words peculiar mainly to English literature and that this probably accounts for its high correlation with its validity criterion, the *Inglis Test of English Vocabulary,* which possesses almost solely literary words and indeed many poetic and some archaic terms. A better measure of whether a pupil has a vocabulary rich enough to enable him to read his school texts efficiently could be derived from a vocabulary test composed of more equal proportions of words from social studies, science, mathematics, and the other subject fields of the curriculum. Perhaps the Educational Records Bureau or some of Traxler's articles offer data bearing upon the matters criticized, but such data are not in the teacher's handbook and consequently are not available for the ordinary test purchaser.

Having set forth criticisms of the test, the reviewer must bring to the attention of schoolmen the following points in its favor. First, directions for administering the rate test emphasize comprehension and the necessity of answering questions about the rate story; these questions are placed where the pupils will see them before reading. Unless the pupils have become "test wise," it is most unlikely therefore that they will read the story superficially for the purpose of gaining a higher test score than their true reading speed merits. This is not intended to be a defense of the vulnerability of the rate test nor an argument against eliminating the excessive weight allotted to it in the calculation of total test scores. Second, the speed story is long and will appeal to pupils. Upon the essentials of the story, not details, the questions are focussed, and thus the pupils are not asked to read rapidly, then confronted with questions demanding information which can be secured only by slow, careful reading. Hence a contradiction inherent in many speed of reading tests is obviated. Third, the stimulus words of the vocabulary items are presented in sentence or phrase context and they are clearly synonymous with their proper response words. Fourth, because the time limit of the power of comprehension test is long, the speed factor is reduced to a degree that makes the test more nearly one of comprehension rather than of speed. All this is a relative matter, of course, for it is impossible to get an index of pure compre-

hension or of pure speed. The power of comprehension paragraphs, moreover, are representative of the materials which the pupil must read and study. Fifth, a "validity" coefficient of .80 between the comprehension parts of the Traxler test and the criterion tests by no means proves the former to be invalid. One of the criterion tests, the Monroe, is no model of perfection: of it Ruch and Stoddard remark that the test "cannot serve to cover even one phase of it [reading] adequately." [1] Likewise a coefficient of .80 does not compare so unfavorably with published correlations between other reading tests that the Traxler test deserves a peremptory condemnation. Sixth, the Traxler test has been employed successfully by the reviewer as a screen test to single out poor readers. It is not a dependable instrument for individual diagnosis when used alone; the reviewer is acquainted with no reading test which is. In the field of education what are called "diagnostic tests" are as common as the ubiquitous white rat of experimental psychology and have an equally high birth rate. Individual diagnosis, nevertheless, still remains a procedure based upon the results of specialized tests of oral reading, vocabulary, etc., and to an even greater extent upon personal observation of the reading method of the retarded child.

Miles A. Tinker, Associate Professor of Psychology, The University of Minnesota. There are many evidences that careful planning entered into the construction of this test. Three aspects of reading performance are measured: (*a*) rate of reading with a check on the story comprehension, (*b*) word meaning in which the word to be defined is presented within a sentence or phrase, and (*c*) power of comprehension for paragraphs varying in difficulty. The two published forms of the test are carefully equated to give practical equivalence. Directions for administration are clear and complete.

The test was standardized on several hundred pupils at each grade level. Unfortunately no measure of deviation is presented with the mean scores so that standard scores cannot be derived for those who might wish to use them. "Tentative" grade norms are given by months for the total score. Norms should be more than tentative. No reading test is entirely adequate unless the cited norms have been soundly established.

The validity of test scores appears adequate. For the rate test, with a composite score from several speed of reading measures as a criterion, the validity coefficient is .81. Similarly for word meaning, it ranges from .76 to .87 with one satisfactory criterion and .78 with another. Comprehension validity (story comprehension plus power of comprehension) with a composite criterion score was found to be .80. Total score validity with a composite score criterion is .88. When compared with school marks the total score has a validity of .56. Analysis of individual items revealed positive validity for all.

Correlation of scores on the two forms of the test yielded reliability coefficients ranging from .61 for story comprehension to .86 for word meaning. For total score, the coefficients ranged from .91 to .95.

In describing the nature of the test the author's statement "that the correlation between the rates of reading any two types of material is high" is misleading. There are ample data which show that such correlations are low.

In general this test may be designated as adequate. It is readily applicable to analysis of reading status and is suitable for research.

Ed Res B 19:59 Ja 17 '40. J. Wayne Wrightstone. * This test . . . has been criticized . . . because the special aspects of comprehension which it measures are not clearly defined or systematically examined by the test items. In this particular respect, however, the test is no better and no worse than many other silent-reading tests. The format of the story-comprehension part of the test could be improved. Despite these and other minor criticisms the test may be recommended as one of the better reading tests for junior-high-school pupils if a survey of the silent-reading skills is desired. The test is not recommended for diagnostic purposes.

For reviews by Frederick B. Davis and Spencer Shank, see 1114.

[1580]

Tyler-Kimber Study Skills Test. Grades 9-16; 1937; 1 form; $2.00 per 25; 15¢ per specimen set; nontimed (60-90) minutes; Stanford University, Calif.: Stanford University Press.

REFERENCES

1 UPSHALL, C. C. "The Study Skills of College Seniors." *Ed Adm and Sup* 26:139-44 F '40.

William A. McCall, Professor of Education, Columbia University. This test is arranged in the following eight parts: (*a*) finding what you want in a book; (*b*) using an index; (*c*) using general reference books; (*d*) recognizing common abbreviations; (*e*) using the library card catalog; (*f*) interpreting maps; (*g*) knowing current periodical literature; and (*h*) interpreting graphs.

Let me sum up its many merits in a sentence and detail what I deem to be its defects, not because I take a natural delight in dwelling on faults but because this is the way of progress.

MERITS. This is the best test of its kind for use in the secondary school and college—an important contribution to our list of useful tests.

DEFECTS. Some of the directions on the test proper appear to me to be unnecessarily difficult. This assumes the presence of the most important study skill, namely, reading ability.

In the case of certain tests, the students are asked not to guess at the answer. In other tests no directions as to guessing are given even though guessing could appreciably increase the score, albeit less so than where the caution is given. This tends to make the test measure degree of daring or willingness to gamble or lack of conscientiousness or something else alien to study skills.

In Test IV—a matching test for abbreviations—there is a startling neglect to disguise items to be matched. Thus the items determine whether a student *recognizes* that *pl.* is an abbreviation for *plural, par.* for *paragraph, obs.* for *obsolete, syn.* for *synonym, ant.* for *antonym, vol.* for *volume,* and *ch.* for *chapter.* Nothing more arduous mentally than simple perception such as that tested in the first grade is required to match these.

Not study skills but *study results* are tested too often. Items 101 to 110 illustrate this defect. For example, consider this item: "On the [outline] map of Europe which number corresponds to London? (1) 1 (2) 2 (3) 3 (4) 4 (5) 5." The difficulty in this item is to know the exact location of London—a knowledge which is the *result* of a study skill. Or consider again this item based on a dot map: "The second state in cattle production was (1) Texas (2) Kansas (3) Nebraska (4) Missouri (5) Iowa." Since the states are not labeled, probably the chief difficulty of this item is to remember which state is Kansas or Nebraska, etc.—a study result. Of course, even study skills are study results, and mere knowledge itself facilitates study, but the authors are obviously not trying to assay the amount of skill by the volume of knowledge produced by it.

As is to be expected of those who lovingly linger in California on their way to Heaven, the authors have given California's fruit industry a boost by basing all but one of their graphs upon it. Far be it from me to decry such loyalty, having been a fortunate guest in that far, fair land, but I do object to the upper half of the Thompson-Muscat-Sultana chart. It is misleading and mislabeled—an excellent example of improper charting technique. Such flaws probably subtract from the validity of the test.

Total scores are transmuted into percentiles, and subtest scores into quartiles. The authors state that they provide quartile scores for subtests because subtest scores are less reliable than total test scores. They seem to have adopted the fallacy, quite common in education, that coarsening the scale makes the scores more reliable. On the contrary it makes the transmuted scores less reliable. It would have been preferable to have kept the finer scale, and stated the probable error of the score (and not the prophecy formula reliability coefficient which is relatively unintelligible to the general consumer).

The authors have shown commendable zeal in determining the reliability of their test, and attempting to establish its validity. The time spent in applying a dubious check on validity should have gone toward freeing test items from faults which inherently impair validity. By and large, we test constructors have erred in giving relatively more attention to statistical considerations than to incisive criticism of the test itself.

Rachel Salisbury, Director of the Junior High School Department, State Teachers College, Platteville, Wisconsin. The *Tyler-Kimber Study Skills Test* is an 8-page booklet (8½ by 11 inches) providing scorable, objective answers to 175 items arranged in eight parts as follows: (*a*) finding what you want in a book (matching, from 10 printed response items); (*b*) using an index (same); (*c*) using general reference books (30 items with a response list of 10 reference books); (*d*) recognizing common abbreviations (2 groups of 10 items each);

(*e*) using the library card catalog (20 true-false questions); (*f*) interpreting maps (20 questions on 4 maps—Mercator, Mollweide, outline, and distribution types); (*g*) knowing current periodical literature (3 groups of 10 questions each); and (*h*) interpreting graphs (35 questions on 5 graphs).

The test is a power test which can ordinarily be taken in 60 to 90 minutes. A convenient cardboard scoring-key accompanies the test. A reliability coefficient of .90 was derived from a random sampling of 105 tests, scored from odd- and even-numbered items separately. Two validity procedures were used. Test scores on the *American Council on Education Psychological Examination for College Freshmen* and on the *Tyler-Kimber Study Skills Test* were correlated with each other and with the grade-point ratio of 343 unselected junior-college seniors, the coefficients ranging from .51 to .65. The study skills test appears to give as good an indication of academic success as either of the other two measures.

Then scores for 100 students with high grade-point ratios were compared with those for 225 students with low ratios. The difference in means between the two groups was found to be greatly in excess of that needed to prove a significant difference.

Both reliability and validity coefficients would be more convincing if a larger number of cases had been used; but the impracticability of isolating many of the factors involved in school success hampers any statistical procedure in this field, so that these values are probably as workable as any that could be obtained.

The diagnostic value of the test is limited. For each of the eight parts the raw scores may be translated only into quarters of a junior-college group. But these are not given by grades and they serve only to show outstanding gaps in training. Percentile norms, based on 2,163 cases, are presented for each of the first four semesters of the junior-college years only. Within this range the test should be definitely useful for placement. The number of cases and the range of norms are being extended by reports submitted by the present users of the test.

To this reviewer it appears unfortunate that the test is so heavily loaded with how-to-use-the-library items. Six of the eight skills measured seem to require more memory than study power. Another, map study, contains too many questions for which there must be factual recall before the study skill can operate (such as, "Which letter applies to the Bay of Bengal?"). The last part is most truly a measure of interpretive skill, testing the pupil's power to find facts from graphs which presumably have zero familiarity; yet one wonders why one-fifth of an eight-part test should be devoted to graphs.

On the whole, the test seems to be more nearly a test of the ability to find materials than of the power to study them. The reviewer misses test items involving the more abstract processes of study: such as (*a*) following directions in mathematical and scientific problems; (*b*) outlining, as evidence of the ability to detect relations among ideas presented in reading; (*c*) drawing inferences or conclusions from data presented; (*d*) combining data from several sources into effective speaking or writing experience; and (*e*) measuring directly or indirectly the student's coefficient of concentration. Lack of attention to some, if not all, of these more psychological aspects of study leaves the teacher with only a partial picture of student ability to study, in which case the name of the test is misleading. The present test, however, seems clearly to be an effective instrument for measuring the eight abilities presented in its pages.

For reviews by Edward S. Jones and C. Gilbert Wrenn, see 1166.

[1581]

Unit Scales of Attainment in Reading. Grades 1B, 1A, 2B, 2A, 3, 3-4, 5-6, 7-8, 9-12; 1932-34; 3 forms, 9 levels; identical to the reading tests in the battery *Unit Scales of Attainment*; 75¢ per 25; 20¢ per specimen set; nontimed (45) minutes; M. J. Van Wagenen; Minneapolis, Minn.: Educational Test Bureau, Inc.

Ivan A. Booker, Assistant Director of the Research Division, National Education Association, Washington, D. C. The comprehensive battery of tests which has been available for several years under the title *Unit Scales of Attainment* was restandardized in 1937. It is a general survey test of pupil achievement, which, in grades beyond the third, is concerned with eight fields: reading, arithmetic, spelling, English usage, literature, history, geography, and elementary science. The parts concerned with reading achievement, *Unit Scales of Attainment in Reading*, are available not only in the comprehensive test booklets designed for

various grade levels but also as separate reading tests. Whether used as part of the test battery or as separate tests, however, the reading scales should be recognized as instruments designed primarily for general survey purposes rather than for diagnosis.

Each of the *Unit Scales of Attainment in Reading* has a narrow grade-level range. There are nine separate booklets—or "Divisions" as they are called. The reading tests employed in grades 1, 2, and 3 measure knowledge of word meaning (or vocabulary) and reading comprehension. In grades 4 to 12 the tests are concerned wholly with reading comprehension. No time limits are set, the expectation being that every pupil will complete the test within a 45-minute period. In this way an attempt is made to measure maximum "power of comprehension," relatively uninfluenced by speed of reading.

Data with respect to the validity and reliability of the *Unit Scales of Attainment in Reading* are given in the manual which accompanies the complete achievement test battery, but virtually no information on these points can be found in the brief booklets which accompany the scales in reading.

In validating the tests, reliance was placed on expert opinion, texts, curricula, and "the discriminatory capacity"—however that ambiguous phrase may have been interpreted by the authors. The reliability of the tests—which compares favorably with that of similar ones—was determined by the usual statistical procedures. From the brief description given, it would seem that these tests have been sufficiently well standardized and carefully scaled so that they may be used with considerable assurance. Discriminating teachers, however, would undoubtedly welcome more information on standardization procedures than is now given in the Directions for Administering and Scoring. Also, many teachers would probably like to have tables of age and grade medians, and tables of quartile and percentile ranks for the various groups, in addition to the table of C-scores now provided.

The *Unit Scales of Attainment in Reading* are highly satisfactory from the standpoint of objectivity and ease of scoring. The multiple-choice technic is employed throughout, with a layout that is unusually favorable for rapid scoring. The directions for administering and scoring the tests are simple and clear, but the explanations and directions for interpreting the tests leave much to be desired with respect to both accuracy in detail and clarity of statement.

The *Unit Scales of Attainment in Reading*, in common with most tests, have some few items that could be improved. For example, some paragraphs seem to call for unwarranted inferences; such as, that a boy was "angry" rather than "sorry" because he could not reach some berries, judging from the remark, "I don't want those berries. I know they are sour." There is at least some reasonable doubt whether this comment indicates either "sorrow" or "anger," or whether it registers only a bit of mild irritation and perhaps some measure of both disappointment and disgust. A few other instances of the same type might be cited, including one case where the reader must infer that a boy is "industrious," either from a casual reference to his return from doing an errand, or from the fact that he wanted very much to attend a new school which was opened in his village. One might readily attribute both to other forms of motivation!

Careful re-editing of the tests, particularly with reference to the spacing and arrangement of the comprehension exercises, would improve their usefulness. One evidence of superficial editing is an occasional "stray" line of bold type. Again, some of the comprehension exercises are needlessly crowded, the introductory questions or phrases running into the multiple-choice answers which follow.

Many of the test paragraphs are used in two or more "Divisions" of the *Unit Scales of Attainment in Reading*. One "Division" is made more difficult than the preceding one by dropping off some of the easier paragraphs and adding a few harder ones, rather than by using wholly new material. Hence, if different "Divisions" of the same form of the test are used with the same pupils within the year, or even from year to year, some degree of "practice effect" should be expected. The amount of overlap in the reading comprehension parts in the four upper "Divisions" of Form A is as follows: (*a*) Of the 10 paragraphs in the test for grades 3-4, 5 are also in the test for grades 5-6; 4, grades 7-8; and 2, grades 9-12. (*b*) Of the 9 paragraphs in the test for grades 5-6, 5 are also in the test for grades 3-4; 6, grades 7-8; and 4, grades 9-12. (*c*) Of the 8 paragraphs in the test for grades 7-8, 4 are also in the test for grades 3-4; 6, grades 5-6; and 6, grades 9-12. (*d*) Of the 8 paragraphs in the test for grades 9-12, 2 are also in the test for grades 3-4; 4, grades 5-6; and 6, grades 7-8.

In situations where a general survey of reading comprehension is desired, the *Unit Scales of Attainment in Reading* should prove quite satisfactory. Where information is wanted on other phases of reading achievement, however, or if one is interested in the specific nature of comprehension difficulties, some other test would probably be selected.

J. Wayne Wrightstone, Assistant Director, Bureau of Reference, Research, and Statistics, Public Schools, New York, New York. The exercises comprising the reading comprehension test of the *Unit Scales of Attainment in Reading* are scaled paragraphs with scaled items following each. These paragraphs overlap somewhat in the forms for succeeding grade levels. Some of the paragraphs used in the grade 5-6 form, for example, are used in the first part of the test grade 7-8 form.

Test items are arranged according to difficulty, and the number of correct responses is transmuted into a C-score, or so-called standard unit of measurement, comparable—according to the authors—to such standard units as inches or pounds in their respective fields. The reliability, or stability, of a C-score for any pupil is variable enough to limit the values claimed for this standard unit score versus a raw, or crude, score. The C-score for an individual pupil has a doubtful value and may influence many teachers to place more confidence in the pupil's score than it deserves. Its limitations as well as its values should be described more fully in the manual, lest the unwary teacher be misled in attempting to ascertain with too much certainty a pupil's progression or regression.

The test for grade three includes a section on vocabulary, or word meaning, and a section on comprehension. From grade four through the remaining series of grade forms, a comprehension section only is provided. Reading comprehension, however, is a general term that has been invested with various meanings in different reading tests. The author of this test has provided no clear designation of the particular aspects of reading comprehension which these scales purport to measure. From an analysis of the items which constitute these tests the reviewer has inferred that the following aspects of comprehension are measured in this series: (*a*) ability to identify the general sense of the paragraph; (*b*) ability to identify details in the paragraph; (*c*) ability to determine whether a definite idea is stated; and (*d*) ability to make simple inferences from the material presented in the paragraph.

Although the reviewer's analysis indicates that some items of the test will provide an index of the ability of pupils to make inferences, most of these items require only superficial inferences and sometimes the reproduction of facts stated directly or indirectly in the reading material rather than inferences drawn from a synthesis of data provided in the paragraph.

The test user who expects this series to provide a measure of such aspects of reading comprehension as reading to understand directions, to predict the outcome of events, to summarize ideas, or to apply these ideas to the solution of a problem will be disappointed. Certainly the author of this test should have stated more precisely the aspects of reading comprehension which his test purports to measure. Moreover, the validity of this test must be inferred from the structure of the items. The author presents no evidence of the validity or validation procedures for these tests, except general statements in the manual. Test authors should provide more adequate data regarding the validation of their tests.

The norms of this test are not clearly defined as to educational conditions of the pupil personnel. The population from which the norms were derived should be more clearly described in terms of educational, social, and economic factors, if the norms are to be used intelligently by teachers and administrators.

These reading comprehension tests are valuable for survey purposes, but do not seem to be especially valuable for diagnostic purposes. Although the author apparently had a general scheme or pattern of items after each paragraph for selected aspects of reading comprehension, the pattern is too vaguely defined to be meaningful in interpreting the results of the test.

As compared with other reading comprehension tests, the *Unit Scales of Attainment in Reading* would seem, in general, to provide as valid measures of selected aspects of reading comprehension as any other test. Many, if not all, of the criticisms made against this test apply equally to most reading comprehension tests. The care that the author has exercised in selecting items and the fact that the norms are apparently revised frequently make this one of the more carefully constructed reading comprehension tests that are available.

For a review by Joseph C. Dewey, see 1115.

[1582]

Use of Library and Study Materials: A Test for High School and College Students. Grades 9-16; 1940; 2 forms; $6 per 100 tests including 100 machine-scorable answer sheets; $1.50 per 100 machine-scorable answer sheets; 10¢ per specimen set; 40(45) minutes; Mary Kirkpatrick, Lola Rivers Thompson, Helen Tomlinson in cooperation with the Texas Commission on Coordination in Education; Austin, Tex.: Steck Co.

[1583]

Work-Study Skills: Iowa Every-Pupil Tests of Basic Skills, Test B. Grades 3-5, 6-8; 1940; Form L, 2 levels; single specimen set free; 30¢ per manual; 12¢ per booklet of norms; 40¢ per 25 record cards; H. F. Spitzer in collaboration with Ernest Horn, Maude McBroom, H. A. Greene, and E. F. Lindquist with the assistance of the faculty of the University Experimental Schools, State University of Iowa; Boston, Mass.: Houghton Mifflin Co.
a) ELEMENTARY BATTERY. Grades 3-5. $1.15 per 25; 44(50) minutes.
b) ADVANCED BATTERY. Grades 6-8. $1.25 per 25; 78 (90) minutes.

[1583.1]

Ypsilanti Reading Test. Grades 6-8; 1940; 1 form; 8¢ per test, 1 to 10 copies; 5¢ per test, 25 or more copies; 35(40) minutes; B. H. Vanden Belt and Thelma McAndless; Hillsdale, Mich.: Hillsdale School Supply Co.

REPRINTED FROM *The Third Mental Measurements Yearbook*

READING—THIRD MMY

REVIEWS BY *Irving H. Anderson, Robert Murray Bear, Paul Blommers, Ivan A. Booker, Marion Monroe Cox, Frederick B. Davis, Robert A. Davis, Ethel M. Feagley, William S. Gray, W. E. Hall, Albert J. Harris, James R. Hobson, Dorothy E. Holberg, Alice N. Jameson, Ruth Lowes, James M. McCallister, Robert L. McCaul, Constance M. McCullough, Margaret G. McKim, Eason Monroe, C. Robert Pace, Holland Roberts, David H. Russell, Douglas E. Scates, Virginia Seavey, George Spache, Herbert F. Spitzer, J. B. Stroud, Edith I. M. Thomson, Robert H. Thouless, Miles A. Tinker, T. L. Torgerson, Francis Oralind Triggs, William W. Turnbull, Carolyn M. Welch, Paul A. Witty, J. Wayne Wrightstone.*

[476]

★Achievement Tests in Silent Reading: Dominion Tests. Grades 1, 2, 2-3, 4-6; 1941–46; 65¢ per 25 of any one test; specimen set must be purchased to obtain the manual for a given test; prepared by the Department of Educational Research, Ontario College of Education, University of Toronto; Vocational Guidance Centre.

a) PRIMARY: TYPE I, WORD RECOGNITION. 1941; Forms A, B; 30¢ per specimen set; 10(20) minutes.

b) PRIMARY: TYPE 2, PHRASE AND SENTENCE READING. 1941; Forms A, B; 30¢ per specimen set; 20(30) minutes.

c) PRIMARY: TYPE 3, PARAGRAPH READING. 1943–45; I form; 30¢ per specimen set; nontimed (35) minutes.

d) PRIMARY: TYPE 4, DIAGNOSTIC TEST IN WORD RECOGNITION. 1943–45; I form; 30¢ per specimen set; nontimed (35) minutes.

e) ADVANCED PRIMARY: TYPE I, VOCABULARY. Grades 2-3; 1943–46; Forms A, B; 30¢ per specimen set; 20 (30) minutes.

f) ADVANCED PRIMARY: TYPE 2, DIAGNOSTIC TEST IN PARAGRAPH MEANING. Grade 2; 1943–46; Forms A, B; 30¢ per specimen set; nontimed (40) minutes.

g) JUNIOR: TYPE I, VOCABULARY. Grades 4-6; 1943–46; Forms A, B; 30¢ per specimen set; 20(30) minutes.

Margaret G. McKim, Assistant Professor of Education, University of Cincinnati, Cincinnati, Ohio. These tests are the first in a series designed for use in Canadian schools. Norms are based on the performance of rural and urban children in selected Canadian schools.

The first-grade tests are similar to the three subtests in the *Gates Primary Reading Test.* The phrase and sentence reading test consists of fifty items, each containing four phrases or sentences, of which the child selects the one matching an accompanying picture. The paragraph reading test provides 28 paragraphs, each accompanied by four pictures, one of which correctly illustrates it. This test seems well adapted to the measurement of paragraph comprehension in the primary grades. The format of the first-grade tests is excellent. The pictures are unusually clear. The directions and the means of indicating the correct answer are simple.

Reliability coefficients for comparable forms of Types I and II of the primary tests are .848 and .909 respectively. Internal estimates of reliability, based on analyses of variance for Types III and IV, for which there are no comparable forms, are .957 and .950. Correlations between Types I and II and the equivalent types of the *Gates Primary Reading Test* were .895 and .884. As the manual of the Dominion Tests indicates, these two types could be considered equivalent forms of the corresponding Gates tests or vice versa.

The Diagnostic Test in Word Recognition is a significant venture. Similar in form to the Word Recognition test, it is so constructed that errors can be classified as related to the beginning, middle, or ending of the word, as reversals, or as choices based on general configuration. A table shows the typical error pattern for a given number of mistakes and the points below which errors might be considered either significant or abnormal. No information is provided as to how these error levels were determined. Furthermore, the proportion of typical errors in each category shows practically no change as the number of total errors decreases. Inasmuch as teaching emphasis in the first stages of word analysis tends to be upon left-to-right orientation and ability to respond to the beginnings of words, one would expect the proportion of errors in these categories and those related to the general configuration of the word to decrease as reading ability improves. If the children who took this test did not give evidence of this growth, it is perhaps because it is geared to a stage before that in which there is much emphasis on word analysis and is therefore not correctly graded to be of greatest service to teachers. Further research seems indicated before teachers are encouraged to rely upon the error scores.

The vocabulary tests at the two upper levels use a key word and four responses. Reliabilities, based on comparable forms, are .927 for grades 2 and 3 combined and .925 for grades 4, 5, and 6 combined.

The Diagnostic Test in Paragraph Reading contains eight paragraphs, each followed by three questions, one related to the general significance of the paragraph, a second calling for an inference, and a third asking for a detail. Error scores are indicated as they were in the Diagnostic Test of Word Recognition, and the same general questions can be raised regarding their validity. The problem of accurate diagnosis is further complicated by the fact that the total test allows for only eight errors of each type. The value of a group test which provides diagnostic information cannot be overemphasized. It is to be hoped that the research will be continued by the authors of the Dominion Tests to the point where the analyses of errors are backed by careful study. The reliability of this test, based on comparable forms, is .830.

Those concerned with the technical aspects of test construction will appreciate the care with which these tests have been built. In addition to the reliabilities, an analysis of variance provides evidence as to the internal consistency of each test, the discrimination between persons, the equivalence of forms, and the effects of the difficulty of the separate items. This careful attention to the statistical bases of test construction seems to be resulting in tests designed to cover only one or two grades instead of the range which is more frequently attempted in one form. This allows for norms which go well below and above the grades for which the test is recommended. There are still gaps in the series, but the tests which have been published are well done and give promise of a strong complete battery.

[477]
Buffalo Reading Test for Speed and Comprehension, Revised. Grades 7-16; 1933–41; Forms A, B; $5 per 100; 10¢ per specimen set; 30(35) minutes; M. E. Wagner; Foster & Stewart Publishing Corporation.

Holland Roberts, Educational Director, California Labor School, Inc., San Francisco, California. This 1941 revision follows the traditional textbook pattern set by the 1936 edition. It is a general survey test of certain abilities needed in understanding the dull mate-rial of unattractive texts, under the pressure of timing. The major revision is the shortening of the test from 40 to 30 minutes.

Each of the two test forms has 16 subdivisions, grouped into two similar 15-minute parts. Each of these two parallel parts consists of 8 selections from text material nearly all published before 1930. The 32 individual selections in the two parallel forms are all essay-type material, distributed as follows among these subject matter fields: geology, paleontology, and biology 9; astronomy 3; physics 2; history 5; sociology 1; economics 2; political science 1; philosophy 3; literary criticism 2; biography 2; and the informal essay 2. As the biographies are both of men of science, the subject matter is divided among the fields in these proportions: (a) biological and physical sciences, 16 out of the total of 32 selections in both forms of the tests, or 50 per cent; (b) social sciences, 12 or 37½ per cent; (c) English, 4 or 12½ per cent. Fiction, poetry, drama, dialog, and mathematics are not represented, and popular nonfiction is included only through token selections. As the material chosen does not represent these five important divisions of the school curriculum, the ability to read in these fields is not directly tested. The absence of fiction which represents such a large part of the reading in the secondary school is particularly noticeable, especially as the abilities needed for reading stories differ in important particulars from those used in understanding heavy textbook content.

Perhaps the key to the many difficulties which this test presents is the author's statement that "Every endeavor was made to select unusual topics so that those tested would be unlikely to have read them." To achieve this standard, the following key features of an effective test have been sacrificed:

(a) The miscellany of textbook scraps which constitute the framework of the test has no unity, and the content consequently has no over-all meaning or purpose and so lacks social significance.

(b) In striving to find material with which young people are unfamiliar, the possibility of giving them a vital learning experience and direction in their lives has been lost. Much of the content chosen could be useful, but it is not assembled and focused on the solution of any particular problem and therefore cannot be assimilated and put to work.

(*c*) The selections are generally uninteresting, lacking in variety, and difficult to read. They deal with subjects that are nearly all outside the experiences of young people, especially students in the high school. The assumption that the reading of informative material, irrespective of its appeal to the reader and of his ability to connect it up with previous experiences in reading or daily living, is an adequate test of reading ability has no established foundation in fact. Motivation has been proved to be a powerful factor in learning, and testmakers who wish to measure reading power cannot disregard it.

(*d*) The selections are without exception humorless and unimaginative.

This test reflects the structure of the educational system and the philosophy of the school systems for which it was designed. In its method and selection of content it is assumed that fact gathering is the business of the school, much as a squirrel garners nuts, and that the student who stores away the most facts is the most highly educated. That society today faces the postwar problems of an atomic age and that it is the key responsibility of the school to help the student learn to solve the basic problems of peace and survival are ignored. Instead, young people who handled machine guns at Bataan and flew bombers over Berlin yesterday and who may, if we fail to build the peace, meet death rays and germ warfare tomorrow are asked to grapple with the social problems of Chinese mandarins in the days before Alexander the Great.

Each of the 16 selections in each form of the test varies from one to three paragraphs of from 200 to 300 words printed on a single right-hand page. The four to six multiple-choice test questions accompanying each selection appear on the following page and are clearly and simply stated. They are primarily fact questions depending upon direct recall of items just read; i.e., "Fossil birds have (1) no teeth (2) reptilian teeth (3) front legs (4) scales rather than feathers." In answering these questions students are not permitted to turn back to the selection, but must recall the facts from a single reading. The ability to remember facts from *one* reading is not of crucial importance in normal study, and in this particular, as in the choice of subject matter, the test situation does not correspond to actual life conditions. The condensed nature of the material selected and the bad writing which characterizes much of it set up additional hurdles that complicate an already specialized, unnatural reading situation.

The test manual for the first edition was carefully prepared and presents directions for giving the test clearly.

William W. Turnbull, Secretary of the Board and Head of the Test Construction Department, College Entrance Examination Board, Princeton, New Jersey. DESCRIPTION. The test consists of sixteen passages (300 to 400 words), each followed by four to seven multiple-choice questions based on its content. The first eight passages (Part I of the test) deal with history, English, economics, sociology, and psychology; the last eight (Part II) with astronomy, physics, geology, biology, and paleontology. The selections, and the questions on each selection, appear in ascending order of difficulty. The student is not allowed to refer to the passage while answering questions about it. The difficulty of the task seems appropriate for students at the senior high school or college freshman levels.

SCORING. With the exception of one question in each form, the test is scored objectively throughout. The student writes the number of his answer choice beside the question; the scorer checks the number against a list of right answers. This is a decidedly tedious process which could easily have been eliminated by arranging the test for stencil scoring, e.g., by use of a separate answer sheet. Three scores are obtained: total right ("raw score"), number of questions up to and including the last question answered ("speed score"), and "raw score" divided by "speed score" ("comprehension score"). Extra credit is given for finishing either part of the test in less than the time allowed (15 minutes).

VALIDITY. No validity data are reported.

RELIABILITY. No reliability data are reported.

NORMS. Percentile norms for the three scores are provided for "college freshmen" on Form A only. Since there is no indication of the number or characteristics of the group on which these norms are based, they are of little or no value. No standardization data are given for Form B, nor is there any indication of the relation between scores on the two forms.

MANUAL. The manual gives directions for administering and scoring the test, and provides the norms mentioned above. There is no statement of the test's purpose, method of construction or standardization, reliability or validity, or of the manner in which the scores should be interpreted.

EVALUATION. This test suffers by comparison with others that are available (e.g., the *Iowa Silent Reading Test,* the *Nelson–Denny Reading Test,* the *Traxler High School Reading Test*). It has already been noted that available data about the test are wholly inadequate. The material itself does not suggest that the data, if available, would be reassuring. Many of the questions deal with unimportant details mentioned in the passages, and a considerable number of items violate common principles of test construction (e.g., clarity, grammatical accuracy, etc.). The proportion of questionable items is unusually large, indicating a need for a thorough re-editing and, most of all, an item analysis. The test user's task is made unnecessarily difficult by use of an awkward scoring system.

[478]

Chicago Reading Tests. Grades 2-4, 4-6, 6-8; 1939–40; 4 levels; 60¢ per specimen set; Max D. Engelhart and Thelma Gwinn Thurstone; E. M. Hale and Co.
a) TEST A. Grades 1-2; Forms 1, 2; 31(40) minutes; $2.50 per 50.
b) TEST B. Grades 2-4; Forms 1, 2, 3; 42(60) minutes; $2.50 per 50.
c) TEST C. Grades 4-6; Forms 1, 2, 3; 45(55) minutes; $3 per 50.
d) TEST D. Grades 6-8; Forms 1, 2, 3; 45(55) minutes; $3 per 50.

REFERENCES
1. ENGELHART, MAX D., AND THURSTONE, THELMA G. "Chicago Reading Tests." *Chicago Sch J* 20:74-81 N '38. *

Ed Res B 20:264 D 17 '41. William J. Jones. The Chicago Reading Tests, purporting to measure comprehension of words, sentences, stories, maps, and paragraphs, and a pupil's rate of reading, follow the usual testing procedures in such measuring. The samples of materials provided in each subtest are inadequate to measure either validly or reliably the status of a pupil in any of the aspects of reading. The samples of materials for measuring comprehension of paragraphs are limited almost exclusively to getting the main idea and noting details in the paragraphs. Other aspects of reading comprehension obviously cannot be measured without an extension of the test. The phases of reading comprehension measured in the test are not adequately defined or explained. No data are provided upon the validity and reliability of these tests. Such tests, however, might well be used in a survey of undifferentiated aspects of reading. It may be presumed that the reliability of scores on subtests are reliable for group interpretation purposes only. For individual diagnosis more carefully constructed reading tests are recommended.

For reviews by Robert Lawrence McCaul and W. J. Osburn, see 40:1531.

[479]

DeVault Primary Reading Test. Grades 1-2; 1931; Forms 1, 2; 60¢ per 25; 25¢ per specimen set, postpaid; (15-20) minutes; Nellie M. DeVault; California Test Bureau.

Alice N. Jameson, Assistant, Child Placement Department, Public Schools, Brookline, Massachusetts. This test purports to measure reading ability in the first and second grades. It contains three tests. The first test measures word recognition. Responses for this first test are registered in four different ways: a cross over a word, a line under a word, a box or a circle around a word or phrase. In the first and third sentences of Test 1 all four marks are employed. By using so many different marks, the child is obliged to concentrate upon both his reading and the type of mark he must use to indicate his response. The use of just one of these marks throughout the test would allow him to concentrate on reading exclusively.

The second test includes 15 short questions which are answered by underlining either Yes or No.

The third test is made up of 15 items. The first seven are sentences giving specific directions to be followed. For example, "Make a ball in the box." The other items are stories of increasing difficulty, each of which is followed by two or three questions to test comprehension.

The *DeVault Primary Reading Test* is to be commended for the following features: (*a*) The content of this test "is based upon a detailed analysis of various courses of study, research concerning word lists, test criteria and reports on children's reading." (*b*) It is well graded. (*c*) Tables in the manual indicate that the DeVault test is "strictly comparable with the Ingraham–Clark Tests, and Gates I, and II in the second grade." (*d*) The test booklet is compact and easy to use. (*e*) The print is clear and the spacing excellent. (*f*) The score sheet contains the answers to all three tests on one page, thereby facilitating correcting and saving the teacher's time.

The DeVault test was "designed to meet the needs of the first and second grade." It accomplishes this purpose.

[480]

Diagnostic Examination of Silent Reading Abilities. Grades 4-6, 7-9, 10-16; 1939-40; IBM in part; 3 levels; 2 parts; 50¢ per specimen set of any one level, postpaid; August Dvorak and M. J. Van Wagenen; Educational Test Bureau.

a) PART I, RATE OF COMPREHENSION TEST AND INDIVIDUAL DIAGNOSTIC READING PROFILE. $1 per 25; 5(15) minutes.

b)PARTS II AND III. IBM; separate answer sheets must be used; $2 per 25; 2¢ per machine-scorable answer sheet; nontimed (105-135) minutes.

REFERENCES

1. HAYTER, WALTER HENRY. *A Survey of Silent Reading Abilities in the State of Oregon.* Unpublished master's thesis, University of Washington, 1941. (*Abstracts of Theses . . . ,* 1941, pp. 46-7.)

2. TRAXLER, ARTHUR E. "A Study of the Van Wagenen-Dvorak Diagnostic Examination of Silent Reading Abilities," pp. 33-41. In *1940 Fall Testing Program in Independent Schools and Supplementary Studies.* Educational Records Bulletin, No. 31. New York: Educational Records Bureau, January 1941. Pp. xi, 41. Paper, lithotyped. $1.00. * (*PA* 15:3580)

Frederick B. Davis, Professor of Psychology, George Peabody College for Teachers; and Director, Test Research Service; Nashville, Tennessee. This test constitutes an ambitious effort to measure ten aspects of silent reading ability for pupils in each of grades 4 through 12 and among college freshmen. Test 1 is a well designed and highly speeded test of ability to comprehend easy material, but the directions do not make it sufficiently clear that the time limit is very short and that individual scores depend mainly on speed. If they did, this test would be one of the most useful of its kind. Test 2 is a verbal analogies test. Specific clues to the answers for some items are provided by differences in the parts of speech of the choices. Test 3 and 4 measure word knowledge. Test 5 includes items of general information, such as "Sugar comes from 26. Louisiana, 27. Hawaii, 28. Florida, 29. Brazil, 30. China." The keyed answer to this item is "Louisiana." According to the 1946 *Statesman's Yearbook,* in 1944 all these areas produced sugar, and all of them except Florida produced more than Louisiana. The item, as worded, has no one correct answer; the better informed the examinee, the worse the item seems to him. These details are cited merely to illustrate the careless construction and keying of some items in the examination. In Part III, for example, several items (e.g., Item 54, Senior Division) begin: "The paragraph is mainly about." The examinee cannot tell whether the main point of the paragraph or the topic discussed at greatest length is wanted.

Tests 6 to 10, inclusive, are composed of items based on reading passages and are administered without time limit. The reading level score derived from Tests 6 to 10 is a weighted combination in which Test 7 (weighted the heaviest) has about twice the weight of Test 6 (weighted the lightest). Whether this relative weighting of the tests, which is determined by the magnitudes of the standard deviations and intercorrelations of the parts, was planned and has any rationale is not stated in the manual. In any case, the writer judges the reading level score to be a reasonably valid measure of level of comprehension. It is unfortunate that the manual makes some inappropriate statements about the means of establishing the validity of any test. What reservations the writer has about the validity of the reading level score are due to the fact that he suspects Tests 6 to 10 (especially Tests 6 and 8) of measuring to an unacceptably great extent the pupils' ability to guess the answers the item writer had in mind in addition to the five skills specified in the manual.

Intercorrelations and reliability coefficients are not presented in the manual, but they have been reported by Traxler (2) on the basis of small, selected samples. In a sample of 116 tenth-grade, independent-school pupils, the intercorrelations of Tests 6 to 10 range from .43 to .70. Corrected for attenuation, the lowest of these becomes .75, and half of them exceed .90. Taken by themselves, these high intercorrelations do not necessarily reflect unfavorably on the validity of the part scores or of the total score. But they do indicate the presence of only small amounts of unique variance in each test.

The reliability coefficients for Tests 2 to 10 in the Senior Division booklet range from .43 (for Test 6) to .79 (for Test 4). Experience with items of these types warrants the conclusion that individual item efficiency in the case of tests like Test 6 is not as high as can be obtained from well-written and well-selected items. However, the standard error of measurement of an obtained reading level score is only about two C-score points at the public school, twelfth-grade level.

All things considered, the examination provides useful reading level and speed of comprehension scores. Its diagnostic value is limited by the unreliability of differences among the separate test scores and the fact that each of them measures little that is unique.

W. E. Hall, Associate Professor of Educational Psychology, The University of Nebraska, Lincoln, Nebraska. It is a quite widely accepted fact among reading experts that the adequacy of a diagnostic reading test rests on three requirements: (*a*) careful analysis of reading skills involved in a reading situation; (*b*) reading material as nearly like a usual reading situation as possible (this requirement is important because we are not sure of our knowledge of what are the reading skills); (*c*) care in selection of criteria of validation and in the subsequent validation. A careful study of the test seems to reveal that it was cleverly constructed, is easy to score, and purports to measure some very important skills in a reading situation.

The reading skills tested are: rate of comprehension, perception of relations, vocabulary in context, vocabulary—isolated words, general information, ability to grasp the central thought, ability to note clearly stated details, interpretation, integration of dispersed ideas, and ability to draw inferences.

All the tests but 1, 2, and 5 are probably measuring skills used in ordinary reading situations. Test 1, rate of comprehension, is not a typical reading situation because it is broken up into small reading units and uses the method of checking extraneous words to determine the rate of comprehension. It would seem that this checking device is very similar to a proofreading type of test rather than to rate of comprehension. Test 2, perception of analogous relationships, contains a type of item common in intelligence tests; and one wonders immediately how frequently this skill occurs in reading and how it is related to reading. Test 5, range of information, appraises the achievement in gathering information, but just how this skill is related to reading would seem to baffle any reading analysis. The only way to justify Tests 1, 2, and 5, or any of the tests, would be validation. The only validation given in the manual is a table of distribution of medians that fall within certain grade levels. It is difficult to see just how such a table can validate these tests as a diagnostic instrument related to the reading tasks that are required of the pupil in school or in our society.

There is no statement of reliability in the manual, which leads one to question reliability in terms of the length of each test. It is now generally conceded that the validity of a measuring instrument is best indicated by its discriminative capacity. It is stated in the manual that this examination has a high degree of discriminative capacity as evidenced by a study of 9,000 cases. The problem still remains—does this examination discriminate between individual skills important to reading and other skills?

J. B. Stroud, Professor of Education and Psychology, The State University of Iowa, Iowa City, Iowa. Part I (Test 1, rate of comprehension) consists of three- and four-line paragraphs, in which some word in the last half disagrees with the meaning of the first half. This word is to be crossed out. The method is similar to that used in the *Chapman–Cook Speed of Reading Test.* The method differs from that used in the reading comprehension part of the *Cooperative English Test* wherein the rate score is the number of items correctly responded to in a given period of time minus a correction; and from the method of computing rate by the number of words read in a length of time, as in Pressey's *Reading Speed and Comprehension,* the *Traxler High School Reading Test,* and the *Iowa Silent Reading Test.* Each of these three methods corrects some fault in the others but in so doing creates some of its own. The last-named method is the most natural, yet gives no evidence of the care with which the piece is read. However, the other two methods mentioned do not separate the time spent in not comprehending from that spent in comprehending. Incidentally, a procedure developed by Blommers * avoids this objection by computing rate scores only from exercises done correctly. On the test here reviewed the student *may* successfully mark most of the paragraphs by reading a portion of the first and last lines only. It would be helpful to know how students actually react to these different testing procedures.

Part II includes Tests 2 through 5. Test 2, perception of relations, is identical with the analogies test commonly found in intelligence tests. Other tests of Part II (vocabulary in context, vocabulary, and general information) are also similar to tests found in intelligence

* Blommers, P. J. "Rate of Comprehension of Reading: Its Measurement and Its Relation to Comprehension." *J Ed Psychol* 35:449-72 N '44.

test batteries. These are excellent tests and may be used as an index of aptitude for comprehension. This is one of the chief diagnostic features of the battery.

Part III (Tests 6-10) in form consists of 100 items based upon reading selections, administered without time limit. By differential scoring, five part scores based upon 20 items each are obtained. The reading exercises are ample in number and variety, and the test items are constructed with care and competence. The scores on Part III should reflect reading power, uncomplicated by rate in so far as this can be controlled by testing procedure. Part III yields the following part scores: grasping central thought, retention of clearly stated detail, integration of dispersed ideas, drawing inferences, and interpreting contents. There is little doubt that the processes suggested by these labels are implicated in effective reading. Utilization of items appropriate to each of these processes certainly should give a more comprehensive account of a student's reading ability than would the use of a smaller number. As a general test of reading, Part III deserves a ranking with the best.

The merit of the diagnostic feature of a reading test depends, among other things, upon the extent to which abilities measured vary independently and upon the extent to which these abilities can and should be developed separately by subsequent instruction. No statistical evidence of the disparateness of the part scores is given. The instructor will wish to decide for himself whether any special use is to be made of the separate scores of Part III in teaching. No information is given about reliability. In using profiles for diagnostic purposes, it is of the greatest importance to keep before teachers the question of the extent to which deviations may be expected by chance. Scores on the three parts of the test—rate, intelligence, and power of comprehension should have considerable diagnostic significance.

For an excerpt from a review by Worth J. Osburn, see 40:1532.

[481]

★**Diagnostic Reading Tests.** Grades 7-13; 1947-48; IBM except for Section IV, Part I; prepared by the Committee on Diagnostic Reading Tests, Inc.: Frances Oralind Triggs (Chairman), Robert M. Bear, Ivan A. Booker, Daniel D. Feder, Constance M. McCullough, A. Eason Monroe, George D. Spache, and Arthur E. Traxler; distributed by Educational Records Bureau.
a) SURVEY SECTION.

b) SECTION I, VOCABULARY.
c) SECTION II, COMPREHENSION.
  1) Part 1, Silent.
  2) Part 2, Auditory.
d) SECTION III, RATES OF READING.
  1) Part 1, General.
  2) Part 2, Social Studies.
  3) Part 3, Science.
e) SECTION IV, WORD ATTACK.
  1) Part 1, Oral.
  2) Part 2, Silent.

REFERENCES

1. TRIGGS, FRANCES ORALIND. "Diagnostic Reading Tests as Aids to Remedial Instruction." *Sch & Soc* 66:42-5 Jl 19 '47. *

[482]

Elementary Reading: Every Pupil Test. Grades 4-6; 1946-47; new form usually issued each April and December; forms December 1946 and April 1947; 2¢ per test; 1¢ per scoring key; Ina Sigworth, Ethel Rudler, and D. S. Gruey; Ohio Scholarship Tests, State Department of Education.
a) GENERAL ABILITY.
b) SPEED AND COMPREHENSION.

[483]

Garrison First Year Reading Test. Grades 1B, 1A; 1938; 1 form; 2 levels; $1 per 25; 20¢ per specimen set; (30-35) minutes; Marie Garrison; C. A. Gregory Co.
a) TEST I, MID-YEAR.
b) TEST II, END OF YEAR.

REFERENCES

1. EVANS, MARIE GARRISON. *The Revision and Standardization of a First Grade Reading Test.* Unpublished master's thesis, University of Michigan, 1938.
2. STONE, CLARENCE, R. "Validity of Tests in Beginning Reading." *El Sch J* 43:361-5 F '43. * (PA 18:2605)

Ruth Lowes, Associate Professor of Education, The West Texas State Teachers College, Canyon, Texas. This is a series of two tests for use in the first grade. One is to be given at midyear and the other at the end of the year. The tests are designed to measure visual discrimination, auditory-visual discrimination, phrase and sentence reading, and comprehension reading. The last-named skill refers to sentence and paragraph comprehension. The present revision is the fourth and was worked out by the author in a course taught by Dr. Arthur I. Gates at Teachers College, Columbia University.

Words used in the first test are those found to be common to twelve primers which were considered leading books at the time the test was published. Words in the second test are those common to ten first readers. Both tests were checked with the vocabulary lists of Thorndike, Gates, and Wheeler and Howell. For purposes of standardization, scores from almost four thousand pupils in schools in from fifteen to seventeen cities were used. For the two tests, reliability coefficients of .84 and validity coefficients of .83 and .80 respectively are reported.

No explanation is made in the manual as to how these coefficients were obtained.

The directions for administering the test are clear-cut and to the point. A strong feature is noted in the directions for giving the part for testing auditory-visual discrimination. Here a row of words is given, and the pupil circles the one pronounced by the examiner. In the trial exercise, precautions are taken to see that the pupil looks at each word before marking one. The test is given in two sittings.

The pictures in both tests are disappointing, and one wonders if the size of the type is not small in comparison with that used in primers and first readers.

The age table showing frequency of individual scores for different chronological ages may be of some value. Grade equivalents and percentile norms would have been helpful. The two tables showing the distribution of scores in the cities in which the tests were standardized contain valuable data but are of little help to the test user.

[484]

Gates Advanced Primary Reading Tests. Grades 2 5-3; 1926-43; revision of *Gates Primary Silent Reading Tests;* Forms 1, 2, 3; 2 parts; $2.70 per 100 of either part; 30¢ per specimen set; 40(50) minutes; Arthur I. Gates; Bureau of Publications, Teachers College, Columbia University.
a) TYPE 1, WORD RECOGNITION.
b) TYPE 2, PARAGRAPH READING.

REFERENCES

1. GATES, ARTHUR I. *The Improvement of Reading: A Program of Diagnostic and Remedial Methods, Third Edition.* New York: Macmillan Co., 1947. Pp. xxi, 657. $4.25. * (PA 22:3195)

Virginia Seavey, Assistant, Child Placement Department, Public Schools, Brookline, Massachusetts. [Review of Form 2.] The *Gates Advanced Primary Reading Tests,* which are recommended for use in the latter part of the second grade and at any time in grade 3, are a carefully constructed and well standardized team of two tests, "designed to measure general competence or power in each of two aspects of reading." Skill in word recognition is tested by the frequently used method of selecting one of four words that accompany a picture. The 48 items increase in difficulty gradually from primer words such as "mother" and "door" to words on an adult level of comprehension like "palatable" and "vaporous." Ability to read with understanding is measured by the paragraph reading test of 24 items directing the child to mark an accompanying set of pictures in certain designated ways, such as

"Draw a line under," or "Put an X on," etc. Both the level and range of vocabulary and comprehension can be determined as there is a very wide range in the difficulty of the items in both tests.

There is much to recommend these tests. They are valuable primarily for survey purposes and as a supplement to the *Gates Primary Reading Tests.* As they have such a high ceiling, they are especially well adapted for use in classes containing a number of superior readers. For second-grade pupils who still have limited reading ability the easier *Gates Primary Reading Tests* are more suitable.

The tests are easily administered and scored. Directions are clear and simple. The time limits are ample enough so that the pupils do not have to work under pressure. The test material is presented in an attractive form with excellent type and spacing. Except for one or two instances, the pictures are free from the ambiguity for which the Gates primary tests have been criticized. Many teachers have remarked that children enjoy these tests, and this has been proved true in the case of a few children with reading difficulty and a high degree of resistance to taking any test. A more technical advantage is the fact that the reading grade and age norms are based on over 5,000 cases. Reliability figures are moderately high. It is also commendable that there are three equivalent forms for each type test so that retesting can be done when necessary.

It must be remembered that the paragraph reading test measures only one narrow reading skill—the ability to follow directions in marking a picture. While total comprehension of reading matter involves more than bearing in mind such details, this kind of exercise is a satisfactory measure of comprehension on the second and third grade levels. We cannot tell, however, whether failure in any specific instance is attributable to lack of power in the mechanics of reading, to carelessness in marking and poor work habits, or to limited mental ability.

George Spache, Rohrer, Hibler and Replogle, New York, New York; formerly Psychologist, Public Schools, Chappaqua, New York. Measures of word recognition and paragraph reading are offered for use in the latter half of the second grade and through the third grade. The word recognition involves associating words and pictures; the paragraph meaning, marking pictures according to instructions inserted in the paragraph.

It is doubtful whether the grade norms given for these tests, which extend from 1.7 to 7.0 or 8.2, represent actual pupil performance above the third grade. Judged by their difficulty, the tests are most effective and discriminatory if used in the range suggested by their author.

The reliabilities for word recognition are given by the author as .89 and .90; those for paragraph meaning as .86 and .88. These are high enough to yield "reasonably reliable results in the individual cases and highly reliable scores for a class," if it is remembered that differences between individuals of less than seven-tenths of a grade are only fairly reliable differences. The norms are expressed in terms of the "average" child, and no cognizance taken of the influence of mental ability upon scores or of the practice effects of utilizing two forms consecutively, as advised by the author when more precise individual appraisal is desired.

Teachers are prone to interpret the grade scores derived from such reading tests as indicating the level of the reading materials that their pupils are competent to handle. When artificially derived norms for grades far above the level where the testing is usually done are given, as here, these grade scores become even more misleading. In a group of 80 third grade children, with median IQ of 103, thirty-one per cent made scores more than a year above their grade placement, implying that they were capable of reading materials more than a year above their actual reading levels. Taken at face value, the inflated scores achieved by these children would have been misinterpreted by the average teacher using the tests preparatory to organizing reading groups. Thus, the norms for these tests tend to give exaggerated estimates of the reading ability of bright children or good readers.

The tests will prove serviceable for screening and diagnostic purposes if used with children of low mentality or poor reading ability. With these pupils they may be interpreted in the common manner as indicating the general level of appropriate reading materials.

[485]

Gates Basic Reading Tests. Grades 3.5-8; 1926-43; revision of *Gates Silent Reading Tests;* Forms 1, 2, 3,

4; 4 parts; $2.70 per 100 of any one part; 30¢ per specimen set; (15) minutes per part; Arthur I Gates; Bureau of Publications, Teachers College, Columbia University.

a) TYPE A, READING TO APPRECIATE GENERAL SIGNIFICANCE.
b) TYPE B, READING TO PREDICT OUTCOME OF GIVEN EVENTS.
c) TYPE C, READING TO UNDERSTAND PRECISE DIRECTIONS.
d) TYPE D, READING TO NOTE DETAILS.

REFERENCES

1-5. *See* 40:1539.
6. GATES, ARTHUR I. *The Improvement of Reading: A Program of Diagnostic and Remedial Methods, Revised Edition.* New York: Macmillan Co., 1935. Pp. xvii, 668. * (PA 9:5252) For latest edition, *see* (7) below.
7. GATES, ARTHUR I. *The Improvement of Reading: A Program of Diagnostic and Remedial Methods, Third Edition.* New York: Macmillan Co., 1947. Pp. xxi, 657. $4.25. * (PA 22:3195)

George Spache, Rohrer, Hibler and Replogle, New York, New York; formerly Psychologist, Public Schools, Chappaqua, New York. The four tests are intended to measure different types of reading such as that for securing a general impression, to predict outcomes, to follow detailed directions, and to recall details. Each consists of 18 to 24 paragraphs and their questions arranged in ascending order of difficulty. As Traxler * has shown, in his survey of reading tests, there is a distinct tendency among testmakers to devise and label reading tests with no evidence whatsoever of their validity. This tendency is present here in that the author gives no proof that his tests actually measure four different types of reading, or that these types even exist. The 57 intercorrelations given by the author range from .66 to .92 with a median of .831. There is certainly little support here for considering the tests as disparate measure of four distinct reading abilities. The self-correlations or reliability coefficients range from .76 to .96 with a median of .889, implying almost as much identity between any two of the four tests as there is between two forms of any one test.

We would seriously question the effectiveness and discriminatory power of these tests in the grade range from 3 to 8 as recommended by their author. There is evidence * from private school testing that above the fourth grade the norms give exaggerated estimates of reading ability. In our own public school experience, 31 per cent of a group of 71 third graders, with median verbal IQ of 110, achieved scores more than a year above their actual grade placement in Type A, Reading for General Significance. Forty-seven per cent were similarly overestimated in Type C, Reading to Un-

* Traxler, Arthur E. *The Nature and Use of Reading Tests.* Educational Records Bulletin, No. 34. New York: Educational Records Bureau, 1941. Pp. 64. Paper.

derstand Precise Directions. None of these children was actually accelerated more than six months in his classroom reading level. These, in our opinion, are typical of the results obtained with these tests in ordinary testing situations.

Norms are also offered for speed in terms of the number of paragraphs attempted and for accuracy in per cent of paragraphs correct. These yield ratings in such terms as very high, medium, very low, etc. Apparently they serve to give an estimate of these aspects of reading.

In our opinion, the tests cannot be recommended for general use for such purposes as screening, organizing reading groups, measuring growth, etc. unless the average score from the use of all four tests is the only result employed in comparing groups and individuals. The tests will also function in individual diagnosis among children of low mentality or poor reading skills, if we accept the author's premise that they are indeed measuring different types of reading.

Herbert F. Spitzer, Associate Professor of Education, The State University of Iowa, Iowa City, Iowa. These tests consist of four separate forms and four types or parts for each form: Type A, Reading to Appreciate General Significance; Type B, Reading to Predict the Outcome of Given Events; Type C, Reading to Understand Precise Directions; and Type D, Reading to Note Details. Each type of the test is printed on a four-page 8½ by 11-inch booklet—one page for title, directions, and pupil's name and three pages of test material. This use of a separate title page for each type seems a waste of paper and test time, for the child in taking the complete tests has to write his name, age, birthday, school, grade, and date of taking the test four times. Since the total working time for the four types is only 38 minutes for grades 3 and 4 and 28 minutes for grade 5 and up, the waste of time resulting from this writing of name and other information appears obvious.

Type A, Reading to Appreciate General Significance, consists of 24 brief paragraphs. The subject is to underline the one of five words which tells something significant about the paragraph. Although this is supposed to be a measure of easy reading, the subject has to move along at a pretty rapid rate, for approximately 1,800 words of reading are presented in

only 6 minutes for upper grades and 8 minutes for lower grades. In fact, 3 pages of test material is a lot of reading for only 24 test items. However, the paragraphs are for the most part interesting and challenging, and the test items bear directly on the paragraph. A few of the paragraphs plunge the reader rather abruptly into a situation in which it is difficult to get the setting, e.g., in Item 17, Form 4, the first sentence is "It was fourteen years before the New World was named." "Fourteen years before what" is the question that normally arises.

In Type B, Reading to Predict the Outcome of Given Events, 24 paragraphs are presented. Four statements follow each paragraph. The subject is to select the statement that represents what is most likely to happen next. Approximately 2,400 words are presented for the 8 or 10 minutes of testing time. The paragraphs are interesting, and the good reader should certainly be able to select more of the best "what happened next" statements than the poor reader would be able to select. This type of test has the very attractive feature of getting away from word matching and other clues. The subject may consult the paragraph but will not find any clues in the form of similar words that will help in selecting the best answer.

In Type C, Reading to Understand Precise Directions, a drawing and word description or explanation is provided. The subject is given directions to draw a line, to make a circle, and the like. There is nothing particularly interesting or challenging about the various test situations. A few attempts to play for interest appear rather weak. For example, after the child has been instructed to draw a circle for the wheel on a water tower, this statement appears, "Now it can begin to pump." The use of such a term as "water tower" rather than "windmill tower" would probably be disturbing to children in the land of windmills. "Water tower" usually refers to the towers and elevated water storage tanks in villages and towns. A similar disturbing misuse of terms is used in connection with kinds of lights. An oil lamp is called a lamp, whereas an electric bulb is called an electric light. Many children refer to their father's desk lamp as a lamp even though it is electric.

In Type D, Reading to Note Details, 24 paragraphs each followed by three incomplete statements or questions about the paragraph are used. Each incomplete statement or question can be answered by underlining one of four words. A minor inconsistency occurs in this test in that the directions state that questions are asked about the paragraph, and then (on Form 4) the first paragraph is followed by three incomplete statements. About one-third of the items of the test consist of incomplete statements rather than questions. The paragraphs used in this test are for the most part interesting, and therefore the best efforts of children should not be as difficult to secure as would be the case for Type C.

A scoring key for the *Gates Basic Reading Tests* is provided in the manual, and the suggestion is made that "a copy of each of the tests should be marked to accord with the key and used to facilitate scoring." Such a key would, of course, require comparison of the key with the paper being scored, a slow and tiring process. Since the tests could easily be arranged so that marks could be counted through use of a stencil-type answer key, the system of scoring recommended in the manual must be considered very poor. Much of the time and energy teachers use in scoring the *Gates Basic Reading Tests* could easily be saved and might be used in doing something in the way of remedial or improved instruction based on the test results.

The manual accompanying the *Gates Basic Reading Tests* provides an excellent discussion of the place and purpose of these tests in an instructional program. There is also a brief description of the different tests and more extensive sections on diagnosis based on raw scores, diagnosis by use of age and grade norms or scales of average achievement, samples of recommended type of diagnosis, appraising a class as a whole, and other uses to be made of the tests.

The notes on reliability in the manual are excellent. The self-correlation on the tests are nearly all within the range .85 to .94. Some of the intercorrelations between two types are as high as .92, an extremely high figure for tests of supposedly different phases of a subject.

Three types of norms are provided in the manual: (*a*) reading age and reading grade, (*b*) accuracy scores, and (*c*) speed or rate norms. The second are provided in the form of five levels for each half grade. The third type of norm is based on the number of paragraphs attempted. This is, of course, not a true speed or rate score since comprehension played a part in determining how fast the pupil read. In this the Gates rate score is no worse than rate scores on other widely used reading tests.

The manual contains an excellent reference list.

The outstanding features of the *Gates Basic Reading Tests* have been presented in the preceding paragraphs, but a few other notes and comments should be made. The wide range of grades (middle third through eighth) for which these tests are recommended is rather surprising when it is a well-known fact that other tests designed for as short a range as grades 3, 4, and 5 have been found to be rather unsuited for some third and some fifth grades. It is difficult to see how a basic reading test can omit such important areas of reading as organization of material read and the skills involved in locating information—the use of the index and sources of information. In the *Gates Basic Reading Tests* use is made of many short unrelated paragraphs, while in normal reading situations several paragraphs on the same topic are the rule rather than the exception. Why not several paragraphs on the same topic is a question that test users should direct to test authors.

The *Gates Basic Reading Tests*, as has been indicated, have relatively simple directions and therefore can be administered without much difficulty. While they are not as easily scored as they might be, the directions for scoring are easily followed. The tests require less than 40 minutes of actual working time, measure important areas of reading, and are provided with three kinds of norms. The wise use of these tests should aid in promoting worthwhile study resulting in improvement of instruction in reading.

T. L. Torgerson, Chairman, Psycho-Educational Clinic, and Professor of Education, The University of Wisconsin, Madison, Wisconsin. This battery is a series of reading tests of high reliability which is easily administered. The series possesses considerable flexibility because of its four types, four forms, and short working time. The manual, on the whole, is very complete and should prove very useful to the user. Scoring would be facilitated if the keys were printed separately and keyed to the test booklets.

One criterion of a valid reading test is the

inability of the pupils to answer the questions without reading the paragraph. Undoubtedly, many of the questions in Tests C and D can be answered by upper-grade pupils without reading the paragraphs because the questions deal with knowledge or information familiar to most pupils.

Do these tests which are designed to measure rate of comprehension utilize a valid technique for measuring rate? The best-answer type of response used in Tests B and C is a useful technique in measuring power of comprehension. Does it yield a valid measure of the rate of reading? The technique of crossing out the absurd or irrelevant word or phrase as employed in the Minnesota and the Michigan speed of reading tests is unquestionably superior. The teacher in using these tests should be aware of the fact that the tests have been designed to determine how much reading material on a third grade level of difficulty pupils in grades 4 to 8 can read and comprehend accurately in a given period of time. In order to determine a measure of a pupil's level of comprehension, a test which consists of reading material which increases in difficulty should be used. The *Gates Reading Survey for Grades 3 to 10* provides such a measure.

For reviews by Joseph C. Dewey and James R. Hobson and an excerpt from an appraisal by Edward William Dolch of the Gates Silent Reading Tests, *see 40:1539.*

[486]
Gates Primary Reading Tests. Grades 1-2.5; 1926–43; revision of *Gates Primary Silent Reading Tests;* Forms 1, 2, 3; 3 parts; $2.70 per 100; 30¢ per specimen set; 50(80) minutes; Arthur I. Gates; Bureau of Publications, Teachers College, Columbia University.
a) TYPE 1, WORD RECOGNITION. 15(25) minutes.
b) TYPE 2, SENTENCE READING. 15(25) minutes.
c) TYPE 3, PARAGRAPH READING. 20(30) minutes.

REFERENCES
1. GATES, ARTHUR I. "The Gates Primary Reading Tests: Their Uses in Measurement, Diagnosis, and Remedial Instruction." *Teach Col Rec* 28:146-78 O '26. * (PA 1:492)
2. GATES, ARTHUR I. *The Improvement of Reading: A Program of Diagnostic and Remedial Methods, Revised Edition.* New York: Macmillan Co., 1935. Pp. xvii, 668. (PA 9:5252) For latest edition, *see* (7) below.
3. FRIDIANA, M. "Achievement in Silent Reading in an Elementary School." *J Ed Res* 34:594-600 Ap '41. * (PA 15:3148)
4. POSTON, FREDA L. *An Evaluation of Techniques of Matching Words and Pictures as Measures of Word Recognition and Word Meaning in First and Second Grades.* Unpublished master's thesis, Ohio University, 1941. Pp. 76. (*Abstracts of Masters' Theses . . .*, 1941, pp. 67-8.)
5. STONE, CLARENCE R. "Validity of Tests in Beginning Reading." *El Sch J* 43:361-5 F '43. * (PA 18:2605)
6. POSTON, FREDA, AND PATRICK, JAMES R. "An Evaluation of Word and Picture Tests for First and Second Grades." *J Appl Psychol* 28:142-52 Ap '44. * (PA 18:2975)
7. GATES, ARTHUR I. *The Improvement of Reading: A Program of Diagnostic and Remedial Methods, Third Edition.* New York: Macmillan Co., 1947. Pp. xxi, 657. $4.25. * (PA 22:3195)

William S. Gray, Professor of Education, The University of Chicago, Chicago, Illinois. These tests are an integral part of a broader program for testing reading throughout the grades which Dr. Gates has developed. They include separate tests designed to measure the level and range of ability of three highly important types of reading in the primary grades. Type 1, Word Recognition, measures the degree to which pupils can identify with reasonable accuracy representative primary words. The test consists of 48 items, each of which includes a picture and four words. The task is to identify and encircle the word that tells most about the picture. All the words used fall within the first 1,000 of the Gates Primary Word List. The first exercises are composed of the easy and most commonly used words, but gradually become more difficult.

Type 2, Sentence Reading, measures ability to read and understand sentences composed of words most commonly used in the primary grades. The test consists of 45 sentences, and comprehension is measured by the pupils' ability to identify and mark one of several pictures which accurately illustrates the meaning of a given sentence. All the words used fall within the first 1,500 of the Gates Primary Word List. The sentences are so arranged that they gradually increase in difficulty, as determined by the decreasing frequency and importance of the words used and by the length of the sentences.

Type 3, Paragraph Reading, measures ability to read thought units with full and exact understanding. There are 26 exercises including one or more sentences accompanied by pictures or drawings. The test of comprehension measures ability to execute accurately the directions in each exercise. Effort has been made to increase the difficulty of the verbal exercises through control of their vocabulary, sentence structure, and length.

VALIDITY. No discussion of validity accompanies the tests. A critical analysis of the test passages led the reviewer to the conclusion that the test exercises were reasonably valid measures of the abilities they purported to measure. In a few exceptional cases, for example, Item 41 in Sentence Reading, the picture assumed to be the right answer represents the meaning of only one word rather than the sentence as a whole.

RELIABILITY. No statistical data on the reliability of the tests are provided. The author rightly points out, however, that the reliability of the results of the tests is determined primarily by the skill of the examiner. The factors of greatest importance in this connection are the explanation of the tasks to the pupils and the management of the group during the test period. Careful directions are provided as an aid to the teacher in giving the tests properly. The reliability of the test for sentence reading may be reduced by the marking device employed. Experience shows that some children are unable to indicate clearly whether they are making one, two, or three parallel lines in harmony with the directions.

NORMS. Tables of grade and age norms are given in the manual. Age and grade norms for each test score are provided, based on records from approximately 250,000 pupils in schools in all parts of the country. Unfortunately, no measure of variability is provided, excepting as suggested by the 75th and 25th percentile scores for various grade levels.

VALUE. It requires 50 minutes to give the tests, not including time for directions. They are easy to administer and can be used either for general survey or diagnostic purposes. The manual which accompanies the tests includes specific suggestions for use in making diagnoses, discusses at length the causes of difficulty in the types of reading measured, and offers suggestions for improving sentence and paragraph reading. Since three forms have been developed, they can be used in measuring the progress of pupils at intervals of a semester or less or for checking individual progress.

George Spache, Rohrer, Hibler and Replogle, New York, New York; formerly Psychologist, Public Schools, Chappaqua, New York. This group of tests includes measures of word recognition, sentence reading, and paragraph reading. The first two involve the association of words and pictures illustrating the test word or sentence. In the third, the child's comprehension is measured by his ability to mark the related pictures in accordance with instructions contained in the paragraph.

The tests are offered for use in the first grade and the first half of the second grade. They are rather sharply scaled in difficulty and discriminate well in their effective range. This we estimate to be from the middle of the first grade through the second grade. The fact that pupils of the first half of the first grade would be able to do less than 15 per cent, or only 2 to 3 items, implies that the tests probably function most discriminatively above the middle of the first grade. There also appears to be adequate ceiling for use of the tests through the second grade.

The author gives no data on validity or reliability other than the comment that "the tests are long enough to yield reasonably reliable results in the individual case and highly reliable scores for a class." If this statement is based upon statistical investigation of the reliability, there seems to be no good reason for withholding the data. The author suggests the use of two forms for "more precise individual appraisals" but gives no information regarding the known effects of practice on two forms. Similarly, although he recognizes the influence of the intellectual ability of the class upon its scores, all norms are expressed in terms of the "average" child. Use of the tests has demonstrated, as the author claims, that they are not unduly influenced by speed. The public school child of normal reading ability will commonly complete the tests in the time allowed.

We believe it is misleading, to say the least, to give norms expressed in units as small as a hundredth of a school year, as is done here. It is highly doubtful whether any test now available has the degree of reliability and discrimination claimed by implication in these norms. Norms in such minute units are not justified for a test in which differences less than eight-tenths of a grade are only "fairly reliable." Another objection to the norms arises from the common practice of teachers of believing that the grade scores obtained from reading tests indicate the actual reading levels of the pupils. It would be much more meaningful in this instance to give norms in terms of the expected performance at preprimer, primer, and first- and second-reader reading levels.

Despite these minor criticisms of standardization, the tests will serve, if interpreted cautiously, in screening and diagnostic testing to indicate pupils who are markedly deficient in the skills of sight word vocabulary, and sentence and paragraph reading. They will serve to rank children in the order of their effectiveness in these skills, an order roughly corresponding to their classroom performance.

[487]
Gates Reading Survey for Grades 3 to 10: Vocabulary, Level of Comprehension, Speed, and Accuracy. Grades 3-10; 1939; Forms I, II; $6.85 per 100; 25¢ per specimen set; (60-90) minutes; Arthur I. Gates; Bureau of Publications, Teachers College, Columbia University.

REFERENCES

1. GATES, ARTHUR I. *The Improvement of Reading: A Program of Diagnostic and Remedial Methods, Third Edition.* New York: Macmillan Co., 1947. Pp. xxi, 657. $4.25. * (PA 22:3195)

Dorothy E. Holberg, Elementary Supervisor and Reading Clinician, Alexis I. duPont Special School District, Wilmington, Delaware. After three years of using this test in grades 3 through 6, the reviewer has reached the following conclusions and suggestions:

(*a*) The printed underlining of the correct answers in the Vocabulary Test, Level of Comprehension Test, and Speed Test should be omitted in order that the student may practice the directions of drawing a line under the correct word before beginning the test. This would enable the examiner to check on the child's ability to follow directions accurately before beginning the test.

(*b*) Include in the oral directions for the Vocabulary Test the statement that the student must not work beyond page 3. Before beginning the Level of Comprehension Test, the examiner should orally stress the fact that the pupil must not work beyond page 7. Printed directions to stop work are included at the *end* of each test, but this does not necessarily impress all students.

(*c*) When used with elementary school students, an additional explanation might be psychologically sound. The students should be informed that this test is used with tenth grade pupils as well as third grade pupils. There may be many parts that they will be unable to read; however, they should work as many as possible. This will tend to eliminate guessing as well as signs of frustration.

(*d*) In order to insure a feeling of success, it might be advisable to administer the Level of Comprehension Test first. Children are generally more successful in reading the Level of Comprehension Test because they are aided by context clues, whereas in the Vocabulary Test the words are in isolation.

(*e*) The directions for both the vocabulary and the level of comprehension tests fail to inform the student that these tests are *not* speed tests. Test-wise students tend to conclude that all standardized tests are speed tests, and one of

the most valuable factors of these power tests is lost unless this misconception is corrected.

(*f*) In power tests such as Tests I and II, students who finish quickly may distract those still working. For the benefit of classroom teachers who might administer these tests it would be advantageous to include in the manual of directions several teaching techniques to avoid the above situation.

(*g*) The size of the print utilized is undesirable for use with elementary school children.

(*h*) This test may be used for analysis on the college level if a reading difficulty has been indicated by other tests such as college entrance examinations.

(*i*) When compared with informal reading testing techniques and teachers' opinions of reading ability, this test overestimates a pupil's ability to read and tends to place him above his true instructional level in reading.

(*j*) It is the writer's opinion that this is the most valuable survey-type reading test at the present time. Where further diagnosis is desired, it may be supplemented by using the *Gates Basic Reading Tests.* Failure by a retarded reader on the Gates Survey Test may be handled by administering the *Gates Advanced Primary Reading Tests,* the *Gates Primary Reading Tests,* or the *Gates Reading Readiness Test* as the case may be. It is suggested that a test similar to the *Durrell–Sullivan Reading Capacity Test* be prepared by Dr. Gates. This would enable a reading clinician to determine a student's retardation in reading by comparing his reading capacity score, i.e., hearing comprehension level, with that of his actual reading achievement level as provided by this test. This would give a complete picture of a student's reading achievement, status within a group, reading strengths and weaknesses, as well as data as to whether or not he is working to full capacity in reading.

Herbert F. Spitzer, Associate Professor of Education, The State University of Iowa, Iowa City, Iowa. According to the manual, this test was developed to complement the *Gates Basic Reading Tests.* This survey test purports to measure vocabulary, level of comprehension, speed, and accuracy. Two scores are obtained from the speed test, one for speed and one for accuracy.

The vocabulary and level of comprehension tests are power tests and therefore do not have fixed limits. However, the directions for administering suggest 20 to 30 minutes for the vocabulary and approximately 30 minutes for the comprehension test. The speed test requires 10 minutes for grades 3, 4, and 5, and 7 minutes for the grades 6 and up.

In the vocabulary test the subject is to select and underline a word similar in meaning to a key word. In the comprehension test, one, two, or three key words are omitted from a short paragraph. The subject is to indicate by underlining which of five words presented would make the best sense when used in the appropriate blank of the paragraph. In the speed and accuracy test the subject reads a short paragraph and is then asked a question which can be answered by underlining a single word, four of which are presented.

The directions for this survey test are simple, although containing a few such indefinite statements as "allow 30 minutes more or less." Directions of that type are frequently a cause of confusion with some teachers, especially when no directions are given regarding what children who finish are to do.

The subjects should have little difficulty in marking the test. A minor inconsistency is found in directions for the speed test. The subject is directed to draw a line under the word that best answers the question. In some instances, however, no question is asked, but an incomplete statement such as "These dogs are very ——" is used. Adequate sample exercises are provided for each section of the test.

A key for scoring consisting of the correct words is provided. Unfortunately this scoring key requires comparison of the subject's underlined word and the key. Since the test requires only the underlining of words, a faster and more accurate method of scoring could be provided by use of a separate answer sheet and a stencil-type key. Even if no answer sheet were used, a stencil-type key for the booklet, which would permit the scorer to count marks instead of having to compare, would be a marked improvement. Time and effort saved in scoring a test is very important, for that time and effort may be used in instruction based on the test results. Too often teachers are so exhausted from scoring a test that they have little desire to do anything about the results they have obtained.

The manual of directions for the *Gates Reading Survey* contains a brief but compre-hensive discussion of each of the parts of the test, a discussion of the function of the test, the interpretation of results, data on reliability, and the like. A section on instruction and remedial work in reading indirectly presents rather significant commentaries on the importance of the areas of reading measured. The following is an illustration: "A limited vocabulary may be due to low intelligence, to meager general experiences, and to little reading of varied materials of real substance." In other words, the author wisely warns the test user to refrain from concluding that a low score is due to a poor reading program.

The suggestions for improvement of reading in the manual are not extensive and not too encouraging to teachers or administrators who are seeking a definite remedial program. The following statement regarding comprehension is illustrative: "The only lasting cure for a low level of comprehension consists in getting the pupil to find and read materials of real interest and suitable difficulty."

The correlations between different forms of the test, which according to the manual are not so high as reliability coefficients reported on many tests, are high enough to be entirely satisfactory and might even be considered high. The range of correlations is from .82 to .92. These high correlations are not surprising when the nature and length of the tests involved are considered. For instance, the vocabulary test consists of 85 items of the same type.

Most of the strong features and minor limitations of the *Gates Reading Survey* have been presented in the preceding discussion. However, a few other points should be noted. An excellent general bibliography is included in the manual. The testing technique, the actual procedures used, do not resemble very closely or approximate normal reading. Perhaps this lack of agreement with the reading process is not a limitation, but the presentation of paragraphs with key words omitted is seldom encountered in everyday reading situations. The speed-of-reading test in the *Gates Reading Survey*, like most speed tests, is a measure of both rate and comprehension, and cannot, therefore, be considered solely as a rate score.

Many test users have found tests designed for only grades 3, 4, and 5 rather difficult for grade 3, and occasionally such tests have insufficient range to measure adequately at even as low a level as fifth grade. In view of the preceding facts it is difficult to see how the *Gates Reading Survey* can be used effectively over as wide range (from middle third through eighth grade) as is assigned to it.

While the manual for this test clearly states that this test was developed as a complement to the *Gates Basic Reading Tests,* its use is not limited to such a combination. It does provide, as the title indicates, a survey test, and if the user keeps in mind its limitations, its use should be valuable in instruction.

[488]
High School Reading Test: National Achievement Tests. Grades 7-12; 1939-45; Forms A, B; $2.50 per 25; 15¢ per specimen set; nontimed (40) minutes; Robert K. Speer and Samuel Smith; Acorn Publishing Co.

Robert L. McCaul, Instructor and Adviser in the College, The University of Chicago, Chicago, Illinois. Presumably the *High School Reading Test* is a publication in separate form of the reading section of the *National Achievement Tests* for the secondary school level. What was said of the whole elementary battery in *The Nineteen Forty Mental Measurements Yearbook (see* 40:1191) can probably be applied, *mutatis mutandis,* to the test being considered here. If the preceding sentences seem vague and noncommittal, the reason is that no information about the test's origin, construction, and standardization is supplied to the user. He gets a single sheet containing directions for administration and scoring, columns for recording class scores, and a set of norms. Consequently, no thorough evaluation of the test can be made.

Although the test is divided into five parts —vocabulary, word discrimination, sentence meaning, noting details, and interpreting paragraphs—there are norms only for the total score. It is impossible, therefore, to determine whether variations in the student's scores on the subtests are produced by differences in the difficulty of the subtests or by differences in the quality of his reading skills. The authors are aware of this flaw and suggest that the student's subtest performance be measured in terms of the accomplishment of his particular class. Such a solution does no more than endow the test with a spurious diagnostic character, for the meaning of the group's achievement upon each of the subtests is just as uncertain as the meaning of the individual's achievement.

The test reveals care in construction and

expression. There are, of course, minor flaws which a captious critic could pounce upon and worry to an extent out of all proportion to their significance. In the sentence meaning part of the test, for example, the longest of the possible responses is usually right. This is true of 10 of the 15 sentence-meaning items in Form A and of 9 of the 15 in Form B. Again, sometimes two of the answers to word-discrimination items could be correct; Item 11, Form A, for instance, is "I can devise no ——— arguments with which to influence your decision," followed by *subtle, salacious, important,* and *revolting.* The right answer according to the key is *subtle,* but is not *important* as good?

The defects pointed out in the previous paragraph are outweighed by the conveniences that the test possesses. It is a power test with no arbitrary time limits. Norms cover a range extending from grade 6 through the sophomore year in college. No scoring key is required—an item is correct if it is designated by a letter in a code word like *master.* Because the test does have these advantages, and the three mentioned are only samples, it is to be hoped that the authors will in the near future provide norms for each of the subtests. They should also furnish the user with more information about the test.

[489]
Iowa Silent Reading Tests: New Edition, Revised. Grades 4-9, 9-13; 1927-43; IBM for grades 9-13; Forms AM (Rev.), BM (Rev.), CM, DM; 2 levels; H. A. Greene, A. N. Jorgensen, and V. H. Kelley; World Book Co.
a) ELEMENTARY TEST. Grades 4-8; 1933-43; $1.60 per 25; 35¢ per specimen set, postpaid; 49(60) minutes.
b) ADVANCED TEST. Grades 9-13; 1927-43; IBM; separate answer sheets need not be used; booklets may be used once without answer sheets and thereafter with answer sheets; $2.20 per 25; $1.35 per 25 machine-scorable answer sheets; 60¢ per set of machine-scoring keys; 35¢ per specimen set, postpaid; 45(60) minutes.

REFERENCES

1-6. *See* 40:1547.
7. HOLCOMB, G. W., AND LASLETT, H. R. "A Prognostic Study of Engineering Aptitude." *J Appl Psychol* 16:107-15 Ap '32 * (PA 7:4722)
8. STUIT, DEWEY B. "Differential Characteristics of Superior and Inferior Students." *Sch & Soc* 46:733-6 D 4 '37. * (PA 12:1640)
9. STUIT, DEWEY B., AND DONNELLY, MARY CARROLL. "Performance in the Iowa Qualifying Examination of Majors in Various Academic Departments With Implications for Counseling." *J Exp Ed* 8:293-9 Mr '40. * (PA 14:4754)
10. ANDERSON, IRVING H., AND DEARBORN, WALTER F. "Reading Ability as Related to College Achievement." *J Psychol* 11:387-96 Ap '41. * (PA 15:3570)
11. LANGSAM, ROSALIND STREEP. "A Factorial Analysis of Reading Ability." *J Exp Ed* 10:57-63 S '41. * (PA 16:1187)
12. PANKASKIE, MARGARET. *Factors in Reading Achievement at the College Level.* Unpublished doctor's thesis, University of Iowa, 1941. (*Doctoral Dissertations . . . 1940 and 1941,* 1944, pp. 336-47.)
13. SMITH, JOSEPHINE M. "The Prognostic Value of Entrance Tests in a Junior College." *J Ed Psychol* 32:584-92 N '41. * (PA 16:2888)

14. RAINIER, RUTH NEELY; REHFELD, FLORENCE WASHBURN; AND MADIGAN, MARIAN E. "The Use of Tests in Guiding Student Nurses." *Am J Nursing* 42:679-82 Je '42. * (*PA* 16:5029)

15. WILKING, S. VINCENT. "Do Our Reading Tests Test the Right Words?" *J Ed Res* 36:35-9 S '42. * (*PA* 17:709)

16. MORGAN, C. L., AND STEINMAN, C. C. "An Evaluation of a Testing Program in Educational Psychology." *J Ed Psychol* 34:495-502 N '43. * (*PA* 18:1891)

17. ADAMS, WILLIAM MICHAEL. "Prediction of Scholastic Success in Colleges of Law: II, An Investigation of Pre-Law Grades and Other Indices of Law School Aptitude." *Ed & Psychol Meas* 4:13-9 sp '44. * (*PA* 18:3271)

18. BLOMMERS, PAUL, AND LINDQUIST, E. F. "Rate of Comprehension of Reading: Its Measurement and Its Relation to Comprehension." *J Ed Psychol* 35:449-73 N '44. * (*PA* 19:1035)

19. PREISCHE, WALTER A. *The Relationship of Certain Measurable Factors to Success in Secondary-School Physics.* Unpublished doctor's thesis, New York University, 1944. (*Abstracts of Theses . . . [School of Education] 1944*, pp. 217-21.)

20. SMITH, HENRY LESTER, AND EATON, MERRILL T. *Analysis of the Proficiency in Silent Reading of 15,206 Sixth Grade Pupils in 648 Schools in Indiana.* Bulletin of the School of Education, Indiana University, Vol. 21, No. 6. Bloomington, Ind.: Indiana University Bookstore, November 1945. Pp. 47. Paper. $0.50. * (*PA* 20:2912)

21. TINKER, MILES A. "Rate of Work in Reading Performance as Measured in Standardized Tests." *J Ed Psychol* 36:217-28 Ap '45. * (*PA* 19:2380)

22. TOWNSEND, AGATHA. "A Study of the Revised New Edition of the Iowa Silent Reading Tests," pp. 31-9. In *1944 Fall Testing Program in Independent Schools and Supplementary Studies.* Educational Records Bulletin, No. 42. New York: Educational Records Bureau, January 1945. Pp. x, 49. Paper, lithotyped. $1.00. * (*PA* 19:1811)

23. KILBY, RICHARD W. "Relation of Iowa Silent Reading Test Scores to Measures of Scholastic Aptitude and Achievement." *J Appl Psychol* 30:399-405 Ag '46. * (*PA* 21:283)

24. PUGH, GLADYS S. "Summaries From 'Appraisal of the Silent Reading Abilities of Acoustically Handicapped Children.'" *Am Ann Deaf* 91:331-49 S '46. * (*PA* 21:290)

25. SMITH, HENRY LESTER, AND EATON, MERRILL T. *Analysis of the Proficiency in Silent Reading of 11,424 Sophomore Pupils in 243 High Schools in Indiana.* Bulletin of the School of Education, Indiana University, Vol. 22, No. 1. Bloomington, Ind.: Indiana University Bookstore, January 1946. Pp. 46. Paper. $0.50. *

26. "A Note on the Correlation Between the Iowa and Cooperative Reading Tests," p. 66. In *1947 Achievement Testing Program in Independent Schools and Supplementary Studies.* Educational Records Bulletin, No. 48. New York: Educational Records Bureau, June 1947. Pp. xii, 66. Paper, lithotyped. $2.00. *

27. KELLEY, VICTOR H., AND GREENE, HARRY A. *Better Reading and Study Habits.* Yonkers, N. Y.: World Book Co., 1947. Pp. iv, 73. Paper. $0.25. *

Frederick B. Davis, Professor of Psychology, George Peabody College for Teachers; and Director, Test Research Service; Nashville, Tennessee. The validity of the total score derived from the *Iowa Silent Reading Tests* as a measure of reading ability depends on the extent to which the subtests adequately sample the important skills involved in reading ability of the work-study type (which is the announced objective, according to the manual of directions). A conscientious effort has been made to measure the skills in reading considered most important, and the reviewer is inclined to believe that the total score is as valid a measure of the work-study type of reading ability as most reading tests are. The tests do not, and do not pretend to, measure the more subtle aspects of comprehension that are measured in some degree by the Cooperative reading comprehension tests.

The writer would be better satisfied with the total comprehension score if the subtests for rate of reading, the use of the index, and the selection of key words were omitted from its computation. Rate of reading is an almost meaningless concept because an individual's rate of reading depends on his immediate purpose and the difficulty of what he is reading. In the *Iowa Silent Reading Tests,* the directions for the rate-comprehension test say, "This is a test to see how well and how rapidly you can read silently. Read the story below very carefully so that you can answer questions about it." The testee has no idea what kind of questions. Penetrating? Superficial? Some testees will rush through and take a chance with the questions. Others will play it safe and digest what comes along. The point is that they will not all set out to do the same thing because the directions are not sufficiently detailed and specific to evoke a closely similar mind-set in each testee. Much more definite instructions would have to be provided in order to standardize the pupils' purposes.

The reviewer tried the 35 comprehension items in Test 1 of Form CM *without* first reading the two passages on which they are based. He got 23 of the 35 items correct on the basis of his general information about cork and city governments. This is better than chance would permit since, if he had marked the answer sheet without reading *either* the passages *or* the items, it would have been most reasonable to have expected him to get 12 correct, or a standard score of 133. This is evidence that the so-called comprehension score involves quite a bit of general information. In all fairness, one should point out that this is a failing of most tests of comprehension in reading.

The reviewer's main criticism of the content of the test is that it never forces a testee to grapple with a difficult passage, to weave an author's ideas together, to understand his overall thought. Every part gave the reviewer the feeling of superficiality, of pecking at the meaning without ever being required to think hard. The reviewer is prepared to defend the statement that the *Iowa Silent Reading Tests* never get at the inner recesses of comprehension and that their use must tend to reward unduly the rapid, superficial reader who is in the habit of skimming along and parroting a phrase or two of the writer if any one presses him regarding the content of what he has read.

In the manual of directions various types of data about the tests are provided. Reliability coefficients obtained by means of the split-half Spearman–Brown procedure and Kuder–Richardson formula No. 21 are presented. The fact is that meaningful reliability coefficients cannot be obtained for speeded tests, like the *Iowa Silent Reading Tests,* by either of these two means. The best way to determine the reliability coefficient (or better, the standard error of measurement at each of several levels on a standard-score scale) of any speeded test is to administer not less than three forms of the test to each one of a sample of testees in a single grade level. The intercorrelations of all three (or more) forms can then be used to get the reliability coefficient of each form *separately* and not the reliability coefficient of the average of a pair of forms (as is commonly done). This is getting reliability coefficients the hard way, but the reviewer is inclined to believe that if they are not worth the labor involved in this procedure they are not worth computing at all.

In summary, the *Iowa Silent Reading Tests* are conscientiously planned tests of the work-study type of reading. The total reading score gives some weight to tests of three mechanical skills: speed of reading, use of an index, and selection of key words. The reviewer does not know how much, if any, weight should be given to these three skills in a total reading score; but he prefers a comprehension score that does not include them. His major criticism of the *Iowa Silent Reading Tests* is that they appear to reward the pupil who reads superficially and who parrots glibly the reading material presented.

A genuine effort has been made to provide helpful, accurate, and complete information in the manual. It is unfortunate that reliability coefficients obtained by means of the split-half Spearman–Brown procedure and Kuder–Richardson formula No. 21 are presented with no warning that meaningful reliability coefficients cannot be obtained for highly speeded tests, such as the *Iowa Silent Reading Tests,* by either of these two means.

William W. Turnbull, Secretary of the Board and Head of the Test Construction Department, College Entrance Examination Board, Princeton, New Jersey. The purpose of the test is to measure rate of reading; comprehension of words, sentences, and passages read; and ability to use skills required in locating information. The Advanced Test has seven subtests and yields nine scores in 45 minutes of testing time (not including time to administer), the Elementary Test has six subtests, giving eight scores in 49 minutes. The tests at both levels include measures of the following: (*a*) rate of reading, (*b*) vocabulary, (*c*) understanding of sentences, (*d*) paragraph comprehension, (*e*) "directed reading," and (*f*) ability to use a simple index. The Elementary Test includes also a test of ability to alphabetize; while the Advanced Test measures ability to select words under which information about a given question might be found in an index. A further addition to the Advanced Test is a measure of comprehension of poetry. In this section the technique is similar to that in the "directed reading" subtest: the student is to identify the parts of a passage which answer certain specific questions.

SCORING. Both the Elementary and the Advanced Tests are scored objectively. The Elementary Tests have the answers indicated (for stencil scoring) in the test booklet, while the Advanced Tests can be given in this manner or with separate answer sheets for scoring by hand or by machine. Each subscore is converted to a standard-score scale, and the median of the subscores provides the total test score.

VALIDITY. From all appearances the test should provide a valid measure of reading ability. Unfortunately the authors rest their case after drawing attention to this fact. No validity coefficients are reported, which to this reviewer seems inexcusable.

RELIABILITY. The total score for each form has a reliability coefficient (computed separately for each grade level by Kuder–Richardson formula No. 21, using over 1,000 cases in all grades but one) of .94 or .95, with a probable error of measurement of 2 points on a scale which has a standard deviation of 13 to 14 for each grade. Thus, the reliability of the total test is high. The coefficients for the subtests range, in general, from .70 to .85 for the Advanced Test (probable error of measurement from 5 to 8 points) and from .70 to .90 (probable error of measurement from 4 to 7 points) for the elementary level forms. Thus, limited reliance can be placed on the subtest scores in individual cases, although their reliability is adequate for group comparisons.

NORMS. The test has been standardized on a national sample of between 1,500 and 2,000 students at each grade level. Percentile norms are given for standard scores on all subtests and on the total test. The standard-score scale for the Advanced Test is continuous with that for the elementary forms, so that direct comparison from one score level to the other is possible. Tables are provided for the purpose of equating scores on this test with those on the 1939 edition.

MANUAL. The directions for giving and scoring the tests are clear and complete. The manual contains relatively full information on reliability, standardization, and interpretation of scores, very little on construction (e.g., the level of discrimination below which items were rejected or revised); and, as already noted, a clearly inadequate treatment of validity.

EVALUATION. Examination of this test suggests that its position of leadership in the field is justified. The material, while perhaps somewhat artificial and academic, is in general appropriate and seems to have been carefully prepared and edited. Standardization appears to have been carried out thoroughly on large samples. The availability of four parallel forms at the two levels is an important advantage where measurement is to be repeated. No data are given on the proportion of students finishing the various subtests, but it is probable that the factor of reading rate enters into all sections of the test, which affects the interpretation of the scores. The comparatively low reliability of individual sections (inevitable in a test of its length) limits its usefulness in diagnosing areas of weakness in individual performance. The test should, however, be found entirely satisfactory for identifying students in need of remedial work, for securing class norms, or as an aid in sectioning classes.

Clearing House 19:322 Ja '45. E(arl) R. G(abler). * an excellent instrument if properly used, for the improvement of instruction.

Teach Col J 12:69 Ja '41. Margaret Pankaskie. * A new edition....is welcomed * The test of rate of reading is doubtless an improvement over the rate test in the earlier edition. * A unique feature of the Iowa tests (both old and new editions) has been the tests of skills required in locating information. This factor is usually omitted in reading tests. The test as a whole has satisfactorily high reliability. What should be desirable is a measure of the reliability of each of the subtests. It is yet to be proven that read-

ing may actually be divided into the number and kinds of skills which are indicated by the authors. If it is true that the seven tests represent separate skills, then each should be tested separately, with the reliability of each test ascertained independently. If there is much overlapping in the skills tested, it would seem that a test with fewer or no sub-tests would be quite as good a test and would in addition be simpler to score. One also wonders, if reading is to be separated into various independent skills, why the reading of technical or scientific material was omitted.

For reviews by Ivan A. Booker and Holland D. Roberts, see 40:1547.

[490]

Lee-Clark Reading Test—Primer, 1943 Edition. Grade 1; 1931–43; Forms A, B; $1.20 per 25; 35¢ per specimen set, postpaid; (15) minutes; J. Murray Lee and Willis W. Clark; California Test Bureau.

Ruth Lowes, Associate Professor of Education, The West Texas State Teachers College, Canyon, Texas. While most primary reading tests are designed for use in from one to three grades, this one is designated as a primer test to be given in the middle of the first school year. The Gates vocabulary list was used as a guide in the selection of words, 80 per cent of the different words being found in the first five hundred of the Gates list. Because of the way in which the words were selected, the authors claim that their tests "provide as valid a measure of reading ability as is available for primary children." No other proof of validity is offered. The coefficients of reliability for the total test are .909 (Form A with Form B) and .952 (total reliability if both forms are used); scores from 232 first grade pupils were used in calculating these coefficients.

Part I of the test measures the pupil's response to auditory stimuli and consists of fifteen rows of words, four words to the row. The pupil underlines the word pronounced by the examiner. Part 2 tests the pupil's ability to recognize eleven words. He draws a line from the word to an appropriate picture. Three minutes is the time allowed for this part. In Part 3 the ability to follow directions is measured by having the pupil mark and color certain objects pictured. Time is allowed for approximately 90 per cent of the class to finish.

The test can be given at one sitting. Scoring is easy. Both grade and age norms are given, but the number of pupils used in establishing the norms is not indicated. A table of percentile norms, based on the results obtained in the first grades in two city school districts, is given. Again the number of pupils tested is not indicated. A brief paragraph of directions for converting raw scores into percentile ranks will prove helpful to teachers who have had no special training in interpreting test results.

There are several mechanical features of this test which merit comment. The blanks on the front page call for a minimum amount of data, and the spaces are wide enough so that most of the pupils can write in the information. Parts 1 and 2 each occupy only one page of space. The left-hand page in each case is blank. This feature will be appreciated by first grade teachers who usually have to help pupils fold the booklet and place it in position so that the correct page is ready for use. Page numbers, large enough for the pupils to read, might prove helpful.

[490a]

Metropolitan Achievement Tests [Reading]. Grades 3-4, 5-6, 7-9.5; 1933–47; Forms R, S; 35¢ per specimen set of any one level, postpaid; 35(45) minutes; Richard D. Allen, Harold H. Bixler, William L. Connor, and Frederick B. Graham; World Book Co.
a) ELEMENTARY READING TEST. Grades 3-4; $1.60 per 25.
b) INTERMEDIATE READING TEST. Grades 5-6; $1.40 per 25.
c) ADVANCED READING TEST. Grades 7-9.5; $1.40 per 25.

For reviews by Ivan A. Booker, Joseph C. Dewey, and D. A. Worcester of an earlier edition, see 38:1105 and 40:1551. For reviews by Jack W. Dunlap, Richard Ledgerwood, Charles W. Odell, E. V. Pullias, and Hugh B. Wood of an earlier edition of the total battery, see 38:874 and 40:1189.

[491]

Minnesota Reading Examination for College Students. Grades 9-16; 1930–35; Forms A, B; $6 per 100; 35¢ per specimen set, postpaid; 46(55) minutes; Melvin E. Haggerty and Alvin C. Eurich; University of Minnesota Press.

REFERENCES

1-3. *See* 40:1554.
4. EURICH, ALVIN C. *An Experimental Study of the Reading Abilities of College Students.* Unpublished doctor's thesis, University of Minnesota, 1929.
5. EURICH, ALVIN C. "A Method for Measuring Retention in Reading." *J Ed Res* 24:202-8 O '31. * (*PA* 6:490)
6. LANGSAM, ROSALIND STREEP. "A Factorial Analysis of Reading Ability." *J Exp Ed* 10:57-63 S '41. * (*PA* 16:1187)

James M. McCallister, Director of Personnel Service, Herzl Branch, Chicago City Junior College, Chicago, Illinois. This test is designed to measure vocabulary and power of comprehension. The section devoted to vocabulary consists of 100 words, each of which is followed by four alternatives. The student selects the alternative that is the best definition of the word. Since few students will be able to finish the vocabulary section in the time allowed, it is an indirect test of speed as well as a measure of vocabulary.

The section that measures power of comprehension consists of ten paragraphs followed by directions for interpretation. These directions are varied so as to include sentence completion, selection of true statements, and selection of false statements. A careful comparison of the paragraph content with the questions reveals the measurement of several aspects of reading ability. The changing instructions require ability to follow directions. The various directions require, in addition to fact selection, some organization of content, occasional formulation of judgments and conclusions, and considerable comparison of ideas. The authors of the test have found correlations of .48 and .54 between the two parts of the test. They interpret these correlations to indicate that the two parts of the test measure the same psychological functions. It appears evident from the analysis mentioned above and these correlations that the test measures a number of the mental processes involved in reading. As the test yields only a single score for power of comprehension, it is in no sense diagnostic but is a composite measure of these various aspects of reading. The time limit in the second section of the test is such that nearly all students will complete it before time is called. Therefore, it is primarily a test of power of comprehension independent of speed of reading.

The validity of the test as a reading examination is implied by the analysis in the preceding paragraphs. The validity of Form A has been studied further by correlating the reading scores with scores on intelligence tests and with measures of scholastic achievement. The correlations obtained with the *Minnesota College Ability Test,* the *Miller Mental Ability Test,* and the *Miller Analogies Test* vary from .52 to .83. In each case the correlation between vocabulary and intelligence was higher than that between reading comprehension and intelligence. The relationship of the test to scholastic achievement was examined by correlating it with ratings of students in educational psychology and with average achievements in all courses taken during one quarter. These correlations were .52 and .46, respectively. The authors express the conclusion that the reading test is as predictive of college achievement as most tests of general intelligence.

Reliability measures are reported in the test manual for Form A only. First, the odd and the even numbered items in the test were compared for a group of 283 high school seniors. The correlation coefficients were .928 for Part I, and .693 for Part II. Second, the test was repeated with a group of 216 college juniors. The reliability coefficient obtained from this group for Part I is .912; for Part II, .780; and for the test as a whole, .865. These correlation coefficients indicate that the test is adequately reliable for group measurements but that it should be used with caution when applied to individuals.

Form A and Form B were not administered to the same population groups in the process of standardization. Form A was administered to 889 college sophomores, juniors, and seniors in 1929 and 1930. Form B was administered to slightly more than 1,000 sophomores, juniors, and seniors in 1933 and 1934. Percentile ranks and scale scores for these two groups reveal only slight differences at various points in the distributions. In so far as these two population groups were comparable, approximately similar scores may be expected from the use of the two forms.

Percentile ranks are published in the manual for high school seniors and for university freshmen, sophomores, juniors, and seniors. Consequently, the test is best adapted for groups at these levels. The arrangement of the test items and the scoring key makes it relatively easy to score. Since it does not provide a direct measure of rate of reading, it must be accompanied by another test if a speed score is desired.

For reviews by W. C. McCall and Ruth Strang, see 38:1106 and 40:1554.

[492]
Nelson Silent Reading Test: Vocabulary and Paragraph: Clapp-Young Self-Marking Tests. Grades 3-9; 1931-39; IBM for Forms A, B; Forms A, B, C; separate answer booklets must be used; $1.98 per 25 sets of test and answer booklet; 90¢ per 25 hand-scored answer booklets; 12¢ per specimen set, postpaid; $1.35 per 25 machine-scored tests; 75¢ per 25 machine-scorable answer sheets; 40¢ per set of machine-scoring stencils; 30(40) minutes; M. J. Nelson; Houghton Mifflin Co.

REFERENCES

1. GRANT, ALBERT. "Results of Nelson Silent Reading Test in Grade IX." *Sch R* 48:34-9 Ja '40. * (*PA* 14:2604)

Constance M. McCullough, Assistant Professor of Education, San Francisco State College, San Francisco, California. This test consists of a 10-minute vocabulary test of 100 words from the Thorndike and Horn lists, and a 20-minute, 25-paragraph test of three types of comprehension: general significance, details, and prediction of outcomes. The first 22 paragraphs, mostly original, contain only words appearing on one of the lists mentioned above. A Clapp–Young marking booklet provides simplified, rapid scoring. Correlations with other tests have run around .8. Reliability coefficients on scores for different forms of the test have been around .9. Norms based upon 41,000 cases from various parts of the country present median scores for various grades, and grade and age equivalents for raw scores. A study by Grant (1) of over 3,000 ninth grade pupils yielded median scores agreeing with the ninth grade norms.

The teachers' manual describes a method of obtaining part scores for the types of comprehension in the paragraph test, and suggests remedial measures. It gives in addition a list of helpful references on reading aids.

The vocabulary test contains useful words of increasing difficulty. Five multiple-choice answers are sometimes synonymous with the words tested; at other times, descriptive of function or attribute. This variation in technique requires continual mental adjustment by the pupil. Some of the words tested are easier than the answers, so that the test becomes a matter of recognizing the form and meaning of the answer rather than of the original word: "Workers receive launches, ships, hospitals, wages, levels." Occasionally two answers are so related as to be eliminated from consideration as possible right answers: "A banker works with stages, *boards,* checks, *saws,* lead." Like many vocabulary tests on the market, this test contains too few easy words to make it very useful or pleasant for its youngest readers. It reveals little about third graders of less than average ability. The ceiling, on the other hand, is challenging for ninth graders.

The paragraph test contains narrative materials with a personal tone. It deals largely with feelings, situations, and motives. The paragraphs are well written for the purpose of testing the three types of comprehension. Like the vocabulary test, however, this test is utterly discouraging to an average third grader. According to the Lorge formula, the first paragraph in Form A is of 3.95 grade difficulty; in Form B, 4.4 grade difficulty. The samples are equally discouraging. In Form A the sentence length averages from about 7 to 30 words per sentence per paragraph. But the first paragraph in Form B averages 11 words per sentence. Thus in certain respects the forms are scarcely comparable.

For some curious reason the authors have mixed the order of types of questions so that they appear in different order for each selection. Considering the importance of setting purposes for reading and considering the fact that the sample already prepares the pupil for the types of question, it seems odd to offer a baffling lack of consistency to the pupil and unnecessary difficulty in scoring to the teacher.

The test, excellent in concept and carefully developed, is unattractive in format, even unpleasant to read, with small type, crowded lines, and poor paper. In its present form the younger readers should not be required to read it. A test as admirably constructed as this test deserves a better appearance.

It is to be hoped that the authors will extend the test downward in difficulty to accommodate the younger readers, rather than continue to disappoint the third grade teacher who accepts the publisher's claim that the test is suitable for grades 3 to 9.

This is not a test of the pupil's ability to read science and social-study textbooks. It is a test of general vocabulary and of major types of comprehension in the reading of story material. It is one of the best available.

For an excerpt from a review by Albert Grant, see 40:1558.

[493]

Primary Reading: Every Pupil Test. Grades 2-3; 1946; new form usually issued each April and December; forms April, December 1946; 2¢ per test; 1¢ per answer key; 13(20) minutes; constructed by primary teachers of Maple Heights (Ohio) schools under the supervision of A. E. Hadfield; Ohio Scholarship Tests, Ohio State Department of Education.

William S. Gray, Professor of Education, The University of Chicago, Chicago, Illinois. [Review of forms for April and December, 1946.] These tests are a part of a battery of reading tests for use in grades 2 to 12, inclusive, in studying the achievement of pupils, primarily in Ohio. They are not standardized tests in the usual sense of the term, different forms being developed twice a year for use throughout the state. As soon as a specific form has been given in local school systems, the scores are sent to the State Department of Education, which prepares special Class Percentile Comparison Forms which make it possible for each class and school to compare the ranking of its pupils with state-wide norms.

The test consists of six parts designed to measure achievement in six types of reading: Type I, Sentence Recognition, consists of ten exercises, each of which includes four sentences and a picture. The pupil is directed to draw a line from the picture to the sentence which belongs with it. Type II, Word Recognition, consists of eight exercises, each of which includes four words and a picture. The pupil is directed to draw a line from a picture to the word that belongs to it. Type III, Following Directions, consists of five exercises, each of which includes a short paragraph followed by a picture and three sentences. Each sentence directs the pupil to do something. Type IV, Details, consists of six exercises, each of which includes a paragraph and two incomplete sentences followed by three words or phrases in each case. The pupil is directed to underline the word or words that make the sentence correct. Type V, Larger and Total Meanings, consists of six exercises similar in form to the exercises in Type IV. The pupil underlines the word or phrase in each case that gives the correct answer. Type VI, Auditory Test, consists of fifteen exercises in which the pupils must discriminate one word heard from three words seen.

The test requires only 22 minutes of actual working time. The fact that it is so brief points to one of its chief weaknesses. Only one minute, for example, is allowed for the test on word recognition. The number of words for which meanings are indicated is eight. This section of the test is too limited, therefore, to insure a reliable measure of a pupil's meaning vocabulary. One of two alternative plans could be adopted: first, to extend the time for each part of the test, thus making more exercises possible; or, second, to reduce the number of types of reading tested.

The exercises to test ability to follow directions are open to the criticism that the right answers can be indicated in many cases without reading the introductory paragraph, for example, "Draw two lines under the mailman." Pupils who merely execute the directions will obviously make a much higher score than the pupil who reads the paragraph first and then does what the directions tell him to do. Similar criticisms may be made of other sections of the test.

The validity of sections of the test is also open to question. For example, in the section on larger and total meanings, the pupils are asked to read a paragraph and then to check the right answer: "What were the shoes made of (wood, cloth, animal skins)?" This measures the recognition of a detail in one sentence only rather than the grasp of a larger or total meaning. Similarly, the auditory test is not a valid measure of auditory discrimination because it is impossible in given cases to determine whether poor auditory or poor visual discrimination is the cause of failure or just lack of word recognition.

Virginia Seavey, Assistant, Child Placement Department, Public Schools, Brookline, Massachusetts. [Review of forms for April and December 1946.] As these two tests were constructed to provide for the needs of the schools in a particular state, they are probably of greatest value when used as originally intended to measure pupil achievement throughout the state of Ohio in December and again in April. The first test is also intended to be used for analyzing reading difficulties and pointing the way toward a remedial program. Teachers are furnished with percentile norms based on 12,000 second grade scores, and 13,000 third grade scores. Any other school system administering these tests should compute its own percentile norms. This is a time-consuming task and a disadvantage to be considered in adopting this testing program in preference to tests that provide national norms. It is also true that teachers in general find it more helpful to know reading age and grade norms than only the percentile rank and that it would be more practicable to compare the December and April scores on that basis. It appears to this reviewer that teachers also need to know how their classes rate before the first of December, particularly if a remedial program is to function effectively. Too little time elapses between the December and April tests for an appreciable amount of progress to take place in the case of average or inferior readers. If the first test were given earlier in the year, it would be necessary to include easier items at the beginning of each section.

Reliability is not reported for these tests,

nor is the method of selection of items described. The vocabulary has been drawn from standard word lists; and while the test has not been scaled, the material in each section increases in difficulty. An item analysis has been made on the difficulty of each item. The table of norms showing the per cent of correct responses to each item indicates that the test has been carefully constructed. The vocabulary is well chosen, particularly from the standpoint of measuring skill in phonetic analysis. The booklet is well planned except that the type is too small for second graders. In a few places the printing is poor with a letter blurred. The pictures, however, are clear and attractive.

A measure of the five types of reading included in this test should give a teacher an excellent picture of her pupils' achievement. As the test now stands with very short time limits, it is definitely a speed test. It is more advisable in the primary grades to allow enough time to obtain a true measure of a child's range and power of reading ability.

[494]

Primary Reading Test. Grade 1; 1939–40; Forms A, B; $1.14 per 25; 15¢ per specimen set, postpaid; (40-55) minutes; Albert G. Reilley; Houghton Mifflin Co.

REFERENCES

1. POSTON, FREDA L. *An Evaluation of Techniques of Matching Words and Pictures as Measures of Word Recognition and Word Meaning in First and Second Grades.* Unpublished master's thesis, Ohio University, 1941. Pp. 76. (*Abstracts of Masters' Theses . . .*, 1941, pp. 67-8.)

Ruth Lowes, Associate Professor of Education, The West Texas State Teachers College, Canyon, Texas. Achievement in word recognition, word meaning, sentence meaning, and paragraph meaning is measured. The test may be given at the end of the first grade or at the beginning of the second. Two sittings are required. Time is allowed for approximately 90 per cent of the class to finish.

Claims that the test is a valid one are based on the fact that the following criteria were used in its construction: (*a*) Vocabulary was selected almost entirely from the first thousand words in the Thorndike list; of the words used nearly 90 per cent are in the Horn–Packer list. (*b*) Concepts used are all familiar to first grade pupils. (*c*) Mechanically the test approximates acceptable primary grade standards. (*d*) The reading content and illustrations are interesting and stimulating. (*e*) All responses are nonverbal. No statement is made concerning the reliability of the test.

For purposes of standardization the test was given to 700 pupils in seventeen carefully selected rural and urban schools. Several states were represented in the selection. A table of percentiles is given. The manual calls attention to the advantage of the graph in comparing class averages or individual scores with the norm established for each part of the test.

An effort has been made to suggest remedial treatment for pupils found weak in sentence and paragraph meaning. The suggestions are not as specific as they might be.

The test folder is large (10 by 12 inches) and difficult to file. The pages devoted to word recognition and word meaning are well filled. One wonders if the pupils, especially the slow readers, would not be discouraged by the layout.

[495]

★**Primary Reading Test: Acorn Achievement Tests.** Grades 2-3; 1943; Forms A, B; $1.50 per 25; 15¢ per specimen set; 31(40) minutes; Winifred E. Stayton, Frances C. Ranson, and Roland L. Beck; Acorn Publishing Co.

Alice N. Jameson, Assistant, Child Placement Department, Public Schools, Brookline, Massachusetts. This test purports to measure word recognition, word meaning, and reading comprehension. Word recognition and reading comprehension are tested as distinct parts. Part A, Reading Vocabulary, comprises the first three tests: (1) Word Recognition, (2) Words—Similar Meaning, and (3) Word Meaning—Opposites. Part B, Reading Comprehension, includes five graded stories each of which measures story, paragraph, and sentence meaning.

This test could be used only for a rough survey and not for analysis or diagnosis. It has been standardized on a very small population about whom no information is given. Furthermore, no data are presented on the reliability of the five part scores. Reliability is based on a wide range of ability—grades 2, 3, 4—which results in a high reliability index.

The data on validity are based on too few cases and upon criteria some of which are of dubious value. It is correlated over a three-grade range, which gives a spuriously high coefficient.

Norms are given for both Forms A and B which range from grades 2 to 7, but no data accompany them to explain their basis.

This examiner would like to comment on the time limit given in Test 1, Word Recogni-

tion. At the beginning of the test it states, "Time limit: 5 minutes." This is superfluous if the later direction is followed—"Watch group and allow 10 seconds for each word."

In Part B, the examiner would question the suitability of the material for second and third grade children.

The test is printed in large, boldface type, and it is well spaced and easy to read.

[496]

Purdue Reading Test. Grades 7-16; 1928; Forms A, B; $2 per 25; 25¢ per manual; 45¢ per specimen set, postpaid; 40(45) minutes; H. H. Remmers and John M. Stalnaker; Lafayette Printing Co.

Albert J. Harris, Assistant Professor of Education, The City College of New York, New York, New York. The content of the silent reading test includes a 40-item sentence reading subtest and nine fairly long selections, taken from books suitable for college use in a variety of fields. Each selection is followed by 10 to 18 questions, for the most part in true-false form. A single score is obtained, which depends partly upon comprehension and partly on rate of reading. Scoring, by means of a key, is completely objective.

The reliability is only fair by today's standards, with an r between the two forms of .855 for a range of eight grades, or about .75 for a single grade. The norms provided include the arithmetic means for each grade, based on a maximum of 237 cases for any one grade, chiefly from consolidated schools in Indiana. A table of percentile scores is also given, in which the scores from all grades are combined.

The test may be considered a commendable pioneering effort, but it does not equal in value such competing tests as the *Nelson–Denny Reading Test* or the Cooperative reading tests.

[497]

★**Reading Comprehension: Cooperative English Test: Lower and Higher Levels, Tests C1 and C2.** Grades 7-12, 13-16; 1941-43; commonly called *Cooperative Reading Comprehension Test;* IBM; Forms R, S, T; 2 levels; $2 per 25; 25¢ per specimen set of either level, postpaid; 40¢ per 25 machine-scorable answer sheets; 15¢ per stencil for scoring answer sheets; 40(45) minutes; Frederick B. Davis, Harold V. King (Form S), and Mary Willis (Form T); Cooperative Test Service.
a) LOWER LEVEL. Grades 7-12.
b) HIGHER LEVEL. Grades 13-16.

REFERENCES

1-2. See 40:1564.
3. RYANS, DAVID G. *The First Step in Guidance: Self-Appraisal: A Report of the 1940 Sophomore Testing Program.* Cooperative Test Service Publications in Measurement and Guidance. Series 3, Vol. 1, No. 1. New York: Cooperative Test Service, January 1941. Pp. 35. Paper. $0.10. * (PA 15:2382)

4. DAVIS, FREDERICK B. "Fundamental Factors of Comprehension in Reading." Abstract. *Psychol B* 39:499-500 Jl '42. * (*PA* 16:5007, title only)

5. DAVIS, FREDERICK B. "Two New Measures of Reading Ability." *J Ed Psychol* 33:364-72 My '42. * (*PA* 17:1337)

6. SIMPSON, R. G. "The Vocabulary Sections of the Cooperative English Tests at the Higher Levels of Difficulty." *J Ed Psychol* 34:142-51 Mr '43. * (*PA* 18:311)

7. DAVIS, FREDERICK B. "Fundamental Factors of Comprehension in Reading." *Psychometrika* 9:185-97 S '44. * (*PA* 19:242)

8. DAVIS, FREDERICK B. "What Do Reading Tests *Really* Measure?" *Engl J* 33:180-7 Ap '44. * (*PA* 18:2250)

9. HENRY, LORNE J. "The Diagnostic Value of a Standardized Reading Test." *Sch, Sec Ed* 32:884-7 Je '44. *

10. DAVIS, FREDERICK B. "A Brief Comment on Thurstone's Note on the Reanalysis of Davis' Reading Test." *Psychometrika* 11:249-55 D '46. * (*PA* 21:978)

11. DAVIS, FREDERICK B. "Fundamental Factors of Reading Comprehension." *Psychometrika* 11:185-8 S '46. *

12. DAVIS, FREDERICK B. "The Factorial Composition of Two Tests of Comprehension in Reading." *J Ed Psychol* 37:481-6 N '46. * (*PA* 21:1632)

13. PEIXOTTO, HELEN E. "The Relationship of College Board Examination Scores and Reading Scores for College Freshmen." *J Appl Psychol* 30:406-11 Ag '46. * (*PA* 21:289)

14. THURSTONE, L. L. "Note on a Reanalysis of Davis' Reading Tests." *Psychometrika* 11:185-8 S '46. * (*PA* 21:295)

15. TRAXLER, ARTHUR E. "Reading and Secondary-School Achievement," pp. 59-63. In *1946 Achievement Testing Program in Independent Schools and Supplementary Studies.* Educational Records Bulletin, No. 45. New York: Educational Records Bureau, June 1946. Pp. x, 63. Paper, lithotyped. $1.50. * (*PA* 20:4354)

16. VOTAW, DAVID F. "A Comparison of Test Scores of Entering College Freshmen as Instruments for Predicting Subsequent Scholarship." *J Ed Res* 40:215-8 N '46. * (*PA* 21:1304)

17. "A Note on the Correlation Between the Iowa and Cooperative Reading Tests," p. 66. In *1947 Achievement Testing Program in Independent Schools and Supplementary Studies.* Educational Records Bulletin, No. 48. New York: Educational Records Bureau, June 1947. Pp. xii, 66. Paper, lithotyped. $2.00. *

Robert Murray Bear, Professor of Psychology and Director of the Reading Clinic, Dartmouth College, Hanover, New Hampshire. Each test has two parts, recognition vocabulary and paragraph reading. The range of difficulty of the 60 vocabulary words is adequate for the grades covered; one subsequent study of a form of the higher level, C2, has confirmed the generally accurate placement of words in order of difficulty. The undesirable influence of speed of recognition on the score is minimized through the use of an ample time limit. The reading paragraphs of Part 2 sample different types of subject matter and are followed by five-choice items testing four main types of skills. As with the vocabulary part, item validity and difficulty were determined by preliminary experimentation. The tests received the benefit of rather careful standardization before publication.

Perhaps the most unusual feature is that the 90 comprehension items are arranged in three repeating scales of equivalent difficulty, each containing 30 questions based upon from 4 to 8 paragraphs per scale. A few paragraphs are as short as three dozen words. Though Part 2 yields scores that differentiate well enough between students with wide differences in reading skill, differentiation is not as satisfactory for others, because of the fact that the scoring

range is very contracted, particularly in the case of students with only one scale completed, of whom there may be as many as 10 per cent in a college freshman class.

While a speed-of-comprehension score is obtained from a count of the total number of items accurately answered, level of comprehension is scored by counting only items of completed scales. This eliminates the influence of speed upon the comprehension score and makes it a better measure of power of comprehension than is obtained in other timed tests. The correlation between level of comprehension and speed of comprehension for the lower level tests is .89 and for the higher level, .87, suggesting a considerable influence of comprehension upon the speed score. The speed score thus is not comparable with rate of reading as the student usually thinks of it or with his performance upon the rate sections of several other tests used in these grades. For example, the correlation between words read per minute on the essay of the Booker *Test of Achievement in Silent Reading* and the speed of comprehension on Form Q of Test C2 was only .317 for 176 college freshmen.

A useful feature in scoring is that by reference to tables all raw scores can be converted into standard scores which are directly comparable and permit comparison of relative proficiency in vocabulary, speed, and level of comprehension.

Reliability coefficients have been computed which show considerable stability at the 50 point of the scaled scores. These range from .75 on C1 and .82 on C2 for level of comprehension with only one scale completed to better than .9 for vocabulary and total scores. For secondary and college groups, correlations of between .7 and .8 with intelligence tests have been reported, and of between .39 and .73 with school marks. Thus, we may conclude that these reading tests have about the same relation to school achievement as do group intelligence tests. Incorporation by the publisher of the findings of these various studies into his descriptive folder would be helpful to users. Directions for administering each test are not supplied separately, but are given in a generalized form to fit all Cooperative tests. One unacquainted with Cooperative test procedure may at first be somewhat puzzled to fit together the directions to be used.

For the grades intended these survey tests

are among the best for measuring reading comprehension of the usual types of subject matter but should be supplemented by some other test if measures of the pupil's usual rates are desired.

J. B. Stroud, Professor of Education and Psychology, The State University of Iowa, Iowa City, Iowa. The test consists of Part I, Vocabulary (15 minutes), and Part II, Reading (25 minutes). The reading test features a speed of comprehension score and a level of comprehension score, obtainable from the same set of exercises. It consists of three comparable scales of 30 items each. The speed of comprehension score is number right minus a fraction of number wrong; maximum raw score is 90. The level of comprehension score is in effect the average number right, minus a correction, on the scales completed; in effect, maximum raw score is 30.

Scaled scores, the size of the unit being one-tenth of a standard deviation of the distribution of scores, are provided for raw scores on vocabulary, speed, level, and total. Standard errors are indicated at various points along the scaled scores in vertical lines extending in both directions, to the distance of twice the standard error. Separate percentile norms based upon scaled scores are provided for 11- and 12-year schools and three types of colleges, which seems justified by the differences obtained.

The test essays separate measurement of rate and comprehension. In this it succeeds as well as any test now available. The level of comprehension score is a particularly fortunate one. The rate of comprehension score is not quite so good as it sounds since in effect the score is influenced by rate of not comprehending. It is the equivalent of the traditional comprehension score and as such is a function both of rate and of comprehension. Perhaps it is in order to say that there is not any one single procedure that is adequate for measuring rate of reading. The level of comprehension score is not complicated by rate except for students who do not complete the first scale and for the possibility that quality may be influenced by the rate set of the student. The advantages of such a score in clinical work, reading instruction, and research are obvious.

In the vocabulary test the examinee is not generally required to make any close discrimination between the correct responses and the foils. The foils contain a good many ruses, words with the same prefixes or suffixes, and other kinds of formal similarity. Use is also made of a kind of second order similarity; e.g., for the word *rudimentary,* the foil *impolite* suggests *rude;* for the word *averse,* the foil *poetry* suggests *verse* and the foil *upside down* suggests *reverse.*

The reading test items are quite good and the reading test is well chosen, although it runs a bit heavily toward literature. The items will probably appeal to English teachers more than to social studies and science teachers. Tests of understanding of mood and purpose and of word meaning in context are featured.

It would be difficult to find a test better conceived and better executed within the limits of its objectives.

For reviews by J. Paul Leonard, Edward S. Noyes, and Robert C. Pooley of the entire battery, see 120.

[498]
Reading Comprehension Test: National Achievement Tests. Grades 3-8; 1938; Forms A, B; $1.50 per 25; 15¢ per specimen set; nontimed (30) minutes; Robert K. Speer and Samuel Smith; Acorn Publishing Co.

James R. Hobson, Director of Child Placement, Public Schools, Brookline, Massachusetts. This test is divided into three parts: I, Following Directions; II, Sentence Meaning; III, Paragraph Meaning. There is nothing to indicate the more specific reading skills which this test is designed to measure. There is no manual worthy of the name and the teacher's directions, class record, answer form and norms are all contained on the two sides of an 8½ by 11 inch sheet of paper. This test is announced as being part of a very ambitious teach-study-test program, whch was to have included achievement tests, diagnostic tests, bulletins for teachers, and bulletins for pupils in every subject practically from the cradle to the grave. If these materials have been developed, this reviewer has not seen them. However, they have little to do with the intrinsic worth of this test.

The defects of this test are so many and so gross that it is difficult to assemble them in any systematic pattern for criticism. To begin with, the material in the test items strikes **this** reviewer as utterly inane and as obviously fabricated for the purpose. It **is** in any event far removed from a normal functional reading situation for any child.

Secondly, the grade range of the test is so extensive as to greatly diminish its actual usefulness if it were otherwise meritorious. Any test which contains enough items of sufficient difficulty to measure the reading abilities of eighth grade children is far too formidable and discouraging for the average third grade child. Conversely, the eighth grade pupils have to wade through too many easy test items which do not discriminate among them before they reach the ones which do. In effect a 30-minute test becomes only about a 15-minute test for the extremes of such a range. Such a test is actually fully effective for only about the middle half of its announced grade range. It follows also that any reliability coefficients based on the entire grade range are spuriously high. The reliability of this test for a single grade is quoted as .92. There is no information as to what grade this is for. This reliability seems very high for what amounts to about a fifteen-minute test at most grade levels.

Another criticism is that in the authors' announced attempt to include "important types of questions that had been ignored or underemphasized in other tests," they appear to have gone too far in the other direction by making 10 of 36 items in the test consist of following directions. This type of item is often used and quite properly belongs in a verbal intelligence test. Its extensive use in a reading test is not justified in the opinion of this reviewer. It is not surprising that the authors have felt constrained to develop norms for high, low, and average IQ's.

The fact that a difference of one item often means a difference of about three months in grade level, combined with the fact that three-choice restricted answer questions, which comprise 26 of the 36 test items, are scored without any correction for chance guessing, not only shows that this test is not very finely graduated but casts doubt upon its basic validity and reliability as well.

The statement made that this test has no time limit is followed by the statement that "the time generally taken is 30 minutes" but that this "will vary according to age and grade." Such directions are much too ambiguous to give to classroom teachers. You cannot make a test a power test merely by eliminating the time limit.

Finally the claims made for this test in almost every aspect are so extravagant and are backed up by so little real data that they immediately alienate anyone who wishes to know the detailed background of instruments he recommends for use.

[499]

★Schonell Reading Tests. 1942; 4 tests; 2s. 6d. per 12 of any test; 20s. per copy of Schonell's *Backwardness in the Basic Subjects,* Third Edition, which serves as the test manual for Tests R2, R3, and R4; Fred J. Schonell; Oliver & Boyd Ltd.
a) TEST R2, SIMPLE PROSE READING TEST. Ages 6-9; also called *My Dog Test;* individual; (3-8) minutes.
b) TEST R3, SILENT READING TEST A. Ages 7-11; 9(15) minutes.
c) TEST R4, SILENT READING TEST B. Ages 9-13; 15(20) minutes.
d) GRADED WORD READING TEST. Ages 5-15; also called *Graded Reading Vocabulary Test;* individual; 6s. per copy of Schonell's *The Psychology and Teaching of Reading,* Second Edition, which serves as the test manual.

REFERENCES
1. SCHONELL, FRED J. *Backwardness in the Basic Subjects,* Third Edition. Edinburgh, Scotland: Oliver and Boyd Ltd., 1946. Pp. xix, 560. 20s. (Toronto, Canada: Clarke, Irwin & Co. Ltd. $7.00.) *
2. SCHONELL, FRED J. *The Psychology and Teaching of Reading,* Second Edition. Edinburgh, Scotland: Oliver & Boyd Ltd., 1946. Pp. 128. 6s. * (Toronto, Canada: Clarke, Irwin & Co. Ltd.)

Edith I. M. Thomson, Lecturer in Education, University of Edinburgh, Edinburgh, Scotland. These tests are intended primarily for the diagnosis of backwardness in reading, the graded reading and simple prose tests being individually administered and the silent reading tests being used mainly for groups, though Test R3 may also be given with individual timing.

The Graded Word Reading Test is similar to Burt's and Vernon's Graded Word Vocabulary Tests, and may be regarded as an alternative version for them. It provides a rapid measure of efficiency in word attack from 5 to 15 years and a useful preliminary to the more detailed tests.

The Simple Prose Test is suitable for pupils from ages 6 to 9 and provides three measurements: speed, accuracy, and comprehension. The study of individual errors is aided by Dr. Schonell's detailed notes in *Backwardness in the Basic Subjects* (1). The test proves interesting and not too alarming for poor readers; the size of print and the arrangement of the paragraphs are planned to resemble the layout of books for six- and seven-year-olds. For the sake of the poorest readers it might be an advantage to have an arrangement like that of Gates in his Oral Context Test, where detailed measurements may be made by the use of the first and easiest paragraphs.

The Silent Reading Tests consist of paragraphs each followed by a question or a multiple-choice problem, and they may be repeatedly used, since the answers are written on a separate paper. It will be noted that this implies writing a word, not merely underlining, and it might be objected that slow writers are penalised.

One would be glad of a separate manual for the tests. Instructions and norms are to be found only in a large book *Backwardness in the Basic Subjects;* and while it is appreciated that the clinic worker will wish to use this book for the study of cases, convenience in testing would be served by having a less cumbersome testing guide.

Again, one would like to know more about the background group on whom the tests were standardised. The Simple Prose Test was based on 650 cases; numbers at each age are not given, and one misses data on reliability. For the Graded Word Reading Test no particulars are given—only norms. The Silent Reading Tests were standardised on 1860 pupils, and again no particulars as to age are given. Correlations between these tests and the *Simplex Junior Group Intelligence Scale* are given in the case of 210 pupils from 8 to 11; the coefficients for number correct with IQ range from .67 to .86, but the number of cases at any age is never above 63. The reliability coefficient of Test B is given as .92. No doubt Dr. Schonell has by this time accumulated more data, and it would be an advantage to have it published.

[500]

Schrammel-Gray High School and College Reading Test. Grades 7-13; 1940–42; Forms A, B; $1.80 per 25; 36¢ per specimen set, postpaid; 25(30) minutes; H. E. Schrammel and W. H. Gray; Public School Publishing Co.

James M. McCallister, Director of Personnel Service, Herzl Branch, Chicago City Junior College, Chicago, Illinois. This test consists of 25 paragraphs, each of which is followed by three or five objective items to be checked true or false. The total number of items is 100. The scoring arrangement provides three measures of reading ability: (*a*) a gross-comprehension score in terms of the number of questions answered correctly, (*b*) rate of reading in terms of words per minute, and (*c*) compre-

hension-efficiency as shown by the ratio of the number of items checked correctly to the number attempted.

A test that covers the range of reading abilities from the seventh grade through college must of necessity contain a variety of materials as to difficulty and interest. The manual states that the paragraphs were selected from a wide variety of sources that would prove interesting to students at each level. Because of the wide range represented, it is important that the validity of the test be established at the various levels. Validity coefficients are reported for the college freshman level only. These coefficients are based on correlations between the test scores and composite decile ranks computed from scores on tests in intelligence, English, vocabulary, spelling, mathematics, reading, and current history. The coefficients, which range from .67 to .97, suggest that the test is valid for the upper levels of the range. Additional data are needed for the lower levels.

Internal analysis of the test paragraphs and the true-false items indicates that the test measures largely apprehension of specific facts. It provides little opportunity for measuring such things as comprehension of main ideas, recognition of relationships and sequences among ideas, or judging relative importance of ideas from the standpoint of the intent of the writers of the passages. The limitations of a test to the measurement of restricted phases of reading ability may be readily justified by the authors, but it must be kept in mind in interpreting the scores as measures of general reading ability.

The test was studied for reliability by comparing alternate forms and by comparing the three measures obtained on single forms. Coefficients of correlation reported for a ninth grade group vary from .63 to .86. The authors also report that "a student's true score, in 50 per cent of the cases, does not diverge from his obtained score by 9.3 points or less in the case of rate, by 4.1 points or less in the case of gross comprehension, and by 4.7 points or less in the case of comprehension efficiency." These data indicate that the test is sufficiently reliable for measurement of group accomplishments, but that it should be used with caution in making individual diagnoses.

The test has the decided advantages of being easily administered and readily interpreted. The meanings attached to the three measurements make the results readily understandable to both students and teachers. The manual contains excellent tables for translating raw scores into percentile ranks and grade norms. It should be particularly valuable in making initial surveys of the reading abilities of large groups for the purpose of screening out students who need further testing and study.

Robert L. McCaul, Instructor and Adviser in the College, The University of Chicago, Chicago, Illinois. The authors declare that this test is an instrument "of considerable diagnostic value." With all due allowance for the pride with which testmakers ordinarily speak of their products, this statement must still be considered an exaggeration. The test is actually of little diagnostic value. It provides only three scores: (*a*) a gross comprehension score consisting of the number of correct answers; (*b*) a rate score of the number of words read per minute; and (*c*) a comprehension-efficiency score which is the ratio between gross comprehension and rate.

When these scores are analyzed, the test's flaws as a diagnostic instrument become manifest. Each of the 25 test paragraphs is followed by three to five true-false items. Since these items are of a factual nature, the gross comprehension score indicates merely that the student is strong, weak, or mediocre in one element of reading—apprehension of facts. We do not know why, nor do we have evidence of the quality of his ability to organize what he reads, select central ideas, follow and evaluate causal relationships, or perform any of the other tasks involved in securing meaning from the printed page.

Similar deficiencies characteristize the speed score derived from the test. The material read includes a poem and paragraphs culled from psychology, music, biology, social science, and general publications. What is obtained from the test, therefore, is a single speed score which represents heterogeneous speeds upon heterogeneous materials. Not only is it impossible to determine how adequate a measure of speed the score is, but it is likewise impossible to estimate how much the speed on each type of material contributes to the total raw score. Yet for diagnosis we should know whether the student read the poem more slowly than he did the paragraph about a frog jumping contest, the paragraph describing Chinese music more slowly than the one about coloring dogs to match women's frocks, etc. It is fair to conclude that there exist

more complete and less ambiguous diagnostic reading tests than the Schrammel–Gray.

Elsewhere in the manual the authors assert that the "test possesses marked predictive value as regards scholastic success." They base this statement upon correlations of .73, .67, and .87 between college-freshman scores on the three parts of their test and composite decile ranks computed from tests of intelligence, English, vocabulary, spelling, mathematics, reading, and current history. Such reasoning seems hazardous. After all, the test correlates an average of .76 with a composite validity criterion which itself probably correlates no more than .70 with teachers' grades. Numerous investigations have proved, moreover, that a single test of a specific trait, aptitude, or achievement does not furnish a trustworthy predictive measure. Thus, the authors' belief in the "marked" prognostic value of their test as well as their faith in its "considerable diagnostic value" must be accepted with reservations.

The Schrammel–Gray High School and College Reading Test suffers more from the extravagant claims of the authors than from any serious weaknesses in construction and content. It does not compare unfavorably with many tests on the market, and it could be a rather useful survey instrument.

Ed Res B 21:47 F 18 '42. William J. Jones. * includes unusually descriptive and informative reading material designed to keep the interest of the students while taking the test. * The test appears to have validity as a predictor of scholastic success. The test has reported reliabilities varying from .63 to .86 on part scores, not high enough to place a lot of confidence in the stability of individual student scores. * a good test * should be examined by those interested in reading.

[501]

Silent Reading Comprehension: Iowa Every-Pupil Tests of Basic Skills, Test A. Grades 3-5, 5-9; 1940-45; IBM, grades 5-9; Forms L, M, N, O; 2 levels; 44¢ per specimen set of either level; H. F. Spitzer in collaboration with Ernest Horn, Maude McBroom, H. A. Greene, and E. F. Lindquist; Houghton Mifflin Co.
a) ELEMENTARY BATTERY. Grades 3-5; $1.50 per 25; 46(50) minutes.
b) ADVANCED BATTERY. Grades 5-9; IBM; separate answer sheets need not be used; $1.60 per 25; 50¢ per 25 machine-scorable answer sheets; 15¢ per machine-scoring stencil; 68(85) minutes.

James R. Hobson, Director of Child Placement, Public Schools, Brookline, Massachusetts.

These tests are the reading tests of a comprehensive achievement test battery measuring the fundamental skills developed in the elementary school. This battery is the outgrowth of the Iowa Every-Pupil Testing Program initiated in 1929 and extended down as far as grade 3 beginning in 1940.

The nation-wide distribution and use of these tests is entirely incidental to their annual use in all Iowa schools and has come about by reason of their intrinsic merit rather than through exploitation by the Iowa State educational authorities.

The four silent reading skills other than vocabulary measured by the elementary reading-comprehension test are paragraph comprehension, noting details, organization of ideas, and grasp of total meaning. The test material ranges from short paragraphs followed by from three to five questions to a 450-word story followed by 15 questions. The restricted answer technique is used with four choices in each instance.

The Advanced Battery is parallel to the Elementary Battery in abilities measured and method of indicating answers. The reading selections used, however, are of much greater length and consist of description, exposition, and historical narrative as contrasted with the simple exposition and fictional narrative of the elementary test. The selections in the advanced test average nearly 700 words in length, and as many as 19 questions are asked about each selection.

The reading selections in both tests appear to be interesting and well chosen. They are obviously the type of reading a child encounters in normal elementary school assignments in various subject matter fields. In both tests the skills to be measured govern the types of questions asked.

The vocabulary test consists of 40 items in the elementary test and 50 items in the advanced test. In some instances the word to be defined is presented in a complete sentence and in others in only a two- or three-word phrase, which in the opinion of this reviewer is less desirable. The four-choice restricted-answer technique is used in both tests.

All of the answers for the advanced test are marked on a single answer sheet on the inside of the front cover, which is perforated for easy detachment. There is no reason why standard IBM answer sheets could not be adapted to this test and machine scoring used.

The manuals for these tests are extremely practical and well arranged for easy understanding by the classroom teacher. The directions for administering and scoring are clear and concise. Three kinds of norms are given: grade equivalents, age equivalents, and grade percentiles, all based, of course, on the performance of Iowa public school children.

The aids to interpretation and practical use of the results of these tests are many and varied. These include the class record, the individual profile and cumulative record, an item analysis of the skills involved, and a particularly complete set of suggestions for developing the reading skills in which pupils may show deficiencies.

No objective data are presented regarding the validity and reliability of these tests. In fact, no particular section of the manual is devoted to these subjects, although the method of developing the tests and selecting the items is given. In spite of the lack of statistical evidence of validity, the use of such criteria in the selection of test items as analysis of course of study, textbooks, and instructional procedures as well as the pooled judgments of the group of authors, most of whom are outstanding figures in the evaluation field, does much to guarantee high validity for this test battery when applied to Iowa children.

Theoretically, this validity will be reduced somewhat when the tests are used outside the Iowa situation. Actually, the nature of reading skills is such as to give this type of test practically nation-wide applicability. Since such a strong point is made of the equivalence of the annual forms of this test and the comparability from year to year which makes a cumulative record and profile really meaningful, consistency would seem to demand some statistical evidence of the reliability of these instruments. None is given.

It goes without saying that none of the three types of norms given will prove very useful outside Iowa except for purposes of comparison and that any school system making use of these tests will have to develop its own norms, which of course is always a good idea. It does appear, however, that a publishing house undertaking the national distribution of tests of this apparent high quality should seek a wider base for their standardization.

Constance M. McCullough, Assistant Professor of Education, San Francisco State College,

San Francisco, California. The test authors have developed the instructions for administering, scoring, interpretation, and remediation, with painstaking care. Their sound insistence, within the test itself, upon comprehension questions that require genuine reading ability and genuine thought is admirable and somewhat unusual in the commercial field.

The paragraph content is science and social studies, sometimes disguised in narrative and conversation form. The elementary battery starts with one paragraph and builds up to a six-paragraph selection; the advanced battery starts with three and builds to six. The number and types of question vary with the content of the selection. The authors profess to be testing four types of comprehension: paragraph, details, organization, and total meaning. But the overlapping of their suggestions for remedial work establishes their failure to select distinct types. For this reason the value of the part scores within the comprehension test is considerably diminished.

Because of their effort to suit the questions to the passages tested, the number of items available to suggest mastery of each type of comprehension is often uneven and inadequate within a given form and extremely irregular between forms. The forms are not at all comparable in this respect. The test is overburdened with detail questions. The authors would have done better, both for scorers and for balance, to construct paragraphs with uniformity of questioning in mind. Aside from this weakness, the excellence of the questions themselves cannot be overemphasized. Someone with a keen appreciation of reading-as-thinking had a hand in this test. A teacher capable of reclassifying the questions as to the comprehension ability tested could draw much of value from her findings.

The difficulty of the paragraphs according to the Lorge formula is not uniform for the different forms or extensive enough for the grades the test claims to cover. In the Elementary Battery, the first paragraph in Form L is of 4.8 grade difficulty; in Form M, 4.0 difficulty. Hardest paragraphs in Form L are about 4.9; in Form M, about 4.6. The range scarcely justifies the claim that the test is suitable for grades 3 to 5. Easier and harder paragraphs are needed.

The elementary vocabulary test contains 40 items; the advanced 50, of general vocabulary. In both cases the words are much too difficult for the younger pupils tested and also in comparison with the vocabulary of the paragraphs in Part 1. In the Elementary Battery, Form L, only 2 of the vocabulary words appear in Dale's list of 769 easy words, and 35 per cent of the right answers are harder words than the ones tested. The norms reflect the fact that the vocabulary section is far out of the reach of many of the children tested. Logically, a good many words in the vocabulary section should have been chosen from the harder words in the paragraphs in Part 1. If the paragraphs were representative of material the children should be able to read, the words they contain would be also. The authors missed the opportunity to make the vocabulary section a tool in the interpretation of the comprehension results.

The elaborate directions in the manual for scoring the test, the perforated answer keys, and the conversion tables on the cover page of the test booklet combine to give the prospective examiner a sense of fear or revulsion. The teacher of 40 children does not want to spend valuable time figuring out the authors' thoughts on how to obtain 40 simple scores on an hour test. It could be wished that there were simple and brief means of obtaining ultimate efficiency and that so much manipulation might be rewarded by a more meaningful, clear-cut diagnosis of separate skills. As it is, the aids to the teacher have far exceeded the point of diminishing returns and are approaching the point of exasperation.

For reviews by Frederic L. Ayer, Gustav J. Froehlich, and Ralph C. Preston of the complete battery, see 10. For reviews by William A. Brownell, J. Murray Lee, and Charles W. Odell of an earlier form of the complete battery, see 38:872.

[502]

★**SRA Reading Record.** Grades 7-12; 1947; 1 form; separate answer pads must be used; 43¢ per test booklet and answer pad; $1.65 per 25 answer pads; 45¢ per 25 profile sheets; 75¢ per specimen set; 28(40) minutes; Guy T. Buswell; Science Research Associates.

Frances Oralind Triggs, Educational Records Bureau, New York, New York. The measurement of reading skills is somewhat difficult because there is no real agreement among authorities on the definition of reading. Buswell defines reading in somewhat narrower terms than do most other reading specialists and his *Reading Record* reflects his thinking. The manual states that the test measures the ten skills "found most essential to satisfactory reading adjustment"— these skills being : rate of reading, reading comprehension, paragraph meaning, directory reading, map-table-graph reading, advertisement reading, index reading, sentence meaning, technical vocabulary, and general vocabulary. The test furnishes a score on rate of reading and total comprehension, as well as scores on nine other skills measured, "a breakdown which is essential to complete reading diagnosis," according to the manual.

The pinprick type of answer sheet accompanies this test; it is scored by counting the holes which appear in the circles printed on the inside of the answer sheet. The answer sheets may be removed from the test booklets and scored by the students, if rescored for checking later. The present edition of the *Record* is not adapted for machine scoring, but it would not be difficult to adapt it. Unless this is done, schools using this test as one of a battery to be scored by a test-scoring service will be handicapped.

The format makes the test physically attractive. It is spirally bound into a seemingly durable, heavy paper cover. The answer sheet is punched to fit easily on to the spiral binding from which it can also be very easily removed. The size of each page of the test booklet varies in accordance with that column on the answer sheet on which the answers are to be punched, making for ease and accuracy of recording. Each test takes up one page. The instructions for each test are printed at the bottom of the preceding test, thus making for ease and accuracy in administering and timing the test.

A number of comments may be made concerning this test. However, it should be noted first that this review is being written before the test is generally available for sale. Thus, the only experimental data available to the reviewer are those furnished by the author in the manual. Comments are based on these data and the experience of the reviewer with other tests in the field.

The test is very closely timed. The manual warns users that "Exact timing of the tests is exceedingly important. Deviation of even five seconds can increase a score ten points. A score on an incorrectly timed test is valueless." Such warning is very pertinent. Excluding the rate of reading test, the number of items varies from 10 to 25 in each subtest; the timing varies from two to three minutes.

The manual gives the median reliabilities for two groups of 1,000 ninth and eleventh grade students. At first glance one wonders, with these short tests, how the reliabilities can be as high as they are: Test 1, Rate of Reading .79 (2 minutes) ; Test 2, Reading Comprehension .75 (2 minutes) (16 items) ; Test 3, Paragraph Meaning .86 (2 minutes) (10 items) ; Test 4, Reading an Alphabetical Directory .96 (3 minutes) (25 items) ; Test 5, Interpretation of Map-Table-Graph Material .86 (3 minutes) (12 items) ; Test 6, Advertising Reading Test .83 (3 minutes) (20 items) ; Test 7, Index Usage .96 (3 minutes) (14 items) ; Test 8, Technical Vocabulary .79 (3 minutes) (23 items) ; Test 9, Sentence Meaning .78 (3 minutes) (19 items) ; Test 10, General Vocabulary .75 (3 minutes) (25 items) ; total score .93 (164 items). While the manual does not so state, the reviewer understands that these reliabilities are Spearman–Brown except for rate of reading, which must be either test-retest (which is not probable as there is only one form of the test) or for which the administration may have been varied to furnish a score for each minute read. It is known that Spearman–Brown reliabilities tend to be overestimates when a test is highly speeded. The reviewer would caution users, therefore, not to put too much emphasis on any one score on this test until more data concerning reliability are available, especially for individual diagnosis. It is probable that the reliabilities on tests which measure specific homogeneous skills— Test 3, Paragraph Meaning; Test 4, Reading an Alphabetical Directory; Test 5, Interpretation of Map-Table-Graph Material; Test 6, Advertisement Reading; and Test 7, Index Usage —are reliable enough for estimating an individual's skills for the specific skills measured by these tests. Reliability of the total score on the test is high enough so that, even though the value is undoubtedly affected by speed, it can be used with confidence that it will not vary markedly on retest.

What of the validity of this test? To what extent does the total score discriminate between efficient and inefficient readers, and to what extent do scores on subtests measure the skills they purport to measure? Also with regard to reliability, it is pertinent to ask to what extent can scores on this test be used to guide a teacher or clinician in remedial work with a student.

It must be stated that validity of a reading test may be judged to some extent on the definition of reading subscribed to. In order to avoid theoretical discussion, it seems wise first to examine the subtests in accordance with the definition of them in the manual.

Test 1 is defined as a measure of rate of reading. Two minutes are allowed for reading a passage of approximately 1,200 words. The topic is of interest, and the vocabulary level would seem to be somewhat simple.

Test 2 is a reading comprehension test. A well-informed reader can answer more than half of the questions without reading the material; most of the questions are questions of detail. The first nine questions are answered in the first six hundred words. This test obviously measures reading comprehension in a very narrow sense—only one question requires any generalization at all, the rest being exactly answered by the content.

Test 3 is called a test of paragraph meaning. Each paragraph is made up of two sentences. One word in the second sentence of each paragraph "spoils the meaning of the paragraph." This test resembles closely a vocabulary test which requires the examinee to recognize the meaning of the word as given by the context.

Test 4 is a measure of ability to read an alphabetical directory. Twenty-five names and addresses are given. The examinee responds by matching correct telephone numbers. This test measures a very specialized, homogeneous skill, which many test specialists would consider clerical, and the reliability reflects this fact. It would be interesting to know the effect which a few short practice periods would have on scores on this test.

Test 5 is a measure of map-table-graph reading. A map, a weather report in tabular form, and a bar graph of average temperature are given. Examinees must find answers to factual questions, based on these pictorial representations. Some questions require reference to more than one of the sources of data. Again, a very specific skill is measured, one that can be learned with very little practice. Though it is true that students do not always have this skill, it can be easily acquired by those who have mastered basic reading skills but probably not by poor readers.

Test 6 is an advertisement reading test. Factual questions are answered by reference to four advertisements of the usual newspaper type. This test probably measures a narrow and specific form of skimming skill. As recognition only, not thought processes, is measured, the skill probably could be attained with a small amount of practice by persons who have mastered basic reading skills.

Test 7 is an index usage test. This test, while of a very specific nature, requires the application of more thought processes than most of the others. The reliability of this test is .96, a surprisingly high value for only 14 items, even though it is probably affected by the highly speeded nature of the test.

Test 8 is called a test of technical vocabulary. The synonym type of item is used. This test is similar to the usual vocabulary test. Test 9 is called a test of sentence meaning but is essentially a measure of vocabulary knowledge. Test 10 is called a test of general vocabulary and utilizes again the usual synonym type of item. It is improbable that the vocabulary tests are difficult enough to discriminate between good and poor readers at the higher level, except as they are very closely timed.

Of these ten subtests, five measure specific skills which may be obtained with practice by good readers but which poor readers would have difficulty attaining until they had mastered the basic reading skills, four measure vocabulary essentially though they are not all entitled vocabulary, and one test measures comprehension and memory of details. This leaves the comprehension of the main thought of a paragraph, ability to draw conclusions and support those conclusions by generalizations and details drawn from reading, ability to read to support generalizations and ability to organize material read almost untouched by this test. These skills are all study-type reading skills needed by students as are the more superficial skills measured by this test. Also, the test does not diagnose the deficiencies of the reader with poor basic reading skills. Few clues for approaching remedial work could be obtained from scores in these cases.

The manual states that "relationships between the tests of the *Record* are moderately high." If these relationships are known, they should have been furnished to users. The point is well taken in the manual that parts which furnish clues for remedial work need not be eliminated just because scores show relationship. There is probably also a close relationship between scores on the types of reading skills which the *Record* does not measure and those measured by the *Record*. However, for a complete diagnosis and for remedial treatment of the usual range of reading deficiencies from the seventh grade through the college freshman year, this test is not broad enough; in other words, it does not measure the types of reading skills most essential to students' everyday reading problems. Four of the tests measure vocabulary skill but do not segregate the skill by specialized fields of knowledge. Five subtests measure skills easily attained by good readers through practice. Therefore, very little of the testing time is left for measuring the type of reading skills most needed by students.

A word should be said about the profile chart. The format is good, and it makes an excellent visual picture of the scores obtained on the test. A study of this profile certainly clearly indicates the extent to which one score point raises a percentile rank. For instance, on Test 5, a score of six is at the 20th percentile and a score of ten is at the 75th percentile, while the ceiling on the test is 12 raw score points. This fact places a great deal of importance on one score point and emphasizes again the effect the speed factor may have on scores in this test.

This reviewer would recommend that this test be used with students known to have the reading skills essential for efficient reading but who may not be using these skills efficiently when applied to the specific skills measured by this test, but not to screen retarded readers or diagnose their deficiencies for the purpose of remedial work.

It would seem that the extent of the use of this test might be affected by its cost. Progress in reading should be measured at least once a year, preferably oftener. There is only one form of this test, a drawback to its frequent use for measuring progress in reading; the cost of frequent testing, however, would be a greater deterrent, since the cost of a single booklet is 43 cents and answer sheets are $1.65 per 25. Profile sheets, which are not absolutely necessary, are 45 cents per 25.

Experience shows that scoring pinprick tests with the clerical help used in a test scoring unit is difficult. It is a slow process, and scorers dislike this type of recording and do not work as accurately as they do with other types of recordings. This is another argument for adapting the test for regular machine-scoring answer sheets.

J Consult Psychol 11:340–1 N-D '47. * The test's greatest value is for use in surveys to discover deficiencies in reading skill, to be followed by a remedial program.

[503]

Stanford Achievement Test [Reading]. Grades 2-3, 4-6, 7-9; 1922–40; same as reading tests in the *Stanford Achievement Test;* 3 levels; $1.20 per 25 of any one level; 35¢ per specimen set of any one level, postpaid; Truman L. Kelley, Giles M. Ruch, and Lewis M. Terman; World Book Co.
a) PRIMARY READING TEST. Grades 2-3; Forms D, E, F; 25(30) minutes.
b) INTERMEDIATE READING TEST. Grades 4-6; Forms D, E, F, G, H; 30(35) minutes.
c) ADVANCED READING TEST. Grades 7-9; Forms D, E, F, G, H; 35(40) minutes.

Margaret G. McKim, Assistant Professor of Education, University of Cincinnati, Cincinnati, Ohio. Forms D to H of the *Stanford Achievement Test* comprise the 1940 revision of this battery. The reading tests contain the sections on paragraph meaning and word meaning from the complete battery. The tests are similar in pattern at all three levels.

The value of these tests lies in their general estimate of paragraph comprehension and vocabulary. The series of short paragraphs comprising the paragraph meaning sections covers a variety of informational materials. A system requiring the reader to write in the word which best fills a blank in the paragraph allows for considerable variation in the type of understanding required. The word meaning sections are equally general in content. A key word in a partial sentence followed by five responses is the form used. Precise time limits make speed a factor in all tests. No information is given as to the bases upon which the test items were chosen.

The primary test, particularly the paragraph meaning section, is the most open to question. Here requiring a written response seems unsuitable. The difficulty is increased by blanks too small for the normal handwriting of the primary child. Few of the paragraphs and few of the items in the word meaning section are simple enough to provide any sure measure of the ability of the poor reader. Extrapolated scores below a grade level of approximately 2.75 are further evidence that this test will not give a satisfactory picture of an entire class much before the end of the third grade.

Standardization was done on a random sample of 50,955 cases drawn from a total population of 300,000 pupils distributed over 173 communities. Spearman–Brown reliability coefficients calculated from odd and even numbered items range from .883 to .969 according to unpublished information supplied by the publishers. Equated scores make it possible to compare the two sections of a test or a test at one level with that at another. Age and grade norms have been calculated using only those children who were at grade for their age. While this does not solve the problem of interpreting norms for a school system in which children are not promoted automatically, it attempts to reduce the influence of varied promotion policies in the norms themselves. Age and grade norms calculated in customary fashion are also provided.

The accompanying manual explains the procedures used to establish the norms and equated scores, and presents evidence regarding reliability. There is no discussion of reading as a skill nor any suggestion of ways in which the test results might be used to improve the reading program other than a general discussion of the use of achievement tests in the manual accompanying the complete battery. The tests will probably be of greatest value as general achievement tests in the intermediate and junior high school grades. They will supplement but not replace the reading tests which provide more specific diagnostic evidence.

For reviews by Walter W. Cook and Ralph C. Preston of the entire battery, see 18.

[504]

Stone-Webster Test in Beginning Reading. Grade 1; 1936–37; Forms 1, 2; 7¢ per test; manual free on request; 40(45) minutes; Clarence R. Stone; Webster Publishing Co.

REFERENCES

1. STONE, CLARENCE R. "Validity of Tests in Beginning Reading." El Sch J 43:361-5 F '43. * (PA 18:2605)

Ruth Lowes, Associate Professor of Education, West Texas State Teachers College, Canyon, Texas. As a guide in selecting words for this test, the author used his own graded vocabulary list based on an analysis of the early reading material of pupils.

The test was standardized on scores made by almost two thousand pupils in town and city schools of eight widely scattered states. A table of median scores with age and grade equivalents is given. Also given are tables of percentile norms for the end of the low first grade and the high first grade. Helpful suggestions for interpreting percentile scores are given. No reliability or validity coefficients are reported.

The test is divided into two parts. Part I measures word recognition. Sixty excellent pictures, simple in detail, are given. Each is accompanied by four words, one of which the pupil circles. Part II consists of twenty-four sen-

tences. With each sentence are four carefully executed drawings. The pupil marks the picture which represents the sentence. Each part requires a sitting of 20 minutes. The test is easily scored.

The manual calls attention to certain diagnostic values of the test. One of the most important is that of determining discriminatory weaknesses when words similar in appearance are presented.

[505]

Techniques in Reading Comprehension for Junior-Senior High School: Every Pupil Test. Grades 7-12; 1943–47; new form usually issued each December and April; forms December 1946, April 1947; 2¢ per test; 17(25) minutes; Ohio Scholarship Tests.

Ivan A. Booker, Assistant Director, Research Division, National Education Association, Washington, D. C. [Review of April and December 1946 forms.] This test is intended as a general measure of reading achievement for junior and senior high school pupils. It is one of the two high school reading tests in the total battery of more than three dozen tests which now constitute the series used in a state-wide testing program. The companion test, *Applied Reading for Junior-Senior High School,* is described elsewhere in this volume.

In *Techniques in Reading Comprehension* the emphasis falls on various aspects of comprehension. However, the element of speed is by no means eliminated. The time limits are short enough that pupils work under pressure, and also short enough that the great majority of scores are affected by rate of work. Like many other reading tests, therefore, this one yields a score in which *rate* and *comprehension* are inseparably tangled. Two students may make identical scores: one a rapid worker but rather inaccurate; the other, a slower but quite accurate reader. From the test scores alone, this difference would not appear.

The test has four parts designed to measure the pupil's ability: (*a*) to identify the central theme of a paragraph; (*b*) to find pertinent details; (*c*) to recognize correct word meanings; (*d*) to interpret common idioms. Each part of the test uses a commonly employed type of test item and response.

The first part, on identifying the central theme, contains ten short paragraphs, several of them usually written about the same general topic, for example, the Holland tunnel in New York City. The pupil selects the main idea of each paragraph from four choices provided. The time limit of six minutes is much more generous for the April test than for the December form. The ten paragraphs of the latter contain thirty-eight more lines of printed material than the former and the multiple-choice items an additional fourteen lines. Apparently the test paragraphs are chosen with little attempt to equate them for length, and the time limit is set arbitrarily irrespective of the reading time involved.

The second part of the test which involves reading (or skimming) for details consists of one or more selections of double-spaced material with words and phrases underlined and numbered. Alongside this material are thirty questions which must be answered by finding the numbered words or phrases which answer them. This seems the least useful of the parts of this test. The response technique, widely criticized as used in the *Iowa Silent Reading Tests,* gains no luster as used in the Ohio test series. Many of the questions can be answered by more than one underscored phrase (and alternate answers are shown in the scoring key). Other items require two numbered items as a correct answer although one could scarcely infer as much from the directions and sample exercises with which the exercise begins. Still another objectionable feature in this part of the test is that several test items appear on a page other than that on which the answers are found, requiring pupils to shift back and forth from one page to another and sometimes to turn a page to find an answer. Again the time limit is six minutes, for reading about eighty-five lines and answering thirty questions. The directions are: "Read the following paragraphs. In the parentheses, write the numbers of the underlined words which correctly answer the question." However, if students proceeded in that order, the slower readers would do relatively few questions. Method of attack undoubtedly has much to do with the pupil's score on this part of the test.

The thirty-word vocabulary test is of standard type. The test words are presented in isolation rather than in a context setting, and for each test word a four-part multiple-choice item is given. The three minutes allowed for this part of the test is a relatively more generous time allowance than that for either of the preceding sections.

The final part of the test, Reading for Phrase Meaning, requires the pupil to interpret such idioms as "in the same boat " "the lion's share," and "put in his oar." According to the manual, an "increment in difficulty is obviously established" in this part of the test. However, according to the test results of the April program, the fifth item was the easiest in the series and the first was about as difficult as any in the list except the last.

The norms provided for the test take the form of percentiles based on the total scores for the four parts of the test. These become available about one month from the time the tests are given in Ohio schools. For this test the norms are given for each grade, instead of merely for junior and senior high school grades, respectively, as is true for some of the Ohio Scholarship Tests. Also, for such help as they may be in diagnostic work, per cents are given in the published reports to show what portion of the pupils answered each test item correctly.

As a general survey of reading achievement, with the emphasis on certain phases of comprehension, this test is a useful measuring instrument. Except for Part II, Reading for Details, the specific skills involved are clearly identified and nicely isolated for the purposes of measurement. For careful evaluations, however, other tests should be used at least in a supplementary way because of the lack of available data with respect to the validity, reliability, and comparability of the various forms of this test.

Teachers who use the Universal Class Error Check Sheets and the Universal Class Percentile Record Blanks which accompany the test will find these charts helpful in planning class activities and in individual pupil guidance even though the test has distinct limitations as a diagnostic instrument.

The directions for administering the test are clear and brief. The test is inexpensive, objective, and easy to score. The availability of similar (if not strictly comparable) forms prepared each year is a real advantage, and the percentile grade norms established on a state-wide basis provide splendid points of reference. The test can be administered within a single class period and, unless other more comprehensive reading tests are already being used in a school, will give a helpful overview of the types of reading ability which this test involves. It will be most useful when used as the initial step in a program of measurement and instruction—least useful when regarded as an adequate and final measure of reading achievement or as a means of accurate, individual diagnosis.

James M. McCallister, Director of Personnel Service, Herzl Branch, Chicago City Junior College, Chicago, Illinois. [Review of April and December 1946 forms.] This test is prepared for use in the state-wide testing program in Ohio. Parallel forms are provided for use in December and April. After the scores are reported to the Ohio State Department of Education, the teacher is furnished with a report of percentile norms and item norms that enables her to ascertain the standing of her class as a whole and the relative standing of each pupil.

According to the printed announcement, this test serves two purposes: "(*a*) to determine the general level of reading comprehension of secondary school pupils, and (*b*) to provide a basis for the improvement of pupils' study through a detailed understanding of their reading strengths and weaknesses." The validity of the test is conditioned by how well it serves these purposes.

An internal analysis of the four parts of the test leaves the impression that it is a good measure of the pupil's ability to apprehend the exact meaning of a passage. The percentile norms indicate the general reading level of each pupil with respect to this ability. In these respects, it accomplishes the first purpose.

It does not appear to serve the second purpose so well, however, because it measures only limited phases of the application of reading to study. It is conceivable that a pupil might succeed well on this test but at the same time be poorly prepared to evaluate the correctness of ideas or detect inconsistencies, to make implications or generalizations based on the material read, to apply ideas gained in the solution of problems, and to perform other study activities that accompany reading. When the test is used as a basis for the improvement of study activities, this limitation must be recognized.

Since tests for state-wide testing programs must of necessity be prepared for immediate use, they cannot be subjected readily to correlational studies as to validity and reliability. Therefore, no studies of these types are reported for the test.

Excellent devices for the diagnostic analysis of the performances of individuals are provided with the test. Among these devices are a class error check sheet and a percentile record blank for diagnosing weaknesses and estimating the progress of individuals. These devices, when used in connection with the report of percentile norms, give a thorough analysis of pupil performances that is especially valuable in ascertaining individual needs.

[506]

★**Thorndike-Lorge Reading Test for Grades 7 to 9.** Grades 7-9; 1945; Forms 1, 2; $5.40 per 100; 35¢ per specimen set; 40(45) minutes; E. L. Thorndike and Irving Lorge; Bureau of Publications, Teachers College, Columbia University.

REFERENCES

1. LORGE, IRVING. "The Thorndike-Lorge Reading Test for Grades 7-9." *Teach Col Rec* 46:453-9 Ap '45. * (*PA* 19:2754)

Robert L. McCaul, Instructor and Adviser in the College, The University of Chicago, Chicago, Illinois. This test follows conventional patterns in validation and standardization. It differs from other reading tests by virtue of the fact that approximately half of the items demand of the pupil thoughtful, creative reading.

The content of the test reflects the authors' belief that "any adequate measure of ability to read will be more or less a measure of intelligence as it operates with language." Form 1, for example, consists of four riddles, twenty-one brief aphorisms from Longfellow, Shakespeare, the Bible, and similar sources, and four relatively long prose selections, one of which is general narrative and the other three expository material from social science and natural history books. While the majority of the questions about the selections solicit a type of rote reproduction of details common to most reading tests, there are included some questions which require comprehension of the whole passage and reasoning with the data presented. To the aphorisms the pupil responds by picking out from a series of sentences the one which "means most nearly the same." Obviously, these items correspond very closely to the proverb tests at the Average Adult and Superior Adult II levels of the *Revised Stanford–Binet Scale.*

Granted that riddles and aphorisms serve a legitimate purpose in a reading test, there still remain several questions to be raised. If, as the authors claim, their test is "planned to include all the important factors in silent reading and give reasonable weight to each of them," are twenty-five riddle and aphorism items out of a total of fifty-five items a "reasonable weight"? Do riddles and aphorisms occur so frequently in children's reading or occupy so important a place that they should comprise nearly half of a "general" reading test? If, on the other hand, these items are intended to provide a measure of how well the pupil's intelligence "operates with language," is the kind of reading exacted by riddles and aphorisms representative of all the complex, diverse elements in thoughtful, creative reading? From a pupil's performance on such items can we generalize safely about how adequately his intelligence "operates with language"? The authors supply no information which will enable the prospective test user to answer these questions.

Because parts of the test sample functions for which no precise nomenclature exists, the diagnostic breakdown of the items is, as the authors imply, unsatisfactory. An item like "He goes where he pleases, low or high, and can walk just as well with his feet to the sky" may measure "knowledge of the meanings of words and phrases in context"; but to answer that *fly* is the word which best fits this sentence requires, in addition, a stroke of constructive imagination, an inference, or an insight much higher in the hierarchy of mental processes than mere knowledge of the meaning of words and phrases. Again, more than a "knowledge of constructions, including idioms" operates when a pupil chooses "To the boiling pot the flies come not" as the appropriate sentence to match with "The busy man has few idle visitors." For this reason the single score—the number of right answers—derived from the test is difficult to interpret.

It should be remarked here that the portion of the test devoted to measuring comprehension of literal meaning and other concrete skills is well and carefully constructed. The reviewer is convinced, nevertheless, that a person's judgment of the whole test will be determined by his attitude toward the sections designed to measure thoughtful, creative reading. If the prospective test user feels that reading is no more than simple apprehension of meaning and recognition of symbols, he may condemn the test as an impractical and inadequate cross of an intelligence test and a reading test. If, conversely, he believes that reading includes all the intellectual and emotional reactions which can possibly be made to the printed page, he may hail the test as almost the only one in its field that attempts to appraise the efficiency with which the higher mental processes function in reading. Actually, the *Thorndike–Lorge Reading Test* undertakes to measure certain factors in reading that are neglected by more pedestrian reading tests. It supplements rather than displaces these tests and may be used most profitably in conjunction with them.

J Bus Ed 20:37 Ap '45. * a general reading such as this....will help to discover shortcomings in word knowledge, understanding and appreciation of the printed page, in ability to concentrate to get thought, or in ability to read fast enough to make reading an asset in other high school subjects. *

[507]

Whipple's High-School and College Reading Test. Grades 9-16; 1925; Forms A, B; $3.60 per 100; 12¢ per specimen set; 10(15) minutes; Guy M. Whipple; Public School Publishing Co.

REFERENCES

1. BOOK, WILLIAM F. "How Well College Students Can Read." *Sch & Soc* 26:242-8 Ag 20 '27. * (*PA* 1:2701)
2. BERNARD, HAROLD W. "Some Relationships of Vocabulary to Scholarship." *Sch & Soc* 51:494-6 Ap 13 '40. * (*PA* 14:4236)
3. ANDERSON, IRVING H., AND DEARBORN, WALTER F. "Reading Ability as Related to College Achievement." *J Psychol* 11:387-96 Ap '41. * (*PA* 15:3570)

Frederick B. Davis, Professor of Psychology, George Peabody College for Teachers; and Director, Test Research Service; Nashville, Tennessee. This test, copyrighted in 1925, has been on the market for over twenty years. At first thought, one would be likely to conclude, with all the research and attention devoted in that time to the problems of reading and to the measurement of achievement, that any reading test published in the last few years would be markedly superior to a test over twenty years old. The facts, however, do not justify such a sweeping conclusion, although there are better reading tests on the market.

Each of the two forms of the *Whipple's High-School and College Reading Test* consists of twenty items based on a single long passage characteristic of a textbook in modern history. These passages are not exactly boring, but they are of the type no normal high school or college student would reread except by necessity. They are, to put it briefly, the type of passages used characteristically for tests of reading comprehension. Except for the Cooperative reading comprehension tests, the writer has yet to find a reading test that contains both humorous passages and excerpts of genuine literary merit.

Since data have been obtained showing that ability to understand passages in the social studies is by no means identical with ability to understand passages taken from other academic fields (such as science), the validity of the Whipple test is at once brought into question.

The twenty items consist of directions to perform some operation and are interpolated at intervals into the content of the passage. Responses are indicated by writing on the test booklet, a procedure which makes it consumable and necessary to score by hand in a rather inconvenient way. Scoring is not entirely objective. The reliability of the scores derived from the test is not stated in the manual. The writer guesses that it might be about .75 in a typical high school grade. If so, the standard error of measurement of an individual raw score would probably work out to be about 1.5. Taking this estimate as better than no data at all (which is what the manual provides), we find that a twelfth-grade student's score could readily vary by sheer chance as much as twenty percentile points if it were close to the mean for the grade. In this connection it is interesting to note the range of raw scores between selected percentile points, say the tenth and ninetieth. For the ninth grade, this range is 7.5; at no grade level is it as great as 10. These data serve to illustrate why a test with so few items cannot be highly discriminative in placing a large group of students in rank order of ability.

SUMMARY. The *Whipple's High-School and College Reading Test* is a reasonably satisfactory survey test of speed of comprehension of material of the kind found in social studies textbooks. It does not appear to measure this ability reliably enough to permit accurate comparisons of individuals at a given grade level. Too limited a range of reading skills and content is presented to warrant confidence in the validity of the test as a measure of general reading ability. The score resulting from the test is a mixture of speed of reading and level of comprehension.

[508]

Williams Primary Reading Test. Grades 1-3; 1926; Forms A, B; $2.40 per 100; 12¢ per specimen set; Allan J. Williams; Public School Publishing Co.

Alice N. Jameson, Assistant, Child Placement Department, Public Schools, Brookline, Massachusetts. This test "was designed to test the ability of the pupils in grades 1-3 to get the thought of the printed page." In 1926 this test may have accomplished its purpose, but today it is inadequate as a measure of reading ability. It is stated that "the material used in the test is common to most of the widely used texts." The books most used today are entirely different in content and construction. It is stated that "the first part of the test is easy enough so that most of the pupils at the end of the first year are able to answer two or more questions." Here again the test is poorly graded, for certainly two or more questions at the end of a

school year are too few to test a whole year's work in grade one.

MISCELLANEOUS

[509]

Examiner's Reading Diagnostic Record for High School and College Students. 1938–39; Forms A, B, C, D; 35¢ per set (includes manual, record blank, and oral reading passages); 30¢ per set, 10 or more; Ruth Strang with the assistance of Margaret E. Martin, Margaret C. McKim, and Mary Alice Mitchell; Bureau of Publications, Teachers College, Columbia University.

Robert Murray Bear, Professor of Psychology and Director of the Reading Clinic, Dartmouth College, Hanover, New Hampshire. The chief value of this instrument lies in its making generally available a record form for a thorough case study of an individual with rather severe reading difficulty. Its various parts, eleven in number, range from personal data, records of scholastic achievement and tests, developmental history, and interests through summary, interpretation, recommendations, and follow-up. An accompanying five and one-half page manual supplies further suggestions for obtaining and recording the data with comments upon their significance.

The *Examiner's Reading Diagnostic Record* performs a special service in calling attention to the values derived from appraisal of oral reading and in providing a rather brief oral test. There are four 100-word paragraphs to be read orally by the student. These are graduated in difficulty, though unfortunately no information is supplied the user regarding their levels of difficulty, either in vocabulary, sentence structure, or ideational complexity. Norms are not provided, though the user is told a number of things which should be observed during the reading. Errors are to be marked in a standard way, but their particular significance as clues to faulty perceptual or mechanical reading habits and the possible use to be made of them in remedial work are not explained.

Experienced workers derive greater value from case histories than do the inexperienced, but the seasoned clinician will probably already have devised a record form containing the items he has found useful in individual diagnosis. It is, therefore, probable that the *Examiner's Reading Diagnostic Record* will hold greater interest for those beginning this work. Quite correctly the manual is written from this standpoint and contains many valuable suggestions for the guidance of the beginner. One wishes it had gone even further and into more detail, as, for example, in suggesting types or even names of reading tests which might be used for various diagnostic purposes, in greater analysis of interests other than reading, in raising questions regarding environmental and emotional factors in poor reading, and in explaining the significance mentioned above of oral reading as an index of silent habits of word recognition.

In summary then, we have here a convenient record form for those without one of their own, a brief, nonstandardized oral reading test suitable for upper class pupils, and a guide for the beginner which should help prevent him from overlooking factors of possible relevance to a diagnosis.

Carolyn M. Welch, Formerly Acting Supervisor, The Reading Clinic, Baltimore, Maryland. This is a form for obtaining information concerning a reading problem at the high school and college levels. The author emphasizes, in the accompanying manual, that the procedure is clinical in nature, an individual approach. The record embraces eleven sections including items to be recorded, suggestions for standardized and informal tests, informal questions, reading material, and directions for the examiner. The manual offers an explanation of the diagnostic procedure and specific directions on how and where to locate information.

The format of the record allots ample space for notation and encourages completeness of analysis. The first section, Identifying Data, reveals home background, reasons for referral, and a statement of the reading problem as recognized by the student and his parents or teachers. The second and third sections, Summaries of Results of Standardized Tests (Intelligence, Achievement, and Reading) and Scholastic Achievement, respectively, give indexes to capacity and achievement relationships; hence, they indicate amount of retardation. The physiological factors are examined in the fourth section, Medical Examination and Reports on Physical Condition. Questions listed in the fifth section, Developmental and Educational History, are particularly helpful as a guide to spotting the initiation of the problem and further defining it. Of significant aid for instructional purposes is the information on pupil interests obtained through the interview

in the sixth section, Present Reading Interests, and in the seventh section, Other Interests and Activities.

In the eighth section, Present Reading Status, the author presents a series of four paragraphs, arranged in order of increasing difficulty, for the analysis of oral reading habits. This appraisal is informal in nature, since the scoring has not been standardized and norms are not presented. However, the manual suggests that in most cases it will not be necessary to administer more than two paragraphs, selected to fit the estimated ability of the examinee. Herein lies a hazy concept of what is meant by "ability." This examiner has inferred that the comprehension of the particular test selections, word recognition skills and abilities, and certain study habits are to be determined through the use of the oral reading and the dictionary tests. No opportunities for determining the instructional level in terms of graded materials are offered. No opportunities for obtaining an informal appraisal of the child's capacity for understanding the material in spite of the reading handicap are suggested.

The ninth, tenth, and eleventh sections provide spaces for summary of results, recommendations, and follow-up. A paragraph in the manual suggests that records be continued during the instructional program.

This diagnostic record presents an analytic procedure for screening and for diagnosing, to a certain degree, a retarded reader at high school and college levels. It leaves for more specific analysis those severe reading disability cases with neurological involvements and with severe emotional aberrations.

This examiner continues to search for a way of recording the relationships of findings in order to determine the specific nature of the reading problem, to define the related and influencing factors, and to determine which procedures to recommend for instruction.

For a review by Henry D. Rinsland and excerpts from reviews by Seth A. Fessenden, Austin G. Schmidt, and one other, see 40:1535.

[510]

Gates Reading Diagnostic Tests, Revised Edition. Grades 1-8; 1926-45; individual; Forms I, II; 20¢ per record booklet; 45¢ per manual; $1.10 per set of oral response test material; 10¢ per set of tachistoscopic cards; (60-90) minutes; Arthur I. Gates; Bureau of Publications, Teachers College, Columbia University.

REFERENCES

1. GATES, ARTHUR I. *The Improvement of Reading: A Program of Diagnostic and Remedial Methods, Revised Edition.* New York: Macmillan Co., 1935. Pp. xvii, 668. * (*PA* 9:5252) For latest edition, *see* (3) below.

2. GATES, A. I.; BOND, G. L.; AND RUSSELL, D. H.; ASSISTED BY EVA BOND, ANDREW HALPIN, AND KATHRYN HORAN. *Methods of Determining Reading Readiness.* New York: Bureau of Publications, Teachers College, Columbia University, 1939. Pp. iv, 55. Paper. Out of print. * (*PA* 13:6466)

3. GATES, ARTHUR I. *The Improvement of Reading: A Program of Diagnostic and Remedial Methods, Third Edition.* New York: Macmillan Co., 1947. Pp. xxi, 657. $4.25. * (*PA* 22:3195)

T. L. Torgerson, Chairman, Psycho-Educational Clinic, and Professor of Education, The University of Wisconsin, Madison, Wisconsin. These tests are available in two forms, consisting of a pupil's record booklet, two sets of cards containing test material for the pupil, and a manual of directions. The 16-page record booklet contains a cover page for recording test scores, 12 pages of test material, a one-page check list of errors and difficulties, and a two-page analytic summary of other tests and observations of vision, hearing, speech, personality, interests, home, and school life. A 35-page manual contains directions, norms, and references to remedial procedures found in the author's *Improvement of Reading* (1).

The series consists of the following eighteen tests: (*a*) oral reading, (*b*) oral vocabulary, (*c*) reversals, (*d*) phrase perception, (*e*) timed word perception, (*f*) untimed word pronunciation, (*g*) spelling, (*h*) syllabication, (*i*) recognition of syllables, (*j*) recognition of phonograms, (*k*) blending letter sounds-visual, (*l*) giving letter sounds, (*m*) reading capital letters, (*n*) reading small letters, (*o*) blending letter sounds-auditory, (*p*) giving letters from sounds, (*q*) giving words with initial sounds, (*r*) giving words with stated final sound.

Both age and grade norms are contained in the manual for each of the tests. Grade norms for the oral reading test, which consists of seven paragraphs, extend from 1.6 to 8.5. The grade norms for the oral meaning vocabulary, consisting of 30 words, extend from 2.0 to 13.0. The grade norms for word perception—timed, phrase perception, pronunciation and syllabication extend to 7.0, 6.5, 6.0, and 4.6 respectively. With the exception of the spelling tests, the norms on all of the remaining tests of basic skills in reading are based on perfect scores at a grade status of 3.0 for giving words with initial sounds and final sounds; 3.7 for reversals, recognition of syllables, and phonograms; and 4.0 for speed of recognizing capital letters and lower-case letters, letter blends, and letter sounds.

Scores on the oral reading test are based upon six types of errors: hesitation of five or more seconds on a word, mispronunciation, omissions, substitutions, insertions, and repetitions. The length of time used by the pupil in reading a paragraph is not taken into consideration in scoring. The seven paragraphs increase in difficulty "at approximately uniform steps of a grade each."

In an unpublished study by the author, the following reliability coefficients are reported: oral reading .86, oral vocabulary .80; these are based upon correlations obtained between the two forms using 90 cases in the third grade. Correlation between odd and even items stepped up by the Spearman–Brown formula yielded coefficients ranging from .88 to .96 for eleven of the tests. Blending letter sounds orally, giving letters for sounds, and giving words with stated initial sounds yielded coefficients of .84, .77, and .63 respectively.

This series of diagnostic tests is the most comprehensive and usable individual test for diagnosis in reading at present available. The classroom teacher can learn to administer the series after a reasonable study of the materials. The administration of both forms to each case studied will insure adequate reliability for most of the tests. The observational check lists of more than 60 specific difficulties in reading, together with the student's developmental history, intelligence, hearing, vision, and speech, will provide an excellent basis for making a diagnosis of a reading disability case.

The oral reading paragraphs provide an interesting story for the pupils. Recall questions which would measure comprehension of these paragraphs would add to the completeness of the diagnosis. Teachers who differ as to the "brand" of phonics emphasized in their teaching may omit the tests that have no curricular validity for them without interfering with the results of the remaining tests. Many teachers would welcome a profile chart that would enable them to record the test scores graphically.

[511]

Inventory of Reading Experiences. Grades 9-16; 1940; 1 form; $1.75 per 25; 15¢ per specimen set; non-timed (15) minutes; Frederick L. Pond; Stanford University Press.

REFERENCES

1. POND, FREDERICK L. "A Qualitative and Quantitative Appraisal of Reading Experiences." *J Ed Res* 33:241-52 D '39. * (*PA* 14:1603)

2. POND, FREDERICK L. *The Qualitative and Quantitative Appraisal of Reading Experience.* Unpublished doctor's thesis, Pennsylvania State College, 1939. Pp. 132.

Albert J. Harris, Assistant Professor of Education, The City College of New York, New York, New York. This inventory is a carefully developed questionnaire intended for use in appraising the quality and quantity of the reading experiences of high school and college students. Part I, Qualitative Inventory, contains 100 items, grouped in ten sections, to be marked on a three-point scale: never, sometimes, often. Part II, Quantitative Inventory, contains 50 items. Most of the items seem relevant and appropriate. Twenty of the qualitative items, however, including 9 with very high weights, deal with radio and moving picture interests; the inclusion of these seems unfortunate. There is one form, administered without time limit. The format is satisfactory. A weighted scoring scheme similar to that used for the Bernreuter *Personality Inventory* is employed. Cardboard stencils are provided, and the use of Veeder counters is recommended for rapidity in scoring.

The inventory seems to have been developed through the use of elaborate research techniques. Reliability is satisfactory: .92 for Part I and .91 for Part II, for a single grade, using the split-half, Spearman–Brown technique. Reliabilities for the 10 sections of Part I are not given but are probably low. Validity data of several kinds are presented, which seem to show that the inventory has low positive correlations with IQ, reading ability, literary knowledge, school marks, and socio-economic status; differentiates between remedial readers and normal readers less satisfactorily than a good vocabulary or reading test does; and correlates highly (above .80) with reading diaries kept by high school students, both for single items and for total scores. It is, of course, subject to any tendencies toward falsification that might also influence reading diaries.

Percentile norms are given by grades for the two main scores, and quartile norms for each of the ten sections. The norms for grades 9, 10, 11, and 12 are based on over 1,000 students in each grade. College norms are based on 187 freshmen, 128 sophomores, and 84 graduate students. No information is provided which allows a judgment about the representativeness of the sampling. The norms must, therefore, be regarded as tentative.

This inventory is the first to provide quantitative scores and norms for the reading interests of high school and college students. It will probably prove useful to instructors in literature and remedial reading courses and in research studies on reading at the high school and college levels.

[512]
Record for Reading Diagnosis. Grades 1-8; 1936; withdrawn from publication; C. R. Stone; Webster Publishing Co.

Carolyn M. Welch, Formerly Acting Supervisor, The Reading Clinic, Baltimore, Maryland. This four-page leaflet was designed to record data and information pertinent to the causes of a reading problem. The record consists of sixteen sections suggesting the gathering of data on intelligence; reading achievement; oral reading habits; word recognition skills and abilities; emotional characteristics; physical status; handedness; eyedness; speech, sight, and hearing deficiencies; handwriting and language habits; school progress; and reading attitudes. Most of the data must be obtained in an individual testing situation.

In general, the record suggests that a number of factors be considered in diagnosing a reading problem. In many sections, responses of correct and incorrect nature are given. For example, under the heading Speech in Section IX, these responses are found: "Normal; baby talk; lisps; stutters; stammers." Those who wish to record more specifically the nature of the speech deficiency will have difficulty enclosing notes in the space provided. The record allots space for hardly more than summary-type recordings of observation.

This user of the record finds the following needs unsatisfied: A column for the chronological age in the first section on intelligence. A definition of the word "easy" as used in the second section describing the type of story to be used for silent reading. (It has been the writer's experience that many children can be given material easy enough so that a satisfactory rate of comprehension exists with satisfactory reading habits, thus resolving the reading problem.) A statement regarding the type and the difficulty of the material to be used for oral reading in the third section. Methods for determining handedness and eyedness. And a section for reporting language handicaps of a structural type, not involving speech deficiencies or foreign language handicaps.

The criteria for analyzing oral reading habits (Section III), word recognition skills and abilities (Section IV), and emotional characteristics (Section V) are very helpful. The fact that the record can in this respect be used at any grade level is a salient feature. The quantity of factors to be considered for diagnosis should be noted. However, the organization of the record presupposes the competence of the examiner in relating the findings for the summary (Section XV) and the recommendations (Section XVI). These latter sections offer very little assistance in recording suggestions for the correction or remediation of reading retardation or disability.

READINESS

[513]

★American School Reading Readiness Test. Grade 1 entrants; 1941; Form A; $4.80 per 100; 30¢ per specimen set, postpaid; nontimed (45) minutes; Robert V. Young, Willis E. Pratt, and Carroll A. Whitmer; Public School Publishing Co.

REFERENCES

1. PRATT, WILLIS E. The Construction of a Group Test of Reading Readiness. Unpublished doctor's thesis, University of Pittsburgh, 1940. (Abstracts of Theses . . . 1940, 1941, pp. 265-73.)

David H. Russell, Professor of Education, University of California, Berkeley, California. This test consists of an above-average number of subtests with a below-average number of items in each subtest. It comprises eight subtests, but the largest number of items in any test is ten and three tests contain only six items. The student of test construction, accordingly, will immediately question the reliability of the subtests. The authors report a split-halves reliability coefficient of .91 for the test as a whole but give no indication of the reliability of the short subtests.

The authors state that the eight subtests were selected from items mentioned in the literature as being related to reading readiness which can be tested by group methods. They include vocabulary (marking pictures), discrimination of letter forms (selecting one letter unlike three others), discrimination of letter combinations (matching one of four combinations with a criterion combination), recognition of words (selecting a letter that does not belong), recognition of words (matching one of four with a criterion word), discrimination of geometric forms (matching as above), following directions (marking pictures), and memory for geometric forms (drawing from memory after a short exposure). The authors report intercorrelations of these subtests ranging from .17 to .61 with a group of children who had been in kindergarten and from .29 to .69 in a nonkindergarten group.

The authors of this test are to be commended for the statement they make in the accompanying manual of their experimental work in developing the test. The description of successive stages of development is succinct and clear. The final validation of the test was accomplished on too small a group to please all test users, but the statement is available to all. The authors found a multiple correlation of .53 between their test and *Gates Primary Reading Tests* given six months later.

Since the predictive value of the test is low, the authors have added a feature not usually found on similar tests. By means of weighting the scores on the subtests and regression equations, they predict "an estimated reading grade on a reading test at the end of the first school year rather than the arbitrary determination of some critical point above which the pupil will succeed and below which he will fail." These predicted grades range from 1.2 to 3.2. In view of the wide variety of factors affecting success in beginning reading, the authors have made a commendable effort to avoid the use of a critical score which has little or no value in dividing the sheep from the goats. If they could improve their total test to give it higher predictive value, their approach would be a very useful one.

Paul A. Witty, Professor of Education, Northwestern University, Evanston, Illinois. This survey test and manual constitute a conscientious effort to meet the need for "a measure of reading aptitude which may be used easily by the regular teacher in the classroom." Tests and studies were examined and the following types of tests were selected for the *American School Readiness Test:* (a) visual discrimination, (b) vocabulary, (c) copying geometric forms from memory, and (d) ability to follow directions. From 143 items which were judged to be discriminatory, 60 items apiece were selected for Form A and for Form B. Experimental work on reliability was based on the study of 226 pupils "in twelve rooms in three typical school districts."

The *American School Reading Readiness Test* is designed as a survey test to be used in examining groups of children. In constructing the test, the predictive value of individual items was considered; the multiple correlation technique was utilized to weight each part of the test. Separate norms were developed for kindergarten and nonkindergarten pupils. Several measures of validity appear to be substantially high. So too are the measures of reliability.

Directions in general are concise and clear. However, lack of time limits proves a handicap to some teachers in giving this test. Directions for some tests should be made more specific. For example, in Test I, the pupils are instructed as follows: " 'Put your piece of paper on the page so that only the first row of pictures is showing. Now put a mark on the boy.' (Show on the board how to make an X.)" This direction is illustrative of several that could be greatly improved. For example, the examiner might be instructed to demonstrate with his own paper how to use the marker. The marker should be designated as a marker rather than as "a piece of paper."

In testing young children, it is best for the examiner to work with them, studying one row of materials at a time (Test II) instead of instructing pupils to follow complex directions such as: "Put aside your piece of colored paper. Look at the rest of the page and you will see more blocks. In each one put a mark on the letter, etc." Test IV is crowded, and instructions for its administration are incomplete. The samples should be made clearer in order that children will not place the marker incorrectly when the teacher says, "Look at the two blocks. In the block on the right. . . ." Here the child may think the block on the right is the large square block at the extreme right which has nothing to do with this test.

The giving of the test would be less confusing if the pictures in Test I were improved; e.g., the rock in row 3 looks like a potato. Children who succeed in such tests do so by a process of elimination rather than discrimination.

Directions for scoring are, on the whole, direct and clear. It is paradoxical that for some of the tests the weighted scores decrease as the raw scores increase. "This phenomenon," mentioned in a footnote on page 11 of the manual, and the fact that for kindergarten children the decrease occurs in Tests I, III, and IV, and for nonkindergarten children it occurs in Tests II and IV, merit further study.

The test can be given by a classroom teacher to approximately 15 children at one time. Moreover, the first test in the series is so easy that good rapport is established and children enjoy taking the test. However, there are some details in giving and scoring which should be remedied. Also, some of the pictures should be improved, and the print for the entire test should be clearer and bolder. One page each should be provided for Tests IV and V.

The *American School Reading Readiness Test* can be used effectively by the classroom teacher. Results secured from its tryout showed that this test is a superior one of its type and is practical to give and use in the typical classroom.

[514]

★**Binion-Beck Reading Readiness Test for Kindergarten and First Grade.** 1945; 1 form; $1.75 per 25; 50¢ per manual; 50¢ per specimen set; (40) minutes; Harriet Seay Binion and Roland L. Beck; Acorn Publishing Co.

REFERENCES
1. BINION, HARRIET SEAY. "Do We Know When a Child is Ready to Read." Abstract. *Proc Okla Acad Sci* 21:139 '41. * (*PA* 16:1153, title only)

Irving H. Anderson, Professor of Education, University of Michigan, Ann Arbor, Michigan. This test is divided into four parts. Part I measures picture vocabulary as well as the ability to detect likenesses and differences in pictures. Part II measures the ability to follow directions. Part III measures picture vocabulary and memory for a story. Part IV is a test of motor control. The reliability of the test as a whole is .95. No reliability coefficients for the individual parts of the test are reported. Validity coefficients were calculated between scores on the reading readiness test given in September and scores on the *Gates Primary Reading Tests* given in May of the same school year. The highest correlation obtained was .80. Correlations between scores on the *Pintner–Cunningham Primary Test* and scores on the *Gates Primary Reading Tests* are also reported. These correlations run lower than the correlations involving the reading readiness test. These results suggest that the reading readiness test is a better predictor of achievement in reading than the Pintner–Cunningham intelligence test. These correlations are based, however, on only 20 cases.

Paul A. Witty, Professor of Education, Northwestern University, Evanston, Illinois. The purposes of the test are: "(1) to aid the teacher in determining whether or not pupils entering first grade are ready to learn to read, and (2) to classify children in particular types of instruction, thus securing the development of right attitudes and habits and the prevention of wrong ones." Furthermore, the makers of the test assert: "The exercises which compose the Reading Readiness Test require the child to bring into use the developed factors in his physical, mental, emotional, and social maturity." Validity is presumably established by measures of agreement with standard reading and mental tests. Coefficients for reliability appear satisfactory.

These tests are somewhat complicated and difficult to administer. The loose sheets found in the testing booklet, the poor drawings, the need for the examiner to assemble materials, and the mimeographed directions suggest the incompleteness of the test and the need for thorough revision.

Some of the pictures are especially crude; for example, the family pictures for Test II, Row 6, and the animal pictures for Test II, Row 7. There is, also, a crowded effect with too much material on some pages. It is burdensome to assemble the materials necessary for administering this test. Test manufacturers should supply the necessary articles. In fact, it might be well to attempt to standardize the test using pictures of objects.

Some of the instructions for giving and scoring the test are inadequate. For example, in Test IV, samples should have been included to show what are considered "best, average, and poor" drawings. The authors state that "This testing technique" (having each picture on the page marked, rather than just one picture in each row) "provides picture-test items at less than one-third the usual cost." But the cost in energy and strain on the part of the teacher and the pupil in giving and taking this test is much too great. Many pictures are so poorly drawn that the child must proceed by the process of elimination to obtain his answer.

The *Binion–Beck Reading Readiness Test* should be considered as an interesting effort to develop a useful test. Thoroughgoing development and revision are needed in the test and the manual before this readiness test can be recommended.

[515]

Classification Test for Beginners in Reading. First grade entrants; 1933; 1 form; 9¢ per test; manual free on request; 14(20) minutes; Clarence R. Stone and Clifford C. Grover; Webster Publishing Co.

REFERENCES

1. WILSON, FRANK T., AND BURKE, AGNES. "Reading Readiness in a Progressive School." *Teach Col Rec* 38:565-80 Ap '37. * (PA 11:3918)
2. GATES, A. I.; BOND, G. L.; AND RUSSELL, D. H.; ASSISTED BY EVA BOND, ANDREW HALPIN, AND KATHRYN HORAN. *Methods of Determining Reading Readiness.* New York: Bureau of Publications, Teachers College, Columbia University, 1939. Pp. iv, 55. Paper. Out of print. * (PA 13:6466)

Marion Monroe Cox, Supervisor of the Reading Division, Psycho-Educational Clinic, The University of Southern California, Los Angeles, California. This test consists of two parts. Part I requires the child to look at a printed word and find it again among four words, three of which are similar in some respect to the test word. Part II requires the child to compare two words and indicate whether they are alike or different. Each part has several preparatory exercises for practice and a time limit of seven minutes.

The test does not require the child to read the words but merely to observe and note their details carefully. The assumption is made that children who can compare and match printed words accurately will become better readers and learn more rapidly than those who cannot do so. To measure the validity of this assumption, the test scores made by children on the *Classification Test for Beginners in Reading* at the beginning of the semester were correlated with scores by them on the *Lee–Clark Reading Test—Primer* at the end of the semester. The correlation coefficient reported by the authors is .62. While the test predicts success in reading in a general way, the prediction for any individual pupil is not very accurate. Many children possess this skill and yet do not learn to read easily because of other reasons, such as physical defects, emotional blockings, personality disturbances, and other factors which may interfere with normal learning.

The *Classification Test for Beginners in Reading* has a reliability coefficient of .97 and is easily administered; items for the test were selected after preliminary study of experimental editions of the test. The norms consist of the scores at the 10th, 25th, 50th, 75th, and 90th percentiles of beginning first grade children. The authors suggest that first grade teachers divide their pupils into three groups on the basis of the test scores: superior, average, and low groups, each to be given a type of instruction suitable to the ability of the group. As a further aid in grouping the children, the authors suggest giving an intelligence test and comparing the mental ages of the children with ratings on the *Classification Test for Beginners.*

The authors recognize that the test has certain limitations of which the teacher should be aware. They caution her to consider the classification of pupils by their test scores as tentative; whenever the teacher is convinced that a child would be better off in another group, she should use her judgment in making the change. Test results, therefore, are not to be adhered to rigidly but are to be supplemented with a generous amount of the teacher's common sense. It takes some time, however, before a teacher can become well enough acquainted with her pupils to estimate their abilities accurately. The authors offer the test as a quick screening device to classify pupils tentatively into fast, slow, and average groups with a fair chance that many pupils will be correctly placed and that the teacher will not need to make a great many changes later.

David H. Russell, Professor of Education, University of California, Berkeley, California. The Stone and Grover *Classification Test for Beginners in Reading* must be given credit for being an early attempt to measure readiness for reading. For example, it appeared three years before Harrison's *Reading Readiness* (Houghton Mifflin Co., 1936), a book which stimulated greater interest in the field. Two other tests were published about the same time, but the Stone and Grover test must be considered one of the pioneers in this area.

The relatively early publication of the test may contribute to its chief weakness as a readiness test, the narrow range of abilities it measures. The two parts of the test both appraise visual perception abilities, similarities and differences in words. The narrow range of abilities tested simplifies procedures and reduces the time for administration of the total test (20 minutes) but, of course, reduces the diagnostic possibilities inherent in the test. It gives a measure of children's word-recognition abilities but gives no information on other factors related to success in beginning reading such as size of understanding vocabulary, ability to follow directions, and ability to complete a story.

The authors of the *Classification Test for Beginners in Reading* give a split-halves reliability of approximately .97 and found a correlation of .62 between scores on the test given at the beginning of a semester and scores on the

Lee–Clark Reading Test—Primer given at the end of the semester. This does not indicate as high a predictive value as is usually found in a test more composite in nature. However, the same coefficient of correlation, .62, was found for this test by Gates, Bond, and Russell (2) to be the highest of the correlations obtained between scores on reading ability at the end of one, two, and three terms and 39 other tests sometimes used as possible predictors of reading success. Accordingly, the test would seem to have little diagnostic value but some administrative value for a tentative grouping of first-graders for purposes of instruction in reading.

[516]

Gates Reading Readiness Tests. Grade 1; 1939; 1 form; $4.85 per 100; 30¢ per specimen set; nontimed (50) minutes; Arthur I. Gates; Bureau of Publications, Teachers College, Columbia University.

REFERENCES

1-5. *See* 40:1537.
6. GATES, ARTHUR I. "A Further Evaluation of Reading Readiness Tests." *El Sch J* 40:577-91 Ap '40. * (*PA* 15:3581)
7. WILSON, FRANK T. "Early Achievement in Reading." *El Sch J* 42:609-15 Ap '42. * (*PA* 16:3816)
8. GATES, ARTHUR I. *The Improvement of Reading: A Program of Diagnostic and Remedial Methods, Third Edition.* New York: Macmillan Co., 1947. Pp. xxi, 657. $4.25. * (*PA* 22:3195)

Marion Monroe Cox, Supervisor of the Reading Division, Psycho-Educational Clinic, The University of Southern California, Los Angeles, California. This test has three main objectives: (*a*) to measure readiness for beginning reading, (*b*) to predict rate of development of reading ability, and (*c*) to diagnose the pupils' needs in several important abilities required in learning to read.

The tests consist of five subtests: Picture Directions, Word Matching, Word-Card Matching, Rhyming, and Reading Letters and Numbers. The first subtest involves hearing, understanding, remembering, interpreting, and following verbal directions. The second and third subtests require observation of printed words. The fourth subtest requires recognition of similar word sounds. The fifth subtest is an achievement test to determine whether the child has already formed associations between printed letters and numbers and their names.

While it is recommended that all five subtests be used, norms are provided separately for each, so that a teacher may omit one or more of the tests and still have a rough measure of readiness. On the other hand, space is provided on the face sheet for recording mental age, vision, hearing, and additional items of information that may add to the diagnostic value of the tests. The reliability coefficients of the separate tests range from .78 to .96, and the coefficient is .97 for the whole test. Validity was measured by correlating the tests given to pupils on entering first grade with the *Gates Primary Reading Tests* at the end of the semester. The correlation coefficients range from .57 to .89 for various groups. The *Gates Reading Readiness Tests* correlate slightly higher with later reading achievement when combined with scores from an intelligence test.

Percentiles are given for each subtest, and a comparison of abilities on the subtests may indicate specific weaknesses of individual pupils. One section of the manual gives helpful suggestions for improving the abilities required by the first four subtests in a prereading program aimed to develop reading readiness. Although the test with the highest predictive value for later reading is the fifth subtest, i.e., ability to read letters and numbers, the author does not suggest that letters and numbers be taught as a prerequisite to later reading. Those children who are interested enough before entering the first grade to learn isolated letters have a drive toward reading which will facilitate rapid progress, but an intensive drill on letters is not recommended as a substitute for a broad reading program out of which the knowledge of letters will gradually, and in due time, emerge.

Dr. Gates warns against using the reading readiness tests as a sole basis for classification of beginners into ability groups. Reading achievement alone is too narrow a criterion for promotion from one grade level to the next in the middle grades. Similarly, promise of ability to read is too narrow a basis for grouping within the first grade. Rather, he suggests, group pupils whose interests and needs are similar, but study the abilities of each child within the groups in order to individualize instruction for effective learning.

Paul A. Witty, Professor of Education, Northwestern University, Evanston, Illinois. On the whole, the mechanical features of the tests are satisfactory. However, pages are not numbered, and tests are not differentiated by titles. These factors produce confusion in some instances, although the clear outlines of the pictures tend to offset this confusion. Time limits are not given. It would be reassuring and helpful to many teachers if time limits were made available. Rows of words and pic-

tures in Tests 2, 3, and 4 are not numbered. Picture labels or numbers would help some children identify the rows.

Twenty cards have to be printed by the examiner to accompany Test 3. Making these cards is time-consuming. Commercial cards might well be made available. In taking this test, the children have to look at examiner's printed card and then match it with a word chosen in their test. This is a tedious process for many children. It might be desirable to have the two words printed on the same page in the child's test booklet and let him identify the required word from his own page. The alphabet and number test is administered individually. This is extremely time-consuming. It might be desirable to attempt to obtain similar results by use of group techniques.

In Tests 2, 3, and 4 suggestions are made as to ways of scoring tests and of making stencils and keys. Many examiners desire to have commercial keys and stencils. In scoring some tests, explicit instructions are offered as to whether credit is given when the crosses and circles are interchanged; in other tests no information is given as to the exactness of the circles or crosses. Hence, some confusion is found.

The *Gates Reading Readiness Tests* conform to acceptable standards for test construction. However, these tests did not consistently hold the attention and interest of some public and private school children to whom they were administered recently. Examiners report that the use of both group and individual methods of administering the test was a most important factor in causing interest to lag. Nevertheless, these tests have proved useful in securing one type of information which, when accompanied by adequate supporting data, seems to indicate a child's readiness for reading.

For excerpts from reviews by Austin G. Schmidt and one other, see 40:1537.

[517]
Lee-Clark Reading Readiness Test, 1943 Revision. Grades kgn-1; 1931–43; 1 form; $1.20 per 25; 35¢ per specimen set, postpaid; J. Murray Lee and Willis W. Clark; California Test Bureau.

REFERENCES

1. LEE, J. MURRAY; CLARK, WILLIS W.; AND LEE, DORRIS MAY. "Measuring Reading Readiness." *El Sch J* 34:656-66 My '34. * (PA 8:4741)
2. WILMORE, WALDO W. *Relative Validity of Three Group Readiness Tests in Predicting Reading Achievement.* Unpublished master's thesis, University of Kansas, 1939.

Marion Monroe Cox, Supervisor of the Reading Division, Psycho-Educational Clinic, The University of Southern California, Los Angeles, California. This test was designed to assist teachers in identifying children who are ready to learn to read. It consists of three parts, each of which measures a skill considered essential to learning to read: (*a*) ability to discriminate printed letter forms; (*b*) ability to select pictures according to verbal descriptions; and (*c*) ability to discriminate printed word forms. Since both the first and third parts of the test involve detecting similarities and differences between printed forms, the test is more heavily weighted with items requiring visual discrimination than with verbal items.

The test is brief enough that first-grade children can usually take the entire test in one sitting without fatigue. Directions are simple and the test is easily given and scored. Norms are interpreted for the teacher in terms that are understandable without special training in statistics or measurements. Because of its ease, simplicity, and brevity the test would appeal to a busy teacher who wants a quick method of grouping children and does not have the time or training for administering a more extensive or diagnostic battery of tests.

The test has a reliability coefficient of .92 and predicts later reading achievement as well as many group intelligence tests do at this level. The correlation coefficients between the *Lee-Clark Reading Readiness Test* and the *Lee-Clark Reading Tests—Primer* are reported to be .67 for unselected first grades and .43 for first grades whose pupils were above average in ability. These correlation coefficients indicate that the skills involved in the tests are related to reading, but that the predictive value for any individual child is not highly accurate. Hence, teachers should interpret the results not too rigidly but supplement the ratings by their own judgment and evaluation of pupils' abilities.

The authors are aware of the limitations of the test as a sole criterion of readiness to read and suggest that an intelligence test also be given. When both his mental age and reading readiness test score indicate sufficient maturity, the child's success in learning to read can be predicted more reliably than by either test alone. The authors also suggest that the teacher investigate many other factors which may impede reading, such as foreign language; visual, hearing, or speech defects; social and personality maladjustments; etc. Children who have any of these difficulties should be studied further in order to give them a type of developmental reading program which is best suited to their needs.

The *Lee-Clark Reading Readiness Test* is useful to teachers who wish to discover quickly and at an early date children who cannot discriminate printed forms or respond accurately to verbal directions. Such children undoubtedly lack important and desirable skills for reading. As a screening device to locate certain types of difficulties, teachers will find this test appropriate and useful, but should not consider it a thorough analysis of readiness to read.

David H. Russell, Professor of Education, University of California, Berkeley, California. This is a revision of a test, first published in 1931, which was a widely used pioneer instrument in the testing of reading readiness. The present form consists of four tests: (*a*) matching letter symbols in two columns, (*b*) crossing out one letter of four which is unlike the other three, (*c*) testing vocabulary and ability to follow directions by marking pictures according to instructions, (*d*) identifying letters and words by marking one of four symbols that is the same as a criterion symbol. The test accordingly gives more place to letter symbols than most other readiness tests. Since Gates reports that "the predictive value of a particular test varies with the teaching method," [*] this may lower the value of the test. Most first-grade teachers today do not give much place to teaching letters at beginning levels of reading.

Unlike a number of readiness tests evaluated elsewhere in this volume, the authors of the *Lee-Clark Reading Readiness Test* give the split-halves reliabilities of their subtests as well as the whole test. These range from .83 to .94. In checking the validity of their test, the authors report a correlation with the *Lee-Clark Reading Tests—Primer* of .67 in two first grades and a lower correlation of .432 with a group of superior children. The correlation of the readiness test with the *California Test of Mental Maturity* is .65, an average figure for such calculations.

[*] Gates, Arthur I. "An Experimental Evaluation of Reading Readiness Tests." *El Sch J* 39:497-508 Mr '39.

The manual accompanying the test lists grade equivalents for various total scores, a unique feature. A number of test users will criticize Table II of the manual stating "Probable Per Cent of Failure" since it assumes that failure is necessary or inevitable. A derivation of this table stating the amount of delay before beginning reading corresponding to various scores gives the first grade teacher a more positive approach to her problems of grouping for instruction. However, there are so many factors affecting the child's early progress in school that setting a definite period for "delay" may be dangerous.

Although it is unfortunate that the authors suggest per cent of failures and length of "delay," they must be given credit for stressing the value of supplementary information about the child such as mental age, vision, speech, and teacher's rating. A short bibliography in the manual should be useful to primary teachers. Finally, the Lee–Clark test achieves some sort of balance between oversimplification and too great complexity of tests, noted elsewhere about certain other readiness tests reviewed in this volume.

[518]

Metropolitan Readiness Tests. Kindergartners and grade 1 entrants; 1933–39; 1 form; $1.55 per 25; 35¢ per specimen set, postpaid; (70) minutes; Gertrude H. Hildreth and Nellie L. Griffiths; World Book Co.

REFERENCES

1-10. *See* 40:1552.
11. NEEB, MARIE MARGUERITE. *The Prognosis of Success in 1A Reading.* Unpublished master's thesis, George Washington University, 1937. Pp. 44.
12. WILSON, FRANK T., AND BURKE, AGNES. "Reading Readiness in a Progressive School." *Teach Col Rec* 38:565-80 Ap '37. * (*PA* 11:3918)
13. DEAN, CHARLES D. "Predicting First-Grade Reading Achievement." *El Sch J* 39:609-16 Ap '39. * (*PA* 13:6458)
14. FITZGERALD, FRANCES. *Predicting Reading Success of First-Grade Entrants.* Unpublished master's thesis, Duke University, 1939. Pp. 96.
15. TRAXLER, ARTHUR E. "Reliability and Predictive Value of the Metropolitan Readiness Tests," pp. 49-58. In *1946 Fall Testing Program in Independent Schools and Supplementary Studies.* Educational Records Bulletin, No. 47. New York: Educational Records Bureau, February 1947. Pp. x, 58. Paper, lithotyped. $1.50. * (*PA* 21:2498)

Irving H. Anderson, Professor of Education, University of Michigan, Ann Arbor, Michigan. The *Metropolitan Readiness Tests* continue to be among the most widely used of the readiness tests. The tests are intended to measure readiness for reading, arithmetic, and even writing and are thus somewhat broader in scope than most other readiness tests, which are rather generally designed to measure readiness for reading alone. The Metropolitan tests are easily administered to first-grade children —more easily than the *Monroe Reading Apti-*

tude Tests, for example. However, the Metropolitan tests are probably not as analytical of readiness for reading as the Monroe tests. The Metropolitan tests require approximately 70 minutes to administer. Percentile norms are available in the manual of directions. These norms show that there is a significant relationship between scores on the test and achievement in the first grade. High correlations exist between scores on the *Metropolitan Readiness Tests* and scores on intelligence tests. These correlations are of approximately the same magnitude as the correlations between scores on different intelligence tests. It would probably be unnecessary to give the pupils both an intelligence test and the *Metropolitan Readiness Tests.* A good intelligence test would serve essentially the same purpose. Readiness for the work of the first grade is not difficult for the observant teacher to determine.

For review by W. J. Osburn, see 40:1552.

[519]

Reading Aptitude Tests. First grade entrants; 1935; individual in part; 1 form; $1.35 per 25; 72¢ per set of testing materials needed by examiner; 10¢ per specimen set; (40-55) minutes; Marion Monroe; Houghton Mifflin Co.

REFERENCES

1. WYLIE, ALICE E. *A Study of the Monroe Reading Aptitude Tests With One Hundred Second- and Third-Grade Children.* Unpublished master's thesis, University of Pittsburgh, 1935. (*Abstracts of Theses . . . 1935,* pp. 363-4.)
2. DEAN, CHARLES D. "Predicting First-Grade Reading Achievement." *El Sch J* 39:609-16 Ap '39. * (*PA* 13:6458)
3. KIRK, SAMUEL A. "Reading Aptitudes of Mentally Retarded Children." *J Psycho-Asthenics* 44:156-62 '39. * (*PA* 14:3552)
4. ROSLOW, SYDNEY. "Reading Readiness and Reading Achievement in First Grade." *J Exp Ed* 9:154-9 D '40. * (*PA* 15:2379)
5. SPACHE, GEORGE. "A Correction in the Administration and Norms of the Monroe Reading Aptitude Tests." *El Sch J* 41:454-8 F '41. * (*PA* 16:770)

Irving H. Anderson, Professor of Education, University of Michigan, Ann Arbor, Michigan. An effort has been made in this test to include items which the literature shows have differentiated between good and poor readers. For example, the literature suggests that children who are successful in beginning reading have better motor control than children who are unsuccessful. A test of motor control, therefore, is included in the examination. The other tests of the battery have been selected in the same way. These other tests cover such things as memory of orientation of forms, ocular-motor control and attention, visual memory, auditory word-discrimination, sound blending, and picture vocabulary. The foregoing are tested on a group basis. A few individual tests are also included. Auditory memory, speed and accuracy of articulation, and speed of association are examples of the individual tests. Teachers like the Monroe test because they consider it to be diagnostic of specific difficulty. The group tests can be administered in 30 to 40 minutes. The individual tests require an additional 10 to 15 minutes per child. Percentile norms are provided in the manual of directions. These norms show that high and low scores on the total test are good predictors of success and failure in beginning reading. The test represents a good effort to apply the results of scientific investigations in the field of reading.

[520]
Reading Readiness Test. First grade entrants; 1932–38; individual; Forms A, B in one booklet; $1.50 per 25 tests; 50¢ per manual and accessories needed by examiner; 50¢ per specimen set, postpaid; (30) minutes; M. J. Van Wagenen; Educational Test Bureau.

REFERENCES
1. WILSON, FRANK T., AND BURKE, AGNES. "Reading Readiness in a Progressive School." *Teach Col Rec* 38:565-80 Ap '37. * (PA 11:3918)
2. HUGGETT, A. J. "An Experiment in Reading Readiness." *J Ed Res* 32:263-70 D '38. *
3. GATES, A. I.; BOND, G. L.; AND RUSSELL, D. H.; ASSISTED BY EVA BOND, ANDREW HALPIN, AND KATHRYN HORAN. *Methods of Determining Reading Readiness.* New York: Bureau of Publications, Teachers College, Columbia University, 1939. Pp. iv, 55. Paper. Out of print. * (PA 13:6466)
4. JOHNSON, NORRIE E. *A Study to Determine the Predictive Accuracy of the Van Wagenen Reading Readiness Test.* Unpublished master's thesis, Indiana State Teachers College, 1942. Pp. 47.

David H. Russell, Professor of Education, University of California, Berkeley, California. Since Van Wagenen's *Reading Readiness Test* is made up of six subtests administered individually it has more diagnostic possibilities than a simpler test such as Stone and Grover's *Classification Test for Beginners in Reading.* This advantage is at least partly offset by the longer time required for administration and a rather elaborate system of scoring.

The six subtests are as follows: (*a*) Range of Information, composed of 30 items of common knowledge such as the number of cents in a dime; (*b*) Perception of Relations, composed of thirty analogies to be completed; (*c*) Vocabulary-Opposites, which requires the child to give the opposites of such words as *empty* and *throw;* (*d*) Memory Span for Ideas, which requires the child to repeat sentences of increasing length; (*e*) Word Discrimination, in which the child picks out from a line of five words (viewed in a slit) one word which is unlike the four others; and (*f*) Word Learning, an associative learning test in which the child

associates an English word with a foreign word (such as *bird* with *mesto*) exposed five different times on a card.

These six tests obviously attempt to measure quite different abilities and agree with the common view that readiness for reading is a complex of factors. The authors, however, give little evidence to suggest that each of these subtests has considerable value in predicting later reading success. The manual quotes only one result, a correlation of .73 between the average of total scores on the two forms of the test (omitting the fifth subtest) given at the beginning of the first grade and an average of four reading tests given at the end of the first grade. Intercorrelations between the subtests and results, including the fifth test, Word Discrimination, are not given. In a study by Gates, Bond and Russell (3) the average correlation between the total score and reading scores after one, two, and three terms was .52 in four New York City classes, and the correlations for the subtests ranged from .23 for the Memory Span for Ideas subtest to .17 for the Perception of Relations subtest. The validity of the parts of the test would accordingly seem to be still in doubt.

The rather elaborate system of scoring the test may discourage some prospective users among teachers but probably will not dissuade testing bureaus or trained test users from employing the test. Conrad (*see* 38:878) has stated clearly some of the disadvantages in using C-scores. However, the use of such scores here has the advantage of giving the child's ability in relation to the difficulty of the tasks in the various scales. In addition, the use of the Aptitude Index (based only on the first four subtests) gives a measure of his probable success, taking into account his chronological age. Van Wagenen recommends a "much slower modified program" for children who have Aptitude Indexes below 90, particularly if they start before six or six and one-half years of age. If the author can establish its validity more clearly, the results of the test can be interpreted, by means of the scores mentioned and the profile chart provided, to provide definite guidance in the child's early reading experiences. The two forms of the test and the provision for incorporating its results into cumulative records are strengths. Because of administration and scoring difficulties, it is probably best used as a follow-up test for diagnostic purposes if a simple test indicates possible difficulties.

[521]

Stevens Reading Readiness Test. First grade entrants; 1938–44; formerly published by American Education Press, Inc.; 1 form; $2.40 per 25; 35¢ per specimen set, postpaid; 10 daily sittings over a 2-week period; Avis Coultas Stevens; World Book Co.

Irving H. Anderson, Professor of Education, University of Michigan, Ann Arbor, Michigan. This test consists of three parts. Part I is designed to measure visual discrimination. Part II is designed to measure the ability to listen to, comprehend, recall, and retell a short story. Part III, which is optional, is designed to measure visual-auditory recall. Other factors related to reading readiness are assessed by means of a detailed individual check list or child study record. The check list is included as a part of the test blank proper. Reliability coefficients are reported for the test as a whole as well as for the individual parts and various combinations of parts. All reliability coefficients are satisfactory for individual diagnosis and prediction. The intercorrelations between the various parts of the test are sufficiently low to suggest that different functions are measured by the separate parts. Satisfactory validation data are reported. The statistical data as a whole are impressive. Norms are presented both in percentiles and standard units. Some teachers will object to the time it takes to administer the test. Several sittings over a period of two weeks are recommended. Part I alone consists of 16 pages involving 120 items. However, the information which the test provides on each individual child is worth having. Teachers will do well to give this reading readiness test careful study.

Marion Monroe Cox, Supervisor of the Reading Division, Psycho-Educational Clinic, The University of Southern California, Los Angeles, California. This test consists of a sixteen-page test booklet encased in a four-page folder which contains a check list of observations about the child; judgments as to his personality, social and emotional behavior, background, and family relationships; and space for recording data from intelligence tests, physical examinations, and kindergarten attendance. The battery of tests includes three parts: (*a*) group tests of ability to discriminate printed letters, words, and phrases; (*b*) an individual

test of ability to reproduce a story heard; and (*c*) an individual test of ability to recall words which have been associated with pictures in a group game played daily for three days previous to the test.

The testing program requires two weeks early in the first grade during which the pupils are given certain sections of the test according to a daily schedule. As the testing proceeds, the teacher becomes acquainted with each child personally and fills out the check list concerning his personality and history. The *Stevens Reading Readiness Test,* therefore, stimulates the teacher to make a brief "case history" of each pupil, to gather together pertinent data, and to observe each pupil's reactions in both group and individual testing.

A teacher who has followed the suggested program carefully undoubtedly discovers many things about each child which will enable her to individualize instruction and adapt to the child's needs in teaching him.

The validity of the test was determined by correlating the total test scores at the beginning of the semester with teachers' reports of achievement in reading at the end of the semester. The correlation coefficient obtained is .80, an unusually high one in the light of the many factors that influence children's ability to learn. The test predicts very well how each child's reading achievement will be rated by his teacher at the end of the semester. However, pupils who scored very low on the tests were not exposed to reading, those who scored low were given only simple charts for reading, and at each level the work was adapted to the children's abilities as shown by the test. A high correlation between test scores and final achievement is, therefore, to be expected.

The manual which accompanies the test contains not only directions for administering the tests, and the norms, but also a number of helpful suggestions and recommendations for improving the child's ability in cases where specific weaknesses have been revealed by the test.

The *Stevens Reading Readiness Test* may require more time in testing and observing children individually than many teachers will be willing to give, and not all the traits listed in the *Check List* are always closely related to reading readiness. An investigation of each child while compiling such a list is illuminating, however, and the teacher may be well repaid for her trouble by a better understanding of each child's problems. In obtaining a history, the cooperation between parents and teachers is essential, and a close parent-teacher relationship may clarify goals and pave the way toward better learning. If teachers using the tests were well trained in mental hygiene or had access to a counselor who could help interpret the data wisely, the individual analysis stimulated by the *Stevens Reading Readiness Test* would be as helpful as or even more helpful than the actual test scores in improving instruction in reading.

SPEED

[522]
Chapman-Cook Speed of Reading Test. Grades 4-8; 1923-24; Forms A, B; 75¢ per 25; 25¢ per specimen set, postpaid; 2½ (10) minutes; J. C. Chapman and Sidney Cook; Educational Test Bureau.

REFERENCES
1. CHAPMAN, J. CROSBY, AND COOK, S. "The Principle of the Single Variable in a Speed of Reading Cross-Out Test." *J Ed Res* 8:389-96 D '23. *

Eason Monroe, Chairman, Language Arts Division, San Francisco State College, San Francisco, California. The *Chapman–Cook Speed of Reading Test,* one of the early tests of its kind, is designed to measure the rate of reading of pupils in grades 4 through 8. This test offers the advantage of a short testing time (two and one half minutes), simplicity and ease of administration, and objective scoring. Norms are furnished for each grade for which the test may be used. Two forms of the test are available.

Very much like the *Michigan Speed of Reading Test,* for which it served as model, the *Chapman–Cook Speed of Reading Test* is composed of thirty-word items. In the latter part of each item one word is inserted which is out of meaning relationship with the rest of the item—"one word which spoils the meaning." The reader is required to find this word in each item and cross it out. The test includes thirty such items. The content of the separate items is unrelated.

The entire test is printed on the two sides of a standard 8½ by 11 inch sheet, the directions and practice exercises on one side and the thirty items arranged in separate paragraphs and in two columns on the reverse side. Type size and format appear to be satisfactory.

The nature of the reading task involved in this test is highly specialized and unusual. It seems questionable, therefore, that the test re-

flects validly those rates of reading which function in the more representative types of reading. (*See* 523 for the reviewer's comments on the *Michigan Speed of Reading Test.*)

The short testing time and the limited number of items raise also the question of whether this test provides a reliable measure of reading rate for all the grade groups for which it is intended.

This test appears to be most useful for teachers who are especially interested in studying the reading rates of intermediate grade pupils. As a survey device, the test may single out those pupils who should receive further testing or other forms of special attention.

[523]
Michigan Speed of Reading Test. Grades 6-16; 1932-37; Forms I, II; $1.75 per 25, postpaid; 35¢ per specimen set, postpaid; 7(15) minutes; Edward B. Greene; Psychological Corporation.

REFERENCES
1-2. See 40:1553.
3. LANGSAM, ROSALIND STREEP. "A Factorial Analysis of Reading Ability." *J Exp Ed* 10:57-63 S '41. * (*PA* 16:1187)

Eason Monroe, Chairman, Language Arts Division, San Francisco State College, San Francisco, California. This test is designed to measure "speed of reading of easy material." Simplicity of organization and procedure and a short testing time (seven minutes) make this test easy and convenient to administer. Two forms of the test are available, with norms for subjects from third grade through the college senior year based upon 3,302 cases. Scoring is objective.

The test is composed of 75 items. Each item consists of 30 words, arranged in two or three short related sentences. There is no continuity of meaning from item to item. With few exceptions, the vocabulary of the items is limited to the first 5,000 words in the *Thorndike Teacher's Word Book.* The content of the items is said to be representative of the school and home situations common to third and fourth grade children (1).

The test items are arranged in five-item paragraphs in double columns on both sides of a standard 8½ by 11 inch sheet. To provide this convenience of format, it has been necessary to use a size of type which is four or six points smaller than intermediate grade pupils are accustomed to read. Otherwise, the test appears to be carefully prepared and presented.

For the purpose of comprehension control, the *Michigan Speed of Reading Test* employs the technique used in the earlier *Chapman–Cook Speed of Reading Test.* In the latter portion of each item a single word has been inserted which is out of meaning with the rest of the item. *As he reads,* the subject is required to "cross out, in the second part of each numbered passage, one word which spoils the meaning."

Reliabilities of this test are reported to vary between .653 and .94, "with the mean reliability of .87 for single age groups" (1). Despite the fact that the vocabulary and concepts of the test are adapted for third and fourth grade pupils, the relatively low reliability of the measure at these grade levels casts doubt upon its appropriateness for these young readers. At the junior high school level and above, however, the test maintains consistently satisfactory reliability.

It is a difficult task to prepare a discrete measure of reading rate which is highly valid and reliable and yet convenient to administer and to score. Frequently, in an effort to provide strongly for one or two of these important elements, test producers introduce shortcomings in other respects. Tests of reading rate which, for the sake of convenient administration or high reliability, involve unusual or non-representative reading tasks may fall seriously short of valid measurement.

Serious question can be raised concerning the extent to which this test measures the types of reading rate which are most representative and significant in general school and life reading. The reading problem involved throughout the entire test—looking for and crossing out in each item the single word which is out of meaning relationship with the remainder of the passage—focuses the reader's attention upon an unusual comprehension task. Instead of reading for the integrated meaning of each item, the reader may find himself scanning the first part of the item for a general clue which he can use merely to identify the misfit word. This specialized process may not be uniformly related to the reader's other reading rate performances and is certainly not a representative reading process. It is likely also that different readers may react variously to the annoyance of interrupting the flow of reading to cross out the inappropriate words.

One of the most serious shortcomings of this test, in the reviewer's opinion, is the complete lack of continuity of meaning throughout the sequence of items. The reader, accustomed in his regular reading to deriving meaning through the continuous process of interpreting relationships, during this test finds that he must make a new reading adjustment for each item. He must demonstrate his rate of reading in a situation which, lacking the dynamic qualities that support efficient efforts in normal reading, actually prevents or inhibits rapid reading. In this respect the test calls for a type of performance which is not commonly involved in general reading and which is perhaps relatively unimportant.

Test users who are interested solely in the measurement of reading rate for junior and senior high school pupils may find this test useful for simple and convenient group screening. Because of the important inadequacies of the test, however, pupils who make unusually high or low scores or who demonstrate in other ways a need for special attention should be checked by means of additional standardized and informal measures of reading.

For reviews by Richard Ledgerwood and M. R. Trabue of an earlier edition, see 38:1171.

[524]

Reading Speed and Comprehension: Ohio Senior Survey Tests. Grade 12; 1935–41; Forms A, B; 3¢ per test; (25) minutes; S. L. Pressey and J. W. Sherburne (Form B); Ohio Scholarship Tests, Ohio State Department of Education.

J. B. Stroud, Professor of Education and Psychology, State University of Iowa, Iowa City, Iowa. Each of two forms of this test, a part of The Ohio Senior Survey Tests battery, consists of a single reading selection of about 2,400 words. The student is given an instructional set to read as rapidly as is consistent with his ability to answer questions over the material after he has read it. At the end of five minutes he marks the line he is then reading. He is then allowed to finish the piece. Presumably the rate score is determined from the number of words read in the five-minute period. The questions are answered without recourse to the reading text.

This sort of test fulfills an important need in testing reading. In some respects it is a more exacting test of ability to read than are the tests in which the student has access to the text when answering the questions. This test requires self-direction. The reader must supply his own set as he must in any natural reading situation. His own perceptual and thought processes rather than the nature of the questions asked determine what elements in the piece shall be reacted to and how he shall react to them. Perhaps the most exacting gauge of the quality of reading is what responses the reader can make about the content after he has read a piece. The criticism that such tests are memory tests is not crucial if the test questions are responded to immediately and if the items are of the kind and quality they should be. After all, items of detail—the kind for which the memory factor would be vitiating— are not good tests of reading ability, except of a very elementary kind, whether they are responded to from memory or from inspection of the text. The items of the two forms of the test in question appear to be adequate.

Miles A. Tinker, Professor of Psychology, The University of Minnesota, Minneapolis, Minnesota. This is one of the tests devised for use with Ohio high school seniors. A case study of a college student constitutes the reading material. Form A is to be administered before remedial training in the senior survey course is begun; Form B, after the program is completed. The student reads as rapidly as possible for ·5 minutes, marks the amount done, and then reads the rest of the material in the test. When finished, the booklet is collected, and a set of 30 multiple-choice comprehension questions is given without time limit. Thus, the test yields a measure of speed in terms of words read per minute and a measure of comprehension. Directions are clear and concise.

There are no data in the manual or in the materials accompanying the test on number of cases employed for standardization or on equivalence of the two test forms. Percentile norms are given for speed and for comprehension scores. Item norms (i.e., per cent answering each item correctly) are also listed for the comprehension questions. Although Form A is printed in uniform line lengths, Form B has exactly five words on each line. This results in a marked variation in length of successive lines, i.e., an undesirable typographical arrangement. Perhaps this explains the fact that Form B was read much slower than Form A although remedial training had intervened. The obvious lack of equivalence in reading rate between the two forms makes interpretation of progress in reading hazardous. One can only note changes in percentile rank from one test to the other. The significance of such shiftings in rank necessarily must remain obscure in the absence of equivalent test forms. For instance, the student who reads 229 words per minute on Form A gets a percentile rank of 40. If, after training, he reads 199 words per minute on Form B, his percentile is 50. Interpretation of the comprehension scores involves similar difficulties.

The materials accompanying the test furnish no information on either the reliability or the validity of the speed of reading and the comprehension scores. The trained worker objects to using tests either for clinical or for survey purposes unless he knows their reliability and validity, since this information is needed for interpreting the significance of the scores.

The typography of the test is very illegible. The print is small, and the letters are blurred as if badly worn type had been used.

This test is constructed in a fundamentally sound way. Rate of reading and comprehension scores are derived from the same material. The reader knows there will be a comprehension check when the test is started, and the timed reading period is of adequate duration. Choice of reading material appears adequate and organization of the comprehension questions well done. Nevertheless, lack of information on standardization and the illegible print are serious obstacles to use of the test. The more adequately standardized *Chapman–Cook Speed of Reading Test* and the *Minnesota Speed of Reading Test for College Students* are more satisfactory for measuring speed of reading and gains in speed of reading than the test reviewed here.

[525]
Reading Speed Test: National Achievement Test. Grades 3-8; 1938–39; Forms A, B; withdrawn from publication in 1947; 3 or 4(10) minutes; Robert K. Speer and Samuel Smith; Acorn Publishing Co.

Eason Monroe, Chairman, Language Arts Division, San Francisco State College, San Francisco, California. This test "has been constructed to test the pupil's speed of reading." The directions for administration are clearly phrased and the test procedure is relatively simple.

Each form of the test consists of a fairly long, somewhat continuous account of children's activities which are likely to be meaningful for elementary school pupils. Normal paragraphing, favorable type size, and doublecolumning of the text increase the readability of the material.

Comprehension is presumably controlled during the reading process by requiring the reader to underline certain sentences throughout the text. In Form A, for example, the pupil is asked to "draw a line under every sentence that tells about John's dog, Fido." In each form, twenty-five sentences should be underlined. These sentences are distributed throughout twenty-two paragraphs in Form A and twenty paragraphs in Form B.

This test offers an important advantage over other rate of reading tests which involve underlining or crossing-out techniques for controlling comprehension. This advantage lies chiefly in the relative continuity of the text, which provides a more representative reading experience and increased pupil interest. Much of this value, however, is seriously reduced by the requirement of underlining the entire sentence in which the key symbols occur. For this reason, the test comes to be a measure not only of speed of reading but also of speed and skill of underlining. Conscientious pupils are likely to sacrifice reading time in their effort to underline in exact accord with the test directions. No score may be given for sentences "incorrectly underlined."

Alert pupils may soon discover that the sentences to be underlined in Form A invariably contain one of three clues—Fido, John's dog, or his dog. Scoring lines beside each paragraph indicate clearly for such pupils the number of sentences to be underlined in each paragraph. Similar clues are evident in Form B. Having made these discoveries, a pupil may shift his method of performance and make satisfactory test responses without continuing the normal process of sequential reading. The scores of individual pupils are likely to be distorted by this possibility.

This test may be used for group survey purposes, but it is important to use additional measures in the case of pupils who make unusually high or low scores or who demonstrate in other ways the need for special study.

SPECIAL FIELDS

[526]

★Interpretation of Reading Materials in the Natural Sciences: Tests of General Educational Development: College Level, Test 3. College; 1944–45; IBM; Form B; separate answer sheets must be used; $3 per 25; 40¢ per 25 machine-scorable answer sheets; 15¢ per scoring key; 25¢ per specimen set, postpaid; worklimit (120) minutes; prepared by the Examinations Staff of the United States Armed Forces Institute; published by the American Council on Education; distributed by the Cooperative Test Service. (Also distributed by Science Research Associates: $3 per 25; 65¢ per 25 machine-scorable answer sheets; 50¢ per key; 50¢ per specimen set.)

For reviews by Herbert S. Conrad and Warren G. Findley of the entire battery, see 20.

[527]

★Interpretation of Reading Materials in the Natural Sciences: Tests of General Educational Development: High School Level, Test 3. High school; 1944–45; IBM; Form B; separate answer sheets must be used; $2 per 25; 40¢ per 25 machine-scorable answer sheets; 15¢ per scoring key; 25¢ per specimen set, postpaid; worklimit (120) minutes; prepared by the Examinations Staff of the United States Armed Forces Institute; published by the American Council on Education; distributed by the Cooperative Test Service. (Also distributed by Science Research Associates: $2 per 25; 65¢ per 25 machine-scorable answer sheets; 50¢ per key; 50¢ per specimen set.)

For reviews by Herbert S. Conrad and Warren G. Findley of the entire battery, see 20.

[528]

★Interpretation of Reading Materials in the Social Studies: Tests of General Educational Development: College Level, Test 2. College; 1944–45; IBM; Form B; separate answer sheets must be used; $3 per 25; 40¢ per 25 machine-scorable answer sheets; 15¢ per scoring key; 25¢ per specimen set, postpaid; worklimit (120) minutes; prepared by the Examinations Staff of the United States Armed Forces Institute; published by the American Council on Education; distributed by the Cooperative Test Service. (Also distributed by Science Research Associates: $3 per 25; 65¢ per 25 machine-scorable answer sheets; 50¢ per key; 50¢ per specimen set.)

REFERENCES
1. BRADLEY, MARY EDITH. "A Study of the Validity of the Armed Forces Institute Tests of General Educational Development in the Field of Social Studies." *Ed & Psychol Meas* 6:265-8 su '46. * (PA 21:595)

W. E. Hall, Associate Professor of Educational Psychology, The University of Nebraska, Lincoln, Nebraska. This test is constructed on a sound basis in terms of the type of reading material presented in the text. This material resembles closely the type of material a college student will be apt to read in the social science area. The questions on the social science reading selections closely resemble the type of questions that will be asked of many students in college courses.

The questions are of a nature to require the student "to dig out" the meaning rather than answer the obvious. There is a novel type of question included in each group of questions following the selection read. The questions can be answered directly out of the general knowledge of the testee rather than from the passage read.

The standardization has been established on the success of high school seniors who have taken the test and who have passed social science courses. Since the three types of percentile tables have been based on the scores made by students who have been classified by the *American Council of Education Psychological Examination* and the tests are constructed on some activity which is practically identical to college work, it would seem that this test goes a long way toward realizing its objective.

It will be hoped that further validation will be published in terms of college success in social science and scores on the test.

C. Robert Pace, Associate Director, Evaluation Service Center, Syracuse University, Syracuse, New York. This test is, for the most part, competently constructed and attempts to measure important and worth-while objectives; its intended use represents a distinct advance from the practice of granting "blanket credits" followed after World War I. Some elements of the test, however, warrant criticism; and the norms given for college populations not only are of doubtful validity but may be misleading.

The test consists of ten paragraphs, one graph, and one table, each followed by a series of questions presumably requiring an interpretation or evaluation of the material. There are 91 items in all, 20 of which are starred as being answerable without reference to the reading materials. In my judgment, however, at least 20 additional items could appropriately be starred, thus making it possible to answer about half of the test items without reference to the reading materials. Further, one may properly object to the "correct" answer which is keyed for some of the questions. Especially in interpretation and evaluation items, testmakers must be on guard to avoid penalizing the individual who is able to bring a great deal of knowledge to bear on a given topic. There may be several good answers rather than one best answer; and the results of item analysis do not prove to the scholars which answer is best. For example, the answer to a question regarding the concentration of economic power is "directors of corporations"; but the student should know that "bankers," even though they are not referred to in the paragraph, hold economic power over the

corporations. Again, social security is considered the correct response to a question about ways in which the United States has lagged in the extension of democracy; the right to vote, however, is also a reasonable choice for we did not obtain women's suffrage until 1921, and we still do not have suffrage for large groups in parts of our society. And again, the correct response to a question about which is the best reply to a prejudiced argument in one of the paragraphs is an argument by analogy (such arguments are always weak from the logician's point of view), whereas a direct and ethical reply is considered "incorrect." Other examples could be cited.

With regard to the college percentile norms, the test authors acknowledge that their meaningfulness is limited and that their uncritical acceptance may be misleading. Percentile norms for Type III institutions offering courses in world history are based on the test performance of 53 students from one institution! For Type I institutions offering general survey courses in social studies, percentile norms are based on 85 students from 3 institutions! These are the two worst examples. In addition to the total inadequacy of these figures (it might have been better not to have published them), a more basic fault lies in the selection of institutions to comprise the norm group. This group is limited to institutions which offer "survey" courses and which also used the ACE psychological examination in 1941. The decision to limit the selection of institutions to those which happen to offer "survey" courses seems to me quite unjustified, especially when the use of the test is practically forced on a nation-wide scale. I would argue that there should have been national college norms, based on a broad sampling of students who had taken any social science course during their first two college years. The composite thus obtained would be representative not only of the kinds of students who take social science courses but also of the variety of social science courses offered in American colleges and universities. In contrast, the high school norms for this and the other tests in the series are based on an excellent national sample.

It should be recognized that the GED tests were constructed to meet a postwar emergency. Within a relatively short time this emergency will have passed. Meanwhile, the GED tests should be compared experimentally with others which might be used to predict ability to carry on advanced college work—such as those of the Cooperative Test Service, the College Entrance Examination Board, the Graduate Record Examination, etc.

The attempt to measure fundamental objectives of understanding and critical judgment deserves every encouragement. It is hoped that the increased familiarity with this type of test which has occurred by virtue of its nation-wide use will encourage local institutions to prepare tests along similar lines for local purposes and will encourage central testing agencies to seek improvements and refinements in future tests designed to measure such basic objectives.

For reviews by Herbert S. Conrad and Warren G. Findley of the entire battery, see 20.

[529]

★Interpretation of Reading Materials in the Social Studies: Tests of General Educational Development: High School Level, Test 2. High school; 1944–45; IBM; Form B; separate answer sheets must be used; $2 per 25; 40¢ per 25 machine-scorable answer sheets; 15¢ per scoring key; 25¢ per specimen set, postpaid; worklimit (120) minutes; prepared by the Examinations Staff of the United States Armed Forces Institute; published by the American Council on Education; distributed by the Cooperative Test Service. (Also distributed by Science Research Associates: $2 per 25; 65¢ per 25 machine-scorable answer sheets; 50¢ per key; 50¢ per specimen set.)

For reviews by Herbert S. Conrad and Warren G. Findley of the entire battery, see 20.

[530]

★Reading Scales in History. Grades 7–12; 1938–39; Forms A, B; $1.25 per 25; 25¢ per specimen set, postpaid; nontimed 45(60) minutes; M. J. Van Wagenen; Educational Test Bureau.

Paul Blommers, Acting Dean of the College of Education and Assistant Professor of Education, The State University of Iowa, Iowa City, Iowa. This test purports to measure power to comprehend the subject matter which is encountered at the junior and senior high school levels in history. The test consists of a series of 15 paragraphs, each followed by from 4 to 6 statements. The students are directed to mark those statements which contain an idea that is either specifically mentioned in or implied by the paragraph. The statements following each paragraph are scored as a unit, the maximum score for no errors being two points. One point is given if one error is made and no points are given if more than one error is made. The paragraphs are graded with respect to difficulty

—difficulty being defined in terms of the proportion of successes on the accompanying statements. A table is provided for converting the total test score into a C-score, which, according to the manual, indicates the difficulty level of the content which the student can understand and mark correctly in 50 per cent of his attempts. Age and grade norms are provided.

The test has been carefully constructed and should be fairly useful as a measure of general reading comprehension. It appears legitimate, however, to question its validity as a measure of the specific ability to comprehend historical material. Consideration of the test statements does not indicate an attempt to measure skills differing from those employed in reading other types of material. It is, of course, true that the content of all paragraphs is historical in nature, but is this in itself sufficient to accomplish the purpose?

In answering this question it must be acknowledged that two individuals equal in reading skill per se may differ in ability to comprehend history. This difference, however, is in a large part due to differences in background knowledge. To the extent that background knowledge enters into the score, the test will differentiate between these individuals. In this test, however, every attempt is made to minimize the effect of background knowledge. The student is told: "there *may be* statements that are *true in themselves,* but do not mark them . . . unless the idea is contained in the paragraph or can be inferred from the facts or ideas in the paragraph." Evidently the student is to come equipped with only his reading cap —his background knowledge being left in the cloakroom. It is difficult to understand how a test which purports to measure an individual's specific ability to comprehend history can be valid for that purpose if it employs such directions. Moreover, such directions are apt to confuse students who take them seriously as the better students are likely to do. At least, there is room for debate on the keying of certain responses when the issue reduces to whether the statements can be inferred from the ideas in the paragraph (e.g., see Statement 2, Paragraph 11, Form B.)

As already indicated, the manual states that the C-score is indicative of the difficulty level of the material the student can understand. Actually the C-score bears little relationship to the difficulty of the content of the paragraph per se. This is evidenced by the different positioning within the two forms of the ten paragraphs common to them. The C-score is more indicative of the type of statement the student can correctly mark, that is, of the depth of his comprehension of the given material rather than of the difficulty of the material itself. This does not constitute an objection to the test and is mentioned in the interest of preventing a misunderstanding of the relationship between the C-score and "difficulty level."

Finally, it should be observed that the overlapping of the content of the two forms is so great as to impair somewhat the value of having the second form.

Albert J. Harris, Assistant Professor of Education, The City College of New York, New York, New York. This test is intended to measure the ability to comprehend historical reading material at the high school level. Similar tests of literary reading and scientific reading have been constructed by the same author.

The test is given as a power test without a specific time limit. Each of the two forms includes fifteen selections followed by four, five, or six true-false items. The selections are supposed to be arranged in ascending order of difficulty. Of the fifteen selections in Form A, ten also appear in Form B, with slightly different questions. Selection 1 in Form A is Selection 5 in Form B; Selection 12 in Form A is Selection 2 in Form B; etc. To make matters even worse, Selection 8 in Form A reappears as Selection 11 in the same form, with a different set of questions based on it! A well-constructed power test should certainly have a more stable order of difficulty than this.

The raw scores are translated into C-scores, a type of scaled score based on the quartile deviation, which is used in several other tests by the same author. Age and grade equivalents are provided for the C-score scale. The reliability is stated as a probable error of 2.6 C-score points. This is the equivalent of between .4 and .5 times the quartile deviation for a single grade and is below what is generally considered good reliability for the measurement of the status of individuals. Norms include age and grade equivalents and the 25th, 50th, and 75th percentiles for grades 9, 10, 11, and 12. No information is given in the brief four-page manual that would allow an evaluation of the adequacy of standardization.

There is no evidence presented that this test would be more helpful than a good general reading comprehension test in assaying a high school student's ability to read historical material. The idea of testing comprehension in a specific field is a good one; the execution, in this case, leaves much to be desired.

[531]
★Reading Scales in Literature. Grades 7-12; 1939; Forms A, B, C; $1.25 per 25; 25¢ per specimen set, postpaid; nontimed (45-60) minutes; M. J. Van Wagenen; Educational Test Bureau.

[532]
★Reading Scales in Science. Grades 7-12; 1938; Form A; $1.25 per 25; 25¢ per specimen set, postpaid; nontimed (45-60) minutes; M. J. Van Wagenen; Educational Test Bureau.

Ivan A. Booker, Assistant Director, Research Division, National Education Association, Washington, D. C. The *Reading Scales in Science* are designed to measure a pupil's ability to comprehend the materials usually encountered in high school science textbooks. They have been developed in such a way and standardized in such manner that the C-scores from this test are said to be comparable to those from the reading scales for junior and senior high schools in the *Unit Scales of Attainment.*

Each form of the *Reading Scales in Science* consists of fifteen paragraphs, each followed by four to six objective test items. The paragraphs typically contain about 150 words. The test items take the form of statements which are to be checked only when "the idea is either contained in the paragraph or can be inferred from the facts or ideas in the paragraph." All other statements are to be left unchecked.

The paragraphs are scaled according to difficulty. However, it is the difference in test items instead of a difference in the difficulty of the test paragraphs which accounts for the paragraph placement. This must be the case in view of the amount of repetition of paragraphs in the tests, with quite different placement of identical paragraphs. The extent to which test paragraphs appear more than once in these scales is indicated in part by the facts that (*a*) three paragraphs are used twice in Form A, and three other paragraphs appear twice in Form B; (*b*) eight paragraphs appear one or more times in one form of the test and also once in the other form; and (*c*) only three paragraphs in Form A and one in Form B are *not* repeated. When a paragraph is repeated, however, every test item used with it is different from the items used elsewhere. Repetition, therefore, merely has the effect of reducing the reading load or holding it within selected limits while increasing the number and difficulty of the test items.

Each paragraph is scored as a unit, irrespective of whether it is accompanied by four, five, or six test items. Each disagreement between the pupil's response and the scoring key (failing to check an item or checking one that should not be checked) is counted as an error. A paragraph is given a score of two if no error occurs, a score of one if there is only one error, and a score of zero if there are two or more errors. Thus, the actual scores must range between zero and thirty. The scoring key used in checking errors is exceptionally well arranged for rapid use. Having to score each paragraph as a unit, however, is time-consuming and greatly increases the hazard of scoring errors. It is difficult to understand how this complicated procedure improves on the total score which would be obtained by simply counting the total number of correct responses for the 70-odd items in the total series. The C-scores, however, are based on the 30-point scale of total scores.

The manual of directions gives no information as to the validity and reliability of the test, neither for the forms when considered as wholes nor for the individual paragraphs and test items which constitute them. Users of this test—as is true for so many other tests also—are given no description of the standardization procedures and no indication of the adequacy of the norms suggested.

The scoring key gives C-scores ranging between 48 and 122 to accompany each actual score of 0 to 30. The manual gives a median and a 25th and 75th percentile C-score for each grade from 8 to 12, inclusive. Norms are not included for grade 7, although the test purports to cover grades 7 to 12.

Lists of C-scores are also given for each form of the test to indicate the relative levels of difficulty of the various paragraphs and items. A part of this scale for Form A follows:

PARAGRAPH:	3	4	....	7	8	9	....	12	13
C-SCORE VALUE:	81	83	....	89	91	92	....	99	102

These are interpreted as follows: a pupil with a C-score of 91 can be expected to do correctly about "half of such paragraphs and sets of statements as paragraph 8; three fourths of such paragraphs and sets of statements as paragraph 3 [ten C-score points lower]; but only about one fourth of such paragraphs and sets of statements as paragraph 13 [ten C-score points higher]." Such interpretation, however, is of doubtful practical value. The teacher has no way to determine whether the content of a given science selection and the pupil's tasks relating to it are more nearly equivalent to Paragraph 3 or Paragraph 13. As has been pointed out, the scaled difficulty is achieved, not through the paragraphs but through the test items. To know, for example, that a pupil can do about three-fourths of the tasks comparable to Paragraph 5 is of little consequence, therefore, when Paragraph 5 is the same as Paragraph 15 except for the test items.

A criticism often voiced against the *Unit Scales of Attainment,* to which these tests are related, seems fully justified here. The C-scores provided with the tests probably are somewhat misleading, especially to teachers not thoroughly grounded in testing procedures. They tend to imply an exactness of pupil placement or an accuracy of measurement which these tests cannot supply.

The unique value in the *Reading Scales in Science* is their use of science content material in a reading comprehension test. Often there is a need for a reading test which will differentiate among the pupils as to their ability to read and understand the materials in a given subject-matter area. And where such a survey of ability to read high school science materials is needed, the *Reading Scales in Science* can be appropriately used. Even the grade norms and C-scores should prove helpful if their limitations are recognized, particularly with respect to the scores of individual pupils. Also, for the teacher who can use tests for something more than merely to obtain a total score, analysis of the kinds of test items on which a pupil made his errors will provide helpful insight as to the kind of guidance needed.

[533]

★Test of Reading Ability for————. College; 1940; 4¢ per reading booklet; 2¢ per test booklet; 10¢ per manual; 40¢ per specimen set; (15) minutes; Francis P. Robinson and Prudence Hall; Ohio State University Press.
a) A TEST OF READING ABILITY FOR ART. 1 form.
b) A TEST OF READING ABILITY FOR GEOLOGY. 1 form
c) A TEST OF READING ABILITY FOR HISTORY. Forms Canada, Russia.
d) A TEST OF READING ABILITY FOR FICTION. 1 form.

REFERENCES

1. ROBINSON, FRANCIS P. *Diagnostic and Remedial Techniques for Effective Study.* New York: Harper & Bros., 1941. Pp. ix, 318. Paper. * (PA 16:352) For latest edition, *see* (3) below.
2. ROBINSON, FRANCIS P., AND HALL, PRUDENCE. "Studies of Higher-Level Reading Abilities." *J Ed Psychol* 32:241-52 Ap '41. * (PA 16:353)
3. ROBINSON, FRANCIS P. *Effective Study.* A revision of *Diagnostic and Remedial Techniques for Effective Study.* New York: Harper & Brothers, 1946. Pp. ix, 262. $3.00. * (PA 21:1658)

STUDY SKILLS

[534]

★Applied Reading for Junior-Senior High School: Every Pupil Test. Grades 7-12; 1946; new form usually issued each April and December; forms April, December 1946; 2¢ per test; 1¢ per answer key; 7(15) minutes; Marion Steele and Margaret Egeland; Ohio Scholarship Tests, Ohio State Department of Education.

Ivan A. Booker, Assistant Director, Research Division, National Education Association, Washington, D. C. [Review of the 1946 forms.] This test is one in the series of Every Pupil Tests designed for use in all the schools of Ohio. More than three dozen tests including two on high school reading are now used in this state-wide testing program which was begun in 1929. New editions are developed each year by committees of teachers working in collaboration with the Testing Division of the State Department of Education for state-wide use in December and April. The two high school reading tests are *Applied Reading for Junior-Senior High School* and *Techniques in Reading Comprehension,* the latter described elsewhere (505) in this volume.

The test of applied reading is designed to measure three selected types of reading skills: (*a*) skill in using an index; (*b*) skill in recognizing, from the running heads used in a dictionary, whether or not a given word is on the page with the heading shown; (*c*) skill in discriminating among word meanings for homonyms and for words with multiple meanings. This is not a test of general level of reading ability, but a test of proficiency in these three specific skills, with emphasis on speed of performance. The over-all time for administering the three-part test in a class is not more than fifteen minutes—the total actual working time, seven minutes.

Part I of the test, on the use of an index, makes use of the usual procedure in testing this skill. Typical index items from A to W are given as a point of reference; the pupils are asked to find the page number or to select the index heading where they would find information about various subjects. The three-minute time limit is not generous, but adequate.

The next part of the test carries seven boxed page headings such as one finds in most dictionaries. Each such heading is followed by four test items consisting of words closely related alphabetically to one of the key words in the heading. The pupils indicate whether or not each test word should be on the page by writing "yes" or "no." The time limit on this part of the test is extremely brief—only two minutes. Those who write slowly are particularly handicapped. Merely to write "yes" and "no" alternately for twenty-eight items, without the slightest pause between items, usually requires from forty-five to sixty seconds for high-school pupils, which means that three-eighths to half of their total working time is used up in handwriting. A system of check (✓) and zero (o) would be just as useful; but of course, if any such plan were followed, it would destroy the comparability of results with pupils who had been forced to write "yes" and "no" to each item. The directions contain no warning against a system of abbreviations, only a positive direction to write "yes" or "no." Do some pupils on their own initiative use a simplified code to save time? If so, are their test papers eliminated? In a state-wide testing program, might some teachers encourage a short cut in marking, believing that the ability to discriminate was the only important part of the test? Where time limits are as brief as in this exercise, any variation in the mechanics of response becomes highly significant.

The final section of the test is focused on the ability to distinguish between word meanings. The words used are quite simple, but in each case two to five different meanings are involved. One series uses the word "contest," giving two definitions of the word when used as a noun and three when used as a verb. Test items then ask the student to indicate which definition would hold in each of several sentences. No writing is required other than to enter the letter of the correct definition in the space provided. Again the time limit is rather brief, which means that speed of performance is rewarded. The slow reader, irrespective of his accuracy in interpreting word meanings, is at a disadvantage on this exercise. A slight difference in content appears between the April and December 1946 editions, which may mean that the two forms are not strictly comparable. The April edition uses homonyms, such as "to," "too," and "two"; and "cite," "sight," and "site." The December edition uses for each unit in the exercise a single word with several meanings, such as "contest" already mentioned. Some students work much faster with the homonyms, knowing the differences in meaning so well that they can do the test items without having to read the definitions. This advantage becomes increasingly great for those in senior high schools.

Taken as a whole the test of *Applied Reading for Junior-Senior High School* undoubtedly is a useful measure of three related reading skills. Especially in classes where practice in the use of the index and practice in dictionary usage are being given—or being considered—this brief test should be quite helpful. When administered according to directions as a timed test, it shows the speed of performance of members of the class in comparison with that of other high school students. It might also be used to advantage in some classes as an untimed test or with individual timing to see how accurately the pupils work when not subjected to time pressures. These results could not be compared with available norms but might give useful diagnostic leads to the teacher.

The manual contains no information as to the procedure followed by the test development committees either to equate the forms in advance of their use or to assure the reliability and item validity of the tests. Perhaps, in view of the purpose of the tests, no elaborate preliminary tryouts and evaluations are feasible. Even the bulletin which reports the results of the 1946 testing program contains no data on reliability or validity, only the percentile scores and a table showing the percentage of pupils who answered each test item correctly. The fact that percentiles are used almost exclusively suggests that exact equality of forms is not expected.

The percentile norms *issued as soon as possible after the state-wide testing program* are based on the total scores—not on the scores for the three parts of the test—which limits its *diagnostic* value. Likewise the percentile norms are published separately only for junior high schools and for senior high schools rather than for individual grades. As stated earlier, there is a table showing the percentage of pupils who answered each test item correctly. This would be of some use in the diagnostic study of indi-

vidual test papers. However, because of the emphasis on speed of performance which the test involves, the number of semichance errors is perhaps too large for individual responses to have real significance.

An excellent class record sheet is included with the test, the Universal Class Error Check Sheet. On it the errors and omissions for an entire class can be recorded to show the parts of the test which were and were not correctly answered by all the pupils. This record sheet would indicate for an entire class and for individual pupils the particular skill or skills on which further work is most desirable.

Those who use the test should be fully aware that it is sharply focused. It is not a general measure of the student's ability to apply reading successfully to all study situations—in spite of the title, *Applied Reading*. It measures only the reader's skill in using an index and in performing two of the processes involved in using a dictionary. Wherever these are the skills for which a brief test is needed, the Ohio tests have many things to commend them, not the least of which are the annual revisions and the state-wide norms. For a comprehensive study of applied reading skills, however, teachers must rely on other tests as well as on these, according to the needs and demands of their respective classes.

[535]

Interpretation of Data. Grades 9-12; 1939-47; revision of *Interpretation of Data*, Test 2.5; IBM; Forms 2.51, 2.52; separate answer sheets must be used; $2 per 25; 40¢ per 25 machine-scorable answer sheets; $1.05 per set of stencils for scoring answer sheets; 75¢ per specimen set, postpaid; worklimit (90) minutes; prepared by the Evaluation Staff of the Eight Year Study, Progressive Education Association under the direction of Maurice L. Hartung; Cooperative Test Service.

REFERENCES

1-9. *See* 40:1544.
10. Teller, James D. "Improving Ability to Interpret Educational Data." *Ed Res B* 19:363-71+ S 25 '40. *
11. Hartung, Maurice L.; Weisman, Leah; McMullen, Harold G.; and Trimble, Harold C. "Interpretation of Data," pp. 38-76, 509-13. In *Appraising and Recording Student Progress.* By Eugene R. Smith, Ralph W. Tyler, and the Evaluation Staff. Progressive Education Association Publications, Commission on the Relation of School and College, Adventure in American Education, Vol. 3. New York: Harper & Brothers, 1942. Pp. xxiii, 550. $3.00. * (PA 16:5033)
12. Neuhof, Mark. "Integrated Interpretation of Data Tests." *Sci Ed* 26:21-6 Ja '42. *
13. Mandell, Milton M., and Adkins, Dorothy C. "The Validity of Written Tests for the Selection of Administrative Personnel." *Ed & Psychol Meas* 6:293-312 au '46. * (PA 21:905)

J. Wayne Wrightstone, Assistant Director, Bureau of Reference, Research and Statistics, Board of Education, New York, New York. Ingenious tests constructed by the staff of

Evaluation in the Eight Year Study of the Progressive Education Association are available through the Cooperative Test Service. The test on interpretation of data is a novel contribution to the measurement of a newer objective of modern education. It is encouraging that the results of experimentation with new test exercises are to be shared more widely.

Commendable features of this test are the breakdown of interpretation of data into various analytical or diagnostic features. These include general accuracy of interpretation, accuracy with probable true and probable false, accuracy with insufficient data, accuracy with true and false data, caution in judgment, generalizing beyond the data, and crude errors in interpretation.

The reliability of the general accuracy score, the beyond data score, the caution in interpretation score, and insufficient data score are sufficiently high so that the results may be used for individual diagnosis. Other subtests, or analytical features, must be used with extreme caution for individual diagnosis because of their lower reliability. The validation of the test against the criteria of pupil behavior defining the objective and against an essay form of the test is adequately described in the manual. The pupil behaviors—described in some detail in the manual—clearly indicate the nature of abilities and skills measured by the test.

One disadvantage of the test is the lack of definitive norms. Interpretation of scores is presented in terms of the percentage of items correctly answered by each pupil for the total test and for the various analytical features of the test. For general use, it is desirable to provide norms achieved by a representative sample of pupils at the various grade levels of the high school. This is in conformity with the usual practice of providing a table for converting raw scores into equivalent scores, such as percentile scores or standard scores.

Considerable time is required for scoring the analytical features of the test unless the International Business Machines electrical test-scoring machine is available. Compared with the usual test, the manual scoring and the arithmetic computations required to convert each score to a percentage of correct responses will present mental hazards for many teachers. Yet it is evident that the authors of the test have attempted to simplify the scoring by the use of a separate answer sheet to be scored by su-perimposing specially punched scoring keys.

For teachers who are accustomed to administer a test in a 40- to 45-minute period, this 90-minute test may arouse hostility because of rearrangement of class schedules, regardless of the inherent values involved and the need for emphasizing thought rather than speed. It is hoped that attitudes of supervisors and teachers will change on the stereotype of the 40-minute testing period.

For teachers who are not conversant with instructional methods for teaching aspects of critical thinking—especially the changes in pupil behavior implicit in this test—detailed suggestions for using the test results wisely must be provided. The authors have not given concrete suggestions required for such a new emphasis in teaching, nor have they cited sources where the teacher may turn for help.

Since these tests were originally designed for use with college-preparatory pupils, it is desirable to try out this test in average public school systems with pupils in all types of courses. This will serve several purposes. One purpose is to define the high school student population that can profitably interpret and use the concepts, vocabulary, and skills involved in the test. Another purpose is to discover the needs of teachers for intelligent use of the test results. Such a tryout may reveal needs for further simplification of the scoring and elaboration of the suggestions on the interpretation and use of the test scores.

This type of test marks a new and promising departure from the conventional types of test exercises. As a pioneer effort, it needs to be evaluated in a variety of school situations. More extensive use may point toward modification or revision of the present edition of the test and its manual. It is a challenge to better teaching and learning.

[536]

★Library Test for Junior High Schools. Grades 7-10; 1942; Forms A, B; $1.25 per 25; 25¢ per specimen set, postpaid; 30(35) minutes; Committee on Tests of the School Library Association of California under the direction of Jeannette Vander Ploeg; California Test Bureau.

Robert A. Davis, Professor of Education, University of Colorado, Boulder, Colorado. Although the subtitle suggests that library skills are measured, the test measures primarily information concerning library materials. It does not measure one's skill in the use of a library.

The test consists of five parts: (a) books, (b) the arrangement of books, (c) card catalog, (d) dictionaries and encyclopedias, and (e) miscellaneous materials. It is designed to reveal the student's information analytically as well as compositely. The various parts of the test consist of multiple-choice, completion, and true-false items, the number of items in each part ranging from 9 to 12, the total number being 51. Inasmuch as some items are of the recall type, scoring is not entirely objective.

The materials of the test are based upon analysis of courses of study and library manuals used in representative schools. These materials were selected for appropriateness by a committee of the School Library Association of California. No data are provided in the manual accompanying the test regarding the specific sources of material examined in formulating items.

The value of this test lies in its ability to reveal the student's knowledge concerning the resources of libraries. When all parts of the test are considered as a unit, it undoubtedly reveals considerable knowledge. The number of items under each part is too few to yield a valid and reliable measure of the student's knowledge of that part. Only total test scores should be considered.

Ethel M. Feagley, Associate Librarian and Assistant Professor of Education, Teachers College, Columbia University, New York, New York. Instruction in the use of the library and its materials varies widely in scope and emphasis and seldom carries course credit. As a first step the librarian always needs to find out how much students already know about the use of the library so that instruction may be planned around real needs and repetition be reduced. Diagnostic tests in this field, therefore, are much more useful than those which measure achievement. The *Library Test for Junior High Schools* definitely states it is designed as a diagnostic test to secure as accurate an indication as possible of each pupil's familiarity with library usage. The results of this test will then be used by teachers or librarians in planning library lessons by showing them which details need attention. The questions are deliberately more general than specific in regard to certain library policies and book collections in order that they may be applicable to many situations. This is a weak point in most library tests, and

it seems a high price to pay for trying to make a test applicable to other than local situations. The manual of directions reports on the content validity, an important item in a diagnostic test. The present form is the result of several revisions. The items for the test were assembled from a careful study of manuals and courses of study. This is a logical and usual procedure. But if the existing manuals and courses of study fail to include many needed items and reflect the viewpoint of librarians rather than library users, the content validity may not be satisfactory. Here is an area demanding attention from all librarians interested in preparing library tests.

The present test is divided into five divisions, the usual ones: (a) the book; (b) arrangement of books; (c) the card catalog; (d) dictionaries and encyclopedias; and (e) miscellaneous reference books. The questions fall in three different forms: matching, multiple choice, and true-false. The type of question varies in the two forms of the test. For instance, questions on the card catalog in Form A are true-false, but in Form B they are multiple choice. In the sections of matching-type questions it might be suggested that the list of choices be given in alphabetical order to make the selecting easier. The questions on the card catalog deal with information about it rather than skill in using it, a far more intricate thing to test. In all library tests the subjects or skills which fall readily into test items are tested again and again while the functional aspects which are difficult to translate into test terms are seldom included.

The directions for administering and scoring the test are clear. Percentile norms are given for each grade. These apparently are based on the results of tests given to California students only. This test should be good for any librarian in a junior high school to use as a survey of needed library instruction and as a guide in planning a more detailed test suitable for the local situation. The weaknesses are basically weaknesses of the existing curriculum in library instruction rather than of the test techniques themselves.

[537]

★Library Usage Test. Grades 11-13; 1940; $1.25 per 25, postpaid; sample test free; 45(50) minutes; Elmer R. Smith; Turner E. Smith & Co.

J. Wayne Wrightstone, Assistant Director, Bureau of Reference, Research and Statistics, Board of Education, New York, New York.

Library usage tests appear in increasing number upon the measurement horizon. Included among these is the *Library Usage Test*. The test has eight subtests on (*a*) Using the Library, (*b*) Using the Card Catalogue, (*c*) Using Books, (*d*) Using the Dictionary, (*e*) Using Reference Books, (*f*) Using Magazine Indexes, (*g*) Using Encyclopedias and (*h*) Library Abbreviations.

The author of the test is attempting to measure too much in too little space and too little time. Three of the subtests have only 10 items; the remainder average 15 items each. Diagnostic or analytical features are defeated by the unreliability of subtests having so few items. The lack of adequate norms and a manual of directions and interpretation is inexcusable in modern tests offered for commercial distribution.

The format of the test does not accord with the best principles in test construction, especially in Subtest 1 where a list of 20 items in column 2 are to be matched with a list of 15 descriptions in column 1. A preferred format would have been to arrange sets of 5 items in column 2 so that 3 of these could be associated with 3 items in column 1. The same criticism holds for the section of the test entitled Finding Books.

In Subtest 2, Using a Card Catalog, the test items are entirely about the identification of different types of catalog cards. The test exercises would have been much more functional and valid if interpretation of catalog cards had been tested rather than mere identification of their types. The section on catalog arrangement, likewise, presents items in isolated and academic statements rather than as approximations to a lifelike situation. It would have been preferable to have stressed interpretation and use rather than mere information about catalog arrangement.

In Subtest 4, Using the Dictionary, the items again pertain to information about a dictionary rather than a measure of skills in the use of the dictionary. This section would have been improved by reproducing a sample page from a dictionary, as in the *Iowa Every-Pupil Tests of Basic Skills: Test B, Work-Study Skills,* which measures the ability of the individual to exhibit skills in a realistic test exercise.

The author has presented realistic test exercises in Subtest 6, Using Magazine Indexes, where he has reproduced typical entries found in a magazine index. These exercises involve a more direct use of the skills in a lifelike testing situation. Their use is commended.

The test reliability would have been increased if the author had omitted certain subtests, namely, using books and abbreviations. These might more validly and logically be included in a test of work-study skills.

[538]

Peabody Library Information Test. Grades 4-8, 9-12, 13-16; 1938-40; Form A; 3 levels; $1.25 per 25 of any one level; 50¢ per specimen set, postpaid; Louis Shores and Joseph E. Moore; Educational Test Bureau.
a) ELEMENTARY LEVEL. Grades 4-8; 1940; 30(35) minutes.
b) HIGH SCHOOL LEVEL. Grades 9-12; 1940; 30(35) minutes.
c) COLLEGE LEVEL. Grades 13-16; 1938; 32(37) minutes.

REFERENCES

1. MOORE, JOSEPH E. "The Relation Between Library Information and Elementary School Attainment." *Peabody J Ed* 18:431-6 Jl '40. * (*PA* 14:6219)
2. DEER, GEORGE H. "The Peabody Library Information Test: A Study of Its Statistical Validity and Reliability." *J Exp Ed* 9:233-6 Mr '41. * (*PA* 15:4385)

Douglas E. Scates, Professor of Education, Duke University, Durham, North Carolina. This test is not for librarians in training but is for regular school pupils, to show their understanding of the role and the use of reference books—or, more generally, of the library itself. As such, the test falls in the general category of study- or work-skills tests. And, as paper-and-pencil tests so frequently do, it relies on knowledge as an indication of these skills. The test, being published separately on three levels, affords an instrument for three grade ranges at which schools may well wish to check on progress.

The test is offered for the purpose of revealing the need for more attention to library knowledge at different points in the curriculum and for assessing the success of teaching in these lines. The reviewer has more confidence in the beneficence of tests which are to be used to help define the responsibilities of the school and to suggest needs to the responsive teacher than he has in tests employed primarily to praise or condemn the student, frequently for attributes which are not of his volition. As educators, we are concerned with evaluation-fitted-into-a-plan-of-action, not simply with scientific assessment which leaves some persons feeling smug and others feeling hopeless.

With this frame of reference the reviewer believes that the Elementary Level of these tests falls in an area of use likely to be constructive. The College Level, when used for freshman orientation and further guidance, also appears salutary. One suggested use of the High School Level, namely, for meeting the requirements of regional accrediting associations, is tinctured with that oversimplification of thought which so quickly falls into machine-like standardization of education and ends in complete formalization. A comprehensive philosophy of education may, however, prevent the tests from having a significant influence in this direction.

When we turn to the construction of the tests, we face another issue. From an inspection of the items in the three levels, the reviewer comes to the following conclusions:

(a) The items evidence some ingenuity in the variety of exercises employed. Certain forms are, however, repeated seemingly without justification, and, in the lower level, certain standard forms which are of value are neglected.

(b) The content of the items is heavily slanted toward technical library information (e.g., the expectancy that the student will have memorized the Dewey Decimal Classification). For special purposes, this heavy emphasis may be desirable; for general use in schools, the reviewer would say it was undesirable. This emphasis is, of course, wholly within the limits of the title of the test.

(c) The workmanship on the items is poor. Far too large a proportion of them are faulty on the surface. In the Elementary Level, Form A, the reviewer is critical of nearly half the items on the basis of faulty construction. Some of the faults are in careless editing; for example, titles to reference books are given in italics in one item, in ordinary roman in the next item, and later in roman with quotes. A catalog card is presented with poor punctuation. A completion item is split at the bottom of the page, with 3 blanks on one page and 5 on the other. And so on. There are similarly numerous defects in the logic of items. One matching item demands recall of the Dewey classification numbers without indicating that they are Dewey. Another matching item has a very heterogeneous set of choices. One multiple-choice item has two reasonably good answers. One completion item asks what a dictionary is about. (One wonders if the key permits "Everything" as an answer.) Most of the defects cannot readily be indicated briefly and so are not

mentioned in detail here. The college level has fewer technical defects but is not perfect.

The three levels of the test give the impression of a fairly good idea poorly executed. Carelessness, or ignorance of what makes a good test item, is too prevalent. Statistical standardization will not rid a test of such faults, and the use cf such tests in schools gives false notions of what is known and what is not because of numerous spurious factors.

Ed Res B 20:114 Ap 16'41. Ruth E. Seeger. * The directions are clear and simple, both for administering and for scoring. * The questions are well chosen to cover desired items and are well worded, making for clarity and exactness of meaning. They are designed to be used primarily to discover which students are in need of library instruction and upon what phases of library instruction they need such instruction. They may also be used as a measure of the effectiveness of such instruction. All forms should be a definite contribution in the field of testing for efficiency in using libraries, particularly since good tests in library usage are not plentiful. They are especially timely in that library instruction is coming to be considered more and more essential in the training of youth by present curricular methods, and that such training is beginning to be considered as one phase of standardization and evaluation of secondary education.

J Higher Ed 12:217-8 Ap '41. Ruth E. Seeger. * an outstanding new library information test * The test presupposed the use of the Dewey decimal classification system *

[539]

Special Reading Test: Ohio Senior Survey Tests. Grade 12; 1934-38; Forms A, B; 3¢ per test; 60(65) minutes; S. L. Pressey and J. W. Sherburne (Form B); Ohio Scholarship Tests, Ohio State Department of Education.

Miles A. Tinker, Professor of Psychology, University of Minnesota, Minneapolis, Minnesota. This is one of the tests devised for use with Ohio high school seniors. The reading abilities measured are: technical vocabulary of English grammar; foreign words, phrases, and abbreviations; use of the dictionary; and getting information from graphs, maps and diagrams. The test is to be used as a point of departure in remedial instruction to locate students deficient in minimum essentials and to diagnose specific student weaknesses. In Ohio,

Form A of the test is given before the remedial work of the senior survey course starts, and Form B after the remedial program is completed to check improvement.

Percentile norms are given for each part and for the total scores on Form A and on Form B separately. Also item norms (i.e., percentage answering each item correctly) are given. There are no data listed on techniques of standardization or on equivalence of the test forms. Examination of the percentile tables reveals that the test forms are not of equal difficulty. Therefore, the interpretation of changes in test scores from Form A to Form B is hazardous. One can only note changes in percentile ranks. Since the two forms are apparently of unequal difficulty and we have no information on reliability, the meaning of the shifting in percentile ranks must remain obscure. No information is given on either the reliability or the validity of the test scores. In the absence of these data, no adequate interpretation of the test results is possible. It is difficult to justify the publication and use of a reading test without making available data on reliability.

The legibility of the print in the test is poor because of blurring of letters as if badly worn type had been used for the printing. In fact, some of the print in the maps and map explanations cannot be read at all. Directions are clearly and concisely worded.

The content of this test is well selected, and the test items are well organized. The reading abilities measured are important both in school and in many of the nonacademic reading activities of the individual.

The organization and content of this test are somewhat similar to those of the *Tyler–Kimber Study Skills Test* and the *Chicago Reading Tests*. Available information indicates more adequate standardization for the Tyler–Kimber and the Chicago tests. None of these tests, however, is entirely adequate. It is desirable that more satisfactory tests of this type be constructed and standardized. They can be very useful in the diagnosis of certain important reading abilities.

Both the lack of data on standardization and the illegible print of this test will be obstacles to its use.

[540]

Study-Habits Inventory, Revised Edition, 1941. Grades 12-16; 1934–41; 1 form; $1.25 per 25; 10¢ per specimen set; nontimed (10-20) minutes; C. Gilbert Wrenn; Stanford University Press.

REFERENCES

1. REEDER, C. W. "Study Habits." *Sch & Soc* 42:413-5 S 21 '35. * (*PA* 10:616)
2. GREENE, J. E., AND STATON, THOMAS F. "Predictive Value of Various Tests of Emotionality and Adjustment in a Guidance Program for Prospective Teachers." *J Ed Res* 32:653-9 My '39. * (*PA* 13:4211)
3. GORDON, H. PHOEBE. "Study Habit Inventory Scores and Scholarship." *J Appl Psychol* 25:101-7 F '41. * (*PA* 15:3149)
4. WRENN, C. GILBERT, AND HUMBER, WILBUR J. "Study Habits Associated With High and Low Scholarship." *J Ed Psychol* 32:611-6 N '41. * (*PA* 16:2801)
5. JOHNSON, A. P. *The Prediction of Scholastic Achievement for Freshman Engineering Students at Purdue University.* Purdue University, Division of Educational Research, Studies in Engineering Education II. Lafayette, Ind.: the Division, May 1942. Pp. 22. Paper. $0.35. * (*PA* 16:5020)
6. JOHNSON, A. P. *The Relationship of Test Scores to Scholastic Achievement for 244 Engineering Freshmen Entering Purdue University in September 1939.* Unpublished doctor's thesis, Purdue University, 1942.
7. MUSSELMAN, JOHN W. "Factors Associated With the Achievement of High School Pupils of Superior Intelligence." *J Exp Ed* 11:53-68 S '42. * (*PA* 17:1363)
8. TRAXLER, ARTHUR E. "A Note on the Wrenn Study Habits Inventory." *J Genetic Psychol* 60:385-6 Je '42. * (*PA* 16:4555)

Douglas E. Scates, Professor of Education, Duke University, Durham, North Carolina. This is a short test (7 or 8 minutes ought to be sufficient for the actual responses), well presented as far as form is concerned, and well described in the accompanying manual. The test is recommended by the maker for clinical use, with the emphasis on an analysis of responses to individual items rather than on the total score.

The reviewer's reaction is much the same as to all personality inventories of this general type. First, the respondent does not know the proper answer (descriptive of himself) on many of the questions; second, different persons will give the same response for widely different reasons; third, such question blanks presume a degree of honesty and frankness on the part of the respondent which is incredible.

The reviewer recalls an early comment of Goodwin Watson to the effect that certain personality questionnaires utterly ignore the conditions under which adolescents will reveal their real problems. And there is also the suggestion by Gordon Hendrickson that full rapport and its opposite (complete lack of concern) probably tend to produce more accurate responses but that in the great middle range of attitudes serious difficulty arises. For the majority of persons, so many factors operate that truth is likely to be not only veiled but effectively screened. Certainly students, like other persons, will seek the most respectable (and probably irrelevant) explanations of their difficulty.

For example, the test affords a number of easy "outs" for the student who lacks the drive and possibly the ability to study. He can find a large number of mechanical or external reasons to check and thus successfully divert the counsellor's attention from the hard truth. Who would not, for example, prefer to take a formal scolding for the prevalent indulging in too much social life (Item 17) instead of facing the difficult job of adequately summarizing, classifying, and systematizing the material learned (Item 23)? Or who would not prefer the apparently blameless "I get 'fussed' and nervous on examinations" (Item 18) as an excuse rather than admit weakness in the intrinsically hard matter of reciting to one's self the material studied and checking all doubtful points (Item 3)? What such natural and nearly universal tendencies to avoid the truth do to the basic validating and standardizing of the test can only be conjectured. What these tendencies do to the responses of particular individuals is to give highly variable and undependable results from one person to another.

Aside from volitional or unconsciously evasive errors of response are the errors of interpretation arising from different bases for the same response. "I have to re-read material several times." Certainly, we all do. What does this response mean? It may be a function of the intrinsic difficulty of the material (as mathematical, detailed description vs. newspaper stories or fiction). The response may be a function of the type of mind (as generally resistant, critical, doubting vs. highly fluid, submissive, credulous). Or the response may arise from one's purpose in reading (as to get a perfectly clear understanding or to memorize vs. to get a sketchy notion). Again, different standards of work will cause different amounts of rereading, and so on. *Why* does the student respond as he does? Who can tell? Again, "I miss important points in the lecture while copying down notes." Of course. With some instructors nobody could help it. But the test is supposed to diagnose the student, not the instructor.

Honest questions will arise in trying to answer the questions. "I spend too much time on some things and not enough on others." Could anyone say no to this one? But apparently some persons are supposed to—who? "I finish my examination papers and turn them in before time is called." Suppose I do on objective tests, but on essay tests I always run over time. Then I will wish study-habit tests did not contain impossible questions!

The statistical procedure for constructing the test is conventional and presumably impeccable. Yet one notes that the scoring weights in more than one-third of the items do not run in a single direction but reverse themselves in a manner difficult to rationalize. For example, "Trouble in picking out the important points" counts -7 if it occurs sometimes; but there is no loss of points if the difficulty occurs often. To "study with others" is all right if it is done always, but the student who does it only occasionally shows poor study habits. Similarly, it is better to engage in bull sessions often than only sometimes. And so on. One wonders a little whether statistics aren't as misleading as some persons claim they are.

The scoring key reveals that only 12 of the 28 items are discriminating in the case of women. Are not women human beings? Do they study or fail to study by means as yet undiscovered by men? Granted that they may perplex and confound members of the opposite sex, but do they also confuse the statistics?

The items are selected and the weights attached on the basis of extreme groups—a technique which is fairly common and generally accepted. But we must bear in mind that the bare fact that a testmaker can get two groups of college students of equal average intelligence, with one group doing well in its studies and the other doing poorly, is not adequate evidence that the two groups are obliging enough to differ markedly and consistently with respect to the trait which the testmaker happens to be thinking of (in this case, study habits). There were, certainly, hundreds or thousands of factors besides study habits which operated to produce differences in college work.

In the reviewer's judgment, validity and other aspects of the standardization of such a test call for the selection of items and the determination of weights only in connection with the most skillful interviews to determine what the response meant to the student and why he gave the response he did. Items found to mean different things would then either be rejected or would be subdivided and defined further; the present test could probably be made four or five times its present length without the addition of a single new question—just by making the present questions more specific. We have been taught now for three decades to utilize and depend on statistical methods. Perhaps the time has come to learn that we cannot rely on statistical methods—at least as they are often used. Statistics suffers most at the hands of its friends.

For reviews by Edward S. Jones and William A. McCall, see 40:1574.

[541]
★**Survey of Study Habits, Experimental Edition.**
Grades 8-12; 1944; 1 form; nontimed (30) minutes; Arthur E. Traxler; Educational Records Bureau.

REFERENCES
1. TRAXLER, ARTHUR E. "Some Results of an Experimental Survey of the Study Habits of Independent-School Pupils," pp. 40-9. In *1944 Fall Testing Program in Independent Schools and Supplementary Studies.* Educational Records Bulletin, No. 42. New York: Educational Records Bureau, January 1945. Pp. x, 49. Paper, lithotyped. $1.00. * (*PA* 19:1812)

[542]
Test of Study Skills. Grades 4-9; 1940; IBM; separate answer sheets must be used; Forms A, B; $1.75 per 30; 1½¢ per machine-scorable answer sheet; 25¢ per specimen set; 60(70) minutes; J. W. Edgar and H. T. Manuel; Steck Co.

Douglas E. Scates, Professor of Education, Duke University, Durham, North Carolina. The test is well put up, makes no false claims, and will probably do as nearly as a paper-and-pencil test can, in a limited time, what it is supposed to do. The first part deals with the use of reference books, indexes, and dictionary and the reading of graphs, tables, and maps. The second part deals with critical inference.

For a basis for comparison, one's thinking turns naturally to the test Work-Study Skills in the *Iowa Every-Pupil Tests of Basic Skills.* The test under review differs at once by giving nearly half of its items to critical thinking rather than all to work skills. And among the latter the present test seems to have certain advantages. In the first place, it avoids the disproportionate emphasis (nearly one-third) of the Iowa test (grades 6 to 8) on interpreting maps. It gives nearly half of the first part to general sources of information, including the use of reference books in general; this emphasis may be somewhat heavy but it is not indefensible. In the second place, the questions on the several aspects of securing information and interpreting technical material are all mixed together, so that they can be arranged spirally as to difficulty. They thus avoid any tendency toward monotony, and, inasmuch as the questions all relate to the same general field, this mixture does not seem to the reviewer to be objectionable.

The second half of the test, concerning "critical thinking in the use of printed materials," represents an adaptation of the evaluation-of-inferences tests, developed during the Eight-Year Study under the influence of Ralph Tyler, in which one is asked to indicate whether certain statements are true, probably true, unsupported, and so on, in the light of facts which are given. The present adaptation offers only three alternatives which include yes, no, and can't tell. The adaptation is probably an advantage, especially for young children, as the five categories of positiveness are difficult even for adults to manage. Another advantage of printing the alternatives for each item is that they can be specially adapted to the wording of the item, and this is done in the test. The reviewer would probably prefer four alternatives, on the basis of a finding by Giles M. Ruch some years back that three-response items were somewhat tricky and erratic.

One cannot fail to think of other important aspects of study skills, such, for example, as outlining and the ability to get the central thought in reading. These are, of course, covered in other tests; but perhaps the name of the present test is somewhat broader than its actual coverage. If that is a sin, it is shared by other tests in this class.

One notes in the sheet of directions the following cautious and salutary statement concerning validity "The claim for validity rests simply upon the careful selection of items in the limited area which the test is designed to measure. It is believed that the test will be useful in individual guidance and in the motivation of learning. It is not designed as a pattern of either the content or the method of teaching pupils how to use printed materials. The test merely samples information and abilities here and there in the total matrix of ability which the pupil has developed." Such frank, honest, and well-oriented statements are refreshing. So also is the following statement on interpretation: "Users of the test . . . should be cautioned against an overemphasis upon comparisons either of individuals or of groups with averages. It is easy to make the erroneous assumption that averages in some way necessarily reflect conditions that are desirable."

These quoted comments are welcome and helpful in mitigating the overemphasis which paper-and-pencil tests unavoidably place on certain formal, highly verbalized aspects of ability. When more testmakers reveal and pass on to the user such insight and understanding, we may have a lessened fear of what commercial tests in the hands of the teacher who lacks the judgment and the self-confidence to see around and beyond them are doing to education. The reviewer welcomes these comments in the manual as evidencing a more than ordinarily mature understanding of the nature and role of standardized tests.

[543]

Use of Library and Study Materials. Grades 9-16; 1939-40; IBM; separate answer sheets must be used; $1.75 per 30 tests; Mary Kirkpatrick, Lola Rivers Thompson, and Helen Tomlinson; Steck Co.

REFERENCES
1. Votaw, David F. "A Comparison of Test Scores of Entering College Freshmen as Instruments for Predicting Subsequent Scholarship." *J Ed Res* 40:215-8 N '46. * (PA 21:1304)

Ethel M. Feagley, Associate Librarian and Assistant Professor of Education, Teachers College, Columbia University, New York, New York. It is always essential to know why a test has been prepared and what use is to be made of its results. The purpose of this test as explained in the manual of directions is to provide some of the necessary instruments for appraising the development of study and library skills. The manual adds that the test may be used as the basis for motivating the learning of the skills which it samples and may also be used as a follow-up test to reveal progress. It is not clear, therefore, whether this test should be considered as diagnostic in nature or as measuring progress. Usually a test is a better instrument if prepared definitely as one type—diagnostic or achievement.

The test is in two main parts. Part I is designed as a measure of a student's ability to locate information; Part II similarly tests certain aspects of his ability to understand the material once it has been found. The questions are all phrased in multiple-choice form. Part I, containing 45 questions, covers the following groups of items: magazines, alphabetizing, call numbers, dictionaries, magazine indexes, the book, classification, card catalog, the library, bibliography, and specific reference books. It is unfortunate that the test is designed for both high school and college students as some of the questions refer to materials which would not usually be found in a high school library, such as the *Art Index, Education Index, International Index,* and the *Union List of Serials.* On the other hand, the questions on reference books are too elementary for college students. For instance, out of eleven such questions three refer to the *World Almanac.* Among these 45 ques-

tions six refer to alphabetizing and six more to call numbers. This seems a large proportion, particularly since the questions are quite similar and do not call for different kinds of analysis. Not all the questions test locating information. Judgment or recalled knowledge is required in four questions about magazines. For example, the student is asked to choose from five magazines that one which "has a regular department dealing with household devices and patents." The questions on magazine indexes are quite limited in scope. More items should be related to the use of the index, subject headings, subdivisions, and other details which enable the student to manipulate the index. Of course such skills are more difficult to test, and at present few good test items of this kind are available. As is so often the case, the questions seem to be phrased from the viewpoint of the librarian rather than the user of the library material.

Part II, Interpreting Information, deserves favorable consideration. It contains some ingenious and useful techniques for testing the student's ability to interpret and handle different types of facts and information. The questions are based on columns of statistics, indexes, graphs, various kinds of maps, a catalog card, and words with diacritical marks. Some of the printing on the map in Form A is difficult to read. The section on indexes needs more detailed questions for college students with perhaps references to an index for a whole set of books. It would be better to have a wider range of questions on the catalog card rather than limit the number by using the multiple-choice form. The last group in this section, dealing with diacritical marks, has two questions, Items 75 and 80, which are based on the recall of learned knowledge rather than on interpretation of given facts.

The directions for administering the test are clear, and the test may be scored by machine although a hand-scoring key is provided. Percentile norms are given for Form A based on 2,356 scores of Texas college freshmen.

By trying to serve both high school and college this test reduces its value to each one. A separate test for each group would be preferable. The test is further weakened by not clearly defining its aim—to diagnose or to measure progress. Usually different test procedures should be employed depending on which type of test is being prepared. An "all purpose" test is seldom very effective. This is one of the weakest phases of library tests at present, together with the uniformity of test items and the small number of skills tested. More thought, study, and experimentation must be devoted to analyzing the facts and skills needed in this area and writing new and effective test items. Here is a task in test construction which still challenges and which will not be solved until librarians and test experts selected from a large number and variety of local situations bend their joint efforts to the undertaking.

[544]

★Watson-Glaser Tests of Critical Thinking. Grades 9-16 and adults; 1942; IBM; Form A; 2 parts; separate answer sheets need not be used; $2.50 per 25 of either part; 35¢ per specimen set, postpaid; 95¢ per 25 machine-scorable answer sheets for either part; nontimed (60) minutes per part; Goodwin Watson and Edward M. Glaser; World Book Co.
a) BATTERY I, DISCRIMINATION IN REASONING.
b) BATTERY II, LOGICAL REASONING.

REFERENCES

1. GLASER, EDWARD M. An Experiment in the Development of Critical Thinking. Columbia University, Teachers College, Contributions to Education, No. 843. Goodwin Watson, faculty sponsor. New York: Bureau of Publications, the College, 1941. Pp. ix, 212. Out of print. * (PA 16:2057)
2. HOWELL, WILLIAM SMILEY. "The Effects of High School Debating on Critical Thinking." Speech Monogr 10:96-103 '43. * (PA 18:2255)
3. BURTON, ARTHUR, AND JOËL, WALTHER. "Adult Norms for the Watson-Glaser Tests of Critical Thinking." J Psychol 19: 43-8 Ja '45. * (PA 19:1180)

Robert H. Thouless, Reader in Educational Psychology, Cambridge University, Cambridge, England. No one who has tried to construct a test of this type will underestimate its difficulties. The authors have succeeded in making a test which should prove useful for measurement and diagnosis and also of educational value to the testees. The tests include the ability to recognise the validity of arguments, the detection of implications of statements, consistency of opinions, etc. In addition to a straightforward assessment of the ability to think critically, there are ingenious methods of assessing qualities of opinions and effects of opinion on the ability to think critically on particular problems.

One of the difficulties of making a good test of reasoning out of material of real significance is that of ensuring an unquestionably right answer as standard. The authors tried to achieve this end by submitting all the items to a jury of 15 persons trained in logic and scientific method, who apparently showed perfect agreement as to the correct responses to all items. I think that a more critical jury might have found fault with some of the remaining items but not many. The battery is perhaps as good in this respect as any that is likely to be made in prac-

tice though it does not appear to be perfect. Scoring is by stencil or by machine scoring.

Norms and estimates of reliability are only tentative. The norms given are calculated from samples of considerably more than average intelligence. More comprehensive norms are to be obtained in the future from reports to the author by users of the test.

Ed Res B 24:139-40 My 16 '45. Harold P. Fawcett. * will be welcomed by all who are interested in the development of this important ability * a helpful and effective means of measuring abilities which are today so essential to competent citizenship. While they relate directly to the stated objectives of teachers in various subject-matter fields, they are particularly suitable for evaluating the extent to which the ability to think has been achieved throughout the school program to which all subject-matters contribute. If they are not used for this purpose, teachers of such subjects as social studies, mathematics, and science will find them useful. They are probably best suited for students on the senior-high school level. *

[545]

Work-Study Skills: Iowa Every-Pupil Tests of Basic Skills, Test B, New Edition. Grades 3-5, 5-9; IBM, grades 5-9; Forms L, M, N, O; 2 levels; 44¢ per specimen set of either level; H. F. Spitzer in collaboration with Ernest Horn, Maude McBroom, H. A. Greene, and E. F. Lindquist (General Editor); Houghton Mifflin Co.
a) ELEMENTARY BATTERY. Grades 3-5; $1.50 per 25; 47(55) minutes.
b) ADVANCED BATTERY. Grades 5-9; IBM; separate answer sheets need not be used; $1.60 per 25; 50¢ per 25 machine-scorable answer sheets; 30¢ per set of machine-scoring stencils; 77(90) minutes.

J. Wayne Wrightstone, Assistant Director, Bureau of Reference, Research and Statistics, Board of Education, New York, New York. ELEMENTARY BATTERY. This battery presents exercises which measure (a) map reading, (b) use of references, (c) use of index, (d) use of dictionary, and (e) alphabetization. The test is the best avaliable in the elementary school field. Its items are carefully constructed, and the test situations are presented so that the skills are measured as closely as possible to the way they function in everyday activities of the modern school. The skills, furthermore, are important in the everyday life of the child.

ADVANCED BATTERY. This battery measures skills of (a) map reading, (b) use of references, (c) use of index, (d) use of dictionary, and (e) reading graphs, charts, and tables. These are skills that function in the modern classroom, and they are measured in lifelike exercises by this test. The authors are to be commended for the manner in which they have approximated real or work sample situations in the test.

Realistic maps are reproduced, and well-chosen questions on interpretation are asked in order to sample skills in map reading. To measure the use of an index, a sample page from an index is reproduced, and interpretations are required by the test items. Similarly, well-constructed items measure interpretation of a sample page from a dictionary, and of reproduction of graphs, charts, and tables in respective subtests. In addition, an ingenious answer sheet and scoring device are used to facilitate the scoring of this test. It is recommended that the publisher print separate answer sheets to avoid mutilating the test booklet by detaching the title page, which includes the answer sheet. While this may not increase the profits of the publisher, it will permit the re-use of the same test booklet by several pupils, who would be supplied with separate answer sheets as required.

GENERAL COMMENTS. The teacher's manual presents concrete suggestions for the interpretation and use of the test results. Specific skills tested are coded for each test item. Norms are presented in terms of equivalent grade scores and percentile scores for the various grade levels.

One disadvantage of the test is the unreliability of subtests for diagnosis of individual pupil achievement. Although the authors state in the manual that the subtests are not reliable enough for individual diagnosis, this assertion is negated by the fact that they recommend an individual profile card, including subtest scores for each child. The unreliability is more readily apparent when it is observed that a raw score change of one point on many of the subtests will account for a grade-equivalent score difference of from three to twelve months.

The published norms for the test are derived mainly from the use of the test in selected communities which are not representative of the nation-wide population. The experience of several cities which have used the test leads to the conclusion that the norms should be revised. This conclusion is based upon the assumption that a test publisher—distributing a test nationally—has a responsibility for providing norms which represent a cross section of the national population. This responsibility cannot be avoided by recommending that it would be a better practice to obtain local norms. Most cities and small school systems are not equipped to carry out effectively such a suggestion. Furthermore, not all purposes in a survey testing program can be achieved by the use of local norms. The method of indicating grade equivalents is somewhat at variance with the usual practice; for example, a grade norm of third grade, fifth month is reported as 35 (without the decimal point) rather than as 3.5. This is a minor point, but the idiosyncrasy of the publisher runs counter to accepted practice, and no advantages are cited for this unique practice, which may cause some confusion for the average classroom teacher.

Teachers and supervisors generally have accepted the work-study skills tests as the most significant contribution of the Iowa Every-Pupil test batteries. The use of lifelike work samples appeals to them. In the modern classroom the newer work-study skills are assuming a position of equality with the more established skills in reading, arithmetic, and the language arts.

For reviews by Frederic L. Ayer, Gustav J. Froehlich, and Ralph C. Preston of the complete battery, see 10. For reviews by William A. Brownell, J. Murray Lee, and Charles W. Odell of an earlier form of the complete battery, see 38:872.

REPRINTED FROM *The Fourth Mental Measurements Yearbook*

READING—FOURTH MMY

REVIEWS BY *Warren R. Baller, Robert Murray Bear, Ivan A. Booker, Harold D. Carter, Frederick B. Davis, Robert L. Ebel, John C. Flanagan, C. M. Fleming, Gustav J. Froehlich, Eric F. Gardner, J. Raymond Gerberich, William S. Gray, J. Thomas Hastings, James R. Hobson, Katherine G. Keneally, Martha E. Layman, Margaret G. McKim, Clarence H. Nelson, Victor H. Noll, Jacob S. Orleans, Worth J. Osburn, M. L. Kellmer Pringle, Henry D. Rinsland, Holland Roberts, Helen M. Robinson, David H. Russell, F. J. Schonell, William D. Sheldon, Louis Shores, Henry P. Smith, Nila Banton Smith, William W. Turnbull, Henry Weitz, and Frederick L. Westover.*

[528]

★A.C.E.R. Silent Reading Test, Form C. Grades 3–6; 1946–50; 3 parts; Form C ['46]; manual ['50]; 8s. 4d. per 10 sets of all parts; 9d. per key; 5s. per manual; 6s. 6d. per specimen set; cash orders postpaid within Australia; Australian Council for Educational Research. *

a) PART I, WORD KNOWLEDGE. 2s. 3d. per 10; 10(20) minutes.
b) PART 2, SPEED OF READING. 2s. 7d. per 10; 6(10) minutes.
c) PART 3, READING FOR MEANING. 4s. per 10; 20(30) minutes.

[529]

*Achievement Tests in Silent Reading: Dominion Tests. Grades 1, 2–3, 3–4, 4–6, 5–6; 1941–50; $1 per 25 of any one test; 25¢ per manual (separate manuals for a and b, c and d, e and f, g, h, and i; postage extra; prepared by the Department of Educational Research, Ontario College of Education, University of Toronto; distributed by Vocational Guidance Centre. *

a) PRIMARY: TYPE I, WORD RECOGNITION. Grade 1; 1941–50; Forms A ('41), B ('41); manual ('41); revised norms ('50); 35¢ per specimen set; 10(20) minutes.
b) PRIMARY: TYPE II, PHRASE AND SENTENCE READING. Grade 1; 1941–50; Forms A ('41); B ('41); manual ('41); revised norms ('50); 35¢ per specimen set; 20 (30) minutes.
c) PRIMARY: TYPE III, PARAGRAPH READING. Grade 1; 1943–49; I form, '43; manual ('45); revised norms ('50); 30¢ per specimen set; 30(40) minutes.
d) PRIMARY: TYPE IV, DIAGNOSTIC TEST IN WORD RECOGNITION. Grade 1; 1943–50; Form A ('43); manual

('45); revised norms ('50); 30¢ per specimen set; 30 (40) minutes.
e) ADVANCED PRIMARY: TYPE I, VOCABULARY. Grades 2–3; 1943–46; Forms A ('43), B ('43); manual ('46); 35¢ per specimen set; 20(30) minutes.
f) ADVANCED PRIMARY: TYPE II, DIAGNOSTIC TEST IN PARAGRAPH READING. Grade 2; 1943–46; Forms A ('43), B ('43); manual ('46); 35¢ per specimen set; 30(40) minutes.
g) TYPE II, DIAGNOSTIC TEST IN PARAGRAPH READING. Grades 3–4; 1946–47; Forms A ('46), B ('46); preliminary manual ('47); 35¢ per specimen set; 30(40) minutes.
h) JUNIOR: TYPE I, VOCABULARY. Grades 4–6; 1943–46; Forms A ('43), B ('43); manual ('46); 35¢ per specimen set; 20(30) minutes.
i) TYPE II, DIAGNOSTIC TEST IN PARAGRAPH READING. Grades 5–6; 1948; Forms A, B; preliminary manual; 35¢ per specimen set; 30(40) minutes.

HENRY P. SMITH, *Associate Professor of Education, and Director of the Reading Laboratory, The University of Kansas, Lawrence, Kansas.*

These tests, designed for use in Canadian schools, show strong relationship to the Gates reading tests in form, vocabulary, and general testing procedure; and the first-grade tests could well be additional forms of the *Gates Primary Reading Tests.*

Norms based on the performance of rural and urban groups of Canadian children are provided. To the extent that the authors have achieved their goal of adapting the vocabulary and action of the reading material to the background and interests of Canadian children, they have a strong case for using these tests in Canadian schools but weaken the value of the tests for use elsewhere. However, the difference in the vocabulary and reading material employed in these tests and in the Gates and similar tests is not so great as to be noticed readily. In certain of the tests, notably the tests of paragraph reading and of vocabulary, rather clever techniques have been employed for identifying the specific reading difficulties of the child.

The quality of paper and printing, clearness of pictures, and general format is excellent. The statistical analysis accompanying the tests is complete and clear.

The care which appears to have gone into the selection of items, the analysis of results, the preparation of norms, and the handling of other details of test construction and standardization is pleasing to the critical user of tests. The battery appears to be a worthwhile contribution.

For a review by Margaret G. McKim, see 3:476.

[530]

*California Reading Test. Grades 1–4.5, 4–6, 7–9, 9–14; 1933–50; a revision of *Progressive Reading Tests* (see 40:1563); a subtest of *California Achievement Tests* (see 2); 3 scores: reading vocabulary, reading comprehension, total; IBM for grades 4–14; 4 levels; Forms AA ('50), BB ('50), CC ('50), DD ('50); manuals ('50); postage extra; 35¢ per specimen set of any one level, postpaid; Ernest W. Tiegs and Willis W. Clark; California Test Bureau. *
a) PRIMARY. Grades 1–4.5; $1.50 per 25; 30(35) minutes.
b) ELEMENTARY. Grades 4–6; $1.50 per 25; separate answer sheets may be used; 4¢ per IBM answer sheet; 7¢ per Scoreze answer sheet; 60¢ per stencil for machine scoring of answer sheets; 20¢ per stencil for hand scoring of answer sheets; 35(40) minutes.
c) INTERMEDIATE. Grades 7–9; prices same as for Elementary; 50(55) minutes.
d) ADVANCED. Grades 9–14; Forms AA, BB, CC only; prices same as for Elementary; 50(55) minutes.

JOHN C. FLANAGAN, *President, American Institute for Research; and Professor of Psychology, University of Pittsburgh; Pittsburgh, Pennsylvania.*

As one step of preparation, this reviewer read previous reviews of earlier editions of this test. It was encouraging to note that a number of points raised by previous reviewers in *The Mental Measurements Yearbook* have now been corrected by the authors and publishers. For example, a review of earlier editions mentioned that standard errors of measurement were not reported. The manual for the 1950 edition reports reliability coefficients for a single grade range and also standard errors of measurement in terms of grade scores. These are given for the reading vocabulary, the reading comprehension, and the total reading scores on the various levels of the test.

Another criticism made by a reviewer of one of the early editions was that there was no warning of the unreliability of the seven subscores used in the Diagnostic Profile. The manual for the 1950 edition states: "Because of the limited number of items (10–30), scores on the seven sections of this test should be used only as guides to indicate the presence of student difficulties in the seven major diagnostic areas."

Although it is likely that the reviewer of the earlier edition would like to have a more specific warning than that quoted above, and would probably also like to see standard errors of measurement for the seven sections of the test which are so prominently featured in the Diagnostic Profile, these additions to the manual should be helpful to those trying to interpret the test results.

The manuals for all four levels contain the following statement: "Careful study of tryouts indicates that most students (about 90%) can respond to the test situation and reveal their skill mastery within the time limits given in each section, and the remaining 10% complete all the items they are capable of comprehending before the time limits are reached; hence, the test is a power rather than a speed test." Earlier editions of the test have been criticized because, although specific time limits were given, the examiner was told to stop the students when 90 per cent of them had finished. Although it has certainly been established that speed and power, or level of test ability, are positively correlated to a substantial extent, the statement that all people not completing the test within the time limits would have finished all the items they were capable of comprehending seemed somewhat arbitrary.

To test this statement in a crude sort of way, an eighth grade student was given Form AA of the Intermediate level. This student was examined under standard conditions, except that at the end of each time limit he was given additional time to attempt any items not previously tried. For the time limits given in the manual, his reading vocabulary score was grade 7.2, and his reading comprehension score was grade 10.0. With additional time he got 11 more vocabulary tems and 9 more comprehension items correct. Thus, his scores under power-test conditions were grade 8.3 and grade 13.5 in vocabulary and comprehension, respectively, and total reading grade score was raised from 8.1 to 9.7 when he was given additional time. This represents a change in his percentile rank in the low eighth grade from below the 50th percentile to above the 85th percentile. Form CC of the Advanced level was given to a high school senior. This student finished practically all of the parts within the time limits allowed. Although the above individual cases cannot be accepted as having demonstrated that the Intermediate level is not a power test for most students, they do suggest that somewhat more objective and specific information about the extent to which students might profit from additional time would be desirable in the manual.

An examination of the test items suggests that they should do fairly well in discriminating between individuals with respect to their knowledge of vocabulary and ability to comprehend what they read. The better students might, however, find some items rather annoying with respect to the instructions given to them. For example, in selecting the second word in a group which means the "opposite or about the opposite" of the first word, the student is asked to pick "solid" as being the opposite of "plane," "obtuse" as being the opposite of "acute," "botany" as the opposite of "zoology," and "cylinder" as the opposite of "prism."

The content of the test appears to have been changed very little from that in the *Progressive Reading Tests* published in 1933, 1937, and 1943. For more detailed comment on the content and other aspects of the test, the reader is referred to the reviews of earlier editions. The norms for the 1950 edition are based on somewhat larger populations than were those for earlier editions. According to the manual, more than 100,000 cases were used in standardizing each of the three higher levels; and the Primary level was standardized on more than 50,000 cases. The manual does not describe the manner in which the school districts were selected, but states that they were "of all sizes and types throughout the United States."

Although the test user might wish for somewhat more precise technical information regarding the test, it is this reviewer's opinion that he will find the *California Reading Test* a valuable tool in appraising the progress of pupils with respect to these important skills of vocabulary and reading comprehension.

JAMES R. HOBSON, *Director of Child Placement, Brookline Public Schools, Brookline, Massachusetts.*

This successful and widely used series of reading tests, appearing under a new name, possesses some general and some specific virtues as well as some of the faults which seem common to most popular standardized tests. The most common of these common faults is the almost total absence of proof of validity. Now, this reviewer has no doubt that these tests are valid within reasonable limits. However, to begin a discussion on validity with the statement, "All levels and forms of the California Achievement Test Series possess a high degree of validity," and to end it with an invitation to write to the California Test Bureau for "further and more detailed data" with little specific information between gives the impression that this subject is to be glossed over. It would be much more to the point to introduce briefly such specific evidence as correlation studies showing the relationship with scores on other widely used reading tests, both group and individual, at specific grade levels; the power of prediction of later school success in such school subjects requiring well developed reading skills as literature or social studies; or even the identification of the recognized experts in the field of reading whose pooled judgments determined what items should be included.

The next important criticism is the grade range covered by each test. The greatest grade range is in the Primary test, where it does the most harm. This covers grades 1 through lower 4. Such a wide range to be covered by the same test results in a spuriously high reliability coefficient so far as any one grade is concerned and, as pointed out by Frederick B. Davis in *The 1940 Mental Measurements Yearbook* (see 40:1563), also results in "unreliability of subtest scores based on only a small number of items." It is obvious that if you include enough items in one test to measure fourth grade ability, you include many which are too difficult and therefore useless to measure first grade ability; conversely, the easy items necessary to measure first grade abilities are useless in the measurement of fourth grade abilities. As a result, the number of items which are valid measures at any one grade level is greatly reduced with a resulting decrease in reliability. It appears that this defect is more serious in an instrument designed for analysis and diagnosis than in one intended only for survey purposes.

Other criticisms and cautions occurring to this reviewer, which have been mentioned in previous reviews and so will not be dwelt upon here, are (a) the direction which instructs the examiner to stop work on a test when 90 per cent of the class have completed it and (b) the caution that in the case of any individual child the analytical profile, improperly referred to as diagnostic, is useful only as a basis for genuine diagnostic testing or as a set of clues for the remedial worker. The former makes it difficult to understand how the test could be truly standardized in the first place, while the latter is a caution which should be emphasized in the manual. Incidentally, there is a distinct paucity of suggestion as to what to do about the class weaknesses disclosed by the analysis.

Fortunately, there are also many entries to be made on the credit side of the ledger regarding this series of reading tests. There is no question that the reading skills measured are among the most important ones we strive to develop. The test materials appear to this reviewer to be well chosen and representative of material encountered by the child in his daily school work. The analytic feature should be a great aid to a teacher in assaying class and, to a lesser extent, individual strengths and weaknesses. The manual, despite the criticisms made above, has much to recommend it, particularly the sections on the diagnostic profile, the uses of test results by administrators, and the adjustment of norms with relation to intelligence quotient medians, although in the last case something should have been said about the desirability of developing one's own norms. Beginning with grade 4, the test user is offered his choice of hand scoring or of using the California Test Bureau's Scoreze answer-sheet or an IBM answer sheet. This is commendable and should serve to widen the usefulness of this test series.

In general, this is a well thought-out series of tests which deserves its wide use. However, this reviewer would like to hold up to its publishers for emulation the statement on validity, reliability, and standardization found in the manual accompanying the *Shank Tests of Reading Comprehension,* and the section on how to provide for and remedy the revealed differences and difficulties found in the manual accompanying

the reading test of the *Iowa Every-Pupil Tests of Basic Skills.*

J Consult Psychol 14:333 Ag '50. Laurance F. Shaffer. [Review of the Intermediate level.] * The test and manual formats, redesigned by Raymond Loewy Associates, are attractive but violate at least a few experimentally determined findings about legibility, such as the use of white letters on a colored background. *

For reviews by Warren G. Findley, Alvin W. Schindler, and J. Harlan Shores of the complete battery, see 2; for a review by Paul A. Witty of an earlier edition of the complete battery, see 3:15; for a review by Frederick B. Davis of an earlier edition, see 40:1563; for reviews by C. W. Odell and Hugh B. Wood of an earlier edition of the complete battery, see 40:1193; for reviews by Ivan A. Booker and Joseph C. Dewey of an earlier edition, see 38:1110; for a review by D. Welty Lefever of an earlier edition of the complete battery, see 38:876.

[531]

*Diagnostic Reading Tests. Grades 7–13; 1947–52; IBM except for Section IV, Part 1; $1.50 per construction and validation booklet ('52—see 19 below); 15¢ per booklet of directions for administering (separate booklets required for each part of each section); $3.15 per specimen set (does not include construction and validation booklet); separate answer sheets may be used except with Section IV, Part 1; postage extra; Committee on Diagnostic Reading Tests, Inc. *

a) SURVEY SECTION. 1947–52; 5 scores: rate of reading, comprehension check, general vocabulary, comprehension, total; IBM; Forms A ('50), B ('47), C ('50), D ('50), E ('50), F ('50), G ('50), H ('50); revised directions for administering ('50); 15¢ per test; 3¢ per IBM answer sheet; (Forms A and B also published by Science Research Associates: 25¢ per test; 15¢ per copy of directions for administering; 3¢ per IBM answer sheet; 60¢ per specimen set; cash orders postpaid); 40 (50) minutes. (Forms A and B were published in the high school and college educational edition of *Reader's Digest* in November 1949 and May 1950 respectively.)

b) SECTION I, VOCABULARY. 1947–52; 5 scores: English, mathematics, science, social studies, total; IBM; Forms A ('51), B ('51); directions for administering ('48); 15¢ per test; 2¢ per IBM answer sheet; 35(40) minutes.

c) SECTION II, COMPREHENSION. 1947–52; IBM; 2 parts; Forms A ('48), B ('48); revised directions for administering ('50).

1) *Part 1, Silent.* 20¢ per test; 2¢ per IBM answer sheet; nontimed (40–60) minutes.

2) *Part 2, Auditory.* Booklet of test paragraphs ('47); 15¢ per test; 20¢ per copy of directions for administering; 50¢ per booklet of test paragraphs (only one copy needed for administrator); 3¢ per IBM answer sheet; (40–60) minutes.

d) SECTION III, RATES OF READING. 1947–52; IBM; 3 parts; Forms A ('47), B ('47); revised directions for administering ('50).

1) *Part 1, General.* 4 scores: normal rate of reading, comprehension at normal rate, maximum rate of

reading, comprehension at maximum rate; 16¢ per test; 2¢ per IBM answer sheet; 30(35) minutes.

2) *Part 2, Social Studies.* 2 scores: rate of reading, comprehension check; 15¢ per test; 2¢ per IBM answer sheet; 15(20) minutes.

3) *Part 3, Science.* 2 scores: same as Part 2; 15¢ per test; 2¢ per IBM answer sheet; 15(20) minutes.

e) SECTION IV, WORD ATTACK. 1947–52; 2 parts.

1) *Part 1, Oral.* 1948–52; individual; Forms A ('48), B ('48); directions for administering ('50); 18¢ per test; (20) minutes.

2) *Part 2, Silent.* 1947–52; 3 scores: identification of sounds, syllabication, total; IBM; Forms A ('47), B ('47); directions for administering ('48); 15¢ per test; 3¢ per IBM answer sheet; nontimed (30) minutes.

REFERENCES

1. BEAR, ROBERT M. "The Development of Diagnostic Tools to Further Remedial Instruction." Abstract. *Am Psychol* 2:291–2 Ag '47. * (*PA* 21:4639, title only)
2. TRIGGS, FRANCES ORALIND. "The Diagnosis of Reading Deficiencies as an Aid to Remedial Work." *Ed & Psychol Meas* 7:638–46 au '47. * (*PA* 22:3614)
3. TRIGGS, FRANCES ORALIND. "Diagnostic Reading Tests as Aids to Remedial Instruction." *Sch & Soc* 66:42–5 Jl 19 '47. *
4. COMMITTEE ON DIAGNOSTIC READING TESTS, INC. "Description of the Purposes and Functions of the Diagnostic Reading Tests." *Ed & Psychol Meas* 8:3–14 sp '48. * (*PA* 22:4123)
5. SPACHE, GEORGE. "The Construction and Validation of a Silent and Auditory Work-Type Comprehension Reading Test." Abstract. *Am Psychol* 3:300 Jl '48. * (*PA* 22:5204, title only)
6. TRIGGS, FRANCES ORALIND. "Better Measurement Service in Reading Diagnosis," pp. 19–23. In *Improving Educational Research:* Official Report, American Educational Research Association, A Department of the National Education Association, Atlantic City, New Jersey, February 21–24, 1948. Washington, D.C.: American Educational Research Association, 1948. Pp. 225. Paper. *
7. TRIGGS, FRANCES ORALIND. "Present Status of Developmental and Remedial Reading Programs at the College Level." *Trans N Y Acad Sci* 10:238–44 My '48. * (*PA* 22:5127)
8. TOWNSEND, AGATHA. "Use of the Survey Section of the Diagnostic Reading Tests in the Independent-School Testing Program," pp. 42–9. (*PA* 23:3422) In *1948 Fall Testing Program in Independent Schools and Supplementary Studies.* Educational Records Bulletin, No. 51. New York: the Bureau, January 1949. Pp. xiii, 72. Paper, lithotyped. *
9. TRAXLER, ARTHUR E. "Correlations Between Scores on Various Reading Tests Administered Several Months Apart," pp. 78–82. (*PA* 24:748) In *1949 Achievement Testing Program in Independent Schools and Supplementary Studies.* Educational Records Bulletin, No. 52. New York: Educational Records Bureau, July 1949. Pp. xiii, 87. Paper, lithotyped. *
10. TRAXLER, ARTHUR E. "Reliability and Intercorrelation of the Vocabulary Section of the Diagnostic Reading Tests," pp. 50–3. (*PA* 23:3423) In *1948 Fall Testing Program in Independent Schools and Supplementary Studies.* Educational Records Bulletin, No. 51. New York: the Bureau, January 1949. Pp. xiii, 72. Paper, lithotyped. *
11. "A Note on the Correlation Between Forms A and B of the Diagnostic Reading Tests: Survey Section, With a Time Interval of Approximately One Year," pp. 67–8. In *1949 Fall Testing Program in Independent Schools and Supplementary Studies.* Educational Records Bulletin, No. 53. New York: Educational Records Bureau, January 1950. Pp. xiii, 70. Paper, lithotyped. * (*PA* 24:3894)
12. SPACHE, GEORGE. "The Construction and Validation of a Work-Type Auditory Comprehension Reading Test." *Ed & Psychol Meas* 10:249–53 su '50. * (*PA* 25:5825)
13. TRIGGS, F. "Report on Measurement of Reading Skills and Reading Therapy." p. 118. Abstract. In *Proceedings and Papers of the Twelfth International Congress of Psychology Held at the University of Edinburgh, July 23rd to July 29th, 1948.* Edinburgh, Scotland: Oliver and Boyd Ltd., 1950. Pp. xxviii, 152. Paper. *
14. TRIGGS, FRANCES, and MEMBERS OF COMMITTEE ON DIAGNOSTIC READING TESTS, INC. "The Relationship of Measured Reading Skills to Mental Abilities as Measured by Paper-and-Pencil Tests." Abstract. *Am Psychol* 5:285–6 Jl '50. * (*PA* 25:1256, title only)
15. TRIGGS, FRANCES ORALIND. "Users Report on Ways in Which Diagnostic Reading Tests Are Used," pp. 27–30. In *The Seventh Yearbook of the National Council on Measurements Used in Education, 1949–1950.* Fairmont, W.Va.: the Council, Fairmont State College, 1950. Pp. v, 55, xi. Paper, mimeographed. *
16. JACKSON, ROBERT. "A Comparison of Diagnostic Reading Tests With Certain Other Criteria." *Ed & Psychol Meas* 11:603–4 w '51. *
17. PRESTON, RALPH C., and BOTEL, MORTON. "Reading Comprehension Tested Under Timed and Untimed Conditions." *Sch & Soc* 74:71 Ag 4 '51. *
18. TRAXLER, ARTHUR E. "Intercorrelations and Validity of

Scores on Three Reading Tests," pp. 79–89. (*PA* 25:6416) In *1950 Fall Testing Program in Independent Schools and Supplementary Studies.* Foreword by Ben D. Wood. Educational Records Bulletin, No. 56. New York: Educational Records Bureau, January 1951. Pp. xiii, 89. Paper, lithotyped. *
19. COMMITTEE ON DIAGNOSTIC READING TESTS, INC. *Diagnostic Reading Tests: A History of Their Construction and Validation.* New York: the Committee, Inc., 1952. Pp. 56. Paper, lithotyped. *

FREDERICK B. DAVIS, *Professor of Education, and Director, Educational Clinic, Hunter College, New York, New York; Director, Test Research Service, Bronxville, New York.*

This series of tests yields a number of scores for which norms (of one sort or another) are provided. The plan for use of the series is to administer the survey section to ascertain the general level of reading competence. Pupils at a low level of proficiency can then be given the longer diagnostic section.

The development of these tests was an ambitious undertaking, and it is obvious from an inspection of the mass of testing materials that have been assembled that a great deal of energy and labor have been expended on this project. As a result, teachers and clinicians have available a useful set of diagnostic tools. Their usefulness would be greatly increased if suitable norms were provided. For a battery of diagnostic tests of this kind, norms should be established by having each child in the sample take all of the tests in the battery. Large representative samples in each one of a wide range of grades should be used. Satisfactory norms are not available for the *Diagnostic Reading Tests,* perhaps because to obtain them is so expensive.

Reliability coefficients have been reported for many of the part scores; some of them are based on reasonably large samples at single grade levels while others are based on as few as 28 cases and on samples not clearly identified as consisting of pupils drawn from a single grade. Parallel forms coefficients are available for certain of the rate tests, but Kuder-Richardson formula No. 21 was used for computing others. Since the latter are not supposed to be speeded, the estimates of reliability for them are probably worth reporting. In general, it must be said that the individual part scores are not sufficiently reliable to identify, with confidence, weaknesses in an individual's ability to read.

The validity of the various part scores can only be determined by subjective judgment. In the reviewer's opinion, the comprehension, vocabulary, and oral reading scores seem acceptably valid measures; the tests of silent word attack do not seem to provide measures of skills that are crucial in this important area; the rate tests are probably about as valid as tests of this kind usually are, but the time and space devoted to them seem to be entirely out of proportion to their very limited meaningfulness or usefulness. If all of Section III were omitted from the battery, the reviewer believes that virtually nothing would be lost. The Committee's intercorrelation data support this belief.

In passing, it should be noted that the reading passages for the rate tests seem interesting and that the comprehension items following them are not generally answerable without reading the passages.

As in almost any test, faulty items can be found; the *Diagnostic Reading Tests* seem to have perhaps a few more than their share. An example of these is Item 32 of the Survey Section, Form A, where choice 5 (perimeter) includes choice 4 (circumference), which is the keyed response. Webster defines circumference as "the perimeter of a circle." Items of this kind tend to reduce test validity.

The publications of the Committee on Diagnostic Reading Tests are written in a labored and clumsy style (See Question 21 in "Questions on Reading") and contain an admixture of information helpful to teachers and test users and misinformation about reading. The answer to Question 11 in "Questions on Reading" will cause statisticians to shudder and will help make percentile norms seem incomprehensible to most teachers.

The format and organization of the tests and manuals are satisfactory for materials in the developmental stage, as these are said to be.

WILLIAM W. TURNBULL, *Vice President, Educational Testing Service, Princeton, New Jersey.*

The *Diagnostic Reading Tests* constitute a well integrated set of instruments for screening students to discover those whose reading skills need special attention and for diagnosing the particular difficulties toward which that attention should be directed. The conception of a survey test supplemented by a set of diagnostic instruments is a sound one, and the tests themselves give evidence of the conscientious work that has gone into bringing them to their present stage of development. The preparation of these tests is an ambitious project, and it has been carried forward energetically.

The tests are designed for use over a wide range: grades 7 to 13 inclusive. The normative material suggests that the tests are reasonably

useful at the two extremes of this widespread group, but the scores are crowding the ends of the scale. In the Survey Section, Form B, for example, the median vocabulary score made by 362 public school students in the seventh grade was 18 out of 60, when the chance score is 12. The 25th percentile for these students was 13—one point above the chance value. Among 1,447 twelfth grade independent school students taking the same form, however, the median vocabulary score was 48 out of 60. The median comprehension score was 33 out of 40 for these students, and the 25th and 75th percentiles were 30 and 35 respectively, indicating a failure of the questions to provide adequate discrimination at this level of ability.

The Survey Section is designed to give a relatively brief (40-minute) overview of general reading ability, yielding separate scores for rate of reading, vocabulary, and comprehension, and a total score summing vocabulary and comprehension. Rate is determined by number of words read in three minutes, using well chosen story type material in the area of natural science. The comprehension score is based on this same material (allowing the student 15 minutes to complete the reading and answer the questions) and on four shorter passages from the natural and social science fields. The rate and comprehension scores are indicated to have reliability coefficients of about .80, while the vocabulary score has a reliability of about .85—fairly satisfactory figures. The reliability of the total comprehension score is about .90.

The skills tested by the comprehension materials are broad and of central importance in reading. Emphasis is given to such questions as "The main idea of the paragraph is...." and "A conclusion which can be drawn is....," rather than to factual memory.

Despite the fact that 30 of the 40 minutes are devoted to comprehension materials, 60 of the 100 items are vocabulary rather than comprehension. While standard deviations are not reported, the quartile figures given suggest that the vocabulary score contributes more heavily to the score called "total comprehension" than does the separate comprehension subscore.

The intercorrelations of the separate scores indicate a median correlation of about .33 between rate and comprehension, showing a degree of independence quite adequate to permit their use in diagnosing the particular area of a student's strength or weakness. The median correlation of .62 between vocabulary and comprehension indicates a less useful degree of independence for these measures, but is as low as could reasonably be asked in view of the close association of the skills involved. The fact that the correlation of the vocabulary score with total comprehension (a composite score summing vocabulary and comprehension) is substantially higher than that of the separate comprehension score with total comprehension indicates that the latter composite depends less heavily on the material termed "comprehension" than its name might imply, and suggests that the composite might benefit from renaming.

A notable feature is the existence of eight parallel forms of the Survey Section, permitting reuse without repetition year after year. The fact that four of these forms (A, B, C, and D) have been published through the Reader's Digest Educational Service detracts from their usefulness in some situations, but should not be a serious disadvantage now that eight forms are available.

The diagnostic reading sections, designed for use with students who do poorly on the Survey Section, are available in parallel editions. The four sections are: I, Vocabulary; II, Comprehension; III, Rates of Reading; and IV, Word Attack (oral and silent).

The Vocabulary Section is 35 minutes in length and is divided into four parts (English grammar and literature, mathematics, science, and social studies) on which separate scores are obtained. The reliabilities of these scores were found to be between .82 and .94, based on a random selection of 100 papers from students in various colleges. This indicates a quite satisfactory degree of stability and reflects the care that has been taken in the construction, analysis, and selection of items. While the reliability of the total score is not reported, it should constitute a useful and highly reliable vocabulary index.

The intercorrelations of the part scores within the vocabulary test range between .43 and .67, and so are well below the reliabilities of the parts. (Since the reliabilities and intercorrelations were established on different samples, both small, one would not push the relations between the two sets of figures too far.) In any case, it seems clear that the part scores are stable and usefully independent.

The Comprehension Section is presented in parallel parts, silent and auditory, in both of which passages from high school texts in sci-

ence, social science, and literature are used. This test is untimed. The provision of an auditory test of comprehension is a distinct contribution in its own right, and teachers may well find scores on this part of the test of real interest. The rationale given for use of the auditory section is that since it is free from the influence of the student's reading skill, it provides an indication of his capacity for understanding the materials of the test and hence of the improvability of his silent comprehension through remedial training. This is an interesting and reasonable hypothesis that remains to be checked. Meanwhile, it seems equally plausible that the silent comprehension section should be considered an indicator of capacity for the improvement of auditory comprehension skills. Neither possibility can be checked in any way from the data given. There are no reported intercorrelations between the silent and auditory parts: Kuder-Richardson reliabilities in the high .80's are reported for both parts.

A circumstance that detracts from the usefulness of this test in the battery is the fact that some of the passages and questions are repeated verbatim from the Survey Section. This will surely result in differential advantage to students who have and those who have not studied the key for the Survey Section in relation to these materials.

Section III, Rates of Reading, is designed to "make it possible to compare....reading abilities in two major areas of study and in situations demanding adjustment in rate of reading." The main purpose for including this section is to provide a measure of flexibility of reading—the degree to which a student adapts his reading rate to the type of material being read and to the amount of pressure under which he is asked to perform.

Two types of material—social studies and science—are used to investigate the differentiation of rates according to content. As the authors point out, however, the intercorrelations of rate scores on the different types of materials "are high, in many cases as high as the reliabilities themselves * To the extent that these tests are accurate, students vary their rate of reading very little according to the content, but instead tend to read all materials at a similar rate." Under the circumstances, it is hard to justify the continuance of separate scores for the two types of material.

Flexibility of rate according to differential time pressure is measured by having the students read first at a leisurely pace for the best possible comprehension and second as rapidly as possible with understanding. Data are presented to show that the second set of instructions does indeed result in increased speed, but correlations of scores under the two conditions are not presented, leaving open the question of whether or not anything concerning an individual's "flexibility" of rate is being measured. It is difficult to obtain reliable scores for such a variable, measured by the difference between two rate scores which are themselves unstable. It remains for the authors to present evidence that their goal has been accomplished.

Since it has not been demonstrated that the test does provide a measure of an individual's flexibility of rate according to time pressure, and since differentiation according to type of material has not been achieved, the authors' decision to retain this section of the test appears unwise to this reviewer. It would seem preferable to omit the section until its value can be demonstrated.

Section IV, Word Attack, is also divided into two parts, oral and silent. The usefulness of the oral part, which constitutes one of the very few tests of its kind available, will depend very heavily on the skill of the teacher giving the test. Several good suggestions for interpretation are provided in the directions, and an alert and interested teacher should find this section rewarding despite the difficulties introduced when a test must be given to pupils individually. The silent part is more readily standardized. The reliabilities of its two parts (rhyming words and division into syllables) are in the .90's, and their intercorrelation is below .60. This test may provide valuable leads to the teacher in individual cases. The correlation between the scores provided by the oral and silent parts is not indicated.

The strength of the entire battery is clearly the fact that it was planned as a unit: one section supports and supplements another. The authors of the plan are to be congratulated upon it. The test materials themselves are reasonably good in the main, with inevitable lapses of detail. A wealth of suggestions for making the test results useful in the teaching situation is provided. The committee's primary intent was to furnish tests that could be translated into guides for teaching, and the consistent orientation of the materials to this end is one of its greatest strengths. From this same aim, however, stems a real difficulty. The material is so finely subdivided, in line with

its diagnostic purpose, that the interpretation of the scores becomes dubious from the technical standpoint of their reliability, and, reliability aside, extremely difficult from the sheer complexity of the battery.

The authors are to be congratulated also on the recently published compilation of extensive and helpful data on the construction and validation of the tests, wherein the user can find information on most aspects of their development and performance. As has been indicated in this review, however, there are still some significant omissions of data—a fact that is understandable and excusable in the early stages of an enterprise of this scope.

In summary, the Survey Section stands already as one of the better instruments for the evaluation of overall reading ability. The Vocabulary and Comprehension sections are likely to be widely useful, and the Word Attack Section should provide valuable information in individual cases. One may hope that the committee responsible for these tests will streamline the battery wherever possible and will persevere in the collection and consolidation of information about them.

HENRY WEITZ, *Director, Bureau of Testing and Guidance, Duke University, Durham, North Carolina.*

I. PURPOSE. These tests were designed to furnish teachers with information about the essential reading skills of students from the seventh grade through the first year of college. The Committee on Diagnostic Reading Tests, Inc. believes that by providing teachers with adequate measures of reading skills, "a large part of the 'remedial' work which has developed widely in our schools could thus be eliminated, because instruction would be individualized to the extent necessary to meet the needs of most students."

II. DESCRIPTION OF THE TEST BATTERY. A. GENERAL. *The Diagnostic Reading Tests* consist of a battery of nine tests grouped into five sections: a Survey Section and four special diagnostic sections. The Committee recommends that the Survey Section of the tests be administered to all students in a class "either as an independent test or as a screening test to segregate those students to whom the total battery or selected portions of [it] should be administered." It is recommended that students scoring below the 30th percentile on the Survey Section be given other appropriate portions of the battery

(Vocabulary, Comprehension, Rates of Reading, and Word Attack) "unless other data are available on factors such as low general ability, which may account for the low scores on a reading test."

An attempt has been made throughout the test battery to relate the various measures of reading skill to subject matter areas: English, mathematics, and the like. Although most of the items on all tests are drawn from typical textbook materials, only the Vocabulary Section yields scores in all the areas from which items are drawn, but these separate vocabulary subtests are generally too unreliable for use in individual measurement. The Rates of Reading Section yields separate scores for rate of general reading and for rate of reading science and social studies materials. The authors report that the correlation between rates of reading different kinds of material is high. If this is so, the separate subject matter tests would appear to be unnecessary. In view of the fact that only two sections yield subject matter scores and that these scores have only limited usefulness, it is unfortunate that the authors have emphasized this subject matter aspect in their discussions of the battery.

B. SURVEY SECTION. The Survey Section of the battery yields measures of reading rate, story comprehension, vocabulary, and general comprehension, and a total reading score. The rate of reading score is not included in computing the total score. Sixty per cent of the total reading items are vocabulary.

While the average reliability for the total score is adequate to permit the use of the test for individual measurement, the subtest scores do not yield such high reliability. Some of the reliabilities reported for the vocabulary subtest approach a satisfactorily high level, but others, for some grade groups, are still so low as to require great caution in the use of the scores. Reliabilities for the other subtests of this section are not sufficiently high to permit measurement of individuals with a high degree of confidence. The Survey Section, therefore, has very limited value as an independent measure of the separate reading skills accounted for in the subtests. However, the use of the total score, as a general device for screening students with reading handicaps is acceptable.

C. SECTION I, VOCABULARY. The Vocabulary Section yields separate measures of general vocabulary and of the vocabulary of English grammar and literature, mathematics, social studies, and science, as well as a total vocabulary score. Most of the items appear to be taken from one or another of the eight forms of the Survey Section. The degree of overlap is not reported although a sample tabulation suggests that it is fairly high. A revised edition of the Vocabulary Section has recently been made available. This revision drops the general vocabulary subtest and increases the length of the remaining subsections by about 50 per cent, thus increasing their reliability.

According to data given in the 1948 edition of Directions for Administering, the unrevised edition of this section seems to provide total scores of fairly high reliability. It should be noted, however, that for two grade groups the reliability of this 150-item test is less than the reliability of the 60-item vocabulary subtest of the Survey Section. The reliabilities of the subtests in the unrevised edition are seriously low, clustering in the .70's, with some falling in the .50's. The diagnostic value of the section is, therefore, seriously impaired. While the revised edition may correct these faults, intercorrelations between the subtests appear to be so high as to raise a question regarding the value of the separate scores anyway.

D. SECTION II, COMPREHENSION. The Comprehension Section consists of two parts: Part 1, Silent, providing a single silent comprehension score, and Part 2, Auditory, providing a single auditory comprehension score. Each part contains reading selections of one or more paragraphs followed by several questions on each selection. These questions are principally of the "What is the main idea?" type. Part 1 is administered in the usual manner with the students reading each selection silently and answering the questions which follow. In Part 2, the selections and questions are read aloud to the students. Each student has a copy of the questions but not of the selections. The student answers the questions either on the test booklet or on a separate answer sheet.

The assumption made by the Committee in presenting these two parts together is that the auditory part gives a measure of the student's "potential" reading ability, his general background of understanding, while the silent part measures his actual comprehension. Remedial instruction is likely to be profitable, the Committee believes, when the auditory score exceeds the silent score. It considers this method of estimating reading potential to be more effective, for this purpose, than the use of intelligence tests. While these hypotheses are intriguing, the Committee offers no evidence to support them. No information is given as to what range of differences between these scores would be necessary to suggest that remedial instruction would be desirable or effective.

The only reliability data supplied for this section indicate reliabilities of .87, .83, and .86 for grades 10, 11, and 12, respectively, on the silent part and reliabilities of .84 and .89 for an eighth grade group on the auditory part. This level of reliability suggests the need for great caution in using these tests for individual diagnosis.

The auditory part has recently been temporarily withdrawn until such time as recorded versions of the material to be read to the students are available. Since both the silent and auditory parts are used together in evaluating a student's comprehension, this temporary withdrawal of the auditory part, in effect, withdraws the entire Section II.

E. SECTION III, RATES OF READING. The Rates of Reading Section consists of three parts : Part I, General, provides measures of "normal" and "speeded" reading rates with comprehension check scores for each rate ; Part 2, Social Studies, and Part 3, Science, provide measures of normal reading rates with the specialized subject matter as well as comprehension check scores for each test.

Although the science and social studies parts represent fairly conventional tests of this type, the general reading rate part introduces an additional element. This part consists of two subparts, each containing a long selection followed by a series of questions. In administering this part, the teacher introduces the first selection to be read with the statement : "Read as rapidly as you can and still understand what you read" ; later this statement is added : "Remember that you are to read the article in this test in the same way you would ordinarily read such materials." The second passage is introduced with this statement, "You were asked to read the first part at your regular everyday rate. Read the next article *as rapidly as you can,* and still understand what you read. *Keep pushing yourself constantly to speed your reading—to get the ideas as quickly as you possibly can.*" Later this statement is added: "*Remember that you are going to try constantly to read the article as rapidly as you can and still understand what you read.*"

These two sets of directions are intended to provide motivation for different reading rates. In terms of the reported norms data, it is doubtful that they do. In the case of two of the seven median scores reported for Form A and three of the seven median scores reported for Form B, the "speeded" rate is slower than the "normal" rate, and in only 4 of the 14 instances reported did the median number of words read per minute at the "speeded" rate exceed the normal rate by more than a line. No evidence is given to support the view that the differences in rate are significant. Therefore, although this approach to measuring reading rate may be promising, the reported evidence suggests that, as presently designed, this section contributes little to the understanding of a student's reading problem.

The estimated reliability of .80 reported for the several parts of the Rates of Reading Section can be achieved only by using both forms of each part, thus doubling the time and cost to achieve a level of reliability still inadequate for individual measurement. This level of reliability is the same as that reported for the rate subtest of the Survey Section.

F. SECTION IV, WORD ATTACK. The Word Attack Section consists of two parts : Part I, Oral, provides a record of the kinds of oral word attack errors made and a count of the total errors ; Part 2, Silent, provides separate measures of the student's skill in recognizing syllable sounds and his ability to recognize the number of syllables in a word, as well as a total silent word attack score. The oral part of this test must be administered individually and is consequently very time consuming. It does, however, offer the teacher a good opportunity to gain some direct insight into the kinds of reading problems being encountered by the student. The silent part also seems promising as a diagnostic device but in a more limited area. Reliability coefficients reported for the oral and silent parts of this section appear to be sufficiently high for individual measurement both by subtests and total score.

III. MANUAL. One of the major handicaps to an adequate evaluation and effective use of this test battery is the absence of a manual. Each of the nine parts of the test has its separate pamphlet on directions for administering, containing a statement of the purpose, a brief description of the construction and standardization procedures, instructions for administration, directions for scoring, a statement about the norms, and some norms data. Much of the material in the instructions for administering, the directions for scoring, and the statement about the norms is repeated from pamphlet to pamphlet. Some of the norms tables present only the three quartiles. Reliability data is frequently either meager or contradictory. Median reliabilities reported in the body of the pamphlets frequently contradict the reliability data reported in the tables. Almost no information is given about the interrelationships of the parts of the battery. These pamphlets are poorly edited as, for example, in the case of the March 1950 Directions for Administering Section III, Part 1, which states on page 2, "Reliabilities of scores are given on each norm table for each grade level for which percentiles are furnished," but which fails to provide these data in the tables.

Recently the Committee prepared a pamphlet which consolidates much of the statistical material published in the older directions for administering and provides a small amount of additional material. The new publication does not replace the directions, nor is it in any sense a manual. Its publication provides relatively little help in understanding the tests and does much to add to the confusion resulting from so much piecemeal material.

The major difficulty of abbreviated directions for administering is that they give insufficient information about the test results, thus making it extremely difficult, if not impossible, for the teacher to apply the results as they were intended as a basis for individualizing instruction. Interpretative data, when it does appear is sketchy, as, for example, in the Directions for Administering Section II, which suggests ways in which the test scores may be interpreted but fails to indicate what levels of scores are to be interpreted in the ways suggested. Nor are the methods of implementing even these sketchy interpretations recommended.

The Committee plans to publish a complete manual in the near future. When it does, and if the manual is adequate, one of the major obstacles to the effective use of this battery will be removed.

IV. NORMS. Tentative percentile norms are available for most parts of the test battery. In some cases, however, only abbreviated norm tables (presenting only the three quartiles) are provided, and in other cases norms are provided on mimeographed inserts to the directions for administering. Not all available norms are pro-

vided. In order to secure certain norms, the test user has to make a special request for them.

The method suggested by the authors for using the norm tables presents an unnecessary problem. They suggest that the teacher compute the three quartiles for each population tested and then match these statistics with those in the norm tables to select the appropriate norms. Since the authors also suggest that the diagnostic portions of the battery be administered only to those students who fall below the 30th percentile on the Survey Section, this method of selecting an appropriate norms group for a diagnostic section administered only to the "screened" students becomes meaningless. More adequate norms are promised for the future.

V. SUMMARY. The *Diagnostic Reading Tests* represent an attempt to provide teachers with measures of essential reading skills in order that they may individualize subject matter instruction to meet the reading needs of students and thereby reduce the need for remedial instruction. Although such a purpose is an entirely desirable one, this test battery does not achieve its purpose. The reliability information supplied by the authors suggests that many subtests are not sufficiently reliable for individual diagnosis; the norms and interpretative information supplied are not adequate to help the teacher translate the test results into meaningful individualized instruction; the intercorrelations between parts of the battery suggest that much of it may be unnecessary overelaboration of a basically simple measurement problem; and some of the sections appear to be based upon hypotheses which are not supported by the data thus far presented.

[532]
*Elementary Reading: Every Pupil Test. Grades 4–6; 1936–51; new form usually published each April and December; 2 parts; form December 1951; no data on reliability and validity; revised manual ['49]; norms ('51); 2½¢ per test; 1¢ per answer key; postpaid; Ohio Scholarship Tests, Ohio State Department of Education. *
a) GENERAL ABILITY. 17(30) minutes.
b) SPEED AND COMPREHENSION. 6(10) minutes.

[533]
*Garvey Primary Reading Test. Grades 1–3; 1931–36; 4 scores: form recognition, vocabulary, comprehension, total; Forms 1 ('36), 2 ('36); manual ['36]; $1.50 per 25, postage extra; 35¢ per specimen set, postpaid; 40(50) minutes; Helen Sue Read and May V. Seagoe; California Test Bureau. *

[534]
*General Reading Test: Ohio Senior Survey Tests. Grade 12; 1935–41; 4 scores: paragraph meaning, general vocabulary, outlining, total; Forms A

('35), B ('37) ; no data on reliability and validity; 3¢
per test; 25¢ per manual ('41) ; postpaid; 60(65) minutes; S. L. Pressey and Maurice E. Troyer (B) ; Ohio
Scholarship Tests, Ohio State Department of Education. *

[535]

Haggerty Reading Examination. Grades 1–3, 6–12;
1920–29; 2 levels; specimen set not available; postage
extra; M. E. Haggerty, Margaret E. Noonan (Sigma
1), and Laura C. Haggerty (Sigma 3) ; World Book
Co. *
a) SIGMA 1. Grades 1–3; 1 form, '20; manual ('29) ;
$1.55 per 25; 25(35) minutes.
b) SIGMA 3. Grades 6–12; Forms A ('20), B ('22) ;
revised manual ('29) ; $1.80 per 25; 20(30) minutes.

REFERENCES

1. HAGGERTY, M. E. Chap. 8, "Basis for Grouping Elementary
School Pupils," pp. 114–57, and Chap. 9, "How Virginia Children are Grouped," pp. 158–93. In *Virginia Public Schools: A
Survey of a Southern State Public School System: Part Two,
Educational Tests.* By the Virginia Education Commission and
the Virginia Survey Staff. Yonkers, N.Y.: World Book Co.,
1921. Pp. xii, 235. *
2. CURRENT, W. F. AND RUCH, G. M. "Further Studies on
the Reliability of Reading Tests." *J Ed Psychol* 17:476–81 O '26.
* (PA 1:196)
3. SYMONDS, PERCIVAL M. *Ability Standards for Standardized
Achievement Tests in the High School.* New York: Bureau of
Publications, Teachers College, Columbia University, 1927. Pp.
x, 91. *
4. BROOM, M. EUSTACE; DOUGLAS, JOSEPHINE; AND RUDD,
MARION. "On the Validity of Silent Reading Tests." *J Appl
Psychol* 15:35–8 F '31. * (PA 5:4288)
5. JACOBSEN, CARLYLE F. "Interest and Attitude as Factors in
Achievement in Medical School." *J Assn Am Med Col* 21:152–9
My '46. *

WILLIAM S. GRAY, *Director of Research in
Reading, and Emeritus Professor of Education,
The University of Chicago, Chicago, Illinois.*

SIGMA 1. This test is designed to measure
reading ability in grades 1–3. The aspects of
reading selected as valid measures in the primary
grades are not discussed in the manual accompanying the test. An analysis of the test exercises shows that the designers of the test concentrated on two basic aspects of silent reading;
namely, sentence meaning and paragraph meaning. The child's grasp of meaning in Part I is
indicated by his ability to perform an act suggested by the sentence or paragraph which is
read; for example, "Make two lines under the
horse." Grasp of meaning is indicated in Part
II of the test by underlining "Yes" or "No" in
response to such a question as, "Are men larger
than boys?" Such tests provide a reasonably
valid measure of grasp of meaning of the kinds
of sentences and paragraphs often read in the
early grades. Since, however, the test is timed,
the final scores represent a composite of capacity
to interpret and speed of performance.

The adequacy of the test is discussed in terms
of two criteria. The first is its value in discriminating the individuals in a group in respect to
reading ability, as measured by the test. In this
connection, two requirements were set up. In

the first place, the scores secured on the test
must distribute themselves over a reasonably
wide range; and in the second place, the test
exercises must vary sufficiently widely in difficulty so that very few, if any, individuals will
make zero scores, a large number will make
average scores, and few or no individuals will
make perfect scores. According to the data presented, Sigma 1 meets these requirements very
well. The reliability of the test was determined
by correlating the results secured on repeated
uses of the test. A reasonably high correlation
(.84) was secured in this way.

Only one form of the test is available. Directions for giving and scoring the test have been
worked out carefully. Grade norms (1–4) and
age norms (6–11) accompany the test. As indicated above, the score is a composite measure of
achievement and therefore has very little diagnostic value.

SIGMA 3. This test is designed to measure
reading ability in grades 6–12. Three aspects of
reading are involved; namely, vocabulary, sentence reading, and paragraph reading. The vocabulary test includes 50 words ranging from
relatively simple words, such as *calm* and *coast*
to relatively difficult words, such as *epaulets* and
chalice. No information is given concerning the
source of the words or the basis of their selection.
Ability to understand sentences is measured by
checking "Yes" or "No" in response to questions. Ability to understand paragraphs is measured by the reader's responses to directions
which are an integral part of the paragraphs read.
The directions are of two kinds: one calls for
underlining, and the other for checking.

No specific discussion of the validity of the
three tests as measures of reading ability is presented. Ability to recognize the meanings of
words, sentences, and paragraphs are indispu-
table aspects of reading ability in junior and senior high schools. Data are presented which show
that the scores on the tests correlate fairly highly
(.61) with a criterion composed of grade location, age, and teachers' estimates of scholarship.
The correlation with intelligence scores is .64.
On the basis of such data, the designers conclude that the "Sigma 3 examination is a really
significant measure." The evidence presented
does not make clear, however, whether the test
is a significant measure of general scholastic
ability, reading competence, general intelligence,
or a combination of the three.

In order to determine if the tests were satisfactory, the same criteria that were used with Sigma 1 were applied. The data presented indicate that the test has adequate discriminative capacity and is highly reliable. Correlations between the scores on repeated use of the test are reported as .88 for the test as a whole, .86 for vocabulary, .77 for sentence meaning, and .81 for paragraph meaning.

Two forms of the test are provided. Grade norms and age norms have been developed for each form, the former extending from grade 5 to grade 12, and the latter, from age 10 to age 20. Carefully prepared directions for giving and scoring the tests are available. Because of the composition of the test, the scores may be used both as gross measures of reading achievement and, to a limited extent, for diagnostic purposes.

The fact that both Sigma 1 and Sigma 3 are still in use and conform reasonably closely to current standards of test construction is a rare tribute to M. E. Haggerty whose pioneer work in the development of tests began almost four decades ago.

[536]

*High School Reading Test: National Achievement Tests. Grades 7–12; 1939–52; 6 scores: vocabulary, word discrimination, sentence meaning, noting details, interpreting paragraphs, total; Forms A ('52), B ('51—same as test copyrighted in 1940); general series manual ['44]; Form A norms ('52), Form B norms ('51); $2.50 per 25; 35¢ per specimen set; postage extra; nontimed (40) minutes; Robert K. Speer and Samuel Smith; Acorn Publishing Co. *

Holland Roberts, *Director, California Labor School, 321 Divisadero St., San Francisco, California.*

The simplicity and clarity of its construction, its reliability, and the ease with which it may be administered have helped this reading test maintain itself beyond the usual term of life. However, it no longer meets today's standards and should be thoroughly revised or replaced. Its major deficiencies include: (*a*) no specific description of its construction; (*b*) no norms for the subtests or for European or Asian foreign language groups, Negroes, Mexican Americans, different geographic areas, and varying socioeconomic levels; (*c*) no specific criteria for the establishment of validity; (*d*) failure to establish relationships between ability to pass the test and the specific reading abilities required in school and in daily life. In particular, those who use this test must assume—without supporting evidence—that it is a valid measure of the reading abilities which pupils need for success in their school work.

In common with all standard measures of reading ability so far developed, the limitations of this test have become standardized. They are not only implicit but explicit in the routine procedures of the schools, the mechanical mass production approach to American education, and the dominant contradictory philosophy of competitive individualism. From its very nature as an objective instrument such a standardized test becomes an important factor in crystallizing the educational process and so serving as a brake on change and development. Unfounded and dangerous conclusions are likely to be drawn from the results of this test by administrators, teachers, pupils, and testmakers. For example, in proposing it as a measure of "the student's mastery of factual material and, especially, his power to use information and skills," and in assuring teachers that in diagnosis it emphasizes "the pupil's ability to judge, appreciate and apply data or principles," the authors state claims which they make no effort to substantiate. What do "mastery of factual material" and "ability to judge, appreciate, and apply data or principles" mean? Certainly the former must include critical examination of the use of "facts" in propaganda to support special interests, while the latter opens up the whole field of moral values. Both these important areas in the development of reading ability are clearly outside the range of this simple reading test.

Teachers who adopt this or any other current reading test for use in their school programs should be aware of these three basic dangers: using the test to measure reading abilities entirely outside its limits; placing the emphasis in reading upon skills and mechanics, and ignoring more significant areas such as appreciation of values and judgment of principles; *assuming* that the important reading abilities needed for successful study in school and for work, recreation, and enjoyment are measured by a reading test of this or any other character. Teachers and administrators can no longer meet their responsibilities by ordering tests by brand names or upon the unsupported assurances of the authors. Rather, test authors must prepare to meet exacting demands for proof that their tests are valid and that they make an essential contribution to the school program.

For a review by Robert L. McCaul, see 3:488.

[537]

★**Holborn Reading Scale.** Ages 5.5–11; 1948; 2 scores: word recognition, comprehension; individual; 1 form; 3s. per 25; 3d. per single copy; 1s. 6d. per manual; postage extra; (20–30) minutes; A. F. Watts; George G. Harrap & Co. Ltd. *

C. M. FLEMING, *Reader in Education, University of London, London, England.*

This scale consists of a set of 33 sentences arranged in order of difficulty in terms of their mechanical elements and their comprehensibility. The sentences were so selected that in the standardisation group of more than 2,000 pupils aged five and a half to ten and a half years the progress shown in mastering the difficulties of reading aloud was at a rate represented by an increase of one sentence every three months. The scale is offered as a means of making valid comparisons between the oral reading of pupils and the degree of their comprehension as assessed by a series of questions on the same sentences read silently.

Apparently no attempt has been made to derive figures for validity or reliability by calculating correlations with other measures of reading ability or by assessing the consistency of scores on split halves of the test or on its repetition on a second occasion. The test, however, bears signs of expert construction.

For the pupil's use the sentences are printed on both sides of a single sheet of paper. The complete test is printed in the manual, together with an account of the construction of the test, directions for administering and scoring the test, and suggestions for interpreting test results. The manual also includes several pages of discussion of reading ability and its assessment, extracted from the author's book on the language and mental development of children. These pages, both interesting and suggestive, serve to present the test not only in its twofold function as a measure of oral and of silent reading but also in its setting of earlier reading researches in America and England.

[538]

Ingraham-Clark Diagnostic Reading Tests. Grades 1–3, 4–8; 1929; 2 levels; 2 parts; Forms 1, 2; $1.50 per 25 of any one level, postage extra; 35¢ per specimen set of any one level, postpaid; Jessie E. Ingraham and Willis W. Clark; California Test Bureau. *
a) PRIMARY: PART I, WORD FORM AND MEANINGS. Grades 1–3; 6 scores: word form, likenesses and differences, auditory stimuli, visual stimuli, opposites, total; 20(25) minutes.

b) PRIMARY: PART II, SENTENCES AND PARAGRAPHS. Grades 1–3; 6 scores: following directions, answering questions, directly stated facts, qualified statements, inferences and conclusions, total; 20(25) minutes.
c) INTERMEDIATE: PART I, WORD FORM AND MEANINGS. Grades 4–6; 6 scores: likenesses and differences, auditory-visual, association, opposites, similarities, total; 30(35) minutes.
d) INTERMEDIATE: PART II, SENTENCES AND PARAGRAPHS. Grades 4–6; 5 scores: relevant and irrelevant statements, true and false deductions, selecting and classifying information, form and mechanics of organization-sequence of events, total; 30(35) minutes.

KATHERINE G. KENEALLY, *Assistant Professor of Psychology, and Director, Remedial Reading Clinic, Catholic University of America, Washington, D.C.*

These tests are intended to measure the instructional needs of individual pupils and to furnish a sufficiently reliable instrument for classification and grouping within the classroom. A valuable feature is a diagnostic outline and profile chart which enables the teacher to locate pupil needs quickly in order to plan corrective or remedial instruction.

When published in 1929, this test was probably a valuable diagnostic instrument for teachers who wished to locate pupil difficulties in order to plan remedial programs. Parts of the test now need revision, however. The test of word form would be strengthened by the inclusion of some capitalized words, italics, and script instead of limiting this exercise to words of lower case letters, as some first grade pupils have difficulty in these areas. Some of the pictures should also be brought up to date.

There is a need for a good diagnostic test of reading, particularly for remedial teachers working at the elementary school level. It is hoped that the authors will consider revision and present new norms in order to compete with the more recent tests now available for the elementary grades.

[539]

Kansas Primary Reading Test. Grades 1–3; 1935; 4 scores: sentence reading, word knowledge, paragraph comprehension, total; Forms A, B; $1.05 per 25; 20¢ per specimen set; postpaid; 12(20) minutes; Alma Hoag, Emma Humble, Bertha Robinson, Adeline Wipf, and H. E. Schrammel; Bureau of Educational Measurements, Kansas State Teachers College of Emporia. *

NILA BANTON SMITH, *Professor of Education, New York University, New York, New York.*

This test is divided into three distinct parts: Part 1, a test of ability to read sentences, consists of 22 yes-no questions; Part 2, a test of word knowledge, consists of 20 multiple choice items; and Part 3 consists of 8 paragraphs, each of which is followed by two multiple choice items. The exercises in all three parts begin with very simple sentences or paragraphs and gradually increase in difficulty.

A helpful manual of directions accompanies the test. It contains explicit directions for administering the test, suggestions for interpreting and using the results, and tables of norms and percentile scores. According to the manual, validity was established by checking each item "against reputable criteria, such as courses of study, text books, word lists, criticisms of teachers and supervisors, and analyses of pupils' test papers." This check, although a valuable safeguard, does not prove that the test measures what it purports to measure. Validity should also have been ascertained through intercorrelations with other reading tests. Reliability coefficients of .81, .93, and .84 are reported for grades 1, 2, and 3, respectively. No reliability coefficients are reported for the part scores. No information is given as to how the reliability coefficients were computed or the numbers of pupils tested.

Very complete information is given in regard to the norms. These norms were computed from scores made by 4,586 pupils at midyear, and 3,960 pupils at end-of-year testing, reported from 159 schools in 19 different states. Percentile tables for interpreting both part and total scores are provided.

The strong points of the test are as follows: (a) The format and organization are excellent. (b) The increments of difficulty within each part appear to be gradual but decisive. (c) The test calls for one type of response only in all three parts—underlining. Because of this simplification pupils are freed from learning new techniques of working and can thus direct their major attention and efforts to the reading situation itself. (d) The scoring is extremely easy.

The disadvantages of the test are these: (a) Data are not presented for intercorrelations of the results of this test with those of other reading tests. (b) More information is needed in regard to the reliability of part scores and methods used in determining reliability coefficients. (c) The norms and percentiles indicate that the test is too difficult for first grade children.

In summary, it might be said that this test has a sufficient number of good features to justify its revision. If the disadvantages mentioned above were removed through further experi-

mentation and revision, this would be an acceptable test for the early grades.

For a review by Alice K. Liveright, see 40: 1549.

[540]

★Lee-Clark Reading Test—First Reader, 1943 Edition. Grades 1–2; 1931–43; 6 scores: auditory stimuli, visual stimuli, following directions, completion, inference, total; Forms A ('43), B ('43); no norms for part scores; manual ('43); $1.25 per 25, postage extra; 35¢ per specimen set, postpaid; nontimed in part (25) minutes; J. Murray Lee and Willis W. Clark; California Test Bureau. *

[541]

Los Angeles Elementary Reading Test. Grades 3–9; 1926–31; Forms 1 ('26), 2 ('26), 3 ('26), 4 ('26); manual ('31); $1 per 25, postage extra; 35¢ per specimen set, postpaid; 30(35) minutes; Jessie E. Ingraham; California Test Bureau. *

HENRY P. SMITH, *Associate Professor of Education, and Director of the Reading Laboratory, The University of Kansas, Lawrence, Kansas.*

This test is now over 25 years old. The age of the test makes the norms of questionable value because of the possible changes in the effectiveness of methods of teaching reading during the 25-year period.

For their time, the care used in selecting the items and in obtaining data concerning the effectiveness of the test is rather remarkable. However, the usefulness of many of these data is lessened by the fact that some of the tests with which comparisons are made are no longer in use. In addition school curriculum and methods for teaching reading have been modified rather greatly in the past 25 years.

While the selections chosen for the test situations offer considerable variety in type of reading demanded, they do not appear typical of the current curriculum in reading. For example, ancient kings and their problems, which are the basis for two selections in each form of the test, and a study of fables which is the basis for one selection in each form is not nearly as typical of reading instruction today as it was in 1926.

It appears that while a reading test with a copyright of 1926, with norms revised in 1931, is not quite so out of date as a chemistry or physics test might be, changes in teaching methods and materials, and general modifications of philosophy of education would serve greatly to reduce its worth.

[542]

Los Angeles Primary Reading Test. Grades 1–3; 1925; Forms 1, 2, 3, 4; manual ['25]; $1 per 25, postage extra; 35¢ per specimen set, postpaid; 10(15) minutes; Jessie E. Ingraham; California Test Bureau. *

REFERENCES

1. BAKER, FLORENCE, AND BROOM, M. E. "Concerning One Criterion for the Choice of Primary Reading Tests." *J Appl Psychol* 16:419–20 Ag '32. * (PA 7:4098)

NILA BANTON SMITH, *Professor of Education, New York University, New York, New York.*

This test purports to measure six reading abilities: (*a*) to follow a simple direction; (*b*) to follow a direction and to make a discrimination; (*c*) to interpret printed material in answering a question and to draw an inference; (*d*) to discriminate between true and false conclusions as to implied facts and characterization; (*e*) to perceive causes; and (*f*) to perceive word meanings.

Each of the four forms consists of a practice exercise and 24 test items. The test items are not grouped according to the abilities to be tested but are arranged miscellaneously. Several different types of responses are called for: marking symbols, underlining, crossing out, and writing answers to questions.

The manual contains information about the test, clear-cut directions for giving and scoring the test, a table of age and grade norms, and a table of percentile ranks.

Information given in the manual concerning the validity of the content is too general to be convincing. This statement is made: "The test materials are based on a careful study of primary courses of study, research concerning word lists, and an examination of studies concerning reading materials and children's reading." It is questionable that a study of primary courses of study would contribute materially to the validation of the content of the test. Research studies in regard to "word lists," "reading materials," and "children's reading" are legion. The content of this test would probably have had greater validity if the vocabulary had been drawn from one thoroughly scientific study or perhaps from a combination of two or three such studies.

According to the manual, validity of function was determined through intercorrelations of the test with eight other reading tests. These intercorrelations, based on the scores of 120 second grade pupils on the several tests, yielded coefficients ranging from .67 to .84, acceptable though not outstandingly high. No data are presented to show that the test actually measures each of the different types of reading ability which it is designed to measure.

The test was originally standardized by giving all four forms, together with the *Haggerty Reading Examination,* Sigma 1, and unnamed intelligence tests to 100 pupils in each of grades 1–3. In this original standardization, the reliabilities of the four test forms varied from .86 to .91 for a two-grade range as determined by intercorrelations. No data are given to support the claim that "extensive use indicates that the four forms are equivalent in difficulty and that the test provides a satisfactory measure of reading." The test is intended for use in grades 1–3. The grade placement norms, however, place a child in grade 1.5 if he makes a score of only 1 on this test of 24 items. The child who gets all 24 items correct is assigned a grade placement of 5.5. The norms confirm the impression that the test is too difficult for first grade children and better suits the second and third grade levels.

In summary, it might be said that (*a*) the test is too ambitious in its attempt to measure so many different reading abilities with the use of only 24 test items; (*b*) it fails to make any distinction among the items designed to measure different abilities either by grouping or labeling, or in scoring procedures; (*c*) it is not carefully graded in increments of difficulty; (*d*) it is much too difficult for first grade pupils in regard to vocabulary, the number of different types of responses which children are required to make, and inferential thinking which is beyond their level of maturity.

On the other hand, the test has some good points. It is printed in large, clear, bold type. It can be given in the relatively short time of 10 minutes. Its validity and reliability as determined through intercorrelations are favorable. It taps some very important reading abilities which have largely been lost sight of in the more recent primary tests, such as drawing inferences, perceiving causes, and perceiving word meanings. As a rough check of general reading ability at second and third grade levels, it still might serve a useful purpose.

[543]

*Metropolitan Achievement Tests [Reading].
Grades 3–4, 5–7.5, 7–9.5; 1933–49; a subtest of *Metropolitan Achievement Tests* (see 18); 3 scores: reading, vocabulary, total; 3 levels; Forms R ('46), S ('47), T ('49); directions for administering ('47); 80¢ per manual ('48); postage extra; 35¢ per specimen set of any one level, postpaid; 35(45) minutes; Richard D. Allen, Harold H. Bixler, William L. Connor, Frederick D. Graham, and Gertrude H. Hildreth; World Book Co. *
a) ELEMENTARY READING TEST. Grades 3–4; 1933–48; Forms R, S only; $1.80 per 25.

b) INTERMEDIATE READING TEST. Grades 5–7.5; 1933–
49; $1.55 per 25.
c) ADVANCED READING TEST. Grades 7–9.5; 1933–49;
$1.55 per 25.

REFERENCES

1–3. See 40:1189.
4–10. See 3:13.
11. SPACHE, GEORGE. "Deriving Comprehension, Rate and
Accuracy of Reading Norms for a Short Form of the Metropolitan Achievement Reading Test." *J Ed Psychol* 32:359–64 My
'41. * (*PA* 16:1207).
12. STONE, CLARENCE R. "Validity of Tests in Beginning
Reading." *El Sch J* 43:361–5 F '43. * (*PA* 18:2605)

JAMES R. HOBSON, *Director of Child Placement,
Brookline Public Schools, Brookline, Massachusetts.*

This series of reading tests is part of a de-
servedly popular series of test batteries introduced in New York City about twenty years
ago. They have undergone three revisions during this period. The 1947 revision and restandardization involved the largest and most complete standardizing population yet used in the
development of a standardized measure of
achievement. The normative material available
in separate Booklets of Norms is the most complete this reviewer has seen. It includes not only
age, grade, percentile, and modal age norms but
also a wide variety of geographical norms as
well as norms for Negro and parochial schools.

The reading sections of the batteries are published as separate tests beginning with the Elementary Reading Test for grades 3–4. It is unfortunate that the reading tests of the Primary I
and Primary II Batteries have not been combined in a Primary Reading Test since their
value has been demonstrated to this reviewer
through 17 years of personal use. In fact, the
three reading tests in the Primary I Battery appear to be more outstanding for their grade level
than are any of the other reading tests in the
battery.

In addition to the three features alluded to
above, the chief virtues of the Metropolitan reading tests appear to be: (*a*) Each test is designed
to cover a narrow grade range. Other things
being equal, the smaller the grade range a test
is designed to cover, the greater the proportion
of the test which is a valid measure for the
achievement of any given grade. (*b*) The authors have done an exceedingly good job of
scaling as to difficulty of items and standardization to produce the optimum degree of comparability from grade to grade and from form
to form. This is exceedingly important if a
cumulative test record from year to year is to be
kept of individuals and classes. (*c*) Finally,
there has been available soon after each revision

an excellent Manual for Interpreting for the
battery of which this reading test is a part. The
present manual, a book of 122 pages, gives extensive data regarding the development and
standardization of the battery, has valuable sections on various aspects of measurement and
evaluation in general, and has a particularly
helpful section on "Improving the Achievement
of Individual Pupils through the Use of Test
Results." Such a manual should be required
reading in teacher training courses in measurement.

While validity has been obtained by the usual
method of adhering rather closely to the results
of surveys of courses of study and the pooled
judgments of "experts," the several revisions
have made it possible to drop test items which
did not distinguish between the capable and the
less capable pupils and thus increase the validity
of the instrument. This is at least a first step
in the experimental determination of validity.

Various minor criticisms of these tests have
been made by previous reviewers, such as confusing directions to examiners in some instances,
low diagnostic value, subjectivity of scoring, and
the lack of fineness in scaling which allows the
difference of one item to make a difference of
from two to six months in grade level. This reviewer and the 200 teachers who have administered these tests or their previous editions for 17
years have not found the directions confusing
although a set of supplementary directions for
each test level is issued annually from the reviewer's office.

These tests could be arranged for analytical
purposes along the lines of the *California Reading Tests* without detracting from their basic
virtues. Many school systems cannot or do not
use more than one standardized instrument in
a grade in any one year. If an analytical feature
based on skills measured were added to the
present class analysis feature, it would be a
boon to many teachers, particularly those with
large classes.

The so-called lack of fineness of scaling occurs only at the upper extremes of the range,
two or more grade levels above the class median
in practically every case. In the middle of the
range it is more likely to take a difference of
two items correct to make one month's difference in grade level. The fact that at the extreme
upper part of the range the norms are able to
show even a rather coarse differentiation of two
or three months in grade level for one item may

be considered indicative of high power of discrimination, since the values were obtained by actual administration of the test at the levels indicated and not by extrapolation.

It is necessary to agree with the criticism of subjectivity in scoring the Paragraph Meaning sections of these tests since many acceptable answers are not included on the keys furnished. In fact, the reviewer has found it advisable, if not necessary, to have all Paragraph Meaning tests scored at a central office to assure some degree of uniformity.

The strongest indictment the writer would make against these tests and the Metropolitan batteries in general is the failure to provide for machine scoring in the cases of those tests which are machine scorable and at the grade levels at which machine scoring is practical and desirable. In school systems which have or which have access to an electric scoring machine, this failure to consider the wishes and convenience of test users will result eventually in deserved loss of business.

To summarize, this reviewer would rate the Metropolitan reading tests as outstanding for general purpose every-pupil measurement and evaluation in reading, although they leave something to be desired in the way of analysis and diagnosis if no other more specialized instruments are to be used.

MARGARET G. McKIM, *Associate Professor of Education, University of Cincinnati, Cincinnati, Ohio.*

The value of these tests lies in their general estimate of paragraph reading ability and word knowledge. Although the questions in the paragraph reading sections call for varied reading skills, there is no way in which definite diagnostic evidence can be obtained. At the elementary level, particularly, the emphasis seems to be on noting details. The vocabulary test is general in content.

At all three levels the tests are easy to administer. The vocabulary test calls for the choice of a correct synonym from four words. The two sections in the paragraph reading part of the elementary test call for the child, first, to select from four possibilities, the correct answer to a question and, second, to write in blanks at the side of the paragraph the words which are needed to complete numbered blanks in the paragraph.

The paragraph reading sections of the intermediate and advanced tests call almost entirely

for written responses. Since the test booklets are about the width of a typical textbook, the space allowed for writing is limited, even for an adult hand. This seems to place an unnecessary hurdle before the immature writer. Children who have spelling difficulties may also be handicapped, although spelling errors are not counted. Scoring the tests will be slow, as time must be taken to check on the correctness of alternate answers. Scoring standards are established so as to allow any reasonable response.

Supplementary booklets of norms provide percentiles, modal age-grade norms based on the proportion of pupils who are considered at grade for their age, and the norms for special population groups, including parochial schools, Negro schools, and selected states or groups of states. These supplementary norms should prove particularly helpful to persons responsible for administering and interpreting city testing programs. They will probably not be used extensively by the classroom teacher.

The manuals accompanying the separate tests provide helpful suggestions to the teacher inexperienced in giving standardized tests. A more extensive battery manual gives detailed suggestions on the planning of a school testing program and the interpreting and reporting of results. Of particular value to teachers is a section discussing general diagnostic and remedial procedures. The battery manual also gives a detailed discussion of the methods used in standardizing all the tests in the battery and developing norms.

Inspection of the norms for the reading tests suggests that the elementary test will prove unduly difficult for a typical class in the early part of the third grade; and that the advanced test is not likely to provide enough challenge for the best readers in a typical class in the first half of the ninth grade. For the greater part of the grade range for which these tests are recommended, however, they should be appropriate. The tests will probably be of greatest value as general achievement tests in reading at the various grade levels; for diagnostic purposes, they will need to be supplemented by reading tests which explore specific skills in more detail.

For a review by Warren G. Findley of the complete battery, see 18; for a review by D. A. Worcester of an earlier edition, see 40:1551; for reviews by E. V. Pullias and Hugh B. Wood of an earlier edition of the complete battery, see

40:1189; for reviews by Ivan A. Booker and Joseph C. Dewey of an earlier edition, see 38: 1105; for reviews by Jack W. Dunlap, Charles W. Odell, and Richard Ledgerwood of an earlier edition of the complete battery, see 38:874.

[544]

The Nelson-Denny Reading Test: Vocabulary and Paragraph: The Clapp-Young Self-Marking Tests. Grades 9–16; 1929–38; 3 scores: vocabulary, paragraph comprehension, total; IBM; Forms A ('29), B ('30); manual ['38]; $1.35 per 25; $2.20 per 25 sets of test and answer booklet; separate answer booklets or sheets must be used; $1 per 25 answer booklets; 50¢ per 25 IBM answer sheets; 20¢ per stencil for machine scoring of answer sheets; 27¢ per specimen set; postage extra; 30(35) minutes; M. J. Nelson and E. C. Denny; Houghton Mifflin Co. *

REFERENCES

1–6. See 40:1557.

7. DAVIS, NELSON W. *A Study in Prediction Based on the Records of First-Year Students of the University of Arizona for 1934–35.* Master's thesis, University of Arizona (Tucson, Ariz.), 1937 and 1938. (*Abstracts of Theses....1938, 1939, p. 19.*)

8. LARSEN, ROBERT P. *Common and Differential Factors in Reading Comprehension and Hearing Comprehension.* Doctor's thesis, University of Iowa (Iowa City, Iowa), 1938.

9. LAWRENCE, WILLIAM A. *An Evaluation of Achievement in the Various Colleges of the Louisiana State University with Special Reference to Certain Aspects of the Junior Division.* Doctor's thesis, Louisiana State University (Baton Rouge, La.), 1939. (*Abstracts of Theses....1939–1940, 1941, pp. 10–11.*)

10. LOTT, HIRAM V. *A Comparative Study of Five Criteria for Predicting Achievement in Freshman History in the Junior Division at Louisiana State University.* Master's thesis, Louisiana State University (Baton Rouge, La.), 1939. (*Abstracts of Theses....1939, 1940, p. 45.*)

11. ROY, ERIC ARTHUR. *Correcting High School Marks as a Means of Better Predicting College Success.* Master's thesis, Clark University (Worcester, Mass.), 1939. (*Abstracts of Dissertations....1939, pp. 170–2.*)

12. VARNADO, GLADYS R. *A Further Study of the Predictive Value of Various Criteria on Achievement in Freshman Mathematics at Louisiana State University for the Session 1938–1939.* Master's thesis, Louisiana State University (Baton Rouge, La.), 1939. (*Abstracts of Theses....1939, 1940, p. 197.*)

13. ANDERSON, IRVING H., AND DEARBORN, WALTER F. "Reading Ability as Related to College Achievement." *J Psychol* 11: 387–96 Ap '41. * (*PA* 15:3570)

14. GREENE, PAUL C. "Some Relationships Between Placement Scores and Scholastic Rating." *Proc Iowa Acad Sci* 48: 361–6 '41. * (*PA* 16:2867)

15. LANGSAM, ROSALIND STREEP. "A Factorial Analysis of Reading Ability." *J Exp Ed* 10:57–63 S '41. * (*PA* 16:1187)

16. CRIDER, BLAKE. "A School of Nursing Selection Program." *J Appl Psychol* 27:452–7 O '43. * (*PA* 18:281)

17. GENTRY, DOROTHY E. *An Attempt to Predict Scholarship From a Variety of Objective Tests: College Ability Test, Nelson-Denny Reading Test, Kuhlmann-Anderson Intelligence Test, and English Placement Test.* Master's thesis, Ohio University (Athens, Ohio), 1943. Pp. 33. (*Abstracts of Masters' Theses.... 1943, 1944, pp. 36–7.*)

18. PORTENIER, LILLIAN G. "Predicting Success in Introductory Psychology." *Ed & Psychol Meas* 8:117–26 sp '48. * (*PA* 22:3730)

19. MURPHY, HAROLD D., AND DAVIS, FREDERICK B. "A Note on the Measurement of Progress in Remedial Reading." *Peabody J Ed* 27:108–11 S '49. *

20. SILVEY, HERBERT M. *Change in Status of Iowa State Teachers College Students as Revealed by Repeating Placement Tests.* Iowa State Teachers College, Research Report No. 58. Cedar Falls, Iowa: Bureau of Research, the College, July 20, 1949. Pp. 27. Paper, lithotyped. *

21. EDMONSON, LAWRENCE DAVIS. *Comparative Analyses of a Test Battery Used for the Prediction of Scholastic Success at the University of Missouri.* Doctor's thesis, University of Missouri (Columbia, Mo.), 1949. Abstract: *Microfilm Abstracts* 9: 64–6 no 3 '50. (*PA* 24:4846, title only)

22. MACDONALD, GORDON LUNDY. *Predicting Collegiate Survival From Pre-Admission Data.* Doctor's thesis, New York University, (New York, N.Y.), 1949. Abstract: *Microfilm Abstracts* 10:42–4 no 1 '50. * (*PA* 24:6663, title only)

23. SILVEY, HERBERT M. "Changes in Test Scores After Two Years in College." *Ed & Psychol Meas* 11:494–502 au '51. *

IVAN A. BOOKER, *Assistant Director, Division of Press and Labor Relations, National Education Association, Washington, D.C.*

For more than 20 years this test has been a familiar tool in the kit of those concerned with the improvement of silent reading among college students. Although designed for use at all grade levels in high school and college, the test probably performs its greatest service when used with high school seniors and college freshmen.

The test is in two parts: a 100-item multiple choice vocabulary test and a 36-item comprehension test consisting of 9 paragraphs, each of which contains about 200 words and is followed by 4 comprehension questions with multiple choice answers. Each vocabulary test item is allowed one point; each comprehension item, two points. The maximum score, therefore, is 172.

This test was quite carefully constructed. Items were selected and scaled in terms of their difficulty, and the two forms of the test were carefully equated. This sound workmanship in constructing the test undoubtedly has been an important factor in its continued popularity and usefulness for more than two decades.

The authors make no claim as to the validity of the test except to explain their purpose in constructing it and their reasons for developing it as they did. Experience has shown, however, that its results correlate well with achievement in academic subjects. Its reliability is approximately .90.

The format of the test makes it economical to use. Students record their answers on separate answer sheets. For test users with machine scoring facilities, IBM answer sheets are provided. For other test users, Clapp-Young Self-Marking answer booklets are provided.

The time limits for the test are rather brief, especially for high school students, 10 minutes for the 100-item vocabulary test and 20 minutes for the comprehension test. This places a premium upon rapid reading, immediate reactions, and lucky guesses. Careful reading, rereading, and deliberation are penalized, thus preventing a great many students from displaying their maximum performance. Yet, norms are invalidated unless strict timing is observed. Since the test yields no rate of reading score, and since the measurement of speed is not one of the specific purposes of the test, the indirect effect of rate of work introduced through the brief timing may be regarded as an extraneous factor. If norms were available for the test administered as a generously timed or as an untimed test, its diagnostic value as a measure of power of vocabulary and comprehension would be increased.

The test manual emphasizes the total score, which is simply the sum of the vocabulary score and the comprehension scores. Grade equivalents are reported only in terms of the total score. Virtually nothing is said about the value of the test as a diagnostic instrument. Although this total score, obtained from the timed administration of the test, provides a useful survey of the general level of reading performance for a group, this reviewer believes that the Nelson-Denny test is of greatest value when used in diagnosis. The manual does give the 1st and 99th percentiles, the deciles, and the quartiles for the vocabulary and comprehension scores. These, like the total score, are affected by the brief time limits but can be helpful if used with discrimination. Moreover, the competent test user can remove the time limits and soon establish local norms for his own diagnostic use. Proper evaluation of the separate vocabulary and comprehension scores, together with analyses of the students' responses to individual test items, will be far more significant, in many cases, than any comparisons of total scores that can be made. The latter, at best, are merely arbitrary combinations of separate elements which lose significance, rather than gain it, when their separate identities are obscured.

Wherever a quick overview of the vocabulary knowledge and comprehension skill of high school seniors or college students is desired, this test is an efficient and dependable device.

For a review by Hans C. Gordon, see 40: 1557.

[545]
The Nelson Silent Reading Test: Vocabulary and Paragraph: The Clapp-Young Self-Marking Tests. Grades 3–9; 1931–39; 5 scores: vocabulary, general paragraph comprehension, ability to note details, ability to predict probable outcome, total; IBM for Forms A, B; Forms A ('31), B ('32), C ('39); manual ['39]; $1.35 per 25; $2.40 per 25 sets of test and answer booklet; separate answer booklets or sheets must be used; $1 per 25 answer booklets; 75¢ per 25 IBM answer sheets; 40¢ per set of stencils for machine scoring of answer sheets; 30¢ per specimen set; postage extra; 30(40) minutes; M. J. Nelson; Houghton Mifflin Co. *

REFERENCES
1. GRANT, ALBERT. "Results of Nelson Silent Reading Test in Grade IX." *Sch R* 48:34–9 Ja '40. * (*PA* 14:2604)

WILLIAM D. SHELDON, *Associate Professor of Education, and Director of the Reading Laboratory, Syracuse University, Syracuse, New York.*

This reviewer would make the same general comments concerning this test as did Constance

M. McCullough (see 3: 492). In addition, he would stress the unattractive format of the test as a feature in need of revision.

Both the advertising literature and the manual for this test indicate the importance of its value as a diagnostic instrument. However, neither statistical validation nor the opinions of competent judges confirm the merits of the test as an aid in diagnosis. There seems to be no evidence that the paragraph reading subtests actually measure the specific aspects of reading comprehension claimed by the author.

The books suggested in the manual as being helpful to the teacher range in publication date from 1931 to 1939. While these older books might be valuable, there are available at least a dozen books and several hundred other references which are more recent. It would be helpful if the publishers of the manual brought their references up to date.

This reviewer suggests that even though the merits of this test as a measure of specific weaknesses in comprehension are questionable, the total scores yielded by the test might be valuable as a general index of a pupil's grade placement in reading.

For a review by Constance M. McCullough, see 3:492; for an excerpt from a review, see 40:1558.

[546]
*Primary Reading: Every Pupil Test. Grades 2–3; 1936–51; new form usually published each April and December; form December 1951; no data on reliability and validity; revised manual ['49]; norms ('51); 2½¢ per test; 1¢ per answer key; postpaid; 19(30) minutes; Ohio Scholarship Tests, Ohio State Department of Education. *

For reviews by William S. Gray and Virginia Seavey of forms for April and December 1946, see 3:493.

[547]
*Reading Comprehension: Cooperative English Test: Lower and Higher Levels, Test C1 and C2. Grades 7–12, 11–16; 1940–51; also called *Cooperative Reading Comprehension Test*; 4 scores: vocabulary, speed of comprehension, level of comprehension, total; IBM; 2 levels; Forms R ('50—same as test copyrighted in 1941), S (Lower Level, '42; Higher Level, '51—same as test copyrighted in 1942), T (Lower Level, '43; Higher Level, '50—same as test copyrighted in 1943), Y ('48); Form Q out of print; no data on validity; no specific manual; descriptive folder ['51]; general Cooperative manual ('51); norms ['40]; $2.50 per 25 of any one level; 50¢ per specimen set of any one level, postpaid; separate answer sheets may be used; 80¢ per 25 IBM answer sheets; 15¢ per stencil for scoring answer sheets; cash orders postpaid; 40(45) minutes; Frederick B. Davis, Harold V.

King (S), Mary Willis (T), Clarence Derrick (Y), Harry R. Neville (Y), Jeanne M. Bradford (Y), and Geraldine Spaulding (Y); Cooperative Test Division, Educational Testing Service. *

REFERENCES

1–2. See 40:1564.
3–17. See 3:497.
18. ARTLEY, A. STERL. *A Study of Certain Relationships Existing Between General Reading Comprehension and Reading Comprehension in a Specific Subject-Matter Area.* Doctor's thesis, Pennsylvania State College (State College, Pa.), 1942.
19. HUMBER, WILBUR J. "The Relationship Between Reading Efficiency and Academic Success in Selected University Curricula." *J Ed Psychol* 35:17–26 Ja '44. * (PA 18:2581)
20. HULT, ESTHER. "Study of Achievement in Educational Psychology." *J Exp Ed* 13:174–90 Je '45. * (PA 19:3494)
21. JONES, RONALD DEVALL. "The Prediction of Teaching Efficiency From Objective Measures." *J Exp Ed* 15:85–99 S '46. * (PA 21:606)
22. LINS, LEO JOSEPH. "The Prediction of Teaching Efficiency." *J Exp Ed* 15:2–60 S '46. * (PA 21:610)
23. ARTLEY, A. STERL. "General and Specific Factors in Reading Comprehension." *J Exp Ed* 16:181–6 Mr '48. * (PA 20:5122)
24. HAVENS, VIRGINIA. "A Prediction of Law School Achievement From High-School Rank, Reading Test Scores, Psychological Test Scores, and Average Grade in Pre-Law Courses." *J Ed Psychol* 39:237–42 Ap '48. * (PA 23:1463)
25. JACOBS, ROBERT. "Public School Testing Project: First Report," pp. 66–72. (PA 23:3446) In *1948 Fall Testing Program in Independent Schools and Supplementary Studies.* Educational Records Bulletin, No. 51. New York: the Bureau, January 1949. Pp. xiii, 72. Paper, lithotyped.
26. JENSEN, RALPH E. *Predicting Scholastic Achievement of First-Year Graduate Students.* Doctor's thesis, University of Pittsburgh (Pittsburgh, Pa.), 1949. (*Abstracts of Doctoral Dissertations....1949, 1950,* pp. 305–13.) (PA 23:2992, title only)
27. MURPHY, HAROLD D., AND DAVIS, FREDERICK B. "College Grades and Ability to Reason in Reading." *Peabody J Ed* 27:34–7 Jl '49. *
28. TRAXLER, ARTHUR E. "Correlations Between Scores on Various Reading Tests Administered Several Months Apart," pp. 78–82. (PA 24:748) In *1949 Achievement Testing Program in Independent Schools and Supplementary Studies.* Educational Records Bulletin, No. 52. New York: Educational Records Bureau, July 1949. Pp. xiii, 87. Paper, lithotyped. *
29. BROTHERS, WILBUR LEO. *The Relationship of Certain Factors to Effectiveness in Student Teaching in the Secondary Schools.* Doctor's thesis, Indiana University (Bloomington, Ind.), 1950. (*Thesis Abstract Series....1950, 1951,* pp. 12–8.)
30. COCHRAN, SAMUEL W., AND DAVIS, FREDERICK B. "Predicting Freshman Grades at George Peabody College for Teachers." *Peabody J Ed* 27:352–6 My '50. *
31. JACOBS, ROBERT. "A Study of the Need for Special Norms on Scholastic Aptitude and Mechanics of English Tests for College Preparatory Students in Public Schools," pp. 52–66. (PA 24:3895) In *1949 Fall Testing Program in Independent Schools and Supplementary Studies.* Educational Records Bulletin, No. 53. New York: Educational Records Bureau, January 1950. Pp. xiii, 70. Paper, lithotyped.
32. JAMES, RICHARD WARREN. *Selection of Graduate Students: (1) The Adequacy of Certain Measures for Differentiating Between Two Groups of Master Candidates (2) The Value of These Measures in Prognosing Graduate Academic Achievement.* Doctor's thesis, New York University (New York, N.Y.), 1950. Abstract: *Microfilm Abstracts* 11:53–4 no 1 '51. * (PA 26:2428, title only)
33. MARTIN, HENRY JOHN. *A Comparison of the Composite Ability Index of College Freshmen With Grades Earned in Different Courses and Departments of Instruction at Indiana University.* Doctor's thesis, Indiana University (Bloomington, Ind.), 1950. (*Thesis Abstract Series....1950, 1951,* pp. 86–90.) (PA 25:7109, title only)
34. TRAXLER, ARTHUR E. "Reading Growth of Secondary-School Pupils During a Five-Year Period," pp. 96–107. (PA 25:569) In *1950 Achievement Testing Program in Independent Schools and Supplementary Studies.* Educational Records Bulletin, No. 54. New York: Educational Records Bureau, July 1950. Pp. xiii, 119. Paper, lithotyped. *
35. FREDERIKSEN, NORMAN. "The Influence of Timing and Instructions on Cooperative Reading Test Scores." Abstract. *Am Psychol* 6:302 Jl '51. *
36. TRAXLER, ARTHUR E. "Intercorrelations and Validity of Scores on Three Reading Tests," pp. 79–89. (PA 25:6416) In *1950 Fall Testing Program in Independent Schools and Supplementary Studies.* Foreword by Ben D. Wood. Educational Records Bureau, January 1951. Pp. xiii, 89. Paper, lithotyped. *
37. WALLACE, W. L. "The Prediction of Grades in Specific College Courses." *J Ed Res* 44:587–97 Ap '51. * (PA 26:5838)

For reviews by Robert Murray Bear and J. B. Stroud, see 3:497; for reviews by J. Paul Leonard, Edward S. Noyes, and Robert C. Pooley of the Forms R, S, and T of the complete battery, see 3:120.

[548]

★Reading: Seven Plus Assessment: Northumberland Series. Ages 7–8; 1951; for complete battery, see 24; 1 form ['51]; no data on reliability; manual ['51]; 7s. 6d. per 25; 6d. per single copy; 1s. per manual; 2s. 6d. per specimen set (includes the other 2 tests in the series); postage extra; (75) minutes; C. M. Lambert; University of London Press Ltd. *

[549]

★Reading Test (Comprehension and Speed): Municipal Tests: National Achievement Tests. Grades 3–6, 6–8; 1938–50; same as reading tests in *Municipal Battery* (see 20); 5 scores: following directions, sentence meaning, paragraph meaning, reading speed, total; 2 levels; Forms A ('50), B ('39); no data on reliability and validity and no description of normative population in manuals; no norms for part scores; Form A manual ('50), Form B manual ('39); $1.75 per 25; 35¢ per specimen set of any one level; postage extra; Robert K. Speer and Samuel Smith; Acorn Publishing Co. *
a) GRADES 3–6. 33(38) minutes.
b) GRADES 6–8. 32(37) minutes.

[550]

SRA Reading Record. Grades 8–13; 1947; 11 scores: reading speed, comprehension, paragraph meaning, directory reading, map-table-graph reading, advertisement reading, index usage, technical vocabulary, sentence meaning, general vocabulary, total; 1 form; 49¢ per set of test and answer pad; separate answer pads must be used; $1.80 per 25 answer pads; 55¢ per 25 profile and norm sheets; 75¢ per specimen set; cash orders postpaid; 28(40) minutes; Guy T. Buswell; Science Research Associates, Inc. *

REFERENCES

1. BUDROW, GLADYS F. "Reading the SRA Reading Record," pp. 141–3. In *Claremont College Reading Conference, Fourteenth Yearbook, 1949: Conference Theme: The Problems and Techniques Involved in Reading Social Relationships.* Claremont, Calif.: Claremont College Curriculum Laboratory, 1949. Pp. viii, 191. Paper. *
2. SELDERS, GILBERT R. W. *A Study of the Academic, Social and Personal Needs of Students of the Pennsylvania State College for the Years 1948–1950 Through an Analysis of Instruments Administered in Education 105.* Doctor's thesis, Pennsylvania State College (State College, Pa.), 1950. (*Abstracts of Doctoral Dissertations....1950, 1951,* pp. 289–97.) (PA 26:2405, title only)

WILLIAM W. TURNBULL, *Vice President, Educational Testing Service, Princeton, New Jersey.*

This is a short, highly speeded test divided into 10 sections, each of which is designed to measure one of 10 "basic skills in reading." Of these, 5 are rather general in nature (rate of reading, reading comprehension, paragraph meaning, sentence meaning, and general vocabulary), 4 are specific applications of reading skills to various kinds of material (directory reading, map-table-graph reading, advertisement reading, index reading), and 1 is technical vocabulary.

The rationale underlying the analysis of reading into this mixture of general functional skills and specific areas of application is not presented. It seems unlikely, however, that a priori agreement on such a classification would be found among authorities in the field. This raises two questions : (*a*) does the test appear to cover most of the reading skills that are usually posited, and (*b*) does it yield reliable and independent measures of the skills it is designed to test?

The test appears to do the most adequate job in the measurement of vocabulary. This seems almost inevitable in view of its brevity : there is time to measure little beyond word knowledge and memory for factual detail. Broader skills such as interpretation, inference, formulation of judgments and conclusions, and comparison of ideas are largely neglected.

The manual presents exceedingly high reliability coefficients for the 11 scores. It fails to point out that such coefficients are spurious when based on sections as highly speeded as these. (Time limits are 3 minutes for each of eight sections, 2 minutes for the other two. The directions warn that a timing error "of even five seconds can increase a score ten points," a huge gain in view of the fact that the number of items in the sections varies from 10 to 25.) Assuming that the coefficients reported were obtained by an internal consistency method rather than by a test-retest method (not specified in the manual, but likely in view of the existence of only one form of the test), the reviewer must conclude that no useful estimate of reliability has as yet been established, since the internal consistency methods give gross overestimates of the reliabilities of highly speeded tests.

Since no intercorrelations of scores on the 10 sections are given, it is impossible to judge the independence of these scores—a vital matter in view of the fact that they are to be plotted in profile form and interpreted differentially. The manual states: "While relationships between the tests of the *Record* are moderate to high, a profile of **specific reading skills** is essential for **complete** diagnosis and remedial treatment of **individual** students." This statement suggests that the Record, in view of its sizeable intercorrelations of parts, will not be found useful as a diagnostic instrument. The prospective user would be able to make a much more intelligent judgment on this point if the intercorrelations, which have apparently been found, were presented.

No statistical data pertaining to validity are reported. The manual contains the unsupported assertion that "the tests have proven successful in differentiating good from poor readers in the skills needed for scholastic and occupational success." In the absence of the evidence on which this comment is based, the power of the test to discriminate between good and poor readers must be guessed at from inspection of the kinds of abilities apparently tested. As indicated earlier, the results of the inspection are not reassuring. It is fair to say, however, that skills in this area tend to be highly correlated, and a test which omits several of them, as this one appears to, may still provide a useful and discriminating overall measure of reading ability.

In format the test is handsome. It is attractively and conveniently printed, as are the manual and the self-interpreting profile. The directions and discussion are clearly and simply written. The use of progressively narrower question sheets to expose successive columns of answer spaces makes for convenience in taking the test.

A stylus is used to mark the answers to the questions by punching holes through the response positions. The key is printed on the reverse of the answer sheet, eliminating the need for a stencil.

In summary, the *SRA Reading Record* is a short, easily administered, highly speeded test of reading ability. It covers a somewhat conglomerate and incomplete group of skills and yields scores of indeterminate reliability and unspecified validity. It is probably of some value in obtaining a level of general reading ability for a group, and to a lesser degree, for an individual. In view of the paucity of data reported, its usefulness in individual diagnosis is questionable.

For a review by Frances Oralind Triggs and an excerpt from a review, see 3:502.

[551]
Sangren-Woody Reading Test. Grades 4–8; 1927–28; 8 scores: word meaning, rate, fact material, total meaning, central thought, following directions, organization, total; Forms A ('27), B ('28); revised manual ('28); $2 per 25, postage extra; 35¢ per specimen set, postpaid; 27(35–40) minutes; Paul V. Sangren and Clifford Woody; World Book Co. *

REFERENCES
1–7. See 40:1565.

DAVID H. RUSSELL, *Professor of Education, University of California, Berkeley, California.*

A complete description of this test is given in *The 1940 Mental Measurements Yearbook* in a review by Liveright (40: 1565) and will not be repeated here. The present review attempts to evaluate the test in light of recent developments in testing and instruction in reading.

A first survey of the test gives the impression that, despite lack of revision, the test follows rather closely modern trends in reading instruction. Its seven subtests suggest that reading is not a unitary ability applicable to all situations but rather a complex process of several abilities or factors. Although these are interdependent variables, the test properly offers separate measures of comprehension and speed in reading. It provides a profile sheet for individual pupils that indicates strengths and weaknesses in seven different areas and which therefore may have more diagnostic value than some more recent reading tests. Furthermore, the accompanying manual gives a clear statement of the steps taken in standardizing the test and in determining its validity by correlations with external criteria. A coefficient of reliability, based on the alternate forms method, is given for each subtest and for the total score.

Further study of the test raises two questions which should be investigated and answered by the authors or the users of the test. The first concerns the selection of factors presumed to make up reading ability. The factors measured, word meaning, rate, and five varieties of comprehension, are often included, in whole or in part, in other reading tests. However, Part I, Word Meaning, is just one more test measuring the superficial recognition of a synonym and neglecting one important aim of vocabulary work and school lessons—the depth and breadth of concepts. In Part II, Rate, the score is based on the child's speed for the first minute only, although he has the opportunity to read for a total of three minutes. An average score on a longer passage might give a more valid result. The comprehension parts deal with getting facts, understanding the main idea, following directions, and stating a sequence of events. These are all important phases of reading ability which should be tested, but other reading abilities which are stated aims in current programs are omitted. For example, the test does not include some of the more creative aspects of reading, such as critical reading of controversial material, reading to interpret motive or character, and reading to predict future or related outcomes. The neglect of some of the more thoughtful forms of reading comprehension is not an omission in the

Sangren-Woody test alone, but is a factor to be considered in relating a testing program to an instructional program.

A second question about the test is the matter of nomenclature. As Cronbach [1] has pointed out, makers of reading tests often develop similar tests but call them by different names. There can probably be no complete agreement as to what a subtest is testing, but the type of exercise presented in Part III, Fact Material, is often called "Reading for Details," and Part IV, Total Meaning, and Part V, Central Thought, seem to overlap considerably in what they measure. Some recent data on the intercorrelations of the various subtests, which are not presented by the authors in the manual, would answer this question of overlap positively or negatively. Finally, Part VII, Organization, seems to be named too generally since it deals only with finding a sequence of ideas or events.

The two questions raised above should not be regarded as fundamental criticisms of what has been a very useful reading test. They point rather to further study and possible revision of a test which is now over twenty years old. In the absence of such study and revision, schools will find that the Sangren-Woody test offers a less intensive diagnosis of reading than individual diagnostic series such as the test batteries of Durrell and of Gates, but that it has survey value combined with more diagnostic value than many other current survey tests.

For a review by Alice K. Liveright, see 40: 1565.

[552]

*The Schonell Reading Tests.** 1942-51; tests are reproduced in full in *Diagnostic and Attainment Testing* ('50—see *3* below) ; tests R5, R6, and R7 not available as separates; 1 form; 2s. 6d. per 12 of any one test; 25s. per copy of *Backwardness in the Basic Subjects,* Third Edition ('46—see *1* below) which serves as the manual for tests R2, R3, R4, R5, R6, and R7 ; 6s. per copy of *The Psychology and Teaching of Reading,* Second Edition ('46—see *2* below) which serves as the manual for the *Graded Word Reading Test;* postage extra; Fred J. Schonell; Oliver & Boyd Ltd. *
a) TEST R2, SIMPLE PROSE READING TEST. Ages 6–9; 1942; also called *My Dog Test;* individual; (3–8) minutes.
b) TEST R3, SILENT READING TEST A. Ages 7–11 ; 1942; 9(15) minutes.
c) TEST R4, SILENT READING TEST B. Ages 9–13; 1942; 15(20) minutes.
d) TEST RI, GRADED WORD READING TEST. Ages 5–15; 1942; also called *Graded Reading Vocabulary Test;* individual; (5–15) minutes.
e) TEST R5, TEST OF ANALYSIS AND SYNTHESIS OF

1 Cronbach, Lee J. *Essentials of Psychological Testing.* New York: Harper and Brothers, 1949. Pp. xiii, 475. *

WORDS CONTAINING COMMON PHONIC UNITS. Individual ; (5–15) minutes.

f) TEST R6, TEST OF DIRECTIONAL ATTACK ON WORDS. Individual ; (5–10) minutes.

g) TEST R7, VISUAL WORD DISCRIMINATION TEST. Individual ; (10–15) minutes.

REFERENCES

1. SCHONELL, FRED J. *Backwardness in the Basic Subjects, Third Edition.* Edinburgh, Scotland: Oliver & Boyd Ltd., 1946. Pp. xix, 560. *

2. SCHONELL, FRED J. *The Psychology and Teaching of Reading, Second Edition.* Edinburgh, Scotland: Oliver & Boyd Ltd., 1946. Pp. 128. *

3. SCHONELL, FRED J., AND SCHONELL, F. ELEANOR. *Diagnostic and Attainment Testing: Including a Manual of Tests, Their Nature, Use, Recording and Interpretation.* Edinburgh, Scotland: Oliver & Boyd Ltd., 1950. Pp. viii, 168. *

M. L. KELLMER PRINGLE, *Lecturer in Education, and Acting Deputy Head, Remedial Education Centre, University of Birmingham, Birmingham, England.*

Together these tests make a comprehensive battery for the measurement of reading attainment levels and for the detailed diagnosis of difficulties. They consist of a test of word recognition skill (R1), three comprehension tests at different levels of difficulty (R2, R3, and R4) and three unstandardised tests for diagnosing different aspects of mechanical failure in reading (R5, R6, and R7). With the exception of R3 and R4, all the tests are administered individually and depend to a considerable degree on the insight of the clinician, though diagnostic pointers are fully discussed in Schonell's *Backwardness in the Basic Subjects* (*1*) in which they first appeared.

The Graded Word Reading Test, R1, consists of 100 words graded in difficulty to give mechanical word recognition levels from 5 to 15 years. It thus supplies a first rapid assessment of reading level. Though similar to Burt's and Vernon's reading vocabulary tests, it differs in one important respect when one is dealing with young or poor readers: R1 is tied to a "look-and-say" approach to reading, whereas the other two presume early phonic teaching. Thus young children will achieve results on Schonell's test which are higher or lower than those on the other two according to the method by which they have been taught.

The Simple Prose Reading Test, R2, primarily measures comprehension. Norms for speed and accuracy of reading as well as for comprehension are provided, adding further diagnostic and attainment pointers. The print, lay-out, and content of this test make it suitable for young children. However, the gradient of difficulty is too steep for weaker readers and is not a sensitive enough measuring device for the

lower ranges of ability. Furthermore, the story would make a better test for measuring comprehension if it contained a greater number of concrete incidents instead of the rather diffuse descriptive sequences of the second half of the test.

The Silent Reading Tests, R3 and R4, which may be given as group or individual tests, consist of short, disconnected paragraphs followed by questions to be answered or instructions to be followed in the case of R3, and by multiple choice vocabulary items, in the case of R4. So that the same test booklets can be used again, separate answer slips are provided. While this is a welcome economy to the hard pressed headmaster, its suitability particularly for Juniors, is in some doubt. It tends to discourage slow and untidy writers and to lead to more confusions than underlining a word in the actual test booklet. The layout of the tests would be improved by more generous spacing between paragraphs and the use of a different type face for the questions or words. But the most serious criticism of R3 and R4 is that the prewar norms for these two tests given in *Backwardness in the Basic Subjects* differ materially from the postwar norms in *Diagnostic and Attainment Testing,* the difference increasing from 9 months at the beginning of the test to 2 years 3 months at the maximum age level. No explanation is offered for this; in fact, the difference in norms is not even mentioned.

Tests R5, R6, and R7 constitute the main diagnostic battery. R5 measures the reader's knowledge of common phonic units and powers of analysis and synthesis of phonic constituents. The whole test consists of 90 words, but it is not necessary to give the test in its entirety in every case. R6 indicates the consistency of the left-right approach, tendencies for reversals or partial reversals, and confusions of similar letters (such as b and d). R7 is concerned with visual perceptual recognition and supplies qualitative information on short-term recall of word patterns.

In addition to these three diagnostic tests, Schonell supplies tests—similar to those suggested by Burt in *The Backward Child* and by Whipple in the *Manual of Mental and Physical Tests*—for assessing auditory and visual recall of nonsense material of different types.

It is very useful and convenient to have all Schonell's reading tests available in a separate handbook; regrettably, however, one is still referred to *Backwardness in the Basic Subjects* and *The Psychology and Teaching of Reading* for the detailed instructions for administering them. Furthermore, although it is over eight years since *Backwardness in the Basic Subjects* was published, data on the standardisation, reliability, and validity of the tests remain inadequate. For the Graded Word Reading Test, R1, only norms are given—no particulars. The Simple Prose Reading Test, R2, is said to be based on 512 cases, but no further details are given. For the Silent Reading Tests, R3 and R4, it is stated that "1,865 cases were used to obtain approximate norms," but no information about the subjects is offered. Estimates of the relationship between silent reading ability and general intelligence, based on the results of 210 children, age 8–11, on R3 and R4 and a verbal group intelligence test are reported; correlation coefficients range from .67 to .86, but the number of cases in each age group is small (from 40 to 63). The reliability coefficient for R4 is given as .92. For the new norms in *Diagnostic and Attainment Testing* no particulars are given at all.

It is worth noting that, in common with almost every diagnostic battery, these tests are constructed rather to indicate superficial defects in acquired skills than to push the diagnosis deeper into the underlying causes of reading difficulties. For this purpose, as Schonell himself indicates in his extensive research, a wide, detailed and subtle study of the child and his environment is necessary. Useful as they are, diagnostic and attainment tests are merely the beginning; they are adjuncts and not substitutes for trained clinical insight and informed judgement. For the purpose for which they were designed, however, the *Schonell Reading Tests*—despite their shortcomings—are the most comprehensive so far available in England.

For a review by Edith I. M. Thomson, see 3:499.

[553]

Shank Tests of Reading Comprehension. Grades 3–6, 7–9, 10–12; 1929; 8 scores: direct details, implied details, general sense of a paragraph, determination of definite ideas, recognition of references, truth of idea, synonyms, total; 3 levels; Forms A, B, C; original manual out of print; $1.60 per 25 of any one level; 15¢ per abbreviated manual ['29—a reprint of Chapter V of the original manual]; postage extra; 10¢ per specimen set of any one level (does not include manual); $1.50 per specimen set of all forms of all levels; postpaid; Spencer Shank; C. A. Gregory Co. *
a) TEST I. Grades 3–6; 18(28) minutes.
b) TEST II. Grades 7–9; 20(30) minutes.
c) TEST III. Grades 10–12; 20(30) minutes.

REFERENCES

1–3. See 40:1567.

WILLIAM D. SHELDON, *Associate Professor of Education, and Director of the Reading Laboratory, Syracuse University, Syracuse, New York.*

This test is designed to measure reading comprehension. Each form of the test provides 10 paragraphs of reading content. In Test I, for grades 3–6, each paragraph is followed by six questions, each of which purports to measure a specific aspect of comprehension, e.g., answering a direct question on content details and determining whether the content stated a given idea. Test II, for grades 7–9, and Test III, for grades 10–12, have, in addition to the six questions measuring comprehension, a question requiring the student to supply a synonym from the paragraph for a word given in the question. The test is hand scored by means of a scoring key, and answers are written on the test booklet. There is no evidence that a machine scored answer sheet is available. A summary statement of data necessary for evaluating scores is provided for teacher use. Correlations with IQ's, but no correlations with other reading tests, have been provided.

Within-grade reliability coefficients between different forms of the test range from .89 to .92. The summary statement provides tables of age and grade norms for each test and subtest, based on a population of approximately 5,000 students.

The difficulty level of the paragraphs has been determined by a system of weights derived from the success of pupils on the various paragraphs. The content of the paragraphs is largely drawn from textbook-type materials from literature, science, mathematics, and history backgrounds.

The material is dated and deals largely with knowledge of specific facts rather than with general ideas or inferential material. There is no statistical evidence presented which would confirm the author's contention that the individual questions do provide measures of specific aspects of comprehension. Hence, the diagnostic value of the test is questionable when success on groups of items is used to measure ability in a specific comprehension skill.

The construction of the test seems to have been quite limited; there is no evidence that either the construction of the items or the statistical evaluation of the test compares in refinement with tests of a later design. There seems to be no reason for a teacher to use this test when others of a superior design such as the *Stanford*

Achievement Test in Reading, the *California Reading Test,* and the *Metropolitan Achievement Test in Reading* are available.

For a review by James R. Hobson, see 40: 1567.

[554]

*Silent Reading Comprehension: Iowa Every-Pupil Tests of Basic Skills, Test A. Grades 3–5, 5–9; 1940–47; for complete battery, see 15; 3 scores: reading comprehension, vocabulary, total; IBM for grades 5–9; 2 levels; Forms L ('40), M ('41), N ('42), O ('43); manual ('45); battery manual ('47); 33¢ per specimen set of any one level; postage extra; H. F. Spitzer in collaboration with Ernest Horn, Maude McBroom, H. A. Greene, and E. F. Lindquist; Houghton Mifflin Co. *
a) ELEMENTARY BATTERY. Grades 3–5; $1.60 per 25; 46(60) minutes.
b) ADVANCED BATTERY. Grades 5–9; IBM; $1.75 per 25; separate answer sheets may be used; 63¢ per 25 IBM answer sheets; 20¢ per stencil for machine scoring of answer sheets; 68(85) minutes.

For reviews by Miriam M. Bryan and Anton Thompson of the complete battery, see 15; for reviews by James R. Hobson and Constance M. McCullough, see 3:501; for reviews by Frederic L. Ayer, Gustav J. Froehlich, and Ralph C. Preston of the complete battery, see 3:10; for reviews by William A. Brownell, J. Murray Lee, and Charles W. Odell of the 1937 form of the complete battery, see 38:872.

[555]

Stanford Achievement Test [Reading]. Grades 2–3, 4–6, 7–9; 1923–43; a subtest of *Stanford Achievement Test* (see 23); 3 scores: paragraph meaning, word meaning, total; 3 levels; Forms D ('40), E ('40), F ('41), G ('42), H ('43); directions for administering ('40); the *Manual for Interpreting* referred to in the directions for administering has not been published; $1.45 per 25 of any one level, postage extra; 35¢ per specimen set of any one level, postpaid; Truman L. Kelley, Giles M. Ruch, and Lewis M. Terman; World Book Co. *
a) PRIMARY READING TEST. Grades 2–3; 1923–41; Forms D, E, F only; 25(30) minutes.
b) INTERMEDIATE READING TEST. Grades 4–6; 1923–43; 30(35) minutes.
c) ADVANCED READING TEST. Grades 7–9; 1923–43; 35 (40) minutes.

REFERENCES

1. CURRENT, W. F., AND RUCH, G. M. "Further Studies on the Reliability of Reading Tests." *J Ed Psychol* 17:476–81 O '26. * (PA 1:196)
2. BAKER, FLORENCE, AND BROOM, M. E. "Concerning One Criterion for the Choice of Primary Reading Tests." *J Appl Psychol* 16:419–20 Ag '32. * (PA 7:4098)
3. MILLARD, CECIL V. "The Nature and Character of Preadolescent Growth in Reading Achievement." *Child Develop* 11:71–114 Je '40. * (PA 14:4797)
4. PFLIEGER, ELMER F. "A Study of Reading Grade Levels." *J Ed Res* 42:541–6 Mr '49. * (PA 23:5752)

JAMES R. HOBSON, *Director of Child Placement, Brookline Public Schools, Brookline, Massachusetts.*

This is the oldest of the reading tests in a widely used achievement test battery and, despite certain basic limitations to be pointed out, remains one of the more satisfactory ones for accomplishing its purpose. Whether it deserves its wide use in the face of its faults and omissions is a moot question.

The Stanford tests have three basic advantages over competing tests: authorship of as yet unparalleled distinction, the earliest start in the field, and the first really adequate job of standardization. These assets have resulted in the general acceptance of the tests as a standard. Several revisions have resulted in such improvements and modernization as the machine scored edition of all tests for grades 4 and over and the publication of an edition of one form of the Partial Battery, Intermediate and Advanced, in extra large type for use in sightsaving classes. (This edition may be obtained from Stanwix House, 336 Fourth Ave., Pittsburgh 22, Pa.)

For obtaining valid and reliable measures of ability in paragraph meaning and word meaning in terms of age or grade norms, between the ages of 7 years 8 months and 15 years, or between the eighth month of the second grade and the beginning of the tenth grade, the Stanford reading tests are entirely adequate. The remainder of this review will be devoted to their inadequacies and unfulfilled functions.

On the debit side of the ledger this reviewer would list the following:

a) There is no reading test covering the skills acquired in grade 1. Yet, several skills whose development is begun in grade 1 can be adequately measured at that level. In most school systems the degree to which a child has acquired these skills is the most important criterion for his grade or class placement. In fact, there is no reliable measure below the eighth month of the second grade since all such values are obtained by extrapolation. This series of tests neglects entirely the most crucial grade levels in beginning reading, consequently preventing the keeping of any cumulative standardized test record based on comparable tests for any child or class until near the end of the second grade.

b) Since there is no manual for interpreting the current edition and forms of these tests, their full and proper use is difficult except for users of long standing who are familiar with the manuals of previous editions. The 2- to 4-page leaflet covering directions for administering which accompanies the various levels of these reading tests neglects to mention reliability or validity data, although several hundred words are devoted to an explanation as to why the age and grade norms on the front of the test booklet are based on modal age groups. This concept is both interesting and worth while. Its practical usefulness in any given school situation is governed, however, by the extent to which the given school's entrance age, and hence its modal age in each grade, coincides with that of the standardization population. This of course points up the desirability of local standardization and norms.

c) There are no suggestions of any kind for making use of individual or class test results in an analytical or remedial way. Perhaps these are to be included in the Manual for Interpreting which remains unpublished after 11 years.

d) This reviewer doubts the validity of a reading test at the second grade level which requires a pupil to write his answers. Incidentally, as mentioned by Margaret McKim in a previous review of these tests (see 3 :503), the spaces provided for writing the omitted words in Test 1 of the Primary Reading Test are too small for some words for some children.

In conclusion and summary, it appears to this reviewer that this series of reading tests, despite distinguished authorship, adequate standardization, and a history of past usefulness is, because of its omissions, somewhat outmoded for present-day classroom uses and needs. For survey purposes and in the hands of experienced users it remains satisfactory within self-set limits.

For reviews by Paul R. Hanna and Claude E. Norcross and Vergil E. Herrick of the complete battery, see 25; for review by Margaret G. McKim, see 3:503; for reviews by Walter W. Cook and Ralph C. Preston of the complete battery, see 3:18.

[556]

*Techniques in Reading Comprehension for Junior-Senior High School: Every Pupil Test. Grades 7–12; 1937–51; new form usually published each April and December; form December 1951; no data on reliability and validity; revised manual ['49]; norms ('51); 2½¢ per test; 1¢ per answer key; postpaid; 18(25) minutes; Ohio Scholarship Tests, Ohio State Department of Education. *

For reviews by Ivan A. Booker and James M. McCallister of April and December 1946 forms, see 3:505.

[557]

★Tests of Reading: Cooperative Inter-American Tests. Grades 1–3, 4–7, 8–13; 1950; 3 scores: vocabulary, comprehension, total; IBM for grades 4 and over; 3 levels; 2 editions; English edition: Forms AE,

BE; Spanish edition: Forms AS, BS; no data on reliability and validity; tentative norms; 50¢ per series manual; cash orders postpaid; 50¢ per specimen set of any one level, postpaid; prepared under the auspices of the Committee on Modern Languages of the American Council on Education, Herschel T. Manuel, Director of Test Construction; Cooperative Test Division, Educational Testing Service. *
a) PRIMARY LEVEL. Grades 1–3; $2.25 per 25; nontimed (25) minutes.
b) INTERMEDIATE LEVEL. Grades 4–7; IBM; $2.50 per 25; separate answer sheets must be used; 80¢ per 25 IBM answer sheets; 15¢ per stencil for scoring answer sheets; 40(50) minutes.
c) ADVANCED LEVEL. Grades 8–13; IBM; prices same as for Intermediate Level.

REFERENCES
1. Bou, Ismael Rodriguez. *A Study of the Parallelism of English and Spanish Vocabularies.* Doctor's thesis, University of Texas (Austin, Tex.), 1944.
2. McCranie, Josephine. *A Study of Four Inter-American Tests Applied to High School Seniors.* Master's thesis, University of Texas (Austin, Tex.), 1944.
3. Kelley, Frances. *A Study of the Inter-American Tests at the High School Level.* Master's thesis, University of Texas (Austin, Tex.), 1945.
4. Fife, Robert Herndon, and Manuel, Herschel T. *The Teaching of English in Puerto Rico,* pp. 171–313, 337–410. Prepared for the American Council on Education. San Juan, P.R.: Department of Education Press, 1951. Pp. xix, 410. *

Jacob S. Orleans, *Professor of Education, and Director of Research and Evaluation, Division of Teacher Education, The College of the City of New York, New York, New York.*

This is a series of reading tests with parallel editions in both English and Spanish. There are three levels. Each level consists of two parts, vocabulary and comprehension. The Primary Level contains 40 vocabulary items (each a picture followed by 4 words) and 30 comprehension items (each containing 4 pictures followed by verbal context). The Intermediate Level contains 65 vocabulary items each in the form of a completion item followed by 4 choices; and 57 comprehension questions (4-response multiple choice) in groups of 3 to 5 questions referring to short paragraphs. The Advanced Level is similar to the Intermediate Level with 70 vocabulary questions and 58 comprehension questions, the latter based on longer and more difficult paragraphs.

The Spanish edition is an exact translation of the English. No evidence is presented that the English context is suitable for testing reading achievement at the levels for which the test is intended, or that the Spanish context is suitable for testing reading achievement at the levels for which it is intended, or that context that is appropriate for measuring reading achievement in English of American children is also appropriate for measuring reading achievement in Spanish of Spanish speaking children. Norms are available for both editions, but the norms represent typical achievement and are not necessarily measures of the suitability of the context. In view of the differences in the cultures of the United States and the Spanish speaking countries of the Americas one may well question the content validity of either or both of the tests for lack of supporting evidence.

One effect of the exact translation from the English to the Spanish edition may be illustrated by Item 3 of Part I (vocabulary) of the Primary Level (Forms AE and AS). It consists of a picture of a woman washing clothes followed in the English edition by the words wash, wake, walk, and call and in the Spanish edition by the words *lavar, despertar, andar,* and *llamar.* In the English edition it is clear that three of the alternates ask the pupil to distinguish among words starting with the same letter. The same is not true in the Spanish translation ("ll" is not the same as "l" in Spanish). There are a number of instances where the same type of distinction (between words starting with the same letter or containing the same group of letters) holds true in the one edition but not in the other. It is possible that such differences in the context of the test, or differences in suitability of the same words, paragraphs, or comprehension questions, make no difference in the validity of the tests for measuring reading achievement in the respective languages; but there is no evidence in the manual to support such an assumption.

Both parts of the Primary Level employ pictures, the same pictures being used in both language editions. Although many of the pictures are recognizable, on the whole they are of rather poor quality. Some would appear to be really difficult to recognize, and it is possible that on occasion the examinee identifies the picture only through a clue given by the verbal context.

Each part of each test is preceded by at least five sample questions. The instructions seem to be clear. All levels of both editions are prepared for machine scoring, although they can also be used for hand scoring. The manual states that at the Primary Level the pupils are to record their answers in the test booklets. It is difficult to see why the booklets at this level are prepared for machine scoring, except perhaps when used by older pupils who are retarded in their reading achievement. The Primary Level is intended for grades 1, 2, and the lower part of grade 3; the Intermediate Level for grades 4–7; and the Advanced Level for grades 8–13. The working time is 16 minutes for the Primary Level, and 40

minutes for each of the other two levels. There is apparently no level appropriate for the upper half of grade 3. The norms indicate that there is no overlapping between the Primary and Intermediate, but a great deal between the Intermediate and Advanced levels which essentially make them a continuous test. The first 33 vocabulary questions of the Advanced Level are the same as the last 33 of the Intermediate Level.

The tests are accompanied by an Examiner's Manual which provides information concerning all five tests in the Cooperative Inter-American Test series, the purposes, levels, uses, administration, applications, validity, reliability, and preliminary interpretative data. There is a separate set of directions for administering and scoring for the Primary Level, and one for both the Intermediate and Advanced Levels. These directions are very detailed.

The manual contains an explanation of the use of the reliability coefficient and the probable and standard errors of a pupil's score, illustrating their meaning with a correlation coefficient of .92, a probable error of 4, and a standard error of 6. A hasty reading may leave the impression that these are the reliability data for the tests. However, the last sentence in this section of the manual reads: "Because the Cooperative Inter-American Tests are being offered for general use for the first time, reliability statistics are not available at present." The user has a right to assume that before the tests are offered for general use they have been adequately validated and standardized, and that therefore the reliability of the tests should have been determined.

In place of the customary "norms" the manual presents "interpretative data." This is a commendable practice since norms, which represent only typical achievement usually of unevaluated quality, are too often used as standards. The data are presented in two tables, one furnishing median scores on the Spanish edition based on 6,000 Mexican children in three cities and 20,000 Puerto Rican children in grades 1 through 12. The data were obtained for experimental forms and "adjusted approximately for changes made in preparing final forms of the tests." The second table furnishes medians based on 10,000 pupils in about 30 cities of the United States, about half in Texas. These medians for the English edition were also "adjusted approximately for changes made in preparing the final forms." The medians are given only for total scores.

For the Primary Level of the English edition a spread of 30 points represents the range of achievement from grade 1 to grade 2 and only 9 points from grade 2 to grade 3. The corresponding values for the Spanish edition are 15 points and 5 points with the median for the second half of each of the first three grades being *lower* than the median for the first half. Obviously the content of the Primary Level is too easy. There was nothing available to the reviewer to explain why the second half of each grade did less well on the Spanish edition than did the lower half. In the case of the Intermediate Level there are large differences between medians for grades 2 to 5 on both editions. Beyond the fifth grade the spread is very much less, again indicating that the tests are too easy for the upper grades. The same condition holds true for the medians for grades 4 through 7 on the English edition of the Advanced Level and grades 4 through 9 of the Spanish edition. Again for the Spanish edition the median for the second half of each grade is lower than the median for the first half of the grade. It is questionable that test scores can have much significance if a difference of 5 points represents two years of achievement—particularly when the probable error of a pupil's score is likely to be at least a year of achievement. No information is furnished concerning the characteristics of the populations for whom the interpretive data were derived other than those indicated above. No evidence is furnished concerning the comparability of the populations.

These tests represent a commendable effort to provide comparable measures of reading achievement in Spanish and English. The manual offers suggestions and cautions concerning the uses of the test results for selection, placement, guidance and counseling, control of learning, motivation, and evaluation. Much work still needs to be done in validating the tests, determining their reliability, furnishing adequate interpretative data, and determining comparability of scores on the two forms.

FREDERICK L. WESTOVER, *Associate Professor of Educational Psychology, University of Alabama, University, Alabama.* [Review of the English edition.]

The unique feature of the series of Cooperative Inter-American Tests is the provision of parallel forms in English and Spanish in order to facilitate comparisons of pupil performance in each of the two languages. The present review considers only the English editions of the tests of reading.

DESCRIPTION OF THE TESTS. The Primary Level test is designed for use in the first three grades. It covers vocabulary and comprehension, and is intended to give a measure of general reading ability. In the vocabulary section, a picture is presented with four accompanying words, and the pupil indicates the word appropriate to the picture. In the comprehension section, the pupil indicates to which of four pictures a given phrase, sentence, or paragraph refers.

The Intermediate Level is designed for use from the fourth through the seventh grade; and the Advanced Level, for use from the eighth grade through the first year of college. These tests, like the Primary Level test, cover vocabulary and comprehension, and are intended to give a measure of general reading ability. The words in the vocabulary section and the paragraphs in the comprehension section are drawn from a wide range of materials.

EVALUATION OF THE TESTS. Some of the drawings in the Primary Level test suffer from crowding and poor detail. This deficiency impairs the appearance of the test and the ease of perception of some of the figures. The usefulness of this test would have been increased for many teachers if the vocabulary section had been modified to give more information about the pupil's word-recognition skills, instead of being principally concerned with the amount of the pupil's word knowledge. The tests at all three levels measure only two aspects of reading: vocabulary and comprehension. The value of the tests at the intermediate and advanced levels would have been enhanced for many users if a measure of reading speed had been included.

All of the tests have been well constructed from a variety of intrinsically interesting materials and appear to possess face validity. However, no statistics on reliability are reported. Norms are based on administration of the tests to 10,000 pupils in cities of the United States, half of them in Texas. The norms provide information only on the median total scores at each level for which each test is scored. The manual is well organized and easy to follow.

SUMMARY. These tests offer satisfactory brief surveys of vocabulary and comprehension in reading. They are of special value to those who wish to use them in connection with the Spanish editions in order to compare the performance of pupils in English and Spanish. Others may find that older established tests possess some advantages, especially in the provision of more adequate norms, diagnostic information, and data on reliability.

[558]

*Thorndike-Lorge Reading Test. Grades 7–9; 1941–47; Forms A Rev. ('47), B Rev. ('47); manual ('47); $5.40 per 100; 35¢ per specimen set; postpaid; 40(45) minutes; E. L. Thorndike and Irving Lorge; Bureau of Publications, Teachers College, Columbia University. *

REFERENCES

1. LORGE, IRVING. "The Thorndike-Lorge Reading Test for Grades 7–9." *Teach Col Rec* 46:453–9 Ap '45. * (PA 19:2754)

IVAN A. BOOKER, *Assistant Director, Division of Press and Radio Relations, National Education Association, Washington, D.C.*

The authors of this test boldly start out to measure "all the important factors in silent reading and to give reasonable weight to each of them." To say that the test falls far short of this ambitious goal is not to condemn it, but merely to look at it more realistically.

The test emphasizes the ability to read and answer fact questions and the ability to read and understand sentences of the proverb or aphorism type. The latter, of course, involves considerable vocabulary skill and the ability to interpret idioms and figures of speech, but the emphasis is not on these subsidiary skills. The test is quite heavily weighted with items that call for the interpretation of proverbs or quotations. In fact, 20 of the 53 to 55 items are of that type. One wonders whether, in a balanced test, two fifths of the items should be of this type. It should be pointed out, too, that for many of these items the difficulty which the reader encounters is in interpreting the supposedly synonymous sentences rather than in interpreting the test items. Perhaps this is not too grave a fault, but some testmakers insist that the test item, not the answer, should constitute the test of skill. Aside from these items, the remainder of the test is devoted quite largely to fact questions. Undoubtedly, both types of items are useful measures of the general level of reading comprehension, but they scarcely give the test that comprehensiveness and balance which the manual claims for it.

The statistical evidence as to the validity and reliability of this test seems satisfactory *as far as it goes.* However, the vague way in which the procedure for checking validity is described and the limited sampling used to establish reliability leave some doubt as to the accuracy of the conclusions drawn. Correlations of about .80 with

scores from "four reputable reading tests" are cited as evidence of validity. The four tests are not named. Moreover, facts are entirely lacking to support the manual's claim that correlations of about .96 would be obtained against "a more reliable criterion of reading ability." If so, why was such a criterion not used? Such probabilities are unconvincing, and many users of the test will prefer to think of it in terms of the demonstrated correlations of about .80 with other reading tests. The reliabilities of about .90 between scores on Forms A and B are based on only four samples of about 200 students each. This is satisfactory, but it would be reassuring to have similar results from a considerably larger number of samples.

The manual suggests a few possible diagnostic uses of the test. In view of the nature of the test, however, it seems highly questionable that it yields any significant results other than those which a discriminating teacher can get from analyzing students' responses to single test items. The test is most valuable as a survey instrument to measure the general level of reading comprehension. It needs no other justification. Used in that way, it should provide a useful measure "of the level of reading comprehension in junior high classes" and should help to identify those in need of careful diagnosis and special instruction in reading.

Each form of the test opens with a short passage followed by 7 fact questions. Items 8 to 27 call for the interpretation of sentences. Finally, there are 3 prose passages, each passage followed by 5 to 12 questions on the content, that are largely fact questions, which call for very little use of reasoning or of the ability to draw conclusions or inferences from what is read.

The time allowance is generous enough to make the test a power test for most junior high school students. The authors estimate that the relative contribution of quality and speed to the students' total scores are in the ratio of 12 to 1. The test gives no measure of reading rate, but students who fail to finish it in the 40 minutes allowed should be suspected of unduly slow reading and should be tested with a good rate test. The directions for administering the test are brief, simple, and clear. Students record their answers to the test questions directly on the test booklets, not on separate answer sheets.

The format of the test is somewhat cumbersome for both student and scorer. For example, the student must read the first test selection at the top of a page, then find and study a series of questions near the middle of the page, select the right answers to those questions from a list at the bottom of the page, and then go back and record the numbers of these answers alongside the questions. The amount of such shifting about from place to place seems unnecessarily great.

For the scorer, the answer keys in the test manual are poorly arranged. They are not set in the form of matching stencils, which can be laid alongside each page of the test for quick comparison. Instead, there is simply a list of the numbered items and the correct responses. The scorer must either move the answer sheet along from one item to the next or construct his own scoring stencil. The manual itself is quite simple and usable, if one disregards its "overselling" claims. Grade and reading age equivalents are given for each score on each form of the test. These are based on approximately 2,000 pupils. No medians, quartiles, percentiles by grades, standard scores, or other interpretative data are included.

For a review by Robert L. McCaul and an excerpt from a review, see 3:506.

[559]

*Traxler High School Reading Test. Grades 10–12; 1938–42; 5 scores: reading rate, story comprehension, main ideas, total comprehension, total; IBM; Forms A ('38), B ('39); $1.80 per 25, postage extra; 12¢ per revised manual ('42); 30¢ per specimen set; postpaid; separate answer sheets (IBM Form I.T.S. 1000 B 108) may be used; IBM answer sheets and scoring stencils must be purchased directly from International Business Machines Corporation; 50(55) minutes; Arthur E. Traxler; Public School Publishing Co. *

REFERENCES

1. TRAXLER, ARTHUR E. "Relationship Between the Length and the Reliability of a Test of Rate of Reading." *J Ed Res* 32:1–2 S '38. (*PA* 12:6660)
2. TRAXLER, ARTHUR E. "One Reading Test Serves the Purpose." *Clearing House* 14:419–21 Mr '40. * (*PA* 14:5233, title only)
3. BLOMMERS, PAUL, AND LINDQUIST, E. F. "Rate of Comprehension of Reading: Its Measurement and Its Relation to Comprehension." *J Ed Psychol* 35:449–73 N '44. * (*PA* 19:1035)
4. PRESTON, RALPH C., AND TUFT, EDWIN N. "The Reading Habits of Superior College Students." *J Exp Ed* 16:196–202 Mr '48. * (*PA* 20:5126)

HAROLD D. CARTER, *Professor of Education, University of California, Berkeley, California.*

This test, designed in two equivalent forms for use in grades 10 through 12, yields a rate score and three comprehension scores. The test requires 50 minutes of working time, a requirement that may be awkward in many school situations.

The manual for the test, written in clear and meaningful style, indicates a fine background of scholarship in the fields of test construction and reading instruction. It contains a description of the test and information concerning its validity and reliability, percentile norms for each score and for each grade level, and practical suggestions for the interpretation of test results.

Face validity of the test is assured by the careful item analysis which preceded selection of the items. The reported reliabilities of .90 for the rate score, .72 for the story comprehension score, and .80 for the paragraph comprehension score are highly satisfactory. The norms are based on the results of over 7,000 pupils.

Among the commendable features of the test are the emphasis upon comprehension of material read at a natural rate chosen by the pupil, and the provision of two nicely equated forms, a convenient device for obtaining the rate score, and the manual packed with essential information. While one might hope for further reports of experimental studies dealing with the use of test results, the test as published appears to furnish the basis for an effective program of reading instruction through providing a high quality instrument for the appraisal of reading ability and achievement.

For reviews by Alvin C. Eurich, Constance M. McCullough, and C. Gilbert Wrenn and excerpts from reviews, see 40:1578.

[560]

*Traxler Silent Reading Test. Grades 7–10; 1934–42; 6 scores: reading rate, story comprehension, word meaning, paragraph meaning, total comprehension, total; IBM; Forms 1 ('34), 2 ('34), 3 ('41), 4 ('42); $1.80 per 25; 18¢ per revised manual ('42), postpaid; 36¢ per specimen set, postpaid; separate answer sheets may be used; 4¢ per IBM answer sheet; 18¢ per stencil for scoring answer sheets; postage extra; 46(55) minutes; Arthur E. Traxler; Public School Publishing Co. *

REFERENCES

1–3. See 40:1579.
4. BLANCHARD, HOWARD L. *A Comparison of Teachers' Marks With an Actual Battery of Aptitude Test Percentile Scores.* Doctor's "Field Study No. 1," Colorado State College of Education (Greeley, Colo.), 1949. (*Abstracts of Field Studies.... 1949, 1950,* pp. 12–5.)
5. TRAXLER, ARTHUR E. "Correlations Between Scores on Various Reading Tests Administered Several Months Apart," pp. 78–82. (*PA* 24:748) In *1949 Achievement Testing Program in Independent Schools and Supplementary Studies.* Educational Records Bulletin, No. 52. New York: Educational Records Bureau, July 1949. Pp. xiii, 87. Paper, lithotyped. *

J. THOMAS HASTINGS, *Associate Professor of Education, Director, Unit on Evaluation, Bureau of Research and Service, College of Education; University Examiner; University of Illinois, Urbana, Illinois.*

In both the 1938 and 1940 *Mental Measurements Yearbooks,* Forms 1 and 2 of this test were thoroughly and critically evaluated. Form 3 (1941) and Form 4 (1942) have since been added. The manual, which was originally published in 1934, was revised in 1942. In addition to these materials a single loose sheet for converting vocabulary scores to mental ages has been added. This sheet, with no explanatory information on validity, reliability, or construction and no suggestions to the user about the dangers involved in use, is likely to be misleading and harmful.

The previous reviews were explicit in both adverse and complimentary criticism. It is quite unfortunate that virtually all the adverse criticisms made at least 11 years ago are still valid. Even though two new forms have been published and the manual has been revised, very little has been done actually to improve the statistics and interpretation.

The "tentative norms" have been replaced in the 1942 revision of the manual by new norms. These consist of (a) some kind of average score given for each grade, 7 through 10, on each test part and total (in the descriptive material relating to this table these averages are called "median scores," but in the table heading they are called "mean scores") ; (b) a table of grade norms by months for the total score; and (c) percentile scores for each part score and the totals by grade level, 7 through 10. The manual says that these new grade norms are based upon scores of about 25,000 pupils. There is no indication of how these cases are distributed according to grade level and no description of the samples in terms of ranges, standard deviations, or chronological ages. These omissions are especially interesting in view of the fact that under the heading "Use of Test Results" the test user is instructed to answer in regard to his pupils' test scores such questions as "What is the range of the scores in each grade?" and "What is the standard deviation of the scores?" He is then told that with the answers to these questions he will know whether the pupils within a grade (in his school) are relatively homogeneous in reading ability. The word "relative" obviously refers to his other classes and not the norm group on which the tests were standardized, since it did not seem important to present such figures on the standardization group.

The data presented in the manual concerning validity, reliability, and equivalence of forms are still insufficient. Surely there has been time to collect new data; yet it appears that old, unsatis-

factory data have been used. For example, the manual presents the following data on the validity of the comprehension scores: a combination score of story comprehension and power comprehension correlated with a composite criterion of other reading tests *for 54 sixth grade pupils.* This is done in spite of the fact that sixth graders were apparently not used in establishing the norms nor for obtaining any of the other data concerning the test. The grade norms by months explicitly state that the grade equivalents below the seventh grade are extrapolated!

Fortunately, the business of not doing much about the material has allowed the test to retain the good points mentioned in the previous reviews: (a) comprehension is properly emphasized in the rate test; (b) the rate test is interesting reading and should appeal to pupils of the age for which it is intended; (c) use of sentences or phrases in the word meaning test is a more meaningful device than the use of words by themselves; (d) the time limits on the various parts are such that it is not likely to be a speeded test at any of the intended grade levels.

In summary, we have here a reading test for the junior high school level—a level at which much attention should be paid to reading—which appears to be relatively good for survey purposes but on which the data presented are extremely scarce even though the test was first copyrighted some 17 years ago. It is discouraging to note that even in the face of sound critical reviews which pointed out serious shortcomings, a decade has been allowed to elapse with little attempt at improvement.

For reviews by Robert L. McCaul and Miles A. Tinker and an excerpt from a review of the 1939 edition, see 40:1579; for reviews by Frederick B. Davis and Spencer Shank of the 1934 edition, see 38:1114.

MISCELLANEOUS

[561]
Durrell Analysis of Reading Difficulty. Grades 1–6; 1933–37; 7 scores: oral reading-comprehension, oral reading-recall, silent reading, word recognition, word pronunciation, spelling, handwriting; individual; 1 form, '37; no data on reliability; manual ('37) ; $2.30 per 25 individual record blanks; stopwatch essential for administration; $1.30 per booklet of reading paragraphs ('37) ; 90¢ per tachistoscope and cards; $1.20 per 30 blank tachistoscope cards; 30¢ per manual; postage extra; $3 per examiner's kit including 5 individual record blanks, postpaid; (40–45) minutes; Donald D. Durrell; World Book Co. *

REFERENCES

1. DURRELL, DONALD D. Chap. 13, "Analysis of Reading Difficulties," pp. 296–315. In his *Improvement of Basic Reading Abilities.* Yonkers, N.Y.: World Book Co., 1940. Pp. viii, 407. * (*PA* 15:1499)
2. SPACHE, GEORGE. "A Comparison of Certain Oral Reading Tests." *J Ed Res* 43:441–52 F '50. * (*PA* 25:562)

HELEN M. ROBINSON, *Associate Professor of Education, and Director of the Reading Clinic, The University of Chicago, Chicago, Illinois.*

This instrument was designed to be used by a skilled observer to detect basic weaknesses in reading. Durrell has chosen to test six phases of both oral and silent reading. Supplementary tests of writing and spelling are provided. The manual states that "a teacher unacquainted with the methods and objectives of teaching reading will find difficulty in using the Analysis intelligently"; it should be used by experienced reading teachers only.

The first subtest implies that comprehension of oral reading is to be tested, yet the norms for this subtest consider only the time required to read each paragraph. Although space is provided for recording the number of errors and the answers to comprehension questions, the former appears to be used only to determine the appropriate paragraphs to be read, while the latter is interpreted qualitatively by such a term as "low." Therefore, the scoring of this subtest appears to be inconsistent with the purpose stated. Furthermore, this test requires only recall of the story read. Many pupils can repeat material without comprehension. This test is of little value in analysis of comprehension of different types, when word recognition is adequate.

Norms for the second subtest, Oral Reading —Unaided Oral Recall, are based on a combination of the number of thought units remembered and the time required for oral reading. The manual suggests that the examiner record both the number of errors made in oral reading and the number of ideas recalled when direct questions are asked, although only a qualitative analysis is made of these data. No standard questions are provided, so that the extent and accuracy of the measure of comprehension depends on the skill of the examiner.

The third subtest, Silent Reading—Unaided Oral Recall, is similar to the second, except that reading errors cannot be noted. These two subtests enable the examiner to compare silent with oral reading since paragraphs are matched in difficulty.

The fourth subtest combines a measure of rapid word recognition with ability to analyze words which are not a part of the pupil's sight vocabulary. The cardboard tachistoscope and shutter are manually operated at a suggested speed of exposure of one half second. The manual states that the purpose for quick exposure is so that the child may have "just one glance without time for an extra eye movement." Considerable practice is required to operate a manual tachistoscope consistently at this speed. Furthermore, studies have shown that several eye movements can be made in a half second.

The Phonetic Inventory is especially useful in determining the nature of the difficulty in one phase of word analysis. The reviewer would question the recommended practice of excusing those who score above third grade on the flash and pronunciation tests, since experience shows that pupils who reach this level nevertheless often exhibit weaknesses which can readily be identified by such an inventory.

The manual is written so that the directions for administration are clear. However, considerable difficulty is experienced in using and interpreting the norms. The latter were established on 1,000 children, but there is no description of the population sampled, or of the methods used in teaching the pupils to read. Furthermore, neither reliability nor validity is mentioned in the manual, and there is no indication of the consistency of the tests.

The author states that "since this test is essentially a method of standard observation of errors and faulty habits in reading, the checklist of errors is more important than the norms." To this end, the checklists for observing errors in oral reading and faulty reading habits are quite complete and detailed. In short, it appears that herein lie the major values of the test.

The Durrell Analysis is not as complete as the *Gates Reading Diagnostic Tests,* but has the advantage of requiring less time to administer. It includes no measures of aptitudes for learning to read by different methods as does the Gates test.

The *Durrell Analysis of Reading Difficulty* provides an excellent opportunity for an experienced reading teacher to observe difficulties in word recognition and oral reading, as the checklist of errors is the best available. However, the silent reading section is of limited value, and the norms must be used with full realization of the limitations pointed out previously.

For reviews by Guy L. Bond and Miles A. Tinker, see 40:1533; for a review by Marion Monroe, see 38:1098.

[562]

*Durrell-Sullivan Reading Capacity and Achievement Tests. Grades 2.5–4.5, 3–6; 1937–45; 5 scores: word meaning, paragraph meaning, spelling (optional), written recall (optional), total; 2 levels; 20¢ per manual ('45); postage extra; 35¢ per specimen set of any one level, postpaid; 30(45) minutes; Donald D. Durrell and Helen Blair Sullivan; World Book Co. *
a) PRIMARY TEST. Grades 2.5–4.5; 2 tests published in 1 booklet; Form A ('37); directions for administering ('39); $2.65 per 25.
　1) *Reading Capacity Test.*
　2) *Reading Achievement Test.*
b) INTERMEDIATE TEST. Grades 3–6; 2 tests.
　1) *Reading Capacity Test.* Form A ('37); directions for administering ('37); $1.70 per 25.
　2) *Reading Achievement Test.* Forms A ('37), B ('44); directions for administering ('45); $2 per 25.

REFERENCES

1. SULLIVAN, HELEN BLAIR. "A New Method of Determining Reading Capacity." *Ed* 59:39–45 S '38. *
2. TIREMAN, L. S., AND WOODS, VELMA E. "Note on the Influence on the Validity of a Vocabulary Test of the Method of Indicating Responses." *J Ed Psychol* 31:153–4 F '40. * (PA 14:3763)
3. ALDEN, CLARA L.; SULLIVAN, HELEN B.; AND DURRELL, DONALD D. "The Frequency of Special Reading Disabilities." *Ed* 62:32–6 S '41. *
4. PUGH, GLADYS S. "Summaries From 'Appraisal of the Silent Reading Abilities of Acoustically Handicapped Children.'" *Am Ann Deaf* 91:331–49 S '46. * (PA 21:290)

HELEN M. ROBINSON, *Associate Professor of Education, and Director of the Reading Clinic, The University of Chicago, Chicago, Illinois.*

Although these tests were first published 14 years ago, they remain unique in their purpose of providing a simple means for identifying poor readers among pupils in grades 2–6. Pupils who have specific reading disabilities often appear to be dull or mentally retarded if they are measured by a group intelligence test requiring them to read. Hence, a reading achievement test shows that such pupils are reading in harmony with their capacities and, as a result, no attempts are made to correct their reading problems. While individual intelligence tests may be more discriminating and more useful, few schools have the number of adequately trained staff members required to administer and interpret them. Authorities estimate that 10 to 20 per cent of pupils in grades 2–6 fall in the category of poor readers; consequently, the need for tests to distinguish pupils with reading deficiencies from those who are intellectually slow in development is urgent.

The *Durrell-Sullivan Reading Capacity and Achievement Tests* meet this need in two ways. First, the tests may be given by a teacher without special psychological training. Second, the tests may be given to groups of children, hence they are an economical means for identifying poor readers without major language deficiencies, who are capable of reading considerably beyond their present achievement level.

The tests were carefully constructed so that the capacity and achievement sections are comparable. It is essential that both sections be administered if a comparison is to be made between the levels of achievement and capacity of a given pupil.

Since these tests include measures of word meaning and paragraph meaning, it is possible to determine whether a pupil's difficulty lies in word recognition or in understanding the meaning of larger speech units. Furthermore, if the latter is the case, clues as to the specific types of comprehension problems are provided by an analysis of the types of questions most frequently answered incorrectly. This is possible because the paragraph meaning section includes questions requiring the reader to understand sentences and words, to note details, to get the central thought, and to locate information. Such hints enable the teacher or reading clinician to select the proper diagnostic tests to investigate these problems more analytically. Supplementary tests of spelling and written recall are available if further information about these areas is needed.

The manual of directions is written clearly and simply. Both age and grade norms are presented for word meaning, paragraph meaning, and the total score. The norms for the Intermediate Test are based upon 6,000 cases in 19 communities. These communities were largely in the East, but this selection shows no limitation so long as the tests are used for comparison purposes. No statement is made concerning the standardization of the Primary Test, but, since it includes the easier items of the Intermediate Test, it is assumed that the same data were used.

The selection of the test items was carefully planned to produce a valid test. Clinical experience has shown a close relationship between the capacity test and scores on individually administered intelligence tests which are heavily weighted with verbal items. The reliability coefficients provided by the authors are highly satisfactory.

In the light of recent studies of the language limitations of underprivileged socio-economic groups, the reviewer questions the assumption that the Capacity Tests are as accurate with these groups as with pupils of the more privileged groups. More probably, they determine whether a pupil has acquired the necessary language facility to make progress in reading. However, they fail to distinguish between pupils who have general language handicaps, with potentialities for rapid increase in language facility and reading improvement, and those who are intellectually dull without these potentialities. The Capacity Tests are really tests of hearing comprehension or language facility and should not be confused with intelligence tests. Further study in this area holds promise for a better understanding of the value of these tests. They can be used with confidence, provided pupils with foreign language backgrounds and those suspected of having language handicaps are given more careful appraisal.

For reviews by William S. Gray and Marion Monroe and an excerpt from a review, see 38: 1099.

[563]

Gates Reading Diagnostic Tests, Revised Edition. Grades 1–8; 1926–45; 21 scores: categories of mispronunciations, speed of reading paragraphs, oral reading total, oral vocabulary, reversals, phrase perception, word perception-flash presentation, word perception and analysis-untimed presentation, spelling, syllabication, recognition of syllables, recognition of phonograms, blending letter sounds, giving letter sounds, speed of reading capital letters, errors in reading capital letters, speed of reading small letters, errors in reading small letters, giving letters for sounds, giving words with stated initial sounds, giving words with stated final sound; individual; Forms I ('42), II ('42); manual ('45); 20¢ per pupil record booklet; 55¢ per oral response test material for any one form; 10¢ per set of tachistoscopic cards; 45¢ per manual; $1.50 per specimen set; postpaid; (60–90) minutes; Arthur I. Gates; Bureau of Publications, Teachers College, Columbia University. *

REFERENCES

1–3. See 3:510.
4. COLLINS, ELIZABETH MARY. *The Measurement of Visual-Visual and Visual-Auditory Association.* Master's thesis, Fordham University (New York, N.Y.), 1939. Pp. 39.
5. GATES, ARTHUR I. "A Correlational Study of a Battery of Reading Diagnostic Tests." *J Ed Res* 40:436–47 F '47. * (*PA* 21:3743)

WORTH J. OSBURN, *Professor of Remedial and Experimental Education, University of Washington, Seattle, Washington.*

These are individual tests designed for use with pupils who have failed or made low scores on group tests. The purpose of the tests is to disclose *why* the pupil has failed to learn to read. They include material on oral reading, vocabulary, reversals, phrase perception, word perception and analysis, spelling, visual perception, and auditory techniques. As a reminder, the booklet in which the tester records the pupil's responses includes blanks for recording results of tests of vision, hearing, and speech, and information about eye movements, emotional tension, special interests and distastes, home and other out-of-school influences, and school history. Since there are two forms of the series, it is possible to measure improvement.

The manual contains explicit aids for those who are relatively inexperienced in diagnosis. Twenty-one tables of norms enable the examiner to ascertain the pupil's grade level in the subelements of the tests. Other tables show degree of retardation, age-grade scores, and the like. Suggestions for appropriate remedial treatment are to be found in the author's *Improvement of Reading (3)*.

No estimate is given in the manual of the time required to administer the entire series of tests individually; however, the author has mentioned elsewhere that 60 to 90 minutes should be a reasonable allowance. Even if the author's estimate is not too conservative, the testing time required is still long enough so that it seems doubtful that the ordinary school system will have anyone around who has sufficient time to use the series to any great extent. The tests were apparently designed to diagnose everything that ever gets wrong with any child anywhere. All such tests need some device by which the tester can find quickly just which part of the series is needed for a given child and thus effect the saving of badly needed time.

In the estimation of the reviewer, more attention should have been given to reading rate and to emotional blocks. In spite of these adverse elements the tests are well worth using.

For related reviews, see 564; for a review by T. L. Torgerson, see 3:510.

[564]

[Re Gates Reading Diagnostic Tests.] GATES, ARTHUR I. **The Improvement of Reading: A Program of Diagnostic and Remedial Methods, Third Edition.** New York: Macmillan Co., 1947. Pp. xxi, 657. $4.75. * (*PA* 22:3195)

J Consult Psychol 12:124 Mr–Ap '48. Laurance F. Shaffer. * rewritten entirely * An appendix gives full directions and norms for the *Gates Diagnostic Reading Tests.* These tests have progressed markedly, since their first publication in 1927, toward a wholistic approach to reading functions in place of the original compartmented approach.

J Ed Res 42:76–7 S '48. Miles A. Tinker. *

primarily a manual of directions for diagnosing and remedying reading defects. It describes the author's series of reading achievement and diagnostic tests. More space has been devoted to discussions of reading activities, especially comprehension, than in earlier editions. * Only a few of the many excellent features of this text can be mentioned here: (1) Heavy emphasis is properly placed upon motivation as a factor in causing and in correcting difficulties in reading. (2) Adequate weight is given to training in phonetics. (3) Physical disabilities as causes of reading disability are satisfactorily evaluated. (4) Non-verbal intelligence tests are unsatisfactory to use with reading cases. (5) Caution should be exercised in assigning reading difficulty to nervous instability since emotional symptoms are frequently the result of the difficulty and will disappear when the difficulty is remedied. (6) Remedial instruction is the same as regular developmental classroom teaching but involves greater individual prescription for individual needs. (7) Strong emphasis is placed upon training left-to-right sequences of perception. (8) Proper weight is assigned to various clues to word recognition. (9) Mechanical devices are properly de-emphasized. (10) It is unnecessary to photograph eye movements in diagnosing a reading case. (11) Good readers are flexible in their reading attack, modifying it in accordance with the difficulty and complexity of the context. There are a few questions of emphasis and a few errors that may be noted: (1) In several places low mentality is given as a cause of reading deficiency. This will confuse the less careful reader for at no place is it clearly explained that low mentality, although associated with poor reading ability, is not the cause of reading disability. (2) The "eye recognition span" is mistakenly called the "eye voice span." (3) Eight per cent rather than 4 per cent of boys are color-blind, and, contrary to the author's statement, the *Jensen Test for Color-Blindness* does not yield "reliable" evidence of color deficiencies. A recent study shows poor validity for this test. (4) In several instances, emphasis is placed upon identifying little words in big words. This procedure is apt to create many difficulties unless handled with extreme caution. To avoid trouble, it is best to confine the technique to distinguishing parts of compound words and root words in variants and derivatives. (5) Greater emphasis might well be placed upon teaching syllabification. (6) "It

is very useful to learn to count the number of stops per line by observing the pupil's eyes as he is . . . reading . . ." (p. 344). This technique is both inaccurate and useless. Furthermore it is contrary to the view expressed on page 314. (7) There should be more emphasis upon the thinking aspects of reading, especially in discussion of comprehension. (8) On page 543, the term presbyopia is erroneously applied to a child. It is a defect of vision associated with advancing age, i.e., middle-aged people. (9) A boy (p. 566) 6 years, 11 months old and with an I.Q. of 110 is considered deficient because he did not use syllabic divisions in spelling, and because he spelled letter by letter. How skillful a speller is a normal child of less than seven years of age supposed to be? (10) Traxler's two important summaries are unfortunately absent from Gate's bibliography. This book is undoubtedly the best text we have in systematic diagnostic and remedial reading. It is thorough, well written and practical. This revision is a decided improvement over previous editions which in themselves were excellent books.

ORAL

[565]
★Oral Diagnostic Test of Word-Analysis Skills, Primary: Dominion Tests. Grades 1–2; 1947; individual; no data on reliability; 1 form; $1 per 25; 15¢ per set of word slide cards and sleeve; 25¢ per manual; 45¢ per specimen set; postage extra; (20–40) minutes; prepared by the Department of Educational Research, Ontario College of Education, University of Toronto; distributed by Vocational Guidance Centre. *

NILA BANTON SMITH, *Professor of Education, New York University, New York, New York.*

This test is designed primarily to assist the teacher in making a diagnosis of the word recognition and word analysis skills of individual children. It is supposed to supplement the word-recognition and vocabulary test in the *Achievement Tests in Silent Reading: Dominion Tests,* a group test. While these two tests are intended largely for survey purposes, the *Oral Diagnostic Test* is designed to reveal more of specific individual weaknesses. It is intended to answer such questions as: Is the child careless? Are his methods of word-analysis immature? Has he any method? Does he have difficulty with specific sounds and blends?

The test consists of 100 words, printed on two oblong strips, with 25 words on each side. A tagboard sleeve or envelope with an opening cut in the upper part of one side is provided. As the word strips are pulled up through the sleeve, one word at a time is revealed in the opening. A Teacher's Record Sheet and Check List is provided for use in recording errors and methods of attack. Information about the test, directions for administering the test and recording responses, and suggestions for using the check list are included in the manual.

The selection of test items is open to question. The manual states that the 100 words were so chosen that all of the common letter sounds and blends are represented, the more important ones several times. No information is given in regard to the procedure used in determining the commonness or the relative importance of the letter sounds and blends. The manual states further that the words are roughly graded for difficulty, with more than half of them well within the scope of the average child at the end of Grade 1, but that some words are included with which all but exceptionally good primary readers are unfamiliar. No explanation is given of the procedure used in determining the relative difficulty of these words.

No reference is made to any attempts to ascertain the validity or reliability of the test. Norms are not provided.

This test cannot be considered a scientific instrument for use in diagnosing word analysis skills. However, as an informal check device, it would undoubtedly prove valuable to those seeking additional information about an individual's word analysis habits and skills. It is to be commended as a pioneer effort in an aspect of reading which has been little explored in the preparation of standardized tests.

READINESS

[566]

Gates Reading-Readiness Tests. Grade 1; 1939; 5 scores: picture directions, word matching, word-card matching, rhyming, letters and numbers; 1 form; $4.85 per 100; 30¢ per specimen set; postpaid; nontimed (50) minutes; Arthur I. Gates; Bureau of Publications, Teachers College, Columbia University. *

REFERENCES

1–5. See 40:1537.
6–8. See 3:516.

F. J. SCHONELL, *Professor of Education and Head of the Department, University of Queensland, St. Lucia, Brisbane, Australia.* [Review of the Australian adaptation.]

The manual and tests have been reprinted in their entirety by the Australian Council for Educational Research for distribution throughout Australia. In addition, tentative Australian norms are presented based upon 500 children selected at random from 50 different schools in Western Australia.

Evidence gathered in Australia indicates that a weighted combination of the scores in the Gates Subtests 1, 2, 3, and 4 and the IQ obtained from an individual intelligence test gives the best prediction of reading success as measured by the A.C.E.R. *Individual Reading Test.* In the report of the Australian testing it is indicated that "busy teachers with large classes and little time at their disposal might well use only Gates Subtests 2 and 3. The scores in Test 3 should be doubled and added to those of Test 2. A table for determining the percentile rank scores obtained in this manner has been constructed.

The material of the foregoing paragraph indicates in some measure what the reviewer has already urged in his *Psychology and Teaching of Reading* that teachers can obtain an effective indication of the readiness of children for formal reading by use of an intelligence test result together with an estimate of the extent of the meaning vocabulary. But in respect to reading readiness, what is perhaps much more important for Australian schools is the introduction of "look and say" and sentence methods based on vocabulary-controlled readers which are almost universal in American schools. The word whole-sentence method and vocabulary-controlled readers presuppose a preparatory or readiness period in reading instruction, and it is during this time that teachers can so readily determine which group of children is ready to go forward with reading. The lock step use of phonic methods in many Australian schools gives no such chance to determine which children are ready for reading, and which require time to mature intellectually and in vocabulary growth. In other words, readiness tests do not replace the informed estimate of discerning teachers using modern methods of teaching reading which in themselves provide a period to discover individual differences in equipment and to allow for the necessary maturation of some pupils. While state education systems use reading methods that push pupils willy nilly into reading instruction as soon as they enter school, a reading readiness test may be a very useful way of revealing individual differences in equipment.

For reviews by Marion Monroe Cox and Paul A. Witty, see 3:516; for excerpts from reviews, see 40:1537.

[567]

★**Group Test of Reading Readiness: Dominion Tests.** Grades kgn–1; 1949–51; 6 scores: discrimination of objects-symbols-words, listening-remembering-observing, familiarity with word forms, memory for word forms, motor coordination, total; Forms A ('49), B ('49); mimeographed manual ('51); profile chart ('51); $1.50 per 25; 15¢ per set of flash cards for any one form; 25¢ per manual; 65¢ per specimen set; postage extra; 31(45) minutes; prepared by the Department of Educational Research, Ontario College of Education, University of Toronto; distributed by Vocational Guidance Centre. *

[568]

★**The Harrison-Stroud Reading Readiness Tests.** Grades kgn–1; 1949–50; 6 scores: making visual discriminations (attention span controlled), making visual discriminations (attention span uncontrolled), using the context, making auditory discriminations, using context and auditory clues, using symbols; 1 form, '50; manual ('50); $2.10 per 25, postage extra; 44¢ per specimen set, postpaid; (90) minutes in 3 sessions; M. Lucile Harrison and James B. Stroud; Houghton Mifflin Co. *

WILLIAM S. GRAY, *Director of Research in Reading, and Emeritus Professor of Education, The University of Chicago, Chicago, Illinois.*

The scope and content of this test are based on the assumption that reasonable readiness in learning to read includes the ability to make visual and auditory discriminations, the ability to use context clues in identifying items that are inherent in that context, the ability to use auditory and context clues separately or in combination in identifying ideas represented by words, and the understanding that printed words stand for ideas. No evidence is presented in support of the validity of these assumptions. The test designers draw, rather, on their wide experience and on the extensive body of available scientific literature relating to requisites for progress in learning to read. There is little question about the validity of including tests of these abilities and understandings in a reading readiness test. However, it could be justly argued that the selection of test items should have been preceded by considerable specific research to justify their selection, as contrasted with others' which might have been included.

The tests used in this battery have been carefully designed as measures of the abilities and understandings selected as basic factors in reading readiness. For example, visual discrimination of the pattern used in reading is tested by asking the pupil to identify a given word (do)

in a series of four words. Ability to use content is measured by asking the pupil to choose and mark one of three pictures which best supplies an element missing in oral text. Ability to use auditory clues with context clues is measured by asking the pupil to listen to oral statements which suggest two possible responses illustrated in a group of three pictures. As implied by these examples the designers of the test have been quite successful in selecting test situations which measure capacity to use specific abilities in situations which approach closely the act of reading.

The form in which the test has been prepared is attractive and convenient. The directions for giving and scoring the test have been very carefully prepared. Six different scores are provided, on the basis of which recommendations are proposed as to the placement of a pupil in a reading group which moves rapidly, normally, or slowly, or his retention in a nonreading group in grade one, the kindergarten, or a transition group.

Unfortunately, only one form of the test has been prepared, the norms provided are based on results of experimental tryouts only, and no data relating to the reliability of the test have been published. Furthermore, no data are available concerning the prognostic value of the scores when used alone or in combination with intelligence scores and other available types of information.

[569]

*Lee-Clark Reading Readiness Test, 1951 Revision.** Grades kgn–1; 1931–51; 4 scores: letter symbols, concepts, word symbols, total; 1 form, '51—same as test copyrighted in 1943; manual ('51); $1.25 per 25, postage extra; 35¢ per specimen set, postpaid; nontimed in part (15) minutes; J. Murray Lee and Willis W. Clark; California Test Bureau. *

REFERENCES

1. LEE, J. MURRAY; CLARK, WILLIS W.; AND LEE, DORRIS MAY. "Measuring Reading Readiness." *El Sch J* 34:656–66 My '34. * (PA 8:4741)
2. WILMORE, WALDO W. *Relative Validity of Three Group Readiness Tests in Predicting Reading Achievement.* Master's thesis, University of Kansas (Lawrence, Kan.), 1939.

For reviews by Marion Monroe Cox and David H. Russell of the 1943 edition, see 3:517.

[570]

*Metropolitan Readiness Tests.** End of kgn and first grade entrants; 1933–50; 4 scores: reading readiness, number readiness, drawing-a-man (optional), total; Forms R ('49), S ('50); Form R manual ('49), Form S manual ('50); $2.35 per 25, postage extra; 35¢ per specimen set, postpaid; nontimed in part (65–75) minutes; Gertrude H. Hildreth and Nellie L. Griffiths; World Book Co. *

REFERENCES

1–10. See 40:1552.
11–15. See 3:518.
16. BAGLEY, JESSIE W. *Reading Readiness as Related to Achievement*. Master's thesis, Southern Methodist University (Dallas, Tex.), 1941. (*Abstracts of Theses....., 1941*, pp. 5–7.)
17. HERR, SELMA E. "The Effect of Pre-First-Grade Training Upon Reading Readiness and Reading Achievement Among Spanish-American Children." *J Ed Psychol* 37:87–102 F '46. * (*PA* 20:2076)
18. KOTTMEYER, WILLIAM. "Readiness for Reading." *El Engl* 24:355–66, 528–35 O, D '47. *

ERIC F. GARDNER, *Associate Professor of Education, Syracuse University, Syracuse, New York.*

Two alternate forms, R and S, of the widely used *Metropolitan Readiness Tests* have replaced the single older form. The new forms contain the same subtests as those in the original edition, except that the Similarities Test, which called for identifying dissimilar pairs of pictures, has been replaced by the Matching Test in which one of four objects similar to a given object is selected.

Several improvements in test format, related materials, and procedures have been introduced. Size of the test booklet has been increased, making picture material clearer and working space greater. Recommended time for administration has been reduced by ten minutes, and new forms now require three sittings instead of four. The carefully prepared scoring directions now include such features as special directions for administering the copying test to left-handed children and explicit instructions, with illustrations, for scoring subjective material.

The new forms include new and revised old items, the final items having been selected after item analysis from three experimental forms administered to 2,600 children in the beginning first grade from localities specified in the manual. The comparability of Forms R and S was independently investigated by administering each to randomly selected halves of an independent sample of 1,500 first grade children. This very praiseworthy and conscientious technical refinement is slightly marred by the sole unelaborated conclusion that "Analysis of the data from this experiment showed the two forms to be completely comparable throughout the range of scores in each subtest." The reader is uninformed as to how comparability was demonstrated (i.e., mean item difficulty, mean internal consistency, similar shape of frequency distributions of scores, difficulty indices or internal consistency indices, similar standard errors of measurement at corresponding portions of the distributions of scores, content, etc.) and what evidence was

considered adequate to warrant the term "completely comparable."

Norms are based on 15,081 white children from 56 communities in 26 states. The publisher offers to furnish upon request details regarding the normative sample and recently developed kindergarten norms. As an aid to teachers, tables are provided which permit the translation of the total readiness score (total raw score) into a percentile rank, and the reading readiness, number readiness, and the total readiness scores into letter ratings with verbal descriptions.

Median reliability coefficients (Pearson r's between two forms administered a few days apart) of six determinations, based on groups of from 90 to 273 of beginning first grade pupils, are provided for each subtest, for the sum of scores on Tests 1–4 (reading readiness), and for total score. Unfortunately, no evidence is provided as to the variability of these reliability coefficients. Means, standard deviations, and standard errors of measurement are also presented. The reported reliability of Tests 1–4 is .83; of the Numbers Test, .84; and of the total score, .89. The corresponding standard errors of measurement are 3.7, 1.9, and 4.6.

The manual appropriately advises against the interpretation of each subtest for an individual, pointing out that the reliability warrants the use of only reading readiness, number readiness, and total readiness scores. Would that other test makers would exercise the same technical competence and restraint. Too often, even in very popular achievement tests, do the authors propose individual diagnosis by means of subdivisions containing ten or even fewer items. Computation of the standard error of measurement would clearly show the absurdity of such attempts.

Face validity is claimed for the test, and some statistical data are presented as evidence of validity. Additional validity studies are reported in progress. In a study involving 487 cases, all of 44 pupils rated as "Superior" on the *Metropolitan Readiness Tests* administered in September 1948 were found to be above the national norm in average "reading achievement," and all but one above this norm in Numbers when tested in February 1949 on the appropriate tests of the Primary I Battery of the *Metropolitan Achievement Tests*. Of 46 pupils rated "Poor Risk" (lowest category) in 1948, 22 were found to be below the national norm in average reading achievement and 39 below in Numbers when tested in 1949.

Even if the norm is accepted as a minimal level of competence (which is certainly a debatable issue), it is to be noted that about half of those who were considered "unready" for reading actually reached the norm of achievement. Even so, the reported results are likely to be somewhat optimistic since the group reported was the same group from which the prediction formula was derived. The present interpretation of these data emphasizes even more than does the manual the extremely tentative meaning of the *Metropolitan Readiness Test* scores for individual diagnosis, especially in the more crucial lower range. The importance of additional factors in considering a child's readiness for first grade work cannot be emphasized too strongly.

These and other deficiencies (such as occasional out-dated pictures and poor phrasing of items) do not obscure a general high level of excellence and careful workmanship both with respect to item construction and statistical analysis. From the technical point of view, the *Metropolitan Readiness Tests* are among the superior readiness tests now available.

Teach Col J 21:15–6 O '49. Fay Griffith. * The correlations between the Metropolitan Readiness Tests given in September, 1948, with the reading score and the number score of the Primary I Battery of the Metropolitan Achievement Tests, given in February, 1949, are so startling as to indicate the value of the Metropolitan Readiness Tests in predicting school success of first grade children. The wise teacher will avail herself of their use.

For a review by Irving H. Anderson of the original edition, see 3:518; for a review by W. J. Osburn of the original edition, see 40:1552.

[571]
★**Murphy-Durrell Diagnostic Reading Readiness Test.** First grade entrants; 1949, c1947–49; 3 scores: auditory, visual, learning rate; Part 3 individual in part; 1 form; $1.70 per 25; $1.10 per set of flash cards; postage extra; 35¢ per specimen set, postpaid; Parts 1–2: nontimed (60) minutes; group administration of Part 3: (30–40) minutes; individual administration of Part 3: (5–10) minutes; Helen A. Murphy and Donald D. Durrell; World Book Co. *

REFERENCES
1. MURPHY, HELEN A. *An Evaluation of Exercises for Developing Auditory Discrimination in Beginning Reading.* Master's thesis, Boston University (Boston, Mass.), 1940.
2. BIGGY, M. VIRGINIA. *The Establishment of a Relative Order of Difficulty of Word Elements in Auditory Discrimination.* Master's thesis, Boston University (Boston, Mass.), 1946.

[572]
★**School Readiness Inventory.** Grades kgn–1; 1950; Forms A, B; both forms on 1 sheet; no data on reliability and validity; $1.25 per 25, postage extra; 50¢ per specimen set, postpaid; Katharine M. Banham; Educational Test Bureau, Educational Publishers, Inc. *

DAVID H. RUSSELL, *Professor of Education, University of California, Berkeley, California.*

This inventory is not a standardized test but a checklist of 25 items of "ordinary personal and social accomplishments of six-year-old children, regardless of whether they have attended nursery school or kindergarten." The items have been selected from developmental scales such as those of Gesell, Doll, and Goodenough, with certain items added by the author. They involve "footwork and balance," "handwork and vision," "speech and language," "personal independence," and "social co-operation." Their inclusion is a result of "observations in examining several hundred six-year-old children in school and child guidance clinics."

The author is on firm ground in emphasizing the motor, social, and emotional factors in readiness for the usual school work. The scale is also useful in presenting specific behavior items rather than generalities about six-year-olds' development. However, the author offers no proof that the items listed in the two forms of the scale are any more crucial for school adjustment and success than dozens of other items that could be listed. Even more serious, no evidence is given for the recommendation that children scoring 20 points or over are ready or almost ready to enter first grade, whereas children scoring below 15 points should attend kindergarten or nursery school or have a longer period at home. In a checklist of 25 items, the setting of specific critical points for school placement, particularly when unsupported by statistical evidence, violates both principles of test interpretation and knowledge of the continuity of human abilities. It is true that the author recommends a psychological examination for a more reliable estimate of the mental level of children scoring below 15 points. Throughout the accompanying directions, however, the only other remedy for the low scoring child seems to be postponement of entrance into first grade. The advantages of the child's staying with his age group, with modification of the first grade program, are never mentioned. Most school people would agree that postponement is not the only cure.

No evidence is offered that the inventory has the reliability or validity to predict early school success by itself. However, since it stresses social and emotional factors, it may be used as a supplement to some of the better known readiness tests, such as those of Hildreth, Gates, and others. (This supplemental use is not mentioned in the manual.) Used as a checklist it may help some teachers in understanding their individual pupils better.

SPECIAL FIELDS

[573]

*Ability to Interpret Reading Materials in the Natural Sciences: Iowa Tests of Educational Development, Test 6. Grades 9–13; 1942–51 (first published as a separate in 1951); for complete battery, see 17; Form Y-2 ('51—same as 1949 edition); manual ('51); general manual ('51); $3.75 per 25; separate answer pads or answer sheets must be used; $1.95 per 25 answer pads; $3 per 100 IBM answer sheets; 50¢ per scoring stencil; $2.50 per 25 first semester ('46) or second semester ('48) profiles for any one of grades 9–12; $1 per 25 self-interpreting profiles for students ('51); 25¢ per school summary report ('44); 4¢ per pupil score sheet ('48); 50¢ per specimen set; cash orders postpaid; 60(65) minutes; edited by E. F. Lindquist; K. W. Vaughn; Science Research Associates, Inc. *

For a review by Eric F. Gardner of the total battery, see 17; for reviews by Henry Chauncey, Gustav J. Froehlich, and Lavone A. Hanna of Forms X-1 and Y-1 of the complete battery, see 3:12.

[574]

*Ability to Interpret Reading Materials in the Social Studies: Iowa Tests of Educational Development, Test 5. Grades 9–13; 1942–51 (first published as a separate in 1951); for complete battery, see 17; Form Y-2 ('51—same as 1949 edition); manual ('51); general manual ('51); $3.75 per 25; separate answer pads or answer sheets must be used; $1.95 per 25 answer pads; $3 per 100 IBM answer sheets; 50¢ per scoring stencil; $2.50 per 25 first semester ('46) or second semester ('48) profiles for any one of grades 9–12; $1 per 25 self-interpreting profiles for students ('51); 25¢ per school summary report ('44); 4¢ per pupil score sheet ('48); 50¢ per specimen set; cash orders postpaid; 60(65) minutes; edited by E. F. Lindquist; K. W. Vaughn; Science Research Associates, Inc. *

For a review by Eric F. Gardner of the total battery, see 17; for reviews by Henry Chauncey, Gustav J. Froehlich, and Lavone A. Hanna of Forms X-1 and Y-1 of the complete battery, see 3:12.

[575]

*[Robinson-Hall Reading Tests.] College; 1940–49; 2 scores: rate, comprehension; 4 tests; no description of normative population; manual ('49); 4¢ per reading selection for any one test; 2¢ per any one test; 15¢ per manual; postage extra; 52¢ per specimen set, postpaid; (15) minutes per test; Francis P. Robinson and Prudence Hall; Ohio State University Press. *
a) A TEST OF READING ABILITY FOR ART. 1 form ['41].
b) A TEST OF READING ABILITY FOR GEOLOGY. 1 form ['41].
c) A TEST OF READING ABILITY FOR HISTORY. Forms Canada ['41], Russia ['41].
d) A TEST OF READING ABILITY FOR FICTION. 1 form ['41].

REFERENCES

1–3. See 3:533.
4. EDGERTON, HAROLD A., AND THOMSON, KENNETH F. "Test Scores Examined With the Lexis Ratio." *Psychometrika* 7:281–8 D '42. * (*PA* 17:1032)
5. HALL, WILLIAM E. AND ROBINSON, FRANCIS P. "An Analytical Approach to the Study of Reading Skills." *J Ed Psychol* 36:429–42 O '45. * (*PA* 20:1680)

ROBERT MURRAY BEAR, *Professor of Psychology, and Director of the Reading Clinic, Dartmouth College, Hanover, New Hampshire.*

These tests, devised in experimental studies of reading performance in four subject fields, provide scores for rate in words read per minute and for percentage of comprehension accuracy. Effort was made to achieve high face validity through use of assignment type material and control of testing conditions. Each test consists of one continuous passage of from 3,000 to 4,500 words in length. With the exception of the fiction passage—a story from *Collier's*—the material was taken from *Compton's Pictured Encyclopedia*. The student is instructed to read in his usual manner of reading assignments and told that after ten minutes he will be asked to answer questions of the type generally asked in class on such material. Test questions, chiefly multiple choice in form and dealing with the more important points, are printed on separate answer sheets. These features make the tests superior to those like the *Michigan Speed of Reading Test* which consist of unrelated short paragraphs in which the testee is asked to mark out an incongruous word. The separation between reading and answering questions makes the reading and the testing resemble the school situation and facilitates the ready identification of the shallow fast reader and the accurate plodding one.

One of the arguments for the short unrelated paragraph type of rate test has been the difficulty of securing high reliability for the continuous passage type. The authors state in the manual that for "our test" the reliability of rate over the 10-minute reading period is .91. A potential user should also be told the reliabilities for rate and comprehension accuracy of the individual tests. They are not shown, but the authors warn that the comprehension scores, especially for fiction, are less reliable than for rate and recommend in individual diagnosis the use of several tests in determining comprehension.

While as is often the case, the manual does not describe the standardization, it cites a report (2) by the authors which states that the subjects of the original experiment were 205 students, mostly freshmen and sophomores, in the College of Education in a required educational psychology course. For interpretative purposes, the manual provides tables of percentile ranks for rate and comprehension accuracy based upon the results of Ohio State University freshmen, but no indication is given of the number of cases involved or of how representative the sampling was.

There is only one form each of the tests for art, geology, and fiction. For history, there are two forms, one on Canada and the other on Russia. The history tests are very highly intercorrelated as to rate and as comparable as two forms usually are. While somewhat lower intercorrelations in rate were found between history, geology, and art, indicating some difference in the ways students read the material or in skills and abilities required in the different subject fields, they are high enough to indicate some overlapping. The still lower correlations between fiction rate and rates in art, geology, and Canadian history (.74, .59, and .62) suggest that differences in reading performance between fiction and nonfiction are more substantial. The intercorrelations between comprehension accuracy scores are generally even lower, but lack of knowledge of reliabilities of scores makes uncertain any generalizations. The authors report a factor analysis (5) which showed heavy loadings for what they term "attitude of comprehension accuracy" by all the comprehension tests, for "rate of inductive reading" by the art rate test, and for "rate for unrelated facts" by the geology rate test and to a lesser extent by the art and history rate tests.

The tests will be most useful to those wishing rate of reading tests based upon materials and conditions similar to those faced by college freshmen. They constitute a helpful approach toward what has proved a difficult task for testmakers, i.e., obtaining in a reasonable length of time measures of differences in reading performance in different subject fields. That the difficulty has not been wholly surmounted is apparent from the magnitude of rate intercorrelations. However, because of the length of the passages a more dependable judgment of rate can be obtained than is possible for most other tests of this type and as satisfactory as for any type. Though the comprehension accuracy score is somewhat less reliable than the rate score, comparison may be made between these scores which afford insight into some of the student's reading habits and levels of proficiency. A different type of reading test should be chosen, however, if an analysis of comprehension skills is desired.

[576]

★Tests of Natural Sciences: Vocabulary and Interpretation of Reading Materials: Cooperative Inter-American Tests. Grades 8–13; 1950; 3 scores: vocabulary, interpretation of reading materials, total; IBM; 2 editions; English edition: Forms AE, BE; Spanish edition: Forms AS, BS; no data on reliability and validity; tentative norms; $2.50 per 25; separate answer sheets must be used; 80¢ per 25 IBM answer sheets; 15¢ per scoring stencil; 50¢ per series manual; cash orders postpaid; 50¢ per specimen set, postpaid; 35(45) minutes; prepared under the auspices of the Committee on Modern Languages of the American Council on Education, Herschel T. Manuel, Director of Test Construction; Cooperative Test Division, Educational Testing Service. *

REFERENCES

1. BOU, ISMAEL RODRIGUEZ. A Study of the Parallelism of English and Spanish Vocabularies. Doctor's thesis, University of Texas (Austin, Tex.), 1944.
2. MCCRANIE, JOSEPHINE. A Study of Four Inter-American Tests Applied to High School Seniors. Master's thesis, University of Texas (Austin, Tex.), 1944.
3. KELLEY, FRANCES. A Study of the Inter-American Tests at the High School Level. Master's thesis, University of Texas (Austin, Tex.), 1945.
4. FIFE, ROBERT HERNDON, AND MANUEL, HERSCHEL T. The Teaching of English in Puerto Rico, pp. 171–313, 337–410. Prepared for the American Council on Education. San Juan, P.R.: Department of Education Press, 1951. Pp. xix, 410. *

CLARENCE H. NELSON, Board of Examiners, Michigan State College, East Lansing, Michigan. [Review of the English edition.]

These tests are designed to measure the pupil's ability to select appropriate words in vocabulary exercises and to read and interpret materials in the natural sciences. A feature which is quite unique is that two parallel forms of these tests are also available in the Spanish language.

Each form of the English edition consists of a vocabulary section of 75 four-choice items which progress from very easy to moderately difficult words commonly used in the natural science area. The exercises are presented in the form of sentences in which the task is to select one of the four words listed to fill a blank. The items in this section reflect, on the whole, careful workmanship on the part of the test builder.

The second section of each form employs a

series of well written one-paragraph reading passages, of increasing difficulty, drawn from different sciences. The three to five multiple choice items following each reading passage are intended to measure the accuracy of reading and the degree to which the passage is understood. While the preponderance of the items are designed to elicit responses which will indicate primarily the degree of understanding of the language of the paragraph, in some of the more difficult exercises the answers to the questions are not to be found in the reading material itself but must be based upon inferences from the facts presented. Items of the latter type measure an ability which is especially desirable in the sciences.

According to the manual, the English version of this test is designed for grades 8–13 when given to English-speaking pupils who are doing their school work in English, and the Spanish edition is designed for Spanish-speaking students in the same grades who are doing their school work in Spanish. The tests appear to be very useful in appraising the status of Spanish-speaking students who have enrolled for regular courses given in English in American high schools, colleges, and universities. By giving such students one form of the test in English and the alternate form in Spanish, a standard of comparison is provided whereby it would be possible to ascertain (a) the quality of their science background, (b) their relative proficiency in Spanish and English, and (c) whether any deficiency in performance is due to inadequate science background or aptitude, to lack of facility with the English language, or to a combination of these factors. The parallelism of the English and Spanish editions thus becomes a feature of special value in the orientation of students who wish to transfer from the one language area to the other.

According to the test builder, these tests have validity in the sense that the materials which provide the basis for the items were drawn from different fields within the natural science area. Furthermore, every exercise was selected on the basis of its power to discriminate between those who scored high and those who scored low on the particular section of the test under consideration. Comparable validity of the English and Spanish editions was sought by employing bilingual staff specialists, by using the same exercises in the two languages, by presentation of the exercises in equivalent language, and by

checking against standard word lists, such as the Thorndike list.

No index of reliability appears in the data accompanying this test, presumably because of the recency of the edition. Since it is of crucial importance for the prospective test user to have this information, it is hoped that reliability data will be forthcoming soon.

Quoting from the manual, "The Cooperative Inter-American tests of Natural Sciences represent a first attempt to provide measures which can be used to compare the performance of students from different linguistic and cultural backgrounds. They have been carefully constructed by bilingual specialists to eliminate, insofar as possible, idiomatic and cultural bias from the test materials themselves." These tests conform to the standards of good test construction. The format is attractive and the legibility is good. The tests should function well as measures of vocabulary and interpretation of reading proficiency in the natural science area.

[577]

★Tests of Social Studies: Vocabulary and Interpretation of Reading Materials: Cooperative Inter-American Tests. Grades 8–13; 1950; 3 scores: vocabulary, interpretation of reading materials, total; IBM; 2 editions; English edition: Forms AE, BE; Spanish edition: Forms AS, BS; no data on reliability and validity; tentative norms; $2.50 per 25; separate answer sheets must be used; 80¢ per 25 IBM answer sheets; 15¢ per scoring stencil; 50¢ per series manual; cash orders postpaid; 50¢ per specimen set, postpaid; 35(45) minutes; prepared under the auspices of the Committee on Modern Languages of the American Council on Education, Herschel T. Manuel, Director of Test Construction; Cooperative Test Division, Educational Testing Service. *

REFERENCES

1. Bou, Ismael Rodriguez. A Study of the Parallelism of English and Spanish Vocabularies. Doctor's thesis, University of Texas (Austin, Tex.), 1944.
2. McCranie, Josephine. A Study of Four Inter-American Tests Applied to High School Seniors. Master's thesis, University of Texas (Austin, Tex.), 1944.
3. Kelley, Frances. A Study of the Inter-American Tests at the High School Level. Master's thesis, University of Texas (Austin, Tex.), 1945.
4. Fife, Robert Herndon, and Manuel, Herschel T. The Teaching of English in Puerto Rico, pp. 171–313, 337–410. Prepared for the American Council on Education. San Juan, P.R.: Department of Education Press, 1951. Pp. xix, 410. *

Gustav J. Froehlich, Assistant Director, Bureau of Institutional Research, University of Illinois, Urbana, Illinois. [A review of the English edition.]

This test is part of an inter-American series designed to provide measures of ability and achievement in parallel editions of tests published in English and in Spanish. The Test of Social Studies is essentially a test of reading skills based upon social studies reading materials.

The idea of having comparable bilingual tests

designed to measure progress in a foreign language in relation to achievement in the native tongue is one worthy of development; however, the question as to whether or not the English edition of the *Test of Social Studies* is a valuable link in this development cannot be answered by this reviewer at this time. There is a dearth of objective evidence. The test manual is well written; it contains a certain amount of pertinent theoretical discussion; but it presents no concrete supporting evidence. No experimental data on validity and reliability have been found anywhere by this reviewer. The degree of comparability between the English and Spanish editions can only be inferred from the fact that an imposing array of experts spent many hours in the preparation of both editions.

To date the only available norms for the English edition are a single set of median scores for each grade from the sixth through the twelfth. These norms, furthermore, are highly tentative. They are based upon the data obtained from an administration of a preliminary form, the data being arbitrarily adjusted to obtain a single set of medians to be applied to both final forms in the English edition. This assumes a high degree of correlation between the two English forms, although no evidence is presented to substantiate such an assumption.

The reviewer is dubious of the value of the English edition when used "to discover more accurately the level at which pupils can read"— especially when used to discriminate between adjacent grade levels. The tentative norms show total score differences of only six, seven, and eight points respectively between adjacent grade medians for grades 11 to 12, 10 to 11, and 9 to 10; and differences of ten to twelve points for grades 8 to 9, 7 to 8, 6 to 7.

The mechanics of the test—its format, wording, type, and keys—are well executed, except that some testees might be bothered by finding a question mark splitting each blank in the vocabulary subtest, especially when a single word is the correct answer. A continuous blank without the question mark might be an improvement.

When considered as English tests of reading skills using social studies reading materials, the *Tests of Social Studies* comprise just another reading test, similar in form and content to a number of such tests currently available. When they are considered as a link in a series of bilingual tests of ability and achievement, a judgment of their worth must be held in abeyance until experimental evidence is made available.

MARTHA E. LAYMAN, *Associate Professor, Board of Examiners, Michigan State College, East Lansing, Michigan.*

These tests, utilizing materials from the social studies, have been prepared in parallel English and Spanish editions. Their purpose is to measure achievement in either English or Spanish and to compare achievement in the two languages on the part of bilingual students. In other words, for either Spanish or English speaking students one form would serve as a test of achievement in the social studies. A student with one of these languages as his native language and studying the other one as a foreign language would take Form A in his native language and Form B in the foreign language. By a study of his two scores authors of these tests claim that the teacher would be able to form some estimate of his ability in the foreign language compared to his ability in his native tongue. Thus a teacher of Spanish in the United States might discover that a student reads English at the twelfth grade level but is able to read similar materials in Spanish at only the eighth grade level. Yet the norms provided for this purpose are simply medians by grade levels based on the testing of 26,000 students on the Spanish forms in Mexico and Puerto Rico in 1943 and on the testing of 10,000 students on the English forms in the United States in 1943 and 1945. One is left wondering just how a teacher could determine very accurately how much better a student was reading in one language than in the other one.

The manual states, moreover, that "Because the Cooperative Inter-American Tests are being offered for general use for the first time, reliability statistics are not available at present." This is a most surprising statement in view of the claim on page 3 that the authors have had "several years of experience with the tests" and have made "many studies." Most test users expect authors and publishers to undertake the responsibility of providing such data when tests are offered for use in the schools.

Part I of these tests consists of 75 vocabulary items of the multiple choice variety. They are in the form of sentences, each containing a blank which the student is to fill from four possible options. The manual states that the method of selection depended primarily on subjective judgment as to concepts that were common to the two languages and which could be expressed in English and Spanish of approximately the same difficulty. In addition, use was made of Thorndike's, Buchanan's, and Eaton's word lists, and the test constructors were further aided in their selection by additional evidence as to relative difficulty of the tests within the same language obtained through administration of the items.

The terms are generally well-chosen from the various components of social studies courses. In the easier items there are wide differences among the meanings and sounds of the response words, but in the difficult items the response words are closer to one another in either classification, meaning, or sound. In a few cases the meanings given in the correct response are doubtful. For example Item 72, Part I, of Form AE reads, "The slaves of ancient Greece were known as ————." The correct response is given as "helots" but helots were *serfs* rather than slaves, and the term is accurately applicable only to Sparta, not to Greece as a whole. In the same part, Item 58 calls for "sedition" as the correct response to define "an action which causes a revolt against the government." Social studies teachers can rightly object to the sentence "All citizens have the right to vote because of universal *suffrage.*" Though *suffrage* is obviously the intended response the sentence is misleading, for of course not all citizens have the right to vote even under so-called "universal" suffrage.

Part II consists of several paragraphs drawn from various social studies materials each followed by a series of questions calling for an interpretation or evaluation of the reading passage. The test builders have avoided one of the customary pitfalls of reading tests by placing in almost all of the items one option reading "The question cannot be answered from the facts of the paragraph." Thus they have included very few items which could be answered without reference to the reading material. The passages are generally well selected and the items competently constructed.

The usefulness of these tests could be considerably increased by a simpler set of instructions and by more complete interpretative data.

STUDY SKILLS

[578]

★Bennett Use of Library Test. High school and college; 1947; Forms A, B; $1.15 per 25; 20¢ per specimen set; postpaid; 50(55) minutes; Alma Bennett and H. E. Schrammel; Bureau of Educational Measurements, Kansas State Teachers College of Emporia. *

LOUIS SHORES, *Dean, School of Library Training and Service, Florida State University, Tallahassee, Florida.*

The 130 questions related to "basic accepted rules and practices" in libraries aim to provide an "achievement test for evaluating the knowledge concerning library organization and practice by high school and college students." Content is covered in nine sections: the book (15 questions), the card catalog (14 or 15), decimal classification (10), subject headings (10), library terms (10 or 12), filing and alphabetizing (10), reference books (25), reference questions (24 or 25), and *Readers' Guide* (10). More than one third of the questions are true-false (54 or 55). Multiple choice and matching types are represented by 44 or 45 and 30 or 32 questions respectively. There are clear directions for administering the test in the manual, and there is a printed scoring key. The publishers report a reliability coefficient, under the corrected split half method, of .86.

Although the manual does not indicate how the content was selected, the questions cover most of the units usually included in high school and college freshman courses and orientation periods on "how to use the library." The section sequence, too, is approximately that of the dozen or fewer lessons prescribed for secondary schools by various state and regional accrediting agencies as well as by standard texts, and to that extent the test should fit in with present library-use teaching programs.

Many of the individual questions are well conceived. For example, Part II, Section B provides a good matching exercise for locating book subjects in the decimal classification. Similarly Sections C and E provide excellent practice in consulting a card catalog for specific titles or subjects.

The weakest sections, in this reviewer's opinion, are those which employ the true-false type of question. Perhaps it is only the inherent 50-50 nature of this type of question which appears

READING TESTS AND REVIEWS   [202

to reduce its effectiveness. But another objection
is suggested by Item 4 in Part I (Form B):
"The publisher of a book is the person who has
written it." This should, no doubt, be marked
false, but many a youngster will recall experiences with books in which that statement was
true. ·

Of the three sections in Part III dealing with
reference books, the multiple choice questions
of Section B, requiring the student to select the
best answer to a specific question from five
choices, offer the greatest learning opportunity.
Section A recalls to librarians the old fashioned
questions given to librarians-in-training in library school reference courses. Section C could
be simplified. For example, in Form A, Item
121, "Find an article continued in succeeding
issues of a magazine," it is not clear whether the
answer should be the title of the article, the
reference to the first issue, or the reference to
the second issue.

The word pseudonym has been misspelled in
both forms.

Despite these suggestions on detail, here is
the germ for a useful test in a much neglected
area.

[579]

★Cooperative Dictionary Test. Grades 7–12; 1951–
52; 5 scores: alphabetizing, spelling, pronunciation,
meaning, total; IBM; Form A ('51); manual ('52)
$1.75 per 25; separate answer sheets must be used;
$1.25 per 25 IBM answer sheets; 30¢ per scoring stencil; cash orders postpaid; 50¢ per specimen set, postpaid; 30(40) minutes; S. D. Melville with the editorial
assistance of Clarence Derrick and Anne W. Henry;
Cooperative Test Division, Educational Testing Service. *

[580]

★Edmiston How to Study Test. Grades 7–13;
1947–49; Forms A ('47), B ('47); manual ['48];
norms ['49]; $2 per 25; 35¢ per specimen set; postpaid; nontimed in part (45) minutes; R. W. Edmiston; the Author, Miami University, Oxford, Ohio. *

[581]

*Interpretation of Data Test: General Education Series. Grades 7–12, 12–14; 1939–50; except for
slight changes in wording, Lower Level: Forms A
('50), B ('50) combined are identical to Interpretation
of Data: Test 2.71 ('40), Upper Level: Forms A
('50), B ('50) combined are identical to Interpretation
of Data: Test 2.51 ('39); original tests published by
Evaluation in the Eight Year Study, Progressive
Education Association; 2 levels; data on reliability
and validity based on the 1939–40 tests; no norms;
manual ('50); separate answer sheets must be used;
60¢ per 25 answer sheets for any one level; cash orders postpaid; 50¢ per specimen set of any one level,
postpaid; (40) minutes; Evaluation Staff (Ralph W.
Tyler, Director) of the Eight Year Study of the Progressive Education Association; published in 1950 by
Cooperative Test Division, Educational Testing Service. *

a) LOWER LEVEL. Grades 7–12; 1940–50; 6 scores: general accuracy, accuracy in recognition of true or false
statements, accuracy with insufficient data, overcaution, going beyond data, crude errors; $2.25 per 25;
30¢ per set of scoring stencils.
b) UPPER LEVEL. Grades 12–14; 1939–50; 7 scores:
same as Lower Level, plus accuracy in recognition of
probably true and probably false statements; $2.50 per
25; 60¢ per set of scoring stencils.

REFERENCES

1–9. See 40:1544.
10–13. See 3:535.
14. SMITH, EUGENE R.; TYLER, RALPH W.; AND THE EVALUATION STAFF. Appraising and Recording Student Progress.
Adventure in American Education, Vol. III. New York:
Harper & Brothers, 1942. Pp. xxiii, 550. * (PA 16:5033)
15. WEISMAN, LEAH L. Some Factors Related to the Ability
to Interpret Data in Biological Science. Doctor's thesis, University of Chicago (Chicago, Ill.), 1946. Pp. vii, 176.
16. BROTHERS, WILBUR LEO. The Relationship of Certain
Factors to Effectiveness in Student Teaching in the Secondary
Schools. Doctor's thesis, Indiana University (Bloomington,
Ind.), 1950. (Thesis Abstract Series....1950, 1951, pp. 12–8.)
17. LUDLOW, HERBERT GLENN. An Analysis of the Ability to
Interpret Data and Its Relationship to Certain Other Aspects
of Pupil Status. Doctor's thesis, Indiana University (Bloomington, Ind.), 1950. (Thesis Abstract Series....1950, 1951, pp.
75–80.) (PA 25:7082, title only)
18. PLUMMER, ROBERT HOWARD. Characteristics and Needs
of Selected Ninth Grade Pupils as a Basis for Curricular
Changes to Meet Life Adjustment Needs. Doctor's thesis, Indiana University (Bloomington, Ind.) 1951. (Thesis Abstract
Series....1951, 1952, pp. 113–9.)

J. RAYMOND GERBERICH, *Director, Bureau of
Educational Research and Service, and Professor of Education, University of Connecticut,
Storrs, Connecticut.*

These pilot editions of the *Interpretation of
Data Tests* for the junior high school through
junior college grades are evaluation instruments
of the Eight Year Study issued as part of the
General Education Series of Cooperative Tests.
Forms A and B of the Lower Level test employ
the ten sets of data originally issued as Form
2.71, while Forms A and B of the Upper Level
instrument make use of the ten sets of data
originally found in Form 2.51. Each of the new
forms is therefore half as long as the "parent"
Forms 2.71 and 2.51 and recommended timing
has been reduced to 40 minutes.

Three criteria employed in the selection of
the data to be interpreted—that they be presented in a variety of forms, that they relate to
major problems in various subject areas, and
that they deal with various types of relationships—appear to be well met. At the lower level
pupils are asked to discriminate on a 3-point
scale whether each statement based on the data
presented is true, false, or uncertain as to truth
or falsity because of insufficient information in
the data. At the upper level a 5-point scale provides for two additional types of responses—
probably true and probably false, intermediate
in position between true and indeterminate and
between false and indeterminate.

Unlike the original 2.51–2.52 and 2.71–2.72

forms issued by the Progressive Education Association in 1939 and 1940 and the 2.51 form reproduced by the Cooperative Test Service in 1947, the new instruments are printed from type and they make no provision for machine scoring. Although a separate answer sheet is used with the new editions, it is not machine scorable. Instead it is scored by the use of a set of transparent stencils to be superimposed over the answer sheet. Six of the seven separate scores of the Lower Level test are obtained by the use of three such stencils, whereas six stencils are required in obtaining seven of the eight scores for the Upper Level test. The remaining score, for omissions, is obtained for each test by scanning the answer sheets. The scoring of the answer sheets hence becomes a rather involved and time-consuming process.

The publisher recommends that comparability of results from score to score for purposes of analysis, summarization, and interpretation be obtained by converting each score to a percentage of its possible value. Although the reviewer recognizes the difficulties involved in establishing comparability otherwise, he believes that these percentage scores are somewhat cumbersome, that they may well give those school officials indoctrinated with the percentage basis for marking pupil achievement an opportunity to misinterpret the results, and that the development of some other basis for comparability or the facilitation of the present one may be desirable. If the percentage base is considered preferable to any alternative scale, likelihood of frequent errors in computing percentages could be reduced and much processing time could be saved the test user by printing tables on the answer sheets for converting from raw scores to percentages.

A chart appearing in each manual shows how the results can be interpreted as to their general accuracy, the tendency to be overcautious, the tendency to go beyond the data, and in terms of crude errors. The general accuracy score is also broken down into three parts: accuracy with true-false items, accuracy with probably true or probably false items, and accuracy with items for which the data are insufficient. All are obtainable for the Upper Level test but only the first and last of the specialized accuracy scores are possible for the Lower Level test. Recommendations concerning the setting up of a Sample Data Sheet for summarizing test results also appear in each manual, together with illustra-

tive data and examples of interpretations of sample scores reported in the illustrations. The publisher could do much to insure utility of results for purposes of class analyses if Sample Data Sheet forms were printed and distributed with copies of the test booklets and answer sheets.

Norms are not provided by the publisher. It is true that the tests are definitely not keyed to particular courses or school curricula and that results from their use do not serve traditional purposes. However, these characteristics do not seem sufficient to preclude the use of norms in the interpretation of results. Most test users at the junior and senior high school levels doubtless prefer tests with norms to tests for which they must establish their own bases for comparisons of results. Norms by grades, and perhaps also by types of high school curricula, seem not only practicable and feasible but also likely to be highly useful. It is even possible that separate tests for such subject areas as the biological sciences, physical sciences, and social studies with differentiated norms would supplement these tests by providing somewhat more diagnostic evaluative instruments.

The validity of these instruments was considered by the publisher from two standpoints: (a) as a measure of the student's ability to judge interpretations formulated by others, and (b) as an index of the student's ability to write original interpretations. One validation technique was that of logical analysis, through which the test situations were so chosen as to allow the pupils to demonstrate the behaviors defined by the test objectives. The other, abstracted in the manuals from a more extensive treatment in Smith and Tyler's *Appraising and Recording Student Progress* (14), showed correlations ranging from .44 to .69 for Form 2.71 at the junior high school level and of .72 and .74 for Form 2.52 at the higher grade level between general accuracy scores and scores on an objectively scored essay test designed to measure the same outcomes. It is pointed out in the Upper Level test manual that these validity coefficients are for a test twice as long as each form of the current edition and that comparable coefficients for Forms A and B would necessarily be lower.

The test manuals treat reliability of scores only in two brief paragraphs referring the reader to Smith and Tyler and noting that the test user may obtain reliability data for himself by correlating scores on Form A and Form B.

Smith and Tyler report reliability data of several types for the original 2.71–2.72 and 2.51–2.52 forms. These data are often based on pupils in single schools and in several grades, so they leave much to be desired. They are also scattered through a number of textual pages and presented in tabular form by grades and separate schools in the appendix. It is improbable that the typical test user could adequately summarize or synthesize these reliability data if, which is highly doubtful, the book were available to him and he took the trouble to seek out and consult the reference. If and when he did, he would obtain evidence on tests twice as long as the current editions and data mainly based on pupils attending the progressive schools of the Eight Year Study.

As a means for obtaining further evidence concerning the reliability of scores and other characteristics of these tests, Form A both of the Lower Level and Upper Level test was administered to 99 twelfth grade chemistry pupils in the Crosby High School of Waterbury, Connecticut, in April 1951. Reliability coefficients were estimated for the various scores of both tests by the use of the Kuder-Richardson "Footrule," Formula 21, with raw score data. Reliability coefficients for the Upper Level test can be compared with a composite of the Kuder-Richardson coefficients reported in Smith and Tyler, page 511, for twelfth grade pupils on the original 2.52 form. The Smith-Tyler results for 234 pupils, presented separately for five schools, were weighted by use of Fisher's z-transformation and then transmuted back to Pearson product-moment r values. These in turn were stepped down to obtain reliability coefficient estimates for a test equivalent in length to the current Form A or Form B.

Estimates of reliability coefficients for the Crosby High School pupils and from the adjusted Smith-Tyler data respectively were found to be, for the various scores: .79 and .79 for general accuracy, .57 and .56 for accuracy with true-false items, .81 and .81 for accuracy with probably true or probably false items, .67 and .77 for accuracy with indeterminate items, .85 and .85 for overcaution, .68 and .87 for beyond data, and .62 and .41 for crude errors. In four of the seven comparisons the two estimates are identical or closely similar; only for scores on accuracy with indeterminate items, beyond data, and crude errors are the two estimates markedly different. For two of these—accuracy

with indeterminate items and beyond data—the Crosby coefficients are markedly lower than the adjusted Smith-Tyler estimates. The degree of conformance in results from the two estimates seems sufficient to warrant the belief that the reliabilities of the scores are relatively stable for the pupil groups represented in the two sets of data.

Doubtless more important than the comparability of results, however, are the magnitudes of the estimated reliability coefficients. They range from .85 to .41 for the Smith-Tyler adjusted data, with a mean coefficient of .72, and from .85 to .57 for the Crosby data, with a mean coefficient of .71. That these estimated coefficients are too low to justify the use of results from one form of the current test for individual pupil diagnosis seems inescapable, even for the more reliable overcaution, accuracy with probably true or probably false items, and general accuracy scores. Some of the other scores seem to be too unreliable even to warrant group comparisons when only one form of the test is administered. Adequate reliability for individual pupil diagnosis seems likely on scores for general accuracy, accuracy with probably true or probably false items, and overcaution scores if scores are based on the combined A and B forms, but the crude error score appears to be too unreliable for group comparisons even if results from Forms A and B are combined.

One other type of evidence on reliability of measurement was obtained from the Crosby data—correlations between scores on Form A of the Upper Level and Lower Level tests for the 99 twelfth grade pupils. These were .65 for general accuracy, .45 for overcaution, .44 for beyond data, and .32 for crude errors. When corrected for attenuation the intercorrelations for the same scores were found to be respectively .89, .74, .64, and .64. These results are in essential harmony with those presented above.

The fact should doubtless be borne in mind when interpreting these results that a diminution in reliability may be accompanied by an increase in validity, especially when a test purports to measure relatively intangible as contrasted with more traditional skill and knowledge outcomes. Insurance against overinterpretation of results seems possible through the exercise of proper caution and through the use of Forms A and B in combination when greater reliability than that obtainable from only one form is desired. So employed, these instruments for measuring abilities to interpret data should make possible for many test users a new and refreshing experience in pupil evaluation and the use of results distinctly different from, and more significant than, many of those obtained from traditional tests. These pilot editions can well be used to supplement tests designed primarily for use in those content and skill areas closely tied to school curricula and courses. The availability of such instruments commercially and as part of a significant series may well accomplish much both directly and indirectly in the improvement of school practices.

VICTOR H. NOLL, *Professor of Education, Michigan State College, East Lansing, Michigan.*

The original forms of these tests are now so well known that little description is needed. The 1950 edition of each test consists of Forms A and B made by splitting each original test in half. By so doing, the time required is said to be reduced to 40 minutes per form. In the report by Smith and Tyler (*14*) the Kuder-Richardson reliability of the Lower Level test (2.71) ranges from .80 to .91. For the Upper Level test the reviewer was unable to find comparable reliability coefficients in either the earlier report or the newer manual. Correlations between the original Tests 2.51 and 2.52 range from .65 to .85, for the different part scores obtainable, and the Kuder-Richardson reliability of the part scores on Test 2.52 ranged from .75 to .95. Splitting the original test into the two forms now published would almost certainly reduce the reliabilities. Unfortunately, the manuals give no information on this point. All statistical data on validity of these forms are also based on the earlier tests. Correlations between the general accuracy score of the Lower Level test (2.71) and an essay form of the test ranged from .44 to .69. For the Upper Level test (2.52) correlations between part scores and an essay form ranged from .12 to .80, when corrected for unreliability of the criterion.

Scoring is a rather cumbersome and time-consuming process. Both tests are *hand* scored by use of transparent stencils, the Lower Level test requiring three stencils and the Upper Level test, six. Each stencil yields one or more part scores. Seven part scores are obtainable on the Upper Level test and six on the Lower Level test. Each raw score is then converted to a percentage score.

One can hardly question the contribution of

these tests as new departures in evaluating rarely measured outcomes of instruction and learning. As pioneer attempts in a comparatively uncultivated field they were, and to a lesser extent still are, unique. There can be little doubt also that they have had a good influence on measurement practices. It is a matter of regret, therefore, that after more than a decade statistical data on reliability, validity, norms, and equivalence of forms are still meager or entirely lacking. It is doubtful, moreover, that the new editions will find wide use in schools because of the complications involved in scoring and interpretation. Finally, it has never to the reviewer's knowledge been shown that these tests actually measure unique qualities or abilities. They appear to be different, but it would be most interesting to see such evidence as correlations between scores on these tests and on good standardized tests of achievement in subject matter such as science or mathematics. Perhaps the publication of these tests in these so-called pilot editions will lead to more evaluation of their qualities as measuring instruments.

For a review by J. Wayne Wrightstone, see 3:535.

[582]

Logical Reasoning Test: General Education Series. Grades 10–12; 1939–50; except for slight changes in wording, Forms A ('50), B ('50) combined are identical to *Application of Certain Principles of Logical Reasoning: Test 5.12* ('40), which was a revision of Tests 5.1 ('39) and 5.11 ('39); original tests published by Evaluation in the Eight Year Study, Progressive Education Association; 10 scores: right conclusions, wrong conclusions, relevant judged relevant, irrelevant judged relevant, irrelevant judged irrelevant, relevant judged irrelevant, accuracy with definitions, accuracy with indirect arguments, accuracy with ad hominem arguments, accuracy with if-then arguments; reliability data based on the use of both forms; manual ('50); $2.50 per 25; separate answer sheets must be used; 60¢ per 25 answer sheets; 20¢ per set of scoring stencils; cash orders postpaid; 50¢ per specimen set, postpaid; nontimed (40–50) minutes; Evaluation Staff (Ralph W. Tyler, Director) of the Eight Year Study of the Progressive Education Association; published in 1950 by Cooperative Test Division, Educational Testing Service. *

REFERENCES

1–4. See 40:1528.
5. SMITH, EUGENE R.; TYLER, RALPH W.; AND THE EVALUATION STAFF. *Appraising and Recording Student Progress.* Adventure in American Education, Vol. III. New York: Harper & Brothers, 1942. Pp. xxiii, 550. * (PA 16:5033)

ROBERT L. EBEL, *Director, University Examinations Service, and Associate Professor of Education, State University of Iowa, Iowa City, Iowa.*

The title of this test carries considerable prestige, and the test itself is certain to interest many teachers. Unfortunately it possesses shortcomings which seriously limit its usefulness as a measuring instrument.

In the first place, the test emphasizes the application of several selected principles of rigorous logic, which is not generally useful in everyday thinking. Most practical problems can not be solved by syllogistic reasoning unless one introduces simplifying assumptions which are quite unacceptable on a common sense basis. This is recognized by the authors, who point out in the manual that the test "is recommended only for classes where conscious attention has been directed toward logical reasoning. Students are apt to wonder why they should attempt to reach logical conclusions, which are sometimes contrary to their better judgment, unless they have previously played the logical game." Logical reasoning as commonly understood involves much more than the exercises of this test would seem to indicate.

Secondly, the test places less emphasis on the process of arriving at a logical conclusion than on the logical defense of the conclusion chosen. There are 12 "supporting" statements to be judged relevant or irrelevant for each conclusion chosen. The authors suggest that one type of behavior which characterizes progress toward logical reasoning is "ability to isolate the significant elements in the logical structure of an argument as shown by distinguishing between statements of ideas which are relevant and statements which are irrelevant for explaining why a conclusion follows logically from given assumptions." That this ability is an essential part of logical reasoning, and that it is revealed in the manner suggested above, seem to be highly questionable assumptions.

It is worth mention at this point that the choice of a particular conclusion makes some of the supporting statements obviously relevant and others obviously irrelevant, so that very little analysis of the structure of the argument is involved. In Problem I of Form A, for example, conclusion X and statement 11 clearly favor one party to the dispute, conclusion Y and statements 1, 3, 5, and 9, clearly favor the other, while conclusion C, and statements 2, 7, and 12, are indecisive. This leaves only four of the statements which are not obviously tied to one or the other of the conclusions. If the response to one item in a test determines absolutely (except for chance errors) the responses to any others, no

useful purpose is served by including the others in the test. It is also worth mention that some of the "correct" conclusions can be arrived at by very superficial "logic." In Problem IV of Form B, for example, the examinee is asked to accept certain statements as true. If he then indicates as his conclusion that one of those statements *is* true, he is credited with logically correct reasoning.

In the third place, the test does not provide a single score which can be interpreted as a measure of ability to reason logically. While the data sheets show columns for 11 separate scores, only 6 or 7 are obtained if only one form is used. Moreover, it seems obvious that some of these 6 or 7 scores (e.g., number of right conclusions and number of wrong conclusions) must be highly correlated. Apparently the authors did not intend the test to provide any overall measure of logical reasoning ability.

The complexity of the task of interpreting scores is indicated by this statement from the manual. "The number of patterns of behavior is almost as great as the number of students who take the test. Each pattern should be considered as presenting a unique situation to be interpreted." Apparently the test is to be regarded more as a diagnostic instrument than as a tool for measurement, and the usefulness of the scores is assumed to lie in their stimulation of speculation rather than in the information they provide. It is questionable that the contents of the test merit the elaborate interpretation of scores which has been suggested.

Finally, while norms and analytic data are provided, they are not adequate. The composition of the norm group appears to have been fortuitous rather than deliberately planned. The manual recommends the test only for groups which have "previously played the logical game," but no mention is made of the extent of the game experience of the norm group. The reliabilities reported for the "conclusions scores" are low, as would be expected from the small number of conclusions involved. Reliabilities of the "relevance scores" are surprisingly high. Perhaps this is because the statements to be judged are very much alike, from exercise to exercise. Consistent interpretations of these statements are likely to lead to consistent responses regardless of the reasoning situation.

As a conscientious effort to open up a new field of appraisal of educational outcomes, the test deserves serious consideration. It is not, however, recommended by this reviewer as a valid test of logical reasoning.

[583]

Survey of Study Habits, Experimental Edition. Grades 8–14; 1944; 1 form; mimeographed manual; 5¢ per copy; 25¢ per specimen set; postage extra; non-timed (30) minutes; Arthur E. Traxler; Educational Records Bureau. *

REFERENCES

1. TRAXLER, ARTHUR E. "Some Results of an Experimental Survey of the Study Habits of Independent-School Pupils," pp. 40–9. In *1944 Fall Testing Program in Independent Schools and Supplementary Studies.* Educational Records Bulletin, No. 42. New York: Educational Records Bureau, January 1945. Pp. x, 49. Paper, lithotyped. * (PA 19:1812)

WARREN R. BALLER, *Professor of Educational Psychology and Measurements, University of Nebraska, Lincoln, Nebraska.*

This blank consists of 85 items grouped under 17 heads: keeping in physical condition for study, understanding the assignment, planning a study schedule, efficient finding of the necessary study materials, applying one's self consistently, fixing material in mind, reflecting, working independently, the prompt completion of work, persistence in overcoming difficulties, paying attention in class, participation in class activities, reviewing, memorizing, increasing vocabulary, improvement of reading rate, and maintaining an attitude of study. The survey items are statements which do or do not characterize the pupil and to which he responds by checking "seldom or never," "sometimes," or "usually or always."

The main purpose of the device is to afford the pupil a means of self-analysis of his study habits and a basis for related counseling. This definition of purpose should serve as a caution against the perfunctory use of the blank as a method of rating pupils' proficiency in study. Clearly the "score" which a pupil might obtain from this process of self-estimation would, at best, be a rough index of the satisfactoriness of his habits of study. Norms for grades 7 through 12 are available, however, and are based upon the use of the survey on a population of independent school pupils.

The author reports a split half reliability coefficient of approximately .91 for pupil responses at two different grade levels. But, quite appropriately, the point is made in the manual that this correlation reflects the internal consistency of the survey blank rather than the consistency of response on the part of pupils who filled out the blank. No repetition of the blank with the same group of pupils has yet been reported.

Correlations between pupil response to the blank and such criteria as achievement test performance, school marks, and teacher ratings of study habits make the validity of the instrument seem low. Median coefficients for these several correlations ranged from .14 to .24. (In some instances the correlations were as high as .42 and statistically significant.) It must be observed, however, that evidence of validity thus obtained is inherently capricious. For one thing, one would be over credulous to accept self-estimates as consistently accurate. For example, not every pupil with poor study habits would be likely to appraise his faults well, and not every pupil with good habits would know the extent and degree of his good behavior. Difficulties of this sort with the determination of validity are not unique to the *Survey of Study Habits*. It would be interesting to learn what would result —in line with this method of determining validity—from a carefully planned briefing of pupils about how most effectively to evaluate their study habits.

It is probably unfair to the Survey to place emphasis upon such tests of validity. The important question is whether the blank gets at the essentials of effective study and thus guides the counseling process along profitable lines. The practices which generally are given major attention in organized plans for the improvement of study habits seem to be well represented in the content of the blank. There are reasons for believing that the blank might prove even more effective for follow-up teaching and counseling were the headings, above the classes of items, fewer in number and better adapted to repetitive emphasis which teachers give to main ideas in this area of instruction.

[584]

★**Test of Critical Thinking.** Grades 7–9; 1951; 7 scores: inquiry, interest, relationships, openmindedness, generalizations, accuracy, total; 1 form ['51]; mimeographed; no data on reliability and validity; no norms for part scores; tentative norms; $8 per 100, postage extra; test may be reproduced by users; 25¢ per specimen set (specimen set must be purchased to obtain manual), postpaid; nontimed (45–50) minutes; M. T. Macy and Hugh B. Wood; University of Oregon Press. *

[585]

*****Test on the Use of Books and Libraries: General Education Series.** Grades 7–12; 1939–50; a revision of *Test on the Use of Books and Libraries: Test 7.3* ('39); original test published by Evaluation in the Eight Year Study, Progressive Education Association; 8 scores: the parts of a book, use of encyclopedias, use of the dictionary, sources of information, use of an index, use of the library card catalog, use of the *Readers' Guide to Periodical Literature*, total; Forms A ('50), B ('50); no data on reliability and validity; no norms; manual ('50); $2.50 per 25; separate answer sheets must be used; 75¢ per 25 answer sheets; 20¢ per set of scoring stencils; cash orders postpaid; 50¢ per specimen set, postpaid; nontimed (60) minutes; Evaluation Staff (Ralph W. Tyler, Director) of the Eight Year Study of the Progressive Education Association; published in 1950 by Cooperative Test Division, Educational Testing Service. *

REFERENCES

1. SMITH, EUGENE R.; TYLER, RALPH W.; AND THE EVALUATION STAFF. *Appraising and Recording Student Progress.* Adventure in American Education, Vol. III. New York: Harper & Brothers, 1942. Pp. xxiii, 550. * (*PA* 16:5033)

HENRY D. RINSLAND, *Professor of Education, The University of Oklahoma, Norman, Oklahoma.*

This test is designed to measure a very important objective in education for the fulfillment of which provision is not made in the usual high school subject-matter course—knowledge as to the proper use of books and libraries. Since the test is being issued in a pilot edition and statistical data are not available to show how well it actually achieves its purpose, it would seem to be in order to discuss here certain aspects of its face validity as they impress the reviewer.

The items based on information about the parts of a book, Part I, are well chosen, except that sometimes the author's full name is not given on the title page (Item 1, Form B) and the table of contents does not always contain an outline of the book (Item 2, Form B).

In Part II, Use of Encyclopedias, the student is asked to give the number of the volume in which he would look for information about a particular topic. For Item 20, Form B, the topic "The cause of thunder" is undoubtedly to be found under "Thunder"; but Volume 4 ends with the word "Thrush," and Volume 5 begins with the word "Thyrm," so there is no "Thunder" in the model encyclopedia. In this part an opportunity has been missed to discover whether students are aware that the alphabetical arrangement of topics differs with different encyclopedias—the *Encyclopedia Americana,* for example, using "word by word" order and the *Encyclopaedia Britannica* and the *New International Encyclopedia* listing words in "letter by letter" order. It is easy for a student to overlook a topic in an encyclopedia if he does not know the type of alphabetizing used.

In Part III, Use of the Dictionary, the directions should state that the five choices are not appropriate to *Funk and Wagnalls New Standard Dictionary* or *Webster's Collegiate Dictionary,* so that there will be no misunderstanding that these items primarily measure ability to use *Webster's New International Dictionary.*

In Part IV, Sources of Information, the style of underlining the names of books, as, for example, *Who's Who in American Education,* is not acceptable. These titles should be printed in italics or enclosed in quotation marks. In this part also, the reviewer does not favor the use of such expressions as "Ask an automobile salesman" or "Ask your druggist" as possible choices when what is needed is some real authority.

In Part VI, Use of the Library Card Catalog, the "word by word" method of alphabetizing should be emphasized since card indices in libraries, including the Congressional Library, are listed in "word by word" order—for example, East Moline, Illinois; East Orange; Easter; Eaton.

In spite of the specific shortcomings mentioned, this test has much to offer. In itself, the test represents an excellent outline for a unit on the use of books and libraries. As a test, it can be used equally well as a measure of achievement in this area of knowledge and for diagnostic purposes; in the latter connection, tabulations of items missed might serve as the basis for effective follow-up lessons. In reissuing this test, the Cooperative Test Division is, in the opinion of the reviewer, making a valuable contribution to measurement in a field where little that is really worthwhile has been done to date.

LOUIS SHORES, *Dean, School of Library Training and Service, Florida State University, Tallahassee, Florida.*

The 107 questions in this test are distributed as follows: 10 on the parts of a book, 10 on the use of encyclopedias, 20 on the use of dictionaries, 25 on other reference books, 14 on the use of indexes, 14 on the use of card catalogs, and 14 on the use of the *Readers' Guide.* Items on the use of encyclopedias are matching items; all others are multiple choice items. Since this test has long been out of print and since, despite some changes, the revision is "substantially the same" as the original form, the publishers invite suggestions.

Part I deals quite effectively with the five basic parts of a book, but it neglects preface, introduction, title-page verso (important in connection with Item 4 (both forms) dealing with the date), and even the use of running heads. Furthermore, there is nothing about the care of the physical book, basic in high school library instruction.

Part II, on the encyclopedia, provides 10

questions on one technique of encyclopedia use —guide words on the backs of the volumes. One or two questions would probably suffice for that point. Several questions are needed to test long article indexes versus short article cross references, "dummy" and "see also" references, kinds of illustrations, alphabetizing, and guide words.

Part III is confined to *Webster's New International Dictionary* and misses an opportunity to test dictionary contrasts, especially since most school libraries have *Funk and Wagnalls New Standard Dictionary* and several good abridged dictionaries, some especially designed for high school. Items like 34, 35, and 37, which in both forms are concerned with proper nouns, tend to confuse the pupils, since not all dictionaries provide separate alphabets for persons and places. The very important comparison of definition sequence is omitted entirely, yet high school students are frequently misled to believe that the first definition given is always the most important.

Part IV, on sources of information, needs typographical attention. Underlining of titles instead of italicizing or enclosing in quotation marks gives improper visual emphasis to some possible answers. The reference sources selected need to be reviewed in the light of newer school reference books.

In Part V, there is an error of detail: for example, in Form A the index entry for "oil gushers" is given as "510–12," but the best possible answer to Item 66 is given as "510 *to* 512." This type of error is repeated in several items in both forms.

The above examples indicate that review of details is needed. But even more important is a reconsideration of what constitutes library aptitude. Unquestionably, the skills necessary to use print and audiovisual materials are becoming an increasingly important aspect of student survival in an educational world of growing emphasis on many and varied instructional sources. The old-fashioned library lessons are probably as good a place as any to start, but certainly no point to stop. In terms of the conventional unit on how to use a library, this test is fairly adequate, but from the standpoint of critical literacy something more is needed.

[586]

*The Use of Library and Study Materials. Grades 9–16; 1939–41; 3 scores: finding information, interpreting information, total; IBM; Forms A ('40— same as test copyrighted in 1939), B ('40); norms only for entering college freshmen on Form A; manual

('41); $2.50 per 30; 25¢ per specimen set; separate answer sheets may be used; 1½¢ per IBM answer sheet; 25¢ per stencil for machine scoring of answer sheets; postpaid; 40(50) minutes; Mary S. Kirkpatrick, Lola Rivers Thompson, and Helen Tomlinson; Steck Co. *

REFERENCES

1. VOTAW, DAVID F. "A Comparison of Test Scores of Entering College Freshmen as Instruments for Predicting Subsequent Scholarship." *J Ed Res* 40:215–8 N '46. * (PA 21: 1304)

ROBERT MURRAY BEAR, *Professor of Psychology, and Director of the Reading Clinic, Dartmouth College, Hanover, New Hampshire.*

This test was designed to help teachers appraise student skill in the use of library and study materials. Since in the present state of test development in this field, it is easier to build items that check knowledge rather than the use of that knowledge, it is not surprising to find heavy emphasis upon the former in Part I, which concerns location of information. To a greater extent, use of knowledge is required in Part II, which is intended to test "ability to understand the material once it has been found." The 88 items of the test are all of the multiple choice type. The wide grade range has resulted in the inclusion of some tasks too difficult for many high school pupils and some references too little used or known by them, while for college students intensiveness of questioning is wanting at points and desirable items are omitted.

The items in Part I place more emphasis upon location of information in dictionaries, magazines, and reference books; classification and the card catalog; and using books. Too few of the 45 items in this part are devoted to each of these groupings to enable the teacher to analyze reliably the student's weaknesses, and there seems to be a disproportionate number of quite similar items requiring alphabetizing.

Almost half of the items of Part II belong in the general area of work-study skills. While librarians fortunately have a lively interest in the improvement of these skills, the emphasis given them reduces the amount of time available for the more specialized library usage items. Under the study skills category are some useful items dealing with reading a population growth table, interpreting a pie graph, locating items in the index of a book, reading a map, understanding a bar graph, and interpreting a time zone map of the United States. Of the more specialized sections, three comprise one third of the items in this part: the card catalog, the periodical index, and abbreviations found in books. Included with the latter are two general vocabulary items in

Form A and one in Form B and two items on recognition of diacritical marks in Form A and three in Form B, all of which seem to serve chiefly as space fillers.

In the manual it is stated that the two forms of the test are "thought" to be of equivalent difficulty. Percentile norms are, however, given only for Form A, and these are based upon scores of 2,356 entering freshmen in seven Texas colleges. Since the manual was copyrighted in 1941, there has been ample time to determine the actual equivalence of forms, to secure normative data for Form B, and to provide percentile scores for the other grade levels for which the test is said to be suitable. These the authors and publishers owe to the public.

According to the manual, choice of the content of the test was made in light of the experience of the authors, two of whom are librarians, and of a review of the literature of the field. Selection of most items depended upon whether they discriminated between high and low scorers on the test as a whole, thus ensuring a degree of internal consistency. As is often the case, the manual hesitates between the clinical and the statistical viewpoints. It states that examination of answers to items may be suggestive of individual needs and at the same time warns that "no great reliability is claimed for analytic scores." Doubtless the test does have some value for individual analysis, but the user should be very cautious since the split half reliabilities of even the two major parts are too low to warrant much dependence except in a group study.

In a field where a good test has yet to be published, this test may be useful, especially in senior high school and when the test as a whole is used as a measure of general work proficiency in the library. One wishing more extensive testing in library usage should look elsewhere. If, on the other hand, a satisfactory measure of ability to understand and interpret material is desired, it is necessary to supplement this test with one for reading comprehension.

For a review by Ethel M. Feagley, see 3:543.

[587]

*Use of Sources of Information: Iowa Tests of Educational Development, Test 9. Grades 9–13; 1942–51 (first published as a separate in 1951); for complete battery, see 17; Form Y-2 ('51—same as 1949 edition); manual ('51); general manual ('51); $3.75 per 25; separate answer pads or answer sheets must be used; $1.95 per 25 answer pads; $3 per 100 IBM answer sheets; 50¢ per scoring stencil; $2.50 per 25 first semester ('46) or second semester ('48) profiles for any one of grades 9–12; $1 per 25 self-interpreting profiles for students ('51); 25¢ per school summary report ('44); 4¢ per pupil score sheet ('48); 50¢ per specimen set; cash orders postpaid; 27(32) minutes; edited by E. F. Lindquist; K. W. Vaughn; Science Research Associates, Inc. *

For a review by Eric F. Gardner of the total battery, see 17; for reviews by Henry Chauncey, Gustav J. Froehlich, and Lavone A. Hanna of Forms X-1 and Y-1 of the complete battery, see 3:12.

[588]

*Work-Study Skills: Iowa Every-Pupil Tests of Basic Skills, Test B, New Edition. Grades 3–5, 5–9; 1940–47; for complete battery, see 15; 6 scores: map reading, use of references, use of index, use of dictionary, alphabetizing (Elementary Battery) or graphing (Advanced Battery), total; IBM for grades 5–9; 2 levels; Forms L ('40), M ('41), N ('42), O ('43); manual ('45); battery manual ('47); 33¢ per specimen set of any one level; postage extra; H. F. Spitzer in collaboration with Ernest Horn, Maude McBroom, H. A. Greene, and E. F. Lindquist; Houghton Mifflin Co. *
a) ELEMENTARY BATTERY. Grades 3–5; $1.60 per 25; 47 (55) minutes.
b) ADVANCED BATTERY. Grades 5–9; IBM; $1.75 per 25; separate answer sheets may be used; 63¢ per 25 IBM answer sheets; 40¢ per set of stencils for machine scoring of answer sheets; 77(90) minutes.

For reviews by Miriam M. Bryan and Anton Thompson of the complete battery, see 15; for a review by J. Wayne Wrightstone, see 3:545; for reviews by Frederic L. Ayer, Gustav J. Froehlich, and Ralph C. Preston of the complete battery, see 3:10; for a review by Harriet M. Barthelmess of the 1937 form, see 38:872; for reviews by William A. Brownell, J. Murray Lee, and Charles W. Odell of the 1937 form of the complete battery, see 38:872.

REPRINTED FROM *The Fifth Mental Measurements Yearbook*

READING—FIFTH MMY

REVIEWS BY *Janet G. Afflerbach, Lois Grimes Afflerbach, Joan Bollenbacher, N. Dale Bryant, Reginald R. Dale, James Deese, Clarence Derrick, Jerome E. Doppelt, Lydia A. Duggins, S. S. Dunn, Henry S. Dyer, Robert Ebel, Leonard S. Feldt, Eric F. Gardner, Marvin D. Glock, Neil Gourlay, J. Thomas Hastings, A. N. Hieronymus, Walker H. Hill, James R. Hobson, Carl I. Hovland, Duncan Howie, Russell P. Kropp, Charles R. Langmuir, Roy D. Lewis, R. W. McCulloch, James Maxwell, Louis C. Nanassy, Stanley Nisbet, Victor H. Noll, S. A. Rayner, Maynard C. Reynolds, Helen M. Robinson, Benjamin Rosner, Fred J. Schonell, Donald E. P. Smith, George D. Spache, Russell G. Stauffer, Harry L. Stein, Ruth M. Strang, Agatha Townsend, Arthur E. Traxler, B. H. Van Roekel, Magdalen D. Vernon, Verna L. Vickery, D. K. Wheeler, Stephen Wiseman, C. Gilbert Wrenn, and J. Wayne Wrightstone.*

[616]
A.C.E.R. Silent Reading Tests. Grades 3–8 and adults (Part 1, Form B only); 1933–57; Forms A, B ['33]; 5 tests; 18s. per 10 copies of all tests; 3s. 6d. per manual ['34]; 5s. per specimen set; postpaid within Australia; Australian Council for Educational Research. *
a) PART I, WORD KNOWLEDGE. 3s. per 10 tests; 8(10) minutes. (An Adult Form B ['54, identical to grades 3–8 Form B except for directions] is also available; 9d. per set of mimeographed instructions ['57] and 18-year-old norms ['54].)
b) PART 2, SPEED OF READING. 3s. per 10 tests; 3(5) minutes.
c) PART 3, READING FOR GENERAL SIGNIFICANCE. Optional; 4s. per 10 tests; 6(10) minutes.
d) PART 4, READING TO NOTE DETAILS. 4s. per 10 tests; 10(15) minutes.

e) PART 5, READING FOR INFERENCE. Optional; 4s. per 10 tests; 6(10) minutes.

FRED J. SCHONELL, *Professor of Education, University of Queensland, Brisbane, Australia.*

The standardisation of this test was carried out in 1933 on approximately 33,000 state school children in 469 schools throughout Australia. It would seem that the standardisation was adequately done and that careful statistical measures were employed in connection with the test. However, due to the fact that there is evidence of a slight move forward in silent reading abilities in several Australian states, it would seem that there is a need for a more recent standardisation.

The reliability of each part was determined by retesting 1,800 children in grades 3–8. It seems a pity, however, that the retesting was done on successive days. It is a more realistic procedure to allow a somewhat greater interval on which to base the reliability of a test.

An examination of the intercorrelations among the various parts of the test shows that there is a fairly close correspondence among them; this is a fair indication that they are measuring valid aspects of reading ability. It is also suggested that a shorter form of the test may be given by omitting Parts 3 and 5. The evidence is that these may be omitted without any appreciable decrease in reliability.

Raw scores have been changed to scale scores for each of the five subtests so that educational ages may be obtained. Centile graphs are also given, but, again, it is doubtful whether these are of any great value to the ordinary class teacher. Grade norms are also provided. These may be used for obtaining the position of an individual child in the grade or for determining the standing of a grade as a whole. Norms are given separately for each state.

[617]

A.C.E.R. Silent Reading Test, Form C. Grades 4–6; 1946–50; Form C ['46]; 3 parts; 12s. per 10 tests of all parts; 2s. per scoring key; 5s. per manual ['50]; 8s. per specimen set; postpaid within Australia; Australian Council for Educational Research. *
a) PART 1, WORD KNOWLEDGE. 3s. per 10 tests; 10(20) minutes.
b) PART 2, SPEED OF READING. 4s. per 10 tests; 6(15) minutes.
c) PART 3, READING FOR MEANING. 5s. 6d. per 10 tests; 20(30) minutes.

REFERENCE
1. WHEELER, D. K. "Reading Speed of W.A. Children." *Educand* 2:4–9 N '54.

FRED J. SCHONELL, *Professor of Education, University of Queensland, Brisbane, Australia.*

Part 1, Word Knowledge, is a vocabulary test consisting of 100 words of increasing difficulty in 5-choice multiple choice form. There are eight practice examples. Part 2, Speed of Reading, consists of a story of 2,950 words, preceded by a short practice passage. In each 50 words there are 47 words of prose and 3 words in brackets from which one must be chosen for completion of the sentence. Although the comprehension aspect of this subtest has been kept to a minimum, it is, nevertheless, a test of both speed and comprehension. Part 3, Reading for Meaning, is composed of paragraphs of varied context and increasing difficulty. Testees answer two questions on each paragraph.

It is suggested that the subtests should be given in the order of their standardisation: Speed of Reading, Reading for Meaning, Word Knowledge. They have been carefully compiled and constitute a very useful battery for measuring the reading abilities of children between the ages of 9 and 12. They were standardised in 1946 on 30,000 children from nearly 600 schools in the six states. The only possible weakness may derive from the fact that teachers gave the tests. For purposes of standardisation, it is always advisable to have tests given by trained workers.

The scoring method is straightforward and the form of interpretation of scores sound and well based. Care has been taken in the calculation and presentation of norms. Five types are provided—grade norms, grade medians, age norms, age medians, and age-in-grade norms—separately for each state.

Both age and grade norms are given on a 15-point scale, but it is doubtful whether many primary teachers ever use a 15-point scale in marking. Hence, the scale scores will not be particularly meaningful to them. Again, while results from these tests are extremely useful for those engaged in surveys and counseling work, it is unlikely that teachers make much use of centile grading. The class teacher who wishes to discover the level of attainment of his children in reading wants a readily understood scale presented in terms of reading age or grade level, even if there is a small element of error attachable to such a measure. It is difficult to see why separate norms for boys and girls are given in the age norms, but not in the grade norms—surely the same sex differences still operate.

However, these are minor criticisms and the tests may be strongly recommended. They are sound, reliable measures and the standardisation reveals very thorough statistical work.

D. K. WHEELER, *Senior Lecturer in Education, University of Western Australia, Nedlands, Australia.*

Because of its availability the reviewer has used this test in schools, but with reservations, particularly about Part 1, Word Knowledge. In similar vocabulary tests it is usual, and seems good practice, to follow the test words by similar parts of speech. In at least 40 per cent of these examples this is not done.

Despite the fact that it is not a test of ability to follow instructions, there are items likely to mislead. In many cases, distractors are words which in context could be closely associated with the test word, e.g., "large" (test word) has as one choice "man"; "separate" has "chaff." The test is not one of visual discrimination; yet "thorough" has as choices "trough" and "tough." Finally, there are 17 items where one choice belongs in the schoolboy howler or boner class. "Colt" has as a choice "frozen"; "signature" has "young swan"; "escalator" both "horse-rider" and "Alpine climber"; "surplus" has "clerical collar"; "chicanery" has "inferior coffee." English teachers will object to "lie back" being taken as the correct answer for "recline" when "rest" is also included as a choice, and teachers generally will object to "storehouse" given for "silo" or "brute" for "thug." Purists may well object to other items such as 24, 79, and 93.

Part 2, Speed of Reading, is a 2,950-word selection. Forty-seven words of continuous prose are followed by three words in parentheses under one of which a line must be drawn to make best sense. According to the manual, all words are within the vocabulary of the fourth grade child and the difficulty of comprehension has as far as possible been kept constant throughout. The writer applied the Lorge and the Dale-Chall readability formulas to words 1294–1403 and 2213–2310. Both readability measures indicated a sixth grade level.

Part 3, Reading for Meaning, consists of 30 paragraphs (19 to 83 words long) of varied content and increasing difficulty, each with two multiple choice questions. About half of the questions are concerned with the main idea ("This story tells you about" or "The best name for this story is"). About one sixth are concerned with detail and about one third require inferences to be made. Occasionally, both questions ask much the same thing (e.g., 39 and 40, 45 and 46).

Answers are checked on test papers and marked with a key. Some care should be exercised with the keys, as the one sent for review needed taking to pieces and rearranging before use. The general format of the tests is good, the cover page of each test being devoted to instructions and adequate practice examples.

Part 1 might be better set out to avoid the difficulty for middle school children of following a question clear across the page. The manual is comprehensive and contains descriptions, detailed instructions, and norms.

In the manual it is suggested that "until experimental evidence is available as to whether the order of administration of the tests is important, it is recommended that they be given in the order followed in the original standardization," that is, 2, 3, 1. As 12 years have passed since the test was first published, either this evidence should be forthcoming or the tests should be renumbered in the proper sequence.

The norms were derived in 1946 from a sample of 30,000 children in 600 schools in six Australian states. Raw scores are converted to normalized standard scores. Age and grade norms are adequate and detailed. There is no provision for a total reading score. The speed test has no norms in terms of rate, only in terms of correct answers from which one can derive rate norms, assuming all children get all answers correct.

Three paragraphs in the manual are devoted to validity. For Part 1, no details are given as to how words were "chosen from the Thorndike and other word lists and subjected to experimental testing." "Only the most satisfactory items were retained. The test can therefore be regarded as a valid measure of a child's ability to select synonyms within the range of general vocabulary." In view of previous remarks about Part 1, it would be of interest to know the criteria by which the items were judged satisfactory. Part 2 exhibits face validity for similar material rather self-consciously culture oriented. Reading for meaning is a blanket term which here at least covers reading for main ideas, for detail, and for inference. Whether the weighting in these areas is deliberate or accidental is not known.

Reliability is given as .93 for Part 1 (split-half), .82 for Part 2 (parallel-forms), and .91 for Part 3 (split-half). The numbers on which these reliabilities are based (149, 134, 151) seem small in view of the extensive sampling, and no indication is given of the age and grade ranges of the samples for which they were computed. The inference is that the standard error of measurement is constant over the total range. Experience would suggest it is not.

Parts 1 and 3 could be used anywhere, subject to the objections made to Part 1. Part 2 is so Australian in its flavour and includes so many local words (boomerang, wallaby, bull-roarer, etc.) that its use is restricted to Australian schools.

As the reading test most easily available to Australian teachers, this is, in parts, in need of revision.

[618]

*A.C.E.R. Silent Reading Tests: Standardized for Use in New Zealand. Ages 9–12; 1934–55; 1 form; manual ['55]; 3 parts; 2s. 3d. per specimen set; postage extra; manual by A. E. Fieldhouse; tests by Australian Council for Educational Research; New Zealand Council for Educational Research; distributed by Educational Books. *
a) PART 1, WORD KNOWLEDGE. Same as corresponding part of *A.C.E.R. Silent Reading Test;* Form C ['46]; 6s. 3d. per 25 tests; 10(20) minutes.
b) PART 2, SPEED OF READING. Same as corresponding part of *A.C.E.R. Silent Reading Test;* Form B ['34]; 6s. 3d. per 25 tests; 3(10) minutes.
c) PART 3, READING FOR MEANING. Same as corresponding part of *A.C.E.R. Silent Reading Test;* Form C ['46]; 12s. 6d. per 25 tests; 20(35) minutes.

[619]

*Achievement Test in Silent Reading: Dominion Tests. Grades 1, 2, 2–3, 3–4, 4–6, 5–6; 1941–57; postage extra; Department of Educational Research, Ontario College of Education, University of Toronto; distributed by Guidance Centre. *
a) PRIMARY. Grade 1; 1941–53.
  1) *Type 1, Word Recognition.* 1941–53; Forms A, B ('41); revised manual ('57); $1.10 per 25 tests; 20¢ per complete specimen set; 10(20) minutes.
  2) *Type 2, Phrase and Sentence Reading.* 1941–53; Forms A, B ('41); revised manual ('53); $1.45 per 25 tests; 20¢ per complete specimen set; 20(30) minutes.
  3) *Type 3, Paragraph Reading.* 1943–53; 1 form ('43); $1.35 per 25 tests; 25¢ per manual ('45); 30¢ per specimen set; 30(40) minutes.
  4) *Type 4, Diagnostic Test in Word Recognition.* 1943–53; 1 form ('45); $1 per 25 tests; 25¢ per manual ('45); 30¢ per specimen set; 30(40) minutes.
b) TYPE 1, VOCABULARY. Grades 2–3, 4–6; 1943–56; Forms A, B ('43); 2 levels; $1.10 per 25 tests; 10¢ per manual ('53) for each level; 20¢ per complete specimen set of either level; (30) minutes.
c) TYPE 2, DIAGNOSTIC TEST IN PARAGRAPH READING. Grades 2, 3–4, 5–6; 1943–56; 2 forms; 3 levels; 10¢ per manual ('53) for each level; $1.45 per 25 tests; 25¢ per complete specimen set of any one level; 30(40) minutes.
  1) *Grade 2.* 1943–55; Forms A, B ('43).
  2) *Grades 3–4.* 1946–56; Forms A, B ('46).
  3) *Grades 5–6.* 1948–53; Forms A, B ('48).

HARRY L. STEIN, *Professor of Education, University of British Columbia, Vancouver, British Columbia, Canada.*

This battery was carefully reviewed in *The Third Mental Measurements Yearbook* by Mc-Kim. Since that time three tests have been added: a Diagnostic Test of Word-Analysis Skills for grade 1, administered individually;

a Diagnostic Test in Paragraph Reading for grades 3–4; and a similar test for grades 5–6.

Two important comments should be added to those made by McKim. First, of the 10 tests in the battery, 5 are labeled as diagnostic tests. As such, they should be administered at the beginning of the year rather than at the end, as are the achievement tests. In this way, their diagnostic function could be put to valuable use by teachers through a well designed program of remedial work. To this end, of course, norms should be established for the beginning of the year. Secondly, users of these tests should be careful to note that the fact that the tests are titled "The Dominion Tests" should not be interpreted as meaning that the tests are necessarily standardized on pupils in all provinces of the Dominion of Canada.

The norms for these tests were revised in 1953. Test users may obtain from the publishers an insert for the manual. This insert includes percentile norms, grade norms, and error norms, and replaces two norms tables in the manual. The new norms are based upon the administration of the tests to some 7,000 pupils in the province of Ontario. One might question the adequacy of the sampling for individual grades in both rural and urban schools.

Some attempt has been made in the revised insert (June 1953) to explain how the error levels for the paragraph reading tests were determined. However, for the lay reader, the wording of this explanation is not very clear. In any event, from a normative standpoint, the value for the teacher of this aspect of the test may be very limited. To make a diagnosis by the method suggested entails more than a modest amount of clerical work, and if the reliability of the diagnosis is low because of the rough estimation of level obtained, the game may not be worth the candle. The table of norms should, however, be very valuable for a general diagnosis of the nature of errors crudely classified, as they are in the error norms, as "Beginnings," "Middles," "Endings," "Reversals," and "Configurations." A machine scoring method of counting these errors would save the teacher a good deal of time.

In spite of the limited sampling, the tests in the primary battery are maintaining a high degree of internal consistency. The latest manual reports reliabilities for Types 3 and 4 of .90 and .94. In the earlier manual the reported reliabilities were .96 and .95.

As a whole, the battery is a strong one and should continue to serve a useful purpose. The format continues to be excellent and the curricular validity acceptable. For local use, the norms should be considered only as a rough guide to level of achievement.

MAGDALEN D. VERNON, *Professor of Psychology, University of Reading, Reading, England.*

This battery, which has been prepared for the group testing of silent reading in grades 1–6 in Canadian schools, falls into two parts. The first part, intended to test the achievement of first graders in the mechanics of reading, includes tests of the ability to match pictures against single words, phrases and short sentences, and paragraphs. The words, selected from books in use in some Canadian schools, are arranged in order of difficulty as given in Gates' *Reading Vocabulary for Primary Grades.* This method of selection must make somewhat difficult the comparison of reading performance in schools which do and schools which do not use these books, since some of the words appear far too difficult for 6- and 7-year-old children unless they have been taught them specifically. However, it is probable that written group tests for children of this age can give no more than a very rough assessment of achievement for any individual child, though they may be valuable for measuring the general level of achievement of a whole class or grade.

This criticism applies more strongly to the fourth of the grade 1 tests, the Diagnostic Test in Word Recognition. This is intended to show, from the pattern of errors made by individual children, whether they tend to make most mistakes in the endings, middles, or beginnings of words; to substitute words with the same letters in a different order; or to substitute words of the same general shape. The children may then be given special drill in overcoming a particular type of error. Now, even supposing that the grade 1 child manages to cope with such a group test adequately, there is no evidence that he will consistently make one of these types of error rather than other types, or indeed that this differentiation of types of error has any particular significance with regard to difficulties in reading. Before any remedial measures are applied, any child who makes a large number of errors of any kind should be given individual reading tests designed to diagnose the fundamental nature of his difficulties—to show, for instance, if he has learnt to analyse words phonetically and blend the phonetic units.

The second part of the battery, containing tests for grades 2–6, consists of two types of tests in paragraph reading—vocabulary and diagnostic tests. No information is given as to how the words for the vocabulary tests were selected, except that they were "constructed and standardized with the active assistance and advice of experienced public school teachers." Many of the words are most unlikely to be within the comprehension of children with the ages given. However, since the child has to choose one word out of four that "goes best" with the test word, he can guess to a certain extent from general similarity of meaning.

No explanation is given as to why this type of test was chosen for assessing reading achievement; nor do its results appear to have been correlated with those of the second type, Diagnostic Tests in Paragraph Reading, or with other measures of reading ability. The diagnostic tests, however, appear to be the most valuable type of test in the battery. The child's answers to questions on the paragraphs read are designed to show if he can grasp the general topic of the paragraph, pick out some important details, and make simple inferences from what he reads. Clearly, all these processes are essential to the development of efficient reading once the child has acquired the fundamental mechanics, and it is important to detect whether a child fails in any one of them. But it would seem advisable to supplement these tests by one designed to determine whether failures were due to inability to read a sufficient number of the words of the paragraphs, or to failure to understand the words or sentences contained in them. Again, individual tests for cases of failure would be most desirable to discover the exact cause of difficulty.

It is unfortunate that the directions, score norms, and methods of standardization are given only in separate manuals for each test. There is no general explanation as to how the tests were designed, how they should be used, and what is the general significance of results on the separate tests or of differences in performance on the several tests. There seems to be some danger that individual teachers may use the tests appropriate to the grades they are teaching in a mechanical fashion, chalking up the error scores of each child and then automatically drilling him in the task in which he seems least efficient. It is to be hoped that when the format of all the test instructions has been revised, a comprehensive manual will be prepared explaining just what is the significance of the results of each test in relation to the others, and what conclusions can be drawn from such results. Moreover, such a manual could contain a more systematic presentation of instructions, answer keys, and norms; a description of the standardization process; and a report of calculations of reliability and internal consistency. The standardization appears to have been carried out satisfactorily on an adequate number of rural and urban children, for whom separate norms are given. Reliability and internal consistency are high, but the separate manuals of directions and their supplementations and revisions are so confused and unsystematic in presentation that it is difficult to understand the rationale of the tests and to follow the method and results of their standardization.

This battery of tests, therefore, requires a more systematic presentation of the explanatory material before it can be finally assessed. In particular, we need to know more about how and for what specific purposes the tests were designed and how the material was selected. At the present moment, the Diagnostic Tests in Paragraph Reading are the most satisfactory; the others are open to numerous criticisms.

For a review by Henry P. Smith, see 4:529; for a review by Margaret G. McKim, see 3:476.

[620]

*American School Achievement Tests, Part 1, Reading.** Grades 2–3, 4–6, 7–9; 1941–58; 3 scores: sentence and word meaning, paragraph meaning, total; Forms D ('55), E ('56), F ('57), G ('58); Forms D, E, F essentially the same as Forms A, B, C copyrighted 1941–43; 3 levels; 35¢ per specimen set of any one level; postpaid; Willis E. Pratt and Robert V. Young; Public School Publishing Co. *

a) PRIMARY BATTERY II. Grades 2–3; revised battery manual ('55); $1.75 per 25 tests; 25(35) minutes.
b) INTERMEDIATE BATTERY. Grades 4–6; revised battery manual ('58); $2 per 25 tests; 25(35) minutes.
c) ADVANCED BATTERY. Grades 7–9; revised battery manual ('58); $2 per 25 tests; 30(40) minutes.

RUSSELL G. STAUFFER, *Director, The Reading-Study Center, University of Delaware, Newark, Delaware.* [Review of Forms D, E, F.]

The teachers' manual accompanying Primary Battery II says:

The....tests....are designed to measure pupil achievement as early as the beginning of the second year of school and as late as the end of the third year of school attendance. Results....may serve a 4-fold purpose: (*1*) to measure pupil progress, (*2*) to assist in the classification of pupils, (*3*) to furnish data for remedial programs in the language arts, and (*4*) to diagnose pupil's knowledge of specific computations and problem-solving ability.

A similar statement of purposes appears in the manuals for the Intermediate and the Advanced Batteries. To appraise the extent to which the tests fulfill the purposes, the reviewer not only worked through each test but studied carefully the additional statements about how the test accomplishes the purposes.

The sentence and word meaning and the paragraph meaning items cover a wide range in vocabulary and in interest areas. In the paragraph meaning section certain questions can be answered without reading the story; for example, "The squirrel likes to eat....nuts." Many of the items require answers other than the parroting of facts, and this is good. The strategy is to present paragraphs followed by multiple choice questions. Many alert readers may soon discover not only that reading the questions first makes the reading of the paragraph more purposeful but that some questions can be answered without reading the paragraph. The items seem to do everything the authors claim for them. As is frequently the case with reading tests of this type, the reader has to read as many running words in the questions as he does in the paragraphs.

In the vocabulary section many of the correct answers cannot be obtained unless the sentence introducing the item is read. This is commendable. Some of the items involve opposites and would require no sentence setting. The more difficult items are not merely confusing items, but seem to reflect a good measure of breadth and depth of word knowledge.

The ceiling for Primary Battery II is quite adequate. The grade equivalents of the maximum possible scores are consistently more than two grades above the highest grade level for which the tests are designed. In the Advanced Battery the sentence and word meaning section requires 26 out of 40 items correct to achieve a score of 6.9. Only eight additional items are required to cover the entire grade range for which the battery is designed—grades 7–9. This is mighty thin selecting; it leaves only five additional items with which to run a score from 9.9 to 11.9. The Advanced Battery has enough bottom to test even the poorest student, but not enough top to test even the good student and certainly not the best student. The same is true of the Intermediate Battery.

This might lead one to believe that the Intermediate and Advanced Batteries would be especially useful as aids to remedial instruction, but this is hardly the case. The authors are right when they say the tests "do not purport to be diagnostic tests." As always, however, a study of items missed by a pupil might be helpful as a partial inventory of needs.

The statements made in the manual about how the tests can be used to classify pupils should be interpreted with similar caution. If pupils are to be grouped on the basis of test scores, reading instruction levels would in many instances be either too high or too low. Standardized test scores tend to overrate the instructional level of average and slow learners and underrate that of superior readers. Results could be used, though, as one source of information for grouping. Test constructors should be especially sensitive to false notions about the possibility of homogeneous grouping and should not suggest it even by implication.

Using test results to measure individual pupil progress is fraught with danger as long as the only norms provided are based on results obtained in large group testing situations. There is nothing wrong with this method of standardization if it is understood that the norms are not based on the results of individual testing. Much of the widespread misuse of norms as standards seems directly attributable to erroneous claims made by testmakers, either directly or by implication, for the use of test results.

According to the manual, curricular validation was thought by the authors to be most feasible because of the lack of adequate criteria for other types of validation. Therefore, the vocabulary of all the tests was "checked against widely used word lists and commonly used textbooks." Only the Thorndike Word List is mentioned as having been used, and there is no indication as to which of the Thorndike lists it was. Reference to word lists might have yielded greater validity evidence: those of Rinsland, Gates, Horn, and Spache, for example. Some of the published vocabulary studies of commonly used basal readers might have provided

better validation material than an examination of textbook materials.

The authors state that their "sentences of necessity include many very simple words (a, and, the, to, do, etc.)." What is really meant is frequently occurring words. There is a sharp difference between "simple" and "difficult" words, especially insofar as learning to read is concerned. It is the feeling of this reviewer that it would be helpful if such statements as the following did not occur in test manuals: "Some more difficult words have been included in order fully to test the abilities of better pupils." What test will ever fully test abilities of any student? This is a trap for unsophisticated test users.

Some standardized tests currently on the market have been standardized on populations of half a million pupils, with as many as 100,000 cases at a particular level; the various batteries of the *American School Achievement Tests* were standardized on 1,000 to 10,000 cases only. The manual reports that the population used was stratified according to school size and socioeconomic location—agricultural, industrial, and residential areas. Apparently there was no stratification according to IQ distributions, acceleration and retardation, and ethnic groups. Testmakers in general could render greater service by being more attentive to more accurate measures of worthwhile aspects of the skill processes in reading for meaning and in concept development.

The time allowances for the tests tend to place emphasis on speed. Timed tests make for comparability of scores. However, emphasis on speed of reading is undesirable, especially at the primary level. It would be better to have a separate section on speed of reading if a measure of speed is wanted.

In summary, the reading tests of the *American School Achievement Tests* are useful for a general survey of reading achievement. They are interesting and attractive, and can be administered and scored easily. They can be used to compare large groups, but are of little or no value for diagnostic purposes. This reviewer would recommend that consideration be given to making the vocabulary section more closely related to the comprehension section. This might permit the teacher to note discrepancies between knowledge of terms and ability to use these in context.

AGATHA TOWNSEND, *Associate Professor of Education, State Teachers College, Kutztown, Pennsylvania.* [Review of Forms D, E, F.]

Certain general features of format and layout are common to all three levels. The tests are printed on a carbon-backed sheet which removes the necessity for a separate answer sheet while still retaining some advantages for quick scoring. The pupil is faced with a sheet approximately 10 by 15 inches, printed on both sides. The size may be inconvenient for some pupils to handle, and since the test parts are divided without regard to the size of the sheet, folding the booklet in half will not be a satisfactory solution. The situation for the scorer is even more troublesome. He will need a working space large enough to accommodate a sheet 20 by 15 inches. If he starts to score Form D of the intermediate test, he will probably begin by counting down the columns on the first page; but he must shift to counting only the bottom segment of the columns on the second, without, it may be added, any guide lines or instructions to keep him out of trouble in column three, where the sentence and word meaning score meets the paragraph meaning score with no division whatever. The test must be refolded before the scores can be recorded on the front, and there is no provision for removing the front portion for filing.

The format of the test apparently has been revised several times, though the norms take no cognizance of any effect this revision may have had on pupil performance. Between 1955, when Form D of Primary Battery II was published, and 1956 when Form E was issued, the shift was made to the oversized sheet, the choices in the sentence and word meaning test received identifying letters and were printed in line instead of vertically, and the answering procedure was changed so that instead of marking an answer space immediately after his choice the pupil marked the space corresponding to the letter of his selection. From Form E to Form F a (desirable) change was made from small letters to capitals in this identification. Somewhat similar changes were made in the intermediate and advanced tests, and it is noticeable that the type for Form F of the Advanced Battery is more reduced and compressed than that on the other two current forms. Unfortunately, even close similarity of test content may not be enough to ensure comparability to the extent that the same norms can be applied to different

forms, and this doubt arises especially with respect to the test for grade 2, where the changes are quite marked.

The organization seems to reflect an oversimplified concept of the nature of reading. Only two kinds of skills are tested—word meaning and paragraph meaning. In structure, these tests parallel the reading tests of other widely used batteries. An attempt has been made to improve over the usual synonym type vocabulary test by the use of an incomplete sentence technique, and the authors underline this step by naming this part "Sentence and Word Meaning."

In view of the multiple aims of reading instruction in the primary and intermediate grades, such an approach has definite limitations. The authors recognize these, but it is doubtful whether the test as it stands fulfills their aims of measuring pupil progress in reading achievement. They point out, quite correctly, that the tests are not designed for diagnosis of individual difficulties, but this statement is buried in a paragraph which aims at quite the opposite—a paragraph which implies that the language arts tests permit one "to determine the general disability which a pupil may have." It does seem as if a better reading test would result if some recognition were given to the changing aims and character of reading instruction from the primary, to the intermediate, to the junior high school grades. As it stands, solution to the problem of assuring continuity in measurement has taken the form of "more of the same."

The authors have provided more information about the tryout and selection of items than most producers. Each manual includes details on the selection of words, the appearance of the words in widely used textbook series, and their location on the Gates and Thorndike lists, and similar data on the vocabulary of the paragraphs.

The authors should have eliminated item writing errors like ending a sentence stem with an "a" only to have one of the choices read "engineer" or "office." More serious is the kind of extraneous difficulty introduced when an item is phrased awkwardly or obscurely. Can a second grader handle a sentence like Item 15 in Form D (Primary Battery II) which says, "A minute is the same kind of measure as....an hour"? Is it accurate to say, as in Item 12 of Form E (Advanced Battery) "One who belongs to a land is called a....native"? Test items cannot always be included merely because they seem to meet difficulty standards on tryout.

With all their care for item selection, the authors have evidently not given equal thought to item placement. How, otherwise, would one find Items 31 and 32, with their paragraph, in Form D of the Intermediate Battery, reappearing as Items 47 and 48, at the very end of Form E of the Advanced Battery? In Form D of the Intermediate Battery, again, the last two items (39 and 40) appear as Items 45 and 46, just before the end of Form E of the Advanced Battery.

Normative data are not nearly so complete as are data on item tryout, and it is not clear, either, to what extent normative populations are identical with experimental groups. The manuals for both the intermediate and advanced batteries refer to the norms as "tentative," but no such indication appears on the norms table. Since the number of cases is not given in the table, it is not possible to tell if the entries are based on a rechecking of the norms which occurred in 1955.

Reliability information, based on test-retest with different forms, is given for groups of about 100 to 200 cases for the various levels. These reliabilities are moderately high, and should probably prove adequate for group survey.

Evidence favorable to the test series is found in the careful description of item construction and selection, and in the care with which the different forms have been improved as one followed another. Reliability data are probably satisfactory, though reliability and norms information seem to be based on a rather small number of cases. Scoring should be reasonably easy, though more attention should be given to scoring problems in the manuals.

Some flaws in item construction, possibly inadequate scaling of items, and rather sparsely described norms seem to be the chief technical limitations. When these are added to the basic problem of determining whether or not the concept of reading expressed throughout the test is satisfactory—which is a major question indeed—it is doubtful if the battery can be highly recommended.

For reviews by J. Raymond Gerberich and Virgil E. Herrick of the complete battery, see 1; for a review by Ralph C. Preston of an earlier edition, see 4:1; for reviews by Walter W. Cook and Gordon N. Mackenzie (with Glen Hass), see 3:1.

[621]

★**American School Reading Tests.** Grades 10–13; 1955; various titles used by publisher; 3 scores: vocabulary, reading rate, comprehension; Forms A, B; tentative norms; $2.80 per 25 tests; separate answer booklets may be used; $1.75 per 25 answer booklets; 50¢ per specimen set; postpaid; 65(80) minutes; Willis E. Pratt and Stanley W. Lore; Public School Publishing Co. *

HENRY S. DYER, *Vice President in Charge of Research, Educational Testing Service, Princeton, New Jersey.*

This is a conventional type of reading test which yields three conventional scores—one on vocabulary, one on reading rate, and one on reading comprehension. It contains the usual types of material for this purpose. In selecting the materials for the sections on vocabulary and on reading rate, the authors have paid careful attention to the frequency of the words used as given in the "Thorndike Word List" and have taken account of this information in equating the two forms.

The format of the test itself is good: the type is legible and the directions to students are clear and uncomplicated. The directions for administering and scoring the test are also simple and straightforward.

The content of the test leaves something to be desired. In the opinion of this reviewer, both the vocabulary section and the reading comprehension section are, in general, measuring only the more superficial aspects of the reading process. There is little attempt in the vocabulary section to test the student's sensitivity to the fine shades of meaning which are likely to be of critical importance in differentiating between an adequate student and one who is highly perceptive. Furthermore, too many of the questions in the paragraph reading section depend too heavily on key words in the text itself. A quick glance back often yields the correct answer; there is little attempt to see whether the student has grasped the significance of what he has read or whether he can demonstrate understanding of the concepts given by using them in his own thinking. In short, it seems to this reviewer that this test hardly samples the kinds of student responses that are, or should be, involved in really effective reading.

The technical information given in the manual accompanying the test is in many respects inadequate. There is essentially no evidence presented on the validity of the test. The claim that the test should be useful in selecting students for college, for instance, is not supported by any data to show how well the scores correlate with college performance. The manual reports reliability data based on a sample of 100 cases "from approximately 1,000 cases in typical schools," but gives no information on the range of ability in the sample. The percentile norms are admittedly "tentative"—so tentative, indeed, that they are likely to be of little help in interpreting the scores. No data other than those drawn from the Thorndike list are given on the characteristics of the items.

Finally, there is one serious piece of misdirection in the manual: the user of the test is directed to obtain a total percentile rank on the test by averaging the percentile ranks of the scores on each of the three parts. It is hard to imagine a procedure more unsound or more calculated to give a meaningless result.

DONALD E. P. SMITH, *Chief, Division of Reading Improvement Services, and Associate Professor of Education, University of Michigan, Ann Arbor, Michigan.*

Reading tests which limit their announced coverage to two or three grades are uncommon. Most purport to span five grades or more, thus often yielding poor estimates at either extreme. This test is designed for use with grades 10 through 13. It is very doubtful, however, that it is "sufficiently easy to allow for some success by even the poorest tenth grade pupil." The easiest vocabulary items, for example, are "lattice" and "perjury." The test might better be limited to college freshmen.

Its purposes are three: to provide diagnostic information, to aid in remedial instruction, and to predict college success. No evidence is provided to indicate whether those purposes have been realized. The two equivalent forms each include three sections, a 72-item vocabulary test, a timed reading passage followed by 20 multiple choice questions, and a reading comprehension section of 10 paragraphs and 50 questions. A self-scoring answer sheet is provided. Administration time, with time limits for each part "experimentally determined," is 65 minutes.

The authors report that sample items were tried out with a thousand students in grades 8–13. Of 300 vocabulary items, 144 were retained; of 28 paragraphs, 20 were retained; of 60 questions on the timed readings, 40 were retained. Norms and reliability data are reported on the same population. Without cross validation, such data are spurious, of course, and lead to such inflated reliability coefficients (parallel forms) as .953 and .978.

A number of other problems suggest that "the buyer beware." For example, the manual states that a total score should be derived by averaging the subject's percentile rank on the subtest scores, at best a questionable procedure. The grade norms are apparently based upon less than 200 cases, since the 1,000 normative cases were spread over six grades. One is surprised to find a percentile rank of 100 reported. While the reading paragraphs consist of textbook material, that hardly provides the curricular validity claimed for them.

In general, the manual is well written and the choice of content is very good. Vocabulary items were selected from the "Thorndike Word List" (not otherwise identified) and data are provided to illustrate the broad range of difficulty sampled. With few exceptions, distractors on the vocabulary items are common words, as they should be. Some obvious clues are provided, however. The most flagrant is the difference in length of the choices: in nearly every case, the longest choice is the correct one.

The authors apparently made a good start toward constructing a reading test appropriate for college freshmen, but not for high school students. Its similarity in design to several other well established tests (*e.g.,* the Survey Section of the *Diagnostic Reading Tests*) raises the question of whether it will make any unique contribution to measurement. The answer to that question must wait until the test is properly validated.

[622]

California Reading Test, 1957 Edition. Grades 1–2, 3–4.5, 4–6, 7–9, 9–14; 1933–58; previous edition (see 4:411) still available; subtest of the *California Achievement Tests;* 3 scores: vocabulary, comprehension, total; IBM for grades 4–14; 5 levels; battery manual ('57) for each level; 1957 technical report ['58]; separate answer sheets may be used in grades 4–14; 4¢ per IBM answer sheet; 7¢ per Scoreze answer sheet; 20¢ per hand scoring stencil; 40¢ per machine scoring stencil; 10¢ per survey data sheet ('52); postage extra; 50¢ per specimen set of any one level, postpaid; Ernest W. Tiegs and Willis W. Clark; California Test Bureau. *
a) LOWER PRIMARY. Grades 1–2; Forms W, X ('57); $2.45 per 35 tests; 23(35) minutes.

b) UPPER PRIMARY. Grades 3–4.5; IBM; Forms W, X ('57); $2.80 per 35 tests; 40(50) minutes.
c) ELEMENTARY. Grades 4–6; IBM; Forms W, X, Y, Z ('57); $3.15 per 35 tests; 48–50(60) minutes.
d) JUNIOR HIGH LEVEL. Grades 7–9; IBM; Forms W, X, Y, Z ('57); $3.15 per 35 tests; 66–68(80) minutes.
e) ADVANCED. Grades 9–14; IBM; Forms W, X, Y ('57); $3.15 per 35 tests; 66–68(80) minutes

REFERENCES

1. CARMICHAEL, ANNE, AND REES, ROBERT E. "A Survey of Reading Achievement in Alberta Schools." *Alberta J Ed Res* 1:18–33 Mr '55. *
2. COULL, WILLIAM H. "A Normative Survey of Reading Achievement of Alberta Children in Relation to Intelligence, Sex, Bilingualism, and Grade Placement." *Alberta J Ed Res* 2:18–29 Mr '56. *
3. YOUNG, CAMPBELL. "A Qualitative Analysis of Reading Achievement in Edmonton Schools." *Alberta J Ed Res* 2:135–50 S '56. *
4. LONG, JAMES R. *Academic Forecasting in the Technical-Vocational High School Subjects at West Seattle High School.* Doctor's thesis, University of Washington (Seattle, Wash.), 1957. (*DA* 17:1951)
5. SOPCHAK, ANDREW L. "Prediction of College Performance by Commonly Used Tests." *J Clin Psychol* 14:194–7 Ap '58. *

For reviews by John C. Flanagan and James R. Hobson of the 1950 edition, see 4:530; for a review by Frederick B. Davis of an earlier edition, see 40:1563; for reviews by Ivan A. Booker and Joseph C. Dewey, see 38:1110. For a review by Charles O. Neidt of the complete battery, see 2; for reviews by Warren G. Findley, Alvin W. Schindler, and J. Harlan Shores of the 1950 edition, see 4:2; for a review by Paul A. Witty of the 1943 edition, see 3:15; for reviews by C. W. Odell and Hugh B. Wood of an earlier edition, see 40:1193; for a review by D. Welty Lefever, see 38:876.

[623]

★**Chapman Reading Comprehension Test.** Grades 5–12; 1924–53; formerly called *Chapman Unspeeded Reading Comprehension Test;* Form A ('53, same as test copyrighted in 1924); directions for administering ('53, norms same as in 1924 manual); no data on reliability and validity; $1.30 per 25 tests, postage extra; 40¢ per specimen set, postpaid; 30(40) minutes; J. C. Chapman; Educational Test Bureau. *

RUSSELL P. KROPP, *Associate Professor of Education, Florida State University, Tallahassee, Florida.*

This instrument appraises reading comprehension by presenting to the examinee 31 short statements, each about two sentences in length, in the second half of each of which the examinee crosses out that word that makes the statement absurd.

A 4-page fold accompanying the test includes directions for administering and scoring and a table of norms. No evidence concerning reliability and validity is presented here or elsewhere.

The raw score can be transformed to a verbal rating, a percentile rank, a standard score, or a reading age. The verbal rating is simply an adjectival description of the score in nine classifications from highest to lowest. The verbal ratings correspond to nine percentile ranks ranging from 95 to 5, and to nine standard scores ranging from 126 to 74. Reading age is determined from a separate table.

In addition to the already apparent weaknesses in the norms, the following criticisms can be made. First, the total number of cases in the normative group is not given. Second, the number of cases tested at each grade level is not given. Third, there is no indication of the grade range of the normative group; consequently, one cannot determine whether or not some of the equivalent scores are extrapolated. In fact, the normative group is not identified or described in any way whatsover except for the implication that they were tested during the midyear in grade. The absence of such information nearly renders the instrument useless.

A passage following the table of norms reads, in part, as follows: "Suppose, for example, that a ninth grade pupil gets 22 right. This is a 'Medium high' score, is at the 66th percentile, and is a standard score of 107, which is expected of a ninth grade pupil with a 'Standard IQ' of 107." This interpretation is clearly not warranted. It implies that intelligence and reading comprehension are, or should be, perfectly related. The error is extremely serious since it is the only suggested interpretation.

This test of only 31 items is designed for use over a range of eight grades. If adequate information were presented about its reliability, validity, and norming, the test might be used in screening situations where information concerning only the grossest kind of discrimination was tolerable. The reviewer believes, however, that the instrument would be of extremely limited usefulness under any circumstances.

[624]

★**Commerce Reading Comprehension Test.** Grades 12–16 and adults; 1956–58; IBM; 1 form ('56); mimeographed manual ['58]; tentative norms ['56, '58]; separate answer sheets must be used; $4 per 100 IBM answer sheets; 25¢ per either hand or machine scoring stencil; 20¢ per specimen set; postpaid; 60(65) minutes; Irma T. Halfter and Raymond J. McCall; Department of Psychological Testing, De Paul University. *

[625]

★**Davis Reading Test.** Grades 11–13; 1956–58; IBM; Forms 1A, 1B, 1C, 1D ('57); manual ('58); separate answer sheets must be used; $3.50 per 25 tests; $1.90 per 50 answer sheets; 35¢ per scoring stencil and manual for any one form; 50¢ per specimen set; postpaid;

40(55) minutes; Frederick B. Davis and Charlotte Croon Davis; Psychological Corporation. *

BENJAMIN ROSNER, *Assistant Professor of Education, Rutgers, The State University, New Brunswick, New Jersey.*

The *Davis Reading Test* is a carefully planned and constructed reading comprehension test designed to appraise the overall reading ability of high school students in grades 11 and 12 and college freshmen. The test is an operational extension of the senior author's earlier analysis of the factors involved in reading comprehension. Accordingly, the items have been constructed to measure ability to: (*a*) answer questions explicitly answered in a passage; (*b*) weave together ideas in a passage and grasp its central thought; (*c*) draw inferences from a passage about its contents and the author's point of view, purpose, or intent; (*d*) recognize the tone or mood of a passage and the literary devices used by its author; and (*e*) follow the structure of a passage. In less well constructed tests, the items may degenerate into pure measures of word knowledge. In the *Davis Reading Test* the verbal difficulty level of the items appears to have been carefully controlled so that the items are more clearly measures of the reading skills cited above.

The Davis test is available in four forms, each form yielding two scores—one for speed and one for level of comprehension. While both scores measure essentially the accuracy of understanding (a global interpretation of the reading factors cited above), the speed score also provides an index as to the relative speed with which students can read and understand the passages in the test booklet. Both scores are obtained from a single administration of the test with a single 40-minute time limit. This is accomplished by dividing the 80 items in the test into, in effect, two 40-item subtests. (No statistical evidence is presented to document the equivalence of the two halves, but the test construction procedures adopted in establishing the two subtests would tend to ensure their equivalence.) Because almost all examinees are reported able to reach the first 40 items, the score on the first subtest provides the level score; because very few examinees have sufficient time to complete the total test, the score on the entire test furnishes a measure of speed.

Directions for administering and scoring the tests, and for interpreting the test results are clearly presented in the manual. The single time limit makes the test practically self-administering; however, the additional time required for the distribution and collection of materials and the reading of directions extends the total testing time somewhat beyond the time limits of most regularly scheduled high school classes. From a practical point of view, it would be more convenient to have the time limits such that the test could be administered within the limits of a single class period. Loss in the precision of measurement would probably be negligible.

Percentile norms for grades 11 and 12, and for college freshmen are provided for both level and speed scores. In general, geographical distribution and size of the norming sample are adequate. It is hoped, however, that future manuals will present norms for separate geographical regions and for different kinds of collegiate institutions.

Scores on the *Davis Reading Test* are translated into individual percentiles rather than presented in percentile "bands" as are scores on the STEP reading tests. While the confidence interval presents a more reasonable appraisal of student performance in terms of "true" scores, the current consumer of test information does not possess the minimally necessary statistical sophistication to appreciate this new approach. The point estimate (single percentile rank), together with tables controlling the interpretation of score differences, is probably less confusing. For this reason current consumers are likely to find the Davis scores more easily interpretable.

Mean reliability estimates (alternate-form) of the level score are .74, .77, and .80 for grades 11 and 12, and college freshmen, respectively. These are adequate but not overly impressive. For the speed score the estimates are .84, .85, and .88 for the same grades. These are more acceptable. The averages of the correlations between level and speed (from two different forms) are .74 for grade 11, .77 for grade 12, and .80 for college freshmen. When these correlations are considered in terms of the reliabilities of the two scores, interpretations of differences are rather questionable. Incidentally, inspection of the effective score range at the three grade levels suggests that the test might be useful at the college sophomore level and that appropriate norms should be developed.

Evidence on statistical validity is good. Correlations with high school and college English grades average approximately .5. Congruent validity estimates are much higher; e.g., the correlation with the STEP reading test is about .80. In almost every instance the speed score has greater predictive and congruent validity than does the level score. In all likelihood the greater statistical validity of the speed score is accounted for by its higher reliability. Considering the correlation between speed and level scores and the greater reliability and statistical validity of the speed score, this reviewer questions the need for both scores. On the other hand, the ease with which both scores are obtained may warrant their computation.

Considering the importance of reading comprehension as a determinant of success in high school and collegiate programs, the *Davis Reading Test* should provide useful information for high school and college guidance personnel. The item construction, the clarity of the manual, and the cautious approach of the authors in the interpretation of test score differences are particularly impressive.

[626]

★**Developmental Reading Tests.** Grades 1.5, 1.5–2.5, 2.5–3; 1955; 1 form; 3 parts; 3 levels; no specific manual; no data on reliability; no norms; $2 per 35 tests of any one part of any one level, postage extra; 40¢ per specimen set, postpaid; 10(15), 15(20) minutes for Parts 1, 2–3; [Guy L. Bond, Theodore Clymer, and Cyril Hoyt]; Lyons & Carnahan. *
a) PRIMER READING. Grade 1.5; 3 parts.
  1) *Part 1, Basic Vocabulary.* Form PV-A.
  2) *Part 2, General Comprehension.* Form PG-A.
  3) *Part 3, Specific Comprehension.* Form PS-A.
b) LOWER PRIMARY READING. Grades 1.5–2.5; 3 parts.
  1) *Part 1, Basic Vocabulary.* Form LV-A.
  2) *Part 2, General Comprehension.* Form LG-A.
  3) *Part 3, Specific Comprehension.* Form LS-A.
c) UPPER PRIMARY READING. Grades 2.5–3; 3 parts.
  1) *Part 1, Basic Vocabulary.* Form UV-A.
  2) *Part 2, General Comprehension.* Form UG-A.
  3) *Part 3, Specific Comprehension.* Form US-A.

[627]

★**Diagnostic Reading Test: Pupil Progress Series.** Grades 1.9–2.1, 2.2–3, 4–6, 7–8; 1956–57; various titles used by publisher; some subtests also appear in *Scholastic Diagnostic Reading Test* for Catholic schools; IBM for grades 4–8; 2 forms; 4 levels; manual ('57) for each form of each level; $4.55 per 35 tests; separate answer sheets may be used in grades 4–8; $1.75 per 35 IBM answer sheets; 20¢ per set of scoring stencils; 50¢ per specimen set of any one level; postage extra; Oliver F. Anderhalter, R. Stephen Gawkoski, and Ruth Colestock; Scholastic Testing Service, Inc. *
a) PRIMARY TEST I. Grades 1.9–2.1; 10 scores: vocabulary (3 subscores), rate, comprehension (3 subscores), total; Forms A ('56), B ('57); (40–60) minutes.

b) PRIMARY TEST II. Grades 2.2–3; 11 scores: vocabulary (3 subscores), rate, comprehension (5 subscores), total; Forms A ('56), B ('57); 40(60) minutes.
c) ELEMENTARY TEST. Grades 4–6; 11 scores: vocabulary (3 subscores), rate, comprehension (5 subscores), total; IBM; Forms A ['56], B ('57); (60) minutes.
d) ADVANCED TEST. Grades 7–8; 14 scores: vocabulary (4 subscores), rate, comprehension (6 subscores), total; IBM; Forms A ['56], B ('57); (60) minutes.

[628]

★**Elementary Reading: Every Pupil Scholarship Test.** Grades 4–6, 7–8; 1928–58; new form usually issued each January and April; 2 levels; norms available following testing program; no data on reliability; 4¢ per test; 4¢ per scoring key; postage extra; 15(20) minutes; Bureau of Educational Measurements. *

[629]

*Elementary Reading: Every Pupil Test.** Grades 4–6; 1936–58; new form usually issued each December and April; 2 parts; norms available following testing program; no data on reliability; 3¢ per test; 1¢ per scoring key; cash orders postpaid; Ohio Scholarship Tests. *
a) GENERAL ABILITY. 19(30) minutes.
b) SPEED AND COMPREHENSION. 2 scores: speed, comprehension; 6(10) minutes.

[630]

*Gates Advanced Primary Reading Tests.** Grades 2.5–3; 1926–58; Forms 1, 2, 3 ('58); 2 tests; manual ('58); series supplement ('58); $1.35 per 35 copies; 40¢ per specimen set of either test; cash orders postpaid; 40(60) minutes; Arthur I. Gates; Bureau of Publications, Teachers College, Columbia University. *
a) TYPE AWR, WORD RECOGNITION. 15(25) minutes.
b) TYPE APR, PARAGRAPH READING. 25(35) minutes.

REFERENCES
1. GATES, ARTHUR I. *The Improvement of Reading: A Program of Diagnostic and Remedial Methods, Third Edition.* New York: Macmillan Co., 1947. Pp. xxi, 657. * (PA 22:3195)
2. MILLER, VELMA J. *A Critical Analysis of Standardized Vocabulary Tests to Determine Those Most Valid for Use With the Macmillan Readers.* Master's thesis, Bowling Green State University (Bowling Green, Ohio), 1954.
3. WARE, FLORENCE EDNA. "Effect on Reading Achievement of Under-Testing Pupils in Low Third Grade." *Calif J Ed Res* 7:22–4 Ja '56. * (PA 30:7698)

For reviews by Virginia Seavey and George Spache of an earlier edition, see 3:484.

[631]

*Gates Basic Reading Tests.** Grades 3.5–8; 1926–58; Tests GS, UD, and ND scored for percentage of attempts correct; Forms 1, 2, 3 ('58); 5 tests; manual ('58); series supplement ('58); $1.35 per 35 copies of any one test; 40¢ per specimen set of any one test; cash orders postpaid; 30(85), 24(85) minutes for grades 3–4, 5–8; Arthur I. Gates; Bureau of Publications, Teachers College, Columbia University. *
a) TYPE GS, READING TO APPRECIATE GENERAL SIGNIFICANCE. 10(15), 8(15) minutes for grades 3–4, 5–8.
b) TYPE UD, READING TO UNDERSTAND PRECISE DIRECTIONS. 10(15), 8(15) minutes for grades 3–4, 5–8.
c) TYPE ND, READING TO NOTE DETAILS. 10(15), 8(15) minutes for grades 3–4, 5–8.
d) TYPE RV, READING VOCABULARY. (20) minutes.
e) TYPE LC, LEVEL OF COMPREHENSION. (20) minutes.

REFERENCES
1–5. See 40:1539.
6–7. See 3:485.
8. HARRIS, CHESTER W. "An Exploration of Language Skill Patterns." *J Ed Psychol* 39:321–36 O '48. * (PA 23:1755)

S. S. DUNN, *Officer-in-Charge, Test Division, Australian Council for Educational Research, Melbourne, Australia.*

The series contains three speed and accuracy tests—Reading to Appreciate General Significance (GS), Reading to Understand Precise Directions (UD), and Reading to Note Details (ND). Two additional tests—Reading Vocabulary (RV) and Level of Comprehension (LC) —are power tests. Three forms, stated to be equivalent, are provided for each test, but evidence of equivalence is not given in the manual.

While there is a need to separate the "how to use the test" material from the technical information, the decision to place it in a manual supplement published separately has dangers. If it makes these data less accessible it encourages teachers to use the tests in faith and contributes nothing to their proper understanding of the tests. In any case, statements and recommendations in the manual which are presumably based on technical information should be cross referenced to the appropriate page in the supplement. Only by close reading does one come across the reference to the existence of the supplement on the second last page of the manual.

The decision to use material of fairly uniform difficulty in the three speed tests poses a problem when the test is supposed to be useful over five and a half grades. If it is not too difficult for grade 4 then it must appear somewhat childish for grade 8. Is there any educational advantage in trying to make the same test cover such a large range? A look at the accuracy norms bears witness to the difficulty of the tests for the younger children.

The appearance of the test papers is excellent with type faces that should offer no problems in readability. The bold type used in LC to distinguish questions from paragraphs could have been extended with benefit to GS and ND. Adequate spacing, and the use of blue lines to divide passages, adds to the total appearance.

The directions for administration are not easy to follow. It is not clear in the manual what is required. There is a note on the front of the two power test booklets labeled "To the Teacher" from which one gets an inkling of what to do, but is it desirable for the pupils to read an instruction such as "The pupils should be kept working vigorously, but they should have as much time as they need to try every exercise"?

For Reading Vocabulary and Level of Comprehension, the standard correction for guessing is applied. There is no instruction on how to handle corrections involving one half point. For example, the correction for 14 wrong is one quarter of 14 or 3½. Does one subtract 3 or 4? No reason is given for not correcting tests UD and GS which have multiple choice answers. The use of a separate "accuracy score" (see later comment) is not a substitute if one believes a correction for guessing is desirable.

For the three speed tests two sets of norms are given, one for 8 minutes (recommended administration time for grades 5 and above) and one for 10 minutes (recommended time for grades 3 and 4). The small differences between the norms for lower reading ages leads one to wonder whether the advantages in using the two times are sufficient to compensate for the dangers of looking at the wrong table.

The general discussion on reliability is useful, but the author fails to provide the reader with examples of the use of the standard error of measurement. The standard errors of individual test scores appear only in the technical supplement, and it would probably surprise teachers to realise the size of changes which could occur on retesting, especially amongst the more able older children. Thus, children scoring 38 on test ND have a reading grade of 8.8 and a reading age of 14.0, but on a retest one in three could be expected to score outside the range 38 ± 4, i.e., outside the reading grade range of 7.5 to 10.2 and the reading age range of 12-10 to 15-6. Such changes must be expected when the growth curve for an ability is flattening out. In these circumstances, the use of reading grades and reading ages becomes artificial in the same way the use of mental ages does for adolescents and adults.

Likewise, the discussion on checking the differences between scores on two tests for significance is useful, but the single table dealing with significance of differences is oversimplified and probably misleading. From the information in the supplement, the reliabilities of differences can be estimated for various pairs of tests and range from zero to .60. It is highly improbable that the standard deviations of differences between pairs of tests are such as to compensate for these different reliabilities and produce approximately equal standard errors of differences for different pairs of tests. Nor is the reader given any indication of level of significance used to decide whether differences are "unreliable," "fairly reliable," or "quite reliable."

The use of accuracy scores is interesting, but one wonders whether the reliability of these scores on each test is such as to justify the use of three separate accuracy scores rather than a more reliable combined score. No evidence on the reliability of the accuracy scores is provided.

The section on improving reading abilities is a useful one and draws on Gates' wide experience.

In summary, the tests are attractively presented. The use of the same material over several grades raises problems. The use of grade percentiles is a valuable addition to the reading grades and reading ages, but the use of the latter for higher grades and older ages is of doubtful value. The provision of a table setting out differences needed for significance in variations among test scores is to be commended, but the value of the present table is questionable. The hints on helping children with reading difficulties are helpful.

For reviews by George Spache, Herbert F. Spitzer, and T. L. Torgerson of an earlier edition, see 3:485; for reviews by Joseph C. Dewey and James R. Hobson of the Gates Silent Reading Tests, *see 40:1539 (1 excerpt).*

[632]

*Gates Primary Reading Tests. Grades 1–2.5; 1926–58; 3 scores: word recognition, sentence reading, paragraph reading; Forms 1, 2, 3 ('58); 3 tests; manual ('58); series supplement ('58); $1.35 per 35 copies of any one test; 40¢ per specimen set of any one test; cash orders postpaid; 50(80) minutes; Arthur I. Gates; Bureau of Publications, Teachers College, Columbia University. *
a) TYPE PWR, WORD RECOGNITION. 15(25) minutes.
b) TYPE PSR, SENTENCE READING. 15(25) minutes.
c) TYPE PPR, PARAGRAPH READING. 20(30) minutes.

REFERENCES

1–7. See 3:486.
8. WARE, FLORENCE EDNA. "Effect on Reading Achievement of Under-Testing Pupils in Low Third Grade." *Calif J Ed Res* 7:22–4 Ja '56. * (PA 30:7698)
9. PRINGLE, M. L. KELLMER, AND NEALE, M. D. "A Note on the Use of the Schonell and Gates Reading Tests in the First Year of the Junior School." *Brit J Ed Psychol* 27:135–41 Je '57. *

For reviews by William S. Gray and George Spache of an earlier edition, see 3:486.

[633]

*Gates Reading Survey. Grades 3.5–10; 1939–58; 5 scores: speed and accuracy, accuracy, vocabulary, level of comprehension, total; Forms 1, 2, 3 ('58); manual ('58); series supplement ('58); $2.35 per 35 tests; 40¢

per specimen set; cash orders postpaid; (50–60) minutes; Arthur I. Gates; Bureau of Publications, Teachers College, Columbia University. *

REFERENCES

1. GATES, ARTHUR I. *The Improvement of Reading: A Program of Diagnostic and Remedial Methods, Third Edition.* New York: Macmillan Co., 1947. Pp. xxi, 657. * (PA 22:3195)
2. WEST, DORAL N. "Reducing Chance in Test Selection." *Personnel & Guid J* 36:420–1 F '58. *

For reviews by Dorothy E. Holberg and Herbert F. Spitzer of an earlier edition, see 3:487.

[634]

*High School Reading Test: National Achievement Tests. Grades 7–12; 1939–52; 6 scores: vocabulary, word discrimination, sentence meaning, noting details, interpreting paragraphs, total; Forms A ('52, identical with test copyrighted in 1939 except for minor changes), B ('51, identical with test copyrighted in 1940 except for Item 4, Part 3); directions sheet for Form A ('45), directions sheet for Form B ('51, identical with sheet copyrighted in 1940); general teachers' guide ['44]; no norms for part scores; $3.75 per 25 tests; 50¢ per specimen set; postage extra; (40) minutes; Robert K. Speer and Samuel Smith; Acorn Publishing Co. *

VICTOR H. NOLL, *Professor of Education, Michigan State University, East Lansing, Michigan.*

This test was adequately reviewed in *The Third Mental Measurements Yearbook* (3:488) and *The Fourth Mental Measurements Yearbook* (4:536). As noted above, no changes of any importance have been made since these reviews were written. The present reviewer is in agreement with what was said about the test in the earlier reviews. Consequently, little more need be said except to make a few additional observations. The statement that "these tests were....based primarily upon the National Survey of Instruction in English for Secondary Schools, Bulletin No. 17, U.S. Department of Interior, Office of Education, and publications of the National Council of Teachers of English" as sole evidence of validity is of little or no value to the prospective user. For one thing, the first reference is of doubtful value for anyone constructing a reading test for use in today's schools if for no other reason than that it is now more than a quarter century since it was published. For another, it contains little that would contribute to the validity of a test such as this. The second reference is meaningless in this instance since it gives no information as to *what* publications of the National Council were used.

Another observation of interest to this reviewer has to do with the equivalence of Forms A and B of the test. The norms were established on 9,000 pupils said to be representative of different sizes of schools and parts of the country. These were checked against returns of thousands of additional pupils and "were found to be accurate." A comparison of norms for the two forms raises serious questions regarding this statement. It is obvious that the forms are not eqivalent. Perhaps most disturbing is the fact that at some points in the scale Form A seems the more difficult and at others, the easier. The range of differences between median scores on the two forms at various grade levels is from 4 points in favor of Form A to 13 points in favor of Form B.

As stated in previous reviews, the tests have some attractive features but these are marred by what must be regarded as inexcusable carelessness in their standardization. Poor workmanship makes the critical, discriminating user of standardized tests take a doubting or suspicious attitude toward all of them and hurts most the careful, conscientious producer who is doing his best to develop tests that will not be subject to such criticisms. Unfortunately, the consumer, who is often relatively unsophisticated in these matters and who may not know what to look for, is likely to be unaware of the serious differences between two tests, both appealing in content and format but very unequal in the quality of work and the attention to sound principles that have gone into their development.

For a review by Holland Roberts, see 4:536; for a review by Robert L. McCaul, see 3:488.

[635]

Holborn Reading Scale. Ages 5.5–11.0; 1948; 2 scores: word recognition, comprehension; individual; 1 form ['48] no data on reliability; 3s. per 25 tests; 2d. per single copy; 1s. 6d. per manual; postage extra; [20–30] minutes; A. F. Watts; George G. Harrap & Co. Ltd. *

REFERENCE

1. WATTS, A. F. *The Language and Mental Development of Children.* London: George G. Harrap & Co. Ltd., 1944. Pp. 354. *

STANLEY NISBET, *Professor of Education, University of Glasgow, Glasgow, Scotland.*

This test consists of 33 sentences arranged in increasing order of difficulty with respect both to mechanical elements and to comprehensibility. The sentences have been so chosen that the gradient in mechanical difficulty is steep but linear, each sentence representing a reading age three months higher than the preceding sentence. A child is given the test sheet

and asked to read aloud from the beginning. He is stopped after his fourth mistake, and his reading age determined from figures in the margin opposite the sentence in which the mistake occurs. The scale thus enables the tester to make a rough assessment of a child's reading level in a remarkably short time and without calculations. The same sentences are also used to test comprehension, the manual containing 33 questions, one to be asked about each sentence.

This is quite obviously a sound test. It could hardly be otherwise, taken as it is from Watts' excellent book *The Language and Mental Development of Children* (1). Such a useful measuring instrument, however, deserves a new and more carefully produced manual, specially written for users of the test. As it is, the relevant paragraphs have merely been lifted verbatim from the book. Not only do they read a little unnaturally by themselves but—a much more serious fault—they do not give clear and adequate instructions to the user.

First of all, he is not told how to obtain a score for comprehension. Presumably the reading ages given in the margin opposite the sentences refer only to mechanical reading, and the comprehension score is simply the total number of questions answered correctly. Secondly, no norms are given for comprehension, although it is assumed in the discussion that comparisons can be made between a child's performances in mechanical reading and comprehension. Thirdly, the graph on which are plotted average scores on mechanical reading for some two thousand children is not so clearly interpreted as it might be, and it contains two errrors. Finally, no mention is made in the manual of test reliability or validity, or of the relationship of the test to other tests.

To sum up: this is already a good test, but it could be a better one with a completely new and adequate manual.

For a review by C. M. Fleming, see 4:537.

[636]

★**Kelley-Greene Reading Comprehension Test: Evaluation and Adjustment Series.** Grades 9–13; 1953–55, c1952–55; 5 scores: paragraph comprehension, directed reading, retention of details, reading rate, total; IBM; Forms AM ('53), BM ('55); manual ('53); expectancy chart ['54]; no college norms: separate answer sheets must be used; $5.35 per 35 tests; $1.70 per 35 IBM answer sheets; postage extra; 35¢ per specimen set, postpaid; 63(75) minutes in 2 sessions; Victor H. Kelley and Harry A. Greene; World Book Co. *

REFERENCE

1. CROOK, FRANCES E. "Interrelationships Among a Group of Language Arts Tests." *J Ed Res* 51:305-11 D '57. *

RUSSELL P. KROPP, *Associate Professor of Education, Florida State University, Tallahassee, Florida.*

There are three parts to the *Kelley-Greene Reading Comprehension Test.* Test 1, Paragraph Comprehension, consists of nine paragraphs, each approximately eight sentences in length, dealing with science and social science topics. Five items follow each paragraph and they call for generalization and inference from the paragraph. Twenty minutes are allowed. Test 2, Directed Reading, consists of three reading passages, each 26 to 28 sentences long, dealing with science and social science content. Each passage is timed separately, 3 minutes being provided for the initial reading and 8 minutes for answering the 24 items that follow the passage. The examinee is permitted to refer back to the passage during these 8 minutes. A measure of reading rate can also be obtained from Test 2. Test 3, Retention of Details, consists of 35 items dealing with the passages in Test 2. Ten minutes are allowed.

The total test is built around seven objectives of reading comprehension: skimming to locate answers to specific questions, critical reading to identify details, selecting the central theme of a passage, generalizing from statements, drawing inferences, summarizing passages, and remembering materials that were read for a purpose. These objectives are important in reading comprehension; their appraisal demands a rather carefully constructed test. The reviewer believes that these objectives have been met in large measure by the authors. However, a separate score is not given for each objective. Nevertheless, the test is commendable from the standpoint of carrying out the purposes for which it was built. It is technically adequate with regard to its construction, standardization, and norming. The weakest part is Test 3, Retention of Details. This weakness is due to the utter detail tested.

The directions for administration are complete and clear. The authors recommend that the test be taken on two successive days. They also recommend that when the test is given in one day a break of at least 15 minutes occur between Tests 1 and 2. No information is provided about whether these two kinds of administration lead to different scores, nor is the user informed about the kind of administration used in collecting the normative data.

Two sets of reliability data were computed, one on 10th grade groups and the other on 12th grade groups. Reliabilities are satisfactory except for Test 3, for which the coefficient is lower than one might expect.

The intercorrelations among the three tests are moderately high, thus indicating that each has much in common with the others.

Concurrent validity information is presented dealing with the relationships between the three tests and the *Terman-McNemar Test of Mental Ability* and other tests in the Evaluation and Adjustment Series. Relationships between the Kelley-Greene and other reading comprehension tests in subject matter fields and language sections of intelligence tests would be more useful. The reviewer can understand the value of having available a series of tests normed on the same groups and having available the intercorrelations of these tests, but he is aware too of the value of having information about the relationships between a particular test and other tests of the same kind that are not necessarily published by the same company.

The normative information apparently was gathered with care and thoroughness and it is quite adequate for high school groups. However, no normative data are provided for the interpretation of scores achieved by college freshmen. The Kelley-Greene is a better than average reading comprehension test that will justifiably be used extensively in the public schools.

MAGDALEN D. VERNON, *Professor of Psychology, University of Reading, Reading, England.*

This group test of reading comprehension is designed to test four competencies: (*a*) selecting the central idea and summarizing the gist of a paragraph; (*b*) reading carefully and skimming for details; (*c*) generalizing and drawing inferences from what is read; and (*d*) remembering details for subsequent recall.

The first subtest is mainly concerned with (*a*) and (*c*), but there are also questions about single details. Moreover, since most of the multiple choice questions can be answered by selecting a single sentence from the paragraph, a piecemeal approach to the paragraph is almost inevitable. In the reviewer's opinion, the only satisfactory manner of measuring a reader's ability to summarize or to extract the main argument of a paragraph is to require him to reproduce it in his own words. In the first place, the gist of a paragraph necessarily requires a longer statement than can conveniently be presented in the form of multiple choice questions. Secondly, a reader cannot demonstrate that he has really grasped the gist unless he can formulate it himself. Merely matching one sentence against another can be done without any real assimilation of the content as a coherent whole. Naturally, numerous difficulties are encountered in standardizing the scoring of statements written by the reader; but they are not insuperable. A test of formulation would be immeasurably superior in demonstrating whether the reader had obtained a real idea of the content he has read.

The same comment is equally apposite to the testing of remembering and recall. We know that in some cases the reader may retain a coherent general impression of what he reads; but in others he may forget or modify considerably the ideas of the original, or may retain certain details only. No allowance is made for the different types of error in Test 3. Test 2 requires the reader to locate single sentences that answer questions on the details of three simple passages relating to the social and physical sciences. Test 3 asks him to recall rather similar details from the same passages. In the first place, it is not made clear to the reader whether or not his memory for this material is going to be tested, though the initial instructions hint at it. In the second place, in order to obviate the difficulty that the reader may not have time to read the whole of each of the passages in Test 2, the questions on these passages are rotated in Test 3 (Item 1 is on passage 1, Item 2 on passage 2, and so on). Thus, if he did in fact acquire and retain impressions of the general gist of these passages, these impressions might be hopelessly confused by the rotation of the questions in Test 3. All in all, both these subtests emphasize the mechanical rote remembering of details, rather than an intelligent and coherent grasp of the passages as a whole. It also seems possible that subjects with special knowledge of the contents of the passages might have some advantage over those who have none.

Lastly, norms are given only for the total scores on each of the three subtests, and there are no separate norms for the different types of item in Test 1, relating to (a), (b), and (c)

above. Thus, it would be difficult to ascertain whether a reader was relatively proficient or deficient in understanding the general gist of a passage, or in drawing conclusions and making inferences from it. His final score would be determined mainly by his rote memory for detail.

Split-half reliability coefficients for the three subtests vary from .71 to .96 and the calculated standard errors of measurement are reasonably small. It is stated that validity indices were calculated for each item in the original tryout of the test, and that valid items were selected for the final form; but no measure of validity is quoted. The test was correlated with tests of intelligence, listening comprehension, and written English usage, but naturally the correlations were only moderate.

This test attempts to test comprehension and remembering of the content of simple material relating to the social and physical sciences; but it is doubtful whether it tests adequately anything more than the assimilation and remembering of factual detail.

[637]

★The Kingston Test of Silent Reading. Ages 7–11; 1953–54; 1 form ('53); 5s. per 25 tests; 3d. per single copy; 2s. 6d. per manual ('54); postage extra; 20(30) minutes; M. E. Highfield; George G. Harrap & Co. Ltd. *

NEIL GOURLAY, *Professor of Education, University of the Witwatersrand, Johannesburg, Union of South Africa.*

This test consists of a simple prose passage of about 600 words in which 50 words have been omitted. The task of the testee is to write down as many of these as he can in 20 minutes. Various other methods for measuring reading comprehensions have been used, but at the reading age levels for which the Kingston test is intended (7 to 12 years)—and particularly over the first half of this range—the Kingston technique is probably as good as most.

Since the missing words do not show any apparent increase in difficulty as one proceeds from the beginning to the end of the passage, speed of working must play an important part in performance on this test. It might, therefore, be regarded as more of a speed test than a power test—unlike Schonell's reading comprehension tests, for example, where the provision of a number of short paragraphs of steadily increasing difficulty ensures that test performance is decided more by the intrinsic difficulty of filling in the missing words and less by the speed factor.

The manual's account of the standardisation of the test is far from clear. The author states that the test was standardised on a population of 2,000 children "nearing the end of their second year in the primary junior school." The reader is informed that "the sigma of the raw scores is 13, but the conversion table is based on a sigma of 15" in order to facilitate "a comparison of a pupil's reading quotient, or R.Q., with his I.Q." Apparently the assumption was made that the reading quotients of the 2,000 children were distributed with a standard deviation of 15, and with this assumption it would, of course, be a simple matter to derive the reading age equivalents of all the raw scores 1–50. The assumption, however, is very dubious. The author tries to justify the procedure by claiming that smaller representative groups at age levels from 7 to 10 obtained mean scores comparable to those for the derived reading ages.

Reliability, as measured by the split-half method, is reported as .98 for pupils aged 8½ years or more. A high figure like this is to be expected with a test in which speed plays such a large part. A parallel-forms reliability coefficient would not be so high. The author, however, does not provide a parallel form of the test.

There is no doubt that the chief weakness of the test is the uncertainty which must exist in regard to the accuracy of the standardisation. The test could not be recommended for use in a situation requiring accurate norms.

MAGDALEN D. VERNON, *Professor of Psychology, University of Reading, Reading, England.*

This is a group test of comprehension in silent reading. Children are given a complete story with words missing at intervals; they have to supply the missing words. It is a test of the ability to recognize the words of the story, to comprehend their meaning and that of the sentences in which they occur, to demonstrate the possession of a vocabulary including the missing words, and to reason out which are the most appropriate words to be inserted. Thus, a good performance on the test requires an adequate degree of all these abilities; and indeed test performance correlates fairly highly with performance on word recognition, vocabulary, and intelligence tests. Again, failure on the test may be due to deficiency in any of these abilities, and therefore further testing or study would be necessary to determine where the deficiency lay. The author states that about four per cent of junior school children may be unable to score at all, and that these children should be tested individually with a graded word reading test. But the range of scores up to a reading age of eight years is a narrow one, and children below this reading age should also be given tests of the mechanics of reading.

The format of the test is unsatisfactory, since the text is printed in two columns on each of two pages and the child has to enter his answers in four different columns. The tester is warned that he should check to see whether the answers are being entered opposite the right numbers. There seems to be no reason other than economy of paper why the test should not be printed in a single column, a format much more familiar to most children and much easier to work with.

For British children with reading ages from 8½ to 12 years this test should provide a reasonably satisfactory measure of general proficiency in reading, though it will give little indication as to ability to comprehend the gist of a whole passage. Supplementary testing would be required to estimate this ability as well as to locate deficiencies in word recognition at lower reading ages.

[638]

*Lee-Clark Reading Test, 1958 Revision.** Grades 1, 1–2; 1931–58; Forms A, B ('58); 2 levels; manual ('58) for each level; $2.80 per 35 tests, postage extra; 25¢ per specimen set, postpaid; (20–30) minutes; J. Murray Lee and Willis W. Clark; California Test Bureau. *
a) PRIMER. Grade 1; 4 scores: auditory stimuli, visual stimuli, following directions, total.
b) FIRST READER. Grades 1–2; 6 scores: same as for primer level plus completion, inference.

For a review by Ruth Lowes of an earlier edition of the primer level, see 3:490.

[639]

★**Nelson-Lohmann Reading Test: Coordinated Scales of Attainment.** Grades 4, 5, 6, 7, 8; 1946–54; identical with reading sections of *Coordinated Scales of Attainment;* IBM; Forms A, B ('53, identical with tests copyrighted in 1946 and 1949 except for title); 5 levels; directions for administering ('53); battery manuals (A, '54; B, '49); separate answer sheets must be used; $1.90 per 25 tests; $1 per 25 IBM scorable answer sheets; 25¢ per scoring stencil; postage extra; 75¢ per complete specimen set, postpaid; (45) minutes; Ethel V. Nelson (A), Victor L. Lohmann (A), and Marvin J. Van Wagenen (B); Educational Test Bureau. *

For a review by Alvin W. Schindler of the complete battery, see 4:8; for reviews by Roland L. Beck, Lavone A. Hanna, Gordon N. Mackenzie (with Glen Hass), and C. C. Ross, see 3:6.

[640]

*Primary Reading: Every Pupil Scholarship Test. Grades 1, 2–3; 1935–58; new form usually issued each January and April; 2 levels; norms available following testing program; no data on reliability; 4¢ per test; 4¢ per scoring key; postage extra; (45), 15(20) minutes for grades 1, 2–3; Bureau of Educational Measurements. *

[641]

*Primary Reading: Every Pupil Test. Grades 2–3; 1936–58; new form usually issued each December and April; norms available following testing program; no data on reliability; 3¢ per test; 1¢ per scoring key; cash orders postpaid; 15(30) minutes in 2 sessions; Ohio Scholarship Tests. *

For reviews by William S. Gray and Virginia Seavey of earlier forms, see 3:493.

[642]

*Primary Reading Test: Acorn Achievement Tests. Grades 2–3; 1943–57; 5 scores: word recognition, words-similar meaning, word meaning-opposites, story-paragraph-sentence meaning, total; Forms A ('57, identical with test copyrighted in 1943), B ('43); manual ('43); directions sheet ('43); no norms for part scores; $2.75 per 25 tests; 25¢ per manual; 50¢ per specimen set; postage extra; 31(40) minutes; Winifred E. Stayton, Frances E. Ranson, and Roland L. Beck; Acorn Publishing Co. *

For a review by Alice N. Jameson, see 3:495.

[643]

*The Purdue Reading Test. Grades 7–16; 1928–53; identical with test copyrighted in 1928 except for minor changes; IBM; Forms AM, BM ('52); no manual; no data on reliability; norms ['53]; 10¢ per test; separate answer sheets may be used; 15¢ per specimen set; postpaid; H. H. Remmers, John M. Stalnaker, and P. C. Baker; distributed by State High School Testing Service for Indiana. *

For a review by Albert J. Harris, see 3:496.

[644]

⋆Purdue Reading Test for Industrial Supervisors: Purdue Personnel Tests. Supervisors; 1955; Form A; preliminary manual; $5 per 25 tests, postage extra; 50¢ per specimen set, postpaid; 25(35) minutes; Joseph Tiffin and Roy Dunlap; distributed by University Book Store. *

REFERENCE

1. DUNLAP, ROY D. *A Reading Comprehension Test for Industrial Supervisors.* Doctor's thesis, Purdue University (Lafayette, Ind.), 1955. (*DA* 16:375)

JEROME E. DOPPELT, *Assistant Director, Test Division, The Psychological Corporation, New York, New York.*

The test consists of 14 reading passages with either two or three multiple choice items per passage. The content of the passages centers around factory and industrial situations in an effort to make the material acceptable to the intended examinees. The time limit of 25 minutes is evidently not sufficient to make the test a power measure.

This instrument is described as "particularly useful in identifying supervisors who are in need of developmental reading instruction or, if such instruction cannot be given, as a guide to management in writing material that supervisors are expected to read." Although these two objectives are laudable, there is no evidence that the test is helpful in the accomplishment of either one.

At the present time, there is a preliminary manual which includes a table of norms based on 137 industrial supervisors representing all levels from first line supervisors to plant superintendents. Reliability was estimated by applying the Kuder-Richardson formula 20 to the scores of a group of supervisors who finished the test and then correcting the coefficient for the increased range of scores when all supervisors are included. The resulting coefficient was .83. When a modification developed by Horst was applied to the K-R formula, the coefficient rose to .91. However, it must be noted that the group for which reliability was estimated was very heterogeneous and it is doubtful whether such reliability could be expected in a single plant.

For validity, the manual simply reports a correlation with another reading test. A communication from one of the test authors states that a revised manual will contain the report of a study in which scores on the test were found to be significantly related to job performance ratings.

There is no evidence to indicate this test is more suitable for accomplishing its purposes than a vocabulary test which could be administered in considerably less time. The technical data supporting the test do not resolve doubts as to its value in specific industrial situations. The reviewer feels there is, as yet, no good reason for recommending the use of this instrument.

LOUIS C. NANASSY, *Professor of Business Education, Montclair State College, Upper Montclair, New Jersey.*

This 38-item test is designed to assist in measuring the paragraph comprehension of industrial supervisors. It is self-administering and is easily scored, the score being simply the number of correct answers.

An estimate of the reliability, based on several computations, would seem to indicate that when the test is used with typical industrial supervisors and covers the full range of reading ability found in such a group, the reliability is in the neighborhood of .90. The only estimate of validity presently reported is a correlation of .81 between scores made by 137 supervisors on this test and on the paragraph comprehension part of the *Nelson Silent Reading Test*.

The test is well constructed, with vocabulary and subject matter appropriate for industrial supervisors. The format and copy make for readability and ease in administering. Instructions are exceptionally clear.

The test gives every indication of fulfilling the specific purpose for which it was constructed. When a more comprehensive analysis of reading ability is desired, the use of the *Purdue Word-Meaning Test for Industrial Supervisors* with this test is recommended.

[645]
*****Reading Comprehension: Cooperative English Test: Lower and Higher Levels, C1 and C2.** Grades 7-12, 11-16; 1940-53; 4 scores: vocabulary, speed, level, total; IBM; Forms R ('50, same as test copyrighted in 1941), T (Lower Level, '43; Higher Level, '50—same as test copyrighted in 1943), Y ('48), Z ('53); 2 levels; no specific manual; general Cooperative manual ('51); descriptive folder ['51]; directions for hand scoring ['49]; norms ['40]; separate answer sheets must be used with Form Z, optional with other forms; $3.25 per 25 tests; $1 per 25 IBM answer sheets; 25¢ per scoring stencil; postage extra; 40(45) minutes; Frederick B. Davis, Mary Willis (T), Clarence Derrick (Y), Harry R. Neville (Y), Jeanne M. Bradford (Y), Geraldine Spaulding (Y), and Charlotte Croon Davis (Z); Cooperative Test Division, Educational Testing Service. *

REFERENCES

1-2. See 40:1564.
3-17. See 3:497.
18-37. See 4:547.
38. COCKRUM, LOGAN V. "Predicting Success in Training for the Ministry." *Relig Ed* 47:198-202 My-Je '52. *
39. FREDERIKSEN, NORMAN. "The Influence of Timing and Instructions on Cooperative Reading Test Scores." *Ed & Psychol Meas* 12:598-607 w '52. * (*PA* 27:6741)
40. ARN, ELMER H. R. *The Prediction of Academic Success in Ten Selected Science Areas at the University of Washington.* Doctor's thesis, University of Washington (Seattle, Wash.), 1953. (*DA* 13:495)
41. BARRETT, DOROTHY M. "Correlation of Survey Section of Diagnostic Reading Tests and of Test C2: Reading Comprehension With College History Grades." *J Ed Res* 46:465-9 F '53. * (*PA* 28:1461)
42. JENSON, RALPH E. "Predicting Scholastic Achievement of First-Year Graduate Students." *Ed & Psychol Meas* 13:322-9 su '53. * (*PA* 28:4833)
43. BOLTON, EURI BELLE. "The Predictive Value of the Columbia and the Michigan Vocabulary Tests for Academic Achievement." *Peabody J Ed* 32:9-21 Jl '54. * (*PA* 29:7954)
44. FITZGIBBON, THOMAS J. *The Prediction of Academic Success of Freshmen at Bradley University.* Doctor's thesis, Bradley University (Peoria, Ill.), 1954. (*DA* 14:1170)
45. MUNRO, JAMES J. R. *The Predictive Value of Entrance Reading Test Scores at the University of Washington.* Doctor's thesis, University of Washington (Seattle, Wash.), 1954. (*DA* 14:1179)
46. BOYKIN, LEANDER L. "The Reading Performance of Some Negro College Students." *J Negro Ed* 24:435-41 fall '55. * (*PA* 30:7666)
47. CHAHBAZI, PARVIZ. "The Prediction of Achievement in a College of Agriculture." *Ed & Psychol Meas* 15:484-6 w '55. * (*PA* 30:7754)
48. HAYNES, JERRY O. *Some Predictive Factors of Academic Success in Two Curricula of a Land-Grant College.* Master's thesis, Alabama Polytechnic Institute (Auburn, Ala.), 1955.
49. McGOLDRICK, DAVID T. *A Correlation Between Scores Attained on the Cooperative Reading Test and Grades Achieved in English One and Two by Freshmen Entering the School of Business, Niagara University From 1951 to 1953, to Ascertain the Value of the Test as a Prediction and to Establish Norms.* Master's thesis, Niagara University (Niagara Falls, N.Y.), 1955.
50. BRAGG, EMMA W. "A Study of Student Withdrawal at 'W.U.'" *J Ed Psychol* 47:199-202 Ap '56. *
51. BRESEE, CLYDE W. *Affective Factors Associated With Academic Underachievement in High-School Students.* Doctor's thesis, Cornell University (Ithaca, N.Y.), 1956. (*DA* 17:90)
52. CHAHBAZI, PARVIZ. *Prediction of Achievement in New York State College of Agriculture at Cornell University.* Doctor's thesis, Cornell University (Ithaca, N.Y.), 1956. (*DA* 17:562)
53. HENDERSON, HAROLD L. "Prediction of Academic Success." *Psychol Rep* 2:321-2 S '56. * (*PA* 31:3784)
54. VAN DER JAGT, E. R., AND MESNER, D. M. "Predictability of Success in College Courses, by Accelerating and Non-Accelerating Students as Measured by Scores Made by Entering Freshmen on A.C.E. and Cooperative Reading Test." *Sci Ed* 40:327-32 O '56. *
55. FRICKE, BENNO G. "Speed and Level Versus Rate and Accuracy of Reading." *Yearb Nat Council Meas Used Ed* 14:73-7 '57. *
56. HENDERSON, HAROLD L. "Predictors of Freshmen Grades in a Long Island College." *Ed & Psychol Meas* 17:623-7 w '57. *
57. LARSEN, TORA M. *A Study of the Student Personnel Records at East Carolina College as Relates to Prediction in Elementary Accounting.* Doctor's thesis, University of Minnesota (Minneapolis, Minn.), 1957. (*DA* 18:1304)
58. LOWRY, CARMEN E. *The Prediction of Academic Success in a Private Liberal Arts College for Negroes.* Doctor's thesis, University of Texas (Austin, Tex.), 1957. (*DA* 17:2500)

For reviews by Robert Murray Bear and J. B. Stroud of Forms R, S, and T, see 3:497. For reviews by J. Paul Leonard, Edward S. Noyes, and Robert C. Pooley of Forms R, S, and T of the complete battery, see 3:120.

[646]
*****Reading Comprehension Test: National Achievement Tests [Speer and Smith].** Grades 3-8; 1938-57; 4 scores: following directions, sentence meaning, paragraph meaning, total; Forms A ('57, identical with test copyrighted in 1938), B ('38); directions sheet ('38); no data on reliability; no norms for part scores; $2.50 per 25 tests; 50¢ per specimen set; postage extra; (30) minutes; Robert K. Speer and Samuel Smith; Acorn Publishing Co. *

For a review by James R. Hobson, see 3:498.

[647]
*****Reading Comprehension Test: National Achievement Tests [Crow, Kuhlmann, and Crow].** Grades 4-6, 4-9; 1953-57; Form A ('57); 2 levels; 25¢ per manual ('54); 50¢ per specimen set of either level; postage extra; 30(35) minutes; Lester D Crow, Martha J. Kuhlmann, and Alice Crow; Acorn Publishing Co. *
a) GRADES 4-6. Identical with the first 88 items of the 130-item test for grades 4-9; reliability and normative data based upon the 130-item test for grades 4-9; $2.50 per 25 tests.
b) GRADES 4-9. Form A ('57, identical with test copyrighted in 1953); $3 per 25 tests.

[648]

*Reading Test (Comprehension and Speed): Municipal Tests: National Achievement Tests. Grades 3–6, 6–8; 1938–57; subtest of *Municipal Battery;* 5 scores: following directions, sentence meaning, paragraph meaning, reading speed, total; 2 forms; 2 levels; no data on reliability; no norms for part scores; $2.75 per 25 tests; 50¢ per specimen set of either level; postage extra; Robert K. Speer and Samuel Smith; Acorn Publishing Co. *
a) GRADES 3–6. 1938–57; Forms A ('54), B ('55) identical with tests copyrighted in 1938 and 1939; directions sheets (A, '57; B, '39); 33(38) minutes.
b) GRADES 6–8. 1938–54; Forms A ('50), B ('54) identical with tests copyrighted in 1938 and 1939; directions sheets (A, '38; B, '39); 32(37) minutes.

For a review by J. Murray Lee of the complete battery, see 18; for a review by Ralph C. Preston, see 4:20; for reviews by A. M. Jordan and Hugh B. Wood of the complete battery for grades 6–8, see 40:1191.

[649]

★SRA Achievement Series: Reading. Grades 2–4, 4–6, 6–9; 1954–57; title on some tests for grades 2–6 is *What Is This About?;* 2 scores: comprehension, vocabulary; IBM for grades 4–9; Forms A, B; 3 levels; technical supplement, second edition ('57); separate answer sheets must be used in grades 4–9; 50¢ per teacher's handbook ('55); 50¢ per administrator's manual ('56); $1 per technical supplement; postage extra; Louis P. Thorpe, D. Welty Lefever, and Robert A. Naslund; Science Research Associates. *
a) GRADES 2–4. Forms A ('55), B ('57); examiner's manual, second edition ('57); $1.70 per 20 tests; $1 per scoring stencil; 90(130) minutes in 2 sessions.
b) GRADES 4–6. IBM; Forms A ('54), B ('56); examiner's manual ('56); $2 per 20 tests; $5 per 100 IBM scorable answer sheets; $1 per set of machine scoring stencils; 50¢ per machine scoring stencil; 65(80) minutes.
c) GRADES 6–9. IBM; Forms A ['55], B ('56); examiner's manual ('56); prices same as for grades 4–6; 70(80) minutes.

N. DALE BRYANT, *Associate Professor of Psychology, University of Houston, Houston, Texas.*

Reading is only one of four areas covered by the *SRA Achievement Series.* Like the rest of the tests in series, the reading test has three separate tests that are used at different grade levels. Each test consists of five stories of graduated difficulty. Following each story are two types of questions which yield the two test scores. The first score is Reading Comprehension, and the items contributing to this score require the reader to (*a*) locate specific information and overall meaning, (*b*) locate information in several places and compare the information in order to select a correct response, and (*c*) locate information and draw logical conclusions or inferences from it. The second score is Reading Vocabulary, and items

contributing to it refer to underlined words in the stories. The items require the reader to either (*a*) select the literal meaning of a specific underlined word when only one of the alternatives in the item gives a correct definition, or (*b*) select the correct meaning of the word as it is used in the story when all of the item choices give correct literal definitions of the word but only one has the shade of meaning used in the context.

While the difficulty level of the stories is not given, the Technical Supplement indicates that difficulty was controlled by regulating sentence length, sentence complexity, and concept load, as well as by using standard vocabulary lists. It seems likely that the difficulty of the first story in each test is slightly below the 2.5, 4.5, or 6.5 minimum grade level for which the test is supposed to be appropriate. The Technical Supplement does indicate that *items* are included that are above the highest grade level for which the test is designed, and this logically implies that the difficulty level of the last story is above the upper ranges of 4.9, 6.9, or 9.9 indicated.

Reliabilities are reported only for Form A, and, while considerable care was exercised in developing Form B so that it would be equivalent and would have equivalent norms, there is no direct evidence that a student making a particular score on Form A would make a very similar score on Form B. Evidence does show that both forms give the same general distribution of scores. The reported estimates of Kuder-Richardson formula 21 reliability, particularly the figures for grades 4–6 and 6–9, are high enough to warrant the use of the test scores in dealing with individuals. The subtest coefficients are generally in the .80's. A split-half estimate of reliability would probably be a little higher but an alternate-form reliability estimate might be lower, depending upon the equivalence of the two forms.

The tests are designed to measure reading ability, and this is further defined as reading comprehension and reading vocabulary. Certainly, reading speed is one aspect of reading that is not evaluated, and it is a particularly important aspect at the sixth to ninth grade level. Flexibility in adjusting speed and technique to suit the purpose of reading and the difficulty of the material being read is another aspect of reading, particularly important at this level, which is not covered. In addition to these untested components, which limit the validity of this test of reading, the more specific validity of a test of reading comprehension is also suspect. The task of reading comprehension is generally one of reading and understanding material at the time. When a student is allowed to go back and seek the answer to a question, a different variable is added. This skill is usually called scanning or one type of skimming. The time limits are liberal, and the Technical Supplement states that "It was frequently observed....that pupils were expending considerable effort to secure the answers to items in the reading tests, going back again and again to the stories."

The reading comprehension score is made up of items that the examinee gets correct because he understood the story when he read it and remembers it when he encounters the item; however, it also consists of items dealing with points which are not comprehended during the initial reading but which are answered correctly after rereading, possibly again and again, with the question in mind. To the extent that scanning or rereading contributes to the test score, the test is less valid as a measure of reading comprehension in the day to day sense of understanding what one reads as one reads it. This reduces the validity only partially, however, since pupils may sometimes reread on their own and since the ability to get information when looking for it is probably related to getting information in the normal reading situation. To the extent that reading comprehension is defined to include the ability to locate information that has been used in a question, the test is more valid.

The validity of the reading vocabulary subtest seems to be closely related to the understanding of both the literal meaning and shades of meaning of words in context. Yet, here again, the testing situation, which supplies direction for rereading, tends to produce a variation from the normal reading situation. The result may be a less valid measure of vocabulary use as it occurs in normal reading. However, even for measuring normal vocabulary use, the test appears to be more valid than many vocabulary measures which use words out of context.

In conclusion, the reading comprehension and reading vocabulary subtests of the SRA reading tests are carefully constructed, frequently item analyzed and revised, and rela-

tively reliable measures. However, the equivalence of the Forms A and B should be demonstrated for individuals rather than just for groups. If understanding during normal reading is the ability the test is trying to reflect, high validity for the tests may be questionable. Going from items back to the stories for repeated rereadings could introduce variance not perfectly related to the content validity.

CLARENCE DERRICK, *Associate Professor of English and Humanities, University of Florida, Gainesville, Florida.*

The reading tests in this series are good; the accessories are excellent.

Users of the SRA reading tests obtain two scores—reading comprehension and reading vocabulary. Bargain hunters who expect more scores per penny are warned to ask whether the part scores which some tests purport to yield in multiplicity are sufficiently reliable to be meaningful. The authors of these tests are to be commended for supplying only scores which can be statistically defended.

The tests differ from many reading tests in two respects. First, the reading selections are relatively long—about twice the length of the passages in most reading tests; second, all vocabulary items are based on words in the selections. Both of these characteristics make sense and will undoubtedly be featured in sales promotion. The reviewer, however, through his own research [1] into the effects of passage length upon the measurement of reading comprehension, is convinced that good tests measuring a wide variety of important reading skills can be constructed using short reading selections. Vocabulary in context has advantages, but the technique necessarily limits sampling. A price is paid by using the vocabulary-in-context approach.

The tests are relatively unspeeded and require two class periods to administer. This may be a limitation in some situations. The reading tests in the *Sequential Tests of Educational Progress* also require two periods, but the STEP tests provide a usable score from a single period, a feature lacking in the SRA reading tests. This reviewer's chief criticism is that, at the second to the fourth grade level, pupils are confronted with questions to be answered

[1] DERRICK, CLARENCE. *Three Aspects of Reading Comprehension as Measured by Tests of Different Lengths.* Research Bulletin No. 53-8. Princeton, N.J.: Educational Testing Service, 1953. Pp. vi, 176. *

"Yes," "No," or "We can't tell." The distribution between "No" and "We can't tell" is too sophisticated a concept for the age group.

The six manuals are models of completeness. There is a manual for school administrators featuring a detailed analysis of the skills being tested; a manual for test technicians which discusses the rationale of the series, national standardization, reliability, validity (including factor analysis data), and equating; three manuals for examiners (one for each level) containing instructions for administering and scoring; and a teacher's handbook with a discussion of norms, use of profiles, and some suggested procedures for developing comprehension skills.

Both percentile and grade equivalent norms are available. There are separate percentile norms for each semester of each grade, and the extrapolation of grade equivalents is limited to one year above and below the grades tested. Each test is designed so that it "does not contain easy items suitable for the seriously retarded student to answer correctly, and only a few items for the low-average learner to handle successfully." (The authors recommend, for example, that retarded students in grade 5 be given the test prepared for the grade 2-4 level.) As a result of the gradient selected for these tests, grade equivalents have a stability lacking in less carefully designed tests where an extra item or two correct will greatly increase a pupil's grade placement score. The norming procedures are described in such detail that the sophisticated test user has a clear idea of what the norms mean, and the less sophisticated can appreciate that the authors have done their job thoroughly and well.

The authors of this series have certainly taken seriously the suggestions of the Committee on Test Standards of the American Educational Research Association as set forth in *Technical Recommendations for Achievement Tests,* January 1955. It is hoped that many test users will have the interest and training to make use of the information supplied to them in the manuals and other accessories in this series.

In summary, there are reading tests as good as the SRA reading tests; there are few or none so fully documented and supported by helpful accessory materials.

For reviews by Warren G. Findley and Worth R. Jones of the complete battery, see 21.

[650]

★Scholastic Diagnostic Reading Test. Grades 1–3, 4–6, 7–9; 1953–55; various titles used by publisher; for Catholic schools; some subtests also appear in *Diagnostic Reading Tests: Pupil Progress Series* for non-Catholic schools; IBM for grades 4–9; 2 forms; 3 levels; manual ('55) for each level; no data on reliability for specific grade levels; separate answer sheets may be used in grades 4–9; $1.75 per 35 IBM scorable answer sheets; 50¢ per specimen set of any one level; 24¢ per set of scoring stencils; postage extra; Oliver F. Anderhalter, Ruth Colestock, and R. Stephen Gawkoski; Scholastic Testing Service, Inc. *
a) PRIMARY TEST. Grades 1–3; 1953–55; 12 scores: vocabulary (3 subscores), rate, comprehension (5 subscores), total; Forms A ('53), B ('55); $3.25 per 35 tests; (30–40) minutes.
b) ELEMENTARY TEST. Grades 4–6; 1953–55; 14 scores: knowledge and use of sources (4 subscores), rate, comprehension (6 subscores), total; IBM; Forms A ['53], B ('55); $3.65 per 35 tests; 42(60) minutes.
c) ADVANCED TEST. Grades 7–9; 1935–55; 14 scores: same as for *b;* IBM; Forms A, B ('55); $3.75 per 35 tests; 42(60) minutes.

RUSSELL G. STAUFFER, *Director, The Reading-Study Center, University of Delaware, Newark, Delaware.*

The purpose of this test is twofold: to help the teacher identify students who are deficient in reading and to provide assistance in the establishment of a remediation program by pointing out areas in reading in which students function at a low level.

To this reviewer it seems that the title of the test is faulty. The word "diagnostic" implies an exhaustive analysis of individual differences in ability to use particular skills. Since such an analysis cannot be accomplished with the use of this test, it would be more accurate to call the test a "reading inventory."

Even a cursory examination of the subparts of the test, regardless of levels, quickly shows that the test is not designed as a clinical device for use in diagnosing severe reading disability. Therefore, the reviewer also protests the use of the words "remediation" and "deficient." The former implies "remedial" with all its connotations of disability and the need for special help, while the latter similarly implies major shortcomings.

The purposes might better read then: to help the teacher identify students who need additional training in certain skills, and to provide assistance in more adequately individualizing reading instruction.

That the test is made available in a series is good, especially if users at any one level will become familiar with what skills are tested at the other two levels. The better a teacher grasps the pattern of the hierarchy of skills and the continuity of development, the better she will be able to differentiate instruction. Since the purpose of the test is to encourage teachers to use the results to plan and motivate learning, the additional study would be especially helpful.

The word recognition test at the primary level is not a true measure of a pupil's ability to recognize words on his own. As an experienced first grade teacher can substantiate, beginning pupils can do much better when someone else reads the words and all they need to do is locate the words, as is true in this test. Word to content relation tends to be a better measure of word recognition ability since it requires the pupil to do his own reading. Here, of course, the meaningful picture clues facilitate recognition, so that once again the task is not as demanding as recognizing words in isolation.

To this reviewer it would seem that there are many other skills more useful and necessary at the primary level than rate of reading. Reading is a mental process involving thinking and versatility of adjustment. Judgment about rate is usually determined, at least in part, by the reader's purpose for reading. In this test the pupil is admonished to read "as fast as you can, but try to remember what you read." Given only such a vague purpose, the pupil has no alternative but to try to soak up everything so as to be prepared for the test that follows. Furthermore, he is told that if he finishes all four of the stories before he is told to stop, he may go back and read the stories again. This forecast of comprehension events to follow should slow the pupil down to a rote memorization pace if the previous warning did not. Then, to boot, Recalling Information, which follows, is strictly a measure of facts, most of them unimportant to either plot development or plot outcome.

The Elementary and Advanced Tests are sounder and more useful. The sections covering knowledge and use of sources are especially good. Many teachers may be alerted to skills that need to be taught when they study these sections. Also, the number of items per section is larger than in the Primary Test.

In the higher level tests Rate of Reading for Meaning merits many of the criticisms given about that section in the Primary Test. The instructions do not urge the reader to "remember"; neither do they establish "purposes" for reading. Rereading is again encouraged.

While rereading is an important reading-study skill, it is not what is being appraised here. In Form A of the Elementary Test (grades 4–6), 17 of the 20 questions start with "the chipmunk('s)" and then proceed to ask a fact about chipmunks. The other three questions also ask for factual information but at least vary the style of the question asking. Knowlege of facts is important, it is true, but never that important. Skillful readers need to know how to size up a situation, evaluate a title, make hypotheses, read to confirm or refute conjectures, alter hypotheses, evaluate outcomes or data, and use ideas or information gained. In all of this, facts are important—but getting them is only one part of the process.

A good feature of the Elementary and Advanced Tests is that they offer scores for the same 10 parts, subtotal, and total categories for grades 4–9. This is a good way to stress continuous growth of all students at all grade levels with respect to basic skills.

In summary, the *Scholastic Diagnostic Reading Test* is useful for a more specific survey of some of the skills of reading. It points up certain skills that might be overlooked otherwise As an inventory of needs for improved individualization of instruction, the test may be very useful. It is not a diagnostic test in the same sense that it diagnoses a disability. The Elementary and Advanced Tests are particularly useful. The Primary Test leaves much to be desired.

ARTHUR E. TRAXLER, *Executive Director, Educational Records Bureau, New York, New York.*

The format and typography of the test booklets and manuals are generally good, although a few of the pictures in the Elementary and Advanced Tests are too small and indistinct to be easily read.

Raw scores on all tests and subtests at each level are translated into grade equivalents. These equivalents may be graphed on an individual profile form on the cover page of the test booklets. Each raw score is simply the number right, even in subtests consisting of yes-no items. This procedure allows chance scores to yield substantial grade equivalents. For instance, in Test 1 of the elementary battery, pure guessing would on the average yield a grade equivalent of about 5.5—a rather respectable score for a fourth grade pupil.

The grade equivalents are based on nationwide testing in Catholic schools. No evidence is presented to support the use of the same grade equivalents when responses are entered in booklets and when they are recorded on answer sheets. This procedure may be questioned, since research has often shown that more time is required to record responses on answer sheets than to enter them in the booklets.

Because of their brevity, the grade equivalent scales for some of the subtests are necessarily coarse. In some places, one item makes a difference of more than one grade in a pupil's score.

The deciles and the 5th and 95th percentiles of the grade scores are reported for each half year from the end of grade 1 through the first half of grade 9. Such norms are desirable but their use requires an extreme amount of interpolation by test users. In fact, in certain brief subtests, no percentile ranks may be obtained without interpolation. The presentation of only certain percentiles is common practice, but it causes test users much loss of time. Tables showing all percentiles, or the percentile ranks of all scores, should be prepared.

Since all three levels were administered in the spring for normative purposes, the percentile norms for the first half of each grade must have been found by interpolation—a somewhat hazardous procedure.

The percentile tables for the Primary Test indicate that this test is somewhat too easy for grade 3. In two of the subtests, the grade equivalent which corresponds to a perfect score yields a percentile rank of about 60 in the last half of the third grade.

The small amount of validity data reported is reasonably favorable. A correlation of .67 between comprehension scores and reading grades of sixth grade pupils is rather high for this kind of relationship.

Split-half and alternate-forms reliabilities for single grades are about what one would expect for tests of these lengths. The reliabilities of two of the three main scores average about .90, which may be regarded as satisfactory. The median of the reliability coefficients reported for the rate score is only .76, which is hardly high enough to indicate usefulness of the rate measure in the study of individuals. The probable reason for the rather low reliability of the rate score is the brevity of the rate test. The rate score in the primary test is based on a two-minute interval; the one in the intermediate and advanced tests is derived from a total of one and one-half minutes of reading time. In order to obtain a rate reliability of .80 to .90, at least three minutes of reading time is generally required.

The reliabilities of the subtests, ranging from .62 to .94 with a median of about .77, are as high as could be expected for scores based on 10 to 20 items. Nevertheless, the rather low reliabilities of at least half of the subtests cast doubt upon their value for individual diagnosis. The diagnostic worth of the subtests could more readily be ascertained if information were available about their intercorrelation.

Raw score equivalence data indicate that the means and standard deviations of the scores yielded by Forms A and B tend to be closely similar. There is an obvious error in the mean rate score for grade 4 reported on page 15 of the manual for the Elementary Test. This is the only printing error noted.

SUMMING UP. Since this purportedly diagnostic reading test was standardized on a nationwide sampling of Catholic pupils, it is very probably one of the most useful available reading tests for Catholic schools. The test has a number of desirable features which would commend it to public schools and independent schools outside the Catholic group. The items are well constructed, the directions are clearly written, the tests are well printed, and the manuals contain a good deal of helpful statistical data.

On the other hand, there are several disadvantages for the general user. No public school norms are available; the reliability of one of the main scores, the rate of reading score, is rather low; and the value of the subtest diagnostic scores is open to question because of their somewhat low reliability and doubtful independence. This reviewer recognizes the special contribution made by the *Scholastic Diagnostic Reading Test,* but for general use he questions whether it offers any advantages over such well known tests as *Reading Comprehension: Cooperative English Test,* the *Diagnostic Reading Tests,* and the *Iowa Silent Reading Tests.*

[651]
*The Schonell Reading Tests. Ages 5-15, 6-9, 7-11, 9-13; 1942-55; individual in part; 1 form; tests are

reproduced in full in 6 below; tests R5, R6, and R7 not available as separates; 2s. 9d. per 12 copies of any one test; 1s. 6d. per manual of instructions and norms ['55]; 6s. 6d. per copy of *The Psychology and Teaching of Reading, Third Edition,* ('51, see 5 below) which serves as the complete manual for *a*; 25s. per copy of *Backwardness in the Basic Subjects, Fourth Edition,* ('51, see 4 below) which serves as the complete manual for *b–g*; postage extra; Fred J. Schonell; Oliver & Boyd Ltd. *

a) TEST R1, GRADED WORD READING TEST. Ages 5–15; 1942; also called *Graded Reading Vocabulary Test;* individual; (5–15) minutes.

b) TEST R2, SIMPLE PROSE READING TEST. Ages 6–9; 1942; also called *My Dog Test;* individual; (3–8) minutes.

c) TEST R3, SILENT READING TEST A. Ages 7–11; 1942; 9(15) minutes.

d) TEST R4, SILENT READING TEST B. Ages 9–13; 1942; 15(20) minutes.

e) TEST R5, TEST OF ANALYSIS AND SYNTHESIS OF WORDS CONTAINING COMMON PHONIC UNITS. Individual; (5–15) minutes.

f) TEST R6, TEST OF DIRECTIONAL ATTACK ON WORDS. Individual; (5–10) minutes.

g) TEST R7, VISUAL WORD DISCRIMINATION TEST. Individual; (10–15) minutes.

REFERENCES

1–3. See 4:552.
4. SCHONELL, FRED J. *Backwardness in the Basic Subjects, Fourth Edition.* Edinburgh, Scotland: Oliver & Boyd Ltd., 1951. Pp. xix, 566.
5. SCHONELL, FRED J. *The Psychology and Teaching of Reading, Third Edition.* Edinburgh, Scotland: Oliver & Boyd Ltd., 1951. Pp. 156.
6. SCHONELL, FRED J., AND SCHONELL, F. ELEANOR. *Diagnostic and Attainment Testing: Including a Manual of Tests, Their Nature, Use, Recording and Interpretation, Third Edition.* Edinburgh, Scotland: Oliver & Boyd Ltd., 1956. Pp. viii, 192.
7. PRINGLE, M. L. KELLMER, AND NEALE, M. D. "A Note on the Use of the Schonell and Gates Reading Tests in the First Year of the Junior School." *Brit J Ed Psychol* 27:135–41 Je '57. *

R. W. McCULLOCH, *Chief Psychologist and Superintendent of Special Schools, Tasmanian Education Department, Hobart, Tasmania, Australia.*

The three tests of reading comprehension (Tests R2, R3, and R4) cover successive difficulty levels from age 6 through age 13, while Test R1 is an individual attainment test in word recognition for ages 5–15. Test R1 is composed of 100 words divided into 10 words per year from ages 5–13 and 10 words for the two years 14 and 15. The 100 words were selected from 300 words administered individually to approximately 60 children in each of the 10 age groups. They are arranged in continuous order of difficulty, the easiest word being read correctly by 55 per cent of children aged 5 and the most difficult being read correctly by 45 per cent of children aged 14–15. The words have no special connection with any method of reading teaching. The test appears to be equally useful in schools following the look-and-say, whole sentence, or phonic methods, or a combined method. The test has been used repeat-edly, even at monthly intervals, to check progress, without any practice effect being detected.

Test R2 is designed for pupils of reading age 6–9 and is scored for speed, accuracy, and comprehension. The story to be read is sufficiently interesting to keep average readers of ages 6–9 trying. To its credit, it can also hold the interest of the older backward reader, though the printing and layout are of the type that is usually provided for the younger child. The norms—always weak in reading tests for children near the age at which they begin to read—have been revised by the author to give separate norms for Paragraph 1 (based on a 5- to 6-year-old vocabulary), for Paragraphs 1 and 2, and for Paragraphs 1, 2, and 3. This improves the test's value for use with the very poor reader.

Tests R3 and R4, silent reading tests, consist of a number of paragraphs, each followed by questions, instructions, or multiple choice problems. Answer sheets are separate. The questions in these tests of comprehension come very close to the kinds of questions which arise in natural reading situations. The requirement of writing a single word in answer to some questions has been criticized as possibly penalizing the slow writer. This may be true, but, to the tester, this disadvantage is balanced by the added information given by the nature of the word chosen.

Tests R5, R6, and R7 constitute a set of diagnostic tests aimed at identifying whether or not any or all of a large number of specific difficulties are operative in individual cases. Test R5 is a diagnostic test of graded words containing most of the common phonic combinations and families. The test consists of two parts. The first 60 words contain regular combinations of vowels and consonants together with the common vowel digraphs such as *ai, ee,* and consonantal digraphs like *ck, gr,* and *sh.* The last 30 words are polysyllabic and are designed to reveal the testee's ability to read regular words that require syllabification, such as "forget" and "contented." The test's prime purpose is the diagnosis of weaknesses in the auditory or phonic elements of word recognition. Its value lies in its qualitative rather than its quantitative results; the application of standardisation procedures would have been pointless.

Test R6, designed to cover directional attack on words, consists of 12 groups of words. Each group comprises four words which contain the same letters but in different positions. The test rapidly identifies the pupil who has not stabilized his ability to look at words carefully from left to right and to differentiate among words of similar but slightly different structure. Test R7 is directed at weaknesses in the perception of visual patterns of words. Its usefulness is mainly as a supplement to Tests R1 and R6.

The tests form an integral part of the books mentioned in the test entry preceding this review. This makes it clear that the author designed the tests for teachers and specialists who intended to use them in conjunction with actual reading programs, whether group or individual. He assumes that those administering the tests will have access to considerably more detail about each child than is provided by the tests alone, and he emphasizes (particularly in relation to Tests R5, R6, and R7) that the insight, caution, and background of the tester play as important a part as does the test itself. Viewed in this context the group tests provide a coverage, both in age range and in competences tested, which is adequate for surveys carried out as preliminaries to the design of group instructional programs in reading, or as appraisals of group instructional programs already in operation. The diagnostic tests are sufficiently comprehensive in the aspects of reading which they probe to lead the diagnostician into the careful consideration of personal history and environmental factors which the author rightly sees as an essential part of the diagnostic procedure. The diagnostic tests achieve comprehensiveness in spite of the absence of tests requiring auditory discrimination between words, the matching of printed words and words heard, and the comprehension of ideas differentiated only by punctuation, word position, or choice of phrasing. Although they are adequate in the way mentioned, Tests R5, R6, and R7 are supported in the Schonell books only by the all too brief chapters on the clinical evaluation of the complex factors which may underlie the failures revealed by the tests. This is the most critical weakness in the series of books and tests which the Schonells and their assistants have issued since 1942.

In summary, it may be said that the fulfilment of the overall plan implicit in the series of books and tests has been brought closer by the extra explanatory material and the restandardizations reported in the latest editions of the

books. As they stand, they provide a convenient and reliable testing kit for the teacher or specialist who is experienced and sensitive. For the learner, the tests, particularly the diagnostic tests, require supplementing by more case reports.

For a review by M. L. Kellmer Pringle, see 4:552; for a review by Edith I. M. Thomson, see 3:499.

[652]

★**Sentence Reading Test 1.** Ages 7-6 to 11-1; 1956; 1 form ['56] no data on validity; 1s. 9d. per 12 tests; 2d. per single copy; 1s. per manual; postage extra; 15(25) minutes; A. F. Watts; published for National Foundation for Educational Research in England and Wales; Newnes Educational Publishing Co. Ltd. *

REGINALD R. DALE, *Lecturer in Education, University College of Swansea, Swansea, England.*

This test assesses the ability of children aged 7-6 to 11-1 to read and understand incomplete sentences and to choose the correct completion word out of five supplied. There are 35 graded sentences. The standardisation is well done, though users should be told whether "a specially chosen sample of primary schools" includes schools representing the necessary proportion of educationally subnormal children, etc., and also children from private schools. In tests of the future, even more attention may be paid to proportions of occupational class in the standardisation sample. Reliability is high, but users are rightly warned that errors at the extremes of the range are "not inconsiderable." It would have been valuable and reassuring for users if an item analysis had been provided, as a careful inspection of the items leaves one with the feeling that the grading of both the sentences and the completion words, though by no means absent, might have been improved.

As a child could give one correct answer in five by guessing, the author examined statistically how this effect might be minimised in the scoring. Discarding the total raw score and "rights minus weighted wrongs" methods, he concluded that the best method was to discount "correct" answers occurring after a gap of five consecutive wrong answers. On the whole, the reviewer agrees that, with the given test, this method of marking is an improvement on the raw scores and will give a valid result, but it is overstating the case a little to claim that the gap "successfully segregated 'chance' scores

from scores contributing to a measure of reading ability."

This test is cheap, simple in method, short,
and easy to administer. The answering procedure for the pupils is the same throughout and
should cause no undue difficulties. Marking is
also simple and quick but it would have been
useful for a machine scoring method to have
been provided for users who test very large
numbers of pupils. The imperfections are slight
in relation to the value of the test. Though no
data are provided on the difficult question of
validity, this reviewer is of the opinion that the
test will prove to be a valuable means of assessing the comparative silent reading standards of individuals and groups.

STEPHEN WISEMAN, *Director, School of Education, University of Manchester, Manchester,
England.*

The test consists of 35 (unrelated) incomplete sentences for which the subject has to
choose the correct final word from five alternatives. The response is made by underlining the
correct word. The test is printed on both sides
of a single sheet. The format of the test, although extremely simple and inexpensive by
American standards, is excellent. Fourteen of
the 35 items come on the first side of the sheet,
in adequately bold sans-serif type face. The remaining 21 items are in smaller type. The items
are graded in difficulty and 15 minutes is allowed for the test after two examples have
been worked. The range of difficulty can best
be demonstrated by quoting the first and last
items:

> 1. Come with me to the shops to buy some (fire,
> water, stone, sweets, motors).
> 35. The political dangers of monopoly seem to
> have been much (exasperated, excised, exagger-
> ated, expropriated, expostulated).

Raw scores are converted to standardised
scores with a mean of 100 and a standard deviation of 15—the common British method for
primary school group tests. The standardisation sample consisted of 7,776 boys and girls
aged 7-6 to 11-1. The population was drawn
from a "specially chosen sample of primary
schools"; no other details are given. Clearly, a
large number of schools was involved, since
British primary schools are small by American
standards, and there are relatively few with
more than a three or four stream entry. It
would have been more satisfactory, however,

to give more information about how the sample was drawn, and particularly, about the regions from which it came. Reading ability may
well vary considerably from one area to another and it is not unconnected with dialect and
differences in speech habits. Standardisations
were done for "each year group separately,
after which inconsistencies between the tables
for adjacent months of age, resulting from differences between segregated year groups, were
smoothed out." Although figures are given in
the manual showing that girls in the sample had
a significantly higher mean score than the boys
at each age level, separate conversion tables
are not provided. Inspection of the conversion
table shows that the effect of age on score is
greater at the younger months, being nearly
twice as great at the 8-5 to 8-9 level as at 10-5
to 10-9 (approximately .7 points of standardised score change per month of age as against
.4).

The reliability figures of .91 to .97 (test-retest after one week, $n = 243$), for a test of 35
items and 15 minutes' time, are extremely good,
giving standard errors of score between 2.7
and 4.5. The short interval between test and
retest should, however, be noted. Test-retest
after one year yielded coefficients of .82, .89,
and .88 for groups of seven-, eight-, and nine-
year-olds, respectively. No Kuder-Richardson
coefficient is reported.

One of the most interesting aspects of the
manual is the suggested correction for chance
scoring. An analysis of item responses "indicated that a gap of five consecutive wrong answers successfully segregated 'chance' scores
from scores contributing to a measure of reading ability." Correlations between "corrected"
and "uncorrected" scores were .98 or .99, and
a study of the test-retest results after one year
showed that the correction had no effect on reliability. One could wish that Watts had included more detailed information about the
analysis of answer patterns which led to this
correction. It is a most interesting technique,
one which might perhaps be further developed.
One wonders, however, whether the "gap"
should be constant over the whole of this very
wide ability range, and what the effect on validity would be for different groups of children.
No guidance is given to the test marker as to
what to do with a gap consisting of four wrong
answers and one omitted item. In view of the
instructions to the children ("Do not worry if

you cannot do some of the sentences. Just do what you can."), there might be a certain degree of injustice done to some subjects by varying interpretations of the instructions.

[653]
★**Sequential Tests of Educational Progress: Reading.** Grades 4–6, 7–9, 10–12, 13–14; 1956–57; IBM; Forms A, B('57); 4 levels; manual ('57); battery directions ('57); battery technical report ('57); no data on reliability of Form B; separate answer sheets must be used; $3.95 per 20 tests; $1 per 20 IBM scorable answer sheets; 45¢ per scoring stencil; $1 per manual; $1 per battery technical report; $1.25 per specimen set; postage extra; 70(90–100) minutes; Cooperative Test Division, Educational Testing Service. *
a) LEVEL 4. Grades 4–6; Forms 4A, 4B.
b) LEVEL 3. Grades 7–9; Forms 3A, 3B.
c) LEVEL 2. Grades 10–12; Forms 2A, 2B.
d) LEVEL 1. Grades 13–14; Forms 1A, 1B.

ERIC F. GARDNER, *Professor of Education and Psychology, University of Syracuse, Syracuse, New York.*

The *Sequential Tests of Educational Progress* are a series of achievement tests measuring learning in seven fields (essay writing, listening comprehension, reading comprehension, writing, science, mathematics and social studies) from the fourth grade through the sophomore year of college. This review is restricted to an examination of the reading comprehension test.

The items were constructed with an intent to assess the following skills: ability to reproduce ideas, ability to translate ideas and make inferences, ability to analyze motivation, ability to analyze presentation, and ability to criticize. Fortunately, no attempt to present separate scores for each of these functions was made. A single score based on the number right is obtained.

Each form of the reading test contains a number of passages of various types, such as directions, announcements, letters, poetry, essays, and speeches. Following each passage is a series of items relating to that passage. There are 70 items of the 4-choice multiple choice type at each level.

Reliability coefficients were computed by an estimate of internal consistency obtained from a single administration of each level (battery) to a single grade. Form 1A was administered to grade 13, Form 2A to grade 11, Form 3A to grade 8, and Form 4A to grade 5. The reliability indices (Kuder-Richardson formula 20) were around .90. As pointed out in the Technical Report, these are slight overestimates of

reliability within a classroom. Of special interest is the attempt to incorporate the standard error of measurement in the score itself by advocating the use of a confidence interval rather than a single point to interpret a student's score. This is a very worthwhile emphasis and should assist in helping teachers avoid making decisions on small score differences, which could have readily arisen by chance.

The validity of the STEP reading comprehension test, as well as that of most other reading tests, is essentially content validity. It is based upon the judgment of the people who constructed the items and built the tests. No information on concurrent or predictive validity is reported, although such information is promised as soon as it may become available.

The norms were obtained from a large sample selected with a view to adequate geographical representation. Both percentile norms for individual scores and percentile norms for the means of the schools included in the normative group are presented. Considerable stress is placed upon the construction of local norms.

In conclusion, the STEP reading test appears to be another technically well constructed test whose basic merits have yet to be demonstrated. This reviewer fails to see where the statement "The Sequential Tests of Educational Progress (STEP) are a new set of achievement tests of a *new kind*" has been substantiated. The criteria set forth for STEP are desirable, but they have been accepted by test constructors for many years and utilized in the construction of most of the currently used achievement test batteries.

JAMES R. HOBSON, *Director of Child Placement, Brookline Public Schools, Brookline, Massachusetts.*

These reading tests are at each level one of a battery of tests of basic skills and understandings and ability in applying them in new situations. They more or less cut across narrowly conceived subject matter lines and attempt to measure educational development and progress in fundamental skill areas rather than subject achievement in the usual sense. Earlier test series which have had some of the same goals in mind would include the *Iowa Every-Pupil Tests of Basic Skills,* the *Iowa Tests of Educational Development,* and, to a degree, the *Cooperative English Test* and the *Diagnostic Reading Tests.* The major goal of the last named series is different, of course, but there is considerable similarity in some of the concepts and methods of implementing them.

A careful reading of the Technical Report, the Manual for Interpreting Scores, and the Directions for Administering and Scoring, and, finally, an item by item and form by form perusal of the tests themselves leave this test consumer and critic with two main generalizations: The conception and development of this test series is an excellent illustration of the scientific method in action; and the end result represents an outstanding professional achievement.

There are several aspects of this undertaking and of its finished product which are worthy of comment. To begin with, a planning committee for each skill area to be tested was chosen with the help of national professional organizations. The members of each planning committee in turn surveyed curriculum and course objectives in their respective geographical areas and arrived at some common agreement at to what it was important to measure at each level. They also took the responsibility for choosing other educators to assist in writing the tests, with due consideration to competence, experience level, geographical location, and type of school representation. Finally, for the actual item writing, all groups were assembled in workshop situations. The tremendous advantages engendered by such an approach to the problem and by the face to face writing and evaluation of test items and exchange of ideas are evident in the propriety of the test items at the different levels and the essential harmony in the overall pattern.

The technical steps taken in producing the final test forms leave little to be desired. The planning foresight, and anticipation of flaws and difficulties in the construction of these instruments show what can be expected when specialists in classroom teaching, curriculum planning, and test construction come together in a professional endeavor which is essentially noncommercial in nature. For example, instead of the usual two preliminary administrations for item analysis and standardization there were separate administrations for item analysis, horizontal as well as vertical equating, and norming the final forms. In many test construction endeavors either steps 1 and 2 or steps 2 and 3 are combined.

In the pretesting program for purposes of item analysis, the respective difficulties of all items were determined not only for the grade for which the test was intended, but in some cases for adjacent grades as well. Next, the effectiveness of every item in discriminating between top ranking and low ranking students was determined. This is, of course, the heart of the content validity of any test. Finally, the pretesting item analysis furnished data on the plausibility of the alternatives to the correct answers, which is such an essential factor in the effectiveness of measurement of all test items of the multiple choice type.

An interesting innovation in the interpretation of STEP scores is the percentile band or confidence interval for any score, based upon the standard error of measurement of a specific score in a given test in a particular class. While this doubtless salves the test construction statistician's conscience and sounds a necessary warning to the literal-minded test user, it is not an unmixed blessing in that it can create as many problem as it solves. After working for 25 years to develop instruments and techniques to give teachers and parents practical methods for interpreting percentile ratings, grade norms, and the like, this reviewer shudders at the thought of trying to interpret a converted score of 290 on a level 2 reading test in terms of a percentile band of 44–74 (manual, page 20), although a recently published student report form does a very good piece of work in this respect albeit the illustrated directions deal with percentile bands only one third as large as the one cited above. It is much easier to interpret a percentile rank of 59, emphasizing the importance of the fact that this is only one item of evidence and that no important decision can be made on the basis of such scanty evidence alone. Incidentally, this reviewer was not able to determine from any data presented specifically how the table of intervals for determining percentile bands was derived. Obviously the range of scores, the shape of the distribution, and the size of the standard error of measurement are the important factors. In view of the completeness and excellence of the presentation in every other respect, however, it was not difficult to take this on faith.

It is not clear why a 2-point "score group" was used in all of the individual score norms tables unless it was so that the percentile rank of a score group would *not* fall on a converted score. A 1-point score group, while making the tables twice as long, would narrow the percentile band by 2 to 4 points in the case of any given score, which would seem desirable to this reviewer. In setting up local norms, it would, of course, be easy to do this if desired.

The maintenance of similarity in the nature and overall pattern of the reading tests at all four levels is clearly illustrated by the fact that the tests look exactly alike and that the number of test items, the directions, and the time limits are identical. To anyone who has ever tried to "run a three-ring circus" by testing pupils of different grades, perhaps those new to the system, in the same room, these identities would constitute a great convenience. The content, of course, becomes progressively more difficult, the skills more complex, and the understandings more mature. These factors amply justify the use of the term "sequential."

In summary, the STEP reading tests are a broadly conceived, expertly planned, scientifically executed, efficiently packaged series whose innate validity will be demonstrated in the crucible of use. This series, over its entire grade and area range, may well prove to be the most useful and authoritative scholastic measuring instrument to be developed in many years.

STEPHEN WISEMAN, *Director, School of Education, University of Manchester, Manchester, England.*

The aim of the STEP series is ambitious—to measure, by means of tests at four levels, all grades from 4 to 14 in each of seven learning fields, of which reading is one ; and to do so by "testing ability to apply learning rather than just 'play it back.' " To the British reviewer the format of the tests is impressive, and, to some extent, formidable. In addition to eight tests, with accompanying answer sheets and scoring stencils, he is provided with a prospectus, directions for administering and scoring, a manual for interpreting scores, a technical report, and specimens of a class record, a score distribution sheet, a student profile, a student report, a supplement to the test catalogue, and an order form.

Each of the reading tests consists of 14 comprehension passages, followed by five multiple choice items, each with four alternatives. This makes a very tidy and symmetrical job, but there seems little other virtue in having exactly five questions on each item. Many times when reading the tests, the reviewer was struck by the obvious wealth of other possible items which might stem from a fairly long extract, and marveled at the discipline which sternly rejected all but the chosen.

The reading material is well varied, including extracts from poems and plays as well as letters, children's stories, technical passages, newspaper articles, and the like. The poetry in the lower grades tends to be somewhat sentimental and trite at times, but this is perhaps difficult to avoid. The reviewer particularly admired some of the passages in the level 1 tests, but could not help contrasting the complexity and sophistication of the extracts and the relative simplicity (or even naiveté) of some of the questions. This gives a rather misleading appearance to the tests at this level : it does not follow that because a student gets a good score on Test 1B, he is capable of coping with confidence with such material as "They told me, Heraclitus, they told me you were dead." The reading material in the tests at this level would be admirable for sixth forms in this country, but one suspects that the items would be much too easy to give an adequate ceiling.

The testmakers have endeavoured to divide items equally among "five major reading-for-comprehension skills": ability to reproduce ideas, ability to translate ideas and make inferences, ability to analyse motivation, ability to analyse presentation, and ability to criticise. The reviewer has made no systematic attempt to check this claim of content validity, but he suspects that the last-named skill at least carries less weight than some of the others. It would be surprising if this were not so.

Nine criteria for the selection of passages are listed in the manual. It is unfortunate that in a test manual in the field of English the English usage should be suspect. Criterion 3 reads : "Materials should be crucial in value (e.g., a selection on how to build a model airplane would be preferable to directions for navigating the Yangtze River)." The meaning of "crucial" is (O.E.D.) "decisive, critical."

Directions for administering the reading tests are exactly the same for all tests at all levels. Thus, one can test a "mixed" group containing students taking tests of different forms and at different levels. This is a great convenience, but when one considers the difference in educational level between the dull fourth grader and the bright college sophomore, one wonders whether the same instructions can be equally effective over such a wide range of comprehension. The vocabulary level is not uniformly low enough for the bottom end, while the length and detail of instructions (and the common "example" used) is likely to be irksome to the top end.

The technical report gives a good deal of information about the construction of the series as a whole, but it is not always clear in detail. Three different samples of children were used for pretesting, for equating, and for norming. All these samples were apparently drawn from the school systems of willing superintendents in a "random sample of superintendents of school systems throughout the nation." The lack of representativeness caused by refusal to participate is recognised, and this is a necessary limitation which must be accepted.

In pretesting the reading tests, 4,000 students in each of grades 5, 8, 11, and 13 were given four forms of each level (each form being administered to a random quarter of the sample). Analysis was based on a 200-case random sample for each form in each grade, and items analysed for difficulty and for discrimination between high and low 100-case subgroups. With 1,000 cases for each form one might have expected rather larger samples to be used for analysis. No information is given on the level of discrimination demanded.

Two hundred twenty-two schools and 41 colleges took part in the programme to equate the tests in the series "horizontally" and "vertically," i.e., to determine the comparability of Forms A and B at the same level and the relationship between different levels. For the vertical equating, pairs of successive grades were used, with random halves in each classroom taking successive levels of Form A. In addition, every student took a "link test," parallel in content and "straddling the two levels of difficulty."

The score scale derived for the series from the programme results is a curious one to British eyes. The scores run from the 220's up to 380, with 230 as the "mean chance score" on level 4 and 300 as the score midway between chance and maximum at level 1. No distributions are given of raw scores or standardised scores—a great pity, for the experienced testmaker can learn a great deal from such distributions.

In order to learn more about the score scale, the reviewer plotted raw score against standard score for all forms of the reading tests at all levels. The curves for levels 1, 2, and 3 are broadly similar and roughly parallel ogives. Level 4 is quite different, being practically a straight line from raw score 10 to 50, and then gently curving off to become almost asymptotic to the maximum score level. Thus Forms 4A and 4B do not appear to be of the same test "family" as the others. The difference can, perhaps, best be illustrated by considering what raw score is necessary on each test to give a scaled score of 260:

Level:	1A	1B	2A	2B	3A	3B	4A	4B
Raw Score:	19	17	23	23½	29	31	51	49

Notice the large jump from level 3 to level 4; this means a large jump in difficulty between these levels, large enough indeed to justify an additional test to straddle the gap. This table also shows some small discrepancies between alternative forms. In parts of the score, scale differences are extremely large. The graph lines for Forms 3B and 4B actually cross at a raw score of 68, but this is so near the maximum that one would hesitate to draw strong conclusions from it. The difference between Forms 1A and 1B is, however, most marked. Form 1B is consistently more difficult than Form 1A, and this difference in difficulty increases as we go up the scale. Beyond a raw score of 55, Form 1B appears to be more difficult than Form 1A by an amount greater than the difference in difficulty between Form 1A and Form 2A! This may well prove to be a blessing in disguise, since Form 1B will give a much higher ceiling than Form 1A and thus give the tester more flexibility. It does, however, raise some doubts as to the efficiency of the equating programme.

Content validity is assumed as a result of the method of item selection and analysis. Correlations with verbal, quantitative, and total scores on the *Cooperative School and College Ability Test* (SCAT) are given by grades and test forms, and are of the expected magnitude. They run from .77 to .87, with .51 for SCAT—V, .74 for SCAT—Q, and .71 to .85 for SCAT—T. No factor analysis data or other evidence on construct validity are given.

Reliability data are restricted to Form A (Why?) and to calculations based on Kuder-Richardson formula 20 (Why?). In addition (or subtraction) to this, in calculating K-R 20, smaller samples were used for Σpq than for the test SD. After the care taken in selecting samples for tryout, equating, and norming, the lack of any attempt to estimate alternate forms reliability—and even more so, test-retest reliability—seems extraordinary. The coefficients reported, .91, .92, .90, and .95 for Levels 1–4, respectively, seem low to British eyes for a test of 70 minutes. Here one is handicapped by lack of precise knowledge of the range of ability in grades as compared with age groups; but in view of the suggestion of lack of parallelism between the A and B forms, the omission of *any* reliability check on Form B seems inexcusable.

In summary, these reading tests seem to be useful and efficient, and no doubt will be found acceptable in schools. The scale and level of publication is impressive, and quite incommensurable with the lack of data on reliability and validity. Whether it is worth correcting raw scores to scaled scores in order to arrive at percentile levels seems to the reviewer highly debatable: the time and energy devoted to this could have been better spent, perhaps, on fuller analysis of the finished product before presenting the tests for publication.

For reviews by Robert W. B. Jackson and Wilbur L. Layton of the complete battery, see 24.

[654]

★**Silent Reading Test.** Standards 1–3 (ages 7–10), 4–8 (ages 10–15); 1947–54; 3 tests; manual ['54]; no data on reliability; specimen set not available; National Bureau of Educational and Social Research. *
a) PARAGRAPHS. Standards 1–3, 4–8; 2 forms; 2 levels; 20(30) minutes.
  1) [*Elementary.*] Standards 1–3; Forms A, B ['47]; 13*s.* 10*d.* per 100 tests.
  2) *Junior.* Standards 4–8; Forms A, B ['47]; 16*s.* 10*d.*, 18*s.* 5*d.* per 100 copies of Forms A, B.
b) VOCABULARY. Standards 1–3, 4–8; 3 forms; 2 levels; 10(15) minutes.
  1) [*Elementary.*] Standards 1–3; Forms A, B, C ['47]; 13*s.* 10*d.* per 100 tests.
  2) *Junior.* Standards 4–8; Forms A, B, C ['47]; 15*s.* 1*d.*, 17*s.* 5*d.*, 16*s.* 10*d.* per 100 copies of Forms A, B, C.
c) SPEED. Standards 1–3, 4–8; 2 forms; 2 levels; 4(7) minutes.
  1) [*Elementary.*] Standards 1–3; 1947–54; Forms A, B ['47]; 11*s.* 4*d.*, 13*s.* 4*d.* per 100 copies of Forms A, B.
  2) [*Junior.*] Standards 4–8; 1947–54; Forms A, B ['47]; 16*s.* 10*d.* per 100 tests.

[655]

The Standard Reading Tests. Reading ages up to 9-0; 1958; individual; 1 form; 12 tests; manual (see *1* below); no data on reliability; 8*s.* 6*d.* per 50 record blanks (published by Philip & Tacey Ltd.); 21*s.* per manual; postage extra; administration time not reported for Tests 1–11; J. C. Daniels and Hunter Diack; Chatto & Windus Ltd. *

a) TEST 1, THE STANDARD TEST OF READING SKILL.
b) TEST 2, COPYING ABSTRACT FIGURES.
c) TEST 3, COPYING A SENTENCE. No norms.
d) TEST 4, VISUAL DISCRIMINATION AND ORIENTATION TEST. No norms.
e) TEST 5, LETTER-RECOGNITION TEST. No norms.
f) TEST 6, AURAL DISCRIMINATION TEST. No norms.
g) TEST 7, DIAGNOSTIC WORD-RECOGNITION TESTS. 8 tests; no norms.
h) TEST 8, ORAL WORD-RECOGNITION TEST. No norms.
i) TEST 9, PICTURE WORD-RECOGNITION TEST. No norms.
j) TEST 10, SILENT PROSE-READING AND COMPREHENSION TEST. No norms.
k) TEST 11, GRADED SPELLING TEST.
l) TEST 12, GRADED TEST OF READING EXPERIENCE. (20) minutes.

REFERENCE
1. DANIELS, J. C., AND DIACK, HUNTER. *The Standard Reading Tests.* London: Chatto & Windus Ltd., 1958. Pp. 215. *

[656]

*****Stanford Achievement Test: Reading.** Grades 3–4, 5–6, 7–9; 1922–55; subtest of *Stanford Achievement Test;* 2 scores: paragraph meaning, word meaning; IBM; 2 editions; postage extra; 35¢ per specimen set of any one level of either edition, postpaid; Truman L. Kelley, Richard Madden, Eric F. Gardner, Lewis M. Terman, and Giles M. Ruch; World Book Co. *
a) [HAND SCORING EDITION.] Grades 3–4, 5–6, 7–9; 3 levels; $2.20 per 35 tests; directions for administering ('53).
  1) *Elementary Reading Test.* Grades 3–4; Forms J ('53), K ('53), L ('54); 33(45) minutes.
  2) *Intermediate Reading Test.* Grades 5–6; Forms J ('53), K ('53), L ('54), M ('55); 37(45) minutes.
  3) *Advanced Reading Test.* Grades 7–9; Forms J ('53), K ('53), L ('54), M ('55); 37(45) minutes.
b) [MACHINE SCORING EDITION.] Grades 5–6, 7–9; IBM; Forms JM ('53), KM ('53), LM ('54); 2 levels; $3.35 per 35 tests; $1.25 per 35 IBM answer sheets; 20¢ per machine scoring stencil; 37(40) minutes.
  1) *Intermediate Reading Test.* Grades 5–6.
  2) *Advanced Reading Test.* Grades 7–9.

HELEN M. ROBINSON, *Associate Professor of Education, The University of Chicago, Chicago, Illinois.*

The reading tests are a portion of a larger battery of tests, but are printed separately. They are designed to measure two aspects of reading achievement: comprehension and word meaning. Thus, these tests may be described as survey tests in contrast to diagnostic tests, which offer several subtest scores.

At each level the paragraph meaning section begins with simple sentences and progresses to longer and more difficult paragraphs. In each paragraph one to four words are omitted, and a blank with a number appears in place of the word. Following the paragraph each number is listed with four alternatives to replace it. There are 40 to 50 separate items. The vocabulary section uses sentence completion for 38 to 50 words. The sentences may define the word or ask for a synonym.

The format of the tests is good and the type is clear. Directions for administering and scoring are unambiguous. The latest revision has eliminated the necessity for writing the answers; hence the score is not contaminated by handwriting and spelling.

Norms are based on 350,000 pupils selected from "all areas of the country, all types of school systems, and all socioeconomic levels." Two types of norms are provided: first, modal-age grade norms, recommended for interpretation of the scores of an individual; and second, total-group grade norms for interpretation of group averages. The modal-age norms are given in percentiles for the beginning, middle, and end of the year. The two sets of norms are especially useful to teachers because they permit comparison of a class with a national norms group and comparison of each pupil with others at his grade level. The manual reports that since the norms beyond grade 10.0 are extrapolated, grade scores are to be interpreted with caution.

The claim for validity of the tests is based on the "content of the typical elementary school curriculum," in addition to extensive experimentation prior to publication. While it is always desirable to have a figure representing validity if some criterion is available, the reviewer prefers that a test be based on the curriculum rather than correlated with teacher's marks or with an another reading test which may not be recent. Split-half reliabilities of the two parts for grades 3–9 range from .82 to .92, with half of them over .90. The reliability, therefore, is satisfactory.

Unfortunately, the paragraph meaning section relies entirely on selecting words to fit the context. Hence, pupils who have had considerable experience and instruction in using context clues are likely to earn higher scores, even though they can read less well than other pupils who have had no such instruction. Furthermore, the technique of filling in blanks with words definitely limits the range of comprehension abilities which can be measured. An examination of the skills required in this section reveals that in most cases filling in the blanks correctly depends on getting the facts or details and securing implied meanings. Notably lacking, especially at the upper levels, is the demand for getting main ideas, following directions, drawing conclusions, determining bias, and recognizing the feelings of those who

are described. Surely most reading curricula state broader goals than merely reading for fact and inference. In general, the paragraphs appear to cover content of interest to pupils of the age levels for which the tests are intended; selections from such content areas as arithmetic, social studies, and science are included.

The manual states that "these are not speed tests," but also that "*under no conditions* should the time limits be extended." Even though the time limit may be generous, speed becomes a factor in individual cases. A more accurate measure of comprehension is a power test such as the Gates reading survey tests in which no pupil is penalized by limited time, and in which speed of reading is measured by a separate test for that purpose.

In spite of the limitations noted, these tests are undoubtedly among the best survey tests of reading achievement for the elementary grades. The format and content, the standardization and norms, the ease of administering and scoring—all contribute to the conclusion that this is a dependable gross measure of reading achievement.

AGATHA TOWNSEND, *Associate Professor of Education, State Teachers College, Kutztown, Pennsylvania.*

Long experience marks the Stanford reading test in many ways—experienced authorship, continuity in publication over a period of almost 30 years, a backlog of statistical study probably unequalled by that for any other test, and (decidedly not the least important factor) a group of users fully familiar with the test and its predecessors. In at least one respect maturity has brought conservatism. The test maintains a limited pattern for reading testing —concentrating on word and paragraph meaning. While skillful item writing has inserted a great deal of reasoning into this rather simple situation, test users seeking a broader picture of reading in grades 5 and above may want to supplement the reading test with the study skills tests in the intermediate and advanced batteries or with other similar measures.

In spite of limitations of test content, however, the Stanford holds a position of importance in the testing program which is very hard to duplicate. This position it holds primarily for these reasons: (a) It can be used either with or without the rest of the battery. (b) It exists in five comparable forms for each level.

(c) Its scoring system facilitates the comprehensive longitudinal study of growth in reading skills over a wide grade range. (d) The results within these limits are unusually dependable. They probably justify fully the remark in the manual that "inability to measure all the outcomes of education should not deter one from measuring those functions for which there are suitable measures."

The modal age norms in which the Stanford results are expressed have certain quite well defined characteristics. They are described in a number of published articles on the Stanford, but they are not described in the manuals as clearly and as consistently as they should be. Specifically, the most complete descriptions of the norms are in the manuals for the complete batteries. The manual for the elementary reading test, for instance, reprints the first part of the explanation given in the battery manual, but omits the rest. Moreover, one of the best statements on the norms is not contained in any of the manuals, but in a 4-page folder addressed to school administrators and teachers. The fact that the publishers have recognized the need for the special brochure is perhaps the best indication that some reworking of the descriptions in the manuals is needed.

The test manuals have other limitations. For example, they have omitted the discussion of what is in the reading parts, which is a section of the manual for the whole battery. They also omit much of the careful description of the construction and tryout of the items, the establishment of reliability, the basis for selecting normative populations, and so on. In all these ways, the manuals do not permit the reading test to stand alone in quite the way it should.

In summary, the Stanford reading test has a number of strong advantages. Schools which limit the testing of general achievement to alternate years should take advantage of the separate printing of the reading test in the off-years, in order to provide greater continuity of the record reading progress through the grades. The testing of reading may well be extended beyond this program, of course; but the use of a consistent plan will permit comparison of reading achievement with progress in other fields, and also the measurement of reading growth through a single score system.

For a review by James R. Hobson of the previous edition, see 4:555; for a review by

Margaret G. McKim, see 3:503. For a review by N. L. Gage of the complete battery, see 25; for reviews by Paul R. Hanna (with Claude E. Norcross) and Virgil E. Herrick of the previous edition, see 4:25; for reviews by Walter W. Cook and Ralph C. Preston, see 3:18.

[657]
*Techniques in Reading Comprehension for Junior-Senior High School: Every Pupil Test. Grades 7-12; 1937-58; new form usually issued each December and April; norms available following testing program; no data on reliability; 3¢ per test; 1¢ per scoring key; cash orders postpaid; 32(40) minutes; Ohio Scholarship Tests. *

For reviews by Ivan A. Booker and James M. McCallister of earlier forms, see 3:505.

[658]
*Williams Primary Reading Test. Grades 1, 2-3; 1926-55; Forms C, D ('55); 2 levels; manual ('55); $2 per 25 tests; 30¢ per specimen set of either level; postpaid; (25-35) minutes; Allan J. Williams; Public School Publishing Co. *
a) PRIMARY I. Grade 1.
b) PRIMARY II. Grades 2-3.

For a review by Alice N. Jameson of the original edition, see 3:508.

MISCELLANEOUS

[659]
★Doren Diagnostic Reading Test of Word Recognition Skills. Grades 1-9; 1956; 12 scores: letter recognition, beginning sounds, whole word recognition, words within words, speech consonants, ending sounds, blending, rhyming, vowels, sight words, discriminate guessing, total; 1 form; no norms for subtest scores; $3.50 per 25 tests; $1.25 per manual; postage extra; $1.40 per specimen set, postpaid; (180) minutes in 3 sessions; Margaret Doren; Educational Test Bureau. *

B. H. VAN ROEKEL, *Associate Professor of Teacher Education, Michigan State University, East Lansing, Michigan.*

The most striking characteristic of this instrument is its comprehensiveness and attention to detail. The content of the 11 subtests is based on an analysis of the word recognition skills presented in the first three books of five widely used basic reading series. Although commonly used textbooks are not necessarily the best criterion for the selection of test content, the fact that considerable care is exercised in the selection of content for most basic reading series supports the contention that Doren's procedure for determining test content has considerable merit.

The skills which the test purports to measure include letter recognition, beginning sounds, whole word recognition, words within words, speech consonants, ending sounds, blending, rhyming, vowels, sight words, and discriminate guessing. The subtest measuring each of these skills has two or more parts, which, combined, make a voluminous instrument that requires about 3 hours when administered in its entirety.

The manual discusses a variety of topics, including the nature of diagnosis, the construction and arrangement of the test, instructions for administering and scoring the test, technical data concerning the test, and suggestions for remedial activities. The manual does not include directions for giving the test but states that "the examiner should read those printed on the test form and encourage the children to follow the words from their own papers." The examiner is not restricted to the printed directions and is at liberty to amplify them.

The manual confuses the issue of norms. Doren states: "In an achievement test, the number of correct responses is the measure of the degree of success. In a diagnostic test, it is the mistakes which an individual makes that will indicate his areas of need, and an exact identification of the types of errors will direct the examiner to specific remedial work." The manual has a table of mean scores for each of grades 1–4, supposedly representing the normal rate of growth in reading skills in the first four years. In essence, the mean scores for each grade level are not different from grade norms except that in this case the mean scores are expressed as raw scores rather than as grade norms. The raw score equivalents of grade norms on any achievement test are as much a measure of rate of growth as are the grade level mean scores on this test.

An overall validity coefficient of .90 is reported for the test, with reading achievement scores of children in the first four grades on the *Coordinated Scales of Attainment* serving as a criterion. Validity coefficients are reported for each grade level as well. Reliability coefficients for the various subtests range from .53 to .88. No information is given concerning the normative group or the method of determining reliability.

The design and quality of the test items themselves leave much to be desired. For example, Test B of Unit II, Beginning Sounds, consists of a series of sentences and specifies that pupils must encircle the one of three rhyming words which in each case best completes the sentence. This is as much a matter of context and sight vocabulary as it is of initial sounds. Unit X supposedly checks a child's ability to recognize sight words and his ability to sound out an unfamiliar word. Each item begins with a word of nonphonetic spelling followed by three words or nonsense syllables, one of which represents the phonetic spelling of the initial word. The pupils are to encircle the phonetic spelling of the initial word. This is hardly a measure of a child's fund of sight words. The deficiencies among the items of some of the other units are equally serious.

Many of the limitations of this test are inherent in the fact that this is a group test. Many of the criticisms previously mentioned would not hold if it were an individual test. As a group instrument, it should be used with considerable discretion.

VERNA L. VICKERY, *Associate Professor of Education, Mississippi State University, Starkville, Mississippi.*

This test consists of 390 items divided among 11 units, each unit purporting to measure a specific word recognition skill required for independent reading. The units are said by the author to be arranged in the order of the introduction of word recognition skills into the reading program "insofar as such introduction of skills has a time placement in the teaching of reading." Since the skills tested and the order of their presentation are based on an analysis of the skills taught in five widely used and highly respected series of primary readers, the claim to overall content validity is probably justified.

Norms as generally presented with achievement tests are not available. The author states that since this test is designed to measure deficiencies in specific areas of word recognition, an indication by norms of level of attainment is neither necessary nor desirable. With this point of view the reviewer would disagree, being of the opinion that the availability of more extensive interpretative data would do much to increase the usefulness of the test.

The test booklet is attractive in format. The manual is clearly and simply written and contains a section on remedial techniques for use in correcting the various deficiencies that may be revealed. Administration and scoring of the test and interpretation of the test results require a considerable amount of time; however, since the test is designed to be diagnostic, it would necessarily be longer and more time-consuming than tests of the survey type.

In spite of the deficiencies noted, the test should be of value to primary teachers, and to teachers of children in need of remedial help in the middle grades as well. The test will provide information concerning a child's word recognition problems and suggestions for remediation which the teacher, especially the skillful one, should be able to put to good use.

[660]

*Durrell Analysis of Reading Difficulty, New Edition.** Grades 1–6; 1937–55, c1933–55; individual; 1 form ('55); no data on reliability; reading paragraphs ('55); tachistoscope and cards ('55); manual ('55); $3.70 per examiner's kit including 5 record booklets ('55), postpaid; $3.75 per 35 record booklets, postage extra; (30–90) minutes; Donald D. Durrell; World Book Co. *

REFERENCES

1–2. See 4:561.

JAMES MAXWELL, *Visiting Professor of Education, Teachers College, Columbia University, New York, New York.*

The requirements of diagnostic tests of reading are very largely determined by the nature of the reading task itself, so that all such tests follow much the same pattern. This test does not diverge radically from the established pattern. The core of the test is two sets of paragraphs, one set for oral and the other for silent reading, accompanied by tables of norms and checklists for recording observations of reading difficulties. Norms are expressed for each of grades 1–6 on three levels (low, medium and high), these being sufficiently precise for the purpose of the test. Unfortunately, however, the norms are based upon speed of reading alone; there are no norms for level of comprehension, which is, nevertheless, tested, and the diagnosis of this aspect of reading comes to depend almost entirely on the checklists of difficulties.

A praiseworthy feature is the inclusion of a set of graded paragraphs for listening comprehension, this giving useful information not always included in diagnostic reading tests.

Other major subtests are word and letter recognition exercises, the presentation being mainly by means of a simple tachistoscope included in the test kit. The child's visual recognition of words is adequately tested, as is his auditory recognition of letters, but there are no tests of the child's methods of word attack,

e.g., syllabication or phonic analysis of the complete word. There are also checklists for the pupil's medical, psychological, and educational records.

The test material is thoroughly prepared and well arranged, and the instructions clear. The checklists of difficulties are perhaps rather too extensive for easy recording while the test is being administered, but they are comprehensive and become quite manageable with practice. The reading paragraphs are well chosen and graded, and the word lists are adequately comprehensive. The weakness of the test lies in the unsatisfactory norms for paragraph reading and the inadequacy of standardized tests of word attack.

GEORGE D. SPACHE, *Professor of Education, and Head, Reading Laboratory and Clinic, University of Florida, Gainesville, Florida.*

This is a battery of tests designed for the observation of the reading performances of individuals varying from nonreading to sixth grade levels. The tests are intended for the use of experienced teachers or those specifically trained in their administration and interpretation.

The battery opens with an oral reading test that permits observation of reading errors and reading speed. Comprehension is measured by questions involving merely recall of the details. The author suggests that testing begin at the child's actual reading level and that at least three paragraphs should be used. Since there is only a single paragraph at each reading level, it is impossible to follow these directions and secure an adequate sample with individuals reading below the third grade level. Thus, if we assume that the reading selections represent specific grade levels, which is doubtful, the test will function adequately only as a measure of the simplest type of oral reading above primary levels.

The second subtest, a silent reading test, offers norms for speed and parrot-like recall. No questions involving any type of comprehension are offered. The purpose is to permit direct comparison of oral and silent reading abilities since the child reads selections and answers questions which are presumably comparable to those in the preceding test. As in the oral reading test, the examiner cannot secure an adequate sample for individuals reading below the third grade level. Since many pupils could recall the details of these selections without actual comprehension, the test's adequacy as a measure of silent reading is doubtful, as is its comparability with the oral reading test. Apparently, the author assumes that any type of recall or interpretation is a thorough measure of comprehension and is equivalent to any other type. For some reason, several questions on imagery are offered for two of the eight reading selections. Similar questions are to be phrased by the teacher for the other selections. The purpose of these questions and their significance in cases of reading difficulty is not clear.

The third subtest, a listening test, is really an adaptation of an oral reading test offered in the earlier edition of the battery. In revising the test, the author has merely downgraded each oral reading selection by one grade and devised a group of recall questions. Just how this revision was justified or just what is measured by this test in its present form is not clarified by the author. The directions indicate that if the child can answer all the questions on the single paragraph for his grade level (?), his reading difficulty is not due to lack of comprehension. Apparently this arbitrarily scaled test is intended to function as a measure of potential for reading comprehension.

The next subtest measures quick word recognition and delayed word analysis techniques with the use of a hand tachistoscope. This is probably the most original and functional test in the entire battery, provided the examiner can manipulate it properly.

New tests added to the current edition include six measures of the visual and auditory characteristics of letters and words. These should be useful measures of phonic skills even among individuals of higher reading levels than the primary level for which they are recommended. A new learning rate test is also included, in which the child's ability to learn isolated words by an abbreviated visual method is presumably evaluated. The lack of norms, the ignoring of the influence of the child's intellectual level, and the use of an inadequate number of words to challenge children of higher capacities, all tend to make this test of little practical value in its present form.

Supplementary tests of written spelling and speed of handwriting are offered. Spelling errors are to be noted and combined with those from oral reading, but these errors are not carefully defined or described, nor are all significant types noted.

The nature or size of the population on which these tests were standardized is not revealed, nor are there any data on the reliability or validity of any of the tests. Apparently the user is to assume that all of the tests are highly valid, dependable and consistent, despite the serious limitations we have noted above. As the author suggests, probably the outstanding contributions of this battery are the checklists for guiding the observation of various reading performances. For the most part, these checklists are detailed and fairly complete. They should be particularly useful for relatively inexperienced reading teachers and clinicians. It is regrettable that the accompanying tests with which the checklists are to be used do not offer a more adequate foundation.

For a review by Helen M. Robinson of the original edition, see 4:561; for reviews by Guy L. Bond and Miles A. Tinker, see 40:1533; for a review by Marion Monroe, see 38:1098.

[661]
Durrell-Sullivan Reading Capacity and Achievement Tests. Grades 2.5–4.5, 3–6; 1937–45; 5 scores: word meaning, paragraph meaning, total, spelling (optional), written recall (optional); 2 levels; 2 tests; 25¢ per battery manual ('45); postage extra; 50¢ per specimen set of either level, postpaid; Donald D. Durrell and Helen Blair Sullivan; World Book Co. *
a) PRIMARY TEST. Grades 2.5–4.5; Form A ('37); 2 tests published in 1 booklet; directions for administering ('39); $4.60 per 35 tests.
1) *Reading Capacity Test.* (30–50) minutes.
2) *Reading Achievement Test.* 30(40) minutes; optional tests, (15–20) minutes.
b) INTERMEDIATE TEST. Grades 3–6.
1) *Reading Capacity Test.* Form A ('37); directions for administering ('37); $3 per 35 tests; 35(50) minutes.
2) *Reading Achievement Test.* Forms A ('37), B ('44); directions for administering ('45); $3.50 per 35 tests; 30(40) minutes; optional tests, (15) minutes.

REFERENCES

1–4. See 4:562.
5. MILLER, VELMA J. *A Critical Analysis of Standardized Vocabulary Tests to Determine Those Most Valid for Use With the Macmillan Readers.* Master's thesis, Bowling Green State University (Bowling Green, Ohio), 1954.
6. BLIESMER, EMERY P. "A Comparison of Results Obtained With Various Types of Capacity Tests Used With Retarded Readers." *Yearb Nat Council Meas Used Ed* 12(pt 1):60–2 '55.
7. BOND, GUY L., AND CLYMER, THEODORE W. "Interrelationship of the SRA Primary Mental Abilities, Other Mental Characteristics, and Reading Ability." *J Ed Res* 49:131–6 O '55. * (PA 30:7752)
8. BLIESMER, EMERY P. "A Comparison of Results of Various Capacity Tests Used With Retarded Readers." *El Sch J* 56:400–2 My '56. * (PA 31:5140)
9. OWEN, JASON C. *A Study of the Prognostic Value of Certain Measures of Intelligence and Listening Comprehension With a Selected Group of Elementary Pupils.* Doctor's thesis, University of Missouri (Columbia, Mo.), 1957. (DA 19:484)

JAMES MAXWELL, *Visiting Professor of Education, Teachers College, Columbia University, New York, New York.*

These tests are constructed on the proposition that reading disability can be detected by differences between scores on a test of reading achievement and a parallel test of equivalent difficulty and of similar content that requires no reading. Each test contains a subtest on word meaning and one on paragraph meaning. In the nonverbal, or reading capacity, test, the questions are answered by the selection of the appropriate picture.

The selection of the material, words and paragraphs, seems to be adequate for the purpose and suited to the abilities of the children for whom the tests are intended. Credit must be given for the avoidance of excessive use of nouns in the word list, and for the close correspondence between the verbal and nonverbal material; though the pictures seem rather small (1 inch square), the authors state this gives no difficulty. The test envelopes contain adequate apparatus for administration and the instructions for administering and scoring are detailed and clear.

The least satisfactory feature of the tests is the manual. Objective data and selling points tend to be confused. Reliability coefficients corrected for attenuation (Is this justified?) are given "for a representative sampling of cases." These are of the order of .85 and "should inspire confidence in the use of these tests." The reviewer feels .95 is more inspiring. The vital score is the difference between the two sets of tests, as it is on this that the validity hinges. The data given are rather vague. A correlation of .85 is given for "a population from which all children over age for their grade have been eliminated." This also "inspires confidence...." The lower part of the distribution of differences is given; but the nature of the total distribution of differences and the interpretation of cases whose achievement is higher than their capacity are sidestepped. The authors state that the "true" correlation is still a matter for further research. More extensive and precise data would more effectively inspire confidence in the tests than do the authors' beliefs.

The underlying concept of this test is an interesting one. The exact paralleling of the content and structure of the two tests, one verbal and the other nonverbal, is ingenious and logi-cal, but not necessarily psychologically valid. It is not clearly established that the abilities required to accomplish successfully the nonverbal test are those underlying reading achievement. And is this particular nonverbal test the most valid predictor available? The two component tests are themselves sufficiently well constructed to provide the basis for fuller investigation of the underlying thesis. Perhaps final judgment should be suspended till this thesis is more fully corroborated.

For a review by Helen M. Robinson, see 4:562; for reviews by William S. Gray and Marion Monroe of the original edition, see 38:1099 (1 excerpt).

[662]

*Gates Reading Diagnostic Tests. Grades 1–8; 1926–53; individual; Forms 1, 2 ('42); revised manual ('53); the author's *The Improvement of Reading, Third Edition* (see 3 below) is necessary for administration; no data on reliability and validity; 55¢ per test; 20¢ per record blank ('45); 10¢ per set of tachistoscopic cards; 45¢ per manual; $1.50 per complete specimen set; cash orders postpaid; [60–90] minutes; Arthur I. Gates; Bureau of Publications, Teachers College, Columbia University. *

REFERENCES

1–3. See 3:510.
4–5. See 4:563.

GEORGE D. SPACHE, *Professor of Education, and Head, Reading Laboratory and Clinic, University of Florida, Gainesville, Florida.*

This battery of tests is intended for individual diagnosis of reading difficulties. The tests themselves are of 1942 vintage. The manual bears a 1953 copyright date, but differs in no essential detail from earlier editions.

In general, the tests are simple enough for classroom teachers or inexperienced clinicians to give. Their interpretation is likewise simple and apparently obvious. Thus, ease of administration and interpretation contribute to the face validity of the battery. However, a number of the separate tests are of questionable validity. Moreover, the interpretations suggested by the author are misleading or even erroneous.

The tendency to a superficial interpretation of the child's performance is first found in the opening instructions in the manual. Here the author suggests that the grade score derived from each test may be rated "low" or "very low" when compared to some such criterion as actual grade placement, mental grade level, or average score on a group of the other tests. On page 29 of the manual, the author offers a table to facilitate this rating of test performance.

This tendency to ignore the actual reliability of the tests in the battery is present in the manual in two other instances. Despite published and unpublished data on the various tests, no reliability coefficients are offered. In addition, highly detailed tables of norms are offered for every test, giving the implication that each and every score is highly accurate, dependable, and discriminative. This attitude is in sharp contrast to current test construction practices of interpreting the significance of a difference between two scores only in terms of the accuracy of both scores and the degree of error of estimate present in both measures.

The first section of the battery is an oral reading test of seven paragraphs, the last three of which are highly artificial and stilted. They do not resemble any reading materials this reviewer has ever seen that are commonly used with children. Furthermore, this test is administered without any estimate of comprehension, thus rewarding the child who is skillful in word calling with an excessively high estimate of functional oral reading level. As a result of these limitations, it is probable that the oral reading test functions as a measure of ability to read (?) this esoteric material rather than as a test of general oral reading ability. It is also doubtful that the intensive analysis of reading errors on this test suggested by the author is realistically related to the child's true reading performance with ordinary materials.

The second test offered is called Oral Vocabulary. This is mislabeled since it measures auditory vocabulary, not the usable speaking vocabulary of the child. These vocabularies are not identical in breadth, depth, or fluency. Therefore, the test does not function as a general measure of the child's vocabulary but as an indication of his level of auditory comprehension of word meanings. It would be correctly interpreted as a measure of potential for development of the child's speaking vocabulary rather than as an actual test of this latter ability.

A third test measures the pupil's tendency to make reversals in a series of readily reversible words. It is based on the questionable assumption that this artificial situation is representative of or related to the child's usual reading error tendencies. Current theories of the etiology of reading disability decry the tendency to overemphasize the importance of any one type of reading error. Contrary to the author's suggestions, reversals have not been found to bear any consistent relationship to eye, hand, or cerebral dominance. They are most properly interpreted as an immaturity of the left-to-right orientation in reading found in severely retarded readers functioning on primary levels, regardless of age or neurological conditions.

Another section offers tests of phrase and word perception and word analysis. These may well function, as they are intended to, as measures of phrase reading, sight word vocabulary, and methods of word attack. An oral spelling test is also included. In the reviewer's opinion, a written spelling test would be more valuable in revealing word analysis patterns, knowledge of word structure, and the like, particularly if a careful analysis of written spelling errors were made.

The battery ends with a group of subtests measuring visual and auditory perception techniques. These tests will aid in the analysis of the primary child's phonic skills and knowledge —his ability to recognize, to hear, and to use the sound qualities of words, letters, and letter combinations.

In addition to the specific limitations noted above, there are other serious omissions in this battery of diagnostic reading tests. No attempt is made to measure reading comprehension, to contrast oral and silent reading skills, or to compare oral and silent reading ability with auditory comprehension. No effort is made to evaluate potential for reading growth by measuring comprehension of spoken language. The only suggestion in this connection is a reference to the Stanford-Binet intelligence test, which is of questionable value in reading retardation cases. Finally, the majority of the subtests are useful only with individuals reading at primary levels. In general, the battery is serviceable to those classroom teachers and clinicians who, in working with individuals reading on primary levels, are concerned only with the word calling, word recognition, and phonic skills of their pupils.

For a review by Worth J. Osburn, see 4:563; for related reviews, see 4:564; for a review by T. L. Torgerson, see 3:510.

[663]

Individual Reading Test. Ages 5.6–8.6; 1935–36; individual; 1 form ['35]; 3 tests: oral word reading, comprehension, speed; no data on reliability; *7s. 6d.* per set of cards; *2s. 6d.* per manual ['36]; postpaid within

Australia; administration time not reported; L. W. Allen; Australian Council for Educational Research. *

R. W. McCulloch, *Chief Psychologist and Superintendent of Special Schools, Tasmanian Education Department, Hobart, Tasmania, Australia.*

The 12-page manual includes description, directions, and norms. It is accompanied by a set of cards which comprise all the printed material required for using the test. The purchaser, however, must provide 10 common articles, ranging from a piece of rag to a cardboard box, for use with the printed material.

The norms were derived during 1935 from the performance of 1,000 South Australian children aged 5-6 to 9-11 who had been taught reading according to the curriculum then followed in South Australia. The handbook reproduces that curriculum; it differs only slightly from present-day reading curricula of the various education departments of Australia and New Zealand, though a review of the present-day validity would be timely.

The test has three sections: word reading, reading comprehension, and speed of reading. All sections are administered individually and the speed of reading test has a time limit of one minute. The word reading section is composed of 100 graded words (from "can" to "valetudinarian") arranged in five sizes of print. The reading comprehension section requires the child to carry out the instructions printed on 30 cards, most of which refer to the materials provided by the tester. The speed of reading section is based on a 500-word story entitled "Tom and His Dog."

The norms are given for chronological age and for period of school attendance. For education systems other than those in South Australia the latter is the set of most value.

Because of its brevity, ease of administration, and close relationship to school curricula, the test is the most useful of those available in Australia for those who wish to test only in the first three grades of the elementary school. However, for those whose testing extends over the whole of the elementary school, a test which covers all grade levels is more convenient. The *Schonell Reading Tests* and *Gates Reading Diagnostic Tests* are, therefore, to be preferred by them.

[664]

★McGuffey Diagnostic Reading Test. Grades 4–6; 1955; 5 scores: syllables, sound value recognition, vo-

cabulary, appreciation, understanding; Form A; no data on reliability; $2.50 per 25 tests, postage extra; $1 per specimen set, postpaid; 81(110) minutes in 2 sessions; Ullin W. Leavell; Educational Test Bureau. *

[665]

★Primary Reading Profiles, [Revised Edition]. Grades 1, 2; 1953–57; 6 scores: reading aptitude, auditory association, word recognition, word attack, reading comprehension, total; 1 form ('57); 2 levels; manual ('57) for each level; $3.60 per 35 tests, postage extra; 40¢ per specimen set, postpaid; (95–100) minutes in 3 sessions; James B. Stroud and Albert N. Hieronymus; Houghton Mifflin Co. *

James R. Hobson, *Director of Child Placement, Brookline Public Schools, Brookline, Massachusetts.*

A rather unique feature of these tests is the built-in readiness or aptitude test which is Test 1 at each level. It is assumed that this test is a measure of readiness for the following year's work in reading; otherwise, it would seem somewhat futile to measure aptitude for reading at the close, rather than at the beginning—particularly in first grade.

On the front cover of each test booklet is an individual profile chart on which the pupil's score on each of the five tests and the composite score for Tests 3, 4, and 5 are to be plotted. Each of the levels was standardized on a widely scattered school population of over a thousand pupils, described by the authors as "nationwide."

Previous to the 1956 standardization, tryout administrations for item analysis purposes were given. In each case almost exactly one third of the original test items were discarded as being unsuitable. The items retained were answered correctly by from 25 per cent to 94 per cent of the tryout sample for Level One and by 20 per cent to 89 per cent for Level Two. Reliability coefficients calculated by both the Spearman-Brown and Kuder-Richardson formulas ranged from .86 to .98 for the composite score and for all subtests, with the exception of Test 1 at each level. These are .77 for Level One and .69 for Level Two.

Although about two and one half pages in the manual for each level are devoted to a discussion of various aspects of validity (content, construct, congruent, concurrent), the only actual evidences of validity produced are: (*a*) Fairly complete data on the level of difficulty and commonality of use of the words in the various subtests, according to such recognized criteria as the Gates, Krantz, Stone, and Thorndike-Lorge word lists; (b) Correlation coefficients between raw scores and both IQ and MA, as determined by administration of the *Revised Stanford-Binet Scale* (form not specified). These correlations, based on 130 first grade and 85 second grade pupils, are fairly normal for the first grade, reaching .53 for Test 1 raw score and MA, and .60 for composite raw score (Tests 3, 4, and 5) and MA. For the second grade the coefficients between the same variables were .49 and .48, respectively.

This reviewer does not see the utility of Test 1 as a sort of a built-in aptitude test. It is not stated that it indicates aptitude for reading the following year, which would seem to be its chief claim to usefulness. It lacks both the validity and the reliability to perform the function of picking out potential or actual cases of reading difficulty through the size of the discrepancy between aptitude and achievement scores. This, in the reviewer's opinion, can be done much better by taking stock of the discrepancy between reading achievement and mental age on a good individual intelligence test, together with observation of sensory abilities and development of other skills and concepts—numbers, for example. A separate aptitude or readiness test long enough to have greater reliability and to include other aspects of reading aptitude would serve a more useful purpose. Test 1 correlations with the *Gates Reading Readiness Tests* (.23 for Level One) and with the composite of Tests 3, 4, and 5 of its own battery (.40 and .43 for Levels One and Two, respectively) cast considerable doubt on its essential validity. It would certainly have very little value as a predictor of subsequent reading achievement.

The auditory association test at each level is cleverly designed and measures a most important primary reading skill too often neglected in standardized tests at these levels. Considerable ingenuity is also displayed in devising word attack tests, each item of which requires the child to complete the meaning of a short paragraph by choosing from pictorial or contextual clues a word which is within his oral and meaning vocabulary but which very probably is not yet within his sight recognition vocabulary.

The reliability data have little value. In the case of each level they are based upon a "representative sample" consisting of about a third of the cases in the tryout sample several years ago. The statement is made that "because only the best of the tryout items were selected for the final test, these coefficients are probably lower than they would have been had they been computed on the basis of an odd-even scoring of items on the tests taken by the standardization sample." This is a gratuitous assumption which is not necessarily so. Shortening the test by discarding about one third of the items would tend to reduce the size of the coefficients, other things being equal. On the other hand, if the items were arranged without reference to order of difficulty in the tryout sample and then were arranged in order of difficulty in the final test, such arrangement would tend to raise the coefficients as calculated by the Spearman-Brown formula.

In the opinion of this reviewer, Tests 2, 3, 4, and 5 of each level are good solid tests with essential content validity for the tasks they attempt to perform, as might be expected from such competent authors. The inclusion in each battery of a brief aptitude test of questionable validity, low reliability, and unclear purpose detracts from its essential value. With the exception of the standardization data, which are somewhat on the scanty side, the other technical data do not appear to have been derived in any planned, consistent manner but seem to have been somewhat improvised from data which were already available. The answer to the criticism of the standardization data would, of course, be to standardize on one's own school population.

VERNA L. VICKERY, *Associate Professor of Education, Mississippi State University, Starkville, Mississippi.*

This is a battery of five tests designed to measure a pupil's aptitude for reading and his reading progress. The authors suggest that the battery may be given whenever pupils have completed the appropriate readers described as being in the basal series; the percentile norms, however, are described as being based on the results of children completing the first and second grades, with no reference to the portion of the basal series completed or supplementary reading accomplished.

A distinctive feature of the battery is a listening comprehension test which purports to measure aptitude for reading. This subtest provides a carefully devised set of 32 items measuring the pupil's general information, reasoning ability, memory span, ability to draw conclusions, and ability to arrange events in correct sequence. An examination of the content of this subtest reveals that the authors are tapping an extremely difficult but very significant area for measurement in primary reading.

The chief value of this battery as compared with other reading tests is that reading aptitude and reading achievement are measured within the same test. In addition to the obvious administrative value of this technique, both the aptitude and achievement scores have been standardized on the same population, making for greater comparability of norms.

The technical information in the manual is presented with such clarity as to increase the classroom teacher's understanding and interpretation of test results. The item analysis data indicate that the items selected met the established criteria in regard to content, range of difficulty, and discriminative value. Reasonably adequate reliability and validation data are presented, except that no data are presented to show the relationships between achievement on these tests and on other reading tests.

The *Primary Reading Profiles* constitute a worthwhile contribution to the field of reading aptitude and achievement at the early primary levels. The format of the battery is quite good, and the material used and techniques recommended combine to provide tests which are at once interesting to children and useful to teachers. The provision of the profile makes for ease of interpretation. It should go without saying, of course, that the teacher who considers this battery for use in her own classroom should make a careful study of the content of each subtest to note its validity for her particular program of study.

[666]

*Reading Diagnostic Record for High School and College Students. High school and college; 1938–52; 1 form ('52); directions sheet ('52); 10 or more copies, 30¢ each; 35¢ per single copy; cash orders postpaid; Ruth Strang, Margaret M. Conant, Margaret G. McKim, and Mary Alice Mitchell; Bureau of Publications, Teachers College, Columbia University. *

MARVIN D. GLOCK, *Professor of Educational Psychology, Cornell University, Ithaca, New York.*

This is an individual diagnostic record folder designed for the recording of the various interests, attitudes, and experiences of a student which are related to his reading performance. The booklet is divided into 12 sections and

forms are provided for listing different kinds of data. Typical of these are provisions for biographical history, results of standardized tests, a summary of scholastic achievement, reading interests and attitudes, and information about work-study skills. One section is devoted to oral reading paragraphs for diagnosing specific reading difficulties. There is also space for summarizing data, stating, recommendations, indicating procedures used, and suggesting a follow-up program.

The folder provides a vehicle for the systematic gathering of pertinent information. Sufficient data are mandatory for diagnosis and remediation and the booklet becomes a continuous and convenient permanent record of important information. This information becomes more useful if the clinician uses the sheet of directions. The author presents helpful suggestions for diagnosis.

The inclusion of oral reading paragraphs in the booklet may be questioned, especially since standardized oral reading tests are available. However, their presence makes the results available as a part of the permanent record. Although no norms are given, this is really unimportant in terms of the use to which the paragraphs are put. Oral reading is helpful to determine the reader's deficiencies in such areas as word attack skills, phrasing, and expression. A good reader should make few if any errors.

The record is too lengthy for general use in high school and college. Work involved in recording so much information will probably preclude the busy teacher from using it with groups of students. This is not to say that any part of the record is unnecessary. If there is time for attention to individual students, the record should prove to be an invaluable aid.

DONALD E. P. SMITH, *Chief, Division of Reading Improvement Services, and Associate Professor of Education, University of Michigan, Ann Arbor, Michigan.*

This is a 21-page interview guide, the implied purpose of which is to facilitate the gathering of information relative to the reading problem of high school and college students. Spaces are provided for identification and family data, a summary of intelligence and school achievement test results (to be gathered, presumably, from school records), medical reports (four of the five headings concern vision), reading background and interests, and present reading status. The latter includes an oral reading test designed to reflect the kinds of errors the subject makes. No scoring key or norms are provided. Next a series of questions are asked to test comprehension of the passages read orally. Finally, space is provided for writing in recommendations, procedures used, and follow-up.

The booklet may be useful for training teachers to look for information on correlates of reading difficulty. The authors state that their method for data gathering is "clinical." The term "clinical," as used here, seems to mean an indirect approach to finding answers. For example, take this statement: "In various ways during the interview the counselor will indirectly learn the student's attitude toward reading. It cannot be obtained by asking, 'What is your attitude toward reading?' "

While this reviewer would agree that much of the information to be gathered is interesting, it seems to be largely irrelevant to the reading problem. If one knows that a boy's father is a laborer, that there are no books in his home, that his IQ score is 90, that he doesn't like reading (most poor readers don't and they'll tell you so when you ask them if they think it won't hurt your feelings), and that he has failed English and social studies over the past several years, what, then, does one know about the cause of his reading problems?

When this form was first published in 1938, it probably reflected diagnostic procedures of that day, at least procedures of a "clinically" oriented shop. Today, with the advent of knowledge about the role of cognition in reading, the importance of physical development, the variety of perceptual skills involved, and the interaction between personality structure and reading styles, the present form appears to be dated despite its revision in 1952.

For reviews by Robert Murray Bear and Carolyn M. Welch of the original edition, see 3:509; for a review by Henry D. Rinsland, see 40:1535 (3 excerpts).

[667]

★**Roswell-Chall Diagnostic Reading Test of Word Analysis Skills.** Grades 2–6; 1956–58; individual; Forms 1, 2 ('56); manual ('56); supplement ('58, reprint of 1 below); $2.58 per 35 tests; 50¢ per specimen set; postpaid; [5–10] minutes; Florence G. Roswell and Jeanne S. Chall; Essay Press. *

REFERENCE
1. CHALL, JEANNE S. "The Roswell-Chall Diagnostic Reading Test of Word Analysis Skills." *Reading Teacher* 11:179–83 F '58. *

BYRON H. VAN ROEKEL, *Associate Professor of Teacher Education, Michigan State University, East Lansing, Michigan.*

This test was developed to help teachers identify specific weaknesses of pupils having difficulty with word recognition. It is intended to supplement standardized silent and oral reading tests.

It was the intent of the authors to provide a simple, practical instrument for the classroom teacher and this they have done. The test is administered individually and requires about five minutes per pupil. It is designed primarily for children who are reading at approximately the second to sixth grade level; it is functional for children of any age or grade who have difficulty with word recognition. It is easy to administer and anyone qualified to teach reading in the elementary school should have no difficulty using this instrument.

The scope and content of the five subtests is open to question. The test purports to measure "basic skills" which "provide the teacher with an estimate of the pupil's strengths and weaknesses in word recognition." Herein lies the major weakness of this instrument. It measures knowledge of certain elements which are essential to word attack but it does not measure the ability to apply this knowledge.

Subtest 1 includes all of the consonants, except *q* and *x*, and 10 of the consonant blends. The pupil is asked to give the sound of each of the elements in this section. No rationale or evidence is cited to support the inclusion of certain blends in contrast to others which might have been included. It is unfortunate that some common blends such as *br, bl, cl, fr, gr,* and *gl* have been excluded. More adequate coverage of the blends could have been effected without materially influencing the time or complexity of administration.

Subtest 2 consists of three parts: (*a*) ten monosyllabic words with short vowel sounds, (*b*) two sentences composed of monosyllabic words, a majority of which contain the short vowel sound, and (*c*) the five vowels in isolation. The pupil is to read the words and sentences and say the long and short sounds of the vowels. It is highly conceivable that the words in the first two parts of this subtest would be in the sight vocabulary of pupils reading at low third grade level. Experience tells us that it is not unusual for poor readers to glibly give the long and short vowel sounds. Hence, this test is of little value in determining the ability to apply knowledge of vowel sounds in word attack.

The third subtest consists of five pairs of words such as pin and pine, cut and cute, and supposedly measures the ability to apply the rule of silent *e*. This appears to be as much a measure of sight vocabulary as it is a measure of the ability to apply the rule.

Subtest 4 deals with vowel combinations including both digraphs and diphthongs. Two of the words (*harm* and *cart* in Form 1 and *part* and *hard* in Form 2) represent the influence of the letter *r* on vowel sounds rather than vowel combinations. This section is subject to the same criticism as the third.

The fifth subtest, Syllabication, includes two compound words and six polysyllabic words. The usual rules of syllabication are applicable in the case of each word and the directions provide for diagnosis of errors in pronunciation.

The manual makes no reference to reliability or validity although such information has been published elsewhere (*1*). Reliability coefficients of the subtests, based on scores on equivalent forms, are as follows: Subtest 1, single consonants, .78, consonant combinations, .81; subtest 2, .99; subtest 3, .84; subtest 4, .93; and subtest 5, .86. The reliability of the total test is reported to be .98. These data are based on a limited sample of 52 pupils enrolled in a remedial reading service and ranging in grade placement from third through eleventh grade. Since reliability coefficients are a function of rank, one would naturally expect a poor eleventh grade reader to consistently rank above a poor third grade reader. Hence, it is difficult to say that the individual part scores are sufficiently reliable to identify, with confidence, a pupil's specific weaknesses in word recognition.

Three different populations were used to obtain validity coefficients: (*a*) two second grade classes averaging at grade 2.1 in overall reading ability, (*b*) two fifth grade classes averaging at grade 5.9 in overall reading ability, and (*c*) the 52 clinic cases previously mentioned, averaging at grade 4.3 in overall reading ability. The total scores on the Roswell-Chall for each of the groups were correlated with appro-

priate levels of various standardized silent and oral reading tests. The validity coefficients for the various groups range from .64 for the clinic group to .92 for the second grade group when using standardized silent reading tests as criteria. Since various levels of the reading tests of the *Metropolitan Achievement Tests* were used for the clinic group and the *New York Test of Reading Growth* was used for the second grade group, it is difficult to pass judgment on the discriminative quality of the test. Apparently it is not as valid for the group for which it is intended as it is for children making normal progress in reading.

There are no norms for this test. Scoring is somewhat subjective and the results are qualitative. The manual states that "if a child misses more than half the items on any subtest, it may be assumed either that he has a special deficiency in this area, or has not received instruction and therefore needs systematic work."

The title of this test is a misnomer. In the main, it measures knowledge of certain phonetic elements rather than skills in word analysis. The classroom teacher will find this instrument helpful but incomplete. Although it does not reflect careful test construction, it will function as an informal inventory of certain elements essential to word recognition.

[668]

★SRA Achievement Series: Language Perception. Grades 2–4; 1954–57; title on test is *Are These The Same?*; 3 scores: auditory discrimination, visual discrimination, sight vocabulary; Form A ('55); examiner's manual, second edition ('57); technical supplement. second edition ('57); 40¢ per 20 tests; 50¢ per teacher's handbook ('55); 50¢ per administrator's manual ('56); $1 per technical supplement; $1 per scoring stencil; postage extra; (60) minutes; Louis P. Thorpe, D. Welty Lefever, and Robert A. Naslund; Science Research Associates. *

For reviews by Warren G. Findley and Worth R. Jones of the complete battery, see 21.

[669]

★Silent Reading Diagnostic Tests: The Developmental Reading Tests, Experimental Form. Grades 3 and over; 1955; 20 scores; 1 form; $4 per 20 tests, postage extra; 40¢ per specimen set, postpaid; 39(65) minutes; Guy L. Bond, Theodore Clymer, and Cyril J. Hoyt; Lyons & Carnahan. *

[670]

★Stanford Diagnostic Phonics Survey, Research Edition. High school and college; 1956–58; test of ability to relate printed sounds to spoken sounds; IBM; 1 form ('56); preliminary manual ('58); distribution restricted to research and experimental use; separate answer sheets must be used; $2.75 per 25 tests and 1 examiner's booklet ('56); $1.25 per 50 IBM answer sheets; $1 per manual and hand or machine scoring stencil; postage extra; $1 per specimen set, cash orders postpaid; (30–45) minutes; Grace M. Brown and Alice B. Cottrell; distributed by Consulting Psychologists Press, Inc. *

ORAL

[671]

★Gilmore Oral Reading Test. Grades 1–8; 1951–52; 3 scores: accuracy, comprehension, rate; individual; Forms A, B ('52); $1.70 per set of reading paragraphs ('51); $2.10 per 35 record blanks; 50¢ per manual ('52); postage extra; 50¢ per specimen set, postpaid; (15–20) minutes; John V. Gilmore; World Book Co. *

REFERENCE

1. GILMORE, JOHN V. *The Relationship Between Oral Reading Habits and Oral and Silent Reading Comprehension.* Doctor's thesis, Harvard University (Cambridge, Mass.), 1950.

LYDIA A. DUGGINS, *Associate Professor and Director of Reading Services, University of Bridgeport, Bridgeport, Connecticut.*

This is an instrument designed to measure three aspects of oral reading competency: pronunciation, comprehension, and rate of reading. A separate score is obtained for each of these. The two forms of the test are not exactly equal in difficulty, but tables of equivalent scores are provided for use in comparing initial and final scores.

The test is comprised of 10 paragraphs which form a continuous story about episodes in a family group. Each form is introduced with a picture of the characters, intended to aid the examiner in establishing rapport and in making the testing more like a normal reading activity. There are five comprehension questions on each paragraph, to be asked and answered orally following the reading of the paragraph. A record blank for each pupil provides for the recording and classification of errors as the reading proceeds, the time required for reading each paragraph, and the responses made to the comprehension questions.

According to the manual, three variables were considered in the gradation of the paragraphs: vocabulary, sentence structure, and interest. Vocabulary was regulated by an increase in the number of words per paragraph, the selection of words of appropriate and evenly increasing difficulty, and the controlled use of polysyllabic words. Sentence difficulty was judged by sentence length and per cent of complex sentences. An effort was made to include materials that were within the experiences of and would be of interest to pupils at

the various grade levels. The gradation appears to have been successfully accomplished.

The comprehension questions following each paragraph are of the recall type. The questions refer to information specifically given in the paragraph; no attempt is made to test for interpretation going beyond the paragraph. Increasing skill in comprehension is related to the increasing difficulty of materials rather than to variation in the type of question asked. This, the author assumes, "differentiates readers of varying degrees of comprehension skill." It also enables the teacher to score the responses to the questions with greater objectivity.

The types of errors to be noted on the record blank were arrived at as the result of a study of error frequency based on data obtained from an initial administration of the test to 446 pupils in grades 1 through 8 in a single Massachusetts community and through an analysis of published oral reading tests. Statistical evidence of the validity of the test was obtained from a comparison of the scores made by 24 fifth grade pupils of the same age on this test and on Gray's *Standardized Oral Reading Paragraphs* and the oral reading test from the *Durrell Analysis of Reading Difficulty.* Correlations ranging from .39 to .80 are reported, with the highest correlations for accuracy and the lowest for speed.

Since this test is designed to aid in a detailed analysis of an individual's oral reading ability, emphasis is put on methods of analyzing performance rather than on interpretative data for comparing individual performance with group performance. However, for those desiring such information, performance ratings for accuracy, comprehension, and rate are provided, as are grade equivalents and standard scores for accuracy and comprehension. These data are based on the results of a standardization program involving 1,620 pupils in five states.

One of the outstanding advantages of the *Gilmore Oral Reading Test* is that no special training is required to administer it satisfactorily. The manual contains specific and clear directions for administration and scoring. A basal level is established as the paragraph on which the pupil makes no more than two errors. A ceiling paragraph is established as that on which he makes 10 or more errors.

The reading paragraphs for both Forms A and B are included in the same spiral-bound booklet which is substantial in construction and can be used over and over. The examiner needs only to replace the supply of record blanks, which makes for economy in cost of administering. The record blank is especially well constructed, providing in addition to the items already mentioned, space for comment on test behavior, a summary checklist of difficulties, and space for entering silent reading test data. The provision for recording both oral and silent reading test data in one place facilitates the evaluation of the child's reading needs.

This test can be used, then, for the analysis of individual or group performance in accuracy, comprehension, and rate of oral reading, and for comparison of this performance with a national norm. It can be used also to provide information concerning the specific weaknesses in these three areas for purposes of more efficient small group instruction to meet common needs. The reviewer is of the opinion that the face validity of the test is so obvious that the scanty statistical evidence of validity should not be a deterrent to its use.

MAYNARD C. REYNOLDS, *Associate Professor of Educational Psychology, University of Minnesota, Minneapolis, Minnesota.*

In each of its two forms, the stimulus material of the *Gilmore Oral Reading Test* consists of 10 paragraphs which form a continuous story, and a picture which portrays the characters in the story. The paragraphs are arranged in order of difficulty, from easy to hard. Five recall type comprehension questions, to be asked upon the completion of the reading of each paragraph, are furnished by the author. The examiner makes a detailed record of a pupil's performance on a blank which permits the recording of errors according to eight categories of error type, the computing of "performance rating" for accuracy, comprehension, and rate of reading, and the summarizing of reading difficulties. Norms, in terms of grade equivalents, are provided for accuracy and comprehension.

The extensive manual includes information concerning the development and standardization of the test, details with respect to the vocabulary difficulty and grammatical construction of each of the paragraphs, suggestions for the interpretation of test results, and a selected bibliography of materials useful in planning the oral reading program. The standardization

population included 1,620 pupils from five states in grades 1 through 8. Analysis of the results of a fifth grade sample on the Gilmore test and similar tests by Gray and Durrell indicates that the accuracy scores on these several tests are quite comparable (correlations of .77, .80, and .73 are reported), but that correlations among comprehension and rate scores tend to be low. Alternate-forms correlations for groups of second, fifth, and seventh grade pupils indicate high reliability for the accuracy scores (.89, .85, and .84), and lower reliability for comprehension (.68, .67, and .52) and rate (.95, .72, and .59), particularly for older pupils. Kuder-Richardson coefficients are approximately the same for accuracy (.88, .86, and .89) and somewhat higher for comprehension (.82, .78, and .78).

Teachers and reading diagnosticians will probably prefer this test over most other tests of similar type. The proper use of the test will, of course, depend on the experience and training of the examiner, but as compared with most other oral reading tests, this one can be administered and scored in quite objective fashion.

[672]
★Leavell Analytical Oral Reading Test. Grades 1–10; 1952–53; individual; Forms A, B ('52); manual ('53); no data on reliability; $1.25 per 25 reading booklets, postage extra; 50¢ specimen set, postpaid; administration time not reported; [Ullin W. Leavell]; Educational Test Bureau. *

LYDIA A. DUGGINS, *Associate Professor and Director of Reading Services, University of Bridgeport, Bridgeport, Connecticut.*

The *Leavell Analytical Oral Reading Test* is an individual test designed to yield an oral reading placement that is comparable to that yielded by a silent reading test. It gives, in addition, information regarding the type of errors the child makes in word perception. Provision is made for recording rate of reading and comprehension. The test does not yield separate scores in these three factors, but rather a composite score in which each of these factors is weighted.

The test materials include a reading section and a record section for each of the two forms. The reading section is reusable. Directions for administering and scoring the test are presented in a manual and made clear by examples at each step.

The material of the reading section consists of a series of paragraphs of increasing difficulty built around the history of a horse (Form A) and a dog (Form B). These should have high enough interest value to the child to encourage his best performance on the test. The range of the test (grades 1–10) should increase its usefulness in the evaluation of gifted readers in the primary and elementary grades where the group tests administered often do not measure the superior child's skills.

One of the desirable features of the test is the organization of the record section. Specific directions for recording errors in word perception are given on the front of the individual record, making it possible for a less skilled examiner to refer to them readily. The comprehension section gives acceptable answers to the comprehension questions, making for greater objectivity in scoring these responses. Space is provided at the end of each paragraph for recording reading time, errors in word perception, and correct answers to comprehension questions. A summation of scores is presented for time, errors, comprehension, and total test.

A less desirable feature is the ambiguity of the section of the manual devoted to the standardization of the test and the scantiness of the statistical data given. So far as this reviewer can determine, a group of 25 children, aged 8 to 16, comprised a combined standardization and norms group. The standardization procedure involved individual testing with the Leavell test and an uncertain combination of oral and silent reading tests, and a comparison of the mean scores on the various tests. The publishers base their claims for comparability of forms, comparability of the Leavell test to the silent reading tests, and significance of differences of scores from grade to grade on these mean scores, and present 100-step grade score equivalents! There is no evidence of the reliability of the test for individual children.

It is rather difficult to imagine that the *Leavell Analytical Oral Reading Test* would justify the necessary time of administration by an inexperienced teacher who could secure comparable scores on a silent reading test in much less time. The major value of this test should lie in the observation and analysis of a child's difficulties, and little attention, other than the careful and convenient directions for recording such difficulties, is given to this matter, either in the manual or on the record form. The child's final score represents a composite of achievements and difficulties rather than an

analysis of them. However, in the hands of a skilled observer who understands the significance of the types of errors made by a child, the comparable forms, interesting reading content, and ease and objectivity of administration would make this test a useful supplement to group tests for individual diagnosis and for research purposes. It does not have the subjectivity of scoring of the usual oral reading test; on the other hand, neither does it have the comprehensiveness of diagnostic information such tests are expected to yield.

MAYNARD C. REYNOLDS, *Associate Professor of Educational Psychology, University of Minnesota, Minneapolis, Minnesota.*

The test consists of nine brief paragraphs which are to be read orally by the child. The paragraphs, organized to make a continuous story, range in difficulty from very simple (beginning readers) to difficult (high school students). Following the reading of each paragraph, the child is asked a set of comprehension questions. The examiner must record reading errors, reading time, and responses to the comprehension questions. Each paragraph is assigned three subscores, the sum of which gives a paragraph score. The total score is then converted into a grade score. There are no norms for part scores. Very little information is given regarding the standardization.

Many teachers and reading diagnosticians like to use a brief oral reading test as part of their diagnostic procedure. Others prefer to use selections from a series of graded readers. The consistent use of a simple oral reading test like the *Leavell Analytical Oral Reading Test,* even though the test may be extremely limited, does allow for greater objectivity of analysis than does the simple procedure of "reading from a book." If such a test is used, however, it should be realized that the evaluation of performance is still highly subjective.

A great many weaknesses in the Leavell test can be cited, most of them reflecting gaps in the manual. For example: No clear statement of the difficulty of the paragraphs is given. There are no data on the reliability of individual scores. The analysis and interpretation of errors and of speed and comprehension scores is left entirely to the examiner. The norms provided are little better than none at all. It is reported that the mean grade scores for 25 children ages 8 to 16 on the two forms of the test were closely comparable and that these mean scores were nearer the mean grade score of an unknown mixture of scores on two silent reading tests for the same population than was the mean score on the Gray oral reading test. Unfortunately, no information is given concerning the comparability of scores earned by *individuals* on the various tests.

We must hope that further information will be incorporated in the manual. Until this is done, those who use the Leavell test will need to do so in highly informal, subjective ways.

[673]

Oral Diagnostic Test of Word-Analysis Skills, Primary: Dominion Tests. Grades 1–2; 1947; individual; no data on reliability; no norms; 1 form; $1 per 25 record booklets; 15¢ per set of word slide cards and sleeve; 25¢ per manual; 45¢ per specimen set; postage extra; [20–40] minutes; Department of Educational Research, Ontario College of Education, University of Toronto; distributed by Guidance Centre. *

S. A. RAYNER, *Assistant Registrar, University of Queensland, Brisbane, Australia.*

As Smith pointed out in *The Fourth Mental Measurements Yearbook,* this instrument could best be regarded as an informal checking device worthy of commendation as a pioneer effort. Now that the test has been available for more than a decade, it must be asked whether it has fulfilled its original purpose and what further data on it has been collected.

There is no evidence to show that any development has occurred since 1947. The original manual has not been modified in any way; it does not yet provide norms; and it lacks evidence on reliability and validity. If the criteria suggested by the A.E.R.A.'s *Technical Recommendations for Achievement Tests* were used to evaluate this test, it would not rate highly.

It is not readily apparent from either the manual or the test that this is a diagnostic instrument which will enable the relatively inexperienced teacher to locate the specific difficulties of a particular pupil. The lack of any norms is a major weakness. If the test is used with a child in grade 2, a considerable number of mistakes can apparently be expected; but, without norms, the tester cannot tell whether reading development is normal for a child of this age, grade, and mental ability or whether there is either a specific or a general reading disability.

A second major weakness is that generalizations based on the errors in relatively few items

of the one type will almost certainly be highly unreliable. Since children will answer known words correctly without any formal analysis, the number of words tackled as an exercise in word analysis will be far smaller than the 100 items ostensibly in the test. In addition, children in grade 2 may not make any serious effort at analysis of the longer and more difficult words. It is almost certain that this test attempts to cover too wide a range of material in too few items to be a reliable diagnostic instrument.

The recommended system of coding errors and of analysing the results appears cumbersome and suggestions for remedial work must be found in a list of reference books published between 1935 and 1940.

This reviewer is of the opinion that the following weaknesses make the *Oral Diagnostic Test of Word-Analysis Skills* unsuitable for classroom use by the teacher: (*a*) lack of norms which makes interpretation difficult; (*b*) a cumbersome system of classifying errors; (*c*) lack of modern suggestions for remedial work; and (*d*) the certainty that there will be relatively few discriminating items for any one normal grade group and hence that the reliability for diagnostic purposes will often be low.

However, if any author should be interested in developing a new test of word analysis skills, he might do worse than to use this test as a starting point.

For a review by Nila Banton Smith, see 4:565.

[674]

★**Oral Word Reading Test.** Ages 7–11; 1952; individual; 1 form ['52]; 4s. per set of 1 test, 50 record blanks, and manual ['52]; 2s. 6d. per 50 record blanks; postage extra; specimen set not available; administration time not reported; A. E. Fieldhouse; New Zealand Council for Educational Research; distributed by Educational Books. *

S. A. RAYNER, *Assistant Registrar, University of Queensland, Brisbane, Australia.*

An oral word recognition test is so generally recognized as being among the most valuable means of estimating the language development of children in their first or second year at school that the construction of such a test to suit a particular culture (such as that of New Zealand) is a valuable service to the educational system. However, since it is highly probable that the English speaking children of New Zealand (for whom this test is specifically designed) may not differ greatly in vocabulary from those of Australia or England, consideration should be given to whether the *Oral Word Reading Test* is superior to the best overseas tests.

None of the 50 words chosen for the test is peculiar to New Zealand; in particular, there are none of the Maori words so widely used in that country. Neither the content nor the format of the test gives any obvious clue to the country of origin. Like other word reading tests, the words are arranged in ascending order of difficulty; the size of type becomes smaller as the words become more difficult. Each child's responses are checked on a separate record form.

The 16-page manual contains directions for administration and scoring and also provides norms. These are based on a total of 5,000 children, made up of 200 boys and a similar number of girls from each half-year age group from 6 to 11 years. Norms are provided for each group. Beyond these age ranges there are norms for bright younger children and dull older children. The table of norms suggests that the test is more steeply graded in difficulty than are similar tests from England.

Few details about the construction and standardization of the test are given in the manual. A brief technical appendix on the choice of words and the selection of children for the standardization sample would have added to its value. The stability reliability, based on a sample of 150 children aged 8-6 to 8-11 retested at an interval of one week, was found to be .98; this can be regarded as remarkably high for a test of this length. However, since the test would commonly be used with children a year younger than this, data on the reliability of the test with 7-year-old children should also be obtained.

No specific information is provided on validity. At least two methods are open to the author: test scores could be compared with an external criterion such as teacher's ratings; or the scores could be compared with those on a similar test designed by another person.

The gradient of difficulty of the *Oral Word Reading Test* for Queensland children has been tested by a method devised by Keats. He found that many of the words were rarely used by 9-year-old children in Queensland and that the easiest words on the list were probably at the

7-year-old level. This suggests that the test is more difficult than the best known British tests.

This reviewer is not able to comment on the suitability of the *Oral Word Reading Test* for New Zealand schools. However, the evidence on the gradient of difficulty of the items suggests that the Australian tester should continue to use the Hull or the Schonell test in preference to the New Zealand test.

D. K. WHEELER, *Senior Lecturer in Education, University of Western Australia, Nedlands, Australia.*

This word recognition test consists of 50 words arranged in approximate order of difficulty on a card which the child is required to read to the tester.

The author points out the difficulties of satisfactory discrimination at the highest and lowest levels with a 50-word test and says that it discriminates reasonably well at ages 7 to 11 years but gives a relatively reliable indication only of high attainment at age 6 and of low attainment at age 11. Reliability is given as .98 for test-retest of 150 children aged 8-6 to 8-11. In view of the remarks about lack of consistency at the ends of the distribution in this middle age range, reliability figures for other ages would be welcomed. The manual states that the N.Z.C.E.R. hopes to collect further information to check the norms, which should, meanwhile, be considered as tentative. This statement was made nearly seven years ago but no further information has been received.

For each half-year group from 6 to 11 years inclusive, score ranges are given for each tenth (called "attainment groups" with 10 designating the highest tenth) of the normative population. Norms are given for boys and girls separately on the ground that results suggest consistent sex differences, but there are also combined norms. It might be helpful to indicate to the classroom teacher where sex norms might be used and where composite norms would be appropriate.

The manual gives good and detailed general and particular instructions about giving the test and recording the results on the record form. Furthermore, it is cautious about the interpretation of scores, warning that too much must not be read into a single score.

This test was designed to determine the level of the child's attainment in word recognition. What it does with high reliability is to provide a means of comparing his attainment in recognizing these particular 50 words with that of other children throughout the age range of the test. Whether it does determine the level of attainment in word recognition generally is dependent on the extent to which these words are a representative sample of words which the child is likely to have to recognize. No information is given as to how the original 290 words were selected, on what criteria were used in reducing them to 90, and on how these 90 were in turn reduced to 50. As a test user, the reviewer would like to know for this, as for all such tests, the criteria for selection of words.

For an experienced reading teacher well versed in the literature of his subject, this could be a useful test of word recognition and attack. Being standardized (for New Zealand children whose mother tongue is English), it will serve, with other tests, for grouping for reading instruction and determining disability. Teachers using it would do well to heed the instructions about interpretation.

READINESS

[675]

*American School Reading Readiness Test. First grade entrants; 1941–55; 9 scores: vocabulary, discrimination of letter forms, discrimination of letter combinations, word selection, word matching, discrimination of geometric forms, following directions, memory of geometric forms, total; Form D ('55, identical with Form A except for slight changes in some drawings); manual ('55, identical with manual copyrighted in 1941 except for minor changes); $2.75 per 25 tests; 35¢ per specimen set; postpaid; (45) minutes; Willis E. Pratt, Robert V. Young, and Carroll A. Whitmer; Public School Publishing Co. *

REFERENCES
    1. PRATT, WILLIS E. *The Construction of a Group Test of Reading Readiness.* Doctor's thesis, University of Pittsburgh (Pittsburgh, Pa.), 1940.
    2. PRATT, WILLIS E. "A Study of the Differences in the Prediction of Reading Success of Kindergarten and Non-Kindergarten Children." *J Ed Res* 42:525-33 Mr '49. * (*PA* 23: 5753)
    3. DELANCY, ELMER O. *A Study of Three Psychological Tests as Related to Reading Achievement in Grade One American School Reading Readiness Test, Form A; SRA Primary Mental Abilities, Primary Form; Otis Quick-Scoring Mental Ability Tests, Alpha Test: Form A.* Doctor's thesis, Pennsylvania State University (University Park, Pa.), 1954.

JOAN BOLLENBACHER, *Supervisor of Appraisal Services, Cincinnati Public Schools, Cincinnati, Ohio.*

This test contains 60 items distributed among eight subtests, covering visual discrimination, vocabulary, ability to copy forms from memory, and ability to follow directions. Pupils react favorably toward this test. It can be ad-

ministered conveniently to 10 pupils at a time, and possibly up to 15 if the group is capable. No time limits have been assigned, but the entire test can be given easily within an hour, including time for a 15-minute recess.

The illustrations in the test generally are clear, but minor criticisms can be made of several of the subtests. The varying sizes and shapes of the blocks containing letter combinations and words contribute to a somewhat confusing format on two of the pages. The geometric forms also could be larger.

The test for following directions contains 12 blocks, each with identical pictures of a boy, a girl, a ball, a book, and an airplane. Perhaps the authors had good reason for using the same pictures with varying directions for each item; nevertheless, this test requires special alertness on the part of the examiner to be sure the pupil does not lose his place or does not mark twice in the same block.

The necessity for a child to understand a different set of instructions for each of the eight subtests poses a question as to whether or not the test, with a subtest specifically devoted to ability to follow directions, may be overemphasizing this purpose. Directions could, perhaps, have been simplified to some extent had similar subtests, such as Discrimination of Letter Combinations and Recognition of Words been combined, or had they at least followed one another.

The test manual, in addition to giving the customary directions for administering and scoring, provides some background information on the concept of reading readiness, a description of the procedures used in constructing the test, data on reliability and validity, and norms for interpreting scores. The manual has copyright dates of 1941 and 1945. Since a review of this test in *The Third Mental Measurements Yearbook* refers to the same normative data, apparently no further reliability and validity studies have been made.

Reliability, determined by the odd-even method, is reported as .95. Because of the great variability in performance of young children, information concerning test-retest reliability should also be provided.

Predictive validity data are based on testing 196 kindergarten and nonkindergarten pupils, all of about the same mental age, for reading readiness and intelligence, and testing six months later for reading achievement. A validity coefficient of .53 was found for both kindergarten and nonkindergarten homogeneous groups. By formula, a validity coefficient of .77 was estimated for a heterogeneous kindergarten group and one of .68 for the nonkindergarten heterogeneous group.

On the basis of the validity data, weights were computed for the subtests, and separate tables for kindergarten and nonkindergarten groups provided for converting raw scores into weighted scores. The negative weights which resulted for several of the tests are mentioned in a footnote. A statistical technique, no matter how defensible, in which higher raw scores receive lower predicted reading grades needs more explanation than a mere footnote to satisfy most teachers. It should be noted also that these data are based on test results for 196 pupils. Further validity studies would be appropriate to verify these findings.

Intelligence tests for the normative groups are mentioned, but the data are not reported in the manual. The reader is referred to an unpublished dissertation, a reference which may not be too accessible.

In view of the increasing size of first grade classes, teachers need a reading readiness test which is valid, reliable, and not too time consuming to administer. In spite of some shortcomings, the *American School Reading Readiness Test* might meet this need, especially if additional validity data were gathered. It is regrettable that further validity studies were not made in the period from 1941 to 1955.

HELEN M. ROBINSON, *Associate Professor of Education, The University of Chicago, Chicago, Illinois.*

This test is intended for use at the beginning of the first grade of school before reading instruction has started. The purpose of the test is to predict success in learning to read, and by implication, to locate difficulties which may impede early progress.

The test is composed of eight parts designed to estimate vocabulary development, visual discrimination, ability to follow directions, and skill in copying forms from memory. The content is similar to that of most other tests of reading readiness, except that auditory discrimination and information are not included. However, only 6 to 10 items are used in each subtest, with a total of 60 items. Thus the number of items is too small to provide reliable subtests. This may account for the fact that the manual makes no suggestions for readiness instruction based on weaknesses in areas measured by the subtests.

Form D is essentially the same as Form A, published in 1941. The booklet for form D is somewhat larger and the pictures are clearer; a few substitutions have been made so that all pictures will be of objects and scenes familiar to children today. Slight rearrangements which have been made in the format of some of the tests should make them easier for young children to use. The manual makes no statement concerning the changes or the adequacy of the old norms for the new form.

The first form of the test was validated by comparing scores on the test with reading attainment on the *Gates Primary Reading Tests* administered six months after the readiness test. The manual describes the original sample to which the readiness test was given as including 1,091 pupils in districts "ranging in size from small rural school districts to large urban schools." No further description is given to determine how representative this sample was of the general population. The reading tests were administered to only 196 pupils from 12 rooms in three "typical school districts" in the original sample. Both the size of the validation sample and the lack of information concerning its distribution are limitations which create many doubts concerning the validity of the test and of the norms supplied. Furthermore, the group of 196 appears to have been divided again into pupils who had had kindergarten experience, and those who had had none. The correlation coefficients between each subtest and the criterion test for the kindergarten group ranged from .22 to .43, and from .17 to .46 for the nonkindergarten group.

This reading readiness test is unique in that the total score is not just a sum of the parts. Instead, each subtest has been weighted by the multiple correlation technique. This method of using weighted scores often yields maximal prediction, providing that the sample is sufficiently large. In this instance, there is considerable doubt about the sample size.

A second unique feature of the test is that the norms "predict" actual reading achievement from grades 1.2 to 3.2 plus. While the manual cautions against prediction "with *absolute* accuracy," the norms are given in such a way as to imply such accuracy. Other tests, such as the *Metropolitan Readiness Tests* or Monroe's *Reading Aptitude Tests,* interpret the scores as high, average, and low, or select a cutoff point below which pupils are not likely to learn to read. The gross interpretations of the last two tests seem to be much more realistic. However, a multiple correlation of .53 is reported for homogeneous groups, which represents validity nearly as high as that reported by the other tests using the more flexible interpretations.

A coefficient of reliability of .91 is reported by correlating odd with even items. This figure is higher than those reported by most reading readiness tests.

The *American School Reading Readiness Test* appears to be worth further study because it may be a better predictor than those tests more frequently used in schools. At present, however, school personnel should choose reading readiness tests with more dependable norms, based on samples with wider distributions. Furthermore, teachers should be able to determine specific as well as general weaknesses in order to provide differentiated reading readiness experiences and instruction.

For reviews by David H. Russell and Paul A. Witty, see 3:513.

[676]

***Group Test of Reading Readiness: The Dominion Tests.** Grades kgn, kgn–1; 1949–55; 2 editions; postage extra; Department of Educational Research, Ontario College of Education, University of Toronto; distributed by Guidance Centre. *
a) [LONG FORM.] Grades kgn–1; 1949–51; 6 scores: discrimination of objects-symbols-words, listening-remembering-observing, familiarity with word forms, memory for word forms, motor coordination, total; Forms A, B ('49); mimeographed manual ('51); profile ('51); $1.70 per 25 tests; 25¢ per set of 10 flash cards of either form; 70¢ per specimen set including both forms, flash cards, and manual; (30–50) minutes in 2 sessions.
b) [SHORT FORM.] Grade kgn; 1954–55; 2 editions; $1.10 per 25 tests; 25¢ per specimen set of either edition including all forms and manual.
    1) *Subtest Type.* Forms A, B, C ('54); manual ('54); norms ('54); 11(19) minutes.
    2) *Omnibus Type.* Forms A, B ('54); manual ('55); norms ('54); 12(17) minutes.

N. DALE BRYANT, *Associate Professor of Psychology, University of Houston, Houston, Texas.*

The *Group Test of Reading Readiness* is a name given to three separate tests of the Dominion Tests series. Each of the three is designed to accomplish the same purpose: to predict at the end of kindergarten or at the beginning of the first grade the reading performance each student will achieve by the completion of the first grade.

The first subtest in the Long Form is designed to measure the ability to discriminate objects, symbols, and words. Five letters, objects, symbols, or words are presented, and the child marks an "X" through the one that is different. Subtest 2 is designed to measure ability to listen, remember, and observe well. Each item consists of four pictures from which the child must select and put an "X" on the picture that fits a story told by the test administrator. The third subtest is designed to measure the ability to discriminate between words and familiarity with word forms. In this subtest four words are presented, and the child draws a ring around the two words that are alike. Subtest 4 is planned to measure the ability to observe and remember word forms and to discriminate these forms from memory. Each of these items consists of a picture and six words, one of which is the name of the object in the picture. The examiner holds up a card with the correct word on it. The child is asked to remember the word and, when the card is no longer visible, to draw a ring around the correct word. This subtest gives an advantage to a child with some word familiarity. The final subtest is designed to measure motor coordination and the ability to observe and reproduce details of simple drawings. Each item consists of a simple figure or design. The child is asked to copy it.

The Short Form—Omnibus Type yields a single score obtained from 16 items similar to those in the first and third subtests of the Long Form. Each item consists of four to five symbols or random combinations of letters. The child marks an "X" through the two or three that are alike.

The Short Form—Subtest Type contains items of the same type as those in the omnibus test, but the items are grouped into two homogeneous subtests of eight items each. Separate directions are provided for each subtest, and two subtest scores are obtained.

Scoring of the Long Form is easy except for the fifth subtest which requires judgment of how adequately the child reproduces a drawing. The manual gives specific and rather comprehensive directions, including examples of correct and incorrect reproduction. The short forms are administered item by item, a method which provides closer control over children in their following directions. The type of item is easier to administer and score than items in some sections on the Long Form. Similar items on the Long Form had the highest subtest correlation with the total score.

The reported alternate-forms reliabilities of the Long Form subtest scores suggest that the subtest scores would be more suitable for making group comparisons than for making decisions about specific individuals. The intercorrelations between the subtests are roughly proportional to their reliabilities, and all subtests seem to be reflecting much the same thing. The high degree of internal consistency suggests that when the total score is used alone, there is little loss in information as compared with the use of the subscores. Of course, extreme deficiencies on any subtest should be noted, as such differences might represent misunderstood directions or some actual deficiency. In addition to providing subtest scores, the Long Form is rich in opportunity for clinical interpretation. While over the entire group, subtest scores and clinical interpretation may add little to the prediction achieved by the total score, extreme cases might provide valuable insights and suggestions for remedial work. Similarly, subtest scores averaged for an entire class may provide useful guides to the teacher.

For the Short Form, the manual reports alternate-forms reliabilities of .63 for Omnibus Type and .77 for Subtest Type. The higher reliability of the latter test is borne out in the higher correlations of this test with the Long Form. It seems likely that the higher reliability is due, at least in part, to the fact that the two types of items are separated and separate directions are given with each type. In addition, there are twice as many examples as there are in the Omnibus Type, and two extra minutes are used for administration. Subtest reliabilities for the Subtest Type range from .57 to .80 for Test 1 and from .57 to .72 for Test 2. Once again, equivalence and reliability data warrant the use of the subtest scores for group work, but use of them to make decisions about individuals unsupported by other evidence should be avoided. The total score for the Subtest Type might, however, justifiably be used with individuals. The use of two forms should be considered if higher reliability for individual work is desired.

A correlation of about .50 is reported between the Long Form total score (test administered prior to first grade training) and a measure of reading achievement at the end of the first grade training. In view of the lapse of time, the effect of variation in instruction, and the lack of perfect reliability, this is a substantial validity. However, it does not account for most of the criterion variance.

The manual repeatedly recommends that the test be used only in conjunction with an intelligence test. However, no correlation is reported between the readiness test and an intelligence test, nor are multiple correlations for validity coefficients given. It is quite possible that the test measures much the same thing as an intelligence test, and the use of both this readiness test and an intelligence test may be no better than using one instrument alone. In the various item analyses that have been done on this test, selection of items which show high correlation with the criterion but low correlation with the intelligence test (if such items exist) would have insured the development of a test that fits the stated purpose, "to measure certain factors of reading readiness which are not completely covered by an intelligence test."

No direct validities are reported for the short forms. However, since correlations with the Long Form (.65 to .70 for the Omnibus Type and .74 to .77 for total score on the Subtest Type) are close to the estimated reliability, most of the validity reported for the Long Form is probably retained by the shorter tests.

In conclusion, these tests are useful, moderately valid measures of reading readiness. The Subtest Type of the Short Form appears well suited for use as a quick screening device in conjunction with other data. The major handicap in using and evaluating the tests is the absence of information about how they relate to intelligence measures and other variables used in predicting readiness.

[677]

*The Harrison-Stroud Reading Readiness Profiles. Grades kgn–1; 1949–56; individual in part; 7 scores: using symbols, making visual discriminations (2 parts), using the context, making auditory discriminations, using context and auditory clues, giving the names of letters; 1 form ('56); 6 tests in 4 booklets; manual ('56); no data on reliability; $3.75 per 35 tests, postage extra; 80¢ per specimen set, postpaid; (80–90) minutes in 3 sessions; M. Lucile Harrison and James B. Stroud; Houghton Mifflin Co. *

REFERENCES

1. Mosbo, Alvin O. *A Study of the Harrison-Stroud Reading Readiness Tests in Relation to Achievement in First Grade Reading, and of Pupil Growth in Specific Readiness Skills in the Public Schools of Davenport, Iowa.* Doctor's field study, Colorado State College of Education (Greeley, Colo.), 1953.

2. Spaulding, Geraldine. "The Relation Between Performance of Independent School Pupils on the Harrison-Stroud Reading Readiness Tests and Reading Achievement a Year Later." *Ed Rec B* 67:73–6 F '56. * (PA 31:3812)

S. S. Dunn, *Officer-in-Charge, Test Division, Australian Council for Educational Research, Melbourne, Australia.*

The immediate impression gained by looking at the tests is excellent. The use of coloured boxes and the spacious layout of the questions is likely to attract the child's interest. The general directions to the tester show a good appreciation of the steps necessary to obtain a valid score for an individual, and the specific directions are precise and should cause no difficulties. The provision of scoring stencils independent of the manual would probably speed up marking, but the present method may have the advantage of forcing the teacher to a more detailed study of each individual's performance.

A detailed study of the manual, however, leaves the impression that the authors are more at home with children than with measurement theory. At no place in the manual is there any evidence of the reliability of the tests or of their intercorrelations, yet this evidence is crucial if one is going to try to interpret differences between scores on individual tests as the authors do. In particular, the authors encourage users to give meaning to differences in scores on Test 2a and Test 2b without any indication of the size of difference needed for significance. In practice, the majority of differences would almost certainly be due to "error" in the tests. The interpretation given to the illustrative profile on page 6 of the manual is certainly using differences which are probably chance fluctuations.

Also, when one is making use of a profile approach, the matter of norms is important. In its first edition, this test appeared with norms based on 221 pupils in one middle western city in the United States. The number has been increased to 1,400 pupils—32 communities in 28 states using at least 5 different reading programmes. Does the reading programme have any effect on the norms? We are not told. The desirability of an individual education authority developing its own norms is not mentioned. A local expectancy table would be even better. The discussion about validity is not helpful.

Evidence of high internal consistency discrimination indexes is presented, but this only points to the likelihood of high reliability. One is asked to take on faith the content validity of the test. One would like some evidence that tests labeled Using Symbols, Using the Context, Making Auditory Discriminations, etc. are in fact measuring these abilities as they relate to reading readiness and that they are not unduly influenced by such a factor as ability to follow directions and to understand what the tester wants.

The method given of computing mental age is appropriate only for tests such as the Binet, using an age scale method of norming. For the WISC and most group tests it would be incorrect. And why compute MA at age of entry to the grade and not at the time the readiness test is taken? Presumably it is then that the decision about classifying the children is going to take place. Overseas experience (Scotland, New Zealand, Australia) should lead reading experts to question the validity of the statement that a mental age of 6-4 to 6-6 is necessary for successfully learning to read.

In the section on interpretation of test results no reference is made to the fact that the result on Test 6, Giving the Names of Letters, depends almost entirely on specific teaching whether by teacher or parent and that, in this regard, the test differs from the other five tests. A low score on this test would seem relatively unimportant if the other five scores are high. A high score on the other hand is unlikely without satisfactory scores on the other tests. The result on this test could well be treated as additional information of value in the same way that mental age is.

In practice, then, the test may be found to be useful, but the authors should endeavour to improve the manual by providing evidence on reliability and validity, and they should use this information to help users properly interpret the test profile.

For a review by William S. Gray of an earlier edition, see 4:568.

[678]

Lee-Clark Reading Readiness Test, 1951 Revision. Grades kgn-1; 1931–51; 4 scores: letter symbols, concepts, word symbols, total; 1 form ('51, identical to test copyrighted in 1943); manual ('51); $3.15 per 35 tests, postage extra; 25¢ per specimen set, postpaid; (20) minutes; J. Murray Lee and Willis W. Clark; California Test Bureau. *

James R. Hobson, *Director of Child Placement, Brookline Public Schools, Brookline, Massachusetts.*

The 1931 edition of this test was the first of the better known tests in the field, and the 1943 and 1951 revisions, with two subtests and a diagnostic profile added, have preserved its usefulness and widespread acceptance.

The general purpose of the test is to predict a child's ability to learn to read, with concomitant dividends in the form of data for initial intraclass grouping, some indication of how long formal reading instruction should be deferred if need be, and a rough analysis of the general readiness area in which a child may be deficient. These purposes are accomplished through four subtests measuring recognition of likenesses; discrimination of differences; experiential background, including understanding vocabulary; and ability to discriminate among similar but different letter and word forms. That these purposes are accomplished with as high a degree of validity as is reported in a fairly sizable body of research by a test which takes less than 20 minutes to administer is a tribute to the ability of the authors and their understanding of the field of beginning reading.

Reliability coefficients obtained on split halves by the Spearman-Brown formula range from .83 to .94 on the subtests, with .92 for the total score, as based on 170 entering first grade pupils. Research data reported by others, as well as by the authors of the test, show coefficients of correlation between scores on various editions of the test and other reading tests that are substantial enough to indicate a fair degree of predictive validity. In practically every instance the criterion reading test was also correlated with either teachers' ratings or group intelligence tests, and in every instance but one the *Lee-Clark Reading Readiness Test* yielded a higher coefficient.

Norms for the 1951 Revision are based on 5,000 entering first graders with median CA 6-0 and median IQ 100, with sigma 16. Norms for near the end of the kindergarten year are based on a different population not further described. Considerable supplementary information of value in determining degree of reading readiness—grade placement equivalents of scores, expectation of success and of failure of various scores—are also provided.

This is an excellent test, considering its brevity and ease of administration. After using it for more than 20 years in the last month of kindergarten, this reviewer can report that in practice it is very effective in screening out those children with gross and usually rather obvious hindrances to success in beginning reading, such as mental immaturity, deprivation in experiential background, nervous instability resulting in short interest and attention span, and gross sensory handicaps. It sometimes serves to give evidence of excellent ability and probable success in reading on the part of children who, lacking somewhat in physical size, social forwardness, manual dexterity, or oral verbosity, have not previously been rated high by their teachers.

Neither the test itself nor any of the technical data presented in the manual would appear to support the rather elaborate normative and interpretative tables. These are attractive and logical enough; but in the absence of any experimental support or statistical verification, it must be assumed that they have been more or less subjectively derived and that their validity for such exact and detailed analysis is in question. We have found that a more valid method of diagnosis is to determine a critical score (35 out of 64 in our situation) below which the chances of success in first grade reading have proved to be poor and to follow up the 5 per cent of the children thus screened out with an individual reading aptitude test (Monroe) and an individual psychological examination (Stanford-Binet). These data, together with an individual 4-page personality profile kept from the beginning of the year by the kindergarten teacher, furnish the material for diagnosis. It jars this reviewer to see the term "diagnostic" applied to a profile based on a test measuring three or four rather general aspects of reading readiness and requiring only 12 to 15 minutes of working time. "Analytic" might be a less presumptuous term.

This is a superior screening test with surprising reliability and validity for its purpose, considering its brevity. Its total administration time of 15 to 20 minutes makes it particularly convenient to administer in one sitting in kindergarten or first grade and gives it a definite advantage in this respect over such widely used tests as the Gates, Metropolitan, Harrison-Stroud, and Murphy-Durrell tests, which require from 50 to 90 minutes and two or three sittings to administer. It saves time from those who do not need detailed diagnosis which can be used on those who do. In the absence of other objective data it serves as a good rough measure for initial grouping, but its scores should not be interpreted too minutely and it should be followed up by additional diagnostic instruments.

For reviews by Marion Monroe Cox and David H. Russell of the 1943 edition, see 3:517.

[679]
Murphy-Durrell Diagnostic Reading Readiness Test. First grade entrants; 1949, c1947–49; 3 scores: auditory, visual, learning rate; Part 3 individual in part; 1 form ('47); manual ('49); $3.05 per 35 tests; $2.20 per set of flash cards ['49]; postage extra; 35¢ per specimen set, postpaid; Parts 1–2: (60) minutes; group administration of Part 3: (20) minutes; individual administration of Part 3: (5–10) minutes; Helen A. Murphy and Donald D. Durrell; World Book Co. *

REFERENCES
1–2. See 4:571.
3. NICHOLSON, ALICE. *Background Abilities Related to Reading Success in First Grade.* Doctor's thesis, Boston University (Boston, Mass.), 1957.
4. NICHOLSON, ALICE. "Background Abilities Related to Reading Success in First Grade." *J Ed* (Boston) 140:7–24 F '58. *

JOAN BOLLENBACHER, *Supervisor of Appraisal Services, Cincinnati Public Schools, Cincinnati, Ohio.*

This test is designed to measure what the authors consider three critical areas in learning to read. It is, accordingly, divided into three parts, testing auditory discrimination, visual discrimination, and learning rate, respectively.

It seems appropriate to consider each of the subtests separately, since the manual states that there is no provision for finding a total score on the test. There is, however, space provided on the front cover of the test booklet for recording total score and percentile. An inconsistency of this type is confusing to a teacher.

The auditory test, consisting of 84 picture items, takes about 30 minutes to administer. The manual indicates that the test is for group use, but contains no information as to the appropriate size of the group. The reviewer has found, however, that no more than six children can be handled properly, since the test requires the children to pay close attention in order to distinguish separate sounds in spoken words. In the general directions, the manual suggests that "it is important to enunciate very clearly and follow directions exactly," but fails to stress the effect of variations in administration on the reliability of the test. The manual reports a reliability coefficient of .96, based on correlating the odd and even items. Since this

is a test for young children whose attention wanders easily and since it depends on the ability of the examiner to enunciate, the test user would have more confidence in a reliability coefficient based on a test-retest procedure.

Evidence that inattention is, indeed, a matter for concern was provided in a test tryout conducted by the reviewer. Given to a capable class of 25 pupils by a trained examiner under optimum conditions, the auditory test, which employs the scoring formula of the number of items right minus twice the number of items wrong, yielded zero scores for 12 of the pupils. On the visual test the lowest score for the same group was 30 (49th percentile). The manual admonishes the examiner to check individual pupils who have zero scores, having them respond orally, to determine whether there is an actual weakness or whether inattention was a determining factor in the test result. If such a procedure is necessary, a question as to whether this should be a group or an individual test might legitimately be raised.

The visual test contains 52 items, half of which involve perception of letters and half, perception of words. The items are presented by the examiner on flash cards, and the pupils must select the matching letter or word among five choices for each item. This test takes about 30 minutes. The odd-even reliability is .95.

The learning rate test consists of 10 words presented in a 20-minute teaching situation to groups of 10 pupils. Later the same day each pupil is tested individually three times on his ability to recognize the words. His score is the number of words he recognizes on the third testing. In a first grade class of present-day size, it would take a teacher the greater part of three days to complete the test. The manual suggests that the teacher provide seatwork exercises for pupils while they are not being tested. This is easier said than done. Even in a class where all pupils had attended kindergarten, this would require quite a degree of independence on the pupils' part and quite a quantity of seatwork.

The manual states that the validity of the learning rate test "stems from the closeness with which the test situation resembles the actual typical word-learning situation in the first grade." The manual furnishes no data regarding the relationship of the learning rate scores to subsequent scores on reading achievement tests, commenting that "it is felt that the closeness of the logical relationship between rate of learning words and reading achievement is so great as to make such data superfluous." (This reviewer believes that data on the predictive validity of a test scarcely could be considered superfluous.) Nevertheless, the manual indicates that this test can provide a meaningful evaluation of pupil performance and suggests that pupils be divided into four groups on the basis of their scores on this test. It is regrettable that data regarding the reliability and the error of measurement on this 10-item test have been omitted. Such data are significant, particularly since groupings such as these sometimes become permanent labels, and more often when they are dignified by a somewhat misleading title such as "learning rate."

In brief, this reviewer does not recommend this test for group use in the first grade.

S. S. DUNN, *Officer-in-Charge, Test Division, Australian Council for Educational Research, Melbourne, Australia.*

For this test there is no empirical evidence for validity. The argument for validity runs thus: (a) Clinical studies on 4,000 children show that failure in reading is mainly due to lack of auditory discrimination, lack of visual discrimination, and improper adjustment to learning rate (no reference to any publication is given). (b) Tests of auditory discrimination, visual discrimination, and learning rate are prepared. (c) Low scores on any of these tests is indicative of lack of readiness for reading.

There seems to be fairly general agreement on the importance of visual and auditory discrimination in learning to read. But can we be sure that the Murphy-Durrell tests bearing these names measure these abilities and not irrelevant ones? For instance, in the auditory discrimination test the first practice example requires the pupil to place his finger on a picture of a garden while the examiner says: "Listen—go—garden. Does garden sound like go at the beginning? Yes, so we shall mark it with a large cross, like this!" Now unless the child has already played this "game" before, he could well say that "go" and "gar" are not the same beginning sounds. There are 12 practice examples and one hopes that all children understand the task before starting. But it is quite possible that only the quick learners understand

what is required. Some evidence, then, that this group test is a valid measure of auditory discrimination, in the form of a correlation with a more direct measure of auditory discrimination obtained individually, would be welcome.

In the visual discrimination test the teacher holds up a card with a letter or a word on it and the children find the matching letter or word on the test paper. In a large class the distance from the stimulus of the nearest and furthest child could be of considerable importance in clear recognition. And what of people suffering from some visual defect? Those tests of visual discrimination in which the stimulus is on the child's test would seem to provide more standard conditions.

The learning rate test is most time-consuming. Only 10 subjects are taught at a time and then tested individually three times during the day. The conditions are far from standard for each individual. The other children in the class doing seatwork exercises are going to be most unusual individuals if they pay no attention to the oral, blackboard, and testing activities of the test group. The aim of a simple "work-sample test" is appealing, but surely the classroom teacher can quickly find out who are fast learners and who are slow learners from her normal observations. In any case it would seem a waste of time to use this third test with those whose scores on tests 1 and 2 are low.

Reliability figures are given only for tests 1 and 2 and these are split-half coefficients. With young children test-retest or parallel-forms figures would be more satisfactory. No table of intercorrelations between the tests is given. This is essential information when tests are purporting to be measuring different abilities.

The usefulness of norms for a test of this type is debatable, but the information given is insufficient to enable a teacher to decide whether or not her group can legitimately be compared with the normative group. Would it not be possible and more meaningful to provide some sort of expectancy table which relates readiness scores to ability to read a passage of given difficulty "X" months after the test?

The teacher who uses the test as a learning experience for the children may find that it gives her insights into the state of readiness of individual children and even helps in the development of these skills. Her own observations of her everyday tasks may, however, be just as useful.

[680]

★**Reading Readiness Test.** Grades kgn-1; 1957; 1 form; $2.50 per 25 tests; 25¢ per specimen set; cash orders postpaid; (20) minutes; David F. Votaw and Peggy Lou Moses; Steck Co. *

REFERENCE

I. BANHAM, KATHARINE M. "Maturity Level for Reading Readiness: A Check List for the Use of Teachers and Parents as a Supplement to Reading Readiness Tests." *Ed & Psychol Meas* 18:371–5 su '58. *

[681]

★**Scholastic Reading Readiness Test.** Grades kgn-1; 1953; various titles used by publishers; for Catholic schools; Form A; manual ['53]; $3.20 per 35 tests; 50¢ per specimen set; postage extra; (30–45) minutes; Oliver F. Anderhalter and Ruth Colestock; Scholastic Testing Service, Inc. *

[682]

★**Webster Reading-Readiness Test.** Grades kgn-1.5; 1950; 5 scores: verbal discrimination, memory of word forms, auditory discrimination, vocabulary and comprehension, total; 1 form; manual ['50]; 24¢ per test; 36¢ per manual kit; postpaid; (30–40) minutes; Clarence R. Stone and Mary Nila; Webster Publishing Co. *

SPECIAL FIELDS

[683]

*****Interpretation of Reading Materials in the Natural Sciences.** High school, college; 1944–57; subtest of *Tests of General Educational Development;* IBM; 2 levels; 2 forms: high school, Form B ('44); college, Form B ('43); revised manuals: high school level ('56), college level ('54); $2.50 per 25 tests of either level; separate answer sheets must be used; $1 per 25 IBM answer sheets; 50¢ per specimen set; postage extra; (120) minutes; prepared by Examination Staff of United States Armed Forces Institute; Veterans' Testing Service, American Council on Education. *

For a review by Robert J. Solomon of the complete battery, see 27; for a review by Gustav J. Froehlich of Form B, see 4:26; for reviews by Herbert S. Conrad and Warren G. Findley, see 3:20.

[684]

*****Interpretation of Reading Materials in the Social Studies.** High school, college; 1944–57; subtest of *Tests of General Educational Development;* IBM; 2 levels; 2 forms: high school, Form B ('44), college, Form B ('43); revised manuals: high school level ('56), college level ('54); $2.50 per 25 tests of either level; separate answer sheets must be used; $1 per 25 IBM answer sheets; 50¢ per specimen set; postage extra; (120) minutes; prepared by Examination Staff of United States Armed Forces Institute; Veterans' Testing Service, American Council on Education. *

For reviews by W. E. Hall and C. Robert Pace of the college level, see 3:528. For a review by Robert J. Solomon of the complete battery, see 27; for a review by Gustav J. Froehlich of Form B, see 4:26; for reviews by Herbert S. Conrad and Warren G. Findley, see 3:20.

[685]

*****The Iowa Tests of Educational Development: Test 5, Ability to Interpret Reading Materials in the Social Studies.** Grades 9–13; 1942–58; title on Form Y-3S is *Interpretation—Social Studies;* IBM; Forms X-3S, Y-3S ('52); examiner's manual ('58); battery manual ('54); pupil profile leaflet ('58); profile card (no date); separate answer sheets must be used; $3 per 20 tests; $5 per 100 IBM answer sheets; 50¢ per scoring stencil; $3 per complete specimen set; postage extra; 60(70) or 40(50) minutes; prepared under the direction of E. F. Lindquist; Science Research Associates. *

For reviews by J. Murray Lee and Stephen Wiseman of the complete battery, see 17; for a review by Eric F. Gardner of earlier forms, see 4:17; for reviews by Henry Chauncey, Gustav J. Froehlich, and Lavone A. Hanna, see 3:12.

[686]

*****The Iowa Tests of Educational Development: Test 6, Ability to Interpret Reading Materials in the Natural Sciences.** Grades 9–13; 1942–58; title on Form Y-3S is *Interpretation—Natural Sciences;* IBM; Forms X-3S, Y-3S ('52); examiner's manual ('58); battery manual ('54); pupil profile leaflet, fourth edition ('58); profile card (no date); separate answer sheets must be used; $3 per 20 tests; $5 per 100 IBM answer sheets; $2.15 per 20 answer pads; 50¢ per scoring stencil; $3 per complete specimen set; postage extra; 60(70) or 40(50) minutes; prepared under the direction of E. F. Lindquist; Science Research Associates. *

For reviews by J. Murray Lee and Stephen Wiseman of the complete battery, see 17; for a review by Eric F. Gardner of earlier forms, see 4:17; for reviews by Henry Chauncey, Gustav J. Froehlich, and Lavone A. Hanna, see 3:12.

SPEED

[687]

★**Tinker Speed of Reading Test.** Grades 7–16 and adults; 1955, c1947–55; Forms 1 ('55), 2 ('55); mimeographed manual ('55); norms for college sophomores on 5-, 10-, and 30-minute tests only; $5 per 25 tests; 50¢ per specimen set; postage extra; any time limit from 4(15) to 30(40) minutes; Miles A. Tinker; University of Minnesota Press. *

LEONARD S. FELDT, *Assistant Professor of Education, State University of Iowa, Iowa City, Iowa.*

This test was developed by the author in connection with his long series of experiments on the effects of typographical and illumination variations on reading speed. It is published primarily for other experimenters in this field and for college and high school reading instructors in need of a rate measure. Since the number of potential users in the first category is undoubtedly very small, its publication is of most consequence to those in the second.

The test consists of 450 independent, 30-word items (usually one sentence, sometimes two) set in pseudo-paragraphs of five items each. The student is instructed to read with all possible speed and, as a comprehension check, to look for and cross out the one word near the end of each item which "spoils the meaning." For this technique the author is indebted to the *Chapman-Cook Speed of Reading Test* and the *Michigan Speed of Reading Test*. The comments of the reviewer of these instruments on this technique are worth careful consideration by the potential user of this test.

There are two main strengths to this instrument. First, it provides sufficient homogeneous material to permit a relatively long test (30 minutes), if the user desires one. Second, the author has gone to considerable trouble to produce two forms which were equated item by item in the mean reading time and mean reading errors of a group of 55 subjects. The resultant forms, though not exactly equal in difficulty, are very closely matched. The availability of such equated forms should facilitate the assessment of changes in reading speed, an important measurement problem in remedial reading programs.

The principal weaknesses of the test are the deficient norms, the inadequate reliability data, and the absence of correlations with other types of rate measures. The only norms provided are based on groups of 96 to 135 sophomores of the University of Minnesota. Norms are presented for 5-, 10-, and 30-minute tests, but the data are clearly inadequate for the interpretation of the scores of high school students. Moreover, without additional evidence, one cannot assume that the norms are suitable for college students at other institutions. Since performance on rate tests depends to some extent on the type of comprehension check employed and the nature of the reading material, evaluation of pupil performance in words per minute will not permit the examiner to use normative data available from other sources. Thus, every user must expect to compile his own norms, a responsibility which a publisher might well recommend but should hardly demand.

Parallel-form reliabilities ranging from .76 to .93 are reported for 18 groups which are not described in any respect. Apparently, the coefficients apply to a 30-minute test, although this is not clearly specified. Since 5-minute and 10-minute tests are specifically suggested, reliability data for tests of these lengths should have been made available for all grade levels. It should be noted, in this regard, that recent investigations strongly indicate the Spearman-Brown formula does not provide accurate estimates of the reliability of shortened and lengthened rate tests. Estimates of such reliabilities must be empirically determined.

The author states that the test was constructed to provide a measure of speed of reading uncomplicated by comprehension difficulties —an end achieved by the use of only the most common words and sentences of unsophisticated thought content. Many reading specialists may not consider this a virtue. The goal of many college programs is not the unqualified increase of reading speed, but the selective use of speed, depending upon the nature and purpose of the reading. This test is clearly unsuited for measurement of this objective. High school and college teachers might well be concerned with the relationship of performance on this test to that on rate tests involving other kinds of material and other kinds of comprehension checks. They might also question the relationship to performance on reading materials which do present comprehension problems. The latter situation is our primary concern, after all. No data are presented on these points, however.

The potential user will have to weigh the strengths of this test against its weaknesses. Both are obvious. With more comprehensive norms and more thorough reliability analyses the instrument could be far more useful than it now is.

STUDY SKILLS

[688]

★Brown-Holtzman Survey of Study Habits and Attitudes. High school and college; 1953–56; IBM; 1 form ('53) ; revised manual ('56) ; separate answer sheets must be used; $2 per 25 tests; $1.90 per 50 IBM answer sheets; 50¢ per set of either hand or machine scoring stencils and manual; 60¢ per specimen set; postpaid; (25–35) minutes; William F. Brown and Wayne H. Holtzman; Psychological Corporation. *

REFERENCES
1. HOLTZMAN, WAYNE H., AND BROWN, WILLIAM F. "Study Habits and Attitudes in the Prediction of Academic Success." Abstract. Am Psychol 8:369 Ag '53. *

2. Brown, William F., and Holtzman, Wayne H. "The Importance of Study Habits and Attitudes in the Scholastic Achievement of High School and College Students." Abstract. *Am Psychol* 9:341–2 Ag '54. *

3. Holtzman, Wayne H.; Brown, William F.; and Farquhar, W. G. "The Survey of Study Habits and Attitudes: A New Instrument for the Prediction of Academic Success." *Ed & Psychol Meas* 14:726–32 w '54. * (PA 29:7962)

4. Brown, William F., and Holtzman, Wayne H. "A Study-Attitudes Questionnaire for Predicting Academic Success." *J Ed Psychol* 46:75–84 F '55. * (PA 30:1503)

5. Pauk, Walter J. *An Analysis of Certain Characteristics of Above-Average and Below-Average Male and Female Readers at the Ninth-Grade Level.* Doctor's thesis, Cornell University (Ithaca, N.Y.), 1955. (DA 16:285)

6. Sie, Georgiana D. W. *The Relationship of Two Experimental Measures of Student Motivation to Academic Success in College.* Doctor's thesis, State University of Iowa (Iowa City, Iowa), 1955. (DA 15:1556)

7. Brown, William F., and Holtzman, Wayne H. "Use of the Survey of Study Habits and Attitudes for Counseling Students." *Personnel & Guid J* 35:214–8 D '56. * (PA 31:8766)

8. Ahmann, J. Stanley, and Glock, Marvin D. "The Utility of Study Habits and Attitudes Inventory in a College Reading Program." *J Ed Res* 51:297–303 D '57. *

9. Chansky, Norman M., and Bregman, Martin. "Improvement of Reading in College." *J Ed Res* 51:313–7 D '57. *

10. Kim, Ki Suk. *The Use of Certain Measurements of Academic Aptitude, Study Habits, Motivation, and Personality in the Prediction of Academic Achievement.* Doctor's thesis, Louisiana State University (Baton Rouge, La.), 1957. (DA 18:150)

11. Krumboltz, John D., and Farquhar, William W. "The Effect of Three Teaching Methods on Achievement and Motivational Outcomes in a How-to-Study Course." *Psychol Monogr* 71(14):1–26 '57.

12. Ahmann, J. Stanley; Smith, William L.; and Glock, Marvin D. "Predicting Academic Success in College by Means of a Study Habits and Attitude Inventory." *Ed & Psychol Meas* 18:853–7 w '58. *

13. Feeney, Mary M. *Scores on SAT-V and Survey of Study Habits and Attitudes as Predictors of Achievement in a College for Women.* Master's thesis, Fordham University (New York, N.Y.), 1958.

14. Garcia, Dolores, and Whigham, Neil. "Validity of SSHA Administered Before and After College Experience." *Ed & Psychol Meas* 18:845–51 w '58. *

James Deese, *Associate Professor of Psychology, The Johns Hopkins University, Baltimore, Maryland.*

This inventory is designed to identify students whose study habits and attitudes are not those of students who do well in academic work and, in addition, to provide a basis for aiding such students through counseling and remedial work with study methods. Furthermore, the inventory may be used to predict academic success for high school and college populations.

The 75 items on the inventory differ somewhat from those usually found in study inventories. In preliminary administrations during the selection and validation of items, the authors found that items probing "study attitudes" were in general more highly related to superior grades than items designed to assess the mechanics of studying. The manifest contents of some of the items are aimed at anxiety before and during tests and, in some instances, at general personality characteristics. The result is that the inventory is very heavily pointed in the direction of assessing motivation for study and attitudes towards academic work. This emphasis provides the most unique and valuable aspect of the inventory.

The data accumulated during validation are very encouraging, though the authors themselves are cautious about the test's predictive use because of its dependence upon frankness of responding. Perhaps the most encouraging aspect of these data is not the size of the obtained coefficients, but the indication that, to a surprising degree, what the inventory measures is independent of scholastic aptitude as measured by the *American Council on Education Psychological Examination for College Freshmen.* The inventory substantially increases the correlation with grades when used in conjunction with the ACE. One curious feature of the validation data is that the correlations between single-semester grade-point averages and SSHA scores are consistently higher for college students in Texas (.39 to .66) than for those from other parts of the country (.27 to .37).

The only serious deficiency in the manual is the sketchiness with which information about the counseling keys is given. On the keys themselves we are informed that the items indicated are items to which the student's response is different from that of students who obtain high grades. While little information about the selection of items used for scoring is necessary to the user, most people giving the test will want to know more than they are told in the manual about the items selected for the counseling key. Indeed, many counselors will be interested in the responses to items not included on the counseling keys.

In summary, this inventory or survey is a unique and valuable contribution to the techniques for assessing student habits of work and motivation for study. It is more suited for uncovering attitudinal and motivational difficulties than any other published study inventory, and its use is particularly recommended where such difficulties are the prime concern. In addition, its value for research on counseling and remedial teaching must not be overlooked.

C. Gilbert Wrenn, *Professor of Educational Psychology,* and Roy D. Lewis, *Teaching Assistant, University of Minnesota, Minneapolis, Minnesota.*

This instrument is designed "to furnish an inventory of study habits and attitudes to serve as a foundation for self-improvement." It consists of a series of statements which are to be responded to in terms of the extent to which they represent actions and attitudes of the person responding. In addition to the scoring key, a special counseling key is provided which permits identification of items to which the response given is different from that most frequently given by students of high scholastic achievement.

The instrument has been standardized on high school students and college freshmen. Correlations between scores and one-semester grade-point averages for college freshmen range from .27 to .66 for men, and from .26 to .65 for women. Correlations for the high school students are somewhat lower. Reliability coefficients seem satisfactory, ranging from .79 to .95 for different groups and different methods.

Correlations between this test and the *American Council on Education Psychological Examination for College Freshmen* are consistently low according to the authors. Multiple correlation coefficients based upon the ACE and the SSHA in combination indicate an increase in the predictive efficiency over either instrument used singly. For example, the weighted average coefficient between grades and ACE scores of women college freshmen rose from .53 to .61 when the SSHA was used in combination. If the test were to be used as a selection device it can be assumed that students would tend to respond in the approved direction and that the predictive efficiency of the instrument would be effected.

The recommended uses as seen by the authors, while fairly clear cut, appear to be a bit ambitious. As either a screening instrument or a diagnostic instrument the test must assume both complete frankness of response and a fairly high degree of memory accuracy on the part of the student. In the use of the SSHA for research, an uncontrolled variable of interest or motivation shows up. In one study (3) reported by the authors the correlations between grades and test scores were considerably higher for persons showing interest in their scores than for persons who did not show such interest. Another variable is revealed in a study by Krumboltz and Farquhar (11) in which students showing a preference for cognitive-type, teacher directed instructors *increased* their SSHA scores after taking a how to study course, whereas students in the same course preferring a student-centered type of instruction *lowered* their scores.

The development procedure for this test was extremely well conceived. Items were chosen on the basis of interviews with students and each item was then empirically validated as to its applicability to the problem. The manual is unusually complete with considerable technical data reported for both college and high school groups.

The instructions state that the student can be helped to obtain an understanding of how to study properly and to learn many of his study faults. These reviewers feel that there is an implication in the instructions that the student will be helped simply by responding honestly. Although there is the possibility of insight through exposure to such information, there is no evidence to support such a thesis.

Tenth grade students should be able to read the test readily. The terms used are generally easy to understand. The statements to be responded to are fairly concise and should create no problem.

In general, the reviewers feel that this instrument is well grounded, easy to understand, and can be an excellent source of study habit and attitude information for use by student and counselor. The basis for interpretation, however, assumes that the student will respond frankly and that he is capable of understanding and reporting his own motivations and attitudes toward studying and academic activities. This assumption may be questioned on the basis of present knowledge in this area. While the instrument may be used to advantage since it has been carefully constructed, use of it will require good judgment and a rigorous application of limiting factors inherent in self-reports of any kind. It is *not* a test and any user of it should fully understand the difference between a test and an inventory or a survey of self-reports.

[689]

★California Study Methods Survey. Grades 7–13; 1958; 5 scores: attitudes toward school, mechanics of study, planning and system, total, verification; IBM; 1 form; $3.50 per 35 tests; separate answer sheets may be used; 5¢ per IBM answer sheet; 40¢ per set of hand and machine scoring stencils; postage extra; 50¢ per specimen set, postpaid; scoring service available; (35–50) minutes; Harold D. Carter; California Test Bureau. *

REFERENCES

1. CARTER, HAROLD D. "Methods of Learning as Factors in the Prediction of School Success." *J Psychol* 26:249–58 Jl '48. * (PA 23:1439)
2. CARTER, HAROLD D. "Correlations Between Intelligence Tests, Study Methods Tests, and Marks in a College Course." *J Psychol* 30:333–40 O '50. * (PA 25:3383)
3. CARTER, HAROLD D. "What Are Some of the Basic Prob-

lems in Analysis of Study Techniques?" *Calif J Ed Res* 2:170–4 S '51. *
4. CARTER, HAROLD D. "Cross-Validation of a Study Methods Test." *Calif J Ed Res* 4:32–6 Ja '53. * (*PA* 28:1553)
5. CARTER, HAROLD D. "Development of a Diagnostic Scoring Scheme for a Study Methods Test." *Calif J Ed Res* 6:26–32 Ja '55. * (*PA* 29:7841)
6. CARTER, HAROLD D. "Some Validity Coefficients for Study Test Scores." *Calif J Ed Res* 7:212–6 N '56. * (*PA* 31:8812)
7. CARTER, HAROLD D. "The Mechanics of Study Procedures." *Calif J Ed Res* 9:8–13 Ja '58. *

[690]

Cooperative Dictionary Test. Grades 7–12; 1951–52; 5 scores: alphabetizing, spelling, pronunciation, meaning, total; IBM; Form A ('51); manual ('52); directions sheet ('52); no data on reliability for grades 8, 10–11; no norms for part scores, no norms for grades 8, 10–11; separate answer sheets must be used; $2.50 per 25 tests; $1.50 per 25 IBM answer sheets; 45¢ per scoring stencil; postage extra; 30(40) minutes; S. D. Melville, Clarence Derrick (manual), and Frances Swineford (manual); Cooperative Test Division, Educational Testing Service. *

A. N. HIERONYMUS, *Associate Professor of Education, State University of Iowa, Iowa City, Iowa.*

ORGANIZATION AND CONTENT. This test employs an ingenious, convenient design. The items are printed on both sides of an IBM answer sheet. A 4-page reusable leaflet contains instructions to the student and two composite pages of selected entries from an established dictionary. The entries very adequately represent the many situations for which a dictionary may be used.

The 50 items cover almost every conceivable skill in the use of the dictionary. The first 20 items deal with alphabetization within a framework of four pairs of guide words; this subtest is accompanied by reliability data but no norms. The remaining 30 items yield three scores based on 10 items each, somewhat misleadingly called pronunciation, meaning, and spelling. However, after the teacher obtains these scores, she is at a complete loss as to what to do with them; no norms or other data are provided.

In order to measure most of the uses which people *can* make of the dictionary, many items deal with skills of marginal social utility, such as the meaning of the abbreviations *Colloq.* and *Dial.* On the other hand, people most often use the dictionary for looking up the pronunciation, meaning, and spelling of words. Pronunciation is represented by several items; spelling and meaning are not so well represented. Only one item deals directly with spelling; other items classified under spelling deal with irregular plurals, irregular verb forms, and the like. Only 3 of the 50 items on the test are concerned directly with the interpretation of meaning.

Whether this should be considered a disadvantage depends upon the purposes for which the test is given.

NORMS. Percentile norms, provided for grades 7, 9, and 12 only, are based on results in only seven schools in five communities. The criteria of selection are not provided, nor are any further data which would allow the user to determine whether this is a meaningful normative sample to employ in evaluating the results from his school. Different schools tested pupils at different levels (only three schools tested in grade 7), but the norms were "adjusted so as *to reflect the performance of the students in all seven schools."* The authors recommend the use of local norms. In view of the inadequacy of the normative sample, schools should take this recommendation seriously.

Schools are encouraged to compute class medians and compare them with the medians for the normative groups. This will almost inevitably result in misinterpretations. Class medians are not distributed in the same way as pupil scores. In recommending this type of comparison, the authors are encouraging schools to misinterpret the standing of their classes.

Item analysis data are provided which allow schools to compare group performance on individual items with that of the normative sample. It is suggested that follow-up instructions begin with the types of items missed most frequently by the group, the implication being that these identify the skills which most need attention. The rank order of the difficulty of items in a test depends on many factors. Very often the most difficult items are difficult because of faulty construction or because they represent skills which are seldom used or needed. It is doubtful that follow-up instruction on the use of the dictionary should start, for example, with tracing the etymology of words. Yet, in almost every class, this is quite likely to be the most difficult skill measured by this test. The second suggested criterion for selecting points for study, to begin with items which are fundamental to the use of the dictionary, would seem to be much more defensible.

TECHNICAL DATA. The section in the manual dealing with technical data is quite complete. Kuder-Richardson (formula 20) reliability coefficients are provided for scores which are accompanied by norms. Intercorrelations of part and total scores are shown, as are speededness data. Difficulty and discrimination data are supplied. No statistical evidence of validity is given, but none would seem to be crucial to evaluating the test.

OVERALL EVALUATION. This is a skillfully constructed test, possibly overemphasizing dictionary skills of marginal social utility. The norms must be regarded as inadequate.

[691]

★Evaluation Aptitude Test. Candidates for college and graduate school entrance; 1951-52; 5 scores: neutral syllogisms, emotionally toned syllogisms, total, emotional bias, indecision; 1 form ('52); manual ('52); $1.95 per 20 tests; $1 per specimen set (must be purchased to obtain manual); postage extra; 50(55) minutes; DeWitt E. Sell; Psychometric Affiliates. *

J. THOMAS HASTINGS, University Examiner; Director of Unit on Evaluation in Bureau of Educational Research; Professor of Education, University of Illinois, Urbana, Illinois.

A name like Evaluation Aptitude Test (EAT) demands a brief description of the stimulus-response content before comments or appraisals are meaningful. The task set for the examinee is to evaluate 36 conclusions each of which is based upon two premises. The evaluation (response) consists of checking each conclusion as logically sound or unsound, or of marking "o" to indicate uncertainty. The first 18 of these syllogisms deal with premises and conclusions which are obviously unreal since a nonsense word is used in the second premise. These first 18 are spoken of as "affectively neutral" because one cannot judge the conclusion from prior knowledge of fact. The other 18—matched one for one with the first group on syllogistic mood and keyed response —deal with social, political, and economic statements and are spoken of as "affective" since the examinee's prior opinions presumably may support or conflict with the syllogistic conclusion.

It should be obvious that in either set of 18 (Part A and Part B, respectively) the examinee who knows anything of syllogistic form may convert each to its equivalent type of general statement (e.g., "All A's are B's. Some C's are A's. Therefore,....") and then ignore both the nonsense word and the prior opinion, if any.

The author suggests that the test be used in college or graduate school entrance examination batteries as an aid in diagnosis, educational guidance, and selection. Since the operational attack on the items (conversion to general syllogism of all, some, none) by the respondents

is indeterminable, diagnosis or selection on the basis of logical validity would be a poor risk. Since no data are presented on the effectiveness of this task for predicting deductive reasoning required in educational situations, there is no possibility of diagnosing or selecting on the basis of empirical validity.

If one wants to diagnose or select on critical thinking and problem solving abilities, he is faced with a shortage of instruments with demonstrated validity. Short of developing his own, he may have to use cautiously a published test. However, certain other tests (e.g., Watson-Glaser Critical Thinking Appraisal) should certainly be considered before this one.

Norms are given in terms of percentiles for high school seniors ($n = 165$) and for college seniors ($n = 158$) on Part A, Part B, and the total score. Only two high schools and two colleges (both small) were used in norming. The person considering using the test should recognize that the author's statement that the norms "can be considered reliably indicative of the probable distribution of evaluation aptitude in high school and college seniors" expresses at most a hope—not a well founded claim. The norms for the other two scores—Index of Discrepancy (proportion of responses in Part B which disagree with responses to paired items in Part A) and Index of Indecision (proportion of omits)—are based upon college seniors only. Furthermore, the five scores are so interdependent that use of all five might be more confusing than helpful, especially to the test user who is less than highly trained in measurement.

The EAT is certainly not ready at present for distribution to school and college guidance people or selection officers. Although this reviewer has serious doubt that more data on relevant points will demonstrate that the test is useful for the purposes stated, such data should be collected and presented if the test is to be offered to consumers. Neither the stated general purposes nor the suggested specific applications are supported convincingly in the data currently presented in the manual.

WALKER H. HILL, Associate Professor, Office of Evaluation Services, Michigan State University, East Lansing, Michigan.

"Evaluation aptitude" is defined in the manual as "the capacity to appraise data accurately; to draw correct inferences from given premises; to think 'straight' or without emotional bias." In view of the range of thinking abilities which this definition seems to suggest, it is rather a letdown to find that the *Evaluation Aptitude Test* is simply a 36-item test of ability to judge the validity of syllogisms.

The test is in two parts. Part A includes 18 syllogisms in various moods and figures. The required judgments are: "sound" (conclusion follows), "unsound" (conclusion does not follow), or "uncertain." Part B is a corresponding set of syllogisms, identical in mood and figure, and therefore in keyed answers, but differing in content. The correspondence is such that Parts A and B are printed in parallel columns, with each item directly opposite its counterpart.

The different content of the two parts is the central feature of the test. The syllogisms in Part A deal with supposedly neutral material. They all concern relationships between candies, confections, and "twangs." Students are not expected to have any feelings, biases, or prior knowledge about the relation of twangs and candies. Part B, on the other hand, deals with such terms as politicians, liberals, conservatives, radicals, Communists, and labor leaders, about which students are expected to have biases and preconceptions.

By comparing scores and responses to corresponding items on the two parts, one can presumably judge the effect of emotionally toned material on a student's ability to reason deductively. In addition to the two part scores and a total score, two "indices" are obtained: a "discrepancy index," which represents the percentage of instances in which two corresponding items are answered differently, regardless of correctness, and an "indecision index," which is the percentage of the total number of items answered "uncertain."

On the theory (said by the author to be a "well-recognized" fact) that the ideological biases of most people can be classed as liberal or conservative, the items in Part B are so constructed that half of them are intended as "traps" for unwary liberals and half as "traps" for unwary conservatives.

It is clear that considerable care has gone into the design of the instrument, and not a little ingenuity. One can seriously question, however, whether the result really justifies the effort, for even the most reasonable claims which can be made for it rest on some shaky

assumptions, and claims actually made for it go far beyond what is reasonable.

The author recognizes that some students may have little or no emotional bias concerning the items in Part B. Yet he says that since the two parts are "comparable in every respect other than their affective character," only bias and chance can produce discrepancies between the two parts. There are other possibilities. Surely some Part B items are easier for some people simply because they have meaningful content. In others the content becomes such a tangle of verbiage as to make them quite difficult. Take, for example, this item in Part B:

> If some qualified by education to hold public office are not politicians, and some democratically elected congressional representatives are politicians; then some democratically elected congressional representatives are not qualified by education to hold public office.

This is the corresponding item in Part A:

> If some candies are not confections, and some twangs are confections; then some twangs are not candies.

The former is loaded all right, but there is more than one kind of loading. Is it attitude toward politicians that makes the difference? Indeed, one can even have misgivings about the *neutrality* of Part A. Granted that it has the appearance of having a pretty low emotional level, this reviewer detected in himself an incipient prejudice against "twangs" by the time he had read about them 18 times.

Examination of the test immediately raises the question of how it would be answered by students who have had a course in logic. Might they not apply mechanically the rules for valid and invalid syllogisms, without paying any attention to the content? The author has recognized this possibility and has investigated it. But he seems to overstate the case. Because a group of students made different part scores before they took such a course and equal part scores after its completion, he concludes: "Evaluating syllogisms correctly by the application of rules learned by rote memory does not denote rational comprehension or increased evaluation aptitude. For this reason the EAT as an aptitude test is meaningless for any person who has had training in deductive logic." He does not say how he knows that the application of rules learned by rote memory is the only outcome of the logic course.

There is no evidence of any investigation of the extent to which students may recognize the parallelism of the two parts. Such recognition would, of course, vastly affect the scores. It is more likely for students who have studied logic, but is possible for others as well. This possibility could easily be eliminated by rearranging the sequence so that like items do not appear opposite each other.

The format of the test is otherwise acceptable. However, the manual is published in a lithoprinted form in which the type size is so reduced as to make it almost unreadable.

A test of this kind has potential usefulness, which in the present instance falls regrettably short of realization. It must be recognized, however, that, even if this were a very good test, the kind of reasoning it involves is but a limited aspect of "straight thinking." To equate it with the thinking required of "leaders in the social sciences who can think 'straight' or without emotional bias" is little short of ludicrous.

[692]

*The Iowa Tests of Educational Development: Test 9, Use of Sources of Information.** Grades 9-13; 1942-58; IBM; Forms X-3S, Y-3S ('52); examiner's manual ('58); battery manual ('54); pupil profile leaflet, fourth edition ('58); profile card (no date); separate answer sheets must be used $3 per 20 tests; $5 per 100 IBM answer sheets; 50¢ per scoring stencil; $3 per complete specimen set; postage extra; 27(35) minutes; prepared under the direction of E. F. Lindquist; Science Research Associates. *

For reviews by J. Murray Lee and Stephen Wiseman of the complete battery, see 17; for a review by Eric F. Gardner of earlier forms, see 4:17; for reviews by Henry Chauncey, Gustav J. Froehlich, and Lavone A. Hanna, see 3:12.

[693]

★A Library Orientation Test for College Freshmen, 1955 Edition.** Grade 13; 1950-55; 1 form ('55); manual ['55]; no data on reliability; no norms; separate answer sheets must be used; $4.50 per 35 tests; $1.25 per 35 answer sheets; 50¢ per specimen set; cash orders postpaid; (50-60) minutes; Ethel M. Feagley, Dorothy W. Curtiss, Mary V. Gaver, and Esther Greene; Bureau of Publications, Teachers College, Columbia University. *

JANET G. AFFLERBACH, *Editor, Professional Examination Service, American Public Health Association, New York, New York; and* LOIS GRIMES AFFLERBACH, *Serials Librarian, Queens College, Flushing, New York.*

This little test of only 80 items provides an excellent two-way look: backwards for an assessment of the effectiveness of the high school library program and forwards toward a broadening and strengthening of the college library

program to meet student needs. Strong emphasis is put on the most important tool of the library, the card catalog, three of the nine parts of the test dealing with this subject. Of the six other parts, four deal with specific reference tools and two with definitions of bibliographical terms. Noticeably absent are the dictionary and encyclopedia play type of item. One must assume that college freshmen know some reference tools and these two are probably the most familiar.

Part 1 is an exercise in matching terms and their respective meanings. The range of terms covered is quite wide. There are not only the usual parts-of-a-book terms, but also types-of-books terms, such as anthology, atlas, and gazeteer. Definitions of types of materials, such as biography, document, and periodical, might have been included as well.

Part 2 shows a typical catalog card with its component parts: author, title, publisher, paging, bibliography, tracings, etc. Each of the parts is given a number, and students choose their answers from the numbered "points of information." While the points exhibited are all testworthy, this section could be enlarged to include such problems as ascertaining from the card whether the book is an English translation or deciding from a subject card what the correct call slip entry should be. There may be some confusion for students in the abundance of numerical figures on the sample card and the test item numbers, which are placed immediately below the card. Could the points of information be given letters of the alphabet instead?

Part 3 is designed to test ability to choose from a list of 19 standard subject headings the one heading most appropriate for each of several book topics or titles. The headings are familiar, ordinary, and workable. Of course, students must know how to use the broad and obvious headings and the system of subdivisions of headings. Regrettably, there seems to be no way in objective tests to discover how students would proceed to find material on new, unusual, or specific topics like atomic submarines, witchcraft, or Dead Sea Scrolls.

Part 4 presents a problem in alphabetizing sample card catalog headings, according to filing rules printed at the head of the problem. This is an excellent approach in miniature to the organization of the catalog.

A good review of important reference tools

in a single field is found in Part 5, where students are to indicate in which of eight familiar reference books they would expect to find the answers to several questions about literature. Since the field of literature is so well provided with reference tools, and since the college student's first encounter with the library is usually by way of English composition and literature classes, it is not a bad idea to devote one whole section of the test to this single subject area. However, one wishes that the student's knowledge of reference material in science and social studies could also be tested.

Part 6 presents the same kind of problem as does Part 5, but covers the more general biographical tools. Responses to the questions included should reveal very well whether students have grasped the distinctive features of each reference book.

Knowledge of several periodical indexes, the *Book Review Digest,* and the *Cumulative Book Index* is tested in Part 7. This part deals mainly with general indexes; e.g., although the *Education Index* is listed, nothing so specialized as the *Art Index* or the scientific abstracting and indexing tools is included.

A group of references from a periodical index is reproduced as the problem in Part 8. Certain parts of the references (title, name of periodical, volume number, date, etc.) are numbered and students must answer questions from these numbered parts. The *Readers' Guide to Periodical Literature* inevitably becomes the freshman's favorite reference tool and this section of the test is a good exercise in the use of all periodical indexes of the *Readers' Guide* type.

Part 9 is a matching exercise to test the student's knowledge of general bibliographical abbreviations, such as *ca., ibid.,* and *q.v.* Although the abbreviations are well chosen, one might wish that the emphasis was more on ability to interpret than on ability to recognize them.

All in all, this test should go far in meeting the purposes set by the test authors: to discover to what extent and in what areas college freshmen need instruction in using the resources of the library, to help freshmen recognize their own deficiencies in the use of the library, and to provide data that can be used as a basis for a program of library instruction to meet the needs of the group tested.

J. WAYNE WRIGHTSTONE, *Director, Bureau of Educational Research, New York Public Schools, New York, New York.*

These test exercises were prepared for: (*a*) discovering to what extent and in what areas college freshmen need instruction in using the resources of a college library; (*b*) diagnosing the strengths and weaknesses of college freshmen in the use of the library; and (*c*) providing data that can be used as a basis for a program of library instruction fitted to the needs of the particular student group.

The manual contains no data on reliability and validity and no norms; hence, the test cannot be considered standardized. The test consists of questions requiring definition of terms related to library usage; interpretation of information on a catalog card; selection of appropriate subject headings in a catalog; arrangement of headings in a card catalog; selection of literature reference books appropriate to a given question; knowledge of sources of biographical information; choice of appropriate book and periodical indexes; interpretation of information in periodical indexes; and definition of abbreviations (such as *ibid., et al.,* and *op. cit.*) frequently found in books.

These various test exercises have face validity as measures of important knowledge that a college freshman should acquire in learning how to use the resources of a library. The authors have attempted to make the exercises as closely parallel to real situations in the library as possible by including, for example, a reproduction of an actual catalog card. The reference books, indexes, and sources of biographical information included are those most frequently used. The section dealing with interpretation of information in periodical indexes contains a reproduction of actual references that an individual would find in *Readers' Guide to Periodical Literature.*

Although the test has some shortcomings with respect to the reliability of diagnosing specific library usage skills because of the limited number of exercises, the results would probably be valuable to the librarian or teacher in counseling the student about improving his specific abilities in using the resources of a library. The authors state that colleges which used earlier forms of the test reported it to be useful for excusing from introductory library instruction students who made a satisfactory score (arbitrarily determined) and for discovering the extent of student progress through administering the test at the beginning and at the end of a period of instruction in library skills.

As a nonstandardized test of knowledge about library resources, this test is probably superior to an informal test constructed by a local librarian. It is unfortunate that evidence has not been presented to show that the items have been analyzed by technically accepted methods and that norms and data on reliability and validity have not been collected and presented.

[694]

★Logical Reasoning. Grades 9–16 and adults; 1955; IBM; Form A; no adult norms; separate answer sheets must be used; $3.75 per 25 tests; 20¢ per single copy; 3¢ per IBM answer sheet; 50¢ per scoring stencil; 25¢ per manual; postage extra; 20(25) minutes; Alfred F. Hertzka and J. P. Guilford; Sheridan Supply Co. *

REFERENCE
1. HILLS, JOHN R. "Factor-Analyzed Abilities and Success in College Mathematics." *Ed & Psychol Meas* 17:615–22 w '57. *

DUNCAN HOWIE, *Professor of Psychology, The University of New England, Armidale, Australia.*

This test has resulted from factorial researches at Guilford's laboratory which have confirmed and clarified Thurstone's earlier identification of a factor he called "deduction." The factor may generally be described as involving "sensitivity to logical relationships in the testing of the correctness or incorrectness of a conclusion." The authors call it "logical evaluation." The test consists of two parallel parts, each of 20 items covering "the 15 valid syllogistic forms." Each item presents two propositions and requires the subject to choose from among four alternatives the logically correct conclusion. Considerable care has been taken to insure that the "herrings" have a near-appropriate smell, i.e., that each of them is at least plausible. The general format and conditions of administration make the test a straightforward one to give. The time limit for each of the parts is 10 minutes.

Standardization is based on two populations: the first, 402 high school students distributed over grades 10, 11, and 12 and ranging in age from 14 to 20 years with mean age of 16.5; the second, 509 college students about 90 per cent of whom were below 30 years of age. In view of the wide age scatter, it is unfortunate, particularly in the case of the high school group, that information is not given as to the possible relationships between age level and test score. Norms are presented for each group in standard C scores and in centile ranks equivalent to raw scores.

Reliabilities are reported for both groups at about .90 for the whole test and about .80 for each of the parts. The main evidence of validity is of factorial or internal validity. The test is said to have a loading of .50 in the logical evaluation factor. Evidences of external or criterion validity are somewhat confusing and decidedly less encouraging. For example, correlations are reported with grades in various mathematics courses ranging from .04 to .42 with a mean of .26.

The reviewer agrees with the authors that this aspect of reasoning ability is one that has been almost entirely neglected in intelligence tests and that the time has come to take it seriously. In this perspective, the test is of unquestionable value as a research instrument for further validation studies. That it should be so used is clearly the authors' intention. It is perhaps necessary, however, to caution prospective users that, at this stage, the test cannot be used as other than a research instrument.

CHARLES R. LANGMUIR, *Director of Special Projects, The Psychological Corporation, New York, New York.*

The test consists of 40 formal syllogisms separated into two comparable parts of 20 items. Ten minutes are allowed for each part. An additional 10 minutes are required for students to read the instructions and to become familiar with the item type. A typical item is:

Some women are mothers.
All women are females.

    Therefore:
A. All mothers are females.
B. All females are women.
C. Some females are mothers.
D. Some women are not mothers.

The correct answer is the *one* conclusion which follows from the *two* premises. Statements which reformulate a single premise, statements which are consistent, but not necessary, and statements that are invalid make up the distractors. This reviewer's reasoning found two correct conclusions for Items 14, 23, 27, and 35, a questionable distractor in Item 11, and a questionable introduction of a term in the keyed conclusion which is not in the premises of Item 5. The keyed answers are best in the sense of being "logically stronger," but the instructions ask only for a correct conclusion without revealing the existence of such formal distinctions.

Subjective experience with intensive study of the items suggests that the test may be highly speeded for naive subjects. It would be helpful to have information in the manual about the speed-power element. A little practice with syllogisms and the tricky distractions introduced by common language symbols may have a marked effect on speed and accuracy in taking the test.

Centile equivalents are supplied for 402 San Diego high school students evenly distributed in grades 10, 11, and 12, and, separately, for 509 San Diego State College students, principally freshmen and sophomores. The mean total score for the high school group was 23, with standard deviation of 8. In the college group, the mean was 27; standard deviation, 6.5. Sex differences are reported to have been small. The reliability of scores is estimated to be about .80 for a single part and .90 for the full test. The extent to which these estimates are inflated by speed effects is not discussed. The test is scored by the formula rights plus one quarter of the omits. This algebraic device is used to avoid the "many negative scores" that occur with the formula $R - W/3$.

Some productive research results could develop from experiments with this test and variations of it. The item material is notably homogeneous and might, therefore, be particularly useful in studying the effectiveness of instruction. It would be interesting, for example, to know whether there are individuals who cannot be taught to overcome the distracting influence of semantically loaded common language in syllogisms that are substantively identical, in the logical sense, with syllogisms not containing irrelevant semantic distractions. We can expect to find a distribution of empirical difficulty values for items of identical logical complexity. Some important clues to the components of reasoning abilities might emerge.

[695]

★Pictographic Self Rating Scale. High school and college; 1955–57; Experimental Form A ('55); manual ('57); no college norms; separate answer sheets must be used; $2.50 per 25 tests; $1.25 per 25 answer sheets; 50¢ per specimen set; postage extra; (35) minutes; Einar R. Ryden; Acorn Publishing Co. *

REFERENCES
1. ROMANOWSKI, WALTER V. The Revision and Factor Analysis of a Pictographic Self Rating Scale. Doctor's thesis, Purdue University (Lafayette, Ind.), 1955.
2. SALES, ROBERT C. A Validity Study of a Pictographic Self-Rating Scale. Master's thesis, Purdue University (Lafayette, Ind.), 1955.

[696]

★SRA Achievement Series: Work-Study Skills. Grades 4–6, 6–9; 1954–57; 2 scores: references, charts; IBM; Forms A, B; 2 levels; technical supplement, second edition ('57); separate answer sheets must be used; $2 per 20 tests; $4.50 per 100 IBM scorable answer sheets; 50¢ per hand scoring stencil; 50¢ per teacher's handbook ('55); 50¢ per administrator's manual ('56); $1 per technical supplement; postage extra; specimen set not available; Louis P. Thorpe, D. Welty Lefever, and Robert A. Naslund; Science Research Associates. *
a) GRADES 4–6. Forms A ['54], B ('56); examiner's manual ('56); $1 per set of machine scoring stencils; 92(125) minutes in 2 sessions.
b) GRADES 6–9. Forms A ('55, identical with test copyrighted in 1954 except for change in format), B ('56); examiner's manual ('56); 50¢ per machine scoring stencil; 70(90) minutes.

ROBERT L. EBEL, *Vice President for Testing Programs and Services, Educational Testing Service, Princeton, New Jersey.*

The test for grades 4–6 consists of 82 multiple choice items administered in two periods. It includes 19 items on the use of a table of contents (21 minutes), 17 items on the use of an index (21 minutes), 20 items on the use of reference materials (15 minutes), and 26 items on reading graphs and tables (35 minutes). The test for grades 6–9 consists of 94 items, administered in a single 90 minute period. It includes 20 items on the use of references (10 minutes), 10 items on the use of a table of contents (8 minutes), 15 items on the use of an index (12 minutes), and 49 items on the reading of graphs, tables, and maps (40 minutes).

All of the items are four alternative, multiple choice items. They require the examinee to demonstrate his ability to apply the various work-study skills. Sample tables of contents, indexes, tables, graphs, and maps are used as the basis for the questions. The sample indexes, particularly those in Form A of the tests, are rather highly organized under major headings and subheadings. This disturbs the alphabetical arrangement of the entries. For example, to find a reference on *Television programs* one must look not under *Television,* or *Programs,* but under *Home entertainment.*

Most of the questions on the indexes and the tables of contents require the examinee to use these reference materials as guides to the location of information. This is as it should be. A few questions require the student to draw inferences concerning the nature of that information. One, for example, requires the examinee to infer the name of the inventor of the steamboat from certain entries in an index. Another departure from direct relevance is found in items which, instead of asking where to find certain facts, ask what information will be found on certain pages.

Each section of the tests is provided with one or more fore-exercises designed to explain to the student exactly what the test requires him to do. This is a desirable feature, especially in tests for the lower grades. In the sections on charts, however, these fore-exercises may actually do considerable teaching of the skill which the remainder of the test is designed to measure, and may therefore make the test partly a measure of ability to learn.

The test publishers have provided a very complete and attractive set of reference materials. The examiner's manual includes general instructions for use of the test battery, directions for administration and scoring, and grade and percentile norms for the tests. The inclusion of a list of correct responses was a convenience to the reviewer and should also be helpful to teachers in making effective use of the tests. A manual for the school administrator describes the nature of the tests and presents a classification of items according to the work-study skills being measured. The attempt to provide such a content analysis of the test is highly commendable; however, the authors have not been as successful in their analysis of this test as in other areas covered in the battery. The difficulty appears to be that the listed work-study skills do not correspond closely to the tasks presented in the test items. This results in suggestions that each item is measuring a multiplicity of skills. For example, one question asks on which page one should begin reading to find certain information. This item is listed as measuring five skills:

1. Ability to locate desired information with the aid of a table of contents.
2. Ability to use clues to arrangement and location of reference information, such as the alphabet, guide words as in the dictionary, page, figures, and table numbers, chapter headings, etc.
3. Ability to select and interpret main and subordinate ideas.

4. Ability to infer from and to see implications of facts given.
5. Ability to generalize from facts given.

This analysis of the diverse functions of a fairly simple item seems overelaborated.

A useful teachers' handbook provides aids to the interpretation of test scores and suggestions for follow-up action on the basis of the test results. These essential steps in the effective utilization of test results are too often slighted or omitted entirely from the accessory materials provided with standardized tests.

The excellent technical supplement gives evidence of careful attention to test construction, standardization, and analysis. The raw score quartiles indicate that, in general, the tests are appropriate in difficulty for the groups tested and give reasonably wide distributions of scores.

The section on validity places appropriate emphasis on the importance of content validity. It also presents an extensive and instructive factor analysis of the scores for the entire battery. This is an excellent example of the use of factor analysis to support the construct validity of each of the tests in the battery. The analysis revealed that all four of the tests in the battery were measuring a general achievement factor. Three of them also appeared to be measuring group achievement factors which corresponded to the content of three of the tests. Only the work-study skills did not yield a group factor. This may be a reflection of the diversity of tasks included in the test. It may be a reflection of the fact that no organized curriculum for the development of work-study skills is followed in most schools. It may be due to some other influence. In any case it suggests that scores on a work-study skills test do not have the kind of independence shown by arithmetic, reading, and language test scores. Hence, it raises a question of the appropriateness of work-study skills tests in achievement batteries at this level.

Most teachers and curriculum specialists readily agree that it is an important objective of elementary education to develop work-study skills. But there is thus far little if any evidence that these study skills can be, or are being, developed independently of other achievements. The immediate consequence of this excellent study is to cast some doubt on the desirability of including a study skills test in a general achievement test battery.

RUTH M. STRANG, *Professor of Education, Teachers College, Columbia University, New York, New York.*

As stated in the manual, this test measures ability to select and discriminate among reference sources; to use the table of contents, index, and other clues to the location of information; to see relationships and to infer and generalize from facts given; and to obtain information from, note relationships among, discern trends among, and make inferences from data presented in graphs, maps, and tables.

Emphasis is placed on the true-to-life, situation approach. However, some conflict may be noted between the objectives of providing lifelike situations and meeting the demands of objective measurement; some of the items seem contrived just for test purposes. For example, some of the items dealing with the table of contents pose problems one would not naturally solve by going to the table of contents. Similarly, some of the information that pupils are expected to obtain from graphs and charts seems trivial and too labored.

The tests for grades 4–6 are introduced in story form, followed by clear, simple directions. In the tests for grades 6–9 the directions are given in a brief straightforward way. The time is ample to give every pupil opportunity to demonstrate his ability.

The number and regional distribution of the normative sample seems adequate, except that the proportion of rural to urban is lower than in the general population. It is pointed out, however, that differences between urban and rural have been decreasing in recent years. Since the test is most appropriately used for diagnosing rather than for grading, for teaching rather than for testing, high standards of general reliability are not so necessary as is the establishment of validity.

Efforts to establish validity have included· reference to commonly stated goals and objectives, three minor studies of predictive value, and extensive factorial analysis. Although the content of the test is similar to that of other current tests in this area, it covers only one aspect of study skills—performance of the objective type; it is not at all concerned with the more basic psychological factors involved in effective study methods. For the predictive studies, the manual reports correlations of .66 and .68 between scores obtained by two groups of eighth

grade pupils and grade-point averages computed a half year and a year later, respectively; and .70 between scores obtained by an eighth grade group and composite scores on a battery of achievement tests administered a year later. These limited predictive studies are described as "encouraging."

It is recommended in the manual that, in order to gain a complete picture of the pupil's ability in this area, the test user examine the pupil's responses to items involving study skills in other subtests in the series. The Teacher's Handbook suggests not only an analysis of the kind of errors made by an individual or a class, but also classroom procedures and projects for developing these study skills. It is with respect to the use of this test that the *SRA Achievement Series* is particularly strong.

There is a question, however, as to whether the study skills test is worth taking time to administer. Since the main objective is the understanding of the pupils' study skills, the teacher might obtain similar and more specifically usable information by asking pupils questions based on the tables of contents and indexes of the books they are using. In the same way he could direct pupils' attention to the interpretation of charts, graphs, and tables in the context of the books they are studying. However, as an introduction, the second part of the test, with its appealing situations for analysis, would arouse the pupils' interest in these special study skills, uncover difficulties in perception and seeing relationships, and lead to application to similar tasks in their daily assignments. At best, the teaching of study skills requires a more searching psychological analysis of methods and patterns effectively used by pupils of different ages and abilities. As in so many instances, tests are being constructed before the field has been sufficiently defined and analyzed.

For reviews by Warren G. Findley and Worth R. Jones of the complete battery, see 21.

[697]

★Spitzer Study Skills Test: Evaluation and Adjustment Series. Grades 9–13; 1954–55; 6 scores: dictionary, index, graphs-tables-maps, sources of information, note taking, total for subtests 1–4; IBM; Forms AM ('54), BM ('55); manual ('54); no college norms; separate answer sheets must be used; $5 per 35 tests; $1.65 per 35 IBM answer sheets; postage extra; 35¢ per specimen set, postpaid; 75(90) minutes in 2 sessions for subtests 1–4 only; 105(135) minutes in 3 sessions; Herbert F. Spitzer; World Book Co. *

REFERENCE
1. CROOK, FRANCES E. "Interrelationships Among a Group of Language Arts Tests." *J Ed Res* 51:305–11 D '57. *

JAMES DEESE, *Associate Professor of Psychology, The Johns Hopkins University, Baltimore, Maryland.*

This test is designed to measure achievement in five specific areas of study skills: (*a*) using the dictionary, (*b*) using the index, (*c*) understanding graphs, tables, and maps, (*d*) locating sources of information, and (*e*) organizing facts in note taking. Each of these areas constitutes a subtest; the fifth subtest is specified as "optional." The test can be administered in two ordinary school periods (or three if the fifth subtest is employed).

The manual presents tables for converting raw scores on each of the five subtests to percentile ranks and standard scores. The standard scores are scaled with a mean of 106 and a standard deviation of 13.0. A number of recommendations are presented for the interpretation and use of test scores. The user is cautioned that the norms themselves may represent undesirably low achievement, the implication being that typical high school students do not receive adequate instruction in these particular study skills. Hints for remedial teaching are given for those subtests on which class achievement is very low.

Reasonably complete information concerning the development of the test is presented. Item analysis was accomplished with data obtained from 2,400 high school students in four high schools. Neither the location of these schools nor the distribution of the sample among them is mentioned. Mean values of difficulty and validity indices for items in all but the fifth subtest are presented for each of the final forms. These are the only data reported for the final forms.

For the standardization study 5,000 students in 17 high schools in 14 states were tested with the preliminary forms of the test. Again, there is no information in the manual concerning the distribution of those tested, nor is there any information about the number of cases for whom data were obtained for each of the forms. One very useful aspect of the validation data is that correlations between scores on each of the first four subtests and a number of other measures, including Terman-McNemar IQ's and scores on other tests in the Evaluation and Adjustment Series, are presented. The manual states

that these four subtests "measure substantially different aspects of study skills." The correlations between them, ranging from .26 to .60, are about typical of the correlations between achievement tests at large. Reliability coefficients obtained by the split-half method on preliminary Form 1 (later Form AM) are satisfactory for the first three subtests, but low for the fourth subtest. No data on reliability are presented for the fifth subtest because "interdependence of items in Test 5 made it inappropriate to obtain a measure of reliability by the same method."

While the standardization is less than completely satisfactory, it is not unsatisfactory. The classroom teacher or counselor has something to gain in using the measure of study skills provided by this test rather than a completely unstandardized test. The chief drawback to the test is the considerable time required for administration.

[698]

★Stanford Achievement Test: Study Skills. Grades 5–6, 7–9; 1953–54, c1952–54; items identical to those in study skills section of *Stanford Achievement Test;* IBM; 2 levels; manual ('53); separate answer sheets must be used; $2.75 per 35 tests; $1.25 per 35 IBM answer sheets; 20¢ per machine scoring stencil; postage extra; 35¢ per specimen set of either level, postpaid; 40(50) minutes; Truman L. Kelley, Richard Madden, Eric F. Gardner, Lewis M. Terman, and Giles M. Ruch; World Book Co. *
a) INTERMEDIATE STUDY SKILLS TEST. Grades 5–6; 1953, c1952–53; Forms JM, KM ('53).
b) ADVANCED STUDY SKILLS TEST. Grades 7–9; 1953–54, c1952–54; Forms JM ('53), KM ('53), LM ('54).

ROBERT L. EBEL, *Vice President for Testing Programs and Services, Educational Testing Service, Princeton, New Jersey.*

Almost all of the items in this test are of the application type in which the student must demonstrate his ability to make practical interpretations or uses of the data presented in charts, tables, maps, dictionaries, indexes, and other sources of information. There is one item in each form which requires identification of a root word from among several combined forms. These items can be justified on the ground that the root word entry in a dictionary frequently includes information that is useful in understanding or using the combined form. On the other hand, it seems doubtful that ability to identify the root word (which is always shorter than and part of the combined forms) in these items really indicates possession of the skill in using the dictionary it is intended to test.

A striking characteristic of the items in both forms is the brevity of the responses. Ordinarily they consist of a single word or numerical value. Economy of words in an objective test item is highly commendable, and tends to yield high reliability per unit of testing time. On the other hand, there are certain inferences, conclusions, and recommendations which cannot be expressed adequately in one word responses. The exclusion of such items may limit the sampling of relevant tasks somewhat.

Part I in both tests includes two charts and one table, with five questions based on each. The questions on the line graphs, and to a lesser extent on the bar graphs, tend to be quite similar. Sometimes the effort to make them different leads to rather artificial questions, e.g., "How many papers did Joe sell on Wednesday and Tuesday together?" (The preceding question had asked, "How many papers did Joe sell on Wednesday?") It is reasonable to suppose that scores on such closely related items would be highly related. This raises the question of whether one would not obtain a better indication of ability to interpret charts and graphs by using a wider variety of examples with fewer questions on each. An alternative would be to seek greater complexity in the information presented in the charts.

Excellent norms of two types, modal-age grade norms and total-group grade norms, are available for both tests. The manual makes clear that grade equivalents above 10.0 have been obtained by extrapolation. Since there is no study skills test in the elementary or primary batteries, it seems likely that grade scores below 5.0 were also obtained by extrapolation. Grade scores for the intermediate test in the 5.0 to 6.9 range, and for the advanced test in the 7.0 to 9.9 range were obtained directly. Other grade scores for each test in the 5.0 to 9.9 range were derived from a norm line based on K-score equating.

Percentile norms for the various modal-age groups indicate that both tests are appropriate in difficulty and give good score distributions. Reliability coefficients in the high .80's on both tests are very good for tests of this length. The manual is careful to point out that the reliability of scores for a single class, or even for a single school system, would probably be somewhat lower than the reported values, which are based on pupils from numerous school systems.

The manual has detailed directions for administering and scoring the test, and for interpreting the scores. Reference is made to a more extensive manual for the complete battery which includes test descriptions, suggestions for the use of test results, information on test construction and standardization, and a brief discussion of the K-scores.

The validity of tests of this type depends largely upon the competence and skill of the test constructors. The primary requirement is that the tests possess content validity. This must be built into the tests, and cannot ordinarily be demonstrated convincingly by any routine statistical procedures. In particular, the typical validity study involving a correlation of test scores with school grades is of little value in demonstrating the validity of tests like those under review.

On the other hand, there are troublesome problems of test content and test design which relate to the question of test validity. Is it appropriate and useful to group diverse test items based on graphs, tables, maps, dictionaries, indexes, encyclopedias, and other sources of information into a single test yielding a single score? Study skills seem not to be considered important enough by curriculum builders to deserve substantial direct allocations of time in the school program. Do they, nevertheless, deserve a place on a par with reading, language, and arithmetic in an achievement battery? Is there any evidence that the use of study skills tests contributes to the improvement of these skills? Or, is there evidence that a well worked out program for developing study skills will be reflected by greater than normal score gains on these tests from grade to grade? Is a study skills test something more than a short, indirect indication of general educational achievement?

The asking of these questions is not intended to imply any special shortcomings of the Stanford tests. In comparison with other similar tests they have a number of excellent qualities and few deficiencies. The point is that more attention should be paid by the authors and publishers of all such tests to their basic meaningfulness (construct validity) and educational utility. A section on validity in the manual would provide an opportunity and an incentive to marshal whatever evidence there is on these questions.

RUTH M. STRANG, *Professor of Education, Teachers College, Columbia University, New York, New York.*

The directions for administering the test are precise and definite except for the introductory statement: "This is a test to show how much you have learned"—presumably about study skills. Actually, the test is limited to skills involved in reading graphs, charts, and maps, and several location of information and word recognition skills.

The test has three parts: Part 1, Reading Charts and Tables; Part 2, Map Reading; and Part 3, Using the Dictionary, Sources, and Index. The test does not presume to measure broader psychological aspects of study methods such as approach to an assignment, concentration, and remembering. In fact, we do not have enough understanding of the study process used by different students to construct a satisfactory study test encompassing these factors.

Parts 1 and 2 of the intermediate forms are high in interest. They test relationships as well as separate facts. The choice of content is practical and sound. Part 3 of Form JM is less satisfactory because of the difficulty of understanding the directions. Part 3 of Form KM tests the same kind of location of information and word recognition skills in a less complicated way. The intent is good, but some children who have the study skills may get tangled up in the test directions and form. The skills in Part 3 might be better tested informally through "work samples" rather than forced into the mold of multiple choice tests.

The advanced test measures the same types of study skills and is interesting and ingenuously constructed.

The conversion of raw scores into total-group grade norms, modal-age grade norms, and percentile norms is clearly and adequately described. The variety of norms permits interpretation for various purposes. The percentile norms, expressed in terms of grade scores for modal-age groups, make possible a comparison of the scores of a pupil with scores of other pupils of the same grade status; the modal-age norms permit comparison with scores of pupils of a given age in a given grade. According to the manual, "the use of the total group average as the norm for evaluation of an individual's performance sets an unduly low standard for the majority of pupils and, in the long run, is likely to encourage acceptance of

an unnecessarily low level of achievement." Thus, accelerated pupils and the larger group of retarded pupils are both eliminated from the modal-age norms group.

According to the manual, the corrected split-half reliability coefficients range from .87 to .89 for both the intermediate test and the advanced test. These are single grade coefficients. However, for a small sample ($n = 89$) of fifth graders in independent schools the coefficient of correlation was lower than the reliability reported for the same grade in the manual—.70 as compared with .87. Any group with less than average variability might be expected to have lower correlations.

No attempt seems to have been made to ascertain the validity of the test by comparing test results with pupils' observed functioning in study skills in classroom situations.

In summary, the test is useful for ascertaining a group's ability to interpret certain kinds of maps and graphs, and to locate information and recognize certain words. The title of the test, however, is misleading in that the test does not tap the psychological aspects of study such as motivation, problem solving, and the use of knowledge gained, nor does it measure habits and attitudes of study characteristic of able students.

For a review by N. L. Gage of the complete battery, see 25.

[699]

A Test of Study Skills. Grades 4–9; 1940–41; IBM; Forms A, B ('40); directions sheet ('40); reliability data based on preliminary edition; no norms; separate answer sheets must be used; $2.50 per 30 tests; 1½¢ per IBM answer sheet; 30¢ per scoring stencil; 25¢ per specimen set; cash orders postpaid; 60(70) minutes; J. W. Edgar and H. T. Manuel; Steck Co. *

MARVIN D. GLOCK, *Professor of Educational Psychology, Cornell University, Ithaca, New York.*

The test is in two parts. Part 1, Finding and Understanding Printed Materials, is concerned with the location of sources of information and the intelligent utilization of the type of materials found in common references. Questions are of the 5-response multiple choice type. Part 2, Critical Thinking in the Use of Printed Materials, consists of a series of paragraphs, accompanied by multiple choice questions the pupils' understanding of which is checked by questions that may be answered by Yes or No, or by a phrase to the effect that the answer is impossible to arrive at from the facts given. To label the skill required to answer the questions in this part as critical thinking may well be questioned, since a number of the items do nothing more than check main ideas and details.

A major weakness of the test is its design for such a wide range of grade levels, the sampling for any particular grade being, as a result, severely limited. Much of the test will be so difficult for many fourth graders that little information will be gained about the study habits they should have mastered. Likewise, the test will have too low a ceiling for able pupils in the upper grades.

No norms of any kind are provided either in the manual or elsewhere. Information concerning test reliability is limited to the reporting of a coefficient of .92, determined by correlating the scores of 72 pupils in grades 4, 6, and 8 on two forms of an earlier edition of the test. Content validity is claimed on the basis of the careful selection of items. The authors, however, are frank in acknowledging weaknesses in content. They also acknowledge the fact that certain study processes can be tested only indirectly through a recall of information. It is possible, for example, for a pupil to answer correctly the question "Where should the light be placed for a left-handed boy writing a letter at night?" He might, however, place the light over his left shoulder.

When this test is compared with the study skills tests of some of the newer achievement test batteries, it is difficult to see why any school official would select it. Since the batteries are designed for a much narrower grade range, the study skills tests at the various levels provide a wider sampling of skills in a larger number of study areas; and language, content, format, and size of print can be adjusted from level to level to suit pupils of a particular age. Finally, with most achievement test batteries, pupil profiles are furnished on which strengths and weaknesses in various areas can be easily observed. For the test under consideration profiles are not available.

For a review by Douglas E. Scates, see 3:542.

[700]
*Watson-Glaser Critical Thinking Appraisal. Grades 9–16 and adults; 1942–56; revision of *Watson-Glaser Tests of Critical Thinking*; 6 scores: inference, assumptions, deduction, interpretation, arguments, total; IBM; Forms AM ('52), BM ('52, booklet with printer's mark WGCTA:BM-2 is a slight revision of booklet WGCTA:BM-1) ; manual ('52); no data on reliability of the current forms; norms ('56); separate answer sheets must be used; $4.15 per 35 tests; $1.40 per 35 IBM answer sheets; postage extra; 35¢ per specimen set, postpaid; (40–50) minutes; Goodwin Watson and Edward Maynard Glaser; World Book Co. *

REFERENCES
1–3. See 3:544.
4. BREMBECK, WINSTON L. *The Effects of a Course in Argumentation on Critical Thinking Ability.* Doctor's thesis, University of Wisconsin (Madison, Wis.), 1947.
5. BREMBECK, WINSTON L. "The Effects of a Course in Argumentation on Critical Thinking Ability." *Speech Monogr* 16: 177–89 S '49. * (PA 24:4486)
6. CANTER, RALPH R., JR. "A Human Relations Training Program." *J Appl Psychol* 35:38–45 F '51. * (PA 25:7152)
7. BROWNELL, JOHN ARNOLD. "The Influence of Training in Reading in the Social Studies on the Ability to Think Critically." *Calif J Ed Res* 4:28–31 Ja '53. * (PA 28:1466)
8. BLEDSOE, JOSEPH C. "A Comparative Study of Values and Critical Thinking Skills of a Group of Educational Workers." *J Ed Psychol* 46:408–17 N '55. * (PA 31:3774)
9. COOK, JOHN. "Validity Information Exchange, No. 8-13: D.O.T. Code 0-17.01, Electrical Engineer." *Personnel Psychol* 8:261–2 su '55. *
10. HOLLENBACH, JOHN W., AND DE GRAAF, CLARENCE. "Teaching for Thinking." *J Higher Ed* 28:126–30 Mr '57. *
11. ENNIS, ROBERT H. "An Appraisal of the Watson-Glaser Critical Thinking Appraisal." *J Ed Res* 52:155–8 D '58. *

WALKER H. HILL, *Associate Professor, Office of Evaluation Services, Michigan State University, East Lansing, Michigan.*

This test, compared with the 1942 edition, has been shortened and refined through experimentation and analysis. The five subtests which have been retained are clearly pertinent to most definitions of "critical thinking." The directions are simplified, and the format is greatly improved. An earlier "objectivity score" has been dropped.

Two parallel forms are provided, each containing 99 items. The five subtests are: (*a*) Inference (20 items), (*b*) Recognition of Assumptions (16 items), (*c*) Deduction (25 items), (*d*) Interpretation (24 items), (*e*) Evaluation of Arguments (14 items). The authors properly urge caution in the use of subtest scores, even when both forms of the test are used.

Both "neutral" and "emotionally toned" items are included, but it is recognized that the impact of the latter will vary with different groups. The authors now advise teachers who are interested in studying the effect of feeling or prejudice on critical thinking to identify for themselves those items which are likely to have a loading for their particular groups.

A significant change has been made in the design of the assumptions subtest. Formerly this test called for *selection* of an assumption from three suggested statements, with a fourth alternative: "None of the above assumptions is made." In the new test one must decide for each statement whether it is or is not assumed. This seems to be a change for the better.

As much as the authors have improved the test, they have not solved all the problems inherent in this area of testing. In the inference subtest they feel it necessary to require use of "certain commonly accepted knowledge or information which practically every person knows." This is a loophole which makes it possible to question the key to certain items, depending on what one considers to be commonly accepted knowledge.

The interpretation subtest permits the use of two types of judgment. The pattern here is a short paragraph followed by a number of proposed conclusions. In some cases each conclusion must be judged independently of the others. In other cases the conclusions are alternative explanations of a set of facts. When this is true, and is recognized, it is immediately apparent that none of the conclusions can follow beyond a reasonable doubt, and it is not necessary to judge each one on its own merit. This discrepancy may or may not have been intended, but it seems to introduce a heterogeneity (involving more than one kind of ability) that is questionable in a short subtest.

In the last subtest each argument is given in support of an answer to a question. The testee is instructed to "try not to let counter-arguments or your own attitude toward the question influence your judgment." This is a misleading instruction. Undoubtedly it is intended to mean: Do not let your own answer to the question keep you from recognizing a strong argument on the other side. But it also means something else. One of the questions, for example, is this: "Should infants be fed by regular schedule rather than whenever they seem to be hungry?" The answer "Yes; a regular schedule is easier for the parents" is supposed to be judged a weak argument. Why? Because the welfare of the infant should be considered more important than the convenience of the parents. The reviewer agrees—which is to say that in this respect he shares the authors' attitude toward the question. There are several instances of this kind. While the reviewer finds the keyed answers quite acceptable, he believes they *do* involve attitudes and that this will be recognized by some students, particularly those who are critical thinkers.

Though the keyed answers throughout the test are said to represent the unanimous judgment of 35 selected persons, this reviewer remains unsatisfied with several and would stoutly challenge a few. In part this reflects the above-mentioned loophole in the first subtest; in other cases it involves the interpretation of individual items. And, though the two forms are said to be carefully equated, there seems to be a significantly larger number of questionable items in Form BM than in Form AM.

The authors have prepared an excellent manual for users of the test. In addition to a description of the test and discussion of its uses, the manual includes percentile norms for high school and college students (based, however, on a regrettably limited college population), tables of technical data, and reports on validity and reliability. While reliability data for the current forms are not given, rough estimates can be made from the data reported for preceding experimental editions. A discussion of the meaning of critical thinking and its relation to other abilities is especially valuable. A useful list of references is included.

If, as this reviewer believes, critical thinking is a central goal of education, serious efforts to understand it and appraise it must be encouraged. The number of such efforts has been growing in recent years, and the *Watson-Glaser Critical Thinking Appraisal* is one of the useful instruments for this purpose. The difficulties mentioned in this review concern certain details, but are not intended to obscure the instrument's generally high quality.

CARL I. HOVLAND, *Sterling Professor of Psychology, Yale University, New Haven, Connecticut.*

The Watson-Glaser test is a conscientious, imaginative effort to provide appraisal in a most difficult area—that of "critical thinking." Five subtests are employed to evaluate the capacity of the individual to draw correct inferences, recognize assumptions, draw appropriate deductions, interpret data, and evaluate arguments. The authors vary the subject matter to which the reasoning process is applied in an interesting manner—some of their items employ content which is abstract and noncontroversial, and other items, parallel in logical structure, involve issues of a controversial character to which many individuals react with emotion and prejudice. Critics of the test may still feel, however, that it does not include sufficient representation of the more subtle aspects of critical thinking, such as those involved in identification of one's own latent premises or in the differentiation of sources of information possessing varying degrees of credibility.

The tests have found useful application both for selection purposes in schools and industry and for evaluation of the effectiveness of programs of instruction. The latter application will undoubtedly be of increasing importance in view of present-day emphasis on improving instruction in scientific reasoning. The authors also suggest the utilization of the test for diagnosis of difficulties in thinking and as a teaching aid. References to researches which have used the test for various of these purposes are cited in the test manual.

Within the last few years the authors have reworked many of the items, basing their modifications on criticisms, expert opinion, and experience gained during the last decade of use. About 40 per cent of the items have been changed.

In addition, the authors have accumulated a more substantial collection of cases upon which to base their norms. The norms printed in the manual are quite sketchy, being based on miscellaneous samples of students in various high schools and colleges. Mimeographed materials which supply somewhat more extensive norms, including norms for adult groups and graduate students in various fields, are available from the publisher. There is still, of course, nothing like national norms available, although additional cases are constantly being secured.

While the two forms of the tests were standardized in a manner intended to provide equivalent scores, there are differences ranging up to 6 points between scores on the two forms so that specification of which form was used is a desirable procedure in individual testing. In evaluation work it is also quite critical to take the form used into account because otherwise increases or decreases may spuriously be attributed to the educational experience being evaluated. A dittoed table of equivalent scores is provided by the authors but it is not stated on what basis this was developed or upon what groups the equivalence is based.

Moderately high reliabilities of .79 to .84 are reported on a preliminary edition for small samples of high school students, based on estimates utilizing split-half and interform methods. (The 19 least reliable items were deleted in the final edition.) The size of these correlation coefficients is, of course, a function of the range of scores, and it is possible that for some purposes higher reliability coefficients might be obtained when testing more heterogeneous populations. By the nature of the test, however, the most frequent utilization will probably involve populations of restricted range, and hence only moderate reliability is to be expected. Reliability is a problem particularly in studies evaluating the effectiveness of educational programs where the reliability of change scores will be very low indeed since the range of changes typically represents only a fraction of the range of the test scores themselves.

The assessment of the validity of a test of this type is a most difficult matter. The authors state that "several high school science teachers were asked to identify their students who appeared markedly able or markedly poor in ability to reason accurately and to think logically. The test distinguished significantly between the two groups." Correlations of from .33 to .52 for four different classes are reported between teacher's ratings and total scores on the test. Similarly, with groups of 15 research chemists, 12 biologists, 18 engineers, and 15 accountants, there was a significant difference between those who were rated in the top and bottom halves of the group by their supervisors. Converted into correlation form, this relationship may not be very impressive. It is also true that since the theoretical relationship between critical thinking and other measures of intelligence is not established, it is difficult to assess whether the correlation of .70 reported between this test and the *Terman-McNemar Test of Mental Ability* means that the Watson-Glaser test is measuring a single major aspect of intelligence or is just another form of intelligence test. (The reliability of the critical thinking test itself is only around .80.) The authors themselves state that the test differs considerably from an intelligence test and is not an intelligence test as such.

Practice effects appear to be relatively slight. The average improvement for a group of secondary students retested after a week was only 0.6 points, as compared with the 6 point difference in scores mentioned above for alternate forms of the test.

This is a very promising test for use on an experimental basis for selection purposes and for research on the effects of instructional procedures on critical thinking. Development of tests in this area is an extremely difficult undertaking. As a consequence we cannot expect to find as precise measurement here as in less complex areas. The test is not yet thoroughly enough standardized to permit the use of scores on it in any absolute way for determining the adequacy of a testee's skill in critical thinking.

Nevertheless, compared with other less well developed tests which are springing up on all sides with items selected as measures of critical thinking largely on a priori considerations, the Watson-Glaser test is a quite effective instrument.

For a review by Robert H. Thouless of the original edition, see 3:544 (1 excerpt).

READING—SIXTH MMY

REVIEWS BY *Ira E. Aaron, Mary C. Austin, Thomas C. Barrett, Emmett Albert Betts, L. B. Birch, Emery P. Bliesmer, M. Alan Brimer, Charles M. Brown, N. Dale Bryant, W. V. Clemans, William E. Coffman, Thomas E. Culliton, Jr., Stanley E. Davis, Gabriel M. Della-Piana, Clarence Derrick, William Eller, W. G. Fleming, Edward B. Fry, J. Raymond Gerberich, Albert J. Harris, A. N. Hieronymus, Kenneth D. Hopkins, Worth R. Jones, C. E. Jurgensen, Albert J. Kingston, John D. Krumboltz, Charles R. Langmuir, Paul R. Lohnes, Arthur S. McDonald, Jason Millman, Coleman Morrison, David B. Orr, David A. Payne, M. L. Kellmer Pringle, Alton L. Raygor, H. Alan Robinson, Donald E. P. Smith, George D. Spache, Russell G. Stauffer, Agatha Townsend, Arthur E. Traxler, B. H. Van Roekel, Magdalen D. Vernon, and Morey J. Wantman.*

[782]

*A.C.E.R. Silent Reading Tests, Forms C and D.
Ages 10–13; 1946–63; Forms C ['46], D ['63]; 3 parts; manual ['63, 38 pages]; 13s. per 10 sets of all 3 parts; 2s. 6d. per key; 5s. per manual; 8s. 9d. per specimen set; postpaid within Australia; Australian Council for Educational Research. *
a) PART 1, WORD KNOWLEDGE. 4 pages; 3s. 6d. per 10 tests; 10(20) minutes.
b) PART 2, SPEED OF READING. 8 pages; 4s. 6d. per 10 tests; 6(15) minutes.
c) PART 3, READING FOR MEANING. 8 pages; 6s. per 10 tests; 20(30) minutes.

REFERENCES
1. WHEELER, D. K. "Reading Speed of W. A. Children." *Educand* 2:4–9 N '54.

For reviews by Fred J. Schonell and D. K. Wheeler, see 5:617.

[783]

American School Achievement Tests: Part 1, Reading. Grades 2–3, 4–6, 7–9; 1941–63; subtest of *American School Achievement Tests;* 3 scores: sentence and word meaning, paragraph meaning, total; Forms D ('55), E ('56), F ('57), G ('58, except for Primary Battery 2, '55), (2 sheets); Forms D, E, and F are essentially the same as Forms A, B, and C copyrighted in 1941–43; 3 levels; 50¢ per specimen set of any one level; postage extra; Willis E. Pratt, Robert V. Young, and Clara E. Cockerille (manuals for b and c); Bobbs-Merrill Co., Inc. *
a) PRIMARY BATTERY 2. Grades 2–3; battery manual ('58, c1955–58, 13 pages); $2.75 per 35 tests; 25(35) minutes.
b) INTERMEDIATE BATTERY. Grades 4–6; battery manual ('61, 17 pages); $3 per 35 tests; 25(35) minutes.
c) ADVANCED BATTERY. Grades 7–9; battery manual ('63, 17 pages); $3 per 35 tests; 30(40) minutes.

For reviews by Russell G. Stauffer and Agatha Townsend, see 5:620. For reviews of the complete battery, see 2, 5:1, 4:1, and 3:1.

[784]

California Reading Test, 1957 Edition With 1963 Norms. Grades 1–2, 2.5–4.5, 4–6, 7–9, 9–14; 1933–63; subtest of *California Achievement Tests;* 3 scores: vocabulary, comprehension, total; IBM and Grade-O-Mat for grades 4–14; 2–4 forms ('63, c1957–63, identical with tests copyrighted in 1957 except for profile on all test booklets and revision of junior high level Form X); 5 levels; battery manual ('63, c1957–63, 53–70 pages) for each level; battery technical report ('57, 48 pages) on 1957 edition with 1957 norms; battery individual profile ('63, 2 pages) for each level; no norms for grades 13–14; separate answer sheets or cards may be used in grades 4–14; 5¢ per IBM answer sheet; 9¢ per Scoreze answer sheet; 3¢ per set of Cal-Cards; 4¢ per set of Grade-O-Mat scorable punch-out cards; 20¢ per set of either IBM answer sheet or Cal-Card hand scoring stencils; 40¢ per set of either IBM answer sheet or Grade-O-Mat machine scoring stencils; 2¢ per profile; postage extra; technical report free; 75¢ per specimen set of a or b; $1 per specimen set of c, d, or e; postpaid; Ernest W. Tiegs and Willis W. Clark; California Test Bureau. *
a) LOWER PRIMARY. Grades 1–2; Forms W, X, ('63, c1957–63, 9 pages); $2.80 per 35 tests; 23(35) minutes.
b) UPPER PRIMARY. Grades 2.5–4.5; Forms W, X, ('63, c1957–63, 13 pages); $3.15 per 35 tests; 40(50) minutes.
c) ELEMENTARY. Grades 4–6; IBM and Grade-O-Mat; Forms W, X, Y, Z, ('63, c1957–63, 14 pages); $3.50 per 35 tests; 50(60) minutes.
d) JUNIOR HIGH LEVEL. Grades 7–9; IBM and Grade-O-Mat; Forms W, X, Y, Z, ('63, c1957–63, 18 pages); $3.50 per 35 tests; 68(80) minutes.
e) ADVANCED. Grades 9–14; IBM and Grade-O-Mat; Forms W, X, Y, ('63, c1957–63, 19 pages); $3.50 per 35 tests; 68(80) minutes.

REFERENCES
1–5. See 5:622.
6. BLACK, D. B. "A Study of the Relationship of the Grade IX Principal's Rating to Performance on the Alberta Grade IX Departmental Examinations." *Alberta J Ed Res* 4:227–36 D '58. * (*PA* 34:2089)
7. HANEY, RUSSELL; MICHAEL, WILLIAM B.; AND JONES, ROBERT A. "Identification of Aptitude and Achievement Factors in the Prediction of the Success of Nursing Trainees." *Ed & Psychol Meas* 19:645–7 w '59. * (*PA* 34:6164)
8. MAKLEY, MARGARET. *A Comparison of California Reading Achievement Scores With Reading Performance in Grades Three and Four.* Master's thesis, Fresno State College (Fresno, Calif.), 1959.
9. MICHAEL, WILLIAM B.; JONES, ROBERT A.; AND HANEY, RUSSELL. "The Development and Validation of a Test Battery for Selection of Student Nurses." *Ed & Psychol Meas* 19: 641–3 w '59. * (*PA* 34:6171)
10. HANEY, RUSSELL; MICHAEL, WILLIAM B.; JONES, ROBERT A.; AND GADDIS, L. WESLEY. "Cognitive and Non-Cognitive Predictors of Achievement in Student Nursing." *Ed & Psychol Meas* 20:387–9 su '60. * (*PA* 35:7120)
11. ANDERSON, HARRY E., JR. "The Prediction of Reading

and Language From the California Tests." *Ed & Psychol Meas* 21:1035–6 w '61. *

12. ANDERSON, HARRY E., JR. "A Study of Language and Nonlanguage Achievement." *Ed & Psychol Meas* 21:1037–8 w '61. *

13. JONES, ROBERT A., AND MICHAEL, WILLIAM B. "The Validity of a Battery of Tests in Communication Skills for Foreign Students Attending an American University." *Ed & Psychol Meas* 21:493–6 su '61. * (*PA* 36:2KK93J)

14. MICHAEL, WILLIAM B., AND JONES, ROBERT A. "Linguistic Factors in Several Tests and Criterion Measures Pertaining to Communication Skills." *Ed & Psychol Meas* 21:1011–4 w '61. *

15. MICHAEL, WILLIAM B.; JONES, ROBERT A.; GETTINGER, TED, JR.; HODGES, JOHN D., JR.; KOLESNIK, PETER E.; AND SEPPALA, JAMES. "The Prediction of Success in Selected Courses in a Teacher Training Program From Scores in Achievement Tests and From Ratings on a Scale of Directed Teaching Performance." *Ed & Psychol Meas* 21:995–9 w '61. *

16. HANEY, RUSSELL; MICHAEL, WILLIAM B.; AND GERSHON, ARTHUR. "Achievement, Aptitude, and Personality Measures as Predictors of Success in Nursing Training." *Ed & Psychol Meas* 22:389–92 su '62. * (*PA* 37:3869)

17. MICHAEL, WILLIAM B.; HANEY, RUSSELL; AND GERSHON, ARTHUR. "Intellective and Non-Intellective Predictors of Success in Nursing Training." *Ed & Psychol Meas* 23:817–21 w '63. *

18. SHEPPARD, CHARLES, AND CAMPBELL, WILLIAM J. "An Evaluation of the California Achievement Test, Elementary, Form W, Reading Vocabulary." *J Ed Res* 56:481–3 My–Je '63. *

For reviews by John C. Flanagan and James R. Hobson of the 1950 edition, see 4:530 (1 excerpt); for a review by Frederick B. Davis of an earlier edition, see 40:1563; for reviews by Ivan A. Booker and Joseph C. Dewey, see 38:1110. For reviews of the complete battery, see 3, 5:2, 4:2, 3:15, 40:1193, and 38:876.

[785]

★**Comprehension Test for Training College Students.** Training college students and applicants for admission; 1962; 1 form (8 pages); manual (12 pages); 17s. per 25 tests; 7s. per manual; 7s. per specimen set; prices include purchase tax; postpaid within U.K.; 45(50) minutes; E. L. Black; distributed by National Foundation for Educational Research in England and Wales. *

[786]

*Davis Reading Test. Grades 8–11, 11–13; 1956–62; 2 scores: level of comprehension, speed of comprehension; IBM; 2 levels; manual ('62, c1958–62, 31 pages); separate answer sheets must be used; $3.50 per 25 tests; $2 per 50 IBM answer sheets; 50¢ per set of scoring stencils and manual; 75¢ per specimen set; postpaid; 40(55) minutes; Frederick B. Davis and Charlotte Croon Davis; Psychological Corporation. *

a) SERIES 1. Grades 11–13; 1956–62; Forms 1A, 1B, 1C, 1D, ('57, c1956–57, 10 pages).

b) SERIES 2. Grades 8–11; 1961–62; Forms 2A, 2B, 2C, 2D, ('61, c1960–61, 11 pages).

REFERENCES

1. KETCHAM, HERBERT E., (MRS.) "Reading Tests and College Performance," pp. 63–6. In *Research and Evaluation in College Reading.* Ninth Yearbook of the National Reading Conference for College and Adults. Fort Worth, Tex.: Texas Christian University Press, 1960. Pp. 137. *

2. WEAVER, WENDELL W., AND KINGSTON, ALBERT J. "A Factor Analysis of the Cloze Procedure and Other Measures of Reading and Language Ability." *J Commun* 13:252–61 D '63. * (*PA* 39:188)

WILLIAM E. COFFMAN, *Director of Research and Development, College Board Programs Division, Educational Testing Service, Princeton, New Jersey.*

The modern standardized test is so much the product of a highly developed technology that one is likely to overlook the fact that the central core of every good test is the collection of test questions—products of creative effort by artist-writers. The *Davis Reading Test* is supported by an unusually comprehensive array of technical data. The manual for the test is a 31-page booklet of which more than 19 pages are devoted to technical information. Six pages are needed for such formal aspects as covers and table of contents, three for directions for administration and scoring, and almost two for acknowledgments. There remains only about two pages for the authors to discuss what they are about.

It is only when one actually takes several forms of the test that he becomes conscious of how much these tests carry the mark of the artist-writer. There is a freshness about the stimulus passages and a challenge to the questions which makes the task of marking answers an encounter with an interesting adversary. On a subjective basis alone one concludes that these are unusually effective collections of passages and questions for assessing the ability of adolescents to garner meaning from the printed page.

But one does not need to depend on subjective impressions only. According to the evidence presented in the manual, the test will do what the authors claim and probably more. Data are presented with respect to scaling, reliability, and validity. The user is provided with detailed guidance as to how to use the test to best advantage. The normative data are appropriate. Let me illustrate.

Most published tests which are offered for use over a span of grades are pitched in difficulty at the middle of the range; thus one has to be careful not to exceed the effective range, especially when using the test with atypical groups. The *Davis Reading Test,* in contrast, has its two levels anchored at the ends of the range. Series 1 is of middle difficulty for the grade 13 norms group; Series 2 is ideal for the grade 8 group. And there is a comfortable overlap for the grade 11 sample in the middle. It is likely that the Series 1 forms will be suitable for many upper class college groups and the

Series 2 forms for many groups below eighth grade.

Some users may object to the fact that the norms samples are defined only by the names of the institutions participating in the norms administrations. One may doubt, however, whether a rigorously drawn national sample would have any clear advantage over a sample which is well distributed geographically and which consists of students in schools which are willing to cooperate. The major values of a test of this type depend on the existence of a sound score scale which will permit comparisons within a school system and over a period of time. The scale for the *Davis Reading Test* meets this requirement; a table relating the scaled scores to those for the *College Qualification Tests* provides additional flexibility.

In response to recommendations of professional groups, most test publishers now provide data on the reliability of a test for within-grade samples. The publishers of the *Davis Reading Test* have based their coefficients on 28 carefully designed experiments involving all eight forms. Furthermore, standard errors of measurement are provided, not only for single forms but also for combinations of two, three, and four forms. The experimenter who wishes to achieve high reliability by administering more than one form has the necessary information at his finger tips.

Evidence is provided regarding both predictive and construct validity. Correlations with English grades are presented for 70 different groups. Correlations with six other tests based on Series 1 scores and with eight other tests based on Series 2 scores appear reasonable. As to content validity, the tests seem to speak for themselves. If there is any question regarding validity, it is that there is no objective evidence to support the differentiation of a level and a speed score.

Each form of the test consists of two parallel halves of 40 questions each. Almost all students complete the first half and almost nobody completes the second half. Therefore, score on the first half is taken as a measure of accuracy or depth of comprehension while score on the total test measures both speed and accuracy. It is argued that "Level score indicates the degree of comprehension attained while progressing at a self-determined rate of working as rapidly as possible without making careless mistakes." It

would be enlightening to study the perceptions of test takers regarding the meaning of the instructions to "work as rapidly as you can without making careless mistakes." It would also be worthwhile to search for criteria against which the level score proves more valid than the speed score.

This test is an outstanding example of the test writer's art. Evidence presented in the manual indicates that the several forms meet high standards of reliability and validity and are of appropriate difficulty for the recommended uses. One may wish to look behind differences between speed and level scores to the perceptions which guided the student at the time he took the test, but it is doubtful that one can find a better reading test for use in grades 8–13.

ALTON L. RAYGOR, *Associate Professor of Educational Psychology, and Coordinator, Reading and Study Skills Center, University of Minnesota, Minneapolis, Minnesota.*

One expects good tests from Fred Davis. Editorship of earlier Cooperative reading tests qualifies him as an expert in the field, as do other pieces of evidence concerning his professional life. He has been very much interested in the problem of measuring gain in reading improvement programs; in fact, he includes in the manual for this test a brief discussion of the problem and refers the reader to a more lengthy treatment of it in another source.

These tests and the manual which goes with them testify to the care with which Davis and his wife go about constructing achievement tests. It is gratifying to see that some of the most typical pitfalls of test constructors are avoided, particularly those in which quality is sacrificed to produce ease of administration and scoring. The use of scaled scores to achieve equivalence of forms is a great deal preferable to the technique of some other reading test authors, who use some system for determining the difficulty level of items and then build equivalent forms on the assumption that one can do this as a random process.

The Davis test is also very simple to administer and to score. Hand scoring with the correction formula is made easy by the provision of a table in the manual which even tells the scorer how many to subtract from the right answers in the case of a given number of wrong answers. The test seems well standardized on an adequate number of students representing what seems to be a good selection of schools and colleges. One could always hope that such a standardization sample could be demonstrated to be a stratified random sample of a nationwide population, but the difficulty of achieving such sampling is certainly a major factor to be considered.

The section in the manual on interpretation of scores is clearly written and does a good job of indicating the limits on the accuracy of measurement of an individual score. The discussion on the standard error of measurement is particularly clear. The section in which the reliability of the test is discussed in terms of increases in reliability to be gained by use of more than one form is very useful in that it is likely not only to encourage the realization of the limits of reliability, but might also result in longer and more reliable testing on the part of the typical user.

Concerning validity the manual states, "The content validity of a reading test depends on whether mental activities required to answer the questions constitute a representative sample of those called into play during the process of understanding material of a defined type. * the content of the *Davis Reading Test* has been carefully designed to bring this about. Factoral studies have provided evidence that tests of this kind are excellent measures of verbal aptitude."

The question which bothers this reviewer about the Davis test is why it was built at all. Davis worked very hard on the development of the Cooperative reading tests which measure the same variables except for the exclusion of the vocabulary in the Davis. A strong criticism of the Cooperative test was that the subscores were based on the same items and that they were extremely difficult to interpret. The speed of comprehension score was commonly mistaken for a speed of reading score and it seems to this reviewer that this confusion is fostered by the word "speed" in the name of the score. In the present test, the level of comprehension score uses a varying proportion of items that overlap with the speed of comprehension score. For the subject who does exactly 40 of the items, both scores are computed on precisely the same items. On the other hand, if the subject completes the whole test, only half of the items are used on the level of comprehension score. The statement that the level of compre-

hension score "indicates the depths of understanding displayed by a student in reading the kinds of material he is ordinarily required to read in high school and college" seems to this reviewer to leave a great deal to be desired in the explanation about the scores in a fashion which will enable the user to successfully discriminate between them and understand the factors which produce differences between the speed score and the level score. This is particularly troublesome when one finds that the two scores are correlated with each other at between .74 and .80, close to the limits of reliability for each score.

To summarize, this seems like a very well built test by competent authors, with adequate reliability and validity, and standardized on an adequate sample of what appear to be representative students, but it suffers the same difficulty in interpretation and overlap in measured skills as the earlier reading test constructed by Davis.

For a review by Benjamin Rosner of a, see 5:625.

[787]

*Developmental Reading Tests. Grades 1.5, 1.5–2.5, 2.5–3, 4–6; 1955–61; 4 levels; the 1961 forms of *a–c* are single-booklet printings of the 1955 three-part forms; no specific manual (directions and norms printed on test booklets); no data on reliability; preliminary norms; $5 per 35 tests (except for *d*, $4 per 35 tests); $1 per set of scoring cards; $1 per 50 class records; 40¢ per specimen set of any one level; postage extra; 40(55) minutes in 3 sessions 1–2 days apart for *a–c*, 32(50) minutes for *d*; [Guy L. Bond, Theodore Clymer, and Cyril Hoyt]; Lyons & Carnahan. *
a) PRIMER READING. Grade 1.5; 1955–61; 3 scores: basic vocabulary, general comprehension, specific comprehension; Form P-A ('61, 14 pages).
b) LOWER PRIMARY READING. Grades 1.5–2.5; 1955–61; 3 scores: same as for *a;* Form L-A ('61, 14 pages).
c) UPPER PRIMARY READING. Grades 2.5–3; 1955–61; 3 scores: same as for *a;* Form U-A ('61, 14 pages).
d) [INTERMEDIATE READING.] Grades 4–6; 1959; 6 scores: basic vocabulary, reading to retain information, reading to organize, reading to evaluate-interpret, reading to appreciate, average comprehension; Forms IR-A, IR-B, ('59, 16 pages).

EDWARD B. FRY, *Professor of Education, Rutgers, The State University, New Brunswick, New Jersey.*

The *Developmental Reading Tests* are good examples of tests that do not have a specific purpose.

There are several reasons why a teacher or a school system might want to use a reading achievement test. One is to compare their students' present achievement, either individually or in groups, with other students who have taken the same test (the standardization group). A second reason might be to see how students are progressing through the curriculum. Teachers might want an answer to such a legitimate question as "Is Johnny ready to start using the second grade book?" A third use of such tests might be to better enable teachers to discern relative differences between students. This would answer the questions "Can Johnny read better than Mary?" and "Which students are my best readers?" Finally, the reading achievement test might be diagnostic in certain specified skills, providing such useful information as "Johnny's sight recognition vocabulary is good but his understanding of a paragraph is poor."

Now if these are some of the ultimate purposes of a reading achievement test, how do the *Developmental Reading Tests* fulfill them?

First, the publisher provides no information about the standardization group. Were the norms obtained on children from one rich district where 90 per cent of the fathers are in the professional class? Or were they obtained in two poor rural communities where the teachers, the school buildings, and the parents' incomes are all well below national norms? It is impossible to tell from the teacher's manual (or rather lack of manual). Hence, it is suggested that the norms provided are valueless and do not represent anything but the authors' or publisher's opinion. Nor do the authors state how this test compares with other tests—it might be much easier, it might be much harder.

From a technical standpoint, there is also a serious flaw in that no reliability data are provided. A student might take the test on one day and do very well, only to be an abject failure another time. Hence, the teacher cannot be sure that Johnny can read better than Mary. There is no information about comparability of the alternate forms provided at the intermediate level. Is one form easier than the other?

In short, as standardized tests, these tests fall far short of the mark.

But there is another valid function of tests and that is to show progress through the curriculum. Presumably, this is one function that the *Developmental Reading Tests* could perform admirably, as there is interlocking authorship with the Developmental Reading Series

(textbooks) published by the same publisher. But one looks in vain for such help or statement that this could or should be done. There is one strong hint in some of the publisher's descriptive material to the effect that "The vocabulary of the tests was selected....[from] the same word lists that were used in writing the Developmental Reading Series." But this is not the same as saying that if a student scores 2.5 on the primer level test, he is ready for the upper second grade book. Hence, as purely curriculum development tests, these tests do not give the type of information that is useful.

These tests also suffer from faults common among all too many reading achievement tests: (a) The subtests have meaningless names. What is the difference between "General Comprehension" and "Specific Comprehension"? (b) The subtests are too short. In the intermediate test, for example, Reading to Evaluate—Interpret has 18 items, and Reading to Appreciate has 18 items. Teachers are given grade scores for each of these, and are instructed to plot them on a profile. Statistically, an 18-item subtest is questionable, and logically, the diagnostic value of the stated names is questionable. Wouldn't it be better to use only average comprehension (which is composed of four such subtests)? It would give much more accurate information to teachers and administrators. (c) There is no bottom cutoff score. Anyone who has administered a number of multiple choice tests in a school has seen the dullest child simply go through and mark items at random, often without even bothering to read them. If he did this on the primary form, on the average he would get a 1.45 reading grade score in General Comprehension. But if he managed to sit in the class until the fourth grade where he might be administered the intermediate form, by using the same process he would average 4.7 in Reading to Organize. Now, there is a real measure of reading progress! He grew three years in achievement in three school years—a fact in which the teacher and the superintendent can really take pride. How long are teachers, administrators, and test publishers going to permit this ridiculous situation to exist? (What should be done? For any raw score below 8, the scoring directions should simply state: "This test not valid below grade 5.0; use a lower form.")

The directions for administering and scoring are clear. The printing is good. Graphic profiles of subtest scores are printed on the front of each booklet. In fact, in most respects, the *Developmental Reading Tests* "look" like well-made standardized tests and this is perhaps what is so insidious. The teacher follows the directions, the students mark the booklet, the tests are scored, and Johnny gets a reading grade of 1.9. What on earth does this mean?

If the test authors and publisher would only decide whether they want to have a standardized test or a test that measures curriculum development against some criterion (such as their reading textbooks), the school administrators, teachers, and children would certainly profit by such a decision.

Agatha Townsend, *Consultant, Educational Records Bureau, New York, New York.*

The *Developmental Reading Tests* as now in print could be used as the raw material from which to manufacture a set of acceptable reading tests for the primary and intermediate grades. Basically, the test content is good; the format, although in need of a few modifications, is clear and quite suitable; and the concept of reading which is implicit in the battery is worth more attention than it can receive in its present form. The authors are, of course, highly qualified.

This review will consider briefly the changes which might be made, beginning with the major gaps in the present materials. The lacks, then, seem to lie primarily in the low esteem in which the authors, or perhaps the publishers, hold the classroom teacher. Evidently the elementary school teacher is not willing to bother himself with details such as the basis for grade equivalence tables, the possible reliability of scores, or any information about test construction. There is no test manual. The sole explanatory item furnished appears on the envelope containing the specimen set. After assuring the teacher that the test construction conforms to modern principles, the two pertinent sentences read: "The vocabulary of the tests was selected by use of the Thorndike, Dale-Chall, and other scientific word lists. These are the same word lists that were used in writing the Developmental Reading Series by Bond et al., which is published by Lyons and Carnahan."

The teacher is evidently expected to refer to manuals for the reading series and his own experience in order to improve scores which are not within the "allowable variation." That term is a new one to this reviewer who is accustomed to classes which are allowed to include pupils of a wide range of reading skills (not that this is necessarily an ideal situation). The description of what is allowable variation (four to six months either side of grade placement for the primary grades, six to eight months for higher grades) appears on the cover page of the booklets. Though it does not appear on the booklet for the intermediate grades, one of the statements refers to this grade range: "If the pupil's placement in grade is between 3.5 and 5.4, variation may be 8 months either way." Since, as mentioned earlier, there is no description of the basis for the grade equivalents, it is not clear if this allowable variation is a way of expressing the standard error of scores, or based on the distributions and related to a percentile band interpretation. Probably many teachers using the test interpret it conservatively enough, to mean that if the score falls within these limits it probably reflects about average performance for classes using Lyons and Carnahan readers.

When one turns to the booklet content, the picture of the tests is a far happier one. The primary tests are similar in appearance and in approach to the *Gates Primary Reading Tests.* The three scores, Basic Vocabulary, General Comprehension, and Specific Comprehension, are based on parts which seem long enough and internally consistent enough so that the scores are probably useful. There are no word attack materials, a serious omission. The intermediate test retains the vocabulary part, and has four brief comprehension parts, which are designed to test, and probably do measure, reading to retain information, to organize, to evaluate and interpret, and to appreciate. There is an average comprehension score obtained by averaging these four parts. Part 3, Reading to Organize, is based on 30 items, but the other sections may be too short for adequate reliability.

Throughout, the battery would be improved by some simple steps to make the teacher's task easier. No score boxes are provided. In most of the parts, the items are not numbered in sequence, making checking for accuracy of scoring difficult. It seems cumbersome, especially since there is no place to record the raw scores, to have to refer to the back cover for the grade rating and then to the front in order to enter it on the profile chart. Grade scales could easily be added to the stencil keys. The boxes on the keys through which the answers appear should also be numbered. The intermediate test could easily be adapted to use of a separate answer sheet.

There is only one form for the three tests below the intermediate level. Hence, reteaching on the basis of the scores would have to be evaluated by repeating the same form, or using another measure altogether. The two forms of the intermediate test are not identical in the range of the grade equivalents. Form A is apparently easier. This circumstance should be pointed out to the user, who might wish to start with Form A for grade 4 to take advantage of it.

Lyons and Carnahan is not the only publisher of textbooks to enter the testing field. It would probably be worthwhile for the firm to review similar publications for competing series. Ginn and Company supplement their basic reading series by tests written by McCullough and Russell, who have written adequate manuals for interpretation and have provided at least minimal information on standardization and test construction.

In summary, since the *Developmental Reading Tests* are not inextricably woven into a single reading series, it might be worthwhile to urge their further improvement into a full-fledged reading achievement test. At the present stage, however, this reviewer is convinced that teachers using the Lyons and Carnahan texts would secure better measurement of reading skills by using a more fully standardized battery issued by publishers who are test specialists.

[788]

*Elementary Reading: Every Pupil Scholarship Test. Grades 4–6, 7–8; 1928–64; new form (4 pages) usually issued each January and April; forms from previous testing programs also available; 2 levels; general directions sheet ['63, 2 pages]; no data on reliability; norms for new forms available following testing program; 4¢ per test; 4¢ per key; postage extra; 15(20) or 25(30) minutes; Bureau of Educational Measurements. *

[789]

*Elementary Reading: Every Pupil Test. Grades 4–6; 1936–64; new form (4–8 pages) usually issued each December and April; forms from previous testing programs also available; 2 tests; general directions sheet ('63, 2 pages); no data on reliability; Ohio norms for new forms available following testing program; 5¢ per test; 3¢ per key; postpaid; Ohio Scholarship Tests. *
a) GENERAL ABILITY. 22(40) minutes.
b) SPEED AND COMPREHENSION. 2 scores: speed, comprehension; 6(15) minutes.

[790]

Gates Advanced Primary Reading Tests. Grades 2.5–3; 1926–58; Forms 1, 2, 3, ('58, 4 pages); 2 tests; manual ('58, 12 pages); series supplement ('58, 5 pages); $1.50 per 35 tests; 50¢ per specimen set of both tests; cash orders postpaid; 40(60) minutes; Arthur I. Gates; Bureau of Publications. *
a) TYPE AWR, WORD RECOGNITION. 15(25) minutes.
b) TYPE APR, PARAGRAPH READING. 25(35) minutes.

REFERENCES

1–3. See 5:630.
4. NORTH, ROBERT D. "Difficulty and Reliability of the Gates Primary and Advanced Primary Reading Tests, 1958 Edition, for Independent School Pupils." *Ed Rec B* 76:45–51 F '60. *

KENNETH D. HOPKINS, *Associate Professor of Educational Psychology, University of Southern California, Los Angeles, California.*

The 1958 edition of the *Gates Advanced Primary Reading Tests* is patterned closely after earlier editions. The content has been updated and percentile norms are available for the first time.

ADMINISTRATION AND SCORING. The procedures for administration are clear and explicit. Several practice exercises are included for the examinee, to insure understanding of the directions. The manual recommends that colored pencils be used to facilitate scoring, which seems somewhat impracticable; having the print of the tests a nonblack color would have better served the purpose.

Since the two subtests (Word Recognition and Paragraph Reading) are usually given together, a combined booklet would have been easier to use. The manual indicates that the usual order of the tests can be changed if desired, yet no empirical findings are presented to support the assumed lack of ordering and practice effects.

The suggestions in the manual for practical use of the test results are excellent, e.g., improving word recognition. A supplementary manual gives more detailed and technical information. Unfortunately this is a single composite supplement serving the purposes of all the several Gates tests; consequently the interspersed data are not always clearly and well defined. The reader is not always certain whether a statement applies to a specific test or to all Gates' tests. The tables are especially inadequately labeled and interpreted.

STANDARDIZATION AND NORMS. Twenty carefully selected schools served as the reference group on whom the normative data were obtained. Consideration was given to representative IQ scores and socioeconomic status. The manual appears to claim too much in indicating that the results from this relatively small sample of stratified schools were "for all practical purposes" as good as those which would have been obtained if all of the approximately 100 stratified schools had been used. Although the normative sample is purported to be "fairly representative of the nation's total school population," substantiating descriptive data are omitted. The norms are based, in part, on an actual group who took the tests ($n = 3,300$), and partially inferred from other "key" tests on which interrelationships had been previously established ($n = 2,500$). Greater explanation regarding this process would have been desirable. The assumption of equal correlation with the "key" tests on other groups may not be completely justifiable due to the curricular specificity of school districts.

Reading grade equivalents, reading ages, and percentile norms are provided. Percentile norms are given at grades 2.5, 2.8, 3.2, 3.5, and 3.8, although it is not made clear whether any of the values are interpolated or extrapolated.

The manual indicates that scores on the present edition "differ materially from those used in earlier editions, reflecting the changes in promotion policy." Additional information regarding the extent of the differences should have been provided so that users accustomed to the earlier editions could more appropriately interpret scores on the current forms.

In some cases, grade equivalents are given to the second decimal place. The validity of this procedure is seriously questioned. A false sense of precision is apt to be inferred from such scores.

RELIABILITY. The tests are to be commended on their use of the most rigorous and appropriate method of reliability determination, the alternate form approach. The manual, however, gives no indication as to which of the three forms were used for the reliability coefficients presented. Unfortunately, reliability data are not given for grade 2, although the tests are designed for grades 2.5–3.9. Difficulty factors would almost certainly make coefficients lower than for grade 3. The samples on which the reliabilities were determined were small and they are inadequately described, but the resulting coefficients, although high, would appear to be conservative since the corresponding standard deviations are usually only about one half

the values for the normative sample as estimated from the percentile norms. Data are missing to support the equality of means and standard deviations for the various forms. This is very important since the same conversion table is used for all forms of the tests.

Although the manual states that the tests are diagnostic, its treatment of difference scores is not precise. The values for the difference scores that "may be regarded as both statistically reliable and practically significant" are probably too small; the .15 level of significance is used for these scores. No basis is given for the claim of practical significance.

VALIDITY. The content universe which the items sample is not defined. In fact, no mention of content validity is made, although the items appear to possess face validity. The basis of item selection is given only in general terms; item statistics are not reported.

Although the manual states that the tests are not primarily tests of speed, no empirical data are reported to indicate the influence of speed. The measures are to be commended for not attempting to span several grades with a single test.

No evidence for concurrent or predictive validity appears. No mention is made of the technical recommendations of the AERA or APA. The present tests do not appear to adequately meet the following specifications for achievement tests: A1, B1.2, B1.3, B5, C2.1, C2.3, C3, C4, C4.1, C4.2, C4.6, C5.1, C11, C16.1, D1.2, D1.3, D3, D7, E1, E2, F1, F3, F4, F5, F8, F8.3, F8.6, F8.7, F8.8.

The 15-minute word recognition subtest is composed of attractive drawings from each of which a line is to be drawn to its name. The distributions are skewed positively at grade 2. The 25-minute paragraph reading subtest is composed of 24 items of increasing length in which the examinee performs a straightforward task requiring no inference or abstraction, e.g., "Draw a line under the little book."

SUMMARY. The *Gates Advanced Primary Reading Tests* are attractive, easily administered, and easily scored. Reliability is excellent, although the standardization and norming leave some unanswered questions which limit generalizability and interpretation. More information regarding content validity would have been desirable, yet the tests appear to be useful survey measures.

For reviews by Virginia Seavey and George Spache of the previous edition, see 3:484.

[791]

Gates Basic Reading Tests. Grades 3.5–8; 1926–58; revision of *Gates Silent Reading Tests;* Forms 1, 2, 3, ('58, 4 pages); 5 tests; Types GS, UD, and ND are scored for percentage of attempts correct; manual ('58, 21 pages); series supplement ('58, 5 pages); $1.50 per 35 copies of any one test; 50¢ per specimen set of all 5 tests; cash orders postpaid; Arthur I. Gates; Bureau of Publications. *

a) TYPE GS, READING TO APPRECIATE GENERAL SIGNIFI-CANCE. 10(15) minutes for grades 3–4, 8(15) minutes for grades 5–8.

b) TYPE UD, READING TO UNDERSTAND PRECISE DIREC-TIONS. 10(15) minutes for grades 3–4, 8(15) minutes for grades 5–8.

c) TYPE ND, READING TO NOTE DETAILS. 10(15) minutes for grades 3–4, 8(15) minutes for grades 5–8.

d) TYPE RV, READING VOCABULARY. (20) minutes.

e) TYPE LC, LEVEL OF COMPREHENSION. (20) minutes.

REFERENCES

1–5. See 40:1539.
6–7. See 3:485.
8. See 5:631.
9. CHASE, CLINTON I. "The Position of Certain Variables in the Prediction of Problem-Solving in Arithmetic." *J Ed Res* 54:9–14 S '60. *

ALBERT N. HIERONYMUS, *Professor of Education and Psychology, State University of Iowa, Iowa City, Iowa.*

These tests were very competently reviewed in their present form in *The Fifth Mental Measurements Yearbook.* Some of the minor faults of the manuals which were criticized have apparently been corrected. The major faults of the tests themselves persist.

The most severe limitation of these tests is that they attempt to serve too wide a grade range. Generally speaking, the tests are far too difficult for the lower grades in the intended range (grades 3–8), and not particularly interesting or challenging for the upper grades. In two of the tests only 24 items are used to separate a population which is extremely heterogeneous (grade equivalent range of 2.0 to 12.4 or 12.5) in reading proficiency.

Type GS, Reading to Appreciate General Significance, is presented as requiring "thorough understanding of and real thinking about the content." Yet most of the passages consist of from three to five short sentences which hardly set the stage for very complex understanding. Furthermore, many of the items can be marked without even reading the passage, as for example: "Draw a line under another invention of the kind that usually does not impress people—paper clip, car, airplane, dynamo, camera." For measuring such a complex skill, the form of items is quite inadequate. It is vir-

tually impossible to ask a genuinely searching question about a passage when the question can be answered in one word. The short passages and the one word responses do not do justice to the standards usually set for appreciating general significance of materials which upper grade children are expected to handle.

On Type GS, the median grade 3.4 score is only 5/24, which is chance. With 10-minute time limits, the median grade 8.7 score is 22/24, but the scores at the top are spread considerably with an 8-minute time limit. With an 8-minute time limit, however, children have to average approximately 250 words per minute to complete the test if they read without looking back. This would seem to put quite heavy emphasis upon speed in a test purported to measure thinking and understanding.

Type UD, Reading to Understand Precise Directions, is presented as a test of the "kind of reading the child should be able to do when he reads the instructions for assembling a toy or gadget, operating a television set, [etc.]." This test appears to be misnamed; the only directions used are "put an x on," "draw a line under," "draw a line from [one object] to [another]," and "draw a line around." It is usually, although not always, necessary to read the short selection, but the selections themselves do not constitute directions as such, nor do the items require "exact memory of details in sequential order," as stated in the manual.

In Type ND, Reading to Note Details, most of the 54 items can be marked without reading the passages. This is caused to a large extent by the use of weak distractors. For example, the four responses to the question, "What may air conditioning add to air?" are "radio," "moisture," "mustache," and "pencil"!

If the first three tests are considered primarily as speed tests, these criticisms are less important than if they are regarded as measuring comprehension skills of the types named in the titles. And if they are considered to be speed tests, it is notable that they sample speed under three different explicitly stated purposes.

Type LC, Level of Comprehension, appears to be much better adapted to the grade range than the first three. The test is strictly a power test, untimed, with increasingly difficult passages. The content is interesting and challenging. The items require close reading and a genuine understanding of the content of the passages. As in Type GS, however, the short passages and the one word responses limit the *range* of comprehension skills which can be assessed and do not do justice to a complex definition of comprehension.

Type RV, Reading Vocabulary, is the traditional type of vocabulary test, competently constructed.

The manual and the supplement to the manual are quite complete, well organized, and written in a style understandable to the typical user. As might be expected, the tests are highly intercorrelated, and in some instances the intertest correlations approach very closely the reliabilities of the tests. (In one of the more extreme situations, the correlation between Type RV and Type LC is reported as .89, which value is also reported for the equivalent forms reliability of each of the tests.) It is to the credit of the author that equivalent forms reliabilities, intercorrelations, and critical differences are reported, although the value of the data is somewhat restricted by small n's and lack of comparability of the many samples employed.

In the section on the interpretation of percentile ranks, the recommendation of a percentile band of ±5 percentile ranks seems extremely conservative. On Type GS, at grade 6.2, for example, this would average approximately ±.9 of a raw score unit, which is about one half the standard error of measurement (1.7).

SUMMARY. Three of the five tests put considerable emphasis on speed of comprehension, although they purport to measure thinking and understanding. In addition, the tests appear to be much better suited for use in grades 5 and 6 than in the other grades for which they are intended. Teachers and reading specialists, however, will find the tests useful as a diagnostic supplement to reading tests published as a part of achievement test batteries. The latter generally provide a more satisfactory measure of a greater variety of comprehension skills on longer passages.

ARTHUR E. TRAXLER, *Executive Director, Educational Records Bureau, New York, New York.*

The *Gates Basic Reading Tests,* designed for grades 3.5 to 8, are a second revision of the *Gates Silent Reading Tests,* first published in 1926 and revised in 1943. The present revision, issued in 1958, has evidently taken into account various suggestions made by reviewers in earlier yearbooks, and the resulting tests represent a considerable improvement over the original ones, although certain limitations that still exist will be mentioned in this review.

DESCRIPTION OF THE TESTS. The current edition is published in five separate booklets, each designed to measure a separate type of reading ability. The author recommends that all five be used as a team, although they are available individually or in any combination. The first three —GS, Reading to Appreciate General Significance; UD, Reading to Understand Precise Directions; and ND, Reading to Note Details— are intended to measure speed and accuracy of reading material of approximately uniform difficulty. The last two—RV, Reading Vocabulary, and LC, Level of Comprehension—consist of items of increasing difficulty and are designed as power tests.

All responses are recorded in the test booklets. No provision is made for separate answer sheets or machine scoring, although all except Type UD could readily be adapted to answer sheets. Scoring is done with strip keys except in the case of Type UD, where a transparent overlay key is used.

Each type exists in three forms, known as Forms 1, 2, and 3. The raw scores on these forms are reputed to be comparable, and the same norms are used with all three forms. The test construction procedures, as reported in the manual, should make for close comparability of the forms, but more evidence is needed concerning the relative difficulty of the three forms.

The tests are accompanied by a comprehensive 21-page manual and a 5-page supplement. The manual includes a brief description of the abilities tested, careful and detailed directions for giving and scoring the tests, grade and age norms, accuracy scores (percentages of exercises correct) and norms, percentile norms, instructions for interpreting the scores and ratings, suggestions for improving the abilities tested, a brief statement about the procedure used in the development of the norms, and other information.

The supplement is a more technical document. It gives a longer explanation of the preparation of the tests and the development of norms and discusses reliability coefficients, intercorrelations, standard errors of measurement, and the reliability and significance of differences between test scores. The supplement is a welcome addition to the Gates tests, which in earlier editions were notably lacking in statistical data on reliability and validity.

STRENGTHS OF THIS SERIES. The reading materials in the Gates tests reflect the competence of their author. The passages are well chosen and prepared, as would be expected from a person of Gates' stature in the reading field. Three of the five booklets, RS, UD, and ND, reflect some 35 years of experience in testing reading abilities of these particular types. Although data are not available concerning the importance of the five types of reading which these tests purport to measure, Gates, as a leading authority on reading, is in a favorable position to say what reading abilities are important, and this reviewer believes that the ones he has chosen would find wide acceptance among reading specialists.

Perhaps the greatest single strength of these tests lies in the sections of the manual in which suggestions for diagnosing abilities and deficiencies are made and guidance in improving the tested abilities is given. These sections should be of much help to teachers in interpreting the scores and making effective use of the results.

The normative population was apparently chosen with care, and it is believed that the norms should be representative of reading achievement in a nationwide sampling of public school pupils at these grade levels.

The format of the tests is good. They are clearly printed on paper stock of good quality. Through judicious use of some blue lines on the cover page, the tests are given a bright, attractive appearance, while, at the same time, their appearance is more reserved and professional than that of some of the modern tests prepared for use by elementary and junior high school pupils.

LIMITATIONS. Some essential statistical data for the basic tests either are lacking or are not especially impressive. All reliability coefficients reported in the supplement are above .80, but none reach .90, the point usually regarded as the reliability desirable for tests used in the study of individual pupils. However, since reliability was computed by the alternate form method, which tends to yield lower reliability coefficients

than the split-half method, these coefficients may be regarded as fairly satisfactory.

As already mentioned, statistical evidence concerning the relative difficulty of the three forms of each type seems to be lacking. Since the scores are reported as raw scores and since the same norms are used for all three forms, this is an omission of some importance. Remedial teachers in particular might draw erroneous conclusions concerning progress if they simply assumed all forms to be equivalent without definite evidence concerning this point.

The intercorrelations among the types raise a question as to whether these types of reading ability differ enough to make separate measurement worthwhile. The correlations between Reading Vocabulary and Level of Comprehension, for example, are almost as high as the reliability coefficients. It should be said, parenthetically, that this sort of outcome is by no means unique to the Gates tests; this oneness—this unity of the reading process—is at once the comfort and the despair of every person who has ever constructed a reading test.

Finally, among the limitations must be listed the structure of some of the tests themselves. In all educational measurement, when we have determined the objectives, scope, and relative emphases of the field to be measured, the goodness of a test comes down pretty much to how well prepared and useful the individual items are. In this respect, Type GS and Type LC are superior. The tests of the other three types seem to fare less well. In Type UD, a high score can be obtained simply by responding to the last sentence of each paragraph without reading the rest of the paragraph at all. Likewise, a good many of the questions in Type ND can be answered by a comparatively mature reader from general knowledge, without reading, or by very hastily skimming, the paragraphs. In these times when test taking begins in the cradle and stops only short of the grave, youngsters in the intermediate and upper grades are, one suspects, testwise enough to take full advantage of this situation.

The structure of Type RV, Reading Vocabulary, leaves most to be desired. Space limitations prevent expansion on this point. Suffice it to say that many of the items seem more nearly classification items than items testing incisive knowledge of word meaning and that one can be almost sure without an item analysis that many of the decoys are nonfunctioning. To take just one example from Form 2, item 11: "GIANT (1) big man, (2) fireman, (3) music, (4) bad man, (5) slowly." What eight- or nine-year-old, if he can recognize words at all, is going to choose "music" or "slowly" as a synonym for "giant"? Decoys usually serve the purpose better when they are more attractive than some of these seem to be. Notwithstanding these limitations, the available data indicate that the vocabulary scores are among the more reliable and valid scores yielded by this battery.

OVERALL APPRAISAL. On balance, the strengths of the *Gates Basic Reading Tests* outweigh their limitations. Such limitations as have been mentioned in this review arise partly from the unitary nature of the reading process itself, which tends to defy attempts to analyze it into types, partly from the testing technique used in certain booklets, and partly from one or two noteworthy statistical omissions or seeming inadequacies. The strengths come from the expert knowledge of the test author concerning what the important areas of reading development are and from his insight into the diagnosis and correction of the reading weaknesses indicated by the tests and his ability to convey this understanding to others through discussion in the manual.

For a review by S. S. Dunn, see 5:631; for reviews by George Spache, Herbert F. Spitzer, and T. L. Torgerson of an earlier edition, see 3:485; for reviews by Joseph C. Dewey and James R. Hobson of the original edition, see 40:1539 (1 excerpt).

[792]

Gates Primary Reading Tests. Grades 1–2.5; 1926–58; 3 scores: word recognition, sentence reading, paragraph reading; Forms 1, 2, 3, ('58, 4 pages); 3 tests; manual ('58, 14 pages); series supplement ('58, 5 pages); $1.50 per 35 tests; 50¢ per specimen set of all 3 tests; cash orders postpaid; 50(80) minutes; Arthur I. Gates; Bureau of Publications. *
a) TYPE PWR, WORD RECOGNITION. 15(25) minutes.
b) TYPE PSR, SENTENCE READING. 15(25) minutes.
c) TYPE PPR, PARAGRAPH READING. 20(30) minutes.

REFERENCES

1–7. See 3:486.
8–9. See 5:632.
10. NORTH, ROBERT D. "Difficulty and Reliability of the Gates Primary and Advanced Primary Reading Tests, 1958 Edition, for Independent School Pupils." *Ed Rec B* 76:45–51 F '60. *

WILLIAM ELLER, *Professor of Education, State University of New York at Buffalo, Buffalo, New York.*

In the extensive sequence of reading tests developed by Gates and his associates for use from kindergarten through grade 10, the *Gates Primary Reading Tests* were planned for grade 1 and the first half of grade 2. However, examination of the items and the norms indicates that in many American schools the tests could not profitably be administered earlier than about December of the first grade year.

Three 4-page booklets, each devoted to a certain reading subskill and each available in three equivalent forms, constitute the *Gates Primary Reading Tests*. The first, Type PWR was "designed to sample the ability to read words representative of the primary vocabulary." Each item consists of a picture accompanied by four words, and the pupil's task is to select the one word which "tells the most about the picture." The sight vocabulary tested is restricted to words which can be defined easily with pictures, with the result that about 75 per cent of the correct answers are nouns, and almost another fourth are verbs in each form. While a balanced representation of the different parts of speech may not be important, it is unfortunate that Type PWR cannot include any of the short, abstract words (these, from, was, etc.) which account for a large proportion of word recognition errors in grades 1 and 2.

Type PSR, Sentence Reading, consists of 45 sentences, each of which describes a picture which the child selects from a set of six pictures in a multiple choice arrangement. Typical picture-matched sentences are "Father is mending the gate" and "This is a dog." About a fifth of the sentences begin with "This is a," which means that only the ending poses a unique reading task in such sentences. If the common 3-word beginning had been used fewer times, Type PSR would test a greater variety of sentences, and the examinee would be forced to read all of each sentence.

Although Type PPR is described as a measure of paragraph reading, it could just as reasonably be titled a test of ability to follow printed directions, since each item instructs the reader to carry out some act with his pencil (draw a line, make an X). As in the two preceding tests, the items seem well graduated in difficulty. The manual includes two paragraphs which explain why the reading of paragraphs requires more advanced reading ability than the reading of single sentences as in Type PSR. Yet about 40 per cent of the items in each form of PPR are one-sentence items, although they appear to be more complex and time consuming than the single sentences of Type PSR.

The manual includes rather generous claims for the diagnostic potential of the tests. The author suggests that comparisons of results from Types PWR, PSR, and PPR will reveal the instructional needs of individuals and groups, because "the three tests measure different phases of reading ability." However, the supplement to the manual lists the following intercorrelations: between PWR and PSR, .80; between PWR and PPR, .82; between PSR and PPR, .84. Intercorrelations of these magnitudes indicate that the three tests do not measure three discrete abilities but are very nearly testing the same skill. Further, the reported intercorrelations so nearly approach the alternate forms reliabilities of the three types (.86, .87, and .89) that sizeable grade-level differences between the three types for any given pupil should be interpreted as errors of measurement and not as diagnostic revelations. Because the three types are evidently measuring the same basic ability, they should be perceived as three parts of a single test, and the publisher should provide a scheme for weighting them into one composite score.

Teachers and supervisors who have used the *Gates Primary Reading Tests* for several years report that they are easy to administer because the directions in the manual are clear and complete and because the examiner does not have to possess much sophistication about measurement. Test users in the field also comment that the tests correlate well with other measures of reading ability, including overall appraisals by classroom teachers.

The *Gates Primary Reading Tests* have enjoyed considerable popularity for many years, and it is likely that they will continue to be regarded favorably by teachers and administrators for certain practical reasons: (*a*) All three tests can be administered in a total of 50 minutes (plus explanation time). (*b*) The items require examinee activities that teachers consider to be valid measures of primary reading skill. (*c*) Information concerning norms is plentiful and easy to interpret. (*d*) The manual includes pedagogic suggestions for improving the specific abilities identified by the tests.

COLEMAN MORRISON, *Assistant Professor of Education, Rhode Island College, Providence, Rhode Island.*

Although the general purpose of these tests is described as diagnostic, the end result falls far short of this objective. One of the chief characteristics of a diagnostic test is to provide the tester with some of the causal factors relating to failure. Yet this element is missing as the present tests are designed. Essentially the tests consist of three parts, Word Recognition, Sentence Reading, and Paragraph Reading. The tester can determine the extent to which the student does well or poorly on each of these areas, but in those instances where he does poorly no rationale is available to ascertain why. In this respect the tests might best be labeled as "survey" rather than diagnostic. It is altogether possible, however, that the author had some different concept of diagnosis than the reviewer since the examples of "diagnosis" that are included in the manual merely point up the obvious (e.g., "Pupil B is retarded in reading....and about equally weak in all three abilities").

There is also some question relating to the accuracy of other statements found in the manual—particularly those relating to the paragraph reading and sentence reading subtests. In this respect the contention in the manual that "the third test [paragraph reading] requires the reading of paragraphs" is very misleading. Actually, of the 26 paragraph items, 11 are of the one-sentence variety and of the remaining 15, 8 can be answered by identifying only one sentence (e.g., "A teacher told the boy to jump into the water for the ball. Draw a line from the boy to the ball").

Similarly, in the sentence reading subtest students can, by identifying one word as opposed to the entire sentence, score correct responses. Admittedly this may involve superior intelligence on the part of the testee, but invariably illustrations that accompany such items are so unequivocal as to almost preclude the possibility of the student making any other selection if he can identify one key word.

Although the manual consistently refers to "representative vocabulary," "representative pupils," "representative passages," "representative sentences," without further elaboration, more detailed information is given in a supplementary manual ("for readers who desire a more extended description of norms, the test reliability data, and the standardization procedures"), which helps clarify some of these obscure phrases. Yet one is never really clear as to what the test vocabulary is actually representative of!

On the other hand, the manual does provide some helpful suggestions for teachers to assist children to overcome word recognition and comprehension difficulties. Similarly helpful is the discussion of the conversion of raw scores into age, grade, and percentile scores.

If teachers follow scoring directions as indicated, the process in correcting 30 or more tests could be extremely time consuming since marks must be made for both right and wrong answers for Word Recognition. In addition, for Paragraph Reading, the scorer is asked to indicate the number of test items that the testee attempted although no subsequent use is made of this information in the scoring. Although overlays are provided which facilitate the scoring process, guides to assist in the interpretation of children's marks are complicated and unnecessary.

One minor point—the words "pencil" and "crayon" are used interchangeably, a practice that could conceivably confuse some young children taking the tests. One might also question the standardization of the tests, especially since the tester is given the liberty to "supplement or to alter the directions or illustrative procedures" and to provide "extra time" for some children.

In summary, these tests have certain advantages as survey tests but leave much to be desired as diagnostic instruments.

For reviews by William S. Gray and George Spache of an earlier edition, see 3:486.

[793]

*Gates Reading Survey. Grades 3.5–10; 1939–60; 5 scores: speed and accuracy, accuracy, vocabulary, level of comprehension, total; IBM for grades 4–10; 2 editions; series manual supplement ('58, 5 pages); $2.75 per 35 tests; postpaid; Arthur I. Gates; Bureau of Publications. *
a) HAND SCORED EDITION. Grades 3.5–10; Forms 1, 2, 3, ('58, 8 pages); revised manual ('60, c1958, 15 pages); 50¢ per specimen set; (50–60) minutes.
b) MACHINE SCORED EDITION. Grades 4–10; Forms M1, M2, M3, ('58, 8 pages); revised manual ('60, c1958, 16 pages); separate answer sheets must be used; $1.25 per 35 IBM answer sheets; $1 per set of scoring stencils; $1 per specimen set; (60–70) minutes.

REFERENCES

1. GATES, ARTHUR I. *The Improvement of Reading: A Program of Diagnostic and Remedial Methods, Third Edition.* New York: Macmillan Co., 1947. Pp. xxi, 657. * (*PA* 22:3195)
2. McQUEEN, ROBERT, AND WILLIAMS, KENNETH C. "Predicting Success in Beginning High School Algebra." *Psychol Rep* 4:603–6 D '58. * (*PA* 34:2009)
3. WEST, DORAL N. "Reducing Chance in Test Selection." *Personnel & Guid J* 36:420–1 F '58. *
4. BARRETT, HARRY O. "The Predictive Efficiency of Grade 8 Objective Tests in Terms of Grade 9 Achievement." *Ont J Ed Res* 2:101–7 Ap '60. *
5. CLELAND, DONALD L., AND TOUSSAINT, ISABELLA H. "The Interrelationships of Reading, Listening, Arithmetic Computation and Intelligence." *Reading Teach* 15:228–31 Ja '62. *
6. TRELA, THADDEUS MICHAEL. *A Comparison of Ninth Grade Achievement on Selected Measures of General Reading Comprehension, Critical Thinking, and General Educational Development.* Doctor's thesis, University of Missouri (Columbia, Mo.), 1962. (*DA* 23:2382)
7. FORTENBERRY, WARREN D., AND BROOME, BILLY J. "Comparison of the Gates Reading Survey and the Reading Section of the Wide Range Achievement Test." *J Develop Read* 7:66–8 au '63. *

GEORGE D. SPACHE, *Professor of Education, and Head, Reading Laboratory and Clinic, University of Florida, Gainesville, Florida.*

This version of the *Gates Reading Survey* represents a 1960 revision or, more properly, a 1960 reprinting of the 1958 edition. The most extensive change in the latest edition is a simplification of a table on page 10 of the manual to clarify the significance of differences among subtest scores.

The 1958 test does not differ materially from the edition of 20 years ago in type of content, rationale, and structure. There are still three subtests: a 36-item speed and accuracy test, a 60-item vocabulary test (65 in the hand scoring edition), and a 43-item level of comprehension test. The speed and accuracy test requires the reading of two- to three-sentence paragraphs, all of similar difficulty, each followed by a simple multiple choice question measuring comprehension of the inferential type. The level of comprehension subtest involves very short paragraphs of increasing difficulty in which comprehension is measured by choosing appropriate words to fit two or three blanks in the paragraphs. The vocabulary subtest requires the simple matching of a word with a synonymous word among the five given choices.

Some of the criticisms of the early edition have been recognized in this revision by supplying a printed scoring key and by clarifying directions slightly. Other objections have not been met, such as the need for instructing the student that the vocabulary and level of comprehension tests are not speed tests, or that he is not to proceed to the next subtest if he finishes quickly, or that the range of items extends up to the tenth grade and therefore he may not be expected to do all items. The use of rather vague directions regarding the time limit for the two power type tests has also persisted. Recent research has shown that the use of the cloze procedure (supplying words for blanks in reading material) as used in the level of comprehension test is a valid reading measure, despite earlier objections.

The author has persisted in the use of some reading tasks of a highly artificial nature with the result that estimates of reading ability are yielded which, in the opinion of many users of the earlier edition, exceed or are unrelated to the pupil's classroom functioning. The speed of comprehension test is particularly susceptible to this criticism. The simplicity of the test may permit good, rapid readers of, say, the third and fourth grades to achieve rather exalted scores in this task, in this reviewer's experience. The correction of the accuracy score on this test for possible guessing is only partially successful in combating this tendency.

Both measures of speed and level of comprehension require largely inferential thinking, a legitimate type of comprehension question but one seldom stressed in the average classroom. The relationship between this mode of testing and the skills of immediate recall of details and main ideas is unknown. Thus the value of these tests in predicting classroom performances, as these are commonly judged by the teacher, is questionable.

The assigning of a grade score to a raw score of zero on each test is hardly defensible, even though the manual does suggest caution in interpreting scores at either extreme. Most teachers do not read manuals very carefully, except perhaps for the directions for administering the tests. Furthermore, many teachers are very naïve in their wholehearted acceptance of test scores as accurate reflections of pupil performances.

The reliability coefficients for each of the subtests for each grade from third to eighth are in the .80's and certainly adequate for most testing purposes. In addition, unlike many test authors, Gates supplies a table indicating the minimum differences necessary for significant variations among subtest scores.

The data on the intercorrelations of the three subtests indicate moderate relationships between speed and level of comprehension (.63–.71) and marked relationship between vocabulary and level of comprehension (in the .80's). These facts seem to imply that there is a justification for reporting the two comprehension scores separately. There is no apparent explanation for the high correlations between the vocabulary and level of comprehension tests.

The inherent difficulty of the scaling of the test items, particularly in the level of comprehension and vocabulary subtests, raises some questions regarding the effective range of use of the test. Upper third grade pupils, the youngest for whom the test is offered, will succeed with approximately 25 per cent of the items in each subtest. At this level, the test would appear to be very difficult and discouraging for such pupils. There is also the question of the validity of the scores for these children, or for those third graders of lesser achievement, as the author himself suggests. Since mid-fourth graders will achieve 33–39 per cent of the items of the tests, it would appear that this level is preferable as the lower limit of the range of applicability.

Despite the many minor limitations, this test will probably continue to find wide and profitable use in survey testing and in evaluations of reading programs and of school systems, even though it lacks diagnostic features and may lack close relationships to teacher estimates.

MOREY J. WANTMAN, *Director of Advisory and Instructional Programs, Educational Testing Service, Princeton, New Jersey.*

The stated purpose of the *Gates Reading Survey* is "to reveal specific strengths and weaknesses in reading abilities, and thereby to indicate the type of training most needed by a class or individual pupil. The tests....are, in other words, diagnostic."

The speed and accuracy score is equal to the number of correct answers on 36 reading comprehension type items. The "accuracy" score is equal to the speed and accuracy score divided by the total number of the correct and incorrect responses. The time limit for this test is from four minutes to eight minutes, depending on the grade level and whether the hand scored or machine scored edition is used. The vocabulary score is based on 60 or 65 words, for which "another word....that means the same or nearly the same" is to be determined. The level of comprehension score is based on 21 passages in which two or three blanks are to be filled in with words that make "the best sense" for the passage. The maximum possible score for level of comprehension is 43. Both the vocabulary and level of comprehension tests are untimed, but about 20 to 25 minutes is suggested. The "total" score is an average score and is based on the reading grade scores for speed and accuracy, vocabulary, and comprehension.

CONTENT. The materials for the tests were carefully selected and subjected to tryout, analysis, and revision. Nevertheless, in view of the directions for the vocabulary test, some of the items are questionable and might cause difficulties for good readers at the higher grade levels. The directions for this test (see above) are likely to be interpreted by pupils to mean that they are to supply synonyms for the words in the stem of the questions. In all three forms of the vocabulary test the correct response is not always a synonym of the stem word but sometimes is either a general term for the stem word or a specific example of the stem word. For example, both the words "three" and "sixteen" appear as stem words in Form M2 and the correct answer for each of these is "number"; and for the stem word "animal," the correct answer is "horse." The directions for the vocabulary test should be revised so pupils will not expect the correct response always to be a synonym.

The tests are intended for grades 3.5 to 10; a wide range of difficulty of content material has therefore been included. The questions appearing early in the tests are far too easy for pupils in grades 9 and 10, and the questions at the end of the test are much too difficult for the youngest pupils. This situation, together with evidence cited below regarding the tables of norms, forces one to question the appropriateness of the tests for grades 3, 4, 9, and 10.

FORMAT. The format of the tests is good. The machine scored edition has one continuous numbering system for the questions of the three tests and has different designations for the options in adjacent questions, thus minimizing the chances of a pupil's marking his response in the wrong position on the answer sheet.

Directions to the teacher for administration of the tests also appear on the front cover of the test booklet for all forms. It seems unwise to have material on the test booklet which is not intended for the pupil.

SCORING. The scoring of the tests for the hand scored edition is cumbersome. The method for handling fractional scores for the vocabulary test and the level of comprehension test is not consistent for the hand scored and machine scored editions; it is not clear why the same rounding rules were not used for the two editions.

NORMS. An attempt was made to base the norms for the tests on a nationwide sampling of schools so that representative types of instruction, socioeconomic status, and levels of intelligence are appropriately sampled. The normative figures are based on 23,100 cases. However, the tables of norms contain flaws and inconsistencies which trouble this reviewer.

The maximum possible score on the speed and accuracy test is 36 and there are four options in each question; thus, the "chance score" is 9. Since there is no correction for wrong responses, a score below 10 is not meaningful. Nevertheless, in one of the tables for this test a reading grade score as high as 4.8 is presented as equivalent to a raw score of 9.

For grades 4 and 5 the table of norms for the speed and accuracy test for the machine scored edition is identical to the corresponding table of the hand scored edition even though there are different time allowances for the two editions. On the other hand, for grades 6–10 the machine scored edition norms and the hand scored edition norms are different for this test.

Discrepancies between the machine and hand scored editions also appear in the norms tables of the vocabulary test. The machine scored and hand scored editions are reported to be identical item for item. Actually, there are 65 items in the vocabulary test of the hand scored edition, of which only 60 appear in the machine scored edition. In spite of this difference, it is difficult to understand, in view of the fact that the "items are arranged in order of increasing difficulty," why a raw score of 10 yields a reading grade of 2.8 on the hand scored edition and a reading grade of 3.1 for the machine scored edition. A similar situation occurs for the comprehension test: a raw score of 10 on the hand scored edition yields a reading grade of 3.3, and the same raw score on the machine scored edition yields a reading grade of 3.7. In the case of the comprehension test the items in the hand scored and machine scored editions are identical, and there is no time limit for either edition.

The percentile norms provided are presented in a form which makes their use unnecessarily involved. (a) A conversion of the raw score to a reading grade must be made in one table and then the reading grade converted to a percentile rank by use of a different table. In this connection a description of the use of percentile ranks in the manual implies that the percentile rank is known and that one can interpret something from it about the reading grade level. The situation is just the reverse: the reading grade is known before the percentile rank is obtained. (*b*) The percentile tables provide only data for percentile ranks which are multiples of five. A teacher would therefore sometimes be unable to find the entry he was looking for in the body of the table.

It is not clear from the descriptions in the manuals and supplement exactly how the percentiles were determined. In the percentile tables for the hand scored edition, entries are provided for grade positions from 3.5 through 10.8. There are 23 different grade position sets of percentiles. The data for each grade position is labeled at the top of the column. The entry for the 50th percentile for a given column usually agrees exactly with the column designation, but this is not always the case. The largest discrepancy occurs in Table 6 in the manual for the hand scored edition: for grade position 10.8 of the speed and accuracy test, the 50th percentile is reported as 10.4. Whether or not any such discrepancies could or should occur depends on the method of deriving the percentile ranks and the median reading grades.

The manuals illustrate the averaging of percentile ranks to obtain an overall score for speed, vocabulary, and comprehension. This procedure is highly questionable.

No data are provided for school or group norms, and the manuals' instructions for interpretation of group results imply that the tables for individual norms should be used. Such use could lead to erroneous interpretations.

The description of procedures for the development of norms for the machine scored edition implies that the machine scored edition was not used in the norming process. The norms for the machine scored tests are "adjusted to take account of the differences in the two editions." The discussion of norms for the machine scored edition is again not specific enough to make clear the method by which they were obtained.

RELIABILITY. The reliability figures presented in the supplement are equivalent forms reliabilities. They are presented for five different grade positions for each test and they range from a low of .82 to a high of .89. These reliability coefficients are certainly acceptable. The author rightly points out that competing tests may be reporting split-half reliability figures, which of course would be much higher for his tests if he had reported them. Furthermore, in

a conservative discussion of reliability, the author warns that a wider range of reading ability in given school systems "would probably yield larger standard deviations and standard errors of measurement." Such systems may not in fact "yield larger standard errors of measurement" because the coefficient of reliability may be higher.

In discussing reliability and sources of unreliability, the author consistently omits the factor which is, to this reviewer, the most important—viz., the sampling of questions. In short, the use of different forms of the tests could result in different scores because of this factor alone. In this connection, it should be pointed out that no evidence for the equivalence of forms is presented. The forms are merely stated to be equivalent.

The discussion in the manuals on the reliability of differences with respect to pupil averages at times is excellent and extremely conservative, and the emphasis on practical significance as opposed to statistical significance is commendable. On the other hand, the discussion on reliability of differences is sometimes vague and not always consistent with the figures presented for standard errors of measurement.

Reliability figures are presented in the supplement to the manuals as if the figures applied equally well to the machine and hand scored editions. A question therefore arises as to why the two editions differ in the figures presented for "Smallest Difference Between Reading Grade Scores That May Be Regarded as Both Statistically and Practically Significant."

VALIDITY. Neither the manuals nor the supplement presents any data on the validity of the tests. The supplement makes the claim that studies of the tests have been carried on since 1928 and that the number is so large that listing them all would be prohibitive. A partial list is presented, but the most recent entry is more than 15 years old.

SUMMARY. The *Gates Reading Survey* is a useful instrument for determining the level of competence in reading of a group of pupils. The reliability coefficients are satisfactory, and the material in the tests has face validity. On the other hand, the tests are probably not appropriate for grades 3, 4, 9, and 10, and the scores are not likely to prove very helpful for individual diagnosis. This reviewer would like to see more information presented on the methods for establishing the tables of norms, particularly the percentile tables, and evidence on the equivalence of the different forms of the tests.

For reviews by Dorothy E. Holberg and Herbert F. Spitzer of an earlier edition, see 3:487.

[794]
*Iowa Silent Reading Tests: New Edition. Grades 4–8, 9–14; 1927–56; IBM and (grades 4–8) MRC; Forms AM Revised, BM Revised, ('43, c1927–39), CM, DM, ('43, c1942); 2 levels; manual ('43, 16 pages) for each level; separate answer sheets may be used; $2.45 per 35 IBM answer sheets; 60¢ per set of scoring stencils; 40¢ per specimen set of either level; postage extra; H. A. Greene, A. N. Jorgensen (b), and V. H. Kelley; [Harcourt, Brace & World, Inc.]. *
a) ELEMENTARY TEST. Grades 4–8; 1933–56; IBM and MRC; 4 forms (12 pages); 9 scores: rate, comprehension, directed reading, word meaning, paragraph comprehension, sentence meaning, alphabetizing, use of index, total; supplementary directions ('56, 4 pages) for use with separate answer sheets; $4.10 per 35 tests; $8 per 100 MRC answer sheets; $1.60 per set of MRC stencils for hand scoring (machine scoring service, by Measurement Research Center, Inc., may be arranged through the publisher); 49(60) minutes.
b) ADVANCED TEST. Grades 9–14; 1927–43; IBM; 4 forms (16 pages); 10 scores: rate, comprehension, directed reading, poetry comprehension, word meaning, sentence meaning, paragraph comprehension, use of index, selection of key words, total; $5.40 per 35 tests; 45(60) minutes.

REFERENCES

1–6. See 40:1547.
7–27. See 3:489.
28. TERRY, PAUL W. "The Prognostic Value of Different Types of Tests in Courses in Educational Psychology." *J Appl Psychol* 18:231–40 Ap '34. * (PA 8:5251)
29. TRAXLER, ARTHUR E. "Sex Differences in Rate of Reading in the High School." *J Appl Psychol* 19:351–2 Je '35. * (PA 10:625)
30. GARRISON, K. C. "The Use of Psychological Tests in the Selection of Student-Nurses." *J Appl Psychol* 23:461–72 Ag '39. * (PA 13:6426)
31. SHERMAN, ORPHA. "A Comparative Study of the A.C.E. Test and the Iowa Silent Reading Test." *Proc Iowa Acad Sci* 46:291–3 '39. *
32. MOORE, JOSEPH E. "A Study of Sex Differences in Speed of Reading." *Peabody J Ed* 17:359–63 My '40. * (PA 14:6218)
33. SLOCUM, ROGER LEON. *Reading Status of University of Wisconsin Freshmen.* Doctor's thesis, University of Wisconsin (Madison, Wis.), 1940.
34. LANGSAM, ROSALIND STREEP. *A Factorial Analysis of Reading Ability.* Doctor's thesis, New York University (New York, N.Y.), 1941.
35. ADAMS, MICHAEL. "The Prediction of Scholastic Success in a College of Law." *Proc Iowa Acad Sci* 49:385–9 '42. * (PA 17:2871)
36. GIESECKE, G. E.; LARSEN, R. P.; AND WITTENBORN, J. R. "Factors Contributing to Achievement in the Study of Elementary German." *Mod Lang J* 27:254–62 Ap '43. *
37. HAVIGHURST, ROBERT J., AND JANKE, LEOTA LONG. "Relations Between Ability and Social Status in a Midwestern Community: 1, Ten-Year-Old Children." *J Ed Psychol* 35:357–68 S '44. * (PA 19:476)
38. HUMBER, WILBUR J. "The Relationship Between Reading Efficiency and Academic Success in Selected University Curricula." *J Ed Psychol* 35:17–26 Ja '44. * (PA 18:2581)
39. SOLOMON, LEWIS E. *Some Relationships Between Reading Ability and Degree of Academic Success in College.* Doctor's thesis, University of Colorado (Boulder, Colo.), 1944.
40. GLADFELTER, MILLARD E. "An Analysis of Reading and English Changes That Occur During the Freshman Year in College." *J Am Assn Col Reg* 20:527–43 Jl '45. * (PA 20:2073)
41. JANKE, LEOTA LONG, AND HAVIGHURST, ROBERT J. "Relations Between Ability and Social Status in a Mid-Western Community: 2, Sixteen-Year-Old Boys and Girls." *J Ed Psychol* 36:499–509 N '45. * (PA 20:1999)
42. SMITH, FRANCIS F. "The Use of Previous Record in Estimating College Success." *J Ed Psychol* 36:167–76 Mr '45. * (PA 19:2377)
43. PRESTON, RALPH C., AND TUFT, EDWIN N. "The Reading Habits of Superior College Students." *J Exp Ed* 16:196–202 Mr '48. * (PA 20:5126)
44. *Selection and Training of Shorthand Students in Ontario Secondary Schools.* A study conducted by the Shorthand Survey Committee of the Ontario Commercial Teachers' Association and the Department of Educational Research, Ontario College of Education, University of Toronto. Toronto, Canada: Sir Isaac Pitman & Sons (Canada) Ltd., 1949. Pp. vii, 68. *
45. BUTLER, ALFRED JAMES. *An Analysis of the Iowa Silent Reading Advanced Tests, Form Cm.* Master's thesis, University of British Columbia (Vancouver, B.C., Canada), 1949.
46. PFLIEGER, ELMER F. "A Study of Reading Grade Levels." *J Ed Res* 42:541–6 Mr '49. * (PA 23:5752)
47. TRAXLER, ARTHUR E. "Correlations Between Scores on Various Reading Tests Administered Several Months Apart." *Ed Rec B* 52:78–82 Jl '49. * (PA 24:748)
48. TREUMANN, MILDRED JENKINS, AND SULLIVAN, BEN A. "Use of the Engineering and Physical Science Aptitude Test as a Predictor of Academic Achievement of Freshman Engineering Students." *J Ed Res* 43:129–33 O '49. * (PA 24:2804)
49. TRAXLER, ARTHUR E. "Intercorrelations and Validity of Scores on Three Reading Tests." *Ed Rec B* 56:79–89 Ja '51. * (PA 25:6416)
50. MANSON, WILLIAM Y. *A Survey of the Use of the Iowa Silent Reading Test in Virginia Group III High Schools.* Master's thesis, University of Richmond (Richmond, Va.), 1951.
51. BARBE, WALTER, AND GRILK, WERNER. "Correlations Between Reading Factors and IQ." *Sch & Soc* 75:134–6 Mr 1 '52. *
52. PRESTON, RALPH C., AND BOTEL, MORTON. "The Relation of Reading Skill and Other Factors to the Academic Achievement of 2048 College Students." *J Exp Ed* 20:363–71 Je '52. * (PA 27:2967)
53. RIDLEY, WALTER NATHANIEL. *Prognostic Values of Freshman Tests Used at Virginia State College.* Doctor's thesis, University of Virginia (Charlottesville, Va.), 1953. (DA 14:1042)
54. CHAPMAN, HAROLD M. "The Prediction of Freshman Achievement From a Combination of Test Scores and High School Grades." Abstract. *Am Psychologist* 10:373 Ag '55. *
55. CHAPMAN, HAROLD MARTIN. *The Prediction of Freshman Scholarship From a Combination of Standardized Test Scores and High School Grades.* Doctor's thesis, University of Houston (Houston, Tex.), 1955. (DA 15:1201)
56. DUNGAN, EARL WILLIAM. *An Evaluation of the Orientation Test Battery at Dickinson State Teachers College for Purposes of Prediction and Counseling.* Doctor's field study, Colorado State College of Education (Greeley, Colo.), 1955.
57. ANDERSON, RODNEY EBON. *The Use of Entrance Tests in the Differential Prediction of Freshman College Achievement, and the Effect of an Item Analysis on the Efficiency of the Predictive Batteries.* Doctor's thesis, Indiana University (Bloomington, Ind.), 1956. (DA 16:2344)
58. BONNER, LEON WILLIAM. *Factors Associated With the Academic Achievement of Freshmen Students at a Southern Agricultural College.* Doctor's thesis, Pennsylvania State University (State College, Pa.), 1956. (DA 17:266)
59. SHAW, GERALDINE SAX. "Prediction of Success in Elementary Algebra." *Math Teach* 49:173–8 Mr '56. *
60. GOWAN, J. C. "Intelligence, Interests, and Reading Ability in Relation to Scholastic Achievement." *Psychol Newsl* 8:85–7 Mr–Ap '57. * (PA 32:3346)
61. CAMPBELL, ROBERT J. *An Analysis to Determine the Value of Otis I.Q. Test and the Iowa Silent Reading Test in Predicting Final Academic Success of Adams State College Students.* Master's thesis, Adams State College (Alamosa, Colo.), 1958.
62. CHAMPION, JOHN MILLS. *A Method for Predicting Success of Commerce Students.* Doctor's thesis, Purdue University (Lafayette, Ind.), 1958. (DA 19:2134)
63. NORTON, DANIEL P. "The Relationship of Study Habits and Other Measures to Achievement in Ninth-Grade General Science." *J Exp Ed* 27:211–7 Mr '59. * (PA 35:1283)
64. GARRETT, WILEY S. "Prediction of Academic Success in a School of Nursing." *Personnel & Guid J* 38:500–3 F '60. * (PA 35:3954)
65. SCARBOROUGH, ROSA L. *A Comparative Study of the Results of the Iowa Silent Reading Tests, Forms AM and BM Administered to the 9th and 12th Grades of the Booker T. Washington High School, Reidsville, North Carolina, 1960.* Master's thesis, Agricultural and Technical College (Greensboro, N.C.), 1961.

66. CRANE, WILLIAM J. "Screening Devices for Occupational Therapy Majors." *Am J Occup Ther* 16:131–2 My–Je '62. * (*PA* 37:4078)
67. JONES, KENNETH J. "Predicting Achievement in Chemistry: A Model." *J Res Sci Teach* 1:226–31 S '63. *

WORTH R. JONES, *Professor of Education, University of Cincinnati, Cincinnati, Ohio.*

Except for the supplementary directions for use with machine scored answer sheets, the *Iowa Silent Reading Tests* and manuals have been unchanged since last reviewed by Davis and Turnbull in *The Third Mental Measurements Yearbook* (3:489). The reader should note also the reviews by Booker and Roberts (40:1547). Pertinent comments regarding the content, the validity, and the reliability of these tests have been expressed adequately by these men. The major purpose of this review will be that of attempting to evaluate the role that these tests have today.

Upon examination it soon becomes evident that some of the paragraphs and statements used in the tests contain informational material which is considerably outdated. For example, in the Elementary Test both Forms CM and DM have sections describing dictating machines using revolving wax cylinders. Machines in use today have magnetic tapes, wires, and plastic belts. Several other instances of antiquated material and ambiguous references could be cited in the tests where items pertain to such things as "the League of Nations," "the production of corn," and "The World War." Also, it is felt that the paragraph comprehension subtests are somewhat jumbled, and the sentence meaning subtests contain too many specific determiners which tend to give away the correct answers.

The availability of four alternative forms at each level is a desirable feature of these tests, but it is important to note that the forms were equated, scaled, and standardized in 1942. According to the manuals, the standardization groups were located in communities and states "widely distributed geographically." The manuals fail to give adequate information concerning the identity of these communities and states. The claim is made, however, that "These data represent a wide sampling of the elementary school population [and the high school population] of the United States." The only two communities identified are Salem, Massachusetts, and Rochester, New Hampshire. Furthermore, the lack of representative norms for grade 13 is a decided weakness.

Because of the limitations and weaknesses mentioned, it is the opinion of this reviewer that the *Iowa Silent Reading Tests* should not be used unless they are thoroughly revised. Readers who are primarily interested in selecting a test for high school and college students which measures reading comprehension and speed of comprehension might consider the *Davis Reading Test* or the *Nelson-Denny Reading Test.* Both of these tests can be administered during a regular class period, and adequate standardization data are included in the manuals.

Several of the available achievement test batteries include reading tests which may be used effectively to measure important skills in reading at elementary school grade levels. Some of those containing subtests similar to the ones found in the *Iowa Silent Reading Tests* are the *Iowa Tests of Basic Skills,* the *Stanford Achievement Test,* and the *Metropolitan Achievement Tests.* The *Stanford Achievement Test* (1964 edition) has an attractive, new format and new norms. It seems to offer excellent possibilities for future use.

The *SRA Achievement Series* and the *Sequential Tests of Educational Progress* also include rather good tests of reading comprehension. One limitation of these tests, however, is the fact that they require more than one class period to administer.

In summary, this reviewer is of the opinion that the *Iowa Silent Reading Tests,* in their present form, no longer serve the purpose for which they were intended.

For reviews by Frederick B. Davis and William W. Turnbull, see 3:489 (2 excerpts); for reviews by Ivan A. Booker and Holland D. Roberts of an earlier edition, see 40:1547.

[795]

Lee-Clark Reading Test, 1958 Revision. Grades 1, 1–2; 1931–58; Forms A, B, ('58, 6–8 pages); 2 levels; manual ('58, 12 pages) for each level; $2.80 per 35 tests, postage extra; 25¢ per specimen set, postpaid; (20–30) minutes; J. Murray Lee and Willis W. Clark; California Test Bureau. *
a) PRIMER. Grade 1; 4 scores: auditory stimuli, visual stimuli, following directions, total.
b) FIRST READER. Grades 1–2; 6 scores: same as for primer level plus completion, inference.

THOMAS C. BARRETT, *Assistant Professor of Education, The University of Wisconsin, Madison, Wisconsin.*

The *Lee-Clark Reading Test,* Primer and First Reader, is designed to determine in an objective manner the reading ability of first and second grade students. The Primer has three parts: (a) Auditory Stimuli tests the subject's ability to hear, remember, and select from four alternatives a word pronounced by the teacher; (b) Visual Stimuli measures word recognition by requiring subjects to relate a number of words to a number of pictures; and (c) Following Directions involves the marking of pictures in prescribed ways on the basis of directions given in sentence form. In addition to the three parts just described, the First Reader provides two additional parts: (a) Completion requires the subject to choose from three alternatives a word that best completes a sentence; and (b) Inferences measures the ability to select a word from three choices that best completes the second sentence in a two sentence story.

Reliability coefficients of .83 and .90 were obtained for the Primer and First Reader, respectively, using the K-R 21. The number of subjects, grade placements, means, standard deviations, and standard errors of measurement are reported for both of these studies. Although the magnitudes of the reliability coefficients appear to be adequate, the test user should interpret them with several facts in mind. First, the samples used in the two investigations were relatively small and the process used in selecting the samples is not described. Second, the possibility that the time limits placed on the parts of the tests might produce spuriously high reliability coefficients is open to question. Finally, the forms of the tests used in these reliability studies are not given.

Content validity of the tests was determined through a comparison of the vocabulary used in the tests with the vocabularies found in first and second grade books of three widely used basic reading series and with Gates' *Reading Vocabulary for the Primary Grades*. The results of the analyses indicated that the vast majority of words used in the *Lee-Clark Reading Test* were common to both the criteria used. It should be noted, however, that the Gates Reading Vocabulary was published in 1926 and that no dates are given for the readers used.

Another facet of validity of both the Primer and First Reader tests is demonstrated by comparing results on the tests with the results on a number of other standardized reading achievement tests. Twenty studies involved the Primer,

Form A, while 18 studies utilized an unidentified form of the First Reader. The correlation coefficients range from .35 to .91 for the former and from .64 to .88 for the latter. Adequate information regarding the grade placements, numbers, means, and standard deviations for the subjects involved in each study is reported in the manual. Test users will have to make their own judgments with respect to adequacy of the results of these studies on the basis of their knowledge of the reliability and validity of the criterion measures, since this information is not provided. Furthermore, any judgments should take into consideration the relatively small number of subjects used in the majority of these studies and the lack of information about their selection.

Percentile and grade placement norms are provided for both the Primer and the First Reader. Grade placement norms are based on two groups of students for each test. The first group is described as normal in intelligence and as a representative national sample with respect to the various types of reading instruction encountered throughout the country. Subjects in the second group are pictured as being representative of above average students enrolled in schools where reading instruction is introduced early in first grade. Although the availability of norms for two different groups of first and second grade readers is most worthwhile, there is, unfortunately, no detailed description of the characteristics of the subjects or the means of selecting them. Therefore, the test user must rely on the judgment of the authors with regard to the adequacy of the standardization sample and the resulting norms.

The manuals provide helpful discussions with respect to test interpretation and the use of test results, e.g., the intelligence of subjects as a factor in interpreting test results and the diagnostic value of part scores. The former discussion should be particularly helpful to the test user since it points out the different meanings of norms for different groups of children depending on their intellectual abilities. Regarding an analysis of part scores on either test, teachers may be able to detect gross intra-individual differences for a student, as the authors suggest, but they should be careful about accepting minute differences on the part scores as indicative of definite differences in the reading abilities measured, since the reliability of part scores and the intercorrelations among the parts are not provided.

In general, the Primer and First Reader tests sample the types of reading behavior that are customarily accepted as being representative of first and second grade reading development and appear to provide an adequate survey of these reading skills. Teachers should have no difficulty with the mechanics of administering and scoring the tests. Furthermore, the technical aspects of the tests appear to be relatively adequate when compared to other tests of this nature; however, test users should keep in mind the shortcomings mentioned above, particularly the lack of information about the subjects upon which the norms were based, when test results are interpreted.

COLEMAN MORRISON, *Assistant Professor of Education, Rhode Island College, Providence, Rhode Island.*

Of the several weaknesses inherent in these tests the most outstanding appears to be the difficulty in interpreting test norms. To determine grade placement of children taking either the Primer or the First Reader tests, the testees can be assigned to either of two groups. To be assigned to "group 2" are those "above average" pupils who are introduced to "formal reading" during the first grade (by example this is indicated to be "late in the first semester" in the Primer manual, and "late in the second semester" in the First Reader manual). To be assigned to group 1 are children of "normal intelligence" who as a group begin "formal reading" after children in group 2, by implication, at some undisclosed time *after* the first grade.

Perhaps much of the confusion that ensues in attempting to assign a pupil to a particular group stems from the absence of any clearly defined explanation of what constitutes "formal reading," what is meant by "above average groups of children," and the altogether amorphous starting time when the two "fairly representative groups" of children begin reading. Additionally there would appear to be no norms to determine the grade placement of children who had been taught to read in the kindergarten or very early in the first grade, or for groups of children introduced to reading at various times during grade 1.

Apart from grade placement norms, "age in months" figures are provided, but without any corresponding information as to how such figures should be utilized. Still another table is provided to adjust the grade norms in relation to intelligence quotient medians. This might have been helpful if figures which represent "fractions of a year above ($+$) and below ($-$) the test norms for pupils of average ability" were spelled out more explicitly.

Aside from the need for more adequate information in the areas noted above, it would be desirable to know something of the selective process and representativeness of the original population sample since samples of only 118 and 120 were used in determining the reliability of the Primer and First Reader tests, respectively.

An analysis presented in the manuals of the vocabulary selection used in both tests indicates that all but 8 of the 86 words found in the Primer and all but 16 of the 194 words in the First Reader were also introduced in 21 books (comprised of preprimers, primers, and first and second readers from three basal reading series) used for comparative purposes. No copyright date is given, however, for any of the 21 books used. In any event it is unlikely that many children would be exposed to all such books. Aside from this at least one of the three series (Scott, Foresman) has been revised since the publication of these tests and another (Macmillan) cannot currently be considered to be "widely used" as the manuals report. A further analysis of words was carried out by comparing test vocabulary with the position of the words on the Gates Reading Vocabulary. Since the latter list was compiled in 1926 it is doubtful that such a comparison would provide any valid rationale for determining vocabulary items in 1958.

Of the 38 items tested in the Primer and 59 in the First Reader, 68 and 51 per cent, respectively, involve the identification of words in isolation, a practice of very questionable merit. Furthermore, 15 of the 38 items in the Primer and 15 of the 59 items in the First Reader are pronounced by the test administrator, thereby tending to place excessive emphasis on this particular type of auditory stimuli.

Despite the ease in administering and scoring these tests, the weaknesses noted above far outweigh these advantages and the tests cannot be recommended.

For a review by Ruth Lowes of the 1943 edition of the primer level, see 3:490.

[796]

★Manchester Reading Comprehension Test (Sen.) 1. Ages 13.5–15; 1959; 1 form (8 pages); manual (8 pages); 10s. 6d. per 25 tests; 7d. per single copy; 1s. 6d. per manual; postage and purchase tax extra; 45(50) minutes; Stephen Wiseman and Jack Wrigley (test); University of London Press Ltd. *

REFERENCES

1. WRIGLEY, JACK. "The Factorial Nature of Ability in Elementary Mathematics." *Brit J Ed Psychol* 28:61–78 F '58. * (PA 33:6845)

[797]

*Metropolitan Achievement Tests: [Reading]. Grades 2, 3–4, 5–6, 7–9; 1932–62; subtest of *Metropolitan Achievement Tests;* 2–3 scores: word knowledge, word discrimination (grade 2 only), reading; IBM and MRC for grades 5–9; 4 levels; battery manual for interpreting ('62, 121 pages); 40¢ per specimen set of any one level; $1.20 per manual for interpreting; postage extra; Walter N. Durost, Harold H. Bixler, Gertrude H. Hildreth, Kenneth W. Lund, and J. Wayne Wrightstone; [Harcourt, Brace & World, Inc.]. *

a) UPPER PRIMARY READING TEST. Grade 2; 1932–62; Form C ('61, 12 pages); directions for administering ('59, 12 pages); $5.40 per 35 tests; (79–84) minutes in 3 sessions.

b) ELEMENTARY READING TEST. Grades 3–4; 1932–62; Forms A ('60, c1958), B ('59), C ('61), (8 pages); directions for administering ('59, 8 pages); supplementary directions for use with deaf children available on request; $4.60 per 35 tests; 37(43) minutes.

c) INTERMEDIATE READING TEST. Grades 5–6; 1933–62; IBM and MRC; Forms AM ('60, c1958), BM ('59), CM ('61), (8 pages); combined directions for administering ('59, 11 pages) for this level and the advanced level; $4.60 per 35 tests; separate answer sheets or cards may be used; $1.75 per 35 IBM answer sheets; 20¢ per scoring stencil; $2 per 100 Harbor answer cards (machine scoring service, by Measurement Research Center, Inc., may be arranged through the publisher); 39(46) minutes.

d) ADVANCED READING TEST. Grades 7–9; 1933–62; forms, prices, and administration time same as for intermediate level.

REFERENCES

1. SPACHE, GEORGE. "Deriving Comprehension, Rate and Accuracy of Reading Norms for a Short Form of the Metropolitan Achievement Reading Test." *J Ed Psychol* 32:359–64 My '41. * (PA 16:1207)
2. STONE, CLARENCE R. "Validity of Tests in Beginning Reading." *El Sch J* 43:361–5 F '43. * (PA 18:2605)
3. LLOYD, CLAUDE J. *The Relationship Between the Scores Made by Pupils on the Primary Mental Abilities Test, the Metropolitan Achievement Reading Test, and the Kuhlmann-Anderson Intelligence Test.* Master's thesis, University of Southern California (Los Angeles, Calif.), 1958.
4. WRIGHTSTONE, J. WAYNE; ARONOW, MIRIAM S.; AND MOSKOWITZ, SUE. "Developing Reading Test Norms for Deaf Children." *Am Ann Deaf* 108:311–6 My '63. * (PA 38:1410)

H. ALAN ROBINSON, *Assistant Professor of Education, The University of Chicago, Chicago, Illinois.*

This test, part of a larger battery, is a good survey instrument yielding three scores (Word Knowledge, Word Discrimination, Reading) at the primary level and two scores (Word Knowledge and Reading) at upper levels. Each score is treated separately although this group of subtests is printed in one booklet. The subtest Reading, which should not be confused with the total reading test, is a measure of sentence and paragraph meaning at the primary level, paragraph meaning at the elementary level, and paragraph plus larger selection comprehension at intermediate and advanced levels. Word Knowledge measures vocabulary and word recognition. Word Discrimination is actually a measure of phonic ability.

No clear reason is advanced by the authors for the exclusion of Word Discrimination from the elementary form; according to the manual's description of the total achievement battery, a word discrimination test is part of the elementary level. Nor do the authors indicate why the reading test at intermediate and advanced levels might not also include Language Study Skills and possibly Social Studies Study Skills, both of which subtests are part of the total achievement battery and measure reading skills. Teachers, supervisors, consultants, and administrators particularly interested in evaluating results in reading might want to add such subtests for fuller coverage.

The test is not a diagnostic instrument, nor does it purport to be one. On the other hand, it offers possibilities for analysis of weaknesses and strengths for given individuals and classes. It might have been helpful for the teacher if some device for analysis had been worked into the scoring of the test, a device such as the one used in the *California Reading Test.*

The test has further diagnostic features: (*a*) Reliability for each subtest is good (.79 to .96) and a measure of validity has been obtained through careful study of curricula, judgment of experts, and repeated experimentation (although the measure of validity of the word discrimination subtest is a little vague). Hence, the examiner has some indication of strengths and weaknesses through examination of the subtests included in the reading test. (*b*) The primary subtest Reading includes a section on sentence reading (14 items), and a section on paragraph reading (51 items). Although the 14 items on sentence reading represent a very small sample, a teacher can get some subjective evidence of performance from the two parts. (*c*) At all upper levels the subtest Reading contains questions aimed at the measurement of just four comprehension skills: main thought, details, inferences, and meaning of words from context. Even though the authors of the test do not provide methods of analyzing strengths and weaknesses in the four skills, the teacher can work out a method for doing this on his own.

The diagnostic features of a survey test such as this are, however, a bonus. The test has much to offer in its own right as a rough measurement of reading achievement. Some important considerations are that: (a) The Manual for Interpreting is exceptionally well done; it serves to explain these tests and also provides excellent material about the use of tests in general. (b) Directions for administration and scoring are clear and not complicated. (c) Results are reported in the three most common ways (grade equivalents, percentiles, stanines), and therefore are most flexible and useful for a variety of interpretive purposes. (d) Standardization has been scientifically executed: experimental forms tried with about 27,000 students; item analyses carried out to select items for final forms; tests then administered to about 500,000 students in 225 school systems throughout 49 states; norm sample based on about 25 per cent of the students tested in each class. (e) The test booklets are modern in appearance, well arranged, and simple to follow.

Although the advanced forms of the test do not appear to discriminate well among those students reading at ninth grade level or above, the *Metropolitan Reading Test* is one of the best survey tests of reading achievement on the market today for the elementary grades. It has been carefully planned, carefully tested, and well produced. It serves its purpose as a rough measure of reading achievement for comparative purposes and as a tool of identification upon which further evaluation may be based.

For reviews by James R. Hobson and Margaret G. McKim of the 1947 edition, see 4:543; for a review by D. A. Worcester of an earlier edition, see 40:1551; for reviews by Ivan A. Booker and Joseph C. Dewey, see 38:1105. For reviews of the complete battery, see 15; for reviews of earlier editions, see 4:18, 40:1189, and 38:874.

[798]
*Monroe's Standardized Silent Reading Test. Grades 3-5, 6-8, 9-12; 1919-59; 2 scores: rate, comprehension; 3 levels; no data on reliability; $3.50 per

35 tests of Tests 1 or 2; $2.80 per 35 tests of Test 3; 50¢ per specimen set of any one level; postage extra; Walter S. Monroe; Bobbs-Merrill Co., Inc. *
a) TEST 1. Grades 3-5; 1919-59; self-marking Forms 4, 5, 6, ('58, 4 pages); combined manual ('59, 4 pages) for this test and Test 2 below; no description of normative population; 4(10) minutes.
b) TEST 2. Grades 6-8; 1919-59; details same as for Test 1.
c) TEST 3. Grades 9-12; 1919-21; Forms 1, 2, (no date, 4 pages, same as 1919-20 tests except for directions); instructions-norms sheet ['21, 2 pages]; 5(10) minutes.

REFERENCES
1. MONROE, WALTER S. "Monroe's Standardized Silent Reading Tests." *J Ed Psychol* 9:303-12 Je '18. *
2. WITHAM, ERNEST C. "Scoring the Monroe Silent Reading Test." *J Ed Psychol* 9:516-8 D '18. *
3. PRESSEY, S. L., AND PRESSEY, L. W. "The Relative Value of Rate and Comprehension Scores in Monroe's Silent Reading Test as Measures of Reading Ability." *Sch & Soc* 11:747-9 Je 19 '20. *
4. WEST, PAUL V. "The Monroe Silent Reading Test." *Sch & Soc* 13:510 Ap 23 '21. *
5. BALLENGER, H. L. "A Comparative Study of the Vocabulary Content of Certain Standard Reading Tests." *El Sch J* 23:522-34 Mr '23. *

CHARLES R. LANGMUIR, *Director of Special Projects, The Psychological Corporation, New York, New York.*

There are two points of interest about this set of tests. First, it is an antiquity which reveals the meaning of "standardized" as applied to tests 45 years ago. Second, comparison of the original and the current issue, advertised as "revised" by its new publisher, reveals a classic example of editorial stability which might better be termed total resistance to a half century's development of psychometric concepts, techniques, and standards of professional reporting.

Test 1 for grades 3-5 and Test 2 for grades 6-8 consist of short passages, each followed by a five-choice item. The several forms vary in length from 16 items totaling 825 words to 21 items totaling 1,003 words. The item content is almost identical with the original tests. In the 1920 edition the pupil underlined the word which answered the question. In the new edition the options have been numbered and the pupil marks an "X" in a numbered box. The practice exercises have been changed. That is the extent of the revision.

The original manual supplied some kind of central tendency scores called "standards" for middle of the year and end of the year in each grade, 3 through 12, and it described the table with the heading: "Standards based on 130,000 scores, October, 1920." The new manual for Tests 1 and 2 contains tables of grade equivalent scores for rate and comprehension without any information whatever to support the entries. In short, no data.

Except for the practice exercise, the two forms of Test 3 for grades 9–12 are identical with the original. Each form contains 12 paragraphs averaging about 60 words and one question, generally two-choice, on each passage. The "standards" for middle of the year and end of the year in grades 9–12 are copied from the original manual, along with the assertion that they are "based on 130,000 scores, October, 1920." It is evident from the original manual that the 65,000 pupils were distributed over all grades, 3–12, so that an unknown but certainly large fraction of the 130,000 scores have no relevance whatever to Test 3.

It is not precisely true that the content of Test 3 is exactly the same as the original. In one form the word "parenthesis" is changed to the plural spelling, doubtless to gain grammatical accuracy. The reviewer contrasts this editorial feat with the folly of perpetuating a science paragraph containing the statement: the barometer registered ten degrees lower. It is a curious fact that the author's blue pencil missed this absurdity in 1919; it is fantastic that a test publisher retained the item intact for 45 years.

AGATHA TOWNSEND, *Consultant, Educational Records Bureau, New York, New York.*

Since it seems quite unlikely that any teacher or reading supervisor examining these tests will today select them for use, it seems appropriate to review them as what they are, a landmark in educational history, or—better still—one living specimen representative of an extinct species. Since the tests are still in print, and distributed by the test division of a well-known publisher, it seems impossible to avoid questioning the purpose, even the plausibility, of keeping them on the market, but this will be a secondary aim of the review.

What was reading like in 1920, and how was it tested? What relation exists between norms for those days and for these? A trial administration of the two elementary school levels to a group of sixth graders provides some evidence that the 1920 norms were probably once fairly representative. This statement is based, it is true, on reasoning by analogy from other comments and studies. There seems to be general agreement that the school grades of the early 1920's were reading, on the average,

about one year above the level of grades similarly designated today. The finding is in line with Gates' summary, which indicated that pupils in the early 1960's are just about one year younger at a given grade placement than were their grandparents. At any rate, trial by this reviewer tended to place sixth graders of about average reading skills for modern test norms at about the fifth grade level on Test 1, which is designed for grades 3 to 5, according to the publisher, and at about the median for grade 6 according to the 1920 standards on the higher level, Test 2, for grades 6 to 8.

Placement in the norms, of course, is not the only dislocation for today's pupils trying out the tests. The material, its style and content, seems to reflect a seriousness of purpose, and preference for the literary and moral paragraph, which is unfamiliar today. Whatever one may conclude about the relative values involved, it is undoubtedly true that our sixth graders were faced with problems different from what was difficult for the earlier testees. The first paragraph in one of the upper level tests, for instance, found several pupils grinding to a halt before they were well begun: "It was the garden-land of Antioch. Even the hedges, besides the lure of shade...." To the historian, some of the paragraphs are attractive, though nostalgic, but they must have been almost as distant from the everyday life of yesterday's youngsters as they are from ours. Moreover, the difficulty of the paragraphs does not lie exclusively in wording or setting. Not all the test questions ask for understanding of the details or main ideas presented. Some are aimed at inference, and even though Monroe's insight was generally good, there are misleading paragraphs and responses. An obscure little passage is supposed to be identified as coming from Russia, but the only clue is a reference to reindeer skins; coupled with a proper name, Lars, this tends to lead the child up a blind alley. Several of our sixth graders also boggled when the term "equinox" was used among the choices for items asking them to identify the "season of the year" pictured in a poem.

It is more interesting for the test specialist, however, to compare the characteristics of the two scores on the tests with those of tests made more recently. The test purports to give the teacher information on both rate and comprehension. The rate score for the lower levels of the test is expressed as words read per minute —a figure derived by dividing the total number of words read throughout the working period by four, the total elapsed minutes for the test. It will be seen that this is a far cry from the usual words per minute score based on a connected passage. No account is taken of the varying character (expository prose, narrative, or poetry) of the portions of the test read, the variations in difficulty (for the passages do not very dependably rise in difficulty as one proceeds), or the fact that a pupil may stop longer to ponder one response or another. It is true, of course, that this method of deriving a rate score has its descendants in modern tests. The speed of comprehension score of the *Cooperative English Tests* and that of the *Davis Reading Test* come immediately to mind. In such tests, the speed score is made less misleading by reporting it as a score which must be related to the norms for its interpretation. The Monroe elementary test did not come to grips with the problem of understanding a reading rate which is called by the same name as other words-read-per-minute scores. The rate score can be translated into a grade equivalent but it still was undoubtedly used as rate per minute.

It is apparent that Monroe himself realized some of the difficulties created by the speed score on the elementary school test. The secondary school test still depends for its rate score on the amount of the test completed, but the score itself is expressed by an arbitrary number which must be translated into a grade rating for use.

Comments have been made above about the types of passages used in the elementary school tests. Test 3, designed for grades 9 to 12, departs even farther from the familiar methods used to test understanding of passages. Several of the paragraphs take on the guise of verbal puzzles like: "If he should stand, underline smoke. If he should lie on the floor, underline air." In such cases, the additional answer choices perform no visible function. Other items require the identification of the main idea. Several are really disguised vocabulary items. Each of the two forms of Test 3 includes only 12 items; choice ranges from two to five; there are several write-in items interspersed, and other devices are used. The forms of Tests 1 and 2, which were adapted at some unspeci-

fied date for a self-scoring device using carbon-backed paper, are all made up of standard five-choice items.

It is not surprising, probably, that this early test carries no indication of reliability or validity. An effort was made to equate the two forms of Test 3. The materials for interpretation include directions (misprinted, by the way) for converting the score on one form to that on the other. The only norms are "Standards based on 130,000 scores, October, 1920" and consist of middle-of-the-year scores, which are not identified as means or medians, for each form for grades 9 through 12. There is a similar set of eight scores for "end of the year," though no explanation is given how either mid-year or end-of-year scores were secured in October. The teacher is urged to distribute the rate and comprehension scores for each class, and compute the medians. No directions are given for interpreting the range of results except for the reporting of the "standards" already described.

The interpretation of Tests 1 and 2 is presumably facilitated by tables assigning grade equivalents to the two scores on each form. Absolutely no data are given for the origin of these norms. It seems probable, however, that they bear no relation whatever to the 1959 copyright date carried by the manual.

Reviewing *Monroe's Standardized Silent Reading Test* has proven a fascinating exercise in the history of testing. Teachers of measurement should take advantage of the test's availability to secure copies for use with their classes. This is where educational testing began. Here is a test which in its time was undoubtedly administered to millions of pupils. It bears no data on reliability and validity. Items are not arranged in order of difficulty, in spite of a strikingly brief time limit. There is no consistent pattern of response or method of rationalizing results on completion items, items with different numbers of choices, or other variants. There are no percentile norms, and the character of the groups on which the scanty medians and the grade equivalents are based is nowhere discussed. All these items and others which might be introduced (such as the implications of the rate score) would certainly provide an interesting session.

On the other hand, the availability of the test may actually be dangerous for the unwary school system. It was devised by a distinguished educator (though one teacher ascribed it to Marion Monroe, since Tests 1 and 2 have mercifully dropped the author's full name). Its simplicity of scoring and its unassuming appearance may recommend it to the timid teacher or to the unsympathetic administrator who may feel that tests are getting altogether too elaborate. And, to tell the truth, anyone must be entitled to wonder why a supposedly responsible publisher still keeps it in stock. It belongs in the archives of testing, where it should rest in peace.

[799]

★N.B. Silent Reading Tests (Beginners): Reading Comprehension Test. Standard 1 (grades 1–2); 1961–62; Forms A, B, ['62, 7 pages]; mimeographed manual ['62, 13 pages]; R2.45 per 100 tests of Form A; R2.15 per 100 tests of Form B; postpaid; specimen set not available; Afrikaans edition available; administration time not reported; National Bureau of Educational and Social Research. *

[800]

*The Nelson-Denny Reading Test: Vocabulary-Comprehension-Rate. Grades 9–16 and adults; 1929–60; previous edition (see 4:544) still available; 4 scores: vocabulary, comprehension, total, rate; IBM and MRC; Forms A, B, ('60, 12 pages); manual ('60, 30 pages); supplementary profile-norms sheet ('60) for adults; adult norms based on cut-time administration only; separate answer sheets or cards must be used; $4.20 per 35 tests; $2.49 per 35 self-marking answer sheets; $3.15 per 100 IBM answer sheets; 45¢ per scoring stencil; $2.55 per 100 MRC answer cards (machine scoring service, by Measurement Research Center, Inc., may be arranged through the publisher); $1.20 per 35 adult profile-norms sheets; 75¢ per specimen set; postage extra; 30(35) minutes for regular administration, 22½(27½) minutes for reading efficiency classes; original edition by M. J. Nelson and E. C. Denny; revision by James I. Brown; Houghton Mifflin Co. *

REFERENCES

1–6. See 40:1557.
7–23. See 4:544.
24. FREEHILL, MAURICE F. "Student Self-Estimates as Guidance in Selecting Courses." Col & Univ 27:233–42 Ja '52. *
25. DURNALL, EDWARD J., JR. "A Testing Program for Junior College for Women." Jun Col J 23:261–7 Ja '53. *
26. MUNGER, PAUL F. "Factors Related to Persistence in College of Students Who Ranked in the Lower Third of Their High School Class." J Counsel Psychol 1:132–6 f '54. * (PA 29:6258)
27. VINEYARD, EDWIN E., AND MASSEY, HAROLD W. "The Interrelationship of Certain Linguistic Skills and Their Relationship With Scholastic Achievement When Intelligence Is Ruled Constant." J Ed Psychol 48:279–86 My '57. * (PA 33:2200)
28. FLEMING, W. G. Aptitude and Achievement Scores Related to Immediate Educational and Occupational Choices of Ontario Grade 13 Students. Atkinson Study of Utilization of Student Resources, Report No. 3. Toronto, Canada: Department of Educational Research, Ontario College of Education, University of Toronto, 1958. Pp. xix, 380. *
29. FLEMING, W. G. Ontario Grade 13 Students: Their Aptitude, Achievement, and Immediate Destination. Atkinson Study of Utilization of Student Resources, Report No. 4. Toronto, Canada: Department of Educational Research, Ontario College of Education, University of Toronto, 1958. Pp. ix, 55. *
30. FLEMING, W. G. Personal and Academic Factors as Predictors of First Year Success in Ontario Universities. Atkinson Study of Utilization of Student Resources, Report No. 5. Toronto, Canada: Department of Educational Research, Ontario College of Education, University of Toronto, 1959. Pp. xi, 137. *
31. PALACIOS, JOHN RAYMOND. A Validation Study of Selected Tests for Possible Use in Admission to Professional Education Sequences at Purdue University. Doctor's thesis, Purdue University (Lafayette, Ind.), 1959. (DA 20:2679)
32. SMITH, D. D. "Traits and College Achievement." Can J Psychol 13:93–101 Je '59. * (PA 34:4780)
33. PIPHER, J. A. "An Appraisal of the Use of the Dominion Group Test of Learning Capacity (Advanced) in the Atkinson Study of Utilization of Student Resources." Ont J Ed Res 3:17–23 O '60. *
34. BEAMER, BEN A. The Relative Value of the Nelson-Denny Test and the Cooperative Reading Test in the Freshman Test Battery at Virginia State College. Master's thesis, Virginia State College (Petersburg, Va.), 1961.
35. FLEMING, W. G. The Use of Predictive Factors for the Improvement of University Admission Requirements. Atkinson Study of Utilization of Student Resources, Report No. 9. Toronto, Canada: Department of Educational Research, Ontario College of Education, University of Toronto, 1962. Pp. xi, 76. *
36. ROBINSON, WILLIS. A Validity Study of the Testing Program for the Selection of Students for Teacher Education. Doctor's thesis, Purdue University (Lafayette, Ind.), 1962. (DA 23:2812)

DAVID B. ORR, Senior Research Scientist, American Institute for Research; and Director of School and Survey Research, University of Pittsburgh Project Talent Office; Washington, D.C.

This test represents a revision and improvement of one already well known and widely used. It is composed of a 100-item vocabulary section and a 36-item reading comprehension section, both of traditional multiple choice types. New features of this revision are the addition of a reading rate score, more complete norms, and some attention to the special case of adults studying "efficient" or "rapid" reading.

The test shows evidence of careful construction. Data on the development and standardization of the revised forms are presented along with reliabilities, difficulties, and standard errors of measurement. In general the format is clear and workable, and, with a few exceptions, the items seem well constructed and unambiguous. Earlier criticisms of the form of the norms and of the lack of discussion of diagnostic uses of the test have been taken care of in the new manual.

Both self-scoring and machine scorable answer sheets are available, making the test economical and convenient to use.

One criticism of the content of the reading comprehension portion of the test is that some of the passages draw their difficulty from what is essentially poor writing, i.e., long, involved, and somewhat awkward sentences and constructions. This reviewer feels that the essence of reading comprehension lies more in the reader's ability to grasp ideas and their implications than in his ability to thread his way through grammatical complexities.

There is little to criticize in the standardization of the test, though the total groups employed were relatively small. A stratified random sampling procedure was used for grades 9–12 based on school enrollment by region and community size. Data are presented. For college levels, enrollment by five types of colleges was used as the basis of stratification. Special adult norms are given for administration of the test to adults in "efficient reading" classes in less than the usual time. These are based on 961 adult students in the University of Minnesota Extension Division Efficient Reading Classes (about half for each of the two available forms).

A considerable amount of technical data about the revision is presented in the manual. Since both the vocabulary and comprehension parts of the test tend to be somewhat speeded, the authors have commendably chosen alternate form reliability rather than split-half. Reliabilities for reading rate, vocabulary, and total score are acceptably high (.92 to .93), but comprehension leaves something to be desired (.81), particularly for individual work. However, standard errors of measurement are presented by form by grade and their use explained. Correlations with English and IQ tests are also given, but these, like the reliabilities, are based on unnecessarily small samples and may not be very dependable.

Comparative data are presented with respect to the mean item difficulty and "validity" of Forms A and B original and Forms A and B revised. This reviewer would like to emphasize his dislike for the use of the terms validity, validity index, or validity coefficient to represent the correlation between an item score and a total score. Such a correlation is more properly referred to as an internal consistency coefficient and does not measure validity in the same sense as either item-criterion correlations or test-criterion correlations. However, the data presented do show considerable improvement in the range for these coefficients for both vocabulary and comprehension sections over the original forms. The mean value for the vocabulary section has been raised from about .38 to .47 which is now more comparable to the comprehension sections (.45). Mean difficulties in terms of per cent passing the item

have been made somewhat easier for the revised vocabulary sections (62) and have remained about the same for the comprehension sections (about 71). All of these values seem satisfactory, though the present difficulty indices show that the comprehension sections are a little on the easy side.

Perhaps the most disappointing aspect of the present manual is its failure to include more data on the predictive and concurrent validity of the test. Only one predictive study is cited and the small group correlations with the ACE, "Otis IQ," and "Coop English" (not further identified) do not really fill the latter need. The authors do not even address themselves, except incidentally, to topics of content or construct validity in describing the development of the test. This reviewer considers these to be regrettable lacks in the manual.

A further deficiency in the manual is the fact that, try as he might, this reviewer could find no information on the intercorrelations of the three Nelson-Denny scores. This is an unfortunate omission as the user may well ask to what extent the information provided by these individual scores is being duplicated from one to another.

In summary, in spite of certain defects, this test is one of the better of its kind and represents a useful improvement of an already useful test. Some care should be exercised in the comprehension score for individual diagnosis, and appropriate standard errors should be kept in mind. In general the test may be expected to provide useful information at a reasonable cost and will doubtlessly continue to find a place in the test user's repertoire.

AGATHA TOWNSEND, *Consultant, Educational Records Bureau, New York, New York.*

The current revision of the old standby for college testing, the *Nelson-Denny Reading Test,* will probably be welcomed by the chief clientele for its predecessor, teachers of college-bound pupils in grades 11 and 12, and those of college English classes; it may also be useful for college placement. It is a good test for a limited audience, and it should be stated at the outset that most of the criticisms which it has incurred, some of which are noted below, have arisen because of an attempt made to increase the sale of the test by appeals to other groups.

The simple structure is well adapted to the survey purposes to which the test has always held. It consists of a long (100-item) vocabulary test and a series of reading passages on which comprehension questions are asked. In both the old and revised editions, the raw score on comprehension is multiplied by two and added to the vocabulary score for a total. This weighting of the comprehension factor is probably justifiable since it brings the two scores fairly closely in line, though the total score for a good reader, or at least one answering most of the questions correctly, will be weighted more heavily with vocabulary.

The new test also includes a rate score. This is an approximation of words read per minute, though for some undisclosed reason, it is not based on an accurate count of the words in the rate passage, which also serves as the first comprehension passage. The manual points out quite correctly that the rate score should be regarded like any other piece of raw data, and interpreted through reference to the percentile tables. The teacher using the rate score, however, should also be warned that the rate passages have a Dale-Chall readability index which places them at the college level; hence comparisons with other rate scores should be made very cautiously. One should not be misled by the statement that the grade norms "represent a convenient way of rendering scores on several tests 'comparable.' " It should also be noted that the rate score is based on a testing time of only one minute, although there is considerable evidence to suggest that such a brief sample is not so reliable as rate measurement over a longer interval. Moreover, interestingly enough, the source which the author quotes in justification for a one-minute limit does not report favorable reliability data on limits less than four minutes.

Except for the limitations noted about the rate score, the data on reliability for the test indicate that the part scores may be used with considerable confidence. The confidence is increased by observing that the percentile norms seem to have been carefully constructed and the populations on which they are based carefully described. Standard error of measurement figures are reported in addition to reliability data; this is a valuable and praiseworthy addition to the manual.

Decisions about the usefulness of this test

should be made, in the opinion of this reviewer, only after careful study of both the test and the students with whom it might be employed. Reference has already been made to the measured difficulty of the passage on which the rate score is based. The manual points out that this passage is about median in difficulty for the series of passages—as judged, however, by the difficulty of the comprehension items. This method of estimating difficulty has its obvious shortcomings, and in fact, the fifth of the eight passages in each form (the only one based on general material typical of newspaper or magazine reporting) seems to be markedly easier than the others. The manual makes no mention of controlling difficulty through reference to any readability formula. Both the comprehension passages and the vocabulary part appear to be suitable for colleges but are almost certainly too difficult for average ninth and tenth grades. This statement is borne out indirectly by the norms. The average score for ninth grade pupils is from 15 to 18 (out of 100) in vocabulary, and represents about 12 of the 36 comprehension items answered correctly. Certainly most teachers will seek a test which samples these abilities more adequately for younger students.

Although the manual points out that "reading range at any one grade level is likely to extend over six to eight grades," all grade equivalents below 9.0 are marked "extrapolated" in the norms table, and there is no indication of any tryout below grade 9. This reviewer considers the use of grade equivalents as misleading and unnecessary, at least above grade 6, and is favorably impressed that these tables are not stressed in the interpretation. The grade norms for comprehension and rate, in any event, are so coarse as to have little attractiveness for most users.

Even though the percentile norms appear to indicate an adequate spread of scores and although suitable reliability figures are reported for grade 11 and above, the restricted content may still make the test unsatisfactory for use with any high school groups except those which are clearly college preparatory, and barely suitable for modern programs with those groups. There is a very sparse scattering of terms from science in the vocabulary test, which is chiefly general and somewhat literary in character. The comprehension passages are limited to history, formal economics, semihistorical passages on literature, two extracts in each form which might be called sociology and anthropology, and the one general passage mentioned above. They seem to give adequate representation for standard college textbook materials in a limited number of fields.

The high school or college teacher who turns to the manual for suggestions on the use of scores in instruction will be disappointed. In an essay on reading improvement, "Some Uses of the Test," the author makes some curious statements about the rise in rate and comprehension which can be expected in reading improvement courses (undescribed), offers an obscure comment about the use of high school rank in place of a measure of intelligence, and refers to an unidentified listening test (from internal evidence this is probably the Brown-Carlsen, since the author participated in the construction of this measure) and its relation to Nelson-Denny scores. Although the essay is interesting, it scarcely lives up to its title.

This review should not close without mentioning the striking new material which has been prepared for use of the Nelson-Denny with adult reading improvement classes. The profile and interpretation sheets as they now stand need improvement. It will be seen that Brown's adult classes are unusual, as it is clearly stated that the adult norms are based on highly selected groups of professional people, chiefly students who read better than the average college senior, and "more than half have one or more college degrees." Bearing this limitation clearly in mind, it seems as if the Nelson-Denny might be appropriate for use in some adult courses; additional norms would be needed for many groups, or reference should be made to the existing grade or college norms.

Unfortunately, the recommendation of the author is that when the test is employed for adults, administration time should be shortened to 7½ minutes for vocabulary, and 15 minutes for rate plus comprehension. The surprising statement is added that this cut-time administration adds "sensitivity" to the test. Considering the small number of comprehension items to begin with and the steep difficulty of the vocabulary part, this conclusion seems questionable. Cutting the time will artificially increase the ceiling of the test but will do so by making it farther than ever from a power test.

The suggestions for use in teaching adults are as vague as those for the school and college situation.

In summary, with the new revision, the Nelson-Denny seems to be very much what it was before. It was and is a challenging test with a highly academic flavor, useful for good readers who expect to use their reading in liberal arts fields, though not in the sciences. The rate score may prove useful for college textbook reading. The percentile norms seem adequate for grade 11 and above, and the test may facilitate a survey of a field where we admittedly lack good information—the growth of reading power in the college years. It is not a test which will adequately differentiate among the reading skills of college students, but it has its place for screening. Without further evidence, it can be recommended to only a limited number of teachers working with adult classes, and then only when the character of the adult enrollment is similar to that of the sample on which the norms are based. The question of carryover from this textbook type of reading to business and professional reading remains unanswered. The explanatory materials which accompany the test are not as good as the norms. The suggestions for teaching are not adequate for the instructor with a limited background in reading improvement, and a teacher with adequate preparation will find them unnecessary.

J Counsel Psychol 10:203-4 su '63. John O. Crites. * extensively up-dated and improved * Unusually complete normative data are given for the test, which was standardized upon large numbers of Ss. * Reliabilities for the test ....based upon a carefully conducted study of 110 college students....seem to be adequate for both general screening purposes with the total scale and diagnostic work with the subscales. With respect to the latter, the validity data on the test, which consists primarily of item analyses indicates that it can be used to identify differential difficulties in vocabulary and comprehension. The value of the rate score is less certain, since no data on its correlation with comprehension are reported, but its expected relationship would be high. Although the Manual (p. 22) attempts to convey the impression that the Nelson-Denny usually correlates with scholastic achievement in the .60's, the data which are cited are far from conclusive. The correlation is more likely in the .40's. * a well constructed and excellently standardized measure which can be confidently recommended to counselors. Its scores appear to be quite reliable, and there is some evidence of its validity for a variety of purposes. If there is a shortcoming in the work which has been done on the test, it is in certain unverified statements which are made in the Manual. For example, on page 22, studies on the relationship of the Nelson-Denny and other tests to academic achievement are summarized and then the following conclusion is drawn: "These findings suggest that the inclusion of this test [the Nelson-Denny] in any college entrance battery should noticeably improve its predictive accuracy." There is no basis for this inference, which would require data on the differential contributions of tests to a battery, such as are determined by a procedure like the Wherry-Doolittle. Consequently, the Manual should be read critically and discriminatingly, since parts of it are misleading, but this should not unduly detract from the over-all high quality of the test.

For a review by Ivan A. Booker of the earlier edition, see 4:544; for a review by Hans C. Gordon, see 40:1557.

[801]

Nelson-Lohmann Reading Test: Coordinated Scales of Attainment. Grades 4, 5, 6, 7, 8; 1946–54; identical with reading sections of *Coordinated Scales of Attainment;* IBM; Form A ('53, 4 pages, identical with test copyrighted in 1946 except for title) ; 5 levels; directions for administering ('53, 4 pages) ; battery manual ('54, 24 pages) ; separate answer sheets must be used; $2.35 per 25 tests; $1.45 per 25 IBM scorable answer sheets; 25¢ per scoring stencil; $1.50 per battery manual; postage extra; 75¢ per specimen set, postpaid; (45) minutes; Ethel V. Nelson and Victor L. Lohmann; Educational Test Bureau. *

JASON MILLMAN, *Assistant Professor of Educational Psychology and Measurement, Cornell University, Ithaca, New York.*

The *Nelson-Lohmann Reading Test* is identical to the reading test in the *Coordinated Scales of Attainment.* A separate test of 60 multiple choice items, based upon 10 to 13 one-paragraph episodes, is provided for each of grades 4 through 8. Directions for each test are identical. While the tests are essentially untimed, 45 minutes are suggested as being "sufficient for all but the slower classes."

Inspection of the items suggests that while the majority measure the ability to note details,

a number of them require the ability to grasp the main idea, determine word meanings from context, and interpret beyond the printed word.

To help in the interpretation of the scores, age equivalent, grade equivalent and percentile rank norms are provided, together with profile charts. The charts will be of most value when the reading test is used in conjunction with the other tests in the *Coordinated Scales of Attainment.*

It is difficult to evaluate the test on more technical grounds since the only information provided is that compared to the earlier editions, "The current, revised edition....matches the original one in difficulty, item by item, and is much improved in other respects." We are further assured that "the same norms apply to both the new test as well as the old test."

Because individual items have been matched on difficulty with corresponding items in the older test is no guarantee that the distribution of total scores on which norms are based will be the same. Further, we have no assurance that the high empirical standards of item selection and the satisfactory levels of reliability associated with the first test are to be found with the present edition.

Only items of average or near average difficulty for the grade under consideration were retained for use in the older edition. Because the current edition matches these item difficulty levels, we can be sure each current test also measures a limited range of ability. Thus, the authors should be commended for warning against distorted interpretations of grade equivalents more than one grade above or below the grade for which the test was designed. This reviewer, however, is less pleased with the claim that the test is appropriate to measure a "wide range of individual differences" and that "the variations in attainment found in a typical class are fully taken into account."

In summary, the *Nelson-Lohmann Reading Test* appears to be a good measure of ability to comprehend nontechnical reading material in a situation where reading speed is minimized. This reviewer agrees that *"school norms* and *city or county norms* [should] be developed." The narrow range of difficulty of the items in each test suggests that accurate measurement of the reading ability of individual students who are much above or below the grade norm of the test will not be possible. A technical manual for the test is needed.

For a review by Alvin W. Schindler of the complete battery, see 4:8; for reviews by Roland L. Beck, Lavone A. Hanna, Gordon N. Mackenzie (with Glen Hass), and C. C. Ross of the batteries for grades 4–8, see 3:6.

[802]

*The Nelson Reading Test, Revised Edition: Vocabulary-Paragraph Comprehension.** Grades 3–9; 1931–62; revision of *The Nelson Silent Reading Test: Vocabulary and Paragraph: The Clapp-Young Self-Marking Tests,* which is still available; 3 scores: vocabulary, paragraph comprehension, total; IBM; Forms A, B, ('62, 19 pages) ; manual ('62, 23 pages) ; separate answer sheets must be used; $4.95 per 35 tests; $2.55 per set of 35 self-marking answer sheets and manual; $3.30 per 100 IBM answer sheets; 42¢ per set of scoring stencils; 42¢ per manual; 84¢ per specimen set; postage extra; 30(35) minutes; M. J. Nelson; Houghton Mifflin Co. *

H. ALAN ROBINSON, *Assistant Professor of Education, The University of Chicago, Chicago, Illinois.*

Although the test is said to be designed for grades 3–9, the requirement that separate answer sheets (either self-marking or IBM) be used places third and fourth graders at a disadvantage and makes the test more suitable for grades 5–9. No evidence of experimentation with and without separate answer sheets is reflected in the examiner's manual. In addition, the test is probably not suitable for junior high school students reading at levels beyond grade 9. Grade equivalents are not given above 10.5 and the most difficult passages in the paragraph comprehension section of the test appear to be rather easy for mature readers.

The revision of the test, however, has produced a paragraph comprehension section which contains a little more challenging and varied material than it did in the old test, and a vocabulary section composed of the best items, selected on the basis of item analyses, from the original forms. The fact that the revision resulted in two forms rather than three as in the earlier edition will make more limited the test-retest use of an instrument which spans seven grades.

The test, however, appears to be effective as a rough measure of reading achievement. The standardization procedure was meticulous and comprehensive. The manual contains percentiles and grade equivalents for vocabulary, paragraph comprehension, and total score. The test appears to be reliable and, when compared with other reading tests, gives some evidence of validity.

A better and more comprehensive measure of validity, however, might have included the study of curriculums in grades 3–9. Obviously there are many more important comprehension skills at these levels than the three measured: main thought, details, and prediction of outcome. In fact, the inclusion of "prediction of outcome" for each paragraph means that material needed to be structured for that purpose.

In a number of instances on this test, possible answers can easily be eliminated because they are nonsensical. One such answer is "went home," which occurs repeatedly in the "what do you think happened next?" type of question: "Durovitch went home"; "the man went home"; "Wilbur went home"; "the professor went home." Inspection of test items by a panel of expert judges might have strengthened the total test.

Although a third of the manual consists of norm tables, it also includes information about the test and its uses. A helpful table is provided which permits the teacher to ascertain students' weaknesses and strengths in the three particular comprehension skills. The author does not make claims, however, for diagnostic values over and above an analysis of scores from both parts of the test (vocabulary and paragraph comprehension). On the other hand, too many conclusions about deficiencies and possible remedies for them are drawn on the basis of this one survey test. A teacher would be ill-advised to plan an instructional program on the evidence presented by one test without further testing in specific skill areas.

This is not a diagnostic instrument. It is a test with some flaws, but it does seem to be an adequate gross measure of reading achievement. It is a decided improvement over the earlier edition especially in format and attractiveness.

For a review by William D. Sheldon of the earlier edition, see 4:545; for a review by Constance M. McCullough, see 3:492; see also 40:1558 (1 excerpt).

[803]

*Primary Reading: Every Pupil Scholarship Test.** Grades 1, 2–3; 1935–64; new form (4 pages) usually issued each January and April; forms from previous testing programs also available; 2 levels; special directions for grade 1 administration ['63, 3 pages] ; general directions sheet ['63, 2 pages] ; no data on reliability; norms for new forms available following testing program; 4¢ per test; 4¢ per key; postage extra; (40–60) minutes for grade 1, 15(20) minutes for grades 2–3; Bureau of Educational Measurements. *

[804]

*Primary Reading: Every Pupil Test. Grades 2–3; 1936–64; new form (8 pages) usually issued each December and April; forms from previous testing programs also available; general directions sheet ('63, 2 pages); no data on reliability; Ohio norms for new forms available following testing program; 5¢ per test; 3¢ per key; postpaid; 16(30) minutes; Ohio Scholarship Tests. *

For reviews by William S. Gray and Virginia Seavey of the 1946 forms, see 3:493.

[805]

★Reading Adequacy "READ" Test: Individual Placement Series. Adults; 1961; 3 scores: reading rate, per cent of comprehension, corrected rate; Form C (4 pages); no manual; no data on reliability; no description of normative population; $4 per 25 tests; $1 per key; $2.25 per specimen set; postpaid; [10–15] minutes; J. H. Norman; the Author. *

[806]

*Reading Comprehension: Cooperative English Tests, [1960 Revision]. Grades 9–12, 13–14; 1940–60; separate booklet edition of reading subtest of *Cooperative English Tests, [1960 Revision]*; revision of *Reading Comprehension: Cooperative English Test: Lower and Higher Levels, C1 and C2*; 4 scores: vocabulary, level of comprehension, speed of comprehension, total; IBM; Forms A, B, C, ('60, 10–11 pages); 2 levels (tests labeled, say, for grades 13–14, Form 1A, for grades 9–12, Form 2A); battery directions for administering ('60, 16 pages); battery manual for interpreting ('60, 42 pages); battery technical report ('60, 35 pages); distribution of Form 1C restricted to colleges; separate answer sheets must be used; $4 per 20 tests; $1 per 20 IBM scorable answer sheets for the battery; 25¢ per scoring stencil; $1 per 20 Scribe answer sheets for the battery (scored by the publisher only); $1 per manual for interpreting; $1 per technical report; postage extra; $2 per specimen set of the battery, cash orders postpaid; 40(45) minutes; revision by Clarence Derrick, David P. Harris, and Biron Walker; Cooperative Test Division. * (Australian edition of the Higher Level of the earlier edition: Australian Council for Educational Research.)

REFERENCES

1–2. See 40:1564.
3–17. See 3:497.
18–37. See 4:547.
38–58. See 5:645.
59. STUCKY, MILO O., AND ANDERSON, KENNETH E. *A Study of Persistence in College Attendance in Relation to Placement-Test Scores and Grade-Point Averages.* University of Kansas, School of Education, Kansas Studies in Education, Vol. 9, No. 2. Lawrence, Kan.: the School, April 1959. Pp. 58. *
60. STUCKY, MILO O., AND ANDERSON, KENNETH E. "A Study of the Relationship Between Entrance-Test Scores and Grade-Point Averages and Length of Stay in College." *Yearb Nat Council Meas Used Ed* 16:164–70 '59. *
61. ANDERSON, A. W. "The Relationship of Age to Adult Reading Scores." *J Ed Psychol* 51:334–6 D '60. * (PA 36:1FA34A)
62. CASSEL, RUSSELL N., AND STANCIK, EDWARD J. "Factorial Content of the Iowa Tests of Educational Development and Other Tests." *J Exp Ed* 29:193–6 D '60. *
63. MARKWARDT, FREDERICK CHARLES, JR. *Pattern Analysis Techniques in the Prediction of College Success.* Doctor's thesis, University of Minnesota (Minneapolis, Minn.), 1960. (DA 21:2990)
64. BARNHART, E. L., AND ANDERSON, KENNETH E. *A Study of the Relationships Between Grade-Point Averages, Placement-Test Scores, Semester Hours Earned, and Area of Major Interest for the Group Who Entered the University of Kansas in the Fall of 1954.* University of Kansas, School of Education, Kansas Studies in Education, Vol. 11, No. 1. Lawrence, Kan.: the School, January 1961. Pp. 36. *
65. BEAMER, BEN A. *The Relative Value of the Nelson-Denny Test and the Cooperative Reading Test in the Freshman Test Battery at Virginia State College.* Master's thesis, Virginia State College (Petersburg, Va.), 1961.
66. COOLEY, JOHN C. "A Study of the Relation Between Certain Mental and Personality Traits and Ratings of Musical Abilities." *J Res Music Ed* 9:108–17 f '61. *
67. CAMPBELL, JOEL T.; OTIS, JAY L.; LISKE, RALPH E.; AND PRIEN, ERICH P. "Assessments of Higher-Level Personnel: 2, Validity of the Over-All Assessment Process." *Personnel Psychol* 15:63–74 sp '62. * (PA 37:3908)
68. PRESTON, RALPH C. "A New Approach to Judging the Validity of Reading Comprehension Tests: Summary of an Investigation." *Int Rdg Assn Conf Proc* 7:166–7 '62. *
69. OSBORN, LYNN R. "An Analysis of the Relationship Between Speech Performance and Performance on Written Examinations of Course Content in a Beginning College Speech Course as Reflected in Assigned Grades." *Univ Kans B Ed* 17:68–71 F '63. *
70. RANKIN, EARL F., JR. "Reading Test Reliability and Validity as Function of Introversion-Extroversion." *J Develop Read* 6:106–17 w '63. *

W. V. CLEMANS, *Director, Test Department, Science Research Associates, Inc., Chicago, Illinois.*

The 1960 series of *Cooperative English Tests* continues the format of similar Cooperative tests first developed in the 1930's. The Manual for Interpreting Scores states that "most of the items in the Reading Comprehension tests are simply revisions of items in previous forms, and the 1960 reading passages include a selection of the best passages from previous forms." But it also states that no item in the 1960 series is identical to an item in an earlier form.

The series contains three forms at each of two levels. Forms 2A, 2B, and 2C were designed for grades 9 through 12, and Forms 1A, 1B, and 1C for college freshmen and sophomores. It is suggested in the Directions for Administering and Scoring that for above average twelfth graders the examiner might prefer the upper series. This reviewer takes a much stronger position: the upper series *should* be used in such instances; in fact, a strong argument can be made that it should be used with average twelfth grade students as well, for the lower level forms contain some passages that border on the childish, and lack ceiling for twelfth graders. For example, the range of raw scores for twelfth grade students scoring in the highest quarter on the level of comprehension section of Form 2A is from 27 to the maximum of 30—hardly enough for valid discrimination. Of course, the tests in the lower series can and probably should be used with below average twelfth graders.

Aside from the problem of form selection, the instructions for administration and scoring are explicit and complete.

Raw scores on all forms are converted to a common scale. The statement in the manual that the scores are directly comparable from form to form can be misleading, because the forms do not have the same range of converted scores. But even for that section of the range where pairs of scores exist the claim can be questioned. For example, a student taking 2A must get 30 per cent of the level of comprehension questions correct to earn a converted score equivalent to zero correct on Form 1B. In fact, more than half of the converted score scale for the Form 2A level of comprehension test is related to a raw score performance on Form 1B that is at chance or below. The term "directly comparable" applies better to other sections of the range.

The samples used for norming the tests were well selected and adequately described. Tables are presented by grade giving percentile bands for converted score equivalents. The upper limit of each band corresponds to a score approximately one standard error of measurement above the midpoint of the converted score interval and the lower limit is a like distance below the midpoint. Referring to these bands the Technical Report states, "It is hoped that this form of presentation will encourage more realistic interpretation of scores." This is a worthy goal, but its achievement is impeded by the directions given for interpreting the bands. To illustrate, in the Manual for Interpreting Scores it is stated, "Stanley's score falls between the 75th and 90th percentiles for this group. This means that only about 10 per cent of freshmen in the norms group score higher and about 75 per cent score lower."

This statement is misleading. It confuses two concepts, namely, percentile rank and the probable location of a "true" percentile rank. Percentile rank for an individual will vary between administrations of the same test as well as between parallel forms, and it is important to make this clear. But the percentile rank for *any* individual on *one administration* is a point on the percentile scale. The percentile band could have been made wider—for example, plus and minus two standard errors of measurement. If the wider band were used, this would not mean that a smaller percentage of the norm group scored above and below Stanley. It would merely mean that the band is more likely to include the percentile corresponding to Stanley's "true" score. If Stanley's performance on a single administration of a test is equivalent to a percentile rank of 84, it can be said that on that particular test at a particular point in time he marked more questions correctly than 84 per cent of the norm population. If his percentile band is 75–90 it can also be said that it is likely that the percentile corresponding to the mean score he would obtain based on repeated administrations of similar forms would fall in this range. But it should not be stated nor implied that "only about 10 per cent of freshmen in the norms group score higher and about 75 per cent lower." This statement misinterprets the significance of the band. Earlier in the manual, in a section explaining why the publisher lists percentile bands, a more accurate description of their meaning is presented.

The reliability coefficients (test-retest) reported are very much the same from form to form. Typical are the values reported for Form 1C based on twelfth graders: vocabulary, .88; level, .77; speed, .83; and total, .92. No reliability coefficients are reported for college students.

Because of the nature of the tests, validity is defended largely on the basis of "relying on well-qualified people to construct the tests." A summary of several validity studies relating to earlier forms is given.

In summary, with some exceptions, the manuals are quite good. The tests, on the other hand, leave something to be desired. By the nature of the scores reported, a major purpose seems to be the differentiation of speed and level of comprehension, and yet the data supplied suggest that except for unreliability these two variables are perfectly correlated. Good manuals can help assure that the basic qualities of a test will be realized, but the best of manuals can do nothing to improve those qualities.

W. G. FLEMING, *Assistant Director, Department of Educational Research, Ontario College of Education, University of Toronto, Toronto, Ontario, Canada.*

The *Cooperative English Tests* have been in use for many years. During this time they have undergone substantial revisions, and a great deal of background and interpretative information has been accumulated. A number of critics have commented on successive editions in *The Mental Measurements Yearbook*. It seems reasonable to examine the 1960 edition with particular reference to the points raised by these critics.

There has been frequent comment on the care taken to obtain the services of highly competent people to construct and edit the items. The most up-to-date and appropriate statistical techniques have been applied in the tryout and analysis of the items. As a result, the finished product has been unusually free from the kind of flaw that proves irritating in so many standardized tests.

The new edition gives even more grounds for satisfaction with the competence shown in construction and editing of the items, the format, and the adequacy of instructions for administration and interpretation of results. The Manual for Interpreting Scores should make a real contribution to the education of teacher-users with little training in statistics and measurement. In particular, the explanation of the use of the percentile band should help to improve understanding of the meaning and importance of errors of measurement.

Some of the earlier critics were concerned about the validity of the tests. Perhaps their main apprehensions had to do with the test of English expression, which the present reviewer does not propose to deal with, as a measure of the student's ability in written expression. The question of validity is also very important for the reading comprehension test. Validity coefficients obtained from a number of studies are presented in the Technical Report, not only for total reading, but also for vocabulary, level of comprehension, and speed of comprehension. These studies are based on earlier editions of the tests, but it is claimed, not unreasonably, that the latest edition is enough like these that the findings may be considered relevant. While some of the reported validity coefficients are reasonably high, both in absolute terms and in comparison with those based on other similar test scores, others are not particularly impressive. They tend to reinforce existing evidence that the user of the tests should not rely on them to the exclusion of other forms of examinations, whatever the defects of the latter may be, if he wants to obtain a satisfactory evaluation of the many facets of a student's development in English. Of course it has never been reasonable to complain, and certainly cannot

now be suggested, that the publishers have made exaggerated claims about the meaning or value of the scores.

An area of potentially fruitful study in the continuing process of improving and perfecting the tests has to do with the degree of emphasis on different types of items. One aspect of this problem concerns the optimum balance between vocabulary and reading comprehension items, assuming that there are no other categories that deserve inclusion along with these two. There must necessarily be a degree of arbitrariness in the decision to have 60 items in each of the two subsections. A continuing examination of statistical evidence and of informed opinion on the advisability of maintaining the present arrangement is indicated.

Another aspect of the same problem has to do with the degree of emphasis on different types of reading passages, such as exposition, narration, and argumentation, and, as a parallel in the vocabulary section, on words commonly used as conveyors of objective information as opposed to those generally used to communicate feeling or emotion. It seems to the reviewer that the utilitarian aspects of the language have predominated in the construction of the tests to the extent that teachers who place a high value on reading for inspirational or aesthetic purposes may be somewhat unhappy with the result. Even though it may be validly pointed out that a very large proportion of reading is done for the "practical" purposes of obtaining information or ideas, there are good arguments for a higher proportion of passages intended to produce emotional effects. More feeling-toned words in the vocabulary section might also tend to meet criticism of this type.

Assuming the appropriateness of the chosen frame of reference, the reading passages are quite satisfactory. On the whole, they are good examples of clear, straightforward language. The item writers have avoided resorting to obscurity or muddiness in their search for difficulty.

Past criticisms of inadequacies in information on reliability have been met. Reliability coefficients between alternative forms are presented for different parts of the tests and for different grade groups. These are satisfactorily high.

Norms information was also criticized at one time for lack of sufficient detail on the types of schools selected. Such information cannot now be considered unsatisfactory. The approach has been to use rather small numbers of students from a relatively large number of institutions. Also, the limitations of "national" norms and the advisability of obtaining and using local norms are pointed out.

In general, it is evident that the test producers have been keenly alert for weaknesses suggested by critics and by users of the tests in practical situations, and have gone to considerable lengths to correct these. The latest edition of *Reading Comprehension: Cooperative English Tests* will be welcomed as a definite contribution to the science of measurement.

For reviews by Robert Murray Bear and J. B. Stroud of the earlier edition, see 3:497. For reviews of the complete battery, see 256; for reviews of earlier editions, see 3:120.

[807]

*Reading: Public School Achievement Tests. Grades 3–8; 1928–59; subtest of *Public School Achievement Tests;* Forms 1, 2, ['28, 8 pages]; battery manual ('59, 20 pages, essentially the same—including norms—as 1928 manual); no data on reliability; $3.50 per 35 tests; 25¢ per battery manual; 50¢ per specimen set; postage extra; 40(45) minutes; Jacob S. Orleans; Bobbs-Merrill Co., Inc. *

For reviews of the complete battery, see 40:1194.

[808]

*SRA Achievement Series: Reading. Grades 1–2, 2–4, 4–6, 6–9; 1954–64; subtest of *SRA Achievement Series;* title on tests for grades 2–6 is *What Is This About?;* 2–5 scores: comprehension, vocabulary, verbal-pictorial association (grades 1–2 only), language perception (grades 1–2 only), total (Forms C and D only); 2 editions; battery teacher's handbook ['64, c1955, 47 pages] for both editions; 50¢ per teacher's handbook; postage extra; Louis P. Thorpe, D. Welty Lefever, and Robert A. Naslund; Science Research Associates, Inc. *

a) FORMS A AND B. Grades 1–2, 2–4, 4–6, 6–9; 1954–64; IBM for grades 4–9; 4 levels; battery school administrator's manual ('58, c1955–56, 32 pages); battery technical supplement, second edition ('57, 45 pages); battery pupil progress and profile charts ('59, c1955–59, 4 pages); separate answer sheets must be used in grades 4–9; 90¢ per 20 pupil progress and profile charts; 50¢ per school administrator's manual; $1 per technical supplement; $1.50 per specimen set of any one level of the complete battery.

  1) *Grades 1–2.* 1958–61; Form A ('58, 29 pages); battery examiner's manual ('58, revised '61, 21 pages); mimeographed technical data supplement ('59, 3 pages) for the battery; $3.50 per 20 tests; 120(185) minutes in 4 sessions.

  2) *Grades 2–4.* 1955–60; Forms A ('55), B ('57), (15 pages); battery examiner's manual, third edition ('60, c1955–60, 27 pages); $2 per 20 tests; 50¢

per hand scoring stencil; 90(130) minutes in 2 sessions.

  3) *Grades 4–6.* 1954–60; IBM; Forms A ('54), B ('56), (16 pages); battery examiner's manual, second edition ('56, c1954–56, revised '60, 39 pages); $2.15 per 20 tests; $5 per 100 IBM scorable answer sheets; $1 per set of machine scoring stencils; 50¢ per hand scoring stencil; 65(80) minutes.

  4) *Grades 6–9.* 1954–60; IBM; Forms A ['55], B ('56), (18 pages); battery examiner's manual, second edition ('56, c1955–56, revised '60, 39 pages); $2 per 20 tests; $5 per 100 IBM scorable answer sheets; 50¢ per either hand or machine scoring stencil; 70(80) minutes.

b) FORMS C AND D. Grades 1–2, 2–4; 1955–64; 2 levels; battery test coordinator's manual ('64, c1961–64, 64 pages); battery pupil progress and profile charts ('64, c1955–64, 4 pages); 90¢ per 20 pupil progress and profile charts; 50¢ per test coordinator's manual; $2 per specimen set of both levels of the complete battery.

  1) *Grades 1–2.* 1958–64; Forms C ('58, revised '63), D ('63), (36 pages); Form C is essentially the same as the 1958 Form A except for typography, art work, 1 new item, revision in 13 items, and option order changes in 3 sets of items; battery examiner's manuals (45 pages): Form C ('58, revised '64), Form D ('63, c1958–63, revised '64); $3.50 per 20 tests; 120(185) minutes in 4 sessions.

  2) *Grades 2–4.* 1955–64; Forms C ('55, revised '63), D ('57, revised '63), (25 pages); tests are revisions, with approximately 24 per cent new items, of Forms A and B published in 1955 and 1957, respectively; battery examiner's manual ('64, c1955–64, 43 pages) for each form; $2 per 20 tests; 90(120) minutes in 2 sessions.

EDWARD B. FRY, *Professor of Education, Rutgers, The State University, New Brunswick, New Jersey.* [Review of Forms A and B.]

The reading tests of the *SRA Achievement Series* are carefully thought out, nicely prepared, and widely standardized. They can be recommended for group testing of average and above average pupils subject to the limitations stated below.

The authors have done an excellent job of stating objectives and in attempting to keep them in harmony with well known curriculum committee recommendations. The reading items have been classified according to types of skills required to answer them, and thus the tests go a long way to refute the critics of multiple choice testing who can only see that type of item as valid for examination of simple facts. One might wonder why more use was not made of Bloom's *Taxonomy of Educational Objectives* when classifying items, but nonetheless, a creditable job was done.

However, the fact that the individual items cover a wide range of skills does not justify the statement found in the administrator's manual that "Test Scores provide a basis for discovering and correcting the causes of poor achievement." In fact, only in the broadest sense can this statement be made. A counselor might do a gross kind of diagnosis in certain cases; for example, if all reading scores were down and all or most arithmetic scores were up.

There is apparently much overlap between vocabulary and comprehension, the only two reading scores given above grade 2. Product-moment correlations between vocabulary and comprehension range from .75 to .81 for various grade levels between second and ninth grade. Probably much of this is due to the authors' "holistic approach" which means that comprehension is based on items immediately following the reading of a paragraph or two, and vocabulary is tested on words used (and underlined) in the same sample paragraph. In brief, the vocabulary subtest and the comprehension subtest seem to be measuring much the same thing; this is not necessarily bad, as they are both important reading comprehension skills and taken together they undoubtedly give important information about the student's reading ability. The teacher, however, should not assume that he is measuring two different skills.

These reading tests should not be used with below average pupils. There are several reasons for this. First, the authors state in the Technical Manual:

Each battery has been so constructed that it does not contain easy items suitable for the seriously retarded pupil to answer correctly, and only a relatively few items simple enough for the low-average learner to handle successfully. However, the upper level of each test battery has been extended sufficiently so that it overlaps the next higher battery to a considerable extent.

The second reason for being wary and often, in fact, disregarding low scores, is that these tests, in common with most achievement tests, do not have a cutoff point at the chance guessing probability score. For example, if a student just guessed at each item on the reading vocabulary section for the grades 1–2 test, on the average he would get a raw score of 10 (there are 41 four-choice items) and this would yield a grade level score of 1.6. On the grades 2–4 form his guessing score for vocabulary would place him at grade level 2.1; on the 4–6 form it would be 3.9, and on the 6–9 form his guessing vocabulary score would be 5.7. Notice what nice progress the nonreading student can make by just guessing at higher forms. Is it any wonder that school superintendents refuse to have remedial reading programs based on such evidence?

It seems to this reviewer that publishers and authors should stop putting out this type of misinformation since, unfortunately, some teachers and school administrators will think that a reading vocabulary score of 5.7 is telling them something about the student when in fact it may only mean that the student was adroit enough to fill in one blank for each question. A cutoff point at least one standard error above the guessing probability score would remedy most of this, and the fact that the user was refused a grade level score would more often force him to give the next lower level test, as should be done anyway.

It is very difficult to assess reading ability with nationally standardized tests at the very beginning reading levels (under grade 3) because the child's knowledge of words is so constricted by the particular reading series of textbooks in which he has received instruction. This reviewer, having spent a good many hours with his knees forced under a little table and a primer in hand, was somewhat bothered by the vocabulary used in the grades 1–2 form of the test. The fourth item in the verbal-pictorial association subtest, for example, asks the child to connect one of eight pictures to each of the four following words: "bride, geyser, dairy, incline." This opinion about word difficulty was substantiated by *The Teacher's Word Book of 30,000 Words* by Thorndike and Lorge, who state that those words should be taught at grades 5, 8, 6, and 4, respectively. To a lesser extent this criticism is also true of the other subtests at the 1–2 level. The Spache readability formula for the two longer and more difficult (of five) sample paragraphs used in the comprehension subtest are at difficulty level 2.5 and 3.3.

The supplementary material such as scoring keys and manuals for the examiner, teacher, and administrator, and the Technical Supplement are all well done and helpful.

In summary, the SRA reading tests are good for measuring general reading ability of average and above average students. They are not recommended for below average pupils as the results are sometimes questionable and sometimes worthless unless extreme care is taken in selecting the proper form. A seventh grader with only a very mild reading problem should be given the 4–6 form and even lower if necessary. Similarly, a teacher with an average fourth grade should use the 2–4 form rather than the 4–6 form.

The difference between the reading vocabulary and reading comprehension sections is not very meaningful, but, separately or together, they give a useful measure of silent reading ability.

The use of the tests in first grade is very questionable and their use before the end of the second grade is somewhat questionable.

For reviews by N. Dale Bryant and Clarence Derrick of Forms A and B, see 5:649. For reviews of Forms A and B of the complete battery, see 21 and 5:21.

[809]
*Sentence Reading Test 1. Ages 7-6 to 11-1; 1956–60; 1 form ['60, 4 pages, identical with test published in 1956 except for format]; manual ['56, 8 pages]; 5s. per 12 tests; 6d. per single copy; 1s. per manual; prices include purchase tax; postage extra; 15(25) minutes; A. F. Watts; published for the National Foundation for Educational Research in England and Wales; Newnes Educational Publishing Co. Ltd. *

For reviews by Reginald R. Dale and Stephen Wiseman, see 5:652.

[810]
*Sequential Tests of Educational Progress: Reading. Grades 4–6, 7–9, 10–12, 13–14; 1956–63; IBM, NCS, and Grade-O-Mat; Forms A, B, ('57, c1956–57, 12–18 pages); 4 levels; battery directions ('57, 12 pages); interpretive manual ('57, 30 pages); battery technical report ('57, 58 pages); 1958 SCAT-STEP supplement ('58, 32 pages); 1962 SCAT-STEP supplement ('62, 49 pages); 1963 SCAT-STEP supplement of urban norms ('63, 16 pages); battery teacher's guide ('59, 85 pages); battery profile ('57, 1 page); battery student report ('58, 4 pages); no data on reliability of Form B; separate answer sheets or cards must be used; $4 per 20 tests; $1 per 20 IBM scorable answer sheets; 25¢ per scoring stencil; see 671 for prices of NCS answer sheets and scoring services; see 666 for prices of Grade-O-Mat cards; $1 per 20 profiles; $1 per 20 student reports; $1 per interpretive manual; $1 per technical report; $1 per supplement; $1 per teacher's guide; postage extra; $2 per specimen set, cash orders postpaid; 70(90–100) minutes; Cooperative Test Division. *
a) LEVEL 4. Grades 4–6; Forms 4A, 4B.
b) LEVEL 3. Grades 7–9; Forms 3A, 3B.
c) LEVEL 2. Grades 10–12; Forms 2A, 2B.
d) LEVEL 1. Grades 13–14; Forms 1A, 1B.

REFERENCES
1. MAYER, ROBERT W. "A Study of the STEP Reading, SCAT and WISC Tests, and School Grades." *Reading Teach* 12:117+ D '58. * (*PA* 34:3441)
2. O'SHAUGHNESSY, MARY MICHAEL. *Some Effects of Praise and Reproof on Test Performances on School Ability and Reading Achievement Tests.* Catholic University of America, Educational Research Monograph, Vol. 24, No. 2. Washington, D.C.: Catholic University of America Press, December 2, 1960. Pp. x, 114. *
3. RUDD, JOHN PAUL. *A Study of the Validity of Selected Predictors for Placement in Three-Rail Curricula.* Doctor's

research study No. 1, Colorado State College (Greeley, Colo.) 1962. (*DA* 24:184)
4. TRELA, THADDEUS MICHAEL. *A Comparison of Ninth Grade Achievement on Selected Measures of General Reading Comprehension, Critical Thinking, and General Educational Development.* Doctor's thesis, University of Missouri (Columbia, Mo.), 1962. (*DA* 23:2382)
5. ENDLER, NORMAN S., AND STEINBERG, DANNY. "Prediction of Academic Achievement at the University Level." *Personnel & Guid J* 41:694–9 Ap '63. * (*PA* 39:2888)
6. MICHAEL, WILLIAM B.; CATHCART, ROBERT; ZIMMERMAN, WAYNE S.; AND MILFS, MILO. "Gains in Various Measures of Communication Skills Relative to Three Curricular Patterns in College." *Ed & Psychol Meas* 23:365–74 su '63. * (*PA* 38:1384)

EMMETT ALBERT BETTS, *Research Professor, University of Miami, Coral Gables, Florida.*

One of the special features of the STEP series of tests is the inclusion of both reading and listening tests. This attention to listening permits the teacher to note a discrepancy between reading and listening achievement and to take steps to correct the deficit in reading ability. Moreover, the listening test may reveal causes of low achievement in reading, even among so-called superior students.

STEP Reading provides a wide range of types of material: fiction, poetry, rhymes, plays, letters, directions for doing something, announcements, articles of opinion, explanations, and information. These presentations probably are of sufficient length to provide relatively high reliability and to measure the pupil's achievement in dealing with units of material longer than the paragraph.

The test materials appear to be well written by competent craftsmen and interesting to the pupils. At Level 4, for example, there are selections on history, games (horseshoes), a canary and a whale, a railroad yard, safety, how a camera operates, plants, and Edison's birthday, as well as verse, poetry, and a play.

These reading tests provide an adequate coverage of certain thinking abilities. Moreover, these specific learnings are identified by item numbers under appropriate categories in the Teacher's Guide, permitting the teacher to identify "need" areas for teaching purposes. However, the causes of these deficits are not necessarily identified; for example, low achievement on some time test items may indicate a need for word perception skills rather than for "analyzing motivation" or critical reading. These hazards are not identified in the well written materials for the use and interpretation of the tests. In short, these tests, like other achievement tests, have limited use for diagnostic purposes and, therefore, require considerable sophistication on the part of the teacher who interprets them.

STEP Reading is purported to measure five major categories of comprehension skills, abilities, and attitudes: (*a*) ability to recall ideas, (*b*) ability to translate ideas and make inferences, (*c*) ability to analyze motivation (of the author), (*d*) ability to analyze presentation, and (*e*) ability to criticize (constructively). Specific test items, not always sequentially grouped, deal with mood, intent, and tone (i.e., reader relationship to author), ability to visualize, relevance of ideas, sequence of ideas (e.g., in learning to play horseshoes), idiomatic and figurative expressions, and drawing conclusions (related facts and cause-effect).

The above achievements are quite thoroughly examined; however, many important reading-study learnings are untapped: organization (e.g., outlining, charts, etc.), rate and purpose (e.g., skimming, rapid reading, and study-type reading—except by inference on the part of the interpreter), word perception, vocabulary, etc. In short, very little is done on the concept that "reading is thinking in a language."

Users of these tests need to select them with caution. For example, Level 4 tests purportedly are designed for grades 4, 5, and 6, where the range of reading achievement may be from beginning reading to at least twelfth grade. However, the vocabulary of the first selection in Form 4B includes *holiday, swimming, experiments, discovery, invention,* and a number of other words which, in terms of word perception skills, will frustrate the lowest 15 to 20 per cent of a fourth grade class. On the other hand, the most difficult items may not challenge the upper 10 to 20 per cent. Hence, these tests are not wide range tests and are not designed for estimating either a pupil's independent reading level or his instructional reading level. However, they may be used to compare the performance of groups and to screen out those pupils at the "tails" of a distribution.

Hence, caution should be observed in selecting pupils for the administration of a given test. Users of these tests are given sound advice that "the tests at a given level are designed for *typical* students in the grade range indicated." Unfortunately, no provision is made for testing the lower achievers, especially in grade 4, but this point is not made in the guide materials.

PAUL R. LOHNES, *Associate Professor of Education, State University of New York at Buffalo, Buffalo, New York.*

Excellent previous MMY reviews of STEP Reading provide the background for these supplementary comments and must be consulted (see 5:24 and 5:653). The consensus of earlier opinions seemed to be that these were carefully and skillfully constructed reading tests of high quality and promise, but that ETS had not furnished sufficient research evidence of validities. The usefulness of the converted scores was questioned because all interpretations of scores depended on percentile bands. The failure to provide alternate forms reliabilities was scored. This reviewer concurs with the earlier reviews in general, and will attempt to critique the present adequacy of STEP Reading research, as reported in all manuals now available. Since scores from a particular test are only meaningful when we know how they relate to scores from other sources, the research in question must be concerned with the SCAT-STEP battery and other school achievement measures, and not solely with STEP Reading. Two major deficiencies of the original published SCAT-STEP research which have not been reduced by more recent publications continue to plague users of STEP Reading, and the delineation of these two problems constitutes the burden of this review.

The first deficiency is the total lack of evidence regarding the factorial compositions of the reading tests. It is admitted that the tests measure a complex set of reading skills, but no evidence is forthcoming to support the contention that the chosen "five major reading-for-comprehension skills" are major components of reading ability, or that the STEP reading tests do actually "weight these five kinds of skills approximately equally." All we know is that a committee of authorities agreed on this breakdown of reading into component skills. With due respect for the committee, it would be highly desirable to have their judgments tested and supported by empirical evidence. This reviewer is surprised that ETS researchers who are so productive of sophisticated factor-analytic studies, testifying to their confidence in the significance of such studies, have allowed a major new test program to be launched and continued for years with no indication that factor analysis is considered pertinent to the establishment of the dimensions of school-developed abilities. Specifically, the claim that five components of reading ability are equally weighted in STEP Reading deserves the empirical test of a factor analysis of the item intercorrelations at each level. The meaningfulness of the results would be greater if the SCAT Verbal were also included. This reviewer suspects that ETS has such research results but has not shared them with STEP Reading users. Possibly the results are embarrassing. If positive support for the design of the reading tests is available in factor-analytic studies, ETS may be hesitant to involve users in the complexities of reports of these results. If so, the agency does educators a disservice, for the ability of ETS staffers to write explanations of technical matters which make those matters comprehensible to lay readers is well proven, and here is an opportunity to educate users on a very important matter, the factorial validities of tests. Since an earlier reviewer charged that the SCAT-STEP battery perhaps provided "a set of measures of general intelligence" (R. W. B. Jackson, see 5:24), it would seem that ETS would have moved to close this gap in the research documentation of the series. This earlier critique was based on inspection of reported correlations between SCAT and STEP tests. To date, no STEP manual reports intercorrelations among the STEP tests. ETS should accept responsibility to contribute, through the SCAT-STEP publications, to users' understanding of the trait composition and organization of the domain of school-developed abilities.

Mention of SCAT-STEP intercorrelations supports the charge of a second major deficiency of the research basis for the test battery, which is the failure to demonstrate differential predictive validities for the tests, and especially for STEP Reading versus SCAT Verbal. The correlations between these tests average about .80 (among 26 coefficients reported on page 13 of the 1957 Technical Report the highest is .87 and the lowest is .72), suggesting the possibility of very similar predictive validities. The one study of comparative validities reported (by R. W. Mayer, 1958 SCAT-STEP Supplement, p. 26) showed both tests correlated .70 with average grades for 271 seventh graders. If this result proved generalizable, it would be possible for the STEP Reading manual to pro-

vide instructions for predicting future achievements, making SCAT Verbal scores redundant and unnecessary. This reviewer suspects that little emphasis has been given to predictive validities of STEP Reading in order to avoid raising this question for the user. ETS should accept responsibility to face the challenge of current discussions of school testing programs which imply that the older distinction between aptitude and achievement batteries and the requirement that schools employ both may now be practically unnecessary and theoretically confusing. By describing the SCAT tests as measures of school-developed abilities ETS has moved in this direction, but the question of whether all uses of SCAT could be developed from STEP remains unanswered. A byproduct of a complete merger of scholastic aptitude and achievement tests might be the abandonment of the over- and under-achievement mythology, now fostered by the proposal for comparing STEP Reading and SCAT Verbal scores for individuals (1957 Interpretive Manual, p. 9).

Some other points on STEP Reading: (a) Users should ponder the report of marked sex differences at all grades (1957 Technical Report, p. 23). Should separate sex norms be prepared? (b) Ponder also the excellent report on reliabilities of difference scores (1958 SCAT-STEP Supplement, pp. 27–9) before interpreting profiles, especially reading versus writing differences, where the reported reliability is .04. (c) The report of a study by J. R. Cleary showing high alternate forms reliabilities in a particular situation, although not definitive, is comforting (1962 SCAT-STEP Supplement, p. 30).

This review has not summarized the many positive features of the STEP reading tests and manuals because they have been reviewed before. It has been argued that ETS should document the factorial composition and predictive validities of the tests.

For reviews by Eric F. Gardner, James R. Hobson, and Stephen Wiseman, see 5:653. For reviews of the complete battery, see 25 and 5:24.

*Silent Reading Tests. Standards 1–3 (ages 7–10), 3–8 (ages 10–15), 6–10 (ages 13–17); 1947–63; 3 levels; postpaid; specimen set not available; Afrikaans edition available; National Bureau of Educational and Social Research. *

a) SILENT READING TEST (ELEMENTARY). Standards 1-3; 1947-63; 4 tests; instructions and norms ['62, 13 pages]; no data on reliability; prices range from R1.38 to R2.73 per 100 tests.

  1) *Paragraphs.* Forms A ['63], B ['51], (7 pages, essentially the same as 1947 tests); 20(30) minutes.
  2) *Sentences.* Forms A, B, ['51, 5 pages, essentially the same as 1947 tests]; 15(20) minutes.
  3) *Vocabulary.* Forms A, B, ['61, 4-5 pages, essentially the same as 1947-51 tests]; 10(15) minutes.
  4) *Speed.* Forms A, B, ['51, 4 pages]; 4(7) minutes.

b) SILENT READING TESTS (REVISED EDITION). Standards 3-8, 6-10; 1947-63; 3-4 scores: vocabulary, paragraphs, sentences (junior level only), language usage; items of vocabulary, paragraphs, and sentences subtests taken from 1947 forms of the earlier edition; 2 levels; revised manual ('63, 42 pages); separate answer sheets must be used; Ro.47 per 100 answer sheets; Ro.06 per scoring stencil.

  1) *Junior.* Standards 3-8; 1947-63; Forms A, B, ['58, 25 pages]; R5.00 per 100 tests of Form A; R8.98 per 100 tests of Form B; 90(95) minutes.
  2) *Senior.* Standards 6-10; 1951-63; Forms A, B, ['58, 20 pages]; R5.00 per 100 tests; 72(77) minutes.

[812]

★**Southgate Group Reading Tests.** Ages 6-0 to 7-6, 7-0 to 8-11; 1959-62; 2 tests; postage and purchase tax extra; Vera Southgate; University of London Press Ltd. *

a) TEST 1—WORD SELECTION. Ages 6-0 to 7-6; 1959; Forms A, B, C, (4 pages); manual (23 pages); 6s. 3d. per 25 tests; 4d. per single copy; 2s. 6d. per manual; (15-20) minutes.

b) TEST 2—SENTENCE COMPLETION TEST. Ages 7-0 to 8-11; 1962; Forms A, B, (4 pages); manual (20 pages); 7s. 6d. per 25 tests; 6d. per single copy; 2s. 6d. per manual; 15(30) minutes.

M. L. KELLMER PRINGLE, *Director, National Bureau for Co-operation in Child Care, London, England.*

The aim of Test 1 of the *Southgate Group Reading Tests* is to provide teachers with a simple and speedy method of making a preliminary assessment of the reading ability of young children who are in the initial stages of mastering the subject. The author's purpose was to fill a need which existed in England since there was no group test available with norms extending much below the seven year level. In the manual it is suggested that the test is most useful for average children between the ages of 6 and 7½ years and for older children up to 14 years who are slow in learning to read. Norms are given for reading ages of 5 years 9 months to 7 years 9 months. To facilitate retesting, three parallel forms are provided. They each contain 30 items, which consist of five words, one of which is read aloud by the teacher and ringed by the pupil; 16 of the items are accompanied by a drawing illustrating the correct word. The design and layout are excel-

lent, the printing and the drawings being bold, clear, and well spaced out. The manual states that the 450 words were selected from 676 items on the basis of item analyses. While the words appear to be well within the comprehension of 6- to 8-year-olds, no information is given as to how they were chosen in the first place. Otherwise the manual contains all the required basic information which is set out simply and lucidly. However, one point needs attention when the instructions for administering the test are reprinted: it is stated that the key word is to be repeated twice; in fact, in the first 10 items, for which the instructions are given in full, the key word is repeated three times for three items and four times for one item. Since this applies to all three forms, it appears to be deliberate. There may well be a good reason for this, but in that case it should be given and the wrong instruction deleted.

The standardisation sample consisted of all the children in Worcester's 32 infant and primary schools who were between the ages of 5 years 8 months and 8 years 1 month; the total number was 2,329. Each pupil completed two of the three parallel forms of the test. It is regrettable that the correlation coefficients are not given if they were worked out. Instead, in discussing the reliability of the test, it is stated that a group of 96 children in one school were given two of the parallel forms on different days and that the product-moment correlation coefficient between raw scores was .95.

Test 2 has been designed for use in conjunction with Test 1. Indeed, the author suggests that "when a teacher is in doubt about the ability of the pupils whom he wishes to test, it is kinder to commence by administering Test 1, and to follow it with Test 2 for those who achieve high scores on Test 1, rather than to reverse this procedure." Since each test takes only about a quarter of an hour, this procedure is quite practicable. Norms are given for reading ages of 7 years 0 months to 9 years 7 months. For Test 1 the author recommends that no more than 15 to 20 children should be tested at one sitting. On the other hand, Test 2 can be taken by an entire class of 40 to 50 pupils, but to prevent cheating a simple but ingenious device is used: the practice examples and instructions for administration are identical for the two parallel forms but Form A has been printed on white and Form B on blue paper; thus, when distributing the test booklets the teacher can readily check that children sitting next to each other do not have the same form of the test. The alternative form of the test can of course also be used for retesting but one would have to ensure that children sit in exactly the same position as on the first occasion if the anti-cheating device is to be employed again.

Each form of Test 2 consists of 42 sentences with a choice of five words at the end, from which the child has to choose one to complete the sentence. They are arranged in order of increasing difficulty. Again it is not made clear how the multiple choice items were selected but the author states that "10 separate tests, comprising 584 items, were devised and administered to children within the age range of 6-0 to 10-11 years." It is not clear whether "item" in this context refers to the sentence or to each of the five words accompanying each sentence.

The standardisation of all the tests was carried out in one small cathedral town in the Midlands (population 67,050). "There is no reason to believe," states the author, "that the reading ability of children in Worcester differs markedly from the reading ability of children elsewhere in the country." Since there were no pupils from rural or highly industrialised or metropolitan areas, one would feel more ready to accept this opinion if it were supported by some factual evidence. After all, it is known that there are differences in attainment in different parts of the country.

On all the tests girls tended to achieve higher scores than boys; on Test 2, this difference reached the 5 per cent level of significance on Form B for the age group 8-11. Though the question of establishing separate norms for boys and girls was considered, the author decided against this mainly on the grounds that teachers would find it of greater practical utility to have a level of attainment for their pupils irrespective of sex.

In summary, these reading tests are welcome additions in the armoury of teachers who wish to group large numbers of pupils and to screen for further individual attention those who are backward in the subject. The tests are well presented, statistically adequate, and both easy and quick to administer. Test 1 has the added merit of making possible the group testing of younger or more backward children than has hitherto been feasible in this country, while Test 2 is distinguished for its "anti-cheating" device.

MAGDALEN D. VERNON, *Professor of Psychology, University of Reading, Reading, England.*

These two group tests are intended for British teachers who wish to gain a general idea as to the achievement of children in the early stages of learning to read, and who have no opportunity for individual testing. The first test especially will be of considerable value since there are few if any group tests for beginners available with British norms.

In Test 1, a test for word recognition, the children, who can be tested in groups up to 20, have to select from five alternatives the word spoken to them in each item. In 16 out of 30 items the correct word is also illustrated by a picture. Preliminary examples are given for practice. There is no time limit for the test, but it normally takes 15–20 minutes. Norms are provided for converting scores into reading ages 5-9 to 7-9.

Test 2, a test of reading comprehension, can be used for larger groups by distributing the alternative forms, A and B, so that children sitting side by side have different forms. After preliminary instructions (the same for A and B) as to which word they should choose to complete short sentences, the children work the 42 test items silently within a time limit of 15 minutes. Norms are given for reading ages 7-0 to 9-7. In both tests the norms have been based on the median, not the mean, scores since a number of children on whom the tests were standardized achieved scores of zero or full scores.

The test manuals are extremely clear and readily comprehensible. The author is to be commended for employing no time limit in Test 1, since little children are confused by haste. Presumably she considered that the older children for whom Test 2 is intended are accustomed to speeded performance.

The process of construction appears to have been satisfactory for both tests. Item analysis was carried out with 500–600 trial items, and the items selected with high validity values to cover the required range of difficulty. Reliability for both tests, as calculated by product-moment correlations between alternative forms, is of the order of .95. Mean scores for alternative forms show no significant differences.

The validity of the first test was measured by correlation with performance on five individual word reading tests, the average correlation being .90, and with teachers' estimates of reading ability (rank correlations of .87 and .95 for an earlier duplicated form of the test). The second test was correlated with another sentence completion test and with an individual word reading test, giving correlations of .82 and .88. It is perhaps unfortunate that more tests were not used for validation.

It should be noted that standardization was carried out in one locality only, the city of Worcester. This procedure obviated sampling difficulties since every child in the city schools within the age ranges of 5-8 to 8-1 (2,329 children) for Test 1 and 7-0 to 10-11 (3,751 children) for Test 2 was tested. However, the procedure does raise the question of representativeness. Several investigations have shown that reading achievement varies considerably in different parts of Britain; it is not possible to determine where, other than in Worcester, the norms for these tests are applicable. Again, it is not stated whether the norms were obtained from children taught mainly by look-and-say methods or phonic methods, or both types of methods. It is the reviewer's impression that Test 1 particularly might be easier for children taught by look-and-say since it includes some words, such as "umbrella" and "cigarette," which might be discriminated by length alone, and other words, such as "thought" and "rough," which are so irregular as to be difficult for phonically taught children. Performance on the test might also be affected by differences in familiarity with the test words resulting from the reading books customarily given to the children. Again, we are not informed as to whether a wide or restricted range of these is used in the Worcester schools.

To summarize: The two tests provide a useful coverage for British children in the early stages of learning to read, and they should be valuable to teachers who wish to obtain a general assessment of reading achievement in their classes. Test 1 is probably the best of its kind available. There are other alternatives to Test 2, and its validity is not entirely satisfactory. However, it would certainly be advisable also to apply individual tests to children showing poor achievement, in order to ascertain if they are really backward or were nervous and confused by the group testing situation. Some check on the norms, involving children in other areas and children taught by different methods, would also seem desirable.

Brit J Ed Psychol 30:188 Je '60. P. E. Vernon. [Review of Test 1.] * a useful job * It is a pity, perhaps, that no information is given on the effects of children's familiarity with the tester's pronunciation and of the clarity of his enunciation. The high reliability quoted as between different testers is meaningless, since it is based on a wide age range. However, about half the items are accompanied by pictures; and the correlations of around 0.90 (in a 6-year age group) with individual oral tests, are reassuring. With reading comprehension, as might be expected, the correlation appears to be much lower though the quoted figure—is again—meaningless. The thirty items in each form provide fair discrimination, namely about one to two months per item. Standardisation was based on over two thousand children in the City of Worcester. One wonders whether the assumption that this sample is representative of the country is legitimate, but it had the advantage of being a complete population. The author might also have provided percentiles at successive age levels. She claims, reasonably enough, that teachers do not understand standard scores; but one fears that the absence of indications of spread mean that there is little discrimination among below-average younger, or above-average older, readers.

[813]

Stanford Achievement Test: [Reading Tests]. Grades 4-5.5, 5.5-6.9, 7-9; 1922-64; same as paragraph meaning and (grades 4-6.9 only) word meaning subtests of *Stanford Achievement Test,* [1964 *Revision*]; 1953 revision (see 5:656) still available; IBM and MRC; 3 levels; manual ['64, 8 pages] for each level; supplementary directions ['64, 1 page each] for using IBM answer sheets, Harbor answer cards; separate answer sheets or cards may be used; $1.50 per 35 IBM answer sheets; 20¢ per scoring stencil; $2 per 100 Harbor answer cards (machine scoring service, by Measurement Research Center, Inc., may be arranged through the publisher) ; 40¢ per specimen set of any one level; postage extra; Truman L. Kelley, Richard Madden, Eric F. Gardner, and Herbert C. Rudman; Harcourt, Brace & World, Inc. *
a) INTERMEDIATE 1 READING TESTS. Grades 4-5.5; 2 scores: word meaning, paragraph meaning; Form W ('64, 8 pages) ; $4.30 per 35 tests; 40(48) minutes.
b) INTERMEDIATE 2 READING TESTS. Grades 5.5-6.9; 2 scores: word meaning, paragraph meaning; Form W ('64, 8 pages) ; $4.30 per 35 tests; 42(50) minutes.
c) ADVANCED PARAGRAPH MEANING TEST. Grades 7-9; Form W ('64, 5 pages) ; $4 per 35 tests; 30(35) minutes.

REFERENCES

1–4. See 4:555.
5. TRELA, THADDEUS MICHAEL. *A Comparison of Ninth Grade Achievement on Selected Measures of General Reading Comprehension, Critical Thinking, and General Educational Development.* Doctor's thesis, University of Missouri (Columbia, Mo.), 1962. (*DA* 23:2382)

For reviews by Helen M. Robinson and Agatha Townsend of the 1953 revision, see 5:656; for a review by James R. Hobson of the previous edition, see 4:555; for a review by Margaret G. McKim, see 3:503. For a review of the complete battery, see 26; for a review of the 1953 revision, see 5:25; for reviews of earlier editions, see 4:25 and 3:18.

[814]

★**Survey of Primary Reading Development.** Grades 1–3.5; 1957; Forms A-1, B-1, (15 pages); manual (48 pages); $2.75 per 20 tests; 50¢ per manual; $1 per specimen set; postage extra; (30–60) minutes in 1–2 sessions; J. Richard Harsh and Dorothy Soeberg; Educational Testing Service (Western Office).*

THOMAS C. BARRETT, *Assistant Professor of Education, The University of Wisconsin, Madison, Wisconsin.*

The *Survey of Primary Reading Development* (SPRD) employs six tests to determine the reading ability of primary grade children. Test 1, Form Comparison, and Test 2, Word Form Comparison, require the student to visually discriminate between pairs of geometric forms and words respectively. Tests 3 and 4, Word Recognition and Sentence Recognition, evaluate the child's ability to hear, remember, and select from among several alternatives a word or sentence pronounced by the tester. Test 5, Sentence Comprehension, measures the ability to select from among three alternatives for each item a word or, in one instance on each form, a group of words which best completes a statement. Test 6, Story Comprehension, includes five stories in each of the two forms. Four to nine statements follow each story and the student is asked to designate from these statements the ones that are true on the basis of what was read.

The manual presents the directions for the six tests in a straightforward, easy to follow manner. Scoring procedures are handled in a similar fashion, and the test user should have little difficulty with the correction process with one possible exception, Test 6, Story Comprehension. Regarding this test, the manual states that it is necessary to determine how many stories a subject actually reads. To achieve this

objective, the manual indicates that the subject must circle at least one statement following a story before all the items relating to that story are to be scored. Since only the correct statements are marked by the student, it seems possible that he might read a story and not choose to mark any statements. Potential test users should be alert to this, and the authors might consider altering the directions on this test in future editions so that students will mark both right and wrong statements following the stories.

The SPRD manual presents a discussion of validity under three headings: (*a*) content validity, (*b*) instrumental validity, and (*c*) predictive validity. With respect to content validity, the authors concentrate on the selection of the vocabulary used in the SPRD. They indicate that a composite vocabulary for the SPRD was drawn from samples of dictated stories of primary children and from the most commonly used series of readers. Although this is helpful information, it would have been more useful had the authors stated the number and sources of the experience charts utilized and the number of basic reading series involved, and given a description of the final composite vocabulary. No other information is provided with respect to content validity; therefore, the potential test user is not provided with the authors' rationale for the selection and the weighting of the six tests.

Instrumental validity deals with the concern of the authors to provide the students with a simple and consistent means of indicating responses to the items so that the ability to follow directions does not confound the results. This is commendable; however, as indicated above the simplicity of this means of indicating responses may be detrimental to the scoring of Test 6.

Regarding predictive validity, the manual reports a correlation coefficient of .79 between the SPRD and the assigned levels of reading competency of each child in an unidentified sample of children determined by a reading specialist using a diagnostic battery of reading tests, which is not described in terms of validity and reliability. The lack of information about the sample, the criterion, and the procedures used to obtain the validity coefficient leaves much to be desired.

Three reliability coefficients for the SPRD

are reported in the manual. Two of these are coefficients of internal consistency based on n's of 87 and 304 and obtained by split-half analyses. The coefficients in these two instances are both .91; however, no information about the subjects sampled or the form or forms of the SPRD used in the analyses are provided. A third reliability coefficient of .88 is reported for a test-retest analysis of Form A-1 involving a sample of 128 subjects. In general, the reliability information for the SPRD is inadequate. Moreover, no reliability coefficients regarding the equivalence of the two forms, A-1 and B-1, are made available; thus, comparability of the two forms is left in doubt.

Grade placement norms are provided for both forms. These norms are based on relatively large samples of first, second, and third grade children drawn from eight school systems in Los Angeles County. Although mention is made of the intent to obtain a representative sample in terms of socioeconomic status, community size, population mobility, and scholastic characteristics, the only specific information about the standardization sample offered is: a brief description of six communities used in the sample; a statement that the average age of the sample upon entering first grade was six years and two months; and a statement that the standardization sample had a normal distribution of intelligence with a mean of 101 and a standard deviation of 15 on an unidentified intelligence test. Fortunately, the manual does recommend that communities using the SPRD would benefit if local norms were developed because of the nature of standardization sample.

In addition to the grade placement norms, the manual presents a scale which places students in six descriptive levels of reading development on the basis of their total scores on the SPRD. These levels of reading development are then related to instructional activities presented in the last 13 pages of the manual. Although the levels of reading development and the correlated instructional activities would be helpful to the classroom teacher, the accuracy of the SPRD in indicating such levels is not verified by the technical information in the manual.

In conclusion, the SPRD has a number of apparent technical limitations, e.g., inadequate information concerning reliability and validity, and a standardization sample drawn from a provincial population. Nevertheless the SPRD does sample behaviors that are accepted characteristics of reading development in the primary grades, and it may be useful, at best, as a supplementary instrument for estimating reading development for primary grade students.

RUSSELL G. STAUFFER, *Professor of Education, and Director, The Reading Study Center, University of Delaware, Newark, Delaware.*

The principal use of this test is, as the test name implies, to survey reading development and, as the manual indicates, the survey is for all children in the first, second, and beginning third grade. It is also suggested that the test might be used with special training class pupils, middle and upper grade elementary pupils who are low achievers, and as part of a battery of tests for individual pupil study. To serve in these different ways the test is designed in six parts so as to "offer some success to a child regardless of his level of reading * the variety of exercises allows the child at the beginning level of reading development to complete some items successfully and also provides some challenge for the student at a more advanced level."

The word "survey" as used in this test seems to apply then to the range of skills exemplified by the six parts and not to the range of achievement that might be found in a typical population such as that used in the standardization. The test does not have enough top to allow a capable third grade level pupil to show his achievement. It is a well established fact that pupils at the first grade level typically display a range of reading achievement of five years. This being the case, this test may survey range of achievement only for first grade level pupils, since it does not have enough top to survey the range of pupils at a second or third grade level.

Examination of the six parts shows that the first four parts are not really tests of ability to read. Part one deals with geometric form discrimination and, as the accompanying manual states: "High scores may be made by children ....even though they may be unable to read." The second part requires pupils to recognize whether words, rather than geometrical forms, are alike or different in appearance. Again, good scores may be obtained by children "even though they may be unable to attach meanings to the words." Tests 3 and 4 require the pupil to listen to the examiner pronounce either a word or a short sentence and then mark in the test the word or sentence that says the same thing. This kind of aid to recognition whereby the teacher does the reading orally falls far short of a test in which a pupil must either use a picture as a stimulus or deal on his own with printed words. Parts five and six require pupil ability to read. However, the number of items is limited to nine and five, respectively, and their structure is quite simple.

Each part is scored separately. A total raw score can be converted into a grade placement equivalent. Test users are cautioned about the use of grade placements for individual children because, for example, "a grade placement of 2.3 does not have a statistically significant deviation from 2.4 or 2.2 for an individual child." The manual also says that a total score usually describes a "frustration level" rather than an "instructional level" for a pupil. No evidence is provided to support this claim. A scattergram analysis is provided to allow pupil placement at one of six levels. Each level is briefly described. Again, no evidence is cited to support either the levels or skills listed for instructional purposes at the different levels.

It is claimed that a feature of this test is the suggested instructional activities recommended for use with pupils placing at one or another of the six different levels. These activities are located in the manual of instructions. They are not to be thought of as remedial in nature. Predictive validity for such subclassifications of pupils and recommended instructional activities are based on one validity study conducted by a reading specialist in a summer workshop. This is hardly an adequate means of determining validity.

[815]

★Survey of Reading Achievement: California Survey Series. Grades 7-9, 9-12; 1959; all items from *California Reading Test, 1957 Edition;* IBM; 2 levels; $2.80 per 35 tests; separate answer sheets may be used; 5¢ per IBM answer sheet; 20¢ per scoring stencil; 10¢ per series class record sheet; 2¢ per series individual record sheet; postage extra; 50¢ per specimen set of either level, postpaid; 40(45) minutes with answer sheets, 37(42) minutes without answer sheets; Ernest W. Tiegs and Willis W. Clark; California Test Bureau. *

a) JUNIOR HIGH LEVEL. Grades 7-9; Forms 1, 2, (11 pages); no specific manual; combined manual (20 pages) for this test, test 638, and the junior high level of test 280.

b) ADVANCED. Grades 9-12; Forms 1, 2, (12 pages); no specific manual; combined manual (20 pages) for this test, test 591, and the advanced level of test 280.

CLARENCE DERRICK, *Professor of English, and Chairman, Humanities Department, University of Florida, Gainesville, Florida.*

The *Survey of Reading Achievement,* one of four separate tests adapted from the longer *California Achievement Tests,* is a 40-minute, 100-item test designed to measure achievement in vocabulary and reading comprehension. The items are "spiraled," i.e., arranged in blocks— vocabulary, comprehension, vocabulary, comprehension. A variety of skills are sampled— ability to recognize synonyms and antonyms; ability to follow directions and use the dictionary; ability to interpret graphs, charts, and maps; ability to draw inferences and deductions in reading. A 20-page manual for each level provides information on reliability, validity, and equivalence of forms, and directions for administering, scoring, and interpreting the test results. The normative population is described; and percentile, standard score, grade placement, and age norms tables are supplied.

Test items can always be criticized. The general rule is that no one ever likes an item written by someone else. The items in this series are distinctly above average, but there are flaws. A useful technique is to attempt to answer reading comprehension items *before* reading the selection (I wish the publishers would stop calling their selections "stories"). On Form 1, grades 7-8-9, items 59-67, this reviewer answered correctly 8 out of the 9 questions about Switzerland without looking at the passage. Fortunately, most of the items in the test stood up better when examined by this technique. The map in this same form is too small. Again fortunately, comparable items in the other forms did not have this defect. Some of the "following directions" items have the flavor of aptitude tests. The number of items testing a particular study skill is necessarily small, but this is a survey test reporting only a single score.

The statistical data are reasonably adequate. One might ask whether it is advisable to report scores in such a variety of ways. In the ancient days, grade placement and age norms were used. Standard scores and percentile ranks are improvements. One suspects that the publisher is listening to the voice of the uninformed consumer, but publishers have an obligation to lead, not follow.

These criticisms are minor. All in all, the

Survey of Reading Achievement is a good test which can serve an important and useful function.

J. RAYMOND GERBERICH, *Visiting Professor of Education, University of Maryland, College Park, Maryland.*

In an era of linear and branching programs, it seems appropriate to trace the genealogy of this test in similar terms. The stock goes back to the *Progressive Achievement Tests,* published in 1933 at four different levels. One of the three parts was also published separately as the *Progressive Reading Test.* Two revisions followed according to the same pattern, the second one in 1943. The Progressive series was followed by the *California Achievement Tests,* almost identical to their immediate predecessors, in 1950. A 1957 revision in which four levels of CAT were expanded to five brought the linear phase of the test series to a close up to the present.

Parallelism, a linear concept, is represented in the quarter century of test history recounted above, except for the minor digressions represented by splitting one level into two in the 1957 edition and by putting out an unrevised hand scoring edition for the elementary and intermediate grades, called the *California Basic Skills Tests.* True branching, however, did not occur until the *Surveys of Achievement* appeared in 1959, to place emphasis on a survey as contrasted with a diagnostic function. The *Survey of Reading Achievement* at two levels, covering grades 7 to 12, is paralleled by survey tests in language and mathematics.

An evaluation of the current reading test that does not take this background into account and that fails to recognize differences between the old and the new seems inadequate to this reviewer. Five reviews of the 1933, 1937, and 1950 editions of the reading tests have appeared in earlier yearbooks of the MMY series. Mention of separate tests in reviews of various editions of the batteries brings critical judgments about the reading tests in the MMY to more than a dozen. It seems appropriate here to examine the current reading test first and then to consider why and how the *Survey of Reading Achievement*—the first test under this title—evolved from the earlier tests of receptive language skills.

The current reading test, paralleled by tests in the areas of mathematics and language, appears at two overlapping levels—"Junior High Level" for grades 7 to 9 and "Advanced" for grades 9 to 12, and in Forms 1 and 2 at each level. Why names for the two levels are not more harmonious does not seem clear, in view of the various name patterns that easily come to mind for the lower and upper portions of the grade 7 to 12 span. Each of the forms at each of the levels includes 100 items in an omnibus format that shifts back and forth, in clusters of from 9 to 20 items, from reading vocabulary to reading comprehension. Vocabulary and comprehension items contribute to the total, and only, score in the ratio of 60 to 40, even though the time necessary to respond to items in these two areas of reading proficiency may well be in the reverse ratio of 40 to 60. The test is timed for 40 minutes with answer sheets and 37 minutes when answers are recorded in booklets.

These tests appear in the two-column format and type styles that have characterized tests of this publisher for many years. The print is clear and legible and the format is in general pleasing. Some undesirable by-products result, however. An occasional item, even a short one, is started in one column and finished in the next. The three lines of directions for one group of items dangles at the bottom of one column and the 20 items fill the next column. Some individual test items are nearly a half column in depth, and in one instance five long items occurring together fill an entire page.

In another place, eight of the nine items based on a story appear on page 8 whereas the two-column story on which the items are based appears entirely on page 7. A pupil taking the test will need to waste much time, and will doubtless suffer some annoyance, in turning back and forth from questions to story as he follows the instructions, "You may look back to find the answers." Since the entire unit occupies slightly less than three and a half columns, the entirety of this exercise could have been put in the four columns of a two-page spread. More than a page and a half at the end of the booklet are unused, so there was no need for economizing on space.

Kuder-Richardson 21 reliability coefficients of .94 and .91 are reported for grade 8 and grade 11, respectively, at the two levels. Means, standard deviations, and standard errors of measurement are also reported for these grades, both in terms of raw scores and of grade placement. No such information appears for grades 7, 9, 10, and 12, however.

Correlations between scores on Forms 1 and 2 are given as .86 and .87 at the lower and higher levels and the means of raw scores are shown to differ only in minor degree. Raw score values at the 90th, 75th, 50th, 25th, and 10th percentiles are also given for the two forms; six of the differences are 1 or 0, three are 2, and one is 3. These data are based on pupils in grades 7 to 9 and grades 9 to 12 at the two levels, but neither the sizes of the samples nor the proportions of pupils at the various grade levels are given. It seems likely that the reduction in range of talent if data were presented for single grades would be reflected at least in lower between-forms correlations.

Evidence concerning test validity depends heavily on subject matter objectives, buttressed by opinions of curriculum specialists and other supposedly qualified critics and by data concerning item difficulty and discriminative power. Average percentages of correct responses to test items are reported as 62 and 64 for the lower and upper levels respectively. Average differences of 35 are shown between the percentages of correct responses for the upper and lower 27 per cent groups at both levels of the test. These indices of difficulty and discriminative power are both reported as averages for the range of grades covered by each level of the test. The dependence on content validity and item characteristics represented here seems not to be inappropriate in a test that purports to measure mastery of basic skills, although more attention could well have been directed toward less traditional and more dynamic instructional outcomes, and data on item characteristics could easily have been presented for the more homogeneous grade groups.

Eighteen geographical areas and four sizes of school communities were systematically sampled in setting up the normative group and a neat, two-stage procedure was used in the process. The results are shown in the 100 classes and 3,420 pupils and the 136 classes and 3,770 pupils involved in the samples for grades 7–9 and grades 9–12, respectively. A number of desirable precautions were also taken in the attempt to have the testing done under optimum conditions. Norms are presented in the form of grade equivalents, age equivalents, percentiles by grade levels, and normalized standard scores. The "band" principle of taking unreliability of scores into consideration is represented by a table of percentile ranges in the manual, but the report forms make no direct provision for recording these ranges.

Such supplementary materials as scoring keys, class record sheets, answer sheets, and test manuals are well printed and commendably precise in organization and format. Instructions for administering and scoring the tests, as well as information about reliability, validity, the normative sample, and the norms, are systematically presented in the manuals. However, the manuals fail to fulfill an obligation to test users when they substitute the statement, "the statistics by grades are available upon request" for data about reliability and intercorrelations at each separate grade level. Reliability data for one grade at each level and data on comparability and equivalence of forms for several adjacent grades combined could easily have been replaced by the more definitive and meaningful results for each of the grades that are presumably in the publisher's files.

Individual test items and exercises, consisting of a story or map and many dependent items, are drawn directly, or with minor editorial changes, from various forms of an earlier test in the series. A comparison of Form 2 of the *Survey of Reading Achievement* and Form W of the *California Reading Test,* 1957 edition, both at the junior high level, disclosed that at least 19 individual items and three groups of items totaling 22, two based on stories and one on a map, are either substantially the same or identical. The manual for the survey series points out that Forms 1 and 2 are "produced," respectively, from items in Forms Y and Z and Forms W and X of the longer and more diagnostic 1957 series. It goes on to show how duplication of items can be avoided by selection of the proper forms if pupils take a test in each series.

Two broad trends are evident in the 30-year history of these achievement tests: recognition of new methods of test scoring in their format, accessory materials, and accompanying services; and recognition of the distinction between diagnostic and survey tests in their titles, formats, and score patterns.

The first trend is shown by a progression including hand scoring of booklets, hand scoring of IBM answer sheets, and scoring IBM answer sheets electrically by using the International Test Scoring Machine. Only the first two of these methods are ordinarily practicable in a small school system; the more technical types of scoring services are available from the large-scale scoring centers that are now found in metropolitan areas throughout the country and from the test publisher.

The second trend—away from a professed diagnostic function and toward a survey purpose—may be in some degree a reaction by the authors and publisher to previous MMY reviews. A number of reviewers, both of the Progressive and the California series of achievement tests, pointed out that the tests were analytic rather than diagnostic and that the subtest scores, in the third echelon from the total reading score at the top, were deficient in reliability. It should be noted, however, that the survey tests are an offshoot from the current achievement series at the two upper levels and seem not at all to be designed as replacements for the multiscore tests of achievement.

It is somewhat disturbing to find significant duplication of items, exercises, and even forms among the several recent series of these tests—the 1957 achievement tests, the basic skills tests, and the survey tests. Although the overlaps are admitted in the test manuals, more than ordinary care is required of test users to avoid the possibility of an undesired second use of testing materials. More important, however, is the problem of singling out, from the batteries and tests with overlapping functions as well as content, the test or tests best calculated to fulfill a certain need. It is possible that time and money spent in the development of new forms, tests, and batteries and in greater differentiation among the various components would materially increase the stature and the reputation of this venerable series of achievement tests.

[816]

*Techniques in Reading Comprehension: Every Pupil Test. Grades 7–9, 10–12; 1937–64; test booklet titles vary; new form (8 pages) usually issued each December and April; forms from previous testing programs also available; 2 levels; general directions sheet ('63, 2 pages); no data on reliability; Ohio norms for new forms available following testing program; 5¢ per test; 3¢ per key; postpaid; 40(45) minutes; Ohio Scholarship Tests. *

For reviews by Ivan A. Booker and James M. McCallister of the 1946 forms, see 3:505.

[817]

★Test of Reading Comprehension. Business and industry; 1951–63; 1 form ('51, 8 pages); manual ['63, 10 unnumbered pages]; $5.25 per 25 tests; 10¢ per key; $1 per manual; postage extra; $1.25 per specimen set, postpaid; 20(25) minutes; Richardson, Bellows, Henry & Co., Inc. *

[818]

*Tests of Reading: Cooperative Inter-American Tests. Grades 1–3, 2–3, 4–7, 8–13, 10–13; 1950–63; Levels 2 and 5 (b and e below) called *Test of Reading: Inter-American Series;* a series of parallel tests and manuals in English and Spanish; IBM for grades 4–13; 5 levels; tentative norms (publisher recommends use of local norms); separate answer sheets must be used for grades 4–13; postage extra; 30¢ per specimen set of any one level, postpaid; prepared under the direction of Herschel T. Manuel; Guidance Testing Associates. *

a) PRIMARY LEVEL. Grades 1–3; 1950; 3 scores: vocabulary, comprehension, total; English language Forms AE, BE, ('50, 8 pages); Spanish language Forms AS, BS, ('50, 8 pages); directions ('50, 4 pages); series manual ('50, 18 pages); no data on reliability; no norms for subscores; $2.50 per 25 tests; 30¢ per set of keys; 16(25) minutes.

b) LEVEL 2—PRIMARY. Grades 2.5–3; 1962–63; 4 scores: level of comprehension, speed of comprehension, vocabulary, total; English language Form CE ('62, 12 pages); Spanish language Form CEs ('62, 12 pages); directions ['62, 4 pages]; tentative norms and technical data ['63, 2 pages]; no norms for grade 3; $3.50 per 25 tests; 23(35) minutes.

c) INTERMEDIATE LEVEL. Grades 4–7; 1950; 3 scores: vocabulary, comprehension, total; IBM; English language Forms AE, BE, ('50, 10 pages); Spanish language Forms AS, BS, ('50, 10 pages); combined directions ('50, 5 pages) for this and the advanced level; series manual ('50, 18 pages); no data on reliability; no norms for subscores; $3 per 25 tests; 4¢ per IBM answer sheet; 20¢ per scoring stencil; 40(50) minutes.

d) ADVANCED LEVEL. Grades 8–13; 1950; 3 scores: vocabulary, comprehension, total; IBM; English language Forms AE, BE, ('50, 12 pages); Spanish language Forms AS, BS, ('50, 12 pages); combined directions ('50, 5 pages) for this and the intermediate level; series manual ('50, 18 pages); no data on reliability; no norms for subscores; $3 per 25 tests; 4¢ per IBM answer sheet; 20¢ per scoring stencil; 40(50) minutes.

e) LEVEL 5—ADVANCED. Grades 10–13; 1962–63; 4 scores: level of comprehension, speed of comprehension, vocabulary, total; IBM; English language Form CE ('62, 14 pages); Spanish language Form CEs ('62, 14 pages); directions ['62, 4 pages]; tentative norms and technical data ['63, 7 pages] for this and the Level 5 general ability test of the series; $4 per 25 tests; 4¢ per IBM answer sheet; 20¢ per scoring stencil; 41(50) minutes.

REFERENCES

1–4. See 4:557.
5. CHENAULT, VIVIAN M. *A Study of the Cooperative Inter-American Tests of General Ability and Reading at the Primary Level.* Master's thesis, University of Texas (Austin, Tex.), 1952.
6. MANUEL, HERSCHEL T. "The Use of Parallel Tests in the Study of Foreign Language Teaching." *Ed & Psychol Meas* 13:431–6 au '53. * (*PA* 28:4842)
7. EINSPAHR, MARTIN HARLEY. *The Construction and Validation of Scales for Predicting Academic Success in College.* Doctor's thesis, University of Houston (Houston, Tex.), 1959. (*DA* 20:3366)
8. ZIMMERER, ANN MORGAN. *A Study of Selected Variables for Predicting Success in a College of Engineering.* Doctor's

thesis, University of Houston (Houston, Tex.), 1963. (*DA* 24:842)

For reviews by Jacob S. Orleans and Frederick L. Westover of a and c–d, see 4:557.

[819]
★ **W.A.L. English Comprehension Test.** High school; 1962–63; 4 scores: vocabulary (2 scores), reading comprehension, total; Form 1 ['62, 8 pages]; mimeographed temporary manual in 2 parts: part 1 ['62, 5 pages], part 2 ['63, 11 pages]; no data on reliability; temporary norms; separate answer sheets must be used; 15s. per 10 tests; 3s. 6d. per 10 answer sheets; 3s. per scoring stencil; 4s. per manual; 9s. per specimen set; postpaid within Australia; 70(75) minutes; Australian Council for Educational Research. *

[Other Tests]
For tests not listed above, see the following entries in *Tests in Print*: 1387, 1389–90, 1392–3, 1397, 1399–400, 1406, 1412, 1415–7, 1419, 1422, 1424, 1428, 1431–4, 1437–8, 1440–1, 1443, 1446–7, 1450, 1456, and 1459–62; out of print: 1396, 1411, 1414, 1444, and 1454.

DIAGNOSTIC

[820]
★**California Phonics Survey.** Grades 7–12 and college; 1956–63; shortened version of *Stanford Diagnostic Phonics Survey, Research Edition;* 9 error analysis scores for Form 1 (Form 2 yields total score only): long-short vowel confusion, other vowel confusion, consonants-confusion with blends and digraphs, consonant-vowel reversals, configuration, endings, negatives-opposites-sight words, rigidity, total; IBM; Forms 1, 2, ('62) in a single booklet (8 pages); manual ('63, 44 pages); may be administered by examiner but tape recording is recommended; no data on reliability of subscores; $3.50 per 35 tests; $5.95 per tape; separate answer sheets may be used (must be used if tape recording is used); 5¢ per IBM answer sheet; $1.80 per set of scoring stencils; 9¢ per Scoreze answer sheet for Form 1 (not available for Form 2); 50¢ per specimen set without tape ($6.45 with tape), postpaid; (40–45) minutes; Grace M. Brown and Alice B. Cottrell; California Test Bureau. *

REFERENCES
1. COTTRELL, ALICE B. *A Group Test for Ascertaining Ability in Phonetic Analysis Among College Freshmen.* Doctor's thesis, Stanford University (Stanford, Calif.), 1958. (*DA* 18:1794)

THOMAS E. CULLITON, JR., *Assistant Professor of Education, University of Illinois, Urbana, Illinois.*

The *California Phonics Survey* is the result of one of the pioneer attempts to measure the phonic knowledge of groups of students at the junior high through college level. The development of a group test to measure this basic component of reading and writing skill is a very worthwhile project. The substitution of a system involving evaluation of reading and listening for one based on reading and speaking has provided for the first time the opportunity to measure large groups of children. The reported correlation of .89 between the two testing methods is high.

The 75-item test "is divided into five units largely to provide variety in the mode of presentation and to obviate any fatigue effect." The five units do not measure different kinds of phonic skill but rather include items of different structural types. Provision is made for analysis of an individual's performance according to eight diagnostic categories. The pattern of the errors of an individual, when plotted on the profile sheet and interpreted according to the key given in the manual, is a basis for diagnosis and a starting point for remedial work. A detailed analysis of the phonic skills of individual examinees is made possible by the diagnostic keys. An examination of the profile and of the errors made in each category reveals phonic deficiencies which could hinder academic achievement. It indicates the type and extent of remedial work which might prove helpful in individual cases.

Since each of the 75 items on the test presents the possibility for more than one error, it is the specific wrong choice that is diagnostically significant. The test items in this survey "include all of the common speech sounds of the English language in their more usual spellings." Test items were kept simple by omitting spellings affected by regional pronunciations and by limiting the frequency of spellings that may be pronounced in more than one way. The *California Phonics Survey* may be administered by use of a magnetic tape recording or it may be presented orally by a competent language arts teacher. The authors note that "in areas where regional pronunciations, dialect or other speech differences are strongly noticeable, it is preferable" that the teacher present the test rather than utilize the tape recording. The test can be completed within a 45 minute period of time, a very practical consideration in terms of ordinary high school class period duration.

The directions for administering and scoring the test are clear and complete. The examiner is advised to be familiar with the samples, pronunciation, and pace of presentation, as well as the general instructions, before administering the test. Specific directions are given for administering the test by using the tape recording and by oral presentation by the teacher. Complete, clear, and precise directions are provided for machine or hand scoring and for the interpretation of the test results.

The standard error of measurement is used to establish the cutoff points to separate the students with adequate phonic skills from those with some phonic difficulty and those with serious or gross phonic disability.

The initial work on the *California Phonics Survey* was begun in 1954. Since that time, seven versions of the test have been written, administered, and analyzed both experimentally and diagnostically. The final version, the present test, was used in a national standardization program at various grade levels in both public and private schools to obtain the adequate reliability and validity data which are given.

This test was prepared to furnish teachers of grades 7 through college with essential information about the phonic ability of students at these levels. An individual's results will indicate the adequacy of the phonic skills of the student and provide information regarding the type and degree of disability, if one exists. Much care and attention have gone into the construction of this test. The selection of the test items to include all of the common speech sounds in their usual spelling, the careful analysis of the experimental results, and the analysis of diagnostic implications, the preparation of analytical data, and the other details of test construction and standardization appear to be well done. This diagnostic test is a much needed device for measuring a very important aspect of reading.

[821]

★Diagnostic Reading Scales. Grades 1–8 and retarded readers in grades 9–12; 1963; 10 or 11 scores: word recognition, instructional level (oral reading), independent level (silent reading), rate of silent reading (optional), potential level (auditory comprehension), and 6 phonics scores (consonant sounds, vowel sounds, consonant blends, common syllables, blending, letter sounds); individual; 1 form (28 pages); record booklet (29 pages); manual (27 pages); no data on reliability of rate of silent reading and phonics scores; $1 per test; $8.75 per 35 record booklets and manual; 25¢ per single copy of record booklet; 25¢ per manual; postage extra; (45) minutes; George D. Spache; California Test Bureau. *

N. DALE BRYANT, *Executive Director, Study Center for Learning Disabilities, State University of New York at Albany and Albany Medical College, Albany, New York.*

These scales provide a logical and well organized approach to diagnosis of reading skills and difficulties. Four major scores and some supplementary measures are provided. Administration and scoring of the major scales is simple and takes relatively little time. The word recognition score is based upon one of three word lists of 40–50 words each. The lists are adequately scaled, and of reasonable reliability (.96, .87, .91, Kuder-Richardson formula 21). Word recognition norms provide grade level scores of 1.3 to 6.5. Only *immediate* responses are considered correct. Words correctly pronounced after a few seconds are counted as errors both in scoring and in determining when to stop testing (this latter point is not clear from the manual but was confirmed by the test author in personal communication with the reviewer). The immediate recognition measure used in this test is particularly valuable, but separate norms should also be given for untimed recognition as well.

It is particularly valuable that the other three major scores—oral reading, silent reading, and auditory comprehension—are based upon the same series of reading selections. Two selections are available at each level 1.6, 1.8, 2.3, 2.8, 3.3, 3.8, 4.5, 5.5, 6.5, 7.5, and 8.5, as determined by readability formulas reflecting vocabulary and sentence length.

Oral reading level is determined by the highest level selection an examinee can read with no more than the average number of errors (for children at that reading level) and with 60 per cent comprehension. The number of errors allowed seems very liberal and, in personal communication, the test author supplemented the manual's description by indicating that the average value referred to the mean plus one standard deviation. This is a logical procedure but one that influences interpretation and comparison with other scores. The manual should clarify this point. Oral reading errors include the standard omissions, additions, substitutions, reversals, repetitions (of more than one word), and aided words (given after five seconds delay). The crucial analysis of types of errors is aided by a checklist of difficulties, but it still requires considerable clinical experience and judgment.

Silent reading level and auditory comprehension level are based entirely upon obtaining 60 per cent comprehension (4 out of 7 or 5 out of 8) on the short answer type questions that follow each selection. Performance on a single selection determines level and this may sometimes produce inaccuracies because of variation in interest, background knowledge, attention, and the approach an examinee brings to a particular selection. Children with reading difficulties are often more variable than normal, so the test-retest (4–10 weeks) reliability of .84 or .88 is not completely reassuring. Test-retest is not the most appropriate measure for evaluating the reliability of comprehension measures since memory is an important factor (indicated in part by an increase in mean silent reading score from 3.5 to 4.1 between test and retest).

The experienced examiner will sometimes note that a child's errors in oral reading of a failed selection, or even in the comprehension test, are not consistent with his performance in previous selections and will, therefore, administer a second selection at the failed level. Such bracketing of the failure level, while not spelled out in the manual, is essential in a few cases, but it may use up the selections so that they are not available for determining silent reading levels or auditory comprehension level. Even one additional selection at each level would almost completely prevent this using up of selections and would increase the usefulness of the test.

The assumptions involved in labeling auditory comprehension as "potential reading level" are not well substantiated. However, this is an important clinical measure since it can detect difficulties in retention and organization of information which are independent of reading. In obtaining the auditory comprehension measure, the user should *not* consider the level of a selection as a grade level norm. While the manual does not discuss this problem, data from Table 7 in the manual make it apparent that regular classroom cases can understand material read to them on an average of two grade levels above their grade placement. In testing over 50 cases with this instrument, the reviewer finds that reading disability cases usually have auditory comprehension scores well above their grade placement, and it is clinically useful to treat any auditory comprehension score below grade placement as indicating a real comprehension problem (probably a general one and one which is likely to interfere with reading comprehension).

While no descriptive data are given on the standardization for the rate of silent reading scores, the time for each selection is classified as slow, average, or fast, and this is probably as specific as one should be on this measure.

The supplementary phonics tests are, as their names suggest, merely supplementary. They are probably as useful as comparable measures in other diagnostic reading tests, but they do not provide an adequate or systematic analysis of usable phonic skills. The experienced clinician, however, will obtain a great deal of information from these supplementary tests, particularly Test 4, Common Syllables, and Test 5, Blending.

There is a potpourri of validity and other studies within the manual which suggest that on normal classroom cases the *Diagnostic Reading Scales* give similar results to the *California Reading Test* and to ratings by first grade teachers, but give rather different results from the reading section of the *Metropolitan Achievement Tests* and the paragraph meaning section of the *Stanford Achievement Test*. Data from one study suggest that the mean instructional level (oral reading) is slightly higher than the mean independent level (silent reading) which contradicts assumptions in the manual and administrative directions. Implication of the data in various tables is not fully explored, and a much more systematic study of the test and more comprehensive manual would be extremely valuable to users. The manual should include particularly a description of the sample on which oral errors were tabulated and the mean and standard deviation of such errors. Also useful would be difficulty indices of test items administered without reading the selections as well as difficulty indices when normal administration is used.

In spite of minor difficulties and the need for a more systematic and effective manual, the four major scores (when accompanied by a clinical analysis of errors) provide one of the most quickly obtainable and most meaningful approaches presently available for the diagnosis of reading skills and difficulties.

[822]

*Diagnostic Reading Test: Pupil Progress Series. Grades 1.9–2.1, 2.2–3, 4–6, 7–8; 1956–60; various titles used by publisher; some subtests also appear in *Scholastic Diagnostic Reading Test* for Catholic schools; IBM for grades 4–8; 2 forms; 4 levels; $2.40 per 20 tests; separate answer sheets may be used in grades 4–8; $1 per 20 IBM answer sheets; 12¢ per set of scoring stencils; 50¢ per specimen set of any one level; postage extra; Oliver F. Anderhalter, R. Stephen Gawkoski, and Ruth Colestock; Scholastic Testing Service, Inc. *

a) PRIMARY TEST 1. Grades 1.9–2.1; 1956–57; referred to as Pre-Primary Test in manual for Form A; 9

scores: vocabulary (word recognition, word to content relation, words in use, total), rate of reading for meaning, comprehension (recalling information, locating information, reading for descriptions, total); Forms A ('56, 11 pages), B ('57, 12 pages); separate manuals for Forms A ('56), B ('57), (9 pages); (40–60) minutes.

b) PRIMARY TEST 2. Grades 2.2–3; 1956–57; referred to as Primary Test in manual for Form A above; 10 scores: vocabulary (words in use, word meaning, total), rate of reading for meaning, comprehension (same as for *a* plus following directions, reading for meaning); Forms A ('56, 12 pages), B ('57, 15 pages); separate manuals for Forms A ('56), B ('57), (11 pages); (40–60) minutes.

c) ELEMENTARY TEST. Grades 4–6; 1956–57; 13 scores: knowledge and use of sources (functions, best sources, use of index, use of table of contents, total), rate of reading for meaning, comprehension (same as for *a* plus word meaning, reading for meaning, reading for directions or procedures); IBM; Forms A ['56, 15 pages], B ('57, 18 pages); separate manuals ('57, 16 pages) for each form; 44(65) minutes for Form A, 48(70) minutes for Form B.

d) ADVANCED TEST. Grades 7–8; 1956–60; 13 scores: same as for *c*; IBM; Forms A ['56, 15 pages], B ('57, 18 pages); manual ['60, 8 pages]; 44(65) minutes for Form A, 48(70) minutes for Form B.

AGATHA TOWNSEND, *Consultant, Educational Records Bureau, New York, New York.*

Tests designated for the diagnosis of individual performance as well as for the description of class status in a field must face the most rigorous scrutiny. Not only must the scores obtained be highly reliable measures, but they must be valid in either curricular terms or in terms of the mental factors involved in the field; frequently, both kinds of validity are desirable. Unfortunately, the title of the *Diagnostic Reading Test: Pupil Progress Series* tends to mislead the user who will assume that the parts meet either of these criteria.

Stauffer, in a review (5:650) of the *Scholastic Diagnostic Reading Test* for Catholic schools, which includes most of the subtests used in the test under review here, observed that the analysis of reading functions was not satisfactory for clinical use, though he praised the curricular validity of certain of the tests at the upper level. Traxler, in the same volume, was critical of the reliability of the part scores. These reviews should be consulted; it is unnecessary to repeat the comments here. It is unfortunate that the publisher has not profited from these suggestions for the improvement of the public school edition.

To the criticism that the test does not give a clinically sound picture of reading problems, this reviewer would like to add that the curricular suitability of the series is also questionable. Two points seem particularly serious. No

matter how one conceives the process of learning to read, a good reliable test of word meaning is required in a battery for either survey or diagnostic use. The vocabulary, or word meaning, sections of this series are too short (30–35 items) at the primary 1 and elementary levels, a fact which is noticeable from the reliabilities reported, which average about .88 for each level. At the primary 2 level, however, where there are 65 items in the vocabulary subtests, reliability averages about .95. The brevity of the primary 1 and elementary parts inordinately restricts the word list, particularly at the elementary level. To return to the curricular criterion, I also note that in the absence of any auditory or word attack tests, the teacher is left with no data on the causes for a low word meaning score.

Again, the content of the subtests contributing to the total score related to comprehension, another score which is certainly a minimum requirement, may be questioned. There is undue weight given to factual detail items in all the parts which contribute to this subtotal in all three of the elementary school batteries.

If these two areas of the curriculum are not measured adequately, one is left with the third subtotal, an index of reading rate, which many teachers and reading specialists do not consider of much importance until at least the end of the grade range for the Elementary Test. The reliability of the brief "Rate of Reading for Meaning" part (based on two minutes of testing in grades 1 and 2, and on a sample of 30 seconds length added to another of one minute in the Elementary Test), is about .89 for primary 1, .88 for primary 2, and .94 for elementary.

It will be noted that no statements have as yet been made about the sections of the Advanced Test. While these are designed to continue the outline of the testing done in the primary and elementary levels, no reliability or standard error of measurement data whatever are included in the 1960 manual for the tests for grades 7 to 8 (such data did appear in the earlier, 1957, manuals but they are not repeated). As does the Elementary Test, the Advanced Test has four subtests (60 items) on "Knowledge and Use of Sources." There is much merit in these sections of the tests. Here, the advanced level seems to have greater face validity than the parallel parts of the elementary level. The questions asked are certainly far more realistic. For instance, the elementary level test on the use of the index asks a series of "On which page would you look to find" questions, beginning with (Form A) "how to fill out a job application form" and ending with "something about preparing for a job interview." (The items cited are for grades 4 to 6.) Questions on the advanced level ask "To which page would you turn if" and include such items as "your father was looking for work as a carpenter" and "you wanted to buy a pet rabbit."

The two reviewers for the forms used in Catholic schools also urged extension of the norms to a broader base. It is unfortunate that once again this reviewer must report that the public school forms also have norms based on a very small sampling. They are drawn from 37 schools in 9 states, with total number of pupils going as low as 531 for grade 9, from a high of 1,751 for grade 2.

Much could be done to improve these batteries. The addition of word attack or word analysis materials to the tests below grade 6 seems obvious advice to give. The strengthening of the norms would make it possible to provide fully worked out percentile tables, requiring less interpolation. The two forms could be equated. Most important, interpretive and statistical data could be added to the manual for the advanced level.

Until steps such as these are taken, competing tests should be preferred. Fuller measurement of vocabulary and inclusion of word attack skills is featured by the lower levels of the *Diagnostic Reading Tests,* produced by the Committee on Diagnostic Reading Tests, Inc. Better measurement for interpretation and critical reading is included in the STEP reading test from the Educational Testing Service. More analytical study skills measurement is possible through the *Iowa Tests of Basic Skills.* Moreover, normative data for all these batteries are far more extensive.

[823]

*Diagnostic Reading Tests. Various grades kgn–13; 1947–63; IBM (except for section 4, part 1) for grades 2–13; 3 levels; interpretation booklet ('52, 42 pages); revised norms booklet ('63, 40 pages); $1 per interpretation booklet; 50¢ per norms booklet; postage extra; Committee on Diagnostic Reading Tests, Inc. *
a) DIAGNOSTIC READING TESTS: KINDERGARTEN THROUGH FOURTH GRADES. Various grades kgn–4 (except for section 4, part 1); 1957–63; 2 sections, 5 booklets; 20¢ per copy of any one booklet; 25¢ per key for any one booklet; 25¢ per directions for any one booklet; $2.50 per specimen set of all forms of all 5 booklets and directions for each.

1) *Survey Section.* Grades kgn–1, 1, 2, 3–4; 1957–63; 4 levels.
(*a*) Reading Readiness Booklet. Grades kgn–1; 5 scores: relationships, eye-hand coordination, visual discrimination, auditory discrimination, vocabulary; Form B ('57, 16 pages); mimeographed directions for administering ['57, 8 pages]; administration time not reported.
(*b*) Booklet 1. Grade 1; 12 scores: visual discrimination, auditory discrimination (3 subscores plus total), vocabulary (3 subscores plus total), story reading (2 subscores plus total); Form A ('57, 23 pages); mimeographed directions ['57, 10 pages]; reliability data for total subscores only; administration time not reported.
(*c*) Booklet 2. Grade 2; 3 scores: word recognition, comprehension, total; IBM; Forms A, B, ('57, 15 pages); mimeographed combined directions ['57, 10 pages] for this test and (*d*) below; separate test-answer sheets may be used; 4¢ per IBM answer sheet; 25¢ per scoring stencil; [30] minutes.
(*d*) Booklet 3. Grades 3–4; details same as for (*c*) above.
2) *Section 4: Word Attack, Part 1: Oral.* Grades 1–8; 1958; individual; Forms A, B, (8 pages); revised directions for administering (8 pages) for grades 1–13; no data on reliability; [20] minutes.
b) DIAGNOSTIC READING TESTS: LOWER LEVEL. Grades 4–8; 1947–63; 2 sections, 4 booklets; 25¢ per key for any one booklet; 25¢ per directions for any one booklet; $1.75 per specimen set of all 4 booklets and directions for each.
1) *Survey Section.* Grades 4–8; 1952–63; IBM; 2 booklets; directions for administering ('61, 14 pages, same as directions published in 1958 except for some wording and typographical changes); 20¢ per copy of either booklet; separate answer sheets may be used; 4¢ per IBM answer sheet; 25¢ per scoring stencil; (30) minutes per booklet.
(*a*) Booklet 1: Part 1, Word Recognition and Comprehension. 2 scores: word recognition, comprehension; Forms A, B, C, D, ('57, 12 pages, Form B identical with test copyrighted in 1952 except for format and cover page).
(*b*) Booklet 2: Parts 2 and 3, Vocabulary-Story Reading. 3 scores: vocabulary, rate of reading, story comprehension; Forms A ('52), B ('57, identical with test copyrighted in 1952 except for cover page and, in vocabulary section, revised option order in most items and minor revision in 1 item), C ('57), D ('57), (12 pages).
2) *Section 4: Word Attack.* Various grades 1–13; 1947–63; 2 parts.
(*a*) Part 1, Oral. Grades 1–8; see *a*2 above.
(*b*) Part 2, Silent. Grades 4–13; 1947–63; 3 scores: identification of sounds, syllabication, total; IBM; Forms A, B, ('47, 6 pages); revised directions for administering ('58, 4 pages); 15¢ per test; separate answer sheets may be used; 4¢ per IBM answer sheet; 25¢ per scoring stencil; (30) minutes.
c) DIAGNOSTIC READING TESTS: [UPPER LEVEL]. Grades 7–13; 1947–63; IBM except for section 4, part 1; 5 sections, 6 booklets; separate answer sheets may be used with all except section 4, part 1; 4¢ per IBM answer sheet; 25¢ per scoring stencil; 25¢ per directions for any one booklet; $4.50 per specimen set of all 6 booklets and directions for each.

1) *Survey Section.* 1947–63; 5 scores: rate of reading, comprehension check, vocabulary, total comprehension, total; IBM; Forms A ('52, same as test copyrighted in 1950 except for cover page, revision

in 2 items, and minor change in directions), B ('47), C ('50), D ('50, some printings c1949), E ('52), F ('50), G ('50), H ('50), (22–23 pages); revised directions for administering ('56, c1947, 10 pages); 25¢ per test; 40(50) minutes. (Forms A and B were published in the high school and college educational edition of *Reader's Digest* in November 1949 and May 1950, respectively.)

2) *Section 1: Vocabulary (Revised).* 1947–63; 5 scores: English, mathematics, science, social studies, total; IBM; Forms A, B, ('52, 9 pages); mimeographed directions for administering ('56, 4 pages); no data on reliability of total score; 15¢ per test; 35(40) minutes.

3) *Section 2: Comprehension: Silent and Auditory.* 1947–63; IBM; revised Forms A, B, C, D, ('57, c1948, 28–34 pages); mimeographed directions for administering ('58, 8 pages); may be administered as a listening comprehension test; no norms for grade 13; 25¢ per test; [30] minutes as a silent reading test.

4) *Section 3: Rates of Reading: Part 1, General.* 1947–63; IBM; 4 scores: normal rate of reading, comprehension at normal rate, maximum rate of reading, comprehension at maximum rate; Forms A, B, ('47, 14 pages); directions for administering ('48, 12 pages); 15¢ per test; 30(35) minutes.

5) *Section 4: Word Attack.* 1947–63; 2 parts.
(*a*) Part 1, Oral. 1948–58; individual; Forms A, B, ('48, 15 pages); revised directions for administering ('58, 6 pages) for grades 1–13; no data on reliability; no norms for grades 9–13; 20¢ per test; (20) minutes.
(*b*) Part 2, Silent. Grades 4–13; see *b*2(*b*) above.

REFERENCES

1–19. See 4:531.
20. COMMITTEE ON DIAGNOSTIC READING TESTS, INC. *Diagnostic Reading Tests: Their Interpretation and Use in the Teaching of Reading.* New York: the Committee, Inc., 1952. Pp. 44. * (*PA* 27:6739)
21. TRIGGS, FRANCES ORALIND. "The Development of Measured Word Recognition Skills, Grade Four Through the College Freshman Year." *Ed & Psychol Meas* 12:345–9 au '52. * (*PA* 27:6120)
22. BARRETT, DOROTHY M. "Correlation of Survey Section of Diagnostic Reading Tests and of Test C2: Reading Comprehension With College History Grades." *J Ed Res* 46:465–9 F '53. * (*PA* 28:1461)
23. TRAXLER, ARTHUR E. "Results of the Diagnostic Reading Tests for Grades 4, 5, and 6, Survey Section, Among Independent School Pupils." *Ed Rec B* 60:69–76 F '53. * (*PA* 28:1579)
24. ROGO, ROBERT A. *The Relationship of Scores of the Diagnostic Reading Tests: Survey Section and the American Council on Education Psychological Examination, to First Semester Freshman Honor Point Averages for Students in the College of Arts and Sciences at the University of Detroit.* Master's thesis, University of Detroit (Detroit, Mich.), 1954.
25. TRIGGS, FRANCES ORALIND; CARTEE, J. KEITH; BINKS, VIRGINIA; FOSTER, DESMOND; AND ADAMS, NICHOLAS A. "The Relationship Between Specific Reading Skills and General Ability at the Elementary and Junior-Senior High School Levels." *Ed & Psychol Meas* 14:176–85 sp '54. * (*PA* 28:8005)
26. WARD, LOUIS R. "Diagnostic Reading Tests." Letter. *Col Engl* 15:475–6 My '54. *
27. SAWIN, E. I. "Problems and Projected Plans in Air Force ROTC Evaluation." *Yearb Nat Council Meas Used Ed* 12:1–5 pt 1 '55. *
28. WALL, CLAIRE FRENCH. *The Relationship Between Certain Variables in Reading Improvement and Academic Grades at the College Level.* Master's thesis, Alabama Polytechnic Institute (Auburn, Ala.), 1955.
29. McQUEEN, ROBERT. "Diagnostic Reading Scores and College Achievement." *Psychol Rep* 3:627–9 D '57. * (*PA* 33:4705)
30. TRIGGS, FRANCES ORALIND. "A Comparison of Auditory and Silent Presentations of Reading Comprehension Tests." *Yearb Nat Council Meas Used Ed* 14:1–7 '57. *
31. WALDMAN, JOHN, AND TRIGGS, FRANCES ORALIND. "Measurement of Word Attack Skills." *El Engl* 35:459–63 N '58. *
32. HINTON, EVELYN A. "Doubts About Equivalent Forms." *J Develop Read* 2:59–62 su '59. *
33. TRIGGS, FRANCES ORALIND. "The Relationship of Word Attack Skills as Measured by Silent and Oral Tests." *Yearb Nat Council Meas Used Ed* 16:134–9 '59. *
34. MILLER, ROBERT E. "Selection of Engineering Students for an Abbreviated Mathematics Sequence." *Personnel & Guid J* 39:224–5 N '60. *
35. ROBERTSON, MALCOLM H., AND HARRISON, MILDRED M. "Reading Skill as a Predictor of College Achievement." *J Ed Res* 53:258–62 Mr '60. *
36. BOAG, AUDREY K., AND NEILD, MARGARET. "The Influence of the Time Factor on the Scores of the Triggs Diagnostic Reading Test as Reflected in the Performance of Secondary School Pupils Grouped According to Ability." *J Ed Res* 55:181–3 D–Ja '62. * (*PA* 37:1986)
37. CASH, W. L., JR. "Predictive Efficiency of Freshman Entrance Tests." *J Psychol Studies* 13:111–6 Je '62 [issued F '64]. *
38. DREW, ALFRED STANISLAUS. *The Relationship of General Reading Ability and Other Factors to School and Job Performance of Machinist Apprentices.* Doctor's thesis, University of Wisconsin (Madison, Wis.), 1962. (*DA* 23:1261)
39. RANKIN, EARL F., JR. "Reading Test Reliability and Validity as Function of Introversion-Extroversion." *J Develop Read* 6:106–17 w '63. *
40. SEEGARS, JAMES E., JR., AND ROSE, HARRIETT A. "Verbal Comprehension and Academic Success in College." *Personnel & Guid J* 42:295–6 N '63. *

ALBERT J. KINGSTON, *Professor of Education, University of Georgia, Athens, Georgia.*

The *Diagnostic Reading Tests* consist of three separate test batteries designed to appraise reading abilities at all grade levels from kindergarten through the college freshman year. The basic plan for each battery includes a separate survey test designed to appraise a pupil's general reading proficiency and a number of supplemental tests for appraising specific reading skills. Teachers may employ all of the tests included in a given battery or merely select those they feel to be desirable. Obviously the development of these instruments required considerable ambition, knowledge, and perseverance. A characteristic of the Committee on Diagnostic Reading Tests has been its long term planning and continuous study of the reading process. As a result of the Committee's work, teachers have available for use a series of tests which possess a common design and theoretical basis for measuring longitudinal growth in reading.

The upper level battery was the first published and is widely employed in college and secondary school reading programs. The Survey Section often is employed for identifying pupils who need special assistance and for evaluating the effectiveness of various types of instruction. Eight different forms of the survey section are available. A number of writers, however, have criticized the claim of equivalency of the forms of the Survey Section. The upper level battery also includes tests (with alternate forms) of vocabulary, comprehension, rates of reading, and word attack skills. Generally the selections employed in appraising reading skills are varied and have been carefully selected. A few, however, need revision and should be brought up to date.

The lower level Survey Section, which is in two booklets with four comparable forms of each, yields measures of word recognition, comprehension, vocabulary, and rate of reading. As the Committee believed it was helpful to print both the reading selections and the comprehension questions pertaining to the passages on the same page, the selected passages tend to be crowded at the top of each page. The result is an unattractive and crowded format. The various sections of the lower level tests appear to have sufficient reliability for appraising general reading ability and for individual diagnosis.

At both the intermediate and primary grade levels, the identical test (Section 4: Word Attack, Part 1, which is available in two forms) is used for appraising oral word attack skills. An unusual feature of the oral word attack test is the availability of norms which are reported in terms of the mean number of errors made by pupils in various grades on each of the seven types of errors the test is scored for. How this information is used is uncertain. Presumably a teacher who diagnoses the reading skills of one of her pupils can use this information in determining the progress of a given student.

In the opinion of the reviewer, the battery designed for use in kindergarten through the fourth grade is less satisfactory than either the upper level or lower level batteries. Although two forms of the tests for use in grades 2–4 exist, there is only one form of the readiness test (for kindergarten and grade 1) and Booklet 1 (for grade 1) of this level of the Survey Section. The test booklets are printed on poor quality paper and the format is unattractive. Directions for administering the readiness and other survey tests are offset reproductions of typed copy, printed on a poor grade of paper and stapled in the upper left hand corner. Even if great care is used in handling the direction sheets it is likely that they will have to be restapled after being used once or twice. In addition, the direction sheets received by the reviewer were faintly printed and blurred, and a number of the words along the left margin were illegible. A further shortcoming is the lack of readily available information regarding the reliability and validity of this battery and its subtests. However, the latest norms booklet published in 1963 contains an

insert sheet which presents median reliability coefficients for the various tests in the battery. The insert also suggests that "Test users who care to do so may find research studies in the literature reported both by the Committee and by independent users of the test." While it undoubtedly is difficult for test publishers to provide current information about their instruments, more adequate manuals would save test consumers considerable time and effort.

The norms distributed with the tests are continuously revised, and a revised norms booklet based on the scores of thousands of children was printed in 1963. Unlike many primary and intermediate grade level reading tests, these tests do not present norms in terms of grade-level equivalents. Quartiles and medians are employed for the readiness test and percentiles are reported for the other subtests. Certain primary grade teachers may be somewhat unhappy about this procedure.

The Committee is to be congratulated for its ambitious attempt to measure reading abilities at various grade levels. The *Diagnostic Reading Tests* represent a step in the right direction. One cannot help but feel that the overall planning which has gone into this vast project has been excellent. Unfortunately, a number of important details which would assist the average teacher in using these tests seem to have been overlooked. It is hoped that in the near future the Committee will concern itself with a number of details which would make these tests more usable to the average classroom teacher. Certain test selections and items need revision, and the format of certain tests should be improved. Above all, efforts should be made to develop manuals of instruction which are both complete and inexpensive. These generally useful tests deserve no less than the best manuals.

B. H. VAN ROEKEL, *Professor of Education, Michigan State University, East Lansing, Michigan.*

Readers usually abhor prefatory comment but in this instance such comment seems appropriate.

The literature dealing directly with the administration, interpretation, and application of the *Diagnostic Reading Tests* is exceedingly voluminous and there is more to come, for apparently there are yet two tests to be printed. In sheer bulk, this reviewer examined 56 separate publications, including 11 manuals of directions, 38 test booklets, and 7 assorted pamphlets and bulletins dealing with test norms and the use and interpretation of test results in the teaching of reading.

The previous paragraph is not intended to exalt the dedication and diligence of the reviewer. It should alert the reader to the problems a reviewer faces in organizing and focusing comment in a manner useful to the prospective users of these tests. Especially, the reader should recognize the likelihood of oversight when a reviewer is confronted with so many pages.

The development of the *Diagnostic Reading Tests* represents one of the most ambitious attempts to help schools individualize reading instruction. It is truly a global effort in the sense that it not only purports to measure reading efficiency from kindergarten through college but it also attempts to provide specific suggestions for using the test scores to adapt instruction in reading to the abilities and needs of students. Unfortunately, the hundreds of pages which make up these tests and related literature tend to defeat the purposes for which the tests were built. The following itemizes the reactions of the reviewer to specific elements within the total framework represented by these tests.

a) One gets the impression that these tests are a bit like Topsy—they just grew. Nowhere did this reviewer find any evidence to suggest that the committee started with a clear cut plan which definitively structured the elements which were to make up this testing program. The best that one can do is to say that the Committee on Diagnostic Tests, Inc., began its work in 1943. Among its first efforts it canvassed the opinions of teachers and others actively involved in matters relating to the teaching of reading. From this survey the Committee concluded "that one of the greatest stumbling blocks to efficient teaching of reading was the inability of teachers to recognize the reading level of students and thus to apply the cardinal principle of all teaching, namely, to start where students are and proceed to a well-defined objective. The Committee therefore decided to construct measuring instruments for the skills already defined as the major areas of reading instruction." The Committee specifies that the tests are scored in areas of instruction in reading rather than in terms of "pure factors." The

prospective test user is left to his own in concluding the distinction between instructional areas and "pure factors." The Committee also suggests that new tests will be built as the need arises but there is no specification as to what constitutes a need or how one determines when a need has arisen.

b) The manuals of directions, tables of norms, and other literature accompanying the tests hardly reflect professional standards. The manuals of directions and tables of norms are so poorly duplicated and the format is so cluttered one has difficulty reading them. Much of the literature dealing with the interpretation and application of test scores is clumsily written and, as Davis put it in a previous review (see 4:531), the materials "contain an admixture of information helpful to teachers and test users and misinformation about reading. The answer to Question 11 in 'Questions on Reading' will cause statisticians to shudder and will help make percentile norms seem incomprehensible to most teachers."

c) Many of the test items lack polish and some are faulty. An example is item 11 of Form C, Booklet 1, Survey Section: Lower Level, the stem of which asks "which word or words would help you to say the word *sprinkle?*" Apparently response 2 ("rink") is intended to be the correct response. If "rink" is the appropriate response, children must split a blend (spr) and a unique syllabic unit (kle), and thus violate basic elements of English structure.

d) The norms are inadequate. The variation and size of samples from which normative data for the various parts of the tests have been gathered provide almost no basis for comparability.

SUMMARY. The basic notion underlying the development of these tests is good. But some parts of these tests have now been on the market for at least a decade. One can hardly excuse the lack of refinement by saying that the tests are in the developmental stage. Ten years is long enough to develop them. These tests need a good overhaul.

For reviews by Frederick B. Davis, William W. Turnbull, and Henry Weitz of the tests for grades 7–13, see 4:531.

[824]

Gates-McKillop Reading Diagnostic Tests. Grades 2-0 to 6-0; 1926-62; revision of *Gates Reading*

Diagnostic Tests; 28 scores: omissions, additions, repetitions, 8 mispronunciation scores (reversals, partial reversals, total reversals, wrong beginnings, wrong middle, wrong ending, wrong in several parts, total mispronunciations), oral reading total, words—flash presentation, words—untimed presentation, phrases—flash presentation, recognizing and blending common word parts, giving letter sounds, naming capital letters, naming lower-case letters, 4 scores for recognizing the visual form of sounds (nonsense words, initial letters, final letters, vowels), auditory blending, spelling, oral vocabulary, syllabication, auditory discrimination; individual; Forms 1, 2, ('62, 9 pages); pupil record-response booklet ('62, 16 pages) for each form; manual ('62, 20 pages); no data on reliability; no norms for auditory discrimination score; separate record-response booklets must be used; $1.25 per test; 20¢ per record-response booklet; 10¢ per tachistoscope card for flash presentation subtests; 25¢ per manual; $2.50 per specimen set; postpaid; [30–60] minutes; Arthur I. Gates and Anne S. McKillop; Bureau of Publications. *

REFERENCES

1–3. See 3:510.
4–5. See 4:563.
6. Russell, David H. "Auditory Abilities and Achievement in Spelling in the Primary Grades." *J Ed Psychol* 49:315-9 D '58. * (*PA* 36:2KL15R)
7. Murray, Carol-Faith, and Karlsen, Bjorn. "A Concurrent Validity Study of the Silent Reading Tests and the Gates Reading Diagnostic Tests." *Reading Teach* 13:293-4+ Ap '60. * (*PA* 35:2751)

N. Dale Bryant, *Executive Director, Study Center for Learning Disabilities, State University of New York at Albany and Albany Medical College, Albany, New York.*

This collection of subtests is a minor revision of the *Gates Reading Diagnostic Tests* and, as such, keeps the advantages of being a familiar and widely used instrument. The manual is well organized but lacks needed descriptions of normative samples and studies as well as crucial reliability data.

The oral reading test uses stilted and unrepresentative reading selections at the higher levels and this may handicap some individuals far more than others. The reading selections have no comprehension tests; this not only influences examinee "set" but may also prevent identification of gross comprehension difficulties. One characteristic that is of particular value in the oral reading test is the analysis of types of errors made in the first four paragraphs read. Errors of omission, addition, repetition, and mispronunciations are compared as percentages of the total errors on the four paragraphs. In addition, seven types of mispronunciation (e.g., reversals, wrong beginnings, wrong in several parts, etc.) are analyzed in relation to the total number of mispronunciations in the four paragraphs. These normative values are particularly valuable if a diagnostician is sophisticated enough to associate the

majority of errors of each type with probable causes, e.g., perceptual errors, difficulties with vowel sounds, careless mistakes from tension, and reading too rapidly. The norms provide guide lines of expected errors, and if cautiously used, can aid specific diagnosis of particular defects contributing to the reading difficulties.

Many of the subsequent subtest scores are interpreted with respect to the oral reading level and not to the child's age or grade level. This can be valuable but it can also be misleading (i.e., when no item is answered correctly on the subtest Recognizing and Blending Common Word Parts, a seventh grader, reading at beginning third grade level, may be rated as showing normal progress. This may be correct, but it can lead an unsophisticated teacher to ignore a possible basic difficulty.) An error in the oral test score gives a continual bias in interpreting later scores. Age differences are sometimes important in that an older child who is a poor reader may perform differently on certain subtests than would be expected of a younger child reading at the same oral reading level.

The word recognition subtest appears adequate and there is a checklist of difficulties which is useful. Word Recognition is both timed and untimed, the timed presentation using about a half second exposure through a slotted card. The difference between untimed word recognition and both timed word recognition and timed phrase recognition can help identify defects in rapid perception. The word recognition measures are not a measure of immediate recognition since children may sound out words (even after a flash) rather than recognizing them automatically.

The remaining subtests are useful but provide an incomplete analysis of component reading skills. The subtest Recognizing and Blending Common Word Parts can be particularly valuable. Auditory Blending can be useful for detecting gross blending defects, but the difficulty of administration makes for extreme variability between examiners. Giving letter sounds which are presented singly, as is done in some subtests, is not a good measure of usable phonic skills, especially when testing reading disability cases. Most of the remaining subtests depend upon the examiner pronouncing a word or sound and the examinee picking a response that corresponds to the presentation. Since production of sound from visual symbols (as in reading) is sometimes very different from identifying symbols to fit sounds, these scores may miss the identification of specific difficulties.

The supplementary tests, Spelling and Oral Vocabulary (actually auditory vocabulary), Syllabication, and Auditory Discrimination, are brief but useful in identifying gross defects but not necessarily in providing exact scores.

In summary, this is a well established test with alternate forms and a well organized manual which has a number of deficiencies. The many scores are useful but they can sometimes lead to misinterpretations, and several important aspects, such as comprehension difficulties, could be missed. As in any diagnostic reading test, clinical judgment is needed to get the most from the scores and the test performance, and this diagnostic test appears to require more sophistication than most.

GABRIEL M. DELLA-PIANA, *Associate Professor of Educational Psychology, University of Utah, Salt Lake City, Utah.*

This reading battery for individual diagnosis is a revision of the earlier *Gates Reading Diagnostic Tests* reviewed by Spache in *The Fifth Yearbook.* There are some major changes in the revision, although most of the test is much like the earlier version and Spache's criticisms remain relevant for the present edition, excepting for the reversal test which has been eliminated.

Subtests 1 (Oral Reading), 2 (Words: Flash Presentation), and 3 (Words: Untimed Presentation) are essentially identical to the earlier test except for order of appearance in the battery and an improvement in format of the pupil record booklet, including larger type and greater space between lines allowing greater ease in legibility and recording of pupil responses by the examiner.

The oral reading test is scored for errors but not time or comprehension in arriving at an oral reading grade equivalent. Norms are given for omissions, additions, repetitions, and seven mispronunciation scores for errors on the first four paragraphs. The norms are rough comparisons of the errors of a given child with those made by the average child making the same number of total errors. The norm group, however, is not defined beyond this.

Subtest 4 (Phrases: Flash Presentation), is also essentially the same as in the earlier edition of the test. The procedure for administration is similar to the flash presentation of words in which the examiner covers the word with a card and moves the card past the word for a half second exposure through an opening on the card. It is a little awkward to cover all other words on the page while exposing one, but the procedure can be mastered with a little practice. With the unreliability of exposure time and the doubtful diagnostic value of flash presentation, the reviewer prefers the approach of Spache's *Diagnostic Reading Scales* which omits flash presentation of words or phrases.

Subtest 5 (Knowledge of Word Parts: Word Attack) has four sections. The first section (Recognizing and Blending Common Word Parts) requires the child to read orally a column of nonsense words and if he misses any he tries sounding out and blending the parts presented to him separately. Thus, if "spack" is missed, the child is given *sp* and *ack* and asked to sound them separately and blend them. If performance on this test is good, the next three sections are omitted: 2, Giving Letter Sounds; 3, Naming Capital Letters; and 4, Naming Lower Case Letters. The first section of this subtest is new in this revision but the other three sections are the same as in the earlier edition except for changes in order of presentation of the letters. The rationale for changing order is not given, but it appears that beginning with *s, t,* and *n,* instead of the earlier *u, o,* and *y,* makes the task easier to begin with in the "letter sounds" test. Also, the change to *X, G, O,* and *K,* from the earlier *A, E, I, O, U,* seems to avoid the familiar sequence prompt in the "naming capital letters" test. Norms for these tests compare errors with those of students with like oral reading grade or actual grade level. However, nowhere in the manual is the norm group clearly identified for this subtest or others.

Subtest 6 (Recognizing the Visual Form or Word Equivalents of Sounds) differs from subtest 5 in that the former requires supplying sounds and this test requires recognition of sounds heard and association with their visual forms. Interpretations are wisely treated as hypotheses to be tested in other ways.

Subtest 7 (Auditory Blending) shows some improvement over the earlier version. Thus, "fry" is presented as *fr-i* instead of *f-r-y* and "dance" is *d-an-s* instead of *d-a-n-c-e.*

Subtest 8 includes supplementary tests on spelling (oral spelling of words read to the child from the earlier Words: Untimed Presentation), oral vocabulary (the examiner reads twice a sentence with four alternative completions, such as "A *head* is part of a: coat, saw, man, box"), syllabication (a condensed version of a test from the earlier edition in which the child reads orally nonsense words like "adon," and "ligarind," and auditory discrimination (in which the child is to say "same" or "different" to pairs of words some of which differ in beginning, ending, or middle sounds).

One of the great strengths of this battery is the studding of suggestions for profile analysis throughout the manual. Even the user of other batteries would gain much from these sections. For example, it is suggested that performance on column 3 of subtest 5-1 (reading the middle and final elements of words, such as the *ack* in "spack") be compared with subtest 8-3, syllabication, to see whether "the pupil has more difficulty in finding and combining syllables in words (as in the syllabication test) than in recognizing the syllables when they are presented alone" (as in column 3 of subtest 5-1). Such suggestions improve one's ability in clinical diagnosis.

If this battery is used as intended, the user must interpret norms where the reference group is not entirely clear, needs to make decisions as to whether a test should be given and in what order, and needs to consider alternative interpretations of test scores. Thus, administering and interpreting this battery requires a sophisticated examiner willing to pay the price of considerable training, formal or informal. This judgment also holds for the *Durrell Analysis of Reading Difficulty* and Spache's *Diagnostic Reading Scales*.

Nevertheless, the sophisticated user must make a choice among these three batteries (or possibly others). The reviewer suggests getting experience with all three because of the training value in studying the different approaches of Gates, Durrell, and Spache. And the final choice at the present will depend in part on what other tests are routinely administered. Thus, the Gates-McKillop's lack of a reading comprehension measure is no serious problem if such measures are routinely available on your cases. If complete or self-contained batteries are desired, the Spache and Durrell tests are preferable.

The casual user (whether classroom teacher or psychologist) could, of course, use these tests very informally. In such a case, I would recommend the Durrell because it is easier to get acquainted with and presents a variety of standard reading tasks which cover many facets of the reading process.

For a review by George D. Spache of the earlier edition, see 5:662; for a review by Worth J. Osburn, see 4:563; for related reviews, see 4:564 (2 excerpts); for a review by T. L. Torgerson, see 3:510.

[825]
Group Diagnostic Reading Aptitude and Achievement Tests. Grades 3–9; 1939; 15 scores: reading (paragraph understanding, speed), word discrimination (vowels, consonants, reversals, additions and omissions), arithmetic, spelling, visual ability (letter memory, form memory), auditory ability (letter memory, discrimination and orientation), motor ability (copying text, crossing out letters), vocabulary; 1 form (16 pages); directions (2 pages); key-norms (12 pages); no data on reliability; tentative norms; no description of normative population; 15¢ per test; $1.50 per set of 22 cards for visual tests; 50¢ per key-norms; postage extra; (60–70) minutes; Marion Monroe and Eva Edith Sherman; C. H. Nevins Printing Co. *

[826]
★**McCullough Word-Analysis Tests, Experimental Edition.** Grades 4–6; 1962–63; c1960–63; 10 scores: initial blends and digraphs, phonetic discrimination, matching letters to vowel sounds, sounding whole words, interpreting phonetic symbols, phonetic analysis total, dividing words into syllables, root words in affixed forms, structural-analysis total, total; 1 form ('62, c1960–62, 8 pages); manual ('62, c1960–62, 10 pages); norms manual ('63, 11 pages); individual record ('62, c1960–62, 4 pages); $5.92 per 35 tests; 76¢ per specimen set; postage extra; [70] minutes in 7 sessions; Constance M. McCullough; Ginn & Co. *

EMERY P. BLIESMER, *Director, McGuffey Reading Clinic, University of Virginia, Charlottesville, Virginia.*

This battery consists of seven 30-item tests, five for diagnosing phonetic analysis skills and two for diagnosing structural analysis skills. The first four tests are intended for pupils who have at least fourth grade, and the last three for pupils with at least fifth grade, level reading skill or above. The tests may be given to groups or to individuals, with examinees recording their answers in an 8-page test booklet. The fourth test (Sounding Whole Words) involves ability to blend or apply the separate skills measured in the first three tests (hearing consonant blends or digraphs and vowels and identifying letters which make their sounds).

A pupil's individual record sheet is provided for compiling a record of performance on each specific item on each test. Two "cross-reference interpretation" pages are also included on the individual record sheet. The first cross reference sheet lists each item in Test 4 (Sounding Whole Words) and the specific item in each of the first three tests which relates to the given Test 4 item. In the second cross reference interpretation page each of the items in Test 5 (Interpreting Phonetic Symbols) is listed; and the specific items in Test 2 (Hearing Vowel Sounds) and Test 3 (Matching Letters to Vowel Sounds) is indicated. Illustrations for interpretation for each of the cross reference pages are also provided. Diagnoses for each of the tests are provided with the answer keys in the manual. For most tests, reference is made to "teachers' manuals or reader series" as a source of exercises or possibilities for adaptation for remedial work.

While the test was originally intended for use as an instructional or diagnostic aid in the classroom, requests for normative data apparently led to a "relatively modest, though technically precise" program for establishing norms; and the test is presented, with its norms, as "classroom-tests-plus-norms." Recommendation is made in the norms manual, however, that the test be used primarily as a classroom related device.

Preliminary tryout and analysis of the tests were accomplished by administering them to approximately 400 children in grades 4–6. For establishing norms, approximately 600 children in each of grades 4–6 were tested. One class for each grade was tested in 23 school systems in 21 states, with all classes tested being in schools in which the Ginn Basic Readers were used. Efforts were made to establish a norming sample representative of socioeconomic districts and distribution of mental ability found in the general population.

Norms are presented in terms of percentile ranks for each grade. The finding of a fairly consistent, although slight, difference in mean scores favoring girls led to provision of separate normative data for boys, girls, and total groups. Standard deviations of boys' scores were found to be greater than those of girls' scores on every test in grades 4 and 5, but not in grade 6; a similar dispersion pattern was found with respect to intelligence test scores.

Examination of the various tables of normative data indicates that scores on the various tests tend to cluster near the tops of distributions. For Test 1, for example, a perfect raw score of 30 corresponds to a percentile rank in the 60's. However, pupils in the norm group did not receive such a high proportion of top scores on the other six tests. It is suggested by the publisher that use of separate subtest scores rather than total scores ("total phonetic," "total structural," or "all tests") should lead to better diagnostic use of the tests, with individual scores deviating at least one standard deviation below the mean score for a subtest before being considered significantly low scores.

On Test 2, which requires that the pupil hear the sound of a given letter or pair of letters in a key word, there might be uncertainty in the case of some children as to whether one or two letters are underlined in some of the key words. Circling the key letter or letter pair, or use of some procedure other than underlining, might reduce the possibilities for confusion. On Test 3, more than one answer should be considered correct on several items unless knowing proper spelling of words spoken by the examiner is also required. For example, any one of the letters of item 11, "a," "o," "e," "ou," could precede r in words and have the same sound as er in "her," "were," "term." Several other similar instances could also be pointed out. However, this test seems unusually free of these types of errors or confusion possibilities, particularly when compared with the exercises or practice activities of word attack skills in many workbooks accompanying reading series or in supplementary practice materials used in many reading programs. Each page of the various test materials is an inch longer than the standard size, 8½ by 11 inches. Shortening of pages to a standard length in future editions would facilitate filing of test materials in case folders.

The test appears to be a carefully planned and well constructed one. Administration of the test will permit a more detailed analysis of word attack skill deficiencies than is possible with most other existing diagnostic tests. The relatively unique cross reference feature of the tests should be valuable not only for determining more specific elements or phases of weaknesses in poor readers but also for helping teachers become more aware of the diagnostic possibilities of word errors made in regular classroom situations.

ALBERT J. HARRIS, *Professor of Education, and Director, Office of Research and Evaluation, Division of Teacher Education, The City University of New York, New York, New York.*

This battery of seven subtests is intended to provide a basis for the group or individual measurement of pupil status and needs in word attack skills in the intermediate grades. The tests, designed for group administration without time limits, get at the following abilities: identifying the consonant combinations heard at the beginnings of words; identifying words with similar vowel sounds; deciding which vowel or vowel digraph represents the common vowel sound in three words; recognizing an artificial word that is a phonetic respelling of a meaningful word; using a dictionary-type pronunciation key; dividing words into syllables; and finding the root word in a word consisting of a root with a prefix or suffix. The tests seem well designed for their specific purposes. Four of them (1, 2, 3, and 6) may be given to grade 4 and up, while the other three are for grade 5 and up.

The test form is an 8-page booklet. The manual, scoring keys, and class record sheet are contained in a 12-page booklet, and there is a 4-page folder for use in analyzing an individual pupil's errors. The tentative norms manual was available to this reviewer in manuscript form.

These tests are ingenious in design and provide for group measurement of skills which previously have had to be measured individually, or by group tests so long and cumbersome as to discourage teachers from using them. They seem capable of providing diagnostically useful information about the instructional needs of a class, group, or individual pupil in word recognition skills. Although scoring is likely to be time consuming, it is probable that many teachers will be willing to exert the effort required. The total score and the subscores for phonics and structural analysis are likely to be less useful than the separate subtest scores, and these, in turn, less useful than individual pupil listings of specific items on which further learning is needed.

The norms manual reports a preliminary standardization which is quite respectable. The tests were administered to one class at each grade in 23 school systems, located in 21 states. Approximately 600 children were tested in each

of grades 4–6. Within-grade reliabilities were found to be .94 or higher for total score; .68 to .97 for subtests. Means and standard deviations show slightly higher means and lower variability for girls than for boys; variability at each grade is considerably larger than change from one grade to the next. Percentile norms are given separately for boys and girls for each subtest at each grade; also for total score, and for phonics and structural analysis subscores. The percentile tables show generally skewed distributions; on Tests 1 and 3 the median is a perfect score of 30, indicating that most of the children had learned the skills measured by these tests before entering fourth grade.

The norms are based on classes of children all of whom had used the Ginn Basic Readers. The *Kuhlmann-Anderson Intelligence Tests* were given at about the same time and showed an average IQ of 108.5. The normative population is, therefore, somewhat untypical and the scores on which the norms are based are probably slightly higher than what might be found in a sample truly representative of the total intermediate grade population.

These tests should be welcomed by schools. They can provide diagnostically useful information on a group test basis, both in intermediate grades and in corrective and remedial reading classes in secondary schools. They seem to be well constructed and quite suitable for the uses for which they are intended. The tentative standardization indicates that many pupils need additional instruction in the skills tested, and these tests can be used to sharpen the focus of instructional efforts.

[827]

★OC Diagnostic Syllable Test. Grades 4–6; 1960; 1 form (1 page); directions-key (2 pages); no data on reliability; no norms; 2-100 tests, 6¢ each; 10¢ per directions-key; 25¢ per single copy and directions-key; cash orders (plus postage) only; (15–20) minutes; Katherine O'Connor; [O'Connor Reading Clinic Publishing Co.]. *

[828]

★Phonics Knowledge Survey. Grades 1–6; 1964; individual; content card (2 pages); response record (8 pages); manual (4 pages); no data on reliability; no norms; $3.75 per set of content card, 25 response records, and manual; 50¢ per specimen set; postpaid; (10–30) minutes; Dolores Durkin and Leonard Meshover; Bureau of Publications. *

[829]

*Phonovisual Diagnostic Test. Grades 3–12; 1949–58; formerly called *Phonovisual Diagnostic Spelling Test;* phonetic weaknesses; no data on reliability; no norms; postage extra; [15] minutes; Lucille D.

Schoolfield and Josephine B. Timberlake; Phonovisual Products, Inc. *
a) [1949 EDITION.] 1 form ('49); error analysis sheet ('49, 1 page); instructions ('49, 4 pages); 75¢ per 50 error analysis sheets; 10¢ per single copy.
b) [1958 EDITION.] 1 form ('58); instructions-class error analysis chart ('58, 5 pages); 50¢ per chart.

CHARLES M. BROWN, *Associate Professor of Education, and Director, The Reading Center, University of Southern California, Los Angeles, California.*

That the *Phonovisual Diagnostic Test* should be included in the reading section is perhaps anomalous. Originally published as a spelling test, it is now called a diagnostic test. But diagnostic of what? The brief instructions to the teacher state that this test is "designed to discover [the pupil's] phonetic weaknesses." It appears to test a combination of skills in auditory discrimination and a knowledge of spelling conventions. At the conclusion of the test, however, the user cannot be certain which of these two factors he has measured.

The test is administered in groups to children from the high second grade up by dictating 17–20 words which purport to "test for all consonant sounds, the digraphs wh, th, sh, ch, ng, 9 initial blends, and 17 fundamental vowel sounds." Analysis of all the mistakes is made for each pupil and errors are summarized for the entire class.

No reliability, validity, or normative data are presented.

GEORGE D. SPACHE, *Professor of Education, and Head, Reading Laboratory and Clinic, University of Florida, Gainesville, Florida.*

The 1949 and 1958 editions of this spelling test are offered as a means of determining a pupil's phonic skills. Both editions are currently available and considered equivalent by the authors. Basically, the task is one of writing 17 words (1958) or 20 words (1949) at dictation. The items are very simple, monosyllabic words which can be spelled successfully, according to the authors, by any pupil above the second grade if he is familiar with the most frequently occurring sounds in the English language. The authors further claim that the tests measure all consonant sounds, 5 consonant digraphs, 9 initial blends, and the 17 fundamental vowel sounds.

Inspection of the test items reveals that the average grade placement of the items in the 1949 test is 4.9, and in the 1958 test, 4.0 according to Gates' *List of Spelling Difficulties in 3876 Words.* While Gates' study is admittedly old (1937), any error in the estimate of current grade placement of the test words is probably in the direction of underestimation because of the trend toward simplification of spelling vocabularies in the intervening years. Thus it appears that the score for an average pupil at the lower levels of use proposed for this test, who might not have been taught to spell these words, might not reflect a lack of phonic spelling knowledge.

Corollary questions regarding the validity of the tests are their lack of equivalence and their suitability for secondary or upper elementary pupils. It is quite possible that many such pupils may have learned to spell these very simple words, and yet lack adequate phonic skills.

The validity of the tests as complete diagnostic measures is also questionable since the items *do not* include all consonant sounds, and make no attempt to evaluate the pupil's knowledge of such phonic elements as vowel digraphs or silent consonants. Furthermore, the lists include only 2 or 3 examples of vowels with *r* and about 5 vowel diphthongs of the 25 to 30 such combinations commonly taught in primary reading programs. The consonant sounds tested include only the simplest 18 and omit the very common alternative sounds of *c, s, g,* and *z.* Thus, in all areas of phonic skills covered the tests are incomplete, and their content validity is questionable.

There is, however, a degree of face validity in the purpose of these tests in view of the research evidence of the frequency of weaker phonic skills among poor spellers. In such cases, when the test is not too simple, it may serve to reveal this weakness as it may manifest itself in spelling, at least in those items covered by the test. But the authors assume, as many of the test users would, that the test is diagnostic of phonic skills in both reading and spelling. This assumption will be incorrect in many individual cases, for the two processes are not identical and all pupils are not necessarily handicapped to the same degree in phonic skills in both reading and spelling. Some poor spellers are good readers, and occasionally a pupil who is poor in reading appears to show normal spelling ability. Some are ineffectual in applying phonic skills in the one area, yet seem to be able to do so in the other.

Thorough testing of phonic skills in **reading**

should involve evaluating the child's ability to hear, discriminate among, and identify all phonic elements, as well as the ability to translate mentally or orally a printed symbol into its equivalent sounds. The pupil must also be skilled in blending the separate sounds he may identify into a complete recognizable word. In contrast, the spelling process involves recognizing and discriminating among the auditory sounds which constitute words, knowing the common symbols used to represent these sounds and their frequent variants, and, finally, writing the proper letters to represent these sounds. It is widely recognized that this process may be disrupted by any of a half dozen factors such as poor auditory discrimination, handwriting errors, lapses of attention, poor auditory memory, certain visual defects, and the influence of defective articulation or pronunciation. The *Phonovisual Diagnostic Test* ignores all these contributing factors and assumes that any and all misspellings of the test words are due purely to weak phonic skills.

In summary, the tests appear to be inappropriate in difficulty for the range of grades for which they are offered, unequivalent in difficulty, incomplete in their sampling of phonic skills and facts, and lacking in coverage of the possible causal factors. Furthermore, the mode of testing is questionable for measuring phonic ability in both reading and spelling.

[830]

★Roswell-Chall Auditory Blending Test. Grades 1–4; 1963; individual; orally administered; 1 form (2 pages); manual (4 pages); $2.50 per 35 tests, postpaid; 50¢ per specimen set, prepaid orders only; administration time not reported; Florence G. Roswell and Jeanne S. Chall; Essay Press. *

REFERENCES

1. HUSET, MARTHA K. *Relationship Between Difficulty in Auditory Blending and Some Diagnostic Indicators of Organicity in Children of Average or Superior Intelligence With Reading Disability.* Master's thesis, City College of New York (New York, N.Y.), 1961.
2. CHALL, JEANNE; ROSWELL, FLORENCE G.; AND BLUMENTHAL, SUSAN HAHN. "Auditory Blending Ability: A Factor in Success in Beginning Reading." *Reading Teach* 17:113–8 N '63. *

IRA E. AARON, *Professor of Education, University of Georgia, Athens, Georgia.*

The purpose of this test is to assess a child's ability to blend sounds into whole words. It is suitable for use in grades 1 through 4 and with older children who have difficulty in recognizing words. The test is individual in nature and is presented orally. Though no estimate of administration time is given in the manual, it is

likely that most children will complete the test in less than five minutes.

The test consists of three parts, each of which contains 10 words. The examiner presents the sounds in a word slowly and the child tells him what the word is. The words in Part 1 are divided into two sounds, one of these being the sound of a consonant letter and the other a vowel, vowel digraph, or diphthong sound (as *a-t*). Each word in Part 2 is subdivided into two parts, the sound of the initial consonant letter or consonant combination and the remainder of the word (as *f-at*). Part 3 words are subdivided into three elements with the initial sound being that of a single consonant, the second sound that of the middle vowel or vowel digraph, and the final sound that of a consonant or consonant combination (as *c-a-t*). The child's score is the number of correct words he gives. Instructions for giving the test are easy to follow.

A brief section on interpretation is included in the manual. By use of a table, raw scores may be interpreted as either "inferior" or "adequate." The table is based upon administration of the test to 62 children in the first grade, to 40 of these same children who were retested in grade 2 or 3 and in grade 4, and to a group of reading disability cases in grades 3–5. Auditory blending scores, on the average, increased with the grade, and correlations were found between auditory blending scores and oral reading, silent reading, and word analysis skills.

The dichotomy of "inferior blending" and "adequate blending" is not in keeping with reality. Six correct answers, for instance, is considered inferior for a first grader while seven correct is adequate. A division similar to those offered by some readiness test manuals in which up to five different categories are presented would be an improvement. Interpretation should be in terms of prediction of success in phonics instruction since the authors emphasize the test's suitability for this.

The usefulness of the table of interpretation is restricted further by the nonrepresentativeness of the samples. The longitudinal study involved 62 New York City Negro children thought to be from the lower to lower middle class, and the second sample consisted of 25 severely disabled readers. Though the helpfulness of the table for interpretation is limited, the explanations for poor blending ability and suggestions for fostering this ability are good.

Reliability coefficients, computed by the split-halves method, ranged from .86 to .93 for the children tested in grades 1–4. A coefficient of .94 was found for 25 severely retarded readers, using the same correlation technique. These appear to be the same children used in the development of the interpretation table. Data presented indicate that the test is reliable.

In an attempt to support the validity of the test, the authors computed correlations between the test and an oral reading test (Gray), a silent reading test (Metropolitan), and the *Roswell-Chall Diagnostic Reading Test of Word Analysis Skills*. These data were based upon the 40 children who were tested in grades 1–4. The sizes of the correlation coefficients were unimpressive, ranging from .26 to .66. Validity is specific, and any data on validity should involve the question, "Valid for what?" The only test of the three cited that deals with phonics, to which this test is supposed to be related, is the *Roswell-Chall Diagnostic Reading Test of Word Analysis Skills*. These correlations range from .46 to .66. A child who knows very few phonics skills may still do well on the other tests if he has a large sight vocabulary and uses other word attack skills well. A correlation coefficient of .70 was found between the auditory blending test and the Gray test for the 25 severely disabled readers in grades 3–5. The extent to which knowledge of phonics is related to the Gray test is not discussed in the manual. The authors refer to two additional sources for information about the reliability and validity of the test. One is a paper, available on request, delivered at a meeting of the American Educational Research Association, and the other is an unpublished master's thesis. Any additional data on reliability and validity contained in these two sources should have been included in the manual.

This test, more an informal inventory than a standardized test, is useful for evaluating a pupil's ability to blend sounds he hears into words. Though the authors do not present convincing data to support the validity of the test, the test is probably valid for this one purpose. No norms are offered, but a section on interpretation in the manual gives the examiner some help in interpreting raw scores.

B. H. VAN ROEKEL, *Professor of Education, Michigan State University, East Lansing, Michigan.*

Anyone contemplating using this test must resolve two issues. The first is the usual one of judging the degree to which the technical aspects of the test meet the standards of good test construction. The second is strictly a theoretical consideration where the prospective user must weigh the significance of that which the test purports to measure in relation to the reading act itself.

The term "auditory blending" occurs here and there in the literature and apparently is synonymous with the more commonly used expression "auditory perception." One can perhaps best define auditory blending by describing a child's behavior when he responds correctly to the items on this test.

The test is administered to children individually and all responses are oral. The test consists of 30 items divided equally among three parts. The items are single words which the teacher pronounces slowly so that the phonemes or, in some instances, combinations of phonemes are heard as more or less discrete sounds. To illustrate, the teacher pronounces the word "at" as *a-t,* "cow" as *c-ow,* "time" as *t-ime,* and "toast" as *t-oa-st.* The child's response is scored as correct if, in the first instance he responds with the usual sound people make when they respond orally to the visual stimulus *at,* in the second instance with the usual oral response to *cow,* and so on. The manual of instructions states that "the test is particularly useful for judging the ease or difficulty that pupils will experience in phonics instruction."

Auditory blending, as interpreted by this reviewer, is the mental act which the child performs when he synthesizes the phonemes prior to uttering the whole word vocally. Correct responses to the items in this test are merely manifestations that auditory blending has been accomplished.

The authors must feel that auditory blending is a significant factor in learning to read or they would not have built this test. The *Handbook of Research on Teaching* [1] cites some research which supports the authors of this test but the evidence is contradictory and far from conclusive.

The technical characteristics of the test are even less defensible than the rationale for re-

1 RUSSELL, DAVID H., AND FEA, HENRY R. "Auditory Perception," pp. 873–8. In *Handbook of Research on Teaching.* Edited by N. L. Gage. Chicago, Ill.: Rand McNally & Co., 1963. Pp. xiii, 1218. *

lating its content to the ease or difficulty pupils will experience in phonics instruction. The manual is almost devoid of information a prospective test user needs to make judgments about the usefulness of this test. The manual carries not even a hint regarding the selection of content, and data on the construction of the test are conspicuous by their complete absence. The norming group is described as "children in Grade 1 who were later retested in Grades 2 through 4 and....a group of children with reading disability in Grades 3, 4, and 5." The manual carries two references which provide additional information regarding the reliability and validity of this test.

In summary, the test reflects almost none of the characteristics of good test construction, the norming group is totally inadequate, and the manual of instructions falls far below reasonable technical standards.

[831]

*Roswell-Chall Diagnostic Reading Test of Word Analysis Skills. Grades 2–6; 1956–59; individual; Forms 1, 2, ('59, c1956–59, 4 pages, identical with tests copyrighted in 1956) ; manual ('59, c1956–59, 4 pages, essentially the same as 1956 manual) ; supplement ('58, reprint of 1 below) ; $2.60 per 35 tests; 50¢ per specimen set; postpaid; supplement free on request; [5–10] minutes; Florence G. Roswell and Jeanne S. Chall; Essay Press. *

REFERENCES

1. CHALL, JEANNE S. "The Roswell-Chall Diagnostic Reading Test of Word Analysis Skills." Reading Teach 11:179–83 F '58. *

IRA E. AARON, Professor of Education, University of Georgia, Athens, Georgia.

This test is designed to assess strengths and weaknesses of selected word recognition skills. It is suited for children reading on approximately the second to sixth grade levels. The five subtests deal mainly with phonics skills.

Subtest 1 measures ability to give sounds of (a) consonant letters and (b) consonant combinations. All consonant letters except q and x are included in the first part, but only 10 consonant combinations (blends and digraphs) are used in the second part of the subtest. Equally important consonant combinations are omitted. The second part of subtest 1 is too brief to be of much value in diagnosis though it may serve as a screening device.

Subtest 2, assessing knowledge of vowel sounds, consists of three parts: (a) pronouncing one-syllable words having short vowel sounds, (b) reading sentences containing words with short vowel sounds, and (c) giving the sounds of vowel letters. A child having a large sight vocabulary may perform well on the first two parts of this subtest without knowing the short sounds. The third part indicates the child's knowledge of short sounds but not the extent to which he will use this knowledge in attacking words. Presenting short vowel sounds in nonsense "words" appears a more natural way of assessing the development of this skill.

In Subtest 3, concerned with the silent e rule, five pairs of one-syllable words are presented for pronunciation. The first of each pair contains the short vowel sound (as fin) ; the second of each pair is the same as the first except for final e and the long vowel sound (as fine). A child with a large sight vocabulary may pronounce all the words without knowing the influence of final e on the sound of the preceding vowel. Again, use of nonsense "words" would be more appropriate. No explanation is offered for including the silent e rule while omitting other rules often taught in the primary grades.

Subtest 4 consists of 12 one-syllable words containing vowel combinations. Eight words have vowel digraphs (as feel and paid) in which the long sound of the first vowel is heard ; two words contain the oi diphthong ; and two words, incongruous with what this subtest is purported to evaluate, have ar combinations. This section of the test, like the previous two subtests, would be ineffective with children who have large sight vocabularies.

Subtest 5, labeled "Syllabication," actually combines syllabication with several other skills. Eight multisyllabic words, difficult enough to challenge most children reading on primary grade level, are presented for the child to pronounce. The examiner observes the child as he puts into practice a combination of word recognition skills. If the purpose of this section is to determine how the child attacks unknown words, then it is effective only with children who do not know the words presented.

The manual does not present information on reliability and validity but does cite an article, available upon request from the publisher, that contains such data (1).

Correlation between the total scores of Forms 1 and 2 was found to be .98 for a small sample of 52 children receiving remedial reading instruction. These children ranged from third through eleventh grades in school and from first through eighth grade reading levels with an average reading level of 4.3. For these same subjects, subtest reliabilities were reported to range from .78 to .99. The reliability of the test appears adequate.

Validity data cited are based upon two second grade classes, two fifth grade classes, and the 52 remedial readers used in the reliability study. Correlations between the total scores on the Roswell-Chall test and other tests are presented. The validity coefficients for the clinic sample were lower than those for the second and fifth grades, though the test was designed for use with poor readers. Validity data are weak in that the same silent reading tests were not used at all levels and the number of cases was small. Despite these limitations, the authors have attempted to a greater extent than most authors of informal tests of word recognition to establish validity. However, the only way to check functional use of word attack skills is to confront children with unknown words. Many of the words used in this test would not be unknown to some of the children taking the test.

The manual is easy to follow though information offered on scoring and interpretation is limited. Normative data are not given, but the manual does include a sequence for teaching the skills tested. Both manual and tests appear to have been prepared without careful thought being given to the skills involved in word recognition.

In summary, this test assesses a limited number of word recognition skills and may be administered easily in a short period of time by an experienced teacher who knows the skills being measured. The test is similar to informal inventories of word recognition skills that many clinics and classroom teachers use. This test alone gives insufficient information to evaluate effectively the word recognition skills of a child.

EMMETT ALBERT BETTS, *Research Professor, University of Miami, Coral Gables, Florida.*

These individually administered tests are designed to assess phonic skills: consonants, vowels, syllables. The first subtest, requiring the pupil to produce in isolation the sounds usually represented by consonant letters, indicates a gross lack of linguistic sophistication on the part of the authors. The second subtest requires the pupil to say words illustrating the "short" vowel principle and to read two sentences containing words of this type. However,

the pupil is requested to give the sound of *a,* with provision for only two possible responses. The third subtest requires the pupil to say "pin-pine" and other words contrasting short vowel and final *e* words. The fourth subtest presents mixed items including vowel digraphs, diphthongs, and vowel plus *r*—without help on interpretation. The last part covers syllabication with most of the emphasis on suffixes and inflectional endings.

This so-called standardized test suffers in comparison with both extant inventories and tests of word perception skills offered by publishers of basic textbooks in reading, and teacher-made informal inventories of phonic skills recommended by authors of textbooks on method. In these materials, systematic attention is given to (*a*) generalizations (e.g., the "at-cat-sat," "ate-mate-late," "eat-meat-heat" word patterns), (*b*) usual sounds represented by letters and syllables (e.g., the usual sound represented by *ir* in "bird"), and (*c*) syllable phonics. These types of skills put the "feed" into *feedback* as a factor in learning the relationships between sounds and letters—an everyday need in the classroom.

For a review by Byron H. Van Roekel, see 5:667.

[832]

Silent Reading Diagnostic Tests: The Developmental Reading Tests. Grades 3–8; 1955; 20 scores: recognition pattern (6 scores), error analysis (4 scores), recognition techniques (9 scores), word synthesis; 1 form (23 pages); manual (14 pages); tentative norms; $4 per 20 tests; $2 per set of scoring cards (optional); $1 per 100 tabulation sheets; postage extra; 40¢ per specimen set, postpaid; (90) minutes in 2 sessions; Guy L. Bond, Theodore Clymer, and Cyril J. Hoyt; Lyons & Carnahan. *

REFERENCES
1. MURRAY, CAROL-FAITH, AND KARLSEN, BJORN. "A Concurrent Validity Study of the Silent Reading Tests and the Gates Reading Diagnostic Tests." *Reading Teach* 13:293-4+ Ap '60. * (*PA* 35:2751)

EMERY P. BLIESMER, *Director, McGuffey Reading Clinic, University of Virginia, Charlottesville, Virginia.*

This test, intended for classroom diagnostic use and designed for children of beginning third grade "age" and above, is made up of 11 separate tests: 1, Recognition of Words In Isolation; 2, Recognition of Words In Context; 3, Recognition of Reversible Words In Context; 4, Locating Elements; 5, Syllabication; 6, Locating the Root Word; 7, Word Elements; 8, Beginning Sounds; 9, Rhyming

Sounds; 10, Letter Sounds, and 11, Word Synthesis. The test yields measures of various abilities concerning word recognition techniques and indications of parts of words where errors tend to be made.

Detailed directions for administering the tests are provided in the manual. It is advised that tests be administered in two sessions of approximately 45 minutes each. Administrators are instructed to "allow sufficient time for the children to attempt all items but not more than" a given number of minutes (7 or 5) on Tests 1–6 and 11. No time limits are suggested for Tests 7 through 10, on which tests the administrator has to read words or sound elements.

A great majority of items in Test 4, Locating Elements, which involves finding a little word in a big word below a picture, are ones in which several little words might be found in a big word; however, only one given response is indicated on the key as a correct one for each item. The advisability of permitting several responses to be scored as correct ones is especially highlighted with such words as "fellowship," "forebearance," "crowbar," "notebook," and "hairdressing." "City" as a little word in "scarcity" is also to be questioned. On Test 6, Locating the Root Word, children are instructed only to locate a "little word within the larger word from which the larger one was made"; and "root word" is not mentioned in the instructions. As in the case of Test 4, the key permits only one of several possible responses for a number of items to be considered as the correct one for each of those items, although several little words are to be found in each of a number of items.

Test 11, Word Synthesis, is somewhat unique. The test consists of 12 paragraphs, each followed by several comprehension questions. A number of lines in each paragraph end with a hyphenated word (frequently not divided between syllables). This then requires that the examinee be able to blend the hyphenated words, which words play an important part in answering the comprehension questions.

Scoring keys or stencils are provided for each of the 18 pages of the test booklet on which test questions appear. Only the test page for which the key is intended is designated on each key. Clear and definite designation of the test to which each key applies is desirable and would facilitate scoring and recording. Keys for a number of tests are some-

what cumbersome and awkward to handle. Some of the slots cut out to show a correct answer are large enough to include part of another word or element; this might lead to confusion as to which of two items is the correct one. Aids or cues for aligning answer keys on a page are missing and would be especially helpful in view of the scoring keys being slightly larger than the test pages.

Keys for Tests 1 and 2 indicate not only the correct response for each item but also give indications for the type of error (initial, ending, middle, or orientation) reflected by each of the wrong responses. This is the "error key." Having a larger symbol for the correct response, or using another method to have this symbol stand out more from the incorrect responses, would facilitate scoring on Tests 1 and 2. A considerable amount of time and effort is involved in scoring and analyzing performance on these two tests. Each of the items must be "key marked" in terms of whether it is correct or the type of error made; and a count of the rights, wrongs, omits, and the various key marks must be made.

A detailed graphic profile is to be found at the beginning of the pupil test booklet. This is broken into the following areas: (a) "recognition pattern," based on performance on Tests 1–3; (b) "error analysis," based on performance on Tests 1 and 2; (c) "recognition techniques," based on performance on three visual analysis tests, Tests 4–6, and on four phonetic knowledge tests, Tests 7–10; and (d) "word synthesis," based on performance on Test 11, which calls for finding word elements phonetically. Plotting the graphic profile for a given pupil involves obtaining or computing his grade placement level, chronological "grade," mental "grade," and various reading ability scores and "average reading score" obtained with other standardized reading tests. Grade equivalent reading scores are determined automatically for each of the scores from the *Silent Reading Diagnostic Tests* (individual test scores and scores based on a combination of tests) when the score on a given test or combination is checked on a horizontal scale.

The variations from "average reading" (for an individual) which are considered important range from one half grade when the average reading level is between 1.5 and 2.4, to one and one half grades when the average reading is 5.5 and above. These distances are also to be applied when considering how much below mental "grade" a child's reading grade needs to be before he is considered a remedial case.

Only brief treatment is given in the manual to interpretation of test performance and results (just slightly over a page) and to presentation and discussion of technical data (less than a page). Very meager information is given with regard to establishment of "tentative norms." Reportedly, tests were based upon research and experimental use, with five editions in experimental form having been used in the development of the tests. The only information presented concerning the norming population is that the group included "all children in a typical Midwestern community with a population of approximately 20,000, and two other groups from other representative communities." Reliability coefficients presented for a group of 49 third grade children range from .78 to .97, except for .67 on orientation errors (reversals) and .46 on syllabication. (For the latter test, a reliability coefficient of .84, based on 104 fifth grade children, is also presented.) The method of internal consistency (each item related both logically and statistically to the designated error pattern) was used for developing error keys for Tests 1 and 2.

The *Silent Reading Diagnostic Tests* afford good opportunities for detailed diagnoses of children with elementary grade level reading skills. Diagnosis in the detail or to the extent made possible with these tests will not be needed for all children in many classes; and the time and effort involved in scoring and analyzing some of the tests would preclude wholesale use in all classes in many school systems. As do some other diagnostic tests, these tests have considerable possibility for use as training instruments in graduate training programs in reading and in inservice training programs (partly by making teachers and others using the instruments more definitely aware of various skills, patterns, and relationships involved in some aspects of reading).

ALBERT J. KINGSTON, *Professor of Education, University of Georgia, Athens, Georgia.*

The *Silent Reading Diagnostic Tests* consist of 11 subtests designed for diagnosing the reading skills of pupils in grades 3 and above. One definite advantage of these tests is that, unlike most diagnostic measures, they are group measures. The tests are excellent for appraising word recognition and word attack skills but do not provide a measure of the reader's comprehension or his interpretation of materials in context settings. In order to obtain maximum value from these tests, a teacher must use them in conjunction with another test of reading ability, such as the *Developmental Reading Tests* by the same authors. In interpreting the results of these tests some measure of the pupil's mental ability also is recommended.

The format of the tests is attractive and the instructions for administering and scoring the tests are clearcut and well written. It is recommended that the tests be administered in two separate periods of 45 minutes each, a procedure which limits fatigue and makes their use more feasible in a typical elementary classroom. The first five tests are administered during the first period of testing, and the remainder of the tests are completed during the second testing session. A possible weakness lies in the format of the test. Tests 5 and 6 are printed on the same page. Faster pupils probably work Test 6 mentally while waiting for their classmates to finish the previous subtest. It is impossible to predict the degree to which they may be helped by such practice prior to being tested on Test 6 during the second testing session. However, since time limits for each subtest are generous, this criticism may not be too important.

Test 11, Word Synthesis, might be improved. This section seeks to evaluate the pupil's ability to blend words together both visually and phonetically. In order to achieve this goal words are presented in context, but a number are hyphenated in an artificial fashion. In the first selection, for example, the five test words employed are wagon, play, stick, pull, and with. Each of these words is the last word on a line. They are hyphenated as follows: wag-on, pl-ay, st-ick, p-ull, and w-ith. This format represents a highly artificial reading situation.

The manual which accompanies the tests is clearly written and more than adequate. The reliabilities of the tests are sufficient for individual diagnosis. Scoring is easy and can be accomplished in approximately 15 minutes per booklet. A set of window cards is furnished for scoring purposes. Norms are presented by half-grade intervals and a profile inside the test booklet lends itself to easy interpretation. It is essential, however, that the teacher also appraise the student's comprehension abilities not included in these measures if she is to obtain maximum value from the use of these tests.

In the opinion of the reviewer, these tests can be of great assistance to the elementary teacher. The results are readily obtained and constitute reliable and valid measures on the basis of which individualized reading instruction can be planned.

[833]

The Standard Reading Tests. Reading ages up to 9-0; 1958; individual; 1 form; 12 tests; manual (128 pages, see *1* below) includes all test materials; no data on reliability; norms for Tests 1, 11, and 12 only; 21*s.* per manual, postage extra; administration time not reported; J. C. Daniels and Hunter Diack; Chatto & Windus Ltd. *
a) TEST 1, THE STANDARD TEST OF READING SKILL.
b) TEST 2, COPYING ABSTRACT FIGURES.
c) TEST 3, COPYING A SENTENCE.
d) TEST 4, VISUAL DISCRIMINATION AND ORIENTATION TEST.
e) TEST 5, LETTER-RECOGNITION TEST.
f) TEST 6, AURAL DISCRIMINATION TEST.
g) TEST 7, DIAGNOSTIC WORD-RECOGNITION TESTS.
h) TEST 8, ORAL WORD-RECOGNITION TEST.
i) TEST 9, PICTURE WORD-RECOGNITION TEST.
j) TEST 10, SILENT PROSE-READING AND COMPREHENSION TEST.
k) TEST 11, GRADED SPELLING TEST.
l) TEST 12, GRADED TEST OF READING EXPERIENCE. (20) minutes.

REFERENCES
1. DANIELS, J. C., AND DIACK, HUNTER. *The Standard Reading Tests.* London: Chatto & Windus Ltd., 1958. Pp. 215. *

L. B. BIRCH, *Senior Lecturer in Educational Psychology, Institute of Education, University of Sheffield, Sheffield, England.*

There are 12 tests in this battery, 11 of reading and 1 of spelling. Only 3—the spelling test, a test of reading accuracy, and a comprehension test of the sentence completion type—have norms; the rest are diagnostic tests of visual and auditory discrimination, shape, letter, and word recognition.

Test 1, called the Standard Test of Reading Skill, consists of 36 items in the form of interrogative sentences. The answers to the questions are not important; if the sentence has been correctly read the answer is obvious. The purpose is to ensure that the children concentrate upon extracting the meaning from the words they read and to discourage concentration upon mere word recognition. The authors claim that the items are placed not only in a statistically derived order of difficulty but also in a logical one. Thus, polysyllabic words with digraphs and irregular phonic structure are placed later than monosyllables with single consonants and regular phonic structure. It is

claimed that this arrangement makes it possible to evaluate a child's response in developmental terms as well as in the more familiar reading ages. There are tables of norms by which raw scores can be converted into reading ages from 5.0 to 9.0 years and into seven broad categories or "reading standards." These range from 0 for children having little functional reading skill to VI for those who have mastered the mechanics of reading and now require only practice to develop adult competence. The characteristics of each stage are described in the manual.

The second normed reading test, the Test of Reading Experience (Test 12) is a group test of 50 sentence completion items. The norms cover reading ages 6.0 to 14+, though it is stated that norms above reading age 10 are unreliable. Unfortunately, no standardisation details for any of the normed tests, and no estimates of reliability or validity, are given in the manual. There is no indication in the text where these data are published.

Of the more specifically diagnostic tests, Test 2 consists of four meaningless line diagrams, something like those in Bender's *Visual Motor Gestalt Test,* which have to be copied. In Test 3 the child has to copy a six-word sentence. Test 4 is a test of visual discrimination and orientation, in which the subject has to reorganise a stimulus shape which may be a drawing of a concrete object, an abstract, or group of letters from among four others which include the stimulus shape. Test 5 is a test of letter recognition which can be used in several ways. The children can be asked simply to name the letters, or to give their phonic values, or to indicate the initial and end letters of a list of stimulus words which are orally presented. Test 6 is of aural discrimination; the subject has to recognise which of three objects begins with a particular sound. There are eight subtests to Test 7, the word recognition test. The first part tests recognition of two- and three-letter words of phonically simple structure; subsequent subtests test recognition of more difficult words with various blends of consonants and with complex and irregular structure. Test 8 is a test of oral recognition in which subjects have to pick one orally presented stimulus word from a line of four. Test 9 is similar but the stimulus this time is a picture of a well known object. Test 10 consists of a short passage to be read silently and a set of comprehension questions. The normed spelling test is of 40 words ranging from *on* to *beautiful* and covering spelling ages of 5.0 to 12.3.

Each of the tests has clear instructions for administration and no special training is required. There is no doubt that a considerable clinical picture of a child's strengths and weaknesses may be built up from responses to these tests. Sometimes these findings can be clearly interpreted in the light of experience, at others the classroom teacher for whom the tests are designed will have to seek advice from the interpretations in the manual. These are usually cautiously stated, but often they are based upon the authors' own theories of the nature of the reading process which are not universally held.

[Other Tests]

For tests not listed above, see the following entries in *Tests in Print*: 1445, 1465–7, 1474, and 1476; out of print: 1473.

MISCELLANEOUS

[834]

★**Botel Reading Inventory.** Grades 1–12; 1961; reading instructional level and placement of reading materials; 3 tests; *b* and *c* yield 4 ratings: free reading level, highest instructional level, highest potential level, frustration level; manual (31 pages including class summary sheets); no data on reliability; $15 per set of manual and 100 copies of each test, postage extra; specimen set free; Morton Botel in cooperation with Cora L. Holsclaw and Gloria C. Cammarota; Follett Publishing Co. *

a) PHONICS MASTERY TEST. Individually administered in part; 1 form; 4 parts in one response booklet (4 pages): consonants, vowels, syllabication, nonsense words; nonsense words may be given alone in grades 3 and over as a screening test; [15–25] minutes; $4.20 per 100 tests.

b) WORD RECOGNITION TEST. Individual; 1 form (2 cards); scoring sheet (3 pages); [4–12] minutes; $4.20 per 100 tests.

c) WORD OPPOSITES TEST. May be administered as a reading or listening test; 2 forms: reading (4 pages), listening (2 pages); [20–30] minutes as a listening test; $7.20 per 100 sets of both forms.

IRA E. AARON, *Professor of Education, University of Georgia, Athens, Georgia.*

This three-part informal inventory is designed to aid the teacher in estimating the instructional, independent, and frustration reading levels of children and to evaluate knowledge of selected phonics and related skills. Though it may be used with pupils in grades 1–12, it is appropriate for use only with those whose reading levels are at the fourth or lower grade levels.

The Phonics Mastery Test assesses knowl-

edge of sounds of single consonants, consonant blends, and consonant digraphs; rhyming elements; vowel sounds; and syllabication (number of syllables in words and accent). For parts of this test, the children write the letter or letters representing the beginning or vowel sounds in the words the examiner reads. Pupils also write words rhyming with each of several words presented in the test booklet. They also identify long and short vowel sounds. The fourth subtest, which must be administered individually, consists of nonsense words the child pronounces. If children are thought to be reading beyond third grade level, the examiner may administer this test first and omit the earlier subtests for children who perform well. This section appears to sample adequately the phonics skills.

The Word Recognition Test contains 20 words at each reading level from preprimer through fourth grade. The examiner asks the child to pronounce the words at appropriate levels, starting where he thinks the child can pronounce all words and ending when accuracy drops below 70 per cent at two successive levels. The lists of words appear to have been selected carefully. This test and the Word Opposites Test serve as a basis for estimating reading levels.

The Word Opposites Test is designed to give an estimate of word comprehension. At levels from first reader through senior high school, 10 multiple choice items at each level are presented. Each item consists of four or five words, and the child is asked to find a word in each line that is the opposite of the first word. No evidence is cited to show the degree of relationship between selecting opposite words in multiple choice items and comprehending sentences and paragraphs. The test may also be given as a listening test in order to estimate a potential level for reading.

The manual presents a table of standards for interpreting scores on the reading placement tests. A child who has from 95 to 100 per cent accuracy on the Word Recognition Test and from 90 to 100 per cent accuracy on the Word Opposites Test is at the independent or free reading level, that is, at a level where he can read without teacher assistance. The levels at which the child has from 70 to 90 per cent accuracy on the Word Recognition Test and from 70 to 90 per cent accuracy on the Word Opposites Test are the instructional levels, where the child can be instructed in reading under teacher supervision. Any level at which accuracy falls below 70 per cent on either of the two tests is a frustration level. Children should not be instructed or allowed to read at frustration level. These standards are modifications of those often used in informal inventories in which paragraphs instead of isolated words are read. The manual indicates that research supports the two criteria that have been modified by Botel in setting up the various reading levels. A thorough review of the literature in this area will reveal very little research evidence to support these criteria. However, actual experience on the part of teachers and reading specialists does indicate the appropriateness of these "standards."

The manual includes an interesting and appropriate discussion of the importance of giving each pupil the right book and of how informal tests help the teacher in selecting appropriate books for children. Its recommendation for individualized reading and concentrated word attack instruction during the first four to six weeks of the school year, because of loss during the vacation period, would not be appropriate in those communities in which children engage actively in reading during the summer months. The manual also includes a useful summary chart of the Phonics Mastery Test for class use.

In summary, the *Botel Reading Inventory* is a useful informal test that will give the classroom teacher an economical way to gather information for selecting reading materials for children and for assessing knowledge and use of word recognition skills. Information, however, is needed on reliability and validity.

CHARLES M. BROWN, *Associate Professor of Education, and Director, The Reading Center, University of Southern California, Los Angeles, California.*

Each of the parts of the *Botel Reading Inventory* must be considered separately. The Phonics Mastery Test calls for the pupils to respond in a group situation to a series of spoken words by writing the first letter, the first two letters, or the vowel letters contained in the words; it further calls for the pupil to identify the number of syllables and the accented syllable in a series of spoken words. Beyond this, pupils may be asked in an individual oral situation to pronounce a series of nonsense words. These tests are "scored" by summariz-

ing the particular sound-symbol elements which give trouble to the individual pupils. No norms are presented; 100 per cent mastery is said to be the goal.

The Word Recognition Test is a somewhat formalized individual informal reading inventory using several groups of graded words. The Word Opposites Test, which may be used as a silent reading comprehension estimate or as a listening potential test, consists of a series of graded words with multiple choice alternatives from which the pupil must select a word with the opposite meaning. The score on each grade level of these tests which the pupil completes is to be compared with a table of standards to determine, for each level of material administered, whether the pupil is at the free reading level ("can read with profit without any teacher help"), the instructional level ("usually needs teacher guidance for comprehension and interpretation"), or the frustration level ("cannot read with profit even with teacher help"). From this procedure the teacher is to determine each pupil's highest instructional level (highest grade level of words read at the instructional level) and highest potential level (highest instructional level on word opposites administered as a listening test).

Because there are no normative data, no information on how the standards for the reading level classifications were determined, no data on reliability or validity, and not even any anecdotal data indicative of tryouts, one wonders how this "instrument" would be any better than a simple application of informal reading inventory criteria to the oral and silent reading of graded material. The selection of appropriate instructional and free reading material on the basis of the scores on this inventory would be rather gross at best and, further, would be very dependent upon some evaluation of the readability level of those instructional materials.

[835]
★Functional Readiness Questionnaire for School and College Students. Grades 1–16; 1957; reports by pupil and teacher on physical and emotional problems related to reading difficulties and school problems; individual; 1 form (1 page, must be reproduced locally); manual (23 pages); no data on reliability and validity; $1 per manual (includes copy of questionnaire), postpaid; [5] minutes; Earl A. Taylor and Harold A. Solan; Reading and Study Skills Center, Inc. *

[836]
★Learning Methods Test. Grades kgn, 1, 2, 3; 1954–55; comparative effectiveness of four methods of

teaching new words: visual, phonic, kinesthetic, combination; individual; 1 form ('55); 4 levels: primer (46 cards), grades 1 (120 cards), 2 (114 cards), 3 (130 cards); procedure consists of a pretest to select 40 unknown words, a 15-minute training session on each method, and post-tests of immediate and delayed recall for each method; mimeographed revised manual ('55, 13 pages); record form ('54, 1 page); $6 per set of cards for all 4 levels, 25 record forms, and manual; 25¢ per manual; postage extra; (85–100) minutes in 5 sessions for pretest, training, and post-tests; Robert E. Mills; Mills Center, Inc. *

REFERENCES

1. COLEMAN, JAMES C. "Learning Method as a Relevant Subject Variable in Learning Disorders." *Percept & Motor Skills* 14:263–9 Ap '62. * (*PA* 37:1870)

THOMAS E. CULLITON, JR., *Assistant Professor of Education, University of Illinois, Urbana, Illinois.*

This test was designed "to aid the remedial reading teacher in determining the student's ability to learn new words under different teaching procedures." The four teaching procedures used in this test are: the visual method, the phonic or auditory method, the kinesthetic or tracing method, and the combination method. Actually, the test is a series of teaching lessons with testing to determine immediate and delayed learning and the appropriateness of the various methods for different individuals.

The *Learning Methods Test* consists of four sets of picture word cards including primer, first, second, and third grade words. A test record form, for each child, is used to record the words selected and the results of the immediate and delayed recall tests.

The author's purpose as stated in the manual is to determine the method by which the individual child learns most easily. A pretest for the selection of test items is necessary. An examination of the four sets of words indicates that they would be in the speaking vocabulary (therefore, in the meaning vocabulary) of even kindergarten children. For this reason it seems unnecessary to use graded lists. The grade 3 set could be used with a child reading at a primer level because the words are going to be taught, and the method then tested.

The author suggests that the order of methods used be varied from child to child. There appears to be no valid reason for this since the test is an individual test and it is assumed that other children will not be present during the administration.

The Phonic Method Test as presented in the manual will probably present difficulty to an examiner. The directions to the examiner state,

"Say, 'This is the letter _____. It makes a sound such as _____. The next letter is _____; it makes the sound of _____, etc.' Have the child repeat the separate sounds after you as you do them with each word. Then have the child try the entire word sound by sound, then blending the different sounds into one whole until it is a unified, complete word." One is left with the problem of what to do with silent letters (nos*e*), consonant digraphs (ben*ch*), vowel digraphs (gr*ai*n), vowel-consonant combinations (n*ur*se), and diphthongs (t*ow*el, rainb*ow*). In many of the words the individual letters have no separate sound of their own, but receive their value because of another letter in the word. Another difficulty might be the consonants that have multiple sounds (*c*ircus, *c*andy). If a child had no prior phonetic training, it seems that this might be too complex a task to cover in a 15-minute period. With all of the phonetic inconsistencies in the English language, perhaps a list of more phonetically regular words would be best for use with this test.

The Combination Method Test suggests, "Ask the child to find any common phonograms or little-words-in-big-words." Care must be taken in this exercise to see that children do not pick out little words that have a different pronunciation than that found in the larger word ("am" in game; "on" in pony; "on" in tongue; "on" in onion).

Reliability coefficients were obtained for all four methods by correlating the number of right responses for a particular method with the number of right responses for delayed recall for the same method. One might question the value of studies based on the responses of only 30 subjects. The author states that he administered all the tests, teaching procedures, and retests. The size of the sample and the single examiner may be limitations of the reliability data. A larger sample with other examiners would be advantageous since it would provide the opportunity for an inter-examiner reliability study to be made.

Research findings on the *Learning Methods Test* based on 58 subjects are included in the manual. Specific conclusions are drawn based on sex differences, differences in intelligence (low, average, and high), and differences in age (ages 7, 8, and 9). With the exception of the sex differences study, we have no idea of the number of children in each of these groups.

At one point, the author refers to one method as being the best "in a great number of cases." While the sampling may indicate tendencies, it must be noted that these should not be considered as specific conclusions as the manual implies.

An editorial correction in the manual should be made. The picture word cards are 2 by 4¼ inches rather than 4 by 6 inches.

In summary, the *Learning Methods Test* is a comparatively short, easily administered test to be used by the remedial reading teacher as an aid in determining the most effective method for teaching specific children new words. The criticisms raised here are not fundamental criticisms of the test but rather are directed to further study and analysis of more complete data and possible revision of parts of the current test.

WILLIAM ELLER, *Professor of Education, State University of New York at Buffalo, Buffalo, New York.*

Elementary teachers and reading specialists frequently observe a pupil's tendency to learn more readily from one method of teaching word recognition than from another. However, weeks or months may elapse before a teacher can detect the most efficient method for teaching a given pupil: therefore, Mills devised his *Learning Methods Test* to aid in the identification of the effective procedures for presenting new words to a given child. The four instructional methods compared are the visual, the phonetic (or auditory), the kinesthetic (or tracing), and a combination of all three.

With a large pack of graded word cards the examiner administers a pretest to identify a pool of words not known to the pupil. Forty words are selected at random from this pool and arranged into four sets of 10. Following any one of the four detailed methodologies set forth in the manual, the examiner next spends exactly 15 minutes teaching the first set of 10 unknown words. At the termination of the teaching interval an immediate recall test reveals the number of words learned, and a day or so later a delayed recall test provides a retention score. On subsequent days the other three methods are taught and tested in like manner except for the differences in teaching methodology. After the four delayed recall scores have been averaged, any single score can be compared with this mean to determine the relative efficiency of a certain instructional method for the particular pupil tested.

The distinctive *Learning Methods Test* can be quite useful to teachers of developmental or remedial reading since it provides evidence of a pupil's word learning rate and his retention of new words, in addition to giving an indication of his relative ability to learn from different teaching methods. The test is particularly appropriate for use with remedial cases or with pupils who seem for a time to be learning at a suspiciously low rate. However, the test is not a highly standardized, precision measure in the manner of the majority of instruments described in this yearbook, and it could perhaps more appropriately be titled "Learning Methods Inventory." Much of the lack of precision is attributable to the flexibility of the 15-minute interaction between examiner and examinee while the 10 new words are being taught. Although each teaching method is carefully defined in the test manual, variations in pupil responses interfere with the examiner's effort to develop a uniform procedure. If the test administrator is an experienced teacher, he will detect in himself a tendency to modify the procedure so that an unusually deficient reader will learn at least a few of the 10 words. Pupil deviation from the prescribed technique occurs chiefly when the child has developed one learning method extensively and thus favors that method. For example, if the pupil has considerable phonic ability and tends to attack strange words phonetically, the examiner will observe the learner "sounding" words to himself, no matter which of the four methods he is supposed to be using.

The limited number of items in each of the four subtests further restricts the precision of this instrument. Equivalent forms reliabilities ranging from .91 to .97 are reported for the four methods. Because it seems inconceivable that a test with so few items and so little rigidity of procedure could enjoy a reliability in excess of .95, this reviewer and a doctoral candidate calculated some reliability coefficients based on procedures very much like those described in the manual. Whereas the manual includes a reliability of .97 for the visual method subtest, the Buffalo data yielded .70, which is a more likely figure. Evidently the reliability values in the manual were influenced by factors not ordinarily included in reliability calculations.

[837]

★**The Reader Rater.** Ages 15 and over; 1959; self-administered survey of reading skills; 12 scores: speed, comprehension, reading habits, reading for details, reading for inferences, reading for main ideas and adjusting speed, summarizing, skimming, recall of information read, unspeeded vocabulary, speeded vocabulary, total; Form A (27 pages); no data on reliability; no norms; $3 per booklet containing test, self-marking answer sheet, and profile; postage extra; accessories not necessary; (60–120) minutes; Better Reading Program, Inc. *

[838]

★**The Reading Eye.** Grades 1, 2, 3, 4, 5, 6, 7–8, 9–16 and adults; 1959–60; an eye-movement camera with test materials; 5 reading component scores (fixations, regressions, average span of recognition, average duration of fixation, rate with comprehension), 3 ratings (grade level of fundamental reading skill, relative efficiency, directional attack), and 2 diagnostic categories (visual adjustment, general adjustment to reading); individual; 1 model ['59]; 8 test forms ('59, 1 card each) for each of 8 levels; manual ('60, 107 pages, see 3 below); graph analyzer ('59, 1 card); reliability data and norms for reading component scores only; $460 per camera; $64 per set of 64 cards (all test forms for all levels); $2.10 per graph analyzer; $27 per light box for use in analyzing graphs; $3.75 per manual; $700 per complete set of the preceding materials plus film, developing unit, carrying case, and other accessories; postage extra; [4] minutes; Stanford E. Taylor and [Helen Frackenpohl]; Educational Developmental Laboratories, Inc. * For a related test, see 839.

REFERENCES

1. TAYLOR, STANFORD E. "A Report on Two Studies of the Validity of Eye-Movement Photography as a Measurement of Reading Performance," pp. 240–5. In *Reading in a Changing Society*. Edited by J. Allen Figurel. International Reading Association Conference Proceedings, Vol. 4. New York: Scholastic Magazines, Inc., 1959. Pp. 264. *
2. SPACHE, GEORGE D. "Evaluation of Eye-Movement Photography in Reading Diagnosis and Reading Training," pp. 98–106. In *Research and Evaluation in College Reading*. Ninth Yearbook of the National Reading Conference for College and Adults. Fort Worth, Tex.: Texas Christian University Press, 1960. Pp. 137. *
3. TAYLOR, STANFORD E. *Eye-Movement Photography With the Reading Eye, Second Edition.* Appendices (EDL Research and Information Bulletins Nos. 2 and 3) by Stanford E. Taylor, Helen Frackenpohl, and James L. Pettee. Huntington, N.Y.: Educational Developmental Laboratories, Inc., 1960. Pp. 69, 12, iv, 22. *

ARTHUR S. MCDONALD, *Professor of Education, and Director of Reading Services, Marquette University, Milwaukee, Wisconsin.*

The *Reading Eye* camera serves four main purposes in the diagnostic and assessment procedures of reading. It (*a*) provides a survey of the individual's oculomotor efficiency in the reading act; (*b*) indicates the need for specific types of corrective or remedial treatment; (*c*) indicates the adequacy of visual functioning while reading; and (*d*) permits more finely discriminated research into aspects of the nature of reading performance. The *Reading Eye*

photographic record reveals the efficiency of reading performance in terms of average number of fixations per line, frequency of regressions, duration of fixations, span of recognition, and adequacy of directional attack (consisting of left-to-right eye movements while reading).

Numerous research studies have demonstrated that eye-movement photographic records reflect accurately the individual's customary reading performance and that these oculomotor characteristics do not naturally improve with the reading instruction provided in the typical classroom.

The availability of several test forms and corresponding normative data enables the *Reading Eye* to be used at every level of instruction from first grade through graduate school. Alternate equated forms make retesting and study of progress practicable. The equated forms for measuring reading flexibility enable teachers to plan instruction to provide the specific kinds of developmental or corrective activities required to produce versatile readers and assess progress.

The test selections and comprehension questions were designed to insure equivalence of alternate selections at each level and a consistent increase of difficulty from level to level by use of readability formulae, vocabulary control, review by a number of test specialists, and item analysis based on two validation testings. In addition, general plot complexity and nature of content were matched at each level. The comprehension questions were designed to test all pertinent information presented in each selection. A research validation study showed that more than 30 percentage points separated the scores of those who read the selections and those guessing answers without reading the selections. On the basis of this study, scores below 70 per cent are recommended to be used with caution.

Norms for reading component scores are based on nationwide testing following a plan which seems to insure the representative nature of the samples with special attention to adequacy of geographical distribution, public-private school representation, and (in the case of the flexibility tests) appropriate proportions of students who had completed special developmental or corrective reading programs and those who had not. A commendable feature of the norms is the preparation of separate norms for males and females for each level based on actual testing at that level. This procedure avoids the hazards of statistical extrapolation over a range of grades and allows differential interpretation of reading performance without the obscuring factor of sex.

The test manual reports validity studies involving comparison of photographic measurements with scores on the Survey Section of the *Diagnostic Reading Tests* at the fourth, seventh, and tenth grade levels. Correlations ranging from .83 to .91 (uncorrected for attenuation) were obtained. Validity studies conducted by the reviewer and his associates on groups of high school, college, and adult students comparing photographic record data and performance on a number of standardized tests, including the reading comprehension test of the *Cooperative English Tests* and the Survey Section of the *Diagnostic Reading Tests,* as well as performance in lengthy selections from books on an immediate test-retest basis and on a time lag basis (after 3 months and after 1 year), resulted in correlations ranging from .85 to .93. A number of other research studies reported in the literature agree in indicating that students read similarly before and away from the eye-movement camera. They also agree in concluding that certain aspects of reading performance are difficult to assess without the use of photographic records or other more expensive measures.

Taylor has reported test-retest reliabilities ranging from .83 to .93 for the various component scores of his reading performance efficiency rating. Other researchers, including the reviewer, have found test-retest correlations of .80 to .91 for these components. Inasmuch as span of recognition is a mathematical computation from the fixation score, reliabilities have not been run on it since this score manifestly depends on the reliability of the fixation component.

The directions for using the camera, obtaining data, and interpreting scores are exceptionally clearly written and should enable teachers to correctly and efficiently use the instrument. In addition, for the researcher, a comprehensive bibliography of studies dealing with eye-movement photographic research is provided.

SUMMARY. The *Reading Eye* is a useful diagnostic and evaluative instrument for teachers and researchers at all levels. Characteristics of reading performance revealed by eye-movement photography correlate highly with reading competence and grade placement as judged by other criteria. Further, certain aspects of the functional and perceptual efficiency of a reader can be detected most effectively in the school situation by eye-movement photography. The reliability coefficients of the various component scores are high enough to permit individual diagnosis with confidence. Thus, the eye-movement camera has a number of unique contributions to make to the process of reading diagnosis, assessment, and research.

GEORGE D. SPACHE, *Professor of Education, and Head, Reading Laboratory and Clinic, University of Florida, Gainesville, Florida.*

The *Reading Eye* is a portable 35 mm. camera devised for the purpose of photographing a reader's eye movements. The permanent record obtained by the camera, the reading graph as it is called, serves four basic purposes: (*a*) to analyze in detail the individual's mechanical functioning in the reading act; (*b*) to obtain indications of the need for specific types of corrective instruction; (*c*) to give indications of difficulties in visual functioning in the reading act; and (*d*) to observe the reader's general adjustment to the reading situation.

In actual use, the subject is administered several trial reading selections chosen from among the 64 test selections ranging from first grade to college level. When an appropriate level is found, as measured by comprehension, a test selection is placed in the camera and read by the subject. The camera employs the principle of corneal reflection by which beads of light are reflected into the camera and onto the moving film, thus providing a permanent, objective record of visual behavior during the reading act. The portion of film may be removed from the camera immediately and developed in the processor supplied with the ensemble.

The reading graph is then analyzed in terms of number of fixations and regressions per 100 running words, the average span of recognition, the average duration of fixations, and the rate of reading. Comprehension is measured by 10 post-reading questions. Subsequent analysis of the graph may be made to judge relative efficiency of eye movements (rate divided by fixations plus regressions); and for directional attack (regressions divided by fixations). The individual's performances are then compared with the norms established by the testing of 12,000 cases ranging from first grade to college level.

Studies by Taylor (*1, 3*) support the validity of the technique by indicating high correlations between rate of reading in the camera and in ordinary reading tests. His studies also indicate consistency of performance of individuals reading materials at or below their grade levels, or in reading materials varying significantly in interest values. Consistency of performances was demonstrated in another sample when individuals read at their "usual" rate or when instructed to read carefully for comprehension. The pretesting to determine an appropriate test card further contributes to the reliability of the camera record. Formal data on reliability by test-retest or other means have not yet been established.

For training in the operation of the camera, purchasers are given a prepared list of training materials and instruction by the local EDL representatives. Actually, the technique is so simple that extended training is unnecessary.

In this reviewer's opinion, the *Reading Eye* adds certain dimensions to reading diagnosis and remediation not found in any other approach. It alone will serve to reveal the efficiency of the reader's functioning in the reading act in such details as excessive regressions, abnormal duration of fixation pauses, habitual regressions at recurring points, inaccuracy of return sweep, coordination and vergence problems, the effects of lateral or vertical imbalance and of variations in acuity, tendencies to suppression or monocular reading, and evidences of severe tension. The analysis of the reading graph also yields information regarding the need for training in directional attack, the effectiveness of mechanical training devices, and the outcomes of remedial training in reading.

For an excerpt from a related book review, see B478.

[839]

★**Reading Versatility Test.** Grades 6–10, 11–16 and adults; 1961–62; reading flexibility; 2 levels; manual ('62, 10 pages); no data on reliability; stopwatch or test timer (card booklet for indicating elapsed time) necessary for administration of *a1* and *b*; 80¢ per test timer; postage extra; Arthur S. McDonald, Mary Alodia, George Zimny, Stanford E. Taylor, and James Byrne; Educational Developmental Laboratories, Inc. *
a) BASIC. Grades 6–10; 1961–62; 2 editions.
  1) [*Paper and Pencil Edition.*] 7 scores: rate of

reading (2 scores), comprehension (2 scores), scanning rate, skimming rate (2 scores); Forms A ('61), B ('61), AA ('62), BB ('62), (16 pages); test booklet title of Forms AA and BB is *Appraisal of Reading Versatility (Basic)*; distribution of Forms A and B restricted to schools; 16¢ per test; 50¢ per specimen set of 2 forms; [30] minutes.
  2) [*Reading Eye Edition.*] Administered using the publisher's eye-movement camera (see 838); 29 scores: 5 scores (comprehension, rate, fixations per 100 words, duration of fixation, apparent number of lines) for each of 5 exercises, and 2 scores (regressions per 100 words, span of recognition) for each of 2 exercises; individual; Forms A, B, ('61, 15 pages); record sheet ['62, 2 pages]; separate answer folders must be used; $1 per test; 5¢ per answer folder; $460 per camera; $24 per special platen for this test; specimen set not available; [35] minutes.
b) ADVANCED. Grades 11–16 and adults; 1962; 6 scores: same as for *a1* except only 1 skimming rate score; Forms C, D, CC, DD, (16 pages); test booklet title of Forms CC and DD is *Appraisal of Reading Versatility (Advanced)*; distribution of Forms C and D restricted to schools and colleges; 20¢ per test; 60¢ per specimen set of 2 forms; [30] minutes.

REFERENCES
1. THEOPHEMIA, MARY. "Testing Flexibility in Reading." *Int Rdg Assn Conf Proc* 7:138–9 '62. *

[840]

★**Understanding Communication (Verbal Comprehension).** Industrial employees at the skilled level or below; 1959, c1956–59; 1 form ('56, 4 pages); manual ('59, 13 pages); reliability data based on student group only; $3 per 20 tests, postage extra; $1 per specimen set, postpaid; 15(20) minutes; Thelma G. Thurstone (test) and Measurement Research Division, Industrial Relations Center, University of Chicago (manual); Education-Industry Service. *

C. E. JURGENSEN, *Assistant Vice President, Personnel, Minneapolis Gas Company, Minneapolis, Minnesota.*

This test purports to measure comprehension of verbal material in the form of short sentences and phrases. The items were selected on the basis of an item analysis of a 200-item test administered to over 500 children in grades 7–12. The test has been used in junior and senior high schools and in at least three industrial groups. Although developed on school children, the test is apparently intended for industrial use. Norms indicate that the range of scores allows the test to discriminate adequately between hourly industrial personnel (better between semiskilled than between persons on skilled levels) but not between executives or between professionals.

Validity data are weak, consisting of a correlation of .75 between scores on this test and an unnamed general scholastic achievement test for a group of 200 eighth grade children and correlations of .52 and .48 with a test of verbal reasoning for two groups of industrial employees (*n*'s of 193 and 45). No predictive or concurrent validity coefficients are given in the manual. Though this test is presumably intended for use in business and industry, there is little evidence on what the test measures or how well it measures whatever it does measure. Similarly there is a lack of evidence on relevance of scores to any criteria of job success. The fact that test scores differentiate within or between occupational groups is insufficient; conceivably, age or educational level might differentiate even better than scores on the test.

The manual, in reference to scores on this test, asserts that "speed of reading, vocabulary, and word fluency are of minor importance if the subject has good verbal comprehension," but no supporting evidence is given. Although the test is intended to measure understanding communication, and although the verbal comprehension factor has been identified in various factorial studies, no evidence is presented to the effect that this test will give more or additional or better information than any test of general mental ability, or even a test of reading ability.

In general, the manual is well written and is particularly commendable for its two-page discussion of standard score interpretation. It is unfortunate that the manual does not also present data on the meaning and use of the specific score obtained from this test.

In summary, though the test may be a useful addition to a battery intended for factor analyses in theoretical studies of the nature of cognitive processes, there is no evidence that it should be used in addition to or in place of other tests in a battery for employee selection or placement or for student counseling or guidance.

DONALD E. P. SMITH, *Associate Professor of Education, and Chief, Reading Improvement Service, The University of Michigan, Ann Arbor, Michigan.*

This test of silent reading comprehension runs the risk of being judged by its typography. That would be a mistake. The measuring technique, the content, and the evaluative evidence commend it as a standard for comparison by those who would measure reading skill. It was developed "to measure comprehension of verbal material in the form of short sentences and phrases * Marking the right answer does not depend on [delayed] memory or on recogniz-

ing the answer in the paragraph; rather, it depends on solving a problem presented in verbal form."

To appreciate the author's implied distinction between her strategy and that of other current measures, consider the following item: "The skill attained by the early smith in England is strikingly illustrated in the discovery of ornate hinges, an andiron with an oxhead design, and fragments of: (*a*) crude weapons, (*b*) beautiful tapestry, (*c*) engraved shields, (*d*) horseshoes." An analysis of the semantic and syntactic elements which must be discriminated in this item is inappropriate here, but the item deserves attention as a model for the reading comprehension task.

The test consists of 40 such items selected from 200 sample items tried out on children in grades 7–12. Four choices, consisting of a terminal word or phrase, follow each item. Distractors are excellent. Items appear to be arranged in order of complexity.

Split-half reliability on 300 students is reported as .91, unusually good for a measure of reading skill. Of interest are data gleaned from the norm table. Standard scores (normalized) are provided for a sample of nearly a thousand hourly industrial personnel. Four standard deviations embrace raw scores from 11 to 38 (of 40 possible). Since the score consists of rights only, a chance score (10) would place the subject at or below the 2nd percentile, where he belongs, a desirable though not necessarily common state of affairs.

Coefficients are provided indicating a substantial relationship with "general scholastic achievement scores" (.75), and with a test of verbal reasoning (.63, no reference given). Failure to compare this scale with others is understandable in light of the author's definition of reading comprehension.

The manual is clearly written and includes a simple explanation of standard scores and their interpretation, as well as a number of careful admonitions concerning interpretation. Print and leading are inappropriate. Minor visual problems, particularly tremor, are likely to penalize some subjects.

With improved typography, this scale deserves the widest possible use in high school, college, and industry.

[Other Tests]

For tests not listed above, see the following entries in *Tests in Print*: 1463-4, 1468, and 1471.

ORAL

[841]

★Flash-X Sight Vocabulary Test. Grades 1–2; 1961; 2 scores: sight vocabulary, experience vocabulary; individual; 1 form (3 discs); instruction booklet (9 pages); record sheet (2 pages); manual (12 pages); no data on reliability; $1.60 per test; $2 per 100 record sheets; $7.20 per tachistoscope with manual and demonstration disc; postage extra; [10] minutes; George D. Spache and Stanford E. Taylor; Educational Developmental Laboratories, Inc. *

[842]

★Gray Oral Reading Test. Grades 1–16 and adults; 1963; individual; Forms A, B, C, D; reading passage booklet (15 pages) for each form; record booklet (8 pages) for each form; manual (29 pages); tentative norms; $1.60 per reading passage booklet; $3.20 per set of 35 record booklets and manual; 50¢ per specimen set of record booklet and manual; postage extra; administration time not reported; edited by Helen M. Robinson; William S. Gray; Bobbs-Merrill Co., Inc. *

EMERY P. BLIESMER, *Director, McGuffey Reading Clinic, University of Virginia, Charlottesville, Virginia.*

While a promised "revision" or extension of the pioneer and widely used Gray *Standardized Oral Reading Paragraphs* has long been anticipated and awaited, this test, according to the publisher, represents a new test rather than a revision of the 1915 Gray test. Four forms are provided for this new test instead of only one, with each form containing 13 reading selections or passages. Four comprehension questions, intended to be checks on comprehension of literal meaning rather than accurate or precise measures of high level understanding, and a checklist or tallying column for various types of pronunciation errors accompany each passage. A separate booklet of reading passages for use by the examinee is provided with each form, as is also an 8-page examiner's record booklet. The latter contains the 13 reading passages for a given form, with the front page of the record booklet being a summary page for separate and total passage scores, types of errors, and observations.

The purported functions of the test are, first, to assess oral reading skill and, second, to aid in diagnosing reading difficulties. Detailed directions for administering and scoring the test and for interpreting and recording errors are given in the manual. Time needed for reading each passage, types of errors made, responses to comprehension questions, and other observations and comments are recorded by the examiner during administration of the test. Eight types of errors are noted: aid on words, gross and partial mispronunciations, omissions, insertions, substitutions, repetitions, and inversions. Each passage is scored on the basis of time required for reading it and the number of errors made. A total passage score is then used for converting to a grade equivalent score.

The reading passages were so constructed as to be of progressive levels of difficulty, ranging from a preprimer level to college or adult levels. Purportedly, the average case tested will read at least five passages before a terminal point is reached. One of the unique features of the test is the use of a picture to introduce the first selection, in line with regular classroom practice at beginning reading levels.

The "tentative norms" presented in the manual are based on results obtained by administering all four forms of the test to each of approximately 20 boys and 20 girls in each of grades 1–12. Grade equivalents of total passage scores on each form for each sex reflect slight differences in difficulty among forms. Subjects in the norming population were from two school districts in Florida and several schools in a Chicago suburb and metropolitan Chicago (all public schools). Attempts were made to have "average readers" for each given grade in the norming population; but the average mental level of subjects in each grade tended to be near the upper limit of the normal or average range.

A detailed and careful presentation of "interpretation of the scores" is provided in the manual. Some attention is given to causes for specific types of errors. Detailed interpretation of three illustrative examples or sample records of data is also included.

The size of the record booklet and manual pages is slightly larger than that of the standard 8½ by 11 inch sheet. Since more than ample room for recording errors, responses, and various scores is provided in the record booklet, cutting the booklet down to standard size could be done without detracting from recording and scoring procedures and would greatly facilitate keeping of the booklets in case folders and files.

The *Gray Oral Reading Test* should be viewed as a very welcome and useful addition to the stock of measuring tools in the field of reading. Development and construction of the test appears to have been done rather carefully and soundly. The suggestions in the manual

that the test can be quite useful in giving estimates of oral reading ability, in suggesting difficulties requiring further analysis, and in giving insight in word perception skills, but that
additional tests may be needed before recommendation for correction procedures can be
made, seem rather modest ones. It is likely that
this test will have an even greater use than did
the *Standardized Oral Reading Paragraphs,*
with its greatest use being found in remedial
programs or in other work with youngsters
with reading difficulties. Provision of more
than one form is particularly welcome (especially in view of the apparently widespread
practice of using the earlier Gray test as a
pretest and post-test in remedial programs and
in reported research studies), as is also the
simpler and better explained scoring procedure.

ALBERT J. HARRIS, *Professor of Education,
and Director, Office of Research and Evaluation, Division of Teacher Education, The City
University of New York, New York, New
York.*

The publisher states that the new *Gray Oral
Reading Test* is not a revision of the *Standardized Oral Reading Paragraphs* (first published in 1915), which will remain available.
The 1963 test is new in content and method
of standardization. Nevertheless, a comparison
shows many similarities with the older test.
The similar features include the basic structure
of a series of short selections for oral reading,
ascending in difficulty from first grade through
secondary school, and a scoring procedure in
which raw scores are based on a combination
of errors and rate.

There are, however, several important differences. These include: (*a*) the new test has
four equivalent forms; (*b*) each form has a
picture to introduce the easiest selection; (*c*)
the 13 passages in each form include 3 of first
grade level; (*d*) the material for the subject
to read is printed on stiff, durable paper in a
booklet, each passage on a separate page; (*e*)
a record booklet is provided in which the subject's responses are recorded and scored; (*f*)
four comprehension questions are asked on
each passage, although comprehension is not
included in the score; and (*g*) the new 29-page
manual provides most of the information one
likes to find in a manual.

The major purposes of the test are: "first,
to provide an objective measure of growth in

oral reading from early first grade to college;
and second, to aid in the diagnosis of oral reading difficulties." For the latter purpose, errors
are categorized under eight headings: aid, gross
mispronunciation, partial mispronunciation,
omission, insertion, substitution, repetition, and
inverting word order. Hesitations, self-correc-
tions, and repetitions of less than a word are
not counted as errors, but affect the score by
increasing the time taken.

Directions for administration and scoring are
clear and explicit. One starts with an easy passage and gives enough passages to cover the
range from reading without error to two passages read with seven or more errors each. The
score for each passage is based on a combination of errors and time, with errors the major
factor. The total raw score is the sum of the
passage scores, with full credit given for passages below the one read perfectly.

The four comprehension questions to be
asked after each passage have been intention-
ally limited to the literal meaning and are therefore not comparable to questions usually asked
in silent reading tests of comprehension. For
this reason, it is probably wise that no norms
have been provided for the comprehension
questions.

The content of the passages is varied, and in
general the style of writing is appropriate. Difficulty ascends regularly and in fairly even
steps. The length of the passages is quite similar, except at first grade level. The four forms
seem quite equivalent in content as well as in
form, although small differences in difficulty
are reported.

The test's claim for validity rests on the
steps taken in its construction, and its content.
The steps taken to use appropriate vocabulary
and content, provide steady and sequential progression in difficulty, and construct forms that
are reasonably equivalent in content as well as
statistically, represent test construction at a
high level. The scoring procedure and methods
of analysis provided are appropriate for the
purposes of the test. Perhaps too much weight
is given to time as compared to errors. Face
and construct validity can be accepted as being
high. At the same time, one can hope that data
about this new test's relationship to other established measures of reading skills will be forthcoming.

Information about reliability is given mainly
in terms of standard errors of measurement,

which range from 1.98 raw score points for girls on Form A to 4.59 points for girls on Form B; 4.0 points is conservatively taken as the average value. In grade scores this is about .4 to .5 at first grade, increasing gradually to .6 or .7 at fourth grade, .8 at eighth grade, and more than a year at secondary levels. Although this may seem like a large margin of error, it compares favorably with the available data on other oral reading tests. For the entire range of scores, intercorrelations among forms average .97; reliability coefficients are not given for single grades.

The weakest feature of this test is the norms, which are presented as tentative. They are based on the testing of 502 children, 256 boys and 246 girls, averaging about 40 children per grade, chosen by means of random numbers from representative classes in schools in Florida, Chicago, and a Chicago suburb. Children with speech defects, serious health or emotional problems, or who had been double promoted or retarded were eliminated. Whether any Negro children were included is not stated. The population seems to have been above average intellectually, with average IQ's of 109.1 for boys and 111.6 for girls. Since the girls in general did better than the boys, separate norms are given for boys and girls. The differences are fairly substantial; a raw score of 40 points on Form B provides a grade equivalent of 5.1 for a boy but only 4.3 for a girl.

This reviewer questions the desirability of sex norms on an achievement test, for which one of the purposes is the proper placement of children in instructional groups. It does not seem likely that a boy scoring 5.1 on this test is any more capable of reading a fifth grade reader than a girl scoring 4.3. The use of separate norms by sex seems to reduce the test's possible usefulness in the selection of appropriate learning materials or in assigning children to instructional groups. This reviewer hopes that a set of combined norms will be added to the present separate norms for boys and girls.

Another difficulty in the norms is the severity of the standards for beginning readers. A boy needs a raw score of at least 11 to achieve a grade score above 1.0; on three of the four forms, a girl needs a raw score above 13 to do the same. This means that a child could read the preprimer passage perfectly and get partial credit on the primer passage, and still

score 1.0, the same as a child unable to recognize a single word. It is to be hoped that when further normative studies are carried out, these difficulties with the present tentative norms will be eliminated.

Considering the test as a whole, this reviewer considers it a long-needed and very welcome addition to the very limited number of reasonably satisfactory oral reading tests.

PAUL R. LOHNES, *Associate Professor of Education, State University of New York at Buffalo, Buffalo, New York.*

The appearance of a new set of oral reading tests from a source as eminently qualified as the late William S. Gray and his colleagues at the University of Chicago is a significant event.

The technical preparation of these tests as described in the manual is excellent, as far as it goes. Four forms are provided, with grade norms for grades 1 through 12 for each sex. Although the forms are not equivalent in difficulty, the grade scores based on the various forms are comparable, and a standard error of measurement estimate is given for each grade score for each form and each sex. The norms are described as "tentative" because they are based on a total *n* of only 502, which breaks down to about 22 boys and 22 girls at each grade level, but considerable thought went into the design of the sample and the construction of the norms, which are judged adequate and useful, particularly as they adjust for sex and form differences in raw scores.

The complex analysis of variance by which the significances of these differences are established, the use of moving averages to smooth the curvilinear relationship of raw scores to grade levels, and the regression analysis employing score first-differences as a source of standard error of measurement estimates, all reported in commendable detail in the manual, will repay the closest study. Incidentally, besides locating sex and form problems, the analysis of variance overwhelmingly confirms the ability of the tests to discriminate among grade levels. Finally, intercorrelations among grade scores on the four forms are all in the neighborhood of .98, which leaves no doubt that the tests are measuring something systematically and similarly.

The problems of the Gray tests relate to questions about the nature of oral reading ability, questions which the manual raises but does not resolve. Internally, the tests produce scores which represent a nice blend of speed and accuracy aspects of performance, but the assumed relationship of fluency to accuracy is not explored. Eight types of errors are counted as sources of inaccuracy. A comprehension score is derived but not included as part of the total score. As the writings of Gray [1] testify, oral reading is a complex ability. Since diagnostic use of the tests is to be based on analysis of these details of performance there is a practical as well as a theoretical need for exposition of the precise interrelations among the components of oral reading ability. Externally, the biggest unanswered question concerns the relation of oral to silent reading, since a major justification for concern about oral reading is the claim that it is an important contributor to silent reading ability,[2] but other correlates of oral reading have been suggested and should be explored. For example, Winston [3] has suggested that "there is a direct relation between oral reading and personality development." Not only the manual is silent on the predictive validities and psychological meaning of oral reading ability; the two most recent reviews of reading research in *Review of Educational Research* [4] are also silent on these issues.

These are excellently prepared tests which will be particularly useful in the instrumentation of educational research into reading and its correlates, and in adding the dimension of oral reading scores to the cumulative school record on which research is frequently based. Perhaps a revision of the manual should review the existing research literature.

[843]

★Neale Analysis of Reading Ability. Ages 6–12; 1957–58; 3 scores (accuracy, comprehension, rate of reading) plus 3 optional supplementary tests (names and sounds of letters, auditory discrimination through simple spelling, blending and recognition of syllables); individual; Forms A, B, C, ('58, 46 pages in 1 booklet); individual record sheet ('57, 4 pages) for each

1 GRAY, WILLIAM S. *The Teaching of Reading and Writing: An International Survey.* UNESCO Monographs on Fundamental Education, No. 10. Chicago, Ill.: Scott, Foresman & Co., 1956. Pp. 281. *
GRAY, WILLIAM S. "Reading," pp. 1086–1135. In *Encyclopedia of Educational Research, Third Edition.* Edited by Chester W. Harris. New York: Macmillan Co., 1960. Pp. xxxi, 1564. *
2 HEILMAN, ARTHUR W. *Principles and Practices of Teaching Reading,* pp. 146–9. Columbus, Ohio: Charles E. Merrill Books, Inc., 1961. Pp. xiii, 465. *
3 WINSTON, GERTRUDE C. "Oral Reading and Group Reading." *El Engl* 40:392–3+ Ap '63. *
4 CLYMER, THEODORE, AND ROBINSON, HELEN M. "Reading." *R Ed Res* 31:130–44 Ap '61. *
McCULLOUGH, CONSTANCE M. "Reading." *R Ed Res* 28: 96–106 Ap '58.

form; manual ('58, 36 pages); no data on reliability of rate score and supplementary tests; no norms for supplementary tests; 5s. ($1) per test booklet; 5d. (25¢) per record sheet; 3s. 6d. (35¢) per manual; postage extra; (10–15) minutes; Marie D. Neale; Macmillan & Co. Ltd. * (United States publisher: St Martin's Press, Inc.)

M. ALAN BRIMER, *Senior Research Fellow in Education, University of Bristol, Bristol, England.*

The absence in Britain of an oral, diagnostic, reading test which would yield measures of reading attainment has handicapped teachers of reading for a number of years. It is this deficiency that the Neale test attempts to remedy, and which suggests the particular criteria for evaluating it.

The test booklet is well produced in spirally-bound, firm board. Black and white illustrations introduce the passages without revealing clues to comprehension. The type face is clear and the size and spacing of type is appropriately adjusted to the visual-perceptual skill requisite at the various reading levels. Each form contains six passages of graded difficulty and increasing length, which have been written to produce controlled variation of vocabulary and sentence structure. Each passage is a self-contained anecdote in which interest is coordinated with reading level.

In reference to the methods used to construct the test, the manual states that analysis of word difficulty, sentence structure, and optimum length of the test for each age level took place after preliminary trials and that statistical analysis followed further trials, but no account of the criteria or methods adopted is given. Some discussion of the rationale of securing three different measures from a single reading performance ought to have been included. Rate, accuracy, and comprehension are interdependent in oral reading, but this test allows them to vary together in an uncontrolled way. The child is allowed and encouraged to try words over when he hesitates, but only a limited time is allowed for word attack before the examiner supplies the word and records a refusal. Thus, inaccuracy reduces reading rate and possibly successful attempts at words are limited in the interests of rate. Comprehension is measured entirely through recall. The examiner is told to prevent the child from rereading the passage for clues to the answer. Consequently, the level of comprehension attained depends on the rate that the child adopts. It may be maintained that it is a representative sample of the child's oral reading that is being examined, and that it is more closely relevant to the child's reading in school to secure the three measures in this same context. Nevertheless, such a desirable intention has merit only insofar as the measures retain their distinct characteristics, and insofar as they are obtained in circumstances unequivocal for the child. It would probably have been better to have measured rate separately from accuracy and comprehension.

There are no difficulties in administration, though the classification of errors requires considerable experience if it is to keep pace with the rate of more rapid readers. A practice test would have improved task orientation. The instruction to "remember the story as you read it" is inadequate to induce the appropriate "set." Until the child has experienced the questions following the first passage and has realised that he may not look back (he is not told this), he does not appreciate the nature of the reading task that is being required of him. Scoring takes place as the test proceeds. For each passage, a ceiling level fixed by the accuracy score determines whether or not the child should proceed to the next passage. Such ceiling level decisions are rapidly made, and, apart from the rate score which rather unnecessarily requires the examiner to divide the number of words read by time, the summary scores are quickly obtained. A table relating time to rate for the six possible total numbers of words read would have facilitated rate scoring.

The reliability of the accuracy scores is good, none of the parallel forms reliabilities for year groups falling below .96. The reliabilities for the comprehension scores, while they are lower, are nevertheless adequate. The difference in the reliability levels may be attributable to the relative number of items. There are 100 scorable accuracy items, but only 42 comprehension items. The failure to quote the reliability of the rate scores or to make any reference to it can only be interpreted to the disadvantage of the test.

Validity was established by factor analysis studies of the performances of 9- and 11-year-old children, but details of the methods and results are not given. When criterion variables were selected and combined to form a complex criterion, the concomitant validity found for the test was high.

The standardisation sample consisted of over 2,000 children. While it is stated that size of school, area, social background, age, and sex were controlled, no account is given of the distribution of these characteristics in the sample. The standardisation sample must be judged small, particularly when it is realised that the numbers are distributed over three forms of the test (Form A, 1,221; Form B, 552; Form C, 489) and that the distribution of these over seven year groups results in an average of just under 200 per year group for Form A, and of less than 100 for Forms B and C.

Norms are given in the form of reading ages only, and it is to be regretted that no alternative form of expression is offered to test users. It may be that the numbers involved in standardisation would not have permitted more exact statistical forms. No account is given of the methods used to derive the norms. Such information would be desirable since, although reading ages are shown to ascend reasonably smoothly with score, some difficulty in smoothing the relationship might be expected from the use of discrete ceiling levels, which would tend to produce uneven trends in the increase of score with age.

Neale emphasizes that the objective score must be interpreted in relation to the child's personal history and that practical help is likely to arise from a study of the errors made rather than of the score. It is suggested that standard testing procedure might be abandoned in favour of more insightful pursuit of the child's difficulty. However, no guidance is offered as to the extremity or character of the errors that would warrant this. Similarly, the three supplementary tests are provided without explicit instructions for administration, scoring, or interpretation, and it is likely that an examiner sufficiently trained and experienced to make use of them would have more adequate tests at his disposal.

In summary, there are failings in construction, standardisation, and test reporting which prevent the test from satisfying the need in Britain that the author recognizes. Its best feature is the provision of standard reading passages within which the categories of reading errors can be recorded.

MAGDALEN D. VERNON, *Professor of Psychology, University of Reading, Reading, England.*

This is a test of individual oral reading rate, accuracy, and comprehension, standardized for British children. Each alternative form of the test consists of six passages of prose, graded in length and in difficulty of vocabulary and sentence structure. Each passage is illustrated by a picture to "set the scene" and arouse interest; the contents themselves also seem adequately interesting.

The child is required to read each passage aloud, and is scored for rate and accuracy. After each passage he answers eight questions (but only four on the first passage), the correctness of his answers indicating his degree of comprehension. There is no time limit, but each test should take about 15 to 20 minutes. The child is stopped after any passage in which he has made 16 errors of accuracy.

Though the instructions for this test are clear and comprehensible, the record sheets are not satisfactory. They give no space for recording the answers to the comprehension questions, though these may often be difficult to score while testing. The space for recording errors in reading is inadequate. Yet the tester may need to do this, since he is advised to classify the errors into six subgroups. The author is of the opinion that the type of error has some significance as to the nature of the child's reading processes. To investigate these further, she provides supplementary diagnostic tests of reading isolated letters, spelling, and blending. But no norms or standardized interpretations are given for these, nor any validation as to the particular type of defect they are supposed to indicate. Thus only a tester with extensive knowledge of reading defects can learn much from the child's performance on these supplementary tests. However, he may be able to obtain some useful information by studying discrepancies between accuracy and comprehension scores on the main test.

The main test seems on the whole to have been satisfactorily constructed, except that the sixth passage in each form appears to be far too difficult for even the older children to understand, and it is doubtful if they could score anything on it for comprehension. The forms were standardized on over 2,000 children, the sample being suitably controlled for region and social background. However, no children over 11 years appear to have been tested. The reading ages, given separately for the three scores, are based on extrapolation above age 11-10 for rate and comprehension, and above 11-11 for accuracy. In view of the aforesaid difficulty of the sixth passage, this seems a somewhat doubtful procedure.

Reliability for accuracy scores, which was calculated by correlating these scores on alternative forms of the test, is good (.98), and there is also a close correspondence between the mean scores on alternate forms for accuracy and comprehension at ages 7 to 11. Nothing is stated as to the correspondence of scores for rate, though it is shown that norms for rate are similar to those obtained on Ballard's *One-Minute Reading Test.* Validity was assessed by correlating a pooled score for rate, accuracy, and comprehension with pooled scores on the Ballard test, another word recognition test, and tests for comprehension, for 200 9-year-olds and 200 11-year-olds. The correlations are high (.95), but no explanation is given as to why scores for rate, accuracy, and comprehension were not separately validated. However, in the pilot study, accuracy scores for 9- to 11-year-olds showed correlations of .94 to .95 with scores on Schonell's *Graded Reading Vocabulary Test.*

It is doubtful whether measures of reading rate are of any particular significance for children of this age, and indeed it might be preferable to encourage them to read slowly and carefully. But the test may be found useful by busy clinicians in that it assesses accuracy and comprehension together in a short space of time and affords a direct comparison between these. The use of pictures also is probably valuable for the younger children. But the validation for comprehension is unsatisfactory, and the test is not clearly superior to any of the existing tests. It is not adequate for diagnostic purposes.

Brit J Ed Psychol 28:298 N '58. * a valuable addition to the educational psychologist's diagnostic battery. Indeed, it provides a better *individual* assessment of reading comprehension from R.A. 6½ to 13.0 than any other at present available (an average of six questions per year as contrasted with two questions in "My Dog"). It covers word pronunciation from 6 to 12½, as reliably as the conventional Graded Vocabulary tests. Norms are also provided for reading speed, but this measure is troublesome to record and calculate and is, in any case, discriminative only from R.A. 6½ to 9½. The material consists of three parallel series of six graded passages which, both by their content and their illustrations, should attract the child's interest. The printed record and score sheet seems unwieldy and expensive; and the clinic psychologist, or trained remedial teacher, will probably prefer to make her own analysis of types of reading error. The author claims that testing occupies ten to fifteen minutes per child. The tests have been carefully standardised and shown to have good reliability. It is a pity, however, that the opportunity was not taken to construct percentile or deviation norms for each age group instead of scoring purely in reading ages. The material is well printed, and the manual is clear, though one fears that unsophisticated teachers may sometimes fail to follow it correctly.

[844]

★Slosson Oral Reading Test (SORT). Grades 1-8 and high school; 1963; individual; 1 form (2 pages, test and examiner's directions and norms on a single sheet); no manual; 75¢ per pad of 20 tests, postpaid; (3) minutes; Richard L. Slosson; Slosson Educational Publications. *

[Other Tests]

For tests not listed above, see the following entries in *Tests in Print*: 1483–5 and 1488–91; out of print: 1486.

READINESS

[844a]

★The Anton Brenner Developmental Gestalt Test of School Readiness. Ages 5–6; 1964; individual; 1 form; manual (32 pages plus sample copies of record booklet and number recognition form); record booklet (3 pages); number recognition form (3 pages); $10 per set of 25 record booklets, 1 number recognition form, and manual; $3 per set of wooden cubes, pencil, and crayon (may also be assembled locally); $6.50 per 25 record booklets; $4 per manual; postpaid; (3–10) minutes; Anton Brenner; Western Psychological Services. *

REFERENCES

1. BRENNER, ANTON. "Reality Perception, Perceptual Differentiation and Readiness for School." *Merrill-Palmer Q* 4:196–209 su '58. *
2. HOFMANN, HELMUT. "Children's Drawings as an Indication of Readiness for First Grade." *Merrill-Palmer Q* 4:165–79 sp '58. *
3. VIEWAG, WILLIAM E., JR. "The Albion Study: A Longitudinal Study of Readiness for School Tasks as Measured by the Brenner-Gestalt Test; A Preliminary Report," pp. 75–88. In *Inter-Institutional Seminar in Child Development: Collected Papers, 1958.* Dearborn, Mich.: Educational Department, Henry Ford Museum and Greenfield Village, 1958. Pp. v, 122. *
4. BRENNER, ANTON. "A New Gestalt Test for Measuring Readiness for School." *Merrill-Palmer Q* 6:27–51 f '59. *
5. RALPH, JEAN SMITH. *The Brenner Gestalt Test as a*

Measure of Readiness for School. Master's thesis, Wayne State University (Detroit, Mich.), 1960.
6. LUTTGEN, GERTRUDE. "Use of the Brenner Gestalt Test by a Classroom Teacher," pp. 102–14. In *The Inter-Institutional Seminar in Child Development: Collected Papers, 1960.* Greenfield Village, Mich.: Education Department, Henry Ford Museum, [1961]. Pp. vi, 272. *
7. RALPH, JEAN. "The Brenner-Gestalt Test as a Measure of Readiness for School," pp. 87–101. In *The Inter-Institutional Seminar in Child Development: Collected Papers, 1960.* Greenfield Village, Mich.: Education Department, Henry Ford Museum, [1961]. Pp. vi, 272. *
8. SANDHU, SWARAN SINGH. *Factors of Personality, Home and Culture as Related to the Early Identification of Under-Achievement.* Master's thesis, Wayne State University (Detroit, Mich.), 1963.

[845]

*Gates Reading Readiness Tests. Grade 1; 1939–42; 5 scores: picture directions, word matching, word-card matching, rhyming, letters and numbers; 1 form ('39, 8 pages); revised manual ('42, 31 pages, essentially the same as 1939 manual except for norms); $2.25 per 35 tests; 50¢ per specimen set; postpaid; (50) minutes; Arthur I. Gates; Bureau of Publications. * (Australian edition: Australian Council for Educational Research.)

REFERENCES

1–5. See 40:1537.
6–8. See 3:516.
9. BALOW, IRVING H. "Sex Differences in First Grade Reading." *El Engl* 40:303–6+ Mr '63. *

For a review by F. J. Schonell (Australian edition, identical except for norms), see 4:566; for reviews by Marion Monroe Cox and Paul A. Witty, see 3:516; see also 40:1537 (2 excerpts).

[846]

*Lee-Clark Reading Readiness Test, 1962 Revision. Grades kgn–1; 1931–63; 4 scores: letter symbols, concepts, word symbols, total; 1 form ('62, c1960, 11 pages, identical with tests copyrighted in 1943 and 1951 except for format changes and, in concepts subtest, revision of all art work and half of items); manual ('62, 16 pages); optional tape recorded directions for administration ('63, 3¾ ips); mimeographed manual ['63, 16 pages] for use with tape; $3.50 per 35 tests; $5.95 per tape; postage extra; 25¢ per specimen set without tape, $6.20 per specimen set with tape, postpaid; (20) minutes; J. Murray Lee and Willis W. Clark; California Test Bureau. *

REFERENCES

1. LEE, J. MURRAY; CLARK, WILLIS W.; AND LEE, DORRIS MAY. "Measuring Reading Readiness." *El Sch J* 34:656–66 My '34. * (PA 8:4741)
2. WILMORE, WALDO W. *Relative Validity of Three Group Readiness Tests in Predicting Reading Achievement.* Master's thesis, University of Kansas (Lawrence, Kan.), 1939.
3. HENIG, MAX S. "Predictive Value of a Reading-Readiness Test and of Teachers' Forecasts." *El Sch J* 50:41–6 S '49. * (PA 24:2060)
4. MOREAU, MARGARET. "Long Term Prediction of Reading Success." *Calif J Ed Res* 1:173–6 S '50. *
5. KOPPITZ, ELIZABETH M.; MARDIS, VERDENA; AND STEPHENS, THOMAS. "A Note on Screening School Beginners With the Bender Gestalt Test." *J Ed Psychol* 52:80–1 Ap '61. * (PA 38:3205)
6. PARSLEY, K. M., JR., AND POWELL, MARVIN. "Relationships Between the Lee-Clark Reading Readiness Test and the 1937 Revision of the Stanford-Binet Intelligence Test, Form L." *J Ed Res* 54:304–7 Ap '61. *
7. POWELL, MARVIN, AND PARSLEY, KENNETH M., JR. "The Relationships Between First Grade Reading Readiness and Second Grade Reading Achievement." *J Ed Res* 54:229–33 F '61. *
8. DOBSON, JAMES C., JR. *A Critical Evaluation of the Lee-Clark Reading Readiness Test.* Master's thesis, University of Southern California (Los Angeles, Calif.), 1962.

9. DOBSON, JAMES C., AND HOPKINS, KENNETH D. "The Reliability and Predictive Validity of the Lee-Clark Reading Readiness Test." *J Develop Read* 6:278–81 su '63. * (*PA* 39: 1724)

For a review by James R. Hobson of the 1951 edition, see 5:678; for reviews by Marion Monroe Cox and David H. Russell of the 1943 edition, see 3:517.

[847]

Maturity Level for School Entrance and Reading Readiness. Grades kgn–1; 1950–59; revision of *School Readiness Inventory;* behavior checklist completed by teachers; 2 scores: maturity level, reading readiness; individual; 1 form ('59, 2 pages, essentially a combination of items from the two forms of the original edition); manual ('59, 7 pages); $3 per 50 records; 50¢ per manual; postage extra; 55¢ per specimen set, postpaid; (20) minutes; Katharine M. Banham; [American Guidance Service, Inc.]. *

For a review by David H. Russell of the original edition, see 4:572.

[848]

Perceptual Forms Test. Ages 6–8.5; 1955–63; revision of *Children's Perceptual Achievement Forms;* visual development; 1 form ['58, 8 cards]; teacher's manuals (both including test cards): 1963 edition ('63, 10 pages) for group testing, clinical guide, 1962 edition ('62, 23 pages) for individual testing; procedure manual, educational edition ('63, 52 pages); mimeographed procedure guide, clinical edition ['62, 75 pages]; mimeographed training manual, parents edition ['61, 22 pages]; incomplete forms sheet ['55, 2 pages]; $2 per teacher's manual of either edition; $2 per pad of 100 incomplete forms sheets; $3.50 per procedure manual; $5 per procedure guide; $3 per set of training manual and templates; cash orders postpaid; [10] minutes; Publication Committee, Winter Haven Lions Club; Winter Haven Lions Research Foundation, Inc. *

REFERENCES

1. LOWDER, ROBERT GLENN. *Perceptual Ability and School Achievement: An Exploratory Study.* Doctor's thesis, Purdue University (Lafayette, Ind.), 1956. (*DA* 16:2205)
2. ROBINSON, HELEN M.; LETTON, MILDRED C.; MOZZI, LUCILLE; AND ROSENBLOOM, ALFRED A. "An Evaluation of the Children's Visual Achievement Forms at Grade I." *Am J Optom* 35:515–25 O '58. *
3. KAGERER, RUDOLPH L. *The Relationship of Visual Perception Performance in Early Grades to Reading Level in Grade Four.* Winter Haven, Fla.: Winter Haven Lion's Publication Committee, [1960]. Pp. vii, 31. *
4. ROBINSON, HELEN M.; MOZZI, LUCILLE; WITTICK, MILDRED LETTON; AND ROSENBLOOM, ALFRED A. "Children's Perceptual Achievement Forms: A Three Year Study." *Am J Optom* 37:223–37 My '60. *
5. MANAS, LEO. "A New Method of Scoring Children's Visual Achievement Forms." *J Am Optom Assn* 32:713–8 Ap '61. *
6. HARVEY, JASPER. "Evaluation and Development of Techniques for Testing Visual Acuity of Trainable Mentally Retarded Children." *Am J Optom* 40:745–54 D '63. *

MARY C. AUSTIN, *Professor of Education, Western Reserve University, Cleveland, Ohio.*

This test, primarily intended to discover the child who lacks that degree of hand-eye coordination considered requisite for beginning school tasks, may be given as a group test or as an individual one. Each child is asked to reproduce seven geometric forms, one at a time, on a blank sheet of paper 8½ by 11 inches. Presented in a specific sequence, the figures include circle, cross, square, triangle, divided rectangle, horizontal diamond, and vertical diamond. Following the drawing of these forms, the child turns his paper over for the "Incomplete Forms" test, for which the teacher shows the same test cards to the pupil so he can finish each incomplete picture on the page provided.

The revised 1962 manual provides clearly outlined directions for testing, scoring, and interpreting the results. Nine sample sets of drawings are illustrated and discussed. The scoring scale, developed from an analysis of more than 7,000 sets of children's drawings, indicates that a child whose drawings rate a score of more than 60 can be expected to possess "a sensory-motor-perceptual pattern adequate for the tasks" related to beginning school activities. A total score of "significantly less than 60" indicates that a child "can be expected to achieve in the lowest third of his class." Age characteristics, organization, neatness, and size relationship of drawings are taken into account, along with the total score obtained on the forms. Having identified the child who is likely to experience problems in general school achievement—problems which may be related to perceptual difficulties—the teacher might delay the introduction of formal reading instruction until hand-eye coordination has been improved through template training. The latter is discussed in some detail in the manual.

The development of the *Perceptual Forms Test* began in 1953 when members of the Winter Haven Lions Club expressed concern about reports of reading failures among children. At that time a committee was established to undertake a four year project to gather data on the probable causes of failures in the primary grades. Preliminary editions of the test were tried in the first three grades during the next few years, and a Lions Club employee collected information about a large number of children, their performance on the forms, and their subsequent success in school.

The history of research and experimentation over a period of several years includes studies made at Purdue University under the direction of Newell C. Kephart, a number of classroom experiments, and a group of independent studies. Lowder (*1*) validated the use of the geometric forms as a predictor of school achievement. He found a significant relationship between copying performance and school achievement, with the divided rectangle and horizontal diamond being the best discriminators and the most difficult items. His observations resulted in some revisions of the test itself. He also raised a number of questions about the testing of perceptual ability. Two of these were "Since outline form perception seems to be a learned, developmental phenomenon, will formal, systematic perceptual training result in improved school achievement in the lower grades?" and "What is the relationship of outline form perception to school achievement in grades beyond one, two, and three?" These questions led Kagerer (3) to explore the relationships between visual performance in the early grades and reading level in grade 4. His findings indicated that copying ability in the first grade does not predict reading ability in the fourth grade. There is, however, a relationship between copying performance in the second and third grade and reading achievement in the fourth grade. Kagerer pointed out that the copying tests should not be used to classify children, but rather to identify those who may be exhibiting difficulty with visual perceptual development. He also suggested that the possibility of helping children who demonstrate perceptual difficulty should be investigated.

The results of independent studies (4, 5) seem to indicate that scores below 58 or 60 on the test should be interpreted to mean poor general achievement in the future, rather than specific difficulties in reading or handwriting.

There can be no question regarding the values of measures of copying or reproduction ability as a predictor of school success. Tests of visual discrimination which do not determine simply the child's knowledge of letters and words are offered in several reading aptitude tests. The *Perceptual Forms Test* represents the first generally available test of visual perception or discrimination not found in the readiness tests. In its present form the test can be helpful in evaluating the perceptual ability of school beginners. That revision of the test may be desirable is indicated in some of the studies mentioned previously. It may be advisable, for example, to eliminate the cross and the square and to add more difficult items to improve the predictive ability of the test. The present test

appears less effective above the ages of 8 and 9. Perhaps an extension of its effective age range, coupled with an increased accuracy of discrimination, will result in the kind of test instrument which has a broader range of applicability. The Winter Haven Lions Research Foundation intends to continue its work in this direction.

[849]

Reading Readiness Test. Grades kgn–1; 1957; 1 form (12 pages); manual (8 pages); $3 per 25 tests; 25¢ per specimen set; cash orders postpaid; (20) minutes; David F. Votaw, Sr. and Peggy Lou Moses; Steck Co. *

REFERENCES

1. BANHAM, KATHARINE M. "Maturity Level for Reading Readiness: A Check List for the Use of Teachers and Parents as a Supplement to Reading Readiness Tests." *Ed & Psychol Meas* 18:371–5 su '58. *

DAVID A. PAYNE, *Assistant Professor of Education, Syracuse University, Syracuse, New York.*

This test contains 92 items distributed among 10 logically sequenced subtests. The authors emphasize the necessity of treating the test as a "game." This is highly desirable in light of the lack of test sophistication of elementary students and the need to establish rapport. An evaluation of the directions and test tasks indicates that this purpose has been reasonably approached.

The test items, subtests, and directions are of variable quality and difficulty. Assessment of students' familiarity with names of objects (10 items) is extremely easy, but "contributes but little to the placement of a child on the score scale." Above functioning as an introductory "game" exercise, this subtest serves no purpose. The semantics of test directions are of critical importance in tests intended for use with the very young. The reviewer encountered several items measuring interpretation of spoken sentences (10 items) which are open to question. In one item directions call for the student to make a cross on the picture which shows a girl carrying her doll, when the picture has the girl standing and holding the doll. Superfluous words in the directions may confuse some students. In one item, directions require the selection of a picture where "Joe likes to ride his bicycle." This direction might justifiably apply to any of the four stimulus pictures. Perhaps the statement "Joe is riding his bike" would be sufficient. These kinds of word selection problems, together with sometimes confusing uses of plurals, are not uncommon. The four subtests evaluating visual discrimination (letters, pairs of letters, words, and phrases) are well constructed. Most of the items in the test, however, appear very easy.

The manual lacks adequate statistical data. Some of the data reported lack complete description, others are open to question regarding validity. A more comprehensive manual would seem to be in order.

A split-half reliability coefficient of .92 is reported. Evidence of stability reliability is not presented but would be highly desirable inasmuch as this instrument is offered for predictive purposes.

Discussion of content validity takes the inadequate form of describing the types of items included in the test. The authors define concurrent validity as a correlation of their test with an unnamed intelligence test ($r = .74$, $n = 66$). It would be interestng to know the correlation of the intelligence measure with later reading performance. Perhaps it could function as well or better than this test in evaluating reading readiness. Correlation with accepted reading readiness and performance tests would also yield very useful information.

The norms (reported in centile form) were based on a "rigidly controlled" sample of 703 children, "about evenly divided between boys and girls, of Southwest Texas." This reviewer wonders what variables were rigidly controlled, and whether this norm group could be considered as a representative national sample.

Interpretation of test results is facilitated by the use of a quasi-expectancy table. The table is constructed with six unequal centile limits being coupled with qualitative descriptions (superior readiness, lower average, definitely not ready, etc.). The first author stated in personal correspondence that this table was "empirically determined," but without elaboration on methodology.

Under the heading, Purpose of the Test, a list is provided describing factors which are very important in reading readiness. Few of these appear to be measured by the test. The untested factors are probably more important than the measured ones. If the test is used, a teacher may wish to augment the results with measures of letter knowledge, copying ability, and auditory perception, especially the latter if instruction is primarily phonics oriented.

Due to the uneven quality of test items,

probable lack of an appropriate test ceiling, and insufficient normative and validity data, particularly with regard to interpretation, it is felt that the *Reading Readiness Test* may yield scores which might be considered equivocal, and in its present form it is not recommended for use with individual students.

[850]

*Scholastic Reading Readiness Test. First grade entrants; 1953–60; various titles used by the publisher; for Catholic schools; Form A Revised ('60, 11 pages); revised directions for administering ('60, 6 pages); no data on reliability; $2.40 per 20 tests; 50¢ per specimen set; postage extra; [30–45] minutes; Oliver F. Anderhalter and Ruth Colestock; Scholastic Testing Service, Inc. *

DAVID A. PAYNE, *Assistant Professor of Education, Syracuse University, Syracuse, New York.*

Inasmuch as the first edition (1953) of this test has not been reviewed previously, an attempt will here be made to compare the original and the revised edition (1960). Most of the statistical data reported in this review were obtained in personal correspondence from the first author.

In comparing the manuals of the two editions an alarming fact is noted. Although the revised edition was published after the APA Technical Recommendations, it contains less basic information than the 1953, or pre-APA Recommendations, edition. The manual of the revised edition contains only directions for administering, scoring, and using an expectancy table. Basic information on reliability, validity, and item analysis techniques employed is lacking. Even the sample sizes and demographic data on students used in composing the norms (reported as percentiles) and in constructing the expectancy table of chances for success in formal reading are not presented. Such a failure to provide even the most elementary data must be considered serious.

Both 1953 and 1960 editions of this test contain 80 "items" distributed among six subtests. Thirty three identical items are found in the two editions. The procedure of Tests 4 and 5 has been modified, though the basic content remains the same. Elsewhere, in 13 items one of the stimulus elements has been changed, and 6 items retain the same content but with one or more of the elements changed in form (e.g., redrawing of pictorial stimuli). No data are reported on the comparability of editions. The first author, in personal correspondence, however, stated that one unpublished study yielded a correlation of .94 ($n = 138$). The directions for administering are very well presented in both editions, but no estimate of administration time is given.

Three general areas are tested, with two subtests for each. Items purporting to measure knowledge and understanding of facts and events appear to be very easy. With a great number of easy items, perhaps the only discriminations possible are between the totally inept and all others. The visual discrimination items appear adequate, but one wonders about the effect of changing the stimuli, as is done within subtests, e.g., changing from geometric designs to letters and numbers as the student progresses through the subtest. The last area tested is sound-symbol association ability. Successful performance on these items appears to be very much dependent upon auditory training, which will differentially influence item difficulty. Such an uncontrolled variable might contribute significantly to the errors of measurement. In addition, the use of blends of "*clock*" (subtest 5) and "*dress*" (subtest 6) might be objected to by many contemporary linguists or phonics specialists. The directions call for the examiner to make a "hard C" (subtest 5) sound and a "hard D" (subtest 6). It is unlikely that either consonant sound can be made in isolation; moreover, one wonders how a "hard D" sounds.

Several comments on the nature of the 1960 revision seem appropriate. An attempt was made to provide a higher ceiling to the test by eliminating items with difficulty indices above 93 per cent. No rationale for selecting the 93 per cent cutoff point is presented. There is no evidence that item discrimination was investigated. The effect of this procedure was to lower the mean by 10 raw score points. The restandardization involved data on 17,144 students in 514 elementary schools representing systems in Michigan, California, Maryland, Virginia, Kentucky, Missouri, and New Jersey. It is not known if the 1960 norm group was composed of kindergarten or first grade students, or, if both grades were used, in what proportion. The norm groups for the 1953 and 1960 editions are markedly different, except at the upper end of the distribution. Despite this difference, the expectancy tables are virtually identical. It

is possible that the expectancy table reported in the revised edition was arrived at by interpolation of figures for the first edition.

Corrected estimates of internal consistency (split-half) ranging from .977 to a remarkable .996 are reported for the 1953 edition. A Kuder-Richardson coefficient (no formula number designation) of .91 for the 1960 edition was reported to the reviewer in personal correspondence. Evidence of stability reliability of the total score and of the individual subtests would be highly desirable.

As stated earlier, no validity data are reported in the 1960 manual. Data made available to the reviewer, however, included reports of correlations ranging from .49 to .61 (median = .54) between the *Scholastic Reading Readiness Test* and the *Scholastic Diagnostic Reading Test*. Coefficients of .64 ($n = 89$) with the *Metropolitan Readiness Test*, and .53 ($n = 135$) with end of year reading performance for the 1953 edition were also given. A general intelligence measure would probably yield correlations similar to the above criteria.

Since this test, despite the revision, does not appear to have a high enough ceiling, the user might desire near perfect test performance before initiating formal reading at the pre-primer level. The three readiness areas assessed are those generally accepted as having the greatest prognostic value. It is suggested that future manuals include a somewhat extended discussion of the authors' rationale in developing their test so that the potential user can evaluate the test in terms of his own classroom philosophy. There is no evidence, for instance, that a table of specifications was developed prior to item construction. It might also be fruitful to include items or subtests measuring knowledge of letter names and of handwriting or copying ability. On the basis of available information, this test cannot be recommended for use and its publication must be considered premature. It is hoped that future publications relating to this test will meet the essential principle of the APA Technical Recommendations of reporting sufficient information necessary for sound evaluations of usefulness and interpretation.

[851]

★Watson Reading-Readiness Test. Grades kgn–1; 1960; 3 scores: subjective test (teacher's ratings of physical, social, emotional, and psychological readiness), objective test, total; 1 form (6 pages); manual

(12 pages) ; no data on reliability ; $1.35 per 25 tests ; 15¢ per manual ; 25¢ per specimen set ; postage extra ; [50–60] minutes in 4 sessions 1 day apart for objective test ; G. Milton Watson ; Book Society of Canada Ltd. * (United States publisher : C. S. Hammond & Co.)

[Other Tests]

For tests not listed above, see the following entries in *Tests in Print*: 1492–3, 1496–7, 1500, 1502, and 1504 ; out of print : 1494, 1501, and 1507.

SPECIAL FIELDS

[852]

*The Iowa Tests of Educational Development: Test 5, Ability to Interpret Reading Materials in the Social Studies.** Grades 9–12 ; 1942–61 ; IBM ; Forms X-3S, Y-3S, ('52, 9 pages) ; battery examiner's manual ('58, c1949–57, 23 pages) ; battery general manual ('59, 37 pages) ; student profile leaflet, sixth edition ('61, c1958, 2 pages) ; see the complete battery entry (14b) for other accessories ; no data on reliability ; separate answer sheets must be used ; $2.40 per 20 tests ; $5 per 100 IBM answer sheets ; 50¢ per scoring stencil ; $3 per specimen set of the complete battery ; postage extra ; 60(70) minutes for full length version, 40(50) minutes for class period version ; prepared under the direction of E. F. Lindquist ; Science Research Associates, Inc. *

For reviews of the complete battery, see 14 and 5:17; for reviews of earlier forms, see 4:17 and 3:12.

[853]

*The Iowa Tests of Educational Development: Test 6, Ability to Interpret Reading Materials in the Natural Sciences.** Grades 9–12 ; 1942–61 ; IBM ; Forms X-3S, Y-3S, ('52, 9 pages) ; battery examiner's manual ('58, c1949–57, 23 pages) ; battery general manual ('59, 37 pages) ; student profile leaflet, sixth edition ('61, c1958, 2 pages) ; see the complete battery entry (14b) for other accessories ; no data on reliability ; separate answer sheets must be used ; $2.40 per 20 tests ; $5 per 100 IBM answer sheets ; 50¢ per scoring stencil ; $3 per specimen set of the complete battery ; postage extra ; 60(70) minutes for full length version, 40(50) minutes for class period version ; prepared under the direction of E. F. Lindquist ; Science Research Associates, Inc. *

For reviews of the complete battery, see 14 and 5:17; for reviews of earlier forms, see 4:17 and 3:12.

[854]

★Lorimer Braille Recognition Test: A Test of Ability in Reading Braille Contractions.** Students (ages 7–13) in grade 2 Braille ; 1962 ; individual ; 1 form (2 pages) ; manual (27 pages, available in printed form or Braille) ; 3d. per test ; 3s. per manual ; postpaid ; John Lorimer ; College of Teachers of the Blind. *

REFERENCES

1. "Lorimer Braille Recognition Test." *Teach Blind* 51: 36–7 O '62. *

[855]

★Tooze Braille Speed Test: A Test of Basic Ability in Reading Braille.** Students (ages 7–13) in grades 1 or 2 Braille ; 1962 ; individual ; 1 form (2 pages) ; manual (24 pages, available in printed form or Braille) ; record sheet (1 page) ; 3d. per test ; 3s. per manual ; postpaid ; 1(5) minutes ; F. H. G. Tooze ; College of Teachers of the Blind. *

[Other Tests]

For tests not listed above, see the following entries in *Tests in Print*: 1508–9 and 1512–4.

SPEED

[Other Tests]

For tests not listed above, see the following entries in *Tests in Print*: 1516 and 1518 ; out of print : 1515 and 1517.

STUDY SKILLS

[856]

Brown-Holtzman Survey of Study Habits and Attitudes.** High school and college ; 1953–56 ; IBM ; 1 form ('53, 3 pages) ; revised manual ('56, 11 pages) ; separate answer sheets must be used ; $2.25 per 25 tests ; $2 per 50 IBM answer sheets ; 60¢ per set of scoring stencils and manual ; 75¢ per specimen set ; postpaid ; (25–35) minutes ; William F. Brown and Wayne H. Holtzman ; Psychological Corporation. *

REFERENCES

1–14. See 5:688.
15. ANDERSON, ROBERT P., AND KUNTZ, JAMES E. "The 'Survey of Study Habits and Attitudes' in a College Counseling Center." *Personnel & Guid J* 37:365–8 Ja '59. * (*PA* 35:1207)
16. CALIA, VINCENT FRANK. *The Use of Discriminant Analysis in the Prediction of Performance of Junior College Students in a Program of General Education at Boston University Junior College.* Doctor's thesis, Boston University (Boston, Mass.), 1959. (*DA* 20:3190)
17. REID, JACKSON B.; KING, F. J.; AND WICKWIRE, PAT. "Cognitive and Other Personality Characteristics of Creative Children." *Psychol Rep* 5:729–37 D '59. * (*PA* 34:5632)
18. SMITH, D. D. "Traits and College Achievement." *Can J Psychol* 13:93–101 Je '59. * (*PA* 34:4780)
19. CURRAN, ANN MARIE. *Non-Intellective Characteristics of Freshman Underachievers, Normal Achievers, and Overachievers at the College Level.* Doctor's thesis, University of Connecticut (Storrs, Conn.), 1960. (*DA* 21:2584)
20. LUM, MABEL K. M. "A Comparison of Under- and Overachieving Female College Students." *J Ed Psychol* 51: 109–14 Je '60. * (*PA* 35:3985)
21. POPHAM, W. JAMES. "The Validity of the SSHA With Scholastic Overachievers and Underachievers." *Ed Res B* 39:214–5 N '60. *
22. POPHAM, W. JAMES, AND MOORE, MARY R. "A Validity Check on the Brown-Holtzman Survey of Study Habits and Attitudes and the Borow College Inventory of Academic Adjustment." *Personnel & Guid J* 38:552–4 Mr '60. * (*PA* 35:7094)
23. ANDERSON, THELMA HILL. *Dimensions of the Characteristics Related to the High- and Low-Achievement of a Selected Group of Negro College Students.* Doctor's thesis, University of Oklahoma (Norman, Okla.), 1961. (*DA* 22:1082)
24. SAVAGE, H. W. *An Evaluation of the Brown-Holtzman Survey of Study Habits and Attitudes for Use in Ontario.* Atkinson Study of Utilization of Student Resources, Supplementary Report No. 3. Toronto, Canada: Department of Educational Research, Ontario College of Education, University of Toronto, 1961. Pp. viii, 34. *
25. DE SENA, PAUL AMBROSE. *Identification of Non-Intellectual Characteristics of Consistent Over-, Under-, and Normal-Achievers Enrolled in Science Curriculums at the Pennsylvania State University.* Doctor's thesis, Pennsylvania State University (University Park, Pa.), 1963. (*DA* 24:3144)
26. PEMBERTON, W. A. *Ability, Values, and College Achieve-*

ment. University of Delaware Studies in Higher Education, No. 1. Newark, Del.: the University, 1963. Pp. xii, 77. * *(PA* 38:6573)

For reviews by James Deese and C. Gilbert Wrenn (with Roy D. Lewis), see 5:688.

[857]

California Study Methods Survey. Grades 7–13; 1958; 5 scores: attitudes toward school, mechanics of study, planning and system, total, verification; IBM and Grade-O-Mat; 1 form (8 pages); manual (16 pages); $3.50 per 35 tests; separate answer sheets or cards may be used; 5¢ per IBM answer sheet; 40¢ per set of scoring stencils; 2¢ per Cal-Card; 40¢ per set of hand scoring stencils for Cal-Cards; 2¢ per Grade-O-Mat scorable punch-out card; 6¢ per stylus; 6¢ per backing pad; postage extra; 50¢ per specimen set, postpaid; (35–50) minutes; Harold D. Carter; California Test Bureau. *

REFERENCES

1–7. See 5:689.
8. CARTER, HAROLD D. "Improving the Prediction of School Achievement by Use of the California Study Methods Survey." *Ed Adm & Sup* 45:255–60 S '59. * *(PA* 34:8397)
9. CARTER, HAROLD D. "Over-Achievers and Under-Achievers in the Junior High School." *Calif J Ed Res* 12:51–6 Mr '61. * *(PA* 36:1KL51C)

JOHN D. KRUMBOLTZ, *Associate Professor of Education and Psychology, Stanford University, Stanford, California.*

The CSMS contains 150 "Yes" or "No" questions about study methods and attitudes which discriminate between high achieving and low achieving students. It yields a verification score plus three other subscores: (*a*) attitudes toward school, (*b*) mechanics of study, and (*c*) planning and system.

The CSMS was validated essentially by correlating its items and subscales with academic success. In general, it shows consistently positive correlations, ranging from .32 to .58 against grade-point averages and from .11 to .48 against achievement test scores. To some extent the use of grade-point averages to validate a study methods survey involves some circularity. The very first question on the CSMS is "Are you well satisfied with the grades you get?" The keyed answer is "Yes," indicating that students who get good grades answer "Yes" to that question more often than students who get poor grades. Obviously the students who are doing well in school know that they are doing well and will say so when asked on an inventory. The fact that their answers to these questions correlate with their grades should be no surprise. Using grade-point averages to validate study methods surveys can therefore be questioned. The absurdity can be shown by imagining what would happen if we were to construct a survey that consisted of only one question: "What is your grade-point average?" It could easily be shown that answers to this question correlated very highly with actual grade-point averages, thereby validating the one-item questionnaire. Many of the questions in the CSMS are more indirect ways of asking this one basic question.

We have no way of knowing whether the use of study methods that are keyed actually help students to get better grades. For example, one of the items that makes up the "mechanics of study" subscale (although it sounds more like an attitude item) is as follows: "Do you like to be alone in a room when you study?" Although the question is keyed "Yes," we have no evidence that students do better when they study in a room alone. It is possible, for example, that good students get better grades when they study in a room alone but that poor students get better grades with the added reinforcement of more studious persons present. The study methods that are best for the good students may not necessarily be best for the poor students. The CSMS makes no claim of taking such factors as this into account, but the careful user must understand that the answers characteristic of good students may or may not provide helpful suggestions about study methods for poor students.

The use of the CSMS as a predictive instrument is also advocated in the manual: "The *Survey,* when combined with tests of ability and intelligence, yields better prediction than that obtained from any instrument alone." Of course, the same statement could be made for almost any instrument, especially when the equations have not been subjected to cross validation. However, it has been well established in hundreds of studies that the best predictor of future grade-point average is previous grade-point average. The critical question is this: Does the addition of the CSMS to previous grade-point averages yield a higher cross validated multiple correlation in predicting future grade-point averages than previous grade-point averages alone? The manual presents no information on this point, but Carter (*4*) reports evidence on 129 high school seniors showing that their fall 1949 GPA correlated .88 with their spring 1950 GPA, while a prior edition of the CSMS predicted the same criterion with an *r* of .54. A multiple correlation was not reported. The usefulness of the CSMS as a predictive instrument is established only when it adds significantly to already available predictors known to be highly valid, not when it adds to those predictors which are not as highly valid.

The reliability data include both test-retest and internal consistency information. Exact descriptions of the samples used in these reliability studies are not given nor do we know the interval between test and retest. The reported reliabilities are in the neighborhood of .87 for the total score. Reliabilities of the subscales range from .58 to .76. Since the intercorrelations of the subscales with each other are in the neighborhood of .50, the reliability of differences between subscales is very low. The manual does not point this out, however. In fact, the manual says that "The coefficients reveal some communality among the three scores but not enough to reduce the usefulness of the scales to any appreciable extent." Actually, the intercorrelations between scales approach the reliability of each scale, so that it would be unwise to interpret differences between a person's subscale scores.

Thirty of the 150 items are also keyed for a verification scale. If a student scores less than 17 on this scale, he is to be "questioned individually about his responses to the *Survey*." The manual states that students scoring below this critical score may indicate "the desire to fake an unduly favorable score." Such an interpretation is highly unlikely in view of the nature of the verification scale. If a student were trying to fake an unduly favorable score, he would attempt to give the same kind of answers that would be given by high achieving students. Yet 19 of the 30 verification scale items are keyed in the same way for the verification scale as they are for the high-achieving students. Thus, a student who was trying to fake a highly favorable score would certainly answer at least 19 of the verification scale items in the "right" direction and thus be above the critical cutting score of 17. His faking of a favorable score would go undetected.

A second use for the verification score is to identify indiscriminate or chance marking due to carelessness or a negative attitude. Even here it is doubtful that a high proportion of careless responders would be caught. Completely random responding to the inventory would yield an average score on the verification scale of 15.

Since a score of only 17 is sufficiently high to put one above suspicion, there would be a substantial percentage of random responders who would escape detection. Furthermore, if a careless student had a response set to answer "Yes" to every question, he would obtain a score of 23 on the verification scale and thus be far above suspicion. Thus the user of this inventory cannot use the verification scale to find those students who are trying to fake a favorable score nor to identify a very large percentage of those who are engaging in indiscriminate responding. Perhaps the best way of preventing these occurrences is to administer the inventory under circumstances where students have nothing to gain and something to lose by carelessness or falsification.

Some users may question the appropriateness of having only "Yes" or "No" answers to questions. The manual justifies this procedure on the questionable grounds that "so many of the attitudes and habits operate on an all-or-none basis." Actually, prior editions of the CSMS required responses on a 5-point scale ranging from "Always" to "Never." The manual states that "careful comparative studies reveal that this relatively cumbersome method of responding to questions was not appreciably more effective than a straightforward 'Yes' or 'No' response method."

One use of this inventory that has not been specifically suggested in the manual is as a source of concrete suggestions of study methods to be tried out by an under-achieving student. While no one knows if a specific study method will be best for any given student, many students need some hints and suggestions of methods that are at least worthy of a tryout. Perhaps one of the most constructive uses of the inventory would be to have a student compare his answers with the keyed answers and make a list of the specific study habits that he would like to try out in the future.

In spite of some of the negative factors pointed out above, the CSMS is actually a well constructed instrument for its type. Many of the criticisms mentioned would apply equally well to other study attitudes and methods inventories.

The author has taken the precaution to avoid a bias due to "response set" by keying about an equal number of "Yes" and "No" items in the three subscales. Only the verification scale has a disproportionate balance.

The norms were carefully constructed from a large number of students taking the test in grades 8 through 13. However, recommended use has been extrapolated to grade 7 also. In the grades studied no significant differences were found between different grade levels or between boys and girls, and hence there was no reason to prepare separate sets of norms.

The administrative instructions and the directions for scoring and recording scores appear to be simple, clear, and complete.

In summary, the CSMS appears to be a simple and useful device for calling attention to study methods which pupils might profitably try. The reliability of the total score appears to be satisfactory, but interpretations of differences between subscales should be avoided. Its use as a predictor of grade-point average is questionable, and its verification scale needs to be taken with a grain of salt. Users must remember that the study methods practiced by good students are not necessarily the study methods best for the poor students.

DONALD E. P. SMITH, *Associate Professor of Education, and Chief, Reading Improvement Service, The University of Michigan, Ann Arbor, Michigan.*

This is "a self-report inventory designed to reveal the....study methods and attitudes" of students in high school and college. It consists of 150 items yielding scores: attitudes toward school, mechanics of study, and planning and system. A "verification" or negative lie scale consists of the number of "correct" answers to 30 popular responses.

The scales have been developed over a 10 year period, during which time the several parts have been administered to several thousand students. That extreme care was used in its construction may be inferred from the clarity, precision, and inclusiveness of the manual. With one exception, the manual abounds with evidence concerning construct, content, and concurrent validity. The exception is the verification scale which has not been validated.

In brief, test-retest and K-R 21 reliabilities have a central tendency of .70 for the subscales and .85 for the total. Factoring at one stage of

development yielded a "Mechanics of Study" factor which correlated only .09 with grade-point average, while the other "attitudinal" factors predicted GPA quite well. The author remedied that. He built in a relationship between mechanics of study and GPA by developing a new scale. Study habits items discriminating high from low achievers were identified so that, this time, the items correlated with GPA (about .50). The total score raises the multiple correlation between GPA and intelligence (Henmon-Nelson) from .66 to .75 among high school students.

Use of the results in counseling is discussed. If a school or college counselor has use for a study habits inventory, this is a good one to use. The manual might also be useful in a graduate course on test construction, since it follows APA recommendations remarkably well.

J Consult Psychol 23:471 O '59. Edward S. Bordin. * A good deal of work seems to have gone into the development of this instrument; its reliability seems adequate, and there is encouraging evidence of its validity for use in educational diagnosis with high school students. Little evidence is offered to support the supposed function of the Verification score.

J Counsel Psychol 7:77 sp '60. Laurence Siegel. * The *CSMS* is simple to administer and to score. It may prove to be a useful adjunct to scholastic counseling when improper study habits or scholastic attitudes are suspected. Two unfortunate omissions from the Manual might well be corrected in the future. First, the results of several validity studies at the college level ought to be summarized. Secondly, the Manual makes no mention of studies wherein *CSMS* scores were correlated with scores obtained from other instruments designed to measure similar functions.

[858]

*The Iowa Tests of Educational Development: Test 9, Use of Sources of Information. Grades 9–12; 1942–61; IBM; Forms X-3S, Y-3S, ('52, 4 pages); battery examiner's manual ('58, c1949–57, 23 pages); battery general manual ('59, 37 pages); student profile leaflet, sixth edition ('61, c1958, 2 pages); see the complete battery entry (14b) for other accessories; no data on reliability; separate answer sheets must be used; $2.40 per 20 tests; $5 per 100 IBM answer sheets; 50¢ per scoring stencil; $3 per specimen set of the complete battery; postage extra; 27(35) minutes; prepared under the direction of E. F. Lindquist; Science Research Associates, Inc. *

For reviews of the complete battery, see 14 and 5:17; for reviews of earlier forms, see 4:17 and 3:12.

[859]

*A Library Orientation Test for College Freshmen, 1955 Edition. Grade 13; 1950–61; 1 form ('55, 12 pages); manual ('61, 7 pages); separate answer sheets must be used; $4.50 per 35 tests; 50¢ per specimen set; postpaid; (50–60) minutes; Ethel M. Feagley, Dorothy W. Curtiss, Mary V. Gaver, and Esther Greene; Bureau of Publications. *

REFERENCES

1. JOYCE, WILLIAM D. "A Study of Academic Achievement and Performance on a Test of Library Understandings." *J Ed Res* 54:198–9 Ja '61. *

MOREY J. WANTMAN, *Director of Advisory and Instructional Programs, Educational Testing Service, Princeton, New Jersey.*

The previous reviews of this test in *The Fifth Mental Measurements Yearbook* present a complete description of the content of this instrument. The criticisms of the test in those reviews regarding both content and format still apply because there has been no revision of the instrument itself. This reviewer would add the comment that the number of options in some parts of the test is far too great. In Part 3, for example, there are as many as 19 options for 9 questions. The reading time for these questions could be reduced by splitting the 9 questions into 3 sets of 3 and reducing the number of options per set to 6. The 19 options are obviously not equally attractive for each question. It can be assumed that item discrimination is not improved by the presence of the large number of options. In addition, the key provided for the test is awkward in its present form. Stencil keys for each side of the answer sheet would be more serviceable.

Even though the instrument itself has undergone no revision, some of the gaps in the manual noted by a previous reviewer have been filled. The manual has been expanded to include both norms and reliability data. The table of norms is based on data from 14 colleges in the United States, distributed geographically as follows: "Eastern 6, North Central 4, Far West 3, and South 1." Neither the names nor characteristics of the institutions are provided, so the representativeness of the norms group of college freshmen in the United States is uncertain.

The instructions in the manual for interpreting group means by use of the table of norms supplied may lead to errors of interpretation of group results. Percentiles based on a distribution of means of colleges are necessary for appropriate interpretation of group means. The variability of a distribution of group means will be far less than the variability shown in the table of norms for individuals. The deviation of a group mean from the mean of all scores would therefore be of much greater significance than the table of norms for individual scores would suggest.

In addition to supplying a table of norms, the authors have also added data on reliability. The reliability coefficient reported for the more than 4,000 cases used is .86, estimated by Kuder-Richardson formula 21, and the standard error of an individual score is 4.2 raw score points. The authors wisely recommend to users of the instrument that they compute reliability coefficients and standard errors for their own groups. The reliability coefficient for an individual college might well be lower than the .86 based on data for 14 colleges.

There is still no evidence of statistical validity presented in the manual. The only validity study located (*1*) is based on 64 seniors in a teachers college, for whom the correlation is .41 between "academic rank and performance on the library test."

This reviewer agrees with the previous reviewers that this test is probably superior to an informal test constructed by a local librarian and that it would provide the librarian with some information regarding the areas in and the extent to which college freshmen need instruction in the use of library resources. The authors have increased the instrument's usefulness by supplying a table of norms and reliability data in the present edition of the manual; they are now urged to furnish validity data in the next edition.

For reviews by Janet G. Afflerbach (with Lois Grimes Afflerbach) and J. Wayne Wrightstone, see 5:693.

[860]

*Nationwide Library Skills Examination. Grades 4–12; 1959–63; new form issued each April; norms available following the testing program; 1 form ('63, 2 pages); no manual; mimeographed norms ('63, 1 page); no data on reliability; 10¢ per test, postage extra; (40–45) minutes; [Donald R. Honz]; Educational Stimuli. *

[861]

*OC Diagnostic Dictionary Test. Grades 5–8; 1960; 1 form (1 page, reprinted from *Thorndike-*

Barnhart Junior Dictionary) ; manual (3 pages) ; no key ; no data on reliability ; no norms ; 2–100 tests, 6¢ each ; 15¢ per manual ; 25¢ per single copy and manual ; cash orders (plus postage) only ; (20) minutes ; Katherine O'Connor ; [O'Connor Reading Clinic Publishing Co.]. *

[862]

*SRA Achievement Series: Work-Study Skills. Grades 4–6, 6–9 (grades 4.7–6.6, 6.7–8.3, 8.4–9.9 for Forms C and D) ; 1954–64 ; subtest of SRA Achievement Series; 2–3 scores: references, charts, total (Forms C and D only) ; IBM ; 2 editions ; battery teacher's handbook ['64, c1955, 47 pages] for both editions ; separate answer sheets must be used ; 50¢ per teacher's handbook ; postage extra ; Louis P. Thorpe, D. Welty Lefever, and Robert A. Naslund ; Science Research Associates, Inc. *
a) FORMS A AND B. Grades 4–6, 6–9 ; 1954–64 ; 2 levels ; battery school administrator's manual ('58, c1955–56, 32 pages) ; battery technical supplement, second edition ('57, 45 pages) ; battery pupil progress and profile charts ('59, c1955–59, 4 pages) ; 90¢ per 20 pupil progress and profile charts ; 50¢ per school administrator's manual ; $1 per technical supplement ; $1.50 per specimen set of any one level of the complete battery.
   1) *Grades 4–6.* Forms A ['54], B ('56), (15 pages) ; battery examiner's manual, second edition ('56, c1954–56, revised '60, 39 pages) ; $2.15 per 20 tests ; $5 per 100 IBM scorable answer sheets ; $1 per set of machine scoring stencils ; 50¢ per hand scoring stencil ; 92(125) minutes in 2 sessions.
   2) *Grades 6–9.* Form A ('55), B ('56), (19 pages) ; battery examiner's manual, second edition ('56, c1955–56, revised '60, 39 pages) ; $2 per 20 tests ; $5 per 100 IBM scorable answer sheets ; 50¢ per either hand or machine scoring stencil ; 70(90) minutes.
b) FORMS C AND D. Grades 4.7–6.6, 6.7–8.3, 8.4–9.9 ; 1955–64 ; an optional supplement to the Multilevel Edition of the complete battery ; Forms C, D, ('63, 32 pages) ; 3 levels (called blue, green, and red levels, after color of answer sheet used) in a single booklet ; separate battery examiner's manuals for use with DocuTran answer sheets ('63, 43 pages), IBM 805 answer sheets ('64, c1963–64, 40 pages), IBM 1230 answer sheets ('64, c1963–64, 42 pages) ; battery test coordinator's manual ('64, c1961–64, 64 pages) ; battery manual on how to use the test results ('64, c1961–64, 34 pages) ; battery conversion tables booklet ('64, 38 pages) for each level ; battery pupil progress and profile charts ('64, c1955–64, 4 pages) ; separate IBM or DocuTran answer sheets must be used ; $6 per 20 tests ; $18 per 100 sets of IBM 805 answer sheets for the complete battery ; $3.50 per set of battery scoring stencils and conversion tables booklet for any one level ; $14 per 100 sets of IBM 1230 answer sheets for the complete battery, set of battery master answer sheets for machine scoring, and conversion tables booklet for any one level ; $2 per set of battery hand scoring stencils and conversion tables booklet for any one level ; $8 per 100 DocuTran answer sheets for the complete battery ; $2 per set of battery hand scoring templates and conversion tables booklet for any one level ; 90¢ per 20 pupil progress and profile charts ; 50¢ per examiner's manual ; 50¢ per how-to-use manual ; $3 per specimen set of the complete battery ; scoring service available ; 70(80) minutes.

For reviews by Robert L. Ebel and Ruth M. Strang of Forms A and B, see 5:696. For re-

views of Forms A and B of the complete battery, see 21 and 5:21.

[863]

★**Senior High School Library and Reference Skills Test.** Grades 9–12 ; 1960 ; 8 scores: alphabetization, uses of the dictionary, the card catalogue, research vocabulary, reference books, Dewey Decimal System, periodicals, total ; 1 form (4 pages) ; no manual ; no data on reliability ; no norms ; separate answer sheets must be used ; 5–99 tests with answer sheets, 15¢ each ; 75¢ per 25 answer sheets ; 15¢ per key ; 30¢ per specimen set ; cash orders postpaid ; [40–50] minutes ; Claude E. Stephenson ; Perfection Form Co. *

[864]

Spitzer Study Skills Test: Evaluation and Adjustment Series. Grades 9–13 ; 1954–55 ; 6 scores: dictionary, index, graphs-tables-maps, sources of information, total, note taking ; IBM ; Forms AM ('54), BM ('55), (12 pages) ; manual ('54, 11 pages) ; no college norms ; separate answer sheets must be used ; $6 per 35 tests ; $1.75 per 35 IBM answer sheets ; 40¢ per specimen set ; postage extra ; 105(135) minutes in 3 sessions, 75(90) minutes in 2 sessions for subtests 1–4 only ; Herbert F. Spitzer ; [Harcourt, Brace & World, Inc.]. *

REFERENCES
1. CROOK, FRANCES E. "Interrelationships Among a Group of Language Arts Tests." *J Ed Res* 51:305–11 D '57. *

ALTON L. RAYGOR, *Associate Professor of Educational Psychology, and Coordinator, Reading and Study Skills Center, University of Minnesota, Minneapolis, Minnesota.*

This test consists of five sections claimed to represent achievement in important study skills: (*a*) Using the Dictionary, (*b*) Using the Index, (*c*) Understanding Graphs, Tables, and Maps, (*d*) Knowledge of Sources of Information, and (*e*) Organization of Facts in Note Taking. The fifth test (note taking) is optional.

Relatively little information is given in the manual about the construction of the tests and their standardization. Item analysis was apparently carried out on some 2,400 students in four high schools, but little more than that is said. The note taking test (optional) is particularly slighted, and one has the feeling it was somewhat of an afterthought. It is left out of the table of intercorrelations, the table showing mean item difficulties and "validity" indices, the table of split-half reliabilities, and the table of correlations with other tests. In view of the lack of information concerning this optional test, it would seem that its inclusion should be questioned seriously.

The manual indicates that the test was standardized on more than 5,000 students in 17 high schools in 14 states, but there is no further information about the nature or location of the schools. The authors do give age and IQ means for the various grade levels.

A rather unusual standard score distribution with a mean of 106 and a standard deviation of 13 is used in converting raw scores to standard scores. The standard score distribution was made to correspond to the Terman-McNemar IQ score distribution on the population on which the test was standardized—a very dubious procedure.

The manual states that the difficulty level of items was computed along with estimates of correlations between item and total scores, but only mean values for subtests are given. These internal consistency estimates are unfortunately listed as "validity indices." When one looks for validity information, he finds some correlations with other tests, but nothing else. The obvious criterion—school grades—does not appear anywhere, even though the test is described on the jacket of the specimen set as "a measure of ability to use skills that are fundamental to success in many areas of the high school and college curriculum."

To the potential user this test will probably seem to be better than nothing, but no substitute for an adequately constructed and well standardized instrument. It may be a good test, but one cannot support that conclusion using the information provided in the manual.

For a review by James Deese, see 5:697.

[865]
★The Study Skills Counseling Evaluation. High school and college; 1962; 1 form (4 pages); mimeographed manual (6 pages); $7 per 25 tests and manual; $1.50 per manual; postpaid; specimen set not available; (10–20) minutes; George Demos; Western Psychological Services. *

STANLEY E. DAVIS, *Reading and Study Skills Counseling Director, University Counseling Center, The Ohio State University, Columbus, Ohio.*

The SSCE is intended to "enable students.... to identify rapidly and objectively their study weaknesses," in study time distribution, study conditions, taking notes, handling examinations, and "other habits and attitudes."

There are 50 five-alternative, multiple choice items of the self-report variety. The student is to respond in terms of the frequency (from "very often" to "very seldom") with which he

or she follows the study procedure, or holds the attitude, indicated in the item stem.

Most of the items pertain to study procedures, with a few being primarily concerned with attitudes toward study and school. In light of research by Brown, Holtzman, and others which suggests that attitude items tend to be more effective in differentiating between high and low students, one might wish that more of the items in this inventory dealt with attitudes and fewer with procedures.

Many potential users would probably like to know more than the manual tells about the rationale and procedures used in the selection of items for inclusion in the SSCE. Seventeen of the items were found to discriminate at a statistically significant level between a group of college students with "B" grade averages ($n = 65$) and a group with less than "C" averages ($n = 46$). This is encouraging, but some explanation of the reasons for the inclusion of the other items is needed.

Data on the reliability of the SSCE are promising, though somewhat scanty. Test-retest scores of 74 students in one college, with an interval of one week between testings, yielded a reliability coefficient of .94.

The reported validity data, while very limited, are at least moderately encouraging. A coefficient of .38 was obtained between SSCE total scores and midsemester grades of 172 students in one college. Another study revealed that a group of 65 students with "B" averages made a significantly higher mean total score than did another group of 46 students with grade averages below "C." No information is given about the sex, class level, major field, or other characteristics of the students in these two studies.

No reliability or validity studies with high school students are cited.

Very little information is given about the students comprising the high school and college norm groups.

A few improvements in the format and organization of the SSCE would probably enhance its usefulness. Randomizing the order of response alternatives, instead of having a progression from the most desirable (best score) response on the left to the least desirable on the right in every item, would help to encourage more careful reading and consideration of the items by some students. In addition, the elimination of the headings that are used to group the items and a random order of presentation of the items would probably help toward the same end.

Users of the SSCE could effect a considerable saving by consuming answer sheets rather than the test booklets.

All in all, the SSCE is a promising instrument for use as an aid in study skills counseling and instruction, but it is in need of a great deal of further refinement and validation. At the present time, the *Brown-Holtzman Survey of Study Habits and Attitudes* is a better developed instrument for essentially the same purposes.

W. G. FLEMING, *Assistant Director, Department of Educational Research, Ontario College of Education, University of Toronto, Toronto, Ontario, Canada.*

The contribution to academic success of adequate study habits and of constructive attitudes is pointed out in the manual as a reason for further efforts to improve measurement in this area. The uses of the SSCE, listed rather repetitively, may be summarized as follows: to increase the student's knowledge and understanding of his own weaknesses and problems as a basis for self-improvement; to provide teachers, counselors, and psychotherapists with information which may be used to assist the student; to screen students for certain courses; and to facilitate research. The third point is fortunately not emphasized. A device which cannot be constructed in such a way as to ensure against falsification of responses is of course all too likely to produce unfortunate results if employed for screening.

The SSCE is printed on a four-page folder with instructions on the front page. The five possible responses (VERY OFTEN, OFTEN, SOMETIMES, SELDOM, VERY SELDOM) are shown, and the student is asked to indicate the one most appropriate for each item. He is told that he will have time to finish. It is apparently assumed that he will feel no serious sense of frustration in marking VERY OFTEN when "always" would seem to be the appropriate answer, and VERY SELDOM when he never engages in the practice referred to.

The 50 items are divided into 5 groups: Study-Time Distribution, Study Conditions, Taking Notes, Preparing and Taking Examinations, and Other Habits and Attitudes. The second of these groups contains only three items.

A total score is obtained by assigning to each response a weight of 1 to 5, depending on the degree to which it is supposed to identify good habits and attitudes. Possible scores range from 50, the best possible, to 250. There seems to be no good reason why the weighting system could not have been devised so that a high score represented the positive end of the scale instead of the reverse. An unnecessary source of confusion might have been avoided by adherence to the more common practice.

Some of the items appear to be less than perfectly designed. The very first one is worded as follows: "I distribute my time on my study courses so I do not study more than two hours at a time on a single course." Apart from objections to the use of "so" in this construction, one might wonder what answer to expect from a student who, for reasons other than an unsatisfactory distribution of his time, spends less than two hours at a time on a single course. Item 4 reads as follows: "I study about two hours a week for each unit of class work I take." Students who habitually spend more than this amount of time on each unit would presumably have to give the same response as those who habitually spend less. There appears to be a danger that both these items might group together students with quite dissimilar characteristics.

With reference to items 21 and 22, it is not clear to the casual observer whether taking notes on one side of the paper only or taking notes in ink should be considered under every possible circumstance as either a good or a bad practice. The use of "so" for "so that" recurs in item 23. The meaning of item 28 is ambiguous: "I change my answers when I take a test." Instructors might feel themselves accused of unsystematic work in item 47: "I study in a 'hit or miss' manner, doing what is demanded of me by the instructor."

The impression that some items lack face validity might of course be overruled by evidence of effective discrimination obtained by analyzing the responses of an adequate tryout group. To judge from information in the manual, however, this kind of work was inadequately done. Only two groups, one consisting of 65 college students, each with a "B" average, and the other of 46 college students, each with less than a "C" average, are mentioned in connection with an attempt to measure item discrimination.

A low positive correlation with academic achievement is accepted as evidence of validity. A coefficient of .38 was found between SSCE scores and grade-point averages of 172 college students. There is no indication of the relationship between these two variables with academic aptitude or general intelligence held constant. The reported correlation of .31 with scores on Wrenn's *Study Habits Inventory* is a finding that ought to be considered highly disturbing instead of being dismissed with the view that "since many items in the two scales differ markedly, a high correlation was not expected; nevertheless, a coefficient of correlation of .31 shows some degree of relationship." Even though some of the items are considerably different, two instruments so similar in stated purpose should show a much closer relationship.

The test-retest reliability coefficient on 74 students from one college is reported as .94, a satisfactory figure. A table of norms is provided, but information about how the norms group was selected is lacking.

The manual is poorly written. The following sentences appear under the heading Uses of the SSCE: "A major use of the SSCE is to identify in High School and College students study weaknesses and problems of studying and then assist such students in their study problem areas" and "The SSCE is used in classes designed to improve study habits; in study skills laboratories." In more than one place there appears to be confusion about the use of the colon and semicolon. Short, choppy paragraphs consisting of one or two sentences follow one another in quick succession.

With a number of modifications and additional information, the SSCE could undoubtedly perform a useful service in schools and colleges. Judged on the basis of whether or not it represents an advance over existing instruments of its kind, it should, however, be identified as an ill-considered and unnecessary addition to the clutter of mediocre instruments of measurement already in existence which merely serve to bewilder the teachers and counselors whose interests they are supposed to serve.

[866]

★**A Test on Use of the Dictionary.** High school and college; 1955–63; 6 scores: pronunciation, meaning, spelling, derivation, usage, total; Form A ['55, 4 pages, plus 8-page reprint of material from *Webster's New International Dictionary, Second Edition*]; hectographed manual ['63, 4 pages]; no data on reliability; tentative norms; separate answer sheets must be used; 5¢ per test; 1¢ per mimeographed answer sheet; 25¢ per manual; 35¢ per specimen set; postpaid; (30–40) minutes; George D. Spache; Reading Laboratory and Clinic. *

[867]

*****Watson-Glaser Critical Thinking Appraisal.** Grades 9–16 and adults; 1942–64; 6 scores: inference, recognition of assumptions, deduction, interpretation, evaluation of arguments, total; IBM; 2 editions; separate answer sheets must be used; $1.80 per 35 IBM answer sheets; 40¢ per specimen set of either edition; postage extra; Goodwin Watson and Edward M. Glaser; Harcourt, Brace & World, Inc. *
a) [1952 EDITION.] Form AM ('52, c1949–52, 8 pages); manual ('52, 12 pages); no data on reliability of current form; $4.50 per 35 tests; (44–50) minutes.
b) [1963 REVISION.] Forms YM, ZM, ('64, c1951–61, 8 pages, revision of Form AM and out of print Form BM, respectively); manual ('64, 16 pages); $5 per 35 tests; 20¢ per scoring stencil; (50–60) minutes.

REFERENCES

1–3. See 3:544.
4–11. See 5:700.
12. MOFFETT, CHARLES R. *Operational Characteristics of Beginning Master's Students in Educational Administration and Supervision.* Doctor's thesis, University of Tennessee (Knoxville, Tenn.), 1954.
13. LUTON, JAMES N. *A Study of the Use of Standardized Tests in the Selection of Potential Educational Administrators.* Doctor's thesis, University of Tennessee (Knoxville, Tenn.), 1955.
14. CRAWFORD, C. DELISLE. *Critical Thinking and Personal Values in a Listening Situation: An Exploratory Investigation Into the Relationships of Three Theoretical Variables in Human Communication, as Indicated by the Relation Between Measurements on the Allport-Vernon-Lindzey Study of Values and the Watson-Glaser Critical Thinking Appraisal, and Similar Measurements of Responses to a Recorded Radio News Commentary.* Doctor's thesis, New York University (New York, N.Y.), 1956. (*DA* 19:1845)
15. FRIEND, CELIA M., AND ZUBEK, JOHN P. "The Effects of Age on Critical Thinking Ability." *J Gerontol* 13:407–13 O '58. * (*PA* 33:10067)
16. JUERGENSON, ELWOOD M. *The Relationship Between Success in Teaching Vocational Agriculture and Ability to Make Sound Judgments as Measured by Selected Instruments.* Doctor's thesis, Pennsylvania State University (University Park, Pa.), 1958. (*DA* 19:96)
17. NUNNERY, MICHAEL Y. *A Study in the Use of Psychological Tests in Determining Effectiveness and Ineffectiveness Among Practicing School Administrators.* Doctor's thesis, University of Tennessee (Knoxville, Tenn.), 1958. (*DA* 19: 1276)
18. BASS, JUET CARL. *An Analysis of Critical Thinking in a College General Zoology Class.* Doctor's thesis, University of Oklahoma (Norman, Okla.), 1959. (*DA* 20:963)
19. HERBER, HAROLD L. *An Inquiry Into the Effect of Instruction in Critical Thinking Upon Students in Grades Ten, Eleven, and Twelve.* Doctor's thesis, Boston University (Boston, Mass.), 1959. (*DA* 20:2174)
20. NUNNERY, MICHAEL Y. "How Useful Are Standardized Psychological Tests in the Selection of School Administrators." *Ed Adm & Sup* 45:349–56 N '59. * (*PA* 35:7092)
21. RODD, WILLIAM G. "A Cross-Cultural Study of Taiwan's Schools." *J Social Psychol* 50:3–36 Ag '59. * (*PA* 35:3960)
22. RUST, VELMA IRENE. *Factor Analyses of Three Tests of Critical Thinking.* Doctor's thesis, University of Illinois (Urbana, Ill.), 1959. (*DA* 20:225)
23. BERGMAN, LUCY MAE ERICKSON. *A Study of the Relationship Between Selected Language Variables in Extemporaneous Speech and Critical Thinking Ability.* Doctor's thesis, University of Minnesota (Minneapolis, Minn.), 1960. (*DA* 21:3552)
24. MILTON, OHMER. "Primitive Thinking and Reasoning Among College Students." *J Higher Ed* 31:218–20 Ap '60. *
25. RUST, VELMA I. "Factor Analyses of Three Tests of

Critical Thinking." *J Exp Ed* 29:177–82 D '60. * (*PA* 35:4466)

26. BESSENT, EDGAR WAILAND. *The Predictability of Selected Elementary School Principals' Administrative Behavior.* Doctor's thesis, University of Texas (Austin, Tex.), 1961. (*DA* 22:3479)

27. JACKSON, TEDDY RANDOLPH. *The Effects of Intercollegiate Debating on Critical Thinking Ability.* Doctor's thesis, University of Wisconsin (Madison, Wis.), 1961. (*DA* 21:3556)

28. RUST, VELMA I. "A Study of Pathological Doubting as a Response Set." *J Exp Ed* 29:393–400 Je '61. *

29. CRANE, WILLIAM J. "Screening Devices for Occupational Therapy Majors." *Am J Occup Ther* 16:131–2 My–Je '62. * (*PA* 37:4078)

30. RUST, VELMA I.; JONES, R. STEWART; AND KAISER, HENRY F. "A Factor-Analytic Study of Critical Thinking." *J Ed Res* 55:253–9 Mr '62. *

31. SHOCKLEY, JAMES T. "Behavioral Rigidity in Relation to Student Success in College Physical Science." *Sci Ed* 46:67–70 F '62. *

32. TRELA, THADDEUS MICHAEL. *A Comparison of Ninth Grade Achievement on Selected Measures of General Reading Comprehension, Critical Thinking, and General Educational Development.* Doctor's thesis, University of Missouri (Columbia, Mo.), 1962. (*DA* 23:2382)

33. *Normative Information: Manager and Executive Testing.* New York: Richardson, Bellows, Henry & Co., Inc., May 1963. Pp. 45. *

34. QUINN, PATRICK VINCENT. *Critical Thinking and Openmindedness in Pupils From Public and Catholic Secondary Schools.* Doctor's thesis, Columbia University (New York, N.Y.), 1963. (*DA* 24:2789)

35. SMITH, PAUL M., JR. "Critical Thinking and the Science Intangibles." *Sci Ed* 47:405–8 O '63. *

For reviews by Walker H. Hill and Carl I. Hovland of the 1952 edition, see 5:700; for a review by Robert H. Thouless of the original edition, see 3:544 (1 excerpt).

[Other Tests]

For tests not listed above, see the following entries in *Tests in Print:* 1519–20, 1525, 1529–30, 1536–39, 1541–2, and 1544; out of print: 1523–4, 1528, 1534, and 1540.

MMY Test Index

THIS chapter presents a classified listing of all tests listed in one or more of the six *Mental Measurements Yearbooks*. The title last used in an MMY is presented for each test along with a listing of the names of persons who have reviewed the test in an MMY, the number of reviews excerpted in an MMY from other sources, and the number of references on the construction, validation and use of the test. The MMY Test Index does not indicate whether a test is currently in print; nor does it list tests published since the 6th MMY; it is a master index to the tests, reviews, excerpts, and references to be found in the first six *Mental Measurements Yearbooks*. Within each classification, tests are listed in alphabetical order. If information is wanted about tests in a particular area, consult the following key to the classification used in the MMY Test Index; if information is wanted about a particular test, consult the title index; if information is wanted about the tests reviewed by a particular person, consult the name index.

KEY TO CLASSIFICATION

ACHIEVEMENT BATTERIES

A1. American School Achievement Tests. For additional information and reviews by Robert H. Bauernfeind and Frank B. Womer, see 6:2; for reviews by J. Raymond Gerberich and Virgil E. Herrick, see 5:1; for a review by Ralph C. Preston of an earlier edition, see 4:1; for reviews by Walter W. Cook and Gordon N. Mackenzie (with Glen Hass), see 3:1. For reviews of subtests, see 5:174 (2 reviews), 5:455 (1 review), 5:456 (2 reviews), and 5:620 (2 reviews).

A2. California Achievement Tests. For additional information and reviews by Jack C. Merwin and Robert D. North, see 6:3 (20 references); for a review by Charles O. Neidt, see 5:2 (10 references); for reviews by Warren G. Findley, Alvin W. Schindler, and J. Harlan Shores of an earlier edition, see 4:2 (8 references); for a review by Paul A. Witty, see 3:15 (3 references); for reviews by C. W. Odell and Hugh B. Wood, see 2:1193 (1 reference); for a review by D. Welty Lefever, see 1:876 (1 excerpt). For reviews of subtests, see 6:251 (1 review), 5:177 (2 reviews), 5:468 (1 review), 4:151 (2 reviews), 4:411 (1 review), 4:530 (2 reviews, 1 excerpt), 2:1292 (2 reviews), 2:1459 (2 reviews), 2:1563 (1 review), 1:893 (1 review), and 1:1110 (2 reviews).

A3. California Basic Skills Tests. For additional information and a review by Robert D. North, see 6:4.

A4. California Tests in Social and Related Sciences. For additional information and a review by David R. Krathwohl, see 5:4; for reviews by Harry D. Berg and J. Raymond Gerberich of an earlier edition, see 4:23.

A5. Canadian Test of General Information (CTGI). For additional information and reviews by J. Douglas Ayers and Robert J. Solomon, see 6:5 (2 references).

A6. Closed High School Placement Test. For additional information and reviews by Marion F. Shaycoft and James R. Hayden, see 6:6; for reviews by William C. Cottle and Robert A. Jones of an earlier form, see 5:15.

A7. Comprehensive Testing Program. For additional information and reviews by Richard Ledgerwood, W. J. Osburn, and Ernest W. Tiegs, see 1:869 (2 references).

A8. Cooperative General Achievement Tests [Revised Series]. For additional information and a review by Willard G. Warrington, see 6:7 (4 references); for a review by Max D. Engelhart, see 5:6 (12 references); for a review by Paul L. Dressel of earlier forms, see 4:5 (9 references); for a review by John V. McQuitty, see 3:3. For reviews of individual tests, see 3:316 (1 review), 3:548 (1 review), and 3:596 (1 review).

A9. Cooperative General Achievement Tests [Survey Series]. For additional information and reviews, see 1:870.

A10. Cooperative General Culture Test. For additional information and a review by Benjamin S. Bloom, see 5:7 (9 references); for a review by John V. McQuitty of earlier forms, see 4:6 (10 references); for reviews by Benjamin S. Bloom and H. T. Morse, see 3:4 (14 references); for reviews by Lavone A. Hanna, Edward S. Jones, and Hilda Taba, see 2:1184 (2 references); for a review by F. S. Beers, see 1:871.

A11. Coordinated Scales of Attainment. For additional information and a review by Alvin W. Schindler, see 4:8; for reviews by Roland L. Beck, Lavone A. Hanna, Gordon N. Mackenzie (with Glen Hass), and C. C. Ross, see 3:6.

A12. Eighth Grade Test. For additional information, see 6:8 (1 reference).

A13. Entrance and Classification Examination for Teachers Colleges: Elementary Test. For additional information, see 2:1185.

A14. Essential High School Content Battery. For additional information and reviews by Herbert S. Conrad, J. Thomas Hastings, and Gordon N. Mackenzie (with A. Harry Passow), see 4:9.

A15. Every Pupil Primary Achievement Test.
For additional information and a review by C. C.
Ross, see 3:7.

**A16. General Scholarship Test for High School
Seniors.** For additional information, see 6:8a (2 references) ; for a review by C. C. Ross of an earlier
form, see 3:14.

**A17. Graduate Record Examination Profile
Tests.** For additional information and a review by
Max D. Engelhart, see 4:10 (5 references).

**A18. Graduate Record Examination Tests of
General Education.** For additional information, see
4:11 (1 reference).

**A19. The Graduate Record Examinations: The
Area Tests.** For additional information and reviews
by Paul L. Dressel and Everett B. Sackett, see 6:9
(10 references) ; for reviews by Benjamin S. Bloom
and Frederick B. Davis of earlier forms, see 5:10. For
a review of the testing program, see 5:601.

A20. The Gray-Votaw-Rogers General Achievement Tests. For additional information and reviews
by Kenneth D. Hopkins, Victor H. Noll, and Ellis
Batten Page, see 6:10 ; for reviews by Warren G.
Findley and Douglas E. Scates of an earlier edition,
see 5:11 (1 reference) ; for a review by Oliver F.
Anderhalter, see 4:12 ; for a review by Roland L.
Beck, see 3:9 (3 references) ; for reviews by Joseph
E. Moore and C. C. Ross, see 2:1187 (1 reference).

**A21. Group Achievement Test: Dominion
Tests, 1934 Edition.** For additional information, see
5:12.

**A22. Group Achievement Tests: Dominion
Tests: Niagara Edition.** For additional information,
see 5:13.

**A23. The Harlow Achievement Tests for
Texas.** For additional information, see 4:13.

A24. The Harlow Battery Achievement Test.
For additional information, see 4:14.

A25. High School Classification Examination.
For additional information and reviews by Thomas
W. Mahan, Jr. and David V. Tiedeman, see 6:11 (1
reference).

**A26. High School Fundamentals Evaluation
Test.** For additional information and reviews by
George D. Demos and Jason Millman, see 6:12 (1 reference) ; for reviews by Victor H. Noll and Verner
M. Sims, see 5:14.

A27. Iowa Every-Pupil Tests of Basic Skills.
For additional information and reviews by Miriam M.
Bryan and Anton Thompson, see 4:15 (4 references) ;
for reviews by Frederic L. Ayer, Gustav J. Froehlich, and Ralph C. Preston, see 3:10 (8 references) ;
for reviews by Harriet M. Barthelmess [Morrison],
William A. Brownell, J. Murray Lee, and Charles W.
Odell of an earlier edition, see 1:872 (3 references).
For reviews of subtests, see 3:334 (2 reviews) and
3:501 (2 reviews).

A28. Iowa High School Content Examination.
For additional information and a review by David
V. Tiedeman, see 4:16 (4 references) ; for a review
by Maurice E. Troyer, see 3:11 (7 references).

A29. Iowa Tests of Basic Skills. For additional
information, see 6:13 (17 references) ; for reviews by
Virgil E. Herrick, G. A. V. Morgan, and H. H.
Remmers, see 5:16 (1 excerpt).

A30. The Iowa Tests of Educational Development. For additional information and reviews by El-

lis Batten Page and Alexander G. Wesman, see 6:14
(23 references) ; for reviews by J. Murray Lee and
Stephen Wiseman, see 5:17 (9 references) ; for a review by Eric F. Gardner of earlier forms, see 4:17
(3 references) ; for reviews by Henry Chauncey, Gustav J. Froehlich, and Lavone A. Hanna, see 3:12. For
reviews of separate tests, see 6:579 (1 review), 6:876
(2 reviews), and 6:969 (1 review).

A31. Master Achievement Tests. For additional
information and a review by Clifford Woody, see
1:873.

A32. Metropolitan Achievement Tests. For additional information and reviews by Paul L. Dressel,
Henry S. Dyer, and Warren G. Findley, see 6:15 (16
references) ; for a review by Warren G. Findley of
an earlier edition, see 4:18 (10 references) ; see also
3:13 (7 references) ; for reviews by E. V. Pullias and
Hugh B. Wood, see 2:1189 (3 references) ; for reviews by Jack W. Dunlap, Charles W. Odell, and
Richard Ledgerwood, see 1:874. For reviews of subtests, see 6:627 (2 reviews), 6:797 (1 review), 6:877
(2 reviews), 6:970 (2 reviews), 4:416 (1 review),
4:543 (2 reviews), 2:1458.1 (2 reviews), 2:1551 (1
review), 1:892 (2 reviews), and 1:1105 (2 reviews).

A33. Modern School Achievement Tests. For
additional information and a review by Charles R.
Langmuir, see 4:19 ; for reviews by William A. Brownell, Herbert S. Conrad, and Herschel T. Manuel of
the original edition, see 2:1190 (3 references).

A34. Municipal Battery: National Achievement Tests. For additional information and a review
by J. Murray Lee, see 5:18 ; for a review by Ralph
C. Preston, see 4:20 ; for reviews by A. M. Jordan
and Hugh B. Wood, see 2:1191. For reviews of subtests, see 5:790 (1 review), 4:406 (2 reviews), and
4:664 (1 review).

A35. Myers-Ruch High School Progress Test.
For additional information and reviews by Harl R.
Douglass, August Dvorak, John M. Stalnaker, and
Ernest W. Tiegs, see 2:1192.

A36. National Achievement Tests. For additional information, see 6:16 ; for a review by William
E. Coffman, see 5:19.

A37. National Educational Development Tests.
For additional information and reviews by Willis W.
Clark, Arthur E. Traxler, and Alexander G. Wesman, see 6:17.

**A38. National Merit Scholarship Qualifying
Test.** For additional information and reviews by
Dorothy C. Adkins, George K. Bennett, and J. Thomas
Hastings, see 6:18 (12 references) ; for reviews by
Benno G. Fricke and Roger T. Lennon of the 1958
test, see 5:20.

A39. Public School Achievement Tests. For additional information, see 6:19 (2 references) ; for reviews by Herbert S. Conrad and E. V. Pullias, see
2:1194.

**A40. Public School Attainment Tests for High
School Entrance: Examination of Abilities in
Reading, English, and Mathematics.** For additional information and a review by Benjamin S.
Bloom, see 3:17 ; for reviews by Harold Gulliksen
and C. C. Ross, see 2:1195 (1 reference).

**A41. Public School Correlated Attainment
Scales.** For additional information and reviews by
C. W. Odell and Robert K. Speer, see 2:1196 (1 reference, 2 excerpts) ; for reviews by H. S. Conrad and
H. E. Schrammel, see 1:877.

A42. Pupil Record of Educational Progress. For additional information and reviews by George D. Demos and Jack C. Merwin, see 6:20.

A43. SRA Achievement Series. For additional information and a review by Jacob S. Orleans, see 6:21 (3 references); for reviews by Warren G. Findley and Worth R. Jones, see 5:21. For reviews of subtests, see 6:632 (1 review), 6:808 (1 review), 5:200 (2 reviews), 5:483 (2 reviews), 5:649 (2 reviews), and 5:696 (2 reviews).

A44. SRA High School Placement Test. For additional information and reviews by Walter N. Durost and Charles O. Neidt, see 6:22 (3 references); for reviews by Cyril J. Hoyt (with W. Wesley Tennyson) and William W. Turnbull of earlier forms, see 5:22.

A45. Scholastic Achievement Series. For additional information and reviews by J. Stanley Ahmann and Thomas W. Mahan, Jr., see 6:23; for reviews by William E. Coffman and James R. Hayden, see 5:23. For reviews of subtests, see 5:201 (2 reviews) and 5:484 (2 reviews).

A46. Secondary School Admission Tests: General School Ability and Reading Test. For additional information and reviews by Charles O. Neidt and David V. Tiedeman, see 6:24 (1 reference).

A47. Sequential Tests of Educational Progress. For additional information and reviews by Harold Seashore and John E. Stecklein, see 6:25 (6 references); for reviews by Robert W. B. Jackson and Wilbur L. Layton, see 5:24 (1 excerpt). For reviews of individual tests, see 6:292 (2 reviews, 1 excerpt), 6:590 (2 reviews), 6:810 (2 reviews), 6:882 (2 reviews), 6:971 (2 reviews), 5:206 (3 reviews), 5:207 (3 reviews), 5:438 (3 reviews), 5:578 (2 reviews), 5:653 (3 reviews), 5:716 (3 reviews), and 5:792 (3 reviews).

A48. Seven Plus Assessment: The Northumberland Series. For additional information and a review by Stanley D. Nisbet, see 4:24.

A49. Stanford Achievement Test. For additional information and a review by Miriam M. Bryan, see 6:26 (13 references, 1 excerpt); for a review by N. L. Gage of an earlier edition, see 5:25 (19 references); for reviews by Paul R. Hanna (with Claude E. Norcross) and Virgil E. Herrick, see 4:25 (20 references); for reviews by Walter W. Cook and Ralph C. Preston, see 3:18 (34 references). For reviews of subtests, see 5:656 (2 reviews), 5:698 (2 reviews), 5:799 (1 review), 4:419 (1 review), 4:555 (1 review), 4:593 (2 reviews), 3:503 (1 review), and 3:595 (1 review).

A50. Test for High School Entrants: [National Achievement Tests]. For additional information and a review by Jacob S. Orleans, see 5:26; for a review by Benjamin S. Bloom, see 3:19.

A51. Tests of General Educational Development. For additional information and a review by Robert J. Solomon, see 5:27 (39 references); for a review by Gustav J. Froehlich, see 4:26 (27 references); for reviews by Herbert S. Conrad and Warren G. Findley, see 3:20 (11 references). For reviews of individual tests, see 3:122 (1 review) and 3:528 (2 reviews).

A52. Unit Scales of Attainment. For additional information and a review by D. Welty Lefever, see 2:1197 (2 references); for reviews by Herbert S. Conrad and Ethel L. Cornell, see 1:878. For reviews of subtests, see 2:1315 (2 reviews), 2:1463 (2 reviews), 2:1581 (2 reviews), and 1:1115 (1 review).

A53. Wide Range Achievement Test: Reading, Spelling, Arithmetic From Kindergarten to College. For additional information, see 6:27 (15 references); for reviews by Paul Douglas Courtney, Verner M. Sims, and Louis P. Thorpe, see 3:21.

A54. Wisconsin Composite Achievement Test. For additional information and reviews by Ernest W. Tiegs and Maurice E. Troyer, see 3:22 (4 references).

BUSINESS EDUCATION

B1. Business Backgrounds Test. For additional information, see 2:1478 (1 reference, 1 excerpt).

B2. Business Education: National Teacher Examinations. For additional information, see 6:28. For reviews of the testing program, see 6:700 (1 review), 5:538 (3 reviews), and 4:802 (1 review).

B3. Business Education: Teacher Education Examination Program. An inactive form of B2; for additional information, see 6:29. For a review of the testing program, see 5:543; for references to additional reviews, see B2.

B4. Business Fundamentals and General Information Test: National Business Entrance Tests. For additional information, see 6:30; for reviews by Vera M. Amerson and C. C. Upshall of an earlier form, see 3:369. For reviews of the complete battery, see 6:33 (1 review), 5:515 (3 reviews), and 3:396 (1 review).

B5. Business Relations and Occupations: Midwest High School Achievement Examinations. For additional information, see 5:510.

B6. General Business: Every Pupil Scholarship Test. For additional information and a review by Ray G. Price, see 6:31.

B7. General Clerical: Every Pupil Test. For additional information, see 1:937.

B8. General Office Clerical Test (Including Filing): National Business Entrance Tests. For additional information, see 6:32 (1 reference). For reviews of the complete battery, see 6:33 (1 review), 5:515 (3 reviews), and 3:396 (1 review).

B9. General Test of Business Information. For additional information and reviews by Vera M. Amerson and Herbert A. Tonne, see 3:380.

B10. National Business Entrance Tests. For additional information and a review by Melvin R.

Marks, see 6:33 (6 references) ; for reviews by Edward N. Hay, Jacob S. Orleans, and Wimburn L. Wallace, see 5:515; see also 4:453 (1 reference) ; for a review by Paul S. Lomax of earlier forms, see 3:396; see also 2:1476 (9 references). For reviews of individual tests, see 6:55 (1 review), 5:514 (1 review), 5:522 (1 review), 5:526 (1 review), 3:368 (2 reviews), 3:369 (2 reviews), 3:379 (2 reviews), 3:384 (1 review), 3:391 (2 reviews), and 3:394 (2 reviews).

B11. Thompson Business Practice Test. For additional information and a review by Herbert A. Tonne, see 1:942.

BOOKKEEPING

B12. Bookkeeping: Every Pupil Scholarship Test. For additional information, see 6:34.

B13. Bookkeeping: Minnesota High School Achievement Examinations. For additional information and a review by Harold L. Royer, see 6:35; for a review by I. David Satlow of an earlier form, see 5:504.

B14. Bookkeeping Test: National Business Entrance Tests. For additional information, see 6:36; for reviews by Harvey A. Andruss and Ray G. Price of an earlier form, see 3:368. For reviews of the complete battery, see 6:33 (1 review), 5:515 (3 reviews), and 3:396 (1 review).

B15. Bookkeeping Test: State High School Tests for Indiana. For additional information, see 3:367.

B16. Breidenbaugh Bookkeeping Tests: Single Proprietorship. For additional information, see 2:1477 (1 excerpt).

B17. Examination in Bookkeeping and Accounting. For additional information and a review by Harvey A. Andruss, see 3:373.

B18. First-Year Bookkeeping: Every Pupil Test. For additional information, see 6:37.

B19. Shemwell-Whitcraft Bookkeeping Test. For additional information and a review by Arnold E. Schneider, see 3:387.

MISCELLANEOUS

B20. Clinton-LeMaster Commercial and Business Law Test. For additional information, see 2:1479.

B21. Commercial Law: Every Pupil Scholarship Test. For additional information, see 6:38.

B22. Dictating Machine Transcription Test: National Clerical Ability Tests. For additional information, see 2:1482.

B23. Examination in Commercial Correspondence—College Level. For additional information and reviews by Orrel E. Little and Herbert A. Tonne, see 3:376.

B24. Filing Test: United-NOMA Business Entrance Tests. For additional information and reviews by Arnold E. Schneider and C. C. Upshall, see 3:379.

B25. Machine Calculation Test: National Business Entrance Tests. For additional informa-

tion, see 6:39; for a review by Dorothy C. Adkins, see 5:514; for a review by Elizabeth Fehrer of an earlier form, see 3:384. For reviews of the complete battery, see 6:33 (1 review), 5:515 (3 reviews), and 3:396 (1 review).

B26. Parke Commercial Law Test. For additional information and a review by Ray G. Price, see 3:385.

B27. Qualifying Test for Ediphone Voice Writing. For additional information, see 2:1488.

SHORTHAND

B28. APT Dictation Test. For additional information, see 6:40.

B29. Byers' First-Year Shorthand Aptitude Tests. For additional information and a review by Edward O. Swanson, see 6:41 (1 reference).

B30. Commercial Education Survey Tests: Junior and Senior Shorthand. For additional information, see 1:936 (2 references, 1 excerpt).

B31. E.R.C. Stenographic Aptitude Test. For additional information and reviews by Philip H. DuBois and Edward A. Rundquist, see 3:372 (1 reference).

B32. Examination in Gregg Shorthand. For additional information and a review by Agnes E. Osborne, see 3:377.

B33. First-Year Shorthand: Every Pupil Test. For additional information, see 6:42.

B34. Hiett Simplified Shorthand Test (Gregg). For additional information and a review by Gale W. Clark, see 5:512.

B35. Hiett Stenography Test (Gregg). For additional information and a review by Agnes E. Osborne, see 3:381.

B36. Personnel Research Institute Test of Shorthand Skills. For additional information and a review by Irol Whitmore Balsley, see 6:43.

B37. Revised Standard Graded Tests for Stenographers. For additional information, see 6:44.

B38. SRA Dictation Skills. For additional information and a review by Harold F. Rothe, see 4:454 (1 reference).

B39. The Seashore-Bennett Stenographic Proficiency Tests: A Standard Recorded Stenographic Worksample. For additional information, see 5:519 (2 references) ; for a review by Harold F. Rothe, see 4:455 (1 reference) ; for a review by Ann Brewington, see 3:386.

B40. Shorthand Aptitude Test. For additional information and a review by James Lumsden, see 5:520.

B41. Shorthand Test: Individual Placement Series (Area IV). For additional information, see 6:45.

B42. Shorthand Test: State High School Tests for Indiana. For additional information, see 4:457.

B43. Shorthand II: Every Pupil Test. For additional information, see 4:456.

B44. Stenogauge. For additional information and a review by Beatrice J. Dvorak, see 3:389.

B45. Stenographic Aptitude Test. For additional information and reviews by Philip H. DuBois and Edward A. Rundquist, see 3:390 (1 reference); see also 2:1677 (1 reference).

B46. Stenographic Dictation Test. For additional information, see 6:46.

B47. Stenographic Test: National Business Entrance Tests. For additional information, see 6:47 (1 reference); for a review by Edward B. Greene, see 5:522; for reviews by Ann Brewington and Elizabeth Fehrer of an earlier form, see 3:391. For reviews of the complete battery, see 6:33 (1 review), 5:515 (3 reviews), and 3:396 (1 review).

B48. Test for Stenographic Skill. For additional information and reviews by Reign H. Bittner and Clifford E. Jurgensen, see 4:459.

B49. Test of Dictation Speed. For additional information, see 6:48.

B50. Turse-Durost Shorthand Achievement Test (Gregg). For additional information, see 3:392 (1 excerpt).

B51. Turse Shorthand Aptitude Test. For additional information and a review by Leslie M. Haynes, see 4:460 (5 references); for a review by Philip H. DuBois, see 3:393.

TYPEWRITING

B52. Commercial Education Survey Tests: Junior and Senior Typewriting. For additional information, see 2:1480 (1 excerpt).

B53. Examination in Typewriting. For additional information and a review by E. G. Blackstone, see 3:378.

B54. First-Year Typewriting: Every Pupil Test. For additional information, see 6:49.

B55. Grading Scales for Typewriting Tests. For additional information, see 2:1486 (1 excerpt).

B56. Kauzer Typewriting Test. For additional information and a review by E. G. Blackstone, see 3:382.

B57. Kimberly-Clark Typing Ability Analysis. For additional information, see 5:513 (2 references); for a review by E. G. Blackstone, see 3:383.

B58. [McCann Typing Tests.] For additional information, see 6:50.

B59. SRA Typing Adaptability Test. For additional information and reviews by Gale W. Clark and Edward B. Greene, see 5:518.

B60. SRA Typing Skills. For additional information and reviews by Lawrence W. Erickson and Jacob S. Orleans, see 6:51 (2 references).

B61. The Tapping Test: A Predictor of Typing and Other Tapping Operations. For additional information and reviews by Ray G. Price and Henry Weitz, see 6:52 (2 references).

B62. Test for Typing Skill. For additional information and a review by Bernadine Meyer, see 5:523.

B63. Test of Typing Speed. For additional information, see 6:53.

B64. Typewriting I and II: Every Pupil Scholarship Test. For additional information, see 6:54.

B65. Typewriting Test: National Business Entrance Tests. For additional information and a review by Lawrence W. Erickson, see 6:55 (1 reference); for a review by Clifford E. Jurgensen, see 5:526; for reviews by E. G. Blackstone and Beatrice J. Dvorak of an earlier form, see 3:394. For reviews of the complete battery, see 6:33 (1 review), 5:515 (3 reviews), and 3:396 (1 review).

B66. Typewriting Test: State High School Tests for Indiana. For additional information, see 4:463.

B67. Typewriting II: Every Pupil Test. For additional information, see 1:944.

B68. Typing Test: Individual Placement Series (Area IV). For additional information, see 6:56.

B69. United Students Typewriting Tests. For additional information, see 5:527.

ENGLISH

C1. A.C.E.R. English Usage Tests. For additional information and a review by J. A. Richardson, see 5:173.

C2. Ability for English (Language): Fife Tests of Ability, Test 1. For additional information, see 3:114 (1 reference). For reviews of the complete battery, see 4:713 (1 review) and 3:8 (1 review).

C3. American School Achievement Tests: Part 3, Language and Spelling. For additional information, see 6:248 (1 reference); for reviews by M. A. Brimer and Clarence Derrick, see 5:174. For reviews of the complete battery, see 6:2 (2 reviews), 5:1 (2 reviews), 4:1 (1 review), and 3:1 (2 reviews).

C4. Analytical Survey Test in English Fundamentals. For additional information and reviews by Leonard S. Feldt and Roger A. Richards, see 6:249 (2 references).

C5. Barrett-Ryan English Test. For additional information and a review by Clarence Derrick, see 6:250 (2 references); for a review by J. Raymond Gerberich, see 5:175.

C6. Barrett-Ryan-Schrammel English Test. For additional information and reviews by Leonard S. Feldt and Cleveland A. Thomas, see 5:176 (1 reference); for reviews by G. Frederic Kuder, Robert C. Pooley, and Charles Swain Thomas of the original edition, see 2:1267.

C7. Basic Language Skills: Iowa Every-Pupil Tests of Basic Skills, Test C. For additional information, see 4:150; see also 3:116 (2 references).

For reviews of the complete battery, see 4:15 (2 reviews), 3:10 (3 reviews), and 1:872 (4 reviews).

C8. California Language Test. For additional information and a review by Richard E. Schutz, see 6:251 (1 reference); for reviews by Constance M. McCullough and Winifred L. Post, see 5:177 (3 references); for reviews by Gerald V. Lannholm and Robert C. Pooley of an earlier edition, see 4:151; for reviews by Harry A. Greene and J. Paul Leonard, see 2:1292. For reviews of the complete battery, see 6:3 (2 reviews), 5:2 (1 review), 4:2 (3 reviews), 3:15 (1 review), 2:1193 (2 reviews), and 1:876 (1 review, 1 excerpt).

C9. Canadian Achievement Test in English (CATE). For additional information and a review by Bernard Spolsky, see 6:252 (2 references).

C10. Canadian English Achievement Test (CEAT). For additional information and reviews by J. Douglas Ayers and Bernard Spolsky, see 6:253 (2 references).

C11. The Clapp-Young English Test. For additional information and a review by Gerald V. Lannholm, see 3:117.

C12. Cleveland English Composition and Grammar Test. For additional information and a review by Frank P. De Lay, see 2:1269.

C13. College English Test: National Achievement Tests. For additional information and a review by Osmond E. Palmer, see 5:178; for reviews by Constance M. McCullough and Robert W. Howard, see 2:1269.1.

C14. College Entrance Examination Board Advanced Placement Examination: English. For additional information, see 6:254.

C15. College Placement Test in English. For additional information and a review by Charlotte Croon Davis, see 4:153.

C16. College Preparatory Test in English. For additional information and a review by Charlotte Croon Davis, see 4:154.

C17. Columbia Research Bureau English Test. For additional information and reviews by L. K. Shumaker and Louis C. Zahner, see 2:1270.

C18. Cooperative English Test: Usage, Spelling, and Vocabulary. For additional information and reviews by Margaret F. Lorimer and John M. Stalnaker, see 6:255 (5 references); for reviews by Carleton C. Jones, Jeanette McPherrin, Louis C. Zahner, Henry D. Rinsland, and L. K. Shumaker, see 2:1271 (11 references); for reviews by John M. Stalnaker, Charles S. Thomas, and John H. Thompson of earlier forms, see 1:961.

C19. Cooperative English Tests. For additional information and reviews by Leonard S. Feldt and Margaret F. Lorimer, see 6:256 (52 references, 1 excerpt); see also 5:179 (58 references) and 4:155 (53 references); for reviews by J. Paul Leonard, Edward S. Noyes, and Robert C. Pooley of an earlier edition, see 3:120 (29 references); see also 2:1276 (2 references). For reviews of subtests, see 6:258 (2 reviews), 6:806 (2 reviews), and 3:497 (2 reviews).

C20. Coordinated Scales of Attainment: English. For additional information, see 5:180. For reviews of the complete battery, see 4:8 (1 review) and 3:6 (4 reviews).

C21. Correct English Usage Test. For additional information, see 4:156.

C22. Correctness and Appropriateness of Expression: The Iowa Tests of Educational Development, Test 3. For additional information, see 6:267 (1 reference). For reviews of the complete battery, see 6:14 (2 reviews), 5:17 (2 reviews), 4:17 (1 review), and 3:12 (3 reviews).

C23. Correctness and Effectiveness of Expression: Tests of General Educational Development, Test 1. For additional information, see 5:181; for a review by Charlotte W. Croon [Davis] of the college level, see 3:122. For reviews of the complete battery, see 5:27 (1 review), 4:26 (1 review), and 3:20 (2 reviews).

C24. Cotswold Junior English Ability Test. For additional information and reviews by M. A. Brimer and John C. Daniels, see 5:182.

C25. Cotswold Measurement of Ability: English. For additional information and reviews by M. A. Brimer and S. C. Richardson, see 5:183.

C26. Cross English Test. For additional information and reviews by Roland L. Beck and Edward S. Noyes, see 2:1272 (3 references).

C27. Davis-Schrammel Elementary English Test. For additional information and reviews by Keith Goltry and Rachel Salisbury, see 2:1273.

C28. Diagnostic Tests in English Composition. For additional information and reviews by Harry A. Greene and Jean Hoard, see 2:1274.

C29. "Dingwall" Test in English Usage. For additional information and a review by Robert H. Thouless, see 3:124; for a review by Charles Fox, see 2:1275.

C30. English Classification Test for High Schools and Colleges. For additional information, see 2:1277.

C31. English: Every Pupil Scholarship Test. For additional information, see 6:257 (1 reference).

C32. English Expression: Cooperative English Tests. For additional information and reviews by John C. Sherwood and John M. Stalnaker, see 6:258; for a review by Chester W. Harris of an earlier edition, see 4:155. For reviews of the the complete battery, see 6:256 (2 reviews, 1 excerpt), 4:155 (1 review), and 3:120 (3 reviews).

C33. English Language and Literature: National Teacher Examinations. For additional information and a review by Holland Roberts, see 6:259. For reviews of the testing program, see 6:700 (1 review), 5:538 (3 reviews), and 4:802 (1 review).

C34. English Language and Literature: Teacher Education Examination Program. An inactive form of C33; for additional information, see 6:260; for a reference to a review, see C33. For a review of the testing program, see 5:543.

C35. English No. 4, Grammar and Style: Midland Attainment Tests. For additional information, see 1:962.

C36. English Placement Test. For additional information and reviews by Roland L. Beck and Robert W. Howard, see 2:1278 (2 references).

C37. English Placement Test for Iowa Universities and Colleges. For additional information, see 1:958.

C38. English Progress Tests. For additional information, see 6:261; for reviews by Neil Gourlay and Stanley Nisbet, see 5:187.

C39. English Survey Test: Ohio Scholarship Tests: Ohio Senior Survey Tests. For additional information, see 5:188; for reviews by Charlotte W. Croon [Davis] and J. Paul Leonard of the original edition, see 3:125 (1 reference).

C40. English Test (Adv.). For additional information and a review by A. E. G. Pilliner, see 6:262.

C41. English Test (Four-Year Course): Affiliation Testing Program for Catholic Secondary Schools. For additional information and a review by Henry Chauncey, see 6:263. For a review of the complete program, see 6:758.

C42. English Test: Municipal Tests: National Achievement Tests. For additional information, see 5:190. For reviews of the complete battery, see 5:18 (1 review), 4:20 (1 review) and 2:1191 (2 reviews).

C43. English Test: National Achievement Tests. For additional information, see 5:191; for a review by Winifred L. Post, see 4:162; for a review by Harry A. Greene, see 3:126.

C44. English Test 2. For additional information and reviews by Reginald Edwards, S. C. Richardson, and Cleveland A. Thomas, see 5:192.

C45. English Tests 1, 3–13. For additional information and reviews by Stanley Nisbet and H. J. Sants, see 6:264 (1 reference).

C46. English: Thanet Mental Tests. For additional information and a review by C. Ebblewhite Smith, see 2:1279.

C47. English Usage: Every Pupil Test. For additional information, see 6:265 (2 references); for a review by J. R. Gerberich of the 1946 forms, see 3:127.

C48. Entrance and Classification Examination for Teachers Colleges: English Test. For additional information, see 2:1280.

C49. Essentials of English Tests. For additional information and a review by J. Raymond Gerberich, see 6:266; for reviews by Charlotte W. Croon [Davis] and Gerald V. Lannholm, see 3:128 (1 excerpt).

C50. Examination in Business English—High-School Level. For additional information and a review by Orrel E. Little, see 3:375.

C51. Examination in English—College Level. For additional information and a review by John S. Diekhoff, see 3:129.

C52. Examination in English—High-School Level. For additional information and reviews by Holland Roberts and Louis C. Zahner, see 3:130 (4 references).

C53. Grammar: Public School Achievement Tests. For additional information and reviews of the complete battery, see 2:1194.

C54. Greene-Stapp Language Abilities Test. For additional information and reviews by Richard A. Meade and Osmond E. Palmer, see 5:195 (1 reference).

C55. Gregory Diagnostic Tests in Language. For additional information and reviews by Keith Goltry and J. Paul Leonard, see 2:1282.

C56. Hoyum-Schrammel English Essentials Tests. For additional information and reviews by Worth R. Jones and Ruth Strickland, see 5:196.

C57. Iowa Every-Pupil Test in English Correctness. For additional information, see 1:965.

C58. Iowa Grammar Information Test. For additional information and a review by Robert C. Pooley, see 4:164.

C59. Iowa Language Abilities Test. For additional information and a review by Margaret G. McKim, see 4:165.

C60. Iowa Placement Examinations: English Aptitude. For additional information and reviews by Clarence Derrick and W. C. Kvaraceus, see 4:166 (5 references); for a review by Robert C. Pooley, see 3:115 (9 references).

C61. Iowa Placement Examinations: English Training. For additional information and reviews by Clarence Derrick and W. C. Kvaraceus, see 4:167 (5 references); for a review by Robert C. Pooley, see 3:131 (15 references).

C62. Kentucky English Test. For additional information, see 3:132; for a review by Henry D. Rinsland, see 1:966; see also F96.

C63. Language Arts: Minnesota High School Achievement Examinations. For additional information and a review by Marvin D. Glock, see 6:268; for a review by Roger A. Richards of earlier forms, see 5:186.

C64. Language Essentials Tests. For additional information and a review by Harry A. Greene, see 3:133.

C65. Language Perception Test. For additional information, see 6:269.

C66. Language Usage: Public School Achievement Tests. For additional information and reviews of the complete battery, see 2:1194.

C67. Leonard Diagnostic Test in Punctuation and Capitalization. For additional information and a review by Jean Hoard, see 2:1285 (2 references).

C68. Linguistic Awareness Test. For additional information, see 2:1287.

C69. Los Angeles Diagnostic Tests: Language (A Test in Capitalization, Punctuation and Language Usage). For additional information and a review by Gerald V. Lannholm, see 4:168.

C70. Mechanics of Written English: State High School Tests for Indiana. For additional information, see 4:169.

C71. Metropolitan Achievement Tests: High School Language Tests. For additional information, see 6:270. For reviews of the complete battery, see 6:15 (3 reviews), 4:18 (1 review), 2:1189 (2 reviews), and 1:874 (3 reviews).

C72. Modern English Usage Test. For additional information and a review by Holland Roberts, see 5:198; for a review by Walter N. Durost, see 4:170.

C73. Moray House English Tests. For additional information and a review by M. Alan Brimer, see 6:271 (7 references).

C74. Nationwide English Grammar Examination. For additional information, see 6:272.

C75. Nelson's High School English Test. For additional information and reviews by Frank P. De Lay and Jacob S. Orleans, see 2:1290.

C76. The New Purdue Placement Test in English. For additional information and reviews by Gerald V. Lannholm and M. J. Wantman, see 5:199 (5 references); see also 4:173 (9 references).

C77. Novelty Grammar Tests. For additional information, see 6:273.

C78. Objective Test in Grammar. For additional information, see 4:171.

C79. Objective Tests in English. For additional information, see 4:172.

C80. Pressey English Tests for Grades 5 to 8. For additional information, see 2:1291 (2 excerpts).

C81. The Pribble-Dallmann Diagnostic Tests in Elementary Language Skills. For additional information and reviews by William H. Lucio and George D. Spache, see 6:274.

C82. The Pribble-McCrory Diagnostic Tests in Practical English Grammar. For additional information and a review by Clarence Derrick, see 6:275.

C83. The Purdue High School English Test. For additional information and reviews by Charlotte Croon Davis and Benjamin Rosner, see 6:276.

C84. Purdue Placement Test in English. For additional information, see 4:173 (9 references); for revised edition, see C76.

C85. Rinsland-Beck Natural Test of English Usage. For additional information and reviews by John M. Stalnaker and Charles Swain Thomas, see 2:1293 (3 references, 1 excerpt).

C86. SRA Achievement Series: Language Arts. For additional information and a review by Miriam M. Bryan, see 6:277 (1 reference); for reviews by Constance M. McCullough and Winifred L. Post, see 5:200. For reviews of the complete battery, see 6:21 (1 review) and 5:21 (2 reviews).

C87. SRA Language Skills. For additional information, see 3:388c.

C88. Scholastic Achievement Series: English-Spelling. For additional information, see 6:278 (1 reference); for reviews by Geraldine Spaulding and Ruth Strickland, see 5:201. For reviews of the complete battery, see 6:23 (2 reviews) and 5:23 (2 reviews).

C89. The Schonell Diagnostic English Tests. For additional information and reviews by John Cohen and Robert H. Thouless, see 3:135.

C90. Shepherd English Test. For additional information and a review by Ruth D. Churchill, see 3:136 (2 references).

C91. Stanford Achievement Test [Language Arts]. For additional information, see 4:174 (1 reference).

C92. Stanford Achievement Test: Spelling and Language Tests. For additional information, see 6:279. For reviews of the complete battery, see 6:26 (1 review, 1 excerpt), 5:25 (1 review), 4:25 (2 reviews), and 3:18 (2 reviews).

C93. Survey of Language Achievement: California Survey Series. For additional information and a review by Miriam M. Bryan, see 6:280.

C94. Survey Tests of English Usage. For additional information and a review by Holland Roberts, see 6:281 (1 reference).

C95. T. C. English Test. For additional information, see 6:282.

C96. Test of English Usage [California Test Bureau]. For additional information and a review by John C. Sherwood, see 6:283; for a review by Charlotte Croon Davis, see 4:175.

C97. A Test of English Usage [Manasayan]. For additional information, see 6:284.

C98. Test of Language Skill. For additional information, see 6:285.

C99. Tests of Language Usage: Active Vocabulary and Expression: Cooperative Inter-American Tests. For additional information and a review by Walter V. Kaulfers, see 4:176 (3 references).

C100. Tools of Written English: State High School Tests for Indiana. For additional information, see 4:177.

C101. Tressler English Minimum Essentials Tests. For additional information and reviews by Osmond E. Palmer and Roger A. Richards, see 6:286 (1 reference).

C102. 20th Century Test for English. For additional information, see 4:159 and 4:160.

C103. Wisconsin Language Usage Test. For additional information, see 3:138.

COMPOSITION

C104. College Entrance Examination Board Achievement Test: English Composition. For additional information and reviews by Charlotte Croon Davis, Robert C. Pooley, and Holland Roberts, see 6:287 (6 references); see also 5:204 (14 references); for a review by Charlotte Croon Davis (with Frederick B. Davis) of earlier forms, see 4:178 (6 references). For reviews of the testing program, see 6:760 (2 reviews).

C105. College Entrance Examination Board Advanced Placement Examination: English Composition. For additional information and a review by Robert C. Pooley, see 5:205.

C106. College Entrance Examination Board Placement Tests: English Composition Test. For additional information, see 6:288.

C107. College Entrance Examination Board Writing Sample. For additional information and a review by Robert C. Pooley, see 6:289 (2 references). For reviews of the testing program, see 6:760 (2 reviews).

C108. Diagnostic Test of Letter-Writing Ability. For additional information, see 2:1481 (1 excerpt).

C109. Hudelson's Typical Composition Ability Scale. For additional information and a review by Worth J. Osburn, see 4:179 (7 references).

C110. Judging the Effectiveness of Written Composition: Test 3.8. For additional information, see 2:1283 (1 reference).

C111. Nationwide English Composition Examination. For additional information, see 6:290.

C112. Sequential Tests of Educational Progress: Essay Test. For additional information, see 6:291 (3 references); for reviews by John S. Diekhoff, John M. Stalnaker, and Louis C. Zahner, see 5:206. For reviews of the complete battery, see 6:25 (2 reviews) and 5:24 (2 reviews, 1 excerpt).

C113. Sequential Tests of Educational Progress: Writing. For additional information and reviews by Hillel Black and Albert N. Hieronymus, see 6:292 (3 references, 1 excerpt); for reviews by Charlotte Croon Davis, John M. Stalnaker, and Louis C.

Zahner, see 5:207. For reviews of the complete battery, see 6:25 (2 reviews) and 5:24 (2 reviews, 1 excerpt).

C114. Writing Skills Test. For additional information and reviews by William E. Coffman and Osmond E. Palmer, see 6:293.

LITERATURE

C115. Ability to Interpret Literary Materials: The Iowa Tests of Educational Development, Test 7. For additional information, see 6:300 (1 reference). For reviews of the complete battery, see 6:14 (2 reviews), 5:17 (2 reviews), 4:17 (1 review), and 3:12 (3 reviews).

C116. Alphabetical List of 1000 Fiction Authors Classified by Subject and Maturity Level. For additional information, see 2:1294 (1 reference).

C117. American Literature: Every Pupil Scholarship Test. For additional information, see 5:208.

C118. American Literature: Every Pupil Test. For additional information, see 6:294.

C119. Analytical Scales of Attainment in Literature. For additional information and reviews by Carleton C. Jones and Robert K. Speer, see 2:1295.

C120. An Awareness Test in 20th Century Literature. For additional information, see 4:182; for reviews by H. H. Giles and Ann L. Gebhardt, see 2:1296.

C121. Barrett-Ryan Literature Test. For additional information and a review by Chester W. Harris, see 3:139.

C122. Book Review Tests. For additional information, see 6:295.

C123. Carroll Prose Appreciation Test. For additional information and a review by Chester W. Harris, see 3:140 (4 references).

C124. Catholic Book Tests. For additional information, see 6:296.

C125. Center-Durost Literature Acquaintance Test. For additional information and a review by Holland Roberts, see 5:210 (1 reference).

C126. Check List of Novels. For additional information and a review by John S. Diekhoff, see 4:183 (2 references).

C127. Checklist of One Hundred Magazines. For additional information, see 2:1297.

C128. College Entrance Examination Board Advanced Placement Examination: Literature. For additional information and a review by John S. Diekhoff, see 5:211.

C129. Cooperative Literary Acquaintance Test. For additional information, see 3:141 (1 reference); for reviews by Lou LaBrant and Edward S. Noyes, see 2:1298; for reviews by Carleton C. Jones and John H. Thompson, see 1:970.

C130. Cooperative Literary Comprehension and Appreciation Test. For additional information, see 4:184 (1 reference); for a review by Holland Roberts, see 3:142 (3 references).

C131. Cooperative Literary Comprehension Test. For additional information and reviews by Lou LaBrant and Edward A. Tenney, see 2:1299 (3 references); for reviews by Charles Swain Thomas and John H. Thompson, see 1:971.

C132. Davis-Roahen-Schrammel American Literature Test. For additional information, see 6:297; for reviews by Paul B. Diederich and Violet Hughes, see 2:1300.

C133. The Eaton Book-Report System. For additional information and a review by Paul B. Diederich, see 1:972.

C134. The Eaton Literature Tests. For additional information, see 1:978.

C135. Elementary Literature: Every Pupil Scholarship Test. For additional information, see 5:218.

C136. English Literature: Every Pupil Test. For additional information, see 6:298.

C137. English No. 5, Knowledge of Literature: Midland Attainment Tests. For additional information, see 1:973.

C138. English Tests for Outside Reading. For additional information, see 2:1301.

C139. English: Understanding and Appreciation of Poetry: State High School Tests for Indiana. For additional information and a review by Chester W. Harris, see 3:143.

C140. The Graduate Record Examinations Advanced Tests: Literature. For additional information, see 6:299; for a review by Robert C. Pooley of an earlier form, see 5:215. For a review of the testing program, see 5:601.

C141. Interpretation of Literary Materials: Tests of General Educational Development, Test 4. For additional information, see 5:216. For reviews of the complete battery, see 5:27 (1 review), 4:26 (1 review), and 3:20 (2 reviews).

C142. Interpretation of Literature Test: General Education Series. For additional information and reviews by John S. Diekhoff and John M. Stalnaker, see 4:187.

C143. Inventory of Satisfactions Found in Reading Fiction: General Education Series. For additional information and a review by Holland Roberts, see 4:188 (2 references).

C144. Iowa Every-Pupil Test in Reading Comprehension in Literature. For additional information, see 1:975.

C145. The Jones Book-A-Day Tests: For Checking Outside Reading of High School Pupils. For additional information, see 4:189.

C146. Literary Information Test: American Literature: Test 3.5. For additional information, see 2:1288 (1 reference).

C147. Literary Information Test: English Literature: Test 3.4. For additional information, see 2:1289 (1 reference).

C148. Literature Appreciation Tests. For additional information, see 4:190; for a review by Paul B. Diederich, see 1:976.

C149. Literature: Every Pupil Scholarship Test. For additional information, see 6:301.

C150. Literature Questionnaire: The Drama: Test 3.21. For additional information, see 2:1302 (1 reference).

C151. Literature Questionnaire: The Novel: Test 3.2a. For additional information, see 2:1303 (1 reference).

C152. Literature Test: Municipal Tests: National Achievement Tests. For additional information, see 4:191.

C153. Literature Test: National Achievement Tests. For additional information, see 5:219; for reviews by H. H. Giles and Robert C. Pooley, see 2:1304.

C154. The New Eaton Literature Test. For additional information, see 1:978.

C155. Objective Tests in American Anthology. For additional information, see 6:302.

C156. Objective Tests in English Anthology. For additional information, see 6:303.

C157. Objective Tests in English [Perfection Form Co.]. For additional information, see 6:304.

C158. Objective Tests in English [Turner E. Smith & Co.]. For additional information, see 4:194.

C159. Outside Reading Tests for Freshmen and Sophomores. For additional information, see 6:305.

C160. Outside Reading Tests for Junior High Schools. For additional information, see 6:307.

C161. Outside Reading Tests for Juniors and Seniors. For additional information, see 6:306.

C162. Questionnaire on Voluntary Reading: Test 3.31. For additional information, see 2:1305 (1 reference).

C163. Rigg Poetry Judgment Test. For additional information and reviews by John S. Diekhoff and Louis C. Zahner, see 3:146 (2 references).

C164. Stanford Achievement Test [Literature]. For additional information and a review by Winifred L. Post, see 4:195.

C165. Stanford Test of Comprehension of Literature. For additional information and a review by J. Wayne Wrightstone, see 2:1306 (1 reference).

C166. Survey Test in American Literature. For additional information, see 3:147.

C167. Survey Test in English Literature. For additional information and a review by John S. Diekhoff, see 4:196.

C168. Test of Literary Essentials. For additional information, see 4:217.

C169. Tests for the Appreciation of Literature. For additional information and a review by Ann L. Gebhardt, see 2:1307.

C170. Ullman-Clark Test on Classical References and Allusions. For additional information, see 4:197.

SPEECH

C171. The Arizona Articulation Proficiency Scale. For additional information, see 6:307a (2 references).

C172. Bryan-Wilke Scale for Rating Public Speeches. For additional information, see 2:1308.

C173. Forms From Diagnostic Methods in Speech Pathology. For additional information, see 6:308 (1 reference).

C174. The Graduate Record Examinations Advanced Tests: Speech. For additional information,

see 6:309 (1 reference). For a review of the testing program, see 5:601.

C175. Guidance Questionnaire for Students of Speech. For additional information, see 3:150 (4 references).

C176. The Houston Test for Language Development. For additional information, see 6:310 (1 reference).

C177. An Integrated Articulation Test for Use With Children With Cerebral Palsy. For additional information, see 6:311 (9 references).

C178. Language Modalities Test for Aphasia. For additional information and a review by T. R. Miles, see 6:312 (1 reference).

C179. Nationwide Speech Examination. For additional information, see 6:313.

C180. Oral English Observation Schedule. For additional information, see 1:1094.

C181. The Orzeck Aphasia Evaluation. For additional information, see 6:313a.

C182. Speech Articulation Test for Young Children. For additional information, see 6:314.

C183. Speech Attitude Scale. For additional information, see 3:151 (2 references).

C184. Speech Experience Inventory. For additional information, see 3:152 (2 references).

C185. Templin-Darley Screening and Diagnostic Tests of Articulation. For additional information, see 6:315 (9 references, 2 excerpts).

C186. Verbal Language Development Scale. For additional information, see 6:316 (7 references).

C187. Weidner-Fensch Speech Screening Test. For additional information and a review by Robert S. Cathcart (with Louise B. Scott), see 5:221.

SPELLING

C188. A.C.E.R. Spelling Test (Form C). For additional information and reviews by J. A. Richardson and D. K. Wheeler, see 5:222.

C189. A.C.E.R. Spelling Tests. For additional information and a review by David H. Russell, see 2:1309 (1 reference).

C190. Ayer Standardized Spelling Test. For additional information and a review by Gus P. Plessas, see 6:317; for a review by Harold H. Bixler, see 4:198 (1 reference).

C191. Buffalo Spelling Scale. For additional information and reviews by John C. Almack and M. E. Broom, see 2:1310; for a review by Henry D. Rinsland, see 1:1158.

C192. Coordinated Scales of Attainment: Spelling. For additional information, see 5:223. For reviews of the complete battery, see 4:8 (1 review) and 3:6 (4 reviews).

C193. Davis-Schrammel Spelling Test. For additional information and a review by Anton Thompson, see 4:199; for reviews by Walter W. Cook and Joseph C. Dewey, see 2:1311 (1 reference).

C194. Gates-Russell Spelling Diagnostic Tests. For additional information, see 6:318; for a review by George Spache, see 4:200 (1 reference); for reviews by John C. Almack and Thomas G. Foran, see 1:1159.

C195. Graded Word Spelling Test. For additional information and a review by John Nisbet, see 5:224.

C196. Group Diagnostic Spelling Test. For additional information, see 6:319.

C197. High School Spelling Test. For additional information and a review by Walter W. Cook, see 2:1312 (2 references).

C198. Kansas Spelling Test. For additional information and reviews by Henry D. Rinsland and Guy M. Wilson, see 3:153.

C199. Kelvin Measurement of Spelling Ability. For additional information, see 1:1160.

C200. Lincoln Diagnostic Spelling Tests. For additional information and a review by Gus P. Plessas, see 6:320 (6 references); for reviews by Walter Scribner Guiler and George Spache of the intermediate and advanced tests, see 4:202–3.

C201. The Morgan Spelling Test for Schools and Colleges. For additional information and a review by Harold H. Bixler, see 4:204.

C202. Morrison-McCall Spelling Scale. For additional information and a review by Anton Thompson, see 4:205 (2 references).

C203. Nationwide Spelling Examination. For additional information, see 6:321.

C204. The New Iowa Spelling Scale. For additional information, see 6:322 (1 reference).

C205. The New Standard High School Spelling Scale. For additional information, see 4:206.

C206. Rich-Engelson Spelling Test. For additional information and a review by Henry D. Rinsland, see 4:207.

C207. Spelling and Vocabulary: Every Pupil Test. For additional information, see 6:323.

C208. [Spelling and Word Meaning Tests]. For additional information, see 6:324.

C209. Spelling Errors Test. For additional information, see 5:228 (1 reference).

C210. Spelling: Every Pupil Scholarship Test. For additional information, see 6:325.

C211. Spelling: Public School Achievement Tests. For additional information and reviews of the complete battery, see 2:1194 (2 reviews).

C212. Spelling: Seven Plus Assessment: Northumberland Series. For additional information, see 4:210. For a review of the complete battery, see 4:24.

C213. Spelling Test for Clerical Workers: [Personal Research Institute Clerical Battery]. For additional information and a review by Harold H. Bixler, see 4:211. For reviews of the complete battery, see 4:729 (2 reviews).

C214. Spelling Test: National Achievement Tests. For additional information and a review by James A. Fitzgerald, see 5:230; for a review by W. J. Osburn, see 1:1161.

C215. Standard Elementary Spelling Scale. For additional information, see 2:1313.1.

C216. Traxler High School Spelling Test. For additional information and a review by Gus P. Plessas, see 6:326; for a review by Henry D. Rinsland, see 4:212.

C217. Unit Scales of Attainment in Spelling. For additional information and reviews by John C. Almack and G. M. Wilson, see 2:1315 (1 reference). For reviews of the complete battery, see 2:1197 (1 review) and 1:878 (2 reviews).

C218. Wellesley Spelling Scale. For additional information and a review by Janet G. Afflerbach, see 5:232 (1 reference); for reviews by Henry D. Rinsland and Guy M. Wilson, see 3:157.

VOCABULARY

C219. A.C.E.R. Word Knowledge Test. For additional information, see 6:327 (1 reference).

C220. American Literacy Test. For additional information and a review by Victor H. Noll, see 6:328.

C221. Bruce Vocabulary Inventory. For additional information, see 6:329.

C222. Clinton General Vocabulary Test for High Schools and Colleges. For additional information and a review by Harold H. Bixler, see 3:158.

C223. Columbia Vocabulary Test. For additional information and reviews by Verner M. Sims and Clifford Woody, see 3:159 (4 references).

C224. Cooperative Vocabulary Test. For additional information, see 4:213 (4 references); for reviews by Edgar Dale and Henry D. Rinsland, see 3:160.

C225. Durost-Center Word Mastery Test. For additional information and a review by George P. Winship, Jr., see 6:330; for a review by A. N. Hieronymus, see 5:233.

C226. English No. 2, Vocabulary: Midland Attainment Tests. For additional information, see 1:980.

C227. English Recognition Vocabulary Test. For additional information and reviews by Paul S. Burnham and Edgar Dale, see 3:161 (12 references); see also 2:1319 (3 references).

C228. General Vocabulary: The Iowa Tests of Educational Development, Test 8. For additional information, see 6:332. For reviews of the complete battery, see 6:14 (2 reviews), 5:17 (2 reviews), 4:17 (1 review), and 3:12 (3 reviews).

C229. Gulick Vocabulary Survey. For additional information and a review by George P. Winship, Jr., see 6:331 (1 reference).

C230. High School Vocabulary Test. For additional information and a review by Harold H. Bixler, see 3:162.

C231. Holborn Vocabulary Test for Young Children. For additional information and a review by C. M. Fleming, see 4:215 (1 reference).

C232. The Inglis Tests of English Vocabulary. For additional information, see 5:234 (3 references); for a review by Henry D. Rinsland, see 3:163 (7 references).

C233. Johnson O'Connor English Vocabulary Worksamples. For additional information, see 6:333 (5 references).

C234. Johnson O'Connor Vocabulary Tests. For additional information, see 6:334.

C235. Kansas Vocabulary Test. For additional information and a review by Harold H. Bixler, see 3:164.

C236. Kennon Test of Literary Vocabulary. For additional information and a review by H. H. Remmers, see 3:165 (1 reference).

C237. Michigan Vocabulary Profile Test. For additional information and a review by David Segel, see 4:216 (7 references) ; for a review by Joseph E. King, see 3:166 (6 references) ; for a review by Herbert A. Landry, see 2:1320 (2 references, 1 excerpt) ; for reviews by John G. Darley, Richard Ledgerwood, John M. Stalnaker, M. R. Trabue, and Arthur E. Traxler of an earlier edition, see 1:1171.

C238. Nationwide English Vocabulary Examination. For additional information, see 6:335.

C239. New Standard Vocabulary Test. For additional information, see 6:336; for reviews by Richard A. Meade and Osmond E. Palmer, see 5:236.

C240. Purdue Industrial Supervisors Word-Meaning Test. For additional information and reviews by Jerome E. Doppelt and Bernadine Meyer, see 5:237 (2 references).

C241. Quick-Scoring Vocabulary Test: Dominion Tests. For additional information and a review by Stephen Hunka, see 6:337.

C242. Schrammel-Wharton Vocabulary Test. For additional information and a review by Arthur E. Traxler, see 2:1321.

C243. Survey Test of Vocabulary. For additional information, see 5:239 (3 references) ; for reviews by

Verner M. Sims and Clifford Woody, see 3:167 (1 reference).

C244. A Test of Active Vocabulary. For additional information, see 6:338.

C245. Vocabulary: Every Pupil Scholarship Test. For additional information, see 6:339.

C246. Vocabulary: Parr Skill-Ability Tests. For additional information, see 2:1321.1.

C247. Vocabulary Power Tests. For additional information, see 2:1322.

C248. Vocabulary Test for High School Students and College Freshmen. For additional information, see 6:342a.

C249. Vocabulary Test—GT. For additional information and a review by Robert E. Stake, see 6:342 (6 references).

C250. Vocabulary Test [Management Service Co.]. For additional information, see 6:340.

C251. Vocabulary Test: National Achievement Tests. For additional information, see 5:241; for a review by Clifford Woody, see 3:168.

C252. Vocabulary Test [Richardson, Bellows, Henry & Co.]. For additional information, see 6:341.

C253. Wide Range Vocabulary Test. For additional information and a review by Paul S. Burnham, see 3:169 (1 reference).

C254. Word Clue Test. For additional information, see 6:343.

C255. Word Dexterity Test. For additional information, see 4:218; see also 3:170 (2 references).

FINE ARTS

D1. Graduate Record Examinations Advanced Fine Arts Test. For additional information, see 4:219.

D2. Oberlin Test of Music and Art. For additional information, see 6:344.

ART

D3. Art Education: National Teacher Examinations. For additional information and a review by Harold A. Schultz, see 6:345. For reviews of the testing program, see 6:700 (1 review), 5:538 (3 reviews), and 4:802 (1 review).

D4. Graves Design Judgment Test. For additional information and reviews by William B. Michael and Edwin Ziegfeld, see 4:220 (2 references, 1 excerpt).

D5. Horn Art Aptitude Inventory. For additional information and a review by Orville Palmer, see 5:242; for a review by Edwin Ziegfeld, see 3:171 (1 reference).

D6. Knauber Art Ability Test. For additional information and a review by Edwin Ziegfeld, see

4:222; for a review by Norman C. Meier, see 2:1323 (4 references).

D7. Knauber Art Vocabulary Test. For additional information and a review by Edwin Ziegfeld, see 4:223 (2 references) ; for reviews by Ray Faulkner and Joseph E. Moore, see 2:1324 (4 references).

D8. McAdory Art Test. For additional information and reviews by Norman C. Meier and Edwin Ziegfeld, see 2:1325 (13 references).

D9. Measuring Scale for Freehand Drawing. For additional information, see 1:896.

D10. The Meier Art Tests. For additional information and a review by Harold A. Schultz of test 2, see 6:346 (8 references) ; for a review by Harold A. Schultz of test 1, see 4:224 (9 references) ; for a review by Edwin Ziegfeld, see 3:172 (4 references) ; for reviews by Paul R. Farnsworth and Aulus Ward Saunders of the original edition of test 1, see 2:1326 (15 references).

D11. Practical Drawing Ability Test: Gibson's Attainment Tests. For additional information, see 1:1036.

D12. Selective Art Aptitude Test. For additional information and a review by Edwin Ziegfeld, see 3:173.

D13. Seven Modern Paintings: Test 3.9. For additional information, see 2:1328.

D14. Tests in Fundamental Abilities of Visual Arts. For additional information and reviews by Ray Faulkner and Aulus Ward Saunders, see 2:1329 (6 references).

MUSIC

D15. Aliferis Music Achievement Test: College Level. For additional information, see 6:347 (5 references); for a review by Herbert D. Wing, see 5:243 (5 references).

D16. Aliferis-Stecklein Music Achievement Test: College Midpoint Level. For additional information and reviews by Paul R. Farnsworth and Herbert D. Wing, see 6:347 (5 references).

D17. Beach Music Test. For additional information and a review by James L. Mursell, see 3:174.

D18. Conrad Instrument-Talent Test. For additional information and a review by Herbert D. Wing, see 5:244.

D19. Diagnostic Tests of Achievement in Music. For additional information and reviews by William S. Larson and Herbert D. Wing, see 4:226.

D20. Drake Musical Aptitude Tests. For additional information and reviews by Robert W. Lundin and James Mainwaring, see 5:245 (1 reference). For references to reviews of a subtest, see D21.

D21. Drake Musical Memory Test: A Test of Musical Talent. For additional information and a review by William S. Larson, see 3:175 (2 references); for reviews by Paul R. Farnsworth and James L. Mursell, see 2:1330 (2 references); see also 1:1083 (1 excerpt). For references to additional reviews, see D20.

D22. Ear Tests in Harmony. For additional information and a review by Jay W. Fay, see 1:1084.

D23. The Farnum Music Notation Test. For additional information and reviews by Kenneth L. Bean and William S. Larson, see 5:246 (1 reference).

D24. The Graduate Record Examinations Advanced Tests: Music. For additional information, see 6:348; for a review by William S. Larson, see 5:247. For a review of the testing program, see 5:601.

D25. Hillbrand Sight-Singing Test. For additional information and a review by Alton O'Steen, see 2:1331 (1 reference).

D26. Jones Music Recognition Test. For additional information and a review by Herbert D. Wing, see 6:349.

D27. Knuth Achievement Tests in Music: For Recognition of Certain Rhythmic and Melodic Aspects. For additional information and a review by Carl E. Seashore, see 2:1332 (1 reference); for reviews by Jay W. Fay and James L. Mursell, see 1:1085.

D28. Kwalwasser-Dykema Music Tests. For additional information and a review by William S. Larson, see 3:176 (29 references).

D29. Kwalwasser Music Talent Test. For additional information and reviews by Paul R. Farnsworth and Kate Hevner Mueller, see 5:248.

D30. Kwalwasser-Ruch Test of Musical Accomplishment. For additional information and reviews by William S. Larson and James L. Mursell, see 2:1333 (1 reference).

D31. Kwalwasser Test of Music Information and Appreciation. For additional information and reviews by Raleigh M. Drake and Karl W. Gehrkens, see 2:1334 (1 reference).

D32. McCauley Examination in Public School Music. For additional information and a review by Alton O'Steen, see 2:1335.

D33. Music Education: National Teacher Examinations. For additional information and a review by William S. Larson, see 6:350. For reviews of the testing program, see 6:700 (1 review), 5:538 (3 reviews), and 4:802 (1 review).

D34. Music Education: Teacher Education Examination Program. An inactive form of D33; for additional information, see 6:351. For a review of the testing program, see 5:543; for references to additional reviews, see D33.

D35. Musical Achievement Test. For additional information and a review by Raleigh M. Drake, see 2:1336.

D36. Musical Appreciation Ability Test: Gibson's Attainment Tests. For additional information, see 1:1086.

D37. Musical Aptitude Test. For additional information and a review by Herbert D. Wing, see 6:352 (2 references); for a review by Robert W. Lundin, see 5:250; for a review by William S. Larson, see 4:228.

D38. Providence Inventory Test in Music. For additional information and reviews by William S. Larson and Clara J. McCauley, see 2:1337.

D39. Seashore Measures of Musical Talents. For additional information and reviews by Kenneth L. Bean and Robert W. Lundin, see 6:353 (13 references); see also 5:251 (9 references); for reviews by John McLeish and Herbert D. Wing of the 1939 revision, see 4:229 (16 references); for reviews by Paul R. Farnsworth, William S. Larson, and James L. Mursell, see 3:177 (46 references); see also 2:1338 (60 references).

D40. Strouse Music Test. For additional information and reviews by Clara J. McCauley and Carl E. Seashore, see 2:1339 (1 reference); for a review by Paul R. Farnsworth, see 1:1087.

D41. Test of Musicality. For additional information and reviews by Paul R. Farnsworth and Kate Hevner Mueller, see 5:252 (1 reference).

D42. Watkins-Farnum Performance Scale: A Standardized Achievement Test for All Band Instruments. For additional information and a review by Herbert D. Wing, see 5:253 (2 references).

D43. Wing Standardised Tests of Musical Intelligence. For additional information and reviews by William S. Larson and Robert W. Lundin, see 6:354 (6 references); see also 5:254 (4 references); for a review by John McLeish of an earlier edition, see 4:230 (6 references).

FOREIGN LANGUAGES

E1. Foreign Language Prognosis Test. For additional information and a review by Wayne D. Fisher (with Bertram B. Masia), see 6:355 (1 reference); for a review by William B. Michael, see 4:232; for a review by Walter V. Kaulfers, see 2:1340 (6 references).

E2. The Graduate School Foreign Language Testing Program. For additional information, see 6:356; for a review of the French test, see 6:377; for a review of the German test, see 6:391.

E3. Iowa Placement Examinations: Foreign Language Aptitude. For additional information and a review by H. E. Brogden, see 3:178 (7 references).

E4. Language Aptitude Test: George Washington University Series. For additional information and a review by H. E. Brogden, see 3:179.

E5. Luria-Orleans Modern Language Prognosis Test. For additional information and a review by Walter V. Kaulfers, see 2:1341 (3 references).

E6. Modern Language Aptitude Test. For additional information and reviews by Wayne D. Fisher (with Bertram B. Masia) and Marion F. Shaycoft, see 6:357 (10 references, 4 excerpts).

ENGLISH

E7. Diagnostic Test for Students of English as a Second Language. For additional information and reviews by Nelson Brooks and Herschel T. Manuel, see 5:255.

E8. English Examinations for Foreign Students. For additional information and reviews by Ralph Bedell, John A. Cox, Jr., and Charles R. Langmuir, see 5:256.

E9. English Language Test for Foreign Students. For additional information and a review by John A. Cox, Jr., see 5:257 (1 reference); for a review by Clarence E. Turner, see 4:234 (2 references).

E10. An English Reading Test for Students of English as a Foreign Language. For additional information and reviews by Ralph Bedell and John A. Cox, Jr., see 5:258.

E11. English Usage Test for Non-Native Speakers of English. For additional information, see 6:358.

E12. Examination in Structure (English as a Foreign Language). For additional information, see 5:260.

E13. Listening Test for Students of English as a Second Language. For additional information, see 6:359.

E14. Michigan Test of English Language Proficiency. For additional information and a review by John B. Carroll, see 6:360.

E15. Oral Rating Form for Rating Language Proficiency in Speaking and Understanding English. For additional information, see 6:361.

E16. Test of Aural Comprehension. For additional information and reviews by Herschel T. Manuel and Clarence E. Turner, see 5:261.

E17. Test of Aural Perception in English for Japanese Students. For additional information, see 6:362.

E18. Test of Aural Perception in English for Latin-American Students. For additional information, see 5:262.

E19. A Vocabulary and Reading Test for Students of English as a Second Language. For additional information, see 6:363.

FRENCH

E20. American Council Alpha French Test. For additional information and reviews by C. E. Ficken and Warren S. Holmes, see 2:1342 (9 references).

E21. American Council Alpha French Test: Aural Comprehension. For additional information and a review by Nelson Brooks, see 2:1343 (3 references).

E22. American Council Beta French Test. For additional information and a review by Bateman Edwards, see 2:1344 (2 references).

E23. American Council French Grammar Test. For additional information and reviews by Harry Heller and Charles Holzwarth, see 2:1345 (5 references).

E24. American Council on Education French Reading Test. For additional information and a review by Charles Holzwarth, see 2:1346 (1 reference); for a review by Nelson Brooks, see 1:984.

E25. Baltimore County French Test. For additional information and reviews by Nelson Brooks and Mary E. Turnbull, see 6:364 (1 reference).

E26. Canadian Achievement Test in French (CATF). For additional information and a review by Mary E. Turnbull, see 6:365 (2 references).

E27. Cohen French Test. For additional information and a review by Mary E. Turnbull, see 4:236.

E28. College Entrance Examination Board Achievement Test: French. For additional information, see 6:366 (4 references); see also 5:263 (2 references); for a review by Walter V. Kaulfers of earlier forms, see 4:237 (7 references). For reviews of the testing program, see 6:760 (2 reviews).

E29. College Entrance Examination Board Achievement Test: French Listening Comprehension. For additional information, see 6:367. For reviews of the testing program, see 6:760 (2 reviews).

E30. College Entrance Examination Board Advanced Placement Examination: French. For additional information, see 6:368 (3 references).

E31. College Entrance Examination Board Placement Tests: French Listening Comprehension Test. For additional information, see 6:369.

E32. College Entrance Examination Board Placement Tests: French Reading Test. For additional information, see 6:370.

E33. Columbia Research Bureau Aural French Test. For additional information and a review by Clarence E. Turner, see 2:1347 (1 reference).

E34. Columbia Research Bureau French Test. For additional information and reviews by Joseph F. Jackson and Laura B. Johnson, see 2:1348 (3 references).

E35. Common Concepts Foreign Language Test: French. For additional information, see 6:371.

E36. Cooperative French Comprehension Test. For additional information and reviews by Joseph F. Jackson and Clarence E. Turner, see 3:180; see also E39.

E37. Cooperative French Listening Comprehension Test. For additional information and reviews by Walter V. Kaulfers and Kathleen N. Perret, see 5:265 (1 reference).

E38. Cooperative French Test. For additional information, see 3:181 (3 references); for reviews by C. E. Ficken, Harry Heller, and Joseph F. Jackson of an earlier form of the advanced level, see 2:1349 (4 references); for reviews by Warren S. Holmes and James B. Tharp of an earlier form of the elementary level, see 2:1350 (6 references); for a review by Nelson Brooks, see 1:985; for a review by Walter V. Kaulfers, see 1:986.

E39. Cooperative French Test: Lower and Higher Levels. For additional information and a review by Elton Hocking, see 4:238 (3 references); for reviews by John H. Meyer and Roland Vinette, see 3:182; for reviews of Part 1, see E36.

E40. Examination in French Grammar. For additional information and a review by Nelson Brooks, see 3:183.

E41. Examination in French Reading Comprehension. For additional information and reviews by Joseph F. Jackson and Clarence E. Turner, see 3:184.

E42. Examination in French Vocabulary. For additional information and a review by Nelson Brooks, see 3:185.

E43. First Year French: State High School Tests for Indiana. For additional information, see 1:987.

E44. First Year French Test. For additional information and reviews by Nelson Brooks and Mary E. Turnbull, see 5:266.

E45. Ford-Hicks French Grammar Completion Tests. For additional information, see 6:372.

E46. French, First Year—Second Semester: State High School Tests for Indiana. For additional information and a review by Clarence E. Turner, see 4:240 (1 reference).

E47. French Grammar Test: Dominion Tests. For additional information and a review by John H. Meyer, see 3:186.

E48. French Life and Culture Test. For additional information and reviews by Bateman Edwards and Clarence E. Turner, see 2:1351 (1 reference).

E49. French I and II: Minnesota High School Achievement Examinations. For additional information, see 6:373; for a review by Mary E. Turnbull of earlier forms, see 5:268; for a review by Elton Hocking, see 4:239.

E50. French Reading Test: Dominion Tests. For additional information and a review by Geraldine Spaulding, see 3:187.

E51. French: Teacher Education Examination Program. For additional information, see 6:374. For a review of the testing program, see 5:543.

E52. French Test (Two-Year Course): Affiliation Testing Program for Catholic Secondary Schools. For additional information and a review by Henry Chauncey, see 6:375. For a review of the complete program, see 6:758.

E53. French Vocabulary Test: Dominion Tests. For additional information and a review by Roland Vinette, see 3:188.

E54. The Graduate Record Examinations Advanced Tests: French. For additional information and a review by Nelson Brooks, see 6:376; for a review by Walter V. Kaulfers, see 5:270. For a review of the testing program, see 5:601.

E55. Graduate School Foreign Language Test: French. For additional information and a review by Clarence E. Turner, see 6:377.

E56. Iowa Placement Examinations: French Training. For additional information and a review by Geraldine Spaulding, see 3:189 (4 references).

E57. Lundeberg-Tharp Audition Test in French. For additional information and a review by Nelson Brooks, see 2:1354 (3 references).

E58. MLA-Cooperative Foreign Language Tests: French. For additional information, see 6:378.

E59. MLA Foreign Language Proficiency Tests for Teachers and Advanced Students: French. For additional information and reviews by Paul Pimsleur and James H. Ricks, Jr., see 6:379 (3 references).

E60. Miller-Davis French Test. For additional information and reviews by Walter V. Kaulfers and James B. Tharp, see 2:1355 (1 reference).

E61. Second Year French: State High School Tests for Indiana. For additional information, see 1:988.

E62. Second Year French Test. For additional information and reviews by Geraldine Spaulding and Clarence E. Turner, see 5:271.

E63. Standard French Test: Vocabulary, Grammar, and Comprehension. For additional information and a review by Laura B. Johnson, see 2:1356 (2 references).

E64. A Standardised French Grammar Test. For additional information, see 6:380 (1 reference); for reviews by Nelson Brooks and Donald G. Burns, see 4:242.

E65. A Standardised French Vocabulary Test. For additional information, see 6:381 (1 reference); for reviews by Nelson Brooks and Donald G. Burns, see 4:243.

GERMAN

E66. AATG German Test. For additional information and reviews by Gilbert C. Kettelkamp and Theodor F. Naumann, see 6:382.

E67. American Council Alpha German Test. For additional information and a review by C. H. Handschin, see 2:1357 (3 references).

E68. American Council on Education German Reading Test. For additional information, see 2:1358; for a review by Curtis C. D. Vail, see 1:999.

E69. College Entrance Examination Board Achievement Test: German. For additional information and a review by Gilbert C. Kettelkamp, see 6:383; for a review by Harold B. Dunkel of an earlier form, see 5:272 (3 references); for a review by Herbert Schueler, see 4:244 (3 references). For reviews of the testing program, see 6:760 (2 reviews).

E70. College Entrance Examination Board Achievement Test: German Listening Comprehension. For additional information and reviews by Harold B. Dunkel and Herbert Schueler, see 6:384 (1 reference). For reviews of the testing program, see 6:760 (2 reviews).

E71. College Entrance Examination Board Advanced Placement Examination: German. For additional information, see 6:385 (5 references); for a review by Herbert Schueler of an earlier form, see 5:273.

E72. College Entrance Examination Board Placement Tests: German Listening Comprehension Test. For additional information, see 6:386.

E73. College Entrance Examination Board Placement Tests: German Reading Test. For additional information, see 6:387.

E74. Columbia Research Bureau German Test. For additional information and a review by Harold B. Dunkel, see 2:1359 (1 reference).

E75. Common Concepts Foreign Language Test: German. For additional information, see 6:388.

E76. Cooperative German Test: Advanced Form. For additional information and a review by Herbert Schueler, see 4:245 (3 references); for a review by Harold B. Dunkel, see 3:190; for a review by C. H. Handschin, see 2:1360 (4 references); for a review by Curtis C. D. Vail, see 1:1000.

E77. Cooperative German Test: Elementary Form. For additional information, see 2:1361; for a review by Curtis C. D. Vail, see 1:1001.

E78. Examination in German Grammar—Lower Level. For additional information and a review by Herbert Schueler, see 3:191.

E79. Examination in German Reading Comprehension—Lower Level. For additional information and a review by Herbert Schueler, see 3:192.

E80. Examination in German Vocabulary—Lower Level. For additional information and a review by Herbert Schueler, see 3:193.

E81. First Year German Test. For additional information and a review by Herbert Schueler, see 5:274.

E82. German: Every Pupil Test. For additional information, see 6:389.

E83. German I and II: Minnesota High School Achievement Examinations. For additional information, see 6:390; for a review by Harold B. Dunkel of earlier forms, see 5:276.

E84. Graduate Record Examinations Advanced German Test. For additional information, see 4:247.

E85. Graduate School Foreign Language Test: German. For additional information and a review by Jack M. Stein, see 6:391.

E86. Lundeberg-Tharp Audition Test in German. For additional information and a review by Harold B. Dunkel, see 3:194.

E87. MLA-Cooperative Foreign Language Tests: German. For additional information, see 6:392.

E88. MLA Foreign Language Proficiency Tests for Teachers and Advanced Students: German. For additional information and reviews by Harold B. Dunkel and Herbert Schueler, see 6:393 (3 references).

GREEK

E89. College Entrance Examination Board Achievement Test: Greek. For additional information, see 6:394; for a review by Konrad Gries of an earlier form, see 5:277. For reviews of the testing program, see 6:760 (2 reviews).

E90. College Entrance Examination Board Placement Tests: Greek Test. For additional information, see 6:395.

HEBREW

E91. College Entrance Examination Board Achievement Test: Hebrew. For additional information, see 6:396. For reviews of the testing program, see 6:760 (2 reviews).

E92. Group Test in Siddur Reading. For additional information, see 3:195.

E93. Hebrew Aptitude Test. For additional information, see 3:196 (1 reference).

E94. Hebrew Intermediate Test. For additional information, see 3:197.

E95. Hebrew Primary Test. For additional information, see 3:198.

E96. Test on the Fundamentals of Hebrew. For additional information, see 6:397.

ITALIAN

E97. College Entrance Examination Board Achievement Test: Italian Listening Comprehension. For additional information, see 6:398. For reviews of the testing program, see 6:760 (2 reviews).

E98. College Entrance Examination Board Achievement Test: Italian Reading and Essay. For additional information, see 6:399. For reviews of the testing program, see 6:760 (2 reviews).

E99. College Entrance Examination Board Placement Tests: Italian Listening Comprehension. For additional information, see 6:400.

E100. College Entrance Examination Board Placement Tests: Italian Test. For additional information, see 6:401.

E101. Cooperative Italian Test. For additional information and a review by Elton Hocking, see 3:199.

E102. Examination in Italian Grammar—Lower Level. For additional information, see 3:200.

E103. Examination in Italian Reading Comprehension—Lower Level. For additional information, see 3:201.

E104. Examination in Italian Vocabulary—Lower Level. For additional information, see 3:202.

E105. MLA-Cooperative Foreign Language Tests: Italian. For additional information, see 6:402.

E106. MLA Foreign Language Proficiency Tests for Teachers and Advanced Students: Italian. For additional information, see 6:403 (3 references).

LATIN

E107. Cicero Test. For additional information and a review by S. D. Atkins, see 2:1363.

E108. College Entrance Examination Board Achievement Test: Latin. For additional information, see 6:404; for a review by Konrad Gries of an earlier form, see 5:280 (1 reference); for a review by Harold B. Dunkel, see 4:250 (2 references). For reviews of the testing program, see 6:760 (2 reviews).

E109. College Entrance Examination Board Advanced Placement Examination: Latin. For additional information, see 6:405.

E110. College Entrance Examination Board Placement Tests: Latin Reading Test. For additional information, see 6:406.

E111. Cooperative Latin Test. For additional information, see 3:204 (1 reference); for reviews by Harold B. Dunkel and John Flagg Gummere of an earlier form of the elementary level, see 2:1365; for a review by S. D. Atkins, see 1:1065; for a review by Norman T. Pratt, Jr. of an earlier form of the advanced level, see 1:1064.

E112. Cooperative Latin Test: Lower and Higher Levels. For additional information and a review by Konrad Gries, see 4:251 (3 references); for a review by C. W. Odell, see 3:205; for a review by Hazel M. Toliver of Part 1, see 3:203.

E113. First- and Second-Year Latin: Every Pupil Test. For additional information, see 6:407.

E114. First Year Latin: Every Pupil Scholarship Test. For additional information, see 6:408.

E115. Godsey Latin Composition Test. For additional information and a review by Konrad Gries, see 4:253 (2 references).

E116. Holtz Vergil Test. For additional information and reviews by W. L. Carr and Norman T. Pratt, Jr., see 2:1366.

E117. Hutchinson Latin Grammar Scale. For additional information and a review by S. D. Atkins, see 2:1367 (2 references).

E118. Iowa Every Pupil Test in Latin Reading Comprehension. For additional information, see 1:1069.

E119. Kansas First Year Latin Test. For additional information, see 5:283; for a review by Hazel M. Toliver of an earlier edition, see 3:206; for a review by John Flagg Gummere, see 2:1368 (1 reference).

E120. Kansas Second Year Latin Test. For additional information and a review by W. C. Kvaraceus, see 4:254; for a review by W. L. Carr, see 2:1369 (1 reference).

E121. Latin I and II: Every Pupil Test. For additional information, see 5:285.

E122. Latin I and II: Minnesota High School Achievement Examinations. For additional information, see 6:409; for a review by Mary E. Turnbull of earlier forms, see 5:286.

E123. Latin Test: State High School Tests for Indiana. For additional information, see 4:252 and 4:257.

E124. Latin Test (Two-Year Course): Affiliation Testing Program for Catholic Secondary Schools. For additional information and a review by Henry Chauncey, see 6:410. For a review of the complete program, see 6:758.

E125. Orleans-Solomon Latin Prognosis Test. For additional information and a review by C. W. Odell, see 3:207.

E126. Powers Diagnostic Latin Test. For additional information and reviews by Paul B. Diederich and Norman T. Pratt, Jr., see 2:1370.

E127. Second Year Latin: Every Pupil Scholarship Test. For additional information, see 6:411.

E128. White Latin Test. For additional information and a review by Konrad Gries, see 4:258 (1 reference).

RUSSIAN

E129. College Entrance Examination Board Achievement Test: Russian. For additional information, see 6:412. For reviews of the testing program, see 6:760 (2 reviews).

E130. College Entrance Examination Board Achievement Test: Russian Listening Comprehension. For additional information, see 6:413. For reviews of the testing program, see 6:760 (2 reviews).

E131. College Entrance Examination Board Placement Tests: Russian Listening Comprehension Test. For additional information, see 6:414.

E132. Graduate School Foreign Language Test: Russian. For additional information, see 6:415.

E133. MLA-Cooperative Foreign Language Tests: Russian. For additional information, see 6:416.

E134. MLA Foreign Language Proficiency Tests for Teachers and Advanced Students: Russian. For additional information and a review by Wayne D. Fisher, see 6:417 (3 references).

SPANISH

E135. American Council Alpha Spanish Test. For additional information and reviews by Lawrence Andrus and Christian O. Arndt, see 2:1371 (4 references).

E136. Baltimore County Spanish Test. For additional information and a review by Mariette Schwarz, see 6:418.

E137. College Entrance Examination Board Achievement Test: Spanish. For additional information, see 6:419 (1 reference); see also 5:287 (1 reference) and 4:259 (3 references). For reviews of the testing program, see 6:760 (2 reviews).

E138. College Entrance Examination Board Achievement Test: Spanish Listening Comprehension. For additional information, see 6:420. For reviews of the testing program, see 6:760 (2 reviews).

E139. College Entrance Examination Board Advanced Placement Examination: Spanish. For additional information, see 6:421 (1 reference).

E140. College Entrance Examination Board Placement Tests: Spanish Listening Comprehension Test. For additional information, see 6:422 (1 reference).

E141. College Entrance Examination Board Placement Tests: Spanish Reading Test. For additional information, see 6:423.

E142. Columbia Research Bureau Spanish Test. For additional information and reviews by James C. Babcock and Harry J. Russell, see 2:1372 (7 references).

E143. Common Concepts Foreign Language Test: Spanish. For additional information, see 6:424.

E144. Cooperative Spanish Test: Elementary and Advanced Forms. For additional information and a review by Christian O. Arndt of the elementary level, see 2:1374; for reviews by Lawrence Andrus and Harry J. Russell of the advanced level, see 2:1373 (3 references); for a review by Walter V. Kaulfers of an earlier form of the elementary level, see 1:1156.

E145. Cooperative Spanish Test: Lower and Higher Levels. For additional information and a review by James B. Tharp, see 4:260 (3 references).

E146. Examination in Spanish Grammar—Lower Level. For additional information and a review by Frederick B. Agard, see 3:208.

E147. Examination in Spanish Reading Comprehension—Lower Level. For additional information and a review by Harry J. Russell, see 3:209.

E148. Examination in Spanish Vocabulary—Lower Level. For additional information, see 3:210.

E149. First Year Spanish Test: State High School Tests for Indiana. For additional information, see 4:261.

E150. Furness Test of Aural Comprehension in Spanish. For additional information, see 4:262; for reviews by Frederick B. Agard and Walter V. Kaulfers, see 3:213.

E151. The Graduate Record Examinations Advanced Tests: Spanish. For additional information, see 6:425. For a review of the testing program, see 5:601.

E152. Iowa Placement Examinations: Spanish Training. For additional information and a review by Harry J. Russell, see 3:212 (2 references).

E153. Kansas First Year Spanish Test. For additional information, see 4:264.

E154. Kansas Second Year Spanish Test. For additional information, see 5:290.

E155. Lundeberg-Tharp Audition Test in Spanish. For additional information and reviews by Frederick B. Agard and Walter V. Kaulfers, see 3:211 (1 excerpt).

E156. MLA-Cooperative Foreign Language Tests: Spanish. For additional information, see 6:426.

E157. MLA Foreign Language Proficiency Tests for Teachers and Advanced Students: Spanish. For additional information and a review by Walter V. Kaulfers, see 6:427 (3 references).

E158. National Spanish Examination. For additional information, see 6:428 (8 references).

E159. Spanish and Latin American Life and Culture. For additional information and a review by Kathleen N. Perret, see 5:291.

E160. Spanish Life and Culture. For additional information and a review by James C. Babcock, see 2:1375; for a review by Walter V. Kaulfers, see 1:1157.

E161. Spanish I and II: Minnesota High School Achievement Examinations. For additional information, see 6:429.

E162. Spanish: Teacher Education Examination Program. For additional information, see 6:430. For a review of the testing program, see 5:543.

E163. Spanish Test (Two-Year Course): Affiliation Testing Program for Catholic Secondary Schools. For additional information and a review by Henry Chauncey, see 6:431. For a review of the complete program, see 6:758.

E164. The Stanford Spanish Tests. For additional information and a review by James B. Tharp, see 4:266.

INTELLIGENCE

GROUP

F1. A.C.E.R. Advanced Test B40. For additional information and a review by C. Sanders, see 5:296 (3 references).

F2. A.C.E.R. Advanced Tests AL and AQ. For additional information and a review by Duncan Howie, see 5:295.

F3. A.C.E.R. Higher Tests. For additional information, see 6:432 (1 reference); for a review by C. Sanders, see 5:297.

F4. A.C.E.R. Intermediate Test A. For additional information, see 6:433.

F5. A.C.E.R. Intermediate Test C. For additional information and a review by James Lumsden, see 5:298 (2 references).

F6. A.C.E.R. Intermediate Test D. For additional information and a review by James Lumsden, see 5:298 (2 references).

F7. A.C.E.R. Junior A Test. For additional information, see 6:434; for a review by R. Winterbourn, see 5:299.

F8. A.C.E.R. Junior B Test. For additional information, see 6:435 (1 reference); for a review by R. Winterbourn, see 5:300.

F9. A.C.E.R. Junior Non-Verbal Test. For additional information and a review by D. A. Pidgeon, see 5:301 (1 reference).

F10. A.C.E.R. Non-Verbal Test. For additional information and a review by F. J. Schonell, see 4:272 (2 references).

F11. A.C.E.R. Test L. For additional information, see 4:273.

F12. A.C.E.R. Test W.N.V. For additional information, see 6:436.

F13. APT Performance Test. For additional information, see 5:302.

F14. Academic Alertness "AA": Individual Placement Series (Area I). For additional information, see 6:437.

F15. Academic Aptitude Test: Non-Verbal Intelligence: Acorn National Aptitude Tests. For additional information, see 5:303; for a review by William B. Schrader, see 4:274.

F16. Academic Aptitude Test: Verbal Intelligence: Acorn National Aptitude Tests. For additional information, see 5:304; for a review by William B. Schrader, see 4:275; for a review by Marion A. Bills, see 3:215.

F17. Adaptability Test. For additional information and a review by John M. Willits, see 5:305 (13 references); for reviews by Anne Anastasi and Marion A. Bills, see 3:216 (3 references).

F18. Advanced Personnel Test. For additional information, see 5:306.

F19. Advanced Test N. For additional information and reviews by A. E. G. Pilliner and C. Sanders, see 5:307.

F20. Akron Classification Test. For additional information and a review by Erwin K. Taylor, see 4:276.

F21. The American College Testing Program Examination. For additional information and reviews by Max D. Engelhart and Warren G. Findley, see 6:1 (14 references, 1 excerpt).

F22. American Council on Education Psychological Examination for College Freshmen. For additional information, see 6:438 (96 references); for reviews by Hanford M. Fowler and William B. Michael, see 5:308 (163 references); see also 4:277 (133 references); for reviews by W. D. Commins and J. P. Guilford of an earlier edition, see 3:217 (95 references); for reviews by Jack W. Dunlap and Robert L. Thorndike, see 2:1377 (48 references); for reviews by Anne Anastasi and David Segel, see 1:1037.

F23. American Council on Education Psychological Examination for High School Students. For additional information and a review by William B. Michael, see 5:309 (1 reference); see also 4:278 (2 references); for a review by Carl I. Hovland of an earlier edition, see 3:218 (7 references); for a review by A. H. Turney, see 2:1378 (2 references); for a review by V. A. C. Henmon, see 1:1038.

F24. American School Intelligence Test. For additional information and reviews by David A. Payne and Frank B. Womer, see 6:439 (1 reference).

F25. Analysis of Relationships. For additional information and reviews by Gustav J. Froehlich and Wimburn L. Wallace, see 6:440 (2 references).

F26. The Army Alpha Examination: First Nebraska Revision. For additional information and a review by Robert G. Demaree (with Louis L. McQuitty), see 4:279 (1 reference); for a review by W. D. Commins, see 1:1039 (1 reference).

F27. Army General Classification Test. For additional information and reviews by Bert A. Goldman and Howard B. Lyman, see 6:441 (5 references); see also 5:310 (17 references); for a review by John T. Dailey, see 4:280 (15 references); see also 3:219 (14 references, 1 excerpt).

F28. Army Group Examination Alpha. For additional information and reviews by John T. Dailey and Willis C. Schaefer, see 4:281 (12 references); see also 3:220 (77 references).

F29. Army Group Examination Alpha: Schrammel-Brannan Revision. For additional information, see 3:220 (77 references); for a review by W. D. Commins, see 1:1040.

F30. Auditory Scale for Group Measurement of General Mental Ability. For additional information, see 1:1041.

F31. [Benge Employment Tests.] For additional information and reviews by Brent Baxter and Marion A. Bills, see 3:221.

F32. Bristol Group Reasoning Tests. For additional information and reviews by Charles Fox and Percival Smith, see 2:1381 (1 reference).

F33. The Business Test. For additional information and reviews by Louis C. Nanassy and James H. Ricks, Jr., see 5:311.

F34. California Analogies and Reasoning Test. For additional information and reviews by John R. Hills and Wimburn L. Wallace, see 6:442 (2 excerpts).

F35. California Capacity Questionnaire. For additional information, see 4:282e; for reviews by Anne Anastasi and Emily T. Burr, see 3:222.

F36. California Short-Form Test of Mental Maturity. For additional information and a review by Julian C. Stanley, see 6:443 (11 references); for a review by Cyril Burt of an earlier edition, see 5:313 (15 references); see also 4:282 (1 excerpt). For reference to reviews of the regular edition, see F37.

F37. California Test of Mental Maturity. For additional information, see 6:444 (30 references); for reviews by Frank S. Freeman and John E. Milholland of an earlier edition, see 5:314 (34 references); see also 4:282 (24 references, 1 excerpt); for a review by Henry E. Garrett, see 3:223 (10 references, 2 excerpts); for reviews by Raymond B. Cattell and F. Kuhlmann, see 2:1384 (5 references, 1 excerpt); for reviews by W. D. Commins, Rudolf Pintner, and

Arthur E. Traxler, see 1:1042 (1 excerpt). For references to reviews of the short form, see F36.

F38. Canadian Academic Aptitude Test. (CAAT). For additional information and reviews by Donald B. Black and George A. Ferguson, see 6:445 (2 references).

F39. Cardall-Miles Test of Mental Alertness. For additional information, see 6:446.

F40. The Carlton Picture Intelligence Test. For additional information and reviews by Elizabeth D. Fraser and S. Rachman, see 6:447.

F41. Carnegie Mental Ability Tests. For additional information and reviews by W. D. Commins and Robert L. Thorndike, see 3:224 (3 references).

F42. Cattell Intelligence Tests. For additional information and a review by I. Macfarlane Smith, see 5:315 (9 references); for a review by Godfrey H. Thomson, see 2:1386 (3 references).

F43. Chicago Non-Verbal Examination. For additional information and a review by Raleigh M. Drake, see 5:316 (10 references); for reviews by Robert G. Bernreuter, Myrtle Luneau Pignatelli, and S. D. Porteus, see 2:1387.

F44. Classification Test 40-A. For additional information and reviews by N. M. Downie and David G. Ryans, see 6:448.

F45. Cole-Vincent Group Intelligence Test for School Entrants. For additional information and a review by Ruth W. Washburn, see 3:226.

F46. College Entrance Examination Board Scholastic Aptitude Test. For additional information and reviews by John E. Bowers and Wayne S. Zimmerman, see 6:449 (79 references); for a review by John T. Dailey of an earlier form, see 5:318 (20 references); for a review by Frederick B. Davis, see 4:285 (22 references).

F47. College Placement Test. For additional information and reviews by Gustav J. Froehlich and David V. Tiedeman, see 5:319.

F48. College Qualification Tests. For additional information and reviews by Ralph F. Berdie and Warren G. Findley, see 6:450 (11 references); for reviews by Gustav J. Froehlich, A. E. G. Pilliner, and David V. Tiedeman, see 5:320.

F49. College Transfer Test. For additional information, see 4:286 (1 reference).

F50. Concept Mastery Test. For additional information, see 6:451 (8 references); for reviews by J. A. Keats and Calvin W. Taylor, see 5:321 (4 references).

F51. Cooperative School and College Ability Tests. For additional information and a review by Russel F. Green, see 6:452 (64 references); for reviews by Frederick B. Davis, Hanford M. Fowler, and Julian C. Stanley, see 5:322 (7 references).

F52. Cotswold Junior Ability Tests. For additional information, see 5:323.

F53. Cotswold Measurement of Mental Ability. For additional information and a review by A. W. Heim, see 5:324.

F54. Culture Fair Intelligence Test. For additional information and reviews by John E. Milholland and Abraham J. Tannenbaum, see 6:453 (15 references); for a review by I. Macfarlane Smith, see 5:343 (11 references); for reviews by Raleigh M. Drake and Gladys C. Schwesinger, see 4:300 (2 references).

F55. Culture-Free Test. For additional information and a review by Raleigh M. Drake, see 4:287; for reviews by L. S. Penrose, Walter C. Shipley, and David Wechsler, see 3:228 (4 references).

F56. The D48 Test. For additional information and reviews by Paul C. Davis and S. S. Dunn, see 6:454 (3 references).

F57. Daneshill Intelligence Test. For additional information and reviews by A. W. Heim and F. W. Warburton, see 5:325.

F58. Davis-Eells Test of General Intelligence or Problem-Solving Ability. For additional information and reviews by Cyril Burt, Raleigh M. Drake, and J. P. Guilford, see 5:326 (36 references).

F59. Dawson Mental Test. For additional information and reviews by Raymond B. Cattell and Percival Smith, see 2:1389; see also 1:1043 (2 excerpts).

F60. Deeside Non-Verbal Reasoning Test: English-Welsh Bilingual Version. For additional information, see 6:455.

F61. Deeside Picture Puzzles. For additional information and reviews by Charlotte E. K. Banks and M. L. Kellmer Pringle, see 5:327.

F62. Detroit Advanced First-Grade Intelligence Test. For additional information and a review by A. M. Jordan, see 2:1392.

F63. Detroit Beginning First-Grade Intelligence Test (Revised). For additional information and a review by Psyche Cattell, see 1:1044 (1 excerpt).

F64. Detroit General Intelligence Examination. For additional information, see 5:328.

F65. [Detroit Intelligence Tests.] For additional information, see 5:329 (9 references); see also 4:288 (2 references); for a review by W. Line, see 2:1393.

F66. The Dominion Group Test of Intelligence. For additional information, see 5:330.

F67. Doppelt Mathematical Reasoning Test. For additional information and a review by W. V. Clemans, see 6:456 (2 references).

F68. Duplex Series of Ability Tests. For additional information and reviews by W. G. Emmett and Stanley D. Nisbet, see 4:289 (2 references, 1 excerpt).

F69. Easel Age Scale. For additional information and reviews by Naomi Stewart and Florence M. Teagarden, see 5:332.

F70. The Essential Intelligence Test. For additional information and a review by R. Winterbourn, see 5:333; for a review by F. W. Warburton, see 4:290.

F71. Figure Reasoning Test: A Non-Verbal Intelligence Test. For additional information and a review by A. W. Heim, see 6:457; for reviews by E. J. G. Bradford and James Maxwell, see 4:291 (1 reference, 1 excerpt).

F72. Fiji Test of General Ability. For additional information, see 2:1395 (2 references).

F73. General Intelligence Test for Africans. For additional information, see 2:1396 (4 references).

F74. General Verbal Practice Tests. For additional information, see 6:458.

F75. Gestalt Continuation Test. For additional information, see 6:459 (3 references).

F76. Gibson's Intelligence Tests. For additional information, see 1:1045.

F77. Glick-Germany Scholastic Aptitude Test. For additional information, see 2:1186.

F78. Goodenough-Harris Drawing Test. For additional information, see 6:460 (43 references); see also 5:335 (34 references); for a review by Naomi Stewart of the original edition, see 4:292 (60 references).

F79. The Graduate Record Examinations Aptitude Test. For additional information and reviews by Robert L. French and Warren W. Willingham, see 6:461 (17 references); for a review by John T. Dailey of an earlier form, see 5:336 (7 references); for reviews by J. P. Guilford and Carl I. Hovland, see 4:293 (2 references). For a review of the testing program, see 5:601.

F80. Group Selective Test No. 1. For additional information and a review by T. R. Miles, see 5:337.

F81. Group Test of Learning Capacity: Dominion Tests. For additional information, see 5:341; for a review by W. G. Emmett, see 4:294 (3 references); for a review by F. T. Tyler, see 3:231.

F82. Group Tests 33 and 33B. For additional information, see 5:339 (9 references); see also 4:295 (2 references).

F83. Group Test 36. For additional information, see 4:296.

F84. Group Test 70. For additional information and a review by George Westby, see 4:297 (5 references).

F85. Group Test 75. For additional information, see 5:338.

F86. Group Test 90A. For additional information and a review by John Liggett, see 5:340.

F87. The Henmon-Nelson Tests of Mental Ability. For additional information and a review by Norman E. Wallen of the college level, see 6:462 (11 references, 1 excerpt); for reviews by D. Welty Lefever and Leona E. Tyler of the other levels, see 5:342 (14 references, 1 excerpt); for a review by H. M. Fowler of an earlier edition, see 4:299 (25 references); for reviews by Anne Anastasi, August Dvorak, Howard Easley, and J. P. Guilford, see 2:1398 (1 excerpt).

F88. Inductive Reasoning Test. For additional information and a review by Charles R. Langmuir, see 3:232.

F89. Intelligence Test: Comprehensive Testing Program. For additional information and a review by W. D. Commins, see 1:869 (2 references).

F90. Inventory No. 2. For additional information, see 6:463.

F91. Jenkins Non-Verbal Test. For additional information, see 5:344 (2 references).

F92. Junior Scholastic Aptitude Test. For additional information and a review by Jerome E. Doppelt, see 6:464 (5 references); see also 5:345 (7 references) and 3:233 (3 references).

F93. Junior School Grading Test. For additional information and a review by E. Patricia Hunt, see 2:1400.

F94. Kelvin Measurement of Ability in Infant Classes. For additional information, see 5:346.

F95. Kelvin Measurement of Mental Ability. For additional information, see 1:1047.

F96. Kentucky Classification Battery. For additional information and a review by David V. Tiedeman of an earlier edition, see 4:301 (1 reference); see also 2:1402 (3 references); for reference to reviews of subtests, see C62 and F97.

F97. Kentucky General Ability Test. For additional information, see 3:234; for a review by Richard Ledgerwood, see 1:1048; see also F96.

F98. The Kingston Test of Intelligence. For additional information and a review by H. J. Sants, see 6:465; for a review by A. W. Heim, see 5:347.

F99. Kingsway Intelligence Tests. For additional information, see 3:235 (1 excerpt); see also 2:1403 (1 excerpt).

F100. Kuhlmann-Anderson Intelligence Tests. For additional information and reviews by William B. Michael and Douglas A. Pidgeon, see 6:466 (11 references, 1 excerpt); see also 5:348 (15 references); for reviews by Henry E. Garrett and David Segel of an earlier edition, see 4:302 (10 references); for reviews by W. G. Emmett and Stanley S. Marzolf, see 3:236 (25 references); for a review by Henry E. Garrett, see 2:1404 (15 references); for reviews by Psyche Cattell, S. A. Courtis, and Austin H. Turney, see 1:1049.

F101. Kuhlmann-Finch Tests. For additional information and reviews by Walter N. Durost, Henry E. Garrett, and Charles O. Neidt, see 5:349 (3 references).

F102. Laycock Mental Ability Test. For additional information and reviews by George A. Ferguson and F. T. Tyler, see 3:237.

F103. The Lorge-Thorndike Intelligence Tests. For additional information, see 6:467 (11 references); for reviews by Frank S. Freeman, John E. Milholland, and D. A. Pidgeon, see 5:350 (6 references).

F104. Lowry-Lucier Reasoning Test Combination. For additional information and reviews by Andrew R. Baggaley and Russel F. Green, see 6:468 (6 references).

F105. Maddox Verbal Reasoning Test. For additional information and reviews by T. R. Miles and A. E. G. Pilliner, see 6:469 (1 excerpt).

F106. Manchester General Ability Test (Senior). For additional information and reviews by A. W. Heim and Arthur B. Royse, see 6:470 (1 reference); for a review by A. E. G. Pilliner of the lower level, see 5:351.

F107. Mental Alertness Test: George Washington University Series. For additional information and a review by J. P. Guilford, see 3:238.

F108. Mill Hill Vocabulary Scale. For additional information and a review by Morton Bortner, see 6:471 (16 references); see also 4:303 (7 references); for a review by David Wechsler, see 3:239 (3 references).

F109. Miller Analogies Test. For additional information and reviews by Lloyd G. Humphreys, William B. Schrader, and Warren W. Willingham, see 6:472 (26 references); for a review by John T. Dailey, see 5:352 (28 references); for reviews by J. P. Guilford and Carl I. Hovland, see 4:304 (16 references).

F110. Mitchell Vocabulary Test. For additional information, see 6:473 (1 reference).

F111. Modified Alpha Examination Form 9. For additional information and a review by Dael Wolfle, see 4:305 (5 references).

F112. [Moray House Intelligence Tests.] For additional information, see 6:474 (13 references) ; see also 5:353 (2 references) ; for a review by Patrick Slater of earlier forms, see 3:241 (2 references) ; for a review by C. Ebblewhite Smith, see 2:1409.

F113. Moray House Picture Test 2. For additional information, see 6:475 ; for reviews by Gertrude Keir and M. L. Kellmer Pringle of the earlier test, see 4:306 (5 references).

F114. Multi-Mental Scale. For additional information and a review by D. A. Worcester, see 3:242 (8 references).

F115. Multi-Racial Picture Intelligence Tests Suitable for Use in African and Asian Schools. For additional information, see 6:476.

F116. N.B. Group Tests. For additional information, see 6:477.

F117. New Rhode Island Intelligence Test. For additional information and a review by Raymond C. Norris, see 5:354 (6 references).

F118. New South African Group Test. For additional information, see 5:355.

F119. Non-Language Multi-Mental Test. For additional information and a review by Carroll A. Whitmer, see 3:243 (1 reference).

F120. Non-Verbal Reasoning Test. For additional information and reviews by James E. Kennedy and David G. Ryans, see 6:478.

F121. Non-Verbal Tests 1–5. For additional information and reviews by T. R. Miles and John Nisbet, see 6:479 (1 reference) ; for a review by Cyril A. Rogers, see 5:356 (1 reference) ; for a review by E. A. Peel of the original edition, see 4:307 (3 references).

F122. Northox Group Intelligence Test. For additional information and a review by E. Patricia Hunt, see 2:1410 ; see also 1:1050 (1 excerpt).

F123. The Ohio Penal Classification Test. For additional information and a review by Norman Eagle, see 5:358.

F124. Ohio State University Psychological Test. For additional information and a review by Cyril J. Hoyt (with W. Wesley Tennyson), see 5:359 (29 references) ; for a review by George A. Ferguson, see 4:308 (23 references) ; for a review by J. P. Guilford, see 3:244 (28 references) ; for reviews by Louis D. Hartson, Theos A. Langlie, and Rudolf Pintner, see 1:1051.

F125. An Orally Presented Group Test of Intelligence for Juniors. For additional information and a review by Elizabeth D. Fraser, see 5:360 (2 references).

F126. O'Rourke General Classification Test, Senior Grade. For additional information and a review by Marion A. Bills, see 3:246 (3 references).

F127. The "Orton" Intelligence Test, No. 4. For additional information, see 1:1052.

F128. Otis Classification Test. For additional information, see 3:247 (3 references, 1 excerpt).

F129. Otis Employment Tests. For additional information, see 4:310.

F130. Otis General Intelligence Examination: Designed Especially for Business Institutions. For additional information and a review by Frederic Kuder, see 3:248.

F131. Otis Group Intelligence Scale. For additional information and a review by D. Welty Lefever, see 6:480 (44 references).

F132. Otis Quick-Scoring Mental Ability Tests. For additional information, see 6:481 (24 references) ; for reviews by D. Welty Lefever and Alfred Yates, see 5:362 (33 references) ; for a review by Frederic Kuder of the earlier forms, see 3:249 (9 references) ; for reviews by F. Kuhlmann and C. Spearman, see 2:1413 ; for reviews by Psyche Cattell and R. Pintner, see 1:1053 (2 excerpts).

F133. Otis Self-Administering Tests of Mental Ability. For additional information, see 5:363 (52 references) ; for a review by Frederic Kuder, see 3:250 (71 references). For the Australian edition, see 2:1412.

F134. PTI-Oral Directions Test. A subtest of F143 which see for a review ; for reviews by Charles D. Flory, Irving Lorge, and William W. Turnbull of the original edition, see 3:245.

F135. Pattern Perception Test. For additional information and a review by Alice W. Heim, see 4:312 (3 references).

F136. The Peel Group Tests of Practical Ability. For additional information and a review by George Westby, see 4:313 (2 references).

F137. Perception of Relations Scales. For additional information and a review by Charles D. Flory, see 3:251.

F138. Performance Alertness "PA" (With Pictures): Individual Placement Series (Area 1). For additional information, see 6:482.

F139. Personal Classification Test. For additional information, see 6:483.

F140. Personnel Classification Test [Henderson]. For additional information and reviews by Brent Baxter and John C. Flanagan, see 3:252.

F141. Personnel Research Institute Classification Test. For additional information and reviews by James R. Glennon and Melvin R. Marks, see 6:484 (2 references).

F142. Personnel Research Institute Factory Series Test. For additional information and a review by N. M. Downie, see 6:485.

F143. Personnel Tests for Industry. For additional information and a review by Erwin K. Taylor, see 5:366 ; for reference to reviews of a subtest, see F134.

F144. Picture Test 1. For additional information, see 6:486 ; for reviews by Charlotte E. K. Banks and M. L. Kellmer Pringle, see 5:367.

F145. Pintner General Ability Tests: Non-Language Series. For additional information and a review by Carroll A. Whitmer, see 3:254.

F146. Pintner General Ability Tests: Verbal Series. For additional information, see 5:368 (10 references) ; for reviews by Stanley S. Marzolf and D. A. Worcester, see 3:255 (13 references) ; see also 2:1416 (3 excerpts).

F147. Pintner Non-Language Primary Mental Test. For additional information and reviews by Psyche Cattell and Carroll A. Whitmer, see 3:256 (6 references).

F148. The Preliminary Scholastic Aptitude Test. For additional information and a review by Wayne S. Zimmerman, see 6:487 (2 references).

F149. [Pressey Classification and Verifying Tests.] For additional information and a review by Walter N. Durost, see 6:488 (11 references).

F150. Primary Verbal Tests. For additional information, see 6:489; for reviews by John Nisbet and F. W. Warburton, see 5:369.

F151. Profion Dealltwriaeth Cyfaddasiad Cymbraeg. For additional information, see 3:257.

F152. Progressive Matrices. For additional information and a review by Morton Bortner, see 6:490 (78 references); see also 5:370 (62 references); for reviews by Charlotte Banks, W. D. Wall, and George Westby, see 4:314 (32 references); for reviews by Walter C. Shipley and David Wechsler of the 1938 edition, see 3:258 (13 references); for a review by T. J. Keating, see 2:1417 (8 references).

F153. Proverbs Test. For additional information and reviews by Eugene L. Gaier and Alfred B. Heilbrun, Jr., see 5:371 (4 references).

F154. Psychological Examination. For additional information and reviews by Howard Easley and D. A. Worcester, see 2:1418; for a review by John C. Flanagan, see 1:1054.

F155. Purdue Non-Language Test. For additional information and reviews by John D. Hundleby and Benjamin Rosner, see 6:491.

F156. Quantitative Evaluative Device. For additional information, see 6:492 (1 reference).

F157. Quick-Scoring Group Test of Learning Capacity: Dominion Tests. For additional information and reviews by Donald B. Black and George A. Ferguson, see 6:493.

F158. Reasoning Tests for Higher Levels of Intelligence. For additional information and a review by Reginald R. Dale, see 5:374.

F159. Revised Alpha Examination, Forms 5 and 7. For additional information and a review by Dael Wolfle, see 4:315 (4 references).

F160. Revised Alpha Examination, Form 6. For additional information and reviews by Edwin R. Henry and Dael Wolfle, see 4:316 (1 reference).

F161. Revised Beta Examination. For additional information and a review by Bert A. Goldman, see 6:494 (13 references); see also 5:375 (14 references); for reviews by Raleigh M. Drake and Walter C. Shipley, see 3:259 (5 references); for reviews by S. D. Porteus and David Wechsler, see 2:1419 (4 references).

F162. Revision of Army Alpha Examination. For additional information and reviews by Edward E. Cureton and Edwin R. Henry, see 4:317 (3 references).

F163. The Ryburn Group Intelligence Tests. For additional information, see 2:1421.

F164. SRA College Classification Tests. For additional information, see 5:376.

F165. SRA Non-Verbal Form. For additional information and a review by W. D. Commins, see 4:318; see also 3:261 (1 excerpt).

F166. SRA Tests of Educational Ability. For additional information and reviews by J. Stanley Ahmann and John E. Horrocks, see 6:495 (1 reference, 1 excerpt); for reviews by Joshua A. Fishman, William B. Michael, and E. A. Peel of the tests for grades 9–12, see 5:377.

F167. [SRA] Tests of General Ability. For additional information and reviews by John E. Horrocks and Richard E. Schutz, see 6:496 (1 excerpt).

F168. SRA Verbal Form. For additional information, see 5:378; for reviews by W. D. Commins and Willis C. Schaefer, see 4:319.

F169. Safran Culture Reduced Intelligence Test. For additional information, see 6:497 (1 reference).

F170. The Scholarship Qualifying Test. For additional information and reviews by Lee J. Cronbach and Roger T. Lennon, see 5:379.

F171. Scholastic Mental Ability Tests. For additional information and reviews by Walter N. Durost and Alexander G. Wesman, see 5:380.

F172. School Aptitude Test: Thanet Mental Tests. For additional information and a review by C. Ebblewhite Smith, see 2:1422.

F173. Schrammel General Ability Test. For additional information, see 6:498; for a review by Henry E. Garrett, see 5:381.

F174. Schubert General Ability Battery. For additional information and a review by William B. Schrader, see 5:382.

F175. Scovill Classification Test. For additional information and reviews by Robert G. Bernreuter and Edward E. Cureton, see 4:320 (1 reference).

F176. Secondary Verbal Tests 1–2. For additional information and a review by Stanley Nisbet of test 1, see 6:499.

F177. Ship Destination Test. For additional information and a review by William B. Schrader, see 6:500 (8 references); for a review by C. J. Adcock, see 5:383.

F178. The Simplex GNV Intelligence Tests. For additional information and a review by Philip M. Levy, see 6:501 (2 references).

F179. The Simplex Group Intelligence Scale. For additional information and a review by James Mainwaring, see 5:385.

F180. [The Simplex Junior Intelligence Tests.] For additional information and a review by Arthur B. Royse, see 5:386 (1 reference); see also 4:322 (2 references).

F181. Sleight Non-Verbal Intelligence Test. For additional information, see 6:502 (1 reference); for reviews by John C. Daniels and M. L. Kellmer Pringle, see 5:387.

F182. The Southend Test of Intelligence. For additional information and a review by James Mainwaring, see 5:388; for a review by Gertrude Keir of the original edition, see 4:323 (1 reference); see also 2:1423 (1 excerpt).

F183. Survey of Mental Maturity: California Survey Series. For additional information and a review by Naomi Stewart, see 6:503.

F184. Terman-McNemar Test of Mental Ability. For additional information, see 4:324 (12 references); for reviews by Carl I. Hovland and Robert L. Thorndike, see 3:263 (25 references); for reviews by Anne Anastasi and Howard Easley of the original edition, see 2:1424 (25 references).

F185. Test of General Knowledge. For additional information, see 2:1425 (1 reference).

F186. Test of Learning Ability. For additional information, see 6:504 (2 references).

F187. Test of Non-Verbal Reasoning. For additional information, see 6:505 (3 references).

F188. Test of Word-Number Ability. For additional information and reviews by I. David Satlow and John M. Willits, see 5:389 (1 reference); for a review by Jane Loevinger of an earlier edition, see 4:333.

F189. Tests AH4 and AH5. For additional information and a review by John Liggett, see 6:506; for reviews by George A. Ferguson of Test AH4 and J. A. Keats of Test AH5, see 5:390 (11 references).

F190. Tests of General Ability: Cooperative Inter-American Tests. For additional information, see 6:507; for reviews by Raleigh M. Drake and Walter N. Durost, see 4:325 (8 references).

F191. Thurstone Test of Mental Alertness. For additional information and a review by Joshua A. Fishman, see 5:391; see also 4:326 (3 references); for reviews by Anne Anastasi and Emily T. Burr of an earlier edition, see 3:265.

F192. The Tomlinson Junior School Test. For additional information and a review by John C. Daniels, see 5:392.

F193. Unit Scales of Aptitude. For additional information and a review by Herschel T. Manuel, see 2:1428.

F194. V.G.C. Intelligence Indicator. For additional information and a review by George A. Ferguson, see 4:327.

F195. Verbal and Non-Verbal Test 1. For additional information and a review by T. R. Miles, see 5:393.

F196. Verbal Capacity Sampler. For additional information, see 5:394.

F197. Verbal Intelligence Test. For additional information and a review by John P. Foley, Jr., see 5:395; for a review by William B. Schrader, see 4:329.

F198. The Verbal Power Test of Concept Equivalence. For additional information, see 6:508 (3 references).

F199. Verbal Reasoning. For additional information and reviews by James E. Kennedy and David G. Ryans, see 6:509.

F200. Verbal Test (Adv.). For additional information and reviews by J. S. Lawes and John Nisbet, see 6:510.

F201. Verbal Tests 1-2, 4-13. For additional information and a review by Arthur B. Royse, see 6:511 (1 reference).

F202. Vocabulary Tests. For additional information and a review by John Nisbet, see 5:398.

F203. Wesman Personnel Classification Test. For additional information, see 5:399 (8 references); for reviews by John C. Flanagan and Erwin K. Taylor, see 4:331 (3 references); see also 3:253 (1 excerpt).

F204. The "West Riding" Tests of Mental Ability. For additional information and a review by Ll. Wynn Jones, see 2:1430.

F205. "West Yorkshire" Group Test of Intelligence. For additional information, see 4:332.

F206. The Western Personnel Tests. For additional information and reviews by Lewis E. Albright and Erwin K. Taylor, see 6:512.

F207. Willis-Smith Advanced Mental Test. For additional information and reviews by Harold H. Bixler and F. T. Tyler, see 3:268.

F208. Wonderlic Personnel Test. For additional information and reviews by N. M. Downie and Marvin D. Dunnette, see 6:513 (17 references); see also 5:400 (59 references); for reviews by H. E. Brodgen, Charles D. Flory, and Irving Lorge, see 3:269 (7 references); see also 2:1415 (2 references).

INDIVIDUAL

F209. Alexander Performance Scale: A Performance Scale for the Measurement of Practical Ability. For additional information and a review by H. Gwynne Jones, see 6:514 (3 references); for a review by Charles A. Strickland, see 4:334 (4 references); for a review by John Cohen, see 3:270 (1 reference, 2 excerpts); for a review by J. M. Blackburn, see 2:1376 (3 references).

F210. Arthur Point Scale of Performance Tests. For additional information and a review by William R. Grove, see 4:335 (12 references); for reviews by Andrew W. Brown and Carroll A. Whitmer, see 2:1379 (16 references, 1 excerpt); see also 3:271 (19 references, 1 excerpt).

F211. California First-Year Mental Scale. For additional information and a review by Florence L. Goodenough, see 2:1382 (1 reference).

F212. California Preschool Mental Scale. For additional information and reviews by B. M. Castner and Florence L. Goodenough, see 2:1383 (1 reference).

F213. Canadian Intelligence Examination. For additional information and a review by Gwen F. Arnold, see 4:336; see also 3:272 (1 reference, 2 excerpts).

F214. Carl Hollow Square Scale. For additional information and a review by Grace H. Kent, see 3:273 (3 references); for a review by T. J. Keating, see 2:1385 (2 references).

F215. Cattell Infant Intelligence Scale. For additional information, see 6:515 (22 references); for reviews by Florence M. Teagarden and Beth L. Wellman, see 3:281 (1 excerpt).

F216. Children's Picture Information Test. For additional information and reviews by Dorothy Eichorn and T. Ernest Newland, see 6:516 (2 references).

F217. Columbia Mental Maturity Scale. For additional information and reviews by Marshall S. Hiskey and T. Ernest Newland, see 6:517 (22 references); see also 5:402 (13 references).

F218. Cornell-Coxe Performance Ability Scale. For additional information and reviews by Francis N. Maxfield and Carroll A. Whitmer, see 2:1388 (3 references).

F219. Crichton Vocabulary Scale. For additional information and a review by Morton Bortner, see 6:518 (1 reference); for reviews by Charlotte Banks and W. D. Wall, see 4:337.

F220. Curtis Classification Form. For additional information and a review by Harold G. Seashore, see 4:338.

F221. Dearborn-Anderson Formboards 2 and 2b. For additional information and a review by Grace H. Kent, see 2:1390 (4 references).

F222. Dearborn Formboard 3. For additional information and a review by Grace H. Kent, see 2:1391 (8 references).

F223. Detroit Kindergarten Test. For additional information and reviews by Psyche Cattell and Ruth W. Washburn, see 3:274 (1 reference).

F224. Detroit Tests of Learning Aptitude. For additional information, see 5:403; for a review by F. L. Wells, see 3:275 (1 reference); for reviews by Anne Anastasi and Henry Feinberg of an earlier edition, see 1:1058 (1 excerpt).

F225. Diagnostic Performance Tests. For additional information and a review by H. Gwynne Jones, see 6:519 (1 reference).

F226. English Picture Vocabulary Test. For additional information and reviews by L. B. Birch and Philip M. Levy, see 6:520.

F227. Ferguson Formboards. For additional information and a review by Grace H. Kent, see 2:1394 (12 references).

F228. Full-Range Picture Vocabulary Test. For additional information, see 6:521 (30 references); for reviews by William D. Altus and William M. Cruickshank, see 4:340 (10 references).

F229. Gesell Developmental Schedules. For additional information and a review by Emmy E. Werner, see 6:522 (27 references); see also 4:341 (5 references); for reviews by Nancy Bayley and Florence M. Teagarden, see 3:276 (28 references).

F230. The Griffiths Mental Development Scale for Testing Babies From Birth to Two Years. For additional information and a review by C. B. Hindley, see 6:523 (4 references); for a review by Nancy Bayley, see 5:404 (3 references).

F231. Herring Revision of the Binet-Simon Tests. For additional information and a review by Andrew W. Brown, see 2:1399 (13 references).

F232. The Immediate Test: A Quick Verbal Intelligence Test. For additional information and reviews by Jerome E. Doppelt and Ivan Norman Mensh, see 4:342 (1 reference).

F233. Intelligence Tests for Children. For additional information and reviews by Elizabeth D. Fraser and G. A. V. Morgan, see 5:405 (2 references); see also 4:343 (3 references) and 3:283 (1 excerpt).

F234. Kahn Intelligence Tests. For additional information, see 6:524 (2 references).

F235. Kent Series of Emergency Scales. For additional information and a review by Ivan Norman Mensh, see 4:346 (8 references); for a review by Charles N. Cofer, see 3:284 (26 references).

F236. Kent-Shakow Formboard. For additional information and a review by Milton L. Blum, see 3:660 (11 references); for a review by Lorene Teegarden, see 2:1401 (9 references).

F237. The Leiter Adult Intelligence Scale. For additional information and reviews by Paul C. Davis and Frank B. Jex, see 6:525 (15 references, 1 excerpt); for reviews by Harold A. Delp and Herschel Manuel of the original edition, see 4:350 (4 references, 1 excerpt). For reviews of subtests, see 4:355 (1 review, 1 excerpt), 4:347 (1 excerpt), and 4:348 (1 excerpt).

F238. Leiter International Performance Scale. For additional information and a review by Emmy E. Werner, see 6:526 (10 references); see also 5:408 (17 references); for a review by Gwen F. Arnold, see 4:349 (25 references, 1 excerpt).

F239. Linfert-Hierholzer Scale for Measuring the Mental Development of Infants During the First Year of Life. For additional information and a review by Nancy Bayley, see 3:285 (6 references).

F240. Merrill-Palmer Scale of Mental Tests. For additional information and a review by Marjorie P. Honzik, see 6:527 (16 references); for reviews by Nancy Bayley, B. M. Castner, Florence L. Goodenough, and Florence M. Teagarden, see 2:1406 (13 references).

F241. Minnesota Preschool Scale. For additional information and a review by Marjorie P. Honzik, see 6:528 (3 references); see also 4:351 (2 references); for a review by Beth L. Wellman, see 3:286 (2 references); for reviews by Rachel Stutsman Ball, Nancy Bayley, and Florence M. Teagarden of the original edition, see 2:1407 (3 references).

F242. Modification of the Kent-Shakow Formboard. For additional information, see 2:1408 (3 references).

F243. Nebraska Test of Learning Aptitude. For additional information and a review by William Sloan, see 5:409 (8 references); for a review by Mildred C. Templin of an earlier edition, see 4:353 (1 reference); see also 3:289 (3 references).

F244. Non-Verbal Intelligence Test for Deaf and Hearing Subjects. For additional information and a review by J. S. Lawes, see 6:529 (2 references).

F245. The Northwestern Intelligence Tests: For Measuring Adaptation to the Physical and Social Environment. For additional information and a review by Nancy Bayley, see 5:411; for a review by Mildred C. Templin, see 4:354 (9 references, 1 excerpt).

F246. Ontario School Ability Examination. For additional information and a review by W. Line, see 2:1411 (2 references).

F247. The Passalong Test: A Performance Test of Intelligence. For additional information and reviews by James Drever, T. J. Keating, and Grace H. Kent, see 2:1414 (5 references). For reference to additional reviews, see F209.

F248. Pathways Test. For additional information and a review by George K. Bennett, see 4:355 (1 reference, 1 excerpt).

F249. Peabody Picture Vocabulary Test. For additional information and reviews by Howard B. Lyman and Ellen V. Piers, see 6:530 (21 references).

F250. Performance Tests of Intelligence: A Series of Non-Linguistic Tests for Deaf and Normal Children. For additional information, see 3:290 (2 references).

F251. Pictorial Test of Intelligence. For additional information, see 6:531 (2 references).

F252. Pintner-Paterson Scale of Performance Tests. For additional information and a review by Francis N. Maxfield, see 1:1061 (1 reference).

F253. The Porteus Maze Test. For additional information, see 6:532 (38 references); see also 5:412 (28 references); for reviews by C. M. Louttit and Gladys C. Schwesinger, see 4:356 (56 references).

F254. Preliminary Test of Intelligence: A Brief Test of Adult Intelligence Designed for Psychiatric Examiners. For additional information, see 3:291.

F255. Quick Screening Scale of Mental Development. For additional information and a review by Boyd R. McCandless, see 6:533.

F256. The Quick Test. For additional information and reviews by Boyd R. McCandless and Ellen V. Piers, see 6:534 (3 references).

F257. Slosson Intelligence Test (SIT). For additional information, see 6:535.

F258. Stanford-Binet Intelligence Scale. For additional information and a review by Elizabeth D. Fraser, see 6:536 (110 references, 5 excerpts); for reviews by Mary R. Haworth and Norman D. Sundberg of the second edition, see 5:413 (127 references); for a review by Boyd R. McCandless, see 4:358 (142 references); see also 3:292 (217 references) and 2:1420 (134 references, 3 excerpts); for reviews by Francis N. Maxfield, J. W. M. Rothney, and F. L. Wells, see 1:1062.

F259. Tests of Mental Development. For additional information and reviews by Grace H. Kent, Francis N. Maxfield, Myrtle Luneau Pignatelli, and F. L. Wells, see 2:1426 (1 reference, 2 excerpts).

F260. Van Alstyne Picture Vocabulary Test. For additional information and reviews by Mary R Haworth and Ellen V. Piers, see 6:537 (6 references); for a review by Ruth W. Washburn of the original edition, see 3:296.

F261. Wechsler Adult Intelligence Scale. For additional information, see 6:538 (180 references); for reviews by Nancy Bayley and Wilson H. Guertin, see 5:414 (42 references). For reference to reviews of an earlier edition, see F262.

F262. Wechsler-Bellevue Intelligence Scale. For additional information, see 6:539 (123 references); see also 5:415 (254 references); for reviews by Murray Aborn and William D. Altus, see 4:361 (250 references); for a review by Robert I. Watson, see 3:298 (119 references); for a review by F. L. Wells, see 2:1429 (2 references, 2 excerpts). For reference to reviews of a later edition, see F261.

F263. Wechsler Intelligence Scale for Children. For additional information and a review by Alvin G. Burstein, see 6:540 (155 references); for reviews by Elizabeth D. Fraser, Gerald R. Patterson, and Albert I. Rabin, see 5:416 (111 references); for reviews by James M. Anderson, Harold A. Delp, and Boyd R. McCandless, see 4:363 (22 references, 1 excerpt).

F264. Williams Intelligence Test for Children With Defective Vision. For additional information and a review by T. Ernest Newland, see 6:541 (2 references).

SPECIFIC

F265. Alternate Uses. For additional information, see 6:542 (7 references).

F266. Benton Visual Retention Test. For additional information, see 6:543 (22 references); for a review by Nelson G. Hanawalt, see 5:401 (5 refer-

ences); for reviews by Ivan Norman Mensh, Joseph Newman, and William Schofield of the original edition, see 4:360 (3 references); see also 3:297 (1 excerpt).

F267. Christensen-Guilford Fluency Tests. For additional information and reviews by J. A. Keats and Albert S. Thompson, see 6:544 (4 references).

F268. Closure Flexibility (Concealed Figures). For additional information and a review by Leona E. Tyler, see 6:545 (4 references).

F269. Closure Speed (Gestalt Completion). For additional information and a review by Leona E. Tyler, see 6:546 (3 references).

F270. Consequences. For additional information and a review by Goldine C. Gleser, see 6:547 (13 references).

F271. Decorations. For additional information, see 6:548 (1 reference).

F272. The FR-CR Test. For additional information and a review by William S. Kogan, see 4:339 (1 reference).

F273. Illinois Test of Psycholinguistic Abilities. For additional information, see 6:549 (22 references).

F274. Jensen Alternation Board. For additional information, see 6:550 (2 references).

F275. Kit of Reference Tests for Cognitive Factors. For additional information, see 6:551.

F276. The Leiter Adaptation of Arthur's Stencil Design Test. For additional information, see 4:347 (1 reference, 1 excerpt).

F277. The Leiter Adaptation of the Painted Cube Test. For additional information, see 4:348 (1 reference, 1 excerpt).

F278. Making Objects. For additional information, see 6:552 (1 reference).

F279. Marianne Frostig Developmental Test of Visual Perception. For additional information and reviews by James M. Anderson and Mary C. Austin, see 6:553 (7 references).

F280. Match Problems. For additional information, see 6:554 (7 references).

F281. Nufferno Tests of Speed and Level. For additional information, see 6:555 (4 references); for reviews by John Liggett and E. A. Peel, see 5:357 (3 references).

F282. Perceptual Speed (Identical Forms). For additional information and a review by Leroy Wolins, see 6:556.

F283. Pertinent Questions. For additional information, see 6:557 (3 references).

F284. Possible Jobs. For additional information, see 6:558 (1 reference).

F285. The Rutgers Drawing Test. For additional information, see 6:559 (2 references).

F286. Stencil Design Test. For additional information and a review by Benjamin Balinsky, see 4:359 (4 references); for a review by James M. Anderson, see 3:295.

F287. Subsumed Abilities Test. For additional information and a review by Naomi Stewart, see 6:560.

F288. Time Appreciation Test. For additional information and reviews by E. J. G. Bradford and Charles N. Cofer, see 3:266 (2 references).

F289. Wechsler Memory Scale. For additional information, see 6:561 (9 references); for reviews

by Ivan Norman Mensh and Joseph Newman, see 4:364 (6 references); for a review by Kate Levine Kogan, see 3:302 (3 references).

F290. Word Fluency. For additional information and a review by James E. Kennedy, see 6:562.

MATHEMATICS

G1. Ability to Do Quantitative Thinking: The Iowa Tests of Educational Development, Test 4. For additional information and a review by Peter A. Lappan, Jr., see 6:579. For reviews of the complete battery, see 6:14 (2 reviews), 5:17 (2 reviews), 4:17 (1 review), and 3:12 (3 reviews).

G2. Business Mathematics: Every Pupil Scholarship Test. For additional information, see 6:563.

G3. California Mathematics Test. The advanced level of test G131; for additional information, see 6:564 (9 references); for a review by Robert D. North of test G131, see 5:468. For reviews of the complete battery, see 6:3 (2 reviews), 5:2 (1 review), 4:2 (3 reviews), 3:15 (1 review), 2:1193 (2 reviews), and 1:876 (1 review, 1 excerpt).

G4. Canadian Achievement Test in Mathematics (CATM). For additional information and a review by Frances Crook Morrison, see 6:565 (2 references).

G5. Canadian Achievement Test in Technical and Commercial Mathematics (CATTCM). For additional information and a review by Stanley Clark, see 6:566 (2 references).

G6. Canadian Mathematics Achievement Test (CMAT). For additional information and reviews by Stanley Clark and Frances Crook Morrison, see 6:567 (2 references).

G7. College Entrance Examination Board Achievement Test: Advanced Mathematics. For additional information and a review by Saunders Mac Lane, see 6:568 (3 references); see also 5:417 (3 references); for a review by Paul L. Dressel of earlier forms, see 4:367 (4 references). For reviews of the testing program, see 6:760 (2 reviews).

G8. College Entrance Examination Board Achievement Test: Intermediate Mathematics. For additional information and a review by Paul L. Dressel, see 6:569 (1 reference); see also 5:418 (3 references); for a review by Paul J. Blommers of earlier forms, see 4:368 (2 references). For reviews of the testing program, see 6:760 (2 reviews).

G9. College Entrance Examination Board Advanced Placement Examination: Mathematics. For additional information, see 6:570 (4 references); for a review by Paul L. Dressel of an earlier form, see 5:419.

G10. College Entrance Examination Board Placement Tests: Advanced Mathematics Test. An inactive form of test G7; for additional information, see 6:571; for references to reviews, see G7.

G11. College Entrance Examination Board Placement Tests: Intermediate Mathematics

Test. An inactive form of test G8; for additional information, see 6:572; for references to reviews, see G8.

G12. Cooperative College Mathematics Test for First-Year Courses. For additional information and reviews by Albert A. Bennett and Nathan Morrison, see 3:304.

G13. Cooperative General Achievement Tests: Test 3, Mathematics. For additional information, see 6:573 (4 references); for a review by John F. Randolph of earlier forms, see 3:316. For reviews of the complete battery, see 6:7 (1 review), 5:6 (1 review), 4:5 (1 review), and 3:3 (1 review).

G14. Cooperative General Mathematics Test for College Students. For additional information and a review by Tomlinson Fort; for a review by M. W. Richardson, see 1:1071.

G15. Cooperative General Mathematics Test for High School Classes. For additional information and a review by L. B. Kinney, see 2:1432 (1 reference); for a review by Maurice Hartung of an earlier form, see 1:1072.

G16. Cooperative Mathematics Pre-Test for College Students. For additional information and a review by E. P. Starke, see 4:369; for reviews by M. W. Richardson and S. S. Wilks of earlier forms, see 1:1073.

G17. Cooperative Mathematics Tests for Grades 7, 8, and 9. For additional information and a review by Gordon Fifer, see 5:421 (1 reference); see also 4:370 (2 references); for a review by M. L. Hartung of earlier forms, see 3:305 (1 reference); for reviews by Richard M. Drake, Judson W. Foust, and G. M. Ruch, see 2:1433 (2 references).

G18. Cooperative Test in Secondary School Mathematics: Higher Level. For additional information and a review by E. H. C. Hildebrandt, see 3:303.

G19. Davis Test of Functional Competence in Mathematics. For additional information and reviews by Paul L. Dressel and Tom A. Lamke, see 5:422 (2 references).

G20. ERB Mathematics Tests. For additional information, see 6:574 (2 references).

G21. Foust-Schorling Test of Functional Thinking in Mathematics. For additional information and reviews by William Betz and M. L. Hartung, see 3:306 (1 reference, 2 excerpts).

G22. Functional Evaluation in Mathematics. For additional information and a review by Charles S. Ross, see 4:372.

G23. General Mathematical Ability: Tests of General Educational Development, Test 5. For additional information, see 5:426. For reviews of the complete battery, see 5:27 (1 review), 4:26 (1 review), and 3:20 (2 reviews).

G24. General Mathematics: Every Pupil Scholarship Test. For additional information, see 6:575.

G25. General Mathematics: Every Pupil Test. For additional information, see 6:576.

G26. General Mathematics: Minnesota High School Achievement Examinations. For additional information and a review by Gerald L. Ericksen, see 6:577.

G27. Graded Arithmetic-Mathematics Test. For additional information and a review by Stanley Nisbet, see 5:476.

G28. The Graduate Record Examinations Advanced Tests: Mathematics. For additional information and a review by Paul C. Rosenbloom, see 6:578; for a review by Eric F. Gardner of an earlier form, see 5:427 (1 reference). For a review of the testing program, see 5:601.

G29. Iowa Placement Examinations: Mathematics Aptitude. For additional information and reviews by Edmund P. Churchill and Paul L. Dressel, see 3:308 (18 references).

G30. Iowa Placement Examinations: Mathematics Training. For additional information and reviews by Edmund P. Churchill and Paul L. Dressel, see 3:309 (8 references).

G31. Junior High School Mathematics Test: Acorn Achievement Tests. For additional information and a review by Myron F. Rosskopf, see 5:429; for a review by William Betz, see 3:310.

G32. Junior Math Reasoning Test. For additional information, see 6:580.

G33. Kansas Mathematics Test. For additional information and a review by Paul Blommers, see 5:430.

G34. Kentucky Mathematics Test. For additional information, see 3:311; see also F96.

G35. Mathematical Ability Test. For additional information, see 1:1075.

G36. Mathematical Literacy for High School Seniors: A Test of Basic Skills and Abilities: [Ohio Senior Survey Tests]. For additional information, see 5:431.

G37. Mathematics: Every Pupil Test. For additional information, see 6:581.

G38. Mathematics: Minnesota High School Achievement Examinations. For additional information, see 6:582.

G39. Mathematics: National Teacher Examinations. For additional information and a review by Paul Blommers, see 6:583. For reviews of the testing program, see 6:700 (1 review), 5:538 (3 reviews), and 4:802 (1 review).

G40. Mathematics: Teacher Education Examination Program. An inactive form of test G39; for additional information, see 6:584; for a reference to a review, see G39. For a review of the testing program, see 5:543.

G41. Mathematics Test (Adv.). For additional information and a review by Kenneth Lovell, see 6:585.

G42. Mathematics Test: Ohio Senior Survey Tests. For additional information and a review by William G. Mollenkopf, see 3:313.

G43. Mathematics Test 1. For additional information and a review by Jack Wrigley, see 5:436.

G44. Metropolitan Achievement Tests: High School Mathematics Tests. For additional information, see 6:586. For reviews of the complete battery, see 6:15 (3 reviews), 4:18 (1 review), 2:1189 (2 reviews), and 1:874 (3 reviews).

G45. Minimum Essentials for Modern Mathematics. For additional information and a review by Gerald L. Ericksen, see 6:587.

G46. The Morgan Achievement Test in Mathematics for Employee Selection. For additional information and a review by Marion F. Shaycoft, see 5:437.

G47. Portland Prognostic Tests for Mathematics. For additional information and a review by Cyril J. Hoyt, see 6:588 (1 reference).

G48. Problems in Quantitative Thinking. For additional information, see 1:1077.

G49. Purdue Industrial Mathematics Test. For additional information and reviews by Clyde H. Coombs and C. C. Upshall, see 3:314.

G50. The Purdue Mathematics Training Test: Arithmetic and Algebra. For additional information and a review by Lynnette B. Plumlee, see 6:589 (8 references).

G51. Rasmussen General Mathematics Test. For additional information and a review by William G. Mollenkopf, see 3:315 (1 reference).

G52. Sequential Tests of Educational Progress: Mathematics. For additional information and reviews by Arthur Mittman and Douglas A. Pidgeon, see 6:590 (5 references); for reviews by Paul L. Dressel, Gordon Fifer, and Tom A. Lamke, see 5:438. For reviews of the complete battery, see 6:25 (2 reviews) and 5:24 (2 reviews, 1 excerpt).

G53. Snader General Mathematics Test. For additional information, see 5:439; for reviews by Paul J. Blommers and Howard F. Fehr, see 4:378.

G54. Solution of Mathematical Problems. For additional information, see 1:1078.

G55. Survey of Mathematics Achievement: California Survey Series. For additional information and reviews by William R. Crawford and Arthur Mittman, see 6:591.

G56. Survey Test in Mathematics: Cooperative General Achievement Test, Part 3. For additional information and a review by Paul R. Rider, see 2:1434; for reviews by Arnold Dresden, Palmer O. Johnson, M. W. Richardson, and S. S. Wilks, see 1:870.

G57. T.C. Mathematics Test. For additional information, see 6:592.

G58. Test of Mathematical Fundamentals for Grades 7 to 12. For additional information and a review by Frances E. Crook [Morrison], see 5:440.

ALGEBRA

G59. Ability for Algebra: Fife Tests of Ability, Test 3. For additional information and a review by William G. Mollenkopf, see 4:380 (3 references). For reviews of the complete battery, see 4:713 (1 review) and 3:8 (1 review).

G60. Advanced Algebra: Minnesota High School Achievement Examinations. For additional information and reviews by Lynnette B. Plumlee and James P. Rizzo, see 6:593; for a review by Emma Spaney of earlier forms, see 5:442.

G61. Advanced Algebra Test: State High School Tests for Indiana. For additional information, see 4:382.

G62. Algebra: Cooperative Mathematics Tests. For additional information and a review by Paul Blommers, see 6:594.

G63. Algebra Prognosis Test. For additional information and reviews by Paul J. Blommers and William G. Mollenkopf, see 4:383.

G64. Algebra Readiness Test. For additional information and a review by Harold Gulliksen, see 4:384.

G65. Algebra Test for Engineering and Science: National Achievement Tests. For additional information and a review by Peter A. Lappan, Jr., see 6:595.

G66. Blyth Second-Year Algebra Test. For additional information and reviews by Paul Blommers and Myron F. Rosskopf, see 5:443.

G67. Breslich Algebra Survey Test. For additional information and a review by John R. Clark, see 2:1435.

G68. California Algebra Aptitude Test. For additional information, see 5:444; for a review by William G. Mollenkopf, see 4:385; for a review by David Segel, see 3:320.

G69. Columbia Research Bureau Algebra Test. For additional information and a review by Stanley Clark, see 4:386; for reviews by L. B. Kinney and S. S. Wilks, see 2:1436 (1 reference).

G70. Colvin-Schrammel Algebra Test. For additional information and a review by J. H. Minnick, see 2:1437; for a review by Maurice Hartung, see 1:879.

G71. Cooperative Algebra Test: Elementary Algebra Through Quadratics. For additional information and a review by Stanley Clark, see 4:387 (4 references); for a review by W. C. Brenke of earlier forms, see 3:321; for reviews by Harl D. Douglass and Harold Fawcett, see 2:1438; for reviews by William Betz, Helen Walker, and S. S. Wilks, see 1:880.

G72. Cooperative Intermediate Algebra Test: Quadratics and Beyond. For additional information and reviews by Lucien B. Kinney and E. P. Starke, see 4:388 (3 references); for a review by L. B. Plumlee of earlier forms, see 3:322; for reviews by Albert A. Bennett and Earle R. Hedrick, see 2:1439; for reviews by J. O. Hassler and S. S. Wilks, see 1:881.

G73. Cooperative Mathematics Test for College Students: Comprehensive Examination in College Algebra. For additional information and reviews by Albert A. Bennett and Paul R. Rider, see 2:1440 (1 reference); for reviews by Arnold Dresden, Marion W. Richardson, and Henry L. Rietz, see 1:882.

G74. Diagnostic Test in Basic Algebra. For additional information and a review by Stanley Clark, see 5:445.

G75. Elementary Algebra: Every Pupil Test. For additional information, see 6:596.

G76. Elementary Algebra: Minnesota High School Achievement Examinations. For additional information, see 6:597; for a review by Lynnette B. Plumlee of earlier forms, see 5:448.

G77. Elementary Algebra Test: Affiliation Testing Program for Catholic Secondary Schools. For additional information and a review by Henry Chauncey, see 6:598 (2 references). For a review of the complete program, see 6:758.

G78. Examination in College Algebra. For additional information and reviews by Albert A. Bennett and Edmund P. Churchill, see 3:323 (1 reference).

G79. Examination in Elementary Algebra— High-School Level. For additional information and reviews by Richard M. Drake and John A. Long, see 3:324.

G80. Examination in Second-Year Algebra— High-School Level. For additional information and reviews by L. B. Plumlee and Daniel W. Snader, see 3:325.

G81. First Year Algebra: Every Pupil Scholarship Test. For additional information, see 6:599.

G82. First Year Algebra Test: National Achievement Tests. For additional information and a review by Donald L. Meyer, see 6:600.

G83. First Year Algebra Test: State High School Tests for Indiana. For additional information, see 4:391.

G84. Garman-Schrammel Algebra Test. For additional information and reviews by Paul Blommers and E. H. C. Hildebrandt, see 3:326.

G85. Illinois Algebra Test. For additional information and reviews by Stanley Clark and Theodore E. Kellogg, see 5:450.

G86. Iowa Algebra Aptitude Test. For additional information and reviews by Harold Gulliksen and Emma Spaney, see 4:393; for a review by David Segel, see 3:327 (2 references); for reviews by Richard M. Drake and M. W. Richardson of an earlier edition, see 2:1441 (1 reference).

G87. Iowa Every-Pupil Test in Ninth Year Algebra. For additional information and a review by John R. Clark, see 2:1442.

G88. Lankton First-Year Algebra Test. For additional information and a review by Emma Spaney, see 5:451; for a review by Stanley Clark, see 4:394.

G89. Larson-Greene Unit Tests in First-Year Algebra. For additional information, see 4:395.

G90. Lee Test of Algebraic Ability. For additional information and a review by S. S. Wilks, see 2:1443 (1 reference).

G91. Orleans Algebra Prognosis Test. For additional information and reviews by Harold Gulliksen and Emma Spaney, see 4:396 (1 reference); for a review by S. S. Wilks of the original edition, see 2:1444 (4 references).

G92. Seattle Algebra Test. For additional information and reviews by Sheldon S. Myers and Willard G. Warrington, see 6:601 (1 reference); for a review by Albert E. Meder, Jr., see 5:452.

G93. Survey Test in Elementary Algebra. For additional information and reviews by John A. Long and Daniel W. Snader, see 3:328.

G94. Survey Test of Algebraic Aptitude: California Survey Series. For additional information and reviews by Cyril J. Hoyt and Donald L. Meyer, see 6:602.

G95. 20th Century Test for First Year Algebra. For additional information, see 4:392.

G96. The Votaw Algebra Test: Elementary Algebra. For additional information and a review by Kenneth F. McLaughlin, see 6:603; for reviews by Richard M. Drake and Nathan Morrison of earlier forms, see 3:329.

G97. Wisconsin Algebra Test. For additional information, see 3:330.

ARITHMETIC

G98. A.C.E.R. Arithmetic Tests. For additional information, see 4:398.

G99. A.C.E.R. Arithmetic Tests: Standardized for Use in New Zealand. For additional information, see 5:453 (the 2 references for this test are incorrectly placed and are for 5:454).

G100. A.C.E.R. Number Test. For additional information, see 5:454 (2 references for this test are incorrectly placed under 5:453); for a review by Leslie M. Haynes of the original edition, see 4:399.

G101. American Numerical Test. For additional information and reviews by Marvin D. Glock and Richard T. Johnson, see 6:604.

G102. American School Achievement Tests: Arithmetic Readiness. For additional information and a review by Harold E. Moser, see 5:455. For reviews of the complete battery, see 6:2 (2 reviews), 5:1 (2 reviews), 4:1 (1 review), and 3:1 (2 reviews).

G103. American School Achievement Tests: Part 2, Arithmetic. For additional information, see 6:605 (1 reference); for reviews by Joseph Justman and J. Fred Weaver, see 5:456. For reviews of the complete battery, see 6:2 (2 reviews), 5:1 (2 reviews), 4:1 (1 review), and 3:1 (2 reviews).

G104. Analytical Scales of Attainment: Arithmetic. For additional information and reviews by R. L. Morton, W. J. Osburn, and G. M. Wilson, see 2:1447.

G105. Analytical Survey Test in Computational Arithmetic. For additional information and a review by Emma Spaney, see 5:457.

G106. Arithmetic Computation: Public School Achievement Tests. For additional information, see 6:606. For reviews of the complete battery, see 2:1194 (2 reviews).

G107. Arithmetic: Cooperative Mathematics Tests. For additional information and a review by O. F. Anderhalter, see 6:607.

G108. Arithmetic Essentials Test. For additional information and a review by J. Wayne Wrightstone, see 5:458; for reviews by Foster E. Grossnickle and Charles S. Ross of the original edition, see 4:400.

G109. Arithmetic: Every Pupil Scholarship Test. For additional information, see 6:608.

G110. Arithmetic: Every Pupil Test. For additional information, see 6:609.

G111. Arithmetic Fundamentals Test: State High School Tests for Indiana. For additional information, see 4:402.

G112. Arithmetic: Midland Attainment Tests. For additional information and a review by Fred J. Schonell, see 2:1448.

G113. Arithmetic Progress Tests. For additional information, see 6:610; for reviews by William Curr and John Sutherland, see 5:461.

G114. Arithmetic Reasoning [B. V. Moore]. For additional information and a review by Jacob S. Orleans, see 3:331.

G115. Arithmetic Reasoning: Public School Achievement Tests. For additional information, see 6:612. For reviews of the complete battery, see 2:1194 (2 reviews).

G116. Arithmetic Reasoning [Richardson, Bellows, Henry & Co., Inc.]. For additional information, see 6:611.

G117. Arithmetic Reasoning Test: Personnel Research Institute Clerical Battery. For additional information, see 4:403. For reviews of the complete battery, see 4:729 (2 reviews).

G118. Arithmetic: Seven Plus Assessment: Northumberland Series. For additional information, see 4:404. For a review of the complete battery, see 4:24.

G119. Arithmetic Test: Fundamental Operations: Dominion Tests. For additional information and a review by Harry L. Stein, see 5:462; for a review by C. L. Thiele, see 3:332.

G120. Arithmetic Test (Fundamentals and Reasoning): Municipal Tests: National Achievement Tests. For additional information, see 5:463; for reviews by Foster E. Grossnickle and Charles S. Ross, see 4:406. For reviews of the complete battery, see 5:18 (1 review), 4:20 (1 review), and 2:1191 (2 reviews).

G121. Arithmetic Test: National Achievement Tests. For additional information, see 6:613; for reviews by R. L. Morton and Leroy H. Schnell, see 2:1449; for reviews by William A. Brownell and W. J. Osburn, see 1:889.

G122. Arithmetic Tests 1–2, 4–13. For additional information, see 6:614 (1 reference).

G123. Arithmetic: Thanet Mental Tests. For additional information and reviews by Fred J. Schonell and C. Ebblewhite Smith, see 2:1450.

G124. Arithmetical Reasoning Test. For additional information and a review by William L. Schaaf, see 4:407.

G125. Basic Arithmetic Skills: Iowa Every-Pupil Tests of Basic Skills, Test D. For additional information, see 4:408; for reviews by William A. Brownell and Leroy H. Schnell, see 3:334. For reviews of the complete battery, see 4:15 (2 reviews), 3:10 (3 reviews), and 1:872 (4 reviews).

G126. Basic Number Skills Test for Employee Selection. For additional information and reviews by Dorothy C. Adkins and Marion F. Shaycoft, see 5:466.

G127. Basic Skills in Arithmetic Test. For additional information and reviews by Jacob S. Orleans and F. Lynwood Wren, see 3:335.

G128. Bobbs-Merrill Arithmetic Achievement Tests. For additional information, see 6:615.

G129. A Brief Survey of Arithmetic Skills. For additional information and a review by H. Vernon Price, see 5:467 (1 reference); for reviews by William A. Brownell and Henry Van Engen of the original edition, see 4:409.

G130. [Brueckner Diagnostic Arithmetic Tests.] For additional information and a review by Herbert F. Spitzer, see 4:410.

G131. California Arithmetic Test. A subtest of A2; for additional information, see 6:616 (4 references); for a review by Robert D. North, see 5:468; for a review by Robert L. Burch of an earlier edition, see 4:411; for reviews by C. L. Thiele and Harry Grove Wheat, see 2:1459; for a review by William A. Brownell, see 1:893. For reviews of the complete battery, see 6:3 (2 reviews), 5:2 (1 review), 4:2 (3 reviews), 3:15 (1 review), 2:1193 (2 reviews), and 1:876 (1 review, 1 excerpt).

G132. Cardall Arithmetic Reasoning Test. For additional information, see 6:617; for a review by William L. Schaaf, see 4:407.

G133. Chicago Arithmetic Readiness Test. For additional information and a review by Foster E. Grossnickle, see 3:337 (1 reference).

G134. Chicago Arithmetic Survey Tests. For additional information and reviews by William A. Brownell and Foster E. Grossnickle, see 3:338; see also 2:1453 (1 excerpt).

G135. The Clapp-Young Arithmetic Test. For additional information and a review by Leroy H. Schnell, see 3:339.

G136. Commercial Arithmetic Test: State High School Tests for Indiana. For additional information, see 4:448.

G137. Compass Diagnostic Tests in Arithmetic. For additional information and reviews by William A. Brownell and Foster E. Grossnickle, see 2:1454.

G138. Compass Survey Tests in Arithmetic. For additional information and a review by William A. Brownell, see 2:1455.

G139. Computation Test A/67. For additional information, see 6:618.

G140. Cooperative Commercial Arithmetic Test. For additional information and a review by Bertram Epstein, see 4:449.

G141. Coordinated Scales of Attainment: Arithmetic. For additional information, see 5:469. For reviews of the complete battery, see 4:8 (1 review) and 3:6 (4 reviews).

G142. Cotswold Junior Arithmetic Ability Test. For additional information and reviews by William Curr and George W. Sturrock, see 5:470.

G143. Cotswold Measurement of Ability: Arithmetic. For additional information, see 5:471; for a review by W. L. Sumner, see 4:412.

G144. Diagnostic Arithmetic Tests. For additional information, see 6:619.

G145. Diagnostic Chart for Fundamental Processes in Arithmetic. For additional information and a review by Leo J. Brueckner, see 4:413; for reviews by H. E. Benz and Foster E. Grossnickle, see 2:1456.

G146. Diagnostic Tests and Self-Helps in Arithmetic. For additional information and a review by Harold E. Moser, see 5:472.

G147. Diagnostic Tests in Arithmetic Fundamentals: Dominion Tests. For additional information and a review by John Sutherland, see 5:473; for a review by Leo J. Brueckner of the original edition, see 3:341.

G148. Diagnostic Tests in Money. For additional information and reviews by Kenneth Lovell and G. A. V. Morgan, see 6:620.

G149. Diagnostic Tests in Vulgar Fractions, Decimal Fractions and Percentages. For additional information and a review by Reginald Edwards, see 5:474.

G150. [Essential Arithmetic Tests.] For additional information and reviews by John Cohen and Stephen Wiseman, see 3:342.

G151. Examination in Advanced Arithmetic— High-School Level. For additional information and reviews by Monica M. Hoye and F. Lynwood Wren, see 3:343.

G152. Examination in Business Arithmetic. For additional information, see 3:374.

G153. Gilbert Business Arithmetic. For additional information and a review by William L. Schaaf, see 4:450.

G154. Group Test of Speed and Accuracy in Arithmetic Computation: Dominion Tests. For additional information and reviews by Frances E. Crook [Morrison] and William Harrison Lucow, see 5:477.

G155. Hildreth Arithmetic Achievement Tests. For additional information and reviews by William A. Brownell and Leo J. Brueckner, see 1:890.

G156. Hundred Problem Arithmetic Test. For additional information and a review by William Betz, see 3:344 (2 references, 1 excerpt); for a review by W. J. Osburn of an earlier edition, see 2:1462.

G157. Intermediate Diagnostic Arithmetic Test. For additional information and a review by Stanley Nisbet, see 6:621.

G158. Kansas Arithmetic Test. For additional information and reviews by H. E. Benz and W. J. Osburn, see 2:1457.

G159. Kansas Primary Arithmetic Test. For additional information and reviews by W. J. Osburn and G. M. Ruch, see 2:1458.

G160. Kelvin Measurement of Ability in Arithmetic. For additional information, see 1:891.

G161. Lee-Clark Arithmetic Fundamentals Survey Test: High School Edition. For additional information and reviews by Monica M. Hoye and F. Lynwood Wren, see 3:345.

G162. Los Angeles Diagnostic Tests: Fundamentals of Arithmetic. For additional information, see 6:622.

G163. Los Angeles Diagnostic Tests: Reasoning in Arithmetic. For additional information, see 6:623.

G164. Madden-Peak Arithmetic Computation Test: Evaluation and Adjustment Series. For additional information, see 6:624; for reviews by Theodore E. Kellogg and Albert E. Meder, Jr., see 5:478.

G165. Manchester Mechanical Arithmetic Test (Sen.) 1. For additional information, see 6:625.

G166. Mechanical Arithmetic Tests. For additional information, see 6:626; for reviews by George W. Sturrock and Jack Wrigley, see 5:489.

G167. Metropolitan Achievement Tests: [Arithmetic]. For additional information and reviews by O. F. Anderhalter and E. W. Hamilton, see 6:627 (1 reference); for a review by Robert L. Burch of an earlier edition, see 4:416; for reviews by Peter L. Spencer and Harry Grove Wheat, see 2:1458.1; for reviews by Foster E. Grossnickle and Guy M. Wilson, see 1:892. For reviews of the complete battery, see 6:15 (3 reviews), 4:18 (1 review), 2:1189 (2 reviews), and 1:874 (3 reviews).

G168. Milne Arithmetic Test. For additional information, see 5:479.

G169. [Moray House Arithmetic Tests.] For additional information, see 6:628 (9 references); for a review by John Cohen of earlier forms, see 3:346.

G170. N.B. Arithmetic Tests. For additional information, see 6:629.

G171. New York Test of Arithmetical Meanings. For additional information and a review by Charles S. Ross, see 5:480.

G172. Number Fact Check Sheet. For additional information and a review by Miriam M. Bryan, see 4:417.

G173. Oral Diagnostic Test in Addition: Analysis of Errors in Addition: Dominion Tests. For additional information and a review by Leo J. Brueckner, see 3:348.

G174. Primary Arithmetic: Every Pupil Scholarship Test. For additional information, see 6:630.

G175. Renfrow Survey Tests of Mathematical Skills and Concepts. For additional information and a review by C. L. Thiele, see 3:349.

G176. Retail Arithmetic Worksample. For additional information and a review by William J. E. Crissy, see 4:418 (1 reference).

G177. Revised Southend Attainment Test in Mechanical Arithmetic. For additional information, see 6:631; for a review by Stephen Wiseman of the original edition, see 3:352.

G178. SRA Achievement Series: Arithmetic. For additional information and a review by E. W. Hamilton, see 6:632 (1 reference); for reviews by Robert D. North and J. Fred Weaver, see 5:483. For reviews of the complete battery, see 6:21 (1 review) and 5:21 (2 reviews).

G179. Sangren-Reidy Survey Tests in Arithmetic. For additional information and reviews by Leo J. Brueckner and C. L. Thiele, see 2:1460.

G180. Scale of Problems in Commercial Arithmetic. For additional information, see 2:1489 (3 references, 1 excerpt).

G181. Scholastic Achievement Series: Arithmetic. For additional information, see 6:633; for reviews by Joseph Justman and Charles S. Ross, see 5:484. For reviews of the complete battery, see 6:23 (2 reviews) and 5:23 (2 reviews).

G182. Schonell Diagnostic Arithmetic Tests. For additional information and a review by John Sutherland, see 5:485 (1 reference); see also 3:350 (1 reference); for a review by C. Ebblewhite Smith of an earlier edition, see 2:1461 (2 references).

G183. Schrammel-Otterstrom Arithmetic Test. For additional information, see 6:634; for a review by William A. Brownell, see 3:351.

G184. Seeing Through Arithmetic Tests. For additional information and a review by William H. Lucio, see 6:635.

G185. Shop Arithmetic Test. For additional information, see 6:636 (2 references).

G186. Speed Addition Test. For additional information, see 1:1081.

G187. The Staffordshire Arithmetic Test. For additional information, see 5:486.

G188. Stanford Achievement Test: Arithmetic Tests. For additional information and a review by C. Alan Riedesel, see 6:637 (7 references); for a review by Robert L. Burch of an earlier edition, see 4:419. For reviews of the complete battery, see 6:26 (1 review, 1 excerpt), 5:25 (1 review), 4:25 (2 reviews), and 3:18 (2 reviews).

G189. Survey of Arithmetic Achievement: California Survey Series. For additional information and reviews by C. Alan Riedesel and Harold C. Trimble, see 6:638.

G190. Survey Test of Arithmetic Fundamentals: Dominion Tests. For additional information and a review by Frances E. Crook [Morrison], see 5:488.

G191. Test A/8: Arithmetic. For additional information, see 6:639.

G192. Test in Fundamental Processes in Arithmetic. For additional information, see 1:894.

G193. Test of Arithmetic Fundamentals. For additional information, see 6:640.

G194. Test on Arithmetic Meanings and Vocabulary. For additional information and a review by Foster E. Grossnickle, see 3:353.

G195. The Tiedeman Arithmetical Knowledge and Information Test. For additional information and a review by James H. Ricks, Jr., see 5:490.

G196. Understanding the Meanings in Arithmetic: A Diagnostic Test. For additional information and reviews by Richard T. Johnson and Harold C. Trimble, see 6:641 (2 references).

G197. Unit Scales of Attainment in Arithmetic. For additional information and reviews by W. J. Osburn and Peter L. Spencer, see 2:1463. For reviews of the complete battery, see 2:1197 (1 review) and 1:878 (2 reviews).

G198. The Wirral Mechanical Arithmetic Tests. For additional information and a review by John Sutherland, see 6:642.

G199. Wisconsin Inventory Tests in Arithmetic. For additional information and a review by Leo J. Brueckner, see 2:1464.

G200. Woody-McCall Mixed Fundamentals in Arithmetic. For additional information and a review by William A. Brownell, see 4:421.

CALCULUS

G201. Calculus: Cooperative Mathematics Tests. For additional information, see 6:654.

G202. Examination in Calculus II—Integral Calculus (Following Initial Course Containing No Integration). For additional information and a review by John F. Randolph, see 3:355 (1 reference).

G203. Examination in Differential Calculus. For additional information, see 3:354 (1 reference).

GEOMETRY

G204. Ability for Geometry: Fife Tests of Ability, Test 4. For additional information, see 3:356 (2 references). For reviews of the complete battery, see 4:713 (1 review) and 3:8 (1 review).

G205. Analytic Geometry: Cooperative Mathematics Tests. For additional information, see 6:643.

G206. Becker-Schrammel Plane Geometry. For additional information and reviews by Harold Fawcett and Judson W. Foust, see 2:1465 (1 reference).

G207. Columbia Research Bureau Plane Geometry Test. For additional information and a review by Cyril J. Hoyt (with Theodore E. Kellogg), see 4:422 (1 reference); for reviews by W. Elmer Lancaster and J. H. Minnick, see 2:1466.

G208. Cooperative Plane Geometry Test. For additional information and a review by Cyril J. Hoyt (with Theodore E. Kellogg), see 4:423 (1 reference); for reviews by Harold P. Fawcett and C. O. Oakley of earlier forms, see 3:357; for a review by Leroy H. Schnell, see 2:1467; for reviews by Charles C. Weidemann and S. S. Wilks, see 1:993.

G209. Cooperative Solid Geometry Test. For additional information and reviews by J. O. Hassler and Earle R. Hedrick, see 2:1468.

G210. Diagnostic Test in Basic Geometry. For additional information, see 6:644.

G211. Examination in Analytic Geometry. For additional information and a review by C. O. Oakley, see 3:358 (1 reference).

G212. Examination in Plane Geometry—High-School Level. For additional information and a review by Hale C. Pickett, see 3:359.

G213. Geometry Attainment Test. For additional information and reviews by I. Macfarlane Smith and W. L. Sumner, see 4:424.

G214. Geometry: Cooperative Mathematics Tests. For additional information, see 6:645 (1 reference).

G215. Geometry: Every Pupil Test. For additional information, see 6:646.

G216. Illinois Plane Geometry Test. For additional information and a review by Lynnette B. Plumlee, see 5:491.

G217. Iowa Every-Pupil Test in Plane Geometry. For additional information and a review by J. H. Blackhurst, see 1:994.

G218. Iowa Plane Geometry Aptitude Test. For additional information and a review by Philip H. Du-Bois, see 3:360; for reviews by Edward E. Cureton and Charles C. Weidemann of an earlier edition, see 2:1469.

G219. Lane-Greene Unit Tests in Plane Geometry. For additional information, see 4:426.

G220. Lee Test of Geometric Aptitude. For additional information and reviews by Kenneth F. McLaughlin and Lynnette B. Plumlee, see 6:647 (5 references); for reviews by Edward E. Cureton and Charles C. Weidemann of the original edition, see 2:1470.

G221. Nelson-Richardson Plane Geometry Readiness Test. For additional information, see 1:995.

G222. Orleans Geometry Prognosis Test. For additional information, see 4:427 (2 references); for reviews by Edward E. Cureton and Charles C. Weidemann of the original edition, see 2:1471 (3 references).

G223. Orleans Plane Geometry Achievement Test. For additional information and a review by Harold P. Fawcett, see 3:361.

G224. Plane Geometry: Every Pupil Scholarship Test. For additional information, see 6:648.

G225. Plane Geometry: Minnesota High School Achievement Examinations. For additional information, see 6:649; for a review by Harold P. Fawcett of an earlier form, see 5:495.

G226. Plane Geometry: National Achievement Tests. For additional information, see 6:650.

G227. Plane Geometry Test: Affiliation Testing Program for Catholic Secondary Schools. For additional information and a review by Henry Chauncey, see 6:651. For a review of the complete program, see 6:758.

G228. Plane Geometry Test: State High School Tests for Indiana. For additional information, see 4:429.

G229. Schrammel-Reed Solid Geometry Test. For additional information and a review by H. Vernon Price, see 5:496.

G230. Seattle Plane Geometry Test. For additional information and a review by Harold P. Fawcett, see 5:497.

G231. Shaycoft Plane Geometry Test. For additional information, see 5:498; for reviews by Harold P. Fawcett and Cyril J. Hoyt (with Theodore E. Kellogg), see 4:433.

G232. Solid Geometry: Minnesota High School Achievement Examinations. For additional information, see 6:652.

G233. Solid Geometry: National Achievement Tests. For additional information and a review by Sheldon S. Myers, see 6:653.

G234. Solid Geometry Test: State High School Tests for Indiana. For additional information, see 4:435.

G235. Survey Test in Plane Geometry. For additional information and a review by Harold P. Fawcett, see 4:436.

G236. 20th Century Test for Plane Geometry. For additional information, see 4:430.

G237. The Van Dyke Solid Geometry Test. For additional information, see 4:437.

G238. Wisconsin Geometry Test. For additional information, see 3:362.

MISCELLANEOUS

G239. Structure of the Number System: Cooperative Mathematics Tests. For additional information, see 6:655.

TRIGONOMETRY

G240. American Council Trigonometry Test. For additional information and reviews by J. O. Hassler and G. E. Hawkins, see 2:1473.

G241. Cooperative Plane Trigonometry Test. For additional information, see 4:438; for a review by G. E. Hawkins of an earlier form, see 2:1474 (1 reference); for reviews by J. O. Hassler and S. S. Wilks, see 1:1074.

G242. Examination in Plane Trigonometry. For additional information, see 3:364 (1 reference).

G243. Plane Trigonometry: National Achievement Tests. For additional information, see 6:656.

G244. Rasmussen Trigonometry Test. For additional information and a review by Lynnette B. Plumlee, see 5:501.

G245. Trigonometry: Cooperative Mathematics Tests. For additional information, see 6:657.

G246. Trigonometry: Minnesota High School Achievement Examinations. For additional information, see 6:658.

G247. Trigonometry Test: State High School Tests for Indiana. For additional information, see 4:440.

MISCELLANEOUS

H1. How Well Can You Read Lips? For additional information, see 5:579 (2 references).

H2. Sign-Search Test. For additional information, see 1:1080.

H3. What Do You Know About Photography? For additional information, see 5:580.

AGRICULTURE

H4. Agriculture: Every Pupil Scholarship Test. For additional information, see 6:659.

H.5. Animal Husbandry Test: State High School Tests for Indiana. For additional information, see 3:365.

H6. Clinton-Walker General Farm Mechanics Test. For additional information, see 2:1475.

H7. Farm Shop Tools: Recognition and Use: State High School Tests for Indiana. For additional information and a review by M. Ray Karnes, see 4:441 (1 reference).

H8. Graduate Record Examinations Advanced Agriculture Test. For additional information, see 4:442.

COMPUTATIONAL AND SCORING DEVICES

H9. Age and I.Q. Calculator. For additional information, see 4:464.

H10. The Bowman I.Q. Kalculator. For additional information, see 5:528.

H11. Burnham Correlation Form. For additional information, see 1:946 (1 excerpt).

H12. Chronological Age Computer. For additional information, see 6:660.

H13. The Delp I.Q. Computer. For additional information, see 4:465 (1 excerpt).

H14. Digitek Optical Test Scoring and Document Scanning System. For additional information, see 6:661.

H15. Dominion Table for Converting Mental Age to I.Q. For additional information, see 6:662.

H16. Durost-Walker Correlation Chart: For Machine or Computation. For additional information, see 1:947.

H17. The EB Punch-Key Scoring and Answer Sheet System. For additional information, see 6:663.

H18. [Grade Averaging Charts.] For additional information, see 6:664.

H19. Grade Master. For additional information, see 6:665.

H20. Grade-O-Mat. For additional information, see 6:666.

H21. Hankes' Answer Sheets. For additional information, see 6:667; see also 5:529 (1 reference) and 4:466 (5 references).

H22. IBM Optical Mark Scoring Reader. For additional information, see 6:668.

H23. IBM Test Scoring Machine. For additional information, see 6:669 (3 references); see also 5:530 (15 references); for a review by Arthur E. Traxler, see 3:397 (22 references); for reviews by John G. Darley and H. T. Manuel, see 2:1492 (14 references).

H24. MRC Test Processing Service. For additional information, see 6:670.

H25. Morgan IQ Calculator. For additional information, see 2:1493 (1 excerpt).

H26. The Multiscore Profile Form and Scoring Codes. For additional information, see 4:467.

H27. NCS Digital Test Scoring and Data Processing. For additional information, see 6:671.

H28. Plumb IQ Slide Rule for Use With the Wechsler-Bellevue Intelligence Scale. For additional information, see 4:362 (1 excerpt).

H29. Psychometric Research and Service Chart Showing the Davis Difficulty and Discrimination Indices for Item Analysis. For additional information, see 6:672 (1 excerpt).

H30. The Rapid-Rater. For additional information, see 6:673.

H31. SRA Self-Scorer. For additional information and reviews by James M. Anderson and Arthur E. Traxler, see 4:468 (4 references).

H32. STAR Score Teach Answer Record. For additional information, see 6:674.

H33. Thurstone Scoring Board. For additional information, see 3:398.

H34. The Tweeddale I.Q. Conversion Tables. For additional information, see 4:469.

H35. [V.G.C. Answer Strips and Scoring Sleeves.] For additional information, see 4:470.

COURTSHIP AND MARRIAGE

H36. A Courtship Analysis. For additional information and a review by William R. Reevy, see 6:675.

H37. A Dating Problems Checklist. For additional information and reviews by Clifford R. Adams and Robert A. Harper, see 6:676.

H38. The El Senoussi Multiphasic Marital Inventory. For additional information, see 6:677.

H39. Individual and Marriage Counseling Inventory. For additional information, see 6:678.

H40. The Male Impotence Test. For additional information, see 6:679.

H41. Marital Roles Inventory. For additional information and a review by Robert A. Harper, see 6:680 (3 references).

H42. A Marriage Adjustment Form. For additional information and a review by Lester W. Dearborn, see 6:681 (1 reference).

H43. The Marriage Adjustment Inventory. For additional information and reviews by Clifford R. Adams and Albert Ellis, see 6:682.

H44. The Marriage Adjustment Sentence Completion Survey. For additional information and a review by Albert Ellis, see 6:683.

H45. A Marriage Prediction Schedule. For additional information and a review by Lester W. Dearborn, see 6:684; see also 5:84 (8 references).

H46. Marriage Role Expectation Inventory. For additional information and a review by Robert C. Challman, see 6:685 (6 references).

H47. Otto Pre-Marital Counseling Schedules. For additional information and reviews by Robert C. Challman and William R. Reevy, see 6:686 (2 references).

H48. Sex Knowledge Inventory. For additional information and a review by Clifford R. Adams, see 6:687 (3 references); for a review by Albert Ellis, see 4:488 (1 excerpt).

H49. Sex Knowledge Test. For additional information, see 6:688.

DRIVING AND SAFETY EDUCATION

H50. [American Automobile Association Driver Testing Apparatus.] For additional information, see 4:521.

H51. Auto and Highway Safety Test. For additional information and a review by Harry R. DeSilva, see 2:1521.

H52. Driver Attitude Survey. For additional information, see 6:689.

H53. Examination for Driving Instructors. For additional information, see 4:522.

H54. General Achievement Test in Fire Safety: National Fire Prevention Tests. For additional information, see 4:523.

H55. General First-Aid Test for Senior-High-School Students: National Safety Education Tests. For additional information, see 2:1522.

H56. General Safety Education Test for Junior-High-School Pupils: National Safety Education Tests. For additional information, see 2:1523.

H57. General Test on Traffic and Driving Knowledge. For additional information, see 5:922.

H58. Hannaford Industrial Safety Attitude Scales. For additional information and a review by David O. Herman, see 6:690.

H59. Home Safety Test for High-School Students and Adults: National Safety Education Tests. For additional information, see 2:1524.

H60. An Instructional Test in Safety. For additional information, see 3:457.

H61. Judgment Test on Safe Driving Practices. For additional information and a review by Harry R. DeSilva, see 2:1525 (2 excerpts).

H62. Lauer Driver Reaction Inventory. For additional information, see 5:593 (2 references).

H63. The McGlade Road Test for Use in Driver Licensing, Education and Employment. For additional information, see 6:691 (1 reference).

H64. National Bicycle Tests. For additional information, see 2:1526.

H65. National Test in Driver Education. For additional information, see 6:692.

H66. Rating Scale for Automobile-Driver Skills: The Abercrombie Driver Test. For additional information, see 4:524.

H67. Revere Safety Test. For additional information and reviews by Willard A. Kerr and Harold G. Seashore, see 4:525.

H68. Road Test Check List for Passenger Car Drivers. For additional information, see 5:594.

H69. Rogers-Lauer Driver Rating Inventory. For additional information, see 5:595.

H70. Siebrecht Attitude Scale. For additional information, see 6:693 (3 references).

H71. Student Record in Driver Education. For additional information, see 6:694.

EDUCATION

H72. Academic Freedom Survey. For additional information, see 5:531.

H73. Aptitude Test for Elementary School Teachers-in-Training. For additional information and reviews by Robert M. W. Travers and Edwin Wandt, see 4:792 (2 references, 1 excerpt).

H74. Attitude Toward Student Ratings of Instruction. For additional information, see 5:532.

H75. Barr-Harris Teacher's Performance Record. For additional information, see 4:793.

H76. Brown Rating Profile for Student Teachers and Teachers of Physical Education. For additional information, see 2:1494.

H77. Clinton-Castle Self-Rating Scale for County School Superintendents. For additional information, see 2:1495.

H78. College Efficiency-of-Instruction Index. For additional information, see 2:1496 (1 reference).

H79. College and University Environment Scales (CUES). For additional information, see 6:695 (2 references).

H80. Comprehensive Examination in Secondary Education. For additional information, see 1:953.

H81. Coxe-Orleans Prognosis Test of Teaching Ability. For additional information and reviews by Harl R. Douglass and David G. Ryans, see 3:399 (5 references).

H82. Diagnostic Teacher-Rating Scale. For additional information, see 6:696; for a review by Dorothy M. Clendenen, see 5:534 (5 references); see also 4:795 (2 references).

H83. Educational Aptitude Test: George Washington University Series. For additional information and reviews by A. S. Barr and Harl R. Douglass, see 3:400 (3 references).

H84. Educational Interest Inventory. For additional information, see 5:535.

H85. Exceptional Teacher Service Record. For additional information and reviews by Leo J. Brueckner and Edwin Wandt, see 4:796.

H86. Faculty Morale Scale for Institutional Improvement. For additional information, see 6:697.

H87. The Graduate Record Examinations Advanced Tests: Education. For additional information and a review by D. Welty Lefever, see 6:698 (7 references); for a review by Harry N. Rivlin of an earlier form, see 5:537. For a review of the testing program, see 5:601.

H88. How I Counsel. For additional information and reviews by Clifford P. Froehlich and Milton E. Hahn, see 4:798 (4 references).

H89. How I Teach: Analysis of Teaching Practices. For additional information and reviews by May V. Seagoe and D. A. Worcester, see 4:799 (4 references); for a review by David G. Ryans, see 3:403.

H90. How Teach and Learn in College? For additional information and a review by Dean A. Worcester, see 4:800 (4 references).

H91. Illinois Opinion Inventories. For additional information and a review by Kenneth E. Clark, see 4:52 (1 reference).

H92. Introduction to Education. For additional information, see 1:954.

H93. Minnesota Teacher Attitude Inventory. For additional information, see 6:699 (146 references); for reviews by Dwight L. Arnold and Lee J. Cronbach, see 4:801 (9 references).

H94. Morrison Rating Scale Profile for Teachers. For additional information and a review by Leo J. Brueckner, see 1:955.

H95. National Teacher Examinations. For additional information and a review by Harold Seashore, see 6:700 (5 references); for reviews by William A. Brownell, Walter W. Cook, and Lawrence G. Derthick of earlier forms, see 5:538 (6 references); for a review by Harry N. Rivlin, see 4:802 (43 references). For reviews of individual tests, see 6:259 (1 review), 6:345 (1 review), 6:350 (1 review), 6:583 (1 review), and 6:974 (1 review).

H96. Ohio Teaching Record: Anecdotal Observation Form. For additional information, see 3:402 (1 reference, 1 excerpt).

H97. Pictographic Self Rating Scale. For additional information and reviews by Stanley E. Davis and John D. Krumboltz, see 6:701 (2 references).

H98. A Pupil's Rating Scale of an Instructor. For additional information and a review by James R. Hayden, see 6:702.

H99. Purdue Instructional Television Attitude Scale. For additional information, see 6:703.

H100. The Purdue Instructor Performance Indicator. For additional information and a review by C. Robert Pace, see 6:704 (3 references).

H101. The Purdue Rating Scale for Instruction. For additional information and a review by C. Robert Pace, see 6:705 (5 references); for a review by Kenneth L. Heaton, see 4:803 (26 references).

H102. The Purdue Teacher Morale Inventory. For additional information, see 6:706.

H103. Rating Instrument for the Evaluation of Student Reactions. For additional information, see 2:1497 (2 references).

H104. Rating Instrument for the Evaluation of the Reactions of College Students. For additional information, see 2:1498 (2 references).

H105. Remmlein's School Law Test. For additional information, see 6:707.

H106. SRA Educators Opinion Inventory. For additional information, see 5:540.

H107. Scale for Rating Effective Teacher Behavior. For additional information and reviews by Leo J. Brueckner and Edwin Wandt, see 4:804 (1 reference).

H108. School Practices Questionnaire. For additional information and reviews by Harriet M. Barthelmess [Morrison] and Hilda Taba, see 1:869 (2 references).

H109. A Self Appraisal Scale for Teachers. For additional information, see 5:541.

H110. Sizing Up Your School Subjects. For additional information, see 6:708.

H111. Stanford Educational Aptitudes Test. For additional information and reviews by A. S. Barr and David G. Ryans, see 3:404 (4 references).

H112. Teacher Education Examination Program. For additional information, see 6:709; for a review by Walter W. Cook, see 5:543.

H113. Teacher Opinionaire on Democracy. For additional information and reviews by George W. Hartmann and C. Robert Pace, see 4:805.

H114. Teaching Aptitude Test: George Washington University Series. For additional information and a review by May V. Seagoe, see 4:806; for a review by A. S. Barr, see 3:405 (8 references).

H115. The Teaching Evaluation Record. For additional information, see 5:542.

H116. A Test on Adult Attitudes Toward Children. For additional information and a review by Elizabeth Hagen, see 6:710.

H117. What Would *You* Do? Perplexing Incidents in Human Relations. For additional information, see 5:545.

H118. The Wilson Teacher-Appraisal Scale. For additional information and a review by James R. Hayden, see 6:711.

ETIQUETTE

H119. The Best Thing to Do: A Test of Knowledge of Social Standards. For additional information and a review by Helen Shacter, see 4:471.

H120. Furbay-Schrammel Social Comprehension Test. For additional information and a review by James H. Ricks, Jr., see 4:472 (1 reference).

H121. The New Century Social Conduct Test. For additional information, see 5:547.

H122. Parsons Social Comprehension Test. For additional information, see 5:548.

H123. Test of Etiquette: George Washington University Series. For additional information and a review by James H. Ricks, Jr., see 4:473.

H124. Test of Knowledge of Social Usage. For additional information and a review by Hilda Taba, see 4:474 (1 reference).

H125. Test on Social Usage. For additional information, see 5:549.

HANDWRITING

H126. The American Handwriting Scale. For additional information and a review by Theodore L. Harris, see 6:712.

H127. Ayres Measuring Scale for Handwriting. For additional information, see 5:550; for a review by Worth J. Osburn, see 4:475 (9 references).

H128. Evaluation Scales for Guiding Growth in Handwriting. For additional information and a review by Theodore L. Harris, see 6:713 (2 references).

H129. Normal Handwriting Scale. For additional information and a review by Theodore L. Harris, see 6:714.

H130. The Thorndike Scale for Handwriting of Children. For additional information and a review by Stuart A. Courtis, see 4:477 (4 references).

HEALTH AND PHYSICAL EDUCATION

H131. AAHPER Youth Fitness Test. For additional information, see 6:715 (21 references).

H132. ACH Index of Nutritional Status. For additional information, see 1:1002 (1 reference, 1 excerpt).

H133. Achievement Scales in Physical Education Activities for Boys and Girls in Elementary and Junior High Schools. For additional information, see 1:1003.

H134. Achievement Scales in Physical Education Activities for College Men. For additional information, see 1:1004.

H135. Action-Choice Tests for Competitive Sports Situations. For additional information, see 6:716 (2 references).

H136. Basic Fitness Tests. For additional information, see 6:716a (1 reference).

H137. Belmont Measures of Athletic Performance: Field Hockey Scale. For additional information, see 6:717.

H138. Brewer-Schrammel Health Knowledge and Attitude. For additional information and reviews by John C. Almack and Frederick Rand Rogers, see 2:1499 (1 reference).

H139. Byrd Health Attitude Scale. For additional information and reviews by Mayhew Derryberry and H. H. Remmers, see 3:418 (1 reference, 1 excerpt).

H140. College Health Knowledge Test, Personal Health. For additional information and reviews by James E. Bryan and Peter G. Loret, see 6:718 (4 references); for a review by H. Harrison Clarke, see 4:478.

H141. Cornell Medical Index—Health Questionnaire. For additional information, see 6:719 (31 references).

H142. Cowell Test of Ability to Recognize the Operation of Certain Principles Important to Physical Education. For additional information, see 6:720 (1 reference).

H143. Elementary Health: Every Pupil Scholarship Test. For additional information, see 6:721.

H144. [French Tests for Professional Courses in Knowledge of Sports]: Physical Education Major Examinations. For additional information and a review by H. Harrison Clarke, see 4:480 (2 references).

H145. Gates-Strang Health Knowledge Tests. For additional information and a review by Paul E. Kambly, see 4:481 (2 references); see also 3:419 (1 excerpt); for reviews by Frederick Rand Rogers and A. H. Turney, see 2:1500 (1 excerpt).

H146. Gill-Schrammel Physiology Test. For additional information and a review by Clarence H. Nelson, see 5:554.

H147. The Graduate Record Examinations Advanced Tests: Physical Education. For additional information, see 6:722. For a review of the testing program, see 5:601.

H148. Health and Safety Education Test: National Achievement Tests. For additional information, see 6:724; for a review by Clarence H. Nelson, see 5:555.

H149. Health and Safety Education Test: State High School Tests for Indiana. For additional information, see 3:420.

H150. Health Awareness Test. For additional information and a review by R. Lenox Criswell, see 2:1501 (1 reference, 1 excerpt); for a review by Austin H. Turney, see 1:1006.

H151. Health Behavior Inventory. For additional information and reviews by James E. Bryan and Peter G. Loret, see 6:723.

H152. Health Education and Hygiene: Every Pupil Test. For additional information, see 6:725.

H153. Health Education Test: Knowledge and Application: Acorn National Achievement Tests. For additional information, see 5:557 (1 reference); for reviews by H. H. Remmers and Mabel E. Rugen, see 3:421.

H154. Health Inventories. For additional information and a review by Benjamin Shimberg, see 4:484 (1 reference).

H155. Health Inventory for High School Students. For additional information and reviews by Mayhew Derryberry and Mabel E. Rugen, see 3:422 (1 reference).

H156. Health Knowledge Test for College Freshmen: National Achievement Tests. For additional information and a review by James E. Bryan, see 5:558 (3 references).

H157. Health Practice Inventory. For additional information and a review by James E. Bryan, see 5:559 (2 references); for a review by Thomas Kirk Cureton of the original edition, see 3:423 (2 references).

H158. Health Test: National Achievement Tests. For additional information and a review by Benno G. Fricke, see 5:560; for a review by Jacob S. Orleans, see 4:485.

H159. High School Health: Every Pupil Scholarship Test. For additional information, see 6:726.

H160. Indiana University Motor Fitness Index. For additional information, see 3:424 (4 references).

H161. Kilander Health Knowledge Test. For additional information, see 5:562 (3 references); see also 2:1503 (2 excerpts).

H162. Kilander Nutrition Information Test. For additional information, see 3:425 (1 reference).

H163. Patient's Self-History Form. For additional information, see 4:486.

H164. Personal Health Inventory. For additional information and a review by Willard W. Patty, see 4:487.

H165. Physical Education Achievement Scales for Boys in Secondary Schools. For additional information, see 1:B338 (1 excerpt).

H166. Physical Education: National Teacher Examinations. For additional information, see 6:727. For reviews of the testing program, see 6:700 (1 review), 5:538 (3 reviews), and 4:802 (1 review).

H167. Physical Education: Teacher Education Examination Program. An inactive form of H166;

for additional information, see 6:728. For a review of the testing program, see 5:543.

H168. Physical Education Tests. For additional information, see 5:565 (1 reference).

H169. Physical Examination Record. For additional information, see 2:1504 (1 reference).

H170. Smoking Habits Questionnaire. For additional information, see 6:729.

H171. Trusler-Arnett Health Knowledge Test. For additional information and a review by Thomas Kirk Cureton, see 3:426.

H172. Veenker Health Knowledge Test for the Seventh Grade. For additional information, see 6:730 (1 reference).

H173. [Wetzel Grid Charts.] For additional information and a review by Dorothy Eichorn, see 6:731 (26 references); see also 4:489 (9 references).

H174. Width-Weight Tables. For additional information, see 4:490 (1 reference).

H175. [Winsberg Tests: Examinations for Physical Education Major Students.] For additional information, see 5:567.

HOME ECONOMICS

H176. Assisting With Care and Play of Children: State High School Tests for Indiana. For additional information and a review by Helen C. Dawe, see 3:427.

H177. Assisting With Clothing Problems: State High School Tests for Indiana. For additional information, see 3:428.

H178. Child Development: State High School Tests for Indiana. For additional information and a review by Helen C. Dawe, see 3:429.

H179. Clothing: Every Pupil Scholarship Test. For additional information, see 6:732.

H180. Clothing I: State High School Tests for Indiana. For additional information, see 3:430.

H181. Clothing II: State High School Tests for Indiana. For additional information, see 3:431.

H182. Cooperative Test in Foods and Nutrition. For additional information and a review by Robert L. Ebel, see 4:491 (1 reference).

H183. Cooperative Test in Home Management. For additional information, see 4:492 (1 reference).

H184. Cooperative Test in Household Equipment. For additional information and reviews by Faith Madden and Victor H. Noll, see 4:493 (1 reference).

H185. Cooperative Test in Textiles and Clothing. For additional information, see 4:494 (1 reference).

H186. Engle-Stenquist Home Economics Test. For additional information and reviews by Clara M. Brown [Arny] and Hester Chadderdon, see 2:1505.

H187. Foods: Every Pupil Scholarship Test. For additional information, see 6:733.

H188. Foods I, Food Selection and Preparation: State High School Tests for Indiana. For additional information concerning earlier forms, see 4:495; for a review by Hester Chadderdon, see 1:1029.

H189. Foods II, Planning for Family Food Needs: State High School Tests for Indiana. For additional information concerning earlier forms, see 4:496.

H190. Frear-Coxe Clothing Test. For additional information and reviews by Laura B. Hadley and Esther F. Segner, see 2:1507.

H191. General Home Economics: Clothing, Home Relations, and Social Usage: State High School Tests for Indiana. For additional information and a review by Clara M. Brown [Arny], see 1:1030.

H192. General Home Economics: Foods, the House, and Child Development: State High School Tests for Indiana. For additional information and a review by Clara M. Brown [Arny], see 1:1030.

H193. Graduate Record Examinations Advanced Home Economics Test. For additional information, see 4:497.

H194. Helping With Food in the Home: State High School Tests for Indiana. For additional information and a review by Jean D. Amberson, see 4:498.

H195. Helping With the Housekeeping: State High School Tests for Indiana. For additional information and a review by Hester Chadderdon, see 4:499.

H196. Home Care of the Sick Test: State High School Tests for Indiana. For additional information, see 4:500.

H197. Home Economics Education: National Teacher Examinations. For additional information, see 6:734. For reviews of the testing program, see 6:700 (1 review), 5:538 (3 reviews), and 4:802 (1 review).

H198. Homemaking I and II: Every Pupil Scholarship Test. For additional information, see 6:735.

H199. Housing the Family: State High School Tests for Indiana. For additional information and a review by Jean D. Amberson of an earlier form, see 4:501.

H200. Information Test on Foods: Illinois Food Test. For additional information and reviews by Norma A. Albright and Clara M. Brown [Arny], see 2:1508 (1 reference).

H201. Johnson Home Economics Interest Inventory. For additional information and reviews by John D. Black and Leona E. Tyler, see 5:570 (6 references).

H202. Minnesota Check List for Food Preparation and Serving. For additional information, see 5:571; see also 2:1509 (1 reference, 1 excerpt).

H203. Minnesota Food Score Cards. For additional information, see 3:439.

H204. Minnesota House Design and House Furnishing Test. For additional information and a review by Ray Faulkner, see 1:1031 (1 reference).

H205. Nutrition Information. For additional information, see 4:502.

H206. Nutrition Information Test. For additional information, see 3:425 (1 reference).

H207. Scales for Appraising High School Homemaking Programs. For additional information, see 5:572.

H208. Tests in Comprehension of Patterns. For additional information and reviews by Laura B. Hadley and Berenice Mallory, see 2:1510.

H209. Unit Scales of Attainment in Foods and Household Management. For additional information and reviews by Norma A. Albright and Hester Chadderdon, see 2:1511.

INDUSTRIAL ARTS

H210. Achievement Test in Mechanical Drawing. For additional information and a review by Verne C. Fryklund, see 2:1512 (1 reference).

H211. Drawing Aptitude Test. For additional information, see 2:1512.1.

H212. Examination in Mechanical Drawing. For additional information, see 3:440.

H213. Industrial Arts Education: National Teacher Examinations. For additional information, see 6:736. For reviews of the testing program, see 6:700 (1 review), 5:538 (3 reviews), and 4:802 (1 review).

H214. Industrial Arts: Every Pupil Scholarship Test. For additional information, see 6:737.

H215. Industrial Arts: Teacher Education Examination Program. An inactive form of H213; for additional information, see 6:738. For a review of the testing program, see 5:543.

H216. Mechanical Drawing. For additional information and a review by Dean M. Schweickhard, see 2:1513.

H217. Mechanical Drawing Performance Test. For additional information and a review by Emanuel E. Ericson, see 2:1514 (1 reference); see also 1:1034 (1 excerpt).

H218. Mechanical Drawing Test: State High School Tests for Indiana. For additional information and a review by William J. Micheels, see 4:503.

H219. Mechanical Drawing Tests. For additional information and a review by Emanuel E. Ericson, see 2:1515.

H220. Middleton Industrial Arts Test. For additional information and a review by William J. Micheels, see 4:504.

H221. Newkirk-Stoddard Home Mechanics Test. For additional information and a review by Arthur B. Mays, see 2:1516 (1 reference).

H222. Practical Arts: Every Pupil Test. For additional information, see 1:1035.

H223. Standard Test in Fundamental Mechanical Drawing. For additional information and a review by Verne C. Fryklund, see 2:1517.

LISTENING COMPREHENSION

H224. Brown-Carlsen Listening Comprehension Test. For additional information, see 6:739 (9 references); for reviews by E. F. Lindquist and Irving Lorge, see 5:577 (13 references).

H225. Sequential Tests of Educational Progress: Listening. For additional information, see 6:740 (11 references); for reviews by E. F. Lindquist and Irving Lorge, see 5:578. For reviews of the complete battery, see 6:25 (2 reviews) and 5:24 (2 reviews, 1 excerpt).

PHILOSOPHY

H226. The Graduate Record Examinations Advanced Tests: Philosophy. For additional information, see 6:741. For a review of the testing program, see 5:601.

H227. The Graduate Record Examinations Advanced Tests: Scholastic Philosophy. For additional information, see 6:742 (2 references). For a review of the testing program, see 5:601.

PSYCHOLOGY

H228. The Case of Mickey Murphy: A Case-Study Instrument in Evaluation. For additional information and a review by Dwight L. Arnold, see 5:533 (2 references); for a review by Frank S. Freeman of the second edition, see 4:794.

H229. Case Study Tests in Human Growth and Development. For additional information and reviews by Harold E. Jones and Goodwin Watson of the original edition, see 3:406 (3 references).

H230. Comprehensive Examination in Psychology. For additional information and a review by Edith M. Huddleston, see 4:507.

H231. Engle Psychology Test. For additional information and a review by Harold Seashore, see 5:582.

H232. Examination in Elementary Psychology —College Level. For additional information, see 3:401.

H233. The Graduate Record Examinations Advanced Tests: Psychology. For additional information, see 6:743; for a review by Harold Seashore, see 5:583. For a review of the testing program, see 5:601.

H234. Hogan Psychology Test. For additional information and a review by Harold Seashore, see 5:584.

H235. Psychology Test: Every Pupil Scholarship Test. For additional information, see 6:744.

H236. Toothman Test in Elementary Educational Psychology. For additional information and a review by V. A. C. Henmon, see 1:956.

RECORD AND REPORT FORMS

H237. A/9 Cumulative Record Folder. For additional information, see 6:745.

H238. American Council on Education Cumulative Record Folders. For additional information and reviews by Warren R. Baller and Arthur H. Brayfield, see 4:510; for reviews by Herbert A. Toops, see 3:444-5.

H239. Blum-Fieldsteel Development Charts. For additional information, see 5:585 (1 reference).

H240. [California Cumulative Record and Health Insert.] For additional information and a review by Warren R. Baller of the original edition, see 4:511.

H241. The Cassel Developmental Record. For additional information and a review by William E. Henry, see 5:586.

H242. Comprehensive Individual History Record Form for Infancy Through High School. For additional information and reviews by Charles D. Flory and Chauncey M. Louttit, see 1:1116.

H243. Cumulative Guidance Record. For additional information, see 4:512; for revision, see TIP 1305.

H244. Cumulative Personnel Record. For additional information, see 4:513.

H245. Diagnostic Child Study Record. For additional information and reviews by Charles D. Flory, Chauncey M. Louttit, and J. W. M. Rothney, see 1:1117 (2 references).

H246. [Guidance Cumulative Folder and Record Forms.] For additional information, see 6:746.

H247. Hamilton Cumulative Record Folder. For additional information, see 3:447.

H248. Indiana Psychodiagnostic Blank. For additional information, see 2:1518 (3 references).

H249. Ontario School Record System. For additional information, see 6:747.

H250. Permanent Record Card. For additional information, see 4:515 (1 reference).

H251. [Personnel Record Form.] For additional information and a review by Charles D. Flory, see 1:1120.

H252. [Physical Growth Record.] For additional information, see 6:748 (1 reference).

H253. A Pre-School Record Form. For additional information, see 5:587.

H254. Profile Chart for Individual Diagnosis. For additional information, see 1:1121.

H255. [Pupils' Record Cards.] For additional information, see 2:1519 (1 reference).

H256. Secondary-School Record. For additional information, see 4:516 (1 reference); for revision, see TIP 1318.

H257. Standard Profile Chart. For additional information and a review by Charles R. Langmuir, see 3:448.

H258. Supplementary Entrance Interview Schedule. For additional information, see 1:1122.

H259. V.G.C. Anecdotal Record Form. For additional information, see 3:449; for revision, see TIP 1306.

H260. V.G.C. Cumulative Record Folder. For additional information, see 4:517; for revision, see TIP 1307.

H261. V.G.C. Interview Record Form. For additional information, see 3:451; for revision, see TIP 1308.

H262. V.G.C. Student Information Form. For additional information, see 3:452; for revision, see TIP 1309.

RELIGIOUS EDUCATION

H263. Achievement Test for Weekday Afternoon Congregational Schools. For additional information, see 6:750.

H264. Achievement Test in Jewish History. For additional information, see 6:749.

H265. Attitude Inventory [Concordia]. For additional information, see 5:588 (1 reference).

H266. Bible History Tests. For additional information, see 5:589.

H267. Hebrew School Attitude Test. For additional information, see 3:452a.

H268. Jewish Home Environment Test. For additional information, see 3:453.

H269. Jewish Information Test. For additional information, see 4:518.

H270. Opinion Survey. For additional information, see 4:519.

H271. Peters Biblical Knowledge Test. For additional information and a review by Janet G. Afflerbach, see 5:590.

H272. Religion Essentials Test. For additional information, see 3:455 (2 references).

H273. Religion Test for Grades Two and Three. For additional information, see 5:591.

H274. Religion Test for High Schools. For additional information, see 5:592.

H275. Religion Test (Four-Year Course): Affiliation Testing Program for Catholic Secondary Schools. For additional information and a review by Henry Chauncey, see 6:751. For a review of the complete program, see 6:758.

H276. Scholastic Achievement Series: Religion. For additional information, see 6:752. For reviews of the complete battery, see 6:23 (2 reviews) and 5:23 (2 reviews).

H277. Standardized Bible Content Test. For additional information, see 6:753.

H278. Test in Religious Instruction for High School Students. For additional information, see 2:1520.

H279. Test on Biblical Information. For additional information, see 6:754.

H280. Theological School Inventory. For additional information, see 6:755.

H281. Uniform Achievement Tests. For additional information, see 5:278.

H282. Unit Tests on Luther's Catechism. For additional information, see 6:756 (1 reference).

H283. Wilson Tests of Religious Aptitude. For additional information and a review by Goodwin Watson, see 3:456 (1 reference).

SOCIOECONOMIC STATUS

H284. The American Home Scale. For additional information, see 5:596 (2 references); for reviews by

Henry S. Maas and Verner M. Sims, see 3:417 (7 references).

H285. The Minnesota Home Status Index: A Scale for Measuring Urban Home Environment. For additional information and a review by Verner M. Sims, see 1:983 (1 reference, 4 excerpts).

H286. Sims SCI Occupational Rating Scale. For additional information and a review by Henry Weitz, see 5:597 (10 references).

H287. The Social Status Scale. For additional information, see 5:598 (7 references).

H288. Socio-Economic Status Scale. For additional information, see 6:757 (1 excerpt).

TEST PROGRAMS

H289. The Affiliation Testing Program for Catholic Secondary Schools. For additional information and a review by Henry Chauncey, see 6:758.

H290. College Board Placement Tests. For additional information, see 6:759.

H291. College Entrance Examination Board Admissions Testing Program. For additional information and reviews by Benno G. Fricke and Dean K. Whitla, see 6:760 (12 references); see also 5:599 (3 references) and 4:526 (9 references). For reviews of individual tests, see 6:287 (3 reviews), 6:289 (1 review), 6:383 (1 review), 6:384 (2 reviews), 6:449 (2 reviews), 6:568 (1 review), 6:569 (1 review), 6:914 (1 review), 6:966 (1 review), 6:967 (1 review), 5:272 (1 review), 5:277 (1 review), 5:280 (1 review), 5:318 (1 review), 5:723 (1 review), 5:742 (1 review), 5:749 (1 review), 5:786 (1 review), 4:178 (1 review), 4:237 (1 review), and 4:367 (1 review).

H292. College Entrance Examination Board Advanced Placement Examinations. For additional information, see 6:761 (5 references). For reviews of individual tests, see 6:893 (1 review), 6:1000 (1 review), 5:205 (1 review), 5:211 (1 review), 5:273 (1 review), 5:419 (1 review), 5:724 (1 review), 5:743 (1 review), 5:750 (1 review), and 5:812 (2 reviews).

H293. Cooperative Inter-American Tests. For additional information and reviews of individual tests, see 4:176 (1 review), 4:325 (2 reviews), 4:557 (2 reviews), 4:576 (1 review), and 4:577 (2 reviews).

H294. The Graduate Record Examinations. For additional information, see 6:762 (1 reference); for a review by Harold Seashore, see 5:601 (12 references); see also 4:527 (24 references). For reviews of individual tests, see 6:9 (2 reviews), 6:376 (1 review), 6:461 (2 reviews), 6:578 (1 review), 6:698 (1 review), 6:919 (1 review), 6:931 (1 review), 6:1021 (1 review), 5:10 (2 reviews), 5:215 (1 review), 5:247 (1 review), 5:270 (1 review), 5:336 (1 review), 5:427 (1 review), 5:537 (1 review), 5:583 (1 review), 5:727 (1 review), 5:754 (1 review), 5:818 (1 review), and 5:835 (1 review).

H295. National Guidance Testing Program. For additional information, see 6:763.

H296. Project Talent Test Battery: A National Inventory of Aptitudes and Abilities. For additional information, see 6:764 (5 references).

H297. [Science Talent Search Program.] For additional information, see 6:765.

MULTI-APTITUDE BATTERIES

I1. Academic Promise Tests. For additional information and reviews by Julian C. Stanley and William W. Turnbull, see 6:766.

I2. Aptitude Tests for Occupations. For additional information and a review by Lloyd G. Humphreys, see 5:891; for a review by Clifford P. Froehlich, see 4:710 (1 excerpt).

I3. Detroit General Aptitudes Examination. For additional information, see 5:603; for reviews by G. Frederic Kuder, Irving Lorge, and John Gray Peatman, see 2:1654.

I4. Differential Ability Tests. For additional information, see 5:604.

I5. Differential Aptitude Tests. For additional information and reviews by J. A. Keats and Richard E. Schutz, see 6:767 (52 references); for reviews by John B. Carroll and Norman Frederiksen, see 5:605 (49 references); for reviews by Harold Bechtoldt, Ralph F. Berdie, and Lloyd G. Humphreys, see 4:711 (28 references); see also 3:620 (1 excerpt).

I6. Differential Test Battery. For additional information, see 6:768; for reviews by E. A. Peel, Donald E. Super, and Philip E. Vernon, see 5:606.

I7. Employee Aptitude Survey. For additional information and reviews by Paul F. Ross and Erwin K. Taylor, see 6:769 (4 references, 1 excerpt); for reviews by Dorothy C. Adkins and S. Rains Wallace, see 5:607.

I8. Factored Aptitude Tests. For additional information and reference to reviews, see 6:774; for a review by Harold P. Bechtoldt, see 5:602; for a review by D. Welty Lefever of an earlier edition, see 4:712 (1 reference, 1 excerpt).

I9. Fife Tests of Ability. For additional information and a review by I. Macfarlane Smith, see 4:713 (3 references); for a review by James Maxwell, see 3:8.

I10. Flanagan Aptitude Classification Tests. For additional information and reviews by Norman Frederiksen and William B. Michael, see 6:770 (7 references); for reviews by Harold P. Bechtoldt, Ralph F. Berdie, and John B. Carroll, see 5:608.

I11. General Aptitude Test Battery. For additional information and reviews by Harold P. Bechtoldt and John B. Carroll, see 6:771 (55 references); for reviews by Andrew L. Comrey, Clifford P. Froehlich, and Lloyd G. Humphreys, see 5:609 (176 references); for reviews by Milton L. Blum, Edward B. Greene, and Howard R. Taylor, see 4:714 (33 references).

I12. The Guilford-Zimmerman Aptitude Survey. For additional information, see 6:772 (17 references); for reviews by Anne Anastasi, Harold Bechtoldt, John B. Carroll, and P. E. Vernon, see 4:715 (15 references).

I13. Holzinger-Crowder Uni-Factor Tests. For additional information and reviews by Anne Anastasi, Benjamin Fruchter, and Philip E. Vernon, see 5:610 (3 references).

I14. The Jastak Test of Potential Ability and Behavior Stability. For additional information and reviews by Anne Anastasi and Benjamin Kleinmuntz, see 6:773 (3 references, 2 excerpts).

I15. Job-Tests Program. For additional information and reviews by William H. Helme and Stanley I. Rubin, see 6:774.

I16. Measurement of Skill: A Battery of Placement Tests for Business, Industrial and Educational Use. For additional information and reviews by Dorothy C. Adkins, Lloyd G. Humphreys, and Joseph E. Moore, see 6:775 (2 references).

I17. The Multi-Aptitude Test. For additional information and a review by H. H. Remmers, see 5:612 (1 reference).

I18. Multiple Aptitude Tests. For additional information and reviews by S. S. Dunn and Leroy Wolins, see 6:776 (8 references, 1 excerpt); for reviews by Ralph F. Berdie and Benjamin Fruchter of the original edition, see 5:613.

I19. N.B. Aptitude Tests (Junior). For additional information, see 6:777.

I20. National Institute for Personnel Research High Level Battery. For additional information, see 6:778 (1 reference).

I21. National Institute for Personnel Research Normal Battery. For additional information, see 6:779.

I22. SRA Primary Mental Abilities. For additional information and a review by John E. Milholland, see 6:780 (50 references); for reviews by Norman Frederiksen and Albert K. Kurtz of an earlier edition, see 5:614 (59 references); for reviews by Anne Anastasi, Ralph F. Berdie, John B. Carroll, Stuart A. Courtis, and P. E. Vernon, see 4:716 (42 references); for reviews by Cyril Burt, Florence L. Goodenough, James R. Hobson, and F. L. Wells, see 3:225 (50 references) and 3:264 (2 references); for reviews by Henry E. Garrett, Truman L. Kelley, C. Spearman, Godfrey H. Thomson, and Robert C. Tryon, see 2:1427 (10 references, 3 excerpts).

I23. [United States Employment Service Special Aptitude Tests.] For additional information, see 4:717.

I24. Vocational Guidance Program. For additional information and a review by Leo Goldman, see 6:781.

I25. Yale Educational Aptitude Test Battery. For additional information and reviews by Anne Anastasi and Ruth Churchill, see 5:615 (4 references); see also 4:718 (7 references).

PERSONALITY

NONPROJECTIVE

J1. A-S Reaction Study: A Scale for Measuring Ascendance-Submission in Personality. For additional information and a review by Warren T. Norman, see 6:57 (11 references); see also 5:28 (15 references); for a review by William U. Snyder, see 3:23 (11 references); for a review by Doncaster G. Humm of the 1928 edition, see 2:1198 (19 references).

J2. A-S Reaction Study: Revision for Business Use. For additional information and a review by Doncaster G. Humm, see 2:1199 (4 references).

J3. Activity Vector Analysis. For additional information and reviews by Lewis E. Albright, Alexander W. Astin, and Winton H. Manning, see 6:58 (21 references); for reviews by Brent Baxter and George K. Bennett, see 5:29 (11 references).

J4. The Adjustment Inventory. For additional information and a review by Forrest L. Vance, see 6:59 (11 references, 1 excerpt); see also 5:30 (26 references); for reviews by Nelson G. Hanawalt and Theodore R. Sarbin, see 4:28 (104 references); for reviews by Raymond B. Cattell, John G. Darley, C. M. Louttit, and Percival M. Symonds of the original Student Form, and reviews by S. J. Beck, J. P. Guilford, and Doncaster G. Humm of the Adult Form, see 2:1200 (15 references, 1 excerpt); for a review by Austin H. Turney of the Student Form, see 1:912.

J5. Adjustment Questionnaire. For additional information, see 5:31.

J6. Affectivity Interview Blank. For additional information and reviews by Morris Krugman and Verner M. Sims, see 4:29 (3 references).

J7. The Alcadd Test. For additional information and a review by Dugal Campbell, see 6:60 (6 references); for reviews by Charles Honzik and Albert L. Hunsicker, see 4:30.

J8. Aspects of Personality. For additional information and reviews by C. M. Louttit and P. E. Vernon, see 2:1201 (4 references); see also 1:913 (1 excerpt).

J9. Attitude-Interest Analysis Test. For additional information, see 6:61 (16 references); for a review by Starke R. Hathaway, see 3:24 (20 references).

J10. Attitude Scales for Measuring the Influence of the Work Relief Program. For additional information, see 2:1203 (1 reference).

J11. Attitudes Toward Child Behavior. For additional information, see 2:1204 (2 references).

J12. Attitudes Toward Industrialization. For additional information and a review by Marvin D. Dunnette, see 6:62.

J13. Attitudes Toward Parental Control of Children. For additional information, see 2:1205 (2 references).

J14. The Ayres Space Test. For additional information and reviews by Alvin G. Burstein and Alfred B. Heilbrun, Jr., see 6:63 (2 references).

J15. BEC Personality Rating Schedule. For additional information and reviews by Francis F. Bradshaw and Theos A. Langlie, see 1:915 (1 reference).

J16. Babcock Test of Mental Efficiency. For additional information, see 6:64 (6 references); for reviews by D. Russell Davis and Seymour G. Klebanoff, see 4:31 (10 references); see also 3:71 (21 references) and 2:1248 (16 references).

J17. [The Baxter Group Tests of Child Feeling.] For additional information, see 4:32 (2 references).

J18. Behavior Cards: A Test-Interview for Delinquent Children. For additional information, see 6:65 (1 reference); for reviews by W. C. Kvaraceus and Simon H. Tulchin, see 3:25 (3 references).

J19. Behavior Description. For additional information, see 1:898.

J20. Behavior Maturity Blank. For additional information, see 2:1209 (2 references).

J21. Behavior Maturity Rating Scale for Nursery School Children. For additional information, see 2:1210.

J22. Behavior Preference Record: What Would You Do? (A Study of Some Home and School Problems). For additional information and reviews by J. Thomas Hastings and Edward Landy, see 5:32 (1 excerpt).

J23. Beliefs About School Life: Test 4.6. For additional information, see 2:1211.

J24. Billett-Starr Youth Problems Inventory. For additional information and reviews by Thomas C. Burgess, J. Thomas Hastings, and Henry Weitz, see 6:66 (1 reference).

J25. Biographical Inventory for Students. For additional information, see 6:67 (6 references).

J26. Bonney-Fessenden Sociograph. For additional information and reviews by Åke Bjerstedt and C. Robert Pace, see 5:33.

J27. A Book About Me. For additional information and a review by Florence M. Teagarden, see 5:34.

J28. Bristol Social-Adjustment Guides. For additional information and reviews by G. A. V. Morgan and M. L. Kellmer Pringle, see 6:68 (13 references, 5 excerpts).

J29. Brown Personality Inventory for Children. For additional information, see 5:36 (10 references); for reviews by S. J. Beck and Carl R. Rogers, see 2:1240 (8 references).

J30. C-R Opinionaire. For additional information and a review by George W. Hartmann, see 4:39 (5 references); for a review by Goodwin Watson, see

2:1212 (5 references) ; for a review by H. H. Remmers, see 1:899.

J31. **Cain-Levine Social Competency Scale.** For additional information and a review by Marshall S. Hiskey, see 6:69.

J32. **The California Medical Survey (CMS).** For additional information, see 6:70.

J33. **California Psychological Inventory.** For additional information and a review by E. Lowell Kelly, see 6:71 (116 references) ; for reviews by Lee J. Cronbach and Robert L. Thorndike, see 5:37 (33 references, 1 excerpt).

J34. **The California Q-Set: A Q-Sort for Personality Assessment and Psychiatric Research.** For additional information and reviews by Allen L. Edwards and David T. Lykken, see 6:72 (2 references, 3 excerpts).

J35. **California Test of Personality.** For additional information, see 6:73 (49 references) ; for a review by Verner M. Sims, see 5:38 (93 references) ; for reviews by Laurance F. Shaffer and Douglas Spencer of the original edition, see 3:26 (24 references, 1 excerpt) ; for reviews by Raymond B. Cattell, Percival M. Symonds, and P. E. Vernon of the elementary and secondary levels, see 2:1213 (1 excerpt).

J36. **Case Inventory.** For additional information and reviews by Harold E. Jones and E. G. Williamson, see 2:1214 (1 reference) ; for a review by Richard Ledgerwood, see 1:916.

J37. **The Cassel Group Level of Aspiration Test.** For additional information and reviews by W. Grant Dahlstrom, Harrison G. Gough, and J. P. Sutcliffe, see 5:39 (5 references, 2 excerpts).

J38. **The Cassel Psychotherapy Progress Record.** For additional information and a review by William Schofield, see 6:74.

J39. **Character and Inventory Chart.** For additional information, see 1:917 (1 excerpt).

J40. **Character and Personality Rating Scale.** For additional information and a review by Bessie Lee Gambrill, see 2:1215.

J41. **The Child Behavior Rating Scale.** For additional information, see 6:74a.

J42. **Children's Embedded Figures Test.** For additional information, see 6:74b (2 references).

J43. **The Children's Hypnotic Susceptibility Scale.** For additional information and reviews by C. Scott Moss and John G. Watkins, see 6:75 (2 references, 1 excerpt).

J44. **Client-Centered Counseling Progress Record.** For additional information and a review by William Schofield, see 6:76.

J45. **The College Inventory of Academic Adjustment.** For additional information and a review by Leonard D. Goodstein, see 6:77 (12 references) ; for reviews by Lysle W. Croft and Harrison G. Gough, see 4:34 (3 references).

J46. **Community Improvement Scale.** For additional information and a review by Wimburn L. Wallace, see 5:42.

J47. **Concept Formation Test.** For additional information, see 6:78 (11 references) ; for a review by Kate Levine Kogan (with William S. Kogan), see 4:35 (8 references) ; for a review by O. L. Zangwill, see 3:27 (19 references).

J48. **Constant-Choice Perceptual Maze Attitude of Responsibility Test.** For additional information, see 6:79.

J49. **Cornell Index.** For additional information, see 5:43 (7 references) ; for reviews by Hans J. Eysenck, Nelson G. Hanawalt, and Laurance F. Shaffer, see 4:37 (41 references).

J50. **Cornell Word Form 2.** For additional information and a review by S. B. Sells, see 6:80 (1 reference) ; see also 5:44 (11 references).

J51. **Cotswold Personality Assessment P.A. 1.** For additional information and reviews by Ralph D. Dutch and G. A. V. Morgan, see 6:81 (1 reference).

J52. **The Cowan Adolescent Adjustment Analyzer.** For additional information, see 4:38 (1 reference) ; for reviews by Harold H. Abelson and William U. Snyder, see 3:30 ; for a review by Goodwin Watson of an earlier edition, see 2:1217 (3 references) ; for a review by Harold E. Jones, see 1:918.

J53. **Cowell Personal Distance Scale.** For additional information, see 6:82 (3 references).

J54. **Cowell Social Behavior Trend Index.** For additional information, see 6:83 (2 references).

J55. **Cree Questionnaire.** For additional information and reviews by Allyn Miles Munger and Theodor F. Naumann, see 6:84.

J56. **DF Opinion Survey.** For additional information and reviews by Andrew R. Baggaley, John W. French, and Arthur W. Meadows, see 5:45.

J57. **Detroit Adjustment Inventory.** For additional information and a review by Laurance F. Shaffer, see 5:46 (1 reference) ; for a review by Albert Ellis of the form for grades 7-12, see 3:31.

J58. **Detroit Scale of Behavior Factors.** For additional information, see 3:32 (1 reference).

J59. **Developmental Potential of Preschool Children.** For additional information, see 6:84a (1 reference).

J60. **Diagnosis and Treatment of Pupil Maladjustment.** For additional information and a review by Laurance F. Shaffer, see 3:34 (2 references).

J61. **Diplomacy Test of Empathy.** For additional information and reviews by Arthur H. Brayfield and Richard S. Hatch, see 6:85 (1 reference) ; for a review by Robert L. Thorndike of the earlier test, see 5:99.

J62. **Dunlap Academic Preference Blank.** For additional information and reviews by Lee J. Cronbach, W. C. Kvaraceus, and Edith I. M. Thomson, see 3:35 (6 references, 1 excerpt).

J63. **Dynamic Personality Inventory.** For additional information and a review by S. B. Sells, see 6:86 (7 references).

J64. **Educational Background Questionnaire.** For additional information and a review by Verner M. Sims, see 1:869 (2 references).

J65. **Edwards Personal Preference Schedule.** For additional information and reviews by John A. Radcliffe and Lawrence J. Stricker, see 6:87 (284 references, 1 excerpt) ; for reviews by Frank Barron, Åke Bjerstedt, and Donald W. Fiske, see 5:47 (50 references, 2 excerpts).

J66. **The Ego Strength Q-Sort Test.** For additional information and reviews by Allen L. Edwards and Harrison G. Gough, see 6:88 (3 references).

J67. Embedded Figures Test. For additional information and reviews by Harrison G. Gough and Leona E. Tyler, see 6:89 (24 references); see also 5:49 (9 references).

J68. Emo Questionnaire. For additional information and reviews by Bertram D. Cohen and W. Grant Dahlstrom, see 6:90 (1 reference).

J69. The Empathy Test. For additional information and a review by Wallace B. Hall, see 6:91 (9 references); for a review by Robert L. Thorndike, see 5:50 (20 references).

J70. [Environment Indexes.] For additional information, see 6:92 (19 references).

J71. Environment Inventory for College and University Students. For additional information and a review by E. G. Williamson, see 2:1218 (1 reference).

J72. Euphorimeter. For additional information, see 3:36 (2 references).

J73. Evaluation Modality Test. For additional information and a review by Wilson H. Guertin, see 5:51.

J74. Every-Day Life: A Scale for the Measure of Three Varieties of Self-Reliance. For additional information and a review by Harold E. Jones, see 4:41; for a review by Albert Ellis, see 3:38 (6 references).

J75. Examining for Aphasia: A Manual for the Examination of Aphasia and Related Disturbances. For additional information and a review by T. R. Miles, see 5:52 (3 references, 2 excerpts); for a review by D. Russell Davis, see 4:42 (2 excerpts); for a review by C. R. Strother, see 3:39 (1 excerpt).

J76. Experience Variables Record: A Clinical Revision. For additional information, see 2:1219 (2 references).

J77. Eysenck Personality Inventory. For additional information and a review by James C. Lingoes, see 6:93 (1 reference).

J78. FIRO-B: [Fundamental Interpersonal Relations Orientation—Behavior]. For additional information, see 6:94 (15 references).

J79. Family Adjustment Test. For additional information and a review by John Elderkin Bell, see 6:95; for a review by Albert Ellis, see 5:53 (6 references).

J80. Famous Sayings. For additional information and reviews by Wesley C. Becker and Robert L. Thorndike, see 6:96 (17 references).

J81. Fatigue Scales Kit. For additional information and a review by Richard S. Barrett, see 6:97 (1 reference).

J82. Fels Parent Behavior Rating Scales. For additional information and a review by Dale B. Harris, see 4:43 (15 references).

J83. The Forty-Eight Item Counseling Evaluation Test. For additional information, see 6:98.

J84. The Freeman Anxiety Neurosis and Psychosomatic Test. For additional information and reviews by Gerald A. Mendelsohn and Robert C. Nichols, see 6:99 (4 references); see also 5:55 (3 references).

J85. Friend-Critic Statement. For additional information, see 5:56.

J86. G. C. Personality Development Record. For additional information, see 6:100.

J87. Gardner Behavior Chart. For additional information, see 4:44.

J88. General Goals of Life Inventory: General Education Series. For additional information and reviews by C. Robert Pace and Leona E. Tyler, see 4:45 (10 references).

J89. Generalized Attitude Scales. For reviews by Donald T. Campbell and Kenneth E. Clark, see 4:46 (37 references); for reviews by W. D. Commins and Theodore Newcomb, see 2:1202 (9 references); for a review by Stephen M. Corey, see 1:897. For a later edition, see J222.

J90. Goldstein-Scheerer Tests of Abstract and Concrete Thinking. For additional information and a review by R. W. Payne, see 6:101 (23 references); see also 5:57 (21 references); for reviews by Kate Levine Kogan, C. R. Strother (with Ludwig Immergluck), and O. L. Zangwill, see 3:41 (28 references).

J91. Gordon Personal Inventory. For additional information and reviews by Charles F. Dicken and Alfred B. Heilbrun, Jr., see 6:102 (13 references); for reviews by Benno G. Fricke and John A. Radcliffe, see 5:58 (1 reference, 2 excerpts).

J92. Gordon Personal Profile. For additional information and reviews by Charles F. Dicken and Alfred B. Heilbrun, Jr., see 6:103 (25 references); for reviews by Benno G. Fricke and John A. Radcliffe, see 5:59 (16 references, 1 excerpt).

J93. The Grassi Block Substitution Test: For Measuring Organic Brain Pathology. For additional information, see 5:60 (5 references, 2 excerpts).

J94. The Grayson Perceptualization Test. For additional information and reviews by D. Russell Davis and William Schofield, see 5:61.

J95. Group Cohesiveness: A Study of Group Morale. For additional information and reviews by Eric F. Gardner and Cecil A. Gibb, see 6:104 (1 reference).

J96. Group Dimensions Descriptions Questionnaire. For additional information, see 6:105 (5 references).

J97. Guidance Inventory. For additional information and a review by John W. M. Rothney, see 6:106.

J98. Guilford-Holley L Inventory. For additional information, see 6:107.

J99. The Guilford-Martin Inventory of Factors GAMIN. For additional information, see 6:108 (11 references); see also 5:63 (33 references); for a review by Hubert E. Brogden, see 4:47 (18 references); for a review by H. J. Eysenck, see 3:43 (7 references).

J100. The Guilford-Martin Personnel Inventory. For additional information, see 6:109 (9 references); see also 5:64 (27 references); for a review by Neil Van Steenberg, see 4:48 (20 references); for a review by Benjamin Shimberg, see 3:44 (7 references).

J101. Guilford-Martin Temperament Profile Chart. For additional information and a review by R. A. Brotemarkle, see 3:45.

J102. The Guilford-Zimmerman Temperament Survey. For additional information, see 6:110 (120 references); for a review by David R. Saunders, see

5:65 (48 references) ; for reviews by William Stephenson and Neil Van Steenberg, see 4:49 (5 references, 1 excerpt).

J103. Haggerty-Olson-Wickman Behavior Rating Schedules. For additional information and a review by Harold E. Jones, see 2:1222 (8 references).

J104. The Handicap Problems Inventory. For additional information and a review by Dorothy M. Clendenen, see 6:111.

J105. Harvard Group Scale of Hypnotic Susceptibility. For additional information and a review by Seymour Fisher, see 6:112 (4 references).

J106. Heston Personal Adjustment Inventory. For additional information, see 6:113 (14 references) ; see also 5:66 (11 references) ; for reviews by Albert Ellis, Hans J. Eysenck, and E. Lowell Kelly, see 4:50 (2 references, 1 excerpt).

J107. High School Attitude Scale. For additional information, see 6:168 ; for a review by Lee J. Cronbach, see 3:46.

J108. The Hoffer-Osmond Diagnostic Test (HOD). For additional information and reviews by Maurice Lorr and William Schofield, see 6:114 (6 references).

J109. Holland Vocational Preference Inventory. For additional information and reviews by Robert L. French and H. Bradley Sagen, see 6:115 (13 references).

J110. The Hooper Visual Organization Test. For additional information and reviews by Ralph M. Reitan and Otfried Spreen, see 6:116 (4 references).

J111. Hospital Adjustment Scale. For additional information and a review by Wilson H. Guertin, see 6:117 (3 references) ; for a review by Maurice Lorr, see 5:67 (5 references).

J112. How Well Do You Know Yourself? For additional information and reviews by Lee J. Cronbach and Harrison G. Gough, see 6:118 (2 references, 2 excerpts).

J113. Human Relations Inventory. For additional information, see 6:119 (6 references) ; for reviews by Raymond C. Norris and John A. Radcliffe, see 5:68.

J114. The Humm-Wadsworth Temperament Scale. For additional information and reviews by James R. Glennon and Floyd L. Ruch, see 6:120 (3 references) ; see also 5:69 (20 references) ; for reviews by H. J. Eysenck, H. Meltzer, and Lorenz Misbach of the 1940 edition, see 3:48 (31 references) ; for reviews by Forrest A. Kingsbury and P. E. Vernon, see 2:1223 (13 references) ; for a review by Daniel A. Prescott of an earlier edition, see 1:920.

J115. Hunt-Minnesota Test for Organic Brain Damage. For additional information and a review by Seymour G. Klebanoff, see 4:51 (8 references) ; for reviews by Margaret Ives and O. L. Zangwill, see 3:49 (11 references).

J116. The IPAT Anxiety Scale Questionnaire. For additional information and a review by Jacob Cohen, see 6:121 (23 references) ; for reviews by J. P. Guilford and E. Lowell Kelly, see 5:70 (1 excerpt).

J117. IPAT Children's Personality Questionnaire. For additional information and reviews by Anne Anastasi, Wilbur L. Layton, and Robert D. Wirt, see 6:122 (2 references).

J118. IPAT Contact Personality Factor Test. For additional information, see 6:123 (6 references) ;

for reviews by Cecil D. Johnson and S. B. Sells, see 5:71.

J119. IPAT 8-Parallel-Form Anxiety Battery. For additional information and reviews by Jacob Cohen and Paul M. Kjeldergaard, see 6:124 (4 references).

J120. The IPAT Humor Test of Personality. For additional information and reviews by W. Grant Dahlstrom, Ardie Lubin (with Frank M. Loos), and J. R. Wittenborn, see 4:61 (5 references).

J121. IPAT Music Preference Test of Personality. For additional information and reviews by Kenneth L. Bean and Paul R. Farnsworth, see 6:125 (7 references) ; for a review by Neil J. Van Steenberg, see 5:73 (4 references).

J122. IPAT Neurotic Personality Factor Test. For additional information and reviews by S. B. Sells and William Stephenson, see 5:74.

J123. Information Blank EA: A Questionnaire on Emotional Adjustment. For additional information and a review by Percival M. Symonds, see 3:50 ; for a review by Stanley G. Dulsky, see 2:1224.

J124. Inpatient Multidimensional Psychiatric Scale (IMPS). For additional information, see 6:126 (26 references).

J125. Institute of Child Study Security Test. For additional information and a review by Laurance F. Shaffer, see 5:75.

J126. Interaction Chronograph. For additional information and a review by Cecil A. Gibb, see 5:76 (20 references) ; see also 3:688 (5 references).

J127. Interaction Process Analysis. For additional information and a review by Cecil A. Gibb, see 5:77 (10 references) ; for a review by Launor F. Carter, see 4:56 (3 references).

J128. Interest Analysis. For additional information and a review by Edward B. Greene, see 3:51.

J129. Interest Index: General Education Series. For additional information, see 4:58 (2 references) ; see also 2:1226 (4 references).

J130. Interest Inventory for Elementary Grades: George Washington University Series. For additional information and reviews by Harold D. Carter and Lee J. Cronbach, see 3:52 (1 reference).

J131. Interest Questionnaire: Games and Sports: Test 8.3. For additional information, see 2:1227.

J132. Interest-Values Inventory. For additional information and reviews by E. Lowell Kelly and Paul E. Meehl, see 3:53 (5 references) ; see also 2:1228 (1 excerpt).

J133. Interests and Activities: Tests 8.2b and 8.2c. For additional information, see 2:1225 (7 references).

J134. Interpersonal Check List. For additional information and a review by P. M. Bentler, see 6:127 (39 references).

J135. Inventory of Affective Tolerance. For additional information and reviews by Paul R. Farnsworth, E. Lowell Kelly, and William U. Snyder, see 3:54 (5 references).

J136. An Inventory of Factors STDCR. For additional information, see 6:128 (17 references) ; see also 5:78 (28 references) ; for a review by Hubert E.

Brogden, see 4:59 (17 references); for a review by H. J. Eysenck, see 3:55 (10 references).

J137. Inventory of Personal-Social Relationships: General Education Series. For additional information and reviews by N. L. Gage and Theodore R. Sarbin, see 4:60 (2 references).

J138. It Scale for Children. For additional information and reviews by Philip L. Harriman and Boyd R. McCandless, see 6:129 (18 references).

J139. JNB Psychograph. For additional information, see 3:56 (1 reference).

J140. Johnson Temperament Analysis. For additional information, see 6:130 (10 references); for a review by Albert Ellis, see 4:62 (6 references); for a review by H. Meltzer, see 3:57.

J141. Jones Personality Rating Scale. For additional information, see 2:1230.

J142. Jr.-Sr. High School Personality Questionnaire. For additional information and reviews by C. J. Adcock and Philip E. Vernon, see 6:131 (17 references); see also 5:72 (4 references).

J143. Jurgensen Classification Inventory. For additional information and reviews by Robert G. Demaree (with Louis L. McQuitty) and William J. E. Crissy, see 4:63 (11 references).

J144. KD Proneness Scale and Check List. For additional information and a review by John W. M. Rothney, see 5:79 (6 references); for reviews by Douglas Courtney and Dale B. Harris, see 4:64.

J145. Kuder Preference Record—Personal. For additional information and reviews by Dorothy M. Clendenen and Wilbur L. Layton, see 6:132 (11 references); for a review by Dwight L. Arnold, see 5:80 (5 references); see also 4:65 (4 references, 1 excerpt).

J146. The Leadership Ability Evaluation. For additional information and reviews by John D. Black and Cecil A. Gibb, see 6:133 (4 references).

J147. The Leadership Q-Sort Test (A Test of Leadership Values). For additional information and reviews by Joel T. Campbell, Cecil A. Gibb, and William Stephenson, see 6:134 (6 references).

J148. Lewerenz-Steinmetz Orientation Test: Concerning Fundamental Aims of Education. For additional information and reviews by Frederic L. Ayer and Roger T. Lennon, see 4:66 (3 references).

J149. Life Adjustment Inventory. For additional information and reviews by John W. M. Rothney and Helen Shacter, see 4:67.

J150. Life Experience Inventory. For additional information and reviews by Dan L. Adler and Douglas T. Kenny, see 5:81 (1 reference).

J151. The MACC Behavioral Adjustment Scale: An Objective Approach to the Evaluation of Behavioral Adjustments of Psychiatric Patients. For additional information and a review by Wilson H. Guertin, see 6:135 (2 references); for a review by Maurice Lorr of an earlier edition, see 5:82.

J152. M-B History Record. For additional information, see 6:136 (2 references).

J153. McCleery Scale of Adolescent Development. For additional information and reviews by Eugene L. Gaier and John E. Horrocks, see 5:83 (1 reference).

J154. The Manson Evaluation. For additional information and a review by Dugal Campbell, see 6:137 (5 references); for reviews by Charles H. Honzik and Albert L. Hunsicker, see 4:68 (4 references).

J155. Maudsley Personality Inventory. For additional information and reviews by Arthur R. Jensen, James C. Lingoes, William Stephenson, and Philip E. Vernon, see 6:138 (120 references, 3 excerpts).

J156. Maxfield-Buchholz Scale of Social Maturity for Use With Preschool Blind Children. For additional information, see 6:139 (2 references).

J157. Memory-For-Designs Test. For additional information and a review by Otfried Spreen, see 6:140 (18 references); see also 4:69 (5 references).

J158. Mental Health Analysis. For additional information and a review by J. Robert Williams, see 6:141 (8 references); for reviews by William E. Coffman, Henry E. Garrett, C. M. Louttit, James Maxwell, and Douglas Spencer of the original edition, see 3:59 (1 excerpt).

J159. Minnesota Counseling Inventory. For additional information and reviews by Norman Frederiksen and John W. M. Rothney, see 6:142 (10 references); see also 5:85 (1 excerpt).

J160. The Minnesota Inventory of Social Attitudes. For additional information and a review by Verner M. Sims, see 4:70 (12 references); for reviews by J. P. Guilford and George W. Hartmann, see 1:900.

J161. Minnesota Multiphasic Personality Inventory. For additional information and reviews by C. J. Adcock and James C. Lingoes, see 6:143 (626 references); for reviews by Albert Ellis and Warren T. Norman, see 5:86 (496 references); for a review by Arthur L. Benton, see 4:71 (211 references); for reviews by Arthur L. Benton, H. J. Eysenck, L. S. Penrose, and Julian B. Rotter, see 3:60 (72 references, 1 excerpt).

J162. Minnesota Personality Scale. For additional information, see 5:87 (22 references); for reviews by Philip Eisenberg and John W. French, see 3:61 (9 references).

J163. Minnesota Rating Scale for Personal Qualities and Abilities. For additional information and a review by Dorothy M. Clendenen, see 5:88 (1 reference).

J164. Minnesota Scale for the Survey of Opinions. For additional information and reviews by H. H. Remmers and Goodwin Watson, see 1:901 (1 reference).

J165. Minnesota T-S-E Inventory. For additional information, see 6:144 (5 references); for reviews by Philip Eisenberg and John W. French, see 3:62 (6 references).

J166. Mooney Problem Check List. For additional information and a review by Thomas C. Burgess, see 6:145 (25 references); see also 5:89 (26 references); for reviews by Harold E. Jones and Morris Krugman, see 4:73 (13 references); for reviews by Ralph C. Bedell and Theodore F. Lentz, see 3:67 (17 references).

J167. The Mother-Child Relationship Evaluation. For additional information and reviews by John Elderkin Bell and Dale B. Harris, see 6:146.

J168. Motivation Analysis Test. For additional information, see 6:146a.

J169. Myers-Briggs Type Indicator. For additional information and reviews by Gerald A. Mendelsohn and Norman D. Sundberg, see 6:147 (10 references, 1 excerpt).

J170. Nebraska Personality Inventory. For additional information and reviews by John C. Flanagan and C. M. Louttit, see 1:922 (1 reference).

J171. The Neuroticism Scale Questionnaire. For additional information and reviews by E. Lowell Kelly and Jerome D. Pauker, see 6:148 (1 reference, 2 excerpts).

J172. Northampton Activity Rating Scale. For additional information, see 4:74.

J173. Objective-Analytic (O-A) Anxiety Battery. For additional information and a review by Harold Borko, see 6:149 (5 references, 1 excerpt).

J174. Objective-Analytic Personality Test Batteries. For additional information and a review by H. J. Eysenck, see 5:90 (6 references).

J175. Occupational Personality Inventory. For additional information, see 2:1232 (3 references).

J176. Ohio Guidance Tests for Elementary Grades. For additional information and reviews by M. H. Elliott and John W. M. Rothney, see 3:63 (8 references).

J177. Omnibus Personality Inventory. For additional information and reviews by Paul M. Kjeldergaard and Norman E. Wallen, see 6:150 (11 references, 1 excerpt).

J178. Opinion, Attitude and Interest Survey. For additional information and reviews by John O. Crites and Harold Webster, see 6:151 (4 references).

J179. Organic Integrity Test. For additional information, see 6:152 (1 reference).

J180. The Orientation Inventory. For additional information and reviews by Richard S. Barrett and H. Bradley Sagen, see 6:153 (2 references).

J181. P.Q. or Personality Quotient Test. For additional information and reviews by Douglas Spencer and Simon H. Tulchin, see 2:1233 (5 references); for reviews by C. M. Louttit and Edmund G. Williamson, see 1:921.

J182. P-S Experience Blank: Psycho-Somatic Inventory. For additional information and reviews by Doncaster G. Humm and Charles I. Mosier, see 2:1234 (2 references).

J183. Parents Rating Scale. For additional information, see 2:1235.

J184. Personal Adaptability Test. For additional information and a review by Harold Webster, see 5:91 (1 reference).

J185. Personal Adjustment Inventory. For additional information and reviews by Norman D. Sundberg and Robert D. Wirt, see 6:154 (6 references); for reviews by Dan L. Adler and Harrison G. Gough, see 5:117 (19 references); for a review by C. M. Louttit, see 2:1258.

J186. The Personal and Social Development Program. For additional information and reviews by Edward Landy and C. Gilbert Wrenn (with Roy D. Lewis), see 5:92.

J187. Personal Audit. For additional information and a review by William Seeman, see 4:75 (3 references); for a review by Percival M. Symonds, see 3:64 (9 references).

J188. Personal Data Scale. For additional information, see 1:1119.

J189. Personal History Record [C. H. Stoelting Co.]. For additional information, see 2:1236 (1 reference).

J190. Personal Index. For additional information and reviews by J. B. Maller and Carl R. Rogers, see 2:1237 (5 references).

J191. The Personal Preference Inventory: Student Form. For additional information and reviews by E. Lowell Kelly and C. M. Louttit, see 4:76.

J192. The Personal Preference Scale. For additional information, see 5:93 (2 references).

J193. Personal Qualities Inventory. For additional information, see 6:155 (1 reference).

J194. Personality and Interest Inventory. For additional information, see 6:156; for a review by Stephen M. Corey, see 2:1238 (3 references); for a review by Jack W. Dunlap, see 1:924.

J195. The Personality Evaluation Form: A Technique for the Organization and Interpretation of Personality Data. For additional information and a review by Dorothy H. Eichorn, see 5:94 (1 excerpt).

J196. Personality Index. For additional information and a review by Benjamin Shimberg, see 3:65.

J197. The Personality Inventory. For additional information and reviews by Wesley C. Becker and Donald J. Veldman, see 6:157 (22 references); see also 5:95 (40 references); for a review by Leona E. Tyler, see 4:77 (188 references); for reviews by Charles I. Mosier and Theodore Newcomb, see 2:1239 (71 references).

J198. Personality Rating Chart for Preschool Children. For additional information, see 2:1241 (1 reference).

J199. Personality Rating Scale. For additional information and a review by Laurance F. Shaffer, see 6:158 (4 references); for reviews by Robert H. Bauernfeind and Dale B. Harris, see 5:41 (18 references).

J200. Personality Rating Scale for Preschool Children. For additional information, see 2:1242 (1 reference).

J201. Personality Record (Revised). For additional information and a review by Verner M. Sims of the original edition, see 4:78 (1 reference).

J202. Personality Schedule. For additional information, see 6:159 (38 references); for a review by J. P. Guilford, see 2:1243 (28 references).

J203. Personality Sketches. For additional information and reviews by Henry E. Garrett and J. P. Guilford, see 1:925.

J204. The Personality Survey. For additional information and reviews by Douglas Courtney and John W. M. Rothney, see 4:79 (2 references).

J205. The Philo-Phobe. For additional information and a review by Parker Davis, Jr., see 3:66 (3 references).

J206. Pictorial Study of Values: Pictorial Allport-Vernon. For additional information and reviews by Andrew R. Baggaley and Harrison G. Gough, see 5:96.

J207. Polyfactorial Study of Personality. For additional information and reviews by Bertram D. Cohen and Donald R. Peterson, see 6:160 (1 excerpt).

J208. Position Response Form and Response Form. For additional information, see 6:161.

J209. The Power of Influence Test. For additional information and reviews by Åke Bjerstedt and Eric F. Gardner, see 6:162 (1 reference).

J210. Practical Policy Test. For additional information, see 5:98 (9 references).

J211. Pre-Counseling Inventory. For additional information and a review by Charles H. Honzik, see 4:80 (1 reference).

J212. The Press Test. For additional information and reviews by William H. Helme and Allyn Miles Munger, see 6:163.

J213. Pressey Interest-Attitude Tests. For additional information and a review by Douglas Spencer, see 2:1243.1 (5 references).

J214. Problem Check List: Form for Rural Young People. For additional information, see 4:81 (2 references).

J215. Problem Check List: Form for Schools of Nursing. For additional information, see 4:82 (1 reference).

J216. A Process for In-School Screening of Children With Emotional Handicaps. For additional information and reviews by Alan O. Ross and J. Robert Williams, see 6:164 (3 references).

J217. Progress Assessment Chart (P-A-C). For additional information, see 6:165.

J218. Psychometric Behavior Checklist. For additional information, see 6:166 (1 reference).

J219. The Psychotic Reaction Profile (PRP): An Inventory of Patient Behavior for Use by Hospital Personnel. For additional information and a review by Wilson H. Guertin, see 6:167 (4 references).

J220. Pupil Adjustment Inventory. For additional information and reviews by Robert H. Bauernfeind and John Pierce-Jones, see 5:100 (1 excerpt).

J221. Pupil Portraits. For additional information and a review by Simon H. Tulchin, see 2:1244 (2 references).

J222. The Purdue Master Attitude Scales. For additional information and a review by Donald T. Campbell, see 6:168. For an earlier edition, see J89.

J223. Purdue Rating Scale for Administrators and Executives. For additional information and reviews by John P. Foley, Jr. and Herbert A. Tonne, see 5:101 (1 reference); for a review by Kenneth L. Heaton, see 4:83 (7 references).

J224. Radio Checklist. For additional information, see 2:1245.

J225. Rating Scale for Pupil Adjustment. For additional information and reviews by William E. Henry and Morris Krugman, see 5:102.

J226. Recreation Inquiry. For additional information and reviews by Theodore F. Lentz and Louis Long, see 3:70 (2 references).

J227. Report Form on Temperament and Social Behavior. For additional information, see 2:1247 (1 reference).

J228. Rutgers Social Attribute Inventory. For additional information and reviews by David B. Orr and John Pierce-Jones, see 6:169.

J229. SAQS Chicago Q Sort. For additional information and reviews by William Stephenson and Clifford H. Swensen, Jr., see 5:103 (2 references).

J230. SRA Junior Inventory. For additional information and a review by Warren R. Baller, see 5:104 (2 excerpts); for a review by Dwight L. Arnold, see 4:90.

J231. SRA Youth Inventory. For additional information and a review by Forrest L. Vance, see 6:170 (12 references, 1 excerpt); see also 5:105 (12 references); for reviews by Kenneth E. Clark and Frank S. Freeman, see 4:91 (7 references).

J232. Scale for Evaluating the School Behavior of Children Ten to Fifteen. For additional information, see 1:926 (1 reference, 1 excerpt).

J233. Scale of Beliefs for Junior High School: Tests 4.4 and 4.5. For additional information, see 2:1251 (1 reference).

J234. Scale of Beliefs: Tests 4.21 and 4.31. For additional information, see 2:1250 (7 references).

J235. A Scale to Measure Attitudes Toward Disabled Persons. For additional information, see 6:171.

J236. The School Inventory. For additional information and a review by Ross W. Matteson, see 4:84 (3 references); for reviews by Robert G. Bernreuter and J. B. Maller, see 2:1252 (4 references).

J237. Schrammel-Gorbutt Personality Adjustment Scale. For additional information and reviews by Raleigh M. Drake and Nelson G. Hanawalt, see 3:92.

J238. The Science Research Temperament Scale. For additional information and reviews by John D. Black and David R. Saunders, see 5:106 (1 reference).

J239. Security-Insecurity Inventory. For additional information and reviews by Nelson G. Hanawalt and Harold Webster, see 5:107 (10 references).

J240. Selective Vocabulary Test. For additional information and a review by James Maxwell, see 4:85 (2 references); for reviews by Jack W. Dunlap and Starke R. Hathaway, see 3:93.

J241. Self-Analysis Inventory. For additional information and reviews by Warren R. Baller and John W. Gustad, see 5:108.

J242. Self-Appraisal Schedule. For additional information, see 1:927 (1 reference).

J243. Self-Interview Inventory. For additional information and reviews by Andrew R. Baggaley and David T. Lykken, see 6:172 (1 reference).

J244. Self-Perception Inventory: An Adjustment Survey With Special Reference to the Speech Situation. For additional information and a review by C. R. Strother, see 5:109.

J245. Sense of Humor Test. For additional information, see 3:94.

J246. The Sherman Mental Impairment Test. For additional information and reviews by D. Russell Davis and William Schofield, see 5:110 (1 reference).

J247. Shipley-Institute of Living Scale for Measuring Intellectual Impairment. For additional information, see 6:173 (13 references); see also 5:111

(23 references) ; for reviews by E. J. G. Bradford, William A. Hunt, and Margaret Ives, see 3 :95 (26 references).

J248. Sixteen Personality Factor Questionnaire. For additional information and a review by Maurice Lorr, see 6 :174 (81 references) ; for a review by C. J. Adcock, see 5 :112 (21 references) ; for reviews by Charles M. Harsh, Ardie Lubin, and J. Richard Wittenborn, see 4 :87 (8 references).

J249. Social Attitude Scales. For additional information and reviews by H. H. Remmers and Goodwin Watson, see 1 :902.

J250. A Social Competence Inventory for Adults. For additional information and reviews by William J. Eichman and Jerome D. Pauker, see 6 :175.

J251. Social Distance Scale. For additional information and a review by Donald T. Campbell, see 4 :88 (19 references).

J252. Social Intelligence Test: George Washington University Series. For additional information, see 6 :176 (14 references) ; see also 4 :89 (7 references) ; for reviews by Glen U. Cleeton and Howard R. Taylor, see 3 :96 (9 references) ; for a review by Robert L. Thorndike, see 2 :1253 (20 references).

J253. Social Orientation. For additional information and a review by Charles C. Peters, see 1 :903.

J254. Social Participation Scale. For additional information, see 5 :113.

J255. Social Personality Inventory for College Women. For additional information and a review by Nelson G. Hanawalt, see 3 :97 (10 references).

J256. Social Problems: Test 1.42. For additional information, see 2 :1254 (1 reference).

J257. Spiral Aftereffect Test. For additional information and reviews by William J. Eichman and Ralph M. Reitan, see 6 :177 (43 references).

J258. Stanford Hypnotic Susceptibility Scale. For additional information and reviews by Milton V. Kline and C. Scott Moss, see 6 :178 (17 references).

J259. Stanford Profile Scales of Hypnotic Susceptibility. For additional information and reviews by Seymour Fisher and Eugene E. Levitt, see 6 :179.

J260. Stern Activities Index. For additional information, see 6 :180 (27 references).

J261. Straus Rural Attitudes Profile. For additional information, see 6 :181 (1 reference, 1 excerpt).

J262. Student Questionnaire. For additional information and a review by Simon H. Tulchin, see 3 :98.

J263. Study of Attitudes Toward the Administration of Justice. For additional information, see 2 :1255 (1 reference).

J264. Study of Values: A Scale for Measuring the Dominant Interests in Personality. For additional information and reviews by John D. Hundleby and John A. Radcliffe, see 6 :182 (137 references) ; for a review by N. L. Gage of the second edition, see 5 :114 (57 references) ; for reviews by Harrison G. Gough and William Stephenson, see 4 :92 (25 references, 1 excerpt) ; for a review by Paul E. Meehl of the original edition, see 3 :99 (61 references).

J265. Style of Mind Inventory: Trait, Value and Belief Patterns in Greek, Roman and Judeo-Christian Perspectives. For additional information, see 6 :183.

J266. Survey of Attitudes and Beliefs. For additional information and reviews by Donald T. Campbell and C. Robert Pace, see 5 :116.

J267. Survey of Interpersonal Values. For additional information and reviews by Lee J. Cronbach, Leonard D. Goodstein, and John K. Hemphill, see 6 :184 (12 references, 1 excerpt).

J268. Survey of Personal Attitude "SPA" (With Pictures): Individual Placement Series (Area III). For additional information, see 6 :185.

J269. Syracuse Scales of Social Relations. For additional information and reviews by Åke Bjerstedt and Donald T. Campbell, see 6 :186 (16 references, 1 excerpt).

J270. Teacher's Rating Scales for Pupil Adjustment. For additional information and a review by Bessie Lee Gambrill, see 2 :1256.

J271. Temperament and Character Test. For additional information, see 5 :115.

J272. Temperament Comparator. For additional information and reviews by Lawrence J. Stricker and Robert L. Thorndike, see 6 :187 (1 reference).

J273. Tentative Check List for Determining Attitudes on Fifty Crucial Social, Economic, and Political Problems. For additional information, see 2 :1257.

J274. Test for Developmental Age in Girls. For additional information, see 1 :1140.

J275. Test of Basic Assumptions. For additional information, see 6 :188.

J276. Test of Behavioral Rigidity. For additional information and reviews by Douglas P. Crowne and Benjamin Kleinmuntz, see 6 :189 (9 references).

J277. Test of Social Attitudes. For additional information, see 2 :1260.

J278. Test of Social Insight. For additional information and reviews by John D. Black and John Pierce-Jones, see 6 :190 (4 references, 1 excerpt).

J279. Test of Work Competency and Stability. For additional information, see 6 :191 (2 references).

J280. Tests of the Socially Competent Person. For additional information and reviews by Alvin C. Eurich, Warren G. Findley, and Pedro T. Orata, see 2 :1259 (1 reference) ; for reviews by Douglas E. Scates and Hilda Taba, see 1 :1154.

J281. Thurstone Temperament Schedule. For additional information, see 6 :192 (17 references) ; for a review by Neil J. Van Steenberg, see 5 :118 (12 references) ; for reviews by Hans J. Eysenck, Charles M. Harsh, and David G. Ryans, see 4 :93 (1 excerpt).

J282. Torgerson's Inventories and Record Forms. For additional information and a review by Harold H. Abelson, see 3 :105 (1 reference).

J283. Triadal Equated Personality Inventory. For additional information, see 6 :193.

J284. Tulane Factors of Liberalism-Conservatism. For additional information and reviews by Donald T. Campbell and C. Robert Pace, see 5 :119 (2 references).

J285. V.G.C. Personality Adjustment Indicator. For additional information, see 3 :106.

J286. Vineland Social Maturity Scale. For additional information, see 6 :194 (20 references) ; see also 5 :120 (15 references) ; for reviews by William M.

Cruickshank and Florence M. Teagarden, see 4:94 (21 references); for reviews by C. M. Louttit and John W. M. Rothney, see 3:107 (58 references, 1 excerpt); for reviews by Paul H. Furfey, Elaine F. Kinder, and Anna S. Starr of an experimental form, see 1:1143.

J287. The Visual-Verbal Test: A Measure of Conceptual Thinking. For additional information and reviews by R. W. Payne and Donald R. Peterson, see 6:195 (8 references).

J288. WLW Personal Attitude Inventory. For additional information, see 6:196.

J289. Walther Social Attitudes Test. For additional information, see 2:1261.

J290. Washburne Social-Adjustment Inventory. For additional information and a review by William Seeman, see 4:95 (12 references); see also 3:110 (11 references, 2 excerpts) and 2:1262 (4 references); for a review by Daniel A. Prescott of an earlier edition, see 1:928.

J291. A Weighted-Score Likability Rating Scale. For additional information, see 5:121.

J292. Weitzman's Inventory of Social Behavior. For additional information and reviews by Louis Long and Goodwin Watson, see 3:111 (3 references).

J293. Welsh Figure Preference Test. For additional information and a review by Harold Borko, see 6:197 (20 references, 1 excerpt).

J294. The Western Personality Inventory. For additional information, see 6:198; for reviews of the component tests, see 6:60 (1 review), 6:137 (1 review), 4:30 (2 reviews), and 4:68 (2 reviews).

J295. What Do You Think? For additional information and a review by Ralph K. Watkins, see 2:1263 (3 references, 1 excerpt); for a review by Francis D. Curtis, see 1:1139.

J296. What I Like to Do: An Inventory of Children's Interests. For additional information and reviews by John W. M. Rothney and Naomi Stewart, see 5:122 (1 excerpt).

J297. What Should Our Schools Do? A Poll of Public Opinion on the School Program. For additional information, see 2:1264 (1 excerpt).

J298. What Would You Do? A Survey of Student Opinion. For additional information, see 2:1265 (1 reference).

J299. William, Lynde & Williams Analysis of Personal Values. For additional information, see 6:199.

J300. Willoughby Emotional Maturity Scale. For additional information and a review by Lysle W. Croft, see 4:96 (7 references).

J301. Wilson Scales of Stability and Instability. For additional information and reviews by Paul E. Meehl and Katherine W. Wilcox, see 3:112.

J302. Winnetka Scale for Rating School Behavior and Attitudes. For additional information and a review by Harriet M. Barthelmess [Morrison], see 1:929 (2 references).

J303. The Wishes and Fears Inventory. For additional information, see 4:97.

J304. The Wishing Well. For additional information, see 4:98 (1 reference).

J305. Wittenborn Psychiatric Rating Scales. For additional information and reviews by H. J. Eysenck and Maurice Lorr, see 5:123 (15 references, 1 excerpt).

J306. Work Preference Inventory. For additional information, see 4:99; for reviews by Edwin W. Davis, John C. Flanagan, and Gilbert J. Rich, see 3:113.

J307. Wrightstone Scale of Civic Beliefs. For additional information and reviews by Stephen M. Corey and Harold Gulliksen, see 2:1266 (3 references).

J308. Your Activities and Attitudes. For additional information, see 4:100 (4 references, 1 excerpt).

PROJECTIVE

J309. The African T.A.T. For additional information, see 6:200 (1 reference).

J310. Animal Puzzles. For additional information, see 1:1057.

J311. Association Adjustment Inventory. For additional information and reviews by W. Grant Dahlstrom and Bertram R. Forer, see 6:201 (1 excerpt).

J312. The Auditory Apperception Test. For additional information and reviews by Kenneth L. Bean and Clifford H. Swensen, Jr., see 5:124 (3 references).

J313. The Behavioral Complexity Test: A Test for Use in Research. For additional information and a review by John Elderkin Bell, see 6:202 (4 references).

J314. Bender Gestalt Test. For additional information and a review by C. B. Blakemore, see 6:203 (99 references, 1 excerpt); see also 5:172 (118 references); for reviews by Arthur L. Benton and Howard R. White, see 4:144 (34 references); see also 3:108 (8 references).

J315. The Blacky Pictures: A Technique for the Exploration of Personality Dynamics. For additional information and a review by Bert R. Sappenfield, see 6:204 (34 references); for a review by Kenneth R. Newton, see 5:125 (38 references, 1 excerpt); for a review by Albert Ellis, see 4:102 (7 references, 3 excerpts).

J316. Buttons: A Projective Test for Pre-Adolescent and Adolescent Boys and Girls. For additional information, see 6:205.

J317. Children's Apperception Test. For additional information and reviews by Bernard I. Murstein and Robert D. Wirt, see 6:206 (19 references); for reviews by Douglas T. Kenny and Albert I. Rabin, see 5:126 (15 references); for reviews by John E. Bell and L. Joseph Stone, see 4:103 (2 references, 5 excerpts).

J318. Controlled Projection for Children. For additional information and a review by John Liggett, see 6:207; see also 5:127 (8 references, 3 excerpts); for reviews by Arthur L. Benton and Percival M. Symonds of the original edition, see 3:29 (5 excerpts).

J319. Curtis Completion Form. For additional information and reviews by Irwin G. Sarason and Laurance F. Shaffer, see 6:208 (2 references); for a review by Alfred B. Heilbrun, Jr., see 5:128.

J320. The Draw-A-Person. For additional information, see 6:209.

J321. Draw-A-Person Quality Scale. For additional information and a review by Philip L. Harriman, see 5:129 (3 references).

J322. The Drawing-Completion Test: A Projective Technique for the Investigation of Personality. For additional information, see 5:130 (3 references, 4 excerpts).

J323. The Driscoll Play Kit. For additional information, see 6:210 (2 references).

J324. The Eight Card Redrawing Test (8CRT). For additional information, see 6:211 (4 excerpts); for reviews by Cherry Ann Clark and Philip L. Harriman, see 5:131 (6 references, 1 excerpt).

J325. Expressive Movement Chart. For additional information, see 4:104 (2 references).

J326. "F" [Fluency of Association] Test. For additional information and reviews by J. M. Blackburn, P. E. Vernon, and Ll. Wynn Jones, see 2:1220 (10 references, 1 excerpt).

J327. The Family Relations Indicator: A Projective Technique for Investigating Intra-Family Relationships. For additional information and reviews by C. B. Blakemore and Walter Katkovsky, see 6:212 (1 reference).

J328. Family Relations Test: An Objective Technique for Exploring Emotional Attitudes in Children. For additional information and reviews by John E. Bell, Dale B. Harris, and Arthur R. Jensen, see 5:132 (1 reference).

J329. The Five Task Test: A Performance and Projective Test of Emotionality, Motor Skill and Organic Brain Damage. For additional information and reviews by Dorothy H. Eichorn and Bert R. Sappenfield, see 5:133 (1 excerpt).

J330. The Forer Structured Sentence Completion Test. For additional information and reviews by Charles N. Cofer and Percival M. Symonds, see 5:134 (5 references).

J331. The Forer Vocational Survey. For additional information and reviews by Benjamin Balinsky and Charles N. Cofer, see 5:135 (1 excerpt).

J332. Four Picture Test (1930). For additional information and reviews by S. G. Lee and Johann M. Schepers, see 6:213 (3 references); for reviews by John E. Bell, E. J. G. Bradford, and Ephraim Rosen of the original edition, see 4:105 (3 references, 1 excerpt).

J333. Franck Drawing Completion Test. For additional information and a review by Arthur W. Meadows, see 5:136 (5 references).

J334. The Graphomotor Projection Technique. For additional information and a review by Philip L. Harriman, see 5:137 (7 references, 2 excerpts).

J335. The Group Personality Projective Test. For additional information, see 6:214 (7 references).

J336. Group Projection Sketches for the Study of Small Groups. For additional information and a review by Cecil A. Gibb, see 5:138 (1 reference); for reviews by Robert R. Holt and N. W. Morton, see 4:106.

J337. H-T-P: House-Tree-Person Projective Technique. For additional information and a review by Mary R. Haworth, see 6:215 (32 references);

for a review by Philip L. Harriman, see 5:139 (61 references); for reviews by Albert Ellis and Ephraim Rosen, see 4:107 (14 references, 1 excerpt); for reviews by Morris Krugman and Katherine W. Wilcox, see 3:47 (5 references).

J338. The Hand Test. For additional information and a review by Goldine C. Gleser, see 6:216 (6 references, 1 excerpt).

J339. The Holtzman Inkblot Technique. For additional information and reviews by Richard W. Coan, H. J. Eysenck, Bertram R. Forer, and William N. Thetford, see 6:217 (22 references).

J340. Horn-Hellersberg Test. For additional information, see 6:218 (1 reference); for reviews by Philip L. Harriman and T. W. Richards, see 4:108 (5 references).

J341. The Howard Ink Blot Test. For additional information and reviews by Jesse G. Harris, Jr. and Bernard I. Murstein, see 6:219 (1 reference, 1 excerpt); for a review by C. R. Strother, see 5:141 (3 references, 1 excerpt).

J342. The IES Test. For additional information and reviews by Douglas P. Crowne and Walter Katkovsky, see 6:220 (15 references, 1 excerpt).

J343. An Incomplete Sentence Test. For additional information, see 6:221; for a review by Benjamin Balinsky, see 5:142.

J344. The Industrial Sentence Completion Form. For additional information, see 6:222.

J345. The Insight Test: A Verbal Projective Test for Personality Study. For additional information and a review by Richard Jessor, see 5:143 (8 references).

J346. Interpersonal Diagnosis of Personality. For additional information and a review by Jerry S. Wiggins, see 6:223 (10 references); see also 5:144 (11 references).

J347. Kahn Test of Symbol Arrangement. For additional information, see 6:224 (10 references); for reviews by Cherry Ann Clark and Richard Jessor, see 5:145 (16 references, 1 excerpt); for a review by Edward Joseph Shoben, Jr., see 4:110 (2 references).

J348. The Kell-Hoeflin Incomplete Sentence Blank: Youth-Parent Relations. For additional information, see 6:225 (2 references).

J349. Kent-Rosanoff Free Association Test. For additional information and a review by Jerry S. Wiggins, see 6:226 (82 references).

J350. The Lowenfeld Kaleidoblocs. For additional information and reviews by T. R. Miles and George Westby, see 6:227 (3 references).

J351. Lowenfeld Mosaic Test. For additional information and reviews by T. R. Miles and George Westby, see 6:228 (20 references); for a review by C. J. Adcock, see 5:147 (43 references); see also 4:115 (13 references).

J352. Machover Draw-A-Person Test. For additional information and a review by Philip M. Kitay, see 6:229 (84 references); see also 5:148 (39 references); for reviews by Philip L. Harriman and Naomi Stewart, see 4:111 (13 references).

J353. Make a Picture Story. For additional information and a review by Arthur R. Jensen, see 6:230 (10 references); see also 5:149 (19 references); for reviews by Albert I. Rabin and Charles R. Strother, see 4:113 (19 references).

J354. The Michigan Picture Test. For additional information and reviews by William E. Henry and Morris Krugman, see 5:150 (7 references, 2 excerpts).

J355. Miner Sentence Completion Scale. For additional information, see 6:230a (2 references).

J356. Minnesota Percepto-Diagnostic Test. For additional information and reviews by Richard W. Coan and Eugene E. Levitt, see 6:231 (2 references).

J357. Myokinetic Psychodiagnosis (MKP). For additional information and reviews by Philip L. Harriman and Irwin G. Sarason, see 6:232 (10 references).

J358. The Object Relations Technique. For additional information and a review by H. R. Beech, see 6:233 (7 references, 1 excerpt); for a review by George Westby, see 5:151 (6 references).

J359. Pickford Projective Pictures. For additional information and a review by Stanley J. Segal, see 6:234 (5 references, 3 excerpts).

J360. The Picture Impressions: A Projective Technique for Investigating the Patient-Therapist Relationship. For additional information, see 5:152 (1 reference, 1 excerpt).

J361. The Picture World Test. For additional information and a review by Walter Kass, see 5:153 (1 excerpt).

J362. Plot-Completion Test. For additional information and reviews by Robert C. Challman and Percival M. Symonds, see 4:116 (2 references).

J363. Psychiatric Attitudes Battery. For additional information, see 6:235 (10 references).

J364. Rock-A-Bye, Baby: A Group Projective Test for Children. For additional information, see 6:236 (4 references).

J365. Rorschach. For additional information and reviews by Richard H. Dana, Leonard D. Eron, and Arthur R. Jensen, see 6:237 (732 references); for reviews by Samuel J. Beck, H. J. Eysenck, Raymond J. McCall, and Laurance F. Shaffer, see 5:154 (1078 references); for a review by Helen Sargent, see 4:117 (621 references); for reviews by Morris Krugman and J. R. Wittenborn, see 3:73 (451 references); see also 2:1246 (147 references).

J366. Rosenzweig Picture-Frustration Study. For additional information and a review by Åke Bjerstedt, see 6:238 (61 references); for reviews by Richard H. Dana and Bert R. Sappenfield, see 5:155 (109 references); for reviews by Robert C. Challman and Percival M. Symonds, see 4:129 (77 references).

J367. The Rotter Incomplete Sentences Blank. For additional information, see 6:239 (17 references); see also 5:156 (18 references); for reviews by Charles N. Cofer and William Schofield, see 4:130 (6 references, 1 excerpt).

J368. Self Valuation Test. For additional information, see 5:157 (2 references).

J369. Sentence Completions Test. For additional information, see 5:158 (1 reference); for reviews by Charles N. Cofer and Charles R. Strother of an earlier edition, see 4:131 (3 references, 1 excerpt).

J370. The South African Picture Analysis Test. For additional information and reviews by S. G. Lee and Johann M. Schepers, see 6:240 (1 excerpt).

J371. Structured Doll Play Test. For additional information and reviews by Terence Moore and Alan O. Ross, see 6:241 (6 references).

J372. Structured-Objective Rorschach Test. For additional information and reviews by Jesse G. Harris, Jr. and Boris Semeonoff, see 6:242 (16 references, 2 excerpts).

J373. Symbol Elaboration Test. For additional information and a review by Richard H. Dana, see 5:160 (1 reference).

J374. Symonds Picture-Story Test. For additional information and reviews by Walter Kass and Kenneth R. Newton, see 5:161 (2 references); for a review by E. J. G. Bradford, see 4:132 (2 references, 1 excerpt).

J375. Szondi Test. For additional information, see 6:243 (21 references); see also 5:162 (74 references); for reviews by Ardie Lubin and Albert I. Rabin, see 4:134 (64 references); for a review by Susan K. Deri, see 3:100.

J376. Ten Silhouettes. For additional information, see 6:244 (4 references).

J377. A Test of Family Attitudes. For additional information and a review by John E. Bell, see 5:163 (2 references).

J378. Thematic Apperception Test. For additional information and a review by C. J. Adcock, see 6:245 (287 references); for reviews by Leonard D. Eron and Arthur R. Jensen, see 5:164 (311 references); for a review by Arthur L. Benton, see 4:136 (198 references); for reviews by Arthur L. Benton, Julian B. Rotter, and J. R. Wittenborn, see 3:103 (101 references, 1 excerpt).

J379. Thematic Apperception Test for African Subjects. For additional information and a review by Mary D. Ainsworth, see 5:165 (1 reference).

J380. Thematic Apperception Test: Thompson Modification. For additional information and a review by Mary D. Ainsworth, see 5:166 (4 references); see also 4:138 (5 references, 3 excerpts).

J381. The Tomkins-Horn Picture Arrangement Test. For additional information and a review by Robert C. Nichols, see 6:246 (7 references, 3 excerpts); for reviews by Donald W. Fiske, John W. Gittinger, and Wayne H. Holtzman, see 5:167 (6 references, 1 excerpt).

J382. The Toy World Test. For additional information and a review by L. Joseph Stone, see 5:168 (11 references); see also 4:147 (6 references).

J383. The Travis Projective Pictures. For additional information and a review by Edwin S. Shneidman, see 5:169 (1 reference); for a review by Robert R. Holt of the original edition, see 4:142 (3 references).

J384. The Tree Test. For additional information, see 5:170 (2 references).

J385. Twitchell-Allen Three-Dimensional Personality Test. For additional information, see 5:171 (3 references); for a review by Edward Joseph Shoben, Jr., see 4:143.

J386. Visual Apperception Test '60. For additional information and reviews by Bert R. Sappenfield and Stanley J. Segal, see 6:247.

READING

K1. A.C.E.R. Silent Reading Tests, Forms A and B. For additional information and a review by Fred J. Schonell, see 5:616.

K2. A.C.E.R. Silent Reading Tests, Forms C and D. For additional information, see 6:782 (1 reference); for reviews by Fred J. Schonell and D. K. Wheeler, see 5:617.

K3. A.C.E.R. Silent Reading Tests: Standardized for Use in New Zealand. For additional information, see 5:618.

K4. Achievement Test in Silent Reading: Dominion Tests. For additional information and reviews by Harry L. Stein and Magdalen D. Vernon, see 5:619; for a review by Henry P. Smith, see 4:529; for a review by Margaret G. McKim, see 3:476.

K5. American School Achievement Tests: Part 1, Reading. For additional information, see 6:783; for reviews by Russell G. Stauffer and Agatha Townsend, see 5:620. For reviews of the complete battery, see 6:2 (2 reviews), 5:1 (2 reviews), 4:1 (1 review), and 3:1 (2 reviews).

K6. American School Reading Tests. For additional information and reviews by Henry S. Dyer and Donald E. P. Smith, see 5:621.

K7. Basic Reading Tests. For additional information, see 1:1096.

K8. The "Brighton" Reading Tests. For additional information and a review by Frederick B. Davis, see 2:1529.

K9. Buffalo Reading Test for Speed and Comprehension. For additional information and reviews by Holland Roberts and William W. Turnbull, see 3:477.

K10. California Reading Test. For additional information, see 6:784 (13 references); see also 5:622 (5 references); for reviews by John C. Flanagan and James R. Hobson of an earlier edition, see 4:530 (1 excerpt); for a review by Frederick B. Davis, see 2:1563; for reviews by Ivan A. Booker and Joseph C. Dewey, see 1:1110. For reviews of the complete battery, see 6:3 (2 reviews) and 5:2 (1 review); for reviews of earlier editions, see 4:2 (3 reviews), 3:15 (1 review), 2:1193 (2 reviews), and 1:876 (1 review, 1 excerpt).

K11. Canadian English Achievement Test (CEAT): Part 1, Reading Comprehension. For additional information and reviews of the complete battery, see 6:253 (2 reviews).

K12. Chapman Reading Comprehension Test. For additional information and a review by Russell P. Kropp, see 5:623.

K13. Chicago Reading Tests. For additional information, see 3:478 (1 reference, 1 excerpt); for reviews by Robert Lawrence McCaul and W. J. Osburn, see 2:1531.

K14. Commerce Reading Comprehension Test. For additional information, see 5:624.

K15. Comprehension Test for Training College Students. For additional information, see 6:785.

K16. Davis Reading Test. For additional information and reviews by William E. Coffman and Alton L. Raygor, see 6:786 (2 references); for a review by Benjamin Rosner of the lower level, see 5:625.

K17. DeVault Primary Reading Test. For additional information and a review by Alice N. Jameson, see 3:479.

K18. Developmental Reading Tests. For additional information and reviews by Edward B. Fry and Agatha Townsend, see 6:787.

K19. Diagnostic Examination of Silent Reading Abilities. For additional information and reviews by Frederick B. Davis, W. E. Hall, and J. B. Stroud, see 3:480 (2 references); see also 2:1532 (1 excerpt).

K20. Elementary Reading: Every Pupil Scholarship Test. For additional information, see 6:788.

K21. Elementary Reading: Every Pupil Test. For additional information, see 6:789.

K22. Emporia Silent Reading Test. For additional information and reviews by M. E. Broom and Harriet Barthelmess Morrison, see 2:1534.

K23. English No. 1, Reading Comprehension: Midland Attainment Tests. For additional information, see 1:1101.

K24. Garrison First Year Reading Test. For additional information and a review by Ruth Lowes, see 3:483 (2 references).

K25. Garvey Primary Reading Test. For additional information, see 4:533.

K26. Gates Advanced Primary Reading Tests. For additional information and a review by Kenneth D. Hopkins, see 6:790 (1 reference); see also 5:630 (3 references); for reviews by Virginia Seavey and George Spache of an earlier edition, see 3:484.

K27. Gates Basic Reading Tests. For additional information and reviews by Albert N. Hieronymus and Arthur E. Traxler, see 6:791 (1 reference); for a review by S. S. Dunn, see 5:631 (1 reference); for reviews by George Spache, Herbert F. Spitzer, and T. L. Torgerson of an earlier edition, see 3:485 (2 references); for reviews by Joseph C. Dewey and James R. Hobson, see 2:1539 (5 references, 1 excerpt).

K28. Gates Primary Reading Tests. For additional information and reviews by William Eller and Coleman Morrison, see 6:792 (1 reference); see also 5:632 (2 references); for reviews by William S. Gray and George Spache of an earlier edition, see 3:486 (7 references).

K29. Gates Reading Survey. For additional information and reviews by George Spache and Morey J. Wantman, see 6:793 (7 references); for reviews by Dorothy E. Holberg and Herbert F. Spitzer of an earlier edition, see 3:487.

K30. General Reading Test: Ohio Senior Survey Tests. For additional information, see 4:534.

K31. Haggerty Reading Examination. For additional information and a review by William S. Gray, see 4:535 (5 references).

K32. High School Reading Test: National Achievement Tests. For additional information and a review by Victor H. Noll, see 5:634; for a review by Holland Roberts, see 4:536; for a review by Robert L. McCaul, see 3:488.

K33. Ingraham-Clark Diagnostic Reading Tests. For additional information and a review by Katherine G. Keneally, see 4:538.

K34. Iowa Silent Reading Tests. For additional information and a review by Worth R. Jones, see 6:794 (40 references); for reviews by Frederick B. Davis and William W. Turnbull, see 3:489 (21 references, 2 excerpts); for reviews by Ivan A. Booker and Holland D. Roberts of an earlier edition, see 2:1547 (6 references).

K35. Kansas Primary Reading Test. For additional information and a review by Nila Banton Smith, see 4:539; for a review by Alice K. Liveright, see 2:1549.

K36. Kelley-Greene Reading Comprehension Test. For additional information and reviews by Russell P. Kropp and Magdalen D. Vernon, see 5:636 (1 reference).

K37. Kelvin Measurement of Reading Ability. For additional information, see 1:1103.

K38. The Kingston Test of Silent Reading. For additional information and reviews by Neil Gourlay and Magdalen D. Vernon, see 5:637.

K39. Lee-Clark Reading Test. For additional information and reviews by Thomas C. Barrett and Coleman Morrison, see 6:795; for a review by Ruth Lowes of the 1943 edition of the primer level, see 3:490.

K40. Los Angeles Elementary Reading Test. For additional information and a review by Henry P. Smith, see 4:541.

K41. Los Angeles Primary Reading Test. For additional information and a review by Nila Banton Smith, see 4:542 (1 reference).

K42. Manchester Reading Comprehension Test (Sen.) 1. For additional information, see 6:796 (1 reference).

K43. Metropolitan Achievement Tests: Reading. For additional information and a review by H. Alan Robinson, see 6:797 (4 references); for reviews by James R. Hobson and Margaret G. McKim of an earlier edition, see 4:543; for a review by D. A. Worcester, see 2:1551; for reviews by Ivan A. Booker and Joseph C. Dewey, see 1:1105. For reviews of the complete battery, see 6:15 (3 reviews), 4:18 (1 review), 2:1189 (2 reviews), and 1:874 (3 reviews).

K44. Minnesota Reading Examination for College Students. For additional information and a review by James M. McCallister, see 3:491 (3 references); for a review by W. C. McCall, see 2:1554 (3 references); for a review by Ruth Strang, see 1:1106.

K45. Monroe's Standardized Silent Reading Test. For additional information and reviews by Charles R. Langmuir and Agatha Townsend, see 6:798 (5 references).

K46. N.B. Silent Reading Tests (Beginners): Reading Comprehension Test. For additional information, see 6:799.

K47. The Nelson-Denny Reading Test: Vocabulary and Paragraph. For additional information and a review by Ivan A. Booker, see 4:544 (17 references); for a review by Hans C. Gordon, see 2:1557 (6 references).

K48. The Nelson-Denny Reading Test: Vocabulary-Comprehension-Rate. For additional information and reviews by David B. Orr and Agatha Townsend, see 6:800 (13 references, 1 excerpt); for references to reviews of an earlier edition, see K47.

K49. Nelson-Lohmann Reading Test. For additional information and a review by Jason Millman, see 6:801.

K50. The Nelson Reading Test. For additional information and a review by H. Alan Robinson, see 6:802; for reference to reviews of an earlier edition, see K51.

K51. The Nelson Silent Reading Test: Vocabulary and Paragraph. For additional information and a review by William D. Sheldon of an earlier edition, see 4:545 (1 reference); for a review by Constance M. McCullough, see 3:492; see also 2:1558 (1 excerpt); for reference to a review of a later edition, see K50.

K52. Primary Reading: Every Pupil Scholarship Test. For additional information, see 6:803.

K53. Primary Reading: Every Pupil Test. For additional information, see 6:804; for reviews by William S. Gray and Virginia Seavey of an earlier form, see 3:493.

K54. Primary Reading Test. For additional information and a review by Ruth Lowes, see 3:494 (1 reference).

K55. Primary Reading Test: Acorn Achievement Tests. For additional information, see 5:642; for a review by Alice N. Jameson, see 3:495.

K56. The Purdue Reading Test. For additional information, see 5:643; for a review by Albert J. Harris, see 3:496.

K57. Reading Comprehension: Cooperative English Tests. For additional information and reviews by W. V. Clemans and W. G. Fleming, see 6:806 (12 references); see also 5:645 (21 references) and 4:547 (20 references); for reviews by Robert Murray Bear and J. B. Stroud of an earlier edition, see 3:497 (15 references); see also 2:1564 (2 references); for reviews of the complete battery, see 6:256 (2 reviews, 1 excerpt) and 3:120 (3 reviews).

K58. Reading Comprehension Test: National Achievement Tests [Crow, Kuhlmann, and Crow]. For additional information, see 5:647.

K59. Reading Comprehension Test: National Achievement Tests [Speer and Smith]. For additional information, see 5:646; for a review by James R. Hobson, see 3:498.

K60. Reading: Public School Achievement Tests. For additional information, see 6:807. For reviews of the complete battery, see 2:1194 (2 reviews).

K61. Reading: Seven Plus Assessment: Northumberland Series. For additional information, see 4:548. For a review of the complete battery, see 4:24.

K62. Reading Test (Comprehension and Speed): Municipal Tests: National Achievement

Tests. For additional information, see 5:648. For reviews of the complete battery, see 5:18 (1 review), 4:20 (1 review), and 2:1191 (2 reviews).

K63. SRA Achievement Series: Reading. For additional information and a review by Edward B. Fry, see 6:808; for reviews by N. Dale Bryant and Clarence Derrick, see 5:649. For reviews of the complete battery, see 6:21 (1 review) and 5:21 (2 reviews).

K64. SRA Reading Record. For additional information and a review by William W. Turnbull, see 4:550 (2 references); for a review by Frances Oralind Triggs, see 3:502 (1 excerpt).

K65. Sangren-Woody Reading Test. For additional information and a review by David H. Russell, see 4:551; for a review by Alice K. Liveright, see 2:1565 (7 references).

K66. Schrammel-Gray High School and College Reading Test. For additional information and reviews by James M. McCallister and Robert L. McCaul, see 3:500 (1 excerpt).

K67. Sentence Reading Test 1. For additional information, see 6:809; for reviews by Reginald R. Dale and Stephen Wiseman, see 5:652.

K68. Sequential Tests of Educational Progress: Reading. For additional information and reviews by Emmett Albert Betts and Paul R. Lohnes, see 6:810 (6 references); for reviews by Eric F. Gardner, James R. Hobson, and Stephen Wiseman, see 5:653. For reviews of the complete battery, see 6:25 (2 reviews) and 5:24 (2 reviews, 1 excerpt).

K69. Shank Tests of Reading Comprehension. For additional information and a review by William D. Sheldon, see 4:553; for a review by James R. Hobson, see 2:1567 (3 references).

K70. Silent Reading Comprehension: Iowa Every-Pupil Tests of Basic Skills, Test A. For additional information, see 4:554; for reviews by James R. Hobson and Constance M. McCullough, see 3:501. For reviews of the complete battery, see 4:15 (2 reviews), 3:10 (3 reviews), and 1:872 (4 reviews).

K71. Silent Reading Tests. For additional information, see 6:811.

K72. Southgate Group Reading Tests. For additional information and reviews by M. L. Kellmer Pringle and Magdalen D. Vernon, see 6:812 (1 excerpt).

K73. Stanford Achievement Test: Reading Tests. For additional information, see 6:813 (1 reference); for reviews by Helen M. Robinson and Agatha Townsend of an earlier edition, see 5:656; for a review by James R. Hobson, see 4:555 (4 references); for a review by Margaret G. McKim, see 3:503. For reviews of the complete battery, see 6:26 (1 review, 1 excerpt), 5:25 (1 review), 4:25 (2 reviews), and 3:18 (2 reviews).

K74. Stone-Webster Test in Beginning Reading. For additional information and a review by Ruth Lowes, see 3:504 (1 reference).

K75. Survey of Primary Reading Development. For additional information and reviews by Thomas C. Barrett and Russell G. Stauffer, see 6:814.

K76. Survey of Reading Achievement: California Survey Series. For additional information and reviews by Clarence Derrick and J. Raymond Gerberich, see 6:815.

K77. Techniques in Reading Comprehension: Every Pupil Test. For additional information, see 6:816; for reviews by Ivan A. Booker and James M. McCallister of earlier forms, see 3:505.

K78. Tests of Reading: Cooperative Inter-American Tests. For additional information, see 6:818 (4 references); for reviews by Jacob S. Orleans and Frederick L. Westover, see 4:557 (4 references).

K79. Thorndike-Lorge Reading Test. For additional information and a review by Ivan A. Booker, see 4:558 (1 reference); for a review by Robert L. McCaul, see 3:506 (1 excerpt).

K80. Traxler High School Reading Test. For additional information and a review by Harold D. Carter, see 4:559 (4 references); for reviews by Alvin C. Eurich, Constance M. McCullough, and C. Gilbert Wrenn, see 2:1578 (2 excerpts).

K81. Traxler Silent Reading Test. For additional information and a review by J. Thomas Hastings, see 4:560 (2 references); for reviews by Robert L. McCaul and Miles A. Tinker, see 2:1579 (3 references, 1 excerpt); for reviews by Frederick B. Davis and Spencer Shank, see 1:1114.

K82. Unit Scales of Attainment in Reading. For additional information and reviews by Ivan A. Booker and J. Wayne Wrightstone, see 2:1581; for a review by Joseph C. Dewey, see 1:1115. For reviews of the complete battery, see 2:1197 (1 review) and 1:878 (2 reviews).

K83. W.A.L. English Comprehension Test. For additional information, see 6:819.

K84. Whipple's High-School and College Reading Test. For additional information and a review by Frederick B. Davis, see 3:507 (3 references).

K85. Williams Primary Reading Test. For additional information, see 5:658; for a review by Alice N. Jameson, see 3:508.

K86. Ypsilanti Reading Test. For additional information, see 2:1583.1.

DIAGNOSTIC

K87. California Phonics Survey. For additional information and a review by Thomas E. Culliton, Jr., see 6:820 (1 reference).

K88. Diagnostic Reading Scales. For additional information and a review by N. Dale Bryant, see 6:821.

K89. Diagnostic Reading Test: Pupil Progress Series. For additional information and a review by Agatha Townsend, see 6:822.

K90. Diagnostic Reading Tests. For additional information and reviews by Albert J. Kingston and B. H. Van Roekel, see 6:823 (21 references); for reviews by Frederick B. Davis, William W. Turnbull, and Henry Weitz, see 4:531 (19 references).

K91. Doren Diagnostic Reading Test of Word Recognition Skills. For additional information and reviews by B. H. Van Roekel and Verna L. Vickery, see 5:659.

K92. Durrell Analysis of Reading Difficulty. For additional information and reviews by James Maxwell and George D. Spache, see 5:660; for a review by Helen M. Robinson, see 4:561 (2 references); for reviews by Guy L. Bond and Miles A. Tinker, see 2:1533; for a review by Marion Monroe [Cox], see 1:1098.

K93. Gates-McKillop Reading Diagnostic Tests. For additional information and reviews by N. Dale Bryant and Gabriel M. Della-Piana, see 6:824 (2 references); for a review by George D. Spache of an earlier edition, see 5:662; for a review by Worth J. Osburn, see 4:563 (2 references); for a review by T. L. Torgerson, see 3:510 (3 references).

K94. Group Diagnostic Reading Aptitude and Achievement Tests. For additional information, see 6:825.

K95. Hildreth Diagnostic Reading Record. For additional information, see 2:1541.

K96. Individual Reading Test. For additional information and a review by R. W. McCulloch, see 5:663.

K97. McCullough Word-Analysis Tests. For additional information and reviews by Emery P. Bliesmer and Albert J. Harris, see 6:826.

K98. McGuffey Diagnostic Reading Test. For additional information, see 5:664.

K99. OC Diagnostic Syllable Test. For additional information, see 6:827.

K100. Phonics Knowledge Survey. For additional information, see 6:828.

K101. Phonovisual Diagnostic Test. For additional information and reviews by Charles M. Brown and George D. Spache, see 6:829.

K102. Primary Reading Profiles. For additional information and reviews by James R. Hobson and Verna L. Vickery, see 5:665.

K103. Reading Diagnostic Record for High School and College Students. For additional information and reviews by Marvin D. Glock and Donald E. P. Smith, see 5:666; for reviews by Robert Murray Bear and Carolyn M. Welch of the original edition, see 3:509; for a review by Henry D. Rinsland, see 2:1535 (3 excerpts).

K104. Record for Reading Diagnosis. For additional information and a review by Carolyn M. Welch, see 3:512.

K105. Roswell-Chall Auditory Blending Test. For additional information and reviews by Ira E. Aaron and B. H. Van Roekel, see 6:830 (2 references).

K106. Roswell-Chall Diagnostic Reading Test of Word Analysis Skills. For additional information and reviews by Ira E. Aaron and Emmett Albert Betts, see 6:831 (1 reference); for a review by Byron H. Van Roekel, see 5:667.

K107. Scholastic Diagnostic Reading Test. For additional information and reviews by Russell G. Stauffer and Arthur E. Traxler, see 5:650.

K108. The Schonell Reading Tests. For additional information and a review by R. W. McCulloch, see 5:651 (4 references); for a review by M. L. Kellmer Pringle, see 4:552 (3 references); for a review by Edith I. M. Thomson, see 3:499.

K109. Silent Reading Diagnostic Tests: The Developmental Reading Tests. For additional information and reviews by Emery P. Bliesmer and Albert J. Kingston, see 6:832 (1 reference).

K110. The Standard Reading Tests. For additional information and a review by L. B. Birch, see 6:833 (1 reference).

K111. Stanford Diagnostic Phonics Survey. For additional information, see 5:670.

MISCELLANEOUS

K112. Botel Reading Inventory. For additional information and reviews by Ira E. Aaron and Charles M. Brown, see 6:834.

K113. Durrell-Sullivan Reading Capacity and Achievement Tests. For additional information and a review by James Maxwell, see 5:661 (5 references); for a review by Helen M. Robinson, see 4:562 (4 references); for reviews by William S. Gray and Marion Monroe [Cox] of the original edition, see 1:1099 (1 excerpt).

K114. Functional Readiness Questionnaire for School and College Students. For additional information, see 6:835.

K115. Instructional Reading Tests for the Intermediate Grades. For additional information, see 2:1543.

K116. Inventory of Reading Experiences. For additional information and a review by Albert J. Harris, see 3:511 (2 references).

K117. Learning Methods Test. For additional information and reviews by Thomas E. Culliton, Jr. and William Eller, see 6:836 (1 reference).

K118. The Master Ophthalmograph. For additional information and a review by Miles A. Tinker, see 4:660 (8 references); see also 3:470 (15 references); for a review by G. T. Buswell of an earlier model, see 2:1559 (2 references, 2 excerpts); for reviews by Stella S. Center, David Kopel, Marion Monroe [Cox], Joseph Tiffin, and Miles A. Tinker, see 1:1108 (1 excerpt).

K119. The Reader Rater. For additional information, see 6:837.

K120. The Reading Eye. For additional information and reviews by Arthur S. McDonald and George D. Spache, see 6:838 (3 references).

K121. Reading Versatility Test. For additional information, see 6:839 (1 reference).

K122. SRA Achievement Series: Language Perception. For additional information, see 5:668.

ORAL

K123. Articulation Test With Reading Disability Feature. For additional information and a review by Irving H. Anderson, see 1:1095.

K124. Flash-X Sight Vocabulary Test. For additional information, see 6:841.

K125. Gilmore Oral Reading Test. For additional information and reviews by Lydia A. Duggins and Maynard C. Reynolds, see 5:671 (1 reference).

K126. Gray Oral Reading Test. For additional information and reviews by Emery P. Bliesmer, Albert J. Harris, and Paul R. Lohnes, see 6:842.

K127. Holborn Reading Scale. For additional information and a review by Stanley Nisbet, see 5:635 (1 reference); for a review by C. M. Fleming, see 4:537.

K128. Jenkins Oral Reading Test: Individualized Oral Diagnostic Test for Children With Serious Reading Difficulties. For additional information and reviews by Guy L. Bond, David Kopel, and Clarence R. Stone, see 2:1548.

K129. Kindergarten-Primary Articulation Test. For additional information and a review by Irving H. Anderson, see 1:1104.

K130. Leavell Analytical Oral Reading Test. For additional information and reviews by Lydia A. Duggins and Maynard C. Reynolds, see 5:672.

K131. Neale Analysis of Reading Ability. For additional information and reviews by M. Alan Brimer and Magdalen D. Vernon, see 6:843 (1 excerpt).

K132. Oral Diagnostic Test of Word-Analysis Skills, Primary: Dominion Tests. For additional information and a review by S. A. Rayner, see 5:673; for a review by Nila Banton Smith, see 4:565.

K133. Oral Word Reading Test. For additional information and reviews by S. A. Rayner and D. K. Wheeler, see 5:674.

K134. Slosson Oral Reading Test (SORT). For additional information, see 6:844.

K135. Standardized Oral Reading Check Tests. For additional information and reviews by David H. Russell and Clarence R. Stone, see 2:1570 (1 reference).

K136. Standardized Oral Reading Paragraphs. For additional information and reviews by David Kopel and Clarence R. Stone, see 2:1571 (7 references).

READINESS

K137. American School Reading Readiness Test. For additional information and reviews by Joan Bollenbacher and Helen M. Robinson, see 5:675 (3 references); for reviews by David H. Russell and Paul A. Witty, see 3:513.

K138. The Anton Brenner Developmental Gestalt Test of School Readiness. For additional information, see 6:844a (8 references).

K139. Betts Ready to Read Tests. For additional information and reviews by I. H. Anderson, David Kopel, Marion Monroe [Cox], and Guy Wagner, see 1:1097 (1 reference).

K140. Binion-Beck Reading Readiness Test for Kindergarten and First Grade. For additional information and reviews by Irving H. Anderson and Paul A. Witty, see 3:514 (1 reference).

K141. Classification Test for Beginners in Reading. For additional information and reviews by Marion Monroe Cox and David H. Russell, see 3:515 (2 references).

K142. Gates Reading Readiness Tests. For additional information, see 6:845 (1 reference); for a review by F. J. Schonell, see 4:566; for reviews by Marion Monroe Cox and Paul A. Witty, see 3:516 (3 references); see also 2:1537 (5 references, 2 excerpts).

K143. Group Test of Reading Readiness: The Dominion Tests. For additional information and a review by N. Dale Bryant, see 5:676.

K144. The Harrison-Stroud Reading Readiness Profiles. For additional information and a review by S. S. Dunn, see 5:677 (2 references); for a review by William S. Gray of an earlier edition, see 4:568.

K145. Lee-Clark Reading Readiness Test. For additional information, see 6:846 (9 references); for a review by James R. Hobson of an earlier edition, see 5:678; for reviews by Marion Monroe Cox and David H. Russell, see 3:517.

K146. Maturity Level for School Entrance and Reading Readiness. For additional information, see 6:847; for a review by David H. Russell of the original edition, see 4:572.

K147. Metropolitan Readiness Tests. For additional information and a review by Eric F. Gardner of an earlier edition, see 4:570 (3 references, 1 excerpt); for a review by Irving H. Anderson, see 3:518 (5 references); for a review by W. J. Osburn, see 2:1552 (10 references).

K148. Murphy-Durrell Diagnostic Reading Readiness Test. For additional information and reviews by Joan Bollenbacher and S. S. Dunn, see 5:679 (2 references); see also 4:571 (2 references).

K149. Reading Aptitude Tests. For additional information and a review by Irving H. Anderson, see 3:519 (5 references).

K150. Reading Readiness Test. For additional information and a review by David A. Payne, see 6:849 (1 reference).

K151. Scholastic Reading Readiness Test. For additional information and a review by David A. Payne, see 6:850.

K152. Stevens Reading Readiness Test. For additional information and reviews by Irving H. Anderson and Marion Monroe Cox, see 3:521.

K153. Van Wagenen Reading Readiness Scales. For additional information and a review by David H. Russell of Part 2, see 3:520 (4 references).

K154. Watson Reading-Readiness Test. For additional information, see 6:851.

K155. Webster Reading-Readiness Test. For additional information, see 5:682.

SPECIAL FIELDS

K156. Ability to Interpret Reading Materials in the Natural Sciences: The Iowa Tests of Educational Development, Test 6. For additional information, see 6:853. For reviews of the complete battery, see 6:14 (2 reviews), 5:17 (2 reviews), 4:17 (1 review), and 3:12 (3 reviews).

K157. Ability to Interpret Reading Materials in the Social Studies: The Iowa Tests of Educational Development, Test 5. For additional information, see 6:852. For reviews of the complete battery, see 6:14 (2 reviews), 5:17 (2 reviews), 4:17 (1 review), and 3:12 (3 reviews).

K158. Interpretation of Reading Materials in the Natural Sciences: Tests of General Educational Development, Test 3. For additional information, see 5:683. For reviews of the complete battery, see 5:27 (1 review), 4:26 (1 review), and 3:20 (2 reviews).

K159. Interpretation of Reading Materials in the Social Studies: Tests of General Educational Development, Test 2. For additional information, see 5:684; for reviews by W. E. Hall and C. Robert Pace, see 3:528 (1 reference). For reviews of the complete battery, see 5:27 (1 review), 4:26 (1 review), and 3:20 (2 reviews).

K160. Lorimer Braille Recognition Test: A Test of Ability in Reading Braille Contractions. For additional information, see 6:854 (1 reference).

K161. Mathematics, Biology, Physical Science. For additional information, see 2:1550.

K162. Purdue Reading Test for Industrial Supervisors. For additional information and reviews by Jerome E. Doppelt and Louis C. Nanassy, see 5:644 (1 reference).

K163. RBH Reading Comprehension Test. For additional information, see 6:817.

K164. Reading Adequacy "READ" Test: Individual Placement Series. For additional information, see 6:805.

K165. Reading Scales in History. For additional information and reviews by Paul Blommers and Albert J. Harris, see 3:530.

K166. Reading Scales in Literature. For additional information, see 3:531.

K167. Reading Scales in Science. For additional information and a review by Ivan A. Booker, see 3:532.

K168. [Robinson-Hall Reading Tests.] For additional information and a review by Robert Murray Bear, see 4:575 (2 references); see also 3:533 (3 references).

K169. Southeastern Problems and Prospects: Social Studies and English. For additional information, see 2:1569.

K170. Tests of Natural Sciences: Vocabulary and Interpretation of Reading Materials: Cooperative Inter-American Tests. For additional information and a review by Clarence H. Nelson, see 4:576 (4 references).

K171. Tests of Social Studies: Vocabulary and Interpretation of Reading Materials: Cooperative Inter-American Tests. For additional information and reviews by Gustav J. Froehlich and Martha E. Layman, see 4:577 (4 references).

K172. Tooze Braille Speed Test: A Test of Basic Ability in Reading Braille. For additional information, see 6:855.

K173. Understanding Communication (Verbal Comprehension). For additional information and reviews by C. E. Jurgensen and Donald E. P. Smith, see 6:840.

SPEED

K174. Chapman-Cook Speed of Reading Test. For additional information and a review by Eason Monroe, see 3:522 (1 reference).

K175. Michigan Speed of Reading Test. For additional information and a review by Eason Monroe, see 3:523 (1 reference); see also 2:1553 (2 references); for reviews by Richard Ledgerwood and M. R. Trabue, see 1:1171.

K176. Minnesota Speed of Reading Test for College Students. For additional information and a review by J. R. Gerberich, see 2:1555 (2 references); for reviews by Frederick B. Davis and Ruth Strang, see 1:1107.

K177. Reading Speed and Comprehension: Ohio Senior Survey Tests. For additional information and reviews by J. B. Stroud and Miles A. Tinker, see 3:524.

K178. Reading Speed Test: National Achievement Test. For additional information and a review by Eason Monroe, see 3:525.

K179. Tinker Speed of Reading Test. For additional information and a review by Leonard S. Feldt, see 5:687.

STUDY SKILLS

K180. Analysis of Controversial Writing: Test 5.31. For additional information, see 2:1527.

K181. Application of Certain Principles of Logical Reasoning: Test 5.12. For additional information, see 2:1528.

K182. Applied Reading for Junior-Senior High School: Every Pupil Test. For additional information and a review by Ivan A. Booker, see 3:534.

K183. Bennett Use of Library Test. For additional information and a review by Louis Shores, see 4:578.

K184. California Study Methods Survey. For additional information and reviews by John D. Krumboltz and Donald E. P. Smith, see 6:857 (2 references, 2 excerpts); see also 5:689 (7 references).

K185. Cooperative Dictionary Test. For additional information and a review by A. N. Hieronymus, see 5:690.

K186. Critical Classification of Magazines and Newspapers. For additional information, see 1:1163.

K187. Critical-Mindedness in the Reading of Fiction: Test 3.7. For additional information, see 2:1530 (1 reference).

K188. Edmiston How to Study Test. For additional information, see 4:580.

K189. Evaluation Aptitude Test. For additional information and reviews by J. Thomas Hastings and Walker H. Hill, see 5:691.

K190. Information Concerning Library Processes. For additional information, see 1:1164.

K191. Interpretation of Data Test: General Education Series. For additional information and reviews by J. Raymond Gerberich and Victor H. Noll, see 4:581 (5 references); for a review by J. Wayne Wrightstone, see 3:535 (4 references); see also 2:1544 (9 references).

K192. Interpretation of Data: Test 2.71. For additional information, see 2:1545 (4 references).

K193. A Library Orientation Test for College Freshmen. For additional information and a review by Morey J. Wantman, see 6:859 (1 reference); for reviews by Janet G. Afflerbach (with Lois Grimes Afflerbach) and J. Wayne Wrightstone, see 5:693.

K194. Library Test for Junior High Schools. For additional information and reviews by Robert A. Davis and Ethel M. Feagley, see 3:536.

K195. Library Usage Test. For additional information and a review by J. Wayne Wrightstone, see 3:537.

K196. Logical Reasoning. For additional information and reviews by Duncan Howie and Charles R. Langmuir, see 5:694 (1 reference).

K197. Logical Reasoning Test: General Education Series. For additional information and a review by Robert L. Ebel, see 4:582 (1 reference); see also 2:1528 (4 references).

K198. Nationwide Library Skills Examination. For additional information, see 6:860.

K199. Nature of Proof: Test 5.22. For additional information, see 2:1556 (3 references).

K200. OC Diagnostic Dictionary Test. For additional information, see 6:861.

K201. Parr Skill-Ability Tests. For additional information, see 2:1559.1.

K202. Peabody Library Information Test. For additional information and a review by Douglas E. Scates, see 3:538 (2 references, 2 excerpts).

K203. Poley Precis Test: A Test by Paragraph Summaries of Reading Comprehension. For additional information and a review by Edward A. Tenney, see 2:1561.

K204. Reading and Construction of Tables and Graphs. For additional information, see 1:1165.

K205. SRA Achievement Series: Work-Study Skills. For additional information, see 6:862; for reviews by Robert L. Ebel and Ruth M. Strang, see 5:696. For reviews of the complete battery, see 6:21 (1 review) and 5:21 (2 reviews).

K206. Senior High School Library and Reference Skills Test. For additional information, see 6:863.

K207. Special Reading Test: Ohio Senior Survey Tests. For additional information and a review by Miles A. Tinker, see 3:539.

K208. Spitzer Study Skills Test. For additional information and a review by Alton L. Raygor, see 6:864 (1 reference); for a review by James Deese, see 5:697.

K209. Stanford Achievement Test: Study Skills. For additional information and reviews by Robert L. Ebel and Ruth M. Strang, see 5:698. For reviews of the complete battery, see 6:26 (1 review, 1 excerpt), 5:25 (1 review), 4:25 (2 reviews), and 3:18 (2 reviews).

K210. Student Skills Inventory. For additional information, see 2:1573 (1 reference).

K211. Study Habits Inventory. For additional information and a review by Douglas E. Scates, see 3:540 (8 references); for reviews by Edward S. Jones and William A. McCall, see 2:1574.

K212. Study Outline Test. For additional information and a review by Harriet Barthelmess Morrison, see 2:1575 (1 reference).

K213. The Study Skills Counseling Evaluation. For additional information and reviews by Stanley E. Davis and W. G. Fleming, see 6:865.

K214. Survey of Study Habits. For additional information and a review by Warren R. Baller, see 4:583 (1 reference).

K215. Survey of Study Habits and Attitudes. For additional information, see 6:856 (12 references); for reviews by James Deese and C. Gilbert Wrenn (with Roy D. Lewis), see 5:688 (14 references).

K216. Test of Critical Thinking. For additional information, see 4:584.

K217. A Test of Study Skills. For additional information and a review by Marvin D. Glock, see 5:699; for a review by Douglas E. Scates, see 3:542.

K218. Test on the Use of Books and Libraries: General Education Series. For additional information and reviews by Henry D. Rinsland and Louis Shores, see 4:585 (1 reference).

K219. A Test on Use of the Dictionary. For additional information, see 6:866.

K220. Tyler-Kimber Study Skills Test. For additional information and reviews by William A. McCall and Rachel Salisbury, see 2:1580 (1 reference); for reviews by Edward S. Jones and C. Gilbert Wrenn, see 1:1166.

K221. The Use of Library and Study Materials. For additional information and a review by Robert Murray Bear, see 4:586 (1 reference); for a review by Ethel M. Feagley, see 3:543.

K222. Use of Sources of Information: The Iowa Tests of Educational Development, Test 9. For additional information, see 6:858. For reviews of the complete battery, see 6:14 (2 reviews), 5:17 (2 reviews), 4:17 (1 review), and 3:12 (3 reviews).

K223. Watson-Glaser Critical Thinking Appraisal. For additional information, see 6:867 (24 references); for reviews by Walker H. Hill and Carl I. Hovland of an earlier edition, see 5:700 (8 references); for a review by Robert H. Thouless, see 3:544 (3 references, 1 excerpt).

K224. Work-Study Skills: Iowa Every-Pupil Tests of Basic Skills, Test B. For additional information, see 4:588; for a review by J. Wayne Wrightstone, see 3:545. For reviews of the complete battery, see 4:15 (2 reviews), 3:10 (3 reviews), and 1:872 (4 reviews).

SCIENCE

L1. Ability for Science: Fife Tests of Ability, Test 2. For additional information, see 3:546 (2 references). For reviews of the complete battery, see 4:713 (1 review) and 3:8 (1 review).

L2. Advanced General Science: Cooperative Science Tests. For additional information, see 6:867a.

L3. Analytical Scales of Attainment in Elementary Science. For additional information and reviews by Francis D. Curtis and Victor H. Noll, see 2:1598; see also 1:1123 (1 excerpt).

L4. Application of Principles in Science: Test 1.3b. For additional information, see 2:1599 (2 references); superseded by L42.

L5. Biology and General Science: National Teacher Examinations. For additional information, see 6:868. For reviews of the testing program, see 6:700 (1 review), 5:538 (3 reviews), and 4:802 (1 review).

L6. Chemistry, Physics and General Science: National Teacher Examinations. For additional information, see 6:869. For reviews of the testing program, see 6:700 (1 review), 5:538 (3 reviews), and 4:802 (1 review).

L7. Cooperative General Achievement Tests: Test 2, Natural Science. For additional information, see 6:870 (4 references); for a review by Palmer O. Johnson of earlier forms, see 3:548. For reviews of the complete battery, see 6:7 (1 review), 5:6 (1 review), 4:5 (1 review), and 3:3 (1 review).

L8. Cooperative General Science Test. For additional information and a review by John S. Richardson, see 4:623 (1 reference); for a review by G. W. Hunter of an earlier form, see 2:1601; for reviews by W. B. Meldrum and Alvin W. Schindler, see 1:1125.

L9. Cooperative General Science Test for College Students. For additional information, see 1:1126.

L10. Cooperative Science Test for Grades 7, 8, and 9. For additional information and a review by R. Will Burnett, see 4:624; for reviews by Hans C. Gordon and Herbert A. Thelen of earlier forms, see 3:571.

L11. Coordinated Scales of Attainment: Science. For additional information, see 5:704. For reviews of the complete battery, see 4:8 (1 review) and 3:6 (4 reviews).

L12. Elementary Science and Health: Every Pupil Test. For additional information, see 6:872.

L13. Elementary Science: Every Pupil Scholarship Test. For additional information, see 6:871.

L14. Elementary Science Test: National Achievement Tests. For additional information and a review by William Harrison Lucow, see 5:707.

L15. Examination in General Science—High-School Level. For additional information and reviews by Hans C. Gordon and Victor H. Noll, see 3:573.

L16. Examination in Senior Science—High-School Level. For additional information and a review by Richard H. Jordan, see 3:574.

L17. General Background in the Natural Sciences: The Iowa Tests of Educational Development, Test 2. For additional information and reviews by Lloyd H. Heidgerd and Jacqueline V. Mallinson, see 6:876 (1 review). For reviews of the complete battery, see 6:14 (2 reviews), 5:17 (2 reviews), 4:17 (1 review), and 3:12 (3 reviews).

L18. General Science: Cooperative Science Tests. For additional information, see 6:872a.

L19. General Science: Every Pupil Scholarship Test. For additional information, see 6:873.

L20. General Science: Every Pupil Test. For additional information, see 6:874.

L21. General Science: Minnesota High School Achievement Examinations. For additional information, see 6:875.

L22. General Science Test: Gibson's Attainment Tests. For additional information, see 1:1129.

L23. General Science Test: National Achievement Tests. For additional information and a review by Robert M. W. Travers, see 5:712; for reviews by Francis D. Curtis and G. W. Hunter, see 2:1602.

L24. General Science Test: State High School Tests for Indiana. For additional information, see 4:592.

L25. Iowa Every-Pupil Test in General Science. For additional information and a review by Edward E. Cureton, see 1:1131.

L26. McDougal General Science Test. For additional information and reviews by Hans C. Gordon and Herbert A. Thelen, see 3:576.

L27. Metropolitan Achievement Tests: [Science]. For additional information and reviews by William W. Cooley and George G. Mallinson, see 6:877. For reviews of the complete battery, see 6:15 (3 reviews), 4:18 (1 review), 2:1189 (2 reviews), and 1:874 (3 reviews).

L28. Physical Science Aptitude Examination. For additional information and reviews by Jack W. Dunlap and John C. Flanagan, see 3:547.

L29. Physical Science: Teacher Education Examination Program. An inactive form of test L6; for additional information, see 6:878. For a review of the testing program, see 5:543.

L30. Purdue Physical Science Aptitude Test. For additional information and a review by William W. Cooley, see 6:879 (8 references).

L31. Read General Science Test. For additional information, see 5:715 (1 reference); for reviews by Benjamin S. Bloom and John S. Richardson, see 4:628.

L32. Science Applications Test: Gibson's Attainment Tests. For additional information, see 1:1132.

L33. Science Background: A Science Service Test to Identify Potential Scientific and Technical Talent. For additional information, see 6:880.

L34. Science Information Test. For additional information and reviews by Hans C. Gordon and G. W. Hunter, see 2:1603.

L35. Science: Minnesota High School Achievement Examinations. For additional information and reviews by Elizabeth Hagen and Jacqueline V. Mallinson, see 6:881.

L36. Sequential Tests of Educational Progress: Science. For additional information and reviews by John C. Flanagan and George G. Mallinson, see 6:882 (2 references); for reviews by Palmer O. Johnson, Julian C. Stanley (with M. Jacinta Mann), and Robert M. W. Travers, see 5:716. For reviews of the complete battery, see 6:25 (2 reviews) and 5:24 (2 reviews, 1 excerpt).

L37. Stanford Achievement Test: Science. For additional information, see 6:883; for reviews by Bertram Epstein and Paul E. Kambly of an earlier edition, see 4:593. For reviews of the complete battery, see 6:26 (1 review, 1 excerpt), 5:25 (1 review), 4:25 (2 reviews), and 3:18 (2 reviews).

L38. Survey Test in Introductory Science: California Survey Series. For additional information and reviews by Kenneth E. Anderson and Lloyd H. Heidgerd, see 6:884.

L39. Survey Test in Physical Science: California Survey Series. For additional information and a review by Irvin J. Lehmann, see 6:885.

L40. Survey Test in the Natural Sciences: Cooperative General Achievement Test, Part 2. For additional information, see 2:1604; for a review by Palmer O. Johnson, see 1:870.

L41. T. C. General Science Test. For additional information, see 6:886.

L42. Test of Application of Principles in General Science: General Education Series. For additional information and a review by R. Will Burnett, see 4:629 (3 references).

L43. Test of Application of Principles in Physical Science: General Education Series. For additional information and a review by Palmer O. Johnson, see 4:594 (3 references).

L44. Wisconsin General Science Test. For additional information, see 3:577.

BIOLOGY

L45. Application of Principles in Biological Science: Test 1.33A. For additional information, see 2:1584 (2 references).

L46. Biological Science: Teacher Education Examination Program. An inactive form of test L5; for additional information, see 6:887. For a review of the testing program, see 5:543.

L47. Biology: Cooperative Science Tests. For additional information, see 6:887a.

L48. Biology: Every Pupil Scholarship Test. For additional information, see 6:888.

L49. Biology: Every Pupil Test. For additional information, see 6:889.

L50. Biology: Minnesota High School Achievement Examinations. For additional information and a review by Barbara F. Esser, see 6:890.

L51. Biology Test: Affiliation Testing Program for Catholic Secondary Schools. For additional information and a review by Henry Chauncey, see 6:891. For a review of the complete program, see 6:758.

L52. Biology Test: State High School Tests for Indiana. For additional information, see 4:598.

L53. College Entrance Examination Board Achievement Test: Biology. For additional information, see 6:892 (3 references); for a review by Elizabeth Hagen of an earlier form, see 5:723; for a review by Clark W. Horton, see 4:600. For reviews of the testing program, see 6:760 (2 reviews).

L54. College Entrance Examination Board Advanced Placement Examination: Biology. For additional information and a review by Clarence H. Nelson, see 6:893 (1 reference); for a review by Clark W. Horton of an earlier form, see 5:724.

L55. College Entrance Examination Board Placement Tests: Biology. An inactive form of test L53; for additional information, see 6:894.

L56. Cooperative Biology Test. For additional information and a review by Leland P. Johnson, see 4:601; for a review by C. W. Horton of earlier forms, see 3:550 (1 reference); for a review by Ralph W. Tyler, see 2:1585; for reviews by Francis D. Curtis and George W. Hunter, see 1:907.

L57. Cooperative Biology Test: Educational Records Bureau Edition. For additional information, see 6:895; see also 5:725 (1 reference) and 4:602 (2 references).

L58. Cooperative Botany Test. For additional information and a review by F. C. Jean, see 1:908.

L59. Cooperative College Biology Test. For additional information and reviews by Clarence H. Nelson and Joseph J. Schwab, see 3:551.

L60. Cooperative Zoology Test. For additional information and a review by Dael L. Wolfle, see 1:909.

L61. Examination in Biology—College Level. For additional information and a review by C. W. Horton, see 3:552.

L62. Examination in Biology—High-School Level. For additional information and reviews by C. W. Horton and Richard H. Jordan, see 3:553 (1 reference).

L63. Examination in Botany—College Level. For additional information and reviews by C. W. Horton and Clarence H. Nelson, see 3:554.

L64. General Biology Test: National Achievement Tests. For additional information and reviews by Elizabeth Hagen and Clark W. Horton, see 5:726.

L65. The Graduate Record Examinations Advanced Tests: Biology. For additional information, see 6:896; for a review by Clark W. Horton of an earlier form, see 5:727. For a review of the testing program, see 5:601.

L66. Hanes-Benz Biology Test. For additional information and a review by Clark W. Horton, see 2:1586 (1 reference).

L67. Iowa Every-Pupil Test in Biology. For additional information and a review by George W. Hunter, see 1:910.

L68. Nelson Biology Test. For additional information, see 5:728; for reviews by Clark W. Horton and Leland P. Johnson, see 4:605.

L69. Presson Biology Test. For additional information and reviews by Thomas F. Morrison and Dael L. Wolfle, see 2:1587 (2 references).

L70. Ruch-Cossmann Biology Test. For additional information and reviews by Thomas F. Morrison and Dael L. Wolfle, see 2:1588 (3 references).

L71. Semester Test for Biology. For additional information, see 4:599.

L72. Survey Test in Biological Science: California Survey Series. For additional information and reviews by Barbara F. Esser and Clarence H. Nelson, see 6:897.

L73. Test of Application of Principles in Biology: General Education Series. For additional information and reviews by Clark W. Horton and Clarence H. Nelson, see 4:606 (4 references).

L74. Williams Biology Test. For additional information and reviews by Clark W. Horton, Victor H. Noll, and Dael L. Wolfle, see 2:1589 (1 reference).

L75. Wisconsin Biology Test. For additional information, see 3:555.

CHEMISTRY

L76. A.C.S. Cooperative Examination: Biochemistry. For additional information, see 6:898 (2 references, 1 excerpt).

L77. A.C.S. Cooperative Examination for Graduate Placement in Analytical Chemistry. For additional information, see 6:899 (1 reference).

L78. A.C.S. Cooperative Examination for Graduate Placement in Organic Chemistry. For additional information, see 6:900 (1 reference).

L79. A.C.S. Cooperative Examination for Graduate Placement in Physical Chemistry. For additional information, see 6:901 (1 reference).

L80. A.C.S. Cooperative Examination in General Chemistry. For additional information and reviews by J. A. Campbell and William Hered, see 6:902 (3 references, 1 excerpt); for reviews by Frank P. Cassaretto and Palmer O. Johnson, see 5:732 (2 references); for a review by Kenneth E. Anderson of earlier forms, see 4:610 (1 reference); for reviews by Sidney J. French and Florence E. Hooper, see 3:557 (3 references); see also 2:1593 (5 references).

L81. A.C.S. Cooperative Examination in Physical Chemistry. For additional information, see 6:904 (1 reference); see also 4:612 (1 reference); for a review by Alfred S. Brown of an earlier form, see 3:559.

L82. A.C.S. Cooperative Examination: Inorganic Chemistry. For additional information and a review by Frank J. Fornoff, see 6:903 (1 reference, 1 excerpt).

L83. A.C.S. Cooperative Examination in Quantitative Analysis. For additional information, see 6:907 (1 reference); see also 5:735 (1 excerpt); for reviews by William B. Meldrum and William Rieman III of an earlier form, see 3:563.

L84. [A.C.S. Cooperative Examinations in Organic Chemistry.] For additional information, see 6:905 (4 references, 1 excerpt); for a review by Shailer Peterson of an earlier form, see 3:558 (1 reference).

L85. [A.C.S. Cooperative Examinations in Qualitative Analysis.] For additional information, see 6:906 (4 references, 2 excerpts); for a review by William Rieman III of earlier forms, see 4:608 (2 references); for reviews by William B. Meldrum and William Rieman III, see 3:562.

L86. A.C.S.-N.S.T.A. Cooperative Examination: High School Chemistry. For additional information and reviews by Frank J. Fornoff and William Hered, see 6:908 (5 references, 2 excerpts); for reviews by Edward G. Rietz and Willard G. Warrington, see 5:729.

L87. A.C.S.-N.S.T.A. Cooperative Examination: High School Chemistry [Advanced Level]. For additional information and reviews by Frank J. Fornoff and William Hered, see 6:909.

L88. Anderson Chemistry Test. For additional information and a review by Theo. A. Ashford, see 5:737; for a review by William Rieman III, see 4:613.

L89. Chemistry: Cooperative Science Tests. For additional information, see 6:909a.

L90. Chemistry: Every Pupil Scholarship Test. For additional information, see 6:910.

L91. Chemistry: Every Pupil Test. For additional information, see 6:911.

L92. Chemistry: Minnesota High School Achievement Examinations. For additional information, see 6:912; for a review by Edward G. Rietz of earlier forms, see 5:741.

L93. Chemistry Test: Affiliation Testing Program for Catholic Secondary Schools. For additional information and a review by Henry Chauncey, see 6:913. For a review of the complete program, see 6:758.

L94. Chemistry Test: State High School Tests for Indiana. For additional information, see 4:616;

for a review by Fred P. Frutchey of an earlier form, see 1:931.

L95. Clinton-Osborn-Ware General Chemistry Test. For additional information, see 2:1590.

L96. College Entrance Examination Board Achievement Test: Chemistry. For additional information and a review by William Hered, see 6:914 (4 references); for a review by Max D. Engelhart, see 5:742 (2 references); for a review by Evelyn Raskin, see 4:617 (4 references). For reviews of the testing program, see 6:760 (2 reviews).

L97. College Entrance Examination Board Advanced Placement Examination: Chemistry. For additional information, see 6:915 (1 reference); for a review by Theo. A. Ashford of an earlier form, see 5:743.

L98. College Entrance Examination Board Placement Tests: Chemistry Test. An inactive form of test L96; for additional information, see 6:916; for reference to reviews, see L96.

L99. Columbia Research Bureau Chemistry Test. For additional information and a review by Max D. Engelhart, see 2:1591.

L100. Cooperative Chemistry Test. For additional information and reviews by Frank P. Cassaretto and Willard G. Warrington, see 5:744; see also 4:618 (4 references); for a review by John H. Daugherty of an earlier form, see 3:561; for reviews by Charles L. Bickel and Louis M. Heil, see 2:1592; for reviews by Edward E. Cureton and W. B. Meldrum, see 1:932.

L101. Cooperative Chemistry Test: Educational Records Bureau Edition. For additional information and a review by Kenneth J. Jones, see 6:917; see also 5:745 (1 reference) and 4:619 (2 references).

L102. Cooperative Chemistry Test: Provisional Form. For additional information and a review by Max D. Engelhart, see 1:933.

L103. Cooperative Objective Tests in Organic Chemistry. For additional information, see 2:1595.

L104. Examination in Chemistry—High-School Level. For additional information and a review by Victor H. Noll, see 3:564 (1 reference).

L105. Examination in General Chemistry—College Level. For additional information and reviews by John H. Daugherty and Florence E. Hooper, see 3:565 (1 reference).

L106. General Chemistry Test: National Achievement Tests. For additional information and a review by J. A. Campbell, see 6:918.

L107. Glenn-Welton Chemistry Achievement Test. For additional information and reviews by Max D. Engelhart, Victor H. Noll, and Eugene A. Waters, see 2:1596 (1 excerpt); see also 1:934 (1 excerpt).

L108. The Graduate Record Examinations Advanced Tests: Chemistry. For additional information and a review by Max D. Engelhart, see 6:919. For a review of the testing program, see 5:601.

L109. Intermediate Chemistry Test. For additional information, see 2:1597.

L110. Iowa Placement Examinations: Chemistry Aptitude. For additional information and a review by Kenneth E. Anderson, see 4:621 (5 references); for a review by Theodore A. Ashford, see 3:566 (15 references).

L111. Iowa Placement Examinations: Chemistry Training. For additional information and a review by Kenneth E. Anderson, see 4:622 (1 reference); for a review by Theodore A. Ashford, see 3:567 (14 references).

L112. A Junior Chemistry Test. For additional information and reviews by Roy W. Stanhope and Mervyn L. Turner, see 5:747.

L113. Kirkpatrick Chemistry Test. For additional information and a review by Theodore A. Ashford, see 3:568 (1 reference).

L114. Qualitative Analysis Supplement for General Chemistry. For additional information and reviews by Frank P. Cassaretto and Palmer O. Johnson of the complete test, see 5:732 (2 references).

L115. Toledo Chemistry Placement Examination. For additional information and reviews by Kenneth E. Anderson and William R. Crawford, see 6:920 (1 reference).

L116. Wisconsin Achievement Tests: Chemistry. For additional information and a review by Victor H. Noll, see 3:569.

MISCELLANEOUS

L117. Cause and Effect Relationship Test in Science: Scientific Attitudes, Test 2. For additional information and a review by Louis M. Heil, see 2:1600.

L118. Common Science Vocabulary. For additional information, see 1:1124.

L119. Cooperative Geology Test. For additional information, see 3:579.

L120. Examination in Astronomy—College Level. For additional information, see 3:578.

L121. Examination in Meteorology—High-School Level. For additional information, see 3:580.

L122. The Facts About Science. For additional information, see 6:921.

L123. The Graduate Record Examinations Advanced Tests: Geology. For additional information, see 6:922. For a review of the testing program, see 5:601.

L124. Measurement of Observation and Understanding of Physical Phenomena and Life Processes. For additional information, see 4:631.

L125. The New Air World. For additional information, see 4:632.

L126. Scientific Attitudes. For additional information, see 1:1135.

L127. Scientific Methods: Test 1, Controlled Experimentation Test in Science. For additional information, see 1:1136.

L128. Scientific Thinking: Every Pupil Test. For additional information and a review by Victor H. Noll, see 1:1137.

L129. Steps in Problem Solving. For additional information, see 1:1138.

L130. Test of Chemical Comprehension. For additional information, see 6:923.

L131. Test of Reasoning in Conservation. For additional information, see 6:924 (1 reference).

L132. Test on Understanding Science (TOUS). For additional information, see 6:925 (3 references).

PHYSICS

L133. Application of Principles in Physical Science: Test 1.34. For additional information, see 2:1606 (2 references); for revised edition, see L43.

L134. College Entrance Examination Board Achievement Test: Physics. For additional information, see 6:926 (4 references); for a review by Theodore G. Phillips of an earlier form, see 5:749 (2 references); for a review by Palmer O. Johnson, see 4:633 (3 references). For reviews of the testing program, see 6:760 (2 reviews).

L135. College Entrance Examination Board Advanced Placement Examination: Physics. For additional information, see 6:927 (2 references); for a review by Leo Nedelsky of an earlier form, see 5:750.

L136. College Entrance Examination Board Placement Tests: Physics Test. An inactive form of test L134; for additional information, see 6:928.

L137. Columbia Research Bureau Physics Test. For additional information and a review by Eugene A. Waters, see 2:1607 (1 reference).

L138. Cooperative Physics Test. For additional information and a review by Theodore G. Phillips, see 5:751 (1 reference); see also 4:634 (2 references); for a review by G. P. Cahoon of earlier forms, see 3:581; for reviews by Andrew Longacre, Alvin W. Schindler, and Ralph K. Watkins, see 2:1608; for reviews by Ernest E. Bayles and A. W. Hurd, see 1:1088.

L139. Cooperative Physics Test: Educational Records Bureau Edition. For additional information, see 6:929; see also 5:752 (1 reference) and 4:635 (2 references).

L140. Cooperative Physics Tests for College Students. For additional information and a review by Edgar P. Slack, see 3:582 (1 reference); for a review by Alan T. Waterman, see 2:1609 (4 references); for a review by Paul A. Northrop, see 1:1089.

L141. Dunning Physics Test. For additional information and a review by Robert M. W. Travers, see 5:753; for a review by G. P. Cahoon, see 4:636.

L142. Examination in Electricity and Magnetism—College Level. For additional information, see 3:583.

L143. Examination in Electron Tubes and Circuits. For additional information, see 3:584.

L144. Examination in Physics—College Level. For additional information, see 3:586.

L145. Examination in Physics—High-School Level. For additional information and reviews by G. P. Cahoon and Palmer O. Johnson, see 3:585.

L146. Fulmer-Schrammel Physics Test. For additional information and reviews by Palmer O. Johnson and Alvin W. Schindler, see 2:1610.

L147. General Physics Test: National Achievement Tests. For additional information and a review by Theodore G. Phillips, see 6:930.

L148. The Graduate Record Examinations Advanced Tests: Physics. For additional information and a review by Theodore G. Phillips, see 6:931; for a review by Leo Nedelsky of an earlier form, see 5:754. For a review of the testing program, see 5:601.

L149. Hurd Test in High School Physics. For additional information and reviews by Andrew Longacre and Paul A. Northrop, see 2:1611.

L150. Iowa Every-Pupil Test in Physics. For additional information and reviews by Ernest E. Bayles and Archer W. Hurd, see 1:1091.

L151. Iowa Placement Examinations: Physics Aptitude. For additional information and a review by John W. French, see 4:638 (2 references); for a review by Robert M. W. Travers, see 3:587 (4 references).

L152. Iowa Placement Examinations: Physics Training. For additional information and a review by G. P. Cahoon, see 4:639 (2 references).

L153. A Junior Physics Test. For additional information and reviews by Roy W. Stanhope and Mervyn L. Turner, see 5:755.

L154. Physics: Cooperative Science Tests. For additional information, see 6:931a.

L155. Physics: Every Pupil Scholarship Test. For additional information, see 6:932.

L156. Physics: Every Pupil Test. For additional information, see 6:933.

L157. Physics: Minnesota High School Achievement Examinations. For additional information and a review by Irvin J. Lehmann, see 6:934.

L158. Physics Test: State High School Tests for Indiana. For additional information, see 4:642; for a review by A. W. Hurd of an earlier form, see 1:1092.

L159. Physics Test (Traditional and PSSC): Affiliation Testing Program for Catholic Secondary Schools. For additional information and a review by Henry Chauncey, see 6:935. For a review of the complete program, see 6:758.

L160. Tests of the Physical Science Study Committee. For additional information and reviews by George G. Mallinson and Leo Nedelsky, see 6:936 (1 reference).

L161. Torgerson-Rich-Ranney Tests in High School Physics. For additional information and reviews by Palmer O. Johnson and Paul A. Northrop, see 2:1612.

L162. 20th Century Test for Physics. For additional information, see 4:643.

L163. Wisconsin Physics Test. For additional information, see 3:589 (1 reference); for a review by Louis M. Heil, see 2:1613.

SENSORY-MOTOR

M1. Harris Tests of Lateral Dominance. For additional information, see 5:761 (1 reference); for reviews by William G. Peacher and Miles A. Tinker of an earlier edition, see 4:644; see also 3:466 (1 excerpt).

M2. Leavell Hand-Eye Coordinator Tests. For additional information, see 6:937.

M3. Moore Eye-Hand Coordination and Color-Matching Test. For additional information, see 5:872 (1 reference); for reviews by Norman Frederiksen and Jay L. Otis, see 4:750 (6 references).

M4. Pre-Tests of Vision, Hearing, and Motor Coordination. For additional information, see 4:645.

M5. Robbins Speech Sound Discrimination and Verbal Imagery Type Tests. For additional information and a review by Louis M. DiCarlo, see 6:938.

HEARING

M6. ADC Audiometers. For additional information, see 5:762.

M7. Ambco Audiometers. For additional information, see 6:939.

M8. Auditory Discrimination Test. For additional information and a review by Louis M. DiCarlo, see 6:940 (2 references).

M9. Auditory Tests. For additional information, see 6:941 (20 references).

M10. Audivox Audiometers. For additional information and a review by Louis M. DiCarlo, see 6:942.

M11. Beltone Audiometers. For additional information, see 6:943. For comments by Louis M. DiCarlo on screening audiometers in general and specific comments on Model 9-C and three other portable audiometers, see 6:942.

M12. The Children's Auditory Test. For additional information, see 6:944.

M13. Eckstein Audiometers. For additional information, see 6:945.

M14. Grason-Stadler Audiometers. For additional information, see 6:946 (6 references).

M15. Maico Audiometers. For additional information, see 6:947 (2 references); see also 5:763 (4 references). For comments by Louis M. DiCarlo on screening audiometers in general and specific comments on Model MA-2B and three other portable audiometers, see 6:942.

M16. Maico Hearing Impairment Calculator. For additional information, see 6:948.

M17. The Massachusetts Hearing Test. For additional information, see 6:949 (10 references).

M18. New Group Pure Tone Hearing Test. For additional information, see 6:950 (3 references).

M19. [Rush Hughes (PB 50): Phonetically Balanced Lists 5–12.] For additional information, see 6:951 (6 references).

M20. Sonotone Pure-Tone Audiometers. For additional information, see 6:951a.

M21. Stycar Hearing Tests. For additional information, see 6:952.

M22. Tests for the Hearing of Speech by Deaf People. For additional information, see 2:1526.1 (1 reference, 3 excerpts).

M23. Western Electric Audiometer. For additional information, see 3:475 (9 references); replaced by M10.

M24. Zenith Audiometers. For additional information, see 6:953. For comments by Louis M. DiCarlo on screening audiometers in general and specific comments on Model ZA-100-T and three other portable audiometers, see 6:942.

MOTOR

M25. Brace Scale of Motor Ability. For additional information and a review by Anna S. Espenschade, see 5:766 (17 references).

M26. Edmiston Motor Capacity Test. For additional information, see 4:649.

M27. The Lincoln-Oseretsky Motor Development Scale. For additional information and a review by Anna Espenschade, see 5:767 (10 references). For an earlier edition, see M28.

M28. Oseretsky Tests of Motor Proficiency: A Translation From the Portuguese Adaptation. For additional information and a review by Anna Espenschade, see 4:650 (10 references); see also 3:472 (6 references, 1 excerpt). For a revised edition, see M27.

M29. The Rail-Walking Test. For additional information and a review by William Sloan, see 4:652.

M30. V.D.L. Psychomotor Scale for the Measurement of Manual Ability. For additional information and reviews by Anna Espenschade and William Sloan, see 4:653 (1 reference).

VISION

M31. A-B-C Vision Test for Ocular Dominance. For additional information and a review by Miles A. Tinker, see 4:654; see also 3:459 (5 references).

M32. AO H-R-R Pseudoisochromatic Plates. For additional information, see 5:768 (11 references); see also 4:661 (8 references) and 3:473 (9 references, 1 excerpt).

M33. AO School Vision Screening Test. For additional information, see 5:769 (4 references).

M34. AO Sight Screener. For additional information, see 5:770 (8 references); for reviews by Henry A. Imus and F. Nowell Jones, see 3:460 (7 references).

M35. The Atlantic City Eye Test. For additional information, see 6:954 (1 reference).

M36. Burnham-Clark-Munsell Color Memory Test. For additional information, see 5:771 (1 reference).

M37. The Color Aptitude Test. For additional information, see 5:772.

M38. Dvorine Color Discrimination Screening Test. For additional information, see 3:461a (1 reference).

M39. Dvorine Pseudo-Isochromatic Plates. For additional information, see 6:955 (12 references); see also 5:773 (13 references, 3 excerpts); for the original edition, see 3:462 (4 references, 6 excerpts).

M40. Eames Eye Test. For additional information and a review by Helen M. Robinson, see 6:956 (1 reference); for a review by Magdalen D. Vernon, see 5:774 (2 references); see also 3:463 (5 references).

M41. Farnsworth Dichotomous Test for Color Blindness: Panel D-15. For additional information and a review by Elsie Murray, see 4:656 (2 references); see also 3:464 (1 excerpt).

M42. The Farnsworth-Munsell 100-Hue Test for the Examination of Color Discrimination. For additional information, see 5:775 (1 reference); for a review by Elsie Murray, see 4:657 (2 references).

M43. Freeman Acuity-Tester. For additional information, see 5:776.

M44. Freeman Protometer. For additional information, see 5:777.

M45. Glenn Colorule. For additional information, see 4:658 (1 reference).

M46. The Illuminant-Stable Color Vision Test. For additional information, see 5:778 (2 references); for a review by Elsie Murray of the original edition, see 4:659 (2 references).

M47. Inter-Society Color Council Color Aptitude Test. For additional information, see 5:779 (5 references).

M48. Keystone Occupational Telebinocular. For additional information and a review by F. Nowell Jones, see 3:467 (43 references, 1 excerpt).

M49. Keystone Tests of Binocular Skill: An Adaptation of the Gray Oral Reading Check Tests for Use in the Keystone Telebinocular. For additional information, see 6:957 (1 reference).

M50. Keystone Visual Tests. For additional information, see 5:780 (18 references). For reference to reviews of a subtest, see K139.

M51. Massachusetts Vision Test. For additional information, see 5:781 (14 references); see also 3:468 (5 references, 1 excerpt).

M52. New Test for the Detection of Color-blindness. For additional information, see 3:469 (2 excerpts).

M53. New York School Vision Tester. For additional information and a review by Helen M. Robinson, see 6:958 (2 references).

M54. Ortho-Rater. For additional information, see 5:783 (59 references); for reviews by Henry A. Imus and F. Nowell Jones, see 3:471 (30 references).

M55. Perceptual Forms Test. For additional information and a review by Mary C. Austin, see 6:848 (6 references).

M56. Spache Binocular Reading Test. For additional information and a review by Helen M. Robinson, see 6:959; see also 5:784 (4 references); for a review by Albert J. Harris of the upper level, see 3:461 (4 references).

M57. Stycar Vision Test. For additional information, see 6:960.

M58. T/O Vision Testers. For additional information, see 6:961 (1 reference).

M59. Test for Colour-Blindness. For additional information, see 6:962 (58 references).

M60. Test of Color Blindness. For additional information, see 3:474.

SOCIAL STUDIES

N1. American History—Government—Problems of Democracy: Acorn Achievement Tests. For additional information and a review by Richard E. Gross, see 5:785; for a review by Howard R. Anderson, see 3:590.

N2. American School Achievement Tests: Part 4, Social Studies and Science. For additional information, see 6:963. For reviews of the complete battery, see 6:2 (2 reviews), 5:1 (2 reviews), 4:1 (1 review), and 3:1 (2 reviews).

N3. Beard-Erbe Social Science Tests. For additional information and a review by Kenneth E. Gell, see 2:1614; for a review by Edgar B. Wesley, see 1:1144.

N4. Christian Democracy Test (Civics, Sociology, Economics): Affiliation Testing Program for Catholic Secondary Schools. For additional information and a review by Henry Chauncey, see 6:964. For a review of the complete program, see 6:758.

N5. Citizenship: Every Pupil Scholarship Test. For additional information, see 6:965.

N6. College Entrance Examination Board Achievement Test: American History and Social Studies. For additional information and a review by Howard R. Anderson, see 6:966; for a review by Ralph W. Tyler of an earlier form, see 5:786; for a review by Robert L. Thorndike, see 4:662. For reviews of the testing program, see 6:760 (2 reviews).

N7. College Entrance Examination Board Achievement Test: European History and World Cultures. For additional information and a review by David K. Heenan, see 6:967.

N8. Cooperative General Achievement Tests: Test 1, Social Studies. For additional information, see 6:968; see also 4:668 (3 references); for a review by Harry D. Berg of earlier forms, see 3:596. For reviews of the complete battery, see 6:7 (1 review), 5:6 (1 review), 4:5 (1 review), and 3:3 (1 review).

N9. Cooperative Social Studies Test for Grades 7, 8, and 9. For additional information and a review by Hilda Taba, see 4:663; for reviews by Robert A. Davis and Edgar B. Wesley of earlier forms, see 3:592.

N10. Cooperative Test of Social Studies Abilities. For additional information and a review by Roy A. Price, see 2:1615; for a review by Howard R. Anderson, see 1:1146.

N11. The Greig Social Studies Test. For additional information and a review by David R. Krathwohl, see 5:788.

N12. Historical Development and Cultural Change. For additional information, see 1:1147.

N13. History and Civics Test: Municipal Tests: National Achievement Tests. For additional information and a review by Howard R. Anderson, see 5:790; for a review by Harry D. Berg, see 4:664. For reviews of the complete battery, see 5:18 (1 review), 4:20 (1 review), and 2:1191 (2 reviews).

N14. Illinois Teachers College Cooperative Social Science Test. For additional information and a review by Harry D. Berg, see 3:593.

N15. Indiana History. For additional information, see 4:691.

N16. Melbo Social Science Survey Test. For additional information and reviews by Howard R. Anderson and R. M. Tryon, see 2:1616 (2 references); for a review by Alvin C. Eurich, see 1:1150.

N17. Metropolitan Achievement Tests: [Social Studies]. For additional information and reviews by Richard E. Gross and Robert J. Solomon, see 6:970. For reviews of the complete battery, see 6:15 (3 reviews), 4:18 (1 review), 2:1189 (2 reviews), and 1:874 (3 reviews).

N18. Sequential Tests of Educational Progress: Social Studies. For additional information and reviews by Jonathon C. McLendon and Donald W. Oliver, see 6:971 (1 reference); for reviews by Richard E. Gross, S. A. Rayner, and Ralph W. Tyler, see 5:792. For reviews of the complete battery, see 6:25 (2 reviews) and 5:24 (2 reviews, 1 excerpt).

N19. Shearer Social Studies Test. For additional information and a review by Raymond C. Norris, see 5:793 (1 reference).

N20. Social Situation Interview. For additional information, see 1:1152.

N21. Social Studies: Every Pupil Scholarship Test. For additional information, see 6:972.

N22. Social Studies: Minnnesota High School Achievement Examinations. For additional information, see 6:973.

N23. Social Studies: National Teacher Examinations. For additional information and a review by Harry D. Berg, see 6:974. For reviews of the testing program, see 6:700 (1 review), 5:538 (3 reviews), and 4:802 (1 review).

N24. Social Studies: Teacher Education Examination Program. An inactive form of test N23; for additional information, see 6:975; for a reference to a review, see N23. For a review of the testing program, see 5:543.

N25. Social Studies Test: Acorn National Achievement Tests. For additional information and a review by Edgar B. Wesley, see 4:666.

N26. Social Studies Test: National Achievement Tests. For additional information, see 5:798; for a review by Ray G. Wood, see 3:594.

N27. Social Studies 12 (American Problems): Minnesota High School Achievement Examinations. For additional information, see 6:976.

N28. Stanford Achievement Test: Social Studies Test. For additional information, see 6:977; for a review by Harry D. Berg of an earlier edition, see 5:799; for a review by Ray G. Wood, see 3:595. For reviews of the complete battery, see 6:26 (1 review, 1 excerpt), 5:25 (1 review), 4:25 (2 reviews), and 3:18 (2 reviews).

N29. Survey Test in the Social Studies: Cooperative General Achievement Test, Part 1. For additional information and a review by Hilda Taba, see 2:1618; for a review by Harold Gulliksen, see 1:870.

N30. T.C. Social Studies Test. For additional information, see 6:978.

N31. Test of Critical Thinking in the Social Studies: Elementary School Series. For additional information and reviews by Warren G. Findley, Pedro T. Orata, and G. M. Ruch, see 2:1619 (1 excerpt).

N32. Understanding of Basic Social Concepts: The Iowa Tests of Educational Development, Test 1. For additional information and a review by Morey J. Wantman, see 6:969. For reviews of the complete battery, see 6:14 (2 reviews), 5:17 (2 reviews), 4:17 (1 review), and 3:12 (3 reviews).

N33. Wesley Test in Social Terms. For additional information and a review by Howard R. Anderson, see 2:1622 (3 references).

CONTEMPORARY AFFAIRS

N34. Contemporary Affairs: Every Pupil Test. For additional information, see 6:979.

N35. Cooperative Contemporary Affairs Test for College Students. For additional information and reviews by Benjamin S. Bloom and John V. McQuitty, see 4:4 (4 references); for a review by H. T. Morse, see 3:2 (12 references); for a review by Ralph W. Tyler, see 2:1182 (5 references); for a review by Paul M. Limbert, see 1:948.

N36. Cooperative Contemporary Affairs Test for High School Classes. For additional information and reviews by John M. Stalnaker and R. M. Tryon, see 2:1183; for reviews by Howard R. Anderson and J. Wayne Wrightstone, see 1:950.

N37. Cooperative Current Literature and Arts Test for High School Classes. For additional information and reviews by Walter Barnes and H. H. Giles, see 1:949.

N38. Cooperative Test on Foreign Affairs. For additional information and a review by Christine McGuire, see 6:980 (1 reference, 1 excerpt).

N39. Cooperative Test on Recent Social and Scientific Developments. For additional information and a review by Roger T. Lennon, see 4:7 (2 references); for reviews by Ernest W. Tiegs, Ralph W. Tyler, and Edgar B. Wesley, see 3:5.

N40. Current Affairs: Every Pupil Scholarship Test. For additional information, see 6:981.

N41. Iowa Every-Pupil Test in Understanding of Contemporary Affairs. For additional information and a review by Alvin C. Eurich, see 1:951.

N42. Nationwide Current Events Examination. For additional information, see 6:982.

N43. New York Times Current Affairs Test. For additional information, see 6:983.

N44. New York Times Current Affairs Test for Colleges. For additional information, see 6:984.

N45. Newsweek Current News Test. For additional information, see 6:985.

N46. Newsweek NewsQuiz. For additional information, see 6:986.

ECONOMICS

N47. Cooperative Economics Test. For additional information, see 3:597; for a review by Edgar B. Wesley, see 2:1624.

N48. Economics Test: State High School Tests for Indiana. For additional information, see 4:670.

N49. The Graduate Record Examinations Advanced Tests: Economics. For additional information, see 6:987 (1 reference). For a review of the testing program, see 5:601.

N50. Hills Economics Test. For additional information, see 4:673.

N51. Iowa Every-Pupil Test in Economics. For additional information, see 1:1148.

N52. A Standard Achievement Test in Economic Understanding for Secondary Schools. For additional information, see 6:988.

N53. Test of Economic Understanding. For additional information, see 6:989.

N54. 20th Century Test for Economics. For additional information, see 4:671.

GEOGRAPHY

N55. Analytical Scales of Attainment in Geography. For additional information and a review by Ernest C. Witham, see 2:1625.

N56. Brandywine Achievement Test in Geography for Secondary Schools. For additional information, see 6:990.

N57. Coordinated Scales of Attainment: Geography. For additional information, see 4:8. For reviews of the complete battery, see 4:8 (1 review) and 3:6 (4 reviews).

N58. Economic Geography: Midwest High School Achievement Examinations. For additional information concerning earlier forms, see 5:803.

N59. Emporia Geography Test. For additional information and reviews by Edwin H. Reeder and Agatha Townsend, see 3:598.

N60. Fourth Grade Geography Test. For additional information and reviews by Elaine Forsyth [Cook] and Agatha Townsend, see 3:599 (1 reference).

N61. Geography Ability Test: Gibson's Attainment Tests. For additional information, see 1:990.

N62. Geography: Every Pupil Scholarship Test. For additional information, see 6:991.

N63. [Geography]: Every Pupil Test. For additional information, see 6:992.

N64. Geography Test: Municipal Tests: National Achievement Tests. For additional information, see 5:806; for a review by Edwin H. Reeder, see 4:676. For reviews of the complete battery, see 5:18 (1 review), 4:20 (1 review), and 2:1191 (2 reviews).

N65. Geography Test: National Achievement Tests. For additional information, see 4:677; for a review by Elaine Forsyth [Cook], see 3:600.

N66. Modern Geography and Allied Social Studies. For additional information and reviews by Edith M. Huddleston and Edwin H. Reeder, see 4:678.

N67. Physical Geography: Every Pupil Scholarship Test. For additional information, see 6:993.

N68. Survey Test in Geography: California Survey Series. For additional information and a review by Jonathon C. McLendon, see 6:994.

N69. Tate Economic Geography Test. For additional information and a review by Marguerite Uttley, see 3:601.

N70. Wiedefeld-Walther Geography Test. For additional information and a review by Marguerite Uttley, see 3:602; for reviews by Anna Parsek and Marie E. Trost, see 2:1626.

N71. World Geography: Every Pupil Scholarship Test. For additional information, see 6:995.

N72. World Geography Test: Dominion Tests. For additional information and a review by Edwin H. Reeder, see 3:603.

HISTORY

N73. American Council European History Test. For additional information and a review by S. P. McCutchen, see 2:1628.

N74. American History: Every Pupil Scholarship Test. For additional information, see 6:996.

N75. American History: Every Pupil Test. For additional information, see 6:997.

N76. American History Test: Affiliation Testing Program for Catholic Secondary Schools. For additional information and a review by Henry Chauncey, see 6:998. For a review of the complete program, see 6:758.

N77. American History Test: National Achievement Tests. For additional information, see 5:811; for reviews by Jacob S. Orleans and Wallace Taylor, see 2:1630.

N78. American History Test: State High School Tests for Indiana. For additional information, see 4:682.

N79. Analytical Scales of Attainment in American History. For additional information and reviews by Wilbur F. Murra and Margaret Willis, see 2:1631.

N80. Ancient History: Every Pupil Scholarship Test. For additional information, see 6:999.

N81. Bowman United States History Test. For additional information and a review by W. C. McCall (with Grace Graham), see 2:1632.

N82. College Entrance Examination Board Advanced Placement Examination: American History. For additional information and a review by Harry D. Berg, see 6:1000 (1 reference); for reviews by James A. Field, Jr. and Christine McGuire of an earlier form, see 5:812.

N83. College Entrance Examination Board Advanced Placement Examination: European History. For additional information, see 6:1001 (2 references).

N84. Cooperative American History Test. For additional information and reviews by Dorothy C. Adkins and Martha E. Layman, see 4:684 (2 references); see also 3:604 (3 references); for a review by Margaret Willis of an earlier form, see 2:1633; for a review by Edgar B. Wesley, see 1:1014.

N85. Cooperative Ancient History Test. For additional information, see 4:685; for a review by S. P. McCutchen, see 2:1634; for a review by Wilbur F. Murra of an earlier form, see 1:1015.

N86. Cooperative Modern European History Test. For additional information, see 4:686; for a review by Lavone A. Hanna of an earlier form, see 2:1635; for reviews by A. C. Krey and S. P. McCutchen, see 1:1016.

N87. Cooperative Topical Tests in American History. For additional information, see 6:1002.

N88. Cooperative World History Test. For additional information and a review by David K. Heenan, see 5:814; for a review by Kenneth E. Gell of an earlier form, see 2:1636; for a review by R. M. Tryon, see 1:1017.

N89. Coordinated Scales of Attainment: History. For additional information, see 5:815. For reviews of the complete battery, see 4:8 (1 review) and 3:6 (4 reviews).

N90. Crary American History Test. For additional information and a review by Frederick H. Stutz, see 5:816 (2 references); for a review by Edgar B. Wesley, see 4:688.

N91. Cummings World History Test. For additional information, see 5:817 (1 reference); for reviews by Dorothy C. Adkins and Howard R. Anderson, see 4:689.

N92. Ely-King Interpretation Tests in American History. For additional information and reviews by Clinton C. Conrad and Edgar B. Wesley, see 2:1637.

N93. Emporia History Test. For additional information, see 1:1018.

N94. Examination in American History. For additional information and a review by Howard R. Anderson, see 3:607 (1 reference).

N95. Examination in Modern European History. For additional information and a review by Frederick H. Stutz, see 3:608.

N96. Examination in World History—High-School Level. For additional information and reviews by Dorothy C. Adkins and Wallace W. Taylor, see 3:609.

N97. The Graduate Record Examinations Advanced Tests: History. For additional information, see 6:1003; for a review by Robert H. Ferrell of an earlier form, see 5:818. For a review of the testing program, see 5:601.

N98. History: Every Pupil Scholarship Test. For additional information, see 6:1004.

N99. Information Tests in American History. For additional information and a review by Roy A. Price, see 2:1638.

N100. Iowa Every-Pupil Test in United States History. For additional information, see 1:1020.

N101. Iowa Every-Pupil Test in World History. For additional information, see 1:1021.

N102. Kansas American History Test. For additional information and a review by W. H. Cartwright, see 3:610; for a review by Wilbur F. Murra, see 2:1639.

N103. Kansas Modern European History Test. For additional information and a review by Frederick H. Stutz, see 3:611; for a review by Clinton C. Conrad, see 2:1640.

N104. Kansas United States History Test. For additional information, see 6:1005; for reviews by Wayne A. Frederick and John Manning, see 5:820.

N105. Kniss World History Test. For additional information and reviews by Dorothy C. Adkins and Wallace W. Taylor, see 3:612 (2 references, 2 excerpts).

N106. Medieval History: Every Pupil Test. For additional information, see 1:1022.

N107. Modern History: Every Pupil Test. For additional information, see 1:1023.

N108. Objective Tests in American History. For additional information, see 6:1006.

N109. Objective Tests in World History. For additional information, see 6:1007.

N110. Semester Test for American History. For additional information, see 4:683.

N111. Semester Test for High School World History. For additional information, see 4:697.

N112. Social Studies 10 (American History): Minnesota High School Achievement Examinations. For additional information, see 6:1008; for a review by Howard R. Anderson of earlier forms, see 5:810.

N113. Social Studies 11 (World History): Minnesota High School Achievement Examinations. For additional information, see 6:1009.

N114. Survey Test in Introductory American History: California Survey Series. For additional information and a review by Richard E. Gross, see 6:1010.

N115. Survey Test in United States History. For additional information, see 3:613 (16 references).

N116. Taylor-Schrammel World History Test. For additional information and a review by J. R. Gerberich, see 2:1641.

N117. Test of Factual Relations in American History. For additional information and a review by Robert E. Keohane, see 2:1642 (1 reference); for a review by Wilbur F. Murra, see 1:1024.

N118. Understanding of American History. For additional information and a review by Elizabeth C. Adams, see 4:693.

N119. Wisconsin American History Test. For additional information, see 1:1025.

N120. World History: Every Pupil Scholarship Test. For additional information, see 6:1011.

N121. World History: Every Pupil Test. For additional information, see 6:1012.

N122. World History Test: Acorn National Achievement Tests. For additional information and a review by John Manning, see 5:825.

N123. World History Test: Affiliation Testing Program for Catholic Secondary Schools. For additional information and a review by Henry Chauncey, see 6:1013. For a review of the complete program, see 6:758.

N124. World History Test: State High School Tests for Indiana. For additional information, see 4:696.

POLITICAL SCIENCE

N125. American Civics and Government Tests for High Schools and Colleges. For additional information and a review by John H. Haefner, see 6:1013a.

N126. American Government and Citizenship: Every Pupil Test. For additional information, see 6:1014; for a review by Elizabeth C. Adams of the 1951 form, see 4:699.

N127. American Government: Every Pupil Scholarship Test. For additional information, see 6:1015.

N128. Attitude Toward Politicians Scale. For additional information and a review by Donald T. Campbell, see 5:829.

N129. Civic Vocabulary Test. For additional information and a review by I. G. Meddleton, see 5:830 (1 reference).

N130. Civics: Every Pupil Test. For additional information, see 1:1145.

N131. Constitution: Every Pupil Scholarship Test. For additional information, see 6:1016.

N132. Cooperative American Government Test. For additional information and a review by Frederic L. Ayer, see 4:702.

N133. Cooperative Community Affairs Test. For additional information and reviews by W. H. Cartwright, J. R. Gerberich, and Lavone A. Hanna, see 3:591 (1 reference).

N134. Dimond-Pflieger Problems of Democracy Test. For additional information and reviews by John H. Haefner and Douglas E. Scates, see 5:833 (1 reference).

N135. Duke University Political Science Information Test (American Government). For additional information, see 6:1017.

N136. Examination in Civics. For additional information and a review by Roy A. Price, see 3:616 (1 reference).

N137. Examination in Problems of Democracy —High-School Level. For additional information and a review by Lavone A. Hanna, see 3:617 (2 references).

N138. General Knowledge Test of Local, State, and National Government. For additional information and a review by Wayne A. Frederick, see 5:834.

N139. The Graduate Record Examinations Advanced Tests: Government. For additional information, see 6:1018; for a review by Christine McGuire of an earlier form, see 5:835. For a review of the testing program, see 5:601.

N140. Iowa Every-Pupil Test in American Government. For additional information, see 1:1019.

N141. Junior High School Civics Test: State High School Tests for Indiana. For additional information, see 4:704.

N142. The Kansas Constitution Test. For additional information and a review by David K. Heenan, see 5:836.

N143. Mordy-Schrammel Constitution Test. For additional information and a review by W. H. Cartwright, see 3:618.

N144. Mordy-Schrammel Elementary Civics Test. For additional information and a review by C. Robert Pace, see 3:619.

N145. Newspaper Reading Survey: What Do You Read? For additional information and reviews by Frederick H. Stutz and M. J. Wantman, see 5:837.

N146. Patterson Test or Study Exercises on the Constitution of the United States. For additional information, see 5:838.

N147. Patterson Test or Study Exercises on the Declaration of Independence. For additional information, see 5:839.

N148. Patterson's Tests on the Federal Constitution. For additional information, see 4:705.

N149. Peltier-Durost Civics and Citizenship Test. For additional information and reviews by Howard R. Anderson and Christine McGuire, see 6:1019.

N150. Principles of American Citizenship Test. For additional information and reviews by Howard R. Anderson and M. J. Wantman, see 5:841 (1 reference).

N151. Principles of Democracy Test. For additional information and reviews by William C. Bingham and John H. Haefner, see 6:1020.

N152. Senior High School Civics Test: For a One-Semester Course: State High School Tests for Indiana. For additional information, see 4:706.

N153. Senior High School Civics Test: State High School Tests for Indiana. For additional information, see 4:707.

N154. 20th Century Test for Civics. For additional information, see 4:701.

N155. Wesley Test in Political Terms. For additional information and a review by Howard R. Anderson, see 2:1621 (1 reference).

SOCIOLOGY

N156. Black-Schrammel Sociology Test. For additional information, see 4:708.

N157. Contemporary Problems. For additional information and a review by Harry D. Berg, see 5:832.

N158. The Graduate Record Examinations Advanced Tests: Sociology. For additional information and a review by J. Richard Wilmeth, see 6:1021. For a review of the testing program, see 5:601.

N159. Sare-Sanders Sociology Test. For additional information and a review by J. Richard Wilmeth, see 6:1022.

N160. Sociology: Every Pupil Scholarship Test. For additional information, see 5:844.

VOCATIONS

O1. Airman Qualifying Examination. For additional information, see 6:1023 (1 reference).

O2. [Aptitude Inventory.] For additional information and reviews by Leonard W. Ferguson and C. E. Jurgensen, see 6:1024 (1 reference, 1 excerpt).

O3. ETSA Tests. For additional information and reviews by Marvin D. Dunnette and Raymond A. Katzell, see 6:1025.

O4. General Adaptability Battery. For additional information, see 6:1026 (1 reference).

O5. Individual Placement Series. For additional information, see 6:1027.

O6. Personnel Selection and Classification Test. For additional information and reviews by Dorothy C. Adkins, George K. Bennett, and George A. Ferguson, see 3:690.

O7. Screening Tests for Apprentices. For additional information, see 6:1028.

O8. Steward Personnel Tests (Short Form). For additional information and reviews by Leonard V. Gordon and Lyman W. Porter, see 6:1029.

O9. Vocational Aptitude Examination, Type E-A. For additional information and reviews by D. Welty Lefever and Benjamin Shimberg, see 3:695 (1 reference); for reviews by Harold D. Carter and M. R. Trabue of an earlier edition, see 2:1679 (3 references).

CLERICAL

O10. A.C.E.R. Short Clerical Test. For additional information, see 6:1030.

O11. A.C.E.R. Speed and Accuracy Tests. For additional information, see 6:1031 (2 references); for a review by D. W. McElwain of an earlier form, see 4:719.

O12. Beginner's Clerical Test. For additional information and reviews by Stephen Hunka and Harry L. Stein, see 6:1032.

O13. Cardall Test of Clerical Perception. For additional information, see 6:1033.

O14. Checking Test. For additional information, see 6:1034.

O15. Classifying Test. For additional information, see 6:1035.

O16. Clerical Aptitude Test: Acorn National Aptitude Tests. For additional information, see 5:847 (1 reference); for reviews by Marion A. Bills, Donald G. Paterson, Henry Weitz, and E. F. Wonderlic, see 3:623.

O17. Clerical Perception Test. For additional information and reviews by Edward N. Hay, Raymond A. Katzell, Erwin K. Taylor, and E. F. Wonderlic, see 3:624 (1 excerpt).

O18. Clerical Test D: Extending—Verifying —Checking—Classifying. For additional information and reviews by Donald G. Paterson and John M. Willits, see 3:625.

O19. Clerical Tests 1 and 2. For additional information, see 5:848.

O20. Clerical Tests, Series N. For additional information, see 6:1036.

O21. Clerical Tests, Series V. For additional information, see 6:1037.

O22. Clerical Worker Examination. For additional information, see 6:1038.

O23. Cross Reference Test. For additional information and a review by Philip H. Kriedt, see 6:1039.

O24. Detroit Clerical Aptitudes Examination. For additional information and a review by E. F. Wonderlic, see 3:626 (1 reference); for reviews by Irving Lorge and M. W. Richardson of an earlier edition, see 2:1655.

O25. Group Test 20. For additional information and a review by E. G. Chambers, see 4:723 (2 references).

O26. Group Test 25 (Clerical). For additional information and a review by E. G. Chambers, see 4:724 (1 reference).

O27. Hay Tests for Clerical Aptitude. For additional information, see 5:849 (2 references); for reviews by Reign H. Bittner and Edward E. Cureton, see 4:725 (8 references).

O28. Martin Office Aptitude Tests. For additional information and reviews by D. Welty Lefever and Ross W. Matteson, see 4:726.

O29. Minnesota Clerical Test. For additional information, see 6:1040 (10 references); for a review by Donald E. Super, see 5:850 (46 references); for reviews by Thelma Hunt, R. B. Selover, Erwin K. Taylor, and E. F. Wonderlic, see 3:627 (22 references); for a review by W. D. Commins, see 2:1664 (18 references).

O30. National Institute of Industrial Psychology Clerical Test (North American Revision). For additional information and a review by Harry L. Stein, see 6:1041; for a review by R. B. Selover of the American revision, see 3:628 (4 references); for a review by Donald G. Paterson, see 2:1665 (2 references).

O31. Number Checking Test. For additional information, see 6:1042.

O32. Office Skills Achievement Test. For additional information and reviews by Douglas G. Schultz and Paul W. Thayer, see 6:1043.

O33. Office Worker Test. For additional information and reviews by Ray G. Price and Douglas G. Schultz, see 6:1044.

O34. O'Rourke Clerical Aptitude Test, Junior Grade. For additional information, see 5:851 (1 reference); for a review by Raymond A. Katzell, see 3:629 (3 references).

O35. Personnel Institute Clerical Tests. For additional information, see 5:852.

O36. Personnel Research Institute Clerical Battery. For additional information and reviews by Louise Witmer Cureton and Albert K. Kurtz, see 4:729. For a review of a subtest, see 4:211.

O37. Psychological Corporation General Clerical Test. For additional information and reviews by Edward E. Cureton and G. A. Satter, see 4:730 (4 references); for reviews by Edward N. Hay, Thelma Hunt, Raymond A. Katzell, and E. F. Wonderlic, see 3:630.

O38. Purdue Clerical Adaptability Test. For additional information and reviews by Mary Ellen Oliverio and Donald Spearritt, see 5:853 (2 references); for reviews by Edward N. Hay, Joseph E. Moore, and Alec Rodger of the previous edition, see 4:731.

O39. SRA Clerical Aptitudes. For additional information and reviews by Edward N. Hay and G. A. Satter, see 4:732.

O40. The Short Employment Tests. For additional information and a review by Leonard W. Ferguson, see 6:1045 (9 references); for a review by P. L. Mellenbruch, see 5:854 (16 references).

O41. Short Tests of Clerical Ability. For additional information and reviews by Philip H. Kriedt and Paul W. Thayer, see 6:1046.

O42. Speed Tabulation Test. For additional information, see 1:1082.

O43. Survey of Clerical Skills (SOCS): Individual Placement Series (Area IV). For additional information, see 6:1047.

O44. Survey of Working Speed and Accuracy. For additional information and reviews by Edward N. Hay, Donald G. Paterson, and Erwin K. Taylor, see 3:631.

O45. Thurstone Examination in Clerical Work. For additional information and reviews by John M. Willits and E. F. Wonderlic, see 3:632 (6 references).

O46. Turse Clerical Aptitudes Test. For additional information and reviews by Robert A. Jones and Donald Spearritt, see 5:855 (1 reference).

O47. V.G.C. Clerical Indicator. For additional information and a review by George A. Ferguson, see 4:735.

INTERESTS

O48. ABC Occupational Inventory. For additional information, see 4:736.

O49. Basic Interest Questionnaire: For Selecting Your Vocation or Avocation. For additional information, see 3:633 (1 excerpt).

O50. Brainard Occupational Preference Inventory. For additional information and a review by William C. Cottle, see 5:856 (2 references); for a review by Elmer D. Hinckley, see 4:737 (1 reference); for reviews by Edwin W. Davis and Herschel T. Manuel, see 3:634 (2 references); for reviews by Jack W. Dunlap and M. R. Trabue of the original edition, see 2:1675 (4 references); for a review by Everett B. Sackett, see 1:1176.

O51. Burke Inventory of Vocational Development. For additional information, see 6:1048.

O52. Career Finder. For additional information and reviews by Arthur C. MacKinney and Charles F. Warnath, see 6:1049.

O53. Career Incentive and Progress Blank. For additional information, see 2:1648.

O54. Chatterji's Non-Language Preference Record. For additional information, see 6:1050.

O55. Cleeton Vocational Interest Inventory. For additional information and reviews by Edward B. Greene, C. A. Oakley, and Arthur E. Traxler, see 3:635 (19 references, 1 excerpt); for reviews by Forrest A. Kingsbury and N. W. Morton, see 2:1682 (1 excerpt); for reviews by Albert S. Thompson, M. R. Trabue, and E. G. Williamson of an earlier edition, see 1:1181.

O56. College Planning Inventory, Senior College Edition. For additional information, see 6:1051.

O57. Curtis Interest Scale. For additional information and reviews by Warren T. Norman and Leona E. Tyler, see 6:1052.

O58. Devon Interest Test. For additional information and reviews by Arthur B. Royse and Alfred Yates, see 5:857 (3 references).

O59. Edmiston Inventory of Interest. For additional information and a review by Arthur E. Traxler, see 4:738 (1 reference).

O60. Fowler-Parmenter Self-Scoring Interest Record. For additional information and reviews by David P. Campbell and John W. French, see 6:1053 (2 references).

O61. The Geist Picture Interest Inventory. For additional information and reviews by Milton E. Hahn and Benjamin Shimberg, see 6:1054 (12 references, 2 excerpts).

O62. Geist Picture Interest Inventory: Deaf Form: Male. For additional information, see 6:1055 (1 reference).

O63. Gordon Occupational Check List. For additional information and reviews by John O. Crites and Kenneth B. Hoyt, see 6:1056.

O64. Gregory Academic Interest Inventory. For additional information and reviews by Paul S. Burnham, Lysle W. Croft, and Herbert A. Toops, see 3:636 (1 reference).

O65. The Guilford-Shneidman-Zimmerman Interest Survey. For additional information and reviews by George K. Bennett and Wilbur L. Layton, see 4:739 (2 references).

O66. The Guilford-Zimmerman Interest Inventory. For additional information and a review by Kenneth B. Hoyt, see 6:1057.

O67. Hackman-Gaither Vocational Interest Inventory. For additional information, see 6:1058 (4 references).

O68. Henderson Analysis of Interest. For additional information and reviews by Wilbur L. Layton and Donald E. Super, see 4:740.

O69. How Well Do You Know Your Interests. For additional information and a review by John R. Hills, see 6:1059 (1 reference, 1 excerpt); for reviews by Jerome E. Doppelt and Henry S. Dyer, see 5:859.

O70. Interest Check List. For additional information, see 5:860; for reviews by Milton L. Blum and Howard R. Taylor of the original edition, see 4:741.

O71. Interest Questionnaire for High School Students. For additional information and a review by Lysle W. Croft, see 3:637 (6 references).

O72. Inventory of Vocational Interests: Acorn National Aptitude Tests. For additional information and a review by John W. French, see 6:1060; for reviews by Marion A. Bills, Edward S. Bordin, Harold D. Carter, and Patrick Slater, see 3:638.

O73. Job Choice Inventory. For additional information, see 6:1061.

O74. Job Qualification Inventory. For additional information and reviews by Ralph F. Berdie and Stanley G. Dulsky, see 3:639 (5 references, 2 excerpts).

O75. Kuder General Interest Survey. For additional information, see 6:1061a.

O76. Kuder Preference Record—Occupational. For additional information and a review by David P. Campbell, see 6:1062 (13 references); for reviews by Edward S. Bordin and John W. Gustad, see 5:862.

O77. Kuder Preference Record—Vocational. For additional information and a review by Martin Katz, see 6:1063 (148 references); for reviews by Clifford P. Froehlich and John Pierce-Jones, see 5:863 (211 references); for reviews by Edward S. Bordin, Harold D. Carter, and H. M. Fowler, see 4:742 (146 references); for reviews by Ralph F. Berdie, E. G. Chambers, and Donald E. Super, see 3:640 (60 references, 1 excerpt); for reviews by A. B. Crawford and Arthur E. Traxler of an earlier edition, see 2:1671 (2 references).

O78. Motivation Indicator. For additional information and reviews by Norman Frederiksen and Arthur E. Traxler, see 3:641 (1 excerpt).

O79. Occupational Interest Blank. For additional information and reviews by Stanley G. Dulsky and J. B. Miner, see 2:1666; for reviews by W. V. Bingham and M. R. Trabue, see 1:1174.

O80. Occupational Interest Blank for Women. For additional information and reviews by Gwendolen Schneidler Dickson and Frances Oralind Triggs, see 3:642 (6 references).

O81. Occupational Interest Inventory. For additional information, see 6:1064 (6 references); for reviews by Martin Katz and Wilbur L. Layton, see

5:864 (20 references) ; for a review by Arthur H. Brayfield of the original edition, see 4:743 (20 references) ; for reviews by Edward S. Bordin and Stanley G. Dulsky, see 3:643.

O82. Occupational Interest Survey (With Pictures): Individual Placement Series (Area II). For additional information, see 6:1065.

O83. Occupational Interests: Self Analysis Scale. For additional information and a review by Stanley G. Dulsky, see 3:644.

O84. Picture Interest Inventory. For additional information and reviews by Ralph F. Berdie and Donald E. Super, see 6:1066 (4 references, 1 excerpt).

O85. Primary Business Interests Test. For additional information, see 6:1067 (2 references) ; for reviews by George K. Bennett, Glen U. Cleeton, and George A. Ferguson, see 3:645.

O86. Qualifications Record. For additional information and reviews by Arthur C. MacKinney and Charles F. Warnath, see 6:1068 ; see also O52.

O87. Rothwell-Miller Interest Blank. For additional information, see 5:867.

O88. Safran Vocational Interest Test. For additional information, see 6:1069 (1 reference).

O89. Self-Administering Vocational Interest Locator With Work Interest Picture. For additional information and a review by Donald E. Super, see 4:744.

O90. Strong Vocational Interest Blank for Men. For additional information and reviews by Alexander W. Astin and Edward J. Furst, see 6:1070 (189 references) ; see also 5:868 (153 references) ; for reviews by Edward S. Bordin and Elmer D. Hinckley, see 4:747 (98 references) ; see also 3:647 (104 references) ; for reviews by Harold D. Carter, John G. Darley, and N. W. Morton, see 2:1680 (71 references) ; for a review by John G. Darley of an earlier edition, see 1:1178.

O91. Strong Vocational Interest Blank for Women. For additional information, see 6:1071 (12 references) ; see also 5:869 (19 references) ; for a review by Gwendolen Schneidler Dickson, see 3:649 (36 references) ; for a review by Ruth Strang of an earlier edition, see 2:1681 (9 references) ; for a review by John G. Darley, see 1:1179.

O92. Thurstone Interest Schedule. For additional information and reviews by Norman Frederiksen and Donald E. Super, see 4:745 (1 reference).

O93. VALCAN Vocational Interest Profile (VIP). For additional information, see 6:1072.

O94. The Vocational Apperception Test. For additional information and reviews by Benjamin Balinsky and William E. Henry, see 4:146 (1 reference, 1 excerpt).

O95. Vocational Interest Analyses: A Six-Fold Analytical Extension of the Occupational Interest Inventory. For additional information and a review by Wilbur L. Layton, see 5:870 (1 reference) ; for a review by Julian C. Stanley, see 4:746.

O96. Vocational Interest Schedule. For additional information and a review by Donald E. Super, see 3:653 (8 references) ; for a review by J. B. Miner, see 2:1683 (4 references) ; for reviews by Harold D. Carter and N. W. Morton, see 1:1180.

O97. A Vocational Interest Test for College Women. For additional information and a review by Frances Oralind Triggs, see 3:654 (2 references).

O98. Vocational Inventory. For additional information and reviews by Edward S. Bordin, Harold D. Carter, and Donald E. Super, see 3:655 (4 references, 1 excerpt).

O99. Vocational Sentence Completion Blank. For additional information, see 6:1073 (4 references).

O100. William, Lynde & Williams Analysis of Interest. For additional information, see 6:1074.

O101. Young-Estabrooks Scale for Measuring Studiousness by Means of the Strong Vocational Interest Blank for Men. For additional information and a review by Edmund G. Williamson, see 1:904 (4 references).

O102. Your Educational Plans. For additional information and a review by Leo Goldman, see 6:1075 (1 reference, 1 excerpt).

MANUAL DEXTERITY

O102.1. APT Manual Dexterity Test. For additional information, see 6:1076.

O103. Benge HanDexterity Test. For additional information and reviews by C. H. Lawshe, Jr. and Joseph E. Moore, see 3:656.

O104. Benge Two Hand Coordination Test. For additional information and a review by Milton L. Blum, see 3:657.

O105. Crawford Small Parts Dexterity Test. For additional information and a review by Neil D. Warren, see 5:871 (8 references) ; for a review by Raymond A. Katzell, see 4:752 ; for a review by Joseph E. Moore, see 3:667.

O106. Hand-Tool Dexterity Test. For additional information and reviews by C. H. Lawshe, Jr. and Neil D. Warren, see 3:659 (2 references).

O107. Martin Peg Board (Finger Dexterity Test). For additional information, see 4:749.

O108. Mellenbruch Curve-Block Series. For additional information and reviews by William R. Grove and Willard A. Kerr, see 3:662 (1 reference).

O109. Minnesota Rate of Manipulation Test, [1946 Edition]. For additional information, see 6:1077 (24 references) ; for reviews by Edwin E. Ghiselli and John R. Kinzer, see 3:663 (22 references, 1 excerpt) ; for reviews by Lorene Teegarden and Morris S. Viteles, see 2:1662 (4 references).

O110. O'Connor Finger Dexterity Test. For additional information, see 6:1078 (32 references) ; for a review by Morris S. Viteles, see 2:1659 (15 references).

O111. O'Connor Tweezer Dexterity Test. For additional information, see 6:1079 (23 references) ; for a review by Morris S. Viteles, see 2:1678 (13 references).

O112. Pennsylvania Bi-Manual Worksample. For additional information and reviews by Edwin E. Ghiselli, Thomas W. Harrell, Albert Gibson Packard, and Neil D. Warren, see 3:665 (3 references).

O113. Purdue Hand Precision Test. For additional information, see 6:1080 (2 references).

O114. Purdue Pegboard. For additional information, see 6:1081 (15 references) ; for a review by Neil D. Warren, see 5:873 (11 references) ; see also 4:751

(12 references); for reviews by Edwin E. Ghiselli, Thomas W. Harrell, and Albert Gibson Packard, see 3:666 (3 references).

O115. Stromberg Dexterity Test. For additional information and a review by Julian C. Stanley, see 4:755 (1 reference).

MECHANICAL ABILITY

O116. A.C.E.R. Mechanical Comprehension Test. For additional information and reviews by John R. Jennings and Haydn S. Williams, see 5:874 (2 references); for a review by D. W. McElwain, see 4:756.

O117. A.C.E.R. Mechanical Reasoning Test. For additional information, see 6:1082; for reviews by John R. Jennings and Haydn S. Williams, see 5:875.

O118. Chriswell Structural Dexterity Test. For additional information, see 6:1083 (1 reference); for a review by A. Pemberton Johnson, see 5:876.

O119. College Entrance Examination Board Placement Tests: Spatial Relations Test. For additional information, see 6:1084 (4 references).

O120. College Entrance Examination Board Special Aptitude Test in Spatial Relations. For additional information and a review by Robert L. Thorndike, see 4:808.

O121. [Cox Mechanical and Manual Tests.] For additional information and reviews by C. A. Oakley and Alec Rodger, see 2:1652–3 (4 references).

O122. Crawford Spatial Relations Test. For additional information and a review by William R. Grove, see 3:658 (7 references).

O123. [Curtis Object Completion and Space Form Tests.] For additional information and reviews by Richard S. Melton and I. Macfarlane Smith, see 6:1085.

O124. Detroit Mechanical Aptitudes Examination. For additional information and reviews by Lloyd G. Humphreys and Dewey B. Stuit, see 3:668 (4 references); for a review by Irving Lorge, see 2:1656 (1 excerpt).

O125. Dynamicube Test of Power to Visualize. For additional information, see 1:1167.

O126. Flags: A Test of Space Thinking. For additional information and a review by I. Macfarlane Smith, see 6:1086.

O127. Form Relations Group Test. For additional information and a review by A. T. Welford, see 4:757 (10 references).

O128. Girls' Mechanical Assembly Test. For additional information and a review by Richard Ledgerwood, see 1:1032 (2 references).

O129. Group Test 80A. For additional information and reviews by E. G. Chambers and John Liggett, see 5:877.

O130. Group Test 81. For additional information and a review by E. G. Chambers, see 4:758 (5 references).

O131. Hazlehurst Primary Mechanical Ability Tests. For additional information, see 6:1087.

O132. MacQuarrie Test for Mechanical Ability. For additional information, see 4:759 (15 references);

see also 4:760 (1 excerpt); for reviews by John R. Kinzer, C. H. Lawshe, Jr., and Alec Rodger, see 3:661 (43 references).

O133. Mechanical Aptitude Test: Acorn National Aptitude Tests. For additional information, see 5:878; for reviews by Reign H. Bittner, James M. Porter, Jr., and Alec Rodger, see 3:669.

O134. Mechanical Information Questionnaire. For additional information, see 6:1088.

O135. Mechanical Movements: A Test of Mechanical Comprehension. For additional information and a review by William A. Owens, see 6:1089.

O136. Mellenbruch Mechanical Motivation Test. For additional information and reviews by Arthur H. Brayfield and John B. Morris, see 5:879; for reviews by Lloyd G. Humphreys and C. A. Oakley of the original edition, see 3:670.

O137. Minnesota Assembly Test. For additional information and a review by William R. Grove, see 3:671 (11 references).

O138. Minnesota Spatial Relations Test. For additional information and a review by Milton L. Blum, see 3:664 (18 references); for a review by Lorene Teegarden, see 2:1663 (10 references).

O139. Moray House Space Test 2. For additional information and a review by E. Anstey, see 6:1090 (4 references).

O140. Mutilated Cubes Test of Power to Visualize. For additional information, see 1:1173.

O141. N.I.I.P. Squares Test. For additional information and a review by J. F. Clark, see 5:880 (9 references).

O142. O'Connor Wiggly Block. For additional information, see 6:1091 (27 references).

O143. O'Rourke Mechanical Aptitude Test. For additional information, see 5:882; for reviews by Jay L. Otis and George A. Satter, see 3:672 (8 references); for a review by Herbert A. Landry, see 2:1668.

O144. Perceptual Mechanics Test. For additional information and a review by Charles M. Harsh, see 3:673.

O145. Prognostic Test of Mechanical Abilities. For additional information and reviews by Willard A. Kerr and Douglas G. Schultz, see 4:761 (1 reference); see also 3:674 (1 excerpt).

O146. Purdue Mechanical Adaptability Test. For additional information, see 4:762 (6 references); for reviews by Jay L. Otis and Dewey B. Stuit, see 3:676.

O147. Purdue Mechanical Performance Test. For additional information, see 5:883 (1 reference).

O148. Revised Minnesota Paper Form Board Test. For additional information, see 6:1092 (16 references); for a review by D. W. McElwain, see 5:884 (29 references); for reviews by Clifford E. Jurgensen and Raymond A. Katzell, see 4:763 (38 references); for a review by Dewey B. Stuit, see 3:677 (48 references); for a review by Alec Rodger, see 2:1673 (9 references).

O149. SRA Mechanical Aptitudes. For additional information and reviews by Alec Rodger and Douglas G. Schultz, see 4:764.

O150. Spatial Tests 1, 2, and 3. For additional information, see 6:1093 (4 references); for reviews by E. G. Chambers and Charles T. Myers of tests 1 and 2, see 5:885; for a review by E. A. Peel of test 1, see 4:753.

O151. Staticube Test of Power to Visualize. For additional information, see 1:1177.

O152. Stenquist Assembling Test. For additional information and a review by William R. Grove, see 3:679 (10 references).

O153. Stenquist Mechanical Aptitude Test. For additional information and a review by James M. Porter, Jr., see 3:678 (18 references).

O154. Survey of Mechanical Insight. For additional information and a review by Arthur H. Brayfield, see 5:886 (3 references); for reviews by Reign H. Bittner, Jay L. Otis, and Shailer Peterson of the original edition, see 3:680.

O155. Survey of Object Visualization. For additional information and a review by William J. Micheels, see 5:887 (5 references); for reviews by Charles M. Harsh, Clifford E. Jurgensen, Shailer Peterson, and Patrick Slater of the original edition, see 3:681.

O156. Survey of Space Relations Ability. For additional information and a review by D. W. McElwain, see 5:888 (4 references); for reviews by E. G. Chambers, Clifford E. Jurgensen, and James M. Porter, Jr., see 3:682.

O157. Tests of Mechanical Comprehension. For additional information, see 6:1094 (15 references); see also 5:889 (46 references); for a review by N. W. Morton, see 4:766 (28 references); for reviews by Charles M. Harsh, Lloyd G. Humphreys, and George A. Satter, see 3:683 (19 references).

O158. Three-Dimensional Space Test. For additional information, see 6:1095.

O159. Tool Knowledge Test [Australian Council for Educational Research]. For additional information and reviews by J. F. Clark and I. G. Meddleton, see 5:890.

O160. Tool Knowledge Test [Richardson, Bellows, Henry & Co., Inc.]. For additional information, see 6:1096.

O161. Two-Dimensional Space Test. For additional information, see 6:1097.

O162. V.G.C. Object Visualization Indicator. For additional information, see 4:767.

O163. V.G.C. Space Relations Ability Indicator. For additional information, see 4:768.

O164. The Vincent Mechanical Models Test A (Industrial). For additional information and a review by A. T. Welford, see 4:769 (7 references).

O165. Weights and Pulleys: A Test of Intuitive Mechanics. For additional information and a review by William A. Owens, see 6:1098.

MISCELLANEOUS

O166. Adjusted Graphic Analysis Chart. For additional information, see 2:1644 (1 reference).

O167. Admission Test for Graduate Study in Business. For additional information, see 5:910.

O168. Aids to Self-Analysis and Vocational Planning Inventory. For additional information, see 2:1645 (1 reference).

O169. The Biographical Index. For additional information and reviews by John K. Hemphill and Richard S. Melton, see 6:1099.

O170. Breadth of Information. For additional information, see 6:1100.

O171. Business Judgment Test. For additional information, see 6:1101 (4 references); for a review by Edward B. Greene, see 5:893.

O172. Cancellation Test. For additional information and a review by Herbert A. Tonne, see 5:894; for a review by Joseph E. King, see 3:684.

O173. Cardall Test of Practical Judgment. For additional information, see 6:1102 (4 references); see also 4:784 (6 references); for reviews by Glen U. Cleeton and Howard R. Taylor of an earlier edition, see 3:694.

O174. Check List for Self-Guidance in Choosing an Occupation. For additional information, see 2:1649.

O175. Check List of Occupations. For additional information, see 2:1650.

O176. Conference Meeting Rating Scale. For additional information, see 6:1103.

O177. Dartnell Self-Administered Employee Opinion Unit. For additional information and a review by Raymond A. Katzell, see 6:1104.

O178. Employee Opinion Survey. For additional information, see 6:1105.

O179. Entrance Questionnaire and Experience Record. For additional information, see 2:1658 (1 reference).

O180. Guidance Questionnaire. For additional information, see 2:1659.1.

O181. Guidance Summary Form for Use in Vocational and Educational Counseling. For additional information and a review by Norman Frederiksen, see 3:446 (1 excerpt).

O182. Identical Forms. For additional information, see 5:899.

O183. Individual Guidance Record. For additional information, see 2:1660 (1 reference).

O184. Information Blank: For Obtaining Data About Vocational Plans and Problems of High School Students. For additional information, see 1:1169.

O185. The Jenkins Job Attitudes Survey. For additional information, see 6:1106 (1 reference).

O186. Kahn Career Orientation Questionnaire: A Preliminary to Vocational or Educational Counseling, Student Form. For additional information and a review by Arthur E. Traxler, see 4:777.

O187. Kefauver-Hand Guidance Tests and Inventories. For additional information and a review by E. G. Williamson, see 2:1661; for reviews by Harold D. Carter, Gwendolen Schneidler, and M. R. Trabue, see 1:1170 (2 excerpts).

O188. Mathematical and Technical Test. For additional information and reviews by Charles R. Langmuir and F. W. Warburton, see 4:779.

O189. Michigan Adult Profile. For additional information and reviews by Richard Ledgerwood, M. R. Trabue, John G. Darley, John M. Stalnaker, and Arthur E. Traxler, see 1:1171.

O190. Miles Career Evaluation Inventory. For additional information, see 4:780 (1 reference).

O191. Minnesota Occupational Rating Scales and Counseling Profile. For additional information and a review by M. H. Elliott, see 3:689 (5 references).

O192. Occupational Analysis Form. For additional information, see 2:1665.1.

O193. Occupational Orientation Inquiry. For additional information and reviews by John Gray Peatman and C. Gilbert Wrenn, see 2:1667 (1 reference).

O194. The Organization Survey. For additional information, see 6:1107.

O195. Per-Flu-Dex Tests. For additional information and reviews by Andrew L. Comrey and John W. French, see 5:901.

O196. SRA Employee Inventory. For additional information and reviews by Erwin K. Taylor and Albert S. Thompson, see 5:905 (10 references).

O197. A Self-Rating Scale for Leadership Qualifications. For additional information, see 5:906.

O198. Survey of Company Morale: Job Satisfaction Blank No. 12. For additional information and a review by William W. Waite, see 3:693 (1 reference).

O199. The Tear Ballot for Industry. For additional information and a review by Raymond A. Katzell, see 6:1108 (5 references); for a review by Brent Baxter, see 4:783 (4 references).

O200. [Tests A/9 and A/10.] For additional information, see 6:1109.

O201. Vocational Guidance Questionnaire. For additional information, see 2:1679.1.

O202. Whisler Strategy Test. For additional information and reviews by Jean Maier Palormo and Paul F. Ross, see 6:1110 (1 reference).

O203. Work Information Inventory. For additional information, see 6:1111.

SELECTION & RATING FORMS

O204. APT Controlled Interview. For additional information, see 6:1112.

O205. [Biography Forms]: Application-Interview Series. For additional information, see 5:892.

O206. [Cardall Interviewing Aids.] For additional information, see 6:1114.

O207. Career Counseling Personal Data Form. For additional information, see 6:1113.

O208. Diagnostic Interviewer's Guide. For additional information and a review by Albert K. Kurtz, see 6:1115 (2 references); for reviews by Clyde H. Coombs and Douglas H. Fryer, see 3:685.

O209. Employee Evaluation Form for Interviewers. For additional information and reviews by Douglas H. Fryer and C. H. Ruedisili, see 3:686 (2 excerpts).

O210. Employee Merit Report. For additional information, see 4:771.

O211. Employee Performance Appraisal. For additional information and a review by Jean Maier Palormo, see 6:1116.

O212. [Employee Rating and Development Forms.] For additional information and a review by Richard S. Barrett, see 6:1117; for reviews by Harry W. Karn and Floyd L. Ruch, see 4:781.

O213. [Employee Rating Forms.] For additional information, see 6:1118.

O214. [Employee Selection Forms.] For additional information, see 4:772.

O215. [Executive, Industrial, and Sales Personnel Forms.] For additional information and a review by John P. Foley, Jr., see 6:1119 (1 reference); for a review by Floyd L. Ruch, see 4:773.

O216. Hiring Summary Worksheet. For additional information, see 5:898.

O217. Individual Background Survey. For additional information, see 6:1120.

O218. Interview Rating Scale for Prospective Employees. For additional information and reviews by Jay L. Otis and S. Rains Wallace, Jr., see 4:776.

O219. Job Description Questionnaire. For additional information, see 6:1121.

O220. Lawshe-Kephart Personnel Comparison System. For additional information and a review by Reign H. Bittner, see 4:778 (1 reference).

O221. The McQuaig Manpower Selection Series. For additional information, see 6:1122.

O222. Merit Rating Series. For additional information and a review by Seymour Levy, see 6:1123; for a review by Brent Baxter of the original series, see 4:770 (1 reference).

O223. The Nagel Personnel Interviewing and Screening Forms. For additional information, see 6:1124.

O224. The Performance Record. For additional information and reviews by Albert K. Kurtz and Albert S. Thompson, see 5:902 (1 reference).

O225. [Performance Review Forms.] For additional information, see 6:1125.

O226. Personal Data Blank. For additional information and a review by Arthur E. Traxler, see 5:903; for reviews by Edward S. Jones and Donald G. Paterson of an earlier edition, see 2:1669.

O227. Personal History Record [Richardson, Bellows, Henry & Co., Inc.]. For additional information, see 6:1126.

O228. [Personnel Interviewing Forms.] For additional information, see 6:1127.

O229. Rating Form for Use of Interviewers and Oral Examiners. For additional information and a review by Douglas H. Fryer, see 3:691 (2 references); for a review by Ruth Strang, see 2:1672.

O230. [Selection Interview Forms.] For additional information, see 6:1128.

O231. [Stevens-Thurow Personnel Forms.] For additional information, see 6:1129.

SPECIFIC VOCATIONS

O232. Probst Rating System. For additional information and reviews by Milton M. Mandell and Dale Yoder, see 4:785 (2 references).

ACCOUNTING

O233. Accounting Orientation Test: High School Level. For additional information, see 5:907 (2 references).

O234. American Institute of Certified Public Accountants Testing Programs. For additional information, see 5:911 (6 references); see also 4:787 (15 references).

DENTISTRY

O235. Dental Aptitude Testing Program. For additional information, see 5:916 (6 references); see also 4:788 (2 references).

O236. Dental Hygiene Aptitude Testing Program. For additional information, see 5:917.

ENGINEERING

O237. AC Test of Creative Ability. For additional information and reviews by Samuel T. Mayo, Philip R. Merrifield, and Albert S. Thompson, see 6:1130 (1 reference).

O238. College Entrance Examination Board Test in Pre-Engineering Science Comprehension. For additional information, see 4:809.

O239. Engineering Aide Test. For additional information, see 6:1131.

O240. Engineering and Physical Science Aptitude Test. For additional information and a review by John W. French, see 4:810 (6 references); for reviews by Norman Frederiksen and Robert M. W. Travers, see 3:698.

O241. Examination in Advanced Engineering Electronics. For additional information, see 3:407.

O242. Examination in Advanced Radio Engineering—College Level. For additional information, see 3:414.

O243. Examination in Diesel Engineering. For additional information, see 3:408.

O244. Examination in Engineering Drawing. For additional information, see 3:409.

O245. Examination in Engineering Electronics. For additional information, see 3:410.

O246. Examination in Engineering Mechanics. For additional information, see 3:411.

O247. Examination in Fluid Mechanics. For additional information, see 3:412.

O248. Examination in Machine Design. For additional information, see 3:413.

O249. Examination in Strength of Materials. For additional information, see 3:415.

O250. Examination in Surveying. For additional information, see 3:416.

O251. The Graduate Record Examinations Advanced Tests: Engineering. For additional information, see 6:1132. For a review of the testing program, see 5:601.

O252. Minnesota Engineering Analogies Test. For additional information, see 6:1133 (2 references); for reviews by A. Pemberton Johnson and William B. Schrader, see 5:933 (6 references).

O253. National Engineering Aptitude Search Test: The Junior Engineering Technical Society. For additional information, see 6:1134.

O254. The Owens' Creativity Test for Machine Design. For additional information and reviews by Samuel T. Mayo and Philip R. Merrifield, see 6:1135 (1 reference).

O255. Placement Examination in General Engineering Drawing. For additional information, see 1:1175.

O256. Pre-Engineering Ability Test. For additional information and reviews by Jerome E. Doppelt and Dewey B. Stuit, see 4:812 (11 references).

O257. Purdue Creativity Test. For additional information and reviews by Samuel T. Mayo and Philip R. Merrifield, see 6:1136 (2 references).

O258. Stanford Scientific Aptitude Test. For additional information and reviews by Joseph E. Moore and Dewey B. Stuit, see 4:813 (4 references); for a review by A. B. Crawford, see 2:1676 (3 references).

LAW

O259. Iowa Legal Aptitude Test. For additional information and a review by Alexander G. Wesman, see 4:814 (5 references).

O260. Law School Admission Test. For additional information, see 5:928 (7 references); for a review by Alexander G. Wesman, see 4:815 (6 references).

MEDICINE

O261. Medical College Admission Test. For additional information and reviews by Robert L. Ebel and Philip H. DuBois, see 6:1137 (43 references); for a review by Alexander G. Wesman of forms previously published by Educational Testing Service, see 5:932 (4 references); for a review by Morey J. Wantman, see 4:817 (11 references).

O262. Medical School Instructor Attitude Inventory. For additional information, see 6:1138 (1 reference).

O263. Veterinary Aptitude Test. For additional information, see 6:1139 (3 references); see also 5:957 (3 references).

MISCELLANEOUS

O264. Card Punch Operator Aptitude Test. For additional information, see 6:1140 (2 references).

O265. Chemical Operators Selection Test. For additional information, see 6:1141 (1 reference).

O266. The Diebold Personnel Tests. For additional information, see 6:1142.

O267. Firefighter Test. For additional information, see 6:1143.

O268. [Firefighting Promotion Tests.] For additional information, see 6:1144.

O269. Fireman Examination. For additional information, see 6:1145.

O270. Memory and Observation Tests for Policeman. For additional information, see 6:1146.

O271. Mooseheart Graphic Rating Scale for Housemothers and Housefathers. For additional information, see 1:1172.

O272. [NCR Test Battery for Prospective Check-Out Cashiers.] For additional information and a review by David O. Herman, see 6:1147.

O273. P-L-S Journalism Test. For additional information, see 3:149.

O274. Personnel Service Rating Report. For additional information, see 5:939.

O275. Police Performance Rating System. For additional information, see 6:1148.

O276. Police Promotion Examinations. For additional information, see 6:1149.

O277. Policeman Examination. For additional information, see 6:1150.

O278. Policeman Test. For additional information, see 6:1151.

O279. The Potter-Nash Aptitude Test for Lumber Inspectors and Other General Personnel Who Handle Lumber. For additional information, see 6:1152.

O280. Punched Card Machine Operator Aptitude Test. For additional information, see 5:941.

O281. Revised Programmer Aptitude Test. For additional information, see 6:1153 (2 references).

O282. The Store Personnel Test. For additional information and reviews by Raymond A. Katzell and John B. Morris, see 5:954 (1 reference).

O283. Visual Comprehension Test for Detective. For additional information, see 6:1154.

NURSING

O284. Achievement Tests in Nursing. For additional information, see 6:1155.

O285. Achievement Tests in Practical Nursing. For additional information, see 5:909.

O286. Entrance Examination for Schools of Nursing. For additional information, see 6:1156 (2 references).

O287. Entrance Examinations for Schools of Practical Nursing. For additional information, see 5:920.

O288. George Washington University Series Nursing Tests. For additional information, see 4:818 (2 references); see also 3:699 (6 references).

O289. The Gordon-Douglass Fraction Test for Beginning Students of Nursing. For additional information, see 1:1168 (1 excerpt).

O290. NLN Achievement Tests for Basic Professional Nursing. For additional information, see 6:1157 (1 reference).

O291. NLN Achievement Tests for Psychiatric Aides. For additional information, see 6:1158.

O292. NLN Graduate Nurse Examination. For additional information, see 6:1159 (4 references).

O293. NLN Practical Nurse Achievement Tests. For additional information, see 6:1160.

O294. NLN Pre-Admission and Classification Examination. For additional information, see 6:1161 (1 reference).

O295. NLN Pre-Nursing and Guidance Examination. For additional information, see 6:1162 (8 references).

O296. PSB-Entrance Examination for Schools of Practical Nursing. For additional information, see 6:1163.

RESEARCH

O297. Research Personnel Review Form. For additional information, see 6:1164.

O298. Supervisor's Evaluation of Research Personnel. For additional information and a review by John W. French, see 6:1165 (3 references, 1 excerpt).

O299. Surveys of Research Administration and Environment. For additional information, see 6:1166.

O300. Technical Personnel Recruiting Inventory. For additional information, see 6:1167.

SELLING

O301. Aptitude Index Selection Procedure. For additional information, see 6:1168 (1 reference); see also 5:913 (1 reference); for reviews by Donald G. Paterson and Albert S. Thompson of an earlier form, see 4:825 (14 references); see also 2:1646 (5 references).

O302. Aptitudes Associates Test of Sales Aptitude: A Test for Measuring Knowledge of Basic Principles of Selling. For additional information, see 6:1169 (6 references); for reviews by Milton E. Hahn and Donald G. Paterson, see 4:824. For a revised edition, see O317.

O303. Combination Inventory. For additional information, see 6:1170 (1 reference).

O304. The Dealer Inventory. For additional information, see 6:1171.

O305. Detroit Retail Selling Inventory. For additional information and reviews by Milton E. Hahn and Floyd L. Ruch, see 3:697 (2 excerpts).

O306. The Evaluation Record. For additional information, see 6:1172.

O307. Hall Salespower Inventory. For additional information, see 5:924.

O308. Hanes Sales Selection Inventory. For additional information and reviews by William E. Kendall and Albert K. Kurtz, see 6:1173.

O309. Hiring Kit. For additional information, see 4:826.

O310. Information Index. For additional information, see 6:1174 (1 reference); see also 5:927 (3 references).

O311. Interviewer's Impressions—Sales Applicants. For additional information, see 6:1175.

O312. LIAMA Inventory of Job Attitudes. For additional information, see 5:929.

O313. Measure of Consociative Tendency. For additional information, see 5:931.

O314. Personal History. For additional information, see 2:1670 (5 references).

O315. Personnel Institute Hiring Kit. For additional information, see 6:1176 (3 references).

O316. SRA Sales Attitudes Check List. For additional information and a review by John P. Foley, Jr., see 6:1177.

O317. Sales Comprehension Test. For additional information, see 6:1178 (7 references) ; for a review by Raymond A. Katzell, see 5:947 (10 references) ; for an earlier edition, see O302.

O318. Sales Employee Inventory. For additional information, see 6:1179.

O319. Sales Motivation Inventory. For additional information and a review by S. Rains Wallace, see 5:948 (2 references).

O320. Sales Personnel Description Form. For additional information and a review by Wayne K. Kirchner, see 6:1180 (2 references).

O321. Sales Questionnaire. For additional information and a review by Robert G. Bernreuter, see 3:703 (1 reference).

O322. The Sales Sentence Completion Blank. For additional information and a review by William E. Kendall, see 6:1181 (1 excerpt).

O323. Sales Situation Test. For additional information, see 4:827 (1 reference).

O324. Steward Basic Factors Inventory. For additional information and reviews by Leonard V. Gordon and Lyman W. Porter, see 6:1182.

O325. Steward Life Insurance Knowledge Test. For additional information, see 5:950.

O326. Steward Occupational Objectives Inventory. For additional information, see 5:951.

O327. Steward Personal Background Inventory. For additional information and reviews by Leonard V. Gordon and Lyman W. Porter, see 6:1183; see also 5:952 (1 reference).

O328. Steward Selection System. For additional information and reviews by Donald G. Paterson and Albert S. Thompson, see 4:828 (2 references) ; for reviews by Milton E. Hahn and Floyd L. Ruch, see 3:704 (2 references) ; see also 2:1651 (3 references).

O329. Test for Ability to Sell: George Washington University Series. For additional information, see 4:829; for a review by Floyd L. Ruch, see 3:705.

O330. Test of Sales Judgment. For additional information, see 4:830.

O331. Word Check Forms. For additional information, see 6:1184.

SKILLED TRADES

O332. Automotive Mechanic Test. For additional information, see 6:1185.

O333. The Fiesenheiser Test of Ability to Read Drawings. For additional information and a review by Joseph E. Moore, see 6:1186.

O334. Garage Mechanic Test. For additional information, see 5:573.

O335. Purdue Blueprint Reading Test. For additional information, see 4:782.

O336. Purdue Industrial Training Classification Test. For additional information and reviews by D. Welty Lefever and Charles I. Mosier, see 3:675 (2 references).

O337. Purdue Interview Aids. For additional information and a review by William W. Waite, see 4:775.

O338. Purdue Test for Electricians. For additional information and a review by John W. French, see 3:701.

O339. Purdue Test for Machinists and Machine Operators. For additional information, see 4:816; for a review by William W. Waite, see 3:702.

O340. Purdue Trade Information Test for Sheetmetal Workers. For additional information, see 5:942.

O341. Purdue Trade Information Test in Carpentry. For additional information and a review by P. L. Mellenbruch, see 5:943 (1 reference).

O342. Purdue Trade Information Test in Engine Lathe Operation. For additional information and a review by William J. Micheels, see 5:944.

O343. Purdue Trade Information Test in Welding. For additional information, see 5:945.

O344. Technical Tests. For additional information, see 6:1187.

O345. Written Trade Tests. For additional information, see 6:1188.

SUPERVISION

O346. A Chart for the Rating of a Foreman. For additional information, see 5:915.

O347. How Supervise? For additional information and a review by Joel T. Campbell, see 6:1189 (9 references) ; see also 5:926 (18 references) ; for a review by Milton M. Mandell, see 4:774 (8 references) ; for reviews by D. Welty Lefever, Charles I. Mosier, and C. H. Ruedisili, see 3:687 (5 references).

O348. Leadership Opinion Questionnaire. For additional information and reviews by Jerome E. Doppelt and Wayne K. Kirchner, see 6:1190 (6 references).

O349. Managerial Scale for Enterprise Improvement. For additional information and reviews by Brent Baxter and Edward B. Greene, see 5:930.

O350. Personal Development Record. For additional information, see 6:1191.

O351. Supervisory Index. For additional information and reviews by Arthur H. Brayfield and Albert K. Kurtz, see 6:1192 (1 reference).

O352. Supervisory Inventory on Human Relations. For additional information and a review by Seymour Levy, see 6:1193 (1 reference).

O353. Supervisory Practices Test. For additional information, see 6:1194 (4 references) ; for reviews by Clifford E. Jurgensen and Mary Ellen Oliverio, see 5:955.

O354. Test of Practical Judgment. For additional information, see 4:784 (6 references) ; for reviews by Glen U. Cleeton and Howard R. Taylor, see 3:694.

O355. Test of Supervisory Judgment. For additional information, see 6:1195.

O356. WLW Supervisor Survey. For additional information, see 6:1196.

TRANSPORTATION

O357. [American Transit Association Tests.] For additional information, see 5:912; for reviews by

Harold G. Seashore, Morris S. Viteles, and J. V. Waits, see 3:696 (1 reference).

O358. Driver Selection Forms and Tests. For additional information and a review by Joseph E. Moore, see 6:1197; for a review by S. Rains Wallace, Jr., see 4:789.

O359. McGuire Safe Driver Scale and Interview Guide. For additional information and reviews by Willard A. Kerr and D. H. Schuster, see 6:1198 (1 reference).

O360. Road Test Check List for Testing, Selecting, Rating, and Training Coach Operators. For additional information, see 5:946.

O361. Road Test in Traffic for Testing, Selecting, Rating, and Training Truck Drivers. For additional information and a review of the battery, see 6:1197g.

O362. Traffic and Driving Knowledge for Drivers of Motor Trucks. For additional information and a review of the battery, see 6:1197f.

O363. Truck Driver Test. For additional information and reviews by Willard A. Kerr and D. H. Schuster, see 6:1199.

O364. Wilson Driver Selection Test. For additional information and reviews by Willard A. Kerr and D. H. Schuster, see 6:1200.

Publishers Directory and Index

References are to test entry numbers, not to page numbers. Stars indicate test publishers which issue catalogs devoted entirely or in large part to tests. The phrase "out of print" precedes the entry numbers of out of print tests. Addresses are given only for publishers known to have one or more reading tests in print as of May 1, 1968.

ACORN Publishing Co.: *out of print, 235*. Other tests acquired by Psychometric Affiliates.

★American Guidance Service, Inc., Publishers' Bldg., Circle Pines, Minn. 55014: 122, 189, 241; *out of print, 143, 179*

American Optical Co.: *out of print, 162*

Association of Georgia Colleges: *out of print, 225, 229*

★Australian Council for Educational Research, Frederick St., Hawthorn, Vic., Australia 3122: 1–3, 16–7, 85, 126

BETTER Reading Program, Inc., 230 East Ohio St., Chicago, Ill. 60611: 154

★Bobbs-Merrill Co., Inc. (The), 4300 West 62nd St., Indianapolis, Ind. 46206: 6–7, 45, 51, 62, 67, 82–3, 86–7, 167, 173–4, 180

Book Society of Canada Ltd., 4386 Sheppard Ave., Agincourt, Ont., Canada: 201

Brador Publications, Inc., Livonia, N.Y. 14487: 133

Brown (Wm. C.) Book Co., 135 South Locust St., Dubuque, Iowa 52001: 116

★Bureau of Educational Measurements, Kansas State Teachers College, 1200 Commercial St., Emporia, Kan. 66802: 23–8, 52; *out of print, 102, 258*

Bureau of Publications. See Teachers College Press.

★CALIFORNIA Test Bureau, Del Monte Research Park, Monterey, Calif. 93940: 10, 38–9, 77, 115, 119, 187, 236; *out of print, 93, 97, 101, 103, 267*. (A division of McGraw-Hill Book Co.)

Cal-State Bookstore, 25776 Hillary St., Hayward, Calif. 94542: 188

Chatto & Windus Ltd., 40–42 William IV St., London W.C.2, England: 139

College of Teachers of the Blind, Royal School for the Blind, Westbury-on-Trym, Bristol, England: 212, 223

Committee on Diagnostic Reading Tests, Inc., Mountain Home, N.C. 28758: 121

★Consulting Psychologists Press, Inc., 577 College Ave., Palo Alto, Calif. 94306: 196, 199, 245, 251

Cooperative Book Store: *out of print, 271*

Cooperative Bureau of Educational Research: *out of print, 260, 263, 273*

★Cooperative Test Division, Educational Testing Service, Princeton, N.J. 08540: 56, 70; *out of print, 259, 264, 269, 281*

Curriculum Bulletin: *out of print, 279*

DELAWARE County Reading Consultants Association, c/o Nicholas A. Spennato, Delaware County Public Schools, Court House Annex, Media, Pa. 19063: 19

Denver Public Schools, 414 Fourteenth St., Denver, Colo. 80202: 117

Department of Psychological Testing, De Paul University, 25 East Jackson Blvd., Chicago, Ill. 60604: 12

Developmental Reading Distributors, 1944 Sheridan Ave., Laramie, Wyo. 82070: 41

EDMISTON (R. W.): *out of print, 262*

Education-Industry Service, 1225 East 60th St., Chicago, Ill. 60637: 224

Educational Developmental Laboratories, Inc., Huntington, N.Y. 11743: 155–7, 164. (A division of McGraw-Hill Book Co.)

Educational Records Bureau, 21 Audubon Ave., New York, N.Y. 10032: 249

Educational Stimuli, 2012 Hammond Ave., Superior, Wis. 54880: 239

Educational Test Bureau: for in print tests, see American Guidance Service, Inc.; *out of print, 91, 104, 112, 226–8, 232*

Educational Testing Service. See Cooperative Test Division and Educational Testing Service (Western Office).

Educational Testing Service (Western Office), 1947 Center St., Berkeley, Calif. 94704: 76

Educators Publishing Service, Inc., 75 Moulton St., Cambridge, Mass. 02138: 159

Essay Press, Inc., P.O. Box 5, Planetarium Station, New York, N.Y. 10024: 134–5

Evaluation in the Eight Year Study, Progressive Education Association: *out of print, 255–6, 261, 265, 270*

FOLLETT Publishing Co., 1010 West Washington Blvd., Chicago, Ill. 60607: 148, 183, 217

GARRARD Publishing Co., 1607 North Market St., Champaign, Ill. 61820: 147

General Educational Development Testing Service of the American Council on Education, 1785 Massachusetts Ave., N.W., Washington, D.C. 20036: 210, 211

Gibson (Robert) & Sons (Glasgow), Ltd., 2 West Regent St., Glasgow C.2, Scotland: 36

Ginn & Co. See Personnel Press, Inc.

Gregory (C. A.) Co.: for in print tests, see Bobbs-Merrill Co., Inc.; *out of print*, 96, 108, 177

★Guidance Centre, Ontario College of Education, University of Toronto, 371 Bloor St., West, Toronto 5, Ont., Canada: 5, 11, 31, 170, 185

★Guidance Testing Associates, 6516 Shirley Ave., Austin, Tex. 78752: 80-1, 221-2

HALE (E. M.) & Co.: *out of print*, 92

★Harcourt, Brace & World, Inc., 757 Third Ave., New York, N.Y. 10017: 20, 34-5, 43, 74-5, 123, 140, 150, 165, 190-1, 244, 253; *out of print*, 100, 107, 205, 276

★Harrap (George G.) & Co. Ltd., 182 High Holborn, London W.C.1, England: 37, 168

Heinemann Educational Books Ltd., River House, 24 River St., South Yarra, Vic. 3141, Australia: 29

Hillsdale School Supply Co.: *out of print*, 114

★Houghton Mifflin Co., 2 Park St., Boston, Mass. 02107: 47-50, 71, 79, 132, 186, 193, 254; *out of print*, 106, 160

IBM. See Science Research Associates, Inc.

KENEVAN (B.): *out of print*, 178

Keystone View Co., Meadville, Pa. 16335: 186.1

LAYTON (Wilbur L.), 3604 Ross Road, Ames, Iowa 50010: 246

Lippincott (J. B.) Co., East Washington Square, Philadelphia, Pa. 19105: 187.1

Lyons & Carnahan, 407 East 25th St., Chicago, Ill. 60616: 21, 137

McCARTNEY (William A.), P.O. Box 507, Kaneohe, Hawaii 96744: 57

McGrath Reading Clinic, 15944 West McNichols Road, Detroit, Mich. 48235: 39.1

McGraw-Hill Book Co. See California Test Bureau and Educational Developmental Laboratories, Inc.

Macmillan & Co. Ltd., 10 St. Martin's St., London W.C.2, England: 169

McMenemy (Richard A.), 3028 N.E. Brazee St., Portland, Ore. 97212: 40

Mills Center, Inc., 1512 East Broward Blvd., Ft. Lauderdale, Fla. 33301: 153

Montana Reading Clinic Publications, 517 Rimrock Road, Billings, Mont. 59102: 141, 152

★NATIONAL Bureau of Educational and Social Research, Department of Higher Education, Private Bag 41, Pretoria, Republic of South Africa: 46, 72

National Council of Teachers of English (The), 508 South Sixth St., Champaign, Ill. 61820: 149

★National Foundation for Educational Research in England and Wales, The Mere, Upton Park, Slough, Bucks, England: 13. See also Newnes Educational Publishing Co. Ltd., which distributes most of the Foundation's tests.

Nevins (C. H.) Printing Co., 311 Bryn Mawr Island, Bayshore Gardens, Bradenton, Fla. 33505: 125

New Zealand Council for Educational Research, Education House, 178 Willis St., Wellington, C.2 New Zealand: 4, 171

★Newnes Educational Publishing Co. Ltd., Tower House, 8-11 Southampton St., Strand, London W.C.2, England: 54, 60, 68-9

O'CONNOR Reading Clinic Publishing Co., Box 447, Roscommon, Mich. 48653: 128, 240

Ohio College Association. Tests acquired by Wilbur L. Layton.

Ohio Scholarship Tests. See Ohio Testing Services.

★Ohio Testing Services, State Department of Education, 751 Northwest Blvd., Columbus, Ohio 43212: 129; *out of print*, 94, 99, 105, 110, 234, 257, 275

Oliver & Boyd Ltd., Tweeddale Court, 14 High St., Edinburgh 1, Scotland: 136

PERFECTION Form Co.: *out of print*, 274

Personnel Press, Inc., 20 Nassau St., Princeton, N.J. 08540: 127, 182.1. (A subsidiary of Ginn & Co.)

Personnel Research Associates, Inc., P.O. Box 2994, Dallas, Tex. 75221: 216

Phonovisual Products, Inc., P.O. Box 5625, Friendship Station, Washington, D.C. 20016: 131

Pioneer Printing Co., 306-B Flora, Bellingham, Wash. 98225: 138

Priority Innovations, Inc., P.O. Box 792, Skokie, Ill. 60076: 192.1, 196.1, 197

Programs for Education, Box 85, Lumberville, Pa. 18933: 195

Progressive Education Association. See Evaluation in the Eight Year Study.

★Psychological Corporation (The), 304 East 45th St., New York, N.Y. 10017: 18, 248; *out of print*, 142, 233, 277

Psychological Institute, P.O. Box 1118, Lake Alfred, Fla. 33850: 78

★Psychometric Affiliates, Chicago Plaza, Brookport, Ill. 62910: 33, 53, 58-9, 64, 182, 237, 242

Public School Publishing Co.: for in print tests, see Bobbs-Merrill Co., Inc.; *out of print*, 113, 272, 278

READING and Study Skills Center. See Taylor Center for Controlled Reading and Research.

Reading Laboratory and Clinic, University of Florida, Gainesville, Fla. 32601: 250

★Research Concepts, 1368 East Airport Road, Muskegon, Mich. 49444: 179.1, 195.1 (A division of Test Maker, Inc.)

★Richardson, Bellows, Henry & Co., Inc., 355 Lexington Ave., New York, N.Y. 10017: 214-5

St. MARTIN'S Press, Inc., 175 Fifth Ave., New York, N.Y. 10010: 169

★Scholastic Testing Service, Inc., 480 Meyer Road, Bensenville, Ill. 60106: 8.1, 120, 198, 209; *out of print*, 146, 204

★Science Research Associates, Inc., 259 East Erie St., Chicago, Ill. 60611: 61, 65-6, 158, 207-8, 220, 243, 244.1, 252; *out of print*, 163. (A subsidiary of IBM.)

Scott, Foresman & Co.: *out of print*, 89

★Sheridan Psychological Services, Inc., P.O. Box 837, Beverly Hills, Calif. 90213: 238

Sheridan Supply Co. See Sheridan Psychological Services, Inc.

Sherman (I.): *out of print*, 175, 178

Skandinaviska Testförlaget AB, Sturegatan 56, Stockholm Ö, Sweden: 194

Slosson Educational Publications, 140 Pine St., East Aurora, N.Y. 14052: 172

Smith (Turner E.) & Co.: *out of print*, 268

Stanford University Press: *out of print*, 161

Staples Press Ltd., 1-3 Upper James St., London W.1, England: 9; *out of print*, 176

State High School Testing Service for Indiana, Purdue University, Lafayette, Ind. 47907: 55

Steck Co. See Steck-Vaughn Co.

Steck-Vaughn Co.: *out of print,* 203, 280, 282

★Stoelting (C. H.) Co., 424 North Homan Ave., Chicago, Ill. 60624: 118

TAYLOR Center for Controlled Reading and Research, 75 Prospect St., Huntington, N.Y. 11744: 151

★Teachers College Press, Teachers College, Columbia University, New York, N.Y. 10027: 30, 124, 130, 184; *out of print,* 98, 111, 144, 266

UNIVERSITY Book Store, 360 State St., West Lafayette, Ind. 47906: 213

★University of London Press Ltd., Saint Paul's House, Warwick Lane, London E.C.4, England: 32, 42, 63, 73, 166, 218; *out of print,* 88, 90, 95

University of Minnesota Press, Minneapolis, Minn. 55455: 44, 230–1

University Publications Sales, Ohio State University, 242 West 18th Ave., Columbus, Ohio 43210: 219

VAN WAGENEN Psycho-Educational Research Laboratories, 1729 Irving Ave. South, Minneapolis, Minn. 55411: 14, 15, 22, 84, 200. (This publisher refused to supply information about his tests or to check the accuracy of the entries prepared.)

Veterans' Testing Service. See General Educational Development Testing Service of the American Council on Education.

WAGNER (Mazie Earle), 500 Klein Road, Buffalo, N.Y. 14221: 8

Webster Publishing Co.: *out of print,* 109, 145, 202, 206

★Western Psychological Services, Box 775, Beverly Hills, Calif. 90213: 181, 247

Winter Haven Lions Research Foundation, Inc., P.O. Box 111, Winter Haven, Fla. 33881: 192

World Book Co. See Harcourt, Brace & World, Inc.

Index of Titles

In addition to listing all reading tests known to be in print as of May 1, 1968, this index includes all tests which have been in one or more of the first six *Mental Measurements Yearbooks* or in *Tests in Print*. References are to entry numbers, not to page numbers. Numbers not preceded by a letter refer to reading tests; thus, 156 refers to reading test 156 in the Reading Test Index. Numbers preceded by a single letter refer to tests in the MMY Test Index; thus, F98 refers to test 98 in the F (intelligence) section of the MMY Test Index. Superseded test titles are followed by a "see" reference; thus, for example, "see G86" indicates that the given title has been superseded by the title reported for test 86 in the G (mathematics) section of the MMY Test Index. Entry numbers for tests listed in *Tests in Print* but not in any of the *Mental Measurements Yearbooks* begin with the acronym TIP. In summary, this is an index to all reading tests known to be in print and to all tests which have been listed either in an MMY or TIP.

How'm I Doin'?, see J241
Hoyum-Schrammel English Essentials Tests, C56
Hudelson's Typical Composition Ability Scale, C109
Human Relations Inventory, J113
Humm-Wadsworth Temperament Scale, J114
Hundred Problem Arithmetic Test, G156
Hunt-Minnesota Test for Organic Brain Damage, J115
Hurd Test in High School Physics, L149
Hutchinson Latin Grammar Scale, E117
Hutt Adaptation of the Bender-Gestalt Test, see J314

IBM OPTICAL Mark Scoring Reader, H22
IBM Test Scoring Machine, H23
IES Test, J342
IPAT Anxiety Scale Questionnaire, J116
IPAT Children's Personality Questionnaire, J117
IPAT Contact Personality Factor Test, J118
IPAT Culture Fair Intelligence Test, F54
IPAT Culture Free Intelligence Test, see F54
IPAT 8-Parallel-Form Anxiety Battery, J119
IPAT High School Personality Questionnaire, see J142
IPAT Humor Test of Personality, J120
IPAT Music Preference Test of Personality, J121
IPAT Neurotic Personality Factor Test, J122
IPAT Self Analysis Form, see J116
I.Q. Calculator, TIP 1154
Ideational Fluency, F267
Ideational Fluency (Speed Test 4) : Differential Test Battery, I6
Identical Forms, O182
Identical Pictures Test : Factor P (Perceptual Speed), F275
Illinois Algebra Test, G85
Illinois Food Test, H200
Illinois Inventory of Parent Opinion, H91
Illinois Inventory of Pupil Opinion, H91
Illinois Inventory of Teacher Opinion, H91
[Illinois Opinion Inventories], H91
Illinois Plane Geometry Test, G216
Illinois State Normal University Social Science Test, see N14
Illinois Teachers College Cooperative Social Science Test, N14
Illinois Test of Psycholinguistic Abilities, F273
Illuminant-Stable Color Vision Test, M46
Immediate Test : A Quick Verbal Intelligence Test, F232
Incomplete Sentence Test, J343
Incomplete Sentence Test for Industrial Use, J343
Indiana History, N15
Indiana Psychodiagnostic Blank, H248
Indiana University Motor Fitness Index, H160
Individual and Marriage Counseling Inventory, H39
Individual Background Survey, O217
Individual Guidance Record, O183
Individual Placement Series, O5; separate tests : 216, B41, B68, F14, F138, J268, K164, O43, O82
Individual Reading Test, 126, K96
Inductive Reasoning Test, F88
Industrial Arts Education : National Teacher Examinations, H213
Industrial Arts : Every Pupil Scholarship Test, H214
Industrial Arts : Teacher Education Examination Program, H215
Industrial Safety Attitude Scale for Male Employees, H58; Supervisors, H58
Industrial Sentence Completion Form, J344
Industrial Subjective Fatigue and Euphoria Scales, J81
Infant Intelligence Scale, see F215
Inference Test : Factor RS (Syllogistic Reasoning), F275

Information Blank EA : A Questionnaire on Emotional Adjustment, J123
Information Blank : For Obtaining Data About Vocational Plans and Problems of High School Students, O184
Information Concerning Library Processes, 263, K190
Information Index, O310
Information Test on Foods : Illinois Food Test, H200
Information Test on Human Reproduction, TIP 1288
Information Tests in American History, N99
Ingenuity : Flanagan Aptitude Classification Tests, FACT 16A, I10
Inglis Intelligence Quotient Values, TIP 1155
Inglis Tests of English Vocabulary, C232
Ingraham-Clark Diagnostic Reading Tests, 101, K33
Inpatient Multidimensional Psychiatric Scale (IMPS), J124
Insight Into Friction Between People, TIP 195
Insight Test : A Verbal Projective Test for Personality Study, J345
Inspection : Flanagan Aptitude Classification Tests, I10
Institute of Child Study Security Test, J125
Instructional Reading Tests for the Intermediate Grades, 160, K115
Instructional Test in Safety, H60
Integrated Articulation Test for Use With Children With Cerebral Palsy, C177
Intelligence Test : Comprehensive Testing Program, F89
Intelligence Tests for Children, F233; for Young Children, see F233
Interaction Chronograph, J126
Interaction Process Analysis, J127
Inter-American Series, 81, F190, K78
Inter-American Series : Tests of Reading, K78
Interest Analysis, J128
Interest Check List, O70
Interest Index : General Education Series, J129
Interest Inventory for Elementary Grades : George Washington University Series, J130
Interest-Preference Test for Prospective Nurses, O288
Interest Questionnaire for High School Students, O71
Interest Questionnaire : Games and Sports : Test 8.3, J131
Interest-Values Inventory, J132
Interests and Activities : Tests 8.2b and 8.2c, J133
Intermediate Chemistry Test, L109
Intermediate Diagnostic Arithmetic Test, G157
International Test Scoring Machine, see H23
International Typewriting Tests, TIP 87
Interpersonal Check List, J134
Interpersonal Diagnosis of Personality, J346
Interpersonal Fantasy Test, J346
Interpretation of Data Test : General Education Series, 264, K191
Interpretation of Data : Test 2.71, 265, K192
Interpretation of Literary Materials : Tests of General Educational Development, C141
Interpretation of Literature Test : General Education Series, C142
Interpretation of Reading Materials in the Natural Sciences : Tests of General Educational Development, 210, K158
Interpretation of Reading Materials in the Social Studies : Tests of General Educational Development, 211, K159
Inter-Society Color Council Color Aptitude Test, M47
Interview Aids : Purdue Vocational Series, O337
Interview Rating Scale for Prospective Employees, O218
Interviewer's Impressions—Sales Applicants, O311
Introduction to Education, H92
Introductory Calculus : ERB Mathematics Tests, G20

Index of Names

AARON, Ira E.: *rev,* 6:830-1, 6:834
Abell, E. L.: *exc,* 2:1578
Abelson, Harold H.: *rev,* J52, J282
Aborn, Murray: *rev,* F262
Adair, Normand: *test,* 179.1
Adams, Clifford R.: *rev,* H37, H43, H48
Adams, Elizabeth C.: *rev,* N118, N126
Adams, Michael: *ref,* 6:794(35)
Adams, Nicholas A.: *ref,* 6:823(25)
Adams, William Michael: *ref,* 3:489(17)
Adcock, C. J.: *rev,* F177, J142, J161, J248, J351, J378
Adkins, Dorothy C.: *ref,* 3:535 (13); *rev,* A38, B25, G126, I7, I16, N84, N91, N96, N105, O6
Adler, Dan L.: *rev,* J150, J185
Afflerbach, Janet G.: *rev,* 5:693, C218, H271
Afflerbach, Lois Grimes: *rev,* 5:693
Agard, Frederick B.: *rev,* E146, E150, E155
Ahmann, J. Stanley: *ref,* 5:688(8, 12); *rev,* A45, F166
Ahr, A. Edward: *test,* 196.1, 197
Ainsworth, Mary D.: *rev,* J379-80
Albright, Lewis E.: *rev,* F206, J3
Albright, Norma A.: *rev,* H200, H209
Alden, Clara L.: *ref,* 4:562(3)
Allen, C. H.: *ref,* 2:1570(1)
Allen, L. W.: *test,* 126
Almack, John C.: *rev,* C191, C194, C217, H138
Alodia, Mary: *test,* 157
Altus, William D.: *rev,* F228, F262
Amberson, Jean D.: *rev,* H194, H199

American Optical Company: *test,* 162
Amerson, Vera M.: *rev,* B4, B9
Ames, Louise Bates: *test,* 195
Amstutz, Wade S.: *ref,* 2:1544 (7-8)
Anastasi, Anne: *rev,* F17, F22, F35, F87, F184, F191, F224, I12-4, I22, I25, J117
Anderhalter, Oliver F.: *test,* 120, 146, 204; *rev,* A20, G107, G167
Anderson, A. W.: *ref,* 6:806(61)
Anderson, Harry E., Jr.: *ref,* 6:784 (11-2)
Anderson, Howard R.: *rev,* N1, N6, N10, N13, N16, N33, N36, N91, N94, N112, N149-50, N155
Anderson, Irving H.: *rev,* 1:1095, 1:1097, 1:1104, 3:514, 3:518-9, 3:521; *ref,* 3:489(10), 3:507(3), 4:544(13)
Anderson, James M.: *rev,* F263, F279, F286, H31
Anderson, Kenneth E.: *ref,* 6:806 (59-60, 64); *rev,* L38, L80, L110-1, L115
Anderson, Robert P.: *ref,* 6:856 (15)
Anderson, Rodney Ebon: *ref,* 6:794(57)
Anderson, Thelma Hill: *ref,* 6:856 (23)
Andrus, Lawrence: *rev,* E135, E144
Andruss, Harvey A.: *rev,* B14, B17
Anstey, E.: *rev,* O139
Arn, Elmer H. R.: *ref,* 5:645(40)
Arndt, Christian O.: *rev,* E135, E144
Arnold, Dwight L.: *rev,* H93, H228, J145, J230
Arnold, Gwen F.: *rev,* F213, F238

Arny, Clara M. Brown: *rev,* H186, H191-2, H200
Aronow, Miriam S.: *ref,* 6:797(4)
Artley, A. Sterl: *ref,* 4:547(18, 23)
Ashford, Theodore A.: *rev,* L88, L97, L110-1, L113
Association of Georgia Colleges: *test,* 225, 229
Astin, Alexander W.: *rev,* J3, O90
Atkins, S. D.: *rev,* E107, E111, E117
Austin, John J.: *test,* 195.1
Austin, Mary C.: *rev,* 6:848, F279, M55
Australian Council for Educational Research: *test,* 2-3, 85
Ayer, Frederic L.: *rev,* A27, J148, N132
Ayers, J. Douglas: *rev,* A5, C10

BABCOCK, James C.: *rev,* E142, E160
Baggaley, Andrew R.: *rev,* F104, J56, J206, J243
Bagley, Jessie W.: *ref,* 4:570(16)
Baker, Florence: *ref,* 4:542(1), 4:555(2)
Baker, P. C.: *test,* 55
Balinsky, Benjamin: *rev,* F286, J331, J343, O94
Ball, Rachel Stutsman: *rev,* F241
Ballard, P. B.: *test,* 88
Ballenger, H. L.: *ref,* 6:798(5)
Baller, Warren R.: *rev,* 4:583, H238, H240, J230, J241
Balow, Bruce: *test,* 21
Balow, Irving H.: *ref,* 6:845(9)
Balsley, Irol Whitmore: *rev,* B36
Banham, Katharine M.: *test,* 189; *ref,* 6:849(1)

JACKSON, Joseph F.: *rev*, E34, E36, E38, E41
Jackson, Robert: *ref*, 4:531(16)
Jackson, Robert W. B.: *rev*, A47
Jackson, Teddy Randolph: *ref*, 6:867(27)
Jacobs, Robert: *ref*, 4:547(25, 31)
Jacobsen, Carlyle F.: *ref*, 4:535(5)
James, Richard Warren: *ref*, 4:547(32)
Jameson, Alice N.: *rev*, 3:479, 3:495, 3:508
Janke, Leota Long: *ref*, 6:794(37, 41)
Jean, F. C.: *rev*, L58
Jenkins, Frances: *test*, 177
Jennings, John R.: *rev*, O116-7
Jensen, Arthur R.: *rev*, J155, J328, J353, J365, J378
Jenson, Ralph E.: *ref*, 4:547(26), 5:645(42)
Jessor, Richard: *rev*, J345, J347
Jex, Frank B.: *rev*, F237
Joël, Walther: *ref*, 3:544(3)
Johnson, A. P.: *ref*, 3:540(5-6); *rev*, O118, O252
Johnson, Cecil D.: *rev*, J118
Johnson, Laura B.: *rev*, E34, E63
Johnson, Leland P.: *rev*, L56, L68
Johnson, Norrie E.: *ref*, 3:520(4)
Johnson, Palmer O.: *rev*, G56, L7, L36, L40, L43, L80, L114, L134, L145-6, L161
Johnson, Richard T.: *rev*, G101, G196
Jones, Carleton C.: *rev*, C18, C119, C129
Jones, Edward S.: *rev*, 1:1166, 2:1574, A10, O226
Jones, F. Nowell: *rev*, M34, M48, M54
Jones, H. Gwynne: *rev*, F209, F225
Jones, Harold E.: *rev*, H229, J36, J52, J74, J103, J166
Jones, Kenneth J.: *ref*, 6:794(67); *rev*, L101
Jones, Ll. Wynn: *rev*, F204, J326
Jones, R. Stewart: *rev*, 6:867(30)
Jones, Robert A.: *ref*, 6:784(7, 9-10, 13-5); *rev*, A6, O46
Jones, Ronald DeVall: *ref*, 4:547(21)
Jones, William J.: *exc*, 3:478, 3:500
Jones, Worth R.: *rev*, 6:794, A43, C56
Jordan, A. M.: *rev*, A34, F62
Jordan, F. L.: *test*, 196
Jordan, Richard H.: *rev*, L16, L62
Jorgensen, A. N.: *test*, 34; *ref*, 2:1547(1)
Joyce, William D.: *ref*, 6:859(1)
Juergenson, Elwood M.: *ref*, 6:867(16)
Jurgensen, Clifford E.: *rev*, 6:840, B48, B65, O2, O148, O155-6, O353
Justman, Joseph: *rev*, G103, G181

KAGERER, Rudolph L.: *ref*, 6:848(3)
Kaiser, Henry F.: *ref*, 6:867(30)
Kambly, Paul E.: *rev*, H145, L37
Kanarik, Rosella: *f*, 1:1097

Karlsen, Bjorn: *test*, 129, 140; *ref*, 6:824(7), 6:832(1)
Karn, Harry W.: *rev*, O212
Karnes, M. Ray: *rev*, H7
Kass, Walter: *rev*, J361, J374
Katkovsky, Walter: *rev*, J327, J342
Katz, Martin: *rev*, O77, O81
Katzell, Raymond A.: *rev*, O3, O17, O34, O37, O105, O148, O177, O199, O282, O317
Kaulfers, Walter V.: *rev*, C99, E1, E5, E28, E37-8, E54, E60, E144, E150, E155, E157, E160
Kawin, Ethel: *ref*, 2:1552(9)
Keating, T. J.: *rev*, F152, F214, F247
Keats, J. A.: *rev*, F50, F189, F267, I5
Keir, Gertrude: *rev*, F113, F182
Kelley, Frances: *ref*, 4:557(3), 4:576(3), 4:577(3)
Kelley, Truman L.: *test*, 75, 276; *rev*, I22
Kelley, Victor H.: *test*, 34-5; *ref*, 3:489(27)
Kellogg, Theodore E.: *rev*, G85, G164, G207-8, G231
Kelly, E. Lowell: *rev*, J33, J106, J116, J132, J135, J171, J191
Kendall, William E.: *rev*, O308, O322
Keneally, Katherine G.: *rev*, 4:538
Kenevan, B.: *test*, 178
Kennedy, James E.: *rev*, F120, F199, F290
Kenny, Douglas T.: *rev*, J150, J317
Kent, Grace H.: *rev*, F214, F221-2, F227, F247, F259
Keohane, Robert E.: *rev*, N117
Kerr, Willard A.: *rev*, H67, O108, O145, O359, O363-4
Ketcham, Herbert E. (Mrs.): *ref*, 6:786(1)
Kettelkamp, Gilbert C.: *rev*, E66, E69
Keystone View Co.: *test*, 186.1
Kilby, Richard W.: *ref*, 3:489(23)
Kim, Ki Suk: *ref*, 5:688(10)
Kimber, George C.: *test*, 251
Kinder, Elaine F.: *rev*, J286
King, F. J.: *ref*, 6:856(17)
King, Joseph E.: *rev*, C237, O172
Kingsbury, Forrest A.: *rev*, J114, O55
Kingston, Albert J.: *rev*, 6:823, 6:832; *ref*, 6:786(2)
Kinney, L. B.: *rev*, G15, G69, G72
Kinzer, John R.: *rev*, O109, O132
Kirchner, Wayne K.: *rev*, O320, O348
Kirk, Samuel A.: *ref*, 3:519(3)
Kirkpatrick, Mary S.: *test*, 282
Kitay, Philip M.: *rev*, J352
Kjeldergaard, Paul M.: *rev*, J119, J177
Klaeger, Maximilian L. G.: *test*, 14, 200
Klebanoff, Seymour G.: *rev*, J16, J115
Kleinmuntz, Benjamin: *rev*, I14, J276
Kline, Milton V.: *rev*, J258

Koeninger, Rupert C.: *ref*, 2:1544(8)
Kogan, Kate Levine: *rev*, F289, J47, J90
Kogan, William S.: *rev*, F272, J47
Kolesnik, Peter E.: *ref*, 6:784(15)
Kopel, David: *rev*, 1:1097, 1:1108, 2:1548, 2:1571; *f*, 1:1097
Koppitz, Elizabeth Munsterberg: *ref*, 6:846(5)
Kottmeyer, William: *ref*, 4:570(18)
Krathwohl, David R.: *rev*, A4, N11
Krey, A. C.: *rev*, N86
Kriedt, Philip H.: *rev*, O23, O41
Kropp, Russell P.: *rev*, 5:623, 5:636
Krugman, Morris: *rev*, J6, J166, J225, J337, J354, J365
Krumboltz, John D.: *rev*, 6:857; *ref*, 5:688(11); *rev*, H97
Kuder, G. Frederic: *rev*, C6, F130, F132-3, I3
Kuhlmann, F.: *rev*, F37, F132
Kuhlmann, Martha J.: *test*, 58
Kuntz, James E.: *ref*, 6:856(15)
Kurtz, Albert K.: *rev*, I22, O36, O208, O224, O308, O351
Kvaraceus, W. C.: *rev*, C60-1, E120, J18, J62

LaBRANT, Lou: *rev*, C129, C131
Lafferty, J. Clayton: *test*, 195.1
Lambert, C. M.: *test*, 63
Lamke, Tom A.: *rev*, G19, G52
Lancaster, W. Elmer: *rev*, G207
Landry, Herbert A.: *ref*, 2:1539(5), 2:1547(4); *rev*, C237, O143
Landy, Edward: *rev*, J22, J186
Langlie, Theos A.: *rev*, F124, J15
Langmuir, Charles R.: *rev*, 5:694, 6:798, A33, E8, F88, H257, O188
Langsam, Rosalind Streep: *ref*, 3:489(11), 3:491(6), 3:523(3), 4:544(15), 6:794(34)
Lannholm, Gerald V.: *rev*, C8, C11, C49, C69, C76
Lappan, Peter A., Jr.: *rev*, G1, G65
Larsen, Robert P.: *ref*, 4:544(8), 6:794(36)
Larsen, Tora M.: *ref*, 5:645(57)
Larson, William S.: *rev*, D19, D21, D23-4, D28, D30, D33, D37-9, D43
Laslett, H. R.: *ref*, 3:489(7)
Lawes, J. S.: *rev*, F200, F244
Lawrence, William A.: *ref*, 4:544(9)
Lawshe, C. H., Jr.: *rev*, O103, O106, O132
Lawson, J. W.: *ref*, 2:1565(2)
Layman, Martha E.: *rev*, 4:577, N84
Layton, Wilbur L.: *rev*, A47, J117, J145, O65, O68, O81, O95
Leavell, Ullin W.: *test*, 143, 179
Ledgerwood, Richard: *rev*, 1:1171, A7, A32, C237, F97, J36, O128, O189
Lee, Dorris M.: *ref*, 6:846(1)